89195

La Cita MEXICAN FOODS

REFRIGERATED AIR
STEAKS
CHICKEN
CURIOS

"Recommended by Duncan Hines"
State Highways 104 & 18 . . . TUCUMCARI, NEW MEXIC

Nature's Pulpit, North Dakota Badlands

SCENE ON CADILLAC MOUNTAIN ROAD, ACADIA NATIONAL PARK, MT. DESERT ISLAND, MAINE

MOON

Road Trip USA

Cross-Country Adventures on America's Two-Lane Highways

JAMIE JENSEN

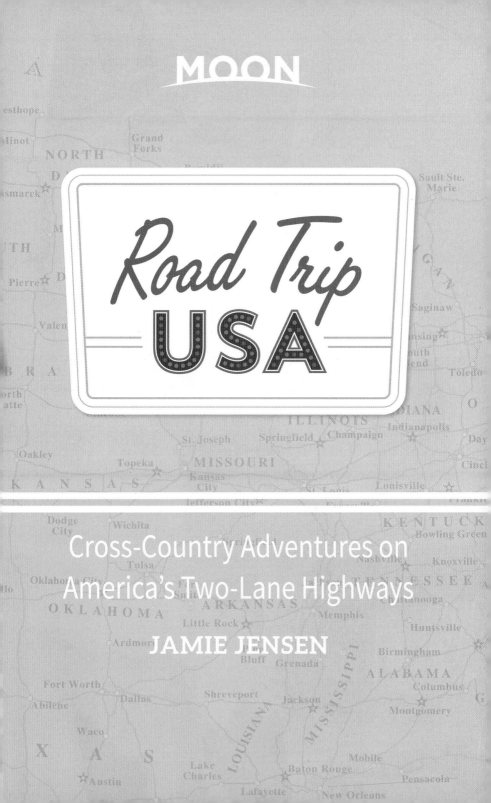

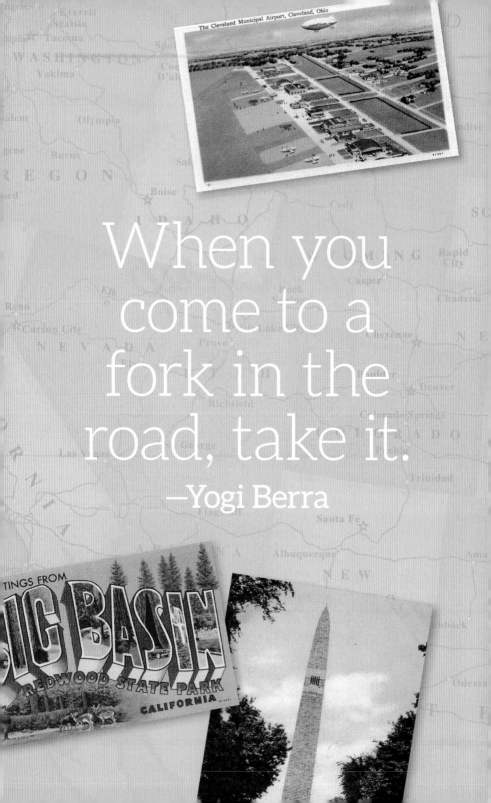

The Cleveland Municipal Airport, Cleveland, Ohio

When you come to a fork in the road, take it.

—Yogi Berra

TINGS FROM

BIG BASIN

REDWOOD STATE PARK

CALIFORNIA

Hit the Road!

The journeys in this book are as wild and varied as the landscapes they traverse. All celebrate the notion that freedom and discovery await us on the open road. American poets and artists from Walt Whitman to Muddy Waters have long sung the praises of rolling down the highway, and no matter how times have changed, we still believe there's nothing more essentially American than hitting the road and seeing the country.

America has always been a nation on the move. From colonial times onward, each generation pushed relentlessly westward until the outward frontier finally closed around the turn of the twentieth century. Taking advantage of the internal combustion engine, and inspired by the slogan "See America First," Americans began to explore a new frontier, the system of highways that developed between the Atlantic and Pacific coasts. The first transcontinental route, the Lincoln Highway from New York to San Francisco, was completed in 1915, and motor courts, diners, and other new businesses soon sprang up along the roadside to serve the passing trade.

The half-century from the 1920s until the arrival of the interstate highway system was the golden age of American motor travel, and while we love shiny diners and neon signs as much as anyone, this book is not especially motivated by nostalgia. Almost all of the places described in *Road Trip USA*—soda fountains and town squares, mom 'n' pop motels and minor league baseball teams—are happily thriving in the modern world, and better yet, they are close at hand. The simple act of avoiding the soulless interstates, with their soggy franchises and identikit chains, opens up a vast, and much friendlier, two-lane world. You'll chance upon monuments marking the actual sites of things you last heard about in high school history classes, or kitschy little souvenir stands flaunting giant dinosaurs outside their doors, and inside still selling the same postcards as they have for decades.

After traveling nearly 500,000 miles in search of the perfect stretches of two-lane blacktop, this is the book I wish I'd had with me all along. So whether you're a biker, an RVer, a road warrior, or a Sunday driver, hop on board, turn the key—and hit the highway.

Jamie Jensen

Contents

Olympic National Park

Seattle

Olympia

WASHINGTON

Portland

370 mi

Cape Perpetua

Salem

OREGON

IDAHO

300 mi

Boise

Avenue of the Giants

235 mi

Sacramento

San Francisco

Carson City

San Francisco

NEVADA

UT

180 mi

Hearst Castle

Las Vegas

Grand Canyon National Park

320 mi

Los Angeles

San Diego

ARIZO

San Diego

Phoen

Pacific Coast

CALIFORNIA
1

The amazing thing about the West Coast is that it is still mostly wild, open, and astoundingly beautiful country, where you can drive for miles and miles and have the scenery all to yourself.

Between Olympic National Park and San Diego, California

For some reason, when people elsewhere in the country refer to the Pacific Coast, particularly **California**, it's apparent that they think it's a land of kooks and crazies, an overbuilt suburban desert supporting only shopping malls, freeways, and body-obsessed airheads. All this

may be true in small pockets, but the amazing thing about the Pacific Coast—from the dense green forests of western **Washington** to the gorgeous beaches of Southern California—is that it is still mostly wild, open, and astoundingly beautiful country, where you can drive for miles and miles and have the scenery all to yourself.

Starting at the northwest tip of the United States at **Olympic National Park,** and remaining within sight of the ocean almost all the way south to the Mexican border, this 1,650-mile, mostly two-lane route takes in everything from temperate rainforest to near-desert. Most of the Pacific Coast is in the public domain, accessible, and protected

from development within national, state, and local parks, which provide habitat for such rare creatures as mountain lions, condors, and gray whales.

Heading south, after the rough-and-tumble logging and fishing communities of Washington State, you cross the mouth of the Columbia River and follow the comparatively peaceful and quiet **Oregon** coastline, where recreation has by and large replaced industry, and where dozens of quaint and not-so-quaint communities line the ever-changing shoreline. At the midway point, you pass through the great redwood forests of Northern California, where the tallest and most majestic living things on earth line the

Avenue of the Giants, home also to some of the best (meaning gloriously kitsch) remnants of the golden age of car-borne tourism: drive-through trees, drive-on trees, houses carved out of trees, and much more. The phenomenally beautiful coastline of Northern California is rivaled only by the incredible coast of **Big Sur** farther south, beyond which stretch the beachfronts of Southern California. The land of palm trees, beach boys, and surfer girls of popular lore really does exist, though only in the southernmost quarter of the state.

Along with the overwhelming scale of its natural beauty, the West Coast is remarkable for the abundance of well-preserved historic sites—most of which haven't been torn down, built on, or even built around—that stand as vivid evocations of life on what was once the most distant frontier of the New World. While rarely as old as places on the East Coast, or as impressive as those in Europe, West Coast sites are quite diverse and include the Spanish colonial missions of California, Russian and English fur-trading outposts, and the place where Lewis and Clark first sighted the Pacific after their long slog across the continent.

Last but certainly not least are the energizing cities—**Seattle** and **Portland** in the north, **San Francisco** in the middle, and **Los Angeles** and **San Diego** to the south—that serve as gateways to (or civilized respites from) the landscapes between them. Add to these the dozens of small and not-so-small towns along the coast, with alternating blue-collar ports and upscale vacation retreats, and you have a great range of food, drink, and accommodations options. Local cafés, seafood grills, and bijou restaurants abound, as do places to stay—from youth hostels in old lighthouses to roadside motels (including the world's first, which still stands in lovely San Luis Obispo, California) to homespun B&Bs in old farmhouses.

WASHINGTON

The coast of Washington is a virtual microcosm of the Pacific Northwest, containing everything from extensive wilderness areas to Native American fishing villages and heavily industrialized lumber towns. Starting at splendid **Port Townsend,** US-101 loops west around the rugged Olympic Peninsula, passing near the northwesternmost point of the continental United States while allowing access to the unforgettable natural attractions—sandy, driftwood-strewn beaches; primeval old-growth forests; and pristine mountain lakes and glaciated alpine peaks, to name just a few—of **Olympic National Park.** The roadside landscape varies from dense woods to clear-cut tracts of recently harvested timber. Innumerable rivers and streams are perhaps the most obvious signs of the immense amount of rainfall (about 12 feet) the region receives every year. Scattered towns, from **Port Angeles** in the north to the twin cities of **Grays Harbor** on the coast, are staunchly blue-collar communities almost wholly dependent on natural resources—not only trees but also salmon, oysters, and other seafood. Though the tourism trade has been increasing steadily, visitor services are still few and far between, so plan ahead.

Although it's not on the ocean, the Puget Sound port city of **Seattle** makes a good starting or finishing point to this Pacific Coast road trip.

Port Townsend

Few places in the world can match the concentration of natural beauty or the wealth of architecture found in tiny **Port Townsend** (pop. 9,113). One of the oldest towns in Washington, Port Townsend was laid out in 1852 and reached a peak of activity in the 1880s. But after the railroads focused on Seattle and Puget Sound as their western terminus, the town sat quietly for most of the next century until the 1960s, when an influx of arts-oriented refugees took over the waterfront warehouses and cliff-top mansions, converting them to galleries, restaurants, and comfy B&Bs while preserving the town's turn-of-the-20th-century character.

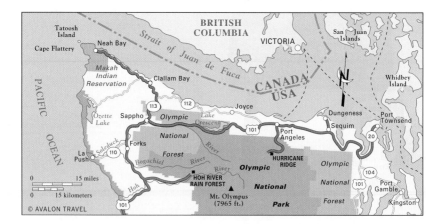

Fort Worden

Port Townsend is neatly divided into two halves: Multistory brick warehouses and commercial buildings line Water Street and the wharves along the bay, while lovely old Victorian houses cover the bluffs above. It's basically a great place to wander, but there are a couple of sights worth seeing, particularly the landmark **City Hall** (250 Madison St.) along the west end of Water Street. Half of this eclectic Gothic pile now houses a local historical museum with two floors of odds and ends tracing Port Townsend history, including the old city jail where Jack London spent a night on his way to the Klondike goldfields in 1897.

On the north side of Port Townsend, **Fort Worden** is a retired military base that served as a location for the Richard Gere movie *An Officer and a Gentleman*. Now home to a wonderful marine science center and natural history museum, the old fort also hosts an excellent series of annual music and arts festivals, ending with October's lively Kinetic Sculpture Race over land and sea and foam. Contact local arts organization **Centrum** (360/385-3102) for schedules and more information.

Port Townsend Practicalities

Not surprisingly, considering the extensive tourist trade, Port Townsend has a number of good restaurants and bars. You'll find many of the best places at the east end of town near the corner of Water and Quincy Streets. For breakfast, try the waterfront **Point Hudson Café** (130 Hudson St., 360/379-

The Waterstreet Hotel

0592), at the far west end of downtown "PT." For lunch or dinner, one of the best seafood places is the **Silverwater Café** (237 Taylor St., 360/385-6448), still going strong after 28 years near the Quincy Street dock. The old waterfront neighborhood also holds a pair of hotels in restored 1880s buildings: **The Waterstreet Hotel** (635 Water St., 360/385-5467 or 800/735-9810, $50 and up) and the quieter **The Palace Hotel** (1004 Water St., 360/385-0773 or 800/962-0741, $89 and up), where the room names play up the building's past use as a brothel.

The most comfortable accommodations in Port Townsend are the many 1880s-era B&Bs dotting the bluffs above the port area, including the ever-popular **The Old Consulate Inn** (313 Walker St., 360/385-6753 or 800/300-6753, $125 and up), where some of the plush rooms come with views of the ocean or the Olympic Mountains. All come with a hearty multicourse breakfast.

Fort Worden (360/344-4400, ext. 304), a mile north of downtown, also offers a wide variety of memorable

The natural cut of the **Hood Canal** on the east side of the Olympic Peninsula is one of the West Coast's prime oyster-growing estuaries, source of the gourmet Quilcenes, Hama Hamas, and other varieties available at roadside stands, shops, and restaurants throughout the region.

accommodations in historic officers quarters, a boutique castle, and converted barracks.

Sequim and Dungeness

Sequim lavender fields

Forty minutes southwest of Port Townsend via Hwy-20 and US-101, **Sequim** (pop. 6,606; pronounced "SKWIM") sits in the rain shadow of the Olympic Mountains and so tends to be much drier and sunnier than spots even a few miles west. Though it retains its rural feel, Sequim's historic farming-and-fishing economy is quickly switching over to tourism, with tracts of new homes filling up the rolling waterfront landscape and a new freeway bypassing the center of town. It's ideal cycling country, for the moment at least, with acres and acres of lavender farms lining quiet country roads.

The Native American-owned **7 Cedars Casino** stands above US-101 at the foot of Sequim Bay, fronted by totem poles.

Coming in from the east on two-lane US-101, the first thing you pass is the large modern John Wayne Marina, built on land donated by The Duke's family. The US-101 frontage through town is lined by the usual franchised fast-food outlets and some unique variations, like the 1950s-themed **HIWAY 101 Diner** (392 W. Washington St., 360/683-3388), in the heart of town.

Sequim's annual **Irrigation Festival,** held every May, is Washington's oldest continuing community celebration. The **Lavender Festival,** in July, is also popular.

Just north of US-101, the **Sequim Museum & Arts Center** (175 W. Cedar St., 360/683-8110, Wed.-Sat. 11am-3pm, donation) houses everything from 12,000-year-old mastodon bones discovered on a nearby farm to exhibits of Native American cultures and pioneer farm implements. From the museum, a well-marked road winds north for 7 miles before reaching the waterfront again at **Dungeness Spit,** where a 5.5-mile-long sand spit, the country's longest, protects a shellfish-rich wildlife refuge.

Cyclists and kayakers in particular like to stay near Sequim at the waterfront **Juan de Fuca Cottages** (182 Marine Dr., 360/683-4433, $120 and up), across from Dungeness Bay on a peaceful road about seven miles northwest of town.

Port Angeles

A busy industrial city at the center of the northern Olympic Peninsula, **Port Angeles** (pop. 19,038) makes a handy base for visiting the nearby wilderness of Olympic National Park. The town is slowly but surely evolving from its traditional dependence on logging, and the waterfront, which once hummed to the sound of lumber and pulp mills, is now bustling with tourists wandering along a 6.5-mile walking trail and enjoying the sealife (sea slugs, starfish, and octopuses) on display at the small but enjoyable **Feiro Marine Life Center** (daily 10am-5pm summer, daily noon-5pm off-season, $5 adults), on the centrally located Port Angeles City Pier.

Malls, gas stations, and fast-food franchises line the US-101 frontage through town, but life in Port Angeles, for locals and visitors alike, centers on the attractive downtown area, two blocks inland from the waterfront around Lincoln Street and 1st Street. Here cafés like **First Street Haven** (107 E. 1st St., 360/457-0352) offer great

TOWARD SEATTLE: PORT GAMBLE

You have a number of options if you're traveling to or from Port Townsend. You can follow US-101 around the western Olympic Peninsula, or take a ferry via Whidbey Island and explore it and the even prettier San Juan Islands to the north. Last, but not least, you can take a middle route across the Kitsap Peninsula, then catch a ferry to **Seattle** (see page 476).

This last route, which includes a trip on the frequent Washington State Ferries between Kingston and Edmonds, has the great advantage of taking you through **Port Gamble,** a slice of New England on the shores of Puget Sound. Owned and run by the Pope & Talbot Lumber Company from the 1850s until the mill shut down in 1995, the entire town is a National Historic Landmark District, with dozens of immaculate Victorian buildings standing along maple tree-lined streets. After wandering past the saltbox houses, have a look inside the large **Port Gamble General Store and Café** (32400 NE Rainier Ave., 360/297-7636), which includes a seashell museum, a local history museum ($4), and a popular café.

breakfasts and good yet inexpensive soup-and-salad lunches, while amiable bars and pubs draw bikers, hikers, and loggers with their pub grub. If you're waiting for a boat, or are fresh off one, more places to eat and drink surround the ferry terminal.

Places to stay in Port Angeles vary. You'll find highway motels, including the **Quality Inn Uptown** (101 E. 2nd St., 360/457-9434, $89 and up), and the **Red Lion Hotel Port Angeles** (360/452-9215, $129 and up), on the water at the foot of Lincoln Street. There are also many characterful B&Bs.

Hurricane Ridge

High above Port Angeles, **Hurricane Ridge** provides the most popular access to Olympic National Park. A paved road twists and turns 17 miles up a steep 7 percent grade to the mile-high summit, where, on a clear day, you can gape at the breathtaking 360-degree views of mountain, valley, and sea. A lodge at the crest provides food and drink, and a concession offers ski and snowshoe rentals on winter weekends. Trails lead down into the backcountry, where you're likely to spot marmots, deer, and bald eagles—and if you're lucky, maybe an elk or a mountain lion. From Hurricane Ridge, thrill-seeking drivers and mountain bikers may get a kick out of Obstruction Point Road, a twisting gravel road that continues (without guardrails!) for another eight miles along the crest from the parking lot. In winter, the snowed-in road becomes a popular cross-country skiing trail.

The peaks and coastal valleys of Olympic National Park receive as much as 200 inches of rainfall each year, while the nearby town of Sequim garners an average of just 15-17 inches annually.

After 20 years of legal wrangling, the Elwah Dam and Lake Aldwell, west of Port Angeles along US-101, were removed in 2011 to enable the river's natural ecosystem and salmon fishery to return.

Apart from the area right around Hurricane Ridge, most of the Olympic National Park backcountry is fairly wet and rugged. If you plan to camp overnight, be prepared, and be sure to get a permit from the Olympic National Park Visitor Center (360/565-3130) in Port Angeles, just south of US-101 on the road up to Hurricane Ridge. This is also the best place to pick up general

OLYMPIC NATIONAL PARK

Olympic National Park, in the heart of the Olympic Peninsula, is a diversely beautiful corner of the country, combining features of Maine's rocky coast and the snow-capped peaks of the Rocky Mountains with the unique rainforests covering the park's Pacific coastal valleys. The rugged, nearly million-acre landscape, ranging from rocky shores to impassably dense forests, resisted exploitation and development until the turn of the 20th century, when local conservationists persuaded Teddy Roosevelt to declare much of the peninsula a national monument, a movement that eventually resulted in the establishment of Olympic National Park in 1938.

There are no roads and few trails across the peninsula, so you have to choose your points of entry depending upon what you want to see. The different areas of Olympic National Park are covered in the surrounding pages, but the most popular part of the park is Hurricane Ridge, which rises high above Port Angeles and offers great views of the silvery peaks and the many glaciers that flank them. (The wildflowers can be spectacular in late spring.)

At the northwestern corner of the park, Lake Crescent sits serenely amid the forests and peaks, while on the western slopes, the temperate rainforests of the usually wet and rainy river valleys hold some of the world's largest trees, all draped with a thick fabric of mosses. At the western edge of the peninsula, the almost completely undeveloped Pacific Ocean coastline, added to the park in 1953, offers miles of sandy beaches and rocky headlands, littered only with driftwood logs and vibrant tide pools.

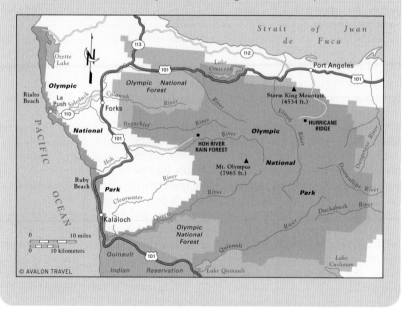

information on the rest of the park, which extends all the way west to the rainforest areas along the coastal valleys.

Lake Crescent

One of the most idyllic spots in the entire Pacific Northwest, the fjord-like **Lake Crescent,** over 8 miles long and some 624 feet deep, lies right alongside two-lane US-101, just 18 miles west of Port Angeles. The placid surface reflects the clouds and surrounding peaks, including 4,537-foot Mt. Storm King. To appreciate the tranquil beauty, rent a rowboat from the Lake Crescent Lodge and float around under your own steam. Starting from the lodge, a popular mile-long hike follows a well-maintained nature trail up to the delicate cascade of 90-foot **Marymere Falls,** while along the north shore an abandoned railroad grade is open to hikers and mountain bikers.

Incomparably situated along US-101 on the lake's southeast shore, **Lake Crescent Lodge** (360/928-3211 or 888/896-3818, open May-Jan. only, except for the Roosevelt Fireplace Cabins, open on the weekends, $156 and up) was originally built in 1915 and has been hosting visitors ever since. Fairly rustic rooms are available in the old lodge, which also has a cozy dining room. Other accommodations are available in the adjacent cabins and motel, though the whole place is booked solid on summer weekends, so reserve as early as you can.

In the forested hills above US-101, **Sol Duc Hot Springs Resort** (866/476-5382, $1 and up) has family-friendly cabins and a restaurant set around a swimming pool and natural hot spring (around $15 for nonguests).

Hwy-112: Strait of Juan de Fuca

The **Strait of Juan de Fuca,** the narrow inlet that links the open Pacific with Puget Sound and divides the United States from Canada, was named for the Greek sailor (real name: Apóstolos Valerianos) who first mapped it while working for the Spanish crown in 1592. On a clear day, you can get some great views across the strait from Hwy-112, which runs along the shore from US-101 all the way to the tip of the Olympic Peninsula at Neah Bay. Though it looks like a great drive on the map, Hwy-112 is a narrow and winding road with some surprisingly steep hills and thick woods that block much of the view, all of which, in addition to the plentiful logging trucks, can make it less than ideal for bicycling or even a scenic drive.

Along Hwy-112, you may pass a pair of fish-headed, human-legged, sneaker-wearing statues. Don't be alarmed.

Neah Bay and Cape Flattery

From the crossroads at **Sappho** on US-101, Hwy-113 leads north, linking up with Hwy-112 on a long and winding 44-mile detour through Clallam Bay to **Cape Flattery,** the northwesternmost tip of the continental United States. The highway is paved as far as the town of **Neah Bay** (pop. 865), a tiny and somewhat bedraggled community that's the center of the Makah Indian Reservation. Salmon and halibut fishing, both by Makah and by visitors, is about the only activity here, although the community does have the impressive and modern **Makah Museum** (360/645-2711, daily, $6), one of the best anthropological museums in the state. Most of the displays are of artifacts uncovered in 1970, when a winter storm exposed the pristine remains of a 500-year-old coastal village that had been buried in a mudslide—the Pompeii of the Pacific Northwest. Other galleries display finely crafted baskets, a full-scale longhouse complete with recorded chants, and a whaling canoe from which fearless Makah harpooners would jump into the surf and sew up the jaws of dying whales to keep them from sinking. The museum gift shop displays and sells a variety of high-quality arts and crafts made by Makah people. For fascinating insights into Makah worldviews, check out Robert Sullivan's thought-provoking book A Whale Hunt: How a Native-American Village Did What No One Thought It Could.

Cape Flattery

The Hwy-112/113 route twists along the rocky and wooded shore of the Strait of Juan de Fuca, but reaching the actual cape itself isn't difficult. From Neah Bay, the well-maintained western half of the Cape Loop Road winds along the Pacific to a parking area that gives access to a trail that brings you to the top of a cliff overlooking the crashing surf and offshore **Tatoosh Island.** On a sunny day it's a gorgeous vista, but if the weather is less than perfect (which it often is), your time would be much better spent inside the Makah Museum.

Forks

Bending southwest along the banks of the Sol Duc River, US-101 passes through miles of green forests under ever-gray skies to reach **Forks** (pop. 3,532), the commercial center of the northwestern Olympic Peninsula. Named for its location astride the Sol Duc and Bogachiel Rivers, Forks is a die-hard lumber town grappling with the inevitable change to more ecologically sustainable alternatives, mainly tourism. Visitors come to fish for steelhead during the late-summer runs, to beachcomb along the rugged coast, or to visit the remarkable rainforests of Olympic National Park. Today, the main attractions are related to the wildly popular teenage vampire novels and films of The Twilight Saga, which were set here in Forks (the movies were filmed elsewhere). You can also visit the quirky **Forks Timber Museum** (360/374-9663, daily, $3), on US-101 on the south edge of town, packed with handsaws, chainsaws, and other logging gear as well as antique cooking stoves and displays telling the town's history. There's also a forest-fire lookout tower perched outside the upper floor gallery.

The old-growth forests of **Olympic National Park** provide prime habitat for the northern spotted owl, an endangered species whose preservation has sparked heated debate throughout the Pacific Northwest.

With three gas stations and five motels, Forks is not a metropolis by any stretch of the imagination, but it does offer the best range of services between Port Angeles and Aberdeen. **Sully's Drive-In** (220 N. Forks Ave.) is a good burger stand on US-101 at the north end of town. There are also a couple of Chinese and

FERRIES TO VICTORIA, BRITISH COLUMBIA

From Port Angeles, the **Black Ball Ferry Line** (360/457-4491, around $64 per car and driver one-way, plus $18.50 per additional person) carries cars and passengers, shuttling across the water to and from pretty Victoria, the provincial capital of British Columbia, one of Canada's most popular destinations. Ships leave Port Angeles at the middle of the attractively landscaped waterfront and arrive near the center of Victoria, making for a great day trip from either place. At the Port Angeles dock there's a helpful information center packed with maps and brochures on Victoria and the rest of BC, or you can call **Tourism Victoria** (800/663-3883).

Mexican places, plus pretty good pies at **Pacific Pizza** (870 S. Forks Ave.). Stay at **The Forks Motel** (351 S. Forks Ave., 360/374-6243, $63 and up) or a more peaceful B&B, the **Miller Tree Inn Bed and Breakfast** (654 E. Division St., 360/374-6806 or 800/943-6563, $125 and up), about half a mile east of US-101.

South of Forks along US-101, **Bogachiel State Park** (360/374-6356, around $25 for tents, $35 for RV hookups) has over 100 forested acres of nice campsites (with showers!) along the Bogachiel River. Sites are first-come, first-served.

For more information, contact the Forks **visitors center** (360/374-2531), next to the Timber Museum, which also serves as clearinghouse for *Twilight*-related tourism.

Hoh Rainforest

If you have time to visit only one of the lush rainforest areas of Washington's northwest coast, head for the **Hoh Rainforest,** 12 miles south of Forks and then 18 miles east along a well-signed and well-paved road. Not only is this the most easily accessible of these incredibly lush old-growth areas, the Hoh Rainforest is also among the least disturbed, with a thick wet blanket of vibrant green ferns, mosses, and lichens covering every inch of the earth at the

Hoh Rainforest

foot of massive hemlocks, cedars, and towering Sitka spruce. Displays inside the visitors center tell all about the forest's flora and fauna and how they are affected by the massive rainfall here—upward of 140 inches every year. There's also a wheelchair-accessible nature trail and a wide range of hiking trails, including the quickest access to the icy summit of 7,965-foot Mt. Olympus, 22 miles away in the glacier-packed alpine highlands at the heart of the park.

The closest services to the Hoh Rainforest are in Forks, but budget travelers may want to take advantage of the $10-a-night bunks at the amiable **Rain Forest Hostel** (360/374-2270), 23 miles south of Forks along US-101 (between mile markers 169

If you're lucky, you might spy one of the rare Roosevelt elk, whose protection was one of the reasons Olympic National Park was established; if you're unlucky, you might come face-to-face with a mountain lion, which can be dangerous but generally avoids contact with humans.

and 170), midway between the Hoh Rainforest and the coast at Ruby Beach.

Kalaloch and the Pacific Beaches

Looping around the northern Olympic Peninsula, US-101 finally reaches the coast 27 miles south of Forks at **Ruby Beach,** where wave-sculpted sea stacks frame a photogenic driftwood-strewn cove. From

Ruby Beach

Ruby Beach, US-101 runs south through the wild coastal section of Olympic National Park, which is almost always foggy and cool, even when the weather is sunny and hot just a mile inland. While almost the entire coast south from Cape Flattery is protected within the national park, this is the only easily accessible stretch. Parking areas along the highway, numbered from Beach 6 to Beach 1 north to south, give access to 20 miles of generally deserted beach, backed by rocky bluffs and packed with tide pools, driftwood castles, and an incredible variety of flotsam and jetsam.

At the southern end of this short but sweet stretch of coastline, between Beach 2 and Beach 3, about 25 miles north of Lake Quinault, **Kalaloch Lodge** (866/662-9969, $1 and up) is a modern resort with a coffee shop and a nice restaurant overlooking a picturesque cove. There's also a gas station, a summer-only **ranger station** across US-101, and an ocean-side **campground** just to the north.

Lake Quinault

Spreading in a broad valley at the southwest corner of Olympic National Park, **Lake Quinault** offers lush rainforest groves within a short walk or drive of most creature comforts. The lake has served for decades as a popular resort destination—cabins, lodges, and stores dating from the 1920s line the southern shore, just outside the park boundary. The old-growth forests here have survived intact, though the naked tracts of clear-cut timber along US-101 north and south of the lake give a good sense of what the area might have looked like had Teddy Roosevelt and friends not stepped in to protect it around the turn of the 20th century.

Before or after the hike, stop at the **U.S. Forest Service ranger station** (360/288-2525) on the south shore, where you can get details of the other excellent hikes in the Lake Quinault

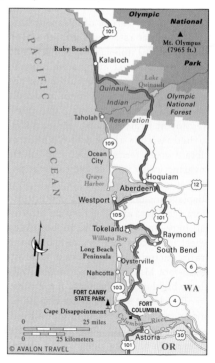

area and pick up a map of the guided driving tour around the lake, including the location of the many record-size trees. The roughly four-mile-long **Quinault Loop Trail** winds on a path from the ranger station along crashing Cascade Creek up through an old-growth rainforest of alders and big-leaf maples, whose leaves grow upward of 12 inches across and provide some splendid fall color. Midway along, the trail crosses a raised wooden boardwalk through a fecund cedar swamp, then drops down again along another creek before returning by way of the lakeshore.

On the lakeshore right next to the ranger station, historic **Lake Quinault Lodge** (360/288-2900, $180 and up) is well worth a look, with a rustic but spacious lobby opening onto lakefront lawns, though the rooms could do with some TLC. The **Rain Forest Resort Village** (360/288-2535, $95 and up), at the east end of the lake, besides offering comfortable and reasonably priced accommodations (from camping to cabins) and good food in the Salmon House Restaurant, also holds the **World's Largest Spruce Tree,** a 191-foot giant.

From US-101 at **Hoquiam,** Hwy-109 runs west and north along the Pacific Ocean through a series of small fishing ports and beach resorts to the heavily logged lands of the Quinault Indian Reservation.

Grays Harbor: Hoquiam and Aberdeen

The Olympic Peninsula is cut off from the southern Washington coast by the spade-shaped bay of **Grays Harbor,** named for an early American sea captain and explorer, Robert Gray. Long the state's prime lumber port, Grays Harbor still processes huge piles of trees, but in many ways what's most interesting is the contrast between the two towns here, Hoquiam and Aberdeen.

At the western end of Grays Harbor, tidy **Hoquiam** (pop. 8,726; kind of rhymes with "requiem") celebrates its lumber-based history with an annual Loggers PlayDay bash, complete with ax-throwing and tree-climbing competitions, in early September. The rest of the year, get a feel for the bygone days of the lumber industry at the grand old timber-magnate mansion now housing **The Polson Museum** (1611 Riverside Ave., 360/533-5862, Wed.-Sun., $4), on US-101. Not surprisingly, it's devoted to local history, with information on logging.

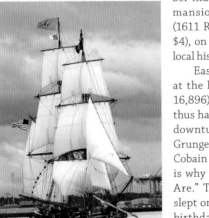

The *Lady Washington* is a replica of one of the first American ships to explore the West Coast.

East of Hoquiam along the Chehalis River at the head of Grays Harbor, **Aberdeen** (pop. 16,896) is much more heavily industrialized and thus has been even harder hit by the continuing downturn in the Northwest timber industry. Grunge-rock hero and Nirvana lead singer Kurt Cobain grew up in and around Aberdeen, which is why the city limits signs say "Come as You Are." There's also a couch Cobain may have slept on, and a mural commemorating his 50th birthday, in Aberdeen's **history museum** (113 E. 3rd St.). Ace road-trip photographer Lee Friedlander is from Aberdeen too. The downtown area has more than a few rough edges, but it also holds one of the more high-profile of the state-sponsored efforts to move from timber to tourism: **Grays Harbor Historical Seaport** (360/532-8611, Mon.-Sun., $5 donation), a mile south of Hwy-12. Reconstructions of American explorer Captain Robert Gray's ships, the *Lady Washington* and *Hawaiian Chieftain,* can be toured when they're not away on regular goodwill cruises. The original *Lady Washington* was the first American vessel to visit the area, way back in 1788, and the replica was completed here in 1989 to celebrate the Washington State centennial.

Hwy-105: Westport and Tokeland

Between Hoquiam and Raymond, US-101 cuts inland from the coast, while an alternative route, Hwy-105, loops to the west past miles of cranberry bogs (and occasional wild elk) through the salmon-fishing town of **Westport.** Once called "The Salmon Capital of the World," and still a prime place for watching migrating gray whales, Westport is a busy port—and one of Washington's few good surfing, clam-digging, and surf-kayaking beaches. The whole place comes to life during the Labor Day seafood festival, but any time of the year the best stop is **Brady's Oysters** (360/268-0077), at the foot of the Hwy-105 bridge from Aberdeen, where you can buy fresh-shucked bivalves by the half gallon.

At the south edge of the peninsula, absorb more coastal character at the **Tokeland Hotel** (360/267-7006, $89-105), off Hwy-105 on the north shore of Willapa Bay, a truly historic landmark that has been welcoming visitors since the 1880s. Expect old-fashioned lodgings (shared baths), a cozy family-style dining room serving classic dishes (pot roast with mashed potatoes and such), and unforgettable ambience.

Willapa Bay: Raymond and South Bend

One of the country's prime oystering grounds, **Willapa Bay** is sheltered from the Pacific by the Long Beach Peninsula and fed by the Nasalle, Willapa, and North Fall Rivers. There are few towns or even villages on this stretch of US-101, which winds past tidal marshes, cattle ranches, and extensively clear-cut forests—which billboards proclaim to be "America's first industrial tree farm," giving dates of harvest, planting, and reharvest on a roughly 40-year cycle.

At the northeast corner of Willapa Bay, on the south bank of the Willapa River, stand two towns that jointly embody the natural resource-based history and economy of the Pacific Northwest: **Raymond** (pop. 2,882) has the lumber mills, while **South Bend** (pop. 1,637) calls itself the "Oyster Capital of the World." South Bend's other claim to fame is its landmark **Pacific County Courthouse** (Mon.-Fri.), which since 1910 has loomed like a mini Taj Mahal on a hill just east of US-101. Step inside for a look at the 30-foot stained-glass dome above the rotunda, and wander through the lushly landscaped park next door.

If you want to stretch your legs, Raymond and South Bend are linked by the nice **Willapa Hills Trail,** a walking and cycling path that follows an old railroad right-of-way along the Willapa River amid some engaging roadside metal sculptures of people canoeing, bird-watching, cycling, fishing, and generally enjoying the great outdoors.

> If the weather's right for a picnic, fresh shellfish can be had at bargain prices—live in the shell, or pre-shucked by the half gallon—from the area's many producers, wholesalers, and roadside stands. Look for them all along US-101 and up the Long Beach Peninsula.

Long Beach Peninsula

On the western side of Willapa Bay, the **Long Beach Peninsula** stretches for 28 miles of hard-packed sandy beaches along the roiling Pacific Ocean. Away from the few small towns, beaches and breakers abound along here, and you won't have any problem finding peace and solitude. The center of activity on the Long Beach Peninsula is the town of **Long Beach,** two miles from US-101, with a wanderable collection of crafts galleries and souvenir shops. A short walk west from "downtown" Long Beach, a wooden boardwalk winds along the coastal dunes, leading to a rare sight: the reconstructed skeleton of a gray whale. Lewis and Clark saw similar bones when they passed by 200-plus years ago, and a **Discovery Trail** linking Corps of Discovery locations runs from here south to Ilwaco, near the mouth of the Columbia River.

"World's Largest Frying Pan"

If you can bear to stretch your budget a little, Long Beach is home to one of the coast's best B&Bs, historic **The Shelburne Inn** (4415 Pacific Way, 360/642-2442, $139 and up), located in the Seaview neighborhood (Pacific Way is also known as Hwy-103, the main road). The Shelburne Inn also houses a friendly pub. Perhaps most appealing of all: Long Beach is also the home of the nearly 10-foot-in-diameter **"World's Largest Frying Pan,"** which sits on a rack across from the one-of-a-kind **Marsh's Free Museum** (409 S. Pacific Ave., 360/642-2188), a totally tacky and wonderfully kitsch collection of postcards, peep shows, and old-time arcade games.

The rest of the slender Long Beach Peninsula is quite quiet, dotted with cranberry bogs and historic fishing and oystering towns. **Oysterville** is the peninsula's oldest community, with some nifty historic homes dating back to the 1850s. The peninsula comes to an end in the north at **Leadbetter Point State Park,** a great place for watching gulls, hawks, eagles, and migratory seabirds passing through on the Pacific Flyway.

Cape Disappointment

The high headland marking the place where the Columbia River finally merges into the Pacific Ocean, **Cape Disappointment** was named by the early explorer Captain John Meares, who in 1788 incorrectly interpreted the treacherous sandbars offshore to mean that, despite reports to the contrary, there was neither a major river nor any mythical Northwest Passage here.

Besides the grand view of the raging ocean, the best reason to visit the cape is to tour the small but worthwhile **Lewis and Clark Interpretive Center** (360/642-3029, daily, $5), incongruously built atop a World War II-era artillery emplacement a short walk from the end of the road. On November 7, 1805, after five months and more than 4,000 miles, the explorers finally laid eyes on the Pacific from this point, and then they sat through nine days of continuous rain before fleeing south to Oregon. Displays inside the museum give the overall context for their journey of discovery, walking you through the different stages of their two-year round-trip. The small **"Cape D" lighthouse** stands atop a cliff, a half-mile walk from the Lewis and Clark museum, which is 200 feet above the Pacific Ocean. The more impressively photogenic **North Head Lighthouse,** on the ocean side of the peninsula a mile north of the museum, was built in 1898.

The entire 1,882-acre area around the cape, including miles of beaches backed by rugged cliffs, is protected from development within **Cape Disappointment State Park** (360/642-3078), which has hiking, camping, and overnight lodgings in historic quarters next to North Head Lighthouse.

The eight-mile **Discovery Trail** heads north to the town of Long Beach and a series of thought-provoking installations by architect Maya Lin (creator of the Washington DC Vietnam Veterans Memorial). Called the **Confluence Project,** and located along the riverfront east as far as Columbia Gorge, these works all deal with the coming together of the natural and artificial worlds, as well as the interaction of explorers and Native Americans. The installations range from driftwood columns, boardwalks, and interpretive trails (lined in places by quotations from Lewis and Clark's diaries) to a sculptural basalt fish-cleaning table.

The nearest services to Cape Disappointment—gas stations and a couple of cafés—are two miles away, back on US-101 in the rough-and-tumble fishing port of **Ilwaco,** where you can also enjoy the sophisticated yet simple and fresh seafood prepared at **Ole Bob's Seafood Market & Grill** (151 Howerton Way, 360/642-4332), on the harbor.

Southeast of Ilwaco, toward the Oregon border, US-101 winds along the north bank of the Columbia River, giving good views of the mighty river's five-mile-wide mouth.

OREGON

Rarely losing sight of the Pacific Ocean during its 340-mile jaunt along the Oregon coast, US-101 winds past rockbound coast, ancient forests, and innumerable towns and villages. While the region also has its share of strip towns and places where the timber boom went bust, the beach loops, historic restorations, and more state parks per mile than any place in the country soften its few hard edges. Every 20 miles or so, you'll pass through attractive, if moderately touristy, towns populated by at most a few thousand people. As a general rule, it's the mileage between these hamlets that explains why most people visit: to take in one of the most dramatic meetings of rock and tide in the world.

Starting in the north along the Columbia River at historic **Astoria,** one of the oldest settlements in the western United States, the route winds along the ocean past the different beachfront hamlets of **Seaside** and **Cannon Beach** before edging slightly inland through the rich dairy lands of **Tillamook County.** Midway along, the popular vacation spots of **Lincoln City, Newport,** and **Florence** form the most developed corridor along the coast, but it's still easy to reach unpeopled stretches, especially at the remarkable **Oregon Dunes** stretching to the south. The dunes end abruptly at the heavily industrial port of **Coos Bay,** beyond which the natural beauty returns with a string of state parks and the diverse coastal towns of **Bandon, Port Orford, Gold Beach,** and **Brookings.**

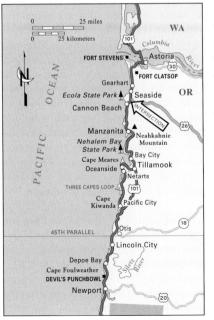

Astoria

The oldest American city west of the Rockies, **Astoria** (pop. 9,477) is an upbeat mix of lovingly preserved past and busy contemporary commerce. Houses perched atop high hills overlook the Columbia River, creating a favorite backdrop for Hollywood movies. Despite its picturesque appearance, Astoria supports an active commercial fishing fleet, and dozens of tugboats guide tankers and container ships across the treacherous sandbars. Founded by and named after fur-trade magnate John Jacob Astor in 1811, Astoria protected the tenuous U.S. claim to the Pacific Coast until the opening of the Oregon Trail brought substantial settlement. By the turn of the 20th century, Astoria was still Oregon's second-largest city, but the downturn in both salmon fishing and logging since the end of World War II has caused an economic decline that town officials have looked to tourism to overcome.

US-101 crosses the Columbia River on the toll-free high-level Astoria-Megler Bridge, completed in 1966, which drops you at the west end of the downtown waterfront. To get a sense of the lay of the land, follow the signs along 16th Street up Coxcomb Hill to the **Astoria Column** (daily dawn-dusk, $5 per car) for a view of the Columbia meeting the ocean, the coastal plain south to Tillamook Head, and the snowcapped Cascade Range (including, on a clear day, Mt. St. Helens) on the eastern horizon. A mosaic chronicling local history is wrapped like a ribbon around the column, tracing the many significant events in the town's past. A spiral staircase climbs to the top.

By state law, there is no self-service gasoline in Oregon; all stations have attendants who pump the gas for you. There's no sales tax, either.

Back downtown, **Flavel House Museum** (441 8th St., daily, $6) is a Queen Anne-style Victorian showplace restored as an elegantly furnished museum of wealthy Columbia River pilot George Flavel. A half mile east, near the foot of 17th Street on the north side of waterfront Marine Drive, the **Columbia River Maritime Museum** (503/325-2323, daily, $14) displays a large and impressive collection that tells the story of the lifeblood of this community: the Columbia River.

Much as Forks, Washington, has benefited from its connections with the *Twilight* books and films, Astoria gets a boost in tourism numbers thanks to its starring role in the 1980s Steven Spielberg teen adventure film *The Goonies*.

Fortify yourself at one of the many good seafood places along the water, starting at the funky and ever-popular **Columbian Café** (1114 Marine Dr., 503/325-2233, breakfast and lunch only), where, for over 37 years, chef Uriah Hulsey has been preparing all sorts of fresh veggie-friendly food in an impossibly cramped galley kitchen. Inspired by the chef's youthful immersion in the Cajun-Creole traditions of Louisiana, meals are massive yet reasonably priced, so be sure to arrive with an appetite. The café has been so popular they've expanded next door with a **Voodoo Room** cocktail bar and pizza joint, which spills over into the restored 1940s movie house next door. There's no better place to get a feel for Astoria, which once promoted itself through the slogan "We Ain't Quaint."

To find out about local issues and current events on the northern Oregon coast, pick up a copy of the excellent Daily Astorian newspaper, or tune to commercial-free **KMUN 91.9 FM** for NPR news and diverse programming.

Another Astoria eating option is the casual **Ship Inn** (503/325-0033), serving halibut fish 'n' chips under the bridge at Marine Drive and 2nd Street. Foodies might want to visit adjacent **Josephson's Smokehouse** (106 Marine Dr., 503/325-2190) to sample the delicious array of smoked salmon and Native American-style salmon jerky, which is prepared on the premises and sold all over the country. One last option for excellent fish 'n' chips is **Bowpicker Fish & Chips** (1634 Duane St.,

503/791-2942), where chunks of fresh beer-battered albacore tuna and more is served up in an old fishing boat moored on the corner of 17th and Duane Streets, a block west of the Maritime Museum. Seating is outdoors at picnic tables, so they close during windy and wet weather (and when they sell out of fish).

To absorb a full portion of Astoria's addictive ambience, stay the night at the river-view **Astoria Crest Motel** (5366 Leif Erickson Dr., 503/325-3141 or 800/421-3141, $69 and up), three miles east of town along US-30, or in town at the luxurious and historic **Hotel Elliott** (357 12th St., 503/325-2222, $129 and up). Astoria also has a handful of nice B&Bs. **Fort Stevens State Park,** off US-101 at the mouth of the Columbia River on the way to Fort Clatsop, was the only continental U.S. fortification bombed during World War II, sustaining a shelling from a Japanese submarine on June 21, 1942. It's now a spacious state park offering camping, cabins, and yurts.

Fort Clatsop

In the conifer forests six miles south of Astoria and three miles east of US-101, and part of the extensive Lewis and Clark National Historical Park, the **Fort Clatsop National Memorial** (503/861-2471, daily, $5 per person) is a credible reconstruction of the encampment Lewis and Clark and company constructed during the winter of 1805-1806. Now the centerpiece of the sprawling multistate Lewis and Clark National Historical Park, Fort Clatsop has been fully (and in many ways more accurately) rebuilt after a 2005 fire destroyed the first circa-1955 replica. The fort itself is joined by a range of exhibits in the visitors center. A longer trail, 13 miles roundtrip, leads down to the coast north of Gearhart. Summertime costumed rangers help conjure the travails of two centuries ago. The expedition spent three miserable months here, mingling occasionally with the indigenous Clatsop and Chinook peoples but mostly growing moldy in the incessant rain and damp while being bitten by fleas, sewing new moccasins, and making salt in preparation for the return journey across the continent.

Gearhart

In between burly Astoria and the boisterous beach resort of Seaside, but a world away from its neighbors in terms of character and ambience, the tiny town of **Gearhart** (pop. 1,462) was the summer vacation home of influential chef and cookbook author James Beard. Beard's culinary legacy lives on in the **Pacific Way Bakery & Café** (601 Pacific Way, 503/738-0245, Thurs.-Mon.), a half mile west of US-101, which offers the coast's best coffees and croissants, along with four-star lunches and dinners. Like many places along the Oregon coast, it's closed Tuesday and Wednesday.

Seaside

Nothing along the Oregon coast prepares you for the carnival ambience of downtown **Seaside** (pop. 6,457), one of Oregon's oldest seafront resorts. Ben Holladay, who built a resort here in the 1870s, included a racetrack, a zoo, and a plush hotel to lure Portlanders to ride his rail line to the beach. Come during spring break, or on a weekend during July or August, and join the 50,000 or more visitors wandering among the saltwater-taffy stands and video-game arcades along Broadway, or cruising the concrete boardwalk (called The Prom) along the beach.

Where Broadway meets the beach, a small traffic circle known locally as The Turnaround is marked by a statue and a sign proclaiming the town "The End of the Lewis and Clark Trail." South of here, between Beach Drive and The Prom, is a replica of the Lewis and Clark salt cairn, where the explorers boiled seawater non-stop for seven weeks to produce enough salt to preserve meat for their return trip east. From the south end of Seaside, you can follow a challenging but rewarding six-mile trail over Tillamook Head to Ecola State Park.

statue of explorers Lewis and Clark at the end of the trail in Seaside

A half mile north of downtown, housed in a wood-shingled old motor court on the banks of the Necanicum River, the **Seaside Lodge & International Hostel** (930 N. Holladay Dr., 503/738-7911) has dorm beds, private rooms, canoes and kayaks, and an espresso bar. There are dozens of motels and a handful of B&Bs in Seaside, booked solid in summer and serene, verging on lonely, come wintertime. The best breakfasts are served up on Broadway just west of US-101 at the **Firehouse Grill** (841 Broadway, 503/717-5502). For fish 'n' chips , head to the south edge of town along US-101, where the no-frills **Bell Buoy** (503/738-6348) has daily fresh seafood and excellent crab cocktails, best eaten on the outdoor deck overlooking the Necanicum River. There are also pizza places and ice cream stands all over Seaside.

This part of the Pacific Coast marks the beginning of our **Oregon Trail** route, which runs east across the country along a combination of US-6, US-20, and US-26. Coverage of the route begins on page 558; **Portland,** just over an hour or so inland from Seaside and Cannon Beach, is covered on page 566.

Ecola State Park

Just north of Cannon Beach, a mile south of the junction of US-101 and US-26 from Portland, the rainforested access road through **Ecola State Park** (503/436-2844, day use only, $5 per car) leads to one of the most photographed views on the coast: Looking south you can see Haystack Rock and Cannon Beach with Neahkahnie Mountain looming above them. Out to sea, the sight of **Tillamook Rock Lighthouse** to the northwest is also striking. Operational from 1881 to 1957, the lighthouse is now used as a repository for the ashes of people who've been cremated.

The rest of Ecola State Park protects a series of rugged headlands stretching for nine miles along the coast, with many forested hiking trails, including some of the most scenic portions of the Oregon Coast Trail system. The park also marks the southernmost extent of Lewis and Clark's cross-country expedition. Clark and a few other members of the Corps of Discovery expedition traversed

Cannon Beach

the area in search of supplements to their diet of hardtack and dried salmon. The word *ecola* means "whale" in the Chinookan tongue and was affixed to this region by the Lewis and Clark expedition, who found one of these leviathans washed up on a beach. They happily bought 300 pounds of tangy whale blubber from local Native Americans, but these days you'd better bring your own lunch to picnic atop bluffs with sweeping views of the rock-strewn Pacific. The view from the top of **Tillamook Head,** which rises 1,200 feet above the sea at the heart of the park, was memorialized by explorer William Clark as "the grandest and most pleasing prospect" he had ever beheld.

Cannon Beach

Unlike many Oregon coast towns, **Cannon Beach** (pop. 1,690) is hidden from the highway, but it's one place you won't want to miss. Though it's little more than a stone's throw south of boisterous Seaside, Cannon Beach has long been known as an artists' colony, and while it has grown considerably in recent years thanks to its popularity as a weekend escape from Portland, it retains a peaceful, rustic atmosphere.

Every summer, Cannon Beach hosts one of the largest and most enjoyable **sand castle competitions** on the West Coast, with some 10,000 spectators and as many as 1,000 participants turning out with their buckets and spades. In terms of traditional tourist attractions, there's not a lot to do, but Cannon Beach is an unbeatable place in which to stop and unwind, or to take long walks along the nine-mile strand and then retreat indoors to the many good galleries, cafés, and restaurants. For breakfast or brunch, fill up on eggs

Haystack Rock

Benedict at **The Lazy Susan Café** (126 N. Hemlock St., 503/436-2816, Wed.-Mon.); it also serves a stupendous array of ice cream at its "scoop shop" up the street. Another great casual gourmet place to eat is **Ecola Seafoods** (208 N. Spruce St., 503/436-9130), a market and restaurant selling and serving locally caught fish and shellfish—including tempura-battered chinook salmon, grilled halibut, smoked mussels, and an excellent $5 chowder.

Reasonably priced rooms near the beach and town can be found at the ocean-front **Sea Sprite at Haystack Rock** (280 S. Nebesna St., 503/436-2266, $129 and up).

South of Cannon Beach, the beach loop runs along a spectacular grouping of volcanic basalt plugs, notably 235-foot-high **Haystack Rock.** Elsewhere along the Oregon coast, there are at least two more geological outcrops called Haystack Rock, a bigger one off Cape Kiwanda and another down near Bandon.

Neahkahnie Mountain and Oswald West State Park

South of Cannon Beach, US-101 rises high above the Pacific. Nowhere else along the Oregon coast does the roadbed offer such a sweeping ocean view. Soaring another thousand feet above the highway is **Neahkahnie Mountain,** which offers unsurpassed views up and down the coast. About 10 miles south of Cannon Beach at **Oswald West State Park** (503/368-3575), a half-mile trail winds beneath the highway through an ancient forest to driftwood-laden (and surfer-friendly) **Short Sands Beach** and the tide pools of **Smuggler's Cove.** Named for an early governor of Oregon who successfully proposed preserving and protecting the beaches of Oregon as state (rather than private) property, Oswald West State Park is a good start for longer hikes, to weather-beaten Cape Falcon or across US-101 to the summit of Neahkahnie Mountain.

South of Neahkahnie Mountain, and thus spared much of the stormy coastal weather (annual rainfall hereabouts averages more than 80 inches), is the upscale resort town of **Manzanita.** Nearby **Nehalem Bay State Park** (503/368-5154) has a large campground with hundreds of sites and plenty of hot showers. US-101 continues through a series of small towns before winding inland past the sloughs and dairy country along Tillamook Bay.

Tillamook

Tillamook (pop. 4,935), where cows outnumber people, sprawls over lush grasslands at the southern end of Tillamook Bay. Its motto, "Land of cheese, trees, and ocean breeze," conjures a clear sense of a place where the high school football team is cheered on by shouts of "Go Cheesemakers!" Tillamook (some say the name is a Salish word meaning "land of many waters") is dominated by the

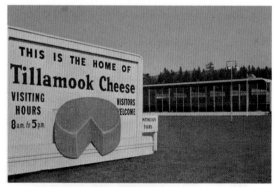
Tillamook Cheese Factory

Tillamook Cheese Factory at the north end of town, one of the busiest tourist draws in the state. Inside, a self-guided tour with informational placards traces Tillamook cheese-making from the last century to the present, and a glassed-in observation area lets you watch the stuff being made and packaged.

Tillamook's other attraction is east of US-101 and south of town. One of the world's largest wooden structures—296 feet wide, 1,072 feet long, and nearly 200 feet tall, enclosing more than seven acres of open-span floor space—has been preserved as the **Tillamook Air Museum** (503/842-1130, Tues.-Sun., $9.50 adults). Built in 1942, the structure is now a museum telling the story of the World War II surveillance blimps kept here by the U.S. Navy. There are also displays about other dirigible craft (like the ill-fated *Hindenburg*) as well as a world-class collection of vintage airplanes (from MiG fighters to an elegant, twin-tailed P-38 Lightning), plus a theater and a restaurant, all making for a fascinating and unusual stop. The building used to be one of a pair of hangars, but the other one burned down in 1992.

Three Capes Loop

US-101 veers inland for 50 miles between Tillamook and Lincoln City, the next sizable town south. If time and weather are on your side, head west along the coast via the well-signed, 40-mile-long **Three Capes Scenic Route.** Running northwest from Tillamook, the loop reaches the mouth of Tillamook Bay at **Cape Meares,** which has a restored 1890 lighthouse and an oddly contorted Sitka spruce known as the Octopus Tree.

Heading south through the coastal villages of **Oceanside** and **Netarts,** the loop proceeds through dairy country until it climbs onto the shoulder of **Cape Lookout,** where a small sign proclaiming "Wildlife Viewing Area" marks the beginning of a 2.5-mile trail that leads through an ancient forest to the tip of the cape, 100-plus feet above the water. Besides the coastal panorama, in winter and spring this is a prime place to view passing gray whales. From the trailhead, the middle path leads to the cape, while others to the left and right lead down to the water. **Cape Lookout State Park** (503/842-4981) has the area's most popular campground, where tent sites, yurts, and cabins come with hot showers and other creature comforts.

> Seven miles south of Tillamook, a turnoff east follows a bumpy, one-mile access road leading to the highest waterfall in Oregon's Coast Range, 319-foot **Munson Creek Falls.** From the parking area at the end of the road, a short trail leads to this year-round cascade.

The Oregon coast's most famous promontory, **Cape Kiwanda,** sees some of the state's wildest surf battering the sandstone headland. Across from the cape is yet another **Haystack Rock,** this one being a 327-foot-tall sea stack, a half mile offshore. Along the beach south of the cape, surfers ride waves while fisherfolk skid their small dories along the sands most afternoons—a sight worth hanging around to see.

The southernmost settlement on this scenic alternative to US-101 is neighboring **Pacific City.**

Otis Café

One of the more unforgettable attractions hereabouts is culinary rather than scenic. It's worth planning your drive around the **Otis Café** (1259 Salmon River Hwy., 541/994-2813, daily breakfast, lunch, and dinner), which immortalizes American road food, including excellent waffles and other breakfast treats, epicurean lunches, and fresh berry pies for dessert. It's located six and a half miles northeast of Lincoln City, just inland off US-101 along Hwy-18, the main road to Portland.

Lincoln City

The most developed section of the Oregon coast stretches for miles along US-101 through **Lincoln City** (pop. 7,930), seven miles of strip malls, outlet stores, fast-food franchises, and motels. With more than 1,000 ocean-side rooms, Lincoln City does offer some of the coast's cheapest lodging, especially in the off-season when sign after sign advertises rooms for as low as $35 a night. Along with inexpensive accommodations, and 24-hour gambling at the Chinook Winds casino, Lincoln City has some great places to eat. After a day on the beach or in the forests, tuck into some four-star fish tacos, chowders, or battered seafood at **J's Fish & Chips** (1800 SE US-101, 541/994-4445).

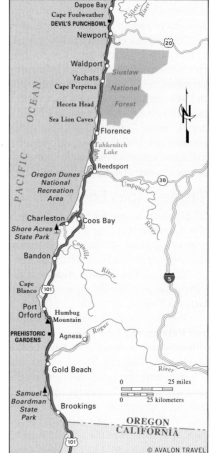

South of Lincoln City, **Siletz Bay** is a bird-watcher's paradise, where hawks and herons and thousands of other seabirds (along with chinook salmon and cutthroat trout) are protected within a federal wildlife refuge.

Depoe Bay

Depoe Bay has an appeal, but so much of its natural beauty is obscured from the highway by gift shops or intruded upon by traffic that you've got to know where to look. In his book *Blue Highways*, William Least Heat-Moon wrote, "Depoe Bay used to be a picturesque fishing village; now it was just picturesque." While it's true that most of the commercial fishing is long gone, you can still park your car along the highway and walk out on the bridge to watch sportfishing boats move through the narrow channel in and out of what the *Guinness Book of Records* rates as the world's smallest navigable natural harbor.

Depoe Bay was originally known as **Depot Bay,** named after a local Siletz Indian who worked at the local U.S. Army depot and called himself Charlie Depot.

Gracie's Sea Hag Restaurant & Lounge (541/765-2734), on US-101 in downtown Depoe Bay, is a time-tested breakfast place—run by the same people for more than 40 years. For a place to stay, try the popular **Inn at Arch Rock** (70 NW Sunset St., 541/765-2560 or 800/767-1835, $89 and up).

Cape Foulweather and the Devil's Punchbowl

Between Depoe Bay and Newport, the roadside scenery along US-101 and the parallel "old road," now signed as the Otter Crest Loop, is dominated by miles of broad beaches and sandstone bluffs, including the 500-foot headland of **Cape**

the Oregon Coast Aquarium

Foulweather, named by Captain James Cook and offering a 360-degree coastal panorama. The Otter Crest Loop has frequently been closed by slides and reconstruction efforts, but you can reach it from many access roads. With fine old bridges and numerous vistas, it's a great drive or bicycle route.

Farther south, midway between Depoe Bay and Newport, the aptly named **Devils Punchbowl** gives a ringside seat on a frothy confrontation between rock and tide. In the parking area you'll find a small lunch café. Other than its famous clam chowder, the claim to fame of this branch of Newport's **Mo's** remains a visit from Bruce Springsteen on June 11, 1987.

Newport

Another old fishing community turned tourist nexus, **Newport** (pop. 9,989) became popular in the 1860s on the strength of sweet-tasting Yaquina Bay oysters, which were in demand from San Francisco to New York City and are still available at local restaurants. Oysters, crabs, and clams, along with sea otters, sea lions, sharks, and seabirds, are the stars of the show at the large and modern **Oregon Coast Aquarium** (541/867-3474, daily, $23 adults), south of Newport across the Yaquina Bay Bridge. The aquarium includes an aquatic aviary, where tufted puffins and other shorebirds cavort in a simulated rockbound coastal habitat, and over 40,000 square feet of similarly ecofriendly exhibits, many of them outdoors.

The coast and inland forests along the Siletz River near Depoe Bay and Newport were the primary location of the Ken Kesey novels and films *One Flew Over the Cuckoo's Nest* and *Sometimes a Great Notion.*

On the north side of the US-101 bridge over Yaquina Bay, turn onto Hurbert Street and head for the bay front, where boatyards and fish-packing plants service a working harbor. Though it's still one of the state's largest fishing ports, much of Newport's bay front has been consumed by souvenir shops, a wax museum, a Ripley's Believe It or Not, and other tourist traps. But you'll also find the original **Mo's** (622 SW Bay Blvd., 541/265-2979), a locally famous seafood restaurant.

North of the harbor is **Nye Beach,** an interesting mélange of old-fashioned beach houses and destination resorts on the western side of US-101. The **Nye Beach Café** (526 NW Coast St., 541/574-1599) serves fresh local fare. The bohemian **Sylvia Beach Hotel** (267 NW Cliff St., 541/265-5428, $105 and up) is *the* place to stay in Newport for anyone of literary bent. All rates include breakfast. Sumptuous dinners are available too.

Waldport

If you want to avoid lines and general tourist bustle, **Waldport** is a nice alternative to the resort towns surrounding it. Tourism is low-key here, and you can still sense the vestiges of the natural resource-based economy, a by-product of the town's proximity to rich timber stands and superlative fishing. Stop along US-101 at the **Alsea Bay Historic Interpretive Center** (541/563-2133) for interesting exhibits on coastal transportation and the local Alsea people, as well as a telescope trained on waterfowl and seals in the bay. The center sits at the southwest foot of the modern span that, in 1995, replaced the historic circa-1936 art deco-style bridge.

Four miles south of Waldport, halfway to Yachats, **Beachside State Recreation Site** (541/563-3220) has a popular campground with hot showers, RV hookups, and a lovely stretch of sandy beach. They also have **yurts** ($45).

Yachats

On the way into **Yachats** (pop. 690; pronounced "YA-hots"), beach loops on either side of the Yachats River give a sense of why the area is called "the gem of the Oregon coast." It's a great place to wander and get lost and found again, especially at the beautiful Ocean Road State Natural Site, where incredible views along a one-mile loop road look out over crashing waves, tide pools, blowholes, and, in winter, gray whales migrating offshore.

Back in town, for the past 30-plus years, **Leroy's Blue Whale** (580 Hwy-101 N., 541/547-3399), on US-101, has been serving breakfast, lunch, and dinner every day, featuring fluffy pancakes, fresh chowders, and fine fish 'n' chips . On US-101 there are a half dozen differ-

Yachats

ent lodging options fronting the beach, including the **Fireside Motel** (1881 US-101 N., 541/547-3636, $95-189) and **The Beachcomber Cottages** (95500 US-101 S., 503/345-9399 or 503/683-7953, $80 and up).

Cape Perpetua

For more than 300 miles along the Oregon coast, US-101 abounds with national forests, state parks, and viewpoints. But unless you have your whole lifetime to spend here, **Cape Perpetua,** two miles south of Yachats, deserves most of your attention. Stop first at the **Cape Perpetua Visitor Center** (541/547-3289), just east of US-101, for seacoast views and exhibits on forestry and area history. From the visitors center, trails lead across the highway past wind-bent trees, piles of seashells and other artifacts left behind by indigenous peoples, excellent tide pools, and two coastal rock formations: the **Devil's Churn,** right on US-101 at the north edge of Cape Perpetua, and the **Spouting Horn,** off US-101 a half mile south of the visitors center. During stormy seas, especially in winter, both are amazing spectacles, with the Spouting Horn shooting huge spouts of foam 50 feet into the air through a hole in the roof of a collapsed underwater lava cave.

You can reach the top of 800-foot-high Cape Perpetua itself by following a two-mile-long road, marked by Cape Perpetua Viewpoint signs and leaving US-101 100 yards or so north of the visitors center. Once atop the cape, walk the **Whispering Spruce Trail,** a half-mile loop around the rim of the promontory that yields, on a clear day, 150-mile views of the Oregon coast from a rustic WPA-built stone observation point.

Heceta Head and the Sea Lion Caves

Halfway between Cape Perpetua and Florence, a small bridge just south of Carl G. Washburne Memorial State Park marks the turnoff to **Heceta Head Lighthouse,** perhaps the most photographed beacon in the United States. Built in 1894, it was named for the Spanish mariner who is credited with being the first European to set foot in the region. You'll have to be content with gazing at it across the cove from a small but rarely crowded beach, unless you stay at the quaint old lighthouse keeper's quarters, restored as an unforgettable **Heceta Lighthouse Bed & Breakfast** (866/547-3696, $215 and up).

A half mile south of Heceta Head Lighthouse, 11 miles north of Florence, traffic along US-101 slows to a stop at the gift shop that serves as the entrance to **Sea Lion Caves** (daily, $1 adults). You can ride an elevator down to the world's largest sea cave, the only mainland rookery for the Steller sea lion. Fall and winter offer the best times to see (and smell!) these animals, which throng together here during mating season. When the weather is nice, you can often watch them swimming in the ocean (for free and without the seal smells) from a viewpoint 100 yards up US-101.

Florence

If first and last impressions are enduring, **Florence** is truly blessed. As you enter the city from the north, US-101 climbs high above the ocean; coming from the south, travelers are greeted by the graceful **Siuslaw River Bridge,** perhaps the most impressive of a handful of WPA-built spans designed by Conde McCullough and decorated with his trademark Egyptian obelisks and art deco stylings. Unfortunately, first impressions feel a little misleading, since much of what you

LOOKING TOWARD TEN MILE LAKE AND SUTTON LAKE

can see from US-101 is a bland highway sprawl of motels, gas stations, and franchised restaurants.

The best part of Florence, **Old Town,** is just upstream from that landmark bridge, along the north bank of the Siuslaw River. Here, among Bay Street's three blocks of interesting boutiques and galleries, you'll find a number of cafés and seafood restaurants, like **Bridgewater Fish House and Zebra**

Bar (1297 Bay St., 541/997-1133, Wed.-Mon.). Old Town Florence is also home to the welcoming **Edwin K Bed and Breakfast** (1155 Bay St., 541/997-8360, $160-240), a lovely white Craftsman-style home built in 1914 by one of the town's founders.

"Dune Country"

For nearly 50 miles south of Florence, US-101 has an extensive panorama of ocean-front dunes. Although the dunes are often obscured from view by forests, roadside signs indicate access roads to numerous dunescapes on both sides of the highway. Coming from the north, the first of these access points is **Jessie M. Honeyman Memorial State Park,** three miles south of Florence, where rhododendrons line a trail leading to a 150-foot-high dune overlooking a mirage-like lake.

Giant rhododendrons and tumbledown shacks that rent out dune buggies and ATVs line US-101 between Florence and Coos Bay. Dune buggy tours ranging from peaceful to exhilarating are offered by **Sandland Adventures** (541/997-8087), less than a mile south of Florence's Siuslaw River Bridge.

Before setting out on any extended exploration, your first stop should be at the heart of the dunes at the U.S. Forest Service-run **Oregon Dunes National Recreation Area Visitors Center** (541/271-6000) at the junction of US-101 and Hwy-38 in **Reedsport,** along the Umpqua River midway between Florence and Coos Bay. The helpful rangers can provide detailed information on hiking and camping throughout the park. Reedsport itself has a line of motels and burger joints—**Don's Main Street Family Restaurant** (2115 Winchester Ave., 541/271-2032), on US-101, has legions of fans for its hearty, inexpensive food and excellent homemade pies.

Perhaps the best introduction to the bewildering geography of the dunes region is **Umpqua Dunes,** nine miles south of the Reedsport visitors center. Another popular walk starts from **Eel Creek Campground,** heading for just under three miles across small marshes and conifer groves en route to the sea, negotiating lunar-like dunes soaring 300 to 500 feet—some of the tallest in the world. Another nice trek leaves from **Tahkenitch Lake,** a popular largemouth bass fishing spot north of Gardiner, and gives a more in-depth look at the dunes' diverse flora and fauna, including swans and (rarely) black bears.

Fans of Frank Herbert's ecological sci-fi saga **Dune** may already know that the stories were inspired by the Oregon Dunes, south of Florence.

Coos Bay

Even if you race right through, it's quite apparent that **Coos Bay** (pop. 15,967), once the world's largest lumber port, retains a core of heavy industry. Many of the big mills have closed, and one has been replaced by **The Mill Casino,** a popular resort complex operated by the Coquille Indian Tribe. You can still watch huge piles of wood chips, the harbor's number-one export, being loaded onto factory ships in the harbor east of US-101. The chips are sent to Asia, where they're turned into paper.

There's good seafood and other meals available at **Sharkbites Café** (240 S. Broadway, 541/269-7475), on southbound US-101. Microbrews and a wide range of beer-friendly German dishes are served at the **Blue Heron Bistro** (100 Commercial Ave., 541/267-3933), across from the visitors bureau. There's no shortage of easy-to-find lodging, including **Motel 6** (1445 N. Bayshore Dr., 541/267-7171, $50 and up) on US-101.

> Behind the Coos Bay visitors bureau, a monument remembers the region's favorite son, middle- and long-distance runner Steve Prefontaine, who electrified the athletic world before his death in a 1975 car wreck at the age of 24. An annual 10K memorial run is held in September.

Shore Acres State Park

The historical antecedents for Coos Bay port development were laid a century ago by the Simpson Lumber Company, whose ships transported Oregon logs around the world. The ships returned with exotic seeds that were planted in the Simpson estate's garden, 12 miles west of Coos Bay via the Cape Arago Highway. Though the Simpson house burned to the ground in 1921, the five acres of formal gardens are still a floral fantasia, now open to the public as **Shore Acres State Park** (daily 8am-dusk). Besides the formal gardens, which are illuminated during the Christmas holiday season, there's an observation building above wave-battered bluffs and a trail down to a delightful beach.

On the way to Shore Acres from Coos Bay is **Sunset Bay State Park,** perhaps Oregon's best swimming beach. South of Shore Acres is **Cape Arago State Park,** complete with tide pools and seals (and seal pups in springtime) lounging on offshore rocks. Mostly level trails lead along the coastline from Shore Acres to Sunset Bay and Cape Arago State Parks. If you're tempted to stay overnight and explore the lovely region, consider taking advantage of one of Oregon's best-kept secrets: the roomy, tent-like **yurts** (800/452-5687, $41-50) available for overnight rental at Sunset Bay and in a dozen other state park beauty spots.

Bandon

There's no sharper contrast on the Oregon coast than the difference between industrial Coos Bay and earthy **Bandon** (pop. 3,066), just 24 miles to the south. Here in

the **Old Town** section along the banks of the Coquille River are several blocks of galleries, crafts shops, and fine restaurants, marked by a gateway arch off US-101. Start a tour of Old Town at the corner of 1st Street and Baltimore Avenue, where Big Wheel General Store houses the **Bandon Driftwood Museum** (daily, free), which gives a good sense of Bandon's back-to-the-land hippie ethos. A more academic introduction to the town and region can be had at the **Bandon Historical Society Museum** (270 Fillmore Ave., 541/347-2164, Mon.-Sat., daily summer, $3 adults), in the old City Hall along US-101. Its exhibits on area history, cranberries, and local color are artfully done, and the building is easy to find, so be sure to stop. South of town, **Beach Loop Drive** runs along a ridge overlooking a fantastic assemblage of coastal monoliths.

Bandon beach

For fish 'n' chips along the waterfront, the **Bandon Fish Market** (249 1st St. SE, 541/347-4282) is cheap, cheerful, and very good; a block to the east, looking more like a tackle shop than a restaurant, **Tony's Crab Shack** (541/347-2875) is another local landmark, famous for fish tacos, chowders, and silky crab sandwiches.

Outside town, the exclusive and expensive (but open to the public) **Bandon Dunes Golf Resort** (541/347-4380 or 888/345-6008, $85-275 per golf round for resort guests) has been drawing raves from golfers, well-heeled vacationers, and landscape architects alike. Designed to preserve and enhance the "natural" scenery in the style of Scottish links courses rather than the anodyne green swaths that characterize most suburban country club courses, Bandon Dunes offers golf, deluxe accommodations, and nice restaurants.

To camp at any of the **Oregon State Parks,** call park system's reservation line: 800/452-5687.

People who keep track of these things say that tiny Port Orford is the "most westerly incorporated city in the continental United States." Others grant it the less welcome title of "rainiest place on the Oregon coast."

South of Bandon, 9.5 miles north of Port Orford, **Cape Blanco** is considered—by Oregonians, at least—the western-most point of land in the contiguous United States. Named by early Spanish explorers for the white shells encrusting the 245-foot cliff face, the cape is also the site of Oregon's oldest (circa 1870) and highest lighthouse. Set back from the cliffs in forested woodlands, **Cape Blanco State Park** (541/332-2973) has hot showers and a few cabins ($41-51), along with a spacious camp-ground ($22). The headland offers great views of the rugged coastline plus a good chance of seeing gray whales spouting and leaping offshore.

Port Orford and Humbug Mountain

Pastoral sheep ranches, cranberry bogs, berry fields, and Christmas tree farms dominate the 25-mile stretch south of Bandon, but as you pull into **Port Orford** (pop. 1,133), you can't help but notice a huge volcanic plug abutting the crescent-shaped shoreline. Known as **Battle Rock,** in memory of a battle (reenacted every 4th of July) in which early settlers fought off a party of hostile Native Americans, the rock is impressive from the harbor below, while a trail climbs up to the windblown summit. Due to the southwestern orientation, which subjects the harbor to turbulent winds and con-stant waves, fishing boats have to be lowered into the water by crane, but surfers (and kite-surfers and windsurfers) don't seem to mind. Port Orford is a great place to pull over and appreciate the coastal scene, especially if you can time it right for an oceanfront meal of chowder, fish 'n' chips , and berry pie at **Griff's on the Dock** (490 Dock Rd., 541/332-8985) at "Graveyard Point."

Six miles south of Port Orford, you'll come to **Humbug Mountain State Park,** whose 1,756-foot elevation flanks the west side of the highway. It's one of the coast's highest peaks, rising directly off the beach. Its steep contours and tree-covered slopes are best appreciated from the steep but well-maintained three-mile trail that climbs to the summit. The mountain's name may have been bestowed by prospectors who found that tales of gold deposits here were just "humbug"—but the views from the top are splendid.

Southern Oregon's coastal forests yield the increasingly rare and disease-threatened Port Orford cedar, a fragrant wood popular for use in Japanese shrines and coffins.

Prehistoric Gardens

On the west side of the highway, midway between Port Orford and Gold Beach, you'll come across one of the Oregon coast's tackiest but most enduring and enjoyable tourist traps, the **Prehistoric Gardens** (541/332-4463, daily, $12 adults). Standing out like a sore thumb on this otherwise unspoiled stretch of US-101, brightly colored, more or less life-size dinosaur sculptures inhabit the evocatively lush green forest. Since 1955, when amateur paleontologist E. V. Nelson sculpted his first concrete *T. rex,* nearly two dozen more have been added to the forest menagerie.

Gold Beach

Gold Beach was named for the nuggets mined from the area's black sands during the mid-19th century. Despite its name, this is one coastal town where the action is definitely *away* from the beach. The **Rogue River** defines the northern city limits and is the town's economic raison d'être. During salmon season, Gold Beach hotels and restaurants fill up with anglers, while **jet-boat tours** of the wild river are also a draw. **Jerry's Rogue Jets** (541/247-4571 or 800/451-3645, $50 and up adults), by the bridge at the north end of town, takes passengers upstream to the isolated hamlet of **Agness,** where a homespun **mountain lodge** (meals around $15) serves family-style fried-chicken lunches and dinners. Other trips head farther upstream to the Rogue River rapids and the roadless wilderness areas of the **Rogue River-Siskiyou National Forest.**

The usual motel rooms are available along US-101, but for a more memorable visit, try the **Tu Tu' Tun Lodge** (96550 North Bank Rogue River Rd., 541/247-6664 or 800/864-6357, $160 and up). Set on a hill above the Rogue River, seven miles upstream from the coast, this upscale fishing lodge (pronounced "ta-TWO-tun") has plushly rustic rooms and a great restaurant.

Samuel H. Boardman State Scenic Corridor

Between Gold Beach and Brookings, US-101's windy, hilly roadbed is studded with the cliff-side ocean vistas, giant conifers, and boomerang-shaped offshore rock formations of **Samuel H. Boardman State Scenic Corridor.** The park covers 12 of the "Fabulous 50" miles between the two towns, and all of the features come together at **Natural Bridges Cove.** Located just north of the **Thomas Creek Bridge** (the highest bridge in Oregon), this turnout is easy to miss despite being well signed because, from the highway, it appears to be simply a parking lot fronting some trees. From the south end of the parking lot, however, a short trail through an old-growth forest leads to a viewpoint several hundred feet above three natural rock archways standing out from an azure cove.

Brookings: Harris Beach State Park

The drive through the malled-over main drag of **Brookings** offers only fleeting glimpses of the Pacific, and if you're hoping for a first or last "Wow!" before or after the 300-plus other miles of coastal Oregon's scenic splendor, these few miles along the California border may be somewhat anticlimactic. That said, Brookings does have beautiful **Azalea Park,** which is gorgeous during the April-June spring bloom. The popular, welcoming beachfront B&B rooms at **Lowden's Beachfront Bed & Breakfast** (14626 Wollam Rd., 541/469-7045, $109 and up), just west of US-101, offer direct access to a driftwood-strewn beach.

Just north of Brookings, one final piece of Oregon's abundant natural beauty has been preserved at **Harris Beach State Park,** across US-101 from the Oregon Welcome Center. Here you can walk down to a driftwood-laden beach and look out at Bird Island, where tufted puffins and other rare birds breed.

Heading south, just over the California border from Brookings, lies **Redwood National Park,** truly one of the West Coast's great places.

CALIFORNIA

Stretching along the Pacific Ocean for roughly a thousand miles from top to tail, the California coast includes virgin wilderness, the cutting edge of cosmopolitan culture, and the full spectrum in between. For almost the entire way, coastal roads give quick and easy access to the best parts, with panoramic views appearing so often you'll simply give up trying to capture it all.

Starting in the north, the green forests of the Pacific Northwest continue well beyond the state border, forming a mountainous seaside landscape that lasts until the edge of metropolitan **San Francisco.** Along this stretch you'll find a number of old logging and fishing towns, varying from the burly blue-collar likes of **Eureka** and **Crescent City** to the upscale ambience of **Mendocino,** in and among endless acres of redwood forest.

At the approximate midpoint of the California coast sits **San Francisco,** deservedly ranked among the world's favorite cities. The 100 miles of coast stretching south from San Francisco hold numerous remnants of the Spanish and Mexican eras, exemplified by the town of **Monterey** and the beautiful mission at **Carmel.** Beyond here is another stretch of wild coastline, the rugged country of **Big Sur.**

Beyond the southern edge of Big Sur, opulent **Hearst Castle** marks the start of what most people consider Southern California, the rivers and trees of the north giving way to golden beaches, grassy bluffs, and considerably denser populations. A pair of pleasant small cities, Midwestern-feeling **San Luis Obispo** and ritzy **Santa Barbara,** make excellent stops in themselves, smoothing the transition into the environs of **Los Angeles,** the unwieldy megalopolis that, seen from the I-5 freeway that links Los Angeles and **San Diego,** seems like one monstrous

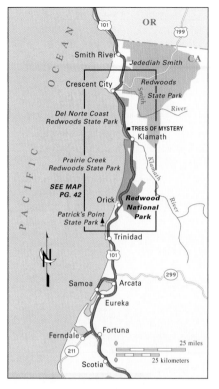

100-mile-long suburb. While it's true that the natural beauty that brought so many people to Southern California in the first place is increasingly endangered, some lovely, almost untouched places remain, hidden away but within easy access of the fast lane. We've pointed them out; enjoy them while they last.

Jedediah Smith Redwoods State Park

The northernmost of the great redwood groves, **Jedediah Smith Redwoods State Park** covers nearly 10,000 acres of virgin forest along the banks of the Smith River. Stretching east of US-101, and most easily accessible from US-199, the park offers over 20 miles of usually uncrowded hiking trails through the pristine wilderness; it is considered by many the most perfect of all the redwood forests. One of the most enjoyable trails leads through **Stout Grove,** past tall trees and a number of summertime swimming holes along the Smith River.

There's also a good **campground** (800/444-7275) with hot showers. For fans of roadside kitsch, there's one unique spot along US-101 in the hamlet of **Smith River,** 15 miles north of Crescent City: **Ship Ashore Resort** (707/487-3141), a gift shop, restaurant, campground, and motel along US-101, marked by a grounded but still handsome 1920s yacht, inside which is a gift shop.

Crescent City

The county seat and only incorporated city in Del Norte County, **Crescent City** (pop. 7,643) is best treated as a base from which to explore the surrounding wilderness. The foggy weather that helps the redwoods thrive makes the city fairly depressing and gray, and what character it developed since its founding in the 1850s has been eroded by storms; a giant tsunami, caused by the 1964 earthquake off Alaska, destroyed much of the city. The more recent tsunami unleashed by the 2011 quake off Sendai, Japan, was less destructive but drowned one man and caused millions of dollars in damage to boats moored in the Crescent City harbor.

Crescent City includes the familiar lineup of motels and restaurants, plus local options like the **CC Diner and Ice Cream**

The **Smith River** and **Jedediah Smith Redwoods State Park** were named in memory of the legendary mountain man Jedediah Strong Smith, who in 1826 at the age of 27 led the first party of American settlers overland to California. Smith also blazed a trail over South Pass through the Rocky Mountains that was later used by the Oregon Trail pioneers.

Outside Crescent City, 3,000 of California's most violent criminals are kept behind bars, and often in solitary confinement, in the notorious Pelican Bay State Prison, which opened in 1989.

(1319 Northcrest Dr., 707/465-5858), on the north side of downtown, a half mile west of US-101. For overnight, one only-in-California option is the **Curly Redwood Lodge** (701 US-101 S., 707/464-2137, $60 and up), a nicely maintained 1950s motel made from a single sawed-up redwood tree.

Del Norte Coast Redwoods State Park

Spreading south from the Jedediah Smith redwoods, **Del Norte Coast Redwoods State Park** runs along the Pacific Ocean (and US-101) for about eight miles, containing more than 6,000 acres of first- and second-growth redwoods as well as brilliant blooms of rhododendrons, azaleas, and spring wildflowers. Del Norte also protects miles of untouched coastline, the best stretch of which is accessible from the end of **Enderts Beach Road,** which cuts west from US-101 just north of the

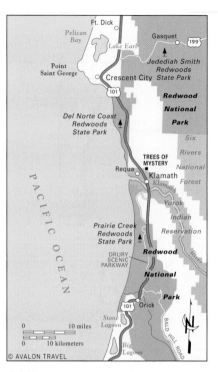

park entrance. From here, a 30-mile trail follows the coast to Prairie Creek. The state park area is bounded on the south by an undeveloped section of **Redwood National Park.**

Trees of Mystery and Klamath

Hard to miss along US-101, thanks to the massive statues of **Paul Bunyan** and **Babe the Blue Ox** looming over the highway, the **Trees of Mystery** (707/482-2251, daily, $16 adults) are literally and figuratively the biggest tourist draws on the Northern California coast. Along the Trail of Tall Tales, chainsaw-cut figures, backed by audiotaped

stories, stand in tableaux at the foot of towering redwoods. There's also a SkyTrail gondola lifting passengers up into the treetop canopy, a huge gift shop, and an excellent, free museum of Native American art and artifacts. Across the highway, **Motel Trees** (707/482-3152, $81 and up) has standard rooms and a café.

Along the banks of the mighty Klamath River, four miles south of the Trees of Mystery, the town of **Klamath** (pop. 779) is a brief burst of highway sprawl, supported by anglers who flock here for the annual fall salmon runs—provided there are any fish left to catch. Fisherfolk, walkers, and kayakers all avail themselves of the enduringly popular **The Historic Requa Inn** (707/482-1425, $95 and up), a friendly, comfortable homestead run by members of the local Yurok Tribe right on the riverfront. At the south end of Klamath town, take a drive right through the

Tour Thru Tree ($5), then cross the Klamath River on a bridge graced by a pair of gilded cement grizzly bears.

Prairie Creek Redwoods State Park

The largest of the trio of north coast state redwood parks, **Prairie Creek Redwoods State Park** is best known for its large herd of endangered Roosevelt elk, which you can usually see grazing in the meadows along US-101 at the center of the park, next to the main **ranger station** (707/465-7347 or visitor center 707/488-2039). A modern freeway carries US-101 traffic around, rather than through, the Prairie Creek redwoods. To reach the best sights, detour along the well-signed Newton B. Drury Scenic Parkway, which follows Prairie Creek along the old US-101 alignment through the heart of the park.

Another elk herd can be spotted among the coastal dunes at **Gold Bluffs Beach,** which stretches for 11 miles through untouched wilderness; there are trails leading from US-101, or you can follow Davison Road northwest from US-101, three miles south of the ranger station. Apart from the elk, Prairie Creek offers a basic campground in a beautiful setting: the usual mix of old-growth redwood trees, which, more than in the other parks, mingle with dense growths of Sitka spruce and Douglas firs here to form a near rainforest of greenery.

All the land along the Klamath River is part of the extensive **Hoopa Valley Reservation,** which stretches for over 30 miles upstream from the Pacific Ocean.

The groves of giant trees in Redwood National Park were used as a location for the Star Wars film *Return of the Jedi,* in which the characters cruised through the forest on airborne cycles. Patrick's Point played a starring role in the 2015 movie *Jurassic World.*

Redwood National Park

Established in 1968 and enlarged since then, **Redwood National Park** protects the last vestiges of the more than two million acres of primeval redwood forest that once covered the entire Northern California coastline. To be honest, alongside the gorgeous groves in the adjacent Smith, Del Norte, and Prairie Creek State Parks, the trees preserved here aren't by any means the oldest, largest, or most beautiful. In fact, much of the federal parkland is second- or third-growth timber, clear-cut as recently as the 1960s. Though redwoods are the fastest-growing softwoods on earth—growing three to five feet a year when young—the groves here can look rather disappointing compared to those in nearby areas. But they do serve a valuable role as an environmental buffer zone even if they're not a tree-lover's pilgrimage site.

That said, Redwood National Park does hold two special sights, including the **Lady Bird Johnson Grove,** on Bald Hill Road two miles east of US-101, where the new park was dedicated in 1969. Ten miles farther up this road, and a long hike beyond that, the **Tall Trees Grove** (free permit required) holds one of the world's tallest trees, the 360-plus-foot Libbey Tree, whose trunk has been measured at 9.5 feet in diameter.

At the south end of the park, the roadside-strip town of

Orick stretches toward the coast, where the main Redwood National Park **Thomas H. Kuchel Visitor Center** (707/465-7765) stands at the mouth of Redwood Creek.

Patrick's Point State Park

If your idea of heaven is sitting on a rocky headland listening to the roar of the Pacific while watching the sunset or looking for passing gray whales, you won't want to pass by **Patrick's Point State Park** (707/677-3570). Three different 200-foot-high promontories at the heart of the park provide panoramic views, while the surrounding acres hold cedar and spruce forests (no redwoods), open pastures bright with wildflowers, great tide pools, a wide dark-sand beach, and three **campgrounds** (800/444-7275) with hot showers. There's also the preserved and restored remnants of a Yurok village, a redwood dugout canoe, and a garden of traditional herbs.

Inland from Arcata along scenic US-299, the town of **Willow Creek** claims to be the heart of Bigfoot Country, boasting a large statue of the furry beast to prove it. One of the state's most scenic drives (or bike rides), US-299 continues east over the coast range through the beautiful **Trinity Alps** to **Weaverville,** with well-preserved relics of a mid-1850s gold rush, before linking up with I-5 at Redding.

Continuing south, US-101 becomes a four-lane freeway along the ocean to Arcata and Eureka, but most of the old US-101 alignment winds along the cliff tops between Patrick's Point and the small town of **Trinidad.** Along this road you'll find some places to stay, like the **Trinidad Inn** (1170 Patrick's Point Dr., 707/677-3349, $105 and up), about three miles south of the park entrance. A little farther down this old stretch of US-101 is **The Larrupin' Café** (1658 Patrick's Point Dr., 707/677-0230), which serves up bountiful portions of fresh all-American food in a friendly, homey ambience—it's California cuisine without the snooty pretense you sometimes find farther south.

Arcata

The most attractive and enjoyable town on the far north coast of California, **Arcata** (pop. 17,231) makes the best first (or last, depending upon the direction you're traveling) overnight stop south of the Oregon border. The presence of Humboldt State University's campus on the hills above US-101 accounts for the town's youthful, nonconformist energy. Cafés, bookstores, bars, and crafts shops surround the lively **Arcata Plaza,** two blocks west of US-101 at 9th and G Streets, incongruously graced by palm trees and a statue of President McKinley. The *Utne Reader* once rated Arcata as the most enlightened town in California. Spending even a little time in this vibrant, cooperative Ecotopia may make you wonder whether or not you really have to race back to the big-city 9-to-5 grind.

You can admire the town's many elaborate Victorian-era cottages, hunt wild mushrooms, clamber over sand dunes, or hike in the redwoods. Afterward, relax with a cup of tea or, better yet, a soak in a hot tub at homey **Café Mokka** (495 J St., 707/822-2228), the coast's only combo sauna and espresso bar. Just off the plaza, **Jambalaya Arcata** (915 H St., 707/822-4766) is a nightclub serving burgers, pizza, microbrew beers, and, of course, jambalaya. More good food, good beer, and good live music are on the menu at the popular "HumBrews," a.k.a. **Humboldt Brews** (856 10th St., 707/826-2739). For a complete selection of foodstuffs and supplies, and more insight into the local community, head to the large and stylish **North Coast Co-op** (811 I St.), a block north of the plaza.

For a place to stay, the centrally located **Hotel Arcata** (708 9th St., 707/826-0217 or 800/344-1221, $97 and up) is right on the plaza, or you can take your pick of the usual motels along US-101.

Eureka

Evolving into a lively artists' colony from its roots as a fairly gritty and industrial port, **Eureka** (pop. 27,191) was well known to fur trappers and traders long before it became a booming lumber and whaling port in the 1850s. Thanks to the lumber trade, Victorian Eureka grew prosperous, building elaborate homes, including the oft-photographed but closed to the public **Carson Mansion** along the waterfront at 2nd and M Streets, two blocks west of US-101.

The author Bret Harte was run out of Arcata by angry townspeople in 1860, after writing an editorial in the local paper criticizing a massacre of local Wiyot people.

One unique thing to see in Eureka is the **Romano Gabriel Sculpture Garden** (315 2nd St.), displayed in a plate-glass showcase. This brilliantly colorful folk-art extravaganza of faces and flowers originally stood in the front yard of local gardener Romano Gabriel, who made them

out of discarded packing crates and other recycled materials over a period of some 30 years before his death in 1977.

Along with dozens of well-preserved Victorian houses, Eureka has done a fine job of finding new uses for its many ornate commercial buildings, most of which have been preserved to house art galleries, cafés, and restaurants in what's now called **Old Town,** a half-dozen blocks between the waterfront and US-101. This historic downtown quarter has a huge number of good places to eat and drink, including **Ramone's Bakery & Café** (209 E St., 707/445-2923) and the pub-like **Café Waterfront** (102 F St., 707/443-9190), serving excellent fish 'n' chips, chowders, and other fresh seafood right on the harbor. And if that's not enough to sate your appetite, for yet more fish 'n' chips and a pint or two of ale, head along to the **Lost Coast Brewery** (1600 Sunset Dr., 707/267-9651).

Accommodation options range from roadside motels to upscale places like the **Carter House Inns & Restaurant 301** (301 L St., 707/444-8062 or 800/404-1390, $189 and up), a recreated Victorian manor with spacious rooms and a big breakfast in the morning.

For further information about Eureka or anywhere in the whole glorious Redwood Empire region, contact the Eureka **Humboldt Visitors Bureau** (322 1st St., 707/443-5097 or 800/346-3482).

KINETIC GRAND CHAMPIONSHIP

Humboldt County's creative community comes alive every Memorial Day weekend for the world-famous **Kinetic Grand Championship,** in which participants pedal, paddle, and otherwise move themselves and their handmade vehicles across land and sea. Part art, part engineering, and part athletic competition, the Kinetic Grand Championship is like nothing you've seen before. Also known as the Kinetic Sculpture Race and the Triathlon of the Art World, the event begins noon Saturday and runs until Monday afternoon, as a mind-boggling array of mobile contraptions make their way over land, sand, and sea from the town square of Arcata to the main street of Ferndale, twice crossing chilly Humboldt Bay. Past winners have included everything from dragons and floating flying saucers to Egyptian pyramids (named *Queen of Denial*) and a Cadillac Coupe de Ville.

Rule Number One of the Kinetic Grand Championship is that all of the "sculptures" must be people-powered; beyond that, imagination is the primary guide. Many "rules" have developed over the years since the race was first run in 1969, including such pearls as: "In the event of sunshine, the race shall proceed," but most of these emphasize the idea that maintaining style and a sense of humor are at least as important as finishing the fastest. Since the grand prizes are valued at somewhere around $14.98, racers take part solely for the glory.

Spectators are expected to be active participants too, so be prepared to shout and scream and applaud the competitors, or even jog or bike or kayak alongside them. There are many great vantage points along the route, but you have to be in the right place on the right day. Before noon on Saturday there's a prerace lineup around Arcata Plaza, from where racers head through the streets of Arcata out toward the Manila Dunes before spending the first night in downtown Eureka. Sunday morning, the racers head across Humboldt Bay from Field's Landing, then camp out overnight on the beach. Monday's trials include another water crossing, and it all culminates in a mad dash down the Main Street of Ferndale, surrounded by cheering multitudes. It's all good fun, and a great focus for a visit to this remarkable corner of the world.

racing along Samoa Peninsula, "Just for the Halibut"

Samoa

Even if you're just passing through, don't miss the chance to visit the old mill town of **Samoa,** across the bay from Eureka but easily reachable via the Hwy-255 bridge. On a narrow peninsula between the bay and the open ocean, the unique **Samoa Cookhouse** (707/442-1659, daily breakfast, lunch, and dinner) was built in 1890 to feed the many hungry men living and working in the "company town" lumber mill here. The mill is long gone now, but the cookhouse remains in operation as a sort of living history center, packed with logging memorabilia and blue-collar character. So take a seat at one of the 20-foot-long tables (redwood, of course, covered in checkered oilcloth), soak up the history, and dig into the family-style feasts (all-you-can-eat!). There are no menus, just huge platters of food at reasonable prices.

Ferndale

Well worth the 10-mile round-trip detour west of US-101, the historic town of **Ferndale** (pop. 1,371) is an odd fish along the woodsy Northern California coast, a century-old dairy town that would look more at home in middle America. The three-block-long franchise-free Main Street includes a fully stocked general store, the **Golden Gait Mercantile** (421 Main St.). Whitewashed farmhouses dot the pastoral valleys nearby. Ferndale's diverse history is well documented inside the **Ferndale Museum** (515 Shaw Ave., 707/786-4466, hours vary).

The area around Ferndale has been hit by numerous earthquakes, including a destructive tremor in April 1992 that registered magnitude 7.2.

Ambling along Main Street is the best way to get a feel for Ferndale, and if you build up an appetite, there are many good places to eat. One of the oldest cafés in the West, **Poppa Joe's** (409 Main St., 707/786-4180), serves great diner food in a no-frills Victorian-era storefront, while one of California's earliest hotels features a family-friendly Italian restaurant, **The Hotel Ivanhoe Restaurant & Saloon** (315 Main St., 707/786-9000, dinner only). On the main road midway between town and US-101 is another fast-foodie landmark: the **No Brand Burger Stand** (1400 Main St., 707/786-9474), where all the tasty patties are hand-formed from local grass-fed beef. There are fab fries and luscious milk shakes too—yum.

Along with its good food options, Ferndale is equally well supplied with places to stay. Right off the heart of Main Street is the clean and tidy **Redwood Suites** (332 Ocean Ave., 707/786-5000, $12 and up), but the real draws are the half-dozen historic B&Bs, including **The Shaw House Inn** (703 Main St., 707/786-9958, $129 and up), an 1854 American Gothic masterpiece.

The Lost Coast

Between Ferndale and Rockport, the main US-101 highway heads inland along the Eel River. But if you have time and a taste for adventure, head west from Ferndale along the narrow, winding Mattole Road, which loops around Cape Mendocino through the northern reaches of the so-called **Lost Coast,** a 100-mile stretch of shoreline justly famous for its isolated

The Lost Coast area was the site of the first oil well in California, which was drilled in the 1860s in the town of **Petrolia,** but is now long gone.

beauty. By road, you can only get close to the ocean at a few points—the few miles south of Cape Mendocino, and again at the fishing resort of **Shelter Cove,** west of Garberville—but hikers can have a field day (or week) exploring the extensive coastal wilderness. Some 50 miles of rugged untouched coastline, packed with tide pools and driftwood-strewn beaches, have been preserved in a pair of parks, the **King Range National Conservation Area** in the north and the **Sinkyone Wilderness State Park** farther south.

Besides Hwy-211/Mattole Road, which makes a 70-mile loop between Ferndale and the Rockefeller Forest section of Humboldt Redwoods State Park, a network of rougher and even more remote routes allows auto access to the Lost Coast, linking the hamlet of **Honeydew** with coastal Hwy-1 near Rockport. If you do explore this wild and rainy region, take a good map and plenty of food and water, and be careful.

For further information on the Lost Coast, contact the **U.S. Bureau of Land Management** (1695 Heindon Rd., 707/825-2300); its office is off US-101 on the north side of Arcata.

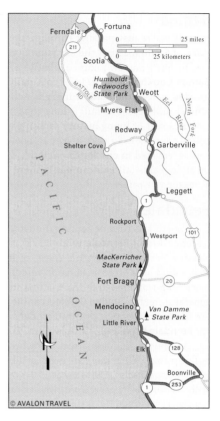

Scotia

Back along US-101, on the banks of the Eel River midway between the coast and the Humboldt Redwoods, **Scotia** was the last true company town left in California. The Pacific Lumber Company (a.k.a. PALCO) built it and, for most of the 20th century, owned and operated everything, from the two huge wood-cutting mills to the 10 blocks of pastel-painted houses, the church, and the schools that constituted this little community of about 1,000 people.

The lumber mills used to be the heart and soul of the town, as well as Scotia's main tourist attraction, but after a 1980s junk-bond leveraged buyout and subsequent asset-stripping, PALCO finally went bankrupt in 2007. Since then the town and the mills have struggled to find a way forward, but Scotia is still a proud and photogenic place, well worth a look and a wander.

Part of the old lumber mill has been reconfigured into a biofueled home for the

excellent (and 100 percent organic) **Eel River Brewery** (1777 Alamar Way, Fortuna, 707/725-2739), which operates a popular tasting room and restaurant at its original location near Ferndale, off US-101 in the hamlet of Fortuna.

In summer, **Scotia Inn** (100 Main St., $75 and up) has B&B rooms and a good restaurant.

Humboldt Redwoods State Park

Sheltering the biggest and best collection of giant coastal redwoods anywhere in the world, **Humboldt Redwoods State Park** is an exceptionally breathtaking corner of an exceptionally beautiful region. Covering more than 53,000 acres along the Eel River, this is the true heart of redwood country, containing the largest and most pristine expanses of virgin forest as well as some of the largest, tallest, and most remarkable trees.

The protection of the mighty redwood forests of Northern California was made possible not by the state or federal governments but primarily by the efforts of the **Save the Redwoods League** (111 Sutter St., 11th Fl., San Francisco, CA 94104, 415/362-2352), a private organization that has raised, since its founding in 1918, millions of dollars to buy or preserve over 185,000 acres of redwood forest. To support these efforts, write or call the league.

Even if you're just passing through, be sure to turn onto the amazing **Avenue of the Giants,** 31 miles of old highway frontage between Pepperwood and Phillipsville. This sinuous old road snakes alongside, and sometimes under, the faster and busier US-101 freeway, which is carried on concrete stilts through the park. In and among the natural wonders along the Avenue of the Giants are a handful of artificial ones: The **Eternal Tree House** (free) in Redcrest, with a friendly and inexpensive café, and the **Shrine Drive-Thru Tree** ($6), in Myers Flat, are just two of the many good-natured "tourist traps" in this neck of the woods. At the north end of the park you'll find an impressive collection of trees in the well-marked **Founder's Grove,** where a half-mile nature trail leads past the 362-foot-tall, possibly 2,000-year-old **Dyerville Giant,** lauded as one of the world's tallest trees before it fell during the winter of 1991.

Once you've done the Avenue of the Giants, if you want to escape the crowds and the freeway rumble, head west from Founder's Grove across US-101 to the 10,000-plus-acre **Rockefeller Forest.** This expansive grove is one of the largest old-growth forests in the world and includes two of the world's champion trees, each over 360 feet tall and some 17 feet in diameter.

The best source of information on the park is the **Visitor Center** (707/946-2263), midway along the Avenue of the Giants in Weott; there's a pleasant state-run **campground** (800/444-7275) with showers right next door. You may have to drive a ways

north (to Ferndale, Eureka, or Arcata) or south (to Garberville) from the park to find an exceptional meal, though there are a few nice places to stay, like the historic **Myers Country Inn** (707/943-3259, $200 and up), midway along the Avenue of the Giants in Myers Flat. Farther south, the hamlet of Miranda holds the pleasant **Miranda Gardens Resort** (6766 Ave. of the Giants,

707/943-3011, $105 and up), with a handy general store and rustic cabins backing onto redwood groves.

Garberville and Redway

Apart from its recurring presence in the national media during the occasional high-profile raids on local marijuana plantations, the redwood country town of **Garberville** is a pretty quiet, peaceful place. The US-101 freeway bypasses the town, and locals walk and talk to each other along the half dozen blocks of Redwood Drive, the well-signed business loop off the highway.

> The Garberville-Redway area is home to a pretty unusual community of old hippies and off-the-grid libertarians, who share their music and politics on noncommercial local radio station KMUD 91.1 FM.

Enjoy an early-morning breakfast with the old-time locals at the **Eel River Café** (801 Redwood Dr., 707/923-3783), or an espresso and healthy food at the **Woodrose Café** (911 Redwood Dr., 707/923-3191), a block south. Garberville also has all the motels you could want, including the **Motel Garberville** (948 Redwood Dr., 707/923-2422, $60 and up).

Two miles west of Garberville on the old highway, **Redway** is worth the short side trip for an burger at **Deb's Great American Hamburgers** (707/923-2244). The Reggae on the River festival, organized by the energetic **Mateel Community Center** (707/923-3368), attracts world-class performers and thousands of fans every August.

Along US-101, four miles south of Garberville, one of the region's most comfortable and characterful places is the stately **Benbow Historic Inn** (707/923-2124 or 800/355-3301, $150 and up), a circa-1926 mock Tudor hotel with a nice restaurant offering afternoon tea and scones on a sunny terrace overlooking the Eel River.

Leggett: The Chandelier Drive-Thru Tree

No longer even a proverbial wide spot in the road since the US-101 freeway was diverted around it, **Leggett** marks the southern end of the Humboldt redwoods. At the south end of "town," a mile from the US-101/Hwy-1 junction along the old highway, stands one of the redwood region's most venerable and worthwhile roadside attractions, the "original" **Chandelier Drive-Thru Tree** (daily dawn-dusk, $5). In addition to the famous tree, which had the six-foot, nine-inch tunnel cut through it in the 1930s, there's an above-average gift shop with a broad range of books, postcards, and schlocky souvenirs.

Nearby, the 14-acre grounds of **Big Bend Lodge** (707/925-2440, summer only, $149-159) has nine quaint riverfront cabins, perfect for lazy days floating, swimming, or fishing. South of Leggett, US-101 runs inland, racing toward San Francisco, while scenic Hwy-1 cuts west over the coastal mountains to Mendocino, winding slowly south along the Pacific.

Westport

From US-101 at Leggett, a narrow stretch of Hwy-1 twists up and over the rugged coastal mountains before hugging the coast through the weather-beaten logging and fishing community of **Westport.** The tiny town has more than you might expect, including a cozy 1970s motel and deli on the ocean side of Hwy-1 called the **Westport Inn** (707/964-5135, $80 and up), and the newer and more upscale **Westport Hotel & Old Abalone Pub** (707/964-3688 or 877/964-3688, Feb.-Nov.) two blocks south, which has a sauna and a restaurant and welcoming pub with

AVENUE OF THE GIANTS

The stretch of historic US-101 through the redwood country of Humboldt County, frequently called the **Avenue of the Giants,** is lined by pristine groves of massive trees and provides boundless opportunities to come face-to-face with your own insignificance in nature's greater scheme of things. If you tire of this display of natural majesty, or simply want to keep it in context with the modern "civilized" world, you're in luck: Every few miles, among the stately trees, you'll come upon shameless souvenir stands selling redwood burl furniture and chainsaw sculptures, as well as wonderfully tacky tourist traps like the Legend of Bigfoot. Many of these hyper-tacky attractions now exist only in memory (and on old postcards), but none of the survivors is big or bold enough to detract from the main event—the big trees—and since they've been in operation since the early days of car-borne tourism, they're as much a part of the redwood experience as the trees themselves. Most charge only a few dollars' admission, so there's not a lot to lose.

While you're encouraged to stop at any and all of them—at least long enough to buy a postcard or two—the most tried-and-true attraction is the **Trees of Mystery,** marked by huge statues of Paul Bunyan and Babe the Blue Ox along US-101 in Klamath, well north of the official Avenue of the Giants. In Myers Flat is the **Shrine Drive-Thru**

at the end of Leggett, the "original" Drive-Thru Tree

Tree, at 13078 Avenue of the Giants (old US-101), which wagon-borne travelers drove through more than a century ago. Two more classics are found in the south: One of the best stops in redwood country, **Confusion Hill** in Piercy is one of those places where water runs uphill and the rules of physics seem not to apply; there's also a little train here that chugs uphill to a nice grove of trees. Finally, at the **Chandelier Drive-Thru Tree,** in Leggett off old US-101 on Drive Thru Tree Road, drive your car through a 315-foot-tall redwood tree, still growing strong despite the gaping hole in its belly.

frequent live music. (Be warned: when the restaurant is closed, it's a half-hour drive to the nearest places to eat, in Fort Bragg.) The small and informal **Howard Creek Ranch Inn** (707/964-6725, $90 and up), three miles north of Westport, offers comfortable B&B rooms, an outdoor hot tub, and easy access to the driftwood-laden beach. Like Westport Hotel, it's a half-hour drive to the nearest restaurants.

Farther south, **MacKerricher State Park** protects seven miles of rocky coast and waterfront pine forest. An old logging railroad right-of-way, called Ten-Mile Haul Road, has been brought back into use as a hiking and cycling path that covers most of the eight miles between the north end of MacKerricher and the town of Fort Bragg, crossing over Pudding Creek on a recently renovated railroad trestle. The park offers the chance to see harbor seals and migrating gray whales (in winter). Ongoing efforts are reclaiming the remnants of the old North Coast logging industry by reconstructing natural dunes and removing nonnative plantlife. There's also a nice **campground** (800/444-7275).

Fort Bragg

Cruising south along Hwy-1, 40 miles from Leggett and US-101, the first real town you come to is **Fort Bragg** (pop. 7,273), whose burly blue-collar edge comes as something of a shock on the otherwise undeveloped and touristy Mendocino coast. Formerly home to a large Georgia-Pacific lumber mill (plans to redevelop it are still in the works and may include ecofriendly housing and a shopping and light industrial complex), and still home to the region's largest commercial fishing fleet, Fort Bragg takes a mostly no-frills approach to the tourist trade, leaving the dainty B&B scene to its upscale neighbor, Mendocino. However, the coastline is lovely, and there are a few down-to-earth places to eat, starting with the good omelets and other eggy dishes at the appropriately named **Egghead's Restaurant** (326 N. Main St., 707/964-5005). Perhaps the most popular place in town is **North Coast Brewing Co.** (455 N. Main St., 707/964-2739), which serves good food and fine pints of its tasty Red Seal Ale among at least a dozen top-notch brews. As you might expect, Fort Bragg has a number of timeworn bars and taverns, like the **Golden West Saloon** (128 E. Redwood Ave.), two blocks south of the brewery. The town also boasts some unexpected treats: **Cowlick's Ice Cream Café** (250 N. Main St., 707/962-9271) and the best pizza for miles at **D'Aurelio & Son** (438 S. Franklin St., 707/964-4227), a block east of Hwy-1.

Fort Bragg also has at least one exemplar of that rare species, the inexpensive (by Mendocino coast standards, at least) motel: the **Beachcomber Motel** (1111 N. Main St., 707/964-2402, $109 and up). Handy for the Ten-Mile Haul Road path, this is pretty much the coast's only beachfront lodging option (apart from camping).

At the south edge of Fort Bragg, near the Hwy-20 junction and eight miles north of the town of Mendocino, 47 acres of intensely landscaped coastal hillsides tumble down between Hwy-1 and the ocean to form the **Mendocino Coast Botanical Gardens** (707/964-4352, daily, $15 adults), a nonprofit public space showing off the abundance of plantlife that thrives in this mild, lush environment. Cultivated varieties like camellias, azaleas, roses, irises, fuchsias, and dahlias share space with native ferns, pines, redwoods, wildflowers, and wetland plants. The garden fronts the ocean, so you can enjoy crashing waves and maybe even watch a gray whale spout offshore.

aerial view of Fort Bragg

From Fort Bragg, the **California Western Railroad** (707/964-6371, $25 and up) runs a number of historic steam- and diesel-powered "Skunk Trains" over the mountains to Willits and back. Half-day and full-day trips run year-round.

Mendocino

One of the prettiest towns on the California coast (as seen in TV shows like *Murder, She Wrote* and numerous movies), **Mendocino** (pop. 894) is an artists and writers community par excellence. Now firmly established as an upscale escape for wage-slaving visitors from San Francisco (hence the local nickname, "Spendocino"), the town was originally established as a logging port in the 1850s. In recent years, Mendocino has successfully pre-served its rugged sandstone coastline—great for wintertime whale-watching—while converting many of its New England-style clapboard houses into super-quaint B&B inns. The area is ideal for leisurely wandering, following the many paths winding through **Mendocino Headlands State Park,** which wraps around the town and offers uninterrupted views across open fields, heathers, and other coastal flora to the crashing

Mendocino

ocean beyond. For field guides, maps, or a look at Mendocino in its lumbering heyday, stop by the visitors center in the historic **Ford House** (45035 Main St., 707/937-5397).

Two miles north of town, one of the north coast's most perfect places is protected as **Russian Gulch State Park** (707/937-5804), where a waterfall, a soaring highway bridge, lush inland canyons, a swimming beach, and an impressive blowhole are yours to enjoy along more than a mile of undisturbed coastline. There's camping too, and sea kayaking, plus a fairly flat three-mile paved bike trail and miles of hiking.

Along with its many fine art galleries and bookshops, the town of Mendocino also has a delicious collection of bakeries, cafés, and restaurants. If you're not getting breakfast at a B&B, come to the friendly **Mendocino Café** (10451 Lansing St., 707/937-6141), where locals have been starting their days for more than 20 years. For a total splurge, try one of California's most famous (and expensive!) restaurants, **Café Beaujolais** (961 Ukiah St., 707/937-5614, lunch and dinner Wed.-Sun., dinner Mon.-Sun.), two blocks from the waterfront, which serves California cuisine delicacies.

Places to stay in Mendocino are rather expensive but generally delightful. The lovely **MacCallum House Inn** (45020 Albion St., 707/937-0289, $159 and up) includes a beautiful garden, good breakfasts, and a cozy nighttime bar and restaurant. Another place to stay is the circa-1878 **Mendocino Hotel & Garden Suites** (45080 Main St., 707/937-0511, $89 and up), on the downtown waterfront.

Mendocino, as you might expect from a well-heeled artists colony, also has a pretty lively music scene. If you just want to drink and unwind after a long day on the road, head to **Dick's Place** (707/937-6010) at the west end of Main Street.

Van Damme State Park

Three miles south of Mendocino at the mouth of the Little River, **Van Damme State Park** stretches along the coastal bluffs and beaches and includes some 1,800 acres of pine and redwood forest. The park's unique attribute is the oddly contorted **Pygmy Forest,** a natural bonsai-like grove of miniature pines, cypress, and manzanita, with a wheelchair-accessible nature trail explaining the unique ecology. There's also a small and popular campground, concession-guided ocean kayak tours, and a seasonal **visitors center** (707/937-4016) housed in a New Deal-era recreation hall.

The nearby hamlet of **Little River** is home to some rural-feeling peaceful alternatives to Mendocino's in-town accommodations. At the comfy **Inn at Schoolhouse Creek & Spa** (707/937-5525, $179 and up), quaint cottages sit in nine acres of dog- and child-friendly gardens around a historic ocean-view home. At the luxurious gourmet food-and-wine indulgence of the **Little River Inn** (707/937-5942, $205 and up during high season), five generations of the same family have been welcoming travelers since 1939.

Anderson Valley

From Hwy-1 south of Mendocino, Hwy-128 cuts diagonally across to US-101 through the lovely **Anderson Valley,** home to numerous fine wineries (including Husch, Navarro, and Kendall-Jackson) and the *Anderson Valley Advertiser,* one of California's most outspoken local newspapers. Anderson Valley also has its own regional dialect, called "Boontling," combining English, Scots-Irish, Spanish, and

vineyard in Anderson Valley

Native American words into a lighthearted lingo created, some say, simply to befuddle outsiders—or "shark the bright-lighters," in the local lingo.

To find out more, stop in the valley's tiny main town, **Boonville,** where the Boont Ferry Farm grocery store is an ad hoc information center. Fans of local food and wine will want to cross the highway to **The Boonville Hotel** (14050 Hwy-128, 707/895-2210, $145 and up), which has a wonderful restaurant (dinner only, alas) and wine bar. The historic building has upstairs rooms filled with art and furniture made by local craftspeople. Beer fans can make a pilgrimage east of town (toward Ukiah) to the partially solar-powered home of the **Anderson Valley Brewing Company** (17700 Hwy-253, 707/895-2337), where you can sample some of the world's best beers, including the legendary Boont Amber Ale.

Elk

While the coastal scenery is stupendous all the way along the Mendocino coast, one place worth keeping an eye out for on the drive along Hwy-1 is the tiny roadside community of **Elk** (pop. 208), 15 miles south of Mendocino. Elk is a wonderful little wide spot in the road, with what must be one of the oldest and most characterful

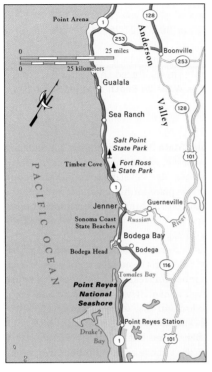

service stations in California—the Elk Garage, in business since 1901—alongside a great little veggie-friendly breakfast-and-lunch road-food stop: **Queenie's Roadhouse Café** (707/877-3285, Thurs.-Mon.). If you have the time and means for a splurge, the peaceful oceanfront **Elk Cove Inn & Spa** (707/877-3321, $145 and up) is a delightful small B&B inn. Elk also boasts a general store and a steep trail leading down to the Pacific shore at Greenwood Cove.

Point Arena and Gualala

With only a few exceptions, the southernmost 40 miles of Mendocino coastline are almost totally undeveloped and virtually uninhabited, with green forests and coastal coves as far as the eye can see. The westernmost point here, **Point Arena,** is about five miles northwest of Hwy-1 via Lighthouse Road (the namesake lighthouse, built in 1870, stands 115 feet tall). Back on Hwy-1, the small town of Point Arena is worth a wander for nice cafés and bakeries; try the fluffy quiches or buttery croissants at the *très* Francophile **Franny's Cup & Saucer** (213 Main St., 707/882-2500), across the street from the lively Arena Theater, which puts on new-run movies nightly and good live music.

Another 15 miles south, situated at the southern edge of Mendocino County, the old logging port of **Gualala** (pop. 2,093) has one truly remarkable feature: the Russian Orthodox domes of **St. Orres** (36601 S. Hwy-1, 707/884-3303), now a B&B inn and $50-plus per person gourmet restaurant glowing with polished wood and stained glass, above Hwy-1 on the north side of town.

If you prefer to hang out with locals rather than well-heeled tourists from San Francisco, head instead to local bakeries like **Trinks Café** (707/884-1713) in the Seacliff Center shopping complex. Great camping and an incredible coastal panorama can be yours at **Gualala Point Regional Park** (707/785-2377, $7 per car, $32-35 camping), a mile south of town along the Gualala River.

Sea Ranch

Midway between Mendocino and the San Francisco Bay Area, the vacation-home community of **Sea Ranch** was laid out in the mid-1960s by a visionary group of architects and planners, including Lawrence Halprin and Charles Moore, who hoped to show that development need not destroy or negatively impact the natural beauty of the California coast. Strict design guidelines, preserving over half the 5,000 acres as open space and requiring the use of muted natural wood cladding and other barn-like features, made it an aesthetic success, which you can appreciate for your-self at the **Sea Ranch Lodge** (707/785-2371 or 800/732-7262, $219 and up), near the south end of the development.

The rest of Sea Ranch, however, is strictly private, which has raised the hackles of area activists, who after years of lawsuits finally forced through a few coastal access trails in the mid-1980s; these, such as **Walk-On Beach** at milepost 56.5, are marked by turnouts along Hwy-1.

Salt Point State Park

The many sheltered rocky coves of **Salt Point State Park** make it ideal for undersea divers, who come to hunt the abundant abalone. Along these six miles of jagged shoreline, pines and redwoods clutch the water's edge, covering some 6,000 acres on both sides of Hwy-1 to make Salt Point a prime place for hiking and camping. For a guide to the 20 miles of trails, or background on the sandstone mortars and other remnants of the Kashaya Pomo Native American village that stood here until the 1850s, contact the **visitors center** (707/847-3221).

One of the few positive effects of cutting down the native redwood forests that once covered the Northern California coast has been the emergence of giant rhodo-dendrons in their place. You'll find the most impressive display at the **Kruse Rhododendron State Natural Reserve,** high above Hwy-1 adjacent to Salt Point State Park, where some 300 acres of rhododendrons, some reaching 14 feet in height, burst forth in late spring, usually peaking around the first week of May.

In between Salt Point and Fort Ross, Beniamino Bufano's 93-foot *Peace* statue looms like a shiny silver missile alongside Hwy-1 above craggy **Timber Cove,** where there's also a nice restaurant and inn at the **Timber Cove Resort** (707/847-3231, $230 and up).

Fort Ross State Historic Park

If you're captivated by California's lively history, one of the most evocative spots in the state is **Fort Ross State Historic Park,** the well-restored remains of a Russian

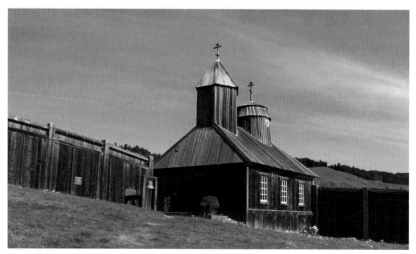

Russian Orthodox chapel at Fort Ross

fur-trapping outpost built here in 1812. During a 30-year residency, the Russians farmed wheat and potatoes, traded with Native Americans, and trapped local seals and sea otters for their furs, which commanded huge sums on the European market. By 1840, the near destruction of the sea otter population caused the company to shut down operations and sell the fort to Sacramento's John Sutter, who financed the purchase on credit. Later, the abandoned fort was badly damaged by the 1906 San Francisco earthquake and later fires, but the state has completed a high-quality restoration and reconstruction project, using hand-hewn lumber and historically accurate building methods to replicate the original barracks and other buildings, including a luminous redwood chapel.

From Hwy-1, Fort Ross spreads west, 20 miles south of Sea Ranch and a dozen miles north of the Russian River. Outside the fort's walls, a modern **visitor center** (707/847-3286, daily summer, Mon.-Fri. winter, $8 per car) traces the site's natural, Native American, and Russian history, and offers information on the park's many fine hiking trails.

Jenner, Guerneville, and the Russian River

South of Fort Ross, Hwy-1 climbs high above the rugged coastline, offering breathtaking vistas of the Pacific Ocean hundreds of feet below. Twelve miles south of Fort Ross, Hwy-1 reaches the low-key resort community of **Jenner** (pop. 139), which stretches along the broad mouth of the Russian River. Harbor seals and sea lions sun themselves on the beach at **Goat Rock,** houses climb the steep hillsides, and there's a gas station, a post office, and the excellent **River's End** (707/865-2484, daily summer, otherwise Thurs.-Tues.), which has a range of great food—everything from burgers to seafood—and ocean-view tables inside and outside, depending on the weather.

Bohemian Grove, the world's most exclusive men's club, covers 2,700 acres of redwood forest just south of the Russian River outside the village of Monte Rio.

From Jenner, Hwy-116 runs east along the river, passing through forests, vineyards, and popular summertime resort towns, the largest of which is **Guerneville,** 13 miles away, with a number of worthwhile cafés and a largely gay

the closing of the Russian River ferry, c. 1931

and lesbian summer population. A more traditional place, with a broad but gravelly beach, boat rentals, cabins, and riverfront camping, is **Johnson's Beach & Resort** (16215 and 16217 1st St., 707/869-2022). After 35-odd miles, Hwy-116 eventually links up with the US-101 freeway to and from San Francisco, providing a faster alternative to coastal Hwy-1.

Sonoma Coast State Park

South of Jenner and the Russian River, Hwy-1 hugs the coast along 10 miles of rocky coves and sandy beaches, collectively protected as **Sonoma Coast State Park** (707/875-3483). Starting with Goat Rock at the southern lip of the Russian River mouth, a bluff-top trail leads south past intriguingly named and usually unpopulated pocket strands like Blind Beach, Schoolhouse Beach, Shell Beach, Wright's Beach (site of the park's main beachfront campground), and Salmon Creek Beach. Take care when hiking along the Sonoma Coast: Many people have been drowned by "sleeper" waves, which rise unannounced and sweep people off the rocky shore.

At the southernmost end, Sonoma Coast State Park broadens to include the wildflower-covered granite promontory of **Bodega Head,** which juts into the Pacific and provides a great vantage point for watching the gray whale migrations in winter.

Bodega Bay

Protected by the massive bulk of Bodega Head, the fishing harbor of **Bodega Bay** has grown into an upscale vacation destination, with Sea Ranch-style vacation homes lining the fairways of golf resorts and deluxe hotels overlooking the still-busy commercial wharves. On the waterfront, the **Lucas Wharf Restaurant & Bar** (595

Bodega's church, used by Alfred Hitchcock in *The Birds*

Hwy-1, 707/875-3522) dishes up fish 'n' chips and clam chowder. Next door, the **Fishetarian Fish Market** (599 S. Hwy-1, 707/875-9092) has fantastic fresh rock cod fish 'n' chips , tasty fries, and a large fresh-fish market. If you've had your fill of fish, continue south to the rustic U.S. Post Office and mini-mall west of the highway, where you can enjoy milk shakes and hot dogs at **The Dog House** (707/875-2441).

South of Bodega Bay, Hwy-1 cuts inland around the marshy coastal estuaries, passing by the photogenic small town of **Bodega,** whose Victorian-era hilltop church was used by Alfred Hitchcock for many of the scariest scenes in his 1963 movie *The Birds*. In 1976, international artists Christo and Jeanne-Claude used Bodega as a key tableau in their installation *Running Fence*, which draped an 18-foot-high, nearly 25-mile-long fabric curtain across the rolling ranchlands of Sonoma County, from the coast to the inland valleys. There's not much sign of Hollywood directors or conceptual art in these parts today, but Bodega is a nice place to wander and explore, and the down-home **Casino Bar & Grill** (17000 Bodega Hwy., 707/876-3185) at the center of "town" is more welcoming than it might look, with a well-worn pool table and excellent locally sourced food most nights.

Valley Ford

Between Bodega Bay and Point Reyes, Hwy-1 veers inland to avoid the marshy lowlands, and midway between the two bigger destinations, the winding two-lane highway brings you to a great road-trip stop. **Valley Ford** is a photogenic community that hosts a great old family-run roadhouse, **Dinucci's Restaurant** (707/876-3260, dinner only Thurs.-Mon., lunch on weekends, $10-28 per person), serving huge portions of unreconstructed Italian food—minestrone, fresh bread, salad, and pasta. More self-consciously stylish, contemporary fare is on the menu next door at quirky **Rocker Oysterfeller's Kitchen + Saloon** (707/876-1983, dinner Thurs.-Fri., late lunch and dinner Sat., brunch and dinner Sun.), inside the Civil War-era **Valley Ford Hotel,** which has been renovated with luxurious rooms while retaining old-time charm (quilts on the beds, rocking chairs on the porch, the whole nine yards).

Point Reyes

Between Bodega Bay and the Golden Gate Bridge, Hwy-1 slices through one of the country's most scenically and economically wealthy areas, **Marin County.** Though less than an hour from San Francisco, the northwestern reaches of the county are surprisingly rural, consisting of rolling dairy lands and a few untouched small towns; Hwy-1 follows a slow and curving route along the usually uncrowded two-lane blacktop.

A sign outside the small white garage on Main Street in Point Reyes Station claims it is the oldest Chevrolet dealer in California.

After looping inland south of Bodega Bay, Hwy-1 reaches the shore again at oyster-rich **Tomales Bay,** around which it winds for a dozen or so miles before reaching the earthy but erudite town of **Point Reyes Station.** Here the excellent **Station House Café** (11180 Hwy-1, 415/663-1515, Thurs.-Tues.) serves incredibly good breakfasts and delicious lunches that include great-tasting local oysters, on the half-shell or barbecued. The bar is lively and well stocked, and it hosts free live music most Sunday afternoons.

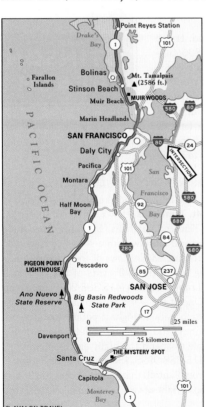

© AVALON TRAVEL

Northwest from town along Sir Francis Drake Boulevard, the 70,000-plus-acre **Point Reyes National Seashore** offers an entire guidebook's worth of hiking and cycling trails, broad beaches, dense forests, and more; stop at the **Bear Valley Visitor Center** (415/464-5100, daily, free) for more information. The photogenic lighthouse at the tip of Point Reyes gives great views over the coast, and in winter and spring (Dec.-June) the steep headland makes an ideal spot for watching migrating gray whales. Eight miles from the visitors center, the **HI Point Reyes Hostel** (1390 Limantour Spit Rd., 415/663-8811) has dorm beds in an old farmhouse on the road to Drake's Bay.

Dozens of delightful inns and restaurants operate in and around Point Reyes, but because they're a mere 35 miles from San Francisco, they're often booked solid weeks in advance.

Everything from treetop rooms to waterfront cabins can be found through the local **chamber of commerce** (415/663-9232, www.pointreyes.org).

Bolinas and Stinson Beach

At the southern end of the Point Reyes peninsula, **Bolinas** is a small town with a well-earned reputation for discouraging tourists. The signs leading you here from Hwy-1 are regularly torn down by locals bent on keeping the place to themselves. It's blessed with one of the coast's best tide-pool areas in **Duxbury Reef,** which curves around the western edge of Bolinas. The town itself is little more than a general store, a bakery, some cafés, and a bar. The 1850s **Smiley's Saloon & Hotel** (41 Wharf Rd., 415/868-1311) offers good food, cold beer, live music, and six upstairs rooms.

In contrast, the broad strands of **Stinson Beach,** four miles south of Bolinas along Hwy-1, are the Bay Area's most popular summertime suntanning spots. A grocery store and deli, the **Live Water Surf Shop** (which rents boards and the essential wetsuits), and a couple of outdoor bar-and-grills along Hwy-1 form a short parade at the entrance to the beach. The best place to eat hereabouts is the **Parkside Café** (43 Arenal Ave., 415/868-1272). If you want to stay overnight, try the pleasant **Sandpiper** Lodging (415/868-1632, $165 and up), just west of Hwy-1.

If you have the chance to plan ahead, try to book a night at the **Steep Ravine Cabins** (800/444-7275, $100), just over a mile south of Stinson Beach on the ocean side of Hwy-1. Now part of Mt. Tamalpais State Park, these nine rustic redwood cabins are basic roof-over-the-head accommodations (bring sleeping bags and food; water faucets are just outside the door) in an absolutely beautiful coastal chasm. These popular cabins (originally owned by Bay Area bigwigs like Dorothea Lange) sleep up to five people.

Mt. Tamalpais, Muir Woods, and Muir Beach

From the coast, a pair of roads—Panoramic Highway and the Shoreline Highway (Hwy-1)—twist up and over the slopes of **Mt. Tamalpais** (elev. 2,586 feet), the signature peak of the San Francisco Bay Area. Known usually as "Mt. Tam," the whole mountain has been protected in a seminatural state within a series of state and national parks, and its voluptuous slopes offer incredible views of the urbanized Bay Area and the untouched coastline. Drive to within 100 yards of the top for a 360-degree panorama, or stop at the Pantoll **ranger station** (415/388-2070) for a map of Mt. Tam's hiking routes and fire roads. One of the world's great trails, the Dipsea Trail between Muir Woods and Stinson Beach, hits its highest points and gives its greatest views within a short stroll of the Pantoll parking lot and walk-in campground.

If you plan ahead, you may also be able to spend the night on the mountain, indoors, in the comfort of **West Point Inn** (415/388-9955, $50 adults), a hiker-centric walk-in-only lodge (two mostly-level miles from Pantoll) that was built back in 1904 as part of a long-vanished scenic railroad, whose right-of-way is now one of Mt. Tam's most popular hiking trails.

A deep, dark valley between the coast and Mt. Tamalpais holds the last surviving stand of Marin County redwoods, preserved for future generations as the **Muir Woods National Monument** (daily 8am-dusk, $10 adults) and named in honor of turn-of-the-20th-century naturalist John Muir. A paved mile-long trail takes in the biggest trees, but since the park is often crowded with busloads of sightseeing hordes making the tour from San Francisco, you may want to explore the farther-flung areas, climbing up Mt. Tamalpais or following Muir Creek two miles downstream to the crescent-shaped cove of **Muir Beach,** along Hwy-1. Besides stunning scenery, Muir Beach is also home to the welcoming **Pelican Inn** (415/383-6000, rooms $224 and up), an Olde English-style pub serving food and fine beers; overnight guests get cozy rooms and access to a delightful room called "The Snug," with a fireplace.

Another enjoyably ersatz experience awaits at the junction of Hwy-1 and the US-101 freeway, where a historic roadside restaurant has been resurrected as the **Buckeye Roadhouse** (15 Shoreline Hwy., 415/331-2600), near Mill Valley on the SF Bay side of the coastal mountains, where you can feast on fine barbecue, great steaks and burgers, and delicious desserts in a lively retro-Route 66 atmosphere.

Marin Headlands

If you can avoid the magnetic pull of the Golden Gate Bridge and San Francisco, take the last turnoff from US-101 (northbound drivers take the second turnoff after crossing the bridge) and head west to the **Marin Headlands,** a former military base that's been turned back into coastal semi-wilderness. A tortuous road twists along the face of 300-foot cliffs, giving incredible views of the bridge and the city behind it. The road continues west and north to the **Visitor Center** (415/331-1540), housed in an old chapel, with a reconstructed Miwok shelter and details on hiking and biking routes. And if you're so inclined, on Wednesday-Friday afternoons and the first Saturday of each month, you can tour a restored Cold War-era **Nike missile silo** (free).

Nearby, the barracks of old Fort Barry have been converted into the peaceful **HI Marin Headlands Hostel** (415/331-2777, dorm beds $31 and up, private rooms $105 and up), which has dorm beds as well as private rooms.

The all-terrain mountain bike, which now accounts for half of all bikes on (and off) the roads, was invented in the late 1970s by a group of daredevil Marin cyclists intent on cruising down the fire roads of Mt. Tamalpais at the highest possible speed.

Every June since 1905, one of the country's wildest foot races, the **Dipsea** (415/331-3550), has followed a rugged 7.4-mile route from the town of Mill Valley to Stinson Beach.

view from atop Mt. Tamalpais

San Francisco

view from inside Fort Point, with the Golden Gate Bridge overhead

San Francisco is easily the most enjoyable city in the United States. Its undulating topography turns every other corner into a scenic vista, while its many distinctive neighborhoods are perfect for aimless wandering. Museums document everything from gold rush history to cutting-edge modern art, while stellar restaurants offer the chance to sample gourmet food from around the world—all in an easily manageable, densely compact small city.

If there's one place in the city you should stop to get your bearings, it's **Fort Point National Historic Site,** a massive photogenic Civil War fort standing along the bay, directly beneath the Golden Gate Bridge. You can wander at will through the honeycomb of corridors, staircases, and gun ports, watch the fearless surfers and windsurfers offshore, and take in a panoramic view of the City by the Bay. From here you can walk up to and across the **Golden Gate Bridge,** or head west to **Land's End** or back into town via a popular bay-front walking and cycling trail. Another great place to get a feel for San Francisco is **Golden Gate Park,** which stretches inland from the western edge of the city, including more than 1,000 acres of gardens, a boating lake, and two landmark museums, featuring the copper-clad art of the **de Young Museum,** and the natural history, aquarium, and planetarium of the grass-roofed **California Academy of Sciences.**

If there's one other place that ought to be on your S.F. itinerary, it's **Alcatraz.** Aptly known as The Rock, this was America's most notorious prison from 1934 until 1963. Now preserved as a historical park, the island is worth a visit as much

the Conservatory of Flowers in Golden Gate Park

view of Alcatraz as seen on approach by boat

for the views of San Francisco as for its grim past. To reach Alcatraz, take one of the ferries that leave throughout the day from Pier 41 at the east end of Fisherman's Wharf.

The **San Francisco Giants** (877/473-4849, tickets $25 and up) play at retro-modern AT&T Park, along the bay in downtown's South of Market district.

PRACTICALITIES

San Francisco is one of the few cities on the West Coast where you don't need a car, since distances are short and public transportation is quite extensive; the grid street plan makes it easy to find your way around. San Francisco's **Municipal Railway** (Muni, 415/673-6864 or 311) network of public transit buses, trams, and cable cars will take you all over the city.

The only problem for visitors in San Francisco is deciding where to eat—there are so many great places that choosing among them can be a painful process. For breakfast, **Sears Fine Foods** (439 Powell St., 415/986-0700) on Union Square is a local institution. Two more SF culinary landmarks are the **Swan Oyster Depot** (1517 Polk St., 415/673-1101 or 415/673-2757, Mon.-Sat. 8am-5:30pm, food service 10:30am-4:45pm), a half block north of the California Street cable car, a simple oyster bar serving the city's freshest shellfish and coldest Anchor Steam beer; and **Sam's Grill & Seafood Restaurant** (374 Bush St., 415/421-0594), downtown, with incredible grilled meat and fish dishes, melt-in-your-mouth shoestring fries, and ancient-looking 1930s wooden booths that seem like set pieces from a Sam Spade mystery.

Given San Francisco's worldwide popularity, it's no surprise that room rates run pretty high—expect to pay $250 a night or more, plus parking and taxes. If you're here for a honeymoon or other romantic reason, the nicest place in town is the swanky **Loews Regency** (222 Sansome St., 415/276-9888, $399 and up), which fills the top floors of a Financial District skyscraper and has 270-degree bay views (even from the bathtubs!). The best budget options are three **HI hostels,** one on the bay at Fort Mason (415/771-7277), another downtown (312 Mason St., 415/788-5604), and a third near Civic Center (685 Ellis St., 415/474-5721). Each one costs about $40 and starts at $110 for a private room. In between there are some nice motels on the outskirts of downtown, like the nouveau retro **Hotel del Sol** (3100 Webster St., 415/921-5520, $199 and up), in the Marina District.

Across San Francisco

From the north, Hwy-1 enters **San Francisco** across the glorious **Golden Gate Bridge,** where parking areas at both ends let you ditch the car and walk across the elegant 1.7-mile-long span. South from the bridge, Hwy-1 follows 19th Avenue across Golden Gate Park, then runs due south through the outer reaches of San Francisco, finally reaching the coast again at the often-foggy town of Pacifica. The most scenic alternative is the **49-Mile Scenic Drive,** the best part

the opening of the Golden Gate Bridge, 1937

of which heads west from the bridge through the **Presidio,** along Lincoln Boulevard and Camino del Mar, following the rugged coastline to **Lands End,** where you can hike around and explore the remains of Sutro Baths, eat a burger or grilled cheese at **Louis'** (415/387-6330), a historic diner with amazing views, or dine at the wonderful (and not all that expensive) **Cliff House** (415/386-3330).

From Lands End, this scenic route runs south along the oceanfront Great Highway, which eventually links back up with Hwy-1 near the small but enjoyable **San Francisco Zoo** (415/753-7080, daily, $20 adults).

Since driving and parking in San Francisco can be frustrating and expensive (Steve McQueen could never make *Bullitt* in today's traffic), consider parking out here in the burbs and taking public transportation into the center of town. The N Judah Muni trolley line runs between downtown and the coast just south of Golden Gate Park, via the Sunset District neighborhood, where parking is comparatively plentiful.

San Francisco is the start of our cross-country road trip along US-50, **The Loneliest Road,** beginning on page 670. The route crosses high mountains and red-rock deserts before winding up at Ocean City, Maryland.

Montara and Princeton

From the San Francisco city limits, Hwy-1 runs along the Pacific Ocean through the rural and almost totally undeveloped coastline of San Mateo County. The first eight miles or so are high-speed freeway, but after passing through the suburban communities of **Daly City** and **Pacifica,** the pace abruptly slows to a scenic cruise. Pacifica, which has a long pier, a popular surfing beach, a bowling alley, an ocean-view Taco Bell, and a handy Holiday Inn Express hotel, makes a good edge-of-town base for seeing the San Francisco area. South of Pacifica, two-lane Hwy-1 hugs the decomposing cliff tops of **Devil's Slide,** where the terrifying old highway has been converted into a cycling and hiking path following completion of the current tunnel.

The first real place south of Pacifica is the ramshackle beach town of **Montara,** where the old but still functioning lighthouse has been partly converted into the **HI Point Montara Lighthouse Hostel** (650/728-7177).

South of Montara, Hwy-1 bends inland around the rugged shores of the **Fitzgerald Marine Reserve** (650/728-3584), a wonderful (but fragile) tide pool area filled with anemones and other delicate sea creatures. The tide pools are visible at low tide only; look, but don't touch! Hwy-1 continues south past the Pillar Point Harbor at **Princeton-by-the-Sea,** where you can enjoy a different sort of sealife appreciation: the fresh fish 'n' chips (plus nice wines and cold beers) at **Barbara's Fishtrap** (650/728-7049, cash only).

Half Moon Bay

The first sizable coastal town south of San Francisco, **Half Moon Bay** (pop. 11,324) is 28 miles from the city but seems much more distant. A quiet farming community that's slowly but surely changing into a Silicon Valley exurb, Half Moon Bay still has an all-American Main Street lined by hardware stores, cafés, bakeries, and the inevitable art galleries and B&Bs. The main event hereabouts is the annual **Art & Pumpkin Festival,** held mid-October, which celebrates the coming of Halloween with a competition to determine the world's largest pumpkin—winning gourds weigh more than 1,500 pounds!

Until the construction of the $550-a-night beachfront Ritz-Carlton golf resort, the coastline of Half Moon Bay was almost completely undeveloped, but it's still pretty nice and accessible, with a four-mile-long string of state park beaches at the foot of bluff-top vegetable farms and horse ranches. The town also retains its rural feel. But thanks to the presence of so many Silicon Valley billionaires just over the hills, it has significantly better restaurants. The best fish tacos (and great fish 'n' chips) can be had at the **Flying Fish Bar & Grill** (211 San Mateo Rd., 650/712-1125), off Hwy-92 at the north end of Main Street. Excellent and not outrageously expensive Italian specialties are on the menu at **Pasta Moon** (315 Main St., 650/726-5125).

Looking for the world's biggest waves? Head down to **Mavericks,** an offshore reef area off Pillar Point, three miles north of Half Moon Bay. In winter, when conditions are right, mega-waves as high as 80 feet draw expert surfers from all over the world. For a report, and a safety advisory to warn off any wannabes, call **Mavericks Surf Company** (650/560-8088); it's located at Pillar Point Harbor, as near as you can get to the offshore breaks.

Pescadero and Pigeon Point Lighthouse

The 50 miles of coastline between Half Moon Bay and Santa Cruz are one of the great surprises of the California coast: The virtually unspoiled miles offer rocky tide pools and driftwood-strewn beaches beneath sculpted bluffs topped by rolling green fields of brussels sprouts, artichokes, and U-pick berry patches. Access to the water is not always easy, and while surfers seem to park along Hwy-1 and walk across the fields to wherever the waves are breaking, for visitors it's best to aim for one of the half-dozen state parks, like San Gregorio, Pomponio, Bean Hollow, or Año Nuevo.

The biggest town hereabouts, **Pescadero** (pop. 643) is a mile or so inland from Hwy-1 and well worth the short detour for a chance to sample the fresh fish, great pies, and other home-cooked treats at **Duarte's Tavern** (202 Stage Rd., 650/879-0464, daily breakfast, lunch, and dinner), at the south end of the block-long downtown.

Less than 10 miles south of Pescadero, the photogenic beacon of **Pigeon Point Light Station** has appeared in innumerable TV and print commercials. The graceful 115-foot-tall brick tower is closed, but the grounds are open for **tours** (at 1pm

Pigeon Point Lighthouse

Thurs.-Mon. 10am-4pm, donation), and the adjacent lighthouse quarters function as the popular **HI Pigeon Point Lighthouse Hostel** (650/879-0633), which has dorms beds, family-friendly private rooms, and a hot tub perched above the crashing surf.

Año Nuevo State Reserve

West of Hwy-1, one of nature's more bizarre spectacles takes place annually at **Año Nuevo State Park** (650/879-2025, daily 8am-dusk), where each winter hundreds of humongous northern elephant seals come ashore to give birth and mate. The males reach up to 13 feet head-to-tail, weigh as much as 4,500 pounds, and have dangling proboscises that inspired their name. These blubbery creatures were hunted almost to extinction for their oil-rich flesh. In 1910, fewer than 100 were left in the world; their resurgence to a current population of more than 100,000 has proved that protection does work.

Every December, after spending the summer at sea, hordes of male elephant seals arrive here at Año Nuevo, the seals' primary onshore rookery, ready to do battle with each other for the right to procreate. It's an incredible show, with the bulls bellowing, barking, and biting at each other to establish dominance; the alpha male mates with most of the females, and the rest must wait till next year. Pups conceived the previous year are born in January, and mating goes on through March. During the mating season (Dec. 15-Mar. 31), ranger-led **tours** (800/444-4445, $10) are the only way to see the seals; these tours are popular, so plan ahead and try to come midweek. Tours start at 8:45am, and end at 2pm. The three-mile walk from the parking area to the shore is worth doing at any time of year, since it's a pretty scene and some of the seals are residents year-round.

The only lodging option along this stretch of coast is three miles south of the lighthouse, or two miles north of the entrance to Año Nuevo, at **Costanoa Lodge** (650/879-1100, $8 and up). A stylish retro-modern eco-minded resort, open since 1999 on the inland side of Hwy-1, Costanoa has everything from a luxurious lodge to tent cabins (complete with saunas). There's also a bar and grill and an adjacent **KOA Campground** (650/879-7302).

South of Año Nuevo State Park, you'll see signs tempting you to stop at **Pie Ranch** (650/879-0995), a rustic roadside attraction selling, you guessed it, fresh pies. They also serve as an ad hoc education center: On the third Saturday of each month they host a farm education program that wraps up with a potluck dinner and barn dance to spread the word to Silicon Valley denizens about good food and old-fashioned ways of life. On most days, visitors can take a self-guided tour of the property. As their T-shirts say, "Pie Ranch. Eat Pie. Repeat."

Davenport

Midway between Año Nuevo State Reserve and Santa Cruz, the tiny roadside hamlet of **Davenport** was the birthplace of Odwalla, the fresh-fruit-juice company, beloved of Apple Computer founder Steve Jobs and now owned and run by beverage giant Coca-Cola. The town is a popular stop for cyclists, motorcyclists, and road-tripping Sunday drivers from all over the Bay Area.

They come for the strong coffee, diner-style breakfasts, and excellent pastries at the friendly **Whale City Bakery Bar & Grill** (490 Hwy 1., 831/423-9009) and the more refined meals and rooms at the neighboring **Davenport Roadhouse Restaurant & Inn** (831/426-8801).

Two miles north of Davenport, **Swanton Berry Farm** (831/469-8804) is one of the last pick-your-own farms on the California coast. Swanton is also a world leader in truly sustainable agriculture, using biodynamic farming practices and paying the workers union wages while partnering with local markets (and the national chain Whole Foods) to provide the freshest, healthiest produce. And if you don't have the time or inclination to get out in the fields, Swanton's has a farm stand where they sell their delicious fresh berries (and kiwis and brussels sprouts, depending upon the season). The famous fruit pies are available year-round.

Big Basin Redwoods State Park

The oldest of California's state parks, **Big Basin Redwoods State Park** (831/338-8860) protects some 18,000 acres of giant coastal redwoods. Established in 1902,

the park has many miles of hiking and cycling trails high up in the mountains. The heart of the park is most easily accessible from Santa Cruz via Hwy-236, but a popular trail winds up from the coast to the crest, starting from Hwy-1 at **Waddell Beach,** a popular haunt for kite-surfers and sailboarders, who sometimes do flips and loops in the wind-whipped waves.

Santa Cruz

The popular beach resort and college town of **Santa Cruz** (pop. 59,946) sits at the north end of Monterey Bay, a 90-minute drive from San Francisco, at the foot of a 3,000-foot-high ridge of mountains. It's best known for its Boardwalk amusement park, which holds the oldest surviving wooden roller coaster on the West Coast, and for the large University of California campus in the redwoods above. The city was named by Spanish explorer Gaspar de Portolà and shares the name Santa Cruz ("holy cross" in Spanish) with the ill-fated mission settlement begun here in 1777.

Modern Santa Cruz was all but leveled by an earthquake in 1989 but has since recovered its stature as one of the more diverting stops on the California coast.

Natural Bridges State Beach, four miles south of Santa Cruz via West Cliff Drive, has a natural wave-carved archway and, in winter, swarms of monarch butterflies.

The downtown area lies a mile inland, so from Hwy-1 follow the many signs pointing visitors toward the wharf and the beach, where plentiful parking is available. Walk, rent a bike, or drive along the coastal Cliff Drive to the world's first **Surfing Museum** (Thurs.-Tues. 10am-5pm July 4-Labor Day, Thurs.-Mon. noon-4pm Sept.-June, donation), which is packed with giant old redwood boards and newer high-tech cutters as well as odds and ends tracing the development of West Coast surfing. Housed in an old lighthouse, it overlooks one of the state's prime surfing spots, Steamer Lane, named for the steamships that once brought day-tripping San Franciscans to the wharf.

A large part of the Santa Cruz economy still depends on visitors, and there are plenty of cafés, restaurants, and lodging options to choose from. Eating and drinking places congregate east of Hwy-1 along Front Street and Pacific Avenue in downtown Santa Cruz, which has a number of engaging, somewhat countercultural book and record shops along with cafés like **Zoccoli's** (1534 Pacific Ave., 831/423-1711), which has great soups and sandwiches. The best burgers, veggie burgers, and fries are a block west of Pacific at **Jack's Hamburgers** (202 Lincoln St., 831/423-4421). More good veggie food can be had at the

Surfboard designs have come a long way.

Saturn Café (145 Laurel St., 831/429-8505), while the stylish **Soif** (105 Walnut Ave., 831/423-2020) has fine wines and tasty tapas-like treats.

Motels line Hwy-1, and some nice-looking Victorian-era B&Bs stand atop Beach Hill, between the Boardwalk and downtown, where the **Seaway Inn** (176 W. Cliff Dr., 831/471-9004, $90 and up) is nice, clean, and reasonably priced. You can also avail yourself of the **HI Santa Cruz Hostel** (321 Main St., 831/423-8304, dorm beds less than $30) in an immaculate 1870s cottage. Among the many nice B&Bs is the rustic **The Babbling Brook Inn** (1025 Laurel St., 831/427-2437 or 800/866-1131, $199 and up).

Santa Cruz Beach Boardwalk

The bay-front **Santa Cruz Beach Boardwalk** (831/423-5590, daily summer, weekends fall-spring, rides vary in cost, all-day ride pass around $37) should be your main stop. Besides the dozens of thrill rides and midway games, it boasts the art deco Cocoanut Grove ballroom and two rides that are such classics of the genre they've been listed as a National Historic Landmark. The biggest thrill is the **Giant Dipper** roller coaster ($7), open since 1924, a senior citizen compared to modern rides but still one of the top coasters in the country—the clattering, half-mile-long tracks make it seem far faster than the 55 mph maximum it reaches. Near the roller coaster is the beautiful Charles Looff **carousel** ($5), one of only six left in the country, with 73 hand-carved wooden horses doing the same circuit they've followed since 1911; grab for the brass rings while listening to music pumped out by the 342-pipe organ, imported from Germany and over 100 years old.

Along with these and many other vintage arcade attractions, the amusement park also features a log flume ride, a sky ride, a two-story miniature-golf course installed inside the old bathhouse, plus a bowling alley and all the shooting galleries, laser tag, and virtual reality machines you could want. The Boardwalk has a concrete concourse but retains a great deal of charm and character.

Santa Cruz Beach Boardwalk

Mystery Spot

In the hills above Santa Cruz, two miles north of Hwy-1, the **Mystery Spot** (465 Mystery Spot Rd., 831/423-8897, daily, $8 per person and $5 per car) is one of those fortunate few tourist traps that actually get people to come back again. Like similar places along the Pacific Coast, the Mystery Spot is a section of redwood forest where the usual laws of physics seem not to apply (trees grow in oddly contorted corkscrew shapes, and balls roll uphill). Among those who study vortexes and other odd geomantic places, the Mystery Spot is considered to be the real thing, but you don't have to take it seriously to enjoy yourself.

Watsonville, Castroville, and Moss Landing

Between Santa Cruz and Monterey, Hwy-1 loops inland through the farmlands fronting Monterey Bay. Part freeway, part winding two-lane road, Hwy-1 races through, and to be honest there's not a lot worth stopping for: The beaches can be dreary, and the two main towns, **Watsonville** and **Castroville,** are little more than service centers for the local fruit and vegetable packers, though Castroville does have one odd sight: the "World's Largest Artichoke," a concrete statue outside a large fruit stand at the center of town.

Back on the coast, midway along Monterey Bay, the port community of **Moss Landing** is a busy commercial fishery, with lots of trawlers and packing plants—not to mention pelicans aplenty. Moss Landing sits alongside **Elkhorn Slough,** the

largest and most wildlife-rich wetlands area in Monterey Bay (a busy nursery for baby seals, baby otters, and baby leopard sharks), which you can see in greatest comfort via **pontoon boat tour** (831/633-5555). Moss Landing is also home to the research arm of the Monterey Bay Aquarium, a nice KOA campground, an obtrusively huge electricity generating plant, and **The Whole Enchilada** (831/633-3038), which has spicy seafood right on Hwy-1, near the power plant. Alternatively, try the sustainable and organic **Haute Enchilada Café** (7902 Moss Landing Rd., 831/633-5843), west of the highway.

Much of the bay front north of Monterey formerly belonged to the U.S. Marine Corps base at Fort Ord. Almost the entire parcel was turned over to the State of California to house the **California State University at Monterey Bay,** which opened its doors in 1994.

San Juan Bautista

Away from the coast, 15 miles inland from Monterey Bay via Hwy-129 or Hwy-156, stands one of California's most idyllic small towns, **San Juan Bautista** (pop. 1,862). It centers on a grassy town square bordered by a well-preserved mission complex, complete with a large church and monastery, standing since 1812. Two other sides of the square are lined by hotels, stables, and houses dating from the 1840s through 1860s, preserved in their entirety within a **state historic park** (831/623-4881, daily).

Completing the living history lesson, the east edge of the square is formed by one of the state's few preserved stretches of El Camino Real, the 200-year-old Spanish colonial trail that linked all the California missions with Mexico. Adding to the interest, the trail runs right along the rift zone of the San Andreas Fault, and a small seismograph registers tectonic activity. (Incidentally, San Juan Bautista was where the climactic final scenes of Hitchcock's *Vertigo* were filmed—though in the movie, they added a much more prominent bell tower with a seemingly endless staircase.)

The town's main street is a block from the mission and is lined by a handful of antiques shops, Mexican restaurants, and cafés like the **Mission Café** (300 3rd St., 831/623-2220).

Coastal farms along Monterey Bay grow about 75 percent of the nation's artichokes, which you can sample along with other produce at stands along Hwy-1.

In 1947, then-unknown Marilyn Monroe reigned as Miss Artichoke during Castroville's Artichoke Festival, still celebrated each May.

Monterey

jellyfish at the Monterey Bay Aquarium

The historic capital of California under the Spanish and Mexican regimes, **Monterey** (pop. 27,810), along with its peninsular neighbors Carmel and Pacific Grove, is one of the most satisfying stops in California. Dozens of significant historical sites have been well preserved, most of them concentrated within a two-mile-long walk called the Path of History that loops through the compact downtown area. Park in the lots at the foot of Alvarado Street, Monterey's main drag, and start your tour at **Fisherman's Wharf,** where bellowing sea lions wallow in the water, begging for popcorn from tourists. Next stop should be the adjacent **Custom House,** the oldest governmental building in the state.

From the Custom House, which is now surrounded by the Portola Hotel & Spa, you can follow the old railroad right-of-way west along the water to **Cannery Row,** where abandoned fish canneries have been gussied up into upscale bars and restaurants—most of them capitalizing on ersatz Steinbeckian themes. The one real attraction here is the excellent **Monterey Bay Aquarium** (886 Cannery Row, 831/648-4800, daily, $50 adults), housed in a spacious modern building and loaded with state-of-the-art tanks filled with over 500 species of local sealife. The aquarium is rated by many as the best in the world: Displays let visitors touch tide-pool denizens, watch playful sea otters, gaze into the gently swaying stalks of a three-story-tall kelp forest, be hypnotized by brilliantly colored jellyfish, or face truly weird creatures that usually live thousands of feet below the surface of the bay.

Hotel Del Monte, California, on Road of a Thousand Wonders

The internationally famous **Monterey Jazz Festival** (831/373-3366) is held every September.

Monterey Practicalities

Because Monterey gets such a considerable tourist trade, there's no shortage of restaurants, though good food at reasonable prices can be hard to find. In the historic center of town, one good bet is the **Old Monterey Café** (489 Alvarado St., 831/646-1021), serving large portions at breakfast and lunch. For breakfast near the aquarium, try **First Awakenings** (125 Oceanview Blvd., 831/372-1125). For seafood, catch an early-bird special (before 6pm) at one of the dozen restaurants on the wharf, or head a mile west along the frontage road to the popular **Monterey's Fish House** (2114 Del Monte Ave., 831/373-4647).

Places to stay vary widely, starting with the **HI Monterey**

Along Hwy-1 on the northwest edge of Monterey, the elegant **Club Del Monte,** a grand resort that attracted the first wealthy tourists in the 1880s when it was called Hotel Del Monte, is now part of the large U.S. Naval Postgraduate School.

Hostel (778 Hawthorne St., 831/649-0375, $32 and up per person), in historic Carpenters Union Hall off Cannery Row, five blocks from the aquarium. Moderate motels line Munras Street along the old US-101 highway frontage south toward Carmel, while prices in downtown Monterey hover in the $200 range, including the refurbished and centrally located **Monterey Hotel** (407 Calle Principal, 831/375-3184, $249 and up).

Many other nice places to stay and eat can be found in neighboring Pacific Grove or Carmel. For additional information on destinations from Monterey south to Big Sur, contact the Monterey County **visitors bureau** (888/221-1010).

Pacific Grove

Perched at the tip of the Monterey Peninsula, **Pacific Grove** (pop. 15,041) is a quiet throwback to old-time tourism, dating from the 1870s when the area was used for summertime Methodist revival meetings. The revivalists' tents and camps later grew

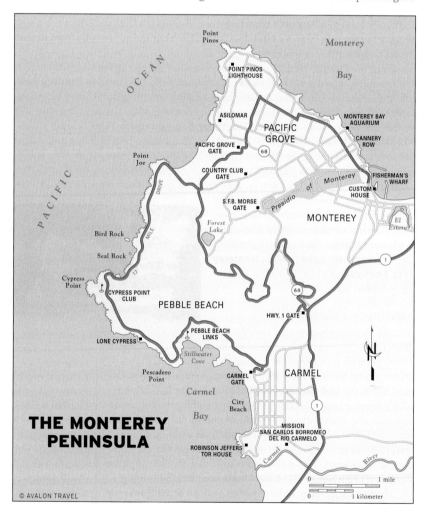

THE MONTEREY PENINSULA

© AVALON TRAVEL

into the West Coast headquarters of the populist Chautauqua educational movement, based in upstate New York. The town still has a curiously Midwestern feel, from its many small churches to the rows of well-maintained Victorian cottages lining its quiet streets. Besides the many fine old buildings, the best reason to come here is the beautiful, fully accessible shoreline, which boasts some of the coast's best tide pools, sunset views, and endless opportunities for winter whale-watching. Pacific Grove is also one of about 20 places in California where thousands of migratory monarch butterflies spend the winter months. From October until March, the butterflies congregate on the Butterfly Trees, a grove of pines on Ridge Road off Lighthouse Avenue, well signed from downtown.

The writer John Steinbeck lived in and around the Monterey Peninsula for many years and set many of his stories here, though things have changed so much in recent years that his beloved **Cannery Row** is hard to recognize. Steinbeck was born and is interred in **Salinas,** east of Monterey on US-101; after spurning him for most of his lifetime, the town in 1998 opened the **National Steinbeck Center** (1 Main St.) as a memorial to its literary son.

Pacific Grove's main street, Lighthouse Avenue, runs through the 15-mph commercial district of cafés, galleries, movie theaters, and a small but excellent **Pacific Grove Museum of Natural History** (Tues.-Sun., $9 adults), which is a great option for kids or when the weather turns bad. Nearby **Peppers Mexicali Café** (170 Forest Ave., 831/373-6892) serves good fresh Mexican food, while a range of fairly priced fish dishes are on the menu at **Fishwife** (1996½ Sunset Dr., 831/375-7107), near Asilomar, overlooking the wet-suited surfers riding the waves at **Asilomar State Beach.**

Places to stay in Pacific Grove are more reasonably priced than in Monterey or Carmel. **Andril Fireplace Cottages** (569 Asilomar Ave., 831/375-0994, $116 and up) is a lovingly maintained set of old-fashioned motor-court cabins, all with fireplaces and just two blocks from the ocean. The real landmark place to stay is the rustic **Asilomar Conference Grounds** (800 Asilomar Ave., 831/372-8016 or 888/635-5310, $143 and up), on the coast, which has a lovely main lobby (with roaring stone fireplace and heirloom pool tables) and some lovely woodsy Julia Morgan-designed cabins and lodge rooms; it is often filled with church groups or convention-goers. For a romantic getaway, it's hard to beat a Victorian-era B&B overlooking the Pacific from Lover's Point: **Seven Gables Inn** (555 Ocean View Blvd., 831/372-4341, $229 and up).

The 17-Mile Drive and Pebble Beach

Spanning the coast between Pacific Grove and Carmel, the **17-Mile Drive** is one of the most famous toll roads in the nation. Opened in the 1880s, the route initially took guests of Monterey's posh Hotel Del Monte on a scenic carriage ride along the coast through the newly planted Del Monte Forest between Carmel and Pacific Grove. Guided by Samuel F. B. Morse, son of the inventor, the formerly wild area underwent development beginning in the 1920s, first with golf courses like Pebble Beach and Cypress Point, and since then with resort hotels and upscale homes.

Enter the drive at any of the gates, where you'll pay the toll (about $10; bicyclists are free, and motorcyclists are banned) and be given a map and guide to the route, pointing out all the scenic highlights, especially the trussed-up old **Lone Cypress,** the legally trademarked subject of so many Carmel postcards. It's definitely worth doing the drive, if only to say you have, but to be honest, the views from the drive are no more or less splendid than they are from the toll-free drives, like Ocean View Boulevard in Pacific Grove, Scenic Road in Carmel, or Hwy-1 through Big Sur. You do, however, get to stop at the lodge, where your toll will be deducted from the price of lunch or dinner. If you're in the mood to splurge on wanton luxury, you can also stay overnight at either of two extremely plush golf and tennis resorts: the modern suburban-style country club of **The Inn at Spanish Bay** (2700 17-Mile Dr., 831/647-7500 or 800/877-0597, $740 and up) or the stately old-money **Lodge at Pebble Beach** (1700 17-Mile Dr., 831/624-3811 or 800/877-0597, $840 and up). for details on accommodations or Pebble Beach golf fees and tee times, call 800/877-0597.

The annual golf tournament hosted by Bing Crosby brought Pebble Beach to national attention. Originally an informal get-together, it grew into one of the main events of the professional circuit and is now the **AT&T Pebble Beach National Pro-Am,** held each winter.

Carmel

The exclusive enclave of **Carmel-by-the-Sea** (to give its complete name) began life in the early years of the 20th century as a small but lively bohemian colony inhabited by the literary likes of Sinclair Lewis, Mary Austin, and Upton Sinclair. However, with a few arts-and-crafts exceptions, by the 1950s Carmel had turned into the archly conservative and contrivedly quaint community it is today—a place where Marie Antoinette would no doubt feel at home, dressing down as a peasant, albeit in Chaps by Ralph Lauren. Preserving its rural feel by banning street addresses (and home mail delivery), Carmel simultaneously loves and abhors the many thousands of tourists who descend on it every weekend to window-shop its many designer boutiques and galleries, which fill the few blocks off Ocean Avenue, the main drag through town.

Every August for more than 60 years, Pebble Beach has drawn classic car collectors from around the world to show off their immaculately restored automobiles at the annual **Pebble Beach Concours d'Elegance.**

Though most of Carmel's many art galleries seem directed at interior decorators, a few are worth searching out, including the **Photography West Gallery** on the southeast corner of Dolores Street and Ocean Avenue, and the **Weston Gallery** on 6th Avenue near Dolores Street, featuring the works of Edward Weston, Ansel Adams, and other Carmel-based photographers.

Though it's easy to be put off by the surface glitz, Carmel does have a lot going for it. The water is too cold and treacherous for swimming, but broad **Carmel Beach City Park** at the foot of Ocean Avenue gleams white against a truly azure cove. To the south, aptly named **Scenic Road** winds along the rocky coast, past poet Robinson Jeffers's dramatic **Tor House** (831/624-1813, tours Fri.-Sat. 10am-3pm, $12). Jeffers, who lived at the house between 1919 and 1962, built much of what you see here out of boulders he hauled up by hand from the beach.

At the south end of the Carmel peninsula, another broad beach, **Carmel River State Beach,** spreads at the mouth of the Carmel River; this usually unpopulated spot is also a favorite spot for scuba divers exploring the deep undersea canyon.

Above the beach, just west of Hwy-1 a mile south of central Carmel, **Carmel Mission** (daily, $9.50 donation), also known as San Carlos Borromeo de Carmelo, was the most important of all the California missions, serving as home, headquarters, and final resting place of Junípero Serra, the Franciscan priest who established Carmel and many of the 20 other California missions, and who is entombed under the chapel floor. The gardens—where on weekends wedding parties alight from limos to take family photos—are beautiful, as is the facade with its photogenic bell tower. This is the mission to visit if you visit only one.

Carmel Practicalities

Dozens of good and usually expensive restaurants thrive in Carmel. One place to see, even if you don't eat there, is the tiny mock-Tudor **The Tuck Box** (831/624-6365, daily 7am-2:30pm), on Dolores Street near 7th Avenue. Dollhouse-cute, it serves up bacon-and-eggs breakfasts and dainty plates of shepherd's pie and meatloaf for lunch. If you'd rather join locals than mingle with your fellow tourists, head to **Katy's Place** (831/624-0199, daily 7am-2pm) on Mission Street between 5th and 6th Avenues, serving delicious waffles and some of the world's best eggs Benedict.

Carmel hotel rates average well over $250, and there isn't any real budget option (apart from nearby Monterey). However, if you want to splurge on a bit of luxury, Carmel is a good place to do it.

Carmel's leading light, Clint Eastwood, seems ever-present: Besides once serving as mayor, he owns the Mission Ranch resort. As a filmmaker, he used Carmel as the location for one of his most disturbing movies, the psychopathic 1970s Play Misty for Me.

Besides the golf course resorts of nearby Pebble Beach, Carmel also has the commodious 1920s-era mission-style **Cypress Inn** (831/624-3871 or 800/443-7443, $279 and up) at Lincoln Street and 7th Avenue, partly owned by dog-loving Doris Day and featuring posters of her movies in the small bar off the lobby. A relaxing spot away from downtown is the historic Clint Eastwood-owned **Mission Ranch** (26270 Dolores St., 831/624-6436 or 800/538-8221, $125 and up), within walking distance of the beach and mission and offering full resort facilities and a good restaurant.

Point Lobos State Natural Reserve

The sculpted headland south of Carmel Bay, now protected as **Point Lobos State Natural Reserve** (831/624-4909, daily, $10 per car), holds one of the few remaining groves of native Monterey cypress, gnarled and bent by the often stormy coastal weather. The name comes from the barking sea lions (*lobos del mar*) found here by early Spanish explorers; hundreds of seabirds, sea lions, sea otters, and—in winter—gray whales are seen offshore or in the many picturesque sea-carved coves.

The entrance to the reserve is along Hwy-1, three miles south of the Carmel Mission. In summer the park is so popular that visitors sometimes have to wait in line outside the gates. If possible, plan to come early or during the week. Whenever you can, come: Point Lobos has been lauded as the greatest meeting of land and sea in the world, and crowded or not it's definitely a place you'll want to see. Point Lobos has endless vistas up and down the rocky coast, and if you don't mind a short hike, there are a number of magical beaches hidden away at its southern end.

Garrapata State Park

The northern stretches of Big Sur are marked by the rugged coves, redwood forests, and sandy beach at **Garrapata State Park,** four miles south of Point Lobos. Though it's just minutes from Carmel, Garrapata could be light-years away from the crowds of shoppers and gallery-goers, but the two-mile-long beach here is pristine and easy to reach, yet generally empty. Winter wildlife-watchers sometimes see gray whales migrating close to shore. The seven-mile Rocky Ridge Trail through **Soberanes Canyon** includes a steep descent (25 percent grade!) and heads east from Hwy-1 into a lush world of redwood groves, springtime wildflowers, seasonal streams, and amazing views.

The highway clings to the coast for a dozen amazing but uneventful miles, passing a few languid cattle and an occasional vacation home before coming upon one of Big Sur's many unique sights, the massive volcanic hump of **Point Sur,** 19 miles south of Carmel. Though it's not exactly scenic or beautiful, it definitely helps you keep your bearings. A symmetrical 361-foot dome, Point Sur is capped by a 128-year-old **lighthouse** (831/625-4419, tours Wed. and Sat.-Sun., $12 adults), which has been preserved as a state historic park.

Andrew Molera State Park

Spreading along the coast at the mouth of the Big Sur River, 20 miles south of Carmel, **Andrew Molera State Park** is a grassy former cattle ranch on the site of one of Big Sur's oldest homesteads. In the 1850s, immigrant Juan Bautista Roger Cooper bought the land; in 1861, he built a cabin, which still stands along Hwy-1 near the park entrance. Well-blazed but sometimes boggy trails wind along both banks of the river down to the small beach, **horses** (831/625-5486) are available for hire, and there are quite a few nice places to camp (walk-in only). In winter, the park is also a popular resting spot for migrating monarch butterflies.

Big Sur Village

South of Andrew Molera, Hwy-1 cuts inland toward the heart of Big Sur, the deep and densely forested valley carved by the Big Sur River. Consisting of little more than three gas stations, a couple of roadside markets, and a number of lodges and restaurants, the mile-long village of **Big Sur** (pop. 1,463) represents the only settlement between Carmel and Hearst Castle.

At the north end of town, the **Big Sur River Inn & Restaurant** (831/667-2700, $150 and up) has a woodsy, warm, and unpretentious restaurant overlooking the river, and rooms upstairs and across the highway. Next door is a small complex that includes crafts galleries, a grocery store with a burrito bar, and the homey **Maiden**

DRIVING BIG SUR

Stretching 90 miles south of Carmel from Point Lobos all the way to Hearst Castle, Big Sur is one of the most memorable sections of coastline on the planet, with 5,000-foot-tall mountains rising up from the Pacific Ocean. Early Spanish missionaries dubbed it El País Grande del Sur (the Big Country of the South), and the rugged land has resisted development or even much population—the current total of around 1,000 is roughly the same as it was in 1900, and for the 3,000 years before that.

Hwy-1, the breathtaking drive through Big Sur, was finally cut across the steep cliffs in 1937 after 20 years of labor and several fatalities. California's longest and most popular scenic route, it's an incredible trip. Like the Grand Canyon and other larger-than-life natural wonders, Big Sur boggles the mind and, in an odd way, can be hard to handle; you have to content yourself with staring in awestruck appreciation, taking pictures, or maybe toasting the natural handiwork with a cold beer or glass of wine at one of the few but unforgettable cafés and restaurants along the way.

However beautiful the drive along Hwy-1, it's also narrow, twisting, packed with sluggish RVers on holiday weekends, and every few years is closed by mud slides and washouts after torrential winter storms and the even more destructive wildfires that have plagued the coast in recent summers.

Big Sur is still a wild place, with little or no cell phone reception. There are few services, with access occasionally limited in recent years due to wildfires, flooding, and landslides alongside the highway. Most of the overnight accommodations booked up solidly during the peak summer season. Spring brings wildflowers, while fall gets the most reliably good weather. No matter when you come, even if you just drive through in an afternoon, be sure to stop whenever possible and get out of the car; scenic viewpoints line the roadside, and dozens of trails lead off into the wilds.

Publick House (831/667-2355), which features good beers and pub grub. Continuing south, the next mile of Hwy-1 holds Big Sur's nicest group of rustic cabins and campgrounds: Besides a handful of quaint cabins in a quiet location, downhill from the highway and right on the riverbanks, **Ripplewood Resort** (831/667-2242) also has a friendly café on the east side of Hwy-1, serving good breakfasts and lunches, as well as a handy gas station and general store.

At the south end of the Big Sur village, a classic 1950s motor court has been updated and restored to its vintage glory (now with free Wi-Fi) as **Glen Oaks Big Sur** (831/667-2105, $225 and up).

Pfeiffer Big Sur State Park

Roughly half a mile south of Big Sur village, **Pfeiffer Big Sur State Park** is the region's main event, a 1,000-acre riverside forest that's one of the most pleasant and popular parks in the state. Besides offering a full range of visitor services—a restaurant, a lodge, a riverside campground, and a grocery store—the park includes one of Big Sur's best short hikes, a three-mile loop on the Valley View trail that takes in stately redwoods, a 60-foot waterfall, and a grand vista down the Big Sur valley to the coast. The park also has the main **ranger station** (831/667-2315) for all the state parks in the Big Sur area. Just south of the park entrance, a U.S. Forest Service **ranger station** (831/667-2423) on the east side of Hwy-1 has information on hiking and camping opportunities in the mountains above Big Sur, including the isolated (but poison oak-ridden) **Ventana Wilderness.**

Pfeiffer Beach

South of Pfeiffer Big Sur State Park, halfway up a long steep incline, a small road turns west and leads down through dark and heavily overgrown Sycamore Canyon, eventually winding up at Big Sur's best beach, **Pfeiffer Beach.** From the lot at the end of the road, a short trail runs through a grove of trees before opening onto the broad white sands, loomed over by a pair of hulking offshore rocks. The water is way too cold for swimming, but the half-mile strand is one of the few places in Big Sur where you can enjoy extended beachcombing strolls. The beach's northern half attracts a clothing-optional crew, even on cool gray days.

The photogenic **Bixby Creek Bridge,** 15 miles south of Carmel, was one of the largest concrete bridges in the world when it was built in 1932. The old coast road runs along the north bank of the creek, linking up again with Hwy-1 near Andrew Molera State Park.

Back along Hwy-1, just south of the turnoff for Sycamore Canyon and Pfeiffer Beach, the excellent **Big Sur Bakery & Restaurant** (831/667-0520) makes its own fresh breads and pastries, brews a rich cup of coffee, and also serves full meals— soups, steaks, and wood-fired pizzas.

Ventana Inn & Spa and the Post Ranch Inn

South of Sycamore Canyon, roughly three miles from the heart of Big Sur village, Hwy-1 passes between two of California's most deluxe small resorts. The larger of the two, **Ventana Inn & Spa** (831/667-2331 or 800/628-6500, $600 and up), covers 243 acres of Big Sur foothills and offers saunas, swimming pools, and four-star accommodations in 1970s-style cedar-paneled rooms and cabins. There's also a fine restaurant, with incredible views and reasonable prices, to which guests are ferried in a fleet of electric carts.

Completed in 1992 and directly across Hwy-1 from Ventana, the **Post Ranch Inn** (831/667-2200 or 800/527-2200, $875 and up), a low-impact but ultra-high-style luxury resort hanging high above the Big Sur coast, is at the forefront of luxury ecotourism. In order to preserve Big Sur's untarnished natural beauty, the Post Ranch

Inn is designed to be virtually invisible from land or sea. The 39 guest rooms and one private house—all featuring a king-size bed and a whirlpool bath with built-in massage table—blend in with the landscape, disguised either as playful tree houses raised up in the branches of the oaks and pines or as underground cabins carved into the cliff top. The Post Ranch restaurant, Sierra Mar, is also excellent.

Nepenthe

One of the most popular and long-lived stopping points along the Big Sur coast, **Nepenthe** (831/667-2345) is a rustic bar and restaurant offering good food and great views from atop a rocky headland some thousand feet above the Pacific. Named for the mythical drug that causes one to forget all sorrows, Nepenthe looks like something out of a 1960s James Bond movie, built of huge boulders and walls of plate glass. The food is plenty good—burgers, steaks, and only two fish dishes dominate the menu—but it's the view you come here for.

The landmark red farmhouse along Hwy-1 at the entrance to Ventana was built in 1877 by pioneer rancher W. B. Post, whose descendants developed the Post Ranch Inn.

Sharing a parking lot, and taking advantage of similar views, the neighboring **Café Kevah** (831/667-2345) serves brunch all day, plus good teas and coffees and microbrews on a rooftop deck. You'll find a gift shop downstairs selling top-quality arts and crafts and knitwear by Kaffe Fassett, whose family owns the place.

Right along Hwy-1, at a sharp bend in the road just south of Nepenthe, **The Henry Miller Memorial Library** (831/667-2574, daily) carries an erratic but engaging collection of books by and about the author, who lived in Big Sur for many years in the 1950s.

A half mile south of Nepenthe on the east side of the highway, one of the oldest and most atmospheric places to stay is **Deetjen's Big Sur Inn** (831/667-2377, $105 and up), a rambling and rustic redwood lodge built by a Norwegian immigrant in the 1930s and now a nonprofit preservationist operation. Though the rooms are not available to families with young children unless you reserve both rooms of a two-room building, Deetjen's also serves Big Sur's best breakfasts and hearty dinners, at which all are welcome.

Thirty years ago, the mighty California condor was all but extinct in the wild. Now, thanks to a successful captive breeding and reintroduction program, these massive birds can be seen soaring over the Ventana Wilderness that rises above Big Sur.

Julia Pfeiffer Burns State Park

If for some untenable reason you only have time to stop once along the Big Sur coast, **Julia Pfeiffer Burns State Park** (daily dawn-dusk) should be the place. Spreading along both sides of Hwy-1, about 14 miles south of Big Sur village, the park includes one truly beautiful sight: a slender waterfall that drops crisply down into a nearly circular turquoise-blue cove. This is the only major waterfall in California that plunges directly into the Pacific. California Condors can be seen here too.

The hilltop where Nepenthe now stands was previously the site of a rustic cabin that Orson Welles and then-wife Rita Hayworth bought in 1944.

From the parking area, east of the highway, a short trail leads under the road to a fine view of the waterfall, while another leads to the remnants of a pioneer mill, complete with a preserved Pelton wheel. Other routes climb through redwood groves up to the chaparral-covered slopes of the Santa Lucia Mountains.

About six miles south of Nepenthe, or a mile north of the parking area at Julia Pfeiffer Burns State Park, a steep fire road drops down to **Partington Cove,** where ships used to moor in the protected anchorage. The last stretch of the route passes through a 60-foot-long tunnel hewn out of solid rock.

Esalen and Lucia

Three miles south of Julia Pfeiffer Burns State Park, the New Age **Esalen Institute** (888/837-2536) takes its name from the Esselen Native Americans who were wiped out by European colonizers. Founded in the early 1960s by free-thinking Stanford University graduates inspired by countercultural pioneers like Gregory Bateson and Alan Watts, and set on a breathtaking cliff-top site overlooking a 180-degree coastal panorama, Esalen offers a variety of religious, philosophical, and psychological workshops, but most visitors are drawn to its incredible set of natural **hot springs** (open to the public 1am-3am, $30 per person, reservations required), right above the ocean. Call for information on overnight "personal retreats," or to make reservations for massages or the hot tubs.

The southern reaches of the Big Sur coast are drier and more rugged, offering bigger vistas but fewer stopping places than the northern half. The road winds along the cliffs, slowing down every 10 miles or so for each of three gas station-café-motel complexes, which pass for towns on the otherwise uninhabited coast. The northernmost of these, 9 miles south of Esalen and 25 miles south of Big Sur village, is **Lucia Lodge** (831/667-2708 or 866/424-4787, $200 and up), which has wonderful ocean views, a small restaurant, and 10 creaky cabins.

High on a hill just south of Lucia, marked by a slender black cross, the Benedictine **New Camaldoli Hermitage** (831/667-2456, $135 and up) is open to interested outsiders as a silent retreat. Rates include private rooms and veggie meals. The mix of contemplative solitude and natural beauty is hard to beat.

> Julia Pfeiffer Burns was a Big Sur pioneer whose family lived near Pfeiffer Beach and homesteaded much of this rugged, isolated area. In 1915, she married John Burns, a Scottish orphan who lived with the nearby Post family, and they continued to live and ranch at what is now Julia Pfeiffer Burns State Park until Julia's death in 1928.

> The roadside along Hwy-1 in the southern half of Big Sur has been invaded by thick bunches of pampas grass that crowd out local flora.

Nacimiento-Fergusson Road and Mission San Antonio de Padua

Five miles south of Lucia, the narrow **Nacimiento-Fergusson Road** makes an unforgettable climb up from Hwy-1 over the coastal mountains. Though ravaged in places by wildfires, it's a beautiful drive, winding through hillside chaparral and dense oak groves before ending up near King City in the Salinas Valley. One real highlight here is **Mission San Antonio de Padua** (831/385-4478, ext. 17, daily 10am-4pm, call to confirm hours), a well-preserved church and monastery that is still in use by a Roman Catholic religious community. Because the road passes through sections of Fort Hunter Liggett Army Base, you may need to show valid car registration and proof of insurance. History note: All the land on which the army base and mission stand belonged at one time to mining magnate George Hearst, whose land stretched from here all the way south and west to the coast at San Simeon, where his only child, William Randolph Hearst, later constructed Hearst Castle.

Near the foot of the Nacimiento-Fergusson Road is one of the few ocean-side campsites in Big Sur, and perhaps the most amazing place to wake up on the West Coast:

Hearst Castle

Kirk Creek Campground (805/434-1996), operated by the U.S. Forest Service. The setting is unforgettable, but so are the dastardly raccoons who are fearless in their efforts to eat your lunch before you do.

Continuing south, Hwy-1 runs past **Pacific Valley,** then passes by a number of small but pretty beaches and coves before reaching **Gorda,** the southernmost stop on the Big Sur coast. Just north of Gorda, tucked away on a knoll just east of the highway, **Treebones Resort** (877/424-4787, $175 and up, basic campsites $95 and up) offers amazing views from its highly rated sushi bar, plus rustic yurts, autonomous tents, human nests, and a swimming pool, all in a spectacular setting.

William Randolph Hearst

San Simeon: Hearst Castle

At the south end of Big Sur, the mountains flatten out and turn inland, and the coastline becomes rolling open-range ranch land. High on a hill above Hwy-1 stands the coast's one totally unique attraction, **Hearst Castle.** Located 65 miles south of Big Sur village and 43 miles northwest of San Luis Obispo, Hearst Castle is the sort of place that you have to see to believe, though simple numbers—115 rooms, including 38 bedrooms in the main house alone—do give a sense of its scale.

Even if Hearst's taste in interior design (or his megalomania, which by all accounts was understated in his fictional portrayal in Orson Welles's *Citizen Kane*) doesn't appeal, Hearst Castle cries out to be seen. One of the last century's most powerful and influential Americans and the Rupert Murdoch of his day, Hearst inherited the land, and most of his fortune, from his mother, Phoebe Apperson Hearst (his father was mining mogul George Hearst), and began work on his castle following the death of

At Piedras Blancas, just north of Hearst Castle, the roadside along Hwy-1 has been taken over by herds of massive bellowing elephant seals, a once threatened but clearly resurgent species of massive pinnipeds who congregate here every winter to fight and procreate.

his mother in 1919. With the help of the great California architect Julia Morgan, who designed the complex to look like a Mediterranean hill town with Hearst's house as the cathedral at its center, Hearst spent more than 25 years working on his "castle"—building, rebuilding, and filling room after room with furniture—all the while entertaining the great and powerful of the era, from Charlie Chaplin to Winston Churchill.

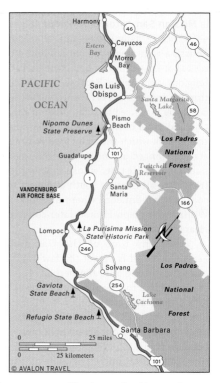

A small **museum** (daily, free) in the visitors center, next to where you board the trams that carry you up to the house, details Hearst's life and times. If you want to go on a **tour** (800/444-4445, $25 and up adults), the Grand Rooms Tour gives the best first-time overview, taking in a few rooms of the main house. There's also an Upstairs Suites Tour and a Cottages & Kitchen Tour; each takes around 45 minutes, not including transit time. All tours also come with the option of watching a 40-minute movie giving the background on Hearst and his house-building. Advance reservations are all but essential, especially in summer.

Since Hearst Castle is rather isolated, it's a good idea to stay the night before or after a visit at nearby **San Simeon,** which has grown into a massive strip of motels. There's a pair of inexpensive overnight options: the **San Simeon Lodge** (9520 Castillo Dr., 805/927-4601, $66 and up) or **Motel 6.**

Cambria

Without Hearst Castle, **Cambria** would be just another farming town, but being next to one of the state's top tourist attractions has turned Cambria into quite a busy little hive. Apart from a few hokey tourist-trapping souvenir shops at the north end of town, it's a casual, walkable, and franchise-free community of arts and crafts galleries, boutiques, and good restaurants; from Hwy-1, Main Street makes a three-mile loop around to the east, running through the heart of town.

Hearty breakfasts are available at the **Redwood Café** (2094 Main St., 805/927-4830), while well-prepared multiethnic and vegetarian food is on the menu at **Robin's** (4095 Burton Dr., 805/927-5007), a half block off Main Street. For barbecue, burgers, and beer, check out the **Main Street Grill** (603 Main St., 805/927-3194, cash only). Places to stay range from nice older motels like the **Bluebird Inn** (1880 Main St., 805/927-4634, $95 and up) to the spacious suites and cabins at **Cambria Pines Lodge** (2905 Burton Dr., 805/927-4200, $115 and up), which has a nice pool high on a hill between town and the beach. For a relaxing overnight, try the lovely little **Bridge Street Inn** (4314 Bridge St.,

805/215-0724), a block from downtown, which offers reasonable B&B rooms as well as shared HI-approved hostel beds.

Five miles south of Cambria, **Harmony** (pop. 18) is a former dairy town turned arts and crafts colony, with a range of galleries and a small wedding chapel.

Cayucos

Though it doesn't look like much from Hwy-1, which has grown into a near freeway to carry all the Hearst Castle traffic, the coastal town of **Cayucos** is definitely worth a look. Sitting along the coast 15 miles south of Cambria, not far from Morro Bay, Cayucos has a nice little beach, a fishing pier, a range of surfing and skateboard shops, and at least two unusual places to eat and drink. If you like tiki-style bars, you'll want to save your thirst for a visit to **Schooners Wharf** (171 N. Ocean Ave., 805/995-3883), with good mojitos and variable food, served up in a landmark barroom downstairs or on an ocean-view terrace above. For great food at fair prices, don't miss **Ruddell's Smokehouse** (101 D St., 805/995-5028), just off the beach, where the no-frills menu features smoked salmon and tuna sandwiches, plus fish, pork, and chicken tacos.

Morro Bay

Marked by the Gibraltar-like monolith of Morro Rock, which was noted by Juan Rodriguez Cabrillo in 1542 and now serves as a peregrine falcon preserve and nesting site, **Morro Bay** (pop. 10,234) surrounds a busy commercial fishing harbor a half mile west of Hwy-1. A thin three-mile-long strip of sand protects the bay from the Pacific Ocean, forming a seabird-rich lagoon that's included within **Morro Bay State Park,** a mile southeast of Morro Rock. There's an excellent **museum** ($3 adults) with displays on local wildlife, and the park also contains the friendly **Bayside Café** (805/772-1465), serving lunch and dinner. Next door, when the weather's nice, you can rent **kayaks** (805/772-8796) and paddle around the estuary.

The rest of Morro Bay is pretty quiet; one unusual sight is a giant **outdoor chessboard** (with waist-high playing pieces) at the foot of Morro Bay Boulevard on the waterfront in City Park. For clam chowder or fish 'n' chips , try **Giovanni's** (1001 Front St., 805/772-2123) in the strollable waterfront neighborhood. Good, fast Mexican-themed fusion food is available at the **Taco Temple** (2680 Main St., 805/772-4965), an often crowded and grandly named fish shack on the land side of the Hwy-1 frontage, a mile north of town.

San Luis Obispo

Located midway between San Francisco and Los Angeles at the junction of Hwy-1 and US-101, **San Luis Obispo** (pop. 45,119) makes a good stopping-off point, at least for lunch if not for a lengthier stay. Like most of the towns along this route, San Luis, as it's almost always called, revolves around an 18th-century mission, here named **Mission San Luis Obispo de Tolosa.** Standing at the heart of town at Chorro and Monterey Streets,

The **James Dean Memorial,** 27 miles east of Paso Robles near the junction of Highways 46 and 41, is a stark stainless-steel sculpture near the site where the talented and rebellious actor crashed in his silver Porsche and died on September 30, 1955. The highway has also been signed in Dean's memory.

The world's first motel opened in 1925 at 2223 Monterey Street, San Luis Obispo. Originally called the Milestone Mo-Tel, the Spanish revival structure was later renamed the Motel Inn, but it went out of business long ago, and its remnants now stand next to US-101 on the grounds of the Apple Farm restaurant and motel.

the mission overlooks one of the state's liveliest small-town downtown districts, with dozens of shops and restaurants backing onto **Mission Plaza,** a two-block park on the banks of Mission Creek.

Besides the mission and the lively downtown commercial district that surrounds it, not to mention the nearly 20,000 students buzzing around the nearby campus of Cal Poly San Luis Obispo, San Luis holds a singular roadside attraction, the **Madonna Inn** (805/543-3000 or 800/543-9666, $209 and up), which stands just west of US-101 at the foot of town. One of California's most noteworthy pop culture landmarks, the Madonna Inn is a remarkable example of what architecturally minded academic types like to call vernacular kitsch. Created by local contractor Alex Madonna, who died in 2004, the Madonna Inn offers 110 unique rooms, each decorated in a wild barrage of fantasy motifs: There's a bright pink honeymoon suite known as "Love Nest," the "Safari" room covered in fake tiger skins with a jungle-green carpet, and the cave-like "Caveman" Room. *Roadside America* rates it as "the best place to spend a vacation night in America," but even if you can't stay, at least stop for a look at the gift shop, which sells postcards of the different rooms. Guys should head down to the men's room, where the urinal trough is flushed by a waterfall.

Though the Madonna Inn has a huge, banquet-ready restaurant—done up in white lace and varying hues of pink—the best places to eat are downtown, near the mission. **Linnaea's Café** (1110 Garden St., 805/541-5888), off Higuera Street, serves coffee and tea and sundry snack items all day and night; there's also the lively veggie-friendly **Big Sky Café** (1121 Broad St., 805/545-5401) and the usual range of beer-and-burger bars you'd expect from a college town. For something special, the heart of SLO holds one of the central coast's great restaurants, **Novo** (726 Higuera St., 805/543-3986), serving locally sourced and fresh Mediterranean-inspired meals on a nice terrace backing onto Mission Plaza. It also has a great bar.

Along with the Madonna Inn, San Luis has a number of good places to stay, with reasonable rates that drop considerably after the summertime peak season. Besides the national chains, try the **Peach Tree Inn** (2001 Monterey St., 800/227-6396, $79 and up) or **La Cuesta Inn** (2074 Monterey St., 800/543-2777, $119 and up). There's also the **HI Hostel Obispo** (1617 Santa Rosa St., 805/544-4678, $32 and up), with 28 beds in a converted Victorian cottage near downtown and the Amtrak station.

A pedestrian walkway in downtown San Luis Obispo, off Higuera Street between Garden and Broad Streets, has become known around the world as **Bubblegum Alley.** Since the 1950s, local kids have written their names and allegiances on the brick walls, using chewing gum rather than the more contemporary spray paint.

Every Thursday evening, the main drag of San Luis Obispo, **Higuera Street,** is closed to cars and converted into a lively farmers market and block party, with stands selling fresh food and good live bands providing entertainment.

Pismo Beach

South of San Luis Obispo, Hwy-1 and US-101 run along the ocean past **Pismo Beach** (pop. 7,655), a family-oriented beach resort where the main attraction is driving or dune-buggying along the sands. Pismo was once famous for its clams, now over-harvested to the point of oblivion. While you may still see people pitchforking a few small ones out of the surf, you won't find any on local menus. Like the rest of Southern California, the Pismo area has grown significantly in the past two decades, thanks mainly to an influx of retired people housed in red-roofed townhouses. Price Street, the old main road running through the heart of the old small town, still offers a wide range of motels and restaurants, like the popular **Cracked Crab** (751 Price St., 805/773-2722), which has fish 'n' chips and a crazy range of fresh crab and other crustaceans (almost all of which come from Alaska). For a close approximation of Pismo's once-abundant clams, walk two blocks from the Cracked Crab, past the bowling alley, to another seafood specialist, the **Splash Café** (197 Pomeroy Ave., 805/773-4653), which is locally famous for clam chowder served up in edible bowls made of freshly baked bread.

While Pismo is most popular for summer fun, every winter a grove of trees just south of downtown turns into a prime gathering spot for migrating monarch butterflies. The largest groupings, numbering in the tens of thousands, though decreasing disturbingly quickly in recent years, are usually found roosting at the North Beach Campground of Pismo State Beach, along Hwy-1 off Dolliver Street.

Guadalupe and Santa Maria

South of Pismo Beach, California's coastal highways again diverge. Hwy-1 cuts off west through the still-agricultural areas around sleepy **Guadalupe** (pop. 7,080), where produce stands sell cabbages, broccoli, and leafy green vegetables fresh from the fields. The town itself feels miles away from modern California, with a four-block Main Street lined by Mexican cafés, bars, banks, and grocery stores.

If you opt to follow US-101, shopping malls and tract-house suburbs fill the inland valleys through rapidly suburbanizing **Santa Maria.** Among barbecue aficionados, the Santa Maria region is famous for its thick cuts of salsa-slathered barbecued beef. These can best be sampled at **Jocko's** (125 N. Thompson Ave., 805/929-3686, Sun.-Thurs. 8am-10pm, Fri.-Sat. 8am-11pm) in **Nipomo,** east of US-101 at the Tefft Street exit. Great steaks and mouthwateringly moist, inch-thick barbecued pork chops highlight the no-frills Jocko's menu. The meats are not soaked in sauces, but simply cooked over smoky oak charcoal.

At the south end of Pismo Beach, beyond the scruffy farmlands that surround the wide mouth of the Santa Maria River, **Guadalupe-Nipomo Dunes National Wildlife Refuge** holds endless acres of windswept beaches, coastal sand dunes, and boggy bird-friendly marshlands, as well as the buried remains of a movie set used in Cecil B. DeMille's *The Ten Commandments.*

In 1936, **Nipomo** was the place where Dorothea Lange took that famous photograph of a migrant mother huddling with her children in a farmworker camp.

EL CAMINO REAL AND THE CALIFORNIA MISSIONS

While the American colonies were busy rebelling against the English crown, a handful of Spaniards and Mexicans were establishing outposts and blazing an overland route up the California coast, along the New World's most distant frontier. Beginning in 1769 with the founding of a fortress and a Franciscan mission at San Diego, and culminating in 1823 with the founding of another outpost at what is now San Francisco, a series of small but self-reliant religious colonies was established, each a day's travel apart and linked by El Camino Real, the King's Highway, a route followed roughly by today's US-101.

Some of the most interesting missions are listed here, north to south, followed by the dates of their founding.

San Francisco Solano (1823): The only mission built under Mexican rule stands at the heart of Sonoma, a history-rich Wine Country town.

San Juan Bautista (1797): This lovely church forms the heart of an extensive historic park, in the town of the same name (see page 70).

San Carlos Borromeo de Carmelo (1771): Also known as **Carmel Mission,** this was the most important of the California missions (see page 75).

San Antonio de Padua (1771): This reconstructed church, still in use as a monastery, stands in an undeveloped valley inland from Big Sur in the middle of Fort Hunter Liggett Army training center. Monks still live, work, and pray here, making for a marvelously evocative visit (see page 81).

Mission San Fernando from Memory Garden, and Father Junipero Serra Statue

San Miguel Arcángel (1797): This is the only mission not to have undergone extensive renovations and restorations—almost everything, notably the vibrantly colorful interior murals, is as it was.

La Purisima (1787): A quiet coastal valley is home to this church, which was restored in the 1930s using traditional methods as part of a New Deal employment and training project (see page 88).

Santa Barbara (1786): Called the Queen of the Missions, this lovely church stands in lush gardens above the upscale coastal city (see page 90).

EL CAMINO REAL BELL
SAN GABRIEL MISSION, CAL.

San Gabriel Arcángel (1771): Once the most prosperous of the California missions, it now stands quietly and all but forgotten off a remnant of Route 66 east of Los Angeles.

San Juan Capistrano (1776): Known for the swallows that return here each year, this mission has lovely gardens (see page 102).

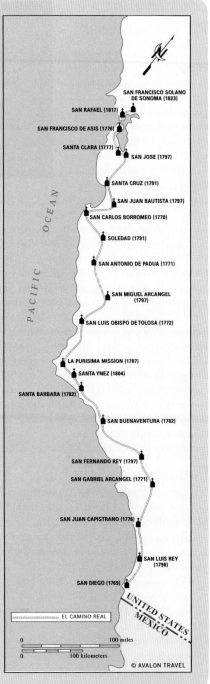

PACIFIC OCEAN

SAN FRANCISCO SOLANO DE SONOMA (1823)
SAN RAFAEL (1817)
SAN FRANCISCO DE ASIS (1776)
SANTA CLARA (1777)
SAN JOSE (1797)
SANTA CRUZ (1791)
SAN JUAN BAUTISTA (1797)
SAN CARLOS BORROMEO (1770)
SOLEDAD (1791)
SAN ANTONIO DE PADUA (1771)
SAN MIGUEL ARCANGEL (1797)
SAN LUIS OBISPO DE TOLOSA (1772)
LA PURISIMA MISSION (1787)
SANTA YNEZ (1804)
SANTA BARBARA (1782)
SAN BUENAVENTURA (1782)
SAN FERNANDO REY (1797)
SAN GABRIEL ARCANGEL (1771)
SAN JUAN CAPISTRANO (1776)
SAN LUIS REY (1798)
SAN DIEGO (1769)

UNITED STATES
MEXICO

EL CAMINO REAL

0   100 miles
0   100 kilometers

© AVALON TRAVEL

Lompoc and La Purisima Mission

The rolling valleys around **Lompoc** are famed for their production of flower seeds, and consequently the fields along Hwy-1 are often ablaze in brilliant colors. Apart from colorful murals adorning downtown buildings, Lompoc as a town is not up to much, despite the unusual nature of the area's two main nonagri-

Lompoc flower fields

cultural employers. One is a minimum-security federal prison; the other is Vandenberg Air Force Base, site of numerous missile tests, the aborted West Coast space shuttle port, and the $60 billion "Son of Star Wars" National Missile Defense program.

With its long arcade reaching across the floor of a shallow grassy valley, **La Purisima Mission** (805/733-7313, Jul.-Aug. Tues.-Sun. 10am-4pm, Mon. 10am-3pm, Sept.-June Tues.-Sun. 10am-4pm, $6 per car) gives a strong first impression of what the missions may have looked like in their prime. Four miles northeast of Lompoc, between Hwy-1 and US-101 on Hwy-246, the mission here was originally built in 1812 but fell to ruin partially due to an earthquake before being totally reconstructed as part of a WPA project in the New Deal 1930s. During the restoration, workers used period techniques wherever possible, hewing logs with hand tools and stomping mud and straw with their bare feet to mix it for adobe bricks. Workers also built most of the mission-style furniture that fills the chapel and the other rooms in the complex. Other features include a functioning aqueduct, many miles of hiking trails, and a small museum.

Buellton and Solvang

The town of **Buellton,** a block west of US-101 at the Solvang exit, holds one of California's classic roadside landmarks, **Pea Soup Andersen's** (376 Ave. of the Flags, 805/688-5581),

advertised up and down the coast. Another Buellton landmark, **The Hitching Post II** (406 E. Hwy-246, 805/688-0676), a little ways east of US-101, starred in the wine-loving road-trip movie *Sideways*.

Four miles east of Buellton and US-101, America's most famous mock-European tourist trap, the Danish-style town of **Solvang** (pop. 5,245), was founded in 1911. Set up by a group of Danish immigrants as a cooperative agricultural community, Solvang found its calling catering to passing travelers. The compact blocks of cobblestone streets and Old World architecture, highlighted by a few windmills and signs advertising the Hamlet Inn, among many more suspicious claims to

The late great pop singer Michael Jackson's **Neverland Ranch** lies here in the foothills of the Santa Ynez Valley, southeast of Solvang via the truly scenic Hwy-154, which loops inland south to Santa Barbara, arriving via a steep and stunning drive over San Marcos Pass.

Danishness, now attract tourists by the busload. Many other U.S. towns (Leavenworth, Washington, and Helen, Georgia, to name two) have been inspired by Solvang's success, but to be honest there's nothing much to do here apart from walking, gawking, and shopping for pastries.

Just east of Solvang's windmills and gables, the brooding hulk of **Old Mission Santa Inés** stands as a sober reminder of the region's Spanish colonial past. Built in 1804, it was once among the more prosperous of the California missions but now is worth a visit mainly for the gift shop selling all manner of devotional ornaments.

Gaviota State Park and Refugio State Beach

Between Solvang and Santa Barbara, US-101 follows the coast past some of California's most beautiful beaches. Dropping through a steep-sided canyon, US-101 reaches the coast at **Gaviota State Park,** where a small fishing pier and campground are overwhelmed by the massive train trestle that runs overhead. Continuing south, US-101 runs atop coastal bluffs past prime surfing beaches, usually marked by a few VWs pulled out along the west side of the highway. Midway along this stretch of coast, some 22 miles north of Santa Barbara, **Refugio State Beach** has groves of palm trees backing a clear white strand. There's also a small **store** (spring weekends, daily summer) and a number of attractive campsites with hot showers. Reservations for **camping** (800/444-7275) at Gaviota or Refugio, or at any California state beach, should be made in advance.

Rancho del Cielo, the former ranch of President Ronald Reagan, spreads along the crest of the coastal hills above Refugio State Beach.

Santa Barbara

The geographical midpoint of California may well be somewhere near San Francisco, but the Southern California of popular imagination—golden beaches washed by waves and peopled by blond-haired surfer gods—has its start, and perhaps best expression, in **Santa Barbara** (pop. 88,410). Around 100 miles north of Los Angeles, Santa Barbara has grown threefold in the last 60 years, but for the moment, at least, it manages to retain its sleepy seaside charm. Much of its character comes from the fact that, following a sizable earthquake in 1925, the town leaders—caught up in the contemporary craze for anything Spanish Revival—required that all buildings in the downtown area exude a mission-era feel, mandating red-tile roofs, adobe-colored stucco, and rounded arcades wherever practicable. The resulting architectural consistency gives Santa Barbara an un-American charm; it looks more like a Mediterranean village than the modern city it is beneath the surface.

For a good first look at the city, head down to the water, where **Stearns Wharf** sticks out into the bay, bordered by palm tree-lined beaches populated by joggers, in-line skaters, and volleyball players. From the wharf area, follow State Street away from the sands to the downtown district, where Santa Barbarans parade among the numerous cafés, bars, and boutiques. At the north end of downtown is the excellent

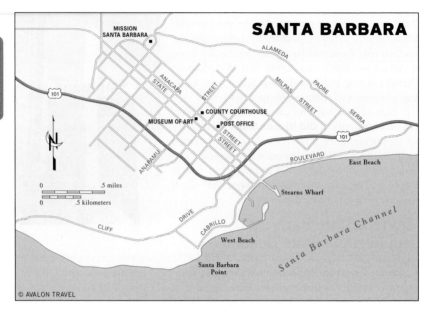

SANTA BARBARA

Santa Barbara Museum of Art (1130 State St., 805/963-4364, Tues.-Sun., $10 adults). A block east on Anacapa Street, the **County Courthouse** is one of the finest public buildings in the state, a handcrafted Spanish Revival monument set in lush semitropical gardens, with an **observation tower** (Mon.-Fri. 8am-5pm, Sat.-Sun. 10am-5pm, free) giving a fine view over the red-tiled cityscape.

Santa Barbara's reigning attraction, **Old Mission Santa Barbara** (805/682-4713, daily, $9 self-guided tours), stands atop a shallow hill that is a well-posted mile up from State Street, looking out over the city and shoreline below. Called the "Queen

of the Missions" by the local tourist scribes, Mission Santa Barbara is undeniably lovely to look at, its rose-hued stone facade perfectly complemented by the roses and bougainvillea that frame the well-maintained gardens and lawns.

Santa Barbara is one of many great places along the coast to go on a **whale-watching cruise** (805/822-0088 or 888/779-4253), on the *Condor Express* or other boats, to see migrating gray whales in winter and jumping humpbacks in summer. Trips take a half day or a full day, and some head out to the Channel Islands; call for details or reservations.

Santa Barbara has perhaps the south coast's best variety of places to eat. State Street holds the most lunch and dinner places, like the old-fashioned burgers and beer on tap in the 1920s dark-wood dining room of **Joe's Café** (536 State St., 805/966-4638). Fans of grilled burgers and Albacore tuna fillet will enjoy the tasty local chain **The Habit** (628 State St., 805/892-5400), which started in collegiate Isla Vista, near UCSB. There's excellent fresh sushi at **Arigato Sushi** (1225 State St.,

805/965-6074), while some of the world's best hole-in-the-wall Mexican food is served a half mile east of State Street at **La Super-Rica** (622 N. Milpas St., 805/963-4940, Thurs.-Tues.), where such distinguished foodies as Julia Child have come to chow down on a variety of freshly made soft tacos and delicious seafood tamales. It's not cheap, but the food is great (fresh tortillas, traditional *adobado*-marinated pork, and spicy chorizo), and the *horchata* is the creamiest you'll taste. Yum.

The city's accommodations, however, are among the central coast's most expensive, especially in summer when even the most basic motel can charge as much as $200 a night. One of the nicest of many motels is **The Franciscan Inn** (109 Bath St., 805/963-8845, $135 and up), just a short walk from the beach and wharf. At the top of the scale, the **Simpson House Inn** (121 E. Arrellaga St., 805/963-7067 or 800/676-1280, $300 and up) offers comfortable, centrally located B&B rooms. Off the scale completely, money's-no-object visitors can enjoy the deluxe facilities of the **San Ysidro Ranch** (805/565-1700, $695 and up), in the hills above neighboring **Montecito,** where Jackie and JFK spent some of their honeymoon. Somewhat ironically, considering the generally high prices here, international budget chain **Motel 6** (443 Corona Del Mar, 805/564-1392, $85 and up) got its start in Santa Barbara, where it now has five area properties, including the recently redesigned original one near the beach.

Channel Islands National Park

South of Santa Barbara, US-101 widens into an eight-lane freeway along the coast. Looking out across the Pacific, beyond the partially disguised offshore oil wells, you can't miss seeing the sharp outlines of the **Channel Islands,** whose rocky tide-pool-packed shores are protected as a national park. Consisting of eight islands, five of which are part of the park, they sit from 12 to about 60 miles off the mainland. Numerous scenic cruises around the Channel Islands start from Santa Barbara, but only the closest, **Anacapa Island,** is easily accessible, via daily trips from Ventura Harbor offered by **Island Packers** (805/642-1393, $59 adults). Bring water, as none is available on the island; camping is possible, but reservations are required.

CAUSEWAY, COAST HIGHWAY, BETWEEN VENTURA AND SANTA BARBARA

Ventura and Oxnard

Midway between Malibu and Santa Barbara, downtown **Ventura** (pop. 106,433) is an offbeat little place, its three-block Main Street lined by enough thrift shops (seven at last count) to clothe a destitute retro-minded army. Apart from searching out vintage couture, the main reason to stop is the small and much-reconstructed **Mission San Buenaventura** (211 E. Main St., daily, $4 adults), standing at the center of Ventura just north of the US-101 freeway. This was the ninth in the California mission chain, and the last one founded by Junípero Serra, in 1782.

Ventura doesn't get anything like the tourist trade that Santa Barbara draws, but it does have the pleasant **Bella**

Ventura is the birthplace and headquarters of the outdoor equipment and clothing company Patagonia, started and still owned by legendary rock climber Yvon Chouinard.

Maggiore Inn (67 S. California St., 805/652-0277 or 800/523-8479, $75 and up), offering good-value B&B rooms in a nicely restored 1920s courtyard hotel between downtown and US-101.

South of Ventura, US-101 heads inland through the San Fernando Valley to Hollywood and downtown Los Angeles, while Hwy-1 heads south through the 10 miles of stop-and-go sprawl that make up the rapidly suburbanizing farming community of **Oxnard** (pop. 197,899), then continues right along the coast through Malibu and West Los Angeles.

As an introduction to the high-style car culture of Southern California, there's no better stop than Oxnard's unexpected treasure trove, the **Mullin Automotive Museum** (1421 Emerson Ave., 805/385-5400, $15). Though it is open barely two days (Saturdays) a month, the chance to appreciate one of the world's finest car collections may be worth planning your trip around.

Simi Valley

If you opt to follow US-101 rather than coastal Hwy-1 into Los Angeles, be sure to check out the somnolent suburb of **Simi Valley,** 30 miles east of Ventura, where the hilltop **Ronald Reagan Presidential Library** (805/522-2977, daily, $23 adults with audio tour) fills 150,000 square feet of Spanish-style stucco with a fascinating array of exhibits and artifacts, most famously a chunk of the Berlin Wall, set in a Cold War-era tableau. Also here, housed in a 200-foot-long glass-walled pavilion, is the actual Boeing 707 used as presidential Air Force One by Nixon, Carter, Ford, Reagan, George H. W. Bush, Clinton, and George W. Bush. The "Great Communicator" was interred here following his death in 2004. To get to the library, take US-101 to Hwy-23 north (a.k.a. the Ronald Reagan Freeway), exit at Olsen Road, and follow the signs.

Grandma Prisbrey's Bottle Village

The other Simi Valley sight to see is **Grandma Prisbey's Bottle Village** (4595 Cochran St., 805/231-2497, $10), a complex of small buildings and sculptures built out of glass bottles, TV sets, hubcaps, and assorted other recycled refuse. The late Tressa Prisbey started building it in 1956. Subject of an ongoing battle between folk-art preservationists and those who think it's a pile of junk, the "village" can be viewed less than a mile south of the Hwy-118/210 freeway between the Tapo Street and Stearns Street exits.

Pacific Coast Highway Beaches

Running right along the beach, the Pacific Coast Highway (Hwy-1) heads south from Oxnard around the rocky headland of **Point Mugu** (pronounced "muh-GOO"), where the U.S. Navy operates a missile testing center and the Santa Monica Mountains rise steeply out of the Pacific Ocean. Most of these chaparral-covered granite mountains have been protected as parkland, with hiking, cycling, and riding trails offering

grand views and a surprising amount of solitude. Before or after a hike in the hills (or a Harley ride along the coast, the preferred mode of arrival), the ramshackle **Neptune's Net** (42505 Pacific Coast Hwy., 310/457-3095) restaurant is a great place to hang out and "star"-gaze while enjoying fresh seafood, served up on paper plates for that down-home Hollywood feel.

South from here, state-owned beaches mark your progress along the coastal road, but this stretch is basically natural wilderness—apart from the highway, of course. Biggest and best of the beaches hereabouts is the lovely **Leo Carrillo State Park** (310/457-8143), which has a sandy strand, some great tide pools, and a sycamore-shaded **campground** (reservations 800/444-7275). Leo Carrillo (1880-1961) was an actor (he played Pancho in *The Cisco Kid* TV show) and preservationist who was instrumental in expanding the California state parks.

South of Leo Carrillo, which marks the Los Angeles County line, there are many more public beach areas, including (in roughly north-to-south order) **Nicholas Canyon County Beach, El Pescador State Beach,** and **El Matador State Beach** (where episodes of TV's *Baywatch* have been filmed). At big, brash **Zuma Beach County Park,** where volleyball courts and snack bars line the sands, the PCH bends inland around the headlands of **Point Dume State Beach,** a great spot for winter whale-watching.

Malibu

South of Zuma Beach, houses begin popping up along Hwy-1 to block the oceanfront views, and more-elaborate multimillion-dollar homes dot the canyons above as well, forming the sprawling exurbia and movie-star playground of **Malibu,** which stretches along Hwy-1 for the next 27 miles to Santa Monica

Malibu Pier at sunset

and metropolitan Los Angeles. Unless TV helicopters are flying overhead to document the latest wildfire or other natural disaster, it's hard to get more than a glimpse of the garage doors or wrought-iron gates of these palaces, but this is the address of choice for the movers and shakers of the entertainment world: If you can name them, they probably own property here. Most of the truly huge estates are hidden away on ranches high up in the mountains.

The main route inland from the coast, Malibu Canyon Road, was the setting of the key murder scene in James M. Cain's thriller *The Postman Always Rings Twice.*

One of these hideaways has been evolving since 1993, when Barbra Streisand donated her 22.5-acre ranch for use as a botanical preserve. Called **Ramirez Canyon Park** (5750 Ramirez Canyon Rd. 310/589-2850), it's managed by the Santa Monica Mountains Conservancy and is open by appointment only, thanks to requests from neighbors. Ramirez Canyon meets the Pacific at the aptly named **Paradise Cove,** a private beach and boat launch that is worth checking out for the excellent little **Paradise Cove Beach Café** (28128 Pacific Coast Hwy., 310/457-9791), serving what may well be the world's best sandwiches. Here they come complete with spectacular ocean views, and frequent activity by film and TV crews. *Baywatch* and *The Rockford Files* were both filmed on the sands and the rustic pier.

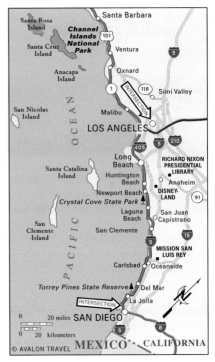

This stretch of coastline holds another great place to eat: **Malibu Seafood** (25653 Pacific Coast Hwy., 310/456-3430), a low-key beach shack drawing local gardeners, pool guys, and Hollywood starlets for BYOB fish 'n' chips.

Continuing south along high-speed Hwy-1, the most prominent sight is the **Pepperdine University** campus, which was described by the late, great architect Charles Moore as "an overscaled motel set in obscenely vivid emerald lawns." Below the bluff-top campus, the legendary **Malibu Colony** of celebrity homes stretches along the coast in high-security splendor. Just north of Pepperdine, a short drive up Corral Canyon Road gives access to Solstice Canyon, part of the **Santa Monica Mountains National Recreation Area,** where a well-marked, mile-long hiking trail leads through scrubby native chaparral up to a delicate spring waterfall, past numerous signs of the frequent fall wildfires (like the 4,900-acre Corral Fire of November 2007, which destroyed Malibu's oldest home; the remains are preserved in situ).

Away from the mountains, about the only place in Malibu proper where it's fun (and legal) to explore is the area around the landmark **Malibu Pier,** which juts into the ocean at the heart of Malibu's short and rather scruffy commercial strip. North of the pier stretches **Surfrider Beach,** site of most of those Frankie Avalon and Annette Funicello *Beach Blanket Bingo*-type movies made during the 1950s. The pier and the beach are part of **Malibu Lagoon State Beach,** which also protects the historic **Adamson House** (23200 Pacific Coast Hwy., 310/456-8432, Thurs.-Sat. 11am-3pm, $7 adults, cash only), a lovely circa-1930 Spanish Revival courtyard home, right on the beach and full of gorgeous tile work and other architectural features. Tours of the house are given throughout the day, and fascinating exhibits portray Malibu history and the Rindge family, who once owned the entire region.

Topanga and the Getty Villa

Between Malibu and Santa Monica, **Topanga Canyon** is one of the last great wild spaces in Los Angeles, with a number of parks, trails, and perhaps the last wild and free waterways—steelhead trout still spawn in the waters of Topanga Creek, which flows down from the mountains to the Santa Monica Bay. Home to an alternative-minded community of some 8,000 hippies and New Agers (Neil Young recorded *After* *the Gold Rush* in his home here), Topanga was first established as an artists' colony in the 1950s by the likes of Woody Guthrie and actor Will Geer, who played Grandpa in TV's *The Waltons,* long after he'd been blacklisted during the anti-Communist McCarthy witch hunts. For over 40 years, Geer's old property has been preserved as the **Theatricum Botanicum** (1419 N. Topanga Canyon Blvd., 310/455-2322), a garden and politically minded 300-seat open-air theater, six miles up the canyon.

South of Topanga and open after a nearly 10-year, $275-million remodeling are the world-famous antiquities of **The J. Paul Getty Museum** (310/440-7300, Wed.-Mon., free, $15 per car, good at both museum sites). Over 1,200 priceless classics are displayed in the pseudo-Pompeiian Getty Villa, where the oil magnate's art collection was housed prior to the construction of the massive Getty Center complex along the I-405 freeway above Brentwood. Admission to the Getty Villa is free, but parking reservations are essential.

From the Getty Villa south to Santa Monica, the Pacific Coast Highway (Hwy-1) runs along the wide-open sands of **Will Rogers State Beach,** gifted to the public by the Depression-era humorist.

Santa Monica marks the western end of legendary **Route 66,** which winds between Chicago and Southern California. Our road trip coverage begins on page 822.

Crossing Los Angeles

From Malibu and Topanga Canyon, Hwy-1 swoops along the shore, running along the beach as far as the landmark Santa Monica Pier before bending inland through a tunnel and metamorphosing quite unexpectedly into I-10, the Santa Monica Freeway. The second exit off this freeway (which has been officially dubbed the Christopher Columbus Transcontinental Highway, running all the way east to Jacksonville, Florida) takes you to Lincoln Boulevard, which carries the Hwy-1 moniker south through Venice and Marina del Rey to Los Angeles International Airport (LAX), where it runs into Sepulveda Boulevard.

After passing through a tunnel under the airport runways—worth the drive just for the experience of seeing 747s taxiing over your head—Sepulveda emerges in the Tarantino-esque communities of LA's South Bay, which utterly lack the glamour of chichi Santa Monica and Malibu. At Hermosa Beach, one of a trio of pleasant if surprisingly blue-collar beach towns, Sepulveda Boulevard changes its name to Pacific Coast Highway, then bends inland to bypass the ritzy communities of the Palos Verdes Peninsula, passing instead through the industrial precincts of San Pedro that border the Los Angeles-Long Beach harbor, one of the busiest on the West Coast.

Since Hwy-1 follows slow-moving Lincoln Boulevard and other surface streets across L.A., if you are in any sort of hurry you should stay on the Santa Monica Freeway (I-10) east to the San Diego Freeway (I-405), and follow that south as far as you're going. Coming from the south, follow these freeways in reverse order—or risk the time-consuming consequences.

Los Angeles

Love it or hate it, one thing you can't do about LA is ignore it. Thanks to Hollywood in all its many guises (movies, television, the music industry), the city is always in the headlines. Without falling too deeply under the spell of its hyperbole-fueled image-making machinery, it's safe to say that LA definitely has something for everyone. In keeping with its car-centered culture, however, our suggested tour ignores the many individual attractions and focuses instead on a pair of quintessential LA drives.

the Los Angeles skyline, as seen from Mulholland Drive

Winding along the crest of the Hollywood Hills, **Mulholland Drive** is the classic LA cruise. Starting in the east within sight of the Hollywood sign and the Hollywood Bowl, this ribbon of two-lane blacktop passes by the city's most valuable real estate, giving great views on both sides, both by day and after dark.

Another classic LA cruise, running from the scruffy fringes of downtown all the way west to the coast, **Sunset Boulevard** gives glimpses into almost every conceivable aspect of Los Angeles life. Starting downtown, the historic core of colonial Los Angeles and now a showcase of contemporary architecture thanks to a stunning new cathedral and concert hall, Sunset Boulevard's 27-mile course then winds west past Echo Park and

Hollywood to West Hollywood, where it becomes the Sunset Strip, still the liveliest nightclub district in town. Continuing west, Sunset winds through Beverly Hills, Brentwood, and Bel Air, lined by the largest mansions you're likely to see, before ending up at the edge of the Pacific Ocean.

The **Los Angeles Dodgers** (866/363-4377) play at beautiful **Dodger Stadium,** on a hill above downtown.

PRACTICALITIES

Most flights to Los Angeles arrive at Los Angeles International Airport (LAX), on the coast southwest of downtown, where you'll find all the usual shuttles and rental car agencies. Other useful LA-area airports include Hollywood Burbank (BUR) in Burbank and John Wayne (SNA) in Orange County.

Before choosing a place to stay, think about where you want to spend your time and settle near there. High-end places abound, but character can be hard to come by. Along the coast, recommended accommodations range from the handy **HI-Santa Monica**

The *Queen Mary*

(1436 2nd St., 310/393-9913, starts at $38 per person), a block from the beach, to the unique *Queen Mary* (877/342-0738, $149 and up) in Long Beach, a hotel offering authentic art deco-era staterooms in the fabulous old luxury liner. Midrange, with a great mid-city location, try the **Farmer's Daughter Hotel** (115 S. Fairfax Ave., 323/937-3930, $210 and up), next to the historic Farmers Market, a friendly 1950s-style motel with tons of charm and the city's hottest new shopping mall and entertainment complex, The Grove, across the street. Downtown, the most fabulous place to stay is the retro-1960s **The Standard Downtown LA** (550 S. Flower St., 213/892-8080, $229 and up), with the world's coolest rooftop poolside bar.

For food, one place I always try to stop is **The Apple Pan** (10801 W. Pico Blvd., 310/475-3585, Tues.-Sun.), an ancient (circa-1947) landmark on the West LA landscape, serving the best hamburgers on the planet—though I'll admit to being biased, since I grew up eating them. Take a seat at the counter, and be sure to save room for a slice of the wonderful fruit pies. Late at night, the huge sandwiches and heart-warming soups at **Canter's Deli** (419 N. Fairfax Ave., 323/651-2030, daily 24 hours) draw all kinds of night owls to a lively New York-style deli in the heart of the predominantly Jewish Fairfax District. Downtown, between Chinatown, historic Olvera Street, and the landmark Union Station, **Philippe the Original** (1001 N. Alameda St., 213/628-3781) serves famous French dip sandwiches in a classic workers' cafeteria, offering good food at impossibly low prices, with character to spare.

The usual array of information about hotels, restaurants, tickets to TV show tapings, and all other LA-area attractions is available through the **Los Angeles Tourism and Convention Board** (6801 Hollywood Blvd., 323/467-6412 or 800/228-2452).

Long Beach

Directly south of downtown Los Angeles, the city of **Long Beach** (pop. 462,257) is the second-largest of LA's constituent cities, but it feels more like the Midwest than the cutting-edge West Coast. Long Beach is probably best known as the home of the cruise ship RMS *Queen Mary* (877/342-0742, tours $27), one of the largest and most luxurious liners ever to set sail. Impossible to miss as it looms over Long Beach harbor, the stately ship is open for self-guided tours. You can also stay overnight in one of the many staterooms and cabins, traveling back to a more elegant time for surprisingly reasonable overnight rates. Across the bay on the main downtown Long Beach waterfront, the **Aquarium of the Pacific** (562/590-3100, daily, $30 adults) explores the diverse ecosystems of the Pacific Ocean, from tropical coral reefs (shown off in an amazing 350,000-gallon display) to the frigid waters of the Bering Sea.

Other Long Beach attractions include a former **"World's Largest Mural,"** a 116,000-square-foot painting of migrating gray whales on the outside of the Long Beach Arena; the self-proclaimed **"Skinniest House in the USA"** (708 Gladys Ave.); and a collection of memorabilia related to brother-and-sister pop singers **Richard and Karen Carpenter,** inside the main concert hall on the CSU Long Beach campus where they went to school.

Long Beach also marks the southern end of LA's reborn rail transit system, and you can ride the Blue Line north to downtown and connect to everywhere else. It's an inexpensive base for exploring the Los Angeles area, especially if you avail yourself of the **Best Western** (1725 Long Beach Blvd., 562/599-5555, $99 and up) right downtown, directly across from a Blue Line train stop.

Huntington Beach

Winding south and east from Long Beach, Hwy-1 continues along the coast past a series of natural marshlands and small-craft marinas. The first real point of interest is the town of **Huntington Beach** (pop. 189,992), one of the largest communities in Orange County. Incorporated in 1909 and developed by Henry Huntington as a stop along his legendary Pacific Electric "Red Car" interurban railway network, Huntington Beach is best known as one of the places where surfing took off on the U.S. mainland. To attract Angelenos down to his new town, Huntington hired Hawaiians to demonstrate the sport, which at the time made use of huge solid wooden boards, 15 feet long and weighing around 150 pounds. Huntington Beach, especially around the pier, is still a popular surfing spot—though contemporary surfers slice through the waves on high-tech foam-core boards, a third the size of the original Hawaiian long boards. The history and culture of West

a surfer at the Huntington Beach Pier

Coast surfing, with examples of boards then and now (plus special collections highlighting surf movies and the creation of surf music by local heroes Leo Fender and Dick Dale), is recounted in the fantastic **International Surfing Museum** (411 Olive Ave., Tues.-Sun. 12pm-5pm, $2), two blocks from the pier in the heart of the lively downtown business district.

Anaheim: Disneyland Resort

Like a little bit of middle America grafted onto the southern edge of Los Angeles, inland Orange County used to feel like a totally different world. Though the area's demographics have changed considerably in the past decade or two, becoming more a part of LA's fast-paced, edgily creative multiethnic stew, Orange County in the 1950s and 1960s was suburban America writ large—mostly white, mostly well-off, and absolutely, totally

The major league baseball **Los Angeles Angels of Anaheim** play at **Angel Stadium** (2000 Gene Autry Way, 714/940-2000).

bland. In short, a perfect place to build the ultimate escapist fantasy, the self-proclaimed "Happiest Place on Earth," **Disneyland** (714/781-4565).

The phenomenon of Disneyland has been done to death by all sorts of social critics, but the truth is, it can be great fun—provided you visit out of season, get there early to avoid the crowds, and immerse yourself in the extroverted mindless joy of it all. (Being here in the company of appreciative 8- to 12-year-olds is probably the best way to maximize your enjoyment.)

If you haven't been before, or not for a while at any rate, here are some useful tidbits of information: Disneyland is 30 miles south of downtown LA, right off I-5 in the city of Anaheim—you can see the Matterhorn from the freeway. The park is open daily; in summer, it remains open until midnight. Admission to the park, which includes all rides, costs $97-124 per person per day.

Disneyland opened in 1955, when there was nothing surrounding it; in intervening years, an entire metropolis has grown up around it. In 2001 the park was joined by the much smaller, more grown-up-oriented **Disney California Adventure**

Angel Stadium

theme park. This billion-dollar park has thrill rides like California Screamin', a 55-mph roller coaster, and the excellent Soarin' Around the World motion simulator, offering an airborne tour of the Golden State from Yosemite Falls to the Malibu beaches. The pièce de résistance is Cars Land, based on the animated Pixar film and featuring the 40-mph Radiator Springs Racers, which simulates a race down Route 66. Disney California Adventure is separate from Disneyland, but a Park Hopper pass allows entry into both.

The whole Disney ensemble includes an upscale resort-hotel complex, surrounded by motels and yet more motels, and it is well worth staying overnight so you can get an early start, go "home" for a while, then come back for the nightly fireworks show. A highly recommended place to stay is the **Sheraton Park Hotel** (1855 S. Harbor Blvd., 714/750-1811, $161 and up), a block from Disneyland, offering spacious modern rooms and a nice pool, with Anaheim Resort Transit running every 20 minutes to and from Disneyland ($5 over age 9, $2 ages 3-9).

Richard Nixon Presidential Library

If you've already done the Disneyland thing, or just want a foil to the empty-headed fun, there is one other Orange County attraction you shouldn't miss: the **Richard Nixon Presidential Library** (18001 Yorba Linda Blvd., 714/993-5075, daily, $15 adults), 10 miles northeast of Disneyland off Hwy-90. The library is built on the very ground where the former president was born in 1913; it's also where he and his wife, Pat, are buried, side by side next to the restored Craftsman-style bungalow where Nixon grew up. No matter what your feelings are toward him, the spare-no-expense displays do a fascinating job of putting his long career into the distorted perspective you'd expect from the only president ever forced to resign from office. Highlights are many, such as the pictures of the pumpkin patch where Whittaker Chambers concealed the microfilm that Nixon used to put Alger Hiss in prison as a Communist spy, next to photos of Nixon and JFK as  chummy freshman U.S. senators sharing sleeping compartments on a train. The best-selling item in the gift shop? Photographs of Nixon greeting Elvis Presley, also available as mousepads, china cups, and fridge magnets.

Newport Beach

Back on the coast, if you want to get a sense of what wealthy Orange Countians do to enjoy themselves, spend some time along the clean white strands of **Newport Beach.** Located at the southern edge of Los Angeles's suburban sprawl, Newport started life in 1906 as an amusement park and beach resort at the southern end of the LA streetcar lines. Since then thousands of Angelenos have spent summer weekends at the **Balboa Pavilion,** at the southern tip of the slender Balboa peninsula, where the Fun Zone preserves a few remnants of the pre-video game amusements—a Ferris wheel, a merry-go-round, and those odd Pokerino games in which you win prizes by rolling rubber balls into a series of numbered holes. If you have some spare time, Newport is also a good base for

taking the unforgettable cruise across the water to **Catalina Island,** a semi-tropical paradise 26 miles off the coast.

Midway along the peninsula, near 23rd Street, Newport Pier is flanked by another holdout from the old days: the dory fleet. For more than a century, small boats have set off from the beach here (often around midnight, landing back around 7am) to catch rock cod and more exotic fish, which are sold fresh off the boats at an outdoor market right on the sands.

A mile southeast of Balboa Pavilion, next to the breakwater at the eastern end of Balboa peninsula, **The Wedge** is one of the world's most popular and challenging bodysurfing spots, with well-formed waves often twice as high as anywhere else on the coast.

To return to Hwy-1 from Balboa Peninsula, you can either backtrack around the harbor or ride the **Balboa Island Ferry,** which shuttles you and your car from the pavilion across the harbor past an amazing array of sailboats, power cruisers, and waterfront homes.

Crystal Cove State Park

Midway between Newport and Laguna Beaches, amid the ever-encroaching Orange County sprawl, **Crystal Cove State Park** (949/494-3539, daily dawn-dusk, $15 per car) protects one of Southern California's finest chunks of coastline. With three miles of sandy beaches and chaparral-covered bluff lined by well-marked walking trails, it's a fine place to enjoy the shoreline without the commercial trappings. Originally home to Native Americans, the land here was later part of Mission San Juan Capistrano and, until 1979 when the state bought it, the massive Irvine Ranch, which once covered most of Orange County.

Crystal Cove State Park

The main parking area for Crystal Cove is at **Reef Point** near the south end of the park, where there are restrooms and showers plus excellent tide pools and a fine beach. You can stay overnight at **Crystal Cove Beach Cottages** (800/444-7275, $35 and up), a well-preserved collection of 1930s-1950s beach bungalows. There is also a large section of the park inland from Hwy-1, through the oak glade of **Moro Canyon,** which gives a vivid sense of Orange County's rapidly vanishing natural landscape.

Laguna Beach

Compared with much of Orange County, **Laguna Beach** (pop. 22,723) is a relaxed and enjoyable place. Bookstores, cafés, and galleries reflect the town's beginnings as an artists' colony, but while the beach and downtown area are still attractive, the surrounding hills have been covered by some of the world's ugliest tracts of "executive homes."

During the annual summertime **Pageant of the Masters** (949/487-6582 or 800/487-3378, $20 and up), Laguna Beach residents recreate scenes from classical and modern art by forming living tableaux, standing still as statues in front of painted backdrops. Proceeds go to good causes. It's a popular event, so get tickets well in advance.

tableau from Laguna Beach's Pageant of the Masters

Right across Hwy-1 from the downtown shopping district, which is full of pleasant cafés and a wide range of art galleries, Laguna's main beach (called simply **Main Beach**) is still the town's main draw, with a boardwalk, some volleyball courts, and a lifeguarded swimming beach with showers.

Many other fine but usually less crowded and quieter beaches are reachable from Cliff Drive, which winds north of downtown Laguna past cove after untouched cove; follow the signs reading "Beach Access."

Laguna Beach has a number of nice places to eat. One place worth searching out is the small **Taco Loco** (640 S. Coast Hwy., 949/497-1635), at the south end of the downtown strip, where the ultra-fresh Mexican food includes your choice of three or four different seafood tacos, from shark to swordfish, in daily-changing specials for about $2-10 each.

Places to stay are expensive, averaging around $199, and include the beachfront **Laguna Riviera** (825 S. Coast Hwy., 949/494-1196). At the top end of the scale, the **Montage** (30801 S. Coast Hwy., 866/271-6953, $595 and up) has everything you could want from a hotel.

South of Laguna Beach, Hwy-1 follows the coast for a final few miles before joining up with the I-5 freeway for the 65-mile drive to San Diego.

San Juan Capistrano

Of the 21 missions along the California coast, **Mission San Juan Capistrano** (949/234-1300, daily, $9 adults) has been the most romanticized. When the movement to restore the missions and preserve California's Spanish colonial past was at its apogee in the late 1930s, its main theme tune was Leon René's "When the Swallows Come Back to Capistrano," popularizing the legend that these birds return

Mission San Juan Capistrano

from their winter migration every St. Joseph's Day, March 19. After wintering in Goya, Argentina, they do come back to Capistrano, along with several thousand tourists, but the swallows are just as likely to reappear a week before or a week after—whenever the weather warms up.

The mission, which has lovely bougainvillea-filled gardens, stands at the center of the small eponymously named town, a short detour inland along I-5 from the coast. Besides the birds, the main attractions include the small **chapel,** the last surviving church where the beatified priest Junípero Serra said mass, widely considered the oldest intact church and perhaps the oldest building of any kind in California, and the ruins of the massive **Great Stone Church,** a finely carved limestone structure that collapsed in an earthquake in 1812, just six years after its completion. Many visitors to the chapel are terminally ill patients saying prayers to Saint Peregrine, the patron saint of cancer patients. To get a sense of the huge scale of the original Great Stone Church, a replica patterned after the fallen building has been constructed next door and now serves as the official Mission Basilica, open to visitors except during religious services.

San Clemente

At the southern tip of coastal Orange County, **San Clemente** marks the midway point between San Diego and Los Angeles. A sleepy beachside community, with frequent Amtrak train service and a nicely undulating stretch of old US-101 (El Camino Real) running through its heart, San Clemente is probably best known as the site of La Casa Pacifica, the one-time "Western White House" of former president Richard Nixon, who lived here following his election in 1968 and during his impeachment in the mid-1970s. The white-walled mission-style house at the south end of Avenida del Presidente (the western frontage road to I-5) is more easily visible from the beach below, though the 25 acres of trees have grown up to obscure it in recent years.

Within a quick walk uphill from the handful of cafés and bars on and around the pier, **Beachcomber Inn** (949/492-5457, $170 and up) is a tidy old-fashioned motor-court motel facing the open ocean. San Clemente also has a couple of low-key coffee shops, like **Rose's Sugar Shack Café** (2319 S. El Camino Real, 949/498-0684), and a great burger place, **The Riders Club** (1701 N. El Camino Real, 949/388-3758, Tues.-Sun.), in the mission-style downtown business district.

Camp Pendleton and Mission San Luis Rey de Francia

South of San Clemente, the northwest corner of San Diego County is taken up by the U.S. Marines Corps's massive **Camp Pendleton** training base, which fills 125,000 acres, running for 17 miles along the coast and about 15 miles inland. (The base motto is "No Beach out of Reach"). Camp Pendleton is the largest undeveloped section of the Southern California coast.

In the sun-bleached hills above the blue Pacific, four miles east of the ocean off I-5 along Hwy-76, **Old Mission San Luis Rey de Francia** (daily, $7 adults) was the

largest and among the most successful of the California missions. Its lands have been taken over by Camp Pendleton, and most of the outbuildings have disappeared, but the stately church at the heart of the complex survives in fine condition, worth a look for the blue-tinted dome atop the bell tower and for the haunting carved stone skull that looks down from the cemetery gate.

A long but worthwhile detour inland from San Luis Rey brings you to one of the least visited but perhaps most evocative of all the California missions, **Mission San Antonio de Pala** (760/742-3317, Wed.-Sun., $2 adults). Located on the Pala Indian Reservation, 20 miles east of San Luis Rey along Hwy-76, then another 100 yards north along a well-marked side road, Mission San Antonio de Pala is the only California mission still serving its original role of ministering to indigenous people, and it gives an unforgettable impression of what California's mission era might have been like.

Oceanside

At the southern edge of 125,000-acre Marine Corps Base Camp Pendleton, **Oceanside** (pop. 167,086) is one of the largest cities between Los Angeles and San Diego, but it offers few tourist attractions—apart from a long fishing pier and guided tours of Camp Pendleton's amphibious-assault training exercises. But if you're in the mood to shop for camouflage gear, watch the muscle cars cruise Hill Street, get a $5 G.I. Joe haircut, or drink beer with a gang of young recruits, this is the right place.

Oceanside is also home to one of the last survivors of the old pre-interstate Coast Highway businesses: The **101 Café** (631 S. Coast Hwy., 760/722-5220) has been open for classic road food since 1928. It often hosts classic car rallies and generally glows with neon-lit nostalgia. Other, more retro-minded all-American roadside favorites include the **Breakfast Club Diner** (228 N. Coast Hwy., 760/722-3124) and a branch of the popular local chain **Ruby's Diner** (760/433-7829), at the far end of the Oceanside Pier.

South from Oceanside, all the way to San Diego, a pleasant alternative to the often-clogged I-5 is the old alignment of US-101, now signed as County Road S21 (and occasionally Coast Highway 101). Slower than the freeway but still in regular use, the old road is now the main drag of quaint beachfront towns like Carlsbad, Leucadia, Encinitas, and Del Mar. If you have the time, it's a great drive, in sight of the ocean for most of the way.

Carlsbad: La Costa and Legoland

Named for the European spa town of Karlsbad, in the Bohemia region of what's now the Czech Republic, **Carlsbad** (pop. 105,328) was established in the 1880s as a spa town and vacation resort. Remnants of the historic resort area still survive along old US-101 in the center of town, and a few flower and strawberry fields have survived the ever-expanding tide of sprawl. These days Carlsbad's spa-town heritage lives on at **Omni La Costa Resort and Spa** (760/438-9111, $299 and up), a 600-plus-room complex of luxurious rooms, health spas, golf courses, and tennis courts covering 400 acres of hills on the inland side of I-5.

Some of the best views of the Southern California coastline can be had from the windows of the frequent Coaster commuter trains, which run right along the shore between Oceanside and downtown San Diego.

Carlsbad's other main attraction is the first American outpost of the popular European children's theme park **Legoland** (877/344-5346, $97 adults, $91 children). Covering 128 acres above the Pacific Ocean, the park is divided into multiple areas, including Miniland USA, where miniature landscapes modeled on New York, New Orleans, New England, and Southern California have all been constructed using millions of the trademark plastic bricks.

South Carlsbad State Beach (760/438-3143, $10-15 per car, seasonal rate), three miles south of town, is one of the nicest and most popular places to camp on the Southern California coast, with its spacious **campsites** ($35-50) with hot showers spread out along a sandstone bluff above a broad beach. However, swimming can be dangerous because of strong riptides. If you don't want to camp or pay the parking fee, leave your car at the park entrance, which is well marked on a surviving stretch of the old US-101 highway.

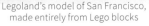

Legoland's model of San Francisco, made entirely from Lego blocks

San Diego

San Diego Zoo

Set along a huge Pacific Ocean harbor at the southwestern corner of the country just a few miles from the Mexican border, San Diego embodies the Southern California ideal. Around the turn of the 20th century, it rivaled Los Angeles as a boomtown based on wild real estate speculation, but while LA continued to expand by leaps and bounds, San Diego grew comparatively slowly. Instead of Hollywood glamour, San Diego's economy has long been based on the U.S. Navy, as evidenced by the massive former USS *Midway* moored right downtown. (San Diego successfully mixed its military and Hollywood influences in the movie *Top Gun*.) Despite a metropolitan population of more than 3 million people, San Diego still feels small and anything but urban.

The main things to see in San Diego are in **Balboa Park,** a lushly landscaped 1,200-acre spread on downtown's northeast edge, which was largely laid out and constructed as part of the 1915 Panama-California Exposition, celebrating the completion of the Panama Canal. The many grand buildings, all built in gorgeous Spanish Revival style by architect Bertram Goodhue, have been preserved in marvelous condition and now house sundry museums, ranging from automobiles to fine art to a functioning replica of Shakespeare's Globe Theatre.

Balboa Park is also home to the **San Diego Zoo** (619/231-1515, daily, $52 adults), one of the largest and most popular in the world with over 3,500 animals kept in settings that simulate their natural habitats. You can see koalas and komodo dragons, panda bears and polar bears, plus gorillas and giraffes. You name it, if it's anywhere outside in the wild, it'll be here amid the zoo's lushly landscaped 100 acres.

Balboa Park

The **San Diego Padres** (619/795-5000) play at popular retro-modern Petco Park, right downtown in the Gaslamp Quarter.

PRACTICALITIES

The city of San Diego bends diagonally around its natural harbor, which makes orientation occasionally confusing. The main airport, Lindbergh Field, is on the waterfront just northwest of downtown—and has one of the swiftest final approaches of any urban American airport. Because it is small and relatively compact, San Diego is easy to get around. Downtown is walkable, and on a bike you could see most everything in a day. Buses operated by **San Diego Metropolitan Transit** (619/557-4555) fan out from downtown, while the light rail **San Diego Trolley** runs south from downtown to the Mexican border.

Though you may feel the need to duck when planes land at nearby Lindbergh Field, for breakfast try the **Hob Nob Hill** (2271 1st Ave., 619/239-8176), a classic 1940s coffee shop with great pecan waffles. For more all-American fare, head west to Ocean Beach, where **Hodad's** (5010 Newport Ave., 619/224-4623), a great old burger joint, awaits you. San Diego's Old Town historic park holds some good old-school Mexican places, like the **Old Town Mexican Café** (2489 San Diego Ave., 619/297-4330). In Balboa Park, soak up San Diego's Spanish Revival splendor while enjoying a meal at **The Prado** (619/557-9441) in the original House of Hospitality.

Places to stay are generally modern, clean, and comfortable, though rates vary with seasons (and conventions). For top-of-the-line accommodations, or just to appreciate the historic architecture, head to the wonderful old **Hotel del Coronado** (1500 Orange Ave., 619/435-6611, $289 and up), across the bridge from downtown on Coronado Island. Rising up in turreted glory, this fabulously grand Victorian-era resort hotel still caters, as it always has, to the four-star trade. It has been seen in many movies, including the great Peter O'Toole flick *The Stunt Man.* It's also where England's King Edward VIII is rumored to have first met the femme fatale who inspired him to give up his throne: Wallis Simpson, whose first husband was first commanding officer of the local Navy base. The cheapest beds are at the **HI San Diego Downtown** (521 Market St., 619/525-1531 or 855/213-0582, $45 and up per person), in the historic downtown Gaslamp Quarter. For more comfort and character, try **The Sofia Hotel** (150 W. Broadway, 619/234-9200, $139 and up), a restored 1920s hotel. For surfer-friendly (and pet-friendly) accommodations near Ocean Beach and Point Loma, try the **Ocean Villa Inn** (5142 W. Point Loma Blvd., 619/224-3481, $99 and up).

Del Mar and Torrey Pines State Natural Reserve

Most of the time, **Del Mar** (pop. 4,161) is a sleepy little upscale suburb of San Diego, with big houses backing onto more than two miles of fine beach. But in late summer, it comes to life for the thoroughbred racing season at beautiful **Del Mar racetrack,** built by Hollywood types like Bing Crosby and seen in *The Grifters* and many other Hollywood movies and TV shows. The waves here are well suited to bodysurfing, but the sands can be hard to reach in summer because of a lack of parking—weekdays it's less of a problem.

A Torrey Pine, San Diego, Cal.—9

South along the Camino Del Mar coast road from Del Mar, hang-gliders, tide-poolers, surfers, and beachcombers flock to the nearly 2,000 acres of bluffs and beaches protected in **Torrey Pines State Natural Reserve.** Named for the long-needled pines that grow naturally only here, the reserve is crisscrossed by hiking trails leading down steep ravines between the bluffs and the sands. Besides hang-gliders, Torrey Pines is prime airspace for remote-controlled model gliders, which float gracefully in the nearly constant onshore breeze. The primary launching spot is the small city park at the south end of the reserve.

Overlooking the Pacific from atop a bluff at the south end of the reserve, the **Salk Institute** is one of the world's most important centers for research in the life sciences. Founded by the late Jonas Salk, designed by Louis Kahn, and modeled in part on the gardens of the Alhambra in Granada, the institute is open for **tours** (858/453-4100, ext. 1287, Mon.-Fri. noon, $15).

Stretching inland and south from the Salk Institute, the hills are covered with faceless business parks around the spacious campus of **University of California at San Diego** (UCSD), beyond which spreads La Jolla and the greater San Diego area. On campus, learn all about local marine biology at the **Birch Aquarium** (858/534-3474, $18.50 adults) of UCSD's Scripps Institution of Oceanography, from where you can amble along the shore to lovely La Jolla.

La Jolla

The wealthiest and most desirable part of San Diego, **La Jolla** sits along the coast northwest of the city proper, gazing out over azure coves to the endless Pacific. Besides the gorgeous scenery, great surfing (head to **Windansea Beach** for the best waves), beachcombing, and diving, tons of good cafés and restaurants have long made La

4569 UNION DEPOT ATCHISON TOPEKA & SANTA FE RY   SAN DIEGO AND ARIZONA RY

SAN DIEGO CALIF

Jolla an all-around great day out, suiting all budgets—especially those with no upper limit. Another big draw here is the **Museum of Contemporary Art San Diego** (700 Prospect St., 858/454-3541, closed Wed., $10 adults), currently closed for renovations expected to be completed by 2020.

Start the day off right at La Jolla's **The Cottage** (7702 Fay Ave., 858/454-8409), where delicious food (including a divine buttermilk coffee cake) is served up on a sunny patio. For an unforgettable, swaddled-in-luxury SoCal experience, stay the night at the elegant Craftsman-style **The Lodge at Torrey Pines** (11480 N. Torrey Pines Rd., 858/453-4420, $400 and up), a modern re-creation of California's turn-of-the-20th-century Golden Age.

At **Belmont Park** (3146 Mission Blvd., 858/228-9283), west of Mission Bay, the Giant Dipper wooden roller coaster survives at the heart of a revived 1920s beachfront amusement park.

Driving San Diego

From La Jolla south, US-101 is pretty well buried by the I-5 freeway. Old US-101 can still be followed, however, by following Pacific Highway past Mission Bay and Lindbergh Field toward San Diego Bay, where it becomes Harbor Drive—where the light rail San Diego Trolley now runs past the hulking USS Midway aircraft carrier.

San Diego is also the beginning of our cross-country **Southern Pacific** route, along US-80, which runs east across Arizona all the way to Tybee Island, Georgia. See page 762.

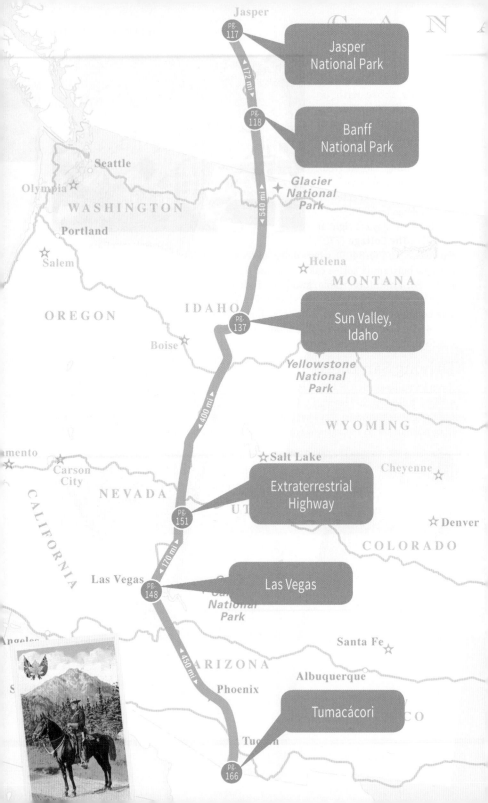

Jasper
pg. 117

Jasper
National Park

▼ 172 mi ▼

pg. 118

Banff
National Park

Seattle

Olympia ☆

WASHINGTON

Portland

☆ Salem

▼ 540 mi ▼

Glacier
National
Park

☆ Helena

MONTANA

OREGON

IDAHO

pg. 137

Sun Valley,
Idaho

Boise ☆

Yellowstone
National
Park

WYOMING

▼ 400 mi ▼

amento

☆ Carson
City

NEVADA

☆ Salt Lake

Cheyenne ☆

UTAH

pg. 151

Extraterrestrial
Highway

☆ Denver

COLORADO

▼ 170 mi ▼

Las Vegas

pg. 148

Las Vegas

National
Park

Angeles

▼ 450 mi ▼

ARIZONA

Santa Fe ☆

Albuquerque

Phoenix

Tumacácori

Tucson

pg. 166

Border to Border

Besides offering up-close looks at mile after mile of almost completely untouched wilderness, US-93 also takes you right through the neon heart of Las Vegas.

93

Between the Canadian Rockies and the Sonoran Desert

the western half of North America is often described as a land of contrasts, and no route across it gives a sharper sense of the region's extremes than US-93. Starting in the north, across the Canadian border at **Jasper National Park** in the heart of the Rocky Mountains, and winding up south of the border in the Sonora Desert twin towns of **Nogales** (one in Arizona, one in Mexico), this route, which retains the number 93 despite the different international jurisdictions, traverses some of the wildest and most rugged lands imaginable: mighty mountains, glaciated valleys, raging rivers, and two very different deserts. Besides offering up-close looks at mile after mile of magnificent and almost completely untouched wilderness, US-93 also takes you right through the neon heart of what is surely the most extreme (and most extremely visual) example of our contemporary "civilization": Las Vegas.

The route divides into two almost unrecognizably different halves. The northern section, from the Canadian Rockies wonderland of **Banff** and

the Columbia Icefield

Jasper south as far as **Sun Valley, Idaho,** is pure alpine majesty. Passing the western flanks of **Glacier National Park,** US-93 runs along river valleys through diverse communities where skiing, hiking, and sightseeing have replaced mining and lumbering as the economic engines. South of **Kalispell,** the highway winds across the **Flathead Reservation** along the western shores of Flathead Lake to **Missoula,** located at the heart of the bountiful country captured in the film *A River Runs Through It.* Western Montana's natural beauty reaches a peak in the **Bitterroot Valley,** which stretches south from Missoula all the way to the Idaho border. Besides scenery, the valley also abounds in history, holding many key sites pertaining to the explorers Lewis and Clark, the first nonnatives to set foot in the region, and other sites related to the epic struggle of Chief Joseph and the Nez Percé people.

As you pass over the Bitterroots into Idaho across the **Continental Divide,** the scenery remains impressive as US-93 winds along the banks of the Salmon River, all the way to its source in the serrated Sawtooth Mountains, then drops down swiftly into Sun Valley, the oldest and most upscale ski resort in the country.

South of Sun Valley, however, everything changes suddenly. Roaring rivers and mountain forests give way to lava flows and empty deserts as US-93 races across the inhospitable landscape of the Snake River Plain. This was the most difficult portion of the historic Oregon Trail, though the biggest difficulty facing today's travelers is the struggle to stay alert—there's little to look for, apart from acres of potato farms reclaimed from the arid desert. The one real sight is the **Snake River** itself, which has carved itself into a deep gorge near Twin Falls.

Continuing south into Nevada, US-93 embarks on what is truly, if not officially, the "Loneliest Road in America," traveling across 500 miles of Great Basin Desert. Though not for the faint-hearted or those with unreliable cars, it's an unforgettably beautiful journey; after hours or days of existential solitude, you drop down into the frenetic boomtown of **Las Vegas.**

Crossing Hoover Dam into Arizona, the route crosses old Route 66 west of the **Grand Canyon**, then races southeast across the lush Sonoran Desert—known as the "world's greenest desert" because of its abundant flora and fauna—through **Phoenix** and **Tucson** to the Mexican border. This last stretch is among the most fascinating 200 miles of highway in the country, taking you past such intriguingly diverse and unique sights as the controversial Biosphere 2 scientific research center, the country's only intact Cold War-era missile silo, and a pair of centuries-old churches, two of the most captivating pieces of architecture in the western United States.

Sonoran Desert

CANADIAN ROCKIES

At its northernmost extreme, high up in the Canadian Rockies, Hwy-93 passes through some of the most famous vacation areas in North America: the Canadian national parks of **Banff** and **Jasper.** Popular with skiers and snowboarders in winter, and hikers and sightseers in summer, these resort areas have been mustsees for over 100 years and remain among the most beautiful places on earth. Between Jasper and **Lake Louise,** Hwy-93 is known as the Icefields Parkway, an amazing drive with endless panoramas of glaciers and towering peaks, and dozens of turnouts and trailheads to tempt you out from behind the wheel. Over 140 miles (225 kilometers) long, the Icefields Parkway runs right alongside the Continental Divide, the rugged crest that separates the Atlantic and Pacific watersheds. South of the Icefields Parkway, our route passes through the world-renowned resort towns of Banff and Lake Louise, taking in their unforgettable alpine scenery—and historic landmark hotels.

Southwest from Lake Louise, Hwy-93 winds through **Kootenay National Park,** another incredible assembly of mountain scenery, before dropping down out of the mountains for the run south to the border, following the broad Kootenay River all the way to Montana.

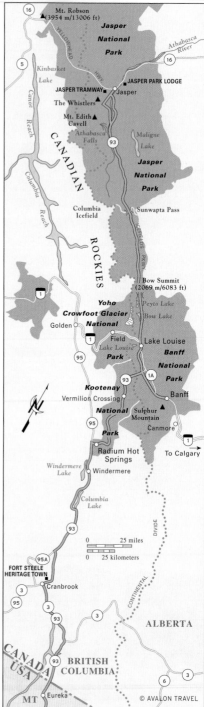

Town of Jasper

The northernmost point on Hwy-93, at the junction of the Icefields Parkway with the cross-country Yellowhead Highway (Hwy-16), which links Edmonton with Prince Rupert, the town of **Jasper** (pop. 5,236) preserves its frontier character intact. Unlike Banff, which exudes wealth and comfort, Jasper, which became an incorporated entity only in 2001 and is officially referred to as the "Town of Jasper" to differentiate it from Jasper National Park, is a rough-and-ready workaday sort of place. Founded on fur trading and mining, Jasper boomed when a cross-Canada railroad came through in 1911, but since the establishment of the national park in 1930, Jasper has served primarily as a handy base for exploring the wilds that surround it.

The main attractions are in the national park, but a few are located close to town. First and foremost of these is probably the **Jasper Skytram** (780/852-3093, daily mid-Mar.-Oct., C$45 adults, C$23 kids), which lifts passengers 3,200 vertical feet up the steep north face of the Whistlers in under 10 minutes. From the upper terminal of the tramway, you can follow a 0.75-mile (1.2-kilometer) path to the 8,100-foot summit for a breathtaking panorama south to the Columbia Icefield and (on a clear day) northwest to Mt. Robson, the highest point of the Canadian Rockies at 12,972 feet (3,954 meters) above sea level.

The other big draw is **Maligne Canyon,** a 100- to 150-foot-deep limestone canyon that's so narrow in places that squirrels can leap from rim to rim. Trails lead around and across it, and in winter you can join a guided **Sundog tour** (888/786-3641, C$65) along the bottom of the narrow, ice-covered gorge.

Beyond Maligne Canyon is one of the prettiest lakes in the Canadian Rockies, **Maligne Lake.** Hiking trails lead along the shore and to panoramic viewpoints, but it is the **cruise to Spirit Island** (888/269-0524, C$65) that attracts most visitors.

Jasper's compact center, sandwiched between the west bank of the Athabasca River and a wide bench of land dotted with forest-encircled lakes, holds all the cafés and gift shops you could want within a block of the main drag, Connaught Drive. The **Bear's Paw Bakery** (4 Pyramid Rd., 780/852-3233), off Connaught has cinnamon buns, great pastries, breakfast sandwiches, and anything else you need to start the day off right. **Jasper Pizza Place** (402 Connaught Dr., 780/852-3225), two blocks north, has wood-fired ovens and walls covered in photos of Jasper in the early days. Another lively spot is the restaurant and lounge on the ground floor of the **Athabasca Hotel** (510 Patricia St., 780/852-3386, C$129-199 peak season, C$129-139 off-season), which also has Jasper's least expensive in-town lodging. Jasper's most expensive place to stay is the **Fairmont Jasper Park Lodge** (780/852-3301, C$195 and up), a grand mountain resort dating back to 1922 but now a mostly modern resort offering 446 rooms, plus golfing and horseback riding, on a lovely site across from town on the other side of the Athabasca River.

Budget travelers may want to take advantage of the hostels around Jasper, including the 75-bed **HI-Jasper Hostel** (C$35 and up per person), five miles south of Jasper on the road to the Jasper Tramway, and the smaller and more rustic **HI-Maligne Canyon Hostel** (C$28 and up per person), a short walk from the canyon.

Prices in the Canadian sections are given in Canadian dollars. At time of writing the Canadian dollar was worth about US$0.75. Also, the colloquial Canadian equivalent of "buck" meaning a dollar is "loonie," thanks to the image of a loon on the Canadian dollar coin. The two-dollar coin is called a "toonie."

THE LAST FRONTIER

The Canadian Rockies are farther north than anything else in *Road Trip USA*, but for indefatigable adventurers there's at least one additional destination: Alaska, "The Last Frontier." It's roughly 1,900 miles from Jasper National Park to Anchorage, via the legendary **Alaska Highway.** Running from the oil- and gas-producing center of Dawson Creek (no connection with the TV show) in British Columbia, the Alaska Highway was constructed in 1942, in just nine months, an amazing engineering feat fueled by fears of a Japanese invasion during World War II. Much improved in the years since, it's now paved all the way but is still quite an adventure, with endless miles (and miles, and miles) of forests, rivers, and mountains.

If you're going, plan ahead carefully and keep a lookout for a few places you won't want to miss. One of these is roughly midway, in Watson Lake, right on the British Columbia-Yukon border and right along the highway: the world-famous **Sign Post Forest,** a collection of city limits signs from around the globe. The "forest" was started in 1942 by Carl Lindley, a U.S. soldier working to build the highway. When ordered to fix an official road sign, he added another of his own making, pointing the way and the distance to his home in Danville, Illinois. Others followed his lead and, over the years, have added sign upon sign to create the current collection, which at

last count totaled in excess of 100,000. The Sign Post Forest earned notoriety in 2009 when it was featured on a Canadian postage stamp.

In the middle of the Sign Post Forest is the helpful **Visitor Interpretive Centre** (867/536-7469, daily 8am-8pm summer) with practical information and historical exhibits.

The four contiguous Canadian Rockies national parks—Jasper, Banff, Yoho, and Kootenay, along with neighboring provincial parks—jointly protect a 7,000-square-mile (18,000-square-kilometer) area that has been declared a UNESCO World Heritage Site for its ecological importance.

Hostel reservations (780/852-3205 or 778/328-2220) for either hostel, and for other hostels in Jasper National Park, can be made by phone. There are also two large **campgrounds,** Whistlers and Wapiti, along Hwy-93 on the south side of Jasper, with over 1,200 sites altogether, some with RV hookups.

For details on hiking and camping options, or to purchase the required entrance passes and backcountry camping permits, go to the Parks Canada **information centre** (780/852-6176) in a lovely old stone building off Connaught Drive in Athabasca Park; for complete accommodations information, including listings of rooms available in private homes, talk to the folks at the **Jasper Visitors Centre** (780/852-6236), which shares the space.

Jasper National Park

Running from the Town of Jasper all the way to Lake Louise, 144 miles (232 kilometers) to the south, this section of Hwy-93 is known as the **Icefields Parkway.** Like many roads in U.S. national parks, the Icefields Parkway was initially built as a relief project during the Great Depression and was completed in 1940. Without a doubt one of the world's great drives, this sinuous ribbon winds along the banks of a series of icy rivers between glaciers and towering Rocky Mountain peaks, with almost no development to mar the views. The northern half of the highway passes through Jasper National Park alongside the milky green Athabasca River.

While the Icefields Parkway makes a great drive, a worthwhile detour follows an older alignment of the highway, Hwy-93A, which runs parallel and slightly to the west. One of the best concentrations of scenery surrounds **Mt. Edith Cavell,** easily reached by Cavell Road, which turns off Hwy-93A about four miles (six kilometers) south of the Town of Jasper. From the winding road, you can choose from fairly short day hikes up to wildflower-rich alpine meadows, with views of Angel Glacier, or longer overnight treks into the backcountry, including the **Tonquin Valley Backcountry Lodge** (780/852-3909), a 15-mile (24-kilometer) hiking or cross-country skiing trip from the trailhead. Right at the trailhead there's the handy **HI-Mount Edith Cavell Wilderness Hostel** (778/328-2220, June-Oct., C$20-29 per person).

About 18 miles (30 kilometers) south of the Town of Jasper, Hwy-93A and the Icefields Parkway rejoin at **Athabasca Falls,** where the river is forced through a narrow gorge and over a cliff into a cauldron of roaring water; numerous viewpoints above and below the falls let you get up close and personal with the thundering torrent. There's a rustic **hostel** (778/328-2220) a short walk away from the falls.

At the southern end of Jasper National Park, 67 miles (108 kilometers) south of the Town of Jasper, the massive Columbia Icefield rises high above the west side of the Icefields Parkway.

Columbia Icefield

Rising to the west of Sunwapta Pass, the dividing line between Banff and Jasper National Parks, the massive **Columbia Icefield** is what the Icefields Parkway is all about: the largest ice field and most accessible glacier in the Canadian Rockies, seemingly endless square miles of solid ice sitting high atop the Continental Divide. Although it has been visibly shrinking for nearly a century, the ice field is still immense, and you can get an up-close look by joining the popular **Glacier Adventure tours** (888/269-0524, C$85) operated by the Brewster company, which leave every 15 to 30 minutes, depending on weather, to travel out onto **Athabasca Glacier.**

Overlooking the ice field from across the Icefields Parkway is the modern **Columbia Icefield Discovery Centre** (daily mid-Apr.-Oct., free), a mini museum of glacial lore operated by Parks Canada. If you want to experience the ice field up close, buy a ticket and take one of the Ice Explorer tours; don't simply walk across the highway and clamber up, since it only takes one false step to fall to your death into one of the deep but invisible crevasses that crisscross the glacier.

Park passes are required for everyone entering any of the Canadian Rockies national parks and are available at park gates and at visitors centers. They're valid for one day (C$10 per person or C$20 per car) or all year (C$70 per person or C$140 per car).

The Icefields Parkway is kept open year-round, but gas, food, and lodging services are available pretty much only near the towns of Banff, Jasper, and Lake Louise. Wide shoulders and frequent HI hostels along the Parkway make it an excellent bicycling route.

Glacier Skywalk

The Columbia Icefield Discovery Centre is also the starting point for visits to the Canadian Rockies' newest attraction, the **Glacier Skywalk** (C$29), a transparent-floor observation deck that juts out over Sunwapta Canyon from alongside the Icefields Parkway. Frequent free shuttle buses make the quick trip from the Icefield Centre, but if you want to walk out onto the vertigo-inducing platform, which hovers 918 feet above the valley floor, you need to pay a pretty steep fee.

Banff National Park

Roughly midway along the Icefields Parkway, the Columbia Icefield and Sunwapta Pass mark the boundary between Jasper and Banff National Parks, and the dividing line between the Arctic and Hudson Bay watersheds. South of the pass, the first worthwhile stop is the **Weeping Wall,** a 330-foot cliff of gray limestone down which a series of waterfalls tumble. Frozen in winter, it's a prime spot for ice-climbing thrill-seekers.

Though it may well sound like empty hyperbole, the list of candidates for the most beautiful sight in **Banff National Park**—and perhaps the entire Canadian Rockies—has to include jewel-like **Peyto Lake,** an iridescently glowing blue-green glacial lake that reflects the surrounding snowcapped peaks. The often mirror-smooth waters of this small oblong lake change color from a deep blue to jade green as the proportion of glacial silt in the water increases with the snowmelt from summer to fall. The short trail to the usually crowded Peyto Lake overlook starts from the parking area along the Icefields Parkway at 6,791-foot **Bow Summit.**

Bow Summit is one of the highest points reachable by road in Canada; south of here, the Icefields Parkway drops down into the **Bow Valley,** which is dominated by the sparkling waters of **Bow Lake** and the views across it to Crowfoot Glacier. At the north edge of the lake, historic **Simpson's Num-Ti-Jah Lodge** (403/522-2167, C$245 and up) is a giant octagonal log cabin, with well-priced rooms and a rustic restaurant; it marks the start of a popular trail to **Bow Glacier Falls.** It's a fairly level, 2.5-mile (four-kilometer) one-way hike.

THE BREWSTER BOYS

Few guides in the Canadian Rockies were as well known as Jim and Bill Brewster. In 1892, at the ages of 10 and 12, respectively, they were hired by the Banff Springs Hotel to take guests on a tour of local landmarks. As their reputations grew, so did their business, which expanded to include a livery and outfitting company, a pair of hotels, and a ski lodge. Today, their legacy lives on in Brewster, where their tour and transportation company has become an integral part of the Canadian Rockies experience for many visitors. The Brewster company operates a fleet of tour buses, a Banff hotel, and the famous Ice Explorers tours, which take tourists out onto the Columbia Icefield.

From the lodge, the Icefields Parkway winds along the east shore of Bow Lake, then along the banks of the Bow River, which flows south through Lake Louise, Banff, and on through Calgary, eventually ending up in Hudson Bay.

Yoho National Park

From the village of Lake Louise, the Trans-Canada Highway (Hwy-1) cuts off from Hwy-93, running west through Kamloops toward Vancouver. The first 25 miles (40 kilometers) of this highway, west from Lake Louise and the Icefields Parkway, passes through **Yoho National Park,** the smallest and least known, but perhaps most feature-packed, of the contiguous Canadian Rockies parks. It's impossible to do justice to the park in a paragraph or two, but if you like the other parks, and particularly if you enjoy backpacking, think about spending some time here too.

From Lake Louise, Hwy-1 climbs quickly over Kicking Horse Pass before reaching the **Lower Spiral Tunnels Viewpoint,** where you can learn about the amazing

Peyto Lake

engineering feat that allowed trains to travel through this rugged region. Heading north on Yoho Valley Road takes you up, and up, and up, along a very tight series of hairpin turns, ending at **Takakkaw Falls,** perhaps the most impressive waterfall in the Canadian Rockies. You can see the 1,260-foot (384-meter) falls from the parking lot, but a short trail leads to the Yoho River, where you can appreciate the view in all its rainbow-refracting glory.

Takakkaw Falls

Farther west along Hwy-1, about a dozen miles (20 kilometers) from the Icefields Parkway in the hamlet of **Field,** you come to the Yoho National Park **information centre** (250/343-6783), which can tell you all about the park's natural attractions. Charming **Truffle Pigs Bistro** serves fresh and inventive meals from the back of the **Truffle Pigs Lodge** (100 Centre St., 250/343-6303, rooms C$115 and up).

Three miles (five kilometers) west of Field, a turnoff to the north leads into the wilderness to the **Emerald Lake Lodge** (403/410-7417 or 800/663-6336, C$375-550, depending on the season), a rustic upscale resort that dates back to 1902. Sitting on the shores of one of the Canadian Rockies' most magnificent lakes, the lodge is open year-round.

Lake Louise

The sight of **Lake Louise,** spreading in a deep aquamarine pool at the foot of silvery snowcapped peaks, is worth traveling around the world to see, which is exactly what many people do: If you come here in summer, you'll be among an international gaggle of tourists for whom Lake Louise is the Canadian Rockies. A small village with the same name sits along Hwy-1, but the 1.2-mile-long (1.9-kilometer-long) lake itself is about 2 miles (3 kilometers) west, at the end of Lake Louise Drive. Besides the summer sightseeing, the Lake Louise area offers world-class downhill skiing and snowboarding: Three mountains (over 3,000 vertical feet, 900 vertical meters) are yours for the price of a Lake Louise **lift ticket** (403/522-3555, C$99 full-day, C$81 half-day). One of the lifts operates throughout the summer as well, offering a grand Canadian Rockies panorama.

Originally built by the Canadian Pacific Railway, the **Fairmont Banff Springs Hotel, Fairmont Chateau Lake Louise,** and **Fairmont Jasper Park Lodge** and some 25 others across Canada are all owned and operated by the same company, **Fairmont Hotels and Resorts** (800/257-7544).

Like the town of Banff to the south, Lake Louise was developed over a century ago as a tourist resort by the Canadian Pacific Railway. As in Banff, the landmark here is a magnificent hotel, the **Fairmont Chateau Lake Louise** (403/522-3511, C$280 and up), which stands eight stories high above the lakeshore. With a Swiss Alps theme—bellhops wear lederhosen, for example—the 552-room Chateau Lake Louise has every service and comfort you could want.

Of course, there's no charge to explore the hotel or walk along the lake and enjoy the views. You can rent canoes and paddle out onto the lake. From the hotel

calm, spectacular Moraine Lake

a popular trail climbs over 1,000 feet (300 meters) in about two miles (three kilometers) to **Bridal Veil Falls,** continuing a short way farther to **Lake Agnes,** where a rustic teahouse serves sandwiches and tea.

Immediately below the lake, the family-owned **Paradise Lodge & Bungalows** (403/522-3595, May-Oct., C$189-409) is smaller and friendlier, with cozy log cabins and modern lodge rooms, many with fireplaces.

Back down in Lake Louise Village, at the northwest end of Village Road, the **HI-Lake Louise Alpine Centre** (403/522-2201 or 866/762-4122, C$30 and up dorm beds) is a large modern log-built lodge. Across the road, the nice **Bill Peyto's Café** (daily 7am-10pm May-Sept., daily 7:30am-9:30pm Oct.-Apr.) is the area's least expensive place to eat. There are gas stations, gift shops, a grocery store, cafés, and the popular **Laggan's Mountain Bakery & Delicatessen** (101 Village Rd., 403/522-2017), serving great pastries and coffee in the hard-to-miss Samson Mall. There's also a large **campground** along the Bow River 0.75 miles (1 kilometer) south of town. The whole place tends to fill up most days despite having around 400 campsites.

Smaller, less visited, but every bit as spectacular as Lake Louise, **Moraine Lake** sits at the end of a summer-only road, six miles (10 kilometers) south of the midpoint of Lake Louise Drive. Despite the name, Moraine Lake is not in fact formed by a glacial moraine, but by a rockfall; nevertheless it's a gorgeous spot, the placid lake reflecting the jagged surrounding peaks. From the lakeside, a three-mile (five-kilometer) trail climbs up to **Larch Valley,** where you can see fall color extraordinaire courtesy of the namesake trees, which are prolific here.

Town of Banff

Fifteen miles (24 kilometers) southeast of Lake Louise, Hwy-93 and the Trans-Canada (Hwy-1) diverge, with Hwy-93 cutting due south through Kootenay National Park across southeastern British Columbia toward the U.S. border. That is the route we follow, all the way south to Mexico, eventually, but anyone in his or her right mind will want to make the 15-mile (24-kilometer) trip southeast along Hwy-1 to visit the beautiful **Town of Banff,** home of the landmark **Fairmont Banff Springs Hotel,** the biggest and most impressive of the grand old Canadian Pacific hotels. When it opened in 1888, this was the largest hotel in the world, with 250 rooms; over the years, the hotel has been rebuilt and expanded to its current 764 rooms, most of which are booked up months in advance. Spreading between the hotel and Hwy-1, the Town of Banff has grown into the tasteful but bustling commercial center of the Canadian Rockies, with a year-round population of some 7,800 people, and many times that many visitors daily during the peak summer season. Though the commercialism can detract from the natural splendor, Banff is definitely a pleasant place to while away some time.

For the most spectacular introduction to Banff, head up Mountain Avenue, where the **Banff Gondola** (403/762-7475, daily, C$49) will take you 2,281 feet up **Sulphur Mountain** for a grand view over the entire Bow Valley. The "springs" in the Fairmont Banff Springs Hotel's name refer to actual hot springs; the original hot springs that

historic Banff Springs Hotel

spurred the growth of Banff have been closed to bathers and converted into the **Cave and Basin National Historic Site** (403/762-1566, daily summer, C$4), west of town at the end of Cave Avenue, where exhibits detail the underlying geology that makes hot springs happen.

The town's main drag, Banff Avenue, has all the cafés, restaurants, and shopping you could want. But if the weather's bad (if it's not, you ought to be outdoors, enjoying Mother Nature!), you can learn about Banff and the Canadian Rockies in the local museums. Best first stop is the **Banff Park Museum** (daily summer, C$4), near the river at the foot of Banff Avenue, a Victorian-era remnant (it was built in 1903) that displays the taxidermied remains of typical park wildlife. Around the corner, a half block down from pleasant riverside Central Park, the **Whyte Museum of the Canadian Rockies** (111 Bear St., daily, C$10 donation) has an expansive collection of historic books, postcards, paintings, and photographs, all capturing various aspects of the mountains and their inhabitants.

One of many cultural events that take place in Banff is the **Banff Mountain Film and Book Festival** (403/762-6100), where the world's best adventure-travel and mountain-climbing films and mountain literature are featured every November.

Town of Banff Practicalities

So long as you plan ahead, and can afford to enjoy some of Canada's most expensive hotels and restaurants, the Town of Banff makes a great place to visit. Because the Town of Banff is located within the confines of Banff National Park, development has been limited—so much so that summertime accommodations here can be hard to come by, and expensive. Throughout the summer, hotels are booked up solidly well in advance, and rates start around C$200 for a basic room. (Winter rates are usually less than half that.) A dozen places are within a short walk of downtown: **Brewster's Mountain Lodge** (208 Caribou St., 403/762-2900, C$165 and up) has spacious rooms, while rooms at the landmark **Fairmont Banff Springs Hotel** (403/762-2211 or 866/540-4406, C$439 and up), when available, climb quickly into the four-digit range.

If you have trouble finding an affordable room in Banff, consider taking a trip farther east to **Canmore,** a lively little city on Hwy-1, just east of the park's boundary, where the nonprofit Alpine Club of Canada operates the **HI-Canmore Hostel** (403/678-3200 ext. 0, C$27).

Restaurants in Banff are plentiful, good, and wide-ranging—there are over 100, which works out to 1 for every 70 or so residents. One of the most popular places with locals and visitors alike is **Melissa's Missteak** (218 Lynx St., 403/762-5511, daily 7am-9:30pm, daily 7am-11pm summer) on the west side of downtown. Housed in a 1928 log building with a nice bar and an outdoor deck, Melissa's serves great pancakes (with real maple syrup) and beefy burgers. The ever-popular **Wild Bill's Saloon** (201 Banff Ave., 403/762-0333) has good food and drink (mostly the latter) right at the center of town. Central Banff also has many Japanese restaurants and a Greek café.

Parks Canada (855/862-1812) operates three **campgrounds** along Tunnel Mountain Road, two miles (three kilometers) east of downtown, which have over 800 sites altogether; all the campgrounds have hot showers, and many sites have full or partial RV hookups. Also on Tunnel Mountain Road is the large **HI-Banff Alpine Centre** (403/762-4123, C$33-105).

For comprehensive information on Banff, head downtown to the large **visitor information centre** (224 Banff Ave.), which is home to both the commercially oriented **Banff-Lake Louise Tourism Bureau** (403/762-8421) and the staff of **Banff National Park** (403/762-1550).

While the Trans-Canada (Hwy-1) is faster, the **Bow Valley Parkway** is a more scenic alternative between Banff and Lake Louise. Running parallel and to the east, it also gives access to some nice spots, including the waterfalls of Johnston Canyon, where **Johnston Canyon Resort** (403/762-2971, C$205-430) has rooms in a quiet woodland setting.

Kootenay National Park

Though Banff and Jasper seem to get all the attention, neighboring **Kootenay National Park** draws travelers who prefer to experience wilderness without having to wait in line. It was originally known as the "Highway Park," since the land was deeded to the federal government in exchange for it building the 65-mile (105-kilometer) Banff-Windermere Highway, which now runs through the heart of the park.

Completed in 1922, this was the first road over the Canadian Rockies, and it linked the prairies and the west coast of British Columbia for the first time. Fortunately for visitors, Hwy-1, which runs through Yoho to the north, now carries most of the through traffic.

Kootenay National Park spreads for five miles (eight kilometers) to either side of the highway. As in all the Canadian Rockies parks, grizzly bears still roam the Kootenay backcountry, and black bears, bighorn sheep, and elk are regularly seen along the roadside. A number of stops along the way offer great short hikes. Two of the most enjoyable, **Marble Canyon** and **Paint Pots,** are at the north end of the park, well signed along the north side of the highway. Marble Canyon is an amazing sight (and sound): a 100-foot-deep, narrow slot canyon carved in the shiny white dolomite limestone by the thundering cascade of

Paint Pots in Kootenay National Park

Tokumm Creek. A half-mile trail leads back and forth on a series of constructed and natural bridges over the gorge. Two miles south, the Paint Pots are much more sedate, displaying a handful of brightly colored mud puddles dyed varying shades of red and yellow by oxidizing minerals in the natural springs.

At **Vermilion Crossing** at the center of the park, about 15 miles south of the Paint Pots and 40 miles from Radium, you'll find the park's only overnight accommodations at **Kootenay Park Lodge** (250/434-9648, C$125-225), which in summer has a handful of cabins, a restaurant, a gas station, an information center, and a general store. From here south, the road follows the broad banks of the Vermilion and Kootenay Rivers before cutting west over **Sinclair Pass,** where a viewpoint offers a stunning high-country panorama. At the southern end of the park, the road winds through the narrow gorge of **Sinclair Canyon** before running suddenly into the roadside sprawl of Radium Hot Springs.

You can drive through Kootenay without charge, but if you want to stop en route you need to buy a **park pass** from the entrance stations. Passes are valid for one day (C$10 per person or C$20 per car) or all year (C$70 per person or $140 per car).

If you're passing through Radium Hot Springs, be sure to stop for a look at the amazing array of signs and sculptures outside Swiss-born artist Rolf Heer's **Radium Woodcarver,** on a hill just east of the Hwy-93/95 junction.

Radium Hot Springs

At the west edge of Kootenay National Park, the town of **Radium Hot Springs** is a swift change from the natural idyll. Motels, cafés, and gas stations line Hwy-93 block after block, and apart from satisfying your fuel-and-food needs, there's not a lot here. The one good place to eat is **Springs Elevation Restaurant,** west of town on the golf course at family-friendly **Radium Resort** (250/347-6200 or 800/667-6444, C$114 and up). Standard motels here include the **Alpen Motel** (250/347-9823, C$79-139).

The actual hot springs from which the town takes its name are just east, inside the park boundary. Unfortunately, the water is heavily chlorinated, and there are no "natural" springs left.

Fort Steele Heritage Town

South of Radium Hot Springs, Hwy-93 runs along the western foot of the Rocky Mountains, but the natural beauty of the national parks doesn't return until you cross the border and visit Glacier National Park, a good 226 miles (362 kilometers) away. That said, it's a wide-open drive, passing a few towns, some golf resorts, and two big lumber mills, following the banks of the Kootenay River all the way.

The one real attraction along this stretch of road is the resurrected frontier community of Fort Steele, roughly midway between Radium and the border crossing. Containing more than 60 preserved and reconstructed buildings, **Fort Steele Heritage Town** (250/417-6000, daily, C$7-27) recreates the boomtown that stood here from 1890 until 1898, servicing the silver, gold, and lead mines of the East

Kootenays. Along with the buildings, which house interpretive exhibits as well as an ice cream store, a bakery and restaurant, and a general store selling top hats and other period essentials, you can enjoy theater performances or ride on a steam train—though there are extra charges for these activities.

MONTANA

From the Canadian border, US-93 runs south and east along the Tobacco River Valley, then cuts through the **Flathead National Forest** to the logging and ski resort towns of **Whitefish** and **Kalispell.** Continuing south along the shores of **Flathead Lake,** the route passes through the college town and cultural nexus of **Missoula,** south of which US-93 passes through some of the most beautiful terrain in the country, winding through broad valleys at the foot of the Bitterroot Mountains, past alpine lakes and snowcapped peaks all the way south to the Idaho border. Quite a lot of the old two-lane route has been upgraded to near-freeway status, but US-93 is still one of either country's great drives.

Eureka

Like British Columbia, Montana's northwest corner, where BC Hwy-93 ends and US-93 begins, is an isolated land of dense forests, broad rivers, and glaciated valleys. Besides providing natural habitat for herds of moose, elk, bison, and bighorn sheep, not to mention mountain lions, wolves, and grizzly bears, the thick groves of cedars, pines, and firs support the Northwest's other endangered species—the logger—whose angular clear-cuts and monocrop tree plantations are also apparent as you pass through the region.

> Hwy-37 is an official Scenic Byway that winds along the Kootenai River and Lake Koocanusa from **Eureka** to the town of **Libby,** where it intersects US-2.

The first sizable town, nine miles south of the border, is **Eureka** (pop. 1,037), a sleepy little place with a pair of gas stations, a couple of cafés, and **Tobacco Valley Historical Village** (406/297-7654, summer only), a fascinating collection of pioneer buildings, preserved and moved to a small park along US-93 at the south end of town.

For a truly unusual experience, spend the night in the former **U.S. Forest Service fire lookout** (around $35) atop Webb Mountain, about 24 miles southwest of Eureka. It's popular; for details and rental availability, contact the **U.S. Forest Service ranger station** (406/296-2536, www.reserveamerica.com) in Eureka.

Whitefish

A major division point on the historic Great Northern Railway, whose tracks are still in use by Amtrak and the Burlington Northern Santa Fe, **Whitefish** (pop. 7,073) was originally known as Stumptown because of the intensive logging operations centered here. Despite its proud industrial history, the blue-collar base has long since been eclipsed by tourism, and the city now calls itself the "Recreational Capital of Montana," with alpine lakes, fishing streams, hiking trails, great skiing, and endless mountain scenery right on its doorstep. The main attraction in Whitefish, for skiing in winter and hiking and mountain biking in summer, is "The Fish," a.k.a. **Whitefish**

bagpipers at the annual Eureka Rendezvous

Mountain Resort, which surrounds the 6,817-foot peak (with a 2,353-foot vertical drop!) that looms over the northwest shore of Whitefish Lake.

Besides giving access to the surrounding great outdoors, Whitefish is a pleasant place to stop and stretch your legs, and it has everything you could want from a resort town—without the rampant tourist-pandering and real estate speculation that has ruined so many other places. A small **museum** (Mon.-Sat., free) inside the rustic Great Northern train station, which stands in a pleasant park at the north end of **Depot Park,** gives a historical overview of Whitefish. Across the park from the station there's a theater, a library, and the **Great Northern Brewing Company,** whose hoppy products you can sample in a small **tasting room** (2 Central Ave.) or in any Whitefish bar.

The heart of town is a few blocks of Central Avenue, running south from the railroad tracks to one of Montana's three Frank Lloyd Wright buildings, an early 1950s bank and office complex on the east side of Central Avenue between 3rd and 4th Streets called, directly enough, the **Frank Lloyd Wright Building.** In between you'll find some great bars and saloons, art galleries, and **Bookworks** (3rd St. and Spokane St.).

The best place to start the day in Whitefish is along 3rd Street, east of Central Avenue, where the **Buffalo Café** (514 E. 3rd St., 406/862-2833) is a popular breakfast and lunch spot, locally famous for its huevos rancheros. Other places line up along Central Avenue, so you can get great burgers or wood-fired pizza or simply quaff a beer or two—all in the same block.

For a place to stay and get to know Whitefish, you can choose from numerous motels along US-93 south of town. The nicest in-town lodging option is walkably close to downtown: the attractive and comfortable **Garden Wall Inn** (504 Spokane Ave., 406/862-3440 or 888/530-1700, $155 and up), a Craftsman cottage.

Kalispell marks the junction of US-93 and **The Great Northern** route along US-2 (see page 489), which runs east through Glacier National Park and west across Idaho and Washington to the Pacific Ocean. Full coverage of this route begins on page 470.

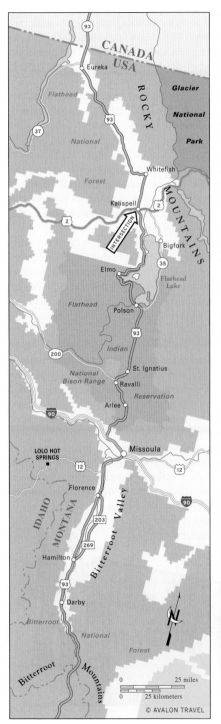

Kalispell

The nearest thing to an urban center in northwestern Montana, **Kalispell** (pop. 22,052) spreads across the northern Flathead Valley at the junction of the Stillwater, Whitefish, and Flathead Rivers. Cut by two main thoroughfares—east-west US-2 and north-south US-93—it ain't quaint by any stretch of the imagination. At first glance it looks like yet another lumber mill and mining town, but the historic downtown area is full of interesting spots, such as the engaging **Hockaday Museum of Art** (302 2nd Ave. E., Tues.-Sat., $5), housed in the old Carnegie Library, two blocks east of Main Street (US-93). Another few blocks east stands the impressive, perfectly preserved **Conrad Mansion** (406/755-2166, tours Tues.-Sun. high season, Wed.-Sun. other seasons, $15), built by pioneer trader and Kalispell founder Charles Conrad in 1895 and now open for guided tours.

Breakfasts don't get much better than those served at **Norm's News** (34 Main St., 406/756-5466), a 1930s soda fountain luncheonette where you can also get killer milk shakes, a wide variety of newspapers and magazines, and more than 800 kinds of candy. Upstairs

Chief Charlo, leader of the Bitterroot Salish, as seen in 1908

is the old Kalispell Opera House. Kalispell also has an above-average range of taverns, including the venerable **Moose's Saloon** (173 N. Main St., 406/755-2337), near the junction of US-2 and US-93, famous for pizza and beer. For good old-fashioned roadside fast food, try the popular local mini chain **Frugals** (1815 S. US-93, 406/257-6710).

There are the usual national motels, but the place to stay in Kalispell is the **Kalispell Grand Hotel** (100 Main St., 406/755-8100 or 800/858-7422, $140 and up), a conveniently located historic downtown hotel with nice clean rooms.

Flathead Lake

The largest natural freshwater lake west of the Mississippi River, deep-blue **Flathead Lake** is a magnet for outdoor recreation in western Montana. US-93 winds along the lake's hilly western shore, passing through a number of state parks and small resort communities that enjoy grand views of the Rocky Mountains to the east and the green foothills of the Flathead National Forest to the west.

Along US-93 at the north end of the lake, **Somers** is a neat old timber town with some well-preserved turn-of-the-20th-century buildings, including an old train depot. From Somers, you can detour east onto Hwy-82 for a trip along the eastern shore of Flathead Lake, where you can enjoy the upscale resort town of **Bigfork** and the acres of cherry orchards that line the lakeshore, flowering in spring and offering delectable treats in early summer.

Polson: Miracle of America Museum

The southern half of Flathead Lake is surrounded by the **Flathead Reservation,** home to a mixed population of Flathead Salish and Kootenai peoples as well as non-indigenous people, who make up around 80 percent of the reservation's population. The large reservation covers a 1.3-million-acre area, roughly 35 by 65 miles, hemmed in by the Mission and Cabinet Mountains. Apart from a few small towns, it's mostly prairie and riverside wetlands.

The largest of these towns, **Polson,** at the bottom end of the lake where the Flathead River flows south, is a predominantly white retirement community, with 24-hour gas stations, the area's only ATMs, a Safeway supermarket, and chain motels. Polson is also home to the deluxe lakefront **Best Western KwaTaqNuk Resort** (49708 US-93 E., 406/883-3636, $205 and up), owned and operated by the Confederated Salish and Kootenai Tribes, with two pools, an on-site casino, a boat dock, and direct access to the lake.

Just two miles south of Polson along US-93, the bizarre but fascinating **Miracle of America Museum** (406/883-6804, daily, $6), which calls itself "Western Montana's Largest Museum," displays kitchen appliances, toys, antique motorcycles, tractors, armored tanks, and framed newspaper clippings to give a unique, to say the least, view of America's industrial, military, and cultural history. If you'd enjoy things like a motorized toboggan or a collection of tractor seats, count on spending an hour at least—twice that long if you also like music, because the museum doubles as the Montana Fiddlers Hall of Fame.

South of Polson, US-93 has been realigned and widened in an eco-sensitive wetlands-friendly fashion, with native plantings, wildlife crossings, and a new name: the Peoples Way.

St. Ignatius and the National Bison Range

The wildly angular Mission Mountains, rising to the east of the Flathead Reservation, were named for a Roman Catholic mission established in the 1850s at **St. Ignatius,** a small town midway between Polson and Missoula. Like most reservation communities, it's a poor and fairly depressed place, worth a look for the imposing **St. Ignatius Mission church** (daily, donation), just east of US-93. Built by Flathead laborers in 1891, the church holds over 55 religious frescoes painted by Joseph Carignano, the mission cook. Along with the church, St. Ignatius holds the **Flathead Indian Museum and Trading Post** (406/745-2951, daily), a large gift shop, a motel, and a drive-through espresso stand right along US-93.

West of St. Ignatius, 18,500 acres of natural rolling prairie have been set aside since 1908 as the **National Bison Range,** protected home of the 500 or so resident

bison grazing at the National Bison Range

bison (a.k.a. buffalo), along with deer, elk, pronghorn, and mountain goats. Allow around two hours to drive a complete circuit of the park; the entrance and visitors center are on the west side of the reserve, off Hwy-200, six miles west of the crossroads town of **Ravalli.** At the southern edge of the Flathead Reservation, **Arlee** hosts an annual 4th of July Powwow, one of the most popular Native American gatherings in Montana.

Missoula

Spreading along the banks of the Clark Fork of the Columbia River at the mouth of Hellgate Canyon, **Missoula** (pop. 71,022) is an engaging mix of college-town sophistication and blue-collar grit. The two industries that built the city, railroads and lumber mills, have both diminished considerably since their turn-of-the-20th-century heyday but still form the foundation of the local economy. The **University of Montana** campus has given Missoula a literate and left-leaning air not usually found in this neck of the woods.

The mountains, rivers, and canyons around Missoula are Montana at its best. Downtown Missoula, stretching along the north bank of the river, contains a large number of elegant turn-of-the-20th-century brick buildings housing a buoyant range of businesses, from department stores to bike shops. Missoula's

The **Missoula Osprey,** the only baseball team with a real live animal mascot in residence, play at **Ogren Park Allegiance Field** (406/543-3300), on the south bank of the river, just west of US-93.

A RIVER RUNS THROUGH IT

Missoula has long been something of a literary center, thanks in part to the writings of Norman Maclean (1902-1990), who grew up in Missoula working in logging camps and later taught English at the University of Chicago. Maclean's 1976 novella *A River Runs Through It* rhapsodizes over the surrounding Rocky Mountain country and the larger-than-life lives lived here. Maclean lovingly uses the art of fly-fishing as an essential metaphor for a life well lived. The book, which was faithfully adapted by director Robert Redford into a 1992 Academy Award-winning film starring a young Brad Pitt and a very young Joseph Gordon Leavitt, makes a great traveling companion. It's full of vivid description and insightful humor. Maclean writes that while growing up he discovered that the world is "full of bastards, the number increasing rapidly the farther one gets from Missoula, Montana."

other social nexus, the University of Montana campus, spreads south of the river at the foot of dusty brown Mt. Sentinel (the one marked with the large "M") and the Sapphire Mountains. It's a pleasant place to walk around—in summer, at least, when cyclists and in-line skaters outnumber pedestrians on the many paths—keeping an eye out for posters advertising local events.

Missoula's number-one attraction, the **Smokejumpers Base Aerial Fire Depot** (406/329-4934, daily 8:30am-5pm summer, donation), is seven miles west of town at the end of Broadway. Displays include dioramas, old photographs, and antique firefighting gear; hourly guided tours are led by the very people who jump out of airplanes to battle raging forest fires.

Missoula Practicalities

Thanks to the student population, Missoula has a wider-than-usual range of places to eat, and a truly phenomenal range of places to drink. Start the day at **Bernice's Bakery** (190 S. 3rd St. W., 406/728-1358), which has good coffee and great pastries. Right downtown, the landmark **Missoula Club** (139 W. Main St., 406/728-3740) is a perfectly preserved 1940s burgers-and-beer bar. For an even grittier Missoula scene, it's hard to beat the round-the-clock **Oxford Saloon** (337 N. Higgins Ave., 406/549-0117), where men and a few women huddle around nightly poker games, brave souls feast on the house special brains-and-eggs, and everyone drinks too much Bud.

There's no shortage of accommodations in Missoula, though it's always a good idea to book a room in advance. The nicest place to stay is **Goldsmith's** (809 E. Front St., 406/204-2535, $89-169), a comfortable downtown B&B along the river. A half dozen motels line I-90 and US-93 (which follows Broadway west of Missoula and Brooks Street south of town), including the usual national chains.

The Bitterroot Valley

Missoula sits at the north end of the **Bitterroot Valley,** where **Lewis and Clark** set up camp at what they called **Traveler's Rest** in September 1805 and again on their return in July 1806. A roadside marker off US-93, just south of the US-12 junction, tells more of the story.

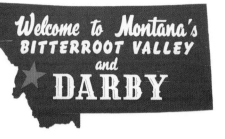

If you're a fan of Lewis and Clark, or hot springs, or want to unwind after a day of cross-country skiing, you won't want to miss the idyllic **Lolo Hot Springs Resort** (406/273-2290), in the mountains 36 miles southwest of Missoula via scenic US-12, which runs along the route Lewis and Clark followed on their way west. Moose wander through the wooded grounds, and the natural hot springs (where Lewis and Clark themselves soaked on their way home from the Pacific Ocean) have been extensively and attractively developed.

Continuing south toward the Idaho border, US-93 runs along the banks of the beautiful Bitterroot River through a broad valley lined by groves of cottonwood trees and bordered by parallel ridges of 8,000-foot peaks. In the hamlet of **Florence, Glen's Café** (406/273-2534), tucked away just west of the highway, is renowned throughout Montana for its carb-loaded pastries, pancakes, and incredibly good, double-crusted, fresh berry pies.

South of Florence, the **Eastside Highway** (Hwy-203 and Hwy-269), a well-marked alternative route, runs parallel to US-93 a half mile to the east, passing rolling ranch lands, pioneer homesteads—some of which are among the oldest in the state—and occasional prefab trailers. This eastern side of the Bitteroot Valley is mostly open countryside, with a few small hamlets like **Stevensville,** Montana's oldest town. It was founded by Jesuits in 1841 around the still intact **St. Mary's Mission** at the end of 4th Street, two blocks west of Main Street.

Hamilton

The Bitterroot Valley's sole sizable town, **Hamilton** (pop. 4,602) stands at the southern end of the valley, where US-93 and the Eastside Highway rejoin. Hamilton was laid out in the 1890s as a planned community by the multimillionaire "Copper King" Marcus Daly. His elegant 56-room **Daly Mansion** (406/363-6004, daily summer, $10) is now a museum, set in 50 acres of lushly landscaped gardens.

Hamilton's other main draw is the large **Ravalli County Museum** (406/363-3338, Tues.-Sat., $3), housed in a 100-year-old former courthouse on the corner of 3rd and Bedford Streets, two blocks south of Main Street. Besides an above-average collection of fishing flies, pioneer clothing, and Native American artifacts, the museum has an entire room dedicated to Rocky Mountain spotted fever ticks—Hamilton, home of the Rocky Mountain Laboratories, was where spotted fever was discovered—and you owe it to yourself to study the two-foot-tall tick model and the diagrams tracing the tick's life cycle.

Hamilton has some great places to eat, like the popular **Coffee Cup Café** (500 S. 1st St., 406/363-3822) on US-93. Great big half-pound burgers ("100% Montana Beef—Best in the Bitterroots") and fresh-cut crispy fries are at **Naps**

Grill (220 N. 2nd St., 406/363-0136), or for something more exotic, look for **Spice of Life** (163 S. 2nd St., 406/363-4433).

One of many highway motels in Hamilton, the **City Center motel** (415 W. Main St., 406/363-1651, $45-80) enjoys a quiet location off US-93. Besides its convenience as a stopover, Hamilton is also the gateway to outdoor activities (mainly hunting, fishing, and riding) in the Bitterroots. For full details on the huge variety of outdoor recreation hereabouts, contact the **Bitterroot Valley Chamber of Commerce** (105 E. Main St., 406/363-2400).

Bitterroot Mountains

South of Hamilton, the serrated peaks and forested foothills of the **Bitterroot Mountains** close in along US-93 as the valley narrows sharply, the towns shrink in size, and woodlands and campgrounds replace farmlands and commerce along the roadside. Just 17 miles south of Hamilton, the pioneer village of **Darby** has a couple of cafés, a log-cabin public library, and a helpful **U.S. Forest Service ranger station** (406/821-3913), the best source of information on hiking and camping in the Bitterroots.

South of Darby, US-93 cuts away from the Bitterroot River at the hamlet of **Sula,** beyond which the highway continues its slow climb up through seven miles of subalpine landscape to another of Montana's many pleasant resorts, **Lost Trail Hot Springs** (283 Lost Trail Hot Springs Rd., 406/821-3574, $95 and up), open year-round with hot springs pools, an attractive variety of moderately priced rooms and cabins, and a good on-site restaurant. Lost Trail is especially popular with cross-country skiers, who can traverse many miles of nearby trails, including the route followed by Chief Joseph and the Nez Percé in 1877 while fleeing from the U.S. Cavalry.

The **Big Hole National Battlefield** (406/689-3155), where 800 Nez Percé warriors, women, and children were attacked by the U.S. Army on August 9, 1877, lies east of the Continental Divide near the hamlet of **Wisdom,** 20 miles east of Lost Trail Pass via Hwy-43.

From Lost Trail Hot Springs, US-93 climbs up to 6,995-foot **Lost Trail Pass,** which Lewis and Clark crossed in 1805 on their return from the impassable Snake River, and which now marks the border with Idaho. The pass also serves as home to **Lost Trail Powder Mountain** (406/821-3211, $42), a low-key downhill ski area with 1,800 vertical feet of groomed runs.

IDAHO

In 1938, the WPA Guide to Idaho described the state's section of US-93 as "miles of beautiful mountains, ranging from soft flanks voluptuously mounded to the lean and glittering majesty of toothed backbones." Though the official US-93 route was redirected around the mountains, not much else has changed since then: The old road is still in place and still gives an unmatched tour of the best of what Idaho has to offer.

Entering the state through a historic pass in the beautiful Bitterroot Mountains, the route drops down to follow the mighty Salmon River to its headwaters over 100 miles away near the frontier resort of **Stanley,** high up in the **Sawtooth Mountains.** South of the Sawtooths, the route plunges into the plush resort community of **Sun Valley,** then races across the Snake River plain through **Twin Falls** to the Nevada border.

Salmon River: North Fork

Beginning at the Montana border, atop Lost Trail Pass, US-93 winds steeply downhill through the 4.3-million-acre **Salmon-Challis National Forest.** Another 25 miles south of the pass, US-93 passes by the village of **North Fork**—where the friendly folks at the **North Fork General Store** (208/865-7001) run a combination café, motel, and post office that has everything a traveler could want, from great pies to an RV park. Here US-93 crosses the **Salmon River,** which is often called the "River of No Return," because without a jet boat to help you along, it is navigable only in a downstream direction. Running swiftly for nearly 300 miles west through one of the most extensive wilderness areas left in the lower 48 states, the Salmon River has carved one of the deepest gorges in North America, a full 1,000 feet deeper than the Grand Canyon.

From North Fork, a paved road leads 18 miles west along the riverside to the tiny hamlet of **Shoup,** beyond which a number of rough roads and hiking trails lead to ghost towns and the **Frank Church-River of No Return Wilderness,** deep in the rugged mountains.

Salmon

Surrounded by ranch lands in a broad valley between the Bitterroot and Yellowjacket Mountains, **Salmon** (pop. 3,036) is a picturesque place that has turned increasingly to tourism and outdoor recreation as its timber and ranching industries have faded. Rafting and fishing guides will take you out into the wilds, so Salmon is both a good base for exploring the surrounding scenery and a destination in itself. Main Street, which US-93 follows through town, has a good variety of places to eat, including the **Salmon River Coffee Shop** (606 Main St., 208/756-3521) and **Bertram's Brewery** (101 S. Andrews, 208/756-3391). There are some motels along US-93, but the best place to stay is the **Syringa Lodge** (13 Gott Lane, 208/756-4424), a log-cabin B&B about a mile west of Main Street, offering panoramic views, reasonable rates, and a warm welcome.

Around Salmon, tune to **KSRA 92.7 FM** or **60 AM** for an eclectic broadcast of oldies, country music, ABC News, and reports on life in the Salmon and Big Hole region.

Salmon River Gorge

South of Salmon, US-93 continues beside the Salmon River, climbing slowly through a landscape that alternates from open meadows to sheer canyons. Nearly 100 miles later, the route arrives at the river's headwaters high up in the Sawtooth Mountains. Apart from a few cottonwoods, there are few trees and no real towns along this stretch of US-93, and traffic still has to stop for the occasional cattle drive. It's a pretty drive, and you can stop almost anywhere for a quick walk or picnic along the river. The appearance of the Salmon River canyon varies tremendously, but for most of the way it is dry and brown—a real shock compared to the dense green forests of Montana, just an hour north.

Challis and the Land of Yankee Fork State Park

The only substantial town for 50 miles in any direction, **Challis** is an old mining camp that has grown into a miniature version of Salmon—albeit without the water or the tourists. Apart from boasting the all-time Idaho record for least rain in a year (seven inches), Challis is a quiet market center for local cattle ranchers, with more bars—and barber shops—than you'd expect of a town this small.

On the south side of Challis, at the junction of US-93 and Hwy-75, the excellent, modern **Land of Yankee Fork State Park visitors center** (208/879-5244, daily summer, Wed.-Sat. fall-spring) has extensive displays on local mining history and maps to guide visitors to many evocative ghost towns and other relics sprinkling the surrounding hills. Gold was first discovered in the region in the 1870s, and nearby mines and mining camps boomed for the next 25 years, though by 1905 the last mine had closed. A few gold mines have reopened in recent years, though all of these are hidden away in isolated areas and protected behind high-security walls and fences; none are open to the public.

US-93: Mackay and the Lost River Valley

At Challis, our main route follows the 1940s alignment of US-93, heading west into the Sawtooth Mountains, but today's US-93 swings southeast toward **Arco** and the **Craters of the Moon National Monument and Preserve** through the **Lost River Valley.** The scenery here remains spectacular, with the mountains towering over the ranches of the valley floor, but it can't compare with the glories of the old road route.

But if you're in a rush, or there's been a recent storm blocking the mountain passes, or you just want to see another corner of Idaho, US-93 will be there for you. Mountaineers follow US-93 on their way to climb 12,662-foot **Mt. Borah,** the highest point in Idaho and a demanding though not technically difficult summit to reach. A popular trailhead is at the end of the well-signed Borah Peak Access Road, roughly halfway between Challis and Mackay. For details, contact the **U.S.**

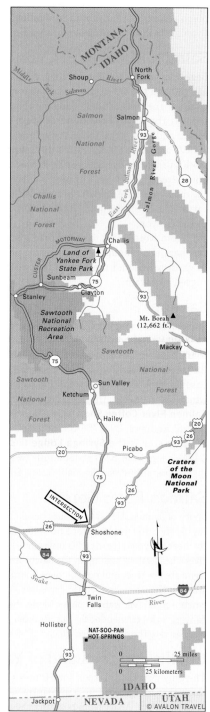

Forest Service ranger station
(208/588-3400) in Mackay.

The rough-and-ready town of **Mackay** (pop. 476; rhymes with "wacky") is the valley's hub. You can stay at the **Wagon Wheel** (809 W. Custer St., 208/588-3331), where rooms with kitchenettes go for as little as $45. Mackay also hosts an annual rodeo and the Custer County Fair, but it's best known for its famous **free barbecue** on the third Saturday in

September, when hundreds of people come here for general fun and games and massive amounts of free food (Tons of Meat—Mackay's Treat, say the signs).

South of Mackay, US-93 continues to Arco, then elbows west through the eerie Craters of the Moon, rejoining Hwy-75 at Shoshone.

Clayton and Sunbeam

Though US-93 swings to the southeast from Challis, the original alignment, now Hwy-75, winds west into the mountains through the more than 2,000-foot-deep canyon carved by the Salmon River. You're deep in the forest by the time you reach **Clayton** (pop. 6), a riverside wide spot with a gas station and a biker-friendly tavern. Farther west, some 45 miles from Challis, you come to the small but pleasant year-round resort of **Sunbeam**, which overlooks the confluence of the Yankee Fork and Salmon Rivers. There's a café and campground at the junction, and just a half mile upstream you'll find the area's greatest attraction: the natural **hot springs**, steaming wildly on cold days and forming rock pools of varying temperatures in the Salmon River, marked by a stone bathhouse built during the New Deal 1930s but no longer in use.

From Sunbeam, it's only another 14 miles to Stanley, heart of the glorious Sawtooth Mountains.

Custer Motorway

If you're here in summer and have a few hours to spare, take the rough (no RVs, please!) but scenic alternative to Hwy-75, built by the Civilian Conservation Corps in the 1930s and called the **Custer Motorway**, which winds west from Challis into the Yankee Fork mining district, passing the remains of old stagecoach stations and stamp mills before reaching the ghost town of **Custer**. Custer now consists of a half-dozen mining shacks and log cabins, the Empire Saloon, and a small but engaging museum housed in the old one-room schoolhouse. Beyond Custer, a well-maintained gravel road follows the Yankee Fork of the Salmon River south to Hwy-75, passing an abandoned gold dredge and other relics of mining operations, past and present, before rejoining the highway at Sunbeam, on the banks of the Salmon River.

In 1805, explorers Lewis and Clark became the first Americans to cross the Continental Divide when they climbed over **Lemhi Pass,** 33 miles southeast of Salmon. Hoping to follow the Salmon River west to the Pacific, they found it was impassable, so they continued north over **Lost Trail Pass,** roughly along the route of US-93.

On October 28, 1983, one of the most powerful earthquakes ever to hit North America rumbled the Lost River Valley, instantly dropping the valley floor as much as 14 feet and forming dramatic escarpments still visible in places throughout the region.

Further details, and free maps of Custer and the Custer Motorway, are available from the **Land of Yankee Fork State Park visitors center** (208/879-5244) in Challis.

Stanley

Set in a broad basin at the eastern foot of the angular Sawtooth Mountains, 58 miles west of Challis, **Stanley** (pop. 68; elev. 6,250 feet) is a tiny, isolated town that makes an excellent base for exploring the surrounding two-million-plus acres of alpine forest. In summertime, the population swells to around 500, including visitors, so although it's just 60 miles north of busy Sun Valley, there's still plenty of room to move. Hikers and mountain bikers in summer, and cross-country skiers in winter, should have no trouble finding solitude among the 10,000-foot peaks; the **ranger station** (208/774-3000), four miles south of town on Hwy-75, can supply details of trails and campgrounds as well as rafting trips along the Middle Fork of the Salmon River.

Places to eat, drink, and be merry stand along Ace of Diamonds Street, the main street of Stanley proper, southwest of the Hwy-21/75 junction. Log cabin breakfasts and great freshly baked goodies are available at **Stanley Baking Co. & Café** (250 Wall St., 208/774-6573). Later in the day, make your way to the **Kasino Club** (34 Ace of Diamonds, 208/774-3516), serving steaks and chops and frequent live music on Friday and Saturday evenings.

Sawtooth National Recreation Area

Stanley and Sunbeam both stand along the northern border of the more than 750,000-acre **Sawtooth National Recreation Area,** which extends south for over 20 miles of untrammeled meadows, forests, and lakes and includes the headwaters of many major Idaho rivers. It also holds one of the nicest places to stay in the Rockies: the historic **Redfish Lake Lodge** (208/774-3536 or 208/644-9096, May-Oct., rooms $76 and up, cabins $138-598), seven miles south of Stanley on Hwy-75 on the east shore of Redfish Lake, which has rustic log-walled rooms in the main lodge and spacious cabins. The lodge also has a good restaurant.

Redfish Lake in Sawtooth National Recreation Area

There are two main **visitors centers** for the Sawtooth NRA: a summer-only one near Redfish Lake and the headquarters (208/727-5000) on the north side of Ketchum.

South of Redfish Lake, Hwy-75 switchbacks steeply up to 8,707-foot **Galena Summit,** which gives a grand view over the surrounding mountains before dropping steeply down toward Sun Valley along the headwaters of the Wood River. About 5 miles south of the pass, 20-odd miles before you reach the resort area, there's one last stop worth making: **Galena Lodge** (208/726-4010), which dates back to the mining era of the 1880s and has been resurrected as a cross-country ski lodge, with food service, ski or snowshoe rentals, and the Sun Valley area's most extensive system of groomed trails. The community-owned lodge also maintains four backcountry **yurts** ($100-165): tentlike structures with wood-burning stoves and bunks for up to eight people.

Sun Valley

The first destination ski resort in the United States, and still among the most famous, **Sun Valley** was developed by Union Pacific railroad tycoon Averell Harriman. In 1936 Harriman built a large mock-Tyrolean chalet, the **Sun Valley Lodge** (1 Sun Valley Rd., 208/622-4111 or 800/786-8259, $339 and up), and began to cultivate Sun Valley's exclusive reputation—reinforced to this day by high prices for lift tickets (over $100 a day) and five-star facilities, including golf courses, tennis courts, and gourmet restaurants. Though Colorado's Vail and other resorts now compete for the top-dollar trade, Sun Valley still attracts well-heeled clientele, if the private jets parked at the local airport are any indication.

Ernest Hemingway is probably the most famous name associated with Sun Valley. Hemingway first came here in the 1930s and worked on **_For Whom the Bell Tolls_** while staying at the Sun Valley Lodge. He returned in 1960, and a year later shot himself; he's now buried in a simple plot in the middle-rear section of Ketchum's small cemetery. Hemingway is also remembered by a small and surprisingly kitschy memorial along Trail Creek Road, a mile east of the resort.

While the resort itself isn't huge, Sun Valley has come to stand for the larger area, including the towns of Ketchum and Hailey and much of the nearby wilderness, much of which is surprisingly barren and treeless—ideal for skiing, perhaps, though not jaw-dropping beautiful. Besides skiers in winter, Sun Valley also draws golfers and mountain bikers in summer and fall, not to mention anglers, who rate the Big Wood River as one of the nation's best trout-fishing streams.

Ketchum

Though both places preexisted Sun Valley, the two old mining and sheep-ranching towns of **Ketchum** (pop. 2,728) and Hailey have more or less lost themselves in the upmarket resort aura of their famous neighbor. Ketchum, the more touristy of the two, has wall-to-wall art galleries and T-shirt shops lining its traffic-jammed streets. It also supports dozens of expensive resort hotels and restaurants that cater to Sun Valley's country club set, plus a handful of more interesting and affordable bar-and-grills along Main Street: try the **Pioneer Saloon** (320 N. Main St., 208/726-3139) or **Whiskey Jacques'** (251 N. Main St., 208/726-5297), which serves good pizzas steaks and strong drinks. The Harley-friendly **Casino Club** (220 N. Main St., 208/726-9901) is a local institution, serving beers and burgers in one of Ketchum's oldest buildings. A block west of Main Street, **Java on Fourth** (191 4th St., 208/726-2882), serves addictive, rich hot chocolate.

The most central and affordable of Ketchum's accommodations line up along Hwy-75, including the clean and convenient **Best Western Plus Kentwood Lodge** (180 S. Main St., 208/726-4114, $179 and up).

Hailey

Hailey, 12 miles south of Ketchum and linked by a popular rail-trail bike path, was founded originally in the 1880s as a supply center for local silver and lead mines and is now the home base of all those workers who make the resorts run smoothly and ski in between shifts. Hailey feels much more friendly and low-key than Ketchum or Sun Valley, and the eating options are much more down-to-earth. For breakfast or lunch, head to diner-style **Shorty's Diner** (126 S. Main St., 208/578-1293), originally built (but no longer owned) by *Die Hard* actor Bruce Willis. (His ex-wife, movie star Demi Moore, is a local mom about town.)

Hailey

In contrast to the civic love affair Sun Valley has with the legacy of Ernest Hemingway, **Hailey** takes little notice of the fact that it was the birthplace (in 1885, in a house that still stands at Pine Street and 2nd Avenue) of another noteworthy literary figure, Ezra Pound. His parents were here working for the U.S. government but fled the snowy winters just two years later.

Shoshone: Ice Caves

South of the Sun Valley area, Hwy-75 runs across 60 miles of south-central Idaho's rocky black lava flows. Halfway between Sun Valley and Twin Falls, 16 miles north of the town of Shoshone, the **Shoshone Indian Ice Caves** (208/886-2058, daily May-Sept., $10) present a series of lava tubes developed into a low-key tourist trap. Just west of the highway, their constant cool temperatures make a pleasant contrast to the often-scorching summer heat. (The "ice" in the name is created by air currents flowing through the tubes, causing subterranean water to freeze.) The only way to explore the caves is through guided tours, which take about 45 minutes. The gift shop and mineral museum, which features lava rocks and local wildlife, will satisfy anyone's needs for tourist-trap trash (and I mean that in the best possible way). Just down the road, **Mammoth Cave** (208/886-7072, daily summer, $10) is much more basic and undeveloped.

Shoshone marks the junction of US-93 with our cross-country **Oregon Trail** route (see page 582), which runs along US-20/26 between Boise and the Craters of the Moon National Monument. Full coverage of this route begins on page 558.

dinosaur at Shoshone Indian Ice Caves

The only town along this stretch of road, **Shoshone** (pop. 1,488) is a ranching and railroad center that marks the junction of Hwy-75 with US-93. Some of its buildings have been constructed from local volcanic rock. Though it's a fairly timeworn place, Shoshone looks great at sunset, when its steel water tower glows and places like the neon-signed **Manhattan Café** (208/886-2142) on the south side of the railroad tracks look especially appealing.

Minidoka Internment National Monument

Between Shoshone and Twin Falls, the potato-growing Snake River plains hold a surprising remnant of a moment in time many Americans would just as soon forget: the forcible arrest and deportation of over 110,000 Americans of Japanese descent during the early 1940s. Moved from their homes in California, Washington, and Oregon, entire families were uprooted and relocated to desolate, middle-of-nowhere places where they were made to live in makeshift shacks. Here at **Minidoka National Historic Site,** 19 miles northeast of Twin Falls, more than 10,000 American citizens were held as prisoners between 1942 and the end of World War II three years later. The 73-acre site preserves a handful of buildings, including the guardhouse, but it's the isolation that endures most. The site has no services and can be hard to reach; head east from US-93 along Hwy-25 for 9.5 miles, then north along Hunt Road for another 2.5 miles. The visitors center is 40 miles away in Hagerman, on US-25.

Twin Falls

Named for a pair of 200-foot cascades on the Snake River, both of which have long been diverted for irrigation or to generate electricity, **Twin Falls** (pop. 47,468) is the heart of the extensive "Magic Valley" of highly productive irrigated croplands that cover half a million acres of south-central Idaho.

341. Twin Falls on the Snake River, near Twin Falls, Idaho.

Best known to people outside Idaho as the place where, in 1974, daredevil Evel Knievel tried and failed to ride a rocket-powered motorcycle across the Snake River Canyon, Twin Falls is both a quiet farming community and a busy highway town—with a barrage of backlit and neon signs around the junction of US-93 and the I-84 freeway.

This lone unique attraction of Twin Falls, the site of **Evel Knievel**'s aborted motorcycle jump, is a mile north of town on US-93, south of I-84. There's a large parking area and a visitors center at the south foot of the delicate Perrine Memorial Bridge, and it's well worth stopping for, not only to see the remains of his launch pad

EVEL KNIEVEL AND THE SNAKE RIVER CANYON

No one who lived through the 1970s could forget the name Evel Knievel (1938-2007), the ultimate thrill seeker who became rich and famous performing dangerous and virtually impossible feats on a motorcycle. Born in Butte, Montana, Knievel dropped out of high school and worked a dozen different jobs before finding his true calling as a motorcycle daredevil. In 1965 he made his first public jump, flying over a caged mountain lion and boxes of rattlesnakes at Moses Lake, Washington. Within a few years he hit the big time: leaping over the fountains at Caesars Palace in Las Vegas and jumping 50 cars at the Los Angeles Coliseum. Though he broke nearly every bone in his body as a result of his numerous crash landings, Knievel's feats were always bigger, better, and more danger-ous than the last; as he liked to say, "Where there's little risk, there's little reward."

Banned by the government from attempting a leap over the Grand Canyon, Knievel set his sights on the Snake River Canyon in southern Idaho, leasing the land so no one could stop him, then building a massive ramp and working out the details of his custom-made, steam-powered Harley-Davidson X-2 Skycycle rocket. On September 8, 1974, some 30,000 people turned out, along with many millions more watching on TV, for Evel's big leap. Unfortunately, one of his parachutes deployed on takeoff, and he floated gently down into the bottom of the gorge, safe and sound and proud of having the guts to try—even if he didn't quite make it. Years later, in 2016, stunt-man Eddie Braun rocketed himself across the Snake River Canyon riding the "Evel Spirit."

(a triangular pile of dirt, on private property a mile or so east of the bridge) or the stone monument that reads "Robert 'Evel' Knievel—Explorer, Motorcyclist, Daredevil." The views down into the 500-foot-deep gorge, the floor of which has been irrigated and filled with a bright green golf course, are also impressive, especially at sunset when the whole scene takes on an otherworldly glow.

Though the town can make a good jumping-off point for Sun Valley and the mountain wilderness farther north, there's not a lot to *do* in Twin Falls. The waterfalls for which the town is named are worth a look if you have the time; **Shoshone Falls,** taller than Niagara, may still impress, especially in spring. Check them out from the park at the end of Champlin Road, seven miles east of US-93. Without its namesake waterfalls, however, Twin Falls has little to offer travelers apart from a chance to fill the gas tank, eat, or get a night's sleep. For breakfast or a burger, head to the **Buffalo Café** (218 W. 4th St., 208/734-0271) or the 24-hour **Depot Grill** (545 S. Shoshone St., 208/733-0710) along down-town's diagonal main drag, where all-you-can-eat fried chicken is served up every Tuesday night. Sleep at your choice of some two dozen motels around the US-93/I-84 junction.

Nat-Soo-Pah Hot Springs

South of Twin Falls, there's a whole lot of nothing in the 47 miles before you reach the Nevada border at Jackpot. One place worth a stop is the summer-only **Nat-Soo-Pah Hot Springs** (208/655-4337, $6), halfway to Nevada, where you'll find a 104106°F hot tub, a giant (125-by-50-foot!) spring-fed swimming pool, a 90-foot water slide, a tree-shaded picnic area and snack bar, and a **campground** ($20). Nat-Soo-Pah is about a mile south of Hollister, then three miles east on a well-signed road. There are a number of other natural springs in the area, so if you enjoy being in hot water, southern Idaho is a great place to explore.

NEVADA

US-93 runs south along the eastern edge of Nevada for 520 miles, 500 of which take you through an exceptional degree of desolation—endless straight and narrow valleys, two-car traffic jams, and towns few and far between. From the gambling oasis of **Jackpot** on the Idaho border to where the highway crosses into Arizona atop Hoover Dam, US-93 is at least as lonely as its Nevada sibling US-50, the official Loneliest Road in America. Towns like **Wells,** along I-80 in the northern half of the state, are big events; south of here it's 140 miles to the next watering hole, **Ely,** beyond which the old mining camp of **Pioche** and the desert hot springs resort of **Caliente** are the only wide spots in the road before you hit the staggering city of **Las Vegas.**

Jackpot

In every respect but one, **Jackpot** (pop. 1,200) belongs more to Idaho than Nevada—a somewhat incongruous introduction to US-93 in the Silver State. Jackpot's visitors and workers mostly come from Idaho, as do its power and water; even its clocks are set to Idaho time. The one little exception, however, is pure Nevada: border-town gambling. Jackpot was founded in 1954, mere months after Idaho banned slot machines, which didn't, to be sure, reduce the demand. In fact, Jackpot has thrived, as a pit stop in any of the town's casinos will attest. Jackpot is compact enough to give long-distance travelers just enough lights, action, and comfort to satisfy more immediate needs and then send them on their way again.

    Cactus Petes (775/755-2321, $89 and up) is the 10-story tower you can see for miles. Along with the big casino, it has a great snack bar, a buffet, a sit-down restaurant, and a showroom, and there's more of the same in the **Horseshu** across the highway. Both casinos are owned and operated by the same firm, Ameristar, which got its start here in Jackpot in the 1950s.

Wells

Some lone peaks, a stretch of badlands and buttes, and a couple of north-south ranges usher US-93 down a long basin toward the little junction town of **Wells** (pop. 1,261). Just under 70 miles from Jackpot at the interchange of US-93 and the I-80 freeway, Wells was named by the Central Pacific Railroad, which chose the site for a depot and town to make use of the plentiful springs in the hills a few miles northeast. Before Wells got hammered by a devastating earthquake in 2008, the old downtown had the most intact abandoned **railroad row** on the entire main line across northern Nevada. Now many of these old landmarks languish. Wells provides an explicit illustration of the Wild West's transition from open range to rail to road to superhighway. The newest action in town is around the east- and westbound exit ramps of I-80, while the 1950s-era "strip" stretches along the old Victory Highway around 6th Street.

East Humboldt Range

The I-80 town of Wells is situated at the northeastern base of the splendidly scenic **East Humboldt Range.** To get into these rugged, glacier-scraped mountains, head briefly west from Wells on I-80 to exit 351, from where Hwy-231 runs 12 miles south and west, climbing to about 8,400 feet before terminating at alluring **Angel Lake.** For details on the abundance of hiking, camping, and outdoor recreation hereabouts, contact the **U.S. Forest Service ranger station** (140 Pacific Ave., 775/752-3357) at the west end of Wells.

Continuing down US-93 affords a different view of the East Humboldts. Ten miles south of Wells, you can head west on Hwy-232, which makes a 14-mile loop through luxuriant **Clover Valley** at the eastern base of the mountains, one of the most bucolic basins in Nevada. About halfway along is a turn leading west up into **Week's Creek Canyon.** Look up to see **Hole-in-the-Mountain Peak** (11,300 feet). The tallest peak in the East Humboldts, it features a 30-by-25-foot natural window in the thin rock 300 feet below its summit, which gives you a spectacular little patch of blue (or silver, orange, or purple, depending on the time of day) right through the top of the range.

Wendover

At I-80, US-93 becomes the hypotenuse of an alternate route, which runs for 60

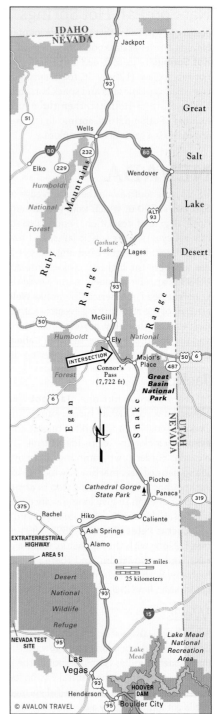

Wendover Will

miles southeast to the Utah border at **Wendover,** then another 60 miles southwest to rejoin the main US-93 at Lages Station. Wendover, like Jackpot, is a bustling border town, with golf course-view subdivisions and at least five major casino-hotels drawing gamblers from Salt Lake City, 120 miles to the east. Wendover's other claims to fame include **Wendover Will,** the more than 60-foot-tall neon cowboy who welcomes you to Nevada along the Utah state line; the **Bonneville Salt Flats** and speedway, where most of the world's early land-speed records were set; and **Wendover Air Force Base,** where in 1945 the crew of the Enola Gay trained to drop an atomic bomb on Japan.

The Ruby Mountains and Elko

It's a long, solitary, 140 miles from Wells to Ely. US-93 shoots down Clover Valley to the southern edge of the East Humboldts, where Hwy-229, a maintained gravel road, cuts off southwest toward the **Ruby Mountains,** also known as the Nevada Swiss Alps. This is one of Nevada's most scenic ranges: 80 miles long, with more than a ten peaks over 10,000 feet.

The best access to the Ruby Mountains is 50 miles west of Wells via I-80, through the engaging small city of **Elko** (pop. 20,279), which enjoys the economic benefits of sitting astride one of North America's largest deposits of gold. Besides mining gold and maintaining its traditional Basque culture, Elko is home to the **Western Folklife Center** (501 Railroad St., 775/738-7508), in the old Pioneer Hotel Building, which hosts the popular National Cowboy Poetry Gathering every January. Eight miles west of town along I-80, history buffs will want to spend some time at the **California Trail Interpretive Center** (775/738-1849, free), a Bureau of Land Management-run museum tracking the old trails that snaked across the Wild West from the 1840s to the coming of the railroads. For a taste of Wild West hospitality, take advantage of some of the fine family-style Basque restaurants, like the **Star Hotel** (246 Silver St., 775/738-9925), near the railroad tracks, which is worth the drive for the delicious lamb chops and other dishes. The Star Hotel has been in business for more than 100 years with few changes, so they must be doing something right.

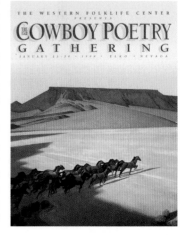

Back on US-93, between Wells and Ely, US-93 bends away from the heart of the Ruby Mountains, running southeast through **Steptoe Valley** on a marathon drive down an elongated basin, hemmed in by the Schell Creek Range on the east and the Egan Range on the west. The only signs of civilization on this stretch are two roadhouses: one at **Lages Station** (78 miles

BONNEVILLE SPEEDWAY

Located in the middle of nowhere, west of the Great Salt Lake on the Utah-Nevada border, the vast salt flats of Bonneville cover some 160 square miles. Since the 1930s, Bonneville's broad, hard, flat, and unobstructed surface has made it a mecca for efforts to set ever-faster land speed records. The earliest speed records were set at Daytona Beach, Florida, but as top speeds increased, racers needed more room to maneuver safely. In 1931, Ab Jenkins set Bonneville's first world record in his bright red Mormon Meteor, and racers have converged on Bonneville's 10-mile-long drag strip in pursuit of record-breaking speed ever since. Burt Munro's motorcycle speed record was set here at Bonneville in 1967, as depicted in the 2005 Anthony Hopkins movie *The World's Fastest Indian.*

Craig Breedlove, in his car named *Spirit of America,* was the first to exceed the 400, 500, and 600 mph marks. In the 1990s, problems with water from nearby mining operations dissolving the salt made Bonneville less than ideal, so racers like Richard Noble, whose team set the current record of 763 mph in 1997, opted for the Black Rock Desert, 110 miles north of Reno, Nevada. In recent years the salt flats have been restored to their historical thickness and size, and once again, hundreds of thrill-seekers descend on Bonneville every August for "Speed Week," racing their vintage cars, hot rods, and motorbikes in a series of time trials.

Mormon Meteor, The World's Greatest Unlimited Speed Record Maker, Bonneville Salt Flats, Utah

Holding All Speed Records from 10 Miles to 7,106 and from One Hour to 48 Hours

The McGill smelter's last skyscraping smokestack was felled in September 1993. At 750 feet, it had been the tallest structure in Nevada.

south of Wells) and the other at **Schellbourne** (40 miles north of Ely), where there's also an old Lincoln Highway marker, all but abandoned in the sagebrush east of US-93.

McGill

Tiny **McGill** (pop. 1,148), 128 miles south of I-80 and 12 miles northeast of Ely, is the classic Nevada company town, its workaday life revolving for the first 50 years of the 20th century around a giant copper smelter. Kennecott Minerals mining company officials lived in the fancy houses around the "Circle" at the top of the hill just below the factory, while workers were housed according to their ethnic origins. The saloon and jail were conveniently built right next door to each other, and steam from the copper furnaces was piped to heat the town's houses. The company has been gone for more than 30 years, but the layout remains, along with acres of fenced-off brick factory buildings painted with fading signs encouraging workers to behave safely. A few of McGill's buildings have been converted to current uses, but most are closed and quite forlorn.

One semi-survivor along this short stretch of US-93 is the **McGill Drugstore Museum** (11 4th St., 775/235-7082 or 775/235-7276, open by appointment or good luck), closed since the 1970s but preserved as an ad hoc museum under the care of the White Pine Public Museum in neighboring Ely. If you can't arrange a tour, peer

US-93 intersects with US-50, the legendary **Loneliest Road** at Ely (see page 691). Full coverage of this route begins on page 670.

in through the windows at a soda fountain and shelves stocked full of Nixon-era merchandise and old uniforms from McGill High School marching bands.

Connors Pass and Majors Place

Southeast of Ely, US-93, spliced together with US-50 and US-6 into a single two-lane highway, continues for 23 miles before crossing the narrow waist of the Schell Creek at **Connors Pass** (elev. 7,722 feet), one of only two areas of Nevada located above the tree line. As you ascend toward the pass, the air cools and freshens, the single-leaf piñon and Utah juniper appear and thicken, and, cresting the summit, the mighty Snake Range, including 13,061-foot Wheeler Peak in Great Basin National Park, comes into view.

At **Majors Place** (where there's a dusty old roadhouse with gas, beer, burgers, and a pool table), US-93 splits off from US-50 and US-6, the latter two heading east toward Utah, while US-93 cuts south, heading 80 long solitary miles to the next contact with humans at Pioche. Once again, the highway rolls along, ushered on its way by the Schell Creek, Fairview, Bristol, and Highland Ranges on the west, and the Snake and Wilson Creek Ranges on the east.

Pioche

The only places that are more than a ghostly outline of civilization in the nearly 300 miles of Great Basin Desert that US-93 crosses between Ely and Las Vegas are the wildly different towns of Caliente, Panaca, and Pioche. The oldest and most northerly of the three, **Pioche** (pop. 1,002; pronounced "pee-OACH," which means "pick-ax" in French) is a onetime mining boomtown that had its heyday well over a century ago. Now bypassed by the main US-93 highway, which runs around the east side of the historic town, Pioche is so remote—back then exponentially more than now—that during the 1870s it descended to a level of anarchy to rival Tombstone, Arizona. Local lore says that in its mining heyday, more than 75 men were killed here before anyone died of natural causes.

Corruption was also the order of the day, and you can tour Pioche's "million-dollar" **Lincoln County Courthouse** on Lacour Street (Hwy-321) for a graphic example of it. Designed in 1871 at an estimated cost of $26,000, the courthouse wasn't completed until 1876, to the tune of $88,000. Then, unable to pay off the principal, the county commissioners kept refinancing the debt, while interest accrued, year after year; by the time it was paid off in 1937, the courthouse had cost a million bucks and been replaced by a more modern structure. Now restored, the old courthouse is open for self-guided **tours** (775/962-5182, daily May-Oct., donation) of the offices, the courtroom, and the old jail.

The eclectic **Lincoln County Historical Museum** (63 Main St., 775/962-5207, daily, free) at the center of town is another good stop, as are nearby historic buildings such as the Thompson's Opera House and the Commercial Club. The rusting remains of the **aerial tramway** that ran through Pioche up through the 1920s, carrying ore to the stamp mills, can be explored—cables, cars, and all—from various points in town. Two state parks to the east (**Echo Canyon** and **Spring Valley,** 13 and 21 miles away, respectively) round out your Pioche-area sightseeing.

Pioche is a pretty long way from anywhere else, so if you want to stay the night, try the characterful **Overland Hotel** (662 Main St., 775/962-5895, $68-105), which has a popular Old West saloon downstairs. The photogenic but ramshackle downtown also has a couple of cafés, including the **Historic Silver Café** (97 Main St., 775/962-5124), convenience stores, and a vital gas station.

Panaca and Cathedral Gorge

Panaca, 11 miles south of Pioche and a mile east of US-93 on Hwy-319, was founded in 1864 by Mormon farmers, attracted to the valley by the plentiful water of Panaca Spring, in what was then a part of Utah. The mining strikes at nearby Bullionville and Pioche disturbed their peace briefly, but Panaca—which has a single gas station-mini mart, plus a school and lots of houses—has a strong sense of tranquility and timelessness rarely felt in the rest of Nevada.

Just west of US-93, two miles north of Panaca, **Cathedral Gorge State Park** is a mini Grand Canyon of eroded mud. A lake once covered this deep gully, and silt and clay were

Cathedral Gorge State Park

washed to the bottom by streams and creeks. The lake dried up, exposing the sediments, and erosion (which never sleeps) sculpted them into the fantastic procession of formations you see today. The **campground** (775/728-4460) here has shade ramadas, flush toilets, and even showers.

Panaca Spring, a fine local swimming hole with warm, sweet water, is found just outside the town of Panaca: Take 5th Street north past the baseball diamond and a rusty old steam engine toward a big cottonwood tree about a half mile beyond where the pavement ends.

Caliente

To Pioche's mining and Panaca's farming, **Caliente** (pop. 1,109), 15 miles south of Panaca, adds railroading. This small town was built around the San Pedro, Los Angeles, and Salt Lake Railroad tracks in the early 1900s, a short while before Las Vegas itself was founded. The **Union Pacific Depot** was built in 1923 and still serves as the nerve center of Caliente, having been restored to house government offices, a local history museum, an art gallery, and a boxcar collection. If you are interested in precolonial Nevada, the Bureau of Land Management office here has a good free map and guide to the Caliente region's fantastic array of Native American rock art.

The town supports two gas stations and the **Mulls' Midway Motel** (251 N. Spring St., 775/726-3199, $40-80), along US-93, but food offerings are limited.

South from Caliente, US-93 bends due west for 43 miles. **Newman Canyon,** just outside town, has high, sheer, smooth volcanic-tuff walls. You twist and climb out of the canyon to cross the Delamar Range at **Oak Springs Summit** (elev. 6,247 feet), where the juniper trees are a welcome change from the low desert scrub. Beyond is a short interface zone in which the junipers grow right next to Joshua trees, an indication of the change from Great Basin Desert, which lies to the north, to the front edge of the Mojave Desert, which spreads south and west. **Pahroc Summit** is next (just under 5,000 feet), then **Six Mile Flat,** and then **Hiko,** where Hwy-318 races north to Ely, and Hwy-375 (a.k.a. "The Extraterrestrial Highway") heads northwest to US-6 and Tonopah.

A nice alternative to US-93 is Hwy-317, south of Caliente through **Rainbow Canyon.** This is one of Nevada's most scenic and least-known drives. Colorful high volcanic-tuff cliffs hold one of the state's preeminent collections of ancient rock art, while railroad trestles, idyllic farms, and ranches line Meadow Wash. The pavement ends after 21 miles, but in dry weather even a rental car can continue 38 miles through Kane Springs Valley to connect back to US-93.

Ash Springs and Alamo

From the Hwy-375 junction, US-93 turns due south again and enters some unexpectedly lush country, in the midst of which three large and faithful springs provide plentiful water for alfalfa farms and cattle ranches, as well as for the only bona fide lake that US-93 encounters in more than 400 miles of its Nevada leg. **Ash Springs**—consisting of a single gas station and convenience store called R Place—is named after the nearby water source, which is believed to be part of a vast aquifer underlying much of eastern Nevada.

Eight miles south of Ash Springs is **Alamo,** whose three motels and two truck stops are the only real services between Caliente and Las Vegas. Four miles south of town is **Upper Pahranagat Lake,** where an old road runs along the eastern shore, with camping, picnic sites, and big cottonwoods—one of the most idyllic spots on the whole Nevada portion of US-93.

Upper Pahranagat Lake is also home to the administration and maintenance facilities for the **Desert National Wildlife Refuge,** at 1.5 million acres the largest refuge in the Lower 48. Elusive desert bighorn sheep enjoy protection within this huge habitat, alongside which US-93 travels for the length of the aptly named Sheep Range. The road descends gradually into rocky and barren desert until finally, 70 miles from Alamo and 125 miles from Caliente, US-93 merges with the I-15 freeway for the high-speed haul into the Big Glow: Las Vegas.

At the crossroads where Hwy-318 joins US-93 near Ely, **Hiko** is the finish line for two high-speed road races. Held for the past 25 years with varying degrees of support from official powers-that-be, the **Nevada Open Road Challenge** (in May) and the **Silver State Challenge** (in September) see racers in varying classes of street-legal and not-so-legal race cars averaging speeds between 100 and 200 mph on the 90-mile course, which is closed to traffic for the day.

Time the drive into Las Vegas so you arrive around dusk, when the western sky sports a purple sunset and the horizon shines brightly from a billion amber streetlights stretching from one end of the valley to the other.

Driving Las Vegas

Las Vegas has to be the easiest city in the world to drive around: Everything lines up along, or in relation to, one big road: **The Strip.** Dubbed an official "All-American Highway," along with such scenic landmarks as the Blue Ridge Parkway and the stretch of Hwy-1 through California's Big Sur, this five-mile traffic-clogged barrage of bright lights and architectural

Las Vegas

Viva Las Vegas! Since its founding more than 100 years ago, Las Vegas has been the biggest, brightest, and brazenest boomtown in the history of the world. Over a dozen major hotels and mega-resorts recreate everything from ancient Egypt to Venice (complete with canals and gondoliers), Paris (a mock Eiffel Tower), and New York City (with a Coney Island roller coaster and fake steam puffing up from fake sidewalks). More numbers: With more than 150,000 rooms, the city has as many as New York and Chicago combined, and 40 million annual visitors lose more than $8 billion in the casinos here every year.

In addition to gambling, Las Vegas casinos have all the rooms, restaurants, and "recreational opportunities" you can imagine, and then some. If you're staying overnight, you'll enter the wacky and somewhat wicked world of Las Vegas lodging. Rooms are no longer the dirt-cheap bargains they were a generation ago; rates vary depending on the time of year, time of the week, and sometimes even the time of day. Count on spending at least $100 for a decent hotel room, and close to five times that for something special. Make reservations as early as you can; on Friday nights, or during a big convention or boxing match, the whole town is often sold

looking up at the Eiffel Tower at Paris, Las Vegas

out. A final note: If you'll be schlepping a lot of luggage, be aware that Las Vegas hotel rooms are a long way from their parking spaces, which are in huge high-rise or underground garages. On the upside, parking is free at most hotels.

Here are a few of the many places you can play:

Caesars Palace (3570 Las Vegas Blvd. S., 702/731-7110 or 866/227-5938): Long before there was a Mirage; a New York, New York; a Bellagio; or a Venetian, there was Caesars Palace. Though ancient by Las Vegas standards (Caesars opened in 1966 as the first "themed" hotel in Las Vegas), this is still one of the classiest and most famous places in town.

Luxor (3900 Las Vegas Blvd. S., 702/262-4000 or 877/386-4658): The most distinctive casino, Luxor is housed inside a mammoth (29-million-cubic-foot) glass pyramid at the southern end of the Strip.

The Mirage (3400 Las Vegas Blvd. S., 702/791-7111 or 800/374-9000): This casino has its own rainforest, a 20,000-gallon saltwater aquarium, and white tigers on display (leftovers from the shows of Siegfried and Roy, who last performed in 2003).

Wynn Las Vegas (3131 Las Vegas Blvd. S., 702/770-7000 or 888/320-7123): Brought to you by the creator of Mirage and Bellagio, on the site of the historic Desert Inn, where billionaire recluse Howard Hughes used to live, this ultra-fashionable 2,700-room oasis is the last word in high-end indulgence, with an on-site Ferrari dealership in case you hit a jackpot or two.

Neon Museum (770 Las Vegas Blvd. N., 702/387-6366): Not a casino or hotel, but a huge and amazing outdoor collection of more than 200 giant neon signs that once lit up Las Vegas. Very popular guided tours are offered day and (even better!) by night.

extravagance is also known as South Las Vegas Boulevard and runs parallel to I-15 between the compact downtown area and the airport. Other roads in Las Vegas are named after the big hotels near their junction with The Strip; hence you have Sahara Avenue, Flamingo Road, and Tropicana Avenue one after another.

Almost everybody who drives into Las Vegas comes by way of the I-15 freeway, which runs between Los Angeles and Salt Lake City and which connects with US-93 some 20 miles northwest of The Strip. From the south and Hoover Dam, use the new I-515 freeway, which carries US-93 and US-95 on a snaking S-figure between Henderson and Fremont Street in downtown Las Vegas.

US-93 actually bypasses The Strip, veering southeast along Fremont Street and the Boulder Highway—or along I-515—but it's all but required that you drive at least a little of The Strip before you can say you've been to Las Vegas. Don't expect to get anywhere quickly, though; The Strip is like one big, slow cruise, with 10 lanes of traffic moving past all those casino lights at about 10 mph, day or night.

The world's highest amusement park stands atop the **Stratosphere Tower,** where thrill rides hang, spin, twirl, and bungie-jump you more than 1,000 feet above the Las Vegas Strip.

Henderson

Southeast of Las Vegas, US-93 joins courses with US-95 along Nevada's newest freeway, I-515, which connects Las Vegas with the rapidly growing industrial city of **Henderson** (pop. 285,667). Henderson itself is relatively young, even by Nevada standards. In 1941 the War Department selected this site, due to its proximity to unlimited electricity generated by the then-six-year-old Hoover Dam, for a giant factory to process magnesium, needed for bombs and airplane components. Within six months, 10,000 workers arrived, and the plant and town were built. After the war ended, the factory was subdivided for private industry, and since then, Henderson has grown to be the second-largest city in Nevada, behind only Las Vegas.

Taking their name from extraterrestrial Area 51, the New York Mets' Triple-A club the **Las Vegas 51s** play their home games at 9,334-seat **Cashman Field** (850 N. Las Vegas Blvd., 702/386-7200).

THE EXTRATERRESTRIAL HIGHWAY

West of US-93, stretching north of Las Vegas nearly to Death Valley and the California border, the U.S. government has turned the multimillion-acre expanse of Nellis Air Force Base into its most top-secret laboratory and testing ground. H-bombs, U-2 spy planes, Stealth bombers, you name it—this is where projects no one is supposed to know about exist. It's not so surprising that, like Roswell, New Mexico, this lonely corner of the world has become the focus of an ongoing controversy pitting government secrecy against allegations that the Air Force has been using a corner of the base known as Area 51 to study UFOs and extraterrestrials. Fueled in part by tabloid stories claiming an ET-like creature is being kept alive at Area 51 in a high-security compound underneath Groom Lake—and also by local businesspeople's realization that UFO tourism could mean big money—the hoopla

has focused on the tiny village of **Rachel** (pop. 54), which has become to UFO-spotters what the grassy knoll is to JFK conspiracy theorists.

Rachel, the only community along the 100-mile stretch of Hwy-375 (now officially known as the Extraterrestrial Highway, promoted by the state along the lines of its "Loneliest Road" campaign), is a block-long strip that holds the lighthearted **Little A'Le'Inn** (775/729-2515), a typical back-of-beyond bar and grill where you can munch on Alien Burgers, down drinks like the Beam Me Up, Scotty (Jim Beam bourbon, 7Up, and Scotch), or peruse UFO-related key chains, fridge magnets, and T-shirts. The Little A'Le'Inn also has small mobile home trailers available overnight for around $50.

The extraterrestrial issues surrounding Area 51 are nothing compared to the actual explosive truth of what has happened there over the years. If you doubt that, spend some time at the **National Atomic Testing Museum** (755 E. Flamingo Rd., 702/794-5151, daily, closed Thanksgiving, Christmas, and New Year's, $22) in Las Vegas, which has a cheesy "Area 51: Myth or Reality?" exhibit alongside extensive documentation and coverage of the U.S. nuclear weapons program.

Though it doesn't even try to compete with the attractions of Las Vegas, Henderson does have a number of casinos, but it's much more of a place to live than it is a tourist destination. The good **Clark County Museum** (1830 S. Boulder Hwy., 702/455-7955, daily, $2), a few miles south of town, has the usual local info plus an enjoyable display on the evolution of motor courts and travel trailers, highlighted by an iconic late 1940s Spartanette.

South of Henderson, US-93/95 climbs up and over 2,367-foot Railroad Pass, and just beyond is the junction where US-95 cuts south, heading along the Colorado River to Laughlin, Nevada; **Needles, California** (see page 892); and **Yuma, Arizona** (see page 770). US-93 continues east and loops a little to the north on its way to Boulder City.

Boulder City

Like Henderson, **Boulder City** (pop. 15,551) was founded and built by the federal government to house workers at Hoover Dam, what was then the largest construction project ever undertaken. Though the dam was completed

See you next time!

in 1935, Boulder City continued under federal ownership and management for another 25 years; in 1960, an act of Congress conferred independent municipal status on the town. Longtime residents purchased their houses, and alcohol consumption was permitted for the first time in the town's history, though gambling remained forbidden. To this day, almost a half century since "independence," Boulder City remains one of the only town in Nevada that expressly prohibits gambling, which may explain why it feels more like the Midwest than a suburb of Sin City.

If you're interested in the men and machines involved in building the dam, spend some time at the **Boulder City-Hoover Dam Museum,** inside the historic restored **Boulder Dam Hotel** (1305 Arizona St., 702/294-1988, $89 and up). The hotel also has a good dining room. The town has a handful of motels and fast-food outlets—1950s-style cafés and motels line the Nevada Highway/US-93 Business Route through town—but the real draws are just below Boulder City: the dam, of course, and the lake behind it.

Heading south past Hoover Dam into Arizona, you'll pass no towns or services in the 78 miles between Boulder City and Kingman on old Route 66, so stock up and fill up here before proceeding on.

Hoover Dam and Lake Mead

Approaching **Hoover Dam** from the Nevada side, in the eight miles from Boulder City you pass a peculiar parade of electrical generators, transformers, and capacitors all secured by cyclone fencing topped by razor wire and barbs to keep out intruders. A major 10-year reconstruction and road-expansion project was completed in 2010, taking traffic off the dam and moving it onto a bypass and concrete-arch bridge over the Colorado River. One of the biggest and highest in the world, the impressive bridge has been named to honor both onetime Nevada governor Mike O'Callaghan and Arizona's pro football star Pat Tillman, who volunteered for duty as an Army Ranger in Afghanistan, where he was killed by friendly fire in 2004. At the parking area at the foot of the bridge, there's a small memorial to Tillman and a detailed explanation of the new bridge's engineering and construction.

Hoover Dam marks the border between Nevada and Arizona, and between the Pacific and Mountain time zones, so set your clocks and watches accordingly—and remember, Arizona does not use daylight saving time.

From there, a pedestrian footpath heads across the canyon, giving good views of the distant lake, the massive dam, and the river below.

Because the main US-93 has been diverted around it, if you want to see Hoover

Dam up close, make your way to the **Visitor Center** (702/494-2517, daily, $15, plus $10 parking), which cost nearly as much as the new bridge. The steep admission price buys you a half-hour film, a self-guided museum tour, and a ride down the $20 million elevators that cut through the rock, ending up inside the dam, where you can gape at the humming turbines, which at peak times generate some 2,000 megawatts of electricity, enough to supply a million homes and still have enough juice left over to light up the Las Vegas Strip. Beyond the visitors center, take a walk across the top of the gargantuan wedge of Hoover Dam: It's nearly a quarter mile across, 726 feet high, 660 feet thick at the base—all accomplished with a mere seven million tons of concrete.

Hoover Dam

Upstream from the dam spreads **Lake Mead,** the largest artificial reservoir in the country. With a capacity of more than 26 million acre-feet or nearly nine trillion gallons, Lake Mead irrigates some 2.5 million acres of land in the United States and Mexico, while helping to control the river's seasonal flooding. However, recent droughts and increased demands for its water have depleted Lake Mead to about half its full capacity, leaving some docks and fishing piers (and potentially the city of Las Vegas) high and dry. Despite these problems, thousands of water-skiers and houseboaters flock to the popular recreation site year-round.

South of Hoover Dam, US-93 runs parallel to the older version of the highway, with numerous old bridges and sections of gravel roadway standing along the modern four-lane freeway.

Laughlin

Between Hoover Dam and Kingman, a detour heads west to the Nevada side of the Colorado River to **Laughlin,** a place that epitomizes the anything-goes character of Nevada gaming. Laughlin, a booming gambling resort that in many ways seems even more mirage-like than Las Vegas, may lack glitz and pizzazz but makes up for it with cheaper rooms ($35 is not uncommon) and the almost unheard-of attraction of river views from the casino floors.

The history of Laughlin—or rather, the lack of it—is impressive even by Nevada standards. Starting with a rundown bait shop he bought in the mid-1960s, Minnesota-born entrepreneur Don Laughlin envisioned the fantasyland you see today, opening his **Riverside Resort Hotel** (702/298-2535 or 800/227-3849, $55 and up), which is still a local favorite, in the late 1970s and drawing visitors from all over Arizona and Southern California. Laughlin's independent mini empire was eclipsed in the 1980s by the big shots and big towers with more than 1,000 rooms. First **Harrah's** came, then Circus Circus opened the steamboat-shaped **Colorado**

Laughlin is one of the hottest inhabited places in the country, with an all-time high temperature of 125°F, registered here in 2005.

Belle, then came the more than 1,900-room palace now known as the **Aquarius** (702/298-5111). Fortunes have ebbed and flowed significantly in recent years, but Laughlin is still well worth a look or an overnight stay.

For further information, contact the **Laughlin Nevada Chamber of Commerce** (702/298-2214).

ARIZONA

Coming into Arizona across the top of Hoover Dam, US-93 cuts southeast across the length, and half the breadth, of the state, covering nearly 500 miles of desiccated desert. Starting at the Nevada border, US-93 makes a diagonal beeline toward the old Route 66 town of **Kingman,** one of the few watering holes in Arizona's northwest quarter. Joshua trees and ghost towns far outnumber

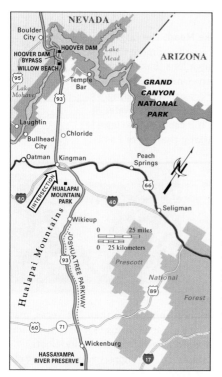

gas stations in this part of the state, so fill up before setting off into these great wide-open spaces. From Kingman, the route cuts south across another huge stretch of desert, passing through the dude-ranch resort town of **Wickenburg.** In the middle of Arizona spreads **Phoenix,** the state's capital and largest city. From this sprawling megalopolis, our route bends east into the mountains, following back roads past the otherworldly Biosphere 2 "space station" before hitting **Tucson,** another hugely horizontal city. South of here you'll enjoy the most feature-packed part of the trip, passing by the historic Spanish colonial communities of **Tubac** and **Tumacácori** before winding up at the enjoyable twin border towns of **Ambos Nogales.**

Before I-40 bypassed it in the 1970s, Kingman was a vital desert oasis. It marks the intersection of US-93 and **Route 66;** coverage of this route begins on page 822. **Kingman** is described on page 889.

Lake Mead

Lake Mead National Recreation Area

Most people come from the Las Vegas area to visit Lake Mead, which covers some 160,000 acres and includes over 750 miles of shoreline, on the extensively developed Nevada side. In contrast, the only access on the Arizona side is from **Temple Bar,** 19 miles south of Hoover Dam, then another 27 miles northeast on a good paved road. Here you'll find a small **marina** (928/767-3211) with boat rentals and lodging.

Stretching to both sides of Hoover Dam, the **Lake Mead National Recreation Area** also incorporates the smaller Lake Mohave, clearly visible from US-93 and accessible at **Willow Beach** on the Colorado River, 17 miles south of Hoover Dam and 4 miles west of US-93.

Chloride

Marked by a big "C" inscribed in the hillside above it, the near-ghost town of **Chloride** (pop. 352), which is 53 miles south of Hoover Dam and 15 miles north of Kingman, then 4 miles east of the highway on a well-marked paved road, is the oldest and among the most evocative former mining camps in Arizona. Following the discovery of silver here in the 1860s, mining activities continued through the 1940s; the town is now preserved by its dedicated residents.

A couple of stores and a restaurant still cling to life, and occasional festivals and flea markets draw sizable crowds of visitors. Mostly what there is to see are the odd bits of "folk art" so often found in the American desert: strange front-yard sculptures made of rusting metal and odd bits of junk, plus comical tributes to the mythology of the Wild West, like a fake "Boot Hill" cemetery with laconic epitaphs and hand-painted signs playing up the apocryphal legacy of the local "Hangin' Judge" Jim Beam.

Joshua Forest Parkway

East from Kingman, US-93 follows I-40 for over 20 miles before turning south, back onto two-lane US-93. Because it's the main route between Phoenix and Las Vegas, US-93 can be busy, and in many places the roadway is being improved and expanded to handle all the trucks and other traffic, but it's one of the great (and least hyped) drives in the desert Southwest. The scenery improves as you head south from I-40, with chocolate-brown boulders and varnished granite cliffs rising to form impressive canyons above forests of saguaro cactus, Joshua trees, and abundant spring wildflowers. The only real "place" along this stretch of US-93 is a wide spot in the road known as **Wikieup,** 30 miles south of I-40, with a pair of gas stations and trading posts.

Between Wikieup and Wickenburg, the 75-odd miles of US-93 are known as the **Joshua Forest Parkway** because the road passes through one of the world's densest concentrations of these odd trees, which were named by Mormon pioneers. Anthropomorphic, multilimbed members of the lily family, and found only here in western Arizona and in southern California, Joshua trees can live to 200 years old and reach 50 feet tall.

Wickenburg

In the middle of the Arizona desert, 65 miles northwest of Phoenix and 130 miles southeast of Kingman, **Wickenburg** (pop. 6,806) grew up as a gold-mining camp in the 1860s and has survived as a low-key resort community. A few crusty prospectors still search for a strike, and cowboys are often seen riding through town, which makes Wickenburg a pleasant place to get a feel for the Old West, especially during the winter months when temperatures are mild and the sun shines nearly every day. If you wander around the compact town, keep an eye out for Gila monsters, tarantulas, and rattlesnakes, but don't worry: If you see one, it's likely made of bronze, part of an art installation that has also populated the streets with metal renditions of Wild West outlaws and schoolteachers.

Wickenburg is also home to the gold-mining ghosts of the **Vulture Mine,** which produced some $200 million before its closure in the 1940s.

Wickenburg's Wild West ambience and reliably good winter weather account for the number of **dude ranches** dotting the surrounding desert, most of which are intended for longer stays rather than passing travelers.

Right where US-93 intersects cross-country US-60 at Wickenburg's only stoplight, the **Desert Caballeros Western Museum** (928/684-2272, daily, $12) gives a

Wickenburg's welcoming Horseshoe Café

SPRING TRAINING:
CACTUS LEAGUE BASEBALL

The arrival of the Arizona Diamondbacks in 1998 culminated a long but limited history of baseball in the Grand Canyon State. Though it never before had a major league team of its own, Arizona has welcomed out-of-state teams for pre-season spring training since 1947, when the Cleveland Indians and New York Giants first trained and played in Tucson. Now every March, ball players at all levels of the game come to Arizona to try out for places on professional teams. The daily workouts and 250-odd exhibition games of what's known as the Cactus League attract thousands of hard-core baseball fans to watch players at all levels compete to earn a spot on professional teams.

The Phoenix metropolitan area hosts the bulk of the teams and the tourists. Though they're not necessarily played to win, Cactus League games are played in modern 10,000-15,000-seat stadia that approach the major leagues in quality. The smaller sizes allow an up-close feel you'd have to pay much more for during the regular season. (Your chances of snagging balls during batting practice are infinitely better too.) Most teams have extensive training facilities adjacent to their home stadia, and morning workouts and practice sessions are usually free and open to the public.

The best central source of Cactus League schedules, information, and tickets is the **Mesa Convention and Visitors Bureau** (480/827-4700, www.cactus-league.com). Tickets for games cost $10-40 and are also available through the teams, online through MLB.com, and at the stadium box offices. March is peak tourist season all over Arizona, so make your lodging arrangements long before game time.

broad overview of regional history and contains a surprisingly good collection of Western art and sculpture (from George Catlin to Charles "Charley" Russell), plus the usual rocks and rusty relics.

Most of the places to eat and sleep are lined up along east-west US-60 (Wickenburg Way). For breakfast and lunch, try the **Horseshoe Café** (207 E. Wickenburg Way, 928/684-7377).

Hassayampa River Preserve

One of Arizona's few stretches of riverside ecology preserved in its natural state, the **Hassayampa River Preserve,** four miles southeast of Wickenburg on US-60/89, is a great place to break a journey. For most of its way, the Hassayampa River runs underground, but here it rises to irrigate a dense forest of willows and cottonwood trees, which in turn shelter an amazing variety of birds—over 200 species, from songbirds to raptors, are listed in the preserve's birders' guide. Lots of lizards are here too, along with bobcats.

The Nature Conservancy, which owns and operates the preserve, runs a small **visitors center** (928/684-2772, Wed.-Sun. 8am-5pm winter, limited hours summer, $5), where you can pick up trail guides and maybe join a guided walk.

Phoenix

More than four million people have settled in and around the Arizona capital, Phoenix, all but obliterating any sense that the land here ever was, and still is, a desert. Golf courses, swimming pools, lakes, and fountains are everywhere, with only a few carefully coiffed cacti remaining here and there to testify to the natural state of things. But there is something oddly charming about the place— an anything-goes, Wild West spirit manifest in one of the highest rates of car theft in the country and a truly phoenix-like ability to grow and thrive despite the almost total lack of natural advantages.

Desert Botanical
Garden's Butterfly Pavilion

Get an unforgettable sense of the desert's natural beauty at the magical **Desert Botanical Garden** (480/941-1225, daily, $25), in Papago Park east of downtown between Scottsdale and Tempe. Especially in spring, when the wildflowers are in bloom and the Butterfly Pavilion is open, the gardens here offer an intense and aesthetic distillation of this harsh but intricate environment.

The best thing about downtown Phoenix is the marvelous **Heard Museum** (2301 N. Central Ave., 602/252-8848, daily, $18), among the best museums anywhere devoted to the indigenous cultures of the Southwestern United States. The permanent galleries trace the history and diversity of prehistoric peoples and contemporary Native Americans, while changing exhibitions focus on specific themes. Don't miss the amazing collection of Hopi kachina dolls, collected by hotelier Fred Harvey and the late U.S. senator Barry Goldwater. Downtown Phoenix is also home to **Chase Field,** the retractable-roofed stadium where the **Arizona Diamondbacks** (602/462-6500) play in the only major league ballpark with its own outfield swimming pool.

Another treat is **Taliesin West** (12345 N. Taliesin Dr., 480/860-2700, daily except major holidays, $34 and up), at the east end of Cactus Road. Every winter from 1937 until his death in 1959, Frank Lloyd Wright lived, worked, and taught here, handcrafting this complex of studios, theaters, and living quarters, which survives as an architecture school.

PRACTICALITIES

Phoenix sprawls some 500 square miles and is expanding by many acres every day—with no end (or beginning or middle, for that matter) in sight. The I-10 freeway cuts through the center, and a spaghetti bowl of local freeways, such as the Hwy-202 Loop, Hwy-51, and the US-60 "Superstition Freeway" complete the high-speed overlay. Though there is a skeletal bus service along with a handy light rail train ($4 all day) connecting downtown's Central Avenue with Mesa and Tempe, trying to get around town without a car is hazardous to your health. In a word, drive.

Phoenix is actually made up of many separate surrounding cities, each of which has its own character. Mesa, for example, was founded by Mormons and is now bigger than Minneapolis and Miami. Not surprisingly, considering its well-deserved reputation as a winter oasis, the Phoenix area is home to a number of gorgeous resort hotels; rates quoted here are for winter, and summer prices are much lower. The historic **Arizona Biltmore** (602/955-6600 or 800/950-0086, $199 and up), on the north side of Phoenix at 24th and Missouri Streets, is an absolutely beautiful, Frank Lloyd Wright-style resort complex tucked away on spacious grounds.

Fun for families can be had at the many water park-style resorts, like the **Pointe Hilton Tapatio Cliffs Resort** (11111 N. 7th St., 602/866-7500, $119 and up), next to the open expanses of North Mountain Park, which has suites and waterslides and eight swimming pools. Downtown, the **Hotel San Carlos** (202 N. Central Ave., 602/253-4121, $169 and up) is a well-maintained older hotel with a rooftop swimming pool. The pleasant **HI-Phoenix The Metcalf House Hostel** (1026 9th St., 602/254-9803, around $30) has dorm beds.

The classic road-food stop in Phoenix is the **Tee Pee** (4144 E. Indian School Rd., 602/956-0178), a characterful and always-crowded place serving cold beer and huge plates of old-style American-Mexican food. For something a bit hotter, brave the salsa at one of **Los Dos Molinos** (8646 S. Central Ave., 602/243-9113) four locations.

On the north side of downtown, next to a Lube 'n' Tune car repair shop, **Sierra Bonita Grill** (6933 N. 7th St., 602/264-0700) is a welcoming, unpretentious restaurant offering an interesting mix of Southwestern and pan-American influences (pork loin alongside *charro* beans and tomato rice) and excellent desserts. Phoenix also boasts an unexpected treat: **Pizzeria Bianco** (623 E. Adams St., 602/258-8300, Mon. 11am-

9pm, Tues.-Sat. 11am-10pm, Sun. noon-7pm), where transplanted New Yorker Chris Bianco cooks up delicious wood-fired designer pizzas in a historic downtown storefront at the original location; there's a second as well as two spin-offs.

Across Phoenix

From the northwest, our route arrives in ever-growing metropolitan **Phoenix** by way of US-60/89, which passes through the retirement communities of **Surprise** and **Sun City.** The historic route follows Grand Avenue all the way to the downtown area, where you can follow the old main road, Van Buren Street. But if you're in a hurry, hop onto the freeway system and hope you don't get too lost—it's a crazy and confusing city, so spread out it can seem to take forever to get anywhere.

Superstition Mountains and the Apache Trail

East of Phoenix, US-60 runs as a four-lane freeway through suburban Tempe and Mesa, but the sprawl fades as you approach the angular **Superstition Mountains,** some 40 miles east of downtown. Protected within the massive **Tonto National Forest,** this area of volcanic crags, desert cactus, and ponderosa pines is best seen by traveling along Hwy-88, the scenic **Apache Trail,** which winds along the Salt River, the

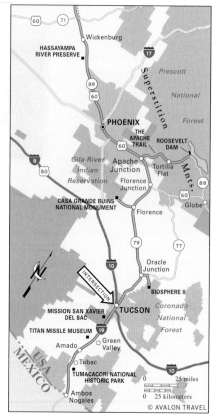
© AVALON TRAVEL

South of Florence, Hwy-79 follows the Pinal Pioneer Parkway, the old main road between Phoenix and Tucson. The route is now lined by a series of signs pointing out palo verde trees, saguaros, and other desert flora. Cowboy actor Tom Mix died here on October 12, 1940, when he crashed his 1937 Cord 812 Phaeton into a ditch along Hwy-79 and was decapitated by his suitcase. The site is marked by a statue of a riderless horse, in a rest area 18 miles south of Florence.

region's lifeblood. Named for the Native Americans who lived in the area a century ago, and now an official National Scenic Byway, the Apache Trail is a 45-mile loop, but even a short trip along it will take you far away from the fast lane.

A mere seven miles north of US-60, the Phoenix suburbs give way to the wild desert of **Lost Dutchman State Park** (480/982-4485, $3 per person or bike, $7 per car), named for a legendary gold mine located nearby. Two miles farther is the overlook for the 4,535-foot phallus of **Weaver's Needle,** beyond which the road passes several reservoirs before reaching the entertaining tourist-trap hamlet of **Tortilla Flat** (pop. 6), 18 miles from US-60 and named after the Steinbeck novella—which has nothing to do with Arizona, but who cares?

Beyond Tortilla Flat, the road turns to dirt and twists and turns through spectacular desert country for the next 27 miles to **Roosevelt Dam,** then heads southeast to rejoin US-60 near **Globe,** at the western edge of the San Carlos Apache Indian Reservation, 87 miles east of Phoenix.

In springtime in particular, another great attraction of the Apache Trail region is the **Boyce Thompson Arboretum State**

Park (520/689-2811, daily, $12.50), the state's oldest and largest botanical exhibit, covering 323 acres with a full array of Sonora Desert cactus and wildflowers. The arboretum is 27 miles west of Globe, right on US-60, near the copper-mining town of Superior.

Picacho Peak

Looming like a giant battleship alongside the I-10 "fast road," 75 miles southeast of Phoenix and 45 miles northwest of Tucson, 3,374-foot **Picacho Peak** has served as a Sonora Desert landmark for as long as there have been people here. Native Americans, Spanish explorers, American pioneers, you name it—they've all used the volcanic peak to keep them on track. Now a **state park** (520/466-3183, $3 per person or bike, $7 per car), Picacho Peak also played a role in the Civil War; the official westernmost battle of the War Between the States was fought here on April 15, 1862, when a dozen Union soldiers skirmished with 17 Confederate cavalrymen. These days, people come here to enjoy the saguaro cactus and the desert wildflowers (mainly in March, when they're at their most colorful), or to hike to the summit for a desert panorama (two miles each way, with roughly 1,500-foot elevation gain). The park is open for day use and camping.

Along the freeway at the foot of Picacho Peak, the sprawling **Rooster Cogburn Ostrich Ranch** ($10 and up) lets you feed the ungainly beasts or purchase a variety of ostrich-derived products. There's also a petting zoo and the unusual chance to take a tour, riding in the back of a massive 4WD "Monster Truck."

Hwy-79: Florence and Casa Grande Ruins National Monument

If you have enough time to avoid the I-10 freeway and follow a slower but more scenic older road, consider Hwy-79, which cuts off south from Apache Junction and US-60. The first stop is **Florence,** one of Arizona's oldest towns, but now best known as the site of the state's largest prison. Florence has a pleasant non-touristy Main Street of bars, general stores, and junk shops, parallel to and a half mile west of the highway. The penal history is documented in gruesome detail at the **Pinal County Historical Museum** (715 S. Main St., 520/868-4382, Sept.-July 15 Tues.-Sat. 11am-4pm, Sun. noon-4pm, donation), where an actual hangman's noose and chairs from the retired gas chamber are displayed along with photos of people put to death.

the "big house" at Casa Grande Ruins National Monument

West of Florence, some of the state's largest and most perplexing prehistoric remains are preserved in the **Casa Grande Ruins National Monument** (520/723-3172, daily, $5), off Hwy-287 midway between Florence and I-10. A small visitors center at the entrance gives some background on the

Tucson

Though it's less than half the size of Phoenix, Tucson (pop. 531,641) is perhaps twice as nice a place to visit. With a lively university community, some of the most beautiful desert landscapes anywhere on earth, and more palpable history than anywhere in the Southwest outside New Mexico, Tucson is well worth taking the time to get to know. It also makes an excellent jumping-off point for visiting the Wild West towns of Tombstone and Bisbee in the state's southeast corner.

However, with daytime temperatures averaging over 100°F, Tucson is hotter than heck during the summer months (early May-late Sept.), so try to visit during the rest of the year. Spring is especially nice, with wildflowers blooming and spring training baseball bashing away, but this is also the most expensive time to be here—room rates in March are easily double those the rest of the year.

Many of Tucson's biggest attractions are outside the city limits and covered under various road trips: Biosphere 2 and Mission San Xavier del Bac are north and south of Tucson along US-93, while the two-part Saguaro National Park is east and west of downtown (and covered with the US-80 Southern Pacific route). But unlike many modern desert cities, downtown Tucson is worth a wander for the many historic buildings that have been spared the redeveloper's wrecking ball, including a wonderfully restored Roaring 1920s movie palace, the Fox Tucson Theatre on Congress Street, which has frequent movies and great live concerts.

The other center of activity is two miles north and east from downtown, where the nicely landscaped 380-acre **University of Arizona** campus spreads between Speedway Boulevard and 6th Street. The campus holds the engaging historical exhibits of the **Arizona State Museum** (520/621-6302, Mon.-Sat., $5) and one of the country's preeminent photography collections in the **Center for Creative Photography** (1030 N. Olive Rd., 520/621-7968, donation).

On the southeast side of Tucson, off I-10 at the Kolb Road exit, Davis-Monthan Air Force Base holds one of the strangest sights in the entire Southwest desert: rows and rows and rows of surplus military aircraft, lined up for what seems like miles. The official name for this desert facility is the Aerospace Maintenance and Regeneration Group (AMARG), but it's best known as **The Boneyard** because of its role as a salvage yard for aircraft long past their production era. You can glimpse dozens of the planes from the highway, but for the full experience you have to sign up for one of the popular **tours** (520/574-0462, Mon.-Fri., $15 and up, reserve online or by phone). The tours are offered by the **Pima Air and Space Museum,** which has another extensive exhibit of aircraft, including JFK's Air Force One, nearby, and also operates the unique Titan Missile Museum south of Tucson.

The foothills of the Santa Catalina Mountains, which rise north of Tucson, are blessed by **Sabino Canyon** (520/749-2327, daily), 12 miles east of downtown (take Tanque Verde Road to Sabino Canyon Road). With its seasonal waterfalls and a nearly year-round creek, Sabino Canyon is a great place to stretch your legs while getting a sense of how pretty and vibrant the desert can be.

West of Tucson, beyond where Speedway Boulevard climbs over Gates Pass, Tucson Mountain is home to a section of **Saguaro National Park** and the excellent **Arizona Sonora Desert Museum** (520/883-2702, daily, $21). Apart from spending a lifetime in the desert, there's no better place to get a sense of the abundant flora and fauna of the Sonora Desert than this creatively presented zoological park.

PRACTICALITIES

The main I-10 freeway runs diagonally from northwest to southeast along the usually dry Santa Cruz River at the western edge of town. Tucson stretches east from here for over 10 miles, and north toward the foothills of the Santa Catalina Mountains. The main east-west route across town is Speedway Boulevard, along with numerous parallel roads.

In addition to the usual highway motels, Tucson has some characterful places to stay, from restored downtown hotels to luxurious vacation resorts. One of the latter is the **Hacienda del Sol** (5501 N. Hacienda del Sol Rd., 520/299-1501, $250

Bird's-Eye View of Tucson, Arizona

and up), a historic guest ranch built as a posh girls' school in the 1920s and now a quiet, intimate getaway with a pool, great sunset views, and one of Tucson's best restaurants (The Grill). Another historic property, the **Arizona Inn** (2200 E. Elm St., 520/325-1541 or 800/933-1093, $129 and up), is perhaps the classic Arizona resort, little changed since the 1930s, when it was a favorite winter haunt of the Rockefellers and other elites. The Arizona Inn offers comfortable accommodations on lovingly landscaped grounds near the university campus.

One of the most enjoyable places to eat in Tucson is the quirky **Café Poca Cosa** (110 E. Pennington St., 520/622-6400), right downtown. Adventurously creative Mexican food, served up in large portions at reasonable prices, is the specialty here—try anything in a mole sauce, and you won't be disappointed. Nearby, the **Little Café Poca Cosa** (151 N. Stone St.) is open for breakfast and lunch versions of the same delicious stuff. On the west side of downtown, **El Charro** (311 N. Court Ave., 520/622-1922) is "the oldest family-operated Mexican restaurant in the USA," so they say, serving up inexpensive food and margaritas since 1922 in a turn-of-the-20th-century house.

Hohokam people, who built the four-story "big house" and the surrounding village, but no one knows what it was used for or why it was abandoned.

Biosphere 2

One of the most ambitious, controversial, and just plain bizarre schemes to hatch at the millennial end of the 20th century was **Biosphere 2,** which stands in the Arizona desert at the northern foot of snowcapped Mt. Lemmon. Developed in the 1990s by a New Age group called Synergia Ranch and funded (to the tune of $200 million) by Texas billionaire Ed Bass, Biosphere 2 was originally intended to simulate the earth's entire ecosystem in order to test the possibility of building self-sustaining colonies on other planets. A crew of four "biospherians" spent two not entirely self-sustained years sealed inside, but amid allegations of corruption and deceit, the project imploded. The University of Arizona eventually took over running the domes, and has since redirected the focus onto research into the effects of greenhouse gases and other ecosystem changes. The surrounding land has been sold and is slated to become yet another upscale housing development, but Biosphere 2 itself should stay open for self-guided **tours** (520/838-6200, daily, $20, kids under 5 free).

To reach Biosphere 2, follow Hwy-79 to Oracle Junction, 25 miles north of Tucson, then turn east onto Hwy-77 for 6 miles and follow the signs.

Across Tucson

The fastest way across Tucson is I-10, which runs diagonally along the western and southern edges of the city. Some of the more interesting "old road" routes around town include the Miracle Mile, north

Biosphere 2

of downtown, and 6th Avenue, the main highway before the interstate was built. South of Tucson, 6th Avenue becomes the Old Nogales Highway, the old road to Mexico, which veers in various alignments among extensive pecan groves while crisscrossing I-19.

Tucson marks the junction of the US-93 route with our cross-country **Southern Pacific** route along US-80 (see page 762). **Saguaro National Park, Tombstone,** and more of the area around Tucson are covered on pages 773-777.

Mission San Xavier del Bac, 1902

Mission San Xavier del Bac

Among the most strikingly memorable of all the Spanish colonial missions in the Southwest, **Mission San Xavier del Bac** (520/294-2624, daily, donation) was built more than 200 years ago and still serves the native Tohono O'odham (a.k.a. Papago) people. Known as the "White Dove of the Desert" because of the gleaming white plaster that covers its adobe walls, balustrades, and twin bell towers—one of which is domed, the other not—this landmark edifice was designed and built by Spanish missionaries beginning in 1783.

Rising up from the flat desert plain, San Xavier presents an impressive silhouette, but what's most unforgettable is the Mexican folk-baroque interior, covered in intensely wrought sculptures and paintings of saints and religious imagery. Currently under restoration, these paintings and figurines are among the country's finest examples of folk art, using painted mud to simulate marble, tiles, and crystal chandeliers.

The environmental activist and author Edward Abbey, who died in 1989, spent his last years living in the Arizona desert near Oracle Junction and Biosphere 2.

The mission is well signed and easy to reach, just 14 miles south of downtown Tucson off I-19 exit 92, then a half mile west. Across the plaza from the church is a small Tohono-owned and operated complex of craft galleries, plus a good taco stand.

Titan Missile Museum

Just 16 miles south of San Xavier, you can travel from the colonial 1700s to the Cold War 1960s by stopping at the **Titan Missile Museum,** the only Intercontinental Ballistic Missile (ICBM) silo preserved intact and open to the public anywhere in the world. On the north side of the sprawling stucco retirement community of **Green Valley** (pop. 23,765), just west from I-19 off exit 69 on Duval Mine Road, the silo was in active use from 1963 until 1982, was declared a National Historic Landmark

the Titan II missile in the silo at the Titan Missile Museum

in 1994, and is now open for **tours** (520/625-7736, daily, $9.50). The tours—the only way to visit—take around an hour, involve donning a hard hat and descending stairs into the control room of the hardened silo, which still contains a 103-foot-tall Titan missile (sans warhead!). If you like these sorts of things, a longer, much more in-depth tour (around $100) lets you climb all the way down into the silo.

Tubac

Another good place to stop between Tucson and the Mexican border is **Tubac,** 50 miles from Tucson, just east of I-19 at exit 34. One of the first European outposts in what's now Arizona, Tubac was established as a Spanish presidio (fort) in 1751, and a century later boomed with the opening of gold mines nearby.

Scattered around a dusty central plaza, just west of the presidio park, Tubac has developed into a small but diverting arts-and-crafts colony, with a number of good shops and cafés. Local artists are frequently showcased in the **Tubac Center for the Arts** on the north side of the plaza, near the peaceful, pleasant **Secret Garden** B&B inn (520/403-6271, $100 and up).

Tumacácori National Historic Park

The preserved ruins of an impressive Spanish colonial mission stand at the center of **Tumacácori National Historic Park** (520/377-5060, daily, $5), which is 52 miles from Tucson, 20 miles north of Nogales, and just 3 miles south of Tubac, off I-19 exit 29. The site was used by missionaries as early as 1691, but it wasn't until 1800 that they set to work building the massive adobe church. Though never finished, thanks to Apache raids and the Mexican Revolution, Tumacácori stands as an impressive reminder of the religious passion of the friars and their efforts to convert local indigenous people.

Directly across the highway from Tumacácori is a rare sight—a Greek café—and a half mile north is **Wisdom's** (520/398-2397), which serves reliable Mexican and American food.

Nogales

Arizona's busiest border crossing, and birthplace of iconoclastic jazz great Charles Mingus (1922-1979), **Nogales** is also perhaps the most pleasant of all the "international" cities along the U.S.-Mexico border. Despite being divided by an ugly corrugated steel fence, it gets promoted as **Ambos Nogales** (Both Nogales). The twin cities (pop. 20,252 on the Arizona side, 212,533 in Mexico) are economically codependent, especially post-NAFTA, as Mexicans come across to shop at Safeway and Walmart, and Americans while away evenings drinking cerveza in south-of-the-border cantinas. The intriguing little **Pimeria Alta Historical Society Museum** (136 N. Grand Ave., 520/287-4621, Tues.-Sat. 11am-4pm, donation), which documents cross-border history in the storefront-size Old City Hall, 400 yards north of the border crossing, is one of the few real sights to see on the Arizona side, but if you just want to spend an hour or two shopping for souvenirs and practicing your Spanish, Nogales, Sonora, Mexico, is a pleasant place in which to do it.

In **Amado,** just west of I-19 at the Arivaca Road exit north of Tubac, you'll notice a huge concrete cow's skull. It's served as the entrance to a long series of businesses that have tried (and mostly failed) to make a go of this unique location.

To save hassle and time crossing the border, drivers should park on the streets or in the $3-a-day-and-up lots on the U.S. side and walk across. Border formalities are minimal, and U.S. dollars are accepted on both sides. There are quite a lot of good taco stands and cantinas, but one place to look for on the Mexican side is the elegant **La Roca** (Calle Elias 91, 520/313-6313), partly carved out of a cave 250 yards southeast of the border crossing, across the train tracks. Good food at fair prices, stiff margaritas, continuous live music, and a lovely ambience await.

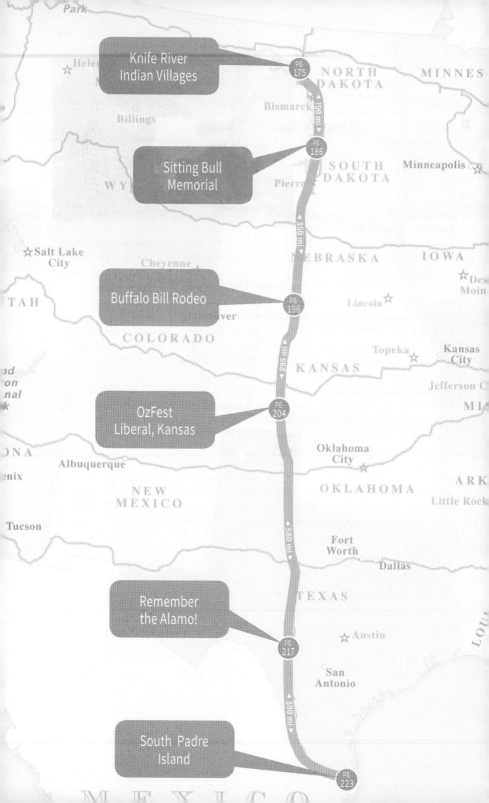

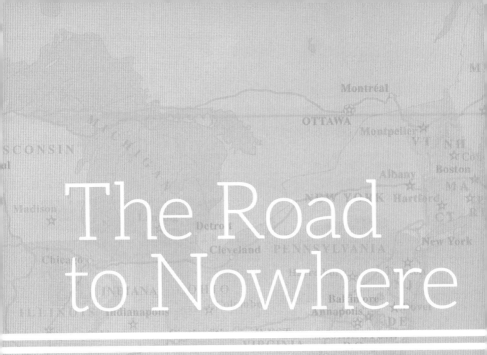

The Road to Nowhere

Cutting across America's heartland, US-83 remains a must-do long-distance byway—transnavigating this broad, odd nation without once grazing a conventional tourist destination.

Between North Dakota and Matamoros, Mexico

Once the only entirely paved route from Canada to "Old Mexico" (as hard-to-find postcards along the route still say), US-83 is still likely the shortest—from Swan River, Manitoba, dead south to Brownsville, Texas, and beyond to Matamoros, Mexico, seemingly without turning once. Its grim moniker, The Road to Nowhere, is alternately unfair and then not severe enough, for the route navigates some of the widest and most aesthetically challenged landscapes in the country—the yawn-inducing rolling grasslands of the northern Great Plains, the beefy expanses of western **Nebraska** and **Kansas,** and the mesmerizing heat of the **Texas-Oklahoma Panhandle**—before following the lower Rio Grande south to the Gulf of Mexico. Yet on US-83 you'll also take in some phenomenal country: verdant farmland dotted with truly small towns, endlessly shifting prairie grassland, winding **Missouri River** roadways, and plain, isolated, where-the-hell-am-I agricultural expanses.

Following roughly along the 100th meridian, US-83 marks the historic divide between the "civilized" eastern United States and the arid western deserts. Physiography aside, this route's cultural landscape centers on small but self-sufficient farm or cattle communities that date back to the last days of the Wild West and that are far enough off the tourist trail to retain an unselfcon-

scious, aw-shucks quaintness. For endless miles in every direction, telephone and power poles provide some of the few signs of life between the highway and the distant horizon, though the towns—where average speeds drop suddenly from 70 mph to radar-enforced 25 mph or slower—are spaced just often enough along the highway to serve your food-and-fuel needs.

Perhaps best of all, US-83 manages to transnavigate this broad, odd nation, albeit north-to-south, without once grazing a conventional tourist attraction. Here along the backbone of the nation, conversations over a daybreak breakfast, afternoons spent cooling off by municipal swimming pools, and twilight American Legion baseball games provide the stuff of truly memorable Road Trip diversions, and for that reason alone, US-83 remains a must-do long-distance byway.

NORTH DAKOTA

Beginning at the U.S. border with Manitoba, Canada, US-83's route across North Dakota is a 265-mile-long rehash of childhood back-of-station-wagon dreams-capes: epic plains too green or golden-hued for your eyes to process rationally, and endless cultivated fields punctuated by umpteen farmers' cooperatives, storage bins, silos, and grain elevators. Hay bales of all shapes and sizes dry peril-ously close to the roadside, and Stetsoned figures in dusty pick-ups or mighty tractors amiably lift their index fingers off steering wheels in back-forty greetings.

US-83 doesn't really follow a straight plumb line south—it just seems that way. After meandering from the border across the fertile residuals of ancient Lake Souris near lonely **Westhope,** the route seems to fall straight down the map while crossing the drift prairie south to **Minot.** Continuing south across the viaduct separating giant **Lake Sakakawea** and the much smaller **Lake Audubon,** US-83 winds across slightly more ambitious hills and plateaus along a historic and hardly changed stretch of the mighty Missouri River to **Bismarck,** the state capital and a better-than-expected place to spend some time. South of Bismarck, US-83 cuts away from the riverfront through a pastry-rich pastoral landscape settled around the turn of the 20th cen-tury by German immigrants—including the parents of dance-meister Lawrence Welk—while a recommended detour follows the Missouri River across the huge, his-toric **Standing Rock Indian Reservation** that stretches into South Dakota.

Westhope

US-83 begins winding its way from the Canadian border at the small **United States Port of Entry** (daily 8am-9pm) six miles north of **Westhope** (pop. 428). Westhope, named by an optimistic Great Northern Railway official, is a good example of North Dakota's small agrarian towns. There are cafés, gas stations, a sparse two-block-long downtown, and that's about it.

Six miles south of Westhope, US-83 zigzags west along Hwy-5 for about 15 miles before sharply banking south. The next 37 miles to Minot are a straight shot south, passing nothing save a sweeping wildlife refuge and a lonely Domino's Pizza, all by itself beneath the occasional B-52s thundering overhead to and from **Minot Air Force Base,** one of the primary bases for the U.S. military's tactical and strategic nuclear forces. Along with bombers and fighter planes, Minot AFB also controls hundreds of nuclear-tipped Minuteman III ICBM missiles, which are housed in high-security underground silos that look like high-security parking lots amid the wheat fields all over the northern Great Plains.

Minot

Snug in the Souris River Valley at the junction of US-2 and US-83, **Minot** (pop. 49,450; rhymes with

Minot Air Force Base logo

"Why not?") grew so rapidly after the Great Northern Railway came through in 1887 that it was dubbed "Magic City." Perhaps "Event Capital" would be more apropos today, for despite the city's importance in other areas, most people visit during the huge **state fair** (near the end of July) and during autumn's burgeoning **Norsk Høstfest,** "North America's Largest Scandinavian Festival." The fairgrounds, along the grandly named Burdick Expressway (Business US-2) a half mile east of downtown, also hold the small **Pioneer Village and Museum** (June-Aug. Tues.-Sat. 12pm-5pm, by appointment the rest of the year) with the usual assembly of turn-of-the-20th-century buildings and artifacts gathered from all over the county.

Minot also has all the traditional homespun attractions of most Great Plains downtowns, with stores selling cowboy hats and Western wear, along with the world-class collectibles (including baseball cards, old magazines, and more than 120,000 classic comics) on sale at **Tom's Coin & Gem Shop** (2 SW 1st St., 701/852-4522).

On US-83 south of town, Minot's newest attraction, **Scandinavian Heritage Park** (1020 S. Broadway) is set in a pleasant, tree-shaded city park and includes all sorts of things tracing—guess what?—Minot's Scandinavian heritage: a 230-year-old house from Sigdal, Norway; a Danish windmill; statues and eternal flame honoring famous Scandinavian skiers Casper Oimoen and Sondre Norheim; a waterfall; and a statue of that famous Viking wanderer, Leif Eriksson. Towering over the whole ensemble is a beautiful (and huge!) wooden replica of the medieval Gol Stave Church in Oslo, Norway, and there's a 25-foot-tall red Dala horse, symbolizing Minot's Swedish heritage.

In summer, when daytime highs hover in the mid-90s, Minot's most enticing attractions are the expansive gardens of **Roosevelt Park,** along the banks of the Souris River between the fairgrounds and downtown Minot. The park, like everything else in North Dakota, is named for Teddy Roosevelt, and there's a larger-than-life statue of him, astride a horse in full Rough Rider regalia. The shady green space also holds a large swimming pool with a 365-foot-long water slide, a slacker's dream of a skateboard park, a rideable miniature train, and a 25-acre zoo with a Northern Plains habitat.

To rent bikes and explore the trails of Roosevelt Park, try **Val's Cyclery** (222 E. Central Ave., 701/839-4817).

East of Minot on US-2, the town of **Rugby** is nearly the geographical center of North America.

In range for an hour or more in all directions, Minot's **KRRZ 1390 AM** broadcasts classic hits along with Minnesota Vikings football games.

Minot Practicalities

Along with the usual crossroads barrage of franchised fast-food places, Minot supports a couple of local cafés, including a retro-styled train car diner, **Kroll's Diner** (1221 SE 20th Ave., 701/839-4111), just off US-2, and a great old 24-hour truck stop, **Schatz Crossroads Restaurant** (1712 SE 20th Ave., 701/852-0810, www.schatzcrossroads.com), farther east on US-2.

Downtown, the longstanding favorite is **Charlie's Main Street Café** (113 S. Main St., 701/839-6500), just a couple of blocks east of US-83, its vinyl booths full of Minot residents catching up on the local gossip.

After dark, choose from over a dozen haunts, from bingo parlors and low-stakes casinos to country-western honky-tonks and low-key beer bars like the **Blue Rider** (118 1st Ave. SE, 701/852-9050), a friendly, smoke-free pub with what may be rural North Dakota's best selection of bottled brews—look for the Grain Belt Beer sign.

Motels are scattered along the congested arteries of both US-83 and US-2, so you shouldn't have trouble finding a place to sleep (except perhaps during the state fair). To cope with the extreme weather on the northern Great Plains (winter cold and summer heat), locals seek relief in the Dakota Square Mall, southwest of downtown, where room rates at the "World's Largest" **Sleep Inn & Suites** (2400 10th St. SW, 701/837-3100, $99 and up) include free use of the **Splashdown Dakota Super Slides** water park, which has 24,000 square feet of water slides, swimming pools, and a 48-person hot tub.

East of downtown Minot near the fairgrounds, there's a nice **Holiday Inn** (2200 E. Burdick Expressway, 701/852-2504 or 888/465-4329, $77 and up).

The Minot **Visitors Center** (1020 S. Broadway, 701/857-8206), on US-83 south of downtown near the Scandinavian Heritage Park, has complete listings and detailed information on events and activities. Being so central to the state, Minot hosts everything from chili cook-offs to the state softball championships, and there's usually something going on.

remnant of Minot's Populist past

Lake Sakakawea and the Garrison Dam

At 178 miles long and with nearly 1,500 miles of shoreline along the dammed Missouri River, **Lake Sakakawea** is the third largest artificial "lake" in the United States. It's one of many places in the northwestern United States named for the legendary Shoshone woman, also known as Sacagawea, who accompanied the Lewis and Clark expedition across the Rocky Mountains. There are countless things to do on the water, most of them involving fishing. The pleasant town of **Garrison** (pop. 1,453), six miles west of US-83 on Hwy-37, has a photogenic fiberglass statue of Wally the 26-Foot Walleye.

Minot (page 172) marks the junction of US-83 and **The Great Northern** route along US-2, which runs cross-country from Seattle to Acadia National Park in Maine. Full coverage of this route begins on page 470.

At the south end of Lake Sakakawea, 12 miles west of US-83 via Hwy-200, the Missouri River backs up behind wide but low-slung **Garrison Dam,** the fifth-largest earth-filled dam in the United States. The powerhouse is enmeshed within a labyrinth of huge power stanchions, high-voltage lines, and transformers. In the adjacent **fish hatchery** on the downstream side of the dam, tanks hold hundreds of thousands of walleyes, pallid sturgeons, and northern pike, plus rainbow and brown trout.

South of Garrison Dam, roadside interest along US-83 focuses on leviathan testimonials to engineering prowess. Huge tractors and bulldozers raise clouds of dust at the extensive coal mining operations around **Underwood.** The whole area on both sides of US-83 has been strip-mined and restored, though current operations are hard to get a good look at. Some 7.5-8 million tons of the valuable black rock each year ends up at the 1,100-megawatt **Coal Creek Station,** six miles north of Washburn and two miles off the roadway but readily apparent. This is one of the largest lignite-fired coal plants in the country.

However, unless you have an abiding interest in fossil fuels, a more interesting alternative to driving this stretch of US-83 is to follow the Missouri River's western bank south of Lake Sakakawea, where it reverts to its naturally broad and powerful self for the next 75 miles.

Knife River Indian Villages National Historic Site

Between Garrison Dam and Washburn, scenic Hwy-200 passes two of North Dakota's most significant historic sites: Fort Clark and the **Knife River Indian Villages National Historic Site** (701/745-3300, daily, free), both of which, though small, saw key scenes of the late-18th and early-19th-century interactions between Native Americans and interloping European traders and explorers. Downstream from Garrison Dam along the west bank of the Missouri River, the Knife River Indian Villages is one of North Dakota's most fascinating historic places, and the only federally maintained site devoted to preservation of the Plains nations' cultures. Standing above the Missouri floodplain, on the site of what was the largest and most sophisticated village of the interrelated Hidatsa, Mandan, and Arikara peoples, the park protects the remains of dozens of terraced fields, fortifications, and earth lodges, remnants of a culture that lived here for thousands of years until the 1830s, when the communities were devastated by smallpox and other diseases within a few short years of European contact.

A highlight of the park is **The Earthlodge,** reconstructed using traditional materials, which gives a vivid sense of day-to-day Great Plains life. Measuring 42 feet across and 15 feet high at its central smoke hole, the earth lodge looks exactly as it would

Lake Sakakawea is one of many places in the northwestern United States named for the legendary Shoshone woman, also known as Sacagawea, who accompanied the Lewis and Clark expedition across the Rocky Mountains.

have when the likes of George Catlin and Karl Bodmer were welcomed by the villagers during the 1830s. Just north of the earth lodge, circular depressions spread in the soil—all that remain of the Hidatsa community where, in 1804, the Lewis and Clark Corps of Discovery was joined by the French fur-trapper Charbonneau and his wife, Sacagawea.

Knife River Indian Villages' Earthlodge

The modern visitors center, well signed off Hwy-200 at the south edge of the park, has archaeological and anthropological summaries that help bring to life these intriguing Native American peoples.

Fort Clark

Seven miles downstream and ten miles by road from the Knife River site, well signed off Hwy-200, **Fort Clark State Historic Site** (701/328-3508, daily May-Sept., free) is as eerily isolated as can be. One of three major fur-trading posts on the upper Missouri River, Fort Clark was founded by the American Fur Company circa 1831, primarily to trade with the Mandan people. The fort was visited by other Native Americans, as well as the usual list of adventurers, explorers, and frontier luminaries, such as Prince Maximilian, George Catlin, and Karl Bodmer; unfortunately, the steamboats that plied the waters to bring supplies also brought smallpox, and in one tragic winter in 1837, the Mandan people's population was cut by 90 percent. After the fur trade declined, Fort Clark was abandoned in 1860.

Today the tranquil site, approached on a narrow gravel-and-dirt road, is devoid of anything—it's a somber, quiet piece of history stretching out on a grassy flat-topped bluff overlooking the Missouri River. Unfortunately, the silence and emptiness of the place are marred by the presence of a smoky Basin Electric Power Company coal plant up the river. A walking trail has markers designating the locations of eight original buildings, and depressions from an earth lodge village and primitive fortifications are still apparent, but you need to use your imagination to see much.

Fort Mandan

Back on the east bank of the Missouri River, north of Washburn and two miles west of US-83, **Fort Mandan** is a reconstruction of Lewis and Clark's winter quarters in

DETOUR: THE ENCHANTED HIGHWAY

Standing out against the badlands of western North Dakota, the world's largest collection of roadside statuary enlivens an otherwise unexciting swath of the northern Great Plains. Standing along a quiet country road outside the town of Regent (pop. 160), some 32 miles south of I-94 exit 72, the unexpected visual delights of the Enchanted Highway have earned it a place in *Guinness World Records* as the World's Largest Scrap Metal Sculpture, as well as in the hearts of many a long-distance roadtripper. Created beginning in 1989 by former schoolteacher and self-taught metal sculptor Gary Greff, these are some of the largest works of art in the world—a flock of geese reaches over 100 feet into the air, while the *Tin Family* stands some 45 feet tall along the roadside. The Enchanted Highway is, well, simply enchanting, and definitely worth the detour.

1804-1805. Arriving here at the end of October after a tediously difficult six-month slog upstream from St. Louis, the expedition set up camp, which consisted of rough-hewn log cabins arranged to form a triangular palisade surrounded by a 16-foot-high wall. Here the 33 men spent the winter, making friendly contact with nearby Native American communities, most significantly those of the Knife River site—where Lewis and Clark hired the French fur-trapper Charbonneau and his young wife, the legendary Sacagawea, who helped guide them across the Rockies.

As it flows across the south-central corner of North Dakota, the **Missouri River** also marks the dividing line between the central (or "east river") and mountain (or "west river") time zones.

The actual site of Lewis and Clark's encampment, some 10 miles upstream across the river from the site of Fort Clark, was long ago washed away by the ever-shifting Missouri River, but this full-scale, historically accurate replica fort was built in the 1970s by local history buffs, and recently restored and expanded as part of the Lewis & Clark Interpretive Center in Washburn. Constructed and furnished,

THE LEWIS AND CLARK EXPEDITION

Following the instructions of President Thomas Jefferson, Meriwether Lewis and William Clark set off across the continent in 1804 to explore the vast territory recently acquired from France in the Louisiana Purchase. Part of their mission was to find a viable trade route from the Mississippi River to the Pacific Ocean.

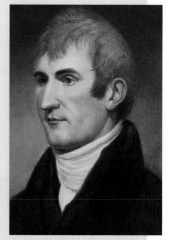

Sharing command of what was officially known as the Corps of Discovery, which included 33 soldiers and experienced "mountain men," plus the legendary Sacagawea, her husband Toussaint Charbonneau, and their infant, Pomp, not to mention Lewis's Newfoundland dog, Seaman, Lewis and Clark blazed a route up the Missouri River, crossed the Rocky Mountains, and made their way west down the Columbia River, returning to St. Louis after 2.5 years and over 8,000 miles of unprecedented travel.

Meriwether Lewis

Along with their copious journals, many good books have been written documenting the Lewis and Clark expedition and tracing their route, which has been declared the **Lewis and Clark National Historic Trail.** Much of the land they traversed has been altered beyond recognition, though thanks to recent bicentennial celebrations, numerous historic sites along the way have been preserved or protected as parks or museums. The best of these are covered here.

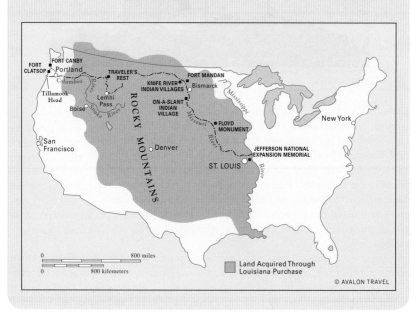

William Clark

Museum of Westward Expansion is an excellent museum underneath the Gateway Arch in St. Louis (see page 262).

The Sergeant Floyd Monument, in Sioux City, is a concrete-core stone obelisk marking the grave of the only expedition member to lose his life—from appendicitis (see page 605).

On-A-Slant Indian Village has been reconstructed atop the remains of a Mandan village (see page 183).

Fort Mandan, where the expedition spent the winter of 1804-1805, has been reconstructed downstream from the original site (see page 176).

Knife River Indian Villages National Historic Site, along the banks of the Missouri River, holds the remains of the Hidatsa village where Sacagawea lived before joining the Corps of Discovery (see page 175).

Lemhi Pass, on the Idaho-Montana border, is where the expedition first crossed the Continental Divide (see page 135).

The River of No Return is an impassable portion of the **Salmon River** (see page 133).

Traveler's Rest, in the Bitterroot Valley south of Missoula, was such an idyllic spot that the Corps of Discovery camped here on both the outbound and return legs of their journey (see page 130).

Fort Canby, now called **Cape Disappointment State Park,** overlooking the mouth of the Columbia River, has a small museum on the spot where the expedition first saw the Pacific Ocean (see page 24).

Fort Clatsop, a full-scale reconstruction of the wooden fort where the expedition spent a miserable winter in 1805-1806, sits in lush forest along the Oregon coast (see page 27).

Tillamook Head, rising high above the Pacific Ocean, is the farthest point the expedition reached (see page 29).

with some original pieces, to look how it did when Lewis and Clark camped here, the fort gives a good sense of the difficulties the explorers faced. History aside, the wild Missouri River frontage is a great place to play Tom Sawyer—on summer afternoons you'll see barefoot kids, shirtless in overalls, fishing and mucking along the banks. Another insight into local life is provided by the visitors center, which is constructed almost entirely out of recycled by-products of the coal-mining industry.

Washburn: Lewis & Clark Interpretive Center

Now a tranquil little highway town, **Washburn** (pop. 1,246) was once a frenetic Missouri River ferry crossing, served by steamboats from St. Louis, the last of which has been mounted on a concrete pedestal at the base of the bridge that helped to make it obsolete. In addition to nearby Fort Clark, across the river, and Fort Mandan, two miles to the northwest, Washburn has the excellent **Lewis & Clark Interpretive Center** (701/462-8535, daily, $7.50). It's at the intersection of US-83 and North Dakota Hwy-200A, an ideal jumping-off point for your exploration of the lower Missouri River valley. Offering the hard-to-find combination of informative exhibits (including a full set of the detailed watercolors painted in the 1830s by explorer-artist Karl Bodmer), great Missouri River views, an excellent gift shop, and impeccably

clean restrooms, this is a place you will want to linger for at least an hour or maybe two. The highly interactive museum exhibits let visitors enjoy Native American sports, sample historic foods, and try heirloom seed gardening.

Part of the promotional campaign for the 2004-2006 bicentennial celebrations of the Corps of Discovery's amazing expedition, billboards all around North Dakota relayed the slogan "Lewis & Clark Slept Here—146 Times."

Cross Ranch State Park

Across the Missouri River, a little more than eight miles south of Washburn via Hwy-1806, **Cross Ranch State Park** ($5 per car) is set among 589 acres of cottonwood-shaded free-flowing Missouri River bottomland with numerous hiking trails, canoe rentals, and fine camping, with sites for RVs and tents. There are also furnished **log cabins and yurts** (cabins around $70, yurts $65). For details, phone the park **visitors center** (701/794-3731 or 800/807-4723), which also has canoe and kayak rentals and information on the annual **Missouri River Bluegrass Festival,** held here in the middle of June.

Across Hwy-1806 from the state park, the remains of the pioneer town of **Sanger** stand as a mute memorial to Great Plains history. Founded in 1879, Sanger was the county seat and a major steamboat and railroad town, with a population of some 400 people. By World War II, Sanger had effectively been bypassed by the modern age, and the post office closed down in the mid-1950s. By 1985, just three residents remained.

From the state park, enticing trails lead into The Nature Conservancy's 5,593-acre **Cross Ranch Preserve** (701/794-8741, daily dawn-dusk, free). One of the richest surviving native Missouri River valley ecosystems, the preserve includes floodplain prairie and riparian forest, plus a resident herd of bison and some undisturbed Native American archaeological sites.

Bismarck

In his best-selling travelogue *Travels with Charley,* writer John Steinbeck wrote about Bismarck:

> *Here is where the map should fold. Here is the boundary between east and west. On the Bismarck side it is eastern landscape, eastern grass, with the look and smell of eastern America. Across the Missouri on the Mandan side it is pure west, with brown grass and water scorings and small outcrops. The two sides of the river might well be a thousand miles apart.*

Like many towns across the Great Plains, **Bismarck** (pop. 61,272) was named after a wealthy European, in this case the chancellor of Germany, in order to lure much-needed capital investment. The town grew exponentially following booms in the railroad industry, Black Hills gold, and most recently, oil, gas, and biofuels, but it's still economically and culturally dependent on its status as North Dakota's state capital. It's one of the smallest of the 50 in the United States, but as state capitals go, Bismarck rates quite highly for its size, with thousands of parkland acres, well-preserved historic districts, and an old-time boat ride along the Missouri River.

Bureaucratic Bismarck seems intent on glossing over its bawdy historical peccadilloes by building monuments to modernity, like the capitol building, 19 stories of angular art deco nicknamed the "Skyscraper on the Prairies." The white limestone and classical symbolism seem out of place on the plains, but free **tours** highlight the ornate interior's woodwork and metalsmithing.

On the grounds you'll find the usual memorial statues of noteworthy North Dakotans, starting with a large statue of **Sacagawea,** the guide of Lewis and Clark, carrying her newborn baby, Pomp, and looking sternly forward. Nearby is another popular subject, a **buffalo,** here rendered out of rusty steel reinforcing rod. A short walk away, the **North Dakota Heritage Center** has an informative array of historical and cultural exhibits, using dinosaurs and tepees to trace the development of North Dakota from its geological underpinnings to its contemporary culture and industry.

Along I-94 in New Salem, 32.5 miles west of Bismarck, stands the **World's Largest Holstein Cow.**

Though Bismarck is the state capital, the selection of places to eat is pretty slim. For a truly otherworldly experience that combines pretty tasty American and Tex-Mex with Jetsons-esque space-age decor, the **Space Aliens Grill & Bar** (1304 E. Century Ave., 701/223-6220), on the US-83 strip north of I-94, is your logical destination. "Earthlings Welcome," proclaims the telltale sign; this lively joint may get a bit too cute with its nomenclature, but it does deliver on flavor with its Planet of the Zombies Taco Burger, Martian Munchies barbecue platter, and Outer Space appetizers. If you want good food rather than a good chuckle, you might be better off at the **Pirogue Grille** (121 N. 4th St., 701/223-3770), near East Broadway.

Between the two state capitals of Bismarck, North Dakota, and Pierre, South Dakota, the Missouri River has been dammed to form 231-mile-long **Lake Oahe.**

Along with the clusters of motels on the northern fringes of US-83 and along I-94, lodging options include a nice **Radisson** (605 E. Broadway, 701/255-6000 and 800/333-3333, $119) about a mile south of the state capitol.

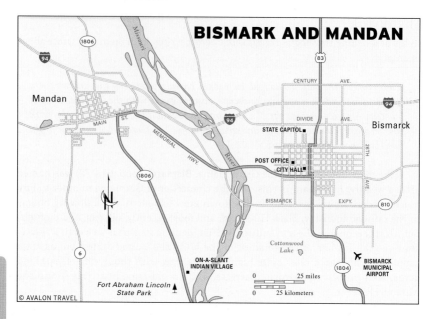

Missouri River Tour: Hwy-1806

An outstanding alternative to US-83 between Bismarck and the South Dakota border is the narrow but well-maintained Hwy-1806, which meanders along the **Missouri River** taking in views of great hillocks and easy bluffs off to the left, and scintillating blue water ribboning beneath stark-white standing-driftwood trees. Round a bend and you'll see a lagoon. Or admire a great panorama of 2,000-foot buttes to the west, all the way across the state line. Be sure to fill up on gas and supplies before you set off, since it's a 100-mile drive with few services along the way.

Mandan

Cross-river sibling to the state capital, **Mandan** (pop. 18,331) is a shipping and warehousing center that grew up swiftly in the years after 1882, when the Northern Pacific railroad completed a bridge from Bismarck. As John Steinbeck pointed out, Mandan marks the beginning of the wild western United States. For a quick trip back to the 1880s, when the Northern Pacific Railroad made its epic push across the Great Plains, visit the **North Dakota State Railroad Museum** (3102 37th St. NW, 701/663-9322, daily 1pm-5pm summer). In addition to a wide array of old railroad photographs, the museum includes restored cabooses, boxcars, tankers, and flatcars from the Soo, Great Northern, and Burlington Northern lines.

Most everything in Mandan, from cafés to beauty parlors, seems to be named after someone related to Lewis and Clark—apart from the string of windowless cowboy-themed beer bars along Main Street (choose among Silver Dollar Bar, the Last Call Bar, and a number of others). The other main things to see in Mandan are two statues, one a 25-foot-tall rendering of a Native American man (601 SE 6th Ave.) carved from a cottonwood tree, the other the requisite Teddy Roosevelt, in front of the train station on Main Street.

Theodore Roosevelt, Rough Rider

Fort Abraham Lincoln State Park

Heading south along Hwy-1806 from Mandan along the west bank of the Missouri River, the first place you'll reach is sprawling **Fort Abraham Lincoln State Park** (701/667-6340, daily, $5 per car), which was originally established as Fort McKeen in advance of the Northern Pacific Railroad expansion. It eventually fell into the hands of the U.S. Army, which in 1872 changed the fort's name to the present one. Soon afterward, General Custer arrived to take over the reins of command, and in 1876 the fort was placed squarely on the map and in the national press as the departure point for the doomed general and his 262 men, who met their demise at Little Big Horn. Abandoned in 1891, the fort was dismantled by settlers who salvaged the wood and bricks to build their own homes, and most everything here today is a reconstruction.

The modern park covers slightly more than 1,000 acres and contains a number of barracks, stables, and stores, plus a replica of **Custer's House** (daily summer, $6), where paid sycophants will lead you around, calling you "General" while conducting guided tours. Best of all is the **On-A-Slant Indian Village,** an excavated Mandan village established about 1575 where you can explore six full-scale recreated earth lodges.

If you like the idea of *not* driving for a change, the **Fort Lincoln Trolley** (depot at 2000 SE 3rd St., daily 1pm-4pm summer, $7 one-way, $9 round-trip) runs along the river between Mandan and Fort Abraham Lincoln, departing every hour or so for the 4.5-mile trip. You can also stay at the park overnight, either in a small sleeping

General George Armstrong Custer

cabin (summer only, $55) or in the adjacent campground (800/807-4723 or 701/667-6340), with cabins and campsites. Make reservations for these well ahead so you don't miss out on the Missouri River sunrise views. Another popular place to stay among these wide-open Great Plains spaces is the glitzy **Prairie Knights Casino and Resort** (800/425-8277), on the Standing Rock Reservation between Mandan and Fort Yates.

Standing Rock Indian Reservation

Huge hills appear around the **Standing Rock Indian Reservation,** home to approximately 8,500 Sioux people and spreading across the state line with a total of 2.3 million acres. In 2016, Standing Rock became a flashpoint in the battle between the "fracking" fossil-fuel industry and environmental activists known as "water protectors," who rallied here to prevent an oil pipeline under the Missouri River. At its peak more than 3,000 protesters set up camp along the Missouri River and Hwy-1806, near the Cannon Ball Bridge.

Along with fantastic roadside views, connections to Sioux traditions, and the travels of Lewis and Clark, the main draw to the reservation is its namesake Standing Rock, which stands in the town of Fort Yates (pop. 184), along the riverfront near the tribal headquarters. In the correct angle of sunlight, the stone resembles a seated woman wearing a shawl. Legend holds that the woman, jealous of her husband's second wife, refused to move when the Sioux decamped; a search party later found her, turned to stone. Fort Yates also once held the original burial site of Sitting Bull, who was killed here in 1890, but the unimpressive site, marked by a boulder on a dusty side road two miles west of Hwy-1806, is certainly not what one would expect for the great Sioux warrior. After his family exhumed his remains in 1953, Sitting Bull is now more suitably interred and memorialized near his birthplace in Mobridge, South Dakota, on the Standing Rock Reservation 50 miles to the south.

South of Fort Yates, the scenery and the driving (or riding) are magnificent. Flawless blacktop winds through valleys and up ambitious swooping hills of grazing land. You'll be confronted by one gorgeous landscape after another, especially at dusk, when the intense Western sun illuminates the bands of sunflower fields, turns the dry and grassy hills a reddish shade of ocher, and casts angular shadows beneath the darting sandpipers, who whisk their brown-and-white forms along the roadway, buzzing the lone car on the road in an extended game of highway tag. You won't even realize you're in South Dakota until you notice the gold border on the highway signs. The actual border between North and South Dakota was marked by 720 stone monuments, each seven feet tall but half-buried in the ground every half mile. They were erected by the federal government around 1892. While many have been destroyed or removed, they are currently the focus of preservation efforts.

US-83: Linton, Strasburg, and the Lawrence Welk Birthplace

While the scenery is superior along the Hwy-1806 detour, for travelers of a certain age, the trek south of Bismarck along US-83 is redeemed by one unique Road Trip destination: the **Welk Homestead** (701/336-7777, Thurs.-Sun. 10am-5pm summer only, $5 adults), boyhood home of Lawrence Welk, a wholesome, middlebrow dance-band maestro who, for more than 20 years, starting in the mid-1950s, had one of the most popular programs on TV. Located a mile north of the town of **Strasburg** (pop. 409), then about two miles west from US-83 following well-signed dirt roads, the preserved homestead where Welk was born in 1903 is one of the top tourist draws in North Dakota (which, to be honest, is not saying a lot; North Dakota is frequently numbered at the bottom of "Favorite States to Visit").

Though the Lawrence Welk connection is the main draw for most visitors, the farm is intended as a memorial to his parents, who, as part of an exodus of Bavarian-born Catholic farmers, fled the Ukraine during the late 1800s, when exemptions from Tsarist military service were threatened, and emigrated to this country in 1893. The promise of land brought the Welks to North Dakota in the

Lawrence Welk leading his band on *The Lawrence Welk Show*

1890s. The clapboard house that stands today began as a sod house—the mud walls can still be seen in places—and is now full of odds and ends of furniture and memorabilia, some of which belonged to the Welk family. There are hand tools in the blacksmith shop, a windmill in the yard, and Lawrence Welk's music plays over the loud speaker for bus tours and during special events.

Much of southern North Dakota is still predominantly populated by descendants of the original wave of these immigrant "Germans from Russia" who homesteaded the region in the 1890s. Their influence is clearly apparent in the town of **Linton** (pop. 1,097), on US-83 around 10.5 miles north of the Welk homestead, where the **Model Bakery** (117 N. Broadway, 701/254-4687, Mon.-Sat.) bakes up delicious, creamy custard kuchen and German cakes and cookies. In Strasburg, Welk's parents are buried in the cemetery behind the absolutely huge Roman Catholic church that dwarfs the tiny town.

SOUTH DAKOTA

US-83 cuts through South Dakota's broad expanse for 254 miles, crossing mostly level but never slate-flat topography, and passing through what's known as the Great Lakes region of the state, most evident in and around **Pierre.** Instead of a multilane transcontinental highway, US-83 across South Dakota resembles a country road, giving an up-close-and-personal look at farming and grazing lands, with an occasional jutting hill, ravine, or serpentine creek bed to break up the monotony. Classic South Dakota—no pretensions.

To either side of the North Dakota border, US-83 is little more than a beeline across the plains. Sadly, the Missouri River is well out of sight, so we strongly recommend following a scenic detour across the river through the huge Standing Rock Indian Reservation, linking up with US-83 again approximately 20 miles east of Mobridge via US-12. After that you'll pass through small farm towns before reaching the state capital, Pierre, at the center of South Dakota.

Mobridge

Since US-83's route across northern South Dakota doesn't offer much stimulation for the senses, if you've got the time to spare, detour west along the Missouri River, leaving North Dakota via the Lewis and Clark Highway, Hwy-1806. This scenic route brings you across the middle of **Standing Rock Indian Reservation,** which falls mainly in South Dakota but stretches about 30 miles over the border.

Wild pheasants and other beautifully plumed game birds scurry about in the grassy verges along US-83 across the Dakotas.

On Hwy-1806, at tiny **Kenel,** a historical marker points out the site of fur-trading Fort Manuel, where Lewis and Clark's guide Sacagawea may have died of fever in 1812, at the age of 25. South of Kenel, the road runs straight south, away from the winding Missouri River and toward imposing 2,200-foot Rattlesnake Butte. After 26 miles or so, you'll cross on sweeping bridges into **Mobridge** (pop. 3,465), the biggest town between the North and South Dakota capitals.

Mobridge, once a village of the Arikara people, is heavily dependent on the anglers who come to pluck the lunkers, wall-eyes, and even 20-pound northern pike from Lake Oahe. The area's earlier history and Native American culture are celebrated on the walls inside the **Scherr-Howe Event Center** (212 N. Main St., Mon.-Fri., free), where bold murals depict Sioux history and culture. These murals were painted as part of the Depression-era Works Progress Administration by Yanktonai Sioux artist Oscar Howe (1915-1983).

The name Mobridge stems from a hasty telegraph message transmitted in 1906 by an operator who needed a quick and clear reference to the area. He chose, at random, "Mo," for the Missouri River, and "bridge," referring to the one then under construction by the Milwaukee Railroad.

The most interesting food option is **Rick's Café** (117 N. Main St., 605/845-5300), in downtown Mobridge, famed for its award-winning chili and tacos. The **Wrangler Inn** (820 W. Grand Crossing, 605/845-3641, $76 and up), a half mile west on US-12, is the best overnight stop on the stretch, with a sports bar and dining room and a heated pool.

Sitting Bull Memorial

A 10-minute trip from Mobridge, back across the Missouri to the Grand River Casino and Resort, then south on Hwy-1806, will bring you to the **Sitting Bull Memorial.** This is the final resting place of the great Sioux leader, after his body was disinterred in 1953 from Fort Yates in a surreptitious and still-controversial move. Whatever injustice or disrespect exhuming his body may have incurred, this magnificent view, high on a palisade hilltop looking southeast over the river, is at least worthier than the previous site. The six-foot granite bust that serves as Sitting Bull's tombstone was carved by the late Korczak Ziolkowski, the sculptor who began the quixotic Crazy Horse Memorial carving near Mt. Rushmore.

US-83: Selby to Pierre

Twenty-odd miles east and slightly south of Mobridge, US-83 passes through diminutive **Selby** (pop. 642), a sleepy middle-American hamlet with grain farming and water towers, populated with children riding bikes home at dusk, families enjoying ice cream cones at **Mr. Bob's Drive-Inn,** and teenagers rumbling down Main Street in their muscle cars.

Between Selby and the state capital at Pierre, there's nothing of dramatic

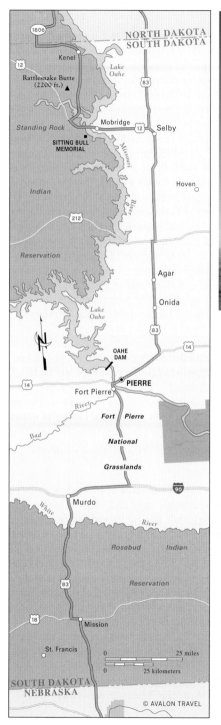

Sitting Bull Memorial

importance. Highway hypnosis is kept at bay by a roadside marker 5 miles south of Selby, standing on the site of the vanished town of Bangor; farther south, then 13 miles east of US-83, the large **Cathedral of the Prairie** looms over the hamlet of **Hoven** (pop. 406).

And then, finally, a town—or at least some grain elevators and a turquoise water tower. **Agar** (pop. 76), "Home of the 1977 State B Track Champions," is a classic single-sidewalk leg-stretch where the Pepsi machine seems as large as the filling station it rests against. The same goes for little **Onida** (pop. 658), with a handsome onion-domed courthouse, a water tower emblazoned with a sunflower, and a cute city park complete with swimming pool and horseshoe courts. You'd hardly guess that this was once a thriving homesteader boomtown, full of transplanted New Yorkers who named it after Oneida, with no apparent reason for the change in spelling.

Pierre

The second-smallest and by far the sleepiest state capital in the country, **Pierre** (pop. 13,646; pronounced "PEER") is an odd amalgam of South Dakota characteristics. Part farm town, part railroad town, and best of all, part river town, Pierre accurately embodies South Dakota's dominant activities. Located at nearly the geographic center of the state, quiet, easy Pierre is filled with natural attractions and totally lacking in the usual power-broker trappings of other state-capital cities.

Pierre's one not-to-be-missed stop is the excellent **South Dakota Cultural Heritage Center** (900 Governors Dr., 605/773-3458, daily, $4 adults), built into the side of a hill on the north side of town. A startling and beautiful structure, it is designed to be a modern evocation of a traditional energy-efficient Native American dwelling. Inside, the museum has the usual interpretive historical displays of indigenous and pioneer cultures, with a focus on the Sioux people and the battles for the Black Hills region. A glass case holds the actual lead plate the brothers Louis-Joseph and François de La Vérendrye, the first Europeans to explore what's now South Dakota, left behind when they claimed the entire territory for France in 1743.

At the center of town, the **state capitol** grounds are a verdant island of tranquility with an arboretum, walking trails, and the Flaming Fountain Memorial, dedicated to South Dakotans who have fought for their country in times of war. The fountain sits on the shore of a lake that is home to thousands of migrating winter waterfowl.

For travel-weary road hogs, especially those traveling with children, the coolest museum has to be the hands-on **South Dakota Discovery Center** (805 W. Sioux Ave., 605/224-8295, daily, $4 adults), in the old Pierre Municipal Power & Light building, with loads of science exhibits.

Museums aside, nature is what draws folks to Pierre. Bordering the town to the south is the long **LaFramboise Island Nature Area,** a perfect place to while away time, recuperating from the drive along the beautiful bay.

About 31 miles northwest of Pierre on Hwy-1806, **Triple U Buffalo Ranch,** locally known as Houck's, spans almost 46,000 acres and supports thousands of bison. Now owned by media mogul Ted Turner, the ranch was featured in the 1990 movie *Dances with Wolves.*

Pierre Practicalities

The nicest place to eat is **La Minestra** (106 E. Dakota Ave., 605/224-8090), a surprisingly cozy and elegant bistro in a restored 1880s building that during its storied history has housed a funeral parlor, a card room, and a country-western saloon. The sophisticated Italian specialties make this one of the nicest restaurants you'll find along the 100th meridian. There's also a pretty good steakhouse next door, **Mad Mary's** (605/224-6469). If beef is what you live for, you'll also want to try the local landmark **Cattleman's Club Steakhouse** (605/224-9774), one of the country's great cowboy haunts, six miles or so east of town along the river via Hwy-34.

There are the usual assorted motels on US-83 as it swoops in from the north and follows the wide landscaped boulevards. West of the state capitol building, you'll find lots of locally owned places: the **Governor's Inn** (700 W. Sioux Ave., 605/224-4200 or 877/523-0080, $72 and up) is at the top end of the price and comfort scale, and this same can't-miss-it main drag holds a popular **Days Inn** (520 W. Sioux Ave., 605/224-0411, $60 and up).

Fort Pierre

South of Pierre, US-83 crosses the Missouri River, then takes you into **Fort Pierre** (pop. 2,078). It's not much now, but it has a rich history. As far back as 1832, it was known as Fort Pierre Chouteau, an American Fur Company trading post, and before that it was Ree and Arikara indigenous lands. Located at the mouth of the Bad (Teton) River, Fort Pierre once was a thriving port, but it is better known as

the site where Joseph La Framboise, a fur trader, stopped and erected a driftwood shelter out of necessity, establishing the area's first nonnative settlement.

Immediately south of Fort Pierre, typical South Dakota topography resumes: rolling black and green hills and twisting creek beds beneath sharp vertical drops of million-year-old geology. Spreading along both sides of US-83, the 116,000 acres of the **Fort Pierre National Grassland** are home to deer, rattlesnakes, antelope, and the most extensive prairie dog towns in the region.

Murdo

One of the duller stretches of US-83 is this 20-mile leg west along the mind-numbing I-90 artery between the Fort Pierre grasslands and **Murdo** (pop. 488). Once a stop on the legendary Texas Cattle Trail and also used by stagecoaches, the town was named for cattle baron Murdo McKenzie, who managed ranches that pushed through some 20,000 head of cattle a year. Today, the town of Murdo still lives on the cattle industry.

The one place that's definitely worth a stop is smack-dab at the diesel-blue polluted confluence of US-83 and I-90, where nostalgists will find the **Pioneer Auto Show** (605/669-2691, daily, $11.50 adults), a 10-acre, 42-building collection of over 275 antique cars, with tons of other great items. There's a rare 1903 Ford Model A, a nifty White Motorhome from 1921, one of the earliest RVs, and the General Lee muscle car from TV's *Dukes of Hazzard*. Star of the show: Elvis Presley's 1976 Harley-Davidson Electra Glide 1200 motorcycle. This is pure Americana.

If you're thinking about driving along US-83 during August, be aware that you may have to share the road with hordes of Harley riders bound for the annual get-together in **Sturgis**, at the edge of the Black Hills.

The Pioneer Auto Show also has a good 1950s-style ersatz diner. The public swimming pool up the hill from the Pioneer will round off your perfectly Middle American Murdo experience.

Rosebud Indian Reservation

There's nothing much south of I-90 and Murdo until you come across a picturesque dale while crossing the White River, sheltering the first grove of trees in too long a time. South of White River, US-83 rolls its way across the **Rosebud Indian Reservation.** After the signing of the Fort Laramie Treaty in 1868, the Sicangu Lakota, under the guidance of Spotted Tail, were moved five times before finally being settled on this reservation, one of the smallest on the Great Plains. The first town you'll encounter is **Mission,** the reservation's trading center, where US-83 zigzags through a strip of gas stations.

WALL DRUG

America's most famous roadside business, **Wall Drug** (510 Main St., 605/279-2175) began with free ice water. Ted Hustead bought this tiny South Dakota town's drugstore in 1931, and for five years Ted and his wife, Dorothy, struggled to survive during the depths of the Depression. Then Dorothy had a brainstorm: Hundreds of people drove past Wall every day on US-16, the main route across South Dakota, battling the dusty dirt road and 90°F summer heat. Why not give them an excuse to stop? Once in the store, maybe they'd buy an ice cream, or an aspirin.

So in the summer of 1936, Ted Hustead erected roadside signs to tempt travelers off the highway and into his store. Spaced at intervals along the highway, like the famous Burma-Shave ads, the signs read:

GET A SODA
GET ROOT BEER
TURN THE CORNER
JUST AS NEAR
TO HIGHWAY 16 AND 14
FREE ICE WATER
WALL DRUG

Before he could return to the store, the tourists were already arriving. And they're coming still: some 20,000 per day in the summer—well over a million a year. Proud South Dakotans have covered foreign landscapes with signs proclaiming the mileage to Wall Drug, and the Husteads themselves have advertised on London buses, Amsterdam canals, and French bistros. Before the 1960s era of "highway

beautification" banned most billboards, Wall Drug touted its free ice water on 3,000 billboards in all 50 states.

But what's waiting at the end of all those billboards? Originally, not much, apart from that glass of water. But today's 50,000-square-foot Wall Drug is a different story: It can feed, clothe, and entertain the entire family for hours. Photo opportunities abound, thanks to the 80-foot-long dinosaur, 6-foot rabbit, giant fiberglass jackalope, Mt. Rushmore replica, a restaurant-café seating more than 520, and shops for everything from postcards to cowboy boots. A younger generation of Husteads still runs Wall Drug, the ice water is still free, and the coffee still costs a nickel. Drop in sometime!

Wall Drug is at the center of Wall, South Dakota (pop. 766), just north of I-90 exit 110. Apart from Wall Drug, one other reason to visit is the chance to tour the **Minuteman Missile National Historic Site** (605/433-5552, daily, free), off I-90 exit 131. The silo and control center are accessible only on the popular guided tours, so sign up as soon as you know you'll be here.

The heart of the reservation is **Rosebud,** 5 miles west of Mission on US-18, then 7 miles southwest on BIA-1. Most of the reservation's activities, including weekend rodeos and powwows, are centered on the reservation headquarters. Another eight miles southwest is tiny **St. Francis,** which has the **Buechel Memorial Lakota Museum** (350 S. Oak St., 605/747-2745, daily summer only, free), a museum dedicated to Sioux culture founded by Eugene Buechel, a German Jesuit priest, avid botanist, and dedicated student of the indigenous people of the Great Plains.

Back on US-83, about 22 miles south of Mission, is the community's most profitable economic endeavor, the **Rosebud Casino,** which sits right on the Nebraska state line, showing where its prospective gamblers are coming from.

NEBRASKA

The 257 miles from South Dakota to Kansas encompass two distinct regions: typical Midwestern wheat and cattle ranches, and the fascinating grass-coated sand dunes of central Nebraska's Sand Hills region. Contrary to a popular belief inspired by the powerhouse college football Cornhuskers nickname, Nebraska isn't mostly corn, but rather beef—lots and lots of it. US-83 passes by more cattle than it does people, with scant few communities along the way. In the northern corner of the state there are trees, trees, and more trees, especially as you drop down from the scorched plains into the evergreen-studded Niobrara River Valley. Coming from South Dakota, your first stop south of the border is **Valentine,** then US-83 crosses the rolling Sand Hills region toward the railroad town of **North Platte,** former home of "Buffalo" Bill Cody. From North Platte, it's a straight shot south to Kansas.

Valentine

Just west of the 100th meridian, the small town of **Valentine** (pop. 2,737) is a center of the extensive cattle-ranching industry of the Sand Hills region, and the kind of tiny but prideful town that makes road-tripping fun. Seat of enormous Cherry County and situated at the northern edge of the 20,000-square-mile Sand Hills region, Valentine, which takes its name from a U.S. congressman, is a broad, well-maintained place that pays its bills with beef cattle fed to tenderness on the hundreds of species of grasses coating the region.

Considering the long stretches of road ahead, it's prudent to check out what the town's got, and there's quite a bit. Downtown, the streetlights are hung with red and

Valentine marks the junction of US-83 and the east-west **Oregon Trail** along US-20 (see page 603). For full coverage of this road trip, see page 558.

white banners emblazoned with wooden hearts and the slogan "Valentine, The Heart City." The facade of the **Security First Bank** (253 N. Main St.) holds the "Largest Brick Mural in Nebraska," with 1,200 square feet of images of longhorn cattle and the building of the transcontinental railroad built out of dark brown bricks.

Four miles southeast of Valentine on US-20/83, an absolutely *huge* old railroad trestle bridges the broad Niobrara River.

Valentine has the usual motels scattered along US-20 and US-83, including the 1960s-era **Trade Winds Motel** (1009 E. US-20/83, 402/376-1600 or 888/376-1601, $75 and up) on the southeast edge of town; there's also a **Comfort Inn.** The place most people go for a sit-down meal is **Peppermill Steakhouse** (502 E. US-20/83, 402/376-2800), featuring steaks and seafood.

Thanks to its name, Valentine is a popular place to mail greeting cards for delivery on February 14. If you want a special "With Love on Valentine's Day" postmark, in early February pack up your stamped, addressed Valentine's cards in a larger envelope and send them to: Valentine's Day Postmark, Postmaster, 239 N. Hall St., Valentine NE 69201-9998.

Fort Niobrara National Wildlife Refuge

One of Valentine's sightseeing highlights is the massive old railroad bridge, called the Cowboy Trail Bridge, over the broad Niobrara River. Just a few miles south of downtown along US-20/83, rising on trestles 150 feet above the water, the bridge now carries the popular Cowboy Trail hiker-biker route, which follows the old railroad right-of-way almost all the way across the state. This stretch of the Niobrara River has been protected for nearly 100 years within the nearly 20,000-acre **Fort Niobrara National Wildlife Refuge** (402/376-3789) and offers top-notch canoeing and tubing. The refuge is named for old Fort Niobrara, semi-famous for never seeing a battle during its 27 years on the Wild West prairie. The diverse environs of the refuge provide a home for a huge variety of native plants and animals; a 3.5-mile self-guided auto tour lets you watch for resident and migratory birds, while herds of elk, bison, and pronghorn roam around the gorgeous green rolling prairies.

Nature-lovers score well at other sites around Valentine. Cyclists and walkers will enjoy the chance to follow the Cowboy Trail right through town, while seasoned canoeists, kayakers, and keen trout anglers will want to tackle the rough **Snake River,** some 23 miles southwest of town, near the short but powerful **Snake River Falls.**

Nebraska Sand Hills

South of Valentine are two fine natural areas, preserving and highlighting the unique ecosystems of the **Nebraska Sand Hills.** The Sand Hills of northwestern Nebraska form one of the largest areas of rolling dune geology in the world. They're also the largest tract of mid- to tallgrass prairie in North America. In the right light

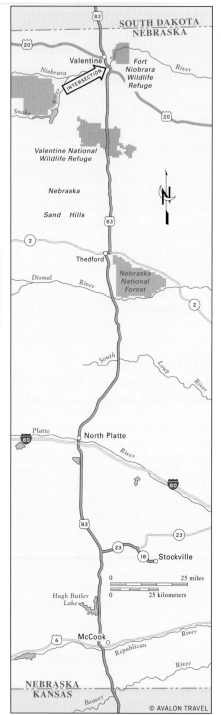

(sunrise or sunset), at the right time of year (spring, especially, before the summer sun saps their color), they are absolutely beautiful.

South of Valentine along US-83 is the large **Valentine National Wildlife Refuge,** which, thanks to water seeping from the world's biggest aquifer, the Ogallala Aquifer, is home to both native rolling dune prairie and lowlands of lake, marsh, and subirrigated meadow. Lots of curlews, sandpipers, terns, and mule deer are found on the drives and hikes through the vaulted hills and long spiny grasses, and along the lakeshores; if you're here in winter, keep an eye for majestic sandhill cranes, which soar overhead on their annual migrations and flock together around lakes and rivers in huge numbers.

Farther south, the Sand Hills occasionally flatten out into simple, absolutely open range, with perhaps a ridge jutting out. Cows fleck the land, as do a few windmills: great stark American Gothic windmills, not the pseudo-efficient energy spinners seen elsewhere. US-83 joins with Hwy-2 approximately 30 miles after leaving the Valentine National Wildlife Refuge. Swinging east will take you to one of the three huge districts of the **Nebraska National Forest,** among the largest artificial forest tracts in the world, with 20,000 acres in total, all planted by hand more than a century ago.

Thedford and Scenic Hwy-2

Sleepy little **Thedford** (pop. 188) stretches west of US-83, lining up along the Burlington Northern Railroad tracks. The town—not much more than a few little houses, some loud cicadas, a motel or two, and a Conoco station—does mark the junction of US-83 and Scenic Hwy-2,

view from the Nebraska Sand Hills over the prairies and forests

which runs west-east across the heart of Nebraska, abounding in wildflowers, ultra-quaint but totally unselfconscious small towns, and pastoral beauty from horizon to horizon.

South of Thedford, US-83 jumps and descends for another 66 miles or so toward North Platte, with little to occupy your time other than scenic overlooks along the Dismal and South Loup Rivers.

At the south edge of the Sand Hills, 123 miles west of Thedford at the end of Hwy-2, the unique **Carhenge**—the finest Detroit wheels, stacked on top of each other to form a steel Stonehenge—stands just outside the town of **Alliance.**

North Platte

It can take some time getting into **North Platte** (pop. 24,733), but despite the heavy-industrial initial appearance, there is a lot here to enjoy. The northern approach along US-83 crosses over the North Fork of the Platte River, taking a leisurely little swoop up and over it, passing scenic bluffs, then flashing back through a living history of the days when the train was king. Rusty old weed-filled tracks and abandoned shops and warehouses lie off to the side, steel and brick remnants of North Platte's blue-collar trade and transportation heyday. From the south the entrance is less memorable, crossing the I-80 strip with its backlit plastic signs and anonymous franchise architecture.

Originally the site of a Union Pacific construction camp, North Platte nearly expired when the workers decamped for Colorado; however, the town's 300 permanent residents were spared when the railroad chose it as a division point, securing its future. The city is still proud of its **Bailey Yard,** in 1995 deemed by *Guinness World Records* as the largest railroad classification yard in the world, at 2,850 acres. A high-tech visitors center, complete with the eight-story Golden Spike Tower ($7), opened on the south side of the tracks in 2008, giving casual visitors and hard-core rail fans a bird's-eye view of the intricate operations. Drive west on Front Street from downtown and you can't miss it.

Many of the city parks feature railroad displays, including 100-acre **Cody Park** along US-83. Within its confines rests the only Challenger 3900 series steam locomotive on public view.

Before the railroad came through, North Platte was a key stop on both the Oregon

Bailey Yard

Trail, which followed the Platte River west past Scotts Bluff and into Wyoming, and the Pony Express. At the dawn of the automobile age, North Platte played a starring role along the historic Lincoln Highway, the first transcontinental road, which followed the Oregon Trail route west along what is now US-30, US-50, and I-80, eventually ending in San Francisco.

But North Platte is most widely known as the home of Buffalo Bill Cody. The huge **Buffalo Bill Ranch State Historical Park** (308/535-8035, daily summer, $5 per car plus $2 adults), also known as Buffalo Bill Scout's Rest Ranch, is four miles northwest via US-30 and Buffalo Bill Avenue. It includes original dwellings on 23 surviving acres of Buffalo Bill's original 4,000-acre spread. Cody's house and some outbuildings look

much the way they did when Buffalo Bill lived here, from 1879 to 1913. This is where Buffalo Bill originated his rodeo with the "Old Glory Blowout" in 1882 and later housed Buffalo Bill's Wild West Show when not on the road. The whole town of North Platte still whoops it up with the **Buffalo Bill Rodeo** in June.

Besides Buffalo Bill memorabilia, North Platte has an interesting World War II canteen mock-up, preserved intact from the days when North Platte was a whistle-stop for troop trains, and a great Railroad Town, both on display at the **Lincoln County Historical Museum** (2403 N. Buffalo Bill Ave., 308/534-5640 daily summer only, $5 adults), adjacent to the Scout's Rest Ranch.

Downtown North Platte, on the south side of the railroad tracks, has largely been superseded by the surrounding interstate sprawl, but the brick-paved streets here still hold some grand old buildings and a few nifty old neon signs, including one for the landmark **Fox Theater, now called the North Platte Community Playhouse** (E. 5th St. and N. Bailey Ave.). Just north of I-80 is one last great Buffalo Bill stop: the giant **Fort Cody Trading Post** (308/532-8081, free), a massive postcard and

Buffalo Bill Cody

souvenir store with a good selection of books on Western Americana and, best of all, a fabulously detailed miniature working model of Buffalo Bill's Wild West Show, complete with dancing bears, jumping horses, and hundreds of cowboys and Indians.

Because I-80 whips through North Platte, there's no shortage of fast food or places to stay. The I-80 route replaced one of the country's first cross-country roads, the Lincoln Highway, and if you've got some time (and an appetite), take a little trip along the old Lincoln Highway (US-30).

Fifty miles east of North Platte, via I-80 or the old Lincoln Highway, the town of **Cozad** has a big sign proudly proclaiming its place along the 100th meridian, the historic dividing line down the middle of America.

The Great Platte River Road Archway Monument

The north-south US-83 route takes you through the heart of North Platte, but historically the main way through was heading west. First along the Oregon Trail, then along the Pony Express, the Union Pacific Railroad, and today's I-80 highway, the Platte River has long been one of the country's most important transportation throughways. Paying tribute to all stages of the river corridor's long history, **The Great Platte River Road Archway** (308/237-1000 and 877/511-2724, daily, $12 adults) is an expansive interactive museum dedicated to America's freedom of mobility. Exhibits cover everything from Lewis and Clark to the Lincoln Highway; one highlight offers a chance to look for speeders on I-80 with a radar gun. The

$59.7 million museum actually spans I-80, just south of the town of Kearney (pronounced "CAR-knee"), 1.5 hours or so east of North Platte.

Some 22.5 miles southeast of Kearney in Minden is another great monument to America: the **Harold Warp Pioneer Village** (800/445-4447, daily, $14.25 adults), a middle-American version of Henry Ford's Greenfield Village with a much better sense of fun. The 20-acre site preserves dozens of historic structures, along with the proclaimed world's oldest steam-powered merry-go-round; 350 classic cars, trucks, and airplanes; and some 50,000 other items of varying historical interest. Almost everything here dates from 1830 to 1950, illustrating Mr. Warp's sense of history:

South of North Platte on US-83, you'll pass a country road, going east and south, that leads to the **Sioux Lookout,** one of the highest points above the Platte Valley. The 1930s statue that used to stand here has been moved to downtown North Platte's Lincoln County Courthouse.

For thousands of years man lived quite simply. Then like a sleeping giant our world was awakened. In a mere hundred and twenty years of eternal time man progressed from open hearth, grease lamps, and oxcarts to television, supersonic speed, and atomic power. We have endeavored to show you the actual development of this astounding progress as it was unfolded by our forefathers and by ourselves.

McCook

Fifteen miles north of the Kansas border, patches of corn grow in the fertile loam of the undulating Republican River Valley around **McCook** (pop. 7,698), the market center for much of southwest Nebraska. With the arrival of the railroad, the town (which is still served by Amtrak's California Zephyr and numerous freight trains) grew into a farm trade center, and now it is a sedate, content-enough place, with at least two good excuses for a brief stop, both of them on the hill above downtown. The **Museum of the High Plains** (421 Norris Ave., 308/345-3661, Tues.-Sat., free), in a large modern building, includes excellent fossil collections, some World War II prisoner-of-war artwork, information on Senator George Norris (1861-1944), and an old drugstore replicated in the very building where Kool-Aid was developed. Up the street, the **George W. Norris Home** (706 Norris Ave., 308/345-8484, call for hours, $3 adults) is a museum devoted to McCook's favorite son, the progressive Nebraska senator who sponsored legislation forming the Tennessee Valley Authority and promoted rural electrification during the New Deal in the 1930s. Norris, who was first elected to Congress as a Republican in 1902, spoke out strongly against U.S. involvement in World War I and was elected to his final term in 1936 as an independent. In between the two museums, at 602 Norris Avenue, stands Nebraska's only Frank Lloyd Wright-designed house. Finished in 1908, it is a private residence, not open for tours.

> McCook sits at the crossroads of US-83 and US-6, which used to be the longest cross-country highway in the United States, running from the tip of Cape Cod all the way to Long Beach, California.

South of McCook, US-83 turns grandly scenic; it's even marked as such on some maps. Just north of the Nebraska-Kansas state line, the highway crosses Beaver Creek, passing over an old trestle bridge.

KANSAS

Kansas is no mere geographical expression, but a "state of mind," a religion, and a philosophy in one.
—Carl Becker, *Kansas* (1910)

I like Kansas—that is, natural Kansas—better than I had expected to.
—Horace Greeley, *An Overland Journey* (1859)

The clichés have told you wrong: US-83 across much of Kansas—surprise, surprise—is actually a treat, not at all the interminable tedium of grain-field stretches you might expect. Yes, the physiography through most of the intrastate span is still predominantly flat, dry northern high plains, but it's compensated for, particularly in the north, with extensive irrigation that coaxes lusher patches of vegetation out of the dark rich soil.

US-83, much of which has been officially proclaimed the "Western Vistas Historic Byway," ushers you along gaping, horizon-filled stretches broken by isolated lakes and occasional oases such as **Oberlin** and **Oakley**. Continuing south across the

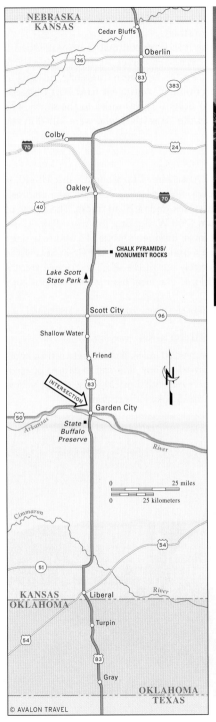

sunflower field in Kansas

windblown plains and limestone hills, US-83 passes through the cow towns of **Scott City** and **Garden City** before crossing the Arkansas River into the baked-clay watercolor that stretches south into Oklahoma and Texas. One final Kansas stop is perhaps the best: **Liberal,** the self-declared home of fictional Dorothy from the celluloid *Wizard of Oz.*

Oberlin

All across northwest Kansas, US-83 sweeps across beautiful rolling farmlands, paralleling railroad tracks and passing through low one-horse towns with towering feed elevators. Funky little **Oberlin,** about 12 miles south of the Nebraska state line, is definitely worth a stop. It's a picture-postcard town, with a Social Realist native limestone statue of a pioneering family marking its northern edge and a mini movie theater called the **Sunflower Cinema** (220 N. Penn Ave., 785/470-2200)—in honor of the

Kansas state flower—playing Hollywood hits amid awning-covered storefronts along the two blocks of redbrick downtown streets.

The peace and quiet of today's Oberlin is in stark contrast to its past: Oberlin was the site of the last Indian raid in Kansas on September 30, 1878, after a fierce skirmish had erupted between Chief Dull Knife's Northern Cheyenne, heading to regain their lands in the Dakotas, and an infantry contingent from Fort Dodge at what is today Lake Scott State Park, near Scott City, 80 miles to the south. The Oberlin cemetery contains a memorial to the 19 settlers who were killed in the Cheyenne attacks.

Oakley

Oakley (pop. 2,045), south and west of I-70 and lined up along historic US-40, is an old big-time ranching and railroad town, featuring lots of utilitarian architecture, massive diesel engines, farm supply stores, and railroad tracks. The big event here, the **Fick Fossil and History Museum** (700 W. 3rd St., 785/671-4839, Mon.-Sat., free), just off US-83, features yet more unique exhibits: 11,000 fossilized shark teeth, a sod house, and some garish mosaics, including the Great Seal of the President of the United States, made entirely out of the aforementioned shark's teeth. It was created by—who else?—Vi Fick. The local history and paleontology exhibits are quite good too.

The I-70 Business Loop (old US-40) offers the usual array of cafés and motels.

Chalk Pyramids/Monument Rocks

South of Oakley, the road bolts straight for over 20 miles, passing between an enormous sea of yellow flowers (in early summer) on one side and expanses of open range on the other. Later, the scenery peters out into a prickly, dry, faintly yellow rocky desolation that signals the fringes of the Smoky Hills region.

Monument Rocks

The prime topographical feature of the Smoky Hills is the surreal **Chalk Pyramids,** also known as **Monument Rocks;** they are referred to in the old WPA *Guide to Kansas* as the "Kansas Pyramids." Whatever you call them, these highly eroded geological formations, which reach heights of 70 feet above the plains, are composed of layers of ancient seabed from the Cretaceous period and were originally formed 80 million years ago. The impressive spires, karst-like formations, and shale cliffs farther on have yielded thousands of excellent fossils of sharks, shark teeth, fish, and reptiles. Although the pyramids are on private land, access is not restricted, but there are no facilities. To get there from Oakley, drive 20 miles south on US-83, then east for 4 miles on Jayhawk Road, around 3 miles south (on Gove 14) and another mile east (on Gove 16). From Scott City, drive 18 miles north, turn east on Dakota Road, and zigzag east and north for around 9 miles. Don't go in wet weather, however, or you'll get stuck in the mud, and you could be there for some time.

West of Oakley, along the I-70 freeway in **Goodland,** Kansas, keep an eye out for an 80-foot easel, which holds the world's largest replica of Van Gogh's painting *Three Sunflowers in a Vase*— in honor of the Sunflower State.

You can get some good maps and directions at the friendly **Keystone Gallery** (620/872-2762), "conveniently located in the middle of nowhere," midway between Oakley and Scott City along US-83; the gallery also has a display of fossils, and you can enjoy a sampling of local art and sculpture as well.

Lake Scott State Park and Scott City

Midway across Kansas, south of the Monument Rocks and west of US-83, **Lake Scott State Park** (620/872-2061, daily Apr.-Sept., $5 per car) is a true spring-fed oasis sheltering cottonwood, ash, hackberry, and willow trees in open high-sky rangeland. Beyond offering a lovely and relaxing spot in which to unwind, Lake Scott includes Kansas's most intriguing historical site, **El Cuartelejo** (The Old Barracks), which was once the home of the only indigenous Puebloan community in Kansas and the farthest north of any in the country.

Originally settled in the 1660s by Taos Pueblo people fleeing the Spanish in New Mexico, the area became home to the Picuris people about 30 years later. Both displaced groups joined with the local Plains Apache clan, but the oasis and the ruined pueblo buildings continued to be used for occasional nomadic squatting by the Pawnee people, and later by Spanish and French explorers and traders, before eventually eroding away. In the late 1880s the site was encountered accidentally by Herbert Steele, who stumbled onto the extensive irrigation ducts leading from spring areas to crop patches. Further excavation eventually revealed the pueblo sites, now considered the first permanent-walled structures in

Traveling US-83 across the Midwest, you'll notice that most of the roadside services are found along the east-west crossroads, especially the major old transcontinental highways like US-6, US-30, or US-40, or today's interstate superslabs. North-south travelers have always been a rare species.

the state. The park has a few other historical points of interest, including a marker by the park's entrance on Hwy-95 at the site of the fateful last battle between the U.S. Cavalry and escaping Cheyenne people led by Chief Dull Knife. The park also has herds of elk and bison, and visitors can see the preserved home of Herbert Steele, full of pioneer furniture and farming implements.

South of Lake Scott State Park, US-83 continues across the high plains, with not a whole lot to disrupt the continuity until Garden City, another 45 miles south. The only town of any size is **Scott City** (pop. 3,816), with its miles and miles of cattle fencing, feedlots, innumerable cattle companies, and patriotic signs dedicated to the All-American City greeting you (or waving good-bye) at the town limits. It's a hardy, industrious place, with everyone busy working.

Garden City stands at the junction of US-83 and coast-to-coast US-50, **The Loneliest Road** in America (see page 717). Full coverage of this route begins on page 670.

Garden City

One of the biggest towns in this part of the Great Plains, **Garden City** (pop. 26,658) is perhaps best known for its huge public **swimming pool:** around 330 feet by 220 feet, with 2.6 million gallons of water. It's south of US-50 at the end of 4th Street, near the Arkansas River in Finnup Park, and it only costs $2. Next to the swimming pool is a small historical museum and the nice **Lee Richardson Zoo** (620/276-1250), with rhinos, elephants, giraffes, and monkeys. The zoo is free for people on foot but costs $10 for a drive-through tour.

At the **Brookover Feed Yards** along US-83 on the northwest side of Garden City, a huge sign standing atop grain elevators reads "Eat Beef Keep Slim." From the comfort of your car you can hear the thousands of cattle burping and mooing up a storm.

North of the zoo in the brick-paved downtown, which, unlike many places, shows few signs of businesses fleeing to the highway frontages, you can window-shop or even buy something at the department stores and antiques shops. Another notable downtown landmark is the **Windsor Hotel,** closed and awaiting refurbishment. After its construction in 1887, this "Waldorf of the Prairies" drew lots of cowpoke-luminaries, including Buffalo Bill Cody.

Garden City supports not only the usual gas stations, motels, and fast food, but also, best of all, the 3,760-acre **Sandsage Bison Range and Wildlife Area,** which may be viewed along the west side of Business US-83, around a half mile south of town.

Farther south, across the often dry-as-a-bone

THE DUST BOWL

Though it may not have been the biggest migration in U.S. history, it was certainly the most traumatic—entire families packing up their few belongings and fleeing the Dust Bowl of the Depression-era Great Plains. Beginning in 1930 and continuing year after year until 1940, a 400-mile-long, 300-mile-wide region roughly bisected by US-83—covering 100 million acres of western Kansas, eastern Colorado, and the panhandles of Oklahoma and Texas—was rendered uninhabitable as ceaseless winds carried away swirling clouds of what had been agricultural land.

The "Dust Bowl," as it was dubbed by Associated Press reporter Robert Geiger in April 1935, was caused by a fatal combination of circumstances. This part of the plains was naturally grassland and had long been considered marginal at best, but the rise in agricultural commodities prices during and after World War I made it profitable to till and plant. Farmers invested in expensive machinery, but when the worldwide economic depression cut crop and livestock prices by as much as 75 percent, many farmers fell deeply into debt. Then, year after year of drought hit the region, and springtime winds carried away the fragile topsoil, lifting hundreds of tons of dust from each square mile and dropping it as far east as New York City.

By the mid-1930s, many of the farmers had been forced to abandon their land, and while some were able to rely on a series of New Deal welfare programs, many more fled for California and the Sunbelt states. In this mass exodus, as recorded by photographers like Dorothea Lange and most memorably in John Steinbeck's 1939 novel *The Grapes of Wrath,* some 100,000 people each year packed up their few possessions and headed west, never to return.

Nowadays, thanks to high-powered pumps that can reach down to the Ogallala Aquifer, much of what was the Dust Bowl is once again fertile farmland, no longer as dependent on the vicissitudes of the weather. Much of the rest of the land was bought up by the U.S. government, and some four million acres are now protected within a series of National Grasslands that maintain the Great Plains in more or less their natural state.

Founded in 1879, **Garden City** was promoted by C. J. "Buffalo" Jones, one of many larger-than-life characters who populated the Wild West. His friend, writer Zane Grey, based the novel *Last of the Plainsmen* on Jones's life. One of Jones's many achievements was the capture and preservation of a small herd of buffalo, the descendants of which populate the bison preserve on the south side of town.

A dozen miles north of Liberal, the majestic **Rock Island Bridge** crosses the Cimarron River. The "Mighty Samson," at 1,269 feet long and 113 feet above the river, is among the largest of its kind.

Arkansas River, oil pumps languidly dip their heads. This is where the stereotypical Kansas landscape comes in: either stark desolation or—thanks to money and modernity—vast irrigation efforts. Prior to the advent of reliable irrigation from the Ogallala Aquifer, overeager farmers almost ruined the region's fortunes plowing up the fragile buffalo grass for a quick cash crop. But the winds then blew the topsoil away, so the hills that stood here prior to the Dust Bowl are gone completely now, and the landscape is endless, see-forever plains, marked by grain elevators and telephone poles.

Liberal

First, the name. It's said that a munificent early settler came and dug a well, and whenever a dusty emigrant would offer money for a drink or the chance to wash his neck, the settler would say, "Water is always free here." One day the reply came, "That is mighty liberal." Rush Limbaugh might not approve of the word choice, but the name stuck, and now the town is stuck with it.

Second, the adjectives: hot, dusty, treeless, flat. The approach into town reveals the drab side of Liberal's oil, gas (the town lies on the eastern edge of an enormous natural gas field), and meatpacking industries.

But the sights do improve, honest. There is one significant draw, the top-notch **Mid-America Air Museum** (2000 W. 2nd St., 620/624-5263, daily, $7 adults), on the site of the old Liberal Army Airfield. It's one of the largest air museums in the United States and has amassed more than 100 different types of aircraft, covering the entire history of flight, including military fighters and bombers from World War II and the Korean and Vietnam Wars.

Otherwise, there's a lot of "Ozmania" in town, since Liberal claims to be the home of Dorothy from *The Wizard of Oz*. Though there's not even the most tenuous connection between Liberal and the film or the book, apart from them all being set in Kansas, every October the annual **OzFest** blowout is held at so-called **Dorothy's House,** also known as the **Coronado Museum** (567 E. Cedar St., 620/624-7624, daily, $7), a block north of US-54. This combination historical museum and re-creation of the movie's Kansas sets displays a mock-up of Dorothy's bedroom from the movie, a mini Yellow Brick Road lined by models of the film's heroes, and a horse bit left behind by the expedition of Francisco

Vázquez de Coronado and his troops, who passed through in 1541 searching for the fabled Seven Cities of Cibola.

The city's most unusual attraction happens annually on Shrove Tuesday (a.k.a. Mardi Gras), when it holds its annual international and soon-to-be-famous **Liberal's International Pancake Day Race,** a competition between local homemakers and their counterparts from Olney, England. No matter how cold or inclement the weather may be, the women of Liberal race a 415-yard S-shaped course, each carrying a frying pan all the way. The Olney event purportedly dates from 1445, when a woman rushed to church with her pan still in her hand; the Liberal race has taken place since 1950.

US-83 and US-54 is known as Pancake Boulevard in Liberal, which may inspire a stop at the popular **Pancake House** (640 E. Pancake Blvd., 620/624-8585). Pancake Boulevard claims the majority of Liberal's places to eat and sleep.

OKLAHOMA

On its beeline to Texas, US-83 doesn't just cross Oklahoma, it forsakes it, merely nipping the panhandle for a 37-mile dash. When crossing the border three miles south of Liberal, among the first things you see are a vape store, a used-car lot, and a bingo hot spot. They're inauspicious sights at best. And

that's not even mentioning the slate-flat, wicked badlands, with temperatures high enough in summer to occlude your vision of the blistering pavement and preclude a drive at top speeds. After a while, you're unable to conjure up synonyms for "endless," though there's plenty of time for it. Even the historical marker you think you eventually see winds up being in Texas.

TEXAS

The old WPA *Guide to Texas* says that "no other route across Texas offers such differences in topography, produce, climate, and people" as does US-83, which is still true today. Starting at the Oklahoma border on the southern edge of the Great Plains, your route winds along the foot of the Caprock Escarpment, then opens out onto the cattle country of Edwards Plateau, where numerous river

canyons provide respite from the mesquite scrubland, and finally ends up some 900 miles later at the Gulf of Mexico. Besides diverse landscapes, US-83 also passes through a virtual survey of Texas history: the prehistoric pictographs of **Paint Rock;** Mexican-American battlegrounds along the **Rio Grande;** and

100-year-old frontier towns built of red brick around their central courthouses. As you'll soon learn if you're perusing other Texas travel literature, this section of the state is, for the most part, ignored. Thus, you're definitely among an elite company, traveling along truly unbeaten paths.

Perryton

Surrounded by wheat fields and ranch lands, agreeable **Perryton** (pop. 8,802) sits seven miles south of the Oklahoma border. The town was formed in 1919 when the Santa Fe Railroad came through; people in nearby towns simply picked up their stuff—buildings included—and shifted them here. Ochilton, eight miles south, off US-83/Hwy-70, was one such town, before some 600 people moved all the infrastructure. If you ignore the industrial oil-industry litter on the outskirts, Perryton is not bad looking, with spacious tree-lined streets. The self-styled "Wheatheart of the Nation," Perryton is also the hometown of Mike Hargrove, 1974 American League Rookie of the Year and later manager of the Cleveland Indians and Seattle Mariners.

Canadian

Exhibiting many of the upsides and downsides of the Texas Panhandle region's boom-and-bust economy, **Canadian** (pop. 2,649) was founded in the 1880s as a railroad town, and later got rich developing oil and gas reserves. After an extended dormancy, Canadian is now hoping to grow again as a center for environmentally sensitive tourism, attracting bird-watchers and history-minded travelers who appreciate the brick-paved streets, 100-year-old buildings, and the delicate, walkable, wooden-decked wagon bridge that spans the Canadian River, two miles north of town.

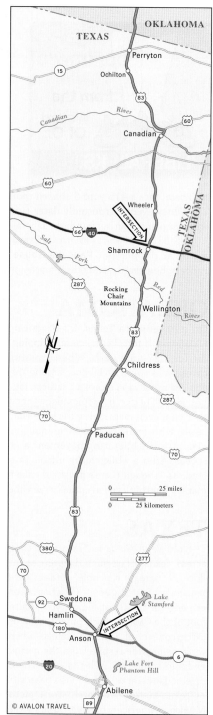

© AVALON TRAVEL

A crossroads town at the junction of US-83 and cross-country US-60, Canadian has dubbed itself "The Oasis of the Texas Panhandle," and its riverside location offers the most trees for miles, as well as opportunities for experiencing some Great Plains hospitality while viewing herds of deer, wild turkeys, and the mating rituals of the odd-looking lesser prairie chicken, a member of the grouse family.

In its 900-mile-plus crossing of Texas, US-83 is also known as the Texas **Vietnam Veterans Memorial Highway.** It forms the longest stretch of U.S. highway through any of the lower 48 states.

A dozen miles northeast of Canadian via paved Hwy-2266, the **Black Kettle National Grassland** maintains one of the few surviving portions of the natural landscape that once covered the Great Plains— where the deer and the antelope once played, and millions of buffalo roamed. Camping and hiking are available at **Lake Marvin** (580/497-2143).

Four miles south of Canadian, along the east side of the suddenly four-lane highway that jointly carries US-60 and US-83, a huge **brontosaurus** stands atop a high bluff. The sculptor, former highway worker Gene Cockrell, named her after his wife, Aud. You may well spot other unique sculptures in and around town.

Shamrock

Once a major oil-pumping and refining center, **Shamrock** is a dusty, rusty old industrial town, off I-40 and a mile south of historic Route 66, which survives as the Business Loop of I-40 through town. Though it's not a particularly lovely place, Shamrock does have at least one real highlight: the lovely old **Tower Station** and **U Drop Inn**, standing together in full art deco glory on the northeast corner of US-83 and Route 66. Following a long-overdue and contentious $1.7-million state-funded restoration, these landmark buildings look great, but instead of selling gas or serving food, they now dispense generous portions of helpful advice, courtesy of the friendly local **visitors center** (806/256-2501).

Playing up the Irish connection, Blarney Stone Plaza in the Route 66 town of Shamrock exhibits a reportedly genuine sliver of the Blarney Stone, encased in a hip-high hunk of green concrete, and there's an annual St. Patrick's Day parade and celebration.

To discover more about Shamrock, visit the old brown-brick Reynolds Hotel, south of Route 66 and east of US-83, where the better-than-you-might-expect **Pioneer West Museum** (204 N. Madden St., 806/256-3941, Mon.-Fri., free) has two dozen rooms full of bygone goodies, including the complete interiors, fixtures, and

fittings of a dentist's office, Wheeler County Military-War Room, and The Old School Room. There's also an exhibit honoring Apollo astronaut Alan Bean, who lived nearby in his youth.

For a bite to eat, it's hard to do better than **Big Vern's Steakhouse** (200 E. 12th St., 806/256-2088), right on old Route 66.

At Shamrock, US-83 crosses the legendary **Route 66** (see page 856). Coverage of the full Chicago-to-LA odyssey begins on page 822.

Wellington

South of Shamrock, US-83 passes over the Salt Fork of the Red River, which definitely deserves its name, running a muddy red throughout the rainy season. West of the highway rise the **Rocking Chair Mountains,** named after a large cattle ranch established west of here in the 1880s by a group of aristocrats, mainly younger sons of noble Scottish families. The only visible sign of their Scotian legacy survives in place-names like Aberdeen, Clarendon, and **Wellington** (pop. 2,189), which is 25 miles south of Shamrock. The center of Wellington is west of the highway, where a nifty 1920s **Ritz Theatre** (902 E. Ave., 806/447-0090, $7) has been brought back to life, but the US-83 frontage holds all the gas stations and cafés.

Childress

A vintage Texas town built around an old Spanish *zócalo* (town square), **Childress** (pop. 6,905) is an important shipping and supply point for surrounding grain and cattle ranches and serves as the market town for area cotton farmers. Located at the junction of US-83 and US-287, Childress was named after George Childress, the principal author of the Texas Declaration of Independence.

The once picturesque downtown still houses the small but engaging **Childress County Heritage Museum** (210 3rd St. NW, Tues.-Sat., free); follow the signs. The downtown is one short step from dry, depressed implosion—the result of every business relocating to the congested annoying fringe highways—but the elaborate 100-year-old facades provide ample opportunities for nostalgic photography and aimless wandering. Depending on your time of arrival, the brick-cobbled streets and empty shells of formerly grand buildings smack more of a ghost town, but there are a few good antiques shops taking advantage of the historic charm.

Virtually every motel in town lines US-287 (Avenue F) east and west of the junction with US-83, but thanks to their highway-side location ("Midway between Amarillo and Wichita Falls"), they all suffer from a lack of quiet and privacy.

The **Goodnight-Loving Trail,** the famed frontier cattle trail, passed through Childress.

Many of the smaller, usually dirt, roads in Texas are labeled "FM," for farm-to-market, or "RM," for ranch-to-market, before their route numbers: e.g., "RM-1208." For simplicity's sake, we have labeled all of them "Hwy-##."

Paducah

South of Childress, US-83 passes through a magnificent landscape of rich red and gold canyon lands covered with vast groves of trees. **Paducah,** 30 or so miles south of Childress at the junction of US-70, is a modest cotton town proudly arrayed around an art deco central courthouse modeled after an Egyptian temple. Brick-paved streets front abandoned stores and the huge old Cottle Hotel, which stands as a dormant reminder of better times, when harvest season or roundup would bring hundreds of transient field hands, cowboys, and card sharps into town. Nowadays Paducah offers little in the way of restaurants other than **Double G** (1112 Easley St., 806/492-3171). You can find a room at two motels west of US-83 along US-70; other options will require more than an hour's drive, so if it's quitting time, check out **The Town House** (1301 Easley, 806/492-3595), the better of the two.

West of Paducah along US-70 spreads the **Matador Ranch,** once one of the largest in Texas, with acres of hunter-friendly pasture and thirsty gullies amid semiarid canyons dotted with cedars and mesquite.

Hamlin and Anson

Deep in the heart of Texas, surrounded by miles and miles of green grass, red earth, mesquite and juniper trees, windmills, pump supplies, and peanut driers, the tidy town of **Hamlin** (pop. 2,124), "Home of the Pied Pipers," is full of charming folks and streets lined by locust trees.

Eighteen miles southeast of Hamlin, at the junction of US-180, sits **Anson,** named in honor of Anson Jones, the last President of the Republic of Texas. Anson was also a stop on the legendary Butterfield Stage U.S. Mail route that ran between St. Louis and San Francisco from 1858 to 1861, but these days it feels more like a stage set for *The Last Picture Show,* with handsome blocks of brick-fronted buildings forming a square around the stately Jones County Courthouse at the center of town. Anson is still a center for the local cotton industry, but its main claim to fame is the **Texas Cowboys' Christmas Ball,** described in an 1890 poem by William Lawrence "Larry" Chittenden and recently revived by country-folk singer Michael Martin Murphey. In 1985 Murphey recorded a hit song also called "The Cowboy Christmas Ball," after which he helped recreate the annual dance here in Anson.

You can see almost all of Anson by driving through on US-83, but if you want to see a scale model of what Anson looked like during its 1900s heyday, or simply want to learn a little something about Texas, stop by the **Anson-Jones Museum** (1300 Ave. K, 325/823-3096, Sun. 2pm-4pm, free), across from the courthouse.

Anson marks the junction of US-83 and US-180, part of the cross-country **Southern Pacific** route (see page 791). Full coverage of this route begins on page 762.

Abilene

At the junction of US-83 and I-20, **Abilene** (pop. 117,063) sits approximately in the geographic center of Texas. Abilene's fundamentalist Christian seminaries and the tame (for Texas) demeanor of its citizens have earned it the much-used nickname, "Buckle of the Bible Belt." Abilene, Texas, originally named after the raucous cowboy town of Abilene, Kansas, grew from nothing once the Texas and Pacific Railway came through in the 1870s. Then, as now, cattle played a predominant economic role, though Abilene's economy has diversified into other classic Texas endeavors, such as a huge U.S. Air Force base and oil refining. Abilene supports big-city amenities, including a symphony, though its indigenous fundamentalism precludes more libertine nocturnal notions; in 1925, the town fathers made it a misdemeanor, in the eyes of the law, to "flirt in a public place."

COWBOYS' CHRISTMAS BALL

All along US-83, but especially in the panhandle area of northern Texas, you pass through town after timeworn town that has clearly seen more prosperous times. Stately courthouse squares, massive old hotels, and blocks of all-but-abandoned storefronts testify to the depopulation of many rural areas in the wake of agricultural mechanization and a myriad of related economic and social changes. Looking at the photogenic remains of these once-bustling towns, it's hard not to imagine what life would have been like here during harvest, roundup, or holiday festivities, when every able-bodied man, woman, and child for miles would come to town to buy supplies, sell their goods, and socialize with friends and neighbors. An excerpt from an entertaining poem written about Anson, Texas, in 1890 by William Lawrence "Larry" Chittenden captures the vitality of these occasions, and gives a strong sense of the creative phraseology that animates cowboy poetry to this day.

Way out in Western Texas, where the Clear Fork's waters flow,
Where the cattle are a-browzin' and the Spanish Ponies grow;
Where the Northers come a-whistlin' from beyond the Neutral Strip;
And the prairie dogs are sneezin,' as though they had the grip;
Where the coyotes come a-howlin' round the ranches after dark,
And the mockin' birds are singin' to the lovely medderlark;
Where the 'possum and the badger and the rattlesnakes abound,
And the monstrous stars are winkin' o'er a wilderness profound;
Where lonesome, tawny prairies melt into airy streams,
While the Double Mountains slumber in heavenly kinds of dreams;
Where the antelope is grazin' and the lonely plovers call,
It was there I attended the Cowboys' Christmas Ball.
The town was Anson City, old Jones' county seat,
Where they raised Polled Angus cattle and waving whiskered wheat;
Where the air is soft and balmy and dry and full of health,
Where the prairies is explodin' with agricultural wealth;
Where they print the Texas Western, that Hall McCann supplies
With news and yarns and stories, of most amazin' size . . .

—Larry Chittenden, *Songs of the Cowboys,* compiled in 1908 by Jack Thorp

Abilene's downtown is not quite gentrified, but obviously galvanized for the attempt. The grand old Hotel Grace has been refurbished as the **Grace Museum** (102 Cypress St., 325/673-4587, Tues.-Sat., $6 adults, free Thurs. evenings), with an art museum, an engaging historical museum, and a children's museum, all air-conditioned and well worth a look. East of downtown, the 16-acre **Abilene Zoo** (daily, $7 adults) houses more than 1,000 animals from 270 different species. You can also get up close to a giraffe and take a ride on the carousel. In between the zoo and downtown Abilene, you'll find **Frontier Texas,** an impressive high-tech historical museum. West of town is the **Dyess Air Force Base** and its "Linear Air

Park," a collection of aircraft from World War II to Desert Storm; it's free, and your parents' tax dollars already paid for it, so you may as well check it out. Dyess AFB is home to the bulk of the Strategic Air Command's potent B-1B bomber fleet. In the 1960s it served as command center for Atlas Missile silos, five of which line the Atlas ICBM Highway (Hwy-604), which loops around the southeast fringes of Abilene.

Abilene Practicalities

Abilene's best place for food is the upscale **Cypress Street Station** (158 Cypress St., 325/676-3463), next to the museums in the heart of downtown. If you'd prefer to search out some local flavor, aim for the classic Texan barbecue of **Joe Allen's** (301 S. 11th St., 325/672-6082), famed for rib-eye steaks cut to order as thick as you want 'em. It's south of downtown in an otherwise unpromising industrial district.

Most of Abilene's lodging options line I-20 or the older US-80 strip along the railroad tracks.

Buffalo Gap

If you're passing through Abilene, don't miss the restored frontier town of **Buffalo Gap** (325/572-3365, daily, $7 adults), 14 miles southwest of town via Hwy-89. It's not completely a tourist trap; cowpokes still reside here, and a courthouse and jail are just 2 of 20-odd buildings dating from the late 1800s, when Buffalo Gap, then the county seat, had over 1,200 residents and Abilene was barely a blip on the map. Other

buildings are done up as Wild West souvenir stands, and there's at least one good restaurant: **Perini Ranch** (3002 Hwy-89, 325/572-3339), for steak and chicken.

Ballinger

Heading south from Abilene, the first real place you come to among the rolling sheepherding hills of the Edwards Plateau is **Ballinger** (pop. 3,767), a lively little town with many of its brick and sandstone buildings dating from its inception in 1886, when the railroad came through. Standing along the banks of the Colorado River, the town now supports itself with agriculture. On the courthouse square are the photogenic **Pompeo Coppini's Charles H. Noyes Statue** and the courthouse itself: a Texas classic, completed in 1889 in opulent, mansard-roofed Second Empire style. Within a block you can get a taste of Ballinger's best enchiladas, either cheese, chicken, or beef at the **Gonzalez Restaurant** (700 Hutchings Ave., 325/365-3781).

Coppini's Charles H. Noyes
statue in Ballinger

Paint Rock Pictographs

Fifteen miles or so south of Ballinger, just west of US-83, the **Paint Rock Pictographs** are the largest concentration of prehistoric drawings in Texas, with well over 1,500 brightly colored images covering a limestone bluff along the north bank of the Concho River. These images, which range in size from a few inches to over five feet tall, are on privately owned ranchland. Many of the paintings were made in the frontier days of the 19th century, when Comanche people lived in the region, but some are believed to date back over 1,000 years, to the time when Kiowa and Apache forebears settled here.

The town of **Paint Rock** is a relic of sorts itself, with photogenic abandoned buildings and a couple of picturesque churches.

Menard

South of Paint Rock, US-83 winds through another 40 miles or so of scrubby hills before reaching the fascinating old wool-products market town of **Menard** (pop. 1,653; pronounced "muh-NARD"), standing in a lush valley along the San Saba River. A trading post and stop on the old cattle trails, Menard was originally founded by Franciscan missionaries in 1757, and many of its early structures survive or have been restored.

It's a picturesque little place, with huge trees, solid old brick storefronts, and a wide bridge over the river. The **Menardville Museum,** housed in the old Santa Fe Railroad Depot, contains a 150-year-old wooden bar from the now-defunct Legal Tender Saloon. A block south of the old main drag, the **Historic Ditch Walk** follows a section of the 10-mile Vaughn Agricultural and Mechanical Canal, a fancy name for an irrigation ditch that has served local farmers since 1876. The canal features an old waterwheel, and the walk passes the 1899 Sacred Heart Catholic Church and a vintage Sinclair filling station before finishing up, appropriately enough, at Menard's summer-only outdoor swimming pool.

Several historic limestone buildings in town date to the turn of the 20th century. The Luckenbach Building (built in 1903) contains the **Burnham Brothers Co.** (325/396-4572), the oldest U.S. retailer of game calls, from simple wooden instruments to state-of-the-art computerized devices that lure turkey, deer, elk, ducks, and other animals.

During Menard's annual **Jim Bowie Days** in late June, visitors and residents gather for arts and crafts shows, live music, and rodeos.

On the main highway there are a couple of moderate motels, like the **Motel 83**

Southwest of Abilene off US-277, about 20 miles beyond Buffalo Gap, Horse Hollow is home to **Horse Hollow Wind Energy Center,** where 421 giant turbines together produce as much as 735 megawatts of ecofriendly, zero-emission electricity. At peak times, the wind farm generates enough power to supply more than 220,600 homes.

South of Ballinger along US-83, keep an eye out for a 100-foot-tall stainless steel cross, set on a hill east of the highway.

(325/396-4549, $45), which is attached to a popular bar, **Shifty's.**

San Sabá Mission

One mile west of Menard, off US-190, a cemetery and foundations of a few buildings are all that's left of **Mission Santa Cruz de San Sabá.** Established in 1757 as Spain's northernmost outpost in the Apache and Comanche lands of what is now Texas, the mission was abandoned in 1768 after repeated Comanche attacks. Now in a county park next to a golf course along Hwy-29, the rebuilt chapel houses a small museum; portions of a later stone fort, named **Real Presidio de San Sabá,** also survive. A simple inscription, "Bouie," on the stone gate is thought to have been carved by Jim Bowie of Alamo fame ("Bouie" was the proper historical inscription of his name). Bowie lived at the presidio ruins while searching for buried Spanish silver during the early 1800s.

Fort McKavett State Historic Site

Farther along US-190, 17 miles west of Menard then another 6 miles south on Hwy-864, **Fort McKavett** (325/396-2358, daily, $4 adults) was called the "prettiest post in Texas" by Civil War General William Sherman. Established in 1852 as the "Camp on the San Saba," Fort McKavett served as a first line of defense against Comanche raids along the Texas frontier and provided protection for travelers along the Upper San Antonio-El Paso Trail. Temporarily abandoned in 1859, the post was reestablished in 1868 after local residents lobbied for Army protection. All four of the Army's African-American units, whose ranks came to be known as **"Buffalo Soldiers"** by the indigenous people, eventually served at McKavett, including the famous 9th and 10th

Cavalries. Twenty-one of the original 40 buildings have been restored, including the officers' quarters, barracks, hospital, school, bakery, and post headquarters. The hospital ward serves as a visitors center and contains interpretive exhibits explaining the natural and military history of the area. A nature trail, passing through pastures of spring wildflowers, leads to a shady dell around the clear waters of Government Springs.

Junction

After passing through the attractively rugged but shallow canyon lands south of Menard, US-83 crosses high-speed I-10 at the aptly named town of **Junction** (pop. 2,574). Once a major crossing where the east-west Chihuahua Trail met a branch of the north-south Chisholm Trail (now I-10 and US-83 respectively), Junction sits at the edge of Texas's famed Hill Country, where the **Edwards Plateau** crumbles into limestone canyons and cliffs along the **Balcones Escarpment.** As in the areas to the immediate north, wool and mohair production are the main means of local livelihood, supplemented by pecan farming (not to mention catering to passing travelers).

From Junction, I-10 heads southeast to San Antonio, passing through the Hill Country town of **Kerrville,** which hosts the popular **Kerrville Folk Festival** (830/257-3600) around Memorial Day.

To continue south along US-83, you can wind along Main Street or follow I-10 southeast for one exit, roughly two miles, to rejoin the old road. Another nice drive is

TEXAS LONG HORN (STEER) WIDTH OF HORNS 8 FT. 8 INCHES.

along US-377, which traces a scenic route along the Llano River southwest of Junction, bisecting typical Edwards Plateau tableaus of limestone arroyos studded with mesquite, oak, prickly pear, and yucca. **South Llano River State Park** (325/446-3994, $5 adults), five miles southwest of Junction off US-377, protects 523 wooded acres and abundant wildlife (white-tailed deer, Rio Grande turkeys, bluebirds, finches, and javelinas) and offers facilities for picnicking, camping, hiking, mountain-biking, canoeing, tubing, and swimming.

Leakey and the Frio Canyon

South of Junction, US-83 continues southward through nearly 62 beautiful miles of rolling ranches and native pecan orchards, entering a verdant spring-filled region that was one of the last strongholds of the Lipan Apache and Comanche people. The rolling hills around **Leakey** (pop. 425; pronounced "LAY-key"; "Home of the 1975 State Football Champions") hold limestone caves, some of which the Confederates mined for bat guano to make saltpeter—an essential ingredient of gunpowder—during the Civil War. At 1,600 feet above sea level, this is one of US-83's prettiest stretches through Texas, as the road follows the clear, cold Frio River through 17 miles of cypress, pecan, live oak, cedar, walnut, wild cherry, piñon, and mountain laurel. Some areas also have big-tooth maples and sycamores, a major tourist attraction in the late fall when the leaves change color. You'll find a dozen or more camps and lodges along this stretch of US-83, including the tin-roofed, wooden-sided **Historic Leakey Inn** (527 S. US-83, 830/232-5246, $79 and up), in the center of Leakey, and the peaceful **River Haven Cabins** (866/232-5400, $85 and up), three miles southeast of town along Hwy-1120.

About 10 miles south of Leakey along US-83, the pretty and popular **Garner State Park** (830/232-6132) offers campgrounds, cabins, hiking trails, kayak rentals, paddle boats, river swimming, and a popular summertime dance terrace on the banks of the Frio River.

The hamlet of **Rio Frio** (pop. 50) boasts the second-largest live oak tree in Texas. The centuries-old tree stands alongside Hwy-1120 on the east side of the Frio River.

Texas Hill Country: Lost Maples and Utopia

While the landscape along US-83 is pleasant, the scenery is much more rugged and beautiful if you detour to the east, into the heart of the Texas Hill Country. East of Leakey via Hwy-337 and then Hwy-187, there's a wonderful drive to **Lost Maples State Natural Area,** where miles of hiking trails take you away from the road into deep canyons carved by the Sabinal River. The "lost maples" of the name refers to a grove of big-leaf maples, which in October provide a taste of New England's famous fall color. The rest of the year, Lost Maples is a real oasis: Texas laurels and wildflowers offer spring blooms, while juniper scent and birdsong fill the air. For the best overview, take the East Trail, a 4.6-mile loop that starts at the maple grove and climbs swiftly over a plateau before dropping down to a pond at the foot of limestone cliffs. The pond is home to snakes and black leeches, so it's not for swimming. **Camping** (800/792-1112, starting at $10) is available, and a couple of nearby ranches offer characterful accommodations, like the **Foxfire Cabins** (830/966-2200, $130 and up, with off-season deals).

South of Lost Maples, 15 miles east of Rio Frio via Hwy-1050, the Sabinal River town of **Utopia** represents a legacy left by frontier circuit preachers who found this

Lost Maples State Natural Area

Lost Maples marks the start of the first official bike route in Texas, the **Utopia 100K,** which follows narrow, winding two-lane roads via Utopia to Garner State Park and back. Another popular cycling road is Hwy-337, which gets especially rugged (and popular with proto-Lance Armstrong cyclists) around Medina, midway to San Antonio.

spot a heavenly place to hold camp meetings and save souls. "A Paradise—Let's Keep it Nice," a sign says. The **Sabinal Canyon Museum** (830/966-2100, Sat. 10am-4pm, Sun. 1pm-4pm) on Main Street displays local arts and crafts, including antique handmade quilts, historic photos, farm implements, arrowheads, spurs, and other artifacts that outline Bandera County history. Across from the museum, Utopia's best place to eat is the **Lost Maples Café** (830/966-2221).

Uvalde

Forty miles south of Leakey, US-83 crosses US-90 (the former San Antonio-El Paso Trail) at **Uvalde** (pop. 15,751), founded in 1855 and still centered on a broad square that originally served as a wagon yard for teamsters and travelers. Uvalde was the home of a Western legend, the late, great celluloid cowgirl Dale Evans. The town's most famous native son, John Nance "Cactus Jack" Garner, served as Franklin Delano Roosevelt's first- and second-term vice president from 1933 to 1941. After retiring from politics, Garner returned to Uvalde and lived here until his death in 1967 at age 98. His home is now owned by the University of Texas and contains the **Briscoe-Garner Museum** (333 N. Park St., 830/278-5018, Tues.-Sat.), a repository of memorabilia from Garner's fascinating political career.

Crystal City

As US-83 continues south from Uvalde, the highway descends farther onto the mostly flat Rio Grande Plain, entering a subtropical zone of seemingly endless chaparral. Amid this scrubby "brush country"—marked by a mixture of thorny cacti, mesquite, dwarf oak, black bush, and huisache—

To get a taste of South Texas culture, tune in to "Tejano y Mas" **KUVA 102.3 FM,** for nonstop Tejano and traditional country-western tunes.

spread large irrigated farms known as the "Winter Garden of Texas" for the bounty of spinach and citrus crops they produce. Nearly 40 miles south of Uvalde sits **Crystal City** (pop. 7,138), the Zavala County seat and self-proclaimed "Spinach Capital of the World," home to a statue of the world's most famous spinach lover, Popeye, in front of the city hall.

Crystal City: "The Spinach Capital of the World"

Laredo

Founded as the first nonmissionary, nonmilitary Spanish settlement in North America in 1755, **Laredo** (pop. 236,091) is surrounded by some of the oldest ranch lands in the United States. With a population that is about 90 percent Hispanic, the city

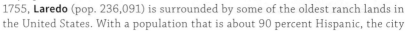

DETOUR: THE ALAMO

One of the great icons of the American Southwest, the Alamo sits at the center of the city of San Antonio. "Remember the Alamo!" was never a question, but a pledge of allegiance that inspired frontier-era Texans to fight and win their independence from Mexico. The significance of the Alamo varies depending upon how you look at it—some see it as the first triumph of Yankee imperialism, others as a sad case of mighty slave-holding Southerners spreading their dominion—but from any angle, the story is quite compelling. The Alamo itself is a small Mexican church, built in 1724 and taken over by a group of Texans and Tejanos, including a band of American mercenaries led by Davy Crockett, in December 1835. Led by Colonel William Travis, the volunteers were besieged and held out several months before they were eventually killed by the Mexican Army. Other Americans then defeated the Mexican Army and established the Republic of Texas, which briefly existed as an independent nation before joining the United States in 1845. The **Alamo Church** (300 Alamo Plaza, 210/225-1391, daily, free), right downtown, still stands much as it has for nearly 300 years and is a pilgrimage spot—one of the most visited sites in the country.

To soak it all up, stay the night at the historic **Menger Hotel** (204 Alamo Plaza, 210/223-4361, $116 and up), across the street. The surrounding city of San Antonio is attractive in its own right, with the lively **River Walk** winding through downtown, and numerous other sights and attractions. **Austin,** the Texas state capital, is just a ways up the road from "San Antone," and between San Antonio and US-83, the **Texas Hill Country** is perhaps the most beautiful part of the Lone Star State.

For more information, contact the **San Antonio visitors bureau** (800/447-3372).

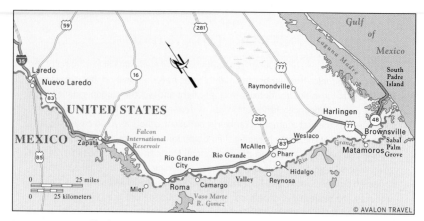

© AVALON TRAVEL

is growing rapidly (more than doubling in the past 20 years) due to its position as the largest international trade center along the U.S.-Mexico border. The I-35 corridor feels as anonymous and fast-paced as anywhere in the United States, but the center of town still holds on to its historic personality.

At the heart of downtown Laredo, a block north of the Rio Grande, is the **San Agustín de Laredo Historic District,** site of the original 1755 Spanish settlement of Villa de San Agustín. Numerous historic buildings surround the plaza, including a small stone building next to La Posada Hotel that served as the capitol of the short-lived Republic of the Rio Grande. It now houses a **museum** (956/727-0977, Tues.-Sat., $2) containing a collection of memorabilia from the separatist movement of 1840.

Built as a high school in 1917, the place to stay to soak up Laredo's substantial if faded character is the plaza's stately **La Posada Hotel** (956/722-1701, $109 and up), which is also home to the Zaragoza Grill and a more expensive Latin American restaurant, the Tack Room.

Eighteen miles north of Laredo, US-83 merges with I-35, then crosses the Rio Grande to meet Mexico 85 (the Pan-American Highway), forming a continuous road between Canada and the Panama Canal, via Mexico and Central America.

Southeast from Laredo: Roma

South of Laredo, US-83 passes through one of the fastest-growing and most Hispanic areas in the United States, following a route parallel to the Rio Grande. The construction from 1950 to 1954 of **Falcon International Reservoir** altered the look and feel of the riverside landscape, but there are still a few places that evoke the past. The surviving 19th-century Spanish- and Creole-style architecture in **Roma,** 40 miles southeast of Zapata, hasn't changed much since it inspired director Elia Kazan to use the town as a film location for the 1952 movie *Viva Zapata!* starring Marlon Brando and Anthony Quinn. Many of the town's buildings have been quietly restored, and the town is *so* quiet you can sometimes hear roosters crowing across the river in the Mexican town of **Ciudad Miguel Alemán,** where the narrow sandstone streets, old churches, and plazas haven't changed in centuries.

Farther south along US-83 comes **Rio Grande City,** where among the historic buildings downtown the **La Borde House** (601 E. Main St., 956/487-5101, $81 and up) is a Creole-style inn designed by Parisian architects in 1893, with construction completed in 1899.

Laredo: "The Gateway to and from Mexico," in 1892

Rio Grande Valley

Southeast of Rio Grande City, the river and US-83 curve eastward toward the Gulf of Mexico through a broad delta region known as the **Rio Grande Valley,** despite the fact there are no nearby mountains to make it a true valley. Compared to the rural stretches US-83 passes through for most of its journey, the Rio Grande Valley is a densely developed, chaotic, and generally poverty-stricken region, with little to recommend it apart from warm winter weather. Citrus orchards line the highway, while lush plantings of bougainvillea and poinsettias drape many of the houses in the string of towns and shantytown colonias that appear every few miles all the way to the gulf. The population of the valley, which sits at approximately the same latitude as the Florida Keys, swells with the arrival each winter of thousands of "winter Texans" fleeing colder climes like Canada and Michigan. This snowbird presence is celebrated by weekly dances, frequent live music jam sessions, and perhaps the nation's highest concentration of RV and mobile home parks.

While US-83 runs as a multilane freeway past one big-box mega-mall after another, the main attractions are to the south and west, along the Rio Grande. The area's unique attraction is **Los Ebanos Ferry** (daily 8am-4pm, $1.25 pedestrians, $4 cars), the last hand-pulled ferry across the Rio Grande. The ferry is about midway between Rio Grande City and McAllen, south and west of Sullivan City. To get there from US-83, drive west on the mazelike El Faro road until you hit the river. The ferry can carry three cars and a small number of pedestrians on each crossing, and you can help pull (if you want to). To be honest, there's not a lot to see or do at either end, but it's a fun ride (passports required!).

Another main draw is the potential for bird-watching: About eight miles southwest of McAllen via Hwy-374 (west) and Hwy-2062 (south), **Bentsen-Rio Grande Valley State Park** (956/584-9156) protects precious acres of Rio Grande riparian ash and elm woodlands. It is home to the World Birding Center, which

On the banks of the Falcon Reservoir, **Zapata, Texas,** has become a popular starting point for long-distance hang-gliders. Many world hang-gliding records have been set from here, with flights traveling over 400 miles.

¡Zapata!

helps bird-watchers find their way around the dozen different wildlife refuges along the lower Rio Grande, where almost 500 different species have been seen and heard.

Harlingen's **Arts and Heritage Museum** (956/216-4901, Tues.-Sun., tours $2), three miles north of town at Boxwood and Raintree near the Harlingen airport, contains exhibits interpreting the history of the valley. At the private Marine Military Academy prep school, next to the airport, the **Iwo Jima Memorial** is the original sculpture (first made of plaster, now protected in fiberglass) from which the famous bronze statue of the flag-raising World War II Marines was made. There's also a small **museum** (956/423-9234, Mon.-Sat., donation) displaying memorabilia from the Battle of Iwo Jima and World War II.

Brownsville

South of Harlingen, US-83 merges with US-77 for the final 26 miles to **Brownsville,** where you may well feel like you've unknowingly crossed the border into Mexico. One of the most historic cities in Texas, Brownsville retains its Spanish and Mexican heritage more than most places, particularly in the architecture of the downtown district around Elizabeth Street, which runs northwest from the 24-hour border crossing at **Matamoros, Mexico.** U.S.-Mexico

Bentsen-Rio Grande Valley State Park

CROSSING THE BORDER

At dozens of sleepy little towns across Southern California, Arizona, New Mexico, and Texas, the temptation to nip across the border and see something of our southern neighbor can be strong. It's only a hop and a skip away, and the crossing is usually simple and hassle-free, but in these days of Homeland Security, it's good to know a few things about international customs—small "c" and big "C"—before you go.

For years, all that a U.S. citizen needed to cross the border for 72 hours or less and be readmitted to the United States afterward was some proof of citizenship. Often, you could get by with just a driver's license, but in this age of increased security, new rules have been implemented, so all travelers returning from Mexico or Canada must have a valid current passport or other documents approved by U.S. Customs and Border Protection to reenter the United States.

If you're thinking of heading south to stock up on Mexican beers or a rug or other handicrafts, be aware that in most cases, merchandise is subject to an $800 duty-free limit, above which U.S. Customs will charge a duty based on fair retail value. Alcohol imports by individuals are limited to a whopping liter every 30 days—less than three cans of beer—and it is illegal to import any knockoff versions of trademarked items (perfumes, watches, even cans of Coke) that are also sold in the United States. So don't risk having to leave something behind at the border—ask before you buy. It's probably a good idea before heading abroad to first go over the U.S. Customs and Border Protection's website (www.cbp.gov).

Because of insurance and other legal concerns, you should definitely leave your car on the United States side of the border and cross into Mexico on foot. Driving is not worth the hassle, especially with the long lines to cross back into the United States.

trade supports the local economy via a Union Pacific rail terminus connected with Mexico's national railway over the Rio Grande; also, a 17-mile deep-sea channel in the river delta links the city with the U.S. Inland Waterway System and the Gulf of Mexico.

Besides the historic downtown, another must-see is **Gladys Porter Zoo** (956/546-2177, daily, $12 adults) at Ringgold and East 6th Streets, with a good show of unexpected and local creatures hailing from around the world.

Sabal Palm Sanctuary

The last remaining grove of the squat endangered sabal palms in the Rio Grande delta (they are the only palm tree native to the continental United States) is protected for future generations in the 527-acre **Sabal Palm Sanctuary** (Thurs.-Tues. 7am-5pm), run by the Gorgas Science Foundation with the National Audubon Society and located about five miles southeast of Brownsville. The palms are nice enough, but the reserve is really for the birds: Bird-lovers flock here to catch a glimpse of the rare green jays, as well as the colorful parakeets and hummingbirds

Rabb Plantation at the Sabal Palm Sanctuary

that make their homes in the dense junglelike growth. Hundreds of species of butterflies are found here as well.

To reach the reserve from Brownsville, take Southmost Boulevard (Hwy-4) east, then turn right (south) on Sabal Palm Grove Road. The small **visitors center** (956/541-8034, Thurs.-Tues., $5 adults) has maps and natural history guides to the sanctuary.

sand dunes on South Padre Island

South Padre Island

Twenty-eight miles or so northeast of Brownsville via Hwy-48 and the Queen Isabella Causeway, the resort town of **South Padre Island** provides a strong contrast to the sleepy historic towns of the Rio Grande Valley.

Multistory hotels and condominiums line white-sand beaches on both the Gulf and Laguna Madre sides of the island. Rooms are easy to come by except during the annual spring break in mid-March, when thousands of college kids from all over Texas and the Midwest fill the hotels and beaches with round-the-clock revelry. Gift shops lining Hwy-100, the main route to "SPI," are fronted by giant sea-shells, giant sharks, and a 40-foot dinosaur. The main daytime activity is sliding down the slippery chutes at the giant **Schlitterbahn Waterpark & Resort** (33261 Hwy-100, 956/761-1160, $51 and up). Drinking is legal on the beaches here—you have been warned. To dive in, try the **Padre Island Brewing Company** (3400 Padre Blvd., 956/761-9585) for great seafood, sports on TV, and microbrews. For spring break mayhem, another popular spot is **Louie's Backyard** (2305 Laguna Blvd., 956/761-6406), a bayside bar "as seen on MTV."

South of McAllen on the Mexican border, the town of **Hidalgo** has proclaimed itself the "Killer Bee Capital of the World" and has a hundred-times-larger-than-life statue of one of these ferocious-looking critters, in front of city hall at the center of town, to prove it.

giant shark on Hwy-100 near South Padre Island

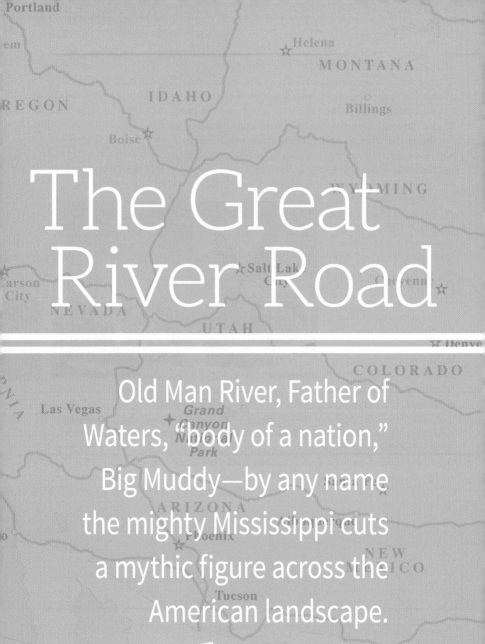

The Great River Road

Old Man River, Father of
Waters, "body of a nation,"
Big Muddy—by any name
the mighty Mississippi cuts
a mythic figure across the
American landscape.

Between Lake Itasca and the Gulf of Mexico

Old Man River, Father of Waters, "body of a nation," Big Muddy: By any name, the mighty **Mississippi River** cuts a mythic figure across the American landscape. Who hasn't read Mark Twain or listened to *Showboat* and not dreamed of a trip down the Mississippi? If you're tired of waiting for somebody to buy you passage aboard the *Delta Queen* or to help you paddle among the 1,500-ton barges, then do what Huck Finn would have done if he'd had a driver's license: Tag alongside the Mississippi on the Great River Road.

Created in 1938 from a network of federal, state, and local roads, the Great River Road—also known as the River Road, and commonly abbreviated to "GRR"—forms a single route along the Mississippi from head to toe. Designed to show off the 10 states bordering the Mississippi from its headwaters to its mouth, the GRR is nothing if not scenic, and anyone who equates the Midwest with the flat Kansas prairie will be pleasantly surprised. Sure, farms line the road, but so do upland meadows, cypress swamps, thick forests, limestone cliffs, and dozens of parks and wildlife refuges.

Of course it isn't all pretty. There's enough industry along the Mississippi for you to navigate the river by the flashing marker lights on smokestacks, and a half-dozen major cities compete with their bigger cousins on the coasts for widest suburban sprawl and ugliest roadside clutter. A pandemic of tacky strip malls has infected the region too, but apart from the astounding growth in casinos (you'll never be more than 100 miles from a slot machine from one end of

stone arch bridge over the Mississippi
in Minneapolis, Minnesota

cypress swamp in Tennessee

the Mississippi to the other), the GRR resists the developers' bulldozers because its meanders were shunned by a century drawn to the straight, fast, and four-lane.

two-lane highway curves along the Mississippi near Brainerd, Minnesota

A full 50 percent longer than the comparable route along the interstates, the GRR changes direction often, crosses the river whenever it can, dallies in towns every other road has forgotten, and altogether offers a perfect analog to floating downstream. If the road itself isn't your destination, *don't* take it. For those who do travel it, the GRR spares you the fleets of hurtling 40-ton trucks and that interstate parade of franchised familiarity, and rewards you with twice the local color, flavor, and wildlife (two- and four-legged) found along any alternative route. Lest these tangibles be taken too much for granted, every so often the GRR will skip over to a freeway for a stretch to help you sort your preferences. Savor, and enjoy.

MINNESOTA

The Great River Road begins in **Lake Itasca State Park** and stair-steps along occasionally unpaved but well-graded backcountry roads through a mix of northern boreal forest, tree farms, and hayfields, all the while staying as close to its namesake as possible. By **Grand Rapids,** only 130 road miles from its source, the Mississippi has been transformed from a grassy brook barely deep enough to canoe to an industry-sustaining river fed by a half dozen of the state's 10,000 lakes. Farther south, the red and white pines, paper birch, and big-tooth aspen give way to more farms while the route breaks from the surveyor's section lines to curve with the river across the glacially flattened state. By St. Cloud, the GRR enters an increasingly developed corridor that culminates in the hugely sprawling Twin Cities of **St. Paul** and **Minneapolis,** south of which the road slips into rural Wisconsin.

If the rivers were being named today, the Mississippi River would flow into the Missouri River and not vice versa, since the Missouri is by far the longer of the two.

Lake Itasca State Park

The GRR begins here among the cattails and tall pines, in the park that protects the headwaters of the mighty **Mississippi River.** The small, clear brook tumbling out of the north end of **Lake Itasca** will eventually carry runoff from nearly two-thirds of the United States and enough silt to make the muddy plume at the river's mouth visible from space. But at its headwaters, 2,550-odd meandering miles from the Gulf of Mexico, you can wade across the Mississippi, and the water is still so clean and clear you can see the bottom.

The Mississippi's humble beginnings were the object of chest-thumping adventurers and the subject of not-so-scholarly debate for decades before explorer Henry Rowe Schoolcraft, led by an Ojibwa warrior named Ozaawindib, determined this lake to be the true source of the nation's most legendary river in 1832. Schoolcraft's story, the tale of the battle to protect the park against logging, and lots of other Mississippi facts are found at the **Visitor Center** (218/699-7251, year-round, $5 per car) just inside the park's north entrance. Skeptics will also find out why professional geographers don't consider the two smaller lakes and the five creeks that feed Itasca competition for the headwaters title.

Throughout the upper Midwest, Friday night is the traditional night for a fish fry. Look for the backlit signboards or hand-lettered banners stuck out in front of the local VFW post or social club for a sample of the truly local variety.

The fact that the lakeshore has been "improved" from its naturally marshy state, the surrounding old-growth pine forest—the most extensive stand of virgin timber left in the state—and outdoorsy amenities such as paved bike trails, boat launches, and a café near the "official headwaters," all contribute to Itasca's popularity. **Bike and boat rentals** (218/266-2150) are available spring through fall.

Accommodations include the rustic **Douglas Lodge** (866/857-2757, rooms $85-145), as well as a number of other lodges and cabins at varying prices. Just steps from the bike path and beach you'll find the immaculate, friendly, and bargain-priced **HI Mississippi Headwaters Hostel** (218/266-3415, starting at $26 per person, plus $28 membership), which has dorms as well as private rooms for four, five, and six people.

NAVIGATING THE GREAT RIVER ROAD

The Great River Road is identified on signs by a green pilot's wheel with a steamboat pictured in the middle. The quality and quantity of route markers varies considerably from state to state; some states, like Minnesota and Illinois, are well marked, with advance warning of junctions and confirmation after turns, while other states, like Louisiana and Mississippi, seem committed to hiding GRR signs miles from where they would serve any conceivable good. Adding to the confusion are the many variations—signposted as "Alternate" or "State Route"—and spurs, denoted by a brown pilot's wheel, which lead off the GRR to various points of interest.

Though most people will be able to find their way along the riverside without too many dead-ends, trying to travel the length of the GRR just by following the signs is not recommended for perfectionists; part of the fun is getting slightly lost and making your own way. To ease your journey, get a detailed map of the entire GRR, along with a guide to local happenings in each of the states along the route, from the **Mississippi River Parkway Commission.** Its helpful ad-free website is www.experiencemississippiriver.com.

When not fishing or foraging for your meals, consider the Douglas Lodge Restaurant, where the menu includes regional blueberries, wild rice, and walleye pike.

No matter when or how long you visit Lake Itasca, or anywhere in Minnesota, really, be sure to pack plenty of potent repellent for ticks and mosquitoes.

Bemidji

Less than a century ago, the northern forests of Minnesota were chock-full of lumber boom camps, with hundreds of mills and lumber works whining night and day, and dozens of saloons, brothels, and boardinghouses catering to the rough-and-tumble logging trade. The ravenous cutting wiped out the stands—virtually nothing remains of Minnesota's primeval pine forests—and the camps disappeared as quickly as they sprang up, but the woods have repeatedly grown back, to be harvested on a more sustainable basis while still providing an eye-pleasing backdrop to the region's literally thousands of lakes.

If you're practicing your Lake Wobegon language skills, be sure to say "You bet" in place of "You're welcome."

For NPR news and other arts and cultural programming, tune in to **KAXE 91.7 FM** in Grand Rapids.

From its boomtown roots, **Bemidji** (pop. 13,431) has long since settled down into a picturesque community—i.e., looking just as it did when Hubert Humphrey first ran for Congress. Its compact and charismatic business district lines the south shore of lovely Lake Bemidji. With large mills still busily turning trees into wood products, Bemidji

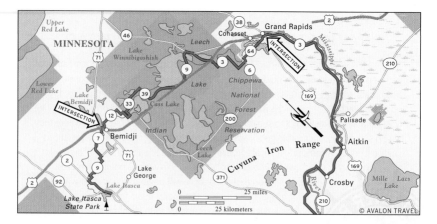

is a typically industrious lumber town, remarkable mainly for having assisted in the birth of that well-loved legendary duo of logging lore, Paul Bunyan and his blue ox, Babe.

The main course of the GRR wraps around downtown Bemidji, so be sure to follow old US-2 onto Hwy-197, which passes up and over both the Mississippi River and Lake Bemidji while winding to downtown and a park where the town's big tourist draws, leviathan statues of **Paul Bunyan** and **Babe the Blue Ox,** have stood along the lakefront since their construction in 1937. Next to that big Paul and Babe on the lakeshore, the **Bemidji Tourist Information Center** (218/444-3541 or 800/458-2223) boasts a fireplace made with 900 stones collected from national parks, the majority of Canadian provinces, every U.S. state (apart from Alaska and Hawaii, which weren't states when the fireplace was constructed), and all 87 Minnesota counties. The Center has displays with odd historical items—including Paul Bunyan's ax and his oversize underwear.

Along with Paul and Babe, Bemidji offers endless opportunities for water-skiing, canoeing, fishing, ice-fishing, and autumnal leaf-peeping; it's also the "Curling Capital of the USA." Downtown, the inviting **Brigid's Irish Pub** (317 NW Beltrami Ave., 218/444-0567) serves good food and great beer, two blocks from the lakefront. A good fast-food option is **Dave's Pizza** (218/751-3225) at 15th Street and Irvine Avenue, on the north side of town.

Bemidji's many motels include the family-oriented **Hampton Inn & Suites** (1019 Paul Bunyan Dr. S., 218/751-3600 or 855/271-3617, $106 and up), situated on the lake, with its own beach and pool.

Walleye pike is a mild whitefish sought by Midwest anglers from May through the cold of February. The walleye found in Minnesota restaurants all come from **Red Lake,** site of the only commercial walleye fishing allowed by law.

Between Bemidji and Grand Rapids, the Great River Road follows a slower but more scenic parallel to transcontinental US-2 (see page 510). Full coverage of his **Great Northern** route begins on page 470.

THE LEGENDS OF PAUL BUNYAN

Like most other myths born on the American frontier, the legend of Paul Bunyan is obscured in the mists of time. Tall tales describe his life: When he was born, it took five storks to deliver him, and it took a whole herd of cows to keep him fed; at just a week old he was big enough to wear his father's clothes; he once bent a crowbar and used it as a safety pin to hold his pants together; he was able to fell trees an acre at a time; and he used to whistle through a hollowed-out log. The stories are impossible to trace, though their widespread popularity is due primarily to a public relations man at the Red River Lumber Company, William Laughead.

Beginning in 1914, and continuing for the next 20 years, Laughead and the lumber company, which was owned by the Walker family, founders of the Walker Art Center in Minneapolis, published a series of illustrated booklets recounting the stories already in general circulation around the logging camps. The booklets bore the full title *The Marvelous Exploits of Paul Bunyan as Told in the Camps of the White Pine Lumberman for Generations, During Which Time the Loggers Have Pioneered the Way through the North Woods from Maine to California, Collected from Various Sources and Embellished for Publication.*

The first large statues of Paul and Babe were built in 1937 in Bemidji, where they now stand along the lake. Statues of Paul and Babe were later built in nearby Brainerd, Minnesota, and others can be found in logging towns from coast to coast, like Klamath, California, and Bangor, Maine.

Bemidji to Grand Rapids: The Big Fish

Leaving downtown Bemidji along the edge of the lake, the GRR makes a series of backcountry loops past tree farms and at least 6 of the state's 10,000 lakes, crossing US-2 twice before snaking into Grand Rapids 100 miles later. The road hugs red pine- and aspen-wooded shores and crosses the ever-widening Mississippi eight times, while numerous signs point to unseen resorts, which in Minnesota don't offer luxury so much as proximity to good fishing. Fishing is serious business hereabouts, as is evident from the frequency of signs advertising "Leeches—Minnows—Nightcrawlers."

If you're just passing through, one place to set aside some time for is about halfway along, in the hamlet of **Bena.** Right along US-2, a 65-foot-long muskie, with a 14-foot-wide mouth, welcomes customers to the popular **Big Fish Supper Club** (218/665-2299, Tues.-Sun.). As seen in that classic Chevy Chase road-trip movie *National Lampoon's Vacation,* the friendly café is open for dinner and drinks year-round.

Big Fish Supper Club

Grand Rapids

Navigational headwaters of the Mississippi River, **Grand Rapids** (pop. 10,869) is a small Frank Capra-esque kind of place, known for its 4 large in-town lakes (there are over 1,000 in this part of the state) and a great bridge over the river. The town—which is proud of its recent rating as the 49th Best Small Town in America—can be a bit confusing in its layout, but its compact size makes sightseeing manageable.

The city sits along the western edge of the famed Mesabi Iron Range and includes viewing sites at a handful of open-pit mines. The iron mines are a thing of the past, but Grand Rapids is still a major lumber town. The impossible-to-miss **UPM Blandin Paper Mill** (218/327-6682, Wed.-Fri. 10am-3pm, free, tours during summer only) stands along the river and US-169. One of the world's largest paper producers, Blandin owns most of the surrounding forests and turns the trees into the stock onto which magazines are printed.

Three miles southwest of Grand Rapids, well signed along the Great River Road and equidistant via US-169 or US-2, the fine **Forest History Center** (218/327-4482, Tues.-Sat. summer, daily fall-spring, $10) is a living-history replica of a 20th-century logging camp, complete with nature trails through the surrounding woods and energetic lumberjacks rolling logs and telling tall tales.

Grand Rapids is very proud of its most famous daughter, Judy Garland, and whoops it up every June with a festival in her honor.

Grand Rapids's real draw is the self-proclaimed "World's Largest Collection of Judy Garland Memorabilia," she of ruby-slipper fame having been born Frances Ethel Gumm in Grand Rapids on June 10, 1922. Truly a cradle-to-grave biographical assembly, the collection displays everything from her first crib to photos of her early performances as part of the Gumm Sisters, a family vaudeville group, to a final shot of her tomb in Hartsdale, New York. There are posters from most of her movies and a copy of her costume from *The Wizard of Oz* (although the ruby slippers were stolen some years ago). All of these artifacts are on display, alongside the house where she was born, at the **Judy Garland Museum** (2727 S. US-169/S. Pokegama Ave., 218/327-9276, $9).

Aitkin

South of Grand Rapids, the land rivals Kansas for flatness, yet the mix of farms and forest continues to lend visual interest to what could otherwise be achingly monotonous. The GRR alleviates boredom with its sinuous irregularity, the curves always hinting at the proximity of the Mississippi. For most of the way the river itself remains hidden, although regular signs for boat landings confirm its presence, and on occasion its broad channel and tree-lined banks roll into view.

For nearly 70 miles south of Grand Rapids you will have this rural road to yourself; then at the single stoplight in **Aitkin** (pop. 2,165), the GRR joins busy Hwy-210, at the edge of the mid-state lakes region. Aitkin is best known as the site of the annual **Fish House Parade,** in which ice fishers show off their one-of-a-kind refuges from the winter cold; this unique event is held every year on the Friday following Thanksgiving.

Crosby

Watch your compass needle for signs of deflection as you proceed to the small but tidy town of **Crosby,** the center of Minnesota's "forgotten" iron range, the Cuyuna. The flood-prone mines have died out, but the surrounding landscape still bears evidence of mining's heyday, with lakes and hills created by subsidence and strip mining, and also by contemporary gravel quarrying. Crosby itself has a nice park fronting onto **Serpent Lake,** complete with a brightly colored 20-foot-high, 25-foot-long sea serpent, while **Croft Mine Historical Park** (218/546-5926, Sat.-Sun. summer, free), well signposted on the edge of Cuyuna Country State Recreation Area, profiles the iron-mining industry, covering immigration and labor issues as well as the actual mining process. Period buildings and a simulated underground self-guided tour round out the site's features.

South of Crosby, the GRR leaves the truck traffic and takes to the cornfields and sumac-laced forests again, passing as many barns as houses, the occasional lakeside hideaway, and some rural town halls. For a thumbnail overview of the area's settlement history, keep an eye peeled for the historical markers along the way.

Brainerd

At roughly the geographical center of the state, **Brainerd** (pop. 13,592) is a medium-size Minnesota town that played a starring role in that offbeat Coen brothers movie *Fargo.*

The economy of this part of the state benefits greatly from recreation. In Minnesota this means lakes: over 400 within a 50-mile radius, with over 150 resorts or campgrounds on their shores. Brainerd, the commercial center of it all, began life in 1870 when the Northern Pacific Railroad chose to cross the Mississippi River here. The rail yards are still in the heart of town beneath the giant water tower, which resembles a Las Vegas-style medieval castle. The historic downtown has been badly "malled" by outlying shopping plazas. But among the discount merchandisers, pawn shops, and empty storefronts, there are still a few points of light, such as **The Barn** (711 Washington St., 218/829-9297), serving all you could want, including breakfasts, burgers, Maid-Rite-style sloppy joes, fries, and fresh fruit pies.

Cass Lake was home to Ka-Be-Nah-Gwey-Wence, whose Anglicized name was John Smith, an Ojibwa man who lived to be somewhere between 129 and 137 years old. It is said he never slept in a bed.

Between Grand Rapids and Brainerd, the official GRR takes a slow and somewhat scenic route along country lanes, though you'll save many hours (and not miss that much) by taking US-169 and Hwy-210.

Twin Cities: Minneapolis and St. Paul

Walker Art Center

The Twin Cities share the Mississippi River but have little else in common. In general, Minneapolis has fashion, culture, and reflective glass, while St. Paul has a greater small-town feel, more enjoyable baseball, and the state capitol. Together, the Twin Cities are a typically sprawling American metropolis with an atypically wholesome reputation: safe, liberal-minded, welcoming to strangers, and inclined to go to bed early. Don't fret; there's enough to keep the visitor fully entertained.

The best place to stop and get a feel for the Twin Cities is at the **Minneapolis Sculpture Garden** (daily 6am-midnight, free), on Lyndale Avenue along I-94. This is one of the city's finer urban oases, with 60 works of art ranging from Henry Moore to Claes Oldenburg's pop art *Spoonbridge and Cherry.* Running over the I-94 freeway, a sculptural footbridge adorned with words from a John Ashbery poem connects the sculpture garden to **Loring Park** and the pedestrian greenway (an in-line skater's heaven) to downtown. Next to the garden is the **Walker Art Center** (612/375-7600, Tues.-Sun., $14), rightfully renowned as one of the nation's finest contemporary art museums and an architectural marvel.

Another advantage of visiting the Twin Cities: Baseball fans have two choices, and both are a blast. The major league **Minnesota Twins** play outdoors at **Target Field,** in the lively Warehouse District on 3rd Avenue, between 5th and 7th Streets. The unaffiliated, independent, and generally anarchic **St. Paul Saints** play at **CHS**

Loring Park

Field (360 Broadway, 651/644-6659) in the reviving neighborhood of Lowertown, near historic Union Station.

PRACTICALITIES

The Twin Cities are on opposite sides of the Mississippi River, at the crossing of the I-35 and I-94 freeways. (It was a bridge along the I-35W freeway that collapsed in August 2007, killing 13 people; in typically cooperative Minnesota fashion, the replacement bridge was finished in just over a year.) Located seven miles south, the Minneapolis-St. Paul International Airport (MSP) is served by 14 airlines, with Delta exercising the home-field advantage. Drivers here, in keeping with Minnesota's reputation, are friendly and helpful, and the city grids are easy enough to navigate by car, although on-street parking becomes more scarce as you approach the downtown areas. There are many parking garages (called "ramps"), and rates vary considerably.

Eating is perhaps the area where the Twin Cities show off their multicultural vitality to best advantage. There are large Central American, Caribbean, Somali, Kurd, and Hmong populations here, and the traditional dominance of meaty northern and eastern European cuisine is being challenged by a bumper crop of new and different places to eat all over town. For a sample, head to **Chino Latino** (2916 S. Hennepin Ave., 612/824-7878), where the Sushi Loco selections capture all the complexity and contradiction underlying the Twin Cities' calm surface.

For a taste of old-style Minnesota, **Kramarczuk's** (215 E. Hennepin Ave., 612/379-3018) has fat wursts and borscht, as well as *varenyky, goulash,* and *holubets* (a.k.a. dumplings, stew, and cabbage rolls), all served up à la carte beneath coffered tin ceilings and the gaze of a giant painted Miss Liberty holding aloft her lamp.

Without doubt, the best road-food place is the decidedly ungentrified 24-hour **Mickey's Dining Car** (36 W. 7th St., 651/222-5633), right in downtown St. Paul. Haute cuisine it ain't, but this 1937 O'Mahony is a fine example of what has become an endangered species since the proliferation of golden arches, its stainless steel sparking with character compared with the anonymous corporate office tower next door.

If you're traveling on an expense account, **The Saint Paul Hotel** (350 Market St., 651/292-9292 or 800/292-9292, $169 and up), across from the beautiful Ordway Music Theatre, is a 1910 gem built for the city's rail and mill tycoons and has a rooftop gym. For a unique stay, try the **Covington Inn** (651/292-1411, $140-265), a towboat B&B moored on the Mississippi opposite downtown St. Paul. Otherwise, look to the interstate beltways for the national chains, particularly I-494 between the airport and Bloomington's 78-acre **Mall of America,** the nation's largest.

The **Minneapolis Visitor Information on Nicollet** (505 Nicollet Mall, Suite 100, 612/397-9275) can provide complete information on hotels, restaurants, and attractions.

East of downtown Brainerd, there is a 26-foot statue of a sitting Paul Bunyan at **Paul Bunyan Land** (17553 Hwy-18, 218/764-2524, daily summer), part of the 23-acre kid-friendly rural-history theme park. The 4th of July in Brainerd is a big event, with marching bands, rock bands, and parades.

Many chain motels are clustered along the GRR (Hwy-371).

Crow Wing State Park

South of Brainerd, the GRR speeds along Hwy-371, which yearns to be an interstate for the 30-odd straight miles it takes to reach Little Falls. Exceedingly flat and awash in a sea of corn, the region gives no hint of the Mississippi River except at **Crow Wing State Park** (218/825-3075, $5 per car). Indigenous people, missionaries, fur trappers, and lumberjacks made Crow Wing a thriving settlement until the 1870s, when the forced removal of the Native Americans and the shift of trade to the rail crossing at Brainerd turned Crow Wing into a ghost town. These days only a cemetery and a single surviving home remain around the old town's site, while trails, a picnic area, and campsites spread out beside the confluence of the Mississippi and Crow Wing Rivers.

Little Falls

At **Little Falls** the GRR neatly misses the fast-food and gas claptrap that has sprung up along the busy Hwy-371 bypass, proceeding instead through the heart of town, which would probably still be recognizable to aviator Charles Lindbergh, who spent his boyhood summers here a century ago. Running along the west bank of the river, the GRR passes by the **Charles A. Lindbergh Historic Site** (1620 Lindbergh Dr. S., 320/616-5421, Thurs.-Sun. summer, $8). The

Charles A. Lindbergh

South of **Little Falls**, the GRR continues on its meandering way. You can switch over to the uglier but much faster US-10 or I-94 freeways for the ride into the Twin Cities without missing anything significant.

house, which sits a mile south of town on a beautiful stretch of the Mississippi, bears the unusual distinction of having been restored with the meticulous guidance of "Lucky Lindy" himself. Lindbergh wanted the site to honor his father, a five-term U.S. congressman, as well as himself, and so it does. Exhibits also illustrate the junior Lindbergh's life and achievements after his historic solo flight across the Atlantic in 1927. There is little mention of Lindy's public admiration for Adolf Hitler, but the museum does display Lindy's 1959 VW Beetle, which he drove more than 170,000 miles on four continents.

Driving the Twin Cities

South of Little Falls, agriculture continues to dominate the landscape, but as our route approaches the junction with I-94 at St. Cloud, the loss of farms foreshadows what is to come downriver. For nearly 100 miles, the GRR does its best to offer a scenic alternative, but sprouting subdivisions and suburban mini-malls make it hard to enjoy. I-94 parallels the GRR and the Mississippi River all the way through the heart of the Twin Cities, and for better or worse it's pretty much the closest you'll get to a riverside highway. If you were hoping to follow the river through this stretch (by car, at least), you're out of luck.

WISCONSIN

Heading out of St. Paul along the industrialized Mississippi riverbanks, the GRR crosses the St. Croix River at Prescott, Wisconsin, and winds south on Hwy-35 across a portion of the glacial plain whose rolling hills, sown in corn, account for an important part of the nation's breadbasket. The fertile soil here, as throughout the Midwestern grain belt, is a product of drift: pulverized soil left by mile-thick ice sheets scouring the ancient sediments of an inland sea for about two million years. Farther south, however, the GRR enters a different landscape, known as the **Driftless Region,** an area of limestone bluffs and rocky uplands bypassed by all that rototilling glaciation. Stretching south into Illinois, and covering an area four times the size of Connecticut, the Driftless Region affords dramatic views, wildlife habitat, and a setting for one of the more painful episodes in Native American history, the devastating Black Hawk War.

Across the Mississippi from Monticello, 2.5 miles downstream from Elk River off US-10, the **Oliver Kelley Farm** living history center preserves the frontier farmhouse where the Patrons of Husbandry, an agricultural education and lobbying organization better known as The Grange, was founded in 1867.

The Burma-Vita Company, based just west of Minneapolis, began erecting advertising signs along Hwy-61 near Red Wing and Hwy-65 near Albert Lea back in 1925. Over the next 38 years, these signs and their witty rhymes appeared in nearly every state and made Burma-Shave one of the most recognized brand names in American business.

The GRR follows two-lane Hwy-35 from Prescott south for nearly 100 miles, staying within closer view of the Mississippi for longer stretches than almost anywhere else on the route.

Hwy-35: Main Street USA

At **Maiden Rock,** about 50 miles southeast of St. Paul, Hwy-35 enters the heart of the Driftless Region, picking its way between steep bluffs and the wide Mississippi. Small towns, populations numbering only in the hundreds, cling to the margin, competing for the distinction of having the longest **Main Street** in the

On the Minnesota side of the Mississippi River, US-61 runs as a fast and fairly scenic freeway, four lanes wide with near-continuous river views almost all the way south to La Crosse, Wisconsin. One place along here worth a linger is the town of **Wabasha,** as seen in the Walter Matthau-Jack Lemmon film *Grumpy Old Men*. Another is **Lake City,** where signs proclaim it the "Birthplace of Water Skiing."

On an island near Red Wing, Minnesota, the **Prairie Island Nuclear Power Plant** is the northernmost of a half dozen uranium-powered generating stations located along the Mississippi.

nation, if not the world; for some of these long hamlets the GRR is nearly the *only* street. These towns wear their age well, too busy with fishing or loading up barges to make themselves pretty for tourists, or to tear down every old building that no longer seems useful. Most of these towns have at least a gas station, open late, and a roadhouse with Old Style or Pabst neon in the windows, open even later. Along with the riverside scenery, most also have a single tourist attraction: Amish crafts in **Stockholm,** a cheese factory in **Nelson**—and **Alma** has an observation platform and a small café overlooking Lock and Dam No. 4, where you can watch river traffic "lock through." In **Pepin,** midway between Maiden Rock and Alma (and roughly midway between Minneapolis and La Crosse), there's a replica of the log cabin where Laura Ingalls Wilder was born in 1867. Her first book, *Little House in the Big Woods,* was set here, though it's hard now to imagine that this was still the wild northwestern frontier back then.

Trempealeau

At the sleepy hamlet of **Trempealeau** (pop. 1,435), the GRR would have you zigzag right through town, but detour a block down toward the river's edge to find the **Historic Trempealeau Hotel, Restaurant & Saloon** (608/534-6898, $46-140), sole survivor of an 1888 downtown fire—maybe that's why the whole joint is smoke-free. The hotel dining room offers a surprisingly eclectic menu, from steak and seafood to burgers and vegetarian dishes; just head for the neon sign reading "Delicious Food." The rooms are nice (and cheap). The hotel also hosts an excellent concert lineup throughout the summer featuring bands you've heard of (Steppenwolf and Asleep at the Wheel have appeared more than a few times) as well as the **Reggae Fest** the second weekend of May. There are more than 100 miles of paved bikeways and rail-trails that pass from town to nearby Perrot State Park, which has lodging to rent or even canoes and kayaks for hardy souls desiring to relax along the five-mile **Long Lake Canoe Trail.**

La Crosse

La Crosse (pop. 51,320) was named by fur traders who witnessed local Winnebago people playing the game. It's an attractive place, but you wouldn't know that coming into town from the north; thanks to the town's location astride the I-90 freeway, miles of food-gas-lodging establishments compete for attention. Successfully run the gauntlet and your reward will be finding the century-old downtown, the tidy residential neighborhoods, and the leafy University of Wisconsin-La Crosse campus. Slap *Spartacus* on the theater marquee and the whole place could easily be mistaken for a giant Eisenhower-era time capsule.

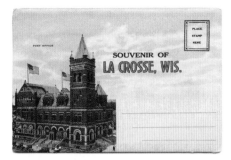

The biggest sight to see in La Crosse is the **World's Largest Six-Pack** (1111 S. 3rd St.), right on the GRR on the south side of downtown. La Crosse-based Heileman was widely recognized around the upper Midwest for its Old Style brand beer, and its brewery was famous for its giant fermentation tanks painted to look like the world's largest six-pack. Alas, about 10 years ago Heileman's brewery was bought out by a multinational company, which immediately whitewashed over what had long been a cherished local landmark. Then a local company, City Brewing, took over operations and brought back the big Six-Pack, which, when full, holds enough beer to fill more than seven *million* real-life cans.

Between Minneapolis and La Crosse, Winona State University's **KQAL 89.5 FM** plays an excellent range of commercial-free pop, punk, and talk radio.

World's Largest Six-Pack

The best overview of La Crosse is two miles east of downtown at the end of Main Street: **Grandad Bluff,** a lofty 600 feet over the city, gives a grand view of the Mississippi and the two states along its opposite shore. In leafy **Riverside Park,** a 20-ton, 25-foot-tall statue of **Hiawatha** greets river traffic with his arms crossed.

La Crosse Practicalities

La Crosse food tends toward the hearty and all-American. For good ol' drive-in burgers, chili dogs, root beers, and milk shakes, nothing beats **Rudy's** (608/782-2200, daily 10am-10pm), northeast of downtown at 10th and La Crosse Streets, where roller-skating carhops feed you, weather permitting. Rudy's sponsors classic car "Cruise Nite" every Tuesday June-September.

The **Pearl Ice Cream Parlor** (207 Pearl St., 608/782-6655), a polished-to-perfection confectionery, offers such indulgences as fluorescent Blue Moon ice cream, while Frank Sinatra croons in the background. More grown-up pleasures, in the shape of nearly 400 bottled beers (plus a dozen microbrews on draft), Wi-Fi, and popcorn await you at the awesome **Bodega Brew Pub** (122 S. 4th St., 608/782-0677), two blocks away. Travelers seeking something wholesome, fresh, and filling should head to the deli of the **People's Food Co-op** (315 S. 5th Ave., 608/784-5798), between Cass and King Streets.

Six miles east of La Crosse, **West Salem** was the boyhood home of Pulitzer Prize-winning novelist Hamlin Garland, whose bittersweet stories of 1860s Wisconsin farm life have earned him a reputation as one of the finest American authors. His honest social-realist books include the autobiographical *A Son of the Middle Border* and an excellent collection of stories, *Main-Travelled Roads*.

For accommodations, look to I-90 for the national chains, while downtown holds the historic **Charmant Hotel** (101 State St., 608/519-8800, $149 and up).

Spring Green

Architect Frank Lloyd Wright's famous country house and studio, Taliesin (pronounced "tally-ESS-en"), is in **Spring Green** (608/588-7900, daily May-Oct., $22-100), 70 miles east of Prairie du Chien via Hwy-60. Fully guided tours of the private residence and architecture school he inspired are offered; ticket prices and times vary, depending on what's included in the tour. Spring Green is also home to the state's biggest tourist trap, the incredible **House on the Rock** (608/935-3639, daily May-Oct., $30, times and rates vary Nov.-Jan. and Mar.-Apr.), with its "World's Largest" merry-go-round, kitschy collections of everything from dolls to replicas of the crown jewels, and the eponymous house, standing atop a 60-foot-high chimney.

Hwy-35

For most of the nearly 60 miles between La Crosse and Prairie du Chien, the GRR (Hwy-35) is again confined to the margin between the tall gray and yellow bluffs and the impressively wide lakelike Mississippi. At times the roadway is so narrow that the few houses have to climb three stories up the irregular wooded slopes, while the railroad tracks on the right

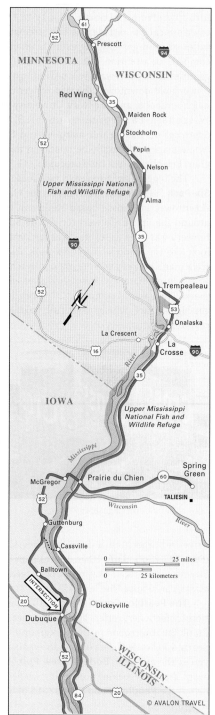

© AVALON TRAVEL

BLACK HAWK WAR

One name recurs frequently as you travel along the northern Mississippi River: Black Hawk was the leader of the Sauk and Mesquakie people of northern Illinois during the feverish era of American expansion into the newly opened Louisiana Purchase in the late 1820s. Native American fighters were held in high esteem by 19th-century Americans; consider that a number of U.S. Army officers sent against Black Hawk later became president, including William Henry Harrison, Zachary Taylor, Abraham Lincoln, and Andrew Jackson. After Jackson rode his Indian-fighter reputation into the White House, Black Hawk and his people were forced to leave their rich Illinois cornfields as settlers and miners moved in.

In 1832, as many newspapers and politicians around the United States demanded the extermination of any and all indigenous people, Black Hawk, who was around 65 years old at the time, moved back to Illinois to regain his nation's lost lands along the Rock River. In response, President Jackson sent in the army, and as Black Hawk and his 300 or so supporters tried to withdraw back across the Mississippi, soldiers and frontier militias attacked them at what became known as the **Battle of Bad Axe,** midway between La Crosse and Prairie du Chien. When Black Hawk and his men came forward under a white flag, an Army gunboat opened fire, while many of the Native American women and children who had succeeded in riding log rafts across the river were slaughtered on the other side. By various accounts, some 150 of Black Hawk's people were killed. Black Hawk himself was soon captured and imprisoned, then paraded around the United States in chains.

statue of Black Hawk in Lowden State Park, near Oregon, Illinois

are suspended over the water on viaducts. About halfway along, there's a maze of small islands around the mouth of the Bad Axe River, with the occasional blue heron poised like a Giacometti sculpture in alga-covered sloughs. Dotting the curves alongside the road are a series of historical markers old enough to be artifacts themselves; most are related to the tragic **Black Hawk War** of 1832.

Midway along this scenic stretch of highway, 31 miles north of Prairie du Chien between the riverside hamlets of De Soto and Genoa, the **Great River Roadhouse**

South of Prairie du Chien, across from McGregor, Iowa, is the spot where Louis Joliet and his Jesuit companion, Jacques Marquette, caught their first sight of what became known as the **Mississippi River.** They were coming down the Wisconsin River in 1673, searching for a route to Asia.

(9660 Hwy-35, 608/648-2045) is a great place to stop and stretch your legs—and your stomach, feasting on the broasted chickens, good pizza, roasted ribs, pasta, Friday night fish fry, and constant cold beers.

Prairie du Chien

Named by early 19th-century French voyageurs, **Prairie du Chien** (pronounced "duh-SHEEN") could be renamed Prairie du Kwik-Stop or Prairie du Pabst by the modern traveler cruising along the GRR on downtown's West Blackhawk Avenue. The town's main attraction is the posh **Villa Louis** (608/326-2721, daily May-Oct., $12.50), which embodies the wealth that could be made in the fur trade back when every European dandy's head sported beaver-pelt hats. Built by the state's first millionaire, the house boasts one of the finest collections of domestic Victoriana in the country; signs point you here from all over town.

IOWA

In its 140-mile course across Iowa, the GRR passes swiftly but unmistakably across the cultural and geographical North-South divide. Separated by the Mississippi River from the rough topography of Wisconsin's Driftless Region, the southeastern corner of Iowa offers instead a taste of the state's trademark rolling plains covered with corn and soybeans. Menus are different too: Cattle here are raised for meat instead of milk, and Iowa is a leading producer of hogs. One of the state lottery games is called Bring Home the Bacon, while radio ads encourage you to "Eat more pork—the other white meat." So say good-bye to walleye and hello to barbecue.

Running along the western bank of the Mississippi, our route tends to the tops of the bluffs rather than to their base, which means the river is often spied from a distance and seems unrelated to the rolling landscape; fortunately it continues to guide the curves of the road. Other than **Dubuque,** our route passes through towns so far from the beaten path they don't even rate a fast-food strip or Walmart—appreciate this while it lasts.

Marquette: Effigy Mounds National Monument

Immediately across, and effectively underneath, the long bridges over the Mississippi from Prairie du Chien, **Marquette** is a homey workaday community that verges on quaint. The main reason to visit is three miles north of Marquette, right along the riverbank: the **Effigy Mounds National Monument** (563/873-3491, ext. 123, daily, free), which preserves 2,500 acres of

aerial view of the Great Bear Mound

Great Bear Mound on the ground

natural riverside ecosystems plus more than 200 distinct burial mounds, many shaped like birds and animals, for example, the Great Bear Mound. The unusual mounds are traces of the people who lived along the Mississippi from around 500 BC to the time of first European contact. The visitors center has exhibits on the archaeology of the mounds, and a dozen miles of hiking trails reach from the river to restored vestiges of the native tallgrass prairie.

McGregor

Just south of Marquette, near the foot of the "original" Pike's Peak—Zebulon Pike came up the Mississippi before he went out west to Colorado—**McGregor** (pop. 871) is a river town whose enticing old saloons and storefronts are a fine reason to stop and stretch your legs, watching the boat and barge traffic or simply wandering along the water. A number of browsable antiques-and-collectibles shops line the GRR through the four-block main business district.

Just south of town, the 500-foot-high limestone bluff known as Pike's Peak is one of the highest points anywhere along the Mississippi River and has been protected at the center of spacious green **Pike's Peak State Park** (563/873-2341), with hiking trails, scenic viewpoints, and a campground with a small store, hot showers, and RV hookups.

Forty-six miles west of McGregor is the Bohemian (as in the Czech Republic, not bearded poets) town of **Spillville,** where Antonin Dvorak completed his symphony *From the New World* in 1893. The Main Street house where he stayed now leads a double life: Displays on Dvorak are upstairs, while downstairs is the **Bily Clock Museum** (563/562-3569), an incredible show of wooden clocks carved by the Bily brothers, depicting everything from the Twelve Apostles to Charles Lindbergh.

Guttenberg

Atop the bluffs, tidy frame farmhouses dot the landscape, with white barns, silos, and farmland aroma accompanying US-18 and US-52 as they loop inland south

toward **Guttenberg** (pop. 1,919), another postcard-pretty old river town whose downtown lines the Mississippi. In fact, it's one of the few Mississippi riverfronts where the river itself is not hidden away behind levees. A long green riverside park, just a quick two blocks east of the main highway, makes the downtown area a particularly pleasant place to stroll.

Guttenberg is indeed named in honor of Johannes Gutenberg, 15th-century inventor of printing from moveable type. Local legend has it that an official of French descent purposely added the extra "t" after German residents won a vote to change the town's name from the original Prairie la Porte. Germanic surnames still predominate in the local phone book, and the two main streets, which run perpendicular to the Mississippi, are named Schiller and Goethe.

McGregor was the hometown of the five children who grew up to found the Ringling Brothers circus.

On the north side of town, the GRR takes an up-close look at the prairie's geological underpinnings as it cuts down to the river's edge. From the downtown area, it's a quick walk upriver to the concrete walls of **Lock and Dam No. 10.** Besides giving a sense of the massive engineering that attempts to tame the Mississippi, the locks are also one block south of an aquarium that offers a quick biology lesson through displays of live specimens of many of the river's fish and invertebrate species.

There are great views to be had in the first few miles of Iowa's GRR route south of Guttenberg. About 10 well-signed miles south of Guttenberg, you can take the Cassville ferry across the Mississippi from Millville and visit the unique Dickeyville Grotto, or stay on the Iowa side and cruise through the Germanic eye-blink towns that dot the rolling uplands between Guttenberg and Dubuque. Midway along, tiny **Balltown** in particular is worth a stop to sample the huge portions and captivating decor at **Breitbach's** (563 Balltown Rd., 563/552-2220), a bar and restaurant that's so old President Millard Fillmore issued the permit allowing it to open.

Dickeyville Grotto

Across the river from Dubuque, the Wisconsin town of Dickeyville is home to one of the most interesting folk-art environments along the Mississippi: the **Dickeyville Grotto** (305 W. Main St., 608/568-3119, donation). Started by the priest Matthias Wernerus in 1925 as a memorial to three local boys killed in World War I, the Dickeyville Grotto consists of a series of caves, alcoves, and shrines made of poured concrete almost completely covered in shells, shards, minerals, and gems. Along with the expected Roman Catholic religious themes, parts of the grotto also exhibit a unique vein of patriotic Americana—highlighted by the "Patriotism in Stone" memorial to Christopher Columbus, George Washington, and Abraham Lincoln. With almost no commercialization, the grotto is open 24 hours every day, adjacent to the Holy Ghost Church, a block west of US-61.

Dickeyville Grotto

Dickeyville can be reached a number of ways. It's a quick shot north along US-151 from Dubuque, or from Prairie du Chien you can follow scenic Hwy-133 along the east bank of the Mississippi. If it's summertime and you want an up-close look at the Mississippi, make your way to **Cassville,** a historic frontier town that holds one of the river's few surviving car ferries. The **ferry** (608/725-5180, daily summer, Sat.-Sun. May and Sept.-Oct., $15 per car) has been running since the 1830s.

Dubuque

At the southern end of an enjoyable ride, cruising up and down sculpted hills and winding past miles of Iowa prairie and river towns, the GRR rolls into **Dubuque** (pop. 57,637), named for the 18th-century French voyageur Julien Dubuque, who unsuccessfully mined lead on land acquired from the Spanish. Finding lead wasn't the problem—Native Americans had dug lead by hand as early as 1680 for trade with the English—but getting it to market was. After the steamboat's invention and forced removal of Native Americans in the late 1820s, mineral wealth became a major catalyst to settlement of the tristate area around Dubuque, as town names

Fenelon Place Elevator

Different towns along the Iowa stretch of the GRR act as the finish line for the trans-Iowa **RAGBRAI,** a 500-mile weeklong mass bike ride that sees thousands of cyclists cruising across the state every July.

like Potosi, Mineral Point, New Diggings, and Lead Mine attest. During the Civil War, just five counties around here supplied all the lead for the entire Union war effort.

On the inland side of the compact downtown, a grand view of the city and the Mississippi valley can be had from the top of the **Fenelon Place Elevator** (daily Apr.-Nov., $3 round-trip), a historic funicular cable car that proudly holds the title of "World's Steepest, Shortest Scenic Railway," a miniature version of those found in the Swiss Alps. Hop on at the east end of 4th Street and ride up to the plush residential district on the hilltop.

On the other side of downtown, the Dubuque waterfront has been recharged by the **National Mississippi River Museum and Aquarium** (350 E. 3rd St., 563/557-9545 or 800/226-3369, daily Mar.-Oct., Tues.-Sun. Nov.-Feb., $15), one of the two biggest and best museums dedicated to the history and culture of Old Muddy (the other one is on River Island in Memphis). A highlight is the steamboat *William M. Black,* an official National Landmark. Other galleries include a National Rivers Hall of Fame, which tells the stories of explorers and adventurers like Lewis and Clark and John Wesley Powell. The introductory film, *River of Dreams,* is narrated by Mr. Lake Wobegon himself, Garrison Keillor.

The museum complex is at the heart of the America's River complex, which also has the inevitable casino plus docks for scenic sightseeing and gambling boats, a nice riverside promenade, and the **Grand Harbor Resort and Waterpark** (563/690-4000, $109 and up), a deluxe hotel and 25,000-square-foot water park.

Dubuque is a meat-and-potatoes place when it comes to food, and as in most of the Midwest, you should plan to dine early to catch restaurants before they close. Near the Fenelon Place Elevator, the **Shot Tower Inn** (390 Locust St., 563/556-1061) is a popular pizza place with an upstairs covered deck and beer by the pitcher. The one standout in Dubuque is the **Pepper Sprout** (378 Main St., 563/556-2167), where the range of dishes (and the big-city prices) proves that "Midwestern fine dining" is not an oxymoron.

East and west of Dubuque, US-20 offers a pair of excellent detours off the Great River Road. The ball field created for the movie *Field of Dreams* has become a minor tourist mecca for rural **Dyersville,** 30 miles due west of Dubuque via US-20 or the surprisingly scenic paved Heritage Trail, which runs along an old railroad right-of-way.

South of Dubuque, the GRR follows US-52 back up the bluffs and across 45 miles of upland farms and wooded bottoms until the next Mississippi crossing at Sabula.

Dubuque Shot Tower

Dubuque marks the junction of the Great River Road and US-20, **The Oregon Trail** (see page 609). Full coverage of this cross-country route begins on page 558.

St. Donatus

Fifteen undulating agricultural miles south of Dubuque, the tiny hamlet of **St. Donatus** (pop. 135) is widely advertised as a historic and picturesque Luxembourg village, mainly thanks to the handsome masonry of the **Gehlen House** (563/773-2480 or 800/280-1177), a 150-year-old home now used as a restaurant and B&B. Other eye-catching structures are the Roman Catholic church and **Pieta Chapel** atop the adjacent Calvary Hill. If you wish to make a pilgrimage up the Way of the Cross to the Chapel, start behind at St. Donatus Catholic Church, east of Kalmes Restaurant. There's a nice view from the top—the other set of spires across the valley belongs to the German Lutheran St. John's Church.

Bellevue and Sabula

The GRR (US-52) returns to the Mississippi valley at **Bellevue,** with its lengthy State Street and Riverview Park beside Lock and Dam No. 12. Bellevue earns its name when you sit on the porch of the restored **Mont Rest Inn** (300 Spring St., 563/872-4220, $150 and up) and take in the sweeping 270-degree panorama over the Mississippi.

Continuing south, the GRR stays in sparsely populated wooded lowlands through **Sabula,** an island of a town created by the Corps of Engineers when the pool above Lock and Dam No. 13, about 16 miles downstream, flooded out the surrounding plains. Sabula takes its name from the Latin *sabulum* (sand). The river here is nearly four miles wide. Sabula's encompassing levees provide fine wetlands birdwatching, especially for bald eagles.

ILLINOIS, IOWA, AND MISSOURI

The Great River Road route along the middle Mississippi starts in northwestern Illinois, at the southern edge of the Driftless Region, and proceeds through sandy floodplain and fertile prairie, nipping back and forth across the ever-locked and dammed Mississippi between Illinois, southern Iowa, and the generally more-developed Missouri uplands. Here, small towns bypassed by much of the 20th century are more likely to be forlorn than quaint, a prelude to those Southern states in which local ordinances appear to require the public display of rusty appliances. With a few exceptions—such as the historic Mormon town of **Nauvoo** or Mark Twain's hometown of **Hannibal**—our route now mostly runs through communities whose best years may have passed. This stretch of the GRR also includes one of the most dramatic sections of the entire route: the 25 miles around **Grafton,** Illinois, at the northern doorstep of **St. Louis.**

South of St. Louis, I-55 is the recommended route, as it bypasses the auto dealerships, appliance stores, shopping centers, and other prefab conveniences lining old US-61. Passing by the enticing old river town of **Sainte Genevieve,** the GRR crosses the Mississippi once again, ambling back to the corn, soybeans, and cicadas of southern Illinois. Accents, "Bar-B-Q" signs, and Baptist churches leave no doubt that our route has entered the South; in summer the heat and humidity confirm this with a vengeance. Fortunately, after leaving the "American Bottom," the GRR skirts the edge of the **Shawnee National Forest,** whose shade brings up to 25°F of relief from the temperatures along the roadside fields on a sunny July day. Occasional levees, raised roadbeds, and brackish seasonal ponds are reminders that the mile-wide Mississippi is only temporarily out of sight of the GRR, which finally crosses into Kentucky beside the giant turbid confluence of the Mississippi and Ohio Rivers at Cairo.

Savanna: Mississippi Palisades

Across the Mississippi from Iowa, **Savanna,** Illinois, is an old railroad town that has grown into an antiques center, offering a large antiques minimall along the main drag. Savanna maintains a few pretty Victorian mansions up on the heights, but for a truly attractive vista, take a detour north along Hwy-84 from the end of the Iowa bridge to the 2,500-acre **Mississippi Palisades State Park** (815/273-2731), with its great eroded bluffs (popular with rock climbers), 13 miles of hiking trails (brilliant fall color in the forested ravines), and fine river views. There's camping too, with hot showers and RV hookups.

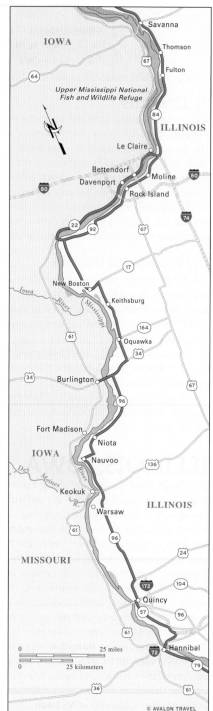

© AVALON TRAVEL

Between Savanna and the I-80 beltway around the Quad Cities are nearly 50 flat miles of river valley, dotted with small historic river and railroad towns mixed in with new commercial and residential construction. Agriculture is conspicuous too, and the sandy soils around Savanna are famous for their melon crops. While the Mississippi for the most part stays invisible from the GRR, the industry on

its banks is clearly evident, especially at night. River access is via a handful of recreation areas in the **Upper Mississippi National Fish and Wildlife Refuge.**

LeClaire, Iowa

On the northeastern edge of the Quad Cities, just off the I-80 freeway, lies the little town of **LeClaire** (pop. 3,765), famous once for its river pilots but now best remembered as William F. "Buffalo Bill" Cody's home. The **Buffalo Bill Museum** (199 N. Front St., 563/289-5580, daily, $5), on the waterfront, is dedicated to Cody's life. LeClaire is also home to the **Faithful Pilot** (117 N. Cody Rd., 563/289-4156), on

Buffalo Bill Museum

LeClaire's main street (US-67). One of the best restaurants in the entire Quad Cities region, the Faithful Pilot has creative high-quality cuisine, a good wine list, fine microbrews, and seating with views over the river.

The Quad Cities

Straddling the Mississippi at its confluence with the Rock River, the **Quad Cities**—Moline and Rock Island, Illinois, and Davenport and Bettendorf, Iowa—encompass an enormous sprawl of some 400,000

residents. While much of the cityscape is dominated by heavy industry, particularly on the Iowa side, points of interest are sprinkled throughout.

Along the river at the heart of the Quad Cities, adjacent to downtown Rock Island, is the former namesake of that city, now called **Arsenal Island** for the U.S. Army facility based there. The island is open to the public. Besides an arsenal museum and Civil War cemeteries, there's a good **Mississippi River Visitor Center** (daily, free) right next to Lock and Dam No. 15, where the operation of the locks can be seen from a penny-pitch away.

The first railroad bridge over the Mississippi linked Rock Island and Davenport in 1856. The railroad was promptly sued by a steamboat company, whose craft was mortally attracted to the bridge piers. The plaintiffs argued that bridges violated their navigation rights; the defense lawyer's elegantly simple—and successful—rebuttal was that a person has as much right to cross a river as to travel upon it. That lawyer was Abraham Lincoln. Today the railroad crosses the river on the upper deck of the old iron **Government Bridge,** which swings open for the tows entering the locks; cars crossing between Rock Island and Davenport can ride the humming lower deck or take the modern concrete highway span below the dam.

If you come to the Quad Cities looking for a slice of old-fashioned middle-American humdrum, you're in for a surprise: one of Midwest's most impressive municipal art museums stands at the heart of unassuming Davenport. The **Figge Art Museum** (225 W. 2nd St., 563/326-7804, Tues.-Sun., $7), overlooking the Mississippi, is housed in a beautiful glass gem designed by noted British architect David Chipperfield. The museum shows off some of the University of Iowa's fine collection of painting and sculpture, the only self-portrait by American Gothic artist Grant Wood, and an excel-

cornetist Leon Beiderbecke, 1924

lent assembly of WPA-era art and Frank Lloyd Wright furniture. The Figge also stages events and educational activities. Another intriguing cultural enterprise is just up the street, where the **River Music Experience** (129 N. Main St., 563/326-1333, Mon.-Fri., free) is a music venue and an interactive museum exploring the many different sorts of music that have grown up along the Mississippi River.

Davenport celebrates the music legacy of native son and cornetist Leon "Bix" Beiderbecke with the annual **Bix Beiderbecke Memorial Jazz Festival,** held each summer. A high-tech "Skybridge" over US-67 links downtown with the riverfront, where a statue of Bix stands along the water. Also here is the wonderful old (circa-1930) but thoughtfully modernized **Modern Woodmen Park,** where the

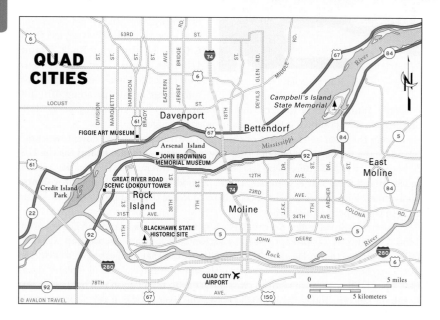

Quad Cities River Bandits (563/324-3000, tickets $5-14) baseball team play their home games. It's a fun time for all, with a Ferris wheel. In a nod to Iowa's famous Field of Dreams, before games the home team players run out from a corn field planted down the left field foul line.

Quad Cities Practicalities

In downtown Davenport, the only large Mississippi River city not cut off from Ol' Muddy by a permanent flood wall, look to the historic downtown area, where you'll find the **Front Street Brewery Pub & Eatery** (208 River Dr., 563/322-1569) and several good restaurants and cafés. Away from downtown Davenport, off I-80 exit 292, the original **Machine Shed Restaurant** (7250 Northwest Blvd., 563/391-2427) draws families from near and far for its huge portions of roast pork and other Midwest faves, like the famously good pies.

In downtown Moline, a half-dozen blocks along 5th Avenue between I-74 and 14th Street hold everything from the unexpectedly excellent Vietnamese fare of **Le Mekong** (1606 5th Ave., 309/797-8660) to the extraordinary **Lagomarcino's** (1422 5th Ave., 309/764-1814), a candy store and soda fountain that serves drinks like phosphates in a setting virtually unchanged since it opened in 1908. Order a hot fudge sundae—it's made with homemade fudge and ice cream.

In Rock Island's old downtown, 2nd Avenue has experienced something of a revival; one pleasant result is The District, centered on the 2nd Avenue pedestrian mall. One great place hereabouts is the **Blue Cat Brew Pub** (113 18th St., 309/788-8247) along the riverside, where salads, seafood, and desserts go way beyond your average pub fare, and the beers range from traditional lagers and ales to more esoteric concoctions.

For a truly regional diner experience, make your way to **Maid-Rite** (2036 16th St., Moline, 309/764-1196). A strictly upper-Midwest phenomenon whose faded logo, "Since 1926," can often be seen on old brick buildings or historic commercial storefronts as far away as Minnesota, the local Maid-Rites are unusually bright and polished, and they come heartily recommended for their "loose meat" sloppy joe sandwiches.

The Yellow Banks

Zigzagging for nearly 100 miles south of the Quad Cities, the GRR picks its way along a series of back roads through Illinois floodplain and prairie, where frequent small farming towns serve as reminders of the need for frequent stops by early stages, steamboats, and railroads. Most of the towns seem not to have changed much since the last steamboat or train whistle blew, although now there's neon in the bars, vinyl and aluminum siding on the houses, and farmers with high-powered four-by-fours on the roads.

Nearly 45 miles south of the Quad Cities beltway, the GRR passes tiny **New Boston,** where the Mississippi is fed by the mouth of the Iowa River. The town is a

historical footnote these days, having been surveyed by the young Abraham Lincoln after his stint in the Army—a tour of duty during which his only combat was against mosquitoes, he later recalled. Along the river farther south, near **Keithsburg,** a sign welcomes travelers to the **Yellow Banks,** named for the deep layer of sand exposed in the river valley in this region. Because of this deposit, visitors can find sandburs and even cactus in the **Big River State Forest** south of town. Keithsburg used to be one of a number of button manufacturing centers located along the middle Mississippi: Freshwater clams were dredged from the river bottom and their shells were used for making pearl buttons.

In **Oquawka, Illinois,** 10 miles northeast of Burlington, Iowa, a roadside marker points out the spot where in 1972 a circus elephant (named Norma Jean Elephant!) was killed by lightning.

Burlington and Niota

Across the Mississippi River via an austere modern suspension bridge, **Burlington** was the frontier capital of Iowa, founded in 1808 and holding many Victorian homes and commercial buildings. In 1887 Burlington gave birth to the great American nature writer Aldo Leopold, then in 2004 the city was awarded "Great American Main Street" status from the National Trust for Historic Preservation. Now it has a fun Class A baseball team (the Bees, a Los Angeles Angels farm team), a casino, a nice bridge over the Mississippi, a great **All-Star Maid-Rite Diner** (112 W. Division St., 319/758-7648), and some busy downtown rail yards—onetime home base of the Burlington Northern Santa Fe (BNSF) railroad conglomerate.

If you have time to wander away from the river and downtown areas, head up to the 6th Street shopping district on **Heritage Hill,** following the twists and turns of **"Snake Alley,"** a section of Washington Street that Ripley's Believe It or Not once called the "Crookedest Street in the World."

At **Niota,** the ghost of a town that marks the next crossing south of Burlington, a nifty old 1920s double-decker swing bridge (trains below, cars on top) crosses the Mississippi, landing on the west bank in the historic town of Fort Madison, Iowa.

Nauvoo

Founded in 1839 by the Church of Jesus Christ of Latter-Day Saints (LDS), the town of **Nauvoo**—a Hebrew-sounding word its founding

Snake Alley, the "Crookedest Street in the World," in Burlington, Iowa

father was told meant "the beautiful location"—was named by Mormon leader Joseph Smith, 12 years after he received the Book of Mormon from the angel Moroni. Smith and many of his followers had spent the previous winter jailed in Liberty, Missouri, and by 1846 they were effectively exiled to Utah, but for a few years Nauvoo was among the largest settlements on the western frontier, with hundreds of log cabins

Mississippi Bridge, Niota

and brick buildings and a population of some 6,000 Mormon believers. After 150 years of relative peace and quiet, in the late 1990s the Mormon church started a massive $30-million program of historic preservation, turning Nauvoo into a top destination for Mormon pilgrims and retirees. The "restoration" of Mormon Nauvoo, and the influx of well-heeled Mormon immigrants, has been on such a big scale that many non-Mormons have felt under siege. Visitors to Nauvoo will certainly have plenty of opportunities to learn about Mormon history and religion, but for the moment at least the part-preserved, part-restored townscape has a broad interest as a mostly noncommercialized reminder of what frontier America looked like in the years before the Wild West was finally "won."

The biggest change in Nauvoo has been the reconstruction of the original Mormon **Nauvoo Temple** (50 N. Wells St.), which, from the time it was finished in 1846 until it was burned down in 1848, was the largest building west of Philadelphia. An exact replica of the original, the new temple took more than three years to complete and was dedicated in 2002. The temple has a remarkable series of stone capitals carved with sunburst motifs and a 165-foot-high steeple capped by a statue of the angel Moroni. Other interesting LDS-related sites include the rebuilt store run by Joseph Smith and the home of Brigham Young. The home and workshop of John Browning, inventor of the repeating rifle, has been restored along Main Street, south of the present downtown area. There's also a massive **outdoor pageant** (217/453-2429, Tues.-Sat. 8:30pm, free) every July, celebrating the early pre-Utah years of the LDS comunity. All summer long you can take part in mostly free nonsectarian activities like blacksmithing and horse-drawn carriage rides.

The Los Angeles Angels' Class A farm team, the **Burlington Bees** (319/754-5705), play all summer long at **Community Field,** on Mount Pleasant Street, two miles west of the Mississippi River.

The annual **Nauvoo Grape Festival,** held each Labor Day weekend at Nauvoo State Park south of town, celebrates the wine business that arose after European immigrants moved onto farms abandoned by the Mormon exodus. Nauvoo also developed a blue-cheese industry in the 1920s, after Prohibition shut down the winemaking trade.

MORMONS IN ILLINOIS

If you're passing through Nauvoo, you'll have plenty of opportunities to learn about Mormon history and religion. Nauvoo is a mecca for Mormons, or Latter-Day Saints (LDS), as church members call themselves. In 1839, a dozen years after receiving their new gospel via the angel Moroni, the Mormons purchased a large tract of swampy land along the Mississippi River, then set about draining swamps and building a city. Within a few years, Nauvoo was not only the largest LDS settlement in America but the 10th-largest city in the United States. The emergence of such a powerful little theocracy with its own well-armed militia generated resentment among outnumbered neighbors, and even some internal dissent. The friction escalated to violence on both sides, finally culminating in the 1844 arrest of Joseph Smith Jr., church founder and president, for having sanctioned the destruction of printing presses used by some church members to question his leadership. While in the nearby Carthage jail, Smith was lynched by a mob and so became one of the Mormons' first martyrs. Amid ensuing disputes over church succession and renewed hostilities with non-Mormon neighbors, most residents followed Brigham Young across the Mississippi on the famous exodus to Salt Lake City.

Given Smith's martyrdom, the fact that he's buried here, and the Brigham Young migration's roots in the town, it's little wonder that Nauvoo attracts Mormon pilgrims by the busload. The Utah-based LDS have sponsored a massive restoration of old Nauvoo buildings, and the town now ranks as one of the leaders in historic preservation in the United States. Most of old Nauvoo is operated essentially as a big museum, totally free and open to non-LDS visitors.

Nauvoo Practicalities

For a map of the town and visitor information, stop by the huge **Nauvoo Tourism Information Center** (1295 Mulholland St., 217/453-6648), opposite the historic Hotel Nauvoo. You can also visit the LDS-run **Historic Nauvoo Visitor Center** (217/577-2603) and the **Joseph Smith Historic Site Visitor Center** (217/453-2246) run by the Community of Christ Church.

Restaurants and lodgings are clustered along Mulholland Street (Hwy-96, a.k.a. the GRR) within the few blocks of downtown Nauvoo. For picnic lunches and cinnamon buns, try **Nauvoo Mill & Bakery** (1530 Mulholland St., 217/453-6734) near the gas station. Near the reconstructed temple, the circa-1840s **Hotel Nauvoo** (1290 Mulholland St., 217/453-2211, rooms $79 and up) is particularly well regarded for its belt-straining buffets; it is also the town's most characterful place to stay.

Warsaw

For a scenic dozen miles south of Nauvoo, the GRR returns after long absence to the banks of the Mississippi, shaded by native hickory and oak, and then sidesteps yet another opportunity to enter Iowa, this time via US-136 west to Keokuk. Staying on the east bank, the GRR follows a series of farm roads past gravel pits and fields for most of the 40-mile run through **Warsaw** down to Quincy.

Warsaw lends its name to a variety of geode found locally in profusion; inside, Warsaw geodes grow calcite crystals. Across the Mississippi, Keokuk geodes grow quartzite crystals inside their stony spheres. South of town, the highway threatens to turn amphibious as it rolls down past a towering grain elevator to the Mississippi's edge, bends south along the base of the bluffs past old house trailers, scruffy fields full of wildlife—including wild turkeys and river turtles waddling along the roadside—and old kilns visible in the limestone. The road passes, finally, back into Illinois's signature cornfields, planted in the river's fertile floodplain.

Quincy

Midway between the Quad Cities and St. Louis, **Quincy** (pop. 40,633) is a modest-size city, Germanic enough in its heritage to consider Pizza Hut an ethnic restaurant. A bastion of abolitionists before the Civil War, Quincy was also home to antiabolitionist Stephen Douglas, the incumbent Illinois senator whose campaign debates with Abraham Lincoln put that tall country lawyer on the path to the White House.

The GRR follows the riverfront, and again the pilot's-wheel signs are missing, but the giant span of the Bayview Bridge over the Mississippi will leave no doubt as to which way to turn to stay on track. However, most of the city perches on the tall bluffs above the GRR and is worth a drive through, if only to sample its textbook variety of residential architecture. Take a walk or drive through the East End, an area roughly bounded by Maine and State Streets between 16th and 24th Streets. Filled with historic mansions along quiet tree-canopied streets, it's the perfect place to practice distinguishing your Queen Anne from your Tudor, and Prairie Style from Gothic Revival.

If you have thus far missed the tried-and-true cooking of the **Maid-Rite** (507 N. 12th St., 217/222-7527) chain, Quincy gives you a chance to fix this oversight:

historic home in Quincy's East End

Perhaps the most intact of all the original Maids is here in Quincy. There's also an exceptionally good Italian place, **Tiramisu** (137 N 3rd St., 217/222-9560). If you plan to spend the night, you'll find the national chains downtown out on Broadway near I-172.

For more information, call or drop by the tourist information center in the **Villa Kathrine** (217/224-3688, free), that hard-to-miss turn-of-the-20th-century Moroccan-style residence on the bluffs overlooking the Mississippi, just south of the US-24 bridge.

Hannibal

It doesn't take a literature professor to figure out who the most famous resident of **Hannibal** (pop. 17,916) was: His name prefaces half the signs in town, and the names of his characters preface the other half. Cross the Mississippi River on the I-72 Mark Twain Memorial Bridge, shop at the Huck Finn Shopping Center, swim at Mark Twain Lake, then spend the night at Injun Joe Campground. Turn onto 3rd Street (the Great River Road) near the Best Western on the River and park yourself in the heart of historic old Hannibal, and visit the Mark Twain Boyhood Home and Museum. Take a ride on the *Mark Twain* riverboat, docked at the Center Street Landing, browse **Becky's Old Fashioned Ice Cream Parlor and Emporium** (318 N. Main St., 573/221-0822), or eat Mark Twain fried chicken at the **Mark Twain Dinette.** Not to detract from the credit due him, but don't look for any subtlety or modesty surrounding Mark Twain's achievements here.

Most of this Twainery is located downtown, within a few blocks of the Mississippi River, and enjoyment requires at least a passing familiarity with (and fondness for) *Tom Sawyer,* Twain's fictionalized memoir of his boyhood here. A statue of Tom and Huck stands at the foot of Cardiff Hill, and two blocks south, the white picket fence featured in that book still stands in front of the **Mark Twain Boyhood Home** (120 N. Main St., 573/221-9010, daily, $11), where young Samuel Clemens (Twain's real name) grew up in the 1840s. The historic site preserves five buildings, including his father's law offices and the drugstore above which the Clemens family also lived. The home of Tom Sawyer's "girl next door," Becky Thatcher, is actually across the street. Tours begin at The **Interpretive Center** (415 N. Main St.) and the **Museum Gallery** (120 N. Main St.) displays artifacts including a steamboat pilot's wheel and numerous first editions, bringing to life scenes from Twain's Mississippi novels.

A pair of high hills bookend Hannibal, and climbing up either (or both) gives a grand overview of the town and the broad Mississippi, its historic lifeblood. On the north side, climb up the staircase from the Tom and Huck statue to the top of Cardiff Hill, where the **Mark Twain Memorial Lighthouse,** built in 1935 to celebrate the centenary of Twain's birth, offers a fine view. South of town, **Lover's Leap** is higher and more breathtaking—best visited by car or bike. Farther south of downtown along the GRR (Hwy-79) is Hannibal's most kid-friendly attraction: the **Mark Twain Cave Complex** (daily, $19), where guides spin tales about Tom and Huck on an hour-long tour.

Samuel Clemens in Hannibal, 1902

The most popular annual festival is **National Tom Sawyer Days,** held around the 4th of July, when children take part in the National Fence Painting Championship (a whitewashing homage to *Tom Sawyer*), a frog-jumping competition (remembering Twain's Gold Rush-era short story, *The Celebrated Jumping Frog of Calaveras County*), and the messy Mississippi Mud Volleyball Championships.

Hannibal Practicalities

The aforementioned Mark Twain Fried chicken and homemade root beer are served all day at the **Mark Twain Dinette** (400 N. 3rd St., 573/221-5300), adjacent to the Mark Twain Home. A step up the culinary scale, **Ole Planters Restaurant** (316 N. Main St., 573/221-4410) has a full range of lunches and dinners; dessert fans will want to sample the German chocolate pie, a specialty of the house. This species, like rhubarb, is predominantly found in pie cases along the middle Mississippi, so if you're planning a scientific sampling, start now.

Consistent with its status as an international tourist attraction, Hannibal has plenty of motels, B&Bs, and campgrounds. The **Best Western on the River** (401 N. 3rd St., 573/248-1150, $82 and up) sits downtown at the foot of the old US-36 bridge. The national chains line up along busy US-61 west of downtown.

For a complete list of lodgings, restaurants, events, and tourist traps, pick up a free guide from the **Hannibal Convention & Visitors Bureau** (505 N. 3rd St., 573/221-2477 or 866/263-4825).

The Twain mania is so overwhelming that little is made of Hannibal's other famous sons. Baseball lovers searching for some mention of Joseph Jefferson "Shoeless Joe" Jackson will look in vain. Neither is there much mention of the inventor of the car radio, the eight-track tape, and the Learjet, Bill Lear, who was born here in 1902.

Louisiana and Clarksville

For the first 20-odd miles south from Hannibal, the GRR ascends and descends the densely wooded tops of bluffs, pausing at scenic turnouts for views across the Mississippi Valley, here many miles wide. In October, the upland forests are blazing with fall color that compares with any outside New England, and if you roll down the windows or stop to stretch your legs during the summer, listen for the omnipresent buzz of cicadas in the tangled undergrowth.

Another icon of the lower Mississippi, one that has extended its range north, like the cicadas (and the fire ant), is the huge and pungent chemical plant on the south side of the town of **Louisiana** (pop. 3,300); ironically, considering current concerns about energy supplies, this plant was originally constructed by the U.S. Army in the 1940s to create synthetic alternatives to fossil fuels. The town itself, like a Hannibal without Mark Twain, has one of the Midwest's most intact Victorian-era streetscapes, full of 125-year-old brick cottages and warehouses, but looks like it has just about lost the battle against extinction.

If you've been keeping track, you'll have noticed that the lock and dam numbering skipped No. 23 between Hannibal and Clarksville. There are 29 Army Corps of Engineers-operated locks and dams on the Mississippi, from the unnumbered ones in the Twin Cities to No. 27 at St. Louis.

A short ways farther south, **Clarksville** (pop. 442) is another GRR town with more of a past than a future, but some optimistic restorers of the riverfront historic block are counting on tourism to improve the town fortunes.

Claiming preeminence as the highest point along this stretch of the Mississippi River, 900-foot **Pinnacle Peak** is also noteworthy for the rusty remains of its old Sky Ride chairlift, which once carried riders over the GRR all the way to the summit. The Sky Ride has been undergoing restoration for about 30 years, without much sign of progress toward reopening. Clarksville also boasts what may be the largest concentration of **bald eagles** in the lower 48 states; in winter months they feed by the hundreds below Lock and Dam No. 24, on the northern edge of town.

Swinging away from the river south of Clarksville, the GRR reenters the corn belt in great straight stretches of road, rising and falling over rolling prairie still hilly enough that you can play peek-a-boo with approaching traffic over the miles of ups and downs, passing towns that often comprise little more than a few houses around a gas station and a grain elevator on a rarely used railroad siding.

The landscape feels far away from urban anything, yet you're less than a half hour from downtown St. Louis.

Calhoun County

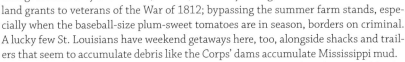

Wedged between the Mississippi and Illinois Rivers, the rural peninsula of **Calhoun County** is one of the best-kept secrets in the state of Illinois. Cut off from the rest of the "Land of Lincoln" and connected to neighboring Missouri by ferry only, Calhoun County is a world of its own. A third of the state's substantial peach crop is grown here on farms that have changed hands only a few times, if at all, since they were given out as land grants to veterans of the War of 1812; bypassing the summer farm stands, especially when the baseball-size plum-sweet tomatoes are in season, borders on criminal. A lucky few St. Louisians have weekend getaways here, too, alongside shacks and trailers that seem to accumulate debris like the Corps' dams accumulate Mississippi mud.

In the town of **Brussels** (pop. 141), whose public phone booth is possibly the town's sole civic improvement since the Coolidge administration, a few cafés and bars are evidence of its popularity with weekenders from St. Louis. The most popular haunt in Brussels is the venerable **Wittmond Hotel Restaurant** (618/883-2345, cash only), across from the water tower and post office at the heart of Brussels. The dining room here serves delicious, all-you-can-eat, family-style meals, popular on Sunday. It no longer rents rooms, but there's still a timeless bar and an even more ancient-looking general store, complete with dusty old merchandise that looks like it dates back to when the enterprise opened in 1847.

Getting to and around Calhoun County is a bit of an adventure. The main access is from near Grafton, Illinois, across the Illinois River via the state-run, round-the-clock, and (best-of-all) free **Brussels Ferry.** There's also a bridge at Hardin, 14 miles upstream. From the Missouri side north of St. Louis, the only access is via the privately operated **Golden Eagle ferry** (618/535-5759), which runs across the Mississippi River from a landing outside St. Charles to **Golden Eagle,** Illinois. A few of the ferries cease operation in the winter, but during summer they run more or less from dawn to midnight, and most sell local maps and can offer basic visitor information. Road signs in Calhoun County are almost nonexistent, but just driving or cycling around, getting lost and found, and lost and found again, is by far the best way to get a feel for this preserved-in-amber island in time.

Pere Marquette State Park

At the south end of Calhoun County, the Brussels Ferry takes all of two or three minutes to cross the narrow **Illinois River,** along which Marquette and Joliet returned to Canada after their failure to find a westward-flowing river to the rich lands of Cathay and the Far East. René-Robert Cavelier, Sieur de La Salle, came down the Illinois eight years later in 1681, on the first expedition to specifically target the Mississippi. It was La Salle who claimed the Mississippi territory for his sponsor, King Louis XIV of France, and who went all the way down to the Gulf of Mexico (Marquette and Joliet turned back after the confluence of the Arkansas River).

If you're equipped for some hiking or biking, **Pere Marquette State Park** is a short, well-signed, and definitely worthwhile three-mile detour upstream from the Brussels Ferry landing. The handsome **park lodge** (618/786-2331, from $89 for two), built by the Civilian Conservation Corps in the late 1930s, is noted for its 700-ton stone fireplace, massive tree-trunk roof supports, decorative ironwork, and out-size chess set. Cabins and lodge rooms are available for reasonable rates. Expect holiday and fall foliage weekends to be booked up a year in advance; **camping** (618/786-3323) is also available.

Following an old railroad route for much of the way, the 21.5-mile **Sam Vadalabene Bike Trail** between Pere Marquette State Park and Alton is unquestionably the best venue for appreciating the scenery, even for a short walk, for Hwy-100 is a fast divided highway whose drivers don't appreciate slowpokes.

Grafton and Elsah

North of St. Louis on the Illinois side of the Mississippi, the high-speed section of the GRR between **Grafton** and Alton is widely considered one of its most scenic stretches. Towering limestone bluffs, their curving faces pocked with caves and overhangs, push the road to the edge of the broad lake formed by Lock and Dam No. 26.

Atop the bluffs over Elsah is the Tudor campus of **Principia College.** A Christian Science institution of higher education, the campus and many buildings were designed by arts-and-crafts master architect Bernard Maybeck.

Speeding along Hwy-100 south of Grafton, it's easy to miss the turnoff for **Elsah,** but even if you have to turn around and come back, it's worth it to check out this tiny hamlet tucked away in a cleft in the palisades. Light years away from St. Louis but only a half-hour's drive away, Elsah is listed in the National Register of Historic Places in its entirety and is an architectural gem, with 19th-century cut-stone and clapboard buildings and narrow lanes reminiscent of some idyllic English country village. Two small B&Bs and the **Green Tree Inn** (618/374-2821, $135-165) offer unexpectedly romantic getaways, a taste of New England in southern Illinois.

South of Elsah, before the bluffs give way to grain elevators at Alton, you'll catch a glimpse of the **Piasa Bird** (pronounced "PIE-a-saw") high on the wall of an old road-side quarry. Marquette and other early explorers mention a pair of huge pictographs on the cliff face, representations of the Illini people's legendary "bird that devours men." Faded by the 1840s, the original site was destroyed by quarrying. The current 20-by-40-foot replica, based on various eyewitness descriptions, resembles

the Great River Road along the Mississippi River, one mile east of Grafton, Illinois

EXCURSION STEAMER "CAPITOL" ON THE MISSISSIPPI.

STRECKFUS STEAMBOAT LINE, SAINT LOUIS.

something from the notebook of an adolescent Dungeons & Dragons fan.

Alton

At **Alton,** 20 miles northeast of St. Louis, the riverfront turns decidedly urban. The GRR races along the water, past busy tugboat docks, sulfurous chemical plants, and towering concrete grain elevators, all along a great protective levee under a thicket of high-tension power lines. The main attraction here is the vivid multicolored (and hugely lucrative) Argosy Alton **casino boat,** formerly the *Alton Belle,* the first in Illinois when riverboat gambling was made legal in 1991.

Inland from the waterfront, however, Alton is surprisingly peaceful and quiet, its redbrick streets lined by mature trees and a range of modest but well-maintained 19th-century houses. Near 5th and Monument Streets at the south end of town, high on a hill above the riverfront, Alton's cemetery is dominated by a large column topped by a winged figure—a monument to one of Alton's most important individuals, the abolitionist newspaper editor Elijah Lovejoy. Widely considered to be the nation's first martyr to freedom of the press and freedom of speech, Lovejoy, a newspaper publisher and preacher, was lynched in Alton in 1837 by a mob of pro-slavery Missourians.

Six miles south of Alton, near the village of Hartford, keep an eye out for the signs to the **Lewis & Clark State Historical Site,** a reconstruction of the winter campsite of the Corps of Discovery in 1803-1804. Recently expanded with a small state-run **museum** (618/251-5811, Wed.-Sun., free), the site sits opposite the confluence of the Missouri and Mississippi Rivers, which roll together in a muddy tide between swampy wooded banks.

A life-size statue of Robert Pershing Wadlow, the world's tallest human, stands on the campus of the Southern Illinois University Dental School, on College Avenue (Hwy-140) a mile or so east of the river. The Alton-born "gentle giant," who enrolled here in what was then a Baptist seminary in 1938, was 8 feet 1 inches tall when he died in 1940, at the age of 22.

In 2010, an Alton fisherman pulled a 125-pound blue catfish out of the Mississippi River, a world-record catch.

The GRR Across St. Louis

The Great River Road has many routes in, around, and across St. Louis, and they're all so poorly marked that you're sure to get lost trying to follow any of them. From Alton, US-67 crosses just below Lock and Dam No. 26, taking first the Clark Bridge (over the Mississippi) and then the Lewis Bridge (over the Missouri River).

casino boats on the Mississippi

St. Louis

the Gateway Arch

Founded by French fur trappers in 1764, St. Louis served for most of its first century as a prosperous outpost of civilization at the frontier of the Wild West. It was the starting point for the explorations of Lewis and Clark, and much later Charles Lindbergh, whose *Spirit of St. Louis* carried him across the Atlantic. Unfortunately, like many other American cities, St. Louis has suffered from years of decline and neglect; the population, which peaked at over 850,000 in 1950, is now less than half that. In recent years the racialized violence in its northern suburb Ferguson made national headlines. Even the sale of the city's iconic beer brand, Budweiser, to the Belgian company InBev was a blow to local pride. Part of the problem may be that, although it has all the cultural and institutional trappings of a major city, not to mention the landmark Gateway Arch, St. Louis is at heart a city of small neighborhoods, such as bluesy Soulard south of downtown, the Italian-American "Hill" (boyhood home of baseball legend Yogi Berra), and the collegiate West End district near verdant Forest Park.

One thing you have to see when in St. Louis (you literally cannot miss it) is the **Gateway Arch** (daily, 877/982-1410), still dominating the city skyline. Eero Saarinen's stunning 630-foot stainless-steel monument, officially called the Jefferson National Expansion Memorial, rises up from the riverfront at the foot of Market Street. A small **tram** ($13) carries visitors to an observation chamber at the top. Under the legs of the arch, the free and fascinating **Museum of Westward Expansion,** under renovation until late 2018, chronicles the human wave that swept America's frontier west to the

Pacific. St. Louis has invested more than $400 million on a "CityArchRiver" project to reconnect the city with its riverfront.

West of downtown around the Washington University campus, in **Forest Park**'s 1,300 beautifully landscaped acres, museums of fine art, history, and science fill buildings that date back to the 1904 World's Fair, St. Louis's world-class swan song.

The **St. Louis Cardinals** (314/345-9600), one of the country's most popular baseball teams, play at retro-modern **Busch Stadium,** right downtown, with views of the river and Gateway Arch. Games are broadcast on **KMOX 1120 AM.**

PRACTICALITIES

Freeways and high-speed arteries reminiscent of Los Angeles make a car handy for navigating the St. Louis area—unless you have oodles of money for cab fares. Thanks to the city's sad history of replacing its landmark buildings with blacktop, you'll find plenty of parking lots around downtown.

For food, The Hill neighborhood is hard to beat: **Gian-Tony's** (5356 Daggett Ave., 314/772-4893) is perhaps the best of a dozen classic neighborhood Italian places. Wherever you go, try the toasted ravioli, a local treat. Near Washington University, another great place is the slightly kitschy **Blueberry Hill** (6504 Delmar Blvd., 314/727-4444), a retro-1950s diner that has an excellent jukebox, good burg-

ers, and enough real-life credibility to have attracted the likes of the late St. Louis-born father of rock 'n' roll, Chuck Berry, to play impromptu gigs.

No one leaves St. Louis without cruising old Route 66 southwest from downtown to **Ted Drewes** (6726 Chippewa Ave., 314/481-2652), a local institution famous for its many flavors of "concrete"—a delicious frozen dairy-and-egg-custard concoction so thick you can turn it upside down and not spill a drop. Nearby, fried chicken fans flock to **Hodak's** (2100 Gravois Ave., 314/776-7292). One last Route 66 place has been going strong for more than 60 years: the **Eat-Rite Diner** (622 Chouteau Ave., 314/621-9621), a plain blue-and-white cube serving up breakfasts and burgers daily 24 hours. As the sign says: "Eat Rite, or Don't Eat at All."

St. Louis doesn't have that much of a tourist trade—the muggy weather here in summer keeps most sensible people far away—so places to stay are relatively cheap. At the Gateway Arch, **Hampton Inn St. Louis-Downtown** (333 Washington Ave., 314/621-7900, $119 and up) is one of the more popular downtown hotels. The **Hyatt Regency at the Arch** (315 Chestnut St., 314/655-1234, $139 and up) is another. In a historic reincarnation, a quartet of stately old warehouses has been converted to house the **Westin St. Louis** (811 Spruce St., 314/621-2000, $136 and up), near the arch, the river, and the baseball stadium.

Get a feel for St. Louis listening habits by tuning in to commercial-free **KDHX 88.1 FM.**

No prizes for guessing what those names refer to, since coming from the north you enter the city on Lewis and Clark Boulevard (Hwy-367).

A good main non-freeway route across St. Louis is Kings Highway, which runs north-south past many of the city's main destinations, including Forest Park and the Missouri Botanical Garden, before ending up at Gravois Avenue, part of old Route 66. From here, numerous roads give direct access to I-55 and US-61, both of which link up with the scenic GRR route south to Sainte Genevieve.

St. Louis is the only city where three of our routes coincide—the Great River Road, the Loneliest Road, and Route 66. For the intersection with US-50, **The Loneliest Road,** see page 731.

For the junction with **Route 66,** see page 834. Where the Great River Road hops onto the I-55 freeway for its final approach to St. Louis, a road clearly marked "GRR Spur" leads to **Cahokia Mounds** (see page 833), the remains of the largest prehistoric American city north of Mexico

Sainte Genevieve

South of St. Louis, to avoid the sprawling suburbia, take I-55 as far as exit 162, where you can rejoin the GRR by picking up US-61 south. If you don't blink, you may even catch sight of one of Missouri's rare pilot's-wheel signs as the busy road ascends a ridge with a fine western panorama. About 55 miles south of St. Louis's I-270/255 beltway, the GRR reaches the outskirts of **Sainte Genevieve,** one of several French trading posts established along the Mississippi in the wake of La Salle's 17th-century expedition. The town's new trade is tourism, as the antiques shops and upscale restaurants clearly illustrate, but the beauty of Sainte Genevieve lies in its restored 18th- to 19th-century remnants, including a brick belle of a **Southern Hotel** (146 S. 3rd St., 573/883-3493, $125 and up), one of the oldest hotels west of the Mississippi River. **Sara's Ice Cream & Antiques** (124 Merchant St., 573/883-5890), down toward the water, provides yet more tasteful distractions, with great ice cream cones, old-fashioned soda fountain drinks, and milk shakes.

Since US-61 doesn't enter town, follow the small blue Tourist Information signs down to the old waterfront to find the area's historic places, like the **Bolduc House Museum.** Visit the **Welcome Center** (66 S. Main St., 800/373-7007, daily, free) to learn about the town's past and present.

Sainte Genevieve also boasts a way across the river: the **Sainte Genevieve-Modoc Ferry** (573/883-7097, daily, $2 one-way for pedestrians, $15 one-way for automobiles) to Modoc, Illinois, is three miles out of town; head down Main Street until it dead-ends at the ferry landing. On the Illinois side, 12 rural crop-lined miles from the Modoc Ferry, we rejoin the GRR, heading south on Hwy-3 toward Chester.

ONE OF THE MAGNIFICENT EIGHT-HORSE HITCHES OF INTERNATIONAL CHAMPION CLYDESDALES USED BY THE LARGEST BREWERY IN THE WORLD — ANHEUSER-BUSCH, INC., ST. LOUIS, MO. — BREWERS OF THE FAMOUS BUDWEISER, KING OF BOTTLED BEER.

Kaskaskia, Illinois

Fifteen miles south of Sainte Genevieve, signposted off US-61, is old **Kaskaskia,** the first Illinois state capital and the only Illinois town now west of the Mississippi, thanks to an 1881 flood. "Town" is a generous overstatement: Originally consisting of only a church and a handful of farmhouses, the community has been all but washed away numerous times in its 250-year history, but there's a preserved fort and moody hilltop cemetery to make it worth a visit. Cut off from the Missouri shore by huge levees and a swampy river channel, Kaskaskia is now a ghost town with an illustrious past: It was here, during the American Revolution, that George Rogers Clark and his tiny force of Kentucky "Long Knives" launched their attack against British control of the huge formerly French territory between the Mississippi and Ohio River valleys, a campaign so stunningly successful that it effectively doubled the size of the United States. After capturing Fort Kaskaskia, the victorious Americans rang the 650-pound bell that hung in the French Catholic church; this bell, now in its own Spartan iron-barred chapel, is called the Liberty Bell of the West.

George Rogers Clark's fame as a war hero, Indian fighter, and explorer put him at the top of Thomas Jefferson's short list for leading an expedition into what became the Louisiana Purchase, but the aging Clark nominated his younger brother instead. Thus did William Clark join Meriwether Lewis for their historic journey to the Pacific.

Chester: Home of Popeye

The GRR neatly skips around **Chester,** "Home of Popeye," via a pleasant riverbank detour, returning to Hwy-3 on the downstream side of town. **Popeye** first appeared in print in 1929, and a memorial to Elzie Segar, local creator of the spinach-guzzling scrapping Sailor Man, stands in a picnic area beside the bridge to Missouri; if you miss it, you'll have to turn around on the other side of the Mississippi. As the story goes, Chester locals Frank "Rocky" Fiegel and William "Windy Bill" Schuchert were the inspiration for Popeye the Sailor and Wimpy the Hamburger Fiend. If you pass through at the beginning of September, drop by the annual **Popeye Picnic,** a weekend full of games, food, shows, and amusement rides.

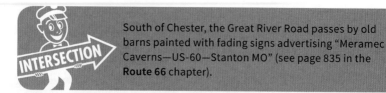

INTERSECTION South of Chester, the Great River Road passes by old barns painted with fading signs advertising "Meramec Caverns—US-60—Stanton MO" (see page 835 in the **Route 66** chapter).

Hwy-3: Shawnee National Forest

No town of any consequence impedes the GRR's 90-mile leg along the southern tip of Illinois. The roadside landscape continues to be fields of heat-loving corn and leafy soybean, while the bluffs of the **Shawnee National Forest** appear to the east. Much of the forested uplands are a botanical crossroads: glacier-borne northern species like the sumac and partridge berry; warmth-seeking southern species like the short-leaf pine; eastern species held back by the Mississippi, such as Virginia willow and silver bell; and western species with a toehold in the east, like Missouri primrose and Ozark coneflower. All count southern Illinois as the edge of their natural ranges. When John James Audubon passed through this region in the early 1800s, he recorded seeing thousands of bright green, red, and yellow-striped parakeets, but these birds are all long extinct.

Jonesboro

Just under 50 miles south of Chester, 8 miles east of the GRR via Hwy-146, the small town of **Jonesboro** hosted the third of seven 1858 U.S. Senate campaign debates between challenger Abe Lincoln and incumbent Stephen Douglas, who tried to portray Lincoln as being out of touch with the people over the issue of slavery. Although Illinois was a designated free state, this area had strong sympathies with the South, something it maintains to this day. For proof, enjoy the down-home ambience and delicious smoked pork barbecue at **Dixie Barbecue** (205 W. Broad St., 618/833-6437). Broad Street, a.k.a. Hwy-146, roughly marks the route of the **Trail of Tears,** the 1838 winter death march of the Cherokee Nation from their homeland west to reservations in Oklahoma.

Back on Hwy-3, just north of I-57 and the town of Cairo, the GRR passes **Horseshoe Lake Conservation Area,** an example of what happens when the river shifts to a new channel and leaves an oxbow lake behind. Now prime winter habitat for over a million migrating geese and ducks, its tupelo gum trees, bald cypress, and swamp cottonwoods foreshadow the scenery found downstream among the bayous of the Mississippi Delta.

Cape Girardeau and the Trail of Tears

If you don't have time to follow the GRR's leisurely wind across southern Illinois, the fastest routes between St. Louis and Memphis are west of the Mississippi, where both US-61 and high-speed I-55 make quick work of the 300-mile drive. Along with Sainte Genevieve, another good stop on the Missouri side is the city of **Cape Girardeau** (pop. 37,941), the biggest and most bustling place for miles. Boyhood hometown of right-wing radio talk-show host Rush Limbaugh, whose father and grandfather were both local lawyers, Cape Girardeau dates its founding back to its days as trading post in the early 1700s, when the area was still in the hands of the French. The long history of the town and surrounding region is engagingly portrayed in a 1,100 foot-long series of

large murals (24 different scenes, totaling nearly 18,000 square feet!), painted on the massive concrete flood walls that protect downtown from Mississippi floods.

You can take in some of the murals, and the whole Cape Girardeau experience, while enjoying a meal at **Port Cape** restaurant (19 N. Water St., 573/334-0954), while more memorable food is on the menu at **Broussard's Cajun Cuisine** (114 N. Main St., 573/334-7235), a block away.

One of many scenes portrayed in the Cape Girardeau murals is a truly tragic one. Six years after wiping out the Native Americans of the upper Mississippi in the Black Hawk War, President Andrew Jackson ordered the "Five Civilized Tribes" of the Cherokee, along with all Native Americans across the southeastern United States, to be forcibly removed from their fertile lands in Florida, Georgia, and Tennessee, where gold had just been discovered. Some 5,000 Cherokee people died along this 1,000-mile journey, during which many of the men, women, and children crossed the Mississippi River here at Cape Girardeau. Ten miles north of town, the 3,400-acre **Trail of Tears State Park** (573/290-5268) preserves the scene of one moment along this marathon tragedy, with a two-mile section of the historic trail and interpretive plaques marking the wooded riverside bluffs.

Cairo

"A grave uncheered by any gleam of promise" was but one of Charles Dickens's unsympathetic descriptions of **Cairo** (pop. 2,831; pronounced "CARE-oh" or "KAY-ro"), the town that presides over—and sometimes under—the meeting of the Mississippi and Ohio Rivers. Routinely submerged by floodwaters until the Corps of Engineers ringed the town with a massive stockade of levees and huge steel floodgates, Cairo's star shone briefly in the steamboat era and during the Civil War, when General Grant quartered his Army of the Tennessee here and Union ironclads were berthed along the waterfront. If you enjoy studying historic buildings (more often than not in Cairo they are empty decaying buildings), you can see many signs of the prosperity that helped Cairo reach a peak population of over 15,000 people: a number of Victorian-era mansions built by merchants and boat captains remain in varying stages of repair, there's a majestic public library, and volunteers have been slowly restoring the stately circa-1872 **Cairo Custom House Museum** (1400 Washington Ave., 618/734-9632, Tues.-Fri., free) into an intriguing if incomplete museum.

Along with the historic remnants, Cairo has something else worth seeing: the confluence of the two mighty rivers. Unless there's a flood in progress (as there was so destructively in the spring of 2011), do your watching from a small platform in

Fort Defiance State Park, at the foot of the bridge that carries US-60 between Missouri and Kentucky, lasting but a quarter mile in Illinois.

While most of Cairo's story is in the past, if you visit you can enjoy one present-day pleasure: the delicious pulled pork sandwiches and other barbecue treats on offer at **Shemwell's** (1102 Washington St., 618/734-0165), just up from the Custom House.

Metropolis: Home of Superman

TRUTH – JUSTICE – THE AMERICAN WAY

The town of **Metropolis, Illinois** (pop. 6,537), along the Ohio River 25 miles northeast of Cairo but most easily accessible via Paducah, Kentucky, takes pride in its adopted superhero son, Superman. An impressive and photogenic 15-foot-tall statue of the Man of Steel stands along Market Street downtown, on a pedestal promoting "Truth—Justice—The American Way," on the north side of the Massac County Courthouse. Nearby are a quick-change telephone booth and the "offices" of the *Daily Planet* newspaper.

Metropolis, Illinois, the hometown of Superman, is also associated with another famous figure: Robert F. Stroud, the "Birdman of Alcatraz," is buried in the Masonic Cemetery.

Every June a festival celebrates the Man of Steel's crime-fighting efforts. For more information, and a look at one of the most extensive collections of Superman artifacts and memorabilia anywhere, visit the **Super Museum** (517 Market St., 618/524-5518, daily, $5), across the street from that selfie-ready statue.

The other big attraction in town is the 40,000-square-foot **Harrah's Metropolis Casino,** down on the banks of the Ohio River at the base of the railroad bridge.

KENTUCKY AND TENNESSEE

Most of the GRR's 60-odd miles across Kentucky are quite scenic, populated by only a handful of small towns, none of which has been overrun by tacky commercial strips. Continuing south across the Tennessee line, the route retains its rural, slow-road feel as it winds along the cultivated bottomlands around earthquake-created **Reelfoot Lake.** Midway to **Memphis,** the GRR comes back to the modern world, crossing the I-55 freeway then rejoining four-lane US-51 as it races to downtown Memphis, passing pine woods and cotton fields mixed with mobile homes, suburban ranch houses, and gas stations.

Wickliffe, Hickman, and New Madrid

Skipping from the banks of the Ohio River, the GRR stays with US-51 southbound through small, thoroughly industrial **Wickliffe** (pop. 688), then takes an attractive 40-mile meander away from the rivers through wooded hill country, returning to the edge of the

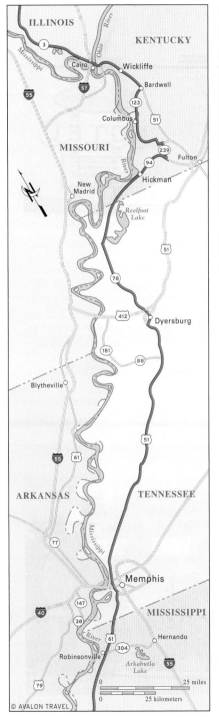

Reelfoot Lake

Mississippi at **Hickman,** a dozen miles from the Tennessee line.

Across from Hickman, on the Missouri side of the river, is the spot where the Army Corps of Engineers blasted a hole in the Mississippi flood wall, taking pressure off the main channel but flooding more than 100,000 acres of riverside farmland around the town of **New Madrid** (pronounced "MAD-rid"). New Madrid, in historical terms, is no stranger to disaster: Besides floods, the town was the epicenter of one of the strongest earthquakes ever to hit the United States, which struck on December 16, 1811. Seismographs weren't around to measure it, but the quake was felt as far away as Boston, and more than 1,000 aftershocks rattled the region for years.

New Madrid conveniently marks the otherwise invisible line between Kentucky and Tennessee, and from here south the GRR follows Hwy-78 across a 40-mile stretch of low-lying bottomlands, passing the roadhouse bars and bait shops near **Reelfoot Lake,** a 25,000-acre recreation area

Memphis

Memphis's gifts to American culture include the supermarket, the drive-in restaurant, the Holiday Inn, Elvis Presley, and Federal Express, and if you detect a pattern here, you'll understand why the city is at once entertainingly kitsch and supremely captivating. This is not to say Memphis (pop. 646,889) lacks a coherent character—just the opposite—but its charms can have unpredictable side effects. Elvis Presley and the Graceland experience are covered on the following pages, but even for those born long after his too-early demise in 1977, Memphis has a lot to offer.

National Civil Rights Museum

Beale Street, downtown between 2nd and 4th Streets, has been Memphis's honky-tonk central ever since native son W. C. Handy set up shop in the early 1900s with the blues he'd learned in Mississippi. Beale Street, and much of downtown Memphis, has been sanitized for your protection, turning it into a (new and improved!) version of its old self. The flashy arena for the Grizzlies basketball team has transformed the entire south side of downtown Memphis. Slap an adhesive name tag on your lapel and you'll fit right in with the tour bus crowds strolling at night along Beale Street's block of clubs—including **B. B. King's** (143 Beale St., 901/524-5464), marked by a giant neon guitar.

Fortunately, a number of other music-related museums and attractions capture a more authentic Memphis: The original **Sun Studio** (706 Union Ave., 800/441-6249, daily, $14), where Elvis, Johnny Cash, Roy Orbison, and many others recorded their historic tracks in the 1950s, is a short walk northeast. Even more satisfying for most

Sun Studio

music obsessives: the site of **Stax Records** studio (926 E. McLemore Ave., 901/942-7685, Tues.-Sun., $13), now an excellent museum documenting the soulful impact of Sam & Dave, Otis Redding, Al Green, and other greats during the 1960s.

If there's one place that shouldn't be missed, it's the eloquent **National Civil Rights Museum** (450 Mulberry St., 901/521-9699, Wed.-Mon., $15), south of Beale Street behind the restored facade of the Lorraine Motel, where Martin Luther King Jr. was assassinated in 1968. Aided by extensive multimedia and life-size dioramas, museum exhibits let you step as far as you like into the powerful struggle of the Civil Rights Movement. Across the street, disturbing displays about King's assassination are housed in the old rooming house where James Earl Ray fired the fatal shot.

On the north side of downtown Memphis, **Mud Island** is a real island in the middle of the Mississippi River, connected to downtown by a pedestrian bridge and a monorail. This 50-acre island holds a five-block-long mock-up of the Mississippi River. Also here is the excellent **Mississippi River Museum.**

Right in downtown Memphis, but just a step away from the majors, the **Memphis Redbirds** (200 Union Ave., 901/721-6000, $9-75), Triple-A farm club for the St. Louis Cardinals, play at **AutoZone Park.**

PRACTICALITIES

As it is with live music, food is one area where Memphis can still surpass just about any other American city, and if your taste buds prefer improvisation and passion to overrefined "perfection," Memphis is sure to satisfy.

Competition among the city's 50 or more rib shacks is fierce. Elvis Presley's favorite barbecue joint, **Charlie Vergos Rendezvous** (52 S. 2nd St., 901/523-2746), right downtown, with its main entrance through a downtown alley, is now something of a tourist trap. Main challengers to the title of "Best Barbecue in the Universe" include **Interstate Bar-B-Que** (2265 S. 3rd St., 901/775-2304), just north of where US-61 crosses I-55, and bare-bones drive-up barbecue stand **Cozy Corner** (735 N. Parkway, 901/527-9158), just east of US-51. For a change of pace from ribs, try the onion rings, burgers, beers, and live blues at another Memphis institution, **Huey's** (77 S. 2nd St., 901/527-2700), right downtown.

Except during the city's many music and food festivals, Memphis accommodations are priced reasonably. The whole alphabet of major chains—from Best Western to Super 8—is spread around the I-240 beltway, and again along I-55 through neighboring Arkansas. One landmark place to stay, the **Peabody Hotel** (149 Union Ave., 901/529-4000, $199 and up) is Memphis's premiere downtown hotel, whose sparkling lobby is home to the Mississippi's most famous mallards: Twice daily, at 11am and 5pm, the red carpet is rolled out for the Peabody ducks to parade (waddle, really) to and from the lobby fountain. And if you're planning a vigil at Graceland, consider **The Guest House at Graceland** (3600 Elvis Presley Blvd., 901/443-3000 or 800/238-2000, $129 and up). Owned by his heirs and next door to his former lair, the upscale lodging opened in 2016 as part of a major overhaul of the Graceland experience, replacing the charming but timeworn old Heartbreak Hotel.

and wildlife refuge created by the New Madrid earthquake. At **Dyersburg** (pop. 17,145), self-described as "friendly, God-fearing, and patriotic citizens living and enjoying big-city conveniences," the Great River Road jumps onto US-51, and from here south to Memphis the route does its level best to mimic an interstate, rendering the final 75 miles a forgettable blur.

Driving Across Memphis

Fans of pop-culture kitsch will love what the GRR offers in Memphis: The main road from the north (US-51) is Danny Thomas Boulevard; south of downtown, this turns into Elvis Presley Boulevard and runs right past the gates of Graceland. (However, if you're continuing on to the Mississippi Delta, from Graceland you should switch onto US-61, which runs about two miles to the west.)

MISSISSIPPI

Ecologically speaking, the Mississippi Delta is the vast alluvial plain between Cairo and the Gulf of Mexico, but "The Delta" of popular myth is much more circumscribed, occupying the 250-mile-long realm of King Cotton between Memphis and Vicksburg. As important as its proper boundaries is its legacy as the cradle of nearly every American musical style from gospel, blues, and jazz to country and rock 'n' roll. The backbone of our route, US-61, is also legendary as the path of the Great Migration, the mass exodus to the industrialized northern United States of some five million black sharecroppers in the decades after World War I.

The word Mississippi comes from the Algonquin word *messipi*, meaning "water from land all over," or "great water."

Mississippi law doesn't require casinos to be riverboats, it merely requires them to float. All appearances to the contrary, the giant Las Vegas-style casinos in Tunica County are indeed floating, mostly in ponds dredged specifically to meet the letter of the law.

As the Great River Road cuts inland and drops like a plumb line across the cotton fields, we recommend a number of side trips to landmarks of this rich cultural heritage. Where the Delta ends at **Vicksburg**'s bluffs, our route begins mingling with ghosts from the South's plantation and Civil War past, then finally rolls into Louisiana.

All across Mississippi, away from the main roads on the sleepier section of the GRR, the towns are filled with shotgun shacks, low-slung Creole-style bungalows, and old trailers that some people have nicknamed "doghouses" without any attempt at irony. What look like oil drums mounted on garden carts in the odd front yard are smokers, for doing barbecue just right; their presence sometimes implies the proximity of a social club or juke joint that may do only weekend business. Local stores, if they exist, are where men in overalls sit and stand in clusters, keeping an eye on the world. In autumn, when the cotton is

IN SEARCH OF ELVIS

Scratch the surface of Memphis and you'll always turn up a little Elvis, like pennies and pocket lint in an old sofa. That guy behind the counter? His mom used to give piano lessons to Elvis's stepbrothers. That woman at the next table? Her after-school job was in the Libertyland amusement park, which Elvis would rent out in its entirety just so he could ride the Zippin' Pippin' roller coaster for hours on end. A frequent Graceland visitor during the Elvis years collected fuzz from the shag carpet to give to friends; maybe the woman paying for her coffee still has her tuft. Even the owner of the greasiest old pizza joint will tell you how Elvis would come in with his band, "back when he was nothin.'" Get used to it: Even decades after his sudden death, Elvis is still everywhere.

The font of all this meta-Elvis-ness is, of course, **Graceland** (3734 Elvis Presley Blvd./US-51, 901/332-3322 or 800/238-2000, daily), about a mile south of I-55 amid a clutter of barbecue joints and muffler shops. At age 21, flush with his early success, Elvis paid $100,000 for Graceland, which was one of the more fashionable houses in Memphis in 1957, and seeing what happens when Elvis's poor-white-boy taste and Hollywood budget run amok is well worth the price of admission, especially since the opening of the expansive new "Elvis: The Entertainer" museum complex in 2017, centerpiece of a $130 million overhaul. Even if you opt out of the $159 VIP Guided Tour, you can buy tickets to each part of Graceland, or splurge on a $57.50 Experience Tour that gives admission to the mansion as well as the other "collections." See the King's private jet or his collection of classic cars, including his famous pink 1955 Cadillac. A room shows off a wall full of gold and platinum records, and the expanded museum traces his love of gospel, blues, and country music.

Elvis is buried on the property, alongside his father and mother, in the Meditation Garden. If you want to pay your respects, his gravesite is free to visit for the first hour every morning.

Elvis's 1955 Cadillac

ready for harvest, huge truck-size bales sit in the cleared muddy margins of the fields, and white fluff accumulates in drifts on the narrow loose shoulder, swirling in small eddies in your wake.

Meanwhile, the Mississippi River does its snaky shuffle off to the Gulf of Mexico behind a continuous line of levees, a bayou here and cut-off lake there, as proof of past indirections.

Casino Country

Leaving Memphis via US-61, the GRR enters DeSoto and Tunica Counties; the place-names memorialize Hernando de Soto, the first European to see the Mississippi, and the combative Tunica people, who forced the Spanish conquistador's

St. Louis likes to claim Tennessee Williams as a native son. While the family did indeed move there when Tom was in the fourth grade, the Mississippi-born playwright hated St. Louis "with a purple passion."

mosquito- and snake-bitten expedition to flee across the river hereabouts in 1542. Outfitted with cannons, priests, slaves, pigs, war dogs, and 1,000 soldiers, de Soto spent years marching through Southern swamps in quest of gold—but he was 450 years too early. Tunica County, long one of the most destitute places in the country, only became a gold mine after the state legalized gambling in 1992. Several billion dollars of investment later, Tunica is the third-largest gambling center in the United States, and every big name in the casino business lines the levee here. Bugsy Siegel would be proud, but as ever, outsiders have benefited much more than the still-poor local residents.

To aid the influx of people anxious to part with their money, US-61 has been turned into a high-volume four-lane highway, and motels, fast-food places, and gas stations have popped up like mushrooms after a spring rain.

Two nongaming benefits of all this investment are the **RiverPark,** where a three-mile hiking trail winds through Mississippi wetlands, giving grand views over the river, and the renovated train depot, which holds the small but scintillating **Gateway to the Blues Museum** ($10) on US-61, where dozens of guitars, historic artifacts, and a small recording studio bring the blues to life in all its tormented and anguished glory.

South of the casino area along US-61, the GRR brings you to another traditional Mississippi experience: the classic grits-and-gravy, steak-and-potatoes **Blue & White Restaurant** (1355 N. US-61, 662/363-1371). Offering a true taste of the Delta with its buffets and local specialties, including flash-fried pickles, the Blue & White has hardly changed since the day it opened at its current location in 1937. South from Tunica, US-61 makes a 35-mile beeline through the cotton fields to Clarksdale.

Moon Lake

Twenty miles south of Tunica's casinos, just west of US-61, **Moon Lake** was home to one of the South's most famous Prohibition landmarks, the Moon Lake Club. Unlike speakeasies associated with thugs and tarts, this club was a family destination where parents could dance and gamble while the kids played by the lake. In a place and time when planes were still so rare the sound of their engines could interrupt work and empty classrooms, the club flew in fresh Maine lobster and Kansas City steak for its clientele of rich white Memphians.

Moon Lake has a literary history too, appearing in a number of Tennessee Williams's dramas. Williams knew it well: Not only was the club property owned by a cousin, but as a boy he had been a frequent guest, accompanying his grandfather, the Reverend Dakin, on parish calls throughout the county.

Thomas Harris, author of The Silence of the Lambs, hails from the tiny hamlet of Rich, just east of the junction of US-61 and US-49.

Helena, Arkansas

About a dozen miles west of the GRR and Moon Lake via US-49 is **Helena, Arkansas,** the deadliest place on the river to Union regiments in the Civil War, stopped in their tracks by the festering malarial swamps that once surrounded the

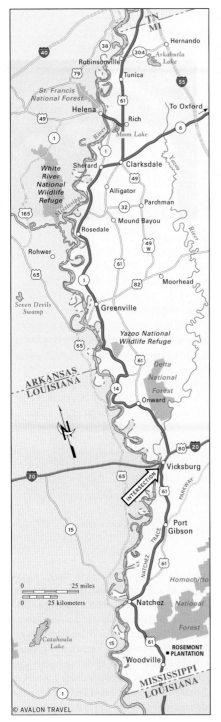

town. It began building a different reputation back in the 1940s when local radio station **KFFA 1360 AM** began broadcasting *King Biscuit Time,* a live blues show hosted by John William "Sonny" Payne; the show is still on the air every weekday at 12:15pm. In early October, the **King Biscuit Blues Festival,** a.k.a. the Arkansas Blues and Heritage Festival, attracts fans by the tens of thousands to hear one of the best lineups of blues in the nation. The **Delta Cultural Center** (141 Cherry St., 870/338-4350, free), in the renovated train depot downtown, with its fine historical displays on the lives of Delta inhabitants, is an equally compelling reason to visit this small river town.

Clarksdale

The blues were born in the Delta, but they grew up in **Clarksdale.** The census rolls for this small town read like a musical hall of fame: Ma Rainey, W. C. Handy, Bessie Smith, Sam Cooke, Ike Turner, Muddy Waters, Wade Walton, John Lee Hooker, Big Jack Johnson, and many others. Their achievements are described—and can be heard—in the **Delta Blues Museum** (662/627-6820, Mon.-Sat., $10) in the circa-1918 railroad depot at the heart of Clarksdale's "Blues Alley" district downtown. Stroll two blocks north to the **Rock & Blues Museum** (113 E. 2nd St., 901/605-8662 or 662/524-5144, hours vary, $5), a more down-home display of memorabilia exploring the international impact of the blues on popular music. Both places offer free maps of the area, calendars of blues events, and all sorts of helpful information and advice. In short, Clarksdale is the best place to start your journey through the Delta blues world.

Ever since W. C. Handy traded his steady gigs in Clarksdale for a career on Beale Street in Memphis, the

GETTING THE BLUES

If serious blues hounds sniff around enough, they can still find the kind of swaggering, sweaty, Saturday-night juke joint that will always be synonymous with real Delta blues. You know the place: bottles of Budweiser on ice in a plastic cooler, clouds of cigarette smoke, some rough customers, hot dancing, and honest gut-wrenching blues played with an intensity that rattles your fillings. Yes, such places exist, and these days they may even have Facebook fan pages, or make the list of area attractions given out by local chambers of commerce.

That said, the homegrown variety announces itself with hand-lettered signs on telephone poles and convenience-store bulletin boards. Ask around, and keep in mind that the blues are rooted in social and economic conditions of the Delta's black community that is no bed of roses; voyeurs slumming as tourists-to-hardship may be politely stonewalled at best. Rest assured, though; with perseverance and the proper attitude (and especially for women, a companion), you'll find what you're looking for. Once you get there, out-of-towners needn't worry about the reception: Blues musicians welcome an appreciative audience, period.

Weekends, again mostly Saturday nights, are also about the only time you'll catch blues in the more commercial juke joints and clubs, simply because so many musicians have other jobs during the week. If you want to be sure of hearing some blues, time your travels to coincide with one of the big annual blues festivals, like these:

Juke Joint Festival (mid-April; Clarksdale, Mississippi)

Sunflower River Blues and Gospel Festival (mid-August; Clarksdale, Mississippi)

Memphis Music and Heritage Festival (Labor Day weekend; Memphis, Tennessee)

Mississippi Delta Blues & Heritage Festival (mid-September; Greenville, Mississippi)

King Biscuit Blues Festival (early October; Helena, Arkansas)

Deep Blues Festival (mid-October; Clarksdale, Mississippi)

Mississippi Delta has exported its blues musicians to places where they receive wider recognition and a living wage, but come on a Friday or Saturday night and you'll see that Clarksdale's juke joints like the resurgent **Red's Lounge** (395 Sunflower Ave.), along the waterfront south of downtown, can still cook up some good hot blues. Many of the most "authentic" juke joints are in dilapidated parts of town, but an infusion of cash by the likes of actor Morgan Freeman has created the more accessible **Ground Zero Blues Club** (662/621-9009), offering meals and music a block west of the Delta Blues Museum. If you're in town during April or August, it would be a shame to miss mid-April's lively **Juke Joint Festival,** or the **Sunflower River Blues and Gospel Festival,** organized by the Blues Association in

partnership with local businesses and organizations and staged every August at venues around town.

The rest of downtown Clarksdale is well worth exploring for its lazy ambience and wealth of history. The old **Delta Cinema** (11 3rd St.), downtown, is closed for most of the year except to host events like the Clarksdale Film Festival and shows during the Juke Joint Festival. There's also a restaurant with a connected steamboat-shaped seating area around the corner, across the street from the Sunflower River. Funky art galleries like **Cat Head Blues & Folk Art** (252 Delta Ave., 662/624-5992) showcase local culture and events while offering an array of hard-to-find CDs, DVDs, and T-shirts. Like the music museums listed above, Cat Head specializes in all things blues, serving as a store, a stage (with frequent free music), a record label, a clearinghouse of information, and a state of mind.

Clarksdale has plenty of fast food, but the barbecue is better: Try **Abe's Bar-B-Q** (616 N. State St., 662/624-9947), in the center of town, cooking up tangy 'cue and hot tamales since 1924. For traditional Deep South diner food mixed with a surprising and comparatively healthy dose of Lebanese-Italian deli items (and fantastic chocolate cream pies), check out **Chamoun's Rest Haven** (419 State St., 662/624-8601, Mon.-Sat.).

US-61, a.k.a. State Street, is also where you'll find Clarksdale's motels, including **Comfort Inn** (818 S. State St., 662/627-5122, $80 and up) at the southern end of town. More adventurous visitors might want to consider Clarksdale's old Afro-American Hospital, where blues vocalist Bessie Smith died in 1937 after a car wreck out on US-61. Now called the **Riverside Hotel** (615 Sunflower Ave., 662/624-9163, $65 and up), it rents a few minimally updated rooms. For a more comfortable but still definitely down-to-earth Delta experience, spend the night in a renovated sharecropper shack at the one-of-a-kind **Shack Up Inn** (662/624-8329, $75 and up), on the grounds of the historic Hopson Plantation three miles south of Clarksdale along Hwy-49. The 19 wooden shacks have plumbing and power but still feel authentic, and you get your own front porch to practice your blues harp or simply take in the Delta dawn; the Shack Up also has other room accommodations, cold beers, and blues music at the on-site **Chapel Bar.**

Oxford

Do you need a break from the Delta yet? Has counting pickup trucks, propane tanks, and barbecued ribs induced a bad imitation drawl? How far would you detour for a well-stocked bookstore, or a restaurant that doesn't immerse everything in boiling oil? Sixty-two miles east of Clarksdale on Hwy-6 is the college town of **Oxford,** whose

Turn off the GRR toward Sam's Town and the Commerce Landing casinos to find the vestiges of **Robinsonville,** hometown of musician Robert Johnson, who, according to blues legend, traded his soul to Satan at "The Crossroads" of Highways 49 and 61 to become king of the blues guitar. In Johnson's day, of course, any guitar-pickin' "musicianer" was thought to be in cahoots with the devil.

Unlike the spreading deltas of the Orinoco or the Nile, the Mississippi cuts a deeper channel as it rolls south, the deceptively smooth surface hiding a flow four times greater than it was at the St. Louis Arch.

About 30 miles south of Clarksdale on US-49 is **Parchman,** infamous home to the state prison farm memorialized in songs like bluesman Bukka White's "Parchman Farm." The "Midnight Special," another oft-heard allusion in Delta blues lyrics, was the weekend train from New Orleans that brought visitors to the prison.

cultural amenities, though common to college towns from Amherst to Berkeley, set it in a world apart from most of Mississippi. The college in question is "Ole Miss," otherwise known as the **University of Mississippi,** whose pleasant yet bustling campus holds the **Center for the Study of Southern Culture** (662/915-5993, Mon.-Fri.), which sponsors exhibits, lectures, and screenings in a renovated antebellum astronomical observatory. The center publishes the excellent Living Blues magazine, and the adjacent J. D. Williams Library holds such treasures as over 8,000 of B. B. King's personal LP collection as well as posters, photos, and more in the **Blues Archive** (Mon.-Fri. 8am-5pm, free), alongside the collected works and first editions of another great Mississippian, William Faulkner. Faulkner was a resident of Oxford for most of his life; readers of his novels will recognize in surrounding Lafayette County (pronounced "luh-FAY-it") elements of Faulkner's fictional Yoknapatawpha. A statue of Faulkner stands in the square at the center of Oxford, and **Rowan Oak** (662/234-3284, Tues.-Sat. 10am-4pm, Sun. 1pm-4pm year-round, Mon. 10am-4pm summer only, $5), his house on Old Taylor Road off South Lamar Avenue, remains as he left it when he died in 1962, with the bottle of whiskey next to the old typewriter in his study almost, but not quite, empty.

Visit Faulkner's gravesite by following the signs from the north side of Courthouse Square. Near the cemetery entrance lie other family members who didn't affect adding the "u" to their surname, including the brother whose untimely death Faulkner mourned in his first novel, *Soldiers' Pay*.

Oxford Practicalities

When respects have been paid to Southern musical and literary culture, and it's time to eat, there's a lot to choose from. The west side of central Courthouse Square is home to two good restaurants, the homespun **Ajax Diner** (118 Courthouse Square, 662/232-8880), with great pies and cobblers, and the eclectic "New Southern" cuisine of the plush **City Grocery** (152 Courthouse Square, 662/232-8080), where

Rowan Oak, former home of William Faulkner

traditional dishes like po'boys and shrimp and grits are complemented by fine wines and a full bar. And thanks to all the Ole Miss students, you can enjoy a range of fast food, pizza places, and live music around Lamar Boulevard, south of the square.

Accommodations in Oxford include a half-dozen large chain hotels and motels, plus a good range of welcoming bed-and-breakfasts like the comfortably worn **5 Twelve** (512 Van Buren Ave., 662/234-8043, $140 and up), formerly the Oliver-Britt House, a circa-1905 B&B.

The **Visit Oxford Visitors Center** (1013 E. Jackson Ave., 662/232-2477) will happily provide more information and a calendar of cultural events. Another good source of information is **Square Books** (662/236-2262), on the south side of the same square. This is one of the country's great independent bookstores, with a full range of local and international authors, plus a nice café.

Hwy-1: Great River Road State Park

Between Clarksdale and Greenville, the Great River Road winds west of the much busier US-61, looping next to the Mississippi River along Hwy-1. It's a rural road, running past soybean, cotton, and "pond cat" farms—catfish farming is big business hereabouts. Midway along, the GRR runs past **Great River Road State Park,** near the town of Rosedale. Located inside the Mississippi River levee, the park offers unique views of the "Father of Waters" from a 75-foot-high overlook tower.

Across the Mississippi from Rosedale in a cotton field off Hwy-1 is **Rohwer, Arkansas,** where about 8,000 Japanese Americans were imprisoned during World War II.

Farther south, at the north edge of Greenville, the 1,000-year-old, 55-foot-high earthen cones next to the highway are the remnants of the prehistoric Mound Builder people who lived here a millennium ago. Now preserved as the **Winterville Mounds,** the 12 ancient mounds that remain are thought to have been sacred ceremonial sites. Little is known about the enigmatic people who built them and hundreds of others along the banks of the Mississippi and Ohio Rivers, but the on-site **museum** (daily, free) shows off a range of pottery and arrowheads recovered here.

Greenville

The Delta's largest city, **Greenville** (pop. 34,400) is one of the largest river ports in the state, but instead of cotton-shipping wharves, its levees are now lined by floating casinos. Hwy-1 through Greenville takes top honors for the least attractive strip of gas stations and minimarts along the GRR, but appearances can be deceiving, as the city has some fine cultural traditions, from the anti-Ku Klux Klan editorializing of Hodding Carter's *Delta-Democrat Times* during the 1950s and 1960s to the great steaks and hot tamales served up since 1941 at **Doe's Eat Place** (502 Nelson St., 662/334-3315). Despite being granted a James Beard "American Classic" award in 2007, Doe's is still housed in the same big white building it started in (follow North Broadway to the brick churches, then turn toward the river).

About 30 miles east of Greenville, **Moorhead** is known in blues geography as the place "where the Southern crosses the Dog," an allusion to the Southern and Yazoo-Delta (a.k.a. Yellow Dog) Railroads. Nearby **Money, Mississippi,** was the location of the notorious 1955 murder of 14-year-old Emmett Till, a key moment in the burgeoning Civil Rights Movement.

It's known for good food and good spirits throughout the state—and all over the South. Several other Doe's Eat Place restaurants have opened, including one in Little Rock, Arkansas, that was made famous by former president Bill Clinton.

Hearing Delta blues live can be as big a challenge as finding it on the radio. Helena, Arkansas's historic **KFFA 1360 AM** plays at least half an hour at lunchtime and on Sunday nights.

Though Doe's looks homespun, its prices are not; steaks will set you back a good $19 or more.

For faster, more affordable food, stop for breakfast at **Jim's Café** (314 Washington Ave., 662/332-5951) or try the chili-cheese combos at **Gino's Hamburgers & Catfish** (128 W. Reed St., 662/378-9655), off South Main Street.

Second to Clarksdale in the Delta blues galaxy, Greenville comes alive in mid-September during the annual **Mississippi Delta Blues and Heritage Festival** (662/335-3523). For accommodations, look along US-82 near the junction with US-61, east of town.

Highway 61 Revisited

Between Greenville and Vicksburg, the GRR contin-ues along Hwy-1 through the cotton-rich bottom-lands, the landscape as unvarying as the country music that dominates the radio dial. Before the Civil War, this land was nearly uninhabitable hardwood forests and fever-riddled swamps, home to snakes, panthers, fire ants, and mosquitoes. After Reconstruction, the valuable oaks, sweetgum, and hickory were logged off, the swamps drained, and levees built. Now just the snakes and mosquitoes remain. It's a long, slow ride, while US-61 races along to the east.

East of Greenville, just west of US-61, the town of **Leland** was the boyhood home of Muppet-master Jim Henson. There's now a small and suitably warm-spir-ited museum, on the north side of US-82 at Deer Creek, honoring him, Kermit the Frog, and his other creations. Another 15 miles farther east, blues great B. B. King was born on a cotton plantation near **Indianola** in 1925, and the town honors its favorite son with an annual festival every summer. After his death in 2015, King had his funeral in Memphis but was buried in a memorial garden at the excellent **B. B. King Museum** (400 2nd St., 662/887-9539, daily, $15),

R.I.P., Robert Johnson

housed in a restored redbrick cotton gin factory where King worked before breaking through as a guitar player and blues singer. King also owned, preserved, and performed an annual concert at Indianola's historic **Club Ebony** (404 Hanna St.), two blocks from the museum, marked by the life-size statue of this larger-than-life bluesman.

The 50 miles of US-82 between Greenville and Greenwood pass through the heart of Delta blues country, and a number of nearby towns feature high on any blues pilgrimage itinerary. **Holly Ridge** holds the grave of **Charley Patton** ("Voice of the Delta," 1891-1934). **Robert Johnson** (1911-1938) is remembered by a burial marker in **Morgan City** (one of three alleged grave sites for the blues legend). Farther south on US-61, **Rolling Fork** was the birthplace of **Muddy Waters** (1915-1983), while the great bass player and songwriter Willie Dixon (1915-1992) was born in Vicksburg.

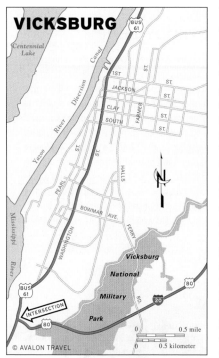

Vicksburg

The "Red Carpet City of the South," **Vicksburg** (pop. 23,856) didn't roll one out for the Union army during the Civil War. Instead, the city so stubbornly opposed Union efforts to win control of the Mississippi River that it became the target of one of the longest sieges in U.S. military history. After the war ended, Vicksburg suffered once again in 1876, when the city woke up to face a mud flat of flopping fish after the Mississippi River found itself a new streambed—overnight. Thanks to the diligence of engineers who redirected the Yazoo River in 1903, Vicksburg has its waterfront back, now complete with several modern-day sharks, whose slot machines and roulette wheels spin 24 hours a day for your entertainment.

Many of the city's posh antebellum houses survived the Civil War with varying degrees of damage, and during the postwar Reconstruction several additional mansions were added to the bluffs overlooking the river. Most of these homes are open to the public (for around $10 each), and during the fortnight-long "Pilgrimages" in mid-spring and mid-fall, slightly discounted multiple-house tours are available. The architecturally varied mansions, many of which Double-As B&Bs, and their copious inventories of fine antiques are more fascinating to decorative arts aficionados than to history buffs, who may find tours illuminating more for what is omitted than included. Stories of deprivation and Union plundering, cannonballs in parlor walls, and other wartime relics are religiously enshrined, yet only rarely is a word spoken about slavery.

The most famous of Vicksburg's antebellum homes turned B&Bs is **Cedar Grove Inn** (2200 Oak St., 601/636-1000, $135 and up), south of downtown, which has a spectacular panorama over lush gardens and railroad yards down the bluffs to the broad Mississippi River. Ironically, Cedar Grove was built for a cousin of General Sherman, who used it as a military hospital. Another grand old mansion, **Anchuca** (1010 E. 1st St., 601/661-0111, $145 and up), preserves a more complete picture of antebellum life, with well-preserved gardens and slave quarters, plus a fine café. Dozens more, dating from the 1870s up through the early 1900s, are found throughout Vicksburg's pleasant cobblestone residential areas.

The downtown commercial district, on the bluffs above the river, offers another, more contemporary glimpse into Southern culture. If you've ever tried to imagine a world without Coke, step into the **Biedenharn Coca-Cola Museum** (1107 Washington St.), smack downtown, and see where one man's ingenuity slew all hopes for such a world. Here, in 1894, Joseph Biedenharn conceived of putting the strictly regional soda-fountain drink into bottles, the better to reach new markets.

BIRTH OF THE TEDDY BEAR

About 30 miles north of Vicksburg along US-61, the hamlet of **Onward** has a historical plaque marking the birthplace of the teddy bear, originally inspired by a cub from the woods near Onward. Tied by a noose to a tree in the canebrakes, the cute fellow was found by President Teddy Roosevelt while hunting here in 1902. His refusal to shoot the defenseless animal, publicized in an editorial cartoon, garnered such popular approval that a New York firm requested the president's permission to name a stuffed toy after him. The only rub is, T. R. didn't actually refuse to shoot—because, in fact, he wasn't there. But neither was the cub! According to members of the hunting party, the president's guide, Holt Collier, an African American veteran of the Confederate cavalry, was challenged to prove he could lasso a bear. So he did, when one came along through the swamp—an old and rather weak one, as it turned out, that splashed around in a slough before they cut him loose. T. R., however, having tired of waiting for game, had returned to camp and missed the whole episode.

The rest, as they say, is history. Toast worldwide domination with some of the classic stuff, straight up or over ice cream, or pay $3.50 to view galleries full of old promotional serving trays and the like.

Vicksburg National Military Park

Though the engineering feat that redirected the Yazoo and Mississippi Rivers (and brought Vicksburg more civil engineers per capita than any other U.S. city) is impressive, it's the story of the Civil War campaign to split the Confederacy in half that dominates history here. The battle for Vicksburg, which was known as the

Vicksburg stands at the junction of the Great River Road and our **Southern Pacific** route along US-80 (see page 800). Coverage of this route, running from San Diego to Savannah, begins on page 762.

"Gibraltar of the Confederacy," reached its dramatic conclusion on July 4, 1863, amid the strategic heights and ravines of the 1,853-acre **Vicksburg National Military Park.** The ins and outs and strategizing behind the 47-day Siege of Vicksburg, and the story behind the 1,300-odd markers and monuments, becomes emotionally compelling after some accounting of the anecdotes of individual valor, of odd courtesies amid the bloodshed, and of the tragedy and humanity that lie behind the 16 winding miles of stone. The **visitors center** (601/636-0583, daily, $15 per car), on the east side of Vicksburg via Clay Street or off I-20 exit 4, has exhibits, maps, brochures, and audio tours with narration and sound effects. Or you can hire a guide to accompany you in your car and explain everything from battle tactics to the symbolism of the monuments. The advantage to a live guide is the opportunity to ask questions and to delve into whatever suits your curiosity, be it stories of the many women who fought incognito, or of the immigrants who enlisted to win citizenship.

Late in the year when the pecan crop is in, you can buy pecans from vans or shacks beside the highway. Buy pre-shelled ones, or spend hours struggling with a nutcracker.

While Vicksburg's surrender allowed President Lincoln to declare that "the Father of Waters now flows unvexed to the sea," local whites stayed vexed for over 80 years: Because the surrender occurred on July 4, until the end of World War II Independence Day in Vicksburg was celebrated only by African Americans.

One of the most unusual sights in the Vicksburg Military Park is the **USS Cairo,** an ironclad paddlewheel battleship that was sunk by a torpedo during the Civil War. Preserved for a century by the Mississippi mud, it was recovered and restored and is now on display in its own museum, above the river at the west end of the park.

Vicksburg also has two military cemeteries, one for each side. The Union cemetery is the largest Civil War burial ground in the country, holding the remains of more than 17,000 soldiers who died here and all over the south; more than 12,000 of the dead are simply marked "unknown." Another 5,000 Confederate dead are buried in the Vicksburg City Cemetery.

Vicksburg Practicalities

Vicksburg has an enormously compelling history, but it's also a pleasant place to spend some time. For a traditional home-style feast, sit down to the communal round table at **Walnut Hills** (1214 Adams St., 601/638-4910, Wed.-Mon.) and dig into the endless supply of classic regional dishes, from fried chicken to fried dill pickles. Given the fresh ingredients (and depending on how much of a pig you can be), the moderate prices are a great value, and the overall ambience embodies the essence of Southern hospitality. Tamale addicts should seek out **Solly's Hot Tamales** (1921 Washington St., 601/636-2020), near the Cedar Grove mansion on US-61 Business.

The icon of Southern gentility and refreshment, the mint julep, was allegedly born in Vicksburg: Water from fragrant Mint Springs in what is now the National Military Park was mixed with good Kentucky bourbon brought to town by riverboat captains. It goes without saying that Kentuckians and Tennesseeans consider this pure fiction.

You won't notice many people lolling about on grassy lawns or parks in the southern Delta, for the simple reason that this has become the realm of the fire ant, whose stinging bite would shame a wasp into adopting some other line of work.

Vicksburg motels, found at the south edge of town along I-20 between the Mississippi River and the Military Park, include a wide selection of the national chains and their local imitators; one of the nicest is the **Deluxe Inn** (2751 N. Frontage Rd., 601/636-5121, $55 and up).

If you're in the mood, you can play Rhett and Scarlett for a night, pampering yourself with canopied beds in one of the dozen camellia-draped antebellum mansions (including Cedar Grove and Anchuca) that Double-As plush B&Bs. Any will have you whistling "Dixie," but true history buffs will want to request the Grant Room at Cedar Grove, which is still furnished with the very bed the general used after Union forces occupied Vicksburg. The staff claims Grant was a bedridden drunk for his entire stay, but pay no attention—he was probably a poor tipper at the bar, and folks around here bear grudges for generations over things like that.

For thorough information on lodging and attractions, contact the friendly **Vicksburg Convention and Visitors Bureau** (52 Old Hwy-27, 601/636-9421 or 800/221-3536) near the entrance to the National Military Park. If your visit falls during Pilgrimage, don't expect easy pickings on rooms: Most B&Bs are booked up months in advance for those weeks.

Port Gibson

One of the many little gems of the GRR is 30 miles south of Vicksburg: **Port Gibson,** the town General Grant found "too beautiful to burn." As they did with Savannah, Georgia, the Union Army spared Port Gibson during the Civil War, and decades of economic doldrums have spared the town from the Walmart sprawl that at times seems to have enveloped the rest of the South. Fine homes still grace the pleasantly shaded main drag, but most eye-catching is the giant Monty Python prop known as the **Church of the Golden Hand** because its steeple is topped by a gold-leafed hand, its index finger pointing the way to heaven. Actually, this is the circa-1859 **First Presbyterian Church** (601/437-5428), whose interior is lit by the gasoliers of the famous steamboat *Robert E. Lee,* the record-setting winner of the Great Steamboat Race of 1870. Newspapers of the day reckoned that millions of dollars were wagered on the outcome of the New Orleans-to-St. Louis race, which attracted international attention. The *Lee*'s three-day, 18-hour, and 14-minute victory was an upset for the favored title holder, the *Natchez.*

Across the street from the Golden Hand, next to an Exxon station, stands another

the Church of the Golden Hand

unusual building, **Temple Gemiluth Chassed,** an elaborate Moorish-arched temple built in 1892 by Port Gibson's then large and prosperous Jewish community.

Ruins of Windsor and Emerald Mound

From Port Gibson, you can race along the 70-mph US-61 to Natchez or follow a quietly scenic 50-mile detour along kudzu-lined country back roads and the serene Natchez Trace Parkway. The great Mississippi writer Willie Morris said "there is no more haunted, complex terrain in America" than this, and traveling through here you can't help but be aware of the region's many ghostly remnants. The looping first part of this route leaves Port Gibson next to the Exxon station, heading west on Rodney Road (Hwy-552) toward the Mississippi River past abandoned homesteads and picturesque old cemeteries rotting in the woods. After about 12 miles, look for a small sign and follow a short gravel road until you spot giant stone columns poking through the treetops. This is the **Ruins of Windsor.** Once the state's most lavish Greek Revival mansion and a landmark to river pilots, it was reduced by an 1890 fire to its bare Corinthian ribs.

Ruins of Windsor

the only known drawing of Windsor before the fire

Another enigmatic ruin is farther south, nearly invisible in the lush growth: **Emerald Mound** (daily), a prehistoric platform over 400 feet wide and 35 feet tall. The second-largest mound in North America, it was built around AD 1250 and was still in use as a ceremonial center when the first Europeans arrived; Emerald Mound is located on Hwy-553 just west of Natchez Trace Parkway milepost 10.3.

For an overview of a nearly vanished Southern culture, spend some time at the **Museum of the Southern Jewish Experience,** with exhibits in the basement of **Temple B'nai Israel** (213 S. Commerce St., 601/362-6357, by appointment only) in Natchez.

Natchez

Before the Civil War, **Natchez** (pronounced "NATCH-iss," rhymes with "matches") had the most millionaires per capita in the United States, and it shows. If luxurious antebellum houses make your heart beat faster, Natchez (which has more than 500 antebellum structures inside the city limits), with its innumerable white columns and rich smorgasbord of Italian marble, imported crystal, and sterling silver, might just put you in the local ICU. That so much antebellum finery still exists is because Natchez, unlike Vicksburg, surrendered to Grant's army almost without a fight. Anti-Yankee sentiment may in fact run higher now than during the war, for Natchez was vehemently opposed to the Confederacy and outspokenly against Mississippi's secession from the Union. Since Natchez was second only to New Orleans as social and cultural capital of a region with two-thirds of the richest people in America, most of whom owed

There are no cotton fields around Natchez, because all the cotton that paid for these mansions was grown across the river in the Louisiana bottomlands.

Across the Mississippi from Natchez, the town of **Ferriday, Louisiana,** was where rocker Jerry Lee "Great Balls of Fire" Lewis and his cousin, evangelist Jimmy Swaggart, grew up.

their wealth to slave-picked cotton, its support of the Union might seem a little incongruous.

Of course, such apparent contradictions should come as no surprise from a community raised with genteel cotillions and the Mississippi's busiest red-light district side-by-side. Once-disreputable Natchez Under-the-Hill, where the most famous brothel in the South was destroyed by a fire in 1992, is today but a single gentrified block of riverfront bars and restaurants.

As befits the place that originated the concept, the annual **Natchez Pilgrimages** (held for four weeks in late spring and around two weeks in the fall) are longer than you will typically find elsewhere. **Antebellum mansions** open to the public, hoop skirts and brass-buttoned waistcoats abound, and musical diversions like the Historic Natchez Tableaux are held almost nightly. Among the most fascinating homes open year-round is the one that didn't get finished: **Longwood,** on Lower Woodville Road, is the nation's largest octagonal house, capped by a red onion dome. Its grounds are fittingly Gothic too, with moss-dripping tree limbs, a sunken driveway, and the family cemetery out in the woods. Information on the Pilgrimages, other **house tours** ($10 and up per house), and the chance to stay in one of many historic B&Bs all comes from the same group, **Natchez Pilgrimage Tours** (601/446-6631 or 800/647-6742), which also runs horse-drawn carriage tours. Southern history doesn't merely comprise those Greek Revival heaps and their *Gone with the Wind* stereotypes. Natchez, for example, had a large population of free blacks, whose story is told in downtown's **Museum of African American History and Culture** (301 Main St., 601/445-0728, Mon.-Fri. 10am-4:30pm), in the old post office, where you'll also find interesting Black Heritage walking-tour brochures. A large Jewish section in the **City Cemetery** (follow signs for the National Cemetery; City Cemetery is along the way) also furnishes evidence of the South's tapestried past. The marble statuary and decorative wrought iron offer a pleasant outdoor respite for weary mansion-goers too.

Dunleith antebellum mansion

Natchez Practicalities

As befits a place with a strong tourism trade, Natchez has some great places to eat. Natchez is almost the southern extremity of the Tamale Belt, and you can sit down to a dish of them at **Fat Mama's** (303 S. Canal St., 601/442-4548, $10 for a dozen tamales). Fat Mama's also serves killer Knock You Naked frozen margaritas, a combination that draws large crowds on summer nights.

Mammy's Cupboard, Natchez

If you prefer fried catfish, po'boys, and chocolate shakes, head down to **The Malt Shop** (601/445-4843), where Doctor Martin Luther King Street (US-61 Business) dead-ends into Homochitto Street. For a change of pace, try **Pearl Street Pasta** (105 S. Pearl St., 601/442-9284), just off Main Street, whose menu is eclectic, reasonably priced, and laced with vegetables that haven't been boiled to oblivion.

Natchez landmark **Mammy's Cupboard** (601/445-8957, Tues.-Sat. 11am-2pm, cash only) is a roadside restaurant in the shape of a five-times-larger-than-life Southern woman, whose red skirts house the small dining room and gift shop. Surviving from an earlier era, the restaurant has adapted to evolving attitudes about cultural racism by changing her skin tone from dark black to light brown. Mammy's offers homemade lunches, daily specials, iced tea, and blueberry lemonade served in mason jars, and a huge range of scrumptious desserts. Mammy's Cupboard can be found along the east side of four-lane US-61, roughly five miles south of downtown Natchez. If Mammy's is closed, you might want to take a look at the building then continue down the road to the modern and spacious **Roux 61** (453 US-61, 601/445-0004) for huge portions of fresh-fried Mississippi catfish and Louisiana Cajun fare.

Accommodations in Natchez include a few familiar names scattered along US-61 and US-84 both north and south of downtown. For a more memorable experience, consider staying the night in one of those historic mansions, many of which do double duty as B&Bs. Top of the line is probably **Dunleith Historic Hotel** (84 Homochitto St., 601/446-8500 or 800/433-2445, $150 and up), preserved as it was in its grand antebellum heyday and set amid acres of lush gardens, with croquet and boccie ball courts and a large but discreetly obscured swimming pool. Keep in mind that the enormous popularity of Pilgrimage may require seriously advanced bookings, especially at weekends.

Woodville: Rosemont Plantation

Rolling and curving past hay fields and woods, the distinctively red earth of southern Mississippi crowding the soft shoulders, the GRR passes quickly over the 45 miles between Natchez and the Louisiana state line. You won't see it from the highway, but just across the Mississippi River is possibly the most significant piece of engineering anywhere along its length: the **Old River Control Project.** More than mere flood control, the project is designed to keep the Mississippi going down to Baton Rouge and New Orleans, rather than finding a new route to the Gulf via the Atchafalaya River. This actually happened during the 1948 flood, and there are hydrologists who predict it is only a matter of time before it will happen again—a potential economic catastrophe for downstream cities along both rivers.

About 10 miles north of the Louisiana border, an unprepossessing intersection

NATCHEZ TRACE PARKWAY

A mile or so south of Port Gibson, US-61 and the GRR cross the much more relaxed Natchez Trace Parkway, which, like the Blue Ridge Parkway, is a scenic route managed by the National Park Service. The parkway follows the route of the old Natchez Trace, a pre-Columbian Native American path that grew into the major overland route between the Gulf Coast and the upper Mississippi and Ohio River Valleys in the years before steamboats provided a faster alternative. The Natchez Trace appeared on maps as early as 1733, and from the 1780s to the 1820s, when steamboats made it obsolete, the Natchez Trace was one of the nation's most traveled routes. Farmers and craftspeople in the Ohio River Valley would transport their products by raft downstream to Natchez or New Orleans, then return on foot, staying at the dozens of inns along the route while doing battle with swamps, mosquitoes, and bands of thieves.

The entire 444-mile length of the parkway, which runs from Nashville south to the edge of Natchez, with a short break around Jackson, is well paved and makes a delightful driving or riding route, with places of interest marked every few miles. Just north of Port Gibson at mile marker 41.5, the Sunken Trace preserves a deeply eroded 200-yard-long section of the trail, the canopy of moss-laden cypress trees offering one of the most evocative five-minute walks you can imagine. Between Port Gibson and Natchez, sights along this short and eminently bikable stretch include the prehistoric **Emerald Mound,** the second-largest ceremonial mound in the United States, which dates from around AD 1250 and offers a commanding view of the woodlands. **Mount Locust,** at mile marker 15.5, is a restored roadhouse and visitors center and the best place to pick up parkway information.

The National Park Police keep the parkway under thorough radar surveillance, by the way, so try to stay within the posted speed limit, generally 50 mph.

of gas stations marks the turnoff west for **Woodville** (pop. 1,096), where a lovely old courthouse sits at the center of a green square full of stately old oak trees, and three historic churches line the somnolent streets.

The biggest attraction of Woodville, however, is a mile east of the GRR on US-24, where a small sign along the highway marks the entrance to **Rosemont Plantation,** the boyhood home of the Confederacy's President Jefferson Davis. Built in 1810 with wooden pegs holding together hand-hewn posts and beams, the house is surrounded by a grove of live oaks and a large rose garden, planted by Davis's mother, after which the plantation takes its name.

LOUISIANA

As the GRR approaches its southern end, land and river begin to merge. With giant levees on one side and standing water on the other, it's easy to imagine the land is sinking—and indeed, by the time you roll off elevated I-10 into New Orleans, you will be four to six feet below sea level.

From the St. Francisville ferry to the interstate bridge just west of New Orleans, the GRR crosses the Mississippi four times, threading along rough back

roads past a series of fine antebellum plantation homes along what's sometimes called **Plantation Alley.** The GRR also runs among a barrage of industrial giants whose toxic discharges have earned the region another sobriquet: Chemical Corridor. The Great River Road across Louisiana is not without its charms—a vividly painted church out in a field, or wrought iron gates framing exquisitely gnarled live oaks festooned with Spanish moss—but these are all too often overshadowed by the specter of a land being poisoned for profit. End of sermon.

St. Francisville

The past is ever-present in this part of the country, so turn west off US-61 at **St. Francisville** and explore the myriad tales of this fascinating community, which grew up around the graveyard of a frontier-era monastery. Stop at the **West Feliciana Historical Society Museum and Tourist Information Center** (11757 Ferdinand St., 225/635-6330, daily 9am-5pm, free), for a sample of the architectural charms that draw visitors to this curious little town. All around St. Francisville are grand old manor homes, most notably at **Rosedown Plantation** (225/635-3332, daily, $12), on Hwy-10 just east of US-61, where a 374-acre state-run historic site preserves an 1830s main house and lush formal gardens. About five miles southeast of St. Francisville on Hwy-965, the **Audubon State Historic Site** (225/635-3739, Wed.-Sun., $10) is also known as the Oakley House, where in 1821 naturalist and illustrator John James Audubon came to work as a resident tutor while he compiled his comprehensive *Birds of America*.

Rosedown Plantation in St. Francisville

Along with the rich history, St. Francisville also has a couple of compelling culinary attractions, including the **Magnolia Café** (225/635-6528), a wonderful little restaurant housed in the old 3V motor court complex at the corner of Commerce and Ferdinand Streets. The café moved here when its original home (a gas station) burned down in 2003, but it's better than ever, still serving some of the best-tasting po'boys in the state that invented them. There's also a coffeehouse-cum-art gallery and cabins for overnight guests; there's no better place to get a feel for this part of Louisiana.

Heading on from St. Francisville, race south down US-61 to Baton Rouge or head west across the river on the John James Audubon Bridge toward Louisiana's legendary Cajun Country.

Baton Rouge

From the lofty vantage point of the I-10 bridge over the Mississippi River, **Baton Rouge** (pop. 229,493) appears to be a largely industrial city, its skyline

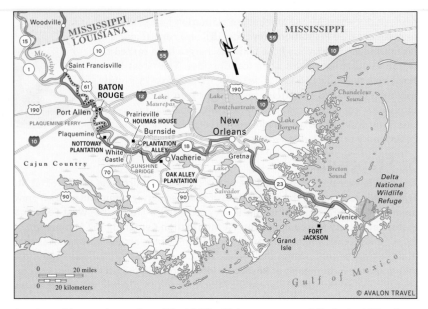

dominated by smokestacks, a World War II destroyer, two Mississippi Riverboat casinos, and the nation's tallest state capitol—essentially a 34-story monument to the populist demagoguery of Huey "Kingfish" Long. Just south of the towering capitol, the state's legendary Depression-era governor dominates the **Old State Capitol** (Tues.-Fri. 10am-4pm, Sat. 9am-3pm, free), that clearly visible white Gothic-style castle—the only thing missing is a moat. Inside the restored 1847 edifice are engaging audio-aided history exhibits, including one about Huey Long's unresolved 1935 assassination: Was the patronage-dealing, road-building, vote-buying potentate the target of premeditated murder, or was then-U.S. Senator Long the victim of his five trigger-happy bodyguards' "friendly fire," aimed at a man who merely punched the boss? Review the evidence and draw your own conclusions.

Another lesson in Louisiana history can be yours at the wonderful **Rural Life Museum** (4560 Essen Lane, 225/765-2437, daily 8am-5pm, $10), managed by Louisiana State University and located east of downtown off I-10 exit 160. This expansive collection of shotgun houses, barns, farming equipment, riverboats, donkey carts, hand tools, and appliances—basically, anything that might have been seen in the state 100 to 200 years ago—was assembled on a former plantation by landscaper Steele Burden. The rest of the 450 acres of land is now picturesque gardens.

Gonzales, just outside Baton Rouge, hosts the **Ascension Hot Air Balloon Championship** (www.ascensionballooning.com) in late September. Besides being a beautiful sight, the hundreds of colorful

balloons take part in a target competition, trying to drop beanbags onto a bull's-eye from 1,000 feet in the air.

The popularity of college football shouldn't be underestimated in Baton Rouge: "Motel No Vacancy" signs light up all over town whenever the **LSU Tigers** (tickets 800/960-8587) play. Basketball, baseball, and other sports are big too.

Baton Rouge Practicalities

If you're looking for a place to eat and absorb a little Baton Rouge ambience, the **Pastime** (252 South Blvd., 225/343-5490), a few blocks from the Old State Capitol, right under the I-10 interchange, is one of those windowless, smoky sports bars ideally suited for discussing political chicanery over po'boys, fried fish, and beer. It has the best pizzas in town, too—try the one topped with crawfish for some local flavor.

Another bunch of good eating and drinking prospects are clustered around the Highland Avenue entrance to Louisiana State University, a couple of miles south of I-10. **Louie's Café** (3322 Lake St., 225/346-8221), is open 24 hours, so there's no excuse to miss it. Facing the North Gates of LSU, **The Chimes** (3357 Highland Rd., 225/383-1754), a restaurant and tap room with over 100 beers and a live music venue next door. Several other bars in the vicinity offer music with some regularity, but be warned that undergraduate projectile vomiting is a serious hazard.

While there are a number of hotels in downtown Baton Rouge and along the highways south and east of town, most of the inexpensive accommodations cluster around exit 151 on I-10, three miles west of the Mississippi in Port Allen. For a memorably characterful overnight, try **The Stockade Bed & Breakfast** (8860 Highland Rd., 225/769-7358, $150 and up), a home-style inn on spacious grounds near LSU.

Louisiana is divided into parishes rather than counties, one of many subtle reminders of the original French Catholic settlement of the state.

The bridge that now carries US-190 over the Mississippi was built during the gubernatorial reign of the notorious "Kingfish," Huey P. Long. The structure was designed to be low enough to prevent oceangoing freighters from passing, thus snuffing out the chances of Vicksburg and other upstream cities to compete with the port of Baton Rouge.

Cajun Country

West of New Orleans and Baton Rouge, a world away from the grand houses lining the Mississippi River, the watery world known as **Cajun Country** spreads along the Gulf of Mexico. If you have the time to explore, the region offers an incredible range of delights for all the senses: antebellum plantation houses and moss-covered monuments set amid groves of stately old oak trees, with all manner of wildlife, from birds to gators, chirping and squawking away in the oddly still bayous, and the sound of accordions and the aroma of boudin sausages and boiling crawfish emanating from what can seem like every other doorway. Cajun Country is also sugarcane country: Over half a million acres are cultivated each year, rising to 10 feet in height by the end of summer, when the cane is chopped down and made into molasses at the many aromatic mills. The name "Cajun" comes from the French-speaking Roman Catholic Acadians, 10,000 of whom were chucked out of Canada when the English took over in 1755. The Acadians were refused entry by the American colonies on the East Coast and had to make their way to this corner of still-French Louisiana, where they absorbed many other cultural influences while retaining their distinct identity.

For a dramatic perspective, take Hwy-70 to cross the Mississippi River on the **Sunshine Bridge,** which runs between Donaldson and I-10. A quick link between Plantation Alley and New Orleans, the Sunshine Bridge was named in honor of "Singing Governor" Jimmie Davis's most famous song, "You Are My Sunshine," now the state's official song.

US-90, the main route through Cajun Country, follows the route of the Old Spanish Trail, the historic cross-country highway that, in the early days of the automobile, linked San Diego and St. Augustine. Though the main route has been widened and "improved" countless times in the past century (it is often signed as "Future I-49"), many wonderful stretches of old country road still wind along shady bayous.

Wandering aimlessly and getting lost amid the many small backwater towns is half the fun of spending time here, but there are a number of places where the whole Cajun Country experience comes together in a concentrated dose. One of your main stops should be the historic town of **St. Martinville,** where the **St. Martin de Tours Catholic Church** (133 S. Main St., 337/394-6021) stands at the center of many blocks of ornate buildings and majestic oak trees, including the one featured in the Cajun-flavored Longfellow poem "Evangeline."

St. Martinville is just north of **New Iberia,** the home of Tabasco sauce, perhaps Cajun Country's most identifiable product, and just south of another great stop in Cajun Country: **Breaux Bridge,** the "Crawfish Capital of the World," located just off the I-10 freeway, about an hour west of Baton Rouge.

Plantation Alley

Between Baton Rouge and New Orleans, if you don't have a stomach strong enough to bear miles of industrial blight, hop onto the I-10 freeway, but if your senses can handle the constant juxtaposition of refined domestic design alongside unsightly industrial complexes, with a few trailer parks, upscale vacation homes, and photogenic aboveground cemeteries thrown in for good measure, the Great River Road is full of treats, and this 100-mile traverse of **Plantation Alley** may well be a highlight of your trip. To 19th-century passengers aboard the packet steamboats traveling the lower Mississippi, the great mansions adorning the river bends between Baton Rouge and New Orleans must have made an impressive sight. The houses are no less grand today, but, sadly, their surroundings have been degraded by the presence of enormous petrochemical refineries. These have, by and large, replaced the antebellum sugarcane fields as the region's economic engine, but in late summer when the cane is 10 feet tall and the smell of molasses fills the air, you can *almost* pretend nothing has changed.

To get a real feel for Louisiana's extensive bayous, you have to get out of the car. A number of outfits offer "swamp tours," including **Swamp Adventures** (504/810-3866).

Giving directions along Plantation Alley is complicated by the winding Mississippi, with its bridges and ferry boats, by the numerous roads and highways, and by the fact that the region is equally easy to explore from Baton Rouge or New Orleans, but it's as a good place as any to get lost and found again, so take your time and enjoy the ride. Nottoway, Houmas House, Oak Alley, and Laura are four of the most popular and memorable plantation estates, but there are many along the way, in varying stages of restoration and decay.

Nottoway

Heading from the north to the south, as the river flows, the first of these riverside manors is **Nottoway** (225/545-2730, daily, $20, $119 and up), among the largest plantation homes in the South. Built in the 1850s, it was also one of the last "big houses" to be built. On the western shore of the Mississippi, along Hwy-1 about two miles north of the town of White Castle, Nottoway is a bright white Greek Revival structure enclosing over an acre of floor space, so you'll be glad you don't have to pay the air-conditioning bills or do the dusting. If you like the look of it all, you can stay for lunch in the grand dining room or overnight in one of many lushly appointed rooms.

Burnside: Houmas House

The most familiar (and easiest to reach) of Louisiana's plantation homes, **Houmas House** (40136 Hwy-942, 225/473-9380, daily, $24), stands on the east bank of the Mississippi amid 38 acres of manicured grounds. Another of Louisiana's grandes dames, Houmas House is a dignified complex of buildings constructed over many generations, mainly between the 1780s and 1840s. The main building is composed of white columns and rich red-ocher walls supporting a central belvedere (like a cupola) from which the antebellum owners could survey their domain. Today, the endless seas of sugarcane have been replaced in part by the monstrous sprawl of the neighboring DuPont plant. Once the seat of a massive 475,000-acre sugarcane plantation, Houmas House may well look strangely familiar: The stately home was used as the setting for Robert Aldrich's 1964 Gothic Southern horror film, *Hush . . . Hush, Sweet Charlotte,* starring Bette Davis, Olivia de Havilland, Joseph Cotten, and Bruce Dern. B&B rooms and a restaurant are also available.

Located on Hwy-942 near the hamlet of Darrow, Houmas House is just five miles southwest of the I-10 freeway via Hwy-22 or Hwy-44, and it is about five miles north of the Sunshine Bridge (Hwy-70) over the Mississippi.

New Orleans

New Orleans has long been famous for its easygoing, live-and-let-live personality, and for placing a high value on the good things in life—food, drink, and music, to name a few.

Royal Street in the French Quarter

With deep roots going back to the earliest days of European settlement in North America, New Orleans is very proud of its multicultural heritage: Its people, its ornate buildings, and especially its food all reflect a uniquely diverse and resilient culture. The focus of New Orleans, for visitors and locals alike, is the **Vieux Carré,** in the French Quarter, which sits on the highest ground in the city and thus escaped the worst of Katrina's floods. Centering on Bourbon Street, lined with tacky souvenir stalls and strip clubs catering to conventioneers, this square mile is full of wrought-iron balconies on picturesque brick buildings. Yes, it's a huge tourist attraction, but it's also the heart of old New Orleans. At the center of the quarter is **Jackson Square,** where a statue of the victor of the Battle of New Orleans, Andrew Jackson, stands in front of St. Louis Cathedral, which was rebuilt in 1850 on top of an original foundation dating back to 1724. The nearby **Old U.S. Mint** (400 Esplanade, 504/568-6968, closed Mon., $5) holds excellent collections tracing the history of two New Orleans institutions: jazz and Mardi Gras.

Jackson Square

After dark, there's live music aplenty in all styles and modes, but one stop you have to make is **Preservation Hall** (726 St. Peter St., 504/522-2841, nightly from 8pm, $15-45), for the redolent ambience and the live traditional Dixieland jazz, still going strong after 50 years.

West of town near the airport, the **New Orleans Baby Cakes** play Triple-A baseball all summer long.

PRACTICALITIES

New Orleans has some of the best and most enjoyable places to eat in the world, so plan to take the time to enjoy yourself here. In the French Quarter, the informal **Acme Oyster House** (724 Iberville St., 504/522-5973) is the place to go for the freshest bivalves, but it closes early by New Orleans standards—around 10pm on weeknights and 11pm on Friday and Saturday. Another very popular spot is **K-Paul's Louisiana Kitchen** (416 Chartres St., 504/596-2530), where Chef Paul Prudhomme, who popularized Cajun-style "blackened" food all over the country, saves the very best examples for his own place. Another world-famous place that merits a meal or two is **NOLA** (534 St. Louis St., 504/522-6652), a comparatively casual setting for celebrated chef Emeril Lagasse's finely crafted Creole fare. For a taste of local character and Cajun comfort food, ride the St. Charles street car west to friendly **Jacques-Imo's Café** (8324 Oak St., 504/861-0886).

No visit to New Orleans is complete without a stop for coffee and beignets (and some serious people-watching) at busy **Café du Monde** (800 Decatur St., 504/525-4544), open 24 hours a day (except on Christmas) on the river side of Jackson Square.

Antoine's Restaurant, 713 St. Louis St., New Orleans

Except during Mardi Gras, Jazz Fest, or Superdome football games, places to stay in New Orleans aren't *all* that expensive. In the French Quarter, the characterful **Olivier House** (828 Toulouse St., 504/525-8456, $139 and up) is a quirky, family-run hotel filling a pair of French Quarter townhouses. Another good bet is **Place d'Armes Hotel** (625 St. Ann St., 504/524-4531 or 800/366-2743, $100 and up), right off Jackson Square at the heart of the French Quarter, with rooms facing onto a quiet courtyard.

Vacherie: Oak Alley and Laura

Traveling along the GRR, moldering concrete mausoleums, houses with loud colors and louvered French doors, and insouciant pedestrians along the levee (not to mention the dangerously large potholes) may arrest your attention briefly, but **Oak Alley** (3645 Hwy-18/Great River Rd., 225/265-2151, daily, $22) will probably stop you in your tracks. This place is to antebellum plantations what Bora Bora is

Oak Alley

to islands, or the Golden Gate is to bridges: Even if you've managed to avoid seeing Oak Alley on tourist brochures, or in the movies *Interview with a Vampire* or *Primary Colors,* it will look familiar—or rather, it will look exactly like it ought to. Plus, no cooling tower or gas flare mars the immediate horizon. For the full effect of the grand quarter-mile-long allée of arching live oaks, which were planted in the 1700s, nearly a century before the current house was built in the late 1830s, drive past the entrance a short ways. Besides the obligatory tour, there's lodging and a restaurant in buildings on the grounds surrounding the main house.

Oak Alley stands on the west bank of the river, about four miles west of Vacherie. The house is about 15 miles south of the Sunshine Bridge and 8 miles west of the Veterans Memorial Bridge (Hwy-3213).

As a colorful antidote to the grand whitewashed privilege on display at Oak Alley, set aside some time for a tour of nearby **Laura Plantation** (2247 Hwy-18, 225/265-7690, daily, $20) as well. Smaller, but seeming more in touch with the realities of sugarcane plantation life, Laura presents itself as a Creole plantation and plays up the myriad of ethnicities and cultures that came together in Louisiana. Laura is three miles downriver from Oak Alley.

From the GRR near Oak Alley, you can see the neighboring plantation, **Felicity,** which was used as a primary location for the 2014 Academy Award-winning Best Picture, *12 Years a Slave.* It's not open for tours.

Continuing south from Vacherie, scattered housing begins to invade the sugarcane, and traffic starts to pick up as the GRR (Hwy-18) works its serpentine way past a pair of ferry landings, a nuclear power plant, and a huge chemical plant with a photogenic cemetery felicitously occupying its front yard. By the time the GRR is within sight of the stylish, rusty-red I-310 bridge, the tentacles of New Orleans's bustle are definitely apparent. Hop on the interstate eastbound, and inside of 25 miles you can be hunting for parking in New Orleans's Vieux Carré, or searching for a Sazerac to celebrate the journey.

Driving New Orleans

Assuming you resisted the industrial-strength charms of US-61 and opted to take the I-10 freeway into town, stay on it until you reach downtown, then get off and

inside Fort Jackson

park the car as soon as you can, and get out and walk. New Orleans rivals Boston for the discomfort it causes drivers, and there are no driving routes that let you see anything you can't see better on foot—or from the St. Charles trolley. Parking in and around the French Quarter is a nightmare, and the small print on the signs can set you up for a ticket or a tow, so play it safe and park in one of the many nearby lots, which typically charge anything from $7 to $10 a day (if you can get an early bird rate) to $10 an hour (if you can't).

Hwy-23: To the Gulf

From downtown New Orleans, if you really, really want to follow the Mississippi River all the way to its mouth at the Gulf of Mexico, you can. (Well, almost . . .) From the Superdome, take the US-90 bridge south across the river to Gretna, where you can join the Belle Chasse Highway (Hwy-23), which follows alongside the river for about 75 miles, ending up at Venice, still a dozen miles from the gulf, on the fringes of the Delta National Wildlife Refuge. Apart from swamps and giant freighters, the main sight along the route is old **Fort Jackson,** eight miles northeast of Venice. Built following the War of 1812 to help protect the river from invasion, Fort Jackson was flooded and badly damaged by the Hurricane Katrina storm surge.

Because the Mississippi in its natural pre-Corps state created a raised channel for itself between embankments of silt, the river sits higher than a third of Louisiana. Much of New Orleans, as the world learned during the Hurricane Katrina disaster, is below sea level, and the river has been dredged to a depth of more than 50 feet.

The Appalachian Trail

This driving route parallels the hiking trail, from the top of New England to the heart of Dixie, taking you through continuous natural beauty—without the sweat, bugs, or blisters.

GREEN MOUNTAINS VERMONT

APPALACHIAN TRAIL
MAINE TO GEORGIA

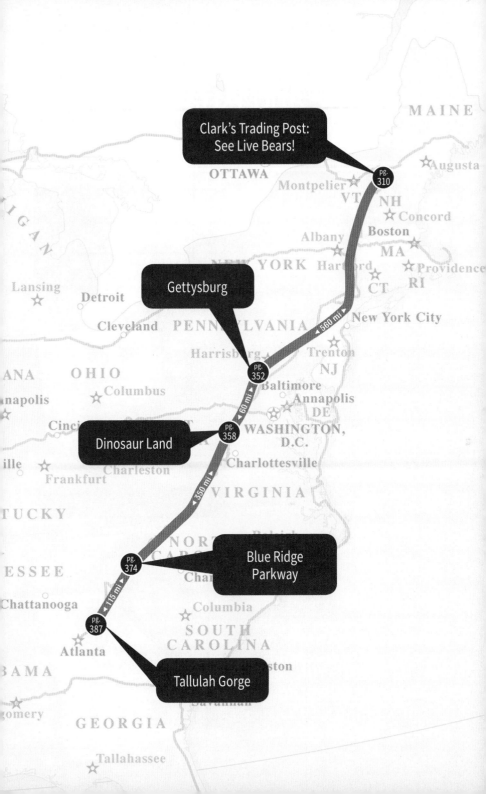

Between the North Woods of Maine and Atlanta, Georgia

The longest and best-known hiking trail in the country, the **Appalachian Trail** winds from the North Woods of Maine all the way south to Georgia. While you won't earn the same kudos driving as you would by walking, the following scenic roads come close to paralleling the pedestrian route, taking you through the almost continuous natural beauty without the sweat and blisters. Best of all, this driving route follows magnificently scenic two-lane roads all the way from the top of New England to the heart of Dixie, running past a wealth of fascinating towns and historic sites.

The Appalachian landscape holds some of the wealthiest, and some of the neediest, areas in the entire country. These contrasting worlds often sit within a few miles of one another: Every resort and retirement community seems to have its alter ego as a former mill town, now as dependent on tourism as they once were upon the land and its resources.

After an extended sojourn through the rugged and buggy

Shenandoah National Park

wilds of northern **Maine**, where the hikers' route winds to the top of Mt. Katahdin, our Appalachian Trail driving tour reaches an early high point atop windswept Mt. Washington in the heart of **New Hampshire's Presidential Range.** From these 6,000-foot peaks, the tallest mountains in New England and some of the hardest and most dura-

Great Smoky Mountains National Park

ble rocks on earth, the route winds through **Vermont's Green Mountains**, taking in the idyllic charms of rural New England, with its summer homes and liberal-arts college communities. Beyond the **Berkshires**, the summer destination of the Boston and New York culture vultures and intelligentsia for most of two centuries, towns become even more prissy and pretty as we approach within commuting distance of New York City.

Skirting the Big Apple, our route ducks down through the **Delaware Water Gap** to enter the suddenly industrial Lehigh Valley, former land of coal and steel that's now struggling to find an economic replacement. South of here, we pass through the heart of the world-famous **Pennsylvania Dutch Country**, where the simple life is under the onslaught of package tourism.

South from Pennsylvania, nearly to the end of the route in **Georgia**, the Appalachian Trail runs through continuous nature, with barely a city to be seen. Starting with Virginia's **Shenandoah National Park**, then following the **Blue Ridge Parkway** across the breathtaking mountains of western **North Carolina**, it's all-American scenic highway all the way, with recommended detours east and west to visit such fascinating historic sights as Thomas Jefferson's home, Monticello, outside Charlottesville, Virginia; the most opulent mansion in America, Asheville's Biltmore; the real-life town that inspired TV's *Mayberry RFD*—Mount Airy, North Carolina; or the white water featured in the film *Deliverance*, north Georgia's Chattooga River.

All in all, the Appalachian Trail is an amazing drive, whether or not you come for fall color.

NEW HAMPSHIRE

"Live Free or Die" is the feisty motto of tiny New Hampshire, the state that hits the national limelight every four years when its political primaries launch the horse race for the White House. During the presidential campaign's opening stretch, locals have to turn into hermits to avoid having their votes solicited by every candidate running and their opinions polled by every reporter. Some of New Hampshire's million residents take the state's motto to heart, however, and when you see the ruggedness of the landscape, you'll appreciate how easy it is to find isolation from the madding crowd.

Though the **Appalachian Trail** runs within day-hiking distance of over 50 million people, most of the route is intensely solitary—only one in four people manage to hike the entire 2,190-mile trail each year.

Despite its apparent brevity, the route across New Hampshire provides a hearty sampling of the topographic spectrum from its start at New England's highest peak, **Mt. Washington,** to neighboring Vermont amid the rolling farmland of the **Connecticut River Valley.**

Although clear-day views from the summit of Mt. Washington are amazing, the summit is more often socked in and cold. Snow can fall any month of the year.

Mt. Washington

The star attraction of the White Mountains' Presidential Range, 6,288-foot **Mt. Washington** stands head and shoulders above every other peak in New England. East of the Mississippi, only Mt. Mitchell and Mt. Craig in North Carolina's Blue Ridge and Clingman's Dome in Tennessee's Great Smokies are taller. Despite its natural defenses—such as notoriously fierce storms that arise without warning—Mt. Washington is accessible to an almost unfortunate degree. The **Mount Washington Auto Road** (603/466-3988, daily May-mid-Oct., weather permitting, $29 car and driver, $9 each additional adult) was first opened for carriages in 1861, earning it the nickname "America's Oldest Man-Made Tourist Attraction." It still switchbacks up the eastern side, climbing some 4,700 feet in barely eight miles. A marvel of engineering, construction, and maintenance, the Mount Washington Auto Road offers a great variety of impressions of the mountain and wonderful views from almost every turn.

historic Tip Top House at the summit of Mt. Washington

If the weather is clear, you can see the Atlantic Ocean from the top of the mountain; in summer, mornings tend to be clearer, and sunny afternoons turn cloudy and stormy on the summit, complete with lightning and thunder. At the top, be prepared for winter weather any time of year (it can and does snow here every month of the year). Stop inside the **Sherman Adams Summit Building,** which

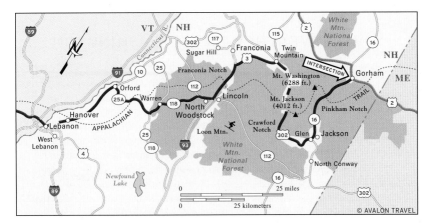

has displays on the historic hotels and taverns that have graced the top over the years, as well as a cafeteria. Visited by hundreds of people every day throughout the summer, since the 1850s the summit of Mt. Washington has sprouted a series of restaurants and hotels—even a daily newspaper. The most evocative remnant of these is the tiny **Tip Top House**, "the oldest mountaintop hostelry in the world," now a state historic site.

> The first automobile ascent of Mt. Washington was made in 1899 by Freelan O. Stanley, piloting one of his namesake Stanley Steamers.

Cyclists, runners, and motorists regularly race each other up the road to the summit, but there is another, much easier ride to the top: the **Mount Washington Cog Railway,** which climbs slowly but surely straight up and down the mountain's western slope from Bretton Woods. While most trains now run on clean, efficient biodiesel, a few of the morning trains still use steam-power.

Pinkham Notch

South from the foot of the Mount Washington Auto Road, Route 16 passes through Pinkham Notch, a mostly undeveloped stretch of the White Mountains lined by forests and a few ski areas. About four miles south of the Auto Road is the area's outdoorsy Grand Central Station: the **Pinkham Notch Visitor Center.** Operated by the venerable Appalachian Mountain Club (AMC), the year-round trailhead facility offers topographical maps, guidebooks, weather updates, and precautionary advice, as well as limited gear. The camp also offers snacks, a dining hall, a 24-hour hikers' pack-up room with restrooms and showers, scheduled shuttle van service, and the **Joe Dodge Lodge** (603/466-2727, about $63 and up per person for bed and board), a modern hostel with shared bunk rooms, a few private doubles and family-rooms, and great views from the library.

Along the northeastern side of the White Mountains, between Grafton Notch and Mt. Washington, the Appalachian Trail parallels **The Great Northern** route of US-2 (see page 550). Full coverage of this route begins on page 470.

SEVERE WEATHER ON MT. WASHINGTON

A mountain barely over 6,000 feet hardly deserves the same respect as Mt. Everest (29,029 feet), or even Mt. McKinley (20,320 feet), yet people get into serious and sometimes fatal trouble on the slopes of New Hampshire's Mt. Washington all the same. Easy access invites complacency and a tendency to ignore trailside warnings advising retreat if you're unprepared for bad weather. But do respect the facts of nature: Simply put, the Presidential Range of the White Mountains experiences some of the worst weather in the world, rivaling both Antarctica and the Alaska-Yukon ranges for consistently raw and bone-numbing combinations of gale-force winds, freezing temperatures, and precipitation. Lashings by 100-mph winds occur year-round on Mt. Washington, whose summit holds the title for highest sustained wind speed on the face of the planet (231 mph in April 1934). Cloudy days outnumber clear ones on the peak, where snowstorms can strike any month of the year, and even in the balmiest summer months the average high temperature at the summit hovers around 50°F. Compounding the weather's potential severity is its total unpredictability: A day hike begun with sunblock and short sleeves can end up in driving rain and temperatures just 10 degrees above freezing—or worse, in a total whiteout above the tree line—even as a group of hikers a couple of miles away on a neighboring peak enjoys lunch under blue skies and warm breezes.

Listen to what your mom and dad always told you: Be careful and don't take chances. Be prepared. Don't hike or ski alone. Carry enough water and food. Learn to recognize and prevent hypothermia. Figure out how to read your trail maps and use your compass *before* you get caught in pelting sleet above tree line. It's better to feel foolish packing potentially unnecessary wool sweaters and rain gear for a hike in July than to have your name added to the body count.

North to Mt. Katahdin

North and east of Mt. Washington, the Appalachian Trail runs through one of its toughest sections, rambling through Mahoosuc Notch into Maine, then passing through **Grafton Notch State Park.** There are no real roads anywhere near here, so drivers wanting a quick taste of this impenetrable country will have to join US-2 for the drive through Gorham, New Hampshire, and Bethel, Maine, then wind along the Bear River on scenic Route 26. Beyond Grafton Notch, the hikers' Appalachian Trail passes through ever more extensive wilderness, with fewer services (and many more mosquitoes and black flies!) the closer you get to the trail's northern finish, atop **Mt. Katahdin.**

In New England, locals call their highways "routes," and we've followed suit, using Route as a generic term (Route 100, for example, rather than Hwy-100). The interstates (I-93) and federal highways (US-3) are abbreviated as usual.

Though the hiking trail and the nearest roads are like strands of a double helix, both routes take you through some memorable country, especially around Rangeley Lakes and Moosehead Lake, in the deep Maine woods.

Mt. Washington Valley: Jackson

Dropping sharply away to the south of Pinkham Notch is the Ellis River, along whose banks sits the northern gateway to the Mt. Washington valley, resort-dominated **Jackson** (pop. 816). Given the number of lodgings among the attractive century-old clapboard homes, it seems the principal village occupation is innkeeper. The porches, gables, and chimneys hint at standard country B&B charms: lazy breakfasts in summer, nooks and crannies brimming with roses, and crackling fires in your room at night. A covered bridge beside Route 16, taverns filled with antiques, and winter sleigh rides complete Jackson's postcard image of Merry Olde New England.

To park a car at any trailhead in the **White Mountain National Forest,** you'll need to buy a pass from one of the information centers or online; these passes cost about $5 and are good for seven days.

The Jackson area is not only pretty but also has a couple of northern New Hampshire's best places to eat, drink, and sleep. At the junction of Route 16 and Route 16A, the **Shannon Door Pub** (603/383-4211) is usually just the right side of crowded—full of skiers, hikers, and other hungry folks enjoying hearty food, good beers, and frequent live, folksy, classic-rock-tinged music in a jovial

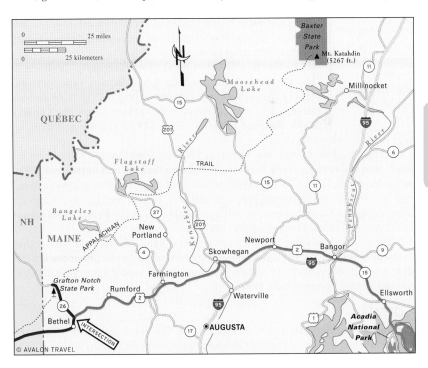

setting. In business for over 60 years, the pub was a main character in John Sayles's first film, *The Return of the Secaucus Seven*. The fanciest restaurant and grandest hotel in Jackson are both in the stately **Wentworth** (603/383-9700, $154 and up) at the heart of the village, welcoming travelers since it was established back in 1869.

Glen

A half mile south of Jackson along Route 16 or Route 16A you pass the picturesque **Jackson Covered Bridge**, where the two alternative routes rejoin at the north edge of tiny **Glen**. In the short stretch between the bridge and the junction with US-302, Glen has one of the more concentrated barrages of roadside clutter in the White Mountains. Glen is best known not for hiking or sightseeing but as home to the children's theme park **Story Land** (603/383-4186, daily summer, $34, free under age 2), where among its many playfully designed and carefully coiffed acres, the highlights include a boat ride, a raft ride, and a fiberglass cow that gives fake milk when you squeeze its fake udders.

A half mile south of Story Land, Route 16 links up with US-302 at a cluster of shops where the **Red Parka Steakhouse & Pub** (603/383-4344), a jolly moderate-to-inexpensive place to eat and drink, has live music most weekend nights.

North Conway

If you're overdue for a little retail therapy, you might consider continuing south on Route 16 from the US-302 junction toward **North Conway** (pop. 2,349), one of the cornerstones of New England's factory-outlet circuit. If you can turn a blind eye to all the retail frenzy, North Conway's central park offers one of the best views of Mt. Washington, and its baseball diamond hosts some pretty intense games.

Besides factory-outlet stores, North Conway is also home to New Hampshire's most popular scenic railroad, running steam engines throughout summer and during the fall color season. Based out of North Conway's downtown depot, the **Conway Scenic Railroad** (603/356-5251, $17.50 and up depending on trip) runs historic trains.

> Just over the Maine border, about 10 miles east of North Conway via US-302, the town of **Fryeburg** hosts a weeklong agricultural fair during the first week in October that is one of the most popular in New England—packed with tractor pulls, horse racing, lots of music, even a pig scramble (a contest involving livestock, not an egg dish).

Although all the tourists may well drive you away from North Conway, there are some good places to eat along Route 16, like **Elvio's Pizzeria and Restaurant** (2888 White Mountain Hwy., 603/356-3208), where you can get slices or full pies, submarine sandwiches, and big salads, plus wine and beer. During the day, the place to eat home-style breakfasts or great sandwiches is family-friendly **Peach's Restaurant** (2506 White Mountain Hwy., 603/356-5860).

There are lots of accommodations on and near Route 16, from old cabin courts to anodyne motels, but the most interesting place has to be the **Cranmore Inn** (80 Kearsarge Rd., 603/356-5502, $79 and up), a quick walk east of Route 16, which has been welcoming travelers since 1863.

Conway

Conway, five miles down Route 16 from North Conway at the south end of the scenic railroad line, is a nicer littler town, with a couple of restaurants, a post

Conway Scenic Railroad

office, and the clean and friendly **White Mountains Hostel** (36 Washington St., 866/902-2521, $34 per person, $64 private rooms), in the heart of town. If you have your doubts about hosteling, this place is sure to dispel them; it's as clean as it is serene, and besides saving money staying here, you're apt to meet like-minded fellow travelers over breakfast or relaxing in the game room.

Up in the hills above Conway, off Route 16, and half a mile south of the Kancamagus Highway at the edge of the White Mountains National Forest, the **Darby Field Inn and Restaurant** (603/447-2181, $165 and up) is a B&B open year-round for skiing, hiking, and great après-outdoors meals.

Kancamagus Highway

Running east-west from Conway over the mountains to Lincoln, the 34-mile **Kancamagus Highway** (Route 112) is a National Scenic Byway and one of the most incredible drives in the White Mountains. Much shorter and a lot less traveled than the prime tourist route along US-302 and US-3 through Crawford and Franconia Notches, The Kanc, as it's often called, takes you up and over the crest of the peaks, giving grand vistas over an almost completely undeveloped landscape—great for fall-color leaf-peeping. Fall is definitely prime time for the drive, but any time of year (except maybe winter, when it can be a bit hairy) it's a lovely trip, lined by lupines in early summer and raging waterfalls in the spring.

The name Kancamagus honors the local Native American chief who controlled the area when the first European settlers began arriving at the White Mountains in the 1680s. The roadway was not paved until 1964 and was declared a National Scenic Byway in 1989.

Near the midpoint of The Kanc, the **Russell-Colbath House** dates from the early 1830s and now houses a small **museum** (Sat.-Sun. summer, free) with an on-site historic interpreter and exhibits describing the lives of the White Mountains' early settlers. From the house, the short loop Rail N' River Trail explores the effects loggers had on this region in the 1890s, when everything you see along The Kanc (and most everywhere else) was devastated by clear-cutting.

Three miles farther west, just east of the crest and an easy half-mile walk from the well-signed parking area, **Sabbaday Falls** is a lovely little waterfall roaring through a narrow gorge. In a series of noisy, splashing cascades, the river drops down through a polished pink granite gorge, barely 10 feet wide but surrounded by dense forest. It's an ideal picnic spot, and only 10 or 15 minutes from the road.

Crawford Notch

US-302 between Glen and Twin Mountain winds west around the southern flank of the Presidential Range, then heads north through **Crawford Notch,** another of the

Fall foliage is at its best when warm clear days are followed by cold nights that stop the essential pigment-producing sugars from circulating out of the leaves. Sugar production is low on cloudy days, when warm nights allow the sugars to disperse before the brightest colors are produced.

White Mountains' high passes and centerpiece of the **Crawford Notch State Park.** The road closely follows the Saco River through new-growth forest; the oaks and white pine of the lower valley give way to more birch and spruce as you gain elevation.

Crawford Notch offers good **day hikes** to various waterfalls and vantage points such as **Frankenstein Cliff,** named for an artist whose work helped popularize the White Mountains, and 140-foot **Arethusa Falls,** the state's second-highest waterfall.

For ambitious and well-prepared hikers, the north end of Crawford Notch is the start of the oldest and perhaps grandest walking trail in the country, the eight-mile **Crawford Path** up towering Mt. Washington. A strenuous, demanding, and potentially dangerous route, the Crawford Path is also breathtakingly beautiful. A walk along it gives an almost complete picture of the White Mountains—sparkling brooks, fields of wildflowers, and glorious mountaintop panoramas.

Mount Washington Hotel and Cog Railway

North of Crawford Notch, the highway joins the Ammonoosuc River headwaters as they flow toward the Connecticut River, passing **Bretton Woods** and the access road for the **Mount Washington Cog Railway** (603/278-5404, spring-fall, adults $69). The giant **Omni Mount Washington Resort** (603/278-1000, $199 and up) dominates the surrounding plain, its Victorian luxury no longer standing in such grand isolation below the peaks of the Presidentials now that a ski resort sits across the highway and motels and condos squat around its skirts. Built at the turn of the 20th century by Pennsylvania Railroad tycoon Joseph Stickney, the Mount Washington Hotel received its most lasting recognition as host of the 1944 United Nations International Monetary Conference, the historic meeting of financiers from 44 nations that established the World Bank and chose the dollar as the global standard for international trade.

Climbing the mountains behind the hotel, the Mount Washington Cog Railway was built in 1869 and has a maximum grade of 37.5 percent, surpassed by only one other non-funicular railroad in the world, high up in the Swiss

Mount Washington Cog Railway

Omni Mount Washington Resort

Alps. One cinder-spewing engine runs on coal, but others have been adapted to run on eco-friendly biodiesel. This historic "Railway to the Moon" takes over an hour to ratchet up the three-mile track to the often windy, cold summit. You can take a round trip, or you can ride up and hike (or ski) back down.

Much more active and exciting than the slow chug up the cog railroad is the **Bretton Woods Canopy Tour** ($89 and up), which takes you up into the top of the trees by way of cables, bridges, and zip-lines.

Franconia and Sugar Hill

Between Twin Mountain (at the junction of US-302 and US-3) and where US-3 merges with I-93, you'll find the aging face of the area's long association with tourism: a variety of motel courts and "housekeeping cottages" at least as old as you are. Despite their outward dowdiness, several make a virtue of the rustic setting, but given their prime location, most are hardly the bargains you might hope for. More interesting and historic lodging may be had on a 200-acre working farm in **Franconia** (pop. 1,104), where, since 1899, the friendly Sherburn family's **Pinestead Farm Lodge** (603/823-8121, $60 and up, shared bath and kitchen), on Route 116 south of town, has offered simple rooms and warm hospitality at reasonable rates.

Just west of Franconia on Route 117 is **Sugar Hill.** The township is aptly named: The sugarbush (a grove of sugar maples) on Hildex Farm contributes its unforgettable essence to breakfasts at the popular **Polly's Pancake Parlor** (603/823-5575, daily 7am-3pm spring-fall). Polly's is located in the farm's

The first known ascent of Mt. Washington was made in 1642 by Darby Field of Durham, New Hampshire, who historians believe followed a route near that of today's Crawford Path.

thrice-expanded 1830 carriage shed. Warning: After trying real maple syrup, you may never be able to go back to Mrs. Butterworth's again.

The most famous farm in the vicinity is certainly **The Frost Place** (603/823-5510, $5 adults) off Route 116 south of the Franconia village intersection. Besides the half-mile Poetry Trail and the displays of Robert Frost memorabilia from his five-year full-time residency and 19 summers here, there's a regular program of readings by the current poet-in-residence during the summer.

> Parking along New Hampshire highways is illegal, so don't be tempted to leave your car beside the road while you take a hike up that nearby hill—you may return to find it's been towed to some town 20 miles away.

Franconia Notch

Franconia Notch is probably the most popular spot in the White Mountains, and, despite the numbers of visitors, it's a fantastic place to spend some time. I-93, the country's only two-lane interstate, offers easy access; a host of attractions—an aerial tram, the state's own "little Grand Canyon," covered bridges, a powerful waterfall called the Flume Gorge, even a trading post with trained bears—make it a great place to linger. If you give yourself the time to hike around or just sit still by a mountain stream, you could easily spend a week or more enjoying it all.

The main draw in Franconia Notch used to be one of the most famous landmarks in New England: the Old Man of the Mountain, a series of five granite ledges 1,200 feet above the valley that seemed to resemble an old man's profile when viewed from certain angles. After years of reconstructive surgery, being held together by epoxies and steel reinforcement, the Old Man came tumbling down on May 3, 2003.

> The hikers' Appalachian Trail crosses the Franconia Notch Parkway and Pemi Trail at **Whitehouse Bridge,** in between the Basin and the Flume.

Fortunately, the other well-known feature of Franconia Notch is still there: **The Flume** ($15) is a granite gorge, 12 to 20 feet wide and nearly 100 feet high, carved by roaring waters at the south end of the notch. To get here, head to the large **visitors center** (603/745-8391, daily 8:30am-5pm May-Oct.), pay the admission fee, and take a short bus ride to near the start of the wooden boardwalk, which runs the length of the 800-foot-long gorge and ends up at the ear-pounding rumble of Avalanche Falls.

Though less famous than the Old Man and The Flume, between the two sits another favorite Franconia Notch stop: **The Basin,** where a lovely waterfall in the thundering Pemigewassett River has polished a 25-foot-deep pothole. Thoreau visited in the 1820s, and thought it was remarkable; it's still a peaceful place to sit and picnic and be soothed by the natural white noise.

Clark's Trading Post

Just south of Franconia Notch along US-3, a barrage of deliciously tacky tourist attractions and old-fashioned roadside Americana awaits you. Well-maintained 1930s motor courts line the highway, setting the stage for one of New England's greatest roadside attractions, **Clark's Trading Post** (603/745-8913, daily summer, $22), where you can enjoy a slice of good ol' cornpone kitsch. At Clark's, you can ride on a genuine old wood-burning railroad over an authentic 1904 covered bridge (and be chased all the way by a hairy, hilarious Wolfman); admire an immaculate 1931 LaSalle in a vintage gas station; or tour a magical mansion.

For the past 50 or so years, the main draw at Clark's has been the chance to **"See Live Bears!"** House-trained black bears perform a series of entertaining tricks—dancing, shooting basketballs through hoops, and riding scooters—and they clearly seem to enjoy their work, not to mention the ice cream cones they're rewarded with. The trainers and caretakers crack jokes and make wry comments about "bear facts" and how the animals are "bearly" able to behave themselves, but they smile and beam every time the bears do what they're supposed to, giving the performances a feel more akin to a school play than to a professional circus. Across from the enclosure where they perform, you can pay respects to the graves of favorite bears who performed here over the years. Spend any time at Clark's and you'll begin to realize that the bears are regarded as family members—albeit seven-foot-tall, 500-pound family members.

Clark's has been in business since 1928, when it was known as Ed Clark's Eskimo Sled Dog Ranch, and everything about it is a family affair. More than a dozen Clarks and close relatives work here throughout the

> Take those moose-crossing signs seriously. Dozens of collisions occur annually, and you can bet your car won't fare too well if it hits an animal that weighs well over a half ton.

summer, doing everything from training and caring for the bears to making milk shakes. The bear shows at Clark's Trading Post are scheduled irregularly (typically in the afternoons, one to three per day, roughly every two hours or so; the schedule is posted online at www.clarkstrading-post.com). You could happily spend most of a day here, making it well worth the price of admission. If you're just racing through, be sure at least to visit the gift shop, which is stocked with all the wonderfully tacky stuff (wind-up toys, funky postcards, snow domes, and the like) that retro-minded road-trippers drive miles to find.

North Woodstock and Lincoln

North Woodstock, 11 miles south of Franconia Notch, is a good example of what White Mountains towns used to look like before vacation condos popped up like prairie dog colonies; neighboring Lincoln is the portrait of "after."

Tiny **North Woodstock** (pop. 528) is a handful of mostly unpretentious businesses at the junction of US-3 and Route 112. In case you're wondering what North Woodstock is north of, there is a much smaller hamlet called **Woodstock**, little more than a collection of cabins, about five miles or so south of North

Woodstock along US-3. **Lincoln** (pop. 1,662) seems to be nothing but a strip of ski-clothing stores, malls, and motels east of I-93 at the base of the Loon Mountain ski resort. Lincoln also sits at the west end of Route 112, the amazing Kancamagus Highway

Diner fans will want to check out the **Sunny Day Diner** (603/745-4833, daily during summer, cash only), a stainless-steel 1950s icon at the north edge of North Woodstock in Lincoln on US-3. A classic breakfast and lunch place, the Sunny Day makes some fine french toast (including a deeply flavored banana variation that goes great with local maple syrup). The Sunny Day is just south of Clark's Trading Post.

Lost River Gorge

With five main roads and countless minor ones connecting the Franconia Notch area with the Connecticut River Valley, there are nearly endless ways to get between these two places while staying more or less on the path of the hikers' Appalachian Trail, which disappears into the woods for most of the way. All of the roads are partly pretty and partly yucky in about equal degrees, but one of the easiest to follow is Route 112, which runs west from North Woodstock along the Lost River, hopping over the crest and dropping down along the Wild Ammonoosuc River. The main stop along this route is the privately owned **Lost River Gorge and Boulder Caves** (603/745-8031, daily mid-May-Oct., $20 adults), where you can explore the jumble of glaciated granite boulders that seem to swallow up the river, giving it its name. Many of the big moss-covered boulders have been given names (Guillotine Rock and Lemon Squeezer, to name two), and you can see these (and smell the fragrant pine trees) from the comfort of a wooden boardwalk, or go wild and explore some of the many caves formed by the huge piles of rocks.

Continuing west from Lost River Gorge, which sits at the top of Route 112's spectacular run through wild Kinsman Notch, the highway drops down into the Connecticut River watershed toward the Vermont town of **Wells River,** which happens to be home to the best truck stop in all New England: the **P&H Truck Stop Café** (802/429-2141) at I-91 exit 17, where you can enjoy charbroiled cheeseburgers and great pies—24 hours a day. After eating here, backtrack 4.5 miles to the river and follow scenic Route 10 along its east bank, winding south toward Hanover. A parallel route along the Vermont side of the river, along old US-5 through the town of **Fairlee** (which has a nice diner and a unique drive-in movie theater-motel), is another nice alternative to the I-91 freeway.

Route 10: North Haverhill and Lyme

While hikers along the Appalachian Trail have to struggle up and over several mountaintops, we drivers get to amble along a few miles to the west, following scenic Route 10 along the east banks of the lazy Connecticut River. Winding past pastures and cornfields, Route 10 is a nonstop pleasure to drive (or cycle); uneventful,

YOU CAN'T GET THERE FROM HERE

One of the first things first-time visitors to New England notice is its compact size: A crow flying 100 miles from almost any treetop outside Maine will end up in the next state, if not Canada. But map distances bear absolutely no relation to travel time, thanks to the mountain ranges pitched up across northern New England. So if you're sitting in your motel room in New Hampshire or Vermont wondering how far to drive for dinner, look to towns north or south. As a rule these will share the same valley since the rivers and mountains are generally aligned north-south, like compass needles. In contrast, that next town to the east or west may as well be on the opposite side of the state so far as convenience is concerned: Whether winding along erratic streambeds or stitching their ways up the sides of passes between high peaks, east-west roads tend to be a slow grind in even the best weather, truly as tortuous as the wiggling lines on the map suggest. Heavy vehicles, cautious drivers, and foul weather can make the going doubly difficult. Keep this in mind as you consider outings and side trips or you too will learn to say, "You can't get there from here."

perhaps, but giving seemingly endless pastoral views framed by white rail fences, occasional farmhouses, and the voluptuous peaks that rise to the east and west. The first hamlet you reach along this part of Route 10, **North Haverhill**, is a real museum piece, with a necklace of distinctive colonial-era homes flanking an oval town green.

On Post Pond, the fine restaurant, rustic lodge, and cabins of **Loch Lyme Lodge** (800/423-2141, $105 and up) have been welcoming generations of New Englanders since 1946. Swim, paddle, or float out on the small lake, which has an idyllic location between the mountains and the river.

Farther south, 10 miles north of Hanover, the tidy town of **Lyme** presents yet another Instagram-worthy scene, with a Civil War Monument standing at the east of a slender green, a large church at one end and an equally large stable behind it.

In case you're worried, **Lyme, New Hampshire,** is not the place the tick-borne disease was named for; that Lyme is in Connecticut. That said, you still need to be on the lookout for these devilish little creatures.

Currier and Ives lithograph of Dartmouth, circa 1834

Hanover: Dartmouth College

Dartmouth College is the principal resident of attractive little **Hanover** (pop. 11,260) and the Ivy League influence shows in the local architecture, fashions, and cultural diversions. When school is in session, the cafés hum with undergraduate discourse, the downtown teems with students, and a varsity air envelops the historic campus and its sturdy neighbors. Between terms, however, the town's metabolism drops toward hibernation levels, which means there's no line for espresso.

Standing out from all the Georgian-style brick buildings is Dartmouth's **Hood Museum of Art** (603/646-2808, Tues.-Sun., free), on the southeast side of the green. Housed in a modern gallery designed in part by Charles Moore, the Hood is undergoing renovation, but hopes to reopen in 2019.

More contentious art can be experienced at the center of Dartmouth, where, in the Orozco Room of **Baker-Berry Library,** the walls are covered with a set of politically charged frescoes, *The Epic of American Civilization* by José Clemente Orozco.

If it's too nice a day to stay indoors and contemplate society's ills, rent a bike and ride north to Lyme and back, or rent a canoe

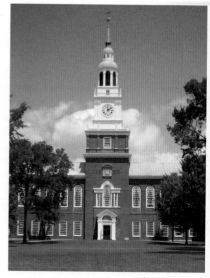
Baker-Berry Library, Dartmouth College

or kayak from Dartmouth's **Ledyard Canoe Club** (603/643-6709, $10 per hour), located on the river just north of the Route 10A bridge, and play Huck Finn for an afternoon. Or you can take a hike—the Dartmouth Outing Club's member club Cabin and Trail maintains hundreds of miles of trails, including a part of the Appalachian Trail (AT) that runs right through town. There's an AT marker embedded in the sidewalk in front of the Hanover Inn, from where the trail runs west across the bridge to Vermont, and east down Main and Lebanon Streets to the town of Etna, before climbing the 2,280-foot peak of Moose Mountain.

Hanover Practicalities

Generations of Dartmouth students have survived their college years thanks in part to the generous portions served up at **Lou's** (30 S. Main St., 603/643-3321). Hardly changed since it opened in 1947, and famed for its magical strawberry rhubarb and other freshly baked pies, Lou's does great big breakfasts, lunchtime soups, and burgers. For dinner, head across the street to the popular **Canoe Club Bistro** (27 S. Main St., 603/643-9660).

For accommodations around Hanover, there's the stately Dartmouth-run **Hanover Inn** (603/643-4300, $150 and up) facing the green; for affordable rooms, however, look in nearby West Lebanon or across the river in White River Junction, Vermont.

Into the Mountains: Norwich, West Hartford, and Pomfret

Just uphill from where the Appalachian Trail crosses the Connecticut River, along Route 10A on a broad low bridge from Hanover, you might want to while away an afternoon in **Norwich** at the interesting **Montshire Museum of Science** (802/649-2200, daily, $17 summer, $15 fall-spring), which has more than 100 educational exhibits focusing on natural history, as well as aquariums showcasing fresh- and saltwater creatures. The next town the AT passes through is **West Hartford,** on the banks of the White River upstream from I-91 along Route 14 and just off I-89.

From West Hartford, you can circle around (on unnumbered and rather rough-surfaced country roads) through **North Pomfret, Pomfret,** and **South Pomfret,** passing dairy farms and quaint barns, coming in through the back door to upscale Woodstock, where this AT route links up with US-4. From South Pomfret, a quaint little hamlet that's also home to the Suicide Six ski area, the hikers' Appalachian Trail heads up into the mountains through a long roadless stretch before crossing US-4 at Sherburne Pass. The only real driving equivalent follows Route 12 south into Woodstock.

Lebanon and West Lebanon

Sitting rather quietly a couple of miles south of Hanover, east of the Connecticut River near the point where US-4 gets submerged beneath the I-89 freeway, historic **Lebanon** (pop. 13,151) has a town green so spacious it seems more like the outskirts of a city park than the center of a town.

Right along the bonny banks of the Connecticut River, three miles or so south of patrician Hanover, the commercial busybody of **West Lebanon** has everything you probably try hard to avoid: shopping plazas, traffic tie-ups, and familiar fast *everything,* all clustered around the two local exits off the I-89 freeway.

Although Ivy League Dartmouth has a $4 billion endowment and a conservative reputation, it also has had some interesting students and supporters, including children's stars Dr. Seuss and Mr. Rogers. Although Captain Kangaroo was not technically a student, both of his children were, and he received an honorary doctorate from the college in 1975. The poet Robert Frost also attended Dartmouth, but dropped out.

VERMONT

Vermont is quintessential New England: picturesque villages still served by cluttered country stores; small farms nestled among the granite ridges of the **Green Mountains;** and needle-sharp white church spires rising above forests ablaze with autumn colors. Precocious from birth—its constitution was the first in the United States to prohibit slavery and establish public schools—Vermont is known for its independent-minded politicians like Jim Jeffords and Bernie Saunders and for its strong liberal traditions (think Howard Dean).

From the Connecticut River, this route across Vermont follows the contours of the land, tagging along fast-running mountain streams or keeping to the valleys between the steep surrounding ridges that carry the Appalachian Trail ever southward.

White River Junction

Across the river from Hanover and Dartmouth, turn-of-the-20th-century **White River Junction** (pop. 2,286) used to echo with the sounds of some 50 trains a day traveling over five separate rail lines. The demise of the railroads and the arrival of the interstate cloverleaf on the outskirts of town effectively mothballed the downtown area, but like good vintage clothing, the photogenic historic center has been rediscovered by an art-smart crowd that doesn't mind the holes and missing buttons.

Freight trains still rumble through White River Junction a few times a day (and night!), and Amtrak stops here on its main Vermonter route. Apart from the trains, the main signs of life here are at breakfast and lunch. The stylish **Tip Top Café** (85 N. Main St., 802/295-3312, Tues.-Sat.) offers delicious soups, sandwiches, and an ever-changing variety of bistro-style meals at lunch and dinner.

If you're looking for lodging with more character than the chain motels along the interstates, consider downtown's **Hotel Coolidge** (39 S. Main St., 802/295-3118 or 800/622-1124, $99 and up). In business since the 1920s, it has a nice café next to the lobby. It is clean, friendly, and definitely a good value. The hotel also offers barebones HI-hostel rooms (around $55 and up per person).

Quechee Gorge

In three miles west from White River Junction and the I-91/I-89 freeways, US-4 climbs upstream into the valley of the Ottauquechee (AWT-ah-KWEE-chee) River. You cross **Quechee Gorge** almost without warning, but adjacent parking on both sides of the gorge gives you a chance to take a longer look at the dramatic little canyon or to stretch your legs along the rim-side hiking trails.

*If you're in the area around mid-June, check out the **Quechee Hot Air Balloon, Craft and Music Festival,** held over Father's Day weekend.*

On the east side of the gorge, **Quechee State Park** (802/295-2990) provides access to the Ottauquechee River and also has camping with hot showers. Next to the park is the nature center of the **Vermont Institute of Natural Science** (802/359-5000, daily, $15 adults), an outdoor education and animal rehabilitation center dedicated to local wildlife, especially raptors. Enclosures let you get up close and personal with hawks, eagles, owls, and falcons.

West of the gorge, you can turn north off US-4 into old **Quechee,** a quaint town famed as the home of renowned glassblower **Simon Pearce**'s woolen mill-cum-art gallery. Norman Rockwell-esque Quechee is a fine example of how pleasant life can be once you turn away from the fast lane. Soak up the ambience with a stay (or just a memorable meal) at the **Quechee Inn** (1119 Quechee Main St., 802/295-3133, $119 and up), a half mile from town.

Woodstock

"The good people of Woodstock have less incentive than others to yearn for heaven," said a 19th-century resident. It's a sentiment readily echoed today. Chartered in 1761, **Woodstock** (pop. 3,232) remains an exceedingly well-preserved example of small-town New England—tidy Federal-style homes, built by wealthy professionals

downtown Woodstock

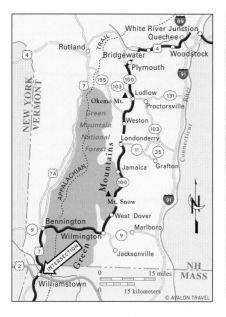

QUECHEE GULF BRIDGE OVER OTTAUQUECHEE RIVER AT DEWEY'S MILLS, VT., HEIGHT 164 FT.

ON COOLIDGE MEMORIAL HIGHWAY BETWEEN WHITE RIVER JUNCTION AND RUTLAND, VT.

of the newborn American republic, still ring the classic village green. Now the historic village is home to wealthy retirees and their fortunate sons and daughters. You'll see the signs of this old money throughout the town: well-stocked wine racks at the general store, shady basketball courts along the river, excellent performing arts at the Town Hall Theatre, and, most importantly, the wherewithal to refuse any compromising commercial development. To put it mildly, expansion of the tax base is not a pressing issue for this community.

As you approach **Woodstock Village Green,** notice that there are no overhead power lines on the two main downtown streets, Central and Elm. Laurance Rockefeller paid to have the lines buried back in 1973.

During summer and fall, walking tours are an excellent way to take stock of the town's history and architecture. Call or visit the **Woodstock Welcome Center** (3 Mechanic St., 802/453-1100) for a schedule. Hiking trails lead up both the summits overlooking the town. A community blackboard at the corner of Central and Elm, a.k.a. the Town Crier, lists local events and activities all year. Even if you're racing through Woodstock, bound for the mountains, be sure to stop long enough to enjoy this quick tour: From the oblong green, cross the Middle Covered Bridge and follow the Ottauquechee downstream along River Street. Then work your way back via Elm Street and **F. H. Gillingham & Sons,**

Vermont's oldest country store, which offers locally made food and crafts.

If you've admired the rolling fields and weathered wooden fences, savored the local apples and sharp cheddar, and enjoyed the scent of mown hay or boiling maple sap, you'll appreciate an even closer look at New England's farms with a visit to the **Billings Farm & Museum** (802/457-2355, daily summer, Sat.-Sun.

DINERS: FAST FOOD
WORTH SLOWING DOWN FOR

A-a-ah, the local diner! Throughout New England, these brightly lit establishments are magnets for folks weary of the dull predictability of the fast-food mega-chains. In contrast to the impersonal nature of those billions-serving burger factories, diners are low-key gathering spots where community gossip is shared and politics debated by a gang of regulars assembling each morning. Where waitresses (frequently named Mildred, Blanche, and Edna) wear lace hankies pinned to their aprons and are quick to offer refills on coffee. Where UPS drivers, Methodist clergy, morticians, and middle-school principals perched on adjacent stools know they can score decent hot roast-beef sandwiches or a great piece of fresh fruit pie. And where autumn leaf-peepers and other passers-through can inquire about local attractions or find out which nearby motels or B&Bs might still have empty rooms for that night.

The diner's lineage can ultimately be traced back to horse-drawn lunch carts selling sandwiches and hot coffee along the streets of cities like Providence and Boston beginning in the 1870s. However, the prototypical New England diners are those built from 1906 through 1961 by the Worcester Lunch Car Company: barrel-roofed with colorful porcelain panels on the exterior and plenty of varnished hardwood inside. Other diners came from manufacturers headquartered in New York (DeRaffele) and especially New Jersey (Mountain View, Fodero, Kullman, Paramount, Silk City, O'Mahony, and many more). Each diner-maker trumpeted its own design innovations: streamlined metal exteriors, artful tile work, bits of elegant stained glass, distinctive built-in clocks, and more efficient floor plans. Some diners even came from the factory with all necessary crockery, flatware, and cooking equipment included, so that new owners could begin serving hungry locals on the very day setup was complete.

Aficionados will be quick to inform you that real diners are roadside eateries

fall-spring, $15), just off Route 12 north of the village. Frederick Billings, better known as the builder of the Northern Pacific Railroad (Billings, Montana, is named for him), began this working dairy farm in the late-19th century. Its restored farmhouse and huge barns illustrate rural life in galleries, demonstrations, and hands-on activities.

Across the road, another historic farm is open to the public as the **Marsh-Billings-Rockefeller National Historical Park** (802/457-3368, tours daily Memorial Day-late Oct., $8 adults), Vermont's only national park. The property, which includes the former home of Laurance Rockefeller (1910-2004), who married Frederick Billings's granddaughter, is a study in conservation practice, and its dense woodlands are living proof of the merits of sustainable agriculture. Some 18

whose component parts were fabricated in a factory, then shipped by road or rail for final assembly on-site. Real diners, they'll insist, always have counters, with at least some cooking done within view of patrons. There'll almost certainly be booths, too, and a definite blue-collar, no-frills ambience. Unlike their urban or roadside truck stop equivalents, few diners are open 24 hours; many in fact serve breakfast and lunch only, opening early in the morning (around 6am) and closing around 2pm or 3pm. But not every place with the word "diner" in its name is the genuine article. Many places that call themselves diners are as far removed from the classic prefab as IKEA furniture is from a handcrafted antique, and mavens regard diner-themed restaurants (like Denny's or Johnny Rockets) with considerable scorn. The smaller, the better, they say, with points deducted for any remodeling that disfigures the original design.

You needn't care about any of this lore, of course, to enjoy yourself. But after visiting your third or fourth diner, you may begin to notice similarities and differences among them. Curious about a particular establishment's history? Quiz the owner—more often than not, he or she will be happy to tell you all about the place, which may have started life with a different name in another town and been moved three or more times before it found its current home. Look for a "tag," the small metal plate (often affixed to the wall over the entry door) listing the manufacturer, date, and serial number. The best and most enjoyable way to get to know diners and diner culture is simply to spend time in them, but if you want to learn more, check the authoritative volume *American Diner Then and Now*, by Richard Gutman, published by Johns Hopkins University Press.

miles of trails are open in the winter for cross-country skiing and snowshoeing from the Nordic center at **The Woodstock Inn & Resort** (802/457-6674, $20).

Woodstock Practicalities

Hungry travelers will find plenty of choices around town. There are also two interesting if rather bare-bones road-food haunts bookending the town along US-4. On US-4 one mile west of the green is the **Woodstock Farmer's Market** (802/457-3658), with top-quality produce and deli fare.

Accommodations run the gamut from moderate motels to deluxe inns; at all of them, expect rates to increase during high season, which in Woodstock is most of summer and fall, along with the winter holidays. The main place right in town, the 142-room Rockefeller-built **Woodstock Inn & Resort** (888/338-2745, $179 and up) sits on the south side of the green, and although it tries hard to look like a stately old place, the inn was actually built from scratch in 1969. **The Village Inn of Woodstock** (41 Pleasant St., 802/457-1255, $169 and up), a lovely Victorian-era B&B, has much more character, yet is still affordable. The modest **Braeside Motel** (908 E. Woodstock Rd., 802/457-1366, $118 and up), along US-4 on the eastern outskirts of town, is about as budget-friendly as you're going to get.

Bridgewater and Killington

The tiny town of **Bridgewater** (pop. 936), stretching along the banks of the Ottauquechee, seems well on the way to the middle of nowhere. But that's what lures many visitors to this region—the fact that so much of it seems to have contentedly hung back with Rip van Winkle. That said, Bridgewater is a gateway to one of the state's most important somewheres: the ski resorts of central Vermont. The large woolen mill here has been converted into the **Bridgewater Mill Mall**, its water-powered turbines and textile machines replaced by small shops and restaurants such as a thrift store, a pizzeria, and showrooms and workshops for furniture and jewelry makers.

Pico Alpine Ski Lift, Rutland, Vermont, in the Green Mts.—99

Through the Bridgewater area, US-4 is generously wide-shouldered and level, making it a popular cycling route, especially during the fall color season, when the dense hardwood forests that climb the slopes above the roadway are blazing with autumn hues. When the leaves have fallen and been replaced by snow, this scenic stretch changes character completely, becoming one of the East Coast's most prominent ski resorts, **Killington** (800/621-6867). The permanent population of Killington is maybe 881 people, but on winter day, as many as 13,000 skiers flock to its six different mountains and many miles of trails. The skiers also support a plethora of real estate agencies, restaurants, and bars, especially off US-4 on the main road to the slopes, Killington Road.

Killington is not as popular in the summer, when the parking lots of the time-share condo complexes are empty and the hills are scarred by clear-cut ski trails, but the lack of crowds also means lower prices for accommodations, from roadside motels to upscale resorts.

Vermont holds more than 100 covered bridges, several good examples of which are to be seen between Quechee and Bridgewater. Look for the 1836 **Taftsville Covered Bridge** west of Quechee, the **Middle Covered Bridge** in Wood-stock (which was totally rebuilt way back in 1969), and the 1877 **Lincoln Covered Bridge** in West Woodstock. The nation's second longest covered bridge, **Cornish-Windsor,** crosses the Connecticut River at Windsor, about 15 miles or so southeast of Woodstock, with a 449-foot span built in 1866.

Gifford Woods State Park

Sitting in the scenic heart of the Green Mountains, at the junction of US-4 and Route 100, **Gifford Woods State Park** (802/775-5354) protects one of the few virgin hardwood forests left in New England, with seven acres of massive sugar maple, birch, and ash trees, some of which are more than 300 years old. There's a nice **campground** (campsites around $20, cabins around $50) with hot showers, four one-room cabins, and access to many fine trails, including the Appalachian Trail and the Long Trail, which run together across US-4 just west of 2,190-foot Shelburne Pass.

Route 100: Rochester and Granville Gulf

Route 100 runs north-south through the geographical and spiritual heart of Vermont, winding from curve to curve past cornfields and fat cows lazing in impossibly green pastures, alongside gurgling streams, up and down switchbacking passes, and generally setting the standard for what scenic roads ought to be. Route 100 runs right at the edge of the Green Mountains National Forest, parallel to Vermont's beloved crest-line Long Trail, and every so often passes by a picturesque gas station-cum-general store, selling everything you'll need to keep you on the road, from gas to maple-syrup milk shakes. Up and down the whole state of Vermont, Route 100 is a wonderful drive, as are just about all of the roads that intersect it.

North of US-4, the first place you come to along Route 100 is **Pittsfield,** an all-in-white hamlet set in a pastoral valley and surrounded by hayfields and acres of corn. From here Route 100 edges east into the White River Valley, passing through Stockbridge, which centers on an ancient-looking Ford dealership, and a couple more places that seem to exist solely on maps. The next stop is **Rochester,** at the junction with Route 73, which heads west over scenic Brandon Gap. Rochester is a proper Vermont town, with a village green, a bandstand, and the excellent **Rochester Café & Country Store** (802/767-4302), serving breakfast and lunch, and bread pudding and milk shakes—yum.

Across the river and away from Route 100, the **Liberty Hill Farm & Inn** (802/767-3926, $139 and up per person) is a family-friendly farm-stay B&B and has a working 261-acre dairy where you can hike, bike, fish, or help feed the cows, chickens, and cats.

North of Rochester, Route 100 passes through a still-working landscape, with ski club cabins sharing the roadside scene with a few barns and remnants of historic sheep pens. The one don't-miss highlight of this middle section of Route 100 is **Granville Gulf State Reservation,** about 30 beautiful miles north from US-4. The Green Mountains rise steeply to either side of the road, and just off the west side of the road, delicate **Moss Glen Falls** tumble down through craggy cliffs to a gurgling stream. A short boardwalk leads to the foot of the falls from a small parking turnout.

Plymouth Notch: Calvin Coolidge Country

Running a twisty seven miles south from US-4 and Bridgewater, Route 100A passes through beautiful scenery and **Plymouth Notch,** birthplace of Calvin

Coolidge, the only U.S. president born on July 4. The small hilltop clutch of buildings is so little changed by modern times, it's a wonder there aren't horses with carriages parked behind the visitors center instead of Subarus. One of the most evocative and simply beautiful historic sites in New England, the **Calvin Coolidge Homestead District** (802/672-3773, daily summer, $9 adults) has been restored to its 1923 appearance, the year Colonel John Coolidge

administered the oath of office to his vacationing son, the vice president, after President Harding died unexpectedly in San Francisco. The house, the general store, and the cheese factory are 3 of the 12 buildings open to the public. There's also a mile-long nature trail offering fine views of Plymouth Notch and its Green Mountain surroundings.

Route 100: The Skiers' Highway

Known as the **Skiers' Highway,** serpentine Route 100 manages to pass the base of nearly every major ski resort in southern Vermont. From Ludlow south through Jamaica, Stratton, and West Dover, any doubt that skiing is the cash cow of the state's most lucrative industry—tourism—is quickly dispelled by the clusters of inns, sportswear shops, vacation real estate offices, and restaurants along the way.

In recent years, downhill mountain-bikers and inn-to-inn cyclists riding Route 100 have made the region more of a year-round recreation center, but overall you still get the sense that, pretty as they are with their village greens, old homes, and hand-carved wooden signs, many of these Route 100 towns spend the warm months convalescing.

Wilmington and Route 9

Route 100 catches a panoramic view of Mt. Snow as the roadway descends into **Wilmington** (pop. 2,225), a picturesque village of 18th- and 19th-century shops and houses built along the Deerfield River. Wilmington also has some great old-fashioned places to eat, like **Dot's Restaurant** (3 W. Main St., 802/464-7284), a white-clapboard Vermont institution, famous for its pancakes, burgers, chili, and pies. Nevertheless, the warmer months see a fair bit of activity in the galleries and antiques shops, and for classical music lovers, the **Marlboro Music Festival** (802/254-2394 summer only) marks summer's zenith at Marlboro College, a dozen miles east toward Brattleboro on Route 9. Between mid-July and mid-August, several score of the world's finest classical musicians perform here in one of the nation's most distinguished annual chamber music series.

Brigham Young, the man who led the Mormon exodus to Utah, was born in **Whitingham,** fewer than 10 miles south of Wilmington on Route 100, at the south end of the Harriman Reservoir. There's a commemorative monument on the Town Hall Common.

Heading westward toward Bennington, you can continue west on Route 9 to Bennington and follow US-7 south through Williamstown, or you can make your way south through the much less developed areas along Route 8 and Route 100, which take you through the heavy-duty mill town of North Adams.

Bennington

By far the largest Vermont town south of Burlington, **Bennington** (pop. 15,764) is a bustling little manufacturing and commercial center. It was the site of a significant victory against the British-paid Hessians in 1777 during the American Revolution, a sweet morale-booster that contributed to the defeat of General "Gentleman Johnny" Burgoyne's army of Redcoats at Saratoga. In the subsequent centuries, Bennington's name became synonymous with art: the decorative arts of the antebellum United States Pottery Company; the liberal arts of **Bennington College,** one of the nation's most expensive and exclusive private colleges; and the folk art of Anna Mary Robertson "Grandma" Moses.

The largest public collection of Grandma Moses's beguiling work is on display in the **Bennington Museum** (75 Main St., daily summer, Thurs.-Tues. Sept.-Dec. and Feb.-Apr., $10 adults), found up the hill on Route 9 in the graceful old part of town. Along with 25 Grandma Moses paintings and the rural schoolhouse she attended two centuries ago, the museum also has a wide variety of historical artifacts, examples of early Bennington pottery, and the sole survivor of the fabulous motor cars once made here in Bennington: a 1925 Wasp.

"Silent Cal" Coolidge was famous—perhaps unjustly—for being a man of few words. A White House dinner guest is said to have bet that she could make the president address her with at least three words; when confronted with this challenge, Coolidge replied, "You lose."

statue of Seth Warner at the Bennington Battle Monument

From the Bennington Museum, walk north toward the 306-foot obelisk that towers over the town: the **Bennington Battle Monument,** completed in 1891 to commemorate the Revolutionary War victory, which actually occurred west of town, over the New York state border. An **elevator** (mid-Apr.-Oct., $5) takes you to an observation room near the top of the tower for a great view up and down the valley.

Bennington is also the final resting place of poet Robert Frost, in the burial ground alongside the **Old First Church,** at Church Lane and Monument Avenue. His tombstone reads, "I had a lover's quarrel with the world."

Whether or not you need gas, those interested in old cars and automobilia will want to stop by the full-service recreated Sunoco filling station and antique car collection at **Hemmings Motor News** (222 Main St., 802/447-9580).

Yum: raspberry and chocolate chip pancakes at the Blue Benn Diner!

When garnished with Vermont-made Ben & Jerry's ice cream, apple pie à la mode is certainly nothing to sneer at, but if you want to try apple pie the Vermont way, ask for a slab of sharp cheddar on the side instead of ice cream.

If anyone starts erecting monuments to good dining instead of old wars or dead poets, this town would have another tower of stone beside the **Blue Benn Diner** (314 North St., 802/442-5140, Mon.-Sat. from 6am, Sun. from 7am), on a bend in US-7 north of town. The fact that it's a vintage 1940s Silk City certainly gives this cozy nonsmoking joint character. But what earns the seven-days-a-week loyalty of its patrons is the top-notch short-order cooking: From baked meat loaf and roast beef to broccoli stir-fry and multigrain pancakes, the food is good, cheap, and served up so fast you'll barely have time to choose your song on the wall-hung jukebox at your table.

Most of Bennington's accommodations are strung along Route 7A to the north and US-7 to the south of downtown, all local names but for the Best Western inn found on Route 7A, and the Hampton Inn on Hannaford Square. If you are in the market for a distinctive B&B, check out the central, historic, and highly regarded **Four Chimneys Inn** (21 West Rd., 802/447-3500, $129 and up), which offers 11 rooms and 11 acres of grounds and gardens, and a full breakfast for overnight guests, along Route 9.

MASSACHUSETTS

Hemmed in by the daunting topography of its surrounding mountains, the Berkshire region of western Massachusetts is a world apart, blessed with abundant nature and an easygoing small-town character. The region's relaxed, rural charms and its location equidistant from Boston and New York City have long made it a magnet for writers and artists as well as a playground for the rich, so be prepared to experience a little of everything from natural splendors to high-society display. And remember, it never

takes more than a few strategic turns to trade plush restaurants and music festivals for splendidly rural forests as deep and undisturbed as any in New England.

North Adams

If you've grown accustomed to the typical tourist New England of village greens and clapboard B&Bs, industrial **North Adams** (pop. 13,708) may come as something of a shock.

Nearly from its inception, North Adams tied its fortunes to major manufacturing plants, churning out printed cotton until textiles went south, then rolling out electronics for everything from the first atomic bomb to the television sets of the 1950s and 1960s. When electronics went solid-state and overseas, North Adams nearly died clinging to the belief that some new assembly line would come fill its sprawling complex of massive Victorian-era mill buildings. Finally, the town's long-awaited salvation seems to have taken shape, in the form of art. The Massachusetts Museum of Contemporary Art, better known as **MASS MoCA** (413/662-2111, daily July-Aug., Wed.-Mon. Sept.-June, $20 adults) fills some 250,000 square feet of heavy-duty industrial buildings with an ever-changing array of cutting-edge art plus the inevitable gift shop, a nice café, frequent live music, and even its own stylish B&B, **The Porches Inn** (231 River St., 413/664-0400, $159 and up).

Susan B. Anthony, circa 1890

North Adams is five miles north of the quaint town of **Adams,** the birthplace of voting rights activist Susan B. Anthony (1820-1906).

For those who are interested in the olden days, the region's historic gravy train is faithfully recollected in the **Western Gateway Heritage State Park** (413/663-6312, daily, free). About a mile southwest of the museum, and occupying the former freight yard of the Boston and Maine Railroad, the park highlights the landmark construction of the 4.75-mile-long Hoosac Tunnel, and North Adams's front-row seat on the Boston-Great Lakes rail connection that it made possible.

Williamstown

To the visitor it appears as if stately **Williamstown** (pop. 7,754) is simply a nickname for the immaculate and graceful campus of Williams College—even the main commercial block is basically the corridor between dorms and gym. From their common 18th-century benefactor, Ephraim Williams (who insisted the town's name be changed from its original West Hoosuck), to the large number of alumni who return in their retirement, "Billsville" and its college are nearly inseparable. The town-gown symbiosis has spawned an enviable array of visual, performing, and edible arts, yet fresh contingents of ingenuous youth keep all the wealth and refinement from becoming too cloying.

Singer Sewing Machine heir Robert Sterling Clark's huge art collection ended up in Williamstown in part because of the Cold War. In the late 1940s and early

In northwestern Massachusetts, this Appalachian Trail route crosses **The Oregon Trail,** a transcontinental road trip along US-20 and other highways (see page 651). Full coverage of the entire route, heading east from North Adams along Route 2 (the Mohawk Trail to Boston and Cape Cod) and west from Williamstown through Albany and beyond, begins on page 558.

1950s, the threat of a Russian nuclear attack seemed real enough that being as distant as possible from likely bomb targets was a critical factor in choosing a permanent repository. Today **Clark Art Institute** (225 South St., 413/458-2303, daily July-Aug., Tues.-Sun. Sept.-June, $20), in a pastoral setting, is the town's jewel, displaying paintings by Winslow Homer and an extraordinary collection of impressionist works, including more than 30 Renoirs. Special exhibitions are held in a gorgeous Tadao Ando-designed gallery built on a nearby hillside. Also worth a look in Williamstown is the excellent and wide-ranging **Williams College Museum of Art** (daily June-Aug., Tues.-Sun. Sept.-May, free) off of Route 2 opposite Thompson Memorial Chapel (that mini-Westminster Abbey).

antique piano at the Clark Art Institute

Williamstown can claim another gem, this time in the natural art of relaxation. Luxurious Cunard Lines used to serve its ocean-going passengers water exclusively from Williamstown's **Sand Springs** (158 Sand Springs Rd., 413/458-6026, Memorial Day-Labor Day, $10). A family-friendly swimming pool has been open every summer since 1907 on the site, on the north side of town.

Williamstown Practicalities

For breakfast, head to US-7 on the north side of town to the popular **Chef's Hat** (905 Simonds Rd., 413/458-5120). The hands-down best takeout pizza joint is **Hot Tomatoes** (100 Water St., 413/458-2722), and in mild weather the nearby stream-side park is well suited to lolling picnickers. Also good: the Indian-inspired food at **Spice Root** (23 Spring St., 413/458-5200).

Nitroglycerin was first used as a construction explosive during the blasting of the Hoosac Tunnel. And just so you know, the river is the Hoosic, but the mountain range is the Hoosac.

Tony continental dining suitable for starched alumni banquets abounds in Williamstown. But if you're looking for truly fresh, interesting food, skip the inns and go to **Mezze Bistro and Bar** (413/458-0123), which outgrew its original downtown home and moved to more spacious digs along US-7 a mile southwest of town. Here the best locally sourced produce, meats, and fish are featured on a stylish dinner-only menu.

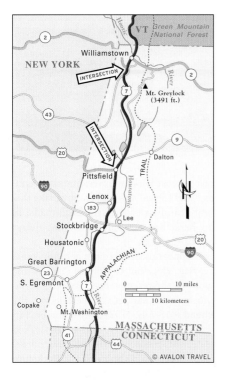

A drive along Main Street (Route 2) will give you a view of most of Williamstown's accommodations, including many small motels out on the eastern edge of town, like the friendly and clean **Maple Terrace Motel** (555 Main St., 413/458-9677, $89 and up). For a real treat, consider **The Guest House at Field Farm** (554 Sloan Rd., 413/458-3135, $200 and up) in South Williamstown, about five miles south along either US-7 or scenic Water Street (Route 43). Occupying the 316-acre former estate of Pacific Northwest lumber tycoon Lawrence Bloedel, the main house, designed in 1948, is a striking example of American mid-20th-century modern architecture. If you have any love of Frank Lloyd Wright or Charles and Ray Eames, you'll be delighted by this live-in museum of contemporary design, with its huge picture windows, proto-Scandinavian furniture, and meadowside swimming pool.

Mt. Greylock

South of Williamstown, Massachusetts's tallest peak is the centerpiece of 12,500-acre **Mount Greylock State Reservation,** one of the state's largest and most popular possessions. More than 70 miles of trails, including some thigh-burning mountain-bike routes, wander along the reforested slopes, most of which were heavily logged for timber and charcoal back in the 19th century. Rock ledges provide great views of the Hoosic River Valley to the east and the Housatonic Valley to the south, when the namesake mists aren't keeping the 3,491-foot summit wadded up in a damp ball of dingy cotton. The $21.3 million reconstruction project has been a complete success, and during warm months, access is a cinch: Century-old Notch Road snakes its way up through the birch and spruce from Route 2 on the north side, while Rockwell Road ascends more gently from US-7 along the flanks of Greylock's southern neighbors; you'll enjoy the most scenic, drivable mountain ascent in New England. Keep in mind that both roads are narrow, enlivened by occasional hairpin turns, and—especially at dusk—prone to wandering wildlife.

By the early 19th century, farmland had replaced 75 percent of Berkshire County's forests. Now forests have reclaimed that 75 percent and more, but innumerable dry stone walls serve as reminders of the once vast cultivated fields.

If you want to see over the forest, climb the 93-foot **Massachusetts Veterans War Memorial Tower** on the summit. If the weather is good, you'll have a panoramic view from New Hampshire to Connecticut. A stone's throw from the granite tower is the **Bascom Lodge** (917/680-0079, private rooms around $125, shared bunks $35 and up per person), a beautiful old stone and timber structure that offers private rooms, shared bunk rooms, and good food (and showers!).

Pittsfield

Compared to the carefully preserved Norman Rockwell simplicity of many of the surrounding small towns, the aging industrial cityscape of **Pittsfield** (pop. 44,737) has made it the place most Berkshire weekenders strenuously try to avoid, despite the fact that its size and the valley's topography make this nearly impossible unless you have a resident's familiarity with the back roads. In contrast to the lives of leisure lived in many Berkshire towns, Pittsfield has always been a busy, hard-working place, resolutely down-to-earth.

Despite Pittsfield's anything-but-quaint appearance, there are actually some good reasons for travelers to pay the place a visit. Head out to Holmes Road, at the city's rural southern edge, and maybe you will see the resemblance between a leviathan and the imposing outline of Mt. Greylock, particularly if you view it from the study window of Herman Melville's **Arrowhead** (413/442-1793, daily summer, $15 adults). That salty masterpiece *Moby Dick* was indeed written in this landlocked locale, where Melville moved in 1850 to be near his mentor, Nathaniel Hawthorne. While foremost a literary shrine, the spacious farm is also home to the **Berkshire County Historical Society,** whose well-curated exhibits are always interesting. Serious pilgrims on the path of Ishmael and the great white whale will also want to

Arrowhead

Herman Melville

visit the Melville Memorial Room on the main floor of the **Berkshire Athenaeum** (1 Wendell Ave.), Pittsfield's public library.

As with its other attractions, Pittsfield has some real unexpected gems when it comes to food, with three great places lining up along East Street between downtown and US-7. If you love hot dogs (and who doesn't?), you've probably been dreaming of someday finding a place like **Teo's Hot Dogs** (1410 East St., 413/447-9592), where you can wash down excellent chili dogs with super-cold $2 beers. For fresh pasta, pizza, and pub grub at a great small-town price, cruise a half-mile farther west down East Street to the **East Side Café** (378 Newell St., 413/447-9405), just off the main road, a neighborhood bar whose comfort food and convivial atmosphere attract a family clientele. Between these two blue-collar haunts is one great full-service dinner place: **Elizabeth's** (1264 East St., 413/448-8244), serving full-flavored Italian classics. All three are cash-only, and popular.

All of the paper used in all of the money printed in the United States comes from a mill here in the backwoods of Massachusetts. Crane & Co. of Dalton makes the 100 percent cotton paper used in United States currency at a series of historic mills along Route 8 just east of Pittsfield.

Lenox: Tanglewood and The Mount

During the late-19th-century Gilded Age, the Berkshires were the inland equivalent of Newport, Rhode Island, with dozens of opulent "cottages" constructed here by newly rich titans of American industry. Built for an era in which "society" was a respectable full-time occupation for folks with names like Carnegie and Westinghouse, some 75 of these giant mansions still stand, especially around the genteel town of **Lenox** (pop. 5,025). Many of the houses have been converted to palatial B&B inns, full-service health spas, or private schools; others are home to organizations whose presence has made Lenox a seasonal mecca for the performing arts.

The lives and times of the Gilded Age elite were well chronicled by Edith Wharton, who lived in Lenox for many years in a 42-room house she designed and built for herself called **The Mount** (413/551-5111, daily summer only, $18 adults). Set in three acres of Italianate gardens and recently restored, The Mount is just south of central Lenox, well signed off Plunkett Street. Wharton, who considered herself better at gardening than writing, was the first woman to win a Pulitzer Prize in the novel category (for her 1920 *The Age of Innocence*). She drew upon local people and incidents in many of her works, including two of her most famous: *The House of Mirth* and *Ethan Frome*.

Lenox is also connected with another great American writer, Nathaniel Hawthorne, who lived here with his family around 1850 and wrote *The House of Seven Gables* at what is now **Tanglewood** (888/266-1200), the summer home of the Boston Symphony Orchestra and visiting pop performers like James Taylor and Earth, Wind and Fire. Besides Tanglewood, the Lenox area also hosts the **Jacob's Pillow Dance Festival** (413/243-0745) in Becket and the **Berkshire Theatre Festival** (413/997-4444) in Stockbridge, so you can understand why such a small town is such a big magnet for East Coast culture vultures.

HANCOCK SHAKER VILLAGE

Just five miles west of Pittsfield on old US-20, Hancock Shaker Village is one of the best-preserved remnants of the religious sect known popularly as Shakers, but formally as the United Society of Believers in Christ's Second Appearing, whose utopian communities flourished in the years before the Civil War. Shakers, as outsiders called them because of their occasional convulsions during wor-

the Round Barn

ship, were dedicated to a communal life conspicuous in its equality between men and women, a natural corollary to their belief in parity between a male God and a female Holy Mother Wisdom.

The English-born leader of the group, Ann Lee, was in fact regarded by Shakers as the female, and second, incarnation of Christ. Although Puritan theocracy was ending, preaching this gospel did not endear her to many New Englanders in the decade following her arrival just prior to the American Revolution. During that war, Lee and her "children" sought their Heaven on Earth, as seen in her visions. Mother Ann died near Albany, New York, in 1784, before any communities based on her precepts could be founded.

Hancock Shaker Village, third among the 24 settlements built in the nation by Lee's followers, was founded in 1783 and survived 177 years, outlasting all but two other Shaker communities. It's been preserved as a **living museum** (413/443-0188 or 800/817-1137, daily Apr.-Nov., $20 adults), with exhibits, tours, and working artisans interpreting the rural lifestyle and famous design skills of the Shakers. Appreciation of the efficiency, simplicity, and perfect workmanship consecrated within the "City of Peace" can quickly fill a couple of days if you let it.

The center of Shaker activities was just west of Hancock, along US-20 across the New York border at New Lebanon, where a few buildings still stand today. Other large Shaker communities in New England included Sabbathday Lake in Maine (the only one still "alive"); one at Enfield, New Hampshire (east of Hanover); and another at Canterbury, New Hampshire (south of Franconia Notch).

Lenox Practicalities

The Berkshires' annual influx of cosmopolitan concertgoers affects everything in southwestern Massachusetts, most obviously the local restaurants, half of which cater to seasonal immigrants from Boston and New York. Try the eclectic menu at the tiny but highly regarded "locavore" **Nudel Restaurant** (37 Church St., 413/551-7183), where the sometimes-exotic tastes from the kitchen come from locally sourced ingredients. Many other contenders for the town's gourmet dining crown lie within the same two-block area.

one of the gardens at The Mount, former home of Edith Wharton

Along with its many good restaurants, Lenox brims with more than 20 handsome B&B inns, all attractively situated amid wide lawns and gardens. Try the historic and cozy **Birchwood Inn** (7 Hubbard St., 413/637-2600, $199 and up), opposite the Church on the Hill, or the **Brook Farm Inn** (15 Hawthorne St., 413/637-3013, $139 and up), which offers more than 700 volumes of poetry in the library, poetry readings on Saturday, and poems *du jour* for perusal before breakfast. Another popular option, right at the center of Lenox, is the always charming **Village Inn** (16 Church St., 413/637-0021), built in 1771 and featuring clean, comfortable rooms, and a good restaurant.

Stockbridge

On the south side of the I-90 Mass Turnpike from Lenox, the other main center of Berkshires cultural life is **Stockbridge** (pop. 1,947). If Main Street feels familiar, perhaps it's because the town made its way onto Norman Rockwell canvases during the final decades of his career, when he lived and worked here. You may dismiss his illustrations as the epitome of contrived sentimentality, but only people with hearts of solid flint won't find themselves grinning after a stroll through the collection of the **Norman Rockwell Museum** (413/298-4100, daily, $18 adults). The modern museum is on Route 183 two miles west of town. The town itself is well worth a stroll, too, particularly past the grand houses along Main Street that seem frozen in an idyllic past.

While most of the large estate homes around Stockbridge are not open to the public, one of the county's more extravagant "cottages" is **Naumkeag** (daily summer, Sat.-Sun. spring and fall, $15 adults), an 1885 mansion on Prospect Hill Road less than a mile north of downtown. The mansion, designed by Stanford White for

Know that Rockwell painting of the runaway kid with the policeman? The lunch-counter setting was inspired by **Joe's Diner** (85 Center St., 413/243-9756) in nearby **Lee,** a Berkshire institution favored by everybody from local factory workers to New York celebrities.

Once upon a time, Stockbridge was home to the eatery immortalized by Arlo Guthrie as the place where "you can get anything you want" in his 1967 folk song, "Alice's Restaurant Massacree."

Joseph Choate, a lawyer who later served as U.S. ambassador to Britain, amply illustrates why this region was regarded as the state's Gold Coast a century ago. The impressively landscaped grounds are an attraction in their own right.

Sculpture is the highlight of **Chesterwood** (daily summer, $18 adults), off Route 183 just south of the Norman Rockwell Museum. The residence was the summer home of Daniel Chester French, one of the most popular contributors to the fin de siècle American renaissance. French arrived on the art scene with a bang, sculpting Concord's *Minute Man* statue at the age of 23 and 24, but he is best remembered for his statue of the seated president at the Lincoln Memorial in Washington DC. A tour of French's studio and house (now a property of the National Trust) or a walk around the 122 wooded acres graced with works of contemporary sculptors quickly confirms why French once called his seasonal visits "six months . . . in heaven."

Tyringham

Route 8, US-20, and the Mass Turnpike all cross the Appalachian Trail at Greenwater Pond, east of Lee, but a much more scenic stretch of the trail can be accessed south of here in the village of **Tyringham** (pop. 327). Site of a Shaker community in the 1800s, and later a popular artist colony, this small hamlet is situated in a delightfully rural landscape of small farms and rolling pastures. The main sight here is an odd one: **Santarella** (413/243-2819), the hand-hewn home and studio of British sculptor Henry Kitson, whose many works include the *Pilgrim Maiden* monument at Plymouth and the *Minuteman* at Lexington Green. His house is a place where Bilbo Baggins of *The Hobbit* would feel at home, with its sculpted rocks, twisting beams, and organic-looking pseudo-thatched roof. Although it's not open for tours, you can stay overnight at its cottages. It is also available for events.

Santarella

Great Barrington

South of Santarella, beyond the ever-quaint center of Tyringham, a signed parking area, which you can follow on a short (three miles round-trip) hike through fields of wildflowers up through Tyringham Cobble to a ridge giving a good view over this pastoral valley, which feels far more remote than it really is.

The first black man ever to earn a Ph.D. from Harvard, writer W. E. B. DuBois, was born in Great Barrington in 1868.

Great Barrington

While most South County towns have been spruced up like precious antiques, **Great Barrington,** with as many hardware stores as chic boutiques, is like Grandma's comfortable old sofa, still too much in daily use to keep under velvet wraps. The town doesn't deplore the few tacky commercial lots around its fringes, perhaps because they can't detract from the handsome buildings at its core. Prime among these buildings, which include stone churches on wide Main Street and imposing Searles Castle, a former Berkshire cottage turned private academy, is the landmark **Mahaiwe Performing Arts Center** (14 Castle St., 413/528-0100), all marble and gilt trim behind its marquee. Built for vaudeville and recently restored, the Mahaiwe still hosts frequent film, theater, and musical theater productions.

The roots of your local utility lie here in the nation's first commercial electrical system, created by transformer inventor William Stanley for Great Barrington's downtown in 1886.

Sheffield: Bartholomew's Cobble

Between Great Barrington and the Connecticut state line, US-7 winds through **Sheffield** and is lined by dozens of antiques stores, earning this stretch the nickname "Antique Alley." Sheffield also has a faded gray covered bridge, just over 100 yards east of US-7 on the north side of town. At the south edge of Sheffield, just west of US-7 off Weatogue Road, the natural rock garden of **Bartholomew's Cobble** ($5) rises up above the west bank of the Housatonic River. Geology and weather

The last battle of Shay's Rebellion, an uprising of farmers demanding reforms to prevent foreclosures after the American Revolution dried up English credit, was fought in a field south of Sheffield village on Sheffield Road. A small stone obelisk marks the spot, coincidentally adjacent to the Appalachian Trail.

The mountainous section of US-20, north of the Mass Turnpike between Huntington and Lee, is one of the oldest auto roads in New England, originally called Jacob's Ladder. Centered on the quaint town of **Chester,** it's older, and in some ways prettier, than the busier and much more famous Mohawk Trail across the state's northwestern tier.

have conspired to produce an outstanding diversity of plants and birds—800 species, including beautiful wildflowers—within a relatively small pocket of fern-covered limestone outcrops and broad meadows. At the center of the 329-acre state-run reserve, a pleasant walk up Hulbert's Hill gives a broad view over the surrounding Berkshire scene.

South Egremont: Bash Bish Falls

While US-7 gets the most tourist traffic, a more pastoral way south into Connecticut follows Route 41 via **South Egremont,** another of those well-preserved villages entirely ensconced in the National Register of Historic Places, which is hardly a rare honor in Massachusetts. At the center of town, **The Old Mill** (53 Main St., 413/528-1421) has been serving great soups, steaks, and more for more than 30 years.

South Egremont is the gateway to the state's remotest corner, the over 4,000 forested acres of **Mount Washington State Forest.** Within its wooded boundaries are miles of hiking trails, including a stretch of the Appalachian Trail climbing up to the 2,624-foot summit of Mt. Everett, but the highlight here is photogenic **Bash Bish Falls,** the highest in Massachusetts. A whopping 60-foot drop, splashing down in a V-shaped pair of cascades, Bash Bish Falls is no Niagara, but it's a nice place to while away a hot summer afternoon.

CONNECTICUT

Anyone who drives its interstates will appreciate why Connecticut enjoys a solid reputation among New Englanders as "the drive-through state." The high-speed route between Boston and New York City, I-95, is something endured rather than enjoyed, but our route through the scenic northwest corner is as different from the coastal megalopolis as a tulip is from a truck tire. Like the neighboring Berkshires, Connecticut's **Litchfield Hills** are a traditional retreat for discerning city dwellers. The area is rich in forests, farms, and picturesque little towns laden with antiques and great restaurants. Fast food and discount shopping are as alien to this landscape as affordability, so if your purse strings are tight, you'll want to keep moving; otherwise, linger a while and enjoy some of the rural charm so prized by those people you might see on the cover of *Business Week*.

North Canaan and Salisbury

Crossing into Connecticut from the north on US-7, the first thing that will catch your eye is the stainless-steel siding of **Collin's Diner** (53 Main St., 860/824-7040) in **North Canaan.** A classic 1940s prefab O'Mahony diner, Collin's has all the usual diner standards, and its big parking lot

(shared with the neighboring historic railroad depot) is frequently full of equally classic cars, whose owners congregate here on summer afternoons. The rest of North Canaan is anything but prissy, a refreshing change of pace from the overly tidy tourist towns that dominate the surrounding region.

From Canaan, US-44 winds east toward Hartford, stopping after 12 miles at another gem of a small town, **Norfolk;** if any town has capitalized on being far removed from trading floors and board meetings, it's this one. With three public parks and the largest nonprofit-owned and operated forest in the state, Norfolk has considered its sheer scenic beauty a stock-in-trade for nearly a century. The town green is worth the drive so that you can see the folksy road sign that points the way with pictures of rabbits and other cute creatures.

After extensive touring around New England, you risk taking white columns, wide porches, picket fences, and the obligatory Congregational steeple for granted.

> Salisbury Furnace, a local foundry, was an armory of the American Revolution, supplying George Washington's troops with almost their entire arsenal of cannons for the duration of the war.

West Cornwall

Rivers are consistently some of the most attractive driving companions you could ask for, a fact proven once again as US-7 rejoins the Housatonic River east of Lime Rock. The highway's scenic miles are further enhanced by the sudden appearance of a barn-red covered bridge, in service since 1864. This is the kind of place that would tar and feather the first vinyl-siding salesperson to walk into town, lest harm befall its antiquarian bookshop or other clapboard buildings bearing signs from previous commercial lives.

South of town in Sharon, **Housatonic Meadows State Park** (860/927-3238) offers riverside camping, perfectly situated for anyone considering a canoe or kayak rental from nearby **Clarke Outdoors** (860/672-6365, canoe trips $50 Mon.-Fri., $60 Sat.-Sun. for two people), on US-7 a mile south of that covered bridge. Clarke's 10-mile and 6-mile canoe trips include a boat, life vests, and all the gear, plus van shuttles and hot showers. Remember to bring bug repellent if you're planning to spend time near the water.

Housatonic Meadows State Park also includes a short 2.41-mile round-trip trail up 1,160-foot Pine Knob, which offers fine views from its summit. South of the park boundary, the hikers' Appalachian Trail crosses US-4 near the hamlet of Cornwall Bridge, then runs alongside the river for some six miles, the longest riverside cruise in the trail's entire 2,100 miles.

Off Route 112 a couple of miles west of US-7, you'll find **Lime Rock Park,** an automobile racetrack made famous by classic car rallies, a mid-summer Grand Prix, the Skip Barber Racing School, and the occasional appearance of celebrity drivers like Tom Cruise. The sharp, twisting descent from nearby Lakeville to the raceway is one of many pretty back-road drives in the area.

Kent

Like many of its Litchfield-area neighbors, **Kent** (pop. 2,962) had a thriving iron industry until competition from larger Pennsylvania mines—with better access to post-Civil War markets—forced the local furnace to close. Now it's a bustling upscale market town, its main street (US-7) lined with antiques shops, galleries, and boutiques that have replaced blacksmith shops and wheelwrights. The area's transition from industry to leisure is implicit in the unusual displays inside the **Eric Sloane Museum** (860/927-3849, Fri.-Sun. 10am-4pm summer, $8), located along US-7, near the ruins of an early American iron foundry.

Kent Falls State Park, along US-7 about four miles north of the museum, is a nice place to take a break from behind the wheel. Along with the namesake cascade, which is most impressive after a rain, the park includes a short path through dense woods.

Beginning in the south of Kent, and parallel to US-7 for about four miles along the west bank of the Housatonic River, Schaghticoke Road is a slower, much more scenic route that gives an up-close look at the rugged geology beneath the trees. The route crosses the Schaghticoke Reservation and passes an old Native American cemetery before rejoining US-7 via a covered bridge on Bulls Bridge Road, three miles north of Gaylordsville.

The Appalachian Trail crosses the New York state line near Bull's Bridge, south of Kent, and so should you, making your way west to Route 22 or the Taconic State Parkway if you want to enjoy a landscape that offers more fields and trees than

Kent Falls State Park

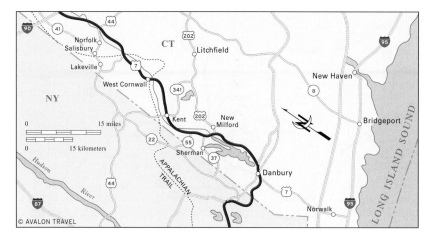

guardrails and parking lots. Technically speaking, there's still a large swath of New England between New York and New Milford, but most of this has more in common with the Indianapolis beltway than with the Vermont countryside.

NEW YORK

According to the map, the Appalachian Trail's corner-cutting path across the southern edge of the state seems well outside **New York City**'s sprawl, but there is no escape from the greater reality of the urban northeast: This part of the Atlantic seaboard is the original megalopolis. The map may not make it obvious that some tens of millions of people live within an hour's drive of this route, but the volume of traffic will.

Between the Connecticut border and the Hudson River, many of the roads along the route of the Appalachian Trail have become heavily developed corridors of suburban malls and park-and-ride lots for Manhattan commuters, but there are also some fascinating parks and other places worth exploring.

West Point

The hikers' Appalachian Trail, and our driving equivalent along old US-6, both cross the Hudson River near **West Point,** the U.S. Army's famous military academy, located at a point on the west bank of the Hudson, naturally. Even if you're not a military buff, there's a lot of fascinating history here: This is the fortress the traitorous U.S. general Benedict Arnold offered to hand over to the British (for cash and a promotion) during the Revolutionary War. There's a small **museum** (daily, free) and guided bus tours of the grounds; walk up to **Trophy Point** for a great view of the river and a display of cannons captured during various U.S. wars.

On the north side of West Point, south of Newburgh off Hwy-32, stretch your legs and enjoy a different outlook on life at the pastoral **Storm King Art Center** (845/534-3115, Wed.-Sun. Apr.-Nov., Wed.-Mon. Sept.-Oct., $18 adults), a fabulous

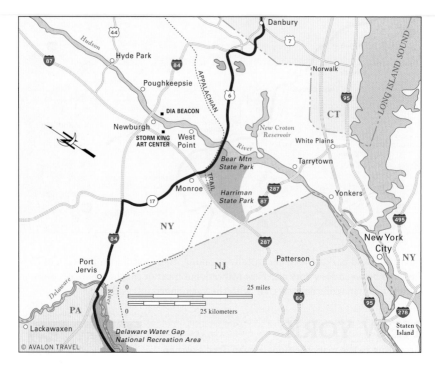

Even if you're racing across New York on the I-84 freeway, there's one place you should stop: the town of **Hyde Park,** where the homes of Franklin D. and Eleanor Roosevelt offer a look back at their admirable lives and challenging times.

500-acre sculpture park that celebrates the dynamic relationship between nature and culture. The artworks include more than a dozen large metal sculptures by the pioneering David Smith (1906-1965), who learned to weld while working in the Studebaker factory in South Bend, Indiana, and became one of the most influential Abstract Expressionists before his death in a car wreck. The Storm King collection also includes pieces by Alexander Calder, Henry Moore, and Louise Nevelson.

Along the east bank of the Hudson River in the town of Beacon, another unexpected art find is the intriguing **Dia:Beacon** (845/440-0100, Thurs.-Mon. Apr.-Dec., Fri.-Mon. Jan.-Mar., $15), a minimally remodeled 1930s factory full of thought-provoking works by Robert Irwin, Dan Flavin, Donald Judd, Louise Bourgeois, and many other influential artists. Metro-North **commuter trains** (about 80 minutes each way, $39.50 round-trip, including museum admission) run right past the windows, heading down the river between Beacon and NYC's Grand Central Station.

West and south of West Point, the hikers' Appalachian Trail closely follows historic US-6 for a scenic foray through Harriman and Bear Mountain State Parks before heading south and west toward New Jersey and Pennsylvania.

Harriman State Park and Bear Mountain

Rising out of the Hudson Valley, **Harriman State Park** is a mountainous oasis with 31 lakes and some 200 miles of hiking trails. The first section of the Appalachian Trail was opened here in 1923. In utter contrast to the get-out-of-my-way style of

Bear Mountain Bridge and the Palisades Parkway

later highway construction, the roads across the park, designed in the 1920s for Sunday afternoon family outings in the newfangled motor car, maximize exposure to the surrounding forests, and even the rustic Romanesque stone arch bridges manage to harmonize with local rock outcroppings.

Closer to the Hudson River, an adjacent state park, **Bear Mountain,** is even more full of old-fashioned pleasures and draws more annual visitors than Yellowstone National Park (no doubt thanks to its location at the north end of the Palisades Parkway). There's a delightful little zoo along a stretch of the hikers' Applachian Trail, and a scenic drive leads near the top of Bear Mountain itself, where a New Deal-era lookout tower

The **Hudson Valley Renegades** (845/838-0094) play Class A baseball in Wappingers Falls, north of I-84 along Route 9D.

gives views over the entire region. In season, there are paddle boats for rent, plus a large swimming pool (or an ice-skating rink). Meals and accommodations are available in the circa-1915 **Bear Mountain Inn** (845/786-2731).

Local literary trivia: At the beginning of Jack Kerouac's *On the Road,* the main character, Sal Paradise, sets off from New York City on an ill-fated attempt to follow US-6 all the way to the West Coast. Hoping to hitch a ride along the "one red line called Route 6 that led from the tip of Cape Cod clear to Ely, Nevada, and there dipped down to Los Angeles," Sal got caught in a rainstorm here at Bear Mountain and had to head home, giving up on the "stupid hearthside idea that it would be wonderful to follow one great line across America instead of trying various roads and routes."

New York City

STATUE OF LIBERTY, NEW YORK CITY

Some people avoid New York City like the plague, but more than eight million others can't bear to leave the glorious buzzing mosaic that makes New York unique in the world. Love it or hate it, New York is New York, and this great metropolis is undeniably the capital of the capitalist world, with some of the best museums, the best shops, the best sights, and the best restaurants in the world.

There's not much point in recommending a select few of New York's huge spectrum of attractions, so here's some practical help. For drivers, to whom all roads must seem to converge upon—and become gridlocked in—New York City, if you value your sanity and your shock absorbers, park your car in a long-term lot and walk or take public transportation. New York's **subway system** ($2.75 per ride, payable via electronic MetroCard), one of the most extensive in the world, is safe, fast, and cheap. City buses are generally slower, but you see more of the sights. Taxis are ubiquitous—except when you want one—and the CitiBike bike-share system makes getting around more fun. And whatever you do, take time to walk: in Central Park, through Chinatown, or along the magical **High Line,** a long-abandoned rail line recently reborn as a stylish pedestrian path, elevated 20 feet above the not-so-mean streets.

The key to a successful visit to New York City is finding a place to stay. Ideally, you'll have an expense account, a friend, or a rich aunt, but lacking that, here are a few that make for a good base. It's hard to beat the **Conrad New York** (102 North

The High Line, formerly a rail line, now serves as a green pedestrian path.

End Ave., 212/945-0100, $349 and up) for location, placed along the Hudson River in peaceful Battery Park City, looking out over the Statue of Liberty, and the rooms are larger than most. The least expensive place in town is probably the large and popular **HI-New York Hostel** (891 Amsterdam Ave., 212/932-2300, $49 and up), on the Upper West Side at 103rd Street. And if money is no object, there are many fabulous hotels in New York City, like the trendy but genteel **Crosby Street Hotel** (79 Crosby St., 212/226-6400, $625 and up), which is surprisingly quiet, considering its heart-of-SoHo location.

Eating out is another way to blow a lot of money quickly, but there are some great places where you can get both a good meal and a feel for New York without going bankrupt. One such place is **Katz's Delicatessen** (205 E. Houston St., 212/254-2246), a Lower East Side landmark that's been serving up huge sandwiches (including great pastrami) since 1888. (For movie buffs, Katz's is where Meg Ryan's famous scene in *When Harry Met Sally* was filmed.) In bohemian Greenwich Village, check out **John's Pizzeria** (278 Bleecker St., 212/243-1680), serving classic thin-crust pizza since 1929. No slices, no reservations. Another affordable all-American experience can be had at the retro-trendy **Shake Shack** (212/889-6600), a high-style burger stand, in leafy Madison Square Park at 5th Avenue and 23rd Street.

The **Statue of Liberty** in New York Harbor marks the beginning of our **Atlantic Coast** trip. See page 394.

New York City skyline

Port Jervis and Bethel

West of Harriman State Park, the Appalachian Trail and US-6 cross the busy I-87 New York Thruway, then wind through the exurbs of the Big Apple, where town after town seems unsure whether this is country living or not.

Farther west, along I-84 on the tristate (New York-New Jersey-Pennsylvania) border, **Port Jervis** is a curious mixture of small-town dereliction and commercial bustle. Transportation has clearly been a major historical force here, with the influence of successive eras—the river, the railroad, and the highway—inscribed in the very layout of the town. Stop inside the old **Erie Hotel and Restaurant** (845/858-4100, around $69 and up) next door to the former depot, which has an ornate bar, a lively restaurant, and rooms upstairs.

About 30 miles northwest of Port Jervis, Max Yasgur's farm outside **Bethel,** New York, welcomed revelers to the August 1969 Woodstock Festival of Music and Art, starring Jimi Hendrix; Crosby, Stills and Nash; and some 300,000 mud-soaked hippies. Starting with a 30th Anniversary concert in 1999, the Woodstock site has been redeveloped into a community-based arts and performance center called the **Bethel Woods Center for the Arts** (866/781-2922), which has a 15,000-seat amphitheater and a good museum tracing the story of the Woodstock generation in pop culture and pop music, self-described as a "destination for anyone who lived through the sixties or wishes they did."

PENNSYLVANIA

The hikers' Appalachian Trail runs across southern New York and western New Jersey, but our road route avoids the Garden State almost entirely, crossing instead the natural chasm of the **Delaware Water Gap,** whose forests, waterfalls, and wildlife are popular with city-dwellers escaping the New York-Philly megalopolis. In its 150-mile length, this route across Pennsylvania passes through a succession of strikingly different places, starting with the densely populated industrial regions of the Lehigh Valley and the historic little town of **Bethlehem,** which plays up its Christmas connections more than its role as a formerly vital steelmaking center. Farther south, modern industry gives way to the traditional agriculture of **Pennsylvania Dutch Country,** world famous for its anti-technology Old Order Christian communities. Continuing southwest across the Susquehanna River, you'll follow the route of the old Lincoln Highway through historic **York,** early capital of the United States, now home to the Harley-Davidson motorcycle assembly plant. The last stop on the Pennsylvania leg of the route is the Civil War battlefields at **Gettysburg,** just shy of the Maryland border.

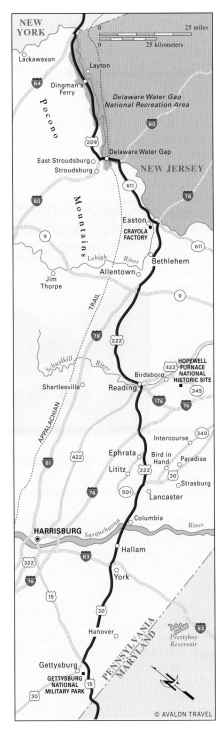

Lackawaxen

The tiny town of **Lackawaxen** (pop. 4,994), along the Delaware River 20 winding, scenic miles northwest of Port Jervis via Hwy-97, holds two fascinating attractions: the preserved home of writer Zane Grey, and a unique suspension bridge completed in 1848 by Brooklyn Bridge designer John Roebling. It comes as something of a surprise to find out that Zane Grey, author of the classic Western novel *Riders of the Purple Sage,* was in fact a fly-fishing, baseball-loving Pennsylvania dentist, but he was. His home was preserved by his family as the **Zane Grey Museum** (135 Scenic Dr., 570/685-4871, Wed.-Sun. 10am-5pm summer, free). Now maintained by the National Park Service, the museum offers an unusually intimate look into his life and works. Zane Grey and his wife (and childhood sweetheart) Dolly are buried side-by-side in the small Lackawaxen graveyard.

The **Roebling Bridge** is about 100 yards downstream from Zane Grey's home and has been preserved by the National Park Service—though it's now used by cars instead of canal boats. For the full experience, stay the night in the circa-1870 canal office, now housing the **Roebling Inn on the Delaware** (570/685-7900, $110 and up).

Milford

At the west end of US-6's pleasant run along the river from Port Jervis, just off I-84 at the northern end of Delaware Water Gap National Recreation Area, **Milford** (pop. 1,021) is a cute little town cashing in on the hordes of rafters, campers, and B&B patrons who make the weekend journey to the surrounding Pocono Mountains from New York or Philadelphia.

Milford was the longtime home of sustainable forestry pioneer and two-term Pennsylvania governor Gifford Pinchot (1865-1946), whose **Grey Towers** (570/296-9630, $8) estate off US-6 is now preserved as a National Historic Site, open in summer for tours. Visitors and locals alike converge on the town's culinary landmarks, the **Milford Diner** (301 Broad St., 570/296-8611, daily 6am-10pm) and the more photogenic **Village Diner** (268 US-6 and 209, 570/491-2819), which sits on the south side of the I-84 freeway, just west of Walmart.

Delaware Water Gap National Recreation Area

Totaling some 67,000 acres of forest on both banks of the Delaware River, the **Delaware Water Gap National Recreation Area** stretches for 35 miles south of the I-84 freeway along two-lane US-209. Established beginning in 1960, the park is still under development, though numerous hiking trails lead through hardwood forests to seasonal waterfalls, and the river itself offers abundant canoeing, swimming, and fishing. Though far from pristine, the natural beauty is surprisingly undisturbed considering the park lies only 50 miles northwest of New York City.

A few remnants of the area's historic agricultural villages have been preserved under the aegis of the park, but the main attraction is the oddly named Delaware Water Gap itself, a deep cleft carved by the river into the solid rock of the Kittatinny Mountains. Artists, sightseers, and rock-climbers have admired this unique feat of geology for centuries, but unfortunately the natural passageway is crisscrossed by all manner of road and railroad, including the six-lane I-80 freeway, which runs right through it.

A stretch of the Appalachian Trail cuts along a 1,200-foot-high ridge at the southeast corner of the park, crossing the Delaware River on an old bridge at the town of **Delaware Water Gap.** Get a feel for the trail at the self-service Appalachian Mountain Club-run **Mohican Outdoor Center** (908/362-5670), which has cabins and a campground on a pretty site outside Blairstown, New Jersey.

The tiny tourist town of Delaware Water Gap, south of I-80 at the far southern end of the park, provides the best views of the gap. A visitors center sits along the river, just off I-80 at the first or last New Jersey exit, and offers exhibits on the geology and history of the region.

The Poconos

The **Pocono Mountains,** which rise to the west of the Delaware River, hold a number of traditional summer resort hotels spread among the golf courses and ski areas. Like the Catskills' "Borscht Belt" of southern New York, the Poconos had their glory days in the 1950s, but some resorts still thrive thanks to the invention here in the 1960s of the couple-friendly, heart- or champagne glass-shaped bathtub, which has turned many a Pocono hotel into a pseudo-Roman honeymoon destination (the *Baltimore Sun* called one a "mini Playboy Mansion"). Many of these passion pits tend to feature all-inclusive package deals (free archery lessons, so

I Brake for Historical Markers

PENNSYLVANIA
Founded 1681 by William Penn
as a Quaker Commonwealth.
Birthplace of
THE DECLARATION OF INDEPENDENCE
and
THE CONSTITUTION OF THE UNITED STATES

Pennsylvania Historical and Museum Commission

you and your beloved can play Cupid with real arrows, etc.). If you're interested, try **Pocono Palace** (866/500-5508) 15 miles northeast of **Stroudsburg** off US-209. To get a feel for the Poconos' working-class charms, head downstream along the Pequest River to **Hot Dog Johnny's** (333 Route 46, 908/453-2882) in Butzville for classic dogs, crunchy fries, frosty mugs of root beer, and all the 1940s old road nostalgia you can want.

By contrast, a classic "old-school" Poconos resort—the rightly named **Skytop Lodge** (855/345-7759)—is about 20 miles northwest of Stroudsburg via Hwy-447. This grand yet family-friendly 1920s hotel, with just 124 rooms and suites but full resort facilities, sits on 5,500 acres of mountaintop forest, with its own golf course, hiking trails, and shooting range.

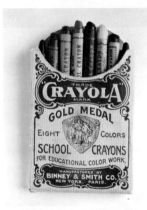

At the southern edge of the Delaware Water Gap park, Stroudsburg has the Poconos' most extensive tourist facilities, clustered along the I-80 freeway.

Easton and Nazareth

South of the Delaware Water Gap, Hwy-611 runs along the Delaware River until its confluence with the Lehigh River, near the town of **Easton.** This historic industrial center is now home to one of the Poconos' most popular family attractions: the **Crayola Experience** (30 Centre Square, 610/515-8000, $20), where you can watch colorful crayons being made and packaged, then scribble away to your heart's content. The actual Crayola factory is a half dozen miles away and not open to the public. The **National Canal Museum** (2750 Hugh Moore Park Rd.) traces the history of the Delaware and Lehigh Canal and other artificial waterways all over the United States. Seasonal canal boat trips are offered.

Another more historic American factory tour is in nearby **Nazareth,** where the venerable **Martin Guitar Company** (510 Sycamore St., 610/759-2837 or 800/633-2060, tours Mon.-Fri. 11am-2:30pm, free) has been in business since 1833. If you've ever enjoyed strumming a six-string, you'll want to take one of the wonderful tours of the family-owned

Martin Guitar Company

factory. The tours include both a look inside the workshops—where you can watch workers as they bend, carve, inlay, and polish the instruments—and displays of classic Martin guitars.

Bethlehem

Upstream from Easton along the Lehigh River and US-222, the remarkable small city of **Bethlehem** (pop. 74,982), famous for its Christmas festivals and as a fun place from which to mail Christmas cards, was originally established in 1741 by a group of Moravian missionaries. The missionaries' chapel, built from 1803 to 1806, still stands at the heart of the compact gaslit downtown district, its cemetery full of 200-year-old headstones laid flat so as not to offend God.

Bethlehem

The **Moravian Museum** (66 W. Church St., 610/691-6055, Sat.-Sun. 11am-4pm, $10) is housed inside the circa-1741 **Gemeinhaus,** the oldest building in Bethlehem. Besides showcasing historic artifacts, the museum also offers guided walking tours of the downtown area. Another engaging historic site is the **Sun Inn** (564 Main St.), a well-preserved former tavern "where the leading figures of the Revolutionary era were entertained," according to a plaque on the wall It now hosts a full bar and microdistillery alongside a rotating menu of gourmet cuisine.

Every May, Bethlehem hosts a hugely popular **Bach Festival** (610/866-4382), rated as one of the best in country.

The Triple-A **Lehigh Valley IronPigs,** the Phillies' top farm club, play at **Coca-Cola Park** (610/841-7447, $8-19), south of US-22 near the Allentown airport. Games are broadcast on **ESPN 1230-1320 AM.**

Across the Lehigh River from the tidy homes and shops of downtown Bethlehem, Lehigh University stands above the rusting remains of the Bethlehem Steel Company. Famous for fabricating engineering marvels such as the towers of the Golden Gate Bridge—cast here in sections, then shipped through the Panama Canal and assembled in San Francisco—the mill was in business for over a century before being closed down in 1995. The **National Museum of Industrial History** is housed inside the mill's electrical building and features two of its cranes. The bulk of the complex has been converted into the massive **Sands Casino Resort** (877/726-3777, $139 and up), where the huge old furnaces are lit up in brightly colored lights as an architectural feature.

Downtown, the bistro-style **Apollo Grill** (85 W. Broad St., 610/865-9600) is perhaps the nicest place in Bethlehem for a bite to eat. For a place to stay, try the large, centrally located **Hotel Bethlehem** (437 Main St., 610/625-5000, $169 and up).

Allentown

The seat of Lehigh County, **Allentown** (pop. 118,032) spreads west of Bethlehem, across a bend in the Lehigh River. The downtown area has two worthwhile stops, the bigger and better of which is the **Allentown Art Museum** (31 N. 5th St., 610/432-4333, Wed.-Sun., $12 adults). After a recent expansion, you'll find a good collection of paintings and photography as well as an entire library moved from the Frank Lloyd Wright-designed Little House. Allentown's other main attraction lies two blocks west at Church and Hamilton Streets: the **Liberty Bell Museum** (610/435-4232, Mon.-Sat. noon-4pm Feb.-Dec., $2), an old church that houses a replica of the famous bell that was hidden here for safekeeping during the Revolutionary War battles at Philadelphia.

Allentown boasts some great places to eat, thanks to the multiple branches of **Yocco's "The Hot Dog King"** (3300 Lehigh St., 610/351-4222; 1930 Catasauqua Rd., 610/264-1884; 2128 Hamilton St.; 610/821-8488). These local landmarks have been serving up chili dogs (and a few burgers) bathed in a top-secret chili sauce since 1922. Allentown also has one of the country's oldest, largest collections of roller coasters and a fine old carousel at **Dorney Park and Wildwater Kingdom** (610/395-3724, daily summer, around $50). There's a water park too.

Reading

Standing along the eastern banks of the Schuylkill River, **Reading** (pop. 88,083) is most famous these days as the childhood home of pop superstar Taylor Swift. Ornately turreted row houses line 5th Street (US-222 Business) through the residential districts, downtown holds a number of well-maintained businesses and signs from the first half of the 20th century, and a photogenic 72-foot, 110-year-old pagoda offers panoramic views from the summit of Mt. Penn, east of town.

For history buffs, two worthwhile places to visit sit southeast of Reading along the Schuylkill River. The closer of these is at **Birdsboro,** 10 miles from town and a mile south of US-422. The **Daniel Boone Homestead** (610/582-4900, Thurs.-Sun., tours $7, self-guided tours $3) marks the site where the great frontiersman was born in 1734.

Well worth the winding five-mile drive south of Birdsboro via Hwy-345, the **Hopewell Furnace National Historic Site** (daily summer, free) preserves intact an entire iron-making community that thrived here from the colonial era until the mid-1880s. Park rangers fire up the furnace and demonstrate the primitive foundry (melting aluminum rather than iron to take the "heat" off

The town of **Jim Thorpe,** in the Lehigh Valley 30 miles northwest of Allentown off the Pennsylvania Turnpike (I-476), 10 miles north of the Appalachian Trail, is a former coal-mining town with many 19th-century buildings. The town changed its name from Mauch Chunk in 1954 to honor the great Olympic athlete Jim Thorpe, whose remains lie in a granite mausoleum along Hwy-903 on the northeast side of town.

Midway between Allentown and Reading, every July the weeklong **Kutztown Folk Festival** celebrates the arts, crafts, and culture of the local Pennsylvania Dutch communities, which are less austere than their Lancaster County counterparts.

Reading is home to a Phillies farm club, the **Reading Fightin Phils,** who play Double-A baseball at the pleasant **FirstEnergy Stadium** (610/375-8469, $7-13).

ROADSIDE AMERICA

One of the quirkiest tourist attractions in the United States, **Roadside America** (610/488-6241, daily, $8 adults) stands alongside the I-78 freeway, 20 miles northwest of Reading in the village of Shartlesville. Built by Reading native Laurence Gieringer, Roadside America is a giant 1:32 scale model of bygone Americana, fleshed out with animated scenes that trace a typical day in the life of the country—circa 1930s, when Roadside America first opened to the public. As you walk around the edges of the 7,450-square-foot exhibit, you can push buttons to make wheels spin, lights flash, and pumps pump, and you'll see a little of everything rural: an 1830s New England village featuring a church and choral music; a canyon and lake complete with waterfalls and resort cabins; a model of Henry Ford's workshop in Dearborn, Michigan, where he built one of the first "horseless carriages"; various turnpikes, canals, highways, and railroads; a coal mine; and a mockup of the San Francisco Bay Bridge, the closest Roadside comes to a city scene.

Though it's definitely a fine example of kitsch, Roadside America is also an oddly compelling place, and only the hardest-hearted road-tripper will be able to hold back the tears when, every half hour or so, the sun sets and Kate Smith bursts into "God Bless America."

The Monopoly Chance card "Take a Ride on the Reading" commemorates the railroad that formerly ran between Reading and Philadelphia.

the ancient tools), and exhibits trace the iron-making process—mining the ore, making charcoal, and fabricating the finished product, which here at Hopewell was primarily pig iron and stoves.

Ephrata and Lititz

South of Reading, US-222 runs along the western edge of the Amish- and Mennonite-influenced Pennsylvania Dutch Country. The heart of this region is due east of Lancaster, but the area north of Lancaster also holds a number of related sites often missed by visitors. The most appealing of these is the **Ephrata Cloister** (632 W. Main St., 717/733-6600, daily summer, $10 adults), just west of the town of **Ephrata.** Founded in 1732 by a communal society of religiously celibate German pietists, the Ephrata Cloister consists of nine log, stone, and fachwerk buildings dating from 1734 to 1837 and which housed dormitories, bakeries, and a printing shop where the commune produced some of the finest illustrated books of the colonial era. Across from the entrance, the **Cloister Restaurant** (607 W. Main St., 717/733-2361) serves good home-style food for breakfast, lunch, and dinner in an overgrown 1950s diner.

Lititz is the unlikely final resting place of John Sutter, the Swiss immigrant who owned huge chunks of pre-gold rush California. He died here in Pennsylvania while battling Washington DC bureaucracy, hoping in vain to receive compensation for his confiscated land.

Ephrata Cloister

If you happen, or can manage, to be in Ephrata on a Friday, there's no more authentic Dutch Country experience than the once-a-week **Green Dragon Farmers Market** (955 N. State St., 717/738-1117), a chaotic complex of some 400 different fresh fruit and vegetable sellers, sausage and hot dog stands, pizza places, and bakery outlets, covering 30 acres in seven buildings, just over a mile north of town. Many people here are truly Amish, so obey the second commandment and resist the urge to take their photo.

West of Ephrata, eight miles north of Lancaster via Hwy-501, the delightful though tiny town of **Lititz** (pop. 9,369) is dominated by the huge **Wilbur Chocolate Candy Store** (45 N. Broad St.), which liberally perfumes the air with the smell of hot chocolate. Lititz, which is packed full of stone buildings and carefully tended gardens, also holds the nation's oldest operating pretzel factory, the **Julius Sturgis Pretzel House** (219 E. Main St.), where you can twist your own. Lititz also holds a huge 4th of July party every year—well worth planning a trip around.

Lancaster

The only place approaching an urban scale in this part of Pennsylvania, **Lancaster** (pop. 59,322) is the region's commercial center, a bustling city that, for a single day during the Revolutionary War, served as capital of the rebellious United States. Though most visitors view it as little more than a handy base for exploring nearby Pennsylvania Dutch Country, Lancaster does have a couple of attractions in its own right, such as the redbrick pseudo-Romanesque **Central Market** (23 N. Market St.) near King and Queen Streets in the center of town. It hosts the nation's oldest publicly

A word to the wise: In Dutch Country, remember that anything claiming to be "authentic Amish" definitely isn't. Respect the Amish you see and refrain from taking photographs. Drive carefully too.

THE PENNSYLVANIA DUTCH COUNTRY

East of Lancaster, toward Philadelphia, the old Lincoln Highway (US-30) runs through the heart of what has become internationally famous as the Pennsylvania Dutch Country. This is a pretty, almost completely rural region, unremarkable apart from the presence here of various Old Order Anabaptist Christian sects, including Amish and Mennonite groups, who eschew most of the trappings and technological advances of the 21st century, including cars, electricity, and irrigation, and retain their simple ways. Long before the Peter Weir movie *Witness* gave Amish low-tech lifestyle the Hollywood treatment, visitors have been coming here to see these anachronistic descendants of German immigrants (Deutsche = Dutch) who settled here in the early 1700s, and to whom all outsiders are known simply as "English."

Amish Boys Out for a Drive, Lancaster County, Pa.

The best way to get a feel for the Amish and Mennonite ways of life is to follow back roads, by bike if possible, through the gently rolling countryside of Lancaster County, keeping an eye out for their horse-drawn buggies (Amish ones are gray, the Mennonites' ones are black). You can cross covered bridges and buy produce, breads, cakes, and shoo-fly pie from the many roadside stands marked by hand-lettered signs.

Most of the many Amish-style restaurants in the region are huge and forbiddingly full of bus-tour hordes. A quintessential road-food place is the **Route 30 Diner** (2575 E. Lincoln Hwy., 717/397-2507, Mon.-Thurs. until 10pm, Fri.-Sat. 24 hours) in Ronks on the north side of US-30, just east of the Hwy-896 intersection.

Though it won't give you any great insight into the Amish, one unique place to stay is the **Red Caboose Motel and Restaurant** (888/687-5005 or 717/687-5000, $85 and up), a mile east of Strasburg on Paradise Lane. All the rooms are built inside old railroad cars, and the on-site restaurant simulates a train journey, with whistles blowing and a gentle rocking vibration to ease your digestion. Strasburg is also home to the **Village Greens Miniature Golf Course** (717/687-6933), which is so fun and challenging that it was featured in *Sports Illustrated*.

owned, continuously operating farmers market, currently held all day Tuesday and Friday as well as Saturday mornings and early afternoons.

Two miles northeast of Lancaster, the state-run and well-signed **Landis Valley Museum** (Tues.-Sun. mid-Mar.-Dec., Wed.-Sun. Jan.-mid-Mar., $12 adults) is a popular living history park of more than 100 acres preserving and interpreting traditional rural lifeways of eastern Pennsylvania.

Hallam: The Shoe House

Many oddball attractions grew up along the old Lincoln Highway, the great cross-country highway that ran coast-to-coast beginning in 1915, and one of the best-beloved is the **Haines Shoe House,** which stands above the modern four-lane US-30 freeway, west of the town of **Hallam.** This landmark of programmatic architecture was built in 1948 by Mahlon "The Shoe Wizard" Haines, who owned a successful shoe company that proudly claimed to make boots "hoof-to-hoof," from raising the cattle to selling the finished products. The seven-room structure is shaped like a giant cartoon boot and can be reached by following Hwy-462 (the old Lincoln Highway, which runs just south of current US-30), to Shoe House Road, then winding north for a quarter mile. The turnoff is easy to miss, so keep an eye out for the Shoe

Midway between Lancaster and York, the town of **Columbia** holds what is arguably the country's best collection of timepieces in the **National Watch and Clock Museum** (514 Poplar St.). Also in Columbia is a beautiful multiarched concrete bridge that used to carry the old Lincoln Highway (US-30) across the broad Susquehanna River.

House Mini-Storage, which stands on the corner. The Shoe House has been bought and sold a number of times over the years. Tours offered weekly from May to October.

Just east of Hallam on US-30, **Jim Mack's Ice Cream** (5745 Lincoln Hwy., 717/252-2013) has been attracting fans for its ice cream—and its adjacent mini-golf course and mini-zoo. Next door is a bowling alley.

York

Though it doesn't look like much from the highway, bypassed by both US-30 and the I-83 freeway, the medium-size town of **York** (pop. 43,718) claims to be the first capital of the United States: Late in 1777, the Articles of Confederation were adopted here by the 13 newly independent former colonies, and (arguably) it's in that document that the name "United States of America" was first used. A significant number of historic buildings still stand in the quiet low-rise downtown area, including the medieval-looking circa-1741 Golden Plough Tavern and other colonial-era structures along Market Street at the west edge of the business district, plus the spacious and popular **Central Market House** (34 W. Philadelphia St.) farmers market.

For all its historic importance, self-proclaimed "Factory Tour Capital of the World" York is best known for its industrial prowess, which is saluted at the **Harley-Davidson assembly plant** (877/883-1450, Mon.-Fri. 9am-2pm, free), a mile east of town off US-30 on Eden Road. The Classic Factory Tour takes about one hour and begin with a brief history of the company,

Two of the main tourist stops in Dutch Country are the towns of **Intercourse** (source of many snickeringly allusive postcards) and **Paradise** (the Paradise post office, just north of US-30 at the west end of town, is a popular place for sending mail).

The town of **Hanover,** south of US-30 between York and Gettysburg, is a prime producer of snack foods, from potato chips to the famed pretzels baked by **Snyder's of Hanover** (1350 York St., 800/233-7125, Tues.-Thurs.), which offers free factory tours.

which is still based in Milwaukee. The tour also gives you the opportunity to sit on current models of the Touring, Softail, SVO, and Trike motorcycles and a chance to visit the shop floor for a close-up (and noisy) look and listen as the bikes get put together: Sheets of steel are pressed to form fenders and fairings, and once assembled, each bike is roll-tested at full throttle on motorcycling's equivalent of a treadmill. A souvenir store is stocked with all manner of things with the Harley-Davidson logo, from T-shirts to leather jackets.

Downtown York has a handful of cafés and restaurants. On the west edge of town, where the US-30 bypass rejoins the old Lincoln Highway (Hwy-462), **Lee's Diner** (4320 W. Market St., 717/792-1300) is a classic early-1950s Mountain View prefab diner, still serving up hearty breakfast all day long.

Gettysburg

Totally overwhelmed by the influx of tourists visiting its namesake battleground, the town of **Gettysburg** (pop. 7,620) has survived both onslaughts remarkably unscathed. Despite the presence of sundry tourist attractions—wax museums, various multimedia reenactments of the bat-

tle and President Lincoln's Gettysburg Address, even a Lincoln Train Museum displaying over a thousand model trains, including a scale replica of the Lincoln's funeral train—once the day-tripping crowds have dispersed, Gettysburg is actually a pleasant place, with rows of brick-fronted buildings lining Baltimore and York Streets at the center of town.

There are, not surprisingly, quite a few places to eat. The atmospheric **Dobbin House Tavern** (89 Steinwehr Ave., 717/334-2100), south of town, serves above-average pub food in Gettysburg's oldest building. Delicious cheesesteaks and burgers are served up at **Hunt's Battlefield Fries & Café** (61 Steinwehr Ave., 717/334-4787). The dozens of places to stay include all the usual national chains, plus the circa-1797 **Gettysburg Hotel** (717/337-2000, $119 and up), on Lincoln Square right at the center of town.

Gettysburg National Military Park

Site of the most famous two-minute speech in U.S. history, and of the bloody Civil War battle that marked the high tide of Confederate fortunes, **Gettysburg National Military Park** surrounds the town of Gettysburg, protecting the scenes of the struggle as they were July 1-3, 1863, when as many as 51,000 of the 165,000 combatants were killed or wounded. Over a thousand monuments mark the various historic sites around the 6,000 acres of rolling green pasture that form the park. The entire battlefield is evocative and interesting, but to make the most of a visit, start your tours at the **visitors center** (1195 Baltimore Pike, 717/334-1124, daily, $9-15), discreetly hidden away near Hunt Avenue east of Taneytown Road, two miles south of town, where an extensive museum puts the battle into context and displays a huge array of period weaponry. Unfortunately, you can no longer watch the battle unfold on the much-loved Electric Map, which looked a lot like a boxing

Abraham Lincoln
Robert E. Lee
George Gordon Meade

ring but has been superseded by more advanced multimedia displays in the digital age. However, the new visitors center has made space for an even older didactic artifact: the famous circular **Cyclorama,** a 42-by-377-foot painting-in-the-round that evocatively portrays the final Confederate assault on July 3, 1863. There are also numerous maps and guides available, including an excellent audio tour of the surrounding battleground.

North from the visitors center, a worthwhile quarter-mile walk leads north to the **Gettysburg National Cemetery,** where President Abraham Lincoln delivered his famous address on November 19, 1863.

A 230-acre farm on the southwest fringe of the Gettysburg battlefields was home to U.S. Army general and later president Dwight D. Eisenhower and his wife, Mamie, and is part of the 690-acre **Eisenhower National Historic Site** (717/338-9114, daily, $9 adults), now open for guided tours that leave from the Gettysburg visitors center.

Gettysburg National Military Park

THE LINCOLN HIGHWAY

The main east-west route through Pennsylvania Dutch Country, US-30 is also one of the best-preserved stretches of the old Lincoln Highway, the nation's first transcontinental route. Conceived in 1912 and named soon afterward, the Lincoln Highway linked New York City's Times Square with the Panama Pacific International Exposition in San Francisco, following over 3,000 miles of country road across 12 states. A thousand miles of the original "highway" were little more than muddy tracks, scarcely more visible on the ground than they were on the still-nonexistent road maps, but by the early 1930s the road was finally fully paved, following present-day US-30 as far as Wyoming, then bending south to follow what's now US-50, "The Loneliest Road in America," along the route of the Pony Express across Nevada and part of California.

In 1928, Boy Scouts placed 2,436 concrete posts and 961 metal signs on the Lincoln Highway. The markers included a bronze profile of Lincoln's face as well as red, white, and blue imagery. As with the later Route 66, the Lincoln Highway was replaced by the interstates, but it does live on, in folk memory as well as the innumerable Lincoln Cafés and Lincoln Motels along its original route, much of which still bears the name Lincolnway. You can become a member of the **Lincoln Highway Association** (815/456-3030), which offers a top-quality quarterly magazine for nominal annual dues.

MARYLAND

Crossing the Mason-Dixon Line from Gettysburg into Maryland on US-15, our route veers west into the Appalachian foothills of **Catoctin Mountain Park,** site of the presidential retreat Camp David. The landscape here is quite rugged, and signs of life few and far between—an oasis of peace and quiet, under an hour by road from Baltimore or Washington DC. Winding south through the mountains of the Maryland Panhandle (the thin strip of land that stretches for some 75 miles between Pennsylvania and West Virginia), this route again meets the hikers' Appalachian Trail, then detours to visit the battlefield of **Antietam,** the well-preserved site of the worst carnage of the Civil War.

Catoctin Mountain Park: Camp David

The Maryland state motto, Fatti Maschii, Parole Femine, is translated roughly as "Manly Deeds, Womanly Words."

US-15 continues south from Gettysburg across the Maryland border, and there's little to stop for until **Thurmont** (pop. 6,170), "Gateway to the Mountains." The green expanse of **Catoctin Mountain Park,** fully recovered after previous centuries of logging activity, protects some 5,810 acres of hardwood forest, a handful of 1,500-foot peaks, and the presidential retreat at

Camp David, hidden away in the woods and strictly off-limits to visitors (for security reasons, Camp David doesn't even appear on park maps). The **Catoctin park visitors center** (301/663-9388, daily) along Hwy-77 a little more than two miles west of US-15 provides information on cabins, camping, and maps of the many hiking trails, including a short trail from the visitors center to the preserved remains of the Blue Blazes whiskey still.

Spreading along the south side of Hwy-77, Maryland-run **Cunningham Falls State Park** offers more natural scenery and a pleasant swimming area in Hunting Creek Lake. There's a snack bar and boats for rent, and a half-mile trail leads to the eponymous cascade.

Washington Monument State Park

From Catoctin Mountain Park, our route heads south on undivided Hwy-6 and two-lane Hwy-17 along the hikers' Appalachian Trail, winding up at **Washington Monument State Park** between the I-70 freeway and the small town of **Boonsboro.** A 30-foot-tall bottle-shaped mound dedicated to the memory of George Washington stands at the center of the park; Boonsboro citizens completed the monument in 1827, making it the oldest memorial honoring the first U.S. president.

Atop a hill south of the park, across an old alignment of the National Road (US-40), the **Old South Mountain Inn** (301/432-6155, dinner Tues.-Sat., brunch and dinner Sun.) opened as a tavern in 1732.

In **Gathland State Park,** on the Appalachian Trail east of Gapland off Hwy-67, the 50-foot stone arch of the **War Correspondents Memorial Arch** was erected in 1896 in honor of journalists killed while covering the Civil War.

The name "David" in Camp David was bestowed by President Eisenhower in celebration of his then five-year-old grandson, who went on to marry Julie Nixon, daughter of Eisenhower's vice president, Richard Nixon. Later in life, young David also inspired John Fogerty of Creedence Clearwater Revival to write the song "Fortunate Son."

Antietam National Battlefield

Between Boonsboro and the Potomac River, which forms Maryland's border with West Virginia, **Antietam National Battlefield** preserves the hallowed ground where over 23,000 men were killed or wounded on the bloodiest single day of the Civil War—September 17, 1862. Atop a shallow hill at the middle of the park, a scant mile north of **Sharpsburg** off Hwy-65, the **visitors center** (301/432-5124, daily, $10 per car) offers a film, museum exhibits, and interpretive programs that put the battle into military and political context. Though there was no clear winner, Antietam is said to have convinced

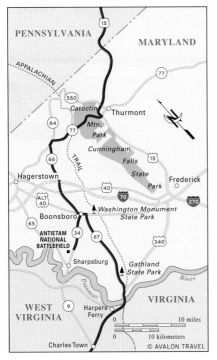

Clara Barton tended the wounded during and after the Civil War's bloodiest battle at Antietam.

Lincoln to issue the Emancipation Proclamation, officially freeing enslaved people in Confederate states and effectively putting an end to British support for the southern side.

WEST VIRGINIA

In its short run across the eastern tip of West Virginia, US-340 passes through one of the most history-rich small towns in the United States: **Harpers Ferry,** located at the confluence of the Shenandoah and Potomac Rivers. Lovely mountain scenery surrounds Harpers Ferry, especially during early autumn when the hardwood forests rival Vermont's for vibrant color. South of Harpers Ferry, the hikers' Appalachian Trail runs directly along the Virginia-West Virginia border, east of the Shenandoah River atop the roadless crest of the **Blue Ridge Mountains.** The best route to follow by car, US-340 swings to the west through the historic mountain resort of **Charles Town** before entering Virginia.

Harpers Ferry

Climbing the steep slopes of the Blue Ridge Mountains, **Harpers Ferry** (pop. 286) embodies the industrial and political history of the early United States. Protected since 1963 as a national park, its many well-preserved wood, brick, and stone buildings are palpable reminders of early American enterprise: Besides the country's first large factory, first canal, and first railroad, scenic Harpers Ferry saw abolitionist John Brown's 1859 rebellion against slavery, and it was later a strategic site during the Civil War. Harpers Ferry was also home to Storer College, an African American college that operated here from the 1860s until 1955.

Small museums, housed in separate buildings along Shenandoah and High Streets along the riverfront in the "Lower Town," trace the various strands of the town's past. From the Shenandoah River, the Appalachian Trail (AT) winds south down what the third president called "one of the most stupendous scenes in Nature," Jefferson's Rock. Crossing the Potomac River to the north, the AT climbs up to Maryland Heights for more spectacular vistas.

Especially in summer, the best first stop is the small **visitors center** (304/535-6029, daily, $5 per person, $10 per vehicle) above the town along US-340. Park here and take one of the frequent free shuttles down to the historic area, as parking elsewhere is limited. Although most of Harpers Ferry is preserved as a historic site, there is considerable pressure to "develop" surrounding lands, so get here while it's still nice. The eastern portions along the Potomac riverfront have remained in private hands, and here you can indulge your taste for American food, wax museums, and schlocky souvenirs. There's excellent cycling, a couple of companies offer white-water rafting trips, and for another sort of adventure, you

downtown Harpers Ferry

can head down to the cute red clapboard depot and hop aboard one of the **Amtrak/ MARC** trains, which run to Washington DC on a limited schedule. To get the most out of a visit, stay overnight at the lovingly restored, circa-1790s, Federal-style brick-fronted **Jackson Rose Bed and Breakfast** (1167 W. Washington St., 304/535-1528, $140 and up).

Charles Town

Founded in 1786, the former colonial resort of **Charles Town** (pop. 5,259) was named in honor of George Washington's younger brother Charles, who surveyed the site on behalf of Lord Fairfax. Many of the streets are named after other family members, over 75 of whom are buried in the cemetery alongside the **Zion Episcopal Church,** on Congress Street on the east side of town. Charles Town, which shouldn't be confused with the West Virginia state capital, Charleston, later played a significant role in John Brown's failed raid on Harpers Ferry. After Brown was captured, he was tried and convicted of treason in the Jefferson County Courthouse at the

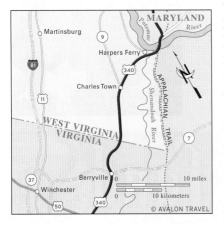

corner of George and Washington Streets and hanged a month later. With his last words, Brown noted the inevitable approach of the Civil War, saying he was "quite certain that the crimes of this guilty land will never be purged away but with blood." A small **museum** (Tues.-Sat. 11am-4pm, $3 adults) operates on the first floor of the town library, a block from the old courthouse on Washington and South Samuel Streets.

South of Charles Town, US-340 winds along the western slopes of the Appalachians for a dozen miles before entering Virginia east of Winchester.

East of Winchester, Virginia, the Appalachian Trail crosses the transcontinental US-50 highway, **The Loneliest Road** in America (see page 752). Full coverage of this route begins on page 670.

VIRGINIA

The Appalachian Trail covers more ground in Virginia than it does in any other state, following the crest of the Blue Ridge Mountains from Harpers Ferry in West Virginia all the way south to the Tennessee and North Carolina borders. In the northern half of the state, the road route closely follows the hikers' route, and the two crisscross each other through the sylvan groves of **Shenandoah National Park.** Midway along the state the two routes diverge, and hikers turn west while the motor route follows the unsurpassed Blue Ridge Parkway along the top of the world.

Most of the time the route follows the mountain crests, though in many places you'll find fascinating towns and cities a short distance to the east or west. Best among these is **Charlottesville,** a history-rich Piedmont town that's best known as the home of Thomas Jefferson and the University of Virginia. Other suggested stops include the Shenandoah Valley town of **Lexington,** the "natural wonder" of **Natural Bridge,** and the engaging city of **Roanoke.**

Dinosaur Land

Located at the intersection of US-340 and US-522, eight miles southeast of Winchester near the hamlet of White Post, **Dinosaur Land** (540/869-2222, daily Jan.-Oct., Fri.-Wed. Nov.-Dec., $6) displays an entertaining and marvelously kitschy collection of constructed sharks, and, of course, dinosaurs. Wry-humored adults will enjoy searching through the large gift shop, which has all manner of cheesy souvenirs.

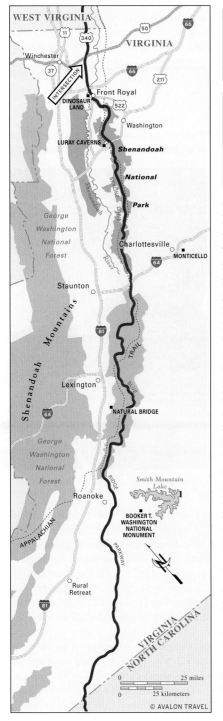

White Post got its name from—you guessed it—a white post, placed here by a young surveyor named George Washington. The post marked the road to the country estate of Lord Fairfax, which was destroyed in 1858.

Until recently housed in an old feed store off I-81 in Middletown, the **Route 11 Potato Chips factory** (11 Edwards Way, 540/477-9664, Mon.-Sat. 9am-5pm) in nearby **Mount Jackson** is said to be the smallest potato chip factory in the country. When it's open, you can watch the spudmasters at work and sample the freshly made chips.

Front Royal and Little Washington

The town of **Front Royal** (pop. 14,440) takes its name, perhaps apocryphally, from a Revolutionary War drill sergeant who, since his troops were unable to tell their left from their right, was forced to shout out "Front Royal Oak" to get them to face the same way. Front Royal sits just south of I-66 at the entrance to Shenandoah National Park. Because of its key location, Front Royal has grown a little unwieldy in past decades but retains some semblance of its 19th-century self along Chester Street, a well-maintained historic district at the center of town, a block east of US-340. You can also rent a boat and float along the South Fork of the Shenandoah River, thanks to the friendly folks at the **Front Royal Canoe Company** (8567 Stonewall Jackson Hwy., 540/635-5440), on US-340.

At the foot of the Blue Ridge Mountains, a bit more than 18 miles southeast of Front Royal via US-522, pristine colonial **Washington** (pop. 135) was surveyed by the future father of the United States, George Washington, who named many of the streets after friends and family. The main attraction here is the **Inn at Little Washington** (540/675-3800) at Main and Middle Streets, which over the past

30 years has grown from modest origins into one of the few Forbes Travel Guide five-star resort hotels in the country. (It has to be said that with room rates starting at $505 and up a night and dinners averaging $200 a head, it's definitely a special-occasion place to stay or eat.) It's worth it, though, especially if someone else is paying the bill: A critic for *The New York Times* said his dinner there was "the most fantastic meal of my life."

Shenandoah National Park

One of the most popular national parks in the east, especially during the fall foliage season when seemingly everyone in the world descends on the place to leaf-peep, **Shenandoah National Park** protects some 300 square miles of hardwood forest along the northernmost crest of the Blue Ridge Mountains. Though the landscape looks natural now, the original forests were logged out and the landscape was heavily cultivated until the 1920s. During the Depression, when the depleted soils could no longer sustain the residents, thousands of farmers and their families moved out and the government began buying up the land to return it to its natural state.

Shenandoah National Park in autumn

Fall foliage in the **Blue Ridge Mountains** can be stunning, though it is not usually as intense as in New England.

Most people experience the park from the top, by driving along the famously beautiful Skyline Drive. This road climbs up from the Shenandoah Valley but mostly runs along the crest, offering grand vistas (when the air is clear, at least). Besides the hardwood forests, the park also protects numerous waterfalls, wildflower meadows, and understory plants like azaleas and mountain laurels, which bloom brightest in late spring. There is considerable development in the park, with rustic lodges and cabins and enough gas stations and restaurants and campgrounds to handle the thousands of visitors who flock here (especially in October for the autumn foliage). Despite the crowds, it's not hard to find peace and quiet, especially if you venture off on even the briefest of hikes.

Pollution from metropolitan areas and from so many car-borne visitors has caused serious problems at Shenandoah National Park, both for the trees—many of which have been poisoned—and for the views people come to see. On an average summer day, the surrounding valleys are often shrouded in smoggy haze.

There is a ranger station at each entrance to the park, where you pay your $25 per car fee (or show your annual parks pass). There's a **visitors center** (540/999-3500) at each end of Skyline Drive. Trails at Big Meadows lead past herds of tame deer to Dark Hollow Falls, which drops 70

SKYLINE DRIVE

Most people experience Shenandoah National Park by driving the spectacular Skyline Drive. The drive, which was plotted and surveyed in 1931 and opened in 1939, runs (at 35 mph!) along the crest over 100 miles, winding between the I-66 and I-64 freeways while giving grand vistas at every bend in the road. Mileposts, arranged in mile-by-mile order from north to south, mark your progress along Skyline Drive. The scenic driving is definitely memorable, but by far the best way to see the park is to get out of the car and walk along the many miles of trails (including more than 100 miles of the Appalachian Trail) that lead through the dense green forests to innumerable waterfalls and overlooks.

A helpful map and brochure is handed out at national park entrance booths along the route—one at either end and two midway. Here are some more great places to look out for:

Milepost 21.1: A roadside parking area marks the trailhead for a lovely three-mile hike to Overall Run Falls, the tallest in the park. You can also reach the falls from Matthews Arm campground, just down the road.

Milepost 31.5: Thornton Gap is the junction with US-211.

Milepost 32.4: Mary's Rock Tunnel is a 670-foot-long, 13-foot-wide bore cut through the granite in 1932. RV drivers beware—it is just 12 feet, 8 inches high.

Milepost 50.7: Near Big Meadows, under a mile from the well-marked trailhead, Dark Hollow Falls tumbles over a 70-foot incline. Outside the Byrd Visitor Center, a macho statue of "Iron Mike" commemorates the efforts of the workers who built the trails, overlooks, and campgrounds as part of the New Deal Civilian Conservation Corps.

Milepost 52.8: Milam Gap marks the start of a two-mile walk to Rapidan Camp, where President Hoover established a trout-fishing retreat in 1929.

Milepost 56.4: A short, steep hike scrambles up to the 3,300-foot-high summit of Bearfence Mountain for a 360-degree panorama.

Milepost 84.1: A parking area marks the trailhead for the rewarding 3.4-mile roundtrip hike to Jones Run Falls, tumbling over a mossy 42-foot cliff.
Near the southern end of Skyline Drive, Calf Mountain provides a grand panorama over the Shenandoah Valley.

THE BLUE RIDGE PARKWAY:
FROM SHENANDOAH NATIONAL PARK TO ROANOKE

Starting at the southern end of Shenandoah National Park and winding along the crest of the Blue Ridge Mountains all the way to Great Smoky Mountains National Park some 469 miles away, the Blue Ridge Parkway is one of the country's great scenic drives. This is especially true during autumn, when the dogwoods and gum trees turn deep red, and the hickories yellow, against an evergreen backdrop of pines, hemlocks, and firs. Spring is wildflower time, with abundant azaleas and rhododendrons blooming orange, white, pink, and red throughout May and June, especially at the higher elevations.

First proposed in the 1920s, the bulk of the Blue Ridge Parkway was constructed in many stages between 1935 and 1967, during which time it grew from a network of local roads to the current route, along which billboards and commercial traffic are both banned. The last section, near Linn Cove Viaduct in North Carolina, was completed in the mid-1980s. While the parkway avoids towns and commercial areas to concentrate on the scenery, many interesting towns and other places along the way are well worth a detour. For ease of use, we've divided the Blue Ridge Parkway into three main sections, starting with the drive between Shenandoah National Park and Roanoke. (For the **Roanoke-North Carolina** section, see page 369; for the final run south to the **Great Smoky Mountains,** see page 374.)

Mile 0: Rockfish Gap, at the southern end of Shenandoah National Park's Skyline Drive, marks the northern start of the Blue Ridge Parkway.

Milepost 6.1: Humpback Rocks has a short but strenuous trail (45 minutes each way), leading through a reconstructed farmstead and a visitors center (visitors center at Milepost 5.9), ending with a 270-degree view over the mountains.

Milepost 34.4: The **Yankee Horse** parking area has an exhibit on an old logging railroad, part of which has been restored, and a short trail to Wigwam Falls.

Milepost 63.6: The **James River Visitor Center** (434/299-5496) offers exhibits and trails along the James River and Kanawha Canal. This is the lowest point on the parkway, at 649 feet, and also the junction with US-501, which runs west along the James River for 15 miles to Natural Bridge.

Milepost 76.5: Great views can be had over both valleys from the highest point on the parkway in Virginia, at 3,950 feet.

Mileposts 84-87: The most popular—and most developed—stretch of the parkway, the Peaks of Otter section includes a **visitors center** (540/586-4496), gas station, restaurant, and pleasant **lodge** (540/586-1081, year-round, $129 and up) Three peaks rise above a small lake and give great sunrise and sunset views; many good trails, including a two-mile loop to Fallingwater Cascades, let you escape the sometimes sizable crowds.

Milepost 105: This section ends at the city of Roanoke.

feet over greenish volcanic stone. The **Big Meadows Lodge** was built in 1939 and retains its cozy feel. There's another lodge to the north, at Skyland (milepost 42), the highest point on Skyline Drive. There are full-service restaurants at both lodges; all food and lodging (and most everything else in the park) is managed by a private concession, **DNC Parks & Resorts** (877/847-1919).

Luray Caverns

Halfway through Shenandoah National Park, US-211 runs west down to **Luray Caverns** (540/743-6551, daily, $27 adults, $14 children), the largest and most impressive in the eastern United States—there are 64 acres of caverns to explore. It also boasts the "World's Only Stalacpipe Organ," where rubber mallets make music by banging on the stone stalactites. There's

also a large antique car museum and the Luray Valley Museum (included in caverns admission), and a **garden maze** ($9 adults, $7 children).

Near the caverns, along US-211 a half mile west of town, the **Luray Zoo** (540/743-4113, daily, $12 adults) is an animal rescue center and zoo that's home to a few hundred animals and one of Virginia's largest collections of scaly creatures. Cobras, alligators, and lemurs coexist with uncommon birds, big cats, and cheerful, playful monkeys. For younger children, there's also a petting zoo.

Luray Caverns

Along with multicolored leaves, the autumn months bring hundreds of hawks, eagles, and other birds of prey to the mountains on their annual migration. You'll spot the greatest numbers of raptors in late September.

Earl Hamner Jr. based his famous 1970s TV series *The Waltons* on vivid memories of growing up during the Depression in the rural village of **Schuyler,** a half hour southwest of Charlottesville. Fans of the show will enjoy visiting the **Walton's Mountain Museum** (434/831-2000, daily 10am-3:30pm Mar.-Nov., $8), which recreates the Waltons' kitchen and living room and John-Boy's bedroom in the Schuyler Community Center—Earl Hamner's old elementary school.

Staunton

West of the mountains from the south end of Shenandoah National Park on I-64, tidy **Staunton** (pop. 23,746; pronounced "STAN-ton") was founded in 1732 as one of the first towns on the far side of the Blue Ridge. Unlike much of the valley, Staunton was untouched during the Civil War and now preserves its many 18th- and early-19th-century buildings in a townscape so perfect it was rated among the dozen most distinctive destinations in the United States by the National Trust for Historic Preservation.

One of Staunton's many sizable historic districts surrounds the boyhood home of favorite son Woodrow Wilson. Son of a Presbyterian minister, Wilson was born in 1856 in a stately Greek Revival townhouse, now established as the **Woodrow Wilson Presidential Library and Museum** (20 N. Coalter St., 540/885-0897, daily, $14),

Detour: Charlottesville

From the southern end of Shenandoah National Park, it's a quick 20 miles east on I-64 to Charlottesville (pop. 48,210), a richly historic college town that's one of the most enjoyable stops in the state. From the rolling green lawns of the University of Virginia campus to neoclassical Monticello on the hills above it, the legacy of Thomas Jefferson

dominates Charlottesville. Jefferson lived and worked here for most of his life—when he wasn't out founding the country or serving as its president.

West of the compact downtown district, the **University of Virginia** campus was Jefferson's pride and joy. Not only did he found it in 1819 and fund its early years, he planned the curriculum and designed the original buildings, a quadrangle of redbrick Palladian villas that the American Institute of Architects declared the most perfect place in the country. Edgar Allan Poe lived and studied here briefly before dropping out in 1826. Poe's room, appropriately, is No. 13 in the West Range, and it's decorated to look like it did a century ago, with a few period belongings visible behind the glass door. When school is in session, free campus tours are offered three times a day by the **University Guides** (434/924-3239).

Charlottesville's other key sight is Jefferson's home, **Monticello** (434/984-9800, tours daily, $28 adults)—the domed

University of Virginia

Monticello, home of Thomas Jefferson

building that fills the back of the nickel coin—well signed off I-64 exit 121. Recently restored and open for tours, Monticello embodies the many different traits of this multifaceted man. The house was designed and built by Jefferson over a period of 40 years (1769-1809) and holds various gadgets he invented—including a double-pen device that made a copy of everything he wrote—and odd things he collected over the years like elk antlers sent to him by Lewis & Clark. Jefferson died here at Monticello on July 4, 1826, and the grounds, which in Jefferson's time formed an extensive plantation worked by slaves, hold his mortal remains in a simple tomb beyond the vegetable gardens.

Down in the valley below Monticello, **Michie Tavern** (434/977-1234, daily, tour $6 adults) is a touristy but interesting inn that opened in 1784 and was moved to the present site in the 1920s. Admission includes a tour of the parlors, bars, and upstairs rooms. Michie Tavern is also a restaurant serving "Old World food" for the bus-tour hordes, at around $18 a head (plus dessert!) for a "colonial buffet" lunch. (Just so you know, Michie is pronounced "MICK-ee.")

PRACTICALITIES

Like most college towns, Charlottesville provides a broad range of good places to eat, including bare-bones cafés like the **White Spot** (1407 University Ave., 434/295-9899), right across from campus. This is the place to satisfy cravings for a cheeseburger with a fried egg on top, known here as a Gus Burger. On the downtown mall, a stretch of Main Street successfully pedestrianized in the 1970s by architect Lawrence Halprin, you'll find places like **Bizou** (119 W. Main St., 434/977-1818), serving upscale diner food. There's more great food, along with live music, next door at **Miller's Downtown** (109 W. Main St., 434/971-8511).

Most of Charlottesville's motels line up along Emmett Street (US-29 Business), near the US-250 freeway, including the well-placed **English Inn** (2000 Morton Dr., 434/971-9900 or 800/786-5400, $110 and up).

Woodrow Wilson

with galleries tracing his life as a scholar—he was president of Princeton University—and as U.S. President during World War I.

Staunton is also the home of the unique **Frontier Culture Museum** (540/332-7850, daily, $12 adults), right off I-81 exit 222 on the southeast side of town. A rural version of Williamsburg, this living history museum consists of four resurrected working farms, incorporating buildings brought over from Germany, England, and Ireland. The fourth farm, dating to antebellum Virginia, shows how various Old World traditions blended in America. The farms are inhabited by interpreters dressed in clean period costumes baking bread, spinning flax, or repairing farm instruments.

Staunton holds a couple of good down-home places to eat, both located on the old US-11 Lee Highway route. For pancakes and waffles, make your way to **Kathy's** (705 Greenville Ave., 540/885-4331), where all of Staunton flocks after church on Sundays. Another classic, **Wright's Dairy-Rite** (346 Greenville Ave., 540/886-0435) serves great burgers, hot dogs, and onion rings to your car or in a dining room decorated with old menus. Enjoy free Wi-Fi and a free Wurlitzer jukebox.

All the usual motels cluster around Staunton's junction of US-250 and I-81.

Just east of the Skyline Drive, three miles northeast of I-64 exit 107, "Virginia's Best Pizza" has been served up for more than 30 years inside barn-red **Crozet Pizza** (5794 Three Notch'd Rd., 434/823-2132) on Hwy-240.

Lexington

Founded in 1778, and named for the then-recent Revolutionary War battleground, photogenic **Lexington** (pop. 7,042) is home to an estimable pair of Virginia

Shenandoah Homestead at the Frontier Culture Museum

institutions, the Virginia Military Institute (VMI) and Washington and Lee University, which meld into one another at the center of town. Numerous old brick buildings, including a typically southern lawyer's row around Courthouse Square, still stand around the town, which you can tour on foot or in one of the horse-drawn carriages that parks across from the downtown visitors center.

Animated by an unusually crew-cut version of typical college-town energy, Lexington is redolent with, and intensely proud of, its military heritage. Generals, in fact, have become the town's stock-in-trade: From 1851 until 1861 when he rode off to fight in the Civil War, **General Thomas "Stonewall" Jackson** lived at 8 East Washington Street, now a small **museum** (540/464-7704, daily, $8 adults). He is buried in the small but well-tended cemetery on the south edge of town. **General Robert E. Lee** spent his post-Civil War years teaching at Washington and Lee, which was named after him (and his wife's ancestor, George). Lee is entombed in a crypt below the chapel, under a famous statue of his recumbent self, with his trusty horse, Traveller, buried just outside. Another influential old warhorse, **General George C. Marshall,** is honored in a large eponymous **museum** (Tues.-Sat. 11am-4pm, $5 adults) on the VMI campus. The museum traces General Marshall's role in planning the D-Day invasions in World War II and salutes his Nobel Peace Prize-winning Marshall Plan for the successful reconstruction of postwar Europe.

Spend a summer night in Lexington at the community-run **Hull's Drive-In** (2367 N. US-11, 540/463-2621, $7 adults), a much-loved local Ozoner drive-in theater still showing Hollywood hits. Before a movie, grab a burger or some fried chicken at **Kenney's** (635 Wadell St., 540/463-5730) off US-11. Or check out the many good bistros and soup-and-sandwich places downtown along Main Street, such as the unusually healthy menu at **Blue Sky Bakery** (125 W. Nelson St., 540/463-6546).

> To get a sense of life in the Shenandoah Valley, tune to **WSVA 550 AM** in Harrisonburg, which broadcasts updated farm and livestock prices once a day between 12:30pm and 1pm.

Natural Bridge, Va.

There are a number of comfortable and captivating places to stay in and around Lexington, like the **Llewellyn Lodge** (603 S. Main St., 540/463-3235 or 800/882-1145, $109 and up). Comfortable, convenient, welcoming, helpful, and within easy walking distance of the campuses and the historic town center, the Llewellyn is everything a B&B should be.

Natural Bridge

Held sacred by the local Monacan people and bought from King George in 1774 by Thomas Jefferson, the 215-foot-high notch of **Natural Bridge** (540/291-1326, daily, $8 adults) is a remarkable piece of geologic acrobatics. Spanning some 90 feet, the thick stone arch bridges Cedar Creek at the bottom of a steeply walled canyon. To see the Natural Bridge, which is heralded as one of the Seven Natural Wonders of the World (others on the list include Niagara Falls, Yellowstone, and Giant's Causeway in Northern Ireland), you have to buy a ticket from the visitors center at the park.

The **Natural Bridge Park Hotel and Conference Center** ($79 and up), located across the street from the state park, has 88 rooms and two suites and a 30-room Veranda Room annex building across the road. The colonial dining room serves breakfast and dinner, with outdoor dining on the veranda and popular weekend buffets.

Roanoke

Apart from Asheville at its southern end, **Roanoke** (pop. 97,032) is the only real city that can claim it's actually *on* the Blue Ridge Parkway. With block after block of brick-fronted business buildings, most of them adorned with neon, metal, and painted signs that seem unchanged since the 1940s, Roanoke contrasts abruptly with the natural verdancy of the rest of the parkway, but you may find it a welcome change after so many trees. Once a busy, belching, industrial Goliath supported by the railroads, Roanoke has evolved into a sophisticated, high-tech city—the commercial, cultural, and medical center of southwest Virginia.

"World's Largest Man-Made Star," on Roanoke's Mill Mountain

Roanoke's main visitor attractions lie right downtown in the **Center in the Square** (540/342-5700) complex, a restored warehouse that holds a wide variety of cultural offerings, including the-aters, an **African American culture museum** ($7 adults), a kid-friendly **science museum** ($15 adults), and a **local history museum** ($6 adults). Also worth a look is the **Virginia Museum of Transportation** (303 Norfolk Ave. SW, 540/342-5670, daily, $11 adults), three blocks west of Center in the Square, which displays lots of old cars and trucks, steam and diesel locomotives, and horse-drawn carriages, plus a complete traveling circus—minus the per-formers, of course. Steam trains, as docu-mented by Roanoke-based photographer O. Winston Link, are the real highlight of the museum. A short walk away, inside Roanoke's streamlined 1930s-era Norfolk & Western Railroad passenger station, the new **O. Winston Link Museum** (101 Shenandoah Ave. NE, 540/982-5465, daily, $6 adults) displays more than 200 of the photogra-pher's indelible black-and-white images. There's also a neat gallery devoted to the building's legendary designer, Raymond Loewy, who created the Coke bottle, the logo for Lucky Strike cigarettes, and hundreds of other all-American icons.

Booker T. Washington

THE BLUE RIDGE PARKWAY: ROANOKE TO NORTH CAROLINA

South from Roanoke, the Blue Ridge Parkway winds another 100 miles before crossing the North Carolina border. This midsection of the parkway, especially the first 25 miles south of Roanoke, runs at a lower elevation across a more settled and cultivated landscape than the rugged ridge tops followed elsewhere. In place of the spectacular vistas, you'll see many more houses and small farms, a few pioneer cabins (preserved and not), miles of split-rail fences, and some picturesque cemeteries. The southern reaches, approaching the North Carolina border, get better and better.

Milepost 122: This section begins at the city of Roanoke.

Milepost 154.5: A 2.6-mile loop trail leads to a pioneer cabin overlooking the **Smart View** for which it's named. Blooming dogwoods abound in May.

Milepost 165.2: At **Tuggles Gap,** the junction with Hwy-8 has a motel, restaurant, gas station, and also a small cemetery right along the parkway.

Mileposts 167-174: The 4,800-acre Rocky Knob area contains a campground (540/745-9664), a visitors center, and a strenuous but rewarding 10-mile round-trip trail (starting at milepost 167.1) leading down through **Rock Castle Gorge** and over 3,572-foot **Rocky Knob.**

Milepost 176.1: A short trail leads to **Mabry Mill,** in use from 1905 to 1935. In summer and fall, interpreters demonstrate blacksmithing and milling skills. A restaurant, open spring through fall, sells old-fashioned pancakes made from stone-ground flour, plus country ham and hamburgers.

Mileposts 199-200: This is the junction with US-52, which runs south to Mount Airy, North Carolina, home of *Mayberry RFD.*

Milepost 216.9: You've reached the Virginia-North Carolina border.

On Mill Mountain, high above Roanoke, the 88.5-foot-tall **Roanoke Star** shines nightly, lit by 2,000 feet of red, white, and blue neon tubing. You can drive up to the base of it and get a grand view over Roanoke.

Southeast of Roanoke, the **Booker T. Washington National Monument** (540/721-2094) is a reconstructed plantation that includes the kitchen cabin where the influential African American leader was born. The 207-acre site, which also includes tobacco fields, is 20 miles or so from Roanoke via Hwy-116 and Hwy-122.

Roanoke Practicalities

Roanoke's most popular place to eat is probably **The Roanoker Restaurant** (2522 Colonial Ave., 540/344-7746, Tues.-Sun.), "The Home of Good Food since 1941," which serves traditional Virginia dishes, two miles south of downtown off I-581 (Colonial Ave. exit). Another candidate for Roanoke's favorite food is the **Texas**

For NPR news and noncommercial arts programming, tune to **WVTF 89.1 FM** in Roanoke.

The soft drink Dr. Pepper, which originated in Waco, Texas, was named for a pharmacist who worked in the town of **Rural Retreat, Virginia,** along I-81 near its intersection with the AT.

The border between Virginia and North Carolina was surveyed in 1749 by a team that included Thomas Jefferson's father, Peter.

Tavern (114 W Church Ave., 540/342-4825), home of "World Famous Chili" and $1.45 cheeseburgers, and open daily 24 hours, seven days a week since 1930. There's also the unexpected world-beat cuisine at **Carlos Brazilian and International Cuisine** (4167 Electric Rd., 540/776-1117) on a hilltop three miles south of town. If you're planning a picnic up in the mountains, be sure to stop first at the historic **farmers market** (free), downtown next to the Center in the Square and active since 1882.

In the mountains west of Roanoke, across I-81 on Hwy-311 in Catawba, excellent home cooking ($15 for three meats, like the popular fried chicken, plus extra for dessert) is served at **The Homeplace Restaurant** (540/384-7252, Thurs.-Sun. lunch and dinner).

Places to stay include the usual interstate motels, lined up along Orange Avenue (US-460). Oldest and best of these is the **Hotel Roanoke** (110 Shenandoah Ave. NW, 540/985-5900 or 866/594-4722, $139 and up), which has anchored downtown for over a century. Now managed as a Hilton, the hotel has outlasted the railroads that financed it. Even if you stay elsewhere, the lobby, with its Florentine marble floors and vaulted ceiling, is worth a look.

Floyd

The town of **Floyd,** west of the Blue Ridge Parkway, about an hour southwest of Roanoke, has only one stoplight, so it's easy to find **The Floyd Country Store** (540/745-4563), which is famous for grilled cheese sandwiches, bowls of chili, and its weekly Jamboree ($5). Every Friday starting at 6:30pm, the display cases are pushed aside for an hour of gospel music, and then the floor is given over to bluegrass music, flat-footing, clogging, two-steps, waltz, square dancing, and shuffling feet.

NORTH CAROLINA

Running along the crest of the Blue Ridge Mountains at the far western edge of the state, this route across North Carolina takes in some of the most beautiful scenery east or west of the Mississippi. Though not as immense as the Rockies or other western landscapes, this part of North Carolina abounds with rugged peaks and deep valleys, pastoral meadows, and ancient-looking mountain villages, some dating back to colonial times. It's all linked by the magnificent Blue Ridge Parkway, perhaps the country's greatest scenic drive.

The region's sole city, **Asheville,** is a proud old resort dominated by the ostentatious Biltmore Estate, the world's largest private house, but everywhere else nature predominates—especially in the majestic **Great Smoky Mountains National Park** in the state's far southwestern corner.

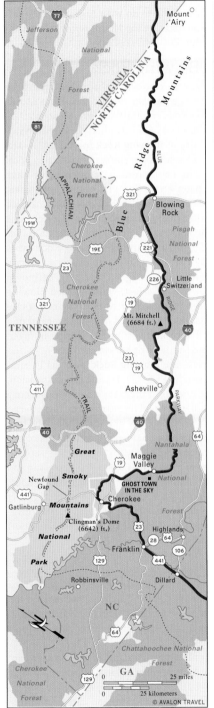

Mount Airy: Mayberry RFD

Along the Virginia-North Carolina border, 12 miles southeast of Blue Ridge Parkway milepost 200 via US-52, **Mount Airy** (pop. 10,388) was the boyhood home of Andy Griffith, who based much of his long-running TV show *The Andy Griffith Show* and the spin-off sitcom *Mayberry RFD* on the region. If you have fond memories of Opie, Andy, Barney, and Aunt Bee, you'll definitely want to visit Mount Airy, which has effectively recreated itself in the image of the show. Take a **Mayberry Squad Car Tour** (336/789-6743) and let a wannabe Barney show you the sights. Eat an ever-tender pork-chop sandwich, raved about by *Gourmet* magazine and Oprah, at the popular **Snappy Lunch** (125 N. Main St., 336/786-4931, closed Sun.) in the compact downtown business district. And don't neglect to admire the "Wall of Fame" comprising thousands of pictures of visitors at Floyd's Barber Shop, next door. Stay the night at the comfortable, clean, and inexpensive **Mayberry Motor Inn** (501 Andy Griffith Parkway/US-52, 336/786-4109, $80 and up) across the highway—just look for the black-and-white Mayberry sheriff's car parked out front.

The Mayberry mania reaches a peak during **Mayberry Days** in late September; details on this (and

the sheriff's car, parked outside Mayberry

In the valley below Mt. Mitchell, off I-40 northeast of Asheville, **Black Mountain College** was a lively intellectual and artistic nexus during the 1930s, 1940s, and 1950s.

anything to do with Andy Griffith) can be found at the **Mount Airy visitors center** (800/948-0949).

Blowing Rock

A quick two miles south of the Blue Ridge Parkway via US-221 from Moses Cone Memorial Park at milepost 291.9 lies the delightful little resort community of **Blowing Rock** (pop. 1,241)—the place to stop if you're only stopping once. The cool summer temperatures have been attracting visitors for centuries, and once you get past the factory outlet mall that welcomes you to town, quaint old Main Street is a great place to stretch your legs while taking in the eclectic range of late Victorian buildings, including some delightful churches. Blowing Rock takes its name from a nearby cliff overlooking John's River Gorge, where updrafts can cause lightweight objects to be blown upward rather than down. This effect, which earned Blowing Rock a mention in *Ripley's Believe It or Not!* as the only place "Where Snow Falls Upside Down," also inspired the Native American legend of a Cherokee warrior who, rather than be forcibly separated from his Chickasaw lover, leapt off the cliff, only to be blown back into the arms of his sweetheart.

North Carolina's oldest tourist attraction, the **Blowing Rock** itself (daily summer, $7 adults), two miles east of town via winding US-321, is worth the admission, whether or not the "magic wind" is blowing. Check out the tremendous views from a platform suspended 3,000 feet above the valley below. The nearby area also offers a couple of enjoyable tourist traps, including an apparently gravity-defying **Mystery Hill,** just off the parkway, and the toddler-friendly coal-fired steam trains of the **Tweetsie Railroad,** four miles north of town on US-321.

Downtown Blowing Rock has a number of good places to eat lined up along and around the quaint few blocks of Main Street. Across US-321 from the Blowing Rock, the storybook **Green Park Inn** (828/414-9230, $89-229) is a large historic resort hotel built in 1882. There's a golf course down the street. More modern conveniences are available at the **Cliff Dwellers Inn** (828/414-9596, $89 and up), right off the parkway on US-321.

Little Switzerland

Another classic mountaintop vacation spot, located midway between Blowing Rock and Asheville, **Little Switzerland** was founded in 1910 around the **Switzerland Inn** (828/765-2153 or 800/654-4026, $79 and up), a peaceful and relaxing old chalet-style resort that also operates a popular restaurant right off the Blue Ridge Parkway at milepost 334.

The inn stands on a crest, but the rest of Little Switzerland sits in the deep canyon to the east, spread out along Hwy-226 and a number of smaller side roads. The main stop is **Emerald Village** (828/765-6463, daily Apr.-Nov., $8 adults), on McKinney Mine Road 2.5 miles from the parkway, where you can tour an old gemstone mine (above and below ground) and museums displaying everything from gemstones to mechanical music makers.

Asheville

What the English country town of Bath was to Jane Austen's 18th-century London, the mountain resort of **Asheville** (pop. 83,393) was to the pre-jet set, pre-air-conditioned Deep South. When summer heat and humidity became unbearable, the gentry headed here to stay cool while enjoying the city's many grand hotels and elaborate summer homes.

The presence here of the world's biggest vacation house, the Vanderbilt family's **Biltmore Estate** (800/411-3812, daily, around $65-75 summer), is proof of Asheville's primary position in the old-school resort pantheon. The estate now covers 8,000 acres on the south side of town, though at the turn of the 20th century it covered 125,000 acres, stretching all the way up to today's Blue Ridge Parkway. Surrounded by a series of flower gardens planned in part by Frederick Law Olmsted, the estate centers on a truly unbelievable French Renaissance-style mansion built in 1895. The 250 rooms hold everything from a palm court to Napoleon's chess set to paintings by Renoir, Sargent, Whistler, and others. Signs aplenty direct you to the estate,

The hikers' **Appalachian Trail** winds west of the Blue Ridge Parkway along the North Carolina-Tennessee border.

The village of **Valle Crucis** holds the original **Mast General Store,** which sells a little of everything, from cookware to Gore-Tex shoes. There are several other locations throughout the region.

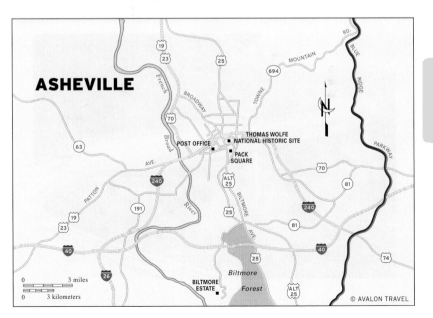

THE BLUE RIDGE PARKWAY: NORTH CAROLINA TO THE SMOKIES

The highest and most memorable parts of the 469-mile Blue Ridge Parkway are the 250 mountainous miles leading along the backbone of North Carolina. Following the southern Blue Ridge Mountains as they fade into the taller and more massive Black Mountains, the parkway skirts three other mountain ranges before ending up at Great Smoky Mountains National Park on the Tennessee border. Spring flowers (including massive rhododendrons), fall colors, songbirds, wild turkeys, numerous waterfalls, and occasional eerie fogs that fill the valleys below all make this an unforgettable trip no matter what the time of year. Take your time and drive carefully, however hard it is to keep your eyes on the road.

A couple of worthwhile detours—to the mountain hamlets of Blowing Rock and Little Switzerland, and to the city of Asheville—are covered in greater detail in the main text. From north to south, here are the mile-by-mile highlights along the North Carolina portion of the Blue Ridge Parkway:

Milepost 216.9: This section starts at the Virginia-North Carolina border.

Milepost 217.5: An easy half-mile trail leads to the top of 2,885-foot **Cumberland Knob.**

Milepost 260.3: An easy mile-long trail leads to the top of **Jumpinoff Rocks** for a sweeping view.

Mileposts 292-295: Moses H. Cone Memorial Park is a 3,500-acre former private estate, with many miles of mountaintop hiking trails. At Mile 294, Southern Highlands Crafts Guild members demonstrate various Appalachian crafts throughout

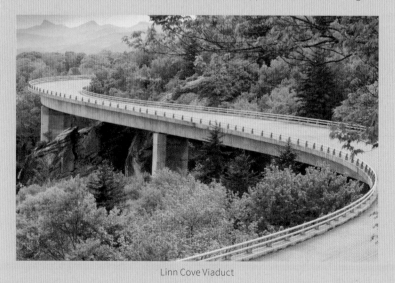

Linn Cove Viaduct

Mile-High Swinging Bridge

the summer at the Parkway Craft Center on the front porch of the former Cone mansion, which is now part of the Southern Highlands Craft Guild nonprofit.

Milepost 304: The marvelous engineering feat of the **Linn Cove Viaduct** carries the parkway around rugged Grandfather Mountain. Completed in 1987, this was the last part of the parkway to be built. Dense walls of rhododendrons border the parkway south of the viaduct.

Milepost 305.1: US-221, which used to carry the parkway before the viaduct was built, leads a mile south to 5,946-foot **Grandfather Mountain** (828/733-4337 or 800/468-7325, daily, $20 adults), the highest peak in Blue Ridge, now a private park with nature trails, a zoo, and the famous **Mile-High Swinging Bridge.**

Milepost 308.2: A half-mile nature trail leads to 3,995-foot Flat Rock for a view of Grandfather Mountain.

Milepost 316.3: Linville Falls crashes through a rugged gorge; short trails lead to scenic overlooks.

Milepost 331: At the junction of Hwy-226, the **Museum of North Carolina Minerals** (828/765-2761, daily 9am-5pm, free) displays all kinds and sizes of local gemstones, which you can watch being polished.

Milepost 355.4: West of the parkway, the 1,650 acres of **Mount Mitchell State Park** include a mountaintop observation tower. Drive to within 200 yards of the weather-beaten 6,684-foot summit, the highest point east of the Mississippi River.

Milepost 364.6: Best seen in late spring when the rhododendrons are in full bloom, the lush greenery of **Craggy Gardens** feels like an Appalachian Shangri-La.

Milepost 382: You can check out exhibits and demonstrations of Appalachian arts and crafts in the **Folk Art Center** (828/298-7928, daily).

Milepost 431: At the highest point on the parkway (6,047 feet in elevation), a self-guided nature trail leads through a first-growth spruce and fir forest.

Milepost 469.1: The southern end of the Blue Ridge Parkway is at the junction with US-441 and the entrance to **Smoky Mountains National Park.**

the Biltmore Estate, "World's Biggest Vacation House"

which stands just north of the I-40 exit 50 off Biltmore Avenue, across from the shops and restaurants in **Historic Biltmore Village,** which originally housed the estate's staff and workshops. It's a true "model village," designed in Gothic style by Richard Morris Hunt.

The rest of Asheville can't compete with the nouveau riche excess of the Biltmore Estate, and, in fact, it's a surprisingly homespun city, with a downtown commercial district filled with 1930s-era storefronts housing thrift stores and offbeat art galleries. One truly worthwhile place to see in downtown Asheville is the nondescript old boardinghouse where author Thomas Wolfe grew up from 1900 to 1920, preserved as it was when Wolfe lived here. The rambling house across from the beige modern Radisson Hotel is officially known as the **Thomas Wolfe Memorial State Historic Site** (52 N. Market St., 828/253-8304, Tues.-Sat., $5 adults). Unfortunately, the house suffered a major fire in 1998, but after restoration it is still one of the most evocative of all American literary sites. In the details and, more importantly, in general ambience, it's identical to the vivid prose descriptions of the house he called "Dixieland," the primary setting of his first and greatest novel, *Look Homeward, Angel.* After Wolfe's death from tubercular meningitis in 1938, the house was made into a shrine to Wolfe by his family, who arranged it to look as it did during his youth; one room contains his desk, typewriter, and other mementos of his life and work. An adjacent museum tells more of his story.

Asheville's long-standing relationship with visitors explains why the local baseball team is called the **Asheville Tourists.** The Colorado Rockies farm club plays at retro-modern **McCormick Field** (828/258-0428), a mile south of downtown. Games are broadcast on **WRES 100.7 FM.**

Two blocks or so south of the Wolfe memorial,

where Broadway becomes Biltmore Avenue, **Pack Square Park** is the center of Asheville, surrounded by the county court-house, the city hall, a small art museum, and the public library. This is where Thomas Wolfe's father ran a stonecutting shop, on whose porch stood the homeward-gazing angel, now recalled by a statue standing on the square's southwest corner.

Asheville Practicalities

The streets around Pack Square hold many good places to eat. There are more good places around the magical, art deco-era Grove shopping arcade west of the square, and yet more cafés and bakeries line Biltmore Avenue south of Pack Square, where you'll also find Asheville's best nightlife. Try the nice outdoor dining area at **Tupelo Honey Café** (12 College St., 828/255-4863). **The Orange Peel** (101 Biltmore Ave., 828/398-1837) gets an enviable array of nationally known musicians in all genres (from Bob Dylan to the Flaming Lips), while the **Fine Arts Theatre** (36 Biltmore Ave., 828/232-1536, $10 adults) up the street shows the latest art-house releases. North of downtown, near the UNC-Asheville campus, good microbrews and $3 evening movies are available at **Asheville Pizza and Brewing Co.** (675 Merrimon Ave., 828/254-1281). Another location is down-town (77 Coxe Ave., 828/255-4077).

The usual chain hotels cluster along the interstates, and some more characterful, older, neon-signed motels line old US-70 between downtown and the Blue Ridge Parkway. For a true taste of Americana, you may prefer the classic 1930s **Log Cabin Motor Court** (330 Weaverville Hwy., 828/645-6546, $94 and up), off the I-26 freeway six miles north of Asheville.

When Vanderbilt types come to Asheville today, they probably stay at **The Omni Grove Park Inn** (290 Macon Ave., 828/252-2711 or 800/438-5800, $139 and up), east of I-26 and north of I-40 and I-240, a lovely rustic inn built in 1913. Newer wings contain the most modern four-star conveniences, but the original lodge boasts rooms filled with authentic Roycroft furniture, making the Grove Park a live-in museum of arts-and-crafts style. There's also a plush **Inn on Biltmore Estate** (866/336-1245, $269 and up), for the full Biltmore Estate experience.

For further information on the Asheville area, contact the **visitors center** (36 Montford Ave., 828/258-6129).

Maggie Valley

The Blue Ridge Parkway swings south from Asheville through Transylvania County on the approach to Great Smoky Mountains National Park, though you'll save an hour or more by following the I-40 freeway to the junction with US-19, which links up with the south end of the parkway. This stretch of US-19, winding through the **Maggie Valley** over the foothills of the Great Smokies, is a pretty drive, and absolutely packed with roadside Americana—miniature golf courses, trout farms, souvenir shops, lookout towers alongside pancake houses, barbecue shacks—you name it, it's here.

For good commercial-free music and NPR news in and around Asheville, tune to **WNCW 88.7 FM** from Spindale.

Novelist F. Scott Fitzgerald stayed at Asheville's **Grove Park Inn and Spa** (now The Omni Grove Park Inn) while visiting his wife, Zelda, who had been committed to the adjacent Highland Hospital sanitarium.

Twenty miles southwest of Asheville, the eponymous peak featured in the book *Cold Mountain* rises amid the **Pisgah National Forest,** but the Academy Award-winning movie version was filmed on location—in distant Romania.

Before its slow demise and final closure in 2016, the **Ghost Town in the Sky** was much more than an old Appalachian ghost town: an amusement park with roller coasters, bumper cars, and all the usual suspects, it was built high on the side of the Great Smoky Mountains in the 1960s. For half a century it managed to stay alive as an odd combo of religious-themed Wild West amusement park, with zip-line adventure parks and quotes from scripture. Fingers crossed, it will find a way to reopen.

You can spot the wild mountains southeast of Asheville in numerous movies, including *Last of the Mohicans,* much of which was filmed around Chimney Rock, east of town along scenic US-64. **Chimney Rock** (800/277-9611) is a great destination, featuring fabulous views and a 26-story elevator carved through solid granite (currently under repair).

Having spent more than 50 years as a living roadside landmark, Cherokee chief Henry Lambert was known as "The World's Most Photographed Indian." Though Chief Henry died in 2007, his image still graces countless Cherokee postcards.

Cherokee

West of Maggie Valley, the Blue Ridge Parkway and US-19 join up 40 miles west of Asheville at touristy **Cherokee** (pop. 2,138), commercial center of the 56,000-acre **Eastern Cherokee Indian Reservation,** which was established here by a small band of Cherokee people in 1866, long after the rest of this once-mighty nation had been forcibly exiled to Oklahoma on the Trail of Tears. Cherokee is a last gasp of commercialism at the edge of the national park, a traffic-clogged gauntlet of places where you can "See Live Bears," "Eat Boiled Peanuts," or ride the "Rudicoaster" at the pricey but kid-friendly **Santa's Land Fun Park and Zoo** (828/497-9191, summer only, $23 adults). The biggest draw hereabouts is the ever-expanding **Harrah's Cherokee Casino Resort** (828/497-7777, $139 and up).

The upscale casino, the region's biggest draw, looms over a fading roadside lined by tacky old-time souvenir stands. But amid the tourist-taunting sprawl is at least one worthwhile stop: the **Museum of the Cherokee Indian** (daily, $11 adults), which traces the history of the Cherokee people from preconquest achievements—the Cherokee used a natural version of aspirin centuries before western chemists "discovered" it, for example—to their forced removal in the 1830s. There's also a living history village and a big outdoor pageant.

Great Smoky Mountains National Park

The most popular park in the United States, **Great Smoky Mountains National Park** offers a taste of wilderness to more than ten million visitors annually. Knoxville, Nashville, and Atlanta are all within a two-hour drive. Day-trippers visit mostly during late October for the annual display of fall color. Crisscrossed by 850 miles of hiking trails, including the Appalachian Trail, the park covers 522,427 acres along the 6,643-foot-high crest of the Great Smoky Mountains, so named for the fogs that fill the deep valleys. Before the park was established, its lands were extensively logged—70 percent of the trees had been clear-cut by 1934, when the lands were protected as a national park. Fortunately, the forests have grown back to obscure any sign of past degradations, and the uncut portions form the most extensive stands of primeval forest in the eastern United States. The region has recently suffered years of drought, culminating in a wind-swept 2016 forest fire that burned from the park's northern border into the neighboring tourist town of Gatlinburg, killing 14 people.

The main route through the park is Newfound Gap Road (US-441), which runs northwest from Cherokee to the even more tourist-traveled Gatlinburg and Pigeon Forge in Tennessee. The road winds steeply through dense forests packed with magnificent giant hardwoods, flowering poplars, dogwoods, azaleas, and rhododendrons, and evergreen pines and firs at the highest elevations. Where the highway reaches the crest, a spur road runs parallel to the Appalachian Trail five miles west to 6,643-foot **Clingmans Dome,** the highest point in the park, where you can take a short but steep trail up to a lookout tower.

One of the most extensive natural areas—unlogged, old-growth forest, full of the park's oldest and tallest trees—lies at the center of the park, off Newfound Gap Road on the north side of the crest. Starting at the popular Chimney Tops picnic area, the well-marked three-quarter-mile **Cove Hardwood Nature Trail** winds through a sampling of the park's most stately maples and other broad-leafed trees—the ones responsible for the best of the fall colors.

Along Little River Road, west of the Sugarlands Visitor Center off US-441 at the park's northern entrance, stands another group of ancient trees. Midway along, trails lead to two marvelous waterfalls, **Laurel Falls** and **Meigs Falls.** Little River Road ends up at **Cades Cove,** where the preserved remnants of a mountain community that existed here from the early 1800s until the 1930s give a strong sense of Appalachian folkways. A church and a number of mills still stand. Self-guiding tour books are available to explain the history and culture of these "hillbilly" people, some 6,000 of whom used to live within the park boundaries. **Bike rentals** (865/448-9034) are available at the **Cades Cove Trading Company** near the Cades Cove campground, and you'll find plenty of opportunities for rides along the old country lanes.

Another popular park destination is **Grotto Falls,** southeast of Gatlinburg via the Roaring Fork Road, where a short, flat trail to the tumbling cascade

Biologists estimate that some 1,500 native black bears live in the backcountry (and campgrounds!) of **Great Smoky Mountains National Park.**

The Appalachian Trail runs along the crest of the Great Smoky Mountains, crossing Newfound Gap Road at the center of the park. West of the park, the AT crosses another great road, US-129, whose winding route takes in more than 300 twisty corners in less than 12 miles. Dubbed the **Tail of the Dragon,** this is one of the country's great driving (and motorcycling) routes.

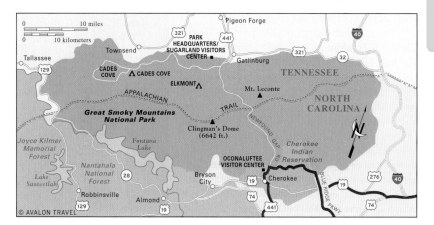

© AVALON TRAVEL

The many different salamanders native to the Great Smokies range from the tiny pygmy to the massive hellbender, which grows up to two feet long, head to tail. These crawling critters have earned the Great Smokies a reputation as the "Salamander Capital of the World."

Just over the mountains on the Tennessee side of the Great Smokies, Dolly Parton owns, runs, and stars at **Dollywood** (800/365-5996), northeast of Pigeon Forge off US-441, the country's biggest autobiographical theme park.

leads through lush hemlock forest—an ideal environment for mushrooms, and for the 27 to 30 different species of salamanders that slither around underfoot.

The only beds available in the park are at the historic **LeConte Lodge** (865/429-5704, $145 and up), built in the 1920s atop 6,593-foot Mt. LeConte, and located a 6.5-mile hike from the nearest road. There are no phones, no TVs, little privacy, and no showers, but the nightly rates do come with "family-style" breakfast and dinner. Ten fairly basic **campgrounds** (877/444-6777, no showers or hookups) operate in the park, with reservations taken only for the largest and most popular ones at Cades Cove, Cataloochee (reservations required), Cosby, Elkmont, and Smokemont. Cades Cove, Elkmont, and Smokemont are accessible to RVs up to 35 feet long; for hikers, there are also bear-proofed backcountry shelters along the Appalachian Trail.

For more information, or to pick up the handy brochures describing the park's array of flora, fauna, trails, and other features, stop by either of the two main visitors centers. North of Cherokee at the south entrance, the **Oconaluftee Visitor Center** (828/497-1904) stands alongside the Mountain Farm Museum, a collection of historic buildings preserved as one pioneer farmstead, where gardening and agricultural demonstrations are given in summer. From the **Sugarlands Visitor Center** (865/436-1200), four miles south of Gatlinburg, Tennessee, you can take a short hike to Cataract Falls.

South to Georgia: Franklin

South from Cherokee and the Great Smoky Mountains, US-441 runs through the giant **Nantahala National Forest,** which stretches all the way to the Georgia border. It's a fast, mostly divided, four-lane freeway, passing through a fairly developed corridor of towns and small cities.

The biggest town in this part of North Carolina, **Franklin** (pop. 3,845) was founded in the mid-1800s on a shallow ridge overlooking the Little Tennessee River. Along with lumber milling, Franklin's main industry has long been the mining of gemstones—garnets, rubies, and sapphires. Now a light industrial center, spread out around the intersection of US-441 and US-64, Franklin has a compact downtown area packed with gemstone and jewelry shops like **Ruby City** (130 E. Main St., 800/821-7829 or 828/524-3967, Tues.-Sat.), which also has a small free museum.

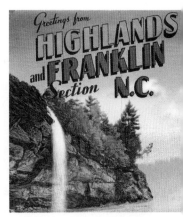

Greetings from HIGHLANDS and FRANKLIN Section N.C.

DETOUR: CHATTANOOGA

Mixing traditional Southern hospitality with fascinating history, cultural vitality, and a stupendous natural setting, Chattanooga is an unexpected treat. Best known to older generations as the home base of Glenn Miller's 1940s big band swing anthem "Chattanooga Choo Choo," this midsize city stretches along the banks of the Tennessee River, where a pleasant promenade of footpaths and bike trails ties an array of tourist attractions into local history. Markers, fountains, and plaques commemorate everything from Civil War battles to the sorry story of the banishment of the native Cherokee westward along the Trail of Tears in the 1830s.

The opening of the ever-expanding **Tennessee Aquarium** (800/262-0695, daily, $30), one of the largest and most popular in the country, was key to Chattanooga's current renaissance. Along with an **IMAX theater,** the excellent **Hunter Museum of American Art,** and a baseball stadium for Double-A **Chattanooga Lookouts,** the aquarium has energized a wholesale reconstruction of the Chattanooga riverfront. On a nice summer's day, cross the river on the **Walnut Street Bridge,** gazing down at kayakers and rock climbers before hopping on the dollar-a-ride historic carousel in idyllic **Coolidge Park.**

While the aquarium and related attractions have given the city a new lease on life, one of the country's most enduring tourist attractions, **Rock City** (800/854-0675 or 706/820-2531, $20), has been tempting travelers here for nearly a century. Standing six miles south of town atop 2,392-foot-tall **Lookout Mountain,** Rock City is one of the most hyped sights in the United States. From the 1930s through the 1960s, hundreds of rural barns from Michigan to Texas were painted with the words "See Rock City," "World's 8th Wonder," and "See 7 States." (The claim that one can see seven states from Rock City is disputed, but in order of distance they would be Georgia, Tennessee, Alabama, North Carolina, South Carolina, Kentucky, and Virginia.) Rock City itself is terrific, with paths winding through oddly shaped limestone canyons at the edge of heart-stopping cliffs. Even better are the other attractions atop Lookout Mountain, especially the beautiful limestone caves, 145-foot-high **Ruby Falls** (423/821-2544, $20), and the historic **Incline Railway** (423/821-4224, $15 adults). All-inclusive tickets are available.

If you've seen the 900-odd barn signs urging you to "See Rock City," you may want to detour west to Chattanooga, where **Lookout Mountain** is a capital of roadside kitsch, giving a supposed 150-mile view over seven states.

The lively **Chattanooga Lookouts,** the Double-A farm club of the Minnesota Twins, play right downtown at riverside **AT&T Field** (423/267-2208).

US-441 races south to Georgia from Franklin, while Hwy-28/US-64 heads southeast through the heart of **Transylvania County,** known as the "Land of Waterfalls" because of its many cascades. The biggest of these is 15 miles or so from Franklin. It's named **Dry Falls** because it's created at the point that the Cullasaja River projects over a cliff, allowing you to walk behind the falls without getting wet. From the well-signed parking area, follow a short trail that ends up underneath and behind the impressively raging torrent, a powerful white-noise generator you can hear long before you reach it. Another waterfall, known as **Bridal Veil Falls,** is less than a mile south from Dry Falls. A portion of old US-64 runs under Bridal Veil Falls, so motorists can drive under the cascade of water.

Two and a half miles south from Bridal Veil Falls, US-64 enters the resort community of **Highlands** (pop. 924). Here Hwy-106 loops back to the southwest, giving grand panoramic views over the forested foothills before rejoining US-441 across the Georgia border in Dillard.

GEORGIA

If Georgia brings to mind endless flat cotton or peanut plantations, you'll be pleasantly surprised by the mountainous wilds of the state's northern tier. The great Appalachian ridge that runs along the East Coast has its southern foot here, high up in the forests of Rabun County, which packs natural wonders, out-door adventures, and down-home Appalachian spirit into the state's small isolated corner. Chattooga River white water—made famous by the movie *Deliverance* and rated among the top 10 river runs in the United States—is the biggest draw, and sightseers can take in the spectacular waterfalls of **Tallulah Gorge.** Christmas-tree farms, dairies, and car graveyards dot the old-time mountain towns, but the ongoing "improvement" of US-441 into a four-lane freeway has resulted in a development boom of golf courses and mountain-view estates, increasing exponentially as the route approaches Atlanta's endless suburbs.

Dillard

Just south of the North Carolina border, the highway hamlet of **Dillard** (pop. 339) is a mini fiefdom of the Dillard family, whose name dates back to the 1700s in these parts. For generations, the Dillards have run a local hospitality empire based around

PARADISE GARDEN

Winding back roads that have run quietly through woodlands or along cotton fields can be suddenly marked by giant crosses or hand-lettered signs. These intensely personal creations, built by eccentric and often outcast individuals, usually spout scripture, warning about Judgment Day.

The best known of these "Gardens of Revelation," as scholar John Beardsley has called them in his excellent book of the same name, is Howard Finster's **Paradise Garden** (200 N. Lewis St., 706/808-0800, Tues.-Sun. 11am-5pm, donation), about an hour south from Chattanooga, down US-27. Famous for his primitivist paintings, which appeared on album covers by R.E.M. and Talking Heads, Finster created a series of Gaudi-esque shrines, embedding seashells, bits of tile, and old car parts into concrete forms. Paintings of Elvis, Jimmy Carter, and Finster himself are arrayed alongside dozens of signs quoting scripture. The spirit of the place is summed up in Finster's own verse: "I built this park of broken pieces / to try to mend a broken world of people / who are traveling their last road."

the sprawling set of bungalows, lodges, and a restaurant all going by the name **Dillard House** (706/746-5348 or 800/541-0671, rooms around $70 and up), on a hill above US-441 at the south edge of town. Heading up the complex is the Dillard House Restaurant, famous for its all-you-can-eat country cooking and its glass-walled dining room, where diners can enjoy plates of classic country ham, fried chicken, vegetables, cornbread, and assorted relishes and desserts. The legendary institution may today impress you as more institution than legend—bus tours dominate the clientele—but you never leave hungry. Rooms are around back in low-slung lodges scattered near a swimming pool, tennis courts, and a petting zoo.

In addition to the rambling inn, the family oligarchy operates a row of roadside businesses off US-441, selling collectible and keepsake souvenirs.

Black Rock Mountain State Park

At the wind-worn summit of 3,640-foot Black Rock Mountain, a flagstone terrace looks out over a grand Appalachian panorama: If there's no fog, you can see clear to the South Carolina Piedmont 80 miles away and as far as the Great Smokies to the north. The highest state park in Georgia, **Black Rock Mountain**

The rocky crest of Black Rock Mountain marks the eastern Continental Divide—from here waters part to follow a path to either the Atlantic Ocean or the Gulf of Mexico.

Atlanta

Gone With the Wind still draws thousands to Atlanta

With an energetic metropolitan population of more than five million people, Atlanta is one of the most dynamic communities in the country. State capital of Georgia, and world headquarters of that flagship of American culture, Coca-Cola, it's the financial and cultural heart of the "New South." Despite the city's sprawling scale, its people are gracious and welcoming, so much that they could seem like walking parodies of Southern hospitality—if they weren't so darn sincere.

Atlanta began as a railroad junction (its original name was simply "Terminus"). That early streetscape has been preserved and restored in **Underground Atlanta** (404/523-2311), a warren of shop fronts underneath the center of the modern city. Abandoned in the 1920s, the buildings were restored in the 1980s as a shopping and entertainment district. On the northwest edge of downtown, building on the efforts of the 1996 Olympics, Atlanta has developed **Centennial Park** as its new center, with the **Georgia Aquarium** (404/581-4000, daily, around $40), the western hemisphere's largest aquarium, alongside a showcase for the city's most successful product, **World of Coca Cola** (800/676-COKE—800/676-2653 or 404/676-5151, daily, $17), recently joined by the ambitious **Center for Civil and Human Rights** (678/999-8990, daily, around $19). The surrounding area holds the world headquarters of another Atlanta product, CNN, along with the Georgia World Congress convention center, the Georgia Dome sports arena, and Georgia Tech university.

On the northwest side of downtown, the powerhouse **Atlanta Braves** (tickets 800/745-3000) play at the new SunTrust Park.

Across the wide I-75 freeway, a half mile east of downtown, the **Martin Luther King Jr. National Historic Site** (450 Auburn Ave. NE, 404/331-5190, daily, free) sits at the heart of the Sweet Auburn neighborhood. The four-block area holds many important landmarks in the life of Dr. King: his birthplace (501 Auburn Ave.); the restored

whale shark at the Georgia Aquarium

Ebenezer Baptist Church (407 Auburn Ave. NE), where he, his father, and his grandfather all served as pastors; and his tomb, emblazoned with the words "Free at Last, Free at Last," sitting on the grounds of the Martin Luther King Jr. Center for Nonviolent Social Change (called the King Center, 449 Auburn Ave. NE).

Atlanta's main museum district is six miles north of downtown, in the upscale Buckhead neighborhood, where the **Atlanta History Center** (130 W. Paces Ferry Rd. NW, 404/814-4000, daily, $16.50) is a don't-miss introduction to the city, the state, and the South in general.

PRACTICALITIES

Atlanta's airport, Hartsfield-Jackson Atlanta International Airport, one of the busiest in the country, is a dozen miles south of downtown, at the junction of the I-85 and I-285 freeways. The usual rental cars, taxis, and shuttle vans are supplemented by the extensive network of Metro Atlanta Rapid Transit Authority (MARTA) trains. The I-75/I-85 freeways cut through the center of the city, while the I-20 freeway skirts its southern edge. Sliced by freeways and spreading in a low-level ooze of mini-malls, housing tracts, and traffic jams, Atlanta's outlying areas are impossible to make sense of, but the downtown area is compact and manageable. Seemingly every other thoroughfare includes the word "Peachtree" in its name, so check twice before getting completely lost.

Midtown Atlanta has a couple of nice places to stay, including the **Hotel Indigo** (683 Peachtree St. NE, 404/874-9200, $109 and up), a historic 1920s building upgraded to boutique status by the InterContinental chain, in a handy location across from the landmark Fox Theatre. The adjacent **Georgian Terrace** (659 Peachtree St. NE, 404/897-1991 or 800/651-2316, $159 and up) is spacious and full of character.

East of Midtown and about two miles northeast of downtown, the lively Virginia-Highland district has Atlanta's best restaurants, cafés, and bars. Atlanta landmark **Mary Mac's Tea Room** (224 Ponce de Leon Ave. NE, 404/876-1800) has served traditional Southern food (fried chicken, peach cobbler, and sweet tea) since 1945. A large, lively (and just a little bit seedy) 1930s-style café, the **Majestic Diner** (1031 Ponce de Leon Ave., 404/875-0276) is open daily 24 hours for great waffles, burgers, and endless cups of java. In between these two landmarks, check out the **Ponce City Market** (675 Ponce de Leon Ave. NE) food hall and amusement center, or take a stroll along the adjacent **BeltLine,** an evolving pedestrian and cyling path that forms a 22-mile loop around the heart of the city.

The Varsity (61 North Ave. NW, 404/881-1706), near Georgia Tech alongside I-75, is the world's largest drive-in, serving up good junk food: chili dogs, onion rings, and more Coca-Cola than anywhere else on this earth. Farther north, within a mile of each other off I-85, are two more Atlanta landmarks: Carnivores and blues fans flock to **Fat Matt's Rib Shack** (1811 Piedmont Ave. NE, 404/607-1622), while The Colonnade Restaurant (1879 Cheshire Bridge Rd., 404/874-5642) has been serving Southern food since 1962 (at the current location, at least—the original location opened in 1927).

After dark, enjoy an alfresco movie at the **Starlight Drive-In** (2000 Moreland Ave. SE, 404/627-5786, $9, $1 under age 10), four miles southeast of downtown. Double features are shown every night, rain or shine, with the first movie starting around 7:30pm.

The usual barrage of tourist information can be had from the **Atlanta Convention and Visitors Bureau** (233 Peachtree St. NE, Suite 1400, 800/285-2682 or 404/521-6600).

The hikers' Appalachian Trail crosses the Georgia-North Carolina border roughly 10 miles west of Dillard, then veers southeast, coming to a finale at the 3,782-foot summit of **Springer Mountain,** where a photogenic sign marks the end of the 2,175-mile trail (or the beginning, since most of the 200 or so annual through-hikers travel south to north).

State Park offers hiking trails and accommodations in addition to the splendid vistas. Set off in a ring at the top of the mountain are 10 fully furnished spacious cottages updated with electricity, heat, and air conditioning. The cottages cost $85-250 per night, sleep 8 to 10 people, and are available for rent mid-March through mid-December. There's also a pair of campgrounds. The park is three miles north of Clayton, well signed to the west of US-441. For information or for reservations for the cabins or the campgrounds, contact the **visitors center** (706/746-2141, reservations 800/864-7275) near the summit.

Mountain City: Foxfire Museum

The monolith of Black Rock Mountain imposes an early twilight on **Mountain City** (pop. 1,088), the community that stretches along US-441. Tucked away on the west side of US-441 just south of the turnoff to Black Mountain State Park, the modest **Foxfire Museum** (706/746-5828, Mon.-Sat., $8 adults) is part of a radical cultural and educational movement that began here in the mid-1960s when local schoolteacher Eliot Wigginton, frustrated in attempts to motivate his uninspired high-school students, assigned them the task of interviewing their elders about how things were in "the old days." The students, inspired with the newly discovered richness of their Appalachian heritage, assembled the written interviews into a magazine, which they named *Foxfire* after a luminescent local fungus.

The magazine expanded to a series of *Foxfire* books, and more than eight million copies have been sold worldwide. The program's twofold success—educational innovation and folk-life preservation—further broadened as the then-emerging back-to-the-land movement seized upon these books as vital how-to manuals for subsistence farming and generally living off the grid. The Foxfire organization still runs classes and events on a 106-acre campus in the hills above town.

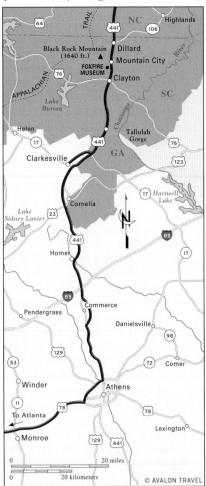

Clayton: *Deliverance*

Slicing through the Appalachian wilderness along the Georgia-South Carolina border, the Chattooga River rates among the nation's top 10 white-water river adventures, attracting some 100,000 visitors a year for rafting, canoeing, kayaking, tubing, swimming, fishing, and riverside hiking. The Wild and Scenic-designated river was seen in the movie *Deliverance,* based on the book by Georgia poet and novelist James Dickey. Ever since the movie was released, authorities have been pulling bodies out of the river—not toothless mountaineers but overconfident river-runners who underestimate the white water's power.

The largest town in the area, the down-home mountain community of **Clayton** (pop. 2,047) is a popular base for excursions into the wild forest and Chattooga River areas. US-441 has grown into an exurban morass of Walmart sprawl, but Main Street is a three-block length of wooden and brick storefronts on a sunny rise just west of the highway.

When you take in the sight of **Tallulah Gorge,** imagine walking a tightrope suspended 1,200 feet above the ground across its breadth. "Professor Leon" managed it (despite a stumble) in 1886, and in 1970, the flying Karl Wallenda replicated the feat, walking across on a wire suspended from the Tallulah Point Overlook, where postcards and photos document his effort.

Tallulah Falls and Gorge

Balanced precariously between the US-441 freeway and the precipitous gorge that once held the thundering cascades of the Tallulah River, tiny **Tallulah Falls** (pop. 168) has an illustrious history. As word of the natural wonder spread, crowds were drawn to the breathtaking sight, and by the turn of the 20th century Tallulah Falls was a fashionable resort, with several elite hotels and boardinghouses catering to lowland sightseers. Fortunes changed when the falls were harnessed for hydroelectricity, but recent compromises have brought the falls back to occasional life. On weekends, usually in spring and fall, the waters are again released and can be

In the mountains northwest of Clarkesville, 15 miles along Hwy-17 and Hwy-75, the tiny town of **Helen** (pop. 510) turned itself into a tourist draw in 1969 by remodeling all the buildings in mock-Bavarian decor and repaving the streets in cobblestones.

downtown Helen

Cornelia, the southernmost Appalachian town, is known for its Big Red Apple monument near Hwy-23 downtown, which pays homage to the apple farmers of the county. If you're here in fall, you can sample them fresh from the tree.

Midway between Athens and Atlanta, just south of I-85, in **Gwinnett,** the Triple-A farm club of the Atlanta Braves plays at **Coolray Field** (678/277-0340).

admired from **Tallulah Gorge State Park** (706/754-7981), a pleasant park with a local interpretive center, camping, showers, hiking trails, and a cool suspension bridge over the river and gorge.

Stretching downstream along the six cascades of Tallulah Falls, the dramatic sheer walls of Tallulah Gorge have both haunted and attracted people for centuries. The wary Cherokee heeded legends that warriors who ventured in never returned, and many a curious settler had a waterfall or pool named in his honor—posthumously, after an untimely slip.

Tallulah Gorge is best seen via staircase-trails leading from the state park, or from the mile-long scenic route (old US-441), which loops off east of the modern highway. Drivers can pull over at numerous parking areas and take one of several rough trails along the gorge's rim, though the best views are from the historic **Tallulah Point Overlook** (daily 9am-6pm, free), a privately owned concession stand midway along the loop.

Clarkesville

The charming little town of **Clarkesville** (pop. 1,733) retains a sophistication dating back to its founding over 150 years ago by lowland Carolina and coastal Georgian plantation families seeking refuge from the oppressive summer heat. Best known as the home of the renowned country resort **Glen-Ella Springs Inn** (888/455-8786 or 706/754-7295, $160 and up), Clarkesville sits at the lower slope of a river valley that stretches northwest to the faux-Bavarian town of Helen and is surrounded by countryside perfect for a leisurely drive or bike tour past an old mill here, a covered bridge there, and old-time country stores in wooden cabins.

Clarkesville tucks urbane delights into its rustic country setting, with over 40 buildings, most of them former summer homes, listed on the National Register of Historic Places. Downtown, three blocks of wooden storefronts, centering on a shaded plaza where numerous festivals take place, hold cafés and crafts shops.

Hundred-year-old Glen-Ella Springs Inn, eight miles or so north of Clarkesville on Bear Gap Road, off US-441, is northern Georgia's premier country inn. Set on 12 lush acres, the historic three-story lodge holds 16 guest rooms, 14 of which open to a wraparound porch with rocking chairs. The top floor's two penthouse suites have private balconies as well as a shared porch.

Athens

If you've got the time and inclination, one of Georgia's most enjoyable destinations is just a slight veer to the east off our route: **Athens,** the coolest college town in the South. Famed for its lively music scene, which gave the world the alternative-rock

"The Tree That Owns Itself"

bands B-52s and R.E.M., Athens is the home of the **University of Georgia,** whose Greek Revival campus sits at the center of town, bordered on the north by a half dozen blocks of cafés, bars, and book and record stores. Besides the dozens of supersize Bulldogs (the UGA mascot) around town, Athens also holds a classic road trip destination: **"The Tree That Owns Itself,"** a second-generation mighty oak tree standing on a small circle of land at the corner of Finley and Dearing Streets west of campus, whose legal autonomy earned it a place in *Ripley's Believe or Not!*

The main music venue is the **40 Watt Club** (285 W. Washington St., 706/549-7871), where R.E.M. played their second gig. Good cheap food is available on the east side of town at **Weaver D's Delicious Fine Foods** (1016 E. Broad St., 706/353-7797), whose enigmatic slogan "Automatic for the People" was enshrined as an R.E.M. album title. R.E.M.'s Michael Stipe owns the building in which you can find the gourmet meat-free restaurant **The Grit** (199 Prince Ave., 706/543-6592). The best restaurant in Athens, is the **Five & Ten** (1073 S. Milledge Ave., 706/546-7300, dinner Mon.-Sat., brunch and dinner Sun.), two miles southwest of downtown. The Five & Ten serves an ever-changing range of seasonal Southern favorites enlivened by inventive, international touches. Stay overnight at the collegiate-themed **Graduate Hotel** (295 E Dougherty St., 706/549-7020, $98 and up), which has comfortable rooms, a coffeehouse, and an on-site bar hosting live music.

On to Atlanta: Stone Mountain

From the foothills of northern Georgia, it's only an hour by freeway southwest to Atlanta, the cultural and commercial center of the New South, and a fascinating (and fun) place to explore. Unfortunately, Atlanta is surrounded by miles and miles of mega-freeway subprime-mortgage sprawl, so you'll have to endure some of the country's craziest driving to get there.

From Athens, Hwy-316 merges into I-85 for the quickest route there, but for a more interesting route follow old US-78 southeast, approaching Atlanta by way of **Stone Mountain** (800/401-2407, daily, $15 per car), 16 miles east of downtown. A Confederate Mt. Rushmore and historic KKK rallying point, Stone Mountain consists of the 20-times-larger-than-life figures of Robert E. Lee, "Stonewall" Jackson, and Jefferson Davis carved into an 825-foot-high hump of granite, which you can walk to the top of on a steep, 1.5-mile trail. A 45-minute patriotic laser-and-fireworks extravaganza is shown nightly in summer (Apr.-Oct.). At the base of Stone Mountain are 3,200 acres of tacky tourist traps: duck-boat tours, a scenic railroad, a reconstructed antebellum town square, a cable car Skylift to the summit, and a tree-top Sky Hike rope course and mini golf course—some of which charge separate fees, or spend $32 and up for an all-inclusive all-day pass. Stone Mountain also holds a number of restaurants and hotels, plus Atlanta's best campground.

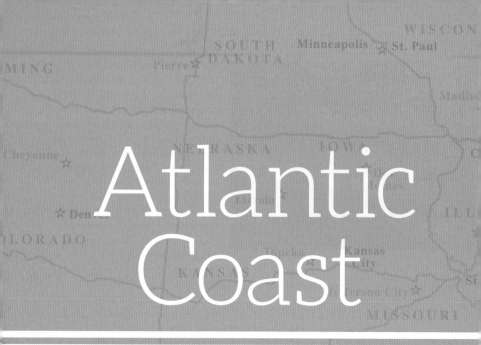

Atlantic
Coast

Starting at the Statue of
Liberty and winding up at
free-wheeling Key West, these
almost 2,000 miles of roadway
run within earshot—and often
within sight—of the
Atlantic Ocean.

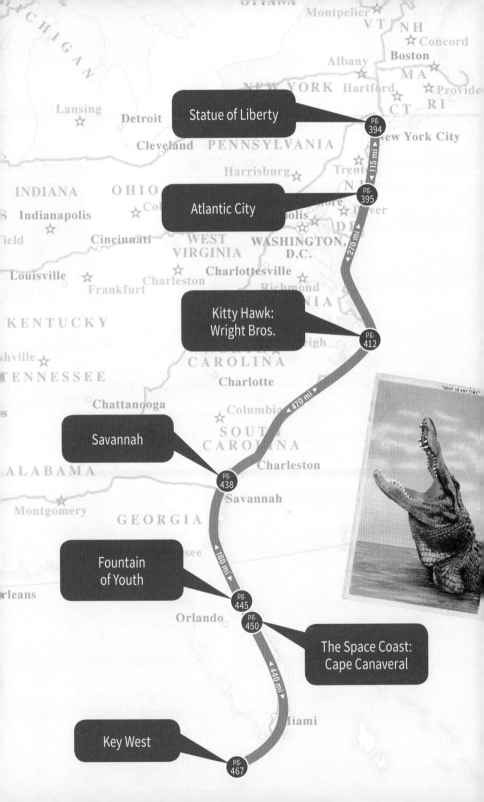

Statue of Liberty
pg. 394

Atlantic City
pg. 395

115 mi

270 mi

Kitty Hawk:
Wright Bros.
pg. 412

470 mi

Savannah
pg. 438

"DROP IN ANY TIME"

Fountain
of Youth
pg. 445

160 mi

The Space Coast:
Cape Canaveral
pg. 450

440 mi

Key West
pg. 467

Between New York City and the Tip of Florida

I f your impressions of the East Coast come from driving along the I-95 corridor through nearly non-stop urban and industrial sprawl, following our Atlantic Coast route will open your eyes to a whole other world. Alternating between wildly differing beach resort areas and lengthy stretches of pristine coastal wilderness, the route runs along almost 2,000 miles of two-lane country roads, within earshot, if not sight, of the Atlantic Ocean almost the entire way. In place of the grimy concrete and soulless netherworld of the interstate, this route passes through innumerable quirky seaside towns and timeless old fishing villages, interspersed with huge swaths of beaches, wetlands, and woodlands that have hardly changed since the European explorers laid eyes on them four centuries ago.

Starting in the north at that all-American icon, the **Statue of Liberty,** and winding up in the south at free-wheeling **Key West,** this route truly offers something for everyone. Those searching for photogenic lighthouses or beachcombing solitude will love the undeveloped and usually deserted strands that stretch for miles along the low-lying islands that make up most of the coast, much of which, as at **Assateague Island** or **Cape Hatteras,** has been protected as national seashore parks. In contrast, the many beach resorts that dot the in-between areas vary from the grand Victorian charms of Cape May to the funky old Coney Island-style attractions of **Ocean City, Maryland,** and **Myrtle Beach, South Carolina,** with their boardwalks full of roller coasters, wax museums, and saltwater taffy stands. And let's not forget the glitzy casino resorts of **Atlantic City.**

Cape Lookout

Alongside the contemporary attractions are many evocative historic sites, including such unique places as **Roanoke Island, North Carolina,** where the first English-speaking colony in North America vanished without a trace in 1587. Lying south of the Mason-Dixon Line for almost all of its length, the route also visits many important Civil War sites, including **Fort Sumter,** where the first shots of the war were fired, and the vital naval battlegrounds at **Hampton Roads** at the mouth of Chesapeake Bay. Midway along, we also pass one of the key sites of modern history: the windy sand dunes at **Kitty Hawk,** where the Wright Brothers first proved that humans could fly.

Although this Atlantic Coast route will bring you to many well-known sights, its real attraction is the traveling, stopping off for fried chicken or barbecue at one of the hundreds of roadside stands, watching the shrimp boats pull into a sleepy dock and unload their day's catch, or simply chatting with locals at the general store or post office in a town that may not even be on the map.

The Overseas Highway

NEW JERSEY

Being so close to New York and Philadelphia, it's not surprising that New Jersey has among the busiest and most densely developed stretches of coastline in the country. It *is* surprising, however, that beyond the boardwalk amusements and flashy gambling casinos of **Atlantic City,** the New Jersey shore offers a whole lot more. As with most of the East Coast, the "shoreline" is actually a series of barrier islands separated from the mainland by wildlife-rich estuaries; these provide fishing and bird-watching opportunities, as well as a break from the ceaseless commercial and residential development along the ocean beaches. Bustling in summer, these beachfront communities—starting with **Margate** near Atlantic City, and running south through vibrant **Wildwood** before winding up at the dainty Victorian-era beach resort of **Cape May**—offer something for everyone, all along a 150-mile stretch of shoreline.

Inspired by the end of slavery following the Civil War, the Statue of Liberty took nearly 20 years to complete. Lady Liberty was sculpted in France, then the 300-plus pieces were put in crates and shipped across the ocean. The statue is just over 150 feet tall, but including her 150-foot stone pedestal, it was the tallest building in New York when dedicated in 1886.

The Statue of Liberty

Raising her lamp beside New York City's immense harbor, the **Statue of Liberty** is one of the most vivid emblems of America. Despite the fact she is French, given to the American people to celebrate the 100th anniversary of the Declaration of Independence, the statue has come to symbolize the Land of the Free and the Home of the Brave. Its spirit has long been evoked by the poem Emma Lazarus wrote in 1883 to help raise funds for installing the Statue of Liberty. Called "The New Colossus," the poem ends with these famous words:

Keep ancient lands, your storied pomp!" cries she with silent lips. "Give me your tired, your poor, your huddled masses yearning to breathe free, the wretched refuse of your teeming shore. Send these, the home-less, tempest-tost to me, I lift my lamp beside the golden door!"

The Statue of Liberty sits on a 12-acre island and can be visited by **ferry** (877/523-9849, daily, $18.50) only. It's about a mile from Manhattan, but much easier to reach from **Liberty State Park** in Jersey City, off New Jersey Turnpike exit 14B. So long as you start your trip before 2pm, both ferry routes also visit Ellis Island, where some 12 million immigrants entered the United States. There is no admission fee for the Statue of Liberty or Ellis Island, but if you want to climb up onto Lady Liberty's pedestal you need a pedestal access ticket (also $18.50) instead.

All pass-holders can explore the base of the Statue of Liberty and gaze up inside her hollow shell, but access up into the small viewing area in the crown on her head requires special tickets ($3 extra) and a climb up more than 350 steps. Her torch has been off-limits since 1916.

The New Jersey Shore

The northernmost stretches of the New Jersey shore are not exactly appealing, and visitors bound for the beaches and vacation spots farther south generally turn a blind eye to the industrial blight of Bayonne, Elizabeth, and Perth Amboy, but once you round Staten Island and hit the Atlantic shoreline, the sights get better and better. Mixed in among gritty blue-collar summer resorts like Bruce Springsteen's **Asbury Park** and **Seaside Heights,** birthplace of MTV's Jersey Shore, there are intriguing Victorian-era resorts like **Spring Lake** and **Avon-by-the-Sea.**

The middle stretch of the Jersey shore is actually the quietest, with the million-acre **Pinelands National Reserve** (609/894-7300, daily, free) covering the inland area with forest and wetlands, and the coastal **Long Beach Island** dotted with sleepy little fishing and retirement communities. The biggest sight hereabouts is at the northern tip of the island: **Barnegat Lighthouse** (609/494-2016, daily summer, $3 adults), "Old Barney," whose image appears on personalized New Jersey license plates.

Atlantic City

Midway along the Jersey Shore, the world-famous beach resort of **Atlantic City** (pop. 39,558) has ridden the ups and downs of history. Home of the world's oldest beachfront boardwalk and the first pleasure pier, Atlantic City also spawned the picture postcard and

INTERSECTION New York City (see page 340) is covered as part of the **Appalachian Trail.** Full coverage of that route begins on page 298.

the Miss America beauty contest. Perhaps most significant of all, the street names for Monopoly were taken from Atlantic City, although the city's layout bears little resemblance to the board game (and there's no "Get Out of Jail Free" card, either).

Atlantic City reached its peak at the turn of the 20th century, when thousands of city-dwellers flocked here from New York and Philadelphia each weekend.

sunset on the beach, Atlantic City

Later on, as automobiles and airplanes brought better beaches and more exotic locales within reach, Atlantic City went into a half century of decline until **gambling** was legalized in the late 1970s, and millions of dollars began to flow into the local economy from tax subsidies for speculating real-estate developers like future president Donald Trump, whose name used to be emblazoned on a number of towering resort hotels. These days, the **Boardwalk** of Atlantic City still attracts millions of annual visitors and millions of dollars daily to its casinos. It's no Monte Carlo, not even a Las Vegas, but the clattering of slot machines and the buzz of the craps tables continues. The Boardwalk runs along the beach

> To enjoy a day on the sands at many of New Jersey's beaches, you need to buy (and wear) a beach badge, which costs $5-10 a day or around $10-25 a week and is available at local tourist offices, shops, and fast-food stands.

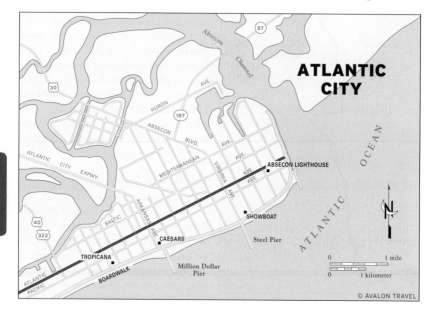

ATLANTIC CITY

© AVALON TRAVEL

In October 2012, the massive hurricane-force winds and 20-foot tidal surge of Superstorm Sandy caused more than $60 billion of damage to the northern East Coast, especially in New York City and here along the New Jersey shore.

for over two miles. Few of the remaining pleasure piers offer much of interest, and only the rebuilt **Steel Pier** holds any sign of the traditional seaside rides and arcade games that people used to come to the shore to enjoy.

Besides constituting Atlantic City's main attractions, the casinos hold most of the places to eat, apart from the dozens of fast-food stands along the Boardwalk. That said, a couple of old favorites stand out from the seedy crowd of ramshackle businesses that fill the nearby streets. One is the birthplace of the submarine sandwich, the chrome **White House Sub Shop** (2301 Arctic Ave., 609/345-8599). A block away, but at the other end of the aesthetic and budgetary spectrum, is **Dock's Oyster House** (2405 Atlantic Ave., 609/345-0092), a white-linen happy-hour and dinner-only restaurant that's been serving great seafood since 1897. Along with a number of national chains, the casinos also control accommodations—expect to pay upward of $100, though off-peak bargains can be found.

Boardwalk at Atlantic City

Margate:
Lucy the Elephant

Immediately south of Atlantic City, tidy **Margate** (pop. 6,354) fans out along the shore, its solidly suburban streets lined by grand houses. Margate utterly lacks the reckless seaside qualities of its larger neighbor but does include one classic remnant of the Jersey shore's glory days: **Lucy the Elephant** (9200 Atlantic Ave., 609/823-6473, daily summer, limited hours fall-spring, $8 guided tour). The six-story wood-and-tin pachyderm, a curiosity built by a Philadelphia real-estate speculator in the 1880s to draw customers to his newly laid-out community, looms over the beach. A National Historic Landmark, the architectural folly was once used around the turn of the 20th century as a tavern. It now holds a collection of old photographs and other memorabilia, including some of the original pieces of Lucy. Visitors walk

Lucy the Elephant

through the museum on the way up to an observation deck, which is disguised as a canopied seat on Lucy's back.

Saved from demolition and restored by community efforts in the 1970s, Lucy is ever in need of repair, kept alive by tour monies, donations, and sales of Lucy souvenirs in the small gift shop.

Ocean Drive: Ocean City and Stone Harbor

A series of local roads collectively known as **Ocean Drive** runs along the south Jersey coast, passing through a number of family-oriented beach resorts, starting at **Ocean City** (pop. 11,701), "America's Greatest Family Resort," 10 miles south of Atlantic City. Ocean City was founded as a religious retreat in the late 1870s and hasn't strayed far from its roots: Every summer morning (at 9:20am on the dot), life on the Boardwalk promenade comes to a standstill as "The Star-Spangled Banner" and "God Bless America" blare out from loudspeakers and the American flag is raised at the beachfront amusement park, which has been owned by the same family for more than a century. Located at 6th Street and known as **Gillian's Wonderland Pier** (609/399-7082, daily summer, Sat.-Sun. spring and fall, free, fees for rides), this old-time funfair has over 30 rides, including a giant Ferris wheel and a 1920s carousel. A block south, you can cool off on a hot summer's day at **OC Waterpark.**

Vacation homes, marinas, miniature golf courses, and a pair of toll bridges mark Ocean Drive for the next 20 miles.

At **Stone Harbor,** six miles north of Wildwood, the **Wetlands Institute** (1075 Stone Harbor Blvd., 609/368-1211, daily summer, Sat.-Sun. fall-spring, $8 adults) is one of the best places to experience the abundant natural life of the New Jersey shore. An observation tower looking over 6,000 acres of saltwater marshland provides excellent bird-watching opportunities, and there's also a museum with a touch-tank and aquarium.

Wildwood

On the Jersey Shore, fun in the sun reaches a peak at raucous **Wildwood,** a trio of interconnected towns housing dozens of nightclubs and New Jersey's biggest beachfront amusement parks. The largest of all, **Mariner's Pier** on the pier at Schellenger Avenue, has 28 rides, including one of the largest Ferris wheels on the East Coast. At 25th Street is **Surfside Pier,** and a little farther south is **Adventure Pier,** which is home to the Great White, the only wooden roller coaster in the U.S. to be built on a pier. All three of these are owned by the Morey family, prime movers behind Wildwood's retro-rediscovery, and an all-ride, all-pier pass (609/522-3900, around $59) is available for a full day's fun. Batting cages, go-karts, and some of the wilder rides are not included in the pass price.

Away from the sands in the local chamber of commerce, the **National Marbles Hall of Fame** (3306 Pacific Ave., 609/729-4000, free) features thousands of glass balls and more marble-shooting paraphernalia than you've ever seen. The city also hosts the **National Marbles Championship** (www.nationalmarblestournament.org) every June.

For many visitors, the best reason to spend time in Wildwood is that the area boasts an extensive collection of 1950s roadside architecture—mainly motel after motel, all sporting exuberant Las Vegas-style neon signs. Many of these motels are closed in the November-May off-season, but in the warmer months you can step back in the past by staying the night in one of these classic "doo-wop" motels—like the **Mango Motel** (209 E. Spicer Ave., 609/522-2067) or the renovated **Lollipop Motel** (2301 Atlantic Ave., 609/729-2800).

Chili dog and coleslaw lovers will want to chow down at **Maui's Dog House** (806 New Jersey Ave., 609/846-0444), at the north end of town, while other retro-minded visitors will want to stop for a meal at the chrome-and-glass **Doo Wop Diner** (4010 Boardwalk, 609/522-7880), two blocks southeast of the main pier. On the boardwalk, look out for the popular burgers-and-pizza diner **Route 66** (2700 Boardwalk, 609/523-6466).

For more details on places to stay and things to do—like late summer-early fall's massive and rowdy **Monsters on the Beach** monster truck rally—contact the **Wildwood visitors center** (1 NJ-47, 800/992-9732).

Cape May

A world away from the carnival atmosphere of the Wildwoods, **Cape May,** the oldest and most serene of the New Jersey beach towns, sits at the southern tip of the state. First settled in the early 1600s, Cape May's glory years ran from the 1850s to the 1890s as an upper-crust summer resort, when it rivaled Newport, Rhode Island, as the destination of choice for the power brokers of Philadelphia and New York City.

At the southern tip of Cape May, an extensive wetland and beachfront nature reserve offer wide-open spaces for beachcombing and bird-watching, while protecting the town from coastal storms. There was a town here until 1944, when a winter storm washed it away. A few modern motels and miniature golf courses spread north along Cape May's broad beaches, while the compact downtown district retains all its

CAPE MAY-LEWES FERRY

Running between the tip of the New Jersey shore and the heart of the Delaware coast, the Cape May-Lewes Ferry carries cars and passengers on a relaxing ride across the mouth of Delaware Bay. The trip ranges in cost depending upon day and season (Friday to Sunday in summer being most expensive), from about $23 to $47 each way for a car and one passenger, plus fares for each additional passenger.

Schedules change seasonally, with boats leaving about every hour in summer and every three hours in winter. Crossings take about 90 minutes, and if the seas are calm you can often see porpoises playing in the swells.

Call for up-to-date times and other **ferry information** (800/643-3779). Reservations ($10 extra) are a good idea at peak travel times and should be made at least one day in advance.

the *Cape May*, one of the five boats in the fleet

overwrought Victorian splendor. Century-old cottages now house cafés, boutiques, and art galleries, and it seems as if every other building has been converted into a quaint B&B. The town's ornate gingerbread mansions were constructed in the aftermath of a disastrous 1878 fire; among the better examples is the elaborate **Emlen Physick Estate** (1048 Washington St.), eight blocks north of downtown, designed by noted Philadelphia architect Frank Furness. It now houses the nonprofit, preservation-oriented **Mid-Atlantic Center for the Arts & Humanities** and is open as a **museum of late Victorian life** (609/884-5404, daily Apr.-Dec., limited hours Jan.-Mar., $12 adults).

Pick up walking-tour maps of some of the town's 600 listed historic buildings and do a taste-test of Cape May's many architecturally magnificent, mostly Victorian-era bed-and-breakfasts. These include the mansard-roofed **Queen Victoria** (102 Ocean St., 609/884-8702, $155 and up) and the **Mainstay Inn** (635 Columbia Ave., 609/884-8690, $175 and up), which has a spacious veranda opening onto gorgeous gardens. Cape May's oldest and most atmospheric place to stay is the Southern Gothic **Chalfonte Hotel** (301 Howard St., 609/884-8409, $70 and up). What the Chalfonte lacks in TVs and telephones it more than makes up for in hospitality: a bank of front-porch rocking chairs, full breakfasts, and huge, down-home dinners.

Places to eat, including a dozen or so bakeries, cafés, restaurants, and bars, can be found along the pedestrian-friendly few blocks of Washington Street at the center of town, while the seafood restaurants, naturally enough, are near the marina and ferry terminal on the north edge of town, off US-9. Two great options are downtown, right across from the water: **George's Place** (301 Beach Ave., 609/884-6088, cash only) mixes diner-style breakfasts with authentic Greek gyros and mezze, while across the street **Uncle Bill's Pancake House** (261 Beach Ave., 609/884-7199) serves thousands of pancakes daily along with waffles, eggs, and french toast.

DELAWARE

Across Delaware Bay from Cape May, the Delaware shore is considerably quieter and more peaceful than New Jersey's. Both shores, originally settled by Scandinavian whalers who established port colonies here in the early 1600s, share a common history. But

because the Delaware shore is that much farther from the urban centers, it has been spared the overdevelopment of much of the rest of the coast. Nevertheless, Delaware's statewide population doubles in summer as visitors from Baltimore and Washington DC descend on its coastal resorts, from historic **Lewes** to lively **Rehoboth Beach** to the untouched sands of **Delaware Seashore State Park,** stretching south to the Maryland border.

Lewes and Cape Henlopen

Sitting at the southern lip of Delaware Bay, **Lewes** is a vacation and sportfishing center that traces its roots back to 1631, when it was settled by the Dutch West India Company as a whaling port. Though this colony lasted only two years, Lewes calls itself the "First Town in the First State," commemorating its history in the false-gabled brick **Zwaanendael Museum** (102 Kings Hwy., 302/645-1148, Tues.-Sun. Apr.-Oct., Wed.-Sat. Nov.-Mar., free) at the center of town. Lewes also harbors huge sand dunes, a fine stretch of beach, and a **campground** with showers in 3,000-acre **Cape Henlopen State Park** (302/645-8983), east of town at the mouth of Delaware Bay. Expect relative peace and quiet here, since many visitors, arriving off the Cape May ferry, simply rush through Lewes to the beach resorts farther south.

Zwaanendael Museum

Rehoboth Beach

Fronting the open Atlantic, **Rehoboth Beach** was founded in the 1870s when church groups bought beachfront land, established the town, and extended a railroad line south from Lewes. The highway frontage along Hwy-1 is over-full of franchise food and factory outlet malls, but the heart of town along Rehoboth Avenue is the

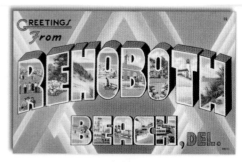

place to go. With its summer-only but lively Sputnik-era **Funland Amusement Park** (302/227-1921, hours vary May-Sept.), where the attractions include bumper cars, a nighttime haunted house, and a tidy boardwalk running along the broad beach, Rehoboth has somehow retained a small-town feel despite the many thousands of bureaucrats and power brokers who descend on the place during the summer, escaping the sweltering heat of Washington DC.

Ever wonder what happens to all those pumpkins that don't get bought by Halloween? In Delaware, they end up as fodder for a unique competition, the **Punkin' Chunkin'** ($10-20), in which the hapless gourds get launched hundreds, even thousands of feet through the air by a variety of mechanical devices. Thousands turn out for the event, which is held in a field in **Bridgeville,** 30 miles west of Lewes, on the last weekend in October or first weekend in November.

The DC connection helps explain the town's profusion of good (and some expensive) restaurants. Lining the main drag are casual, kid-friendly places like **Dogfish Head Brewings & Eats** (320 Rehoboth Ave., 302/226-2739), which has great food and killer beers in Delaware's oldest brewpub. There are also the traditional delights of **Thrasher's French Fries** and sundry beer-and-burger joints along the boardwalk.

Places to stay include some quaint old B&Bs and a barrage of highway chain motels, plus local ones like the **Beach View Hotel** (6 Wilmington Ave., 302/227-2999, $97 and up), on the boardwalk.

Delaware Seashore State Park

South from Rehoboth stretches one of the last long stretches of pristine beach on the whole northern East Coast: **Delaware Seashore State Park** (302/227-2800), which contains six miles of open beach with golden-flecked white sand and 2,825 acres of marshland estuary, thronged in season with migrating birds and bird-watchers, along with campers and anglers. The park's many beaches are all easily accessible from beachfront Hwy-1.

The park has camping and nice new **cottages** ($1,900 a week during prime summer season!) and is book-ended by a pair of densely developed resort towns: **Dewey Beach** in the north draws a younger collegiate crowd, while **Bethany Beach** in the south attracts more families.

Near Maryland, the 1858 **Fenwick Island Lighthouse,** hidden away amid the mini-malls and trailer parks on the bay side of Hwy-1 just south of Hwy-54, marks the state border. This lighthouse is a local landmark, but the waist-high white **Transpeninsular Marker** in front of it may be more significant: Placed in 1751, it marked the boundary between the colonies of Maryland and Pennsylvania, of which Delaware was then a part. Showing respect to the colonial proprietors, the more than 250-year-old marker has the Calvert family coat of arms on the Maryland (south) side, and William Penn's family crest on the other.

MARYLAND

Maryland, the most oddly shaped of the lower 48 states, shares the broad "DelMarVa" peninsula with Delaware and a small piece of Virginia. The inland area along the eastern shore of Chesapeake Bay, with its many inlets and tributary rivers, is filled with dozens of small colonial-era towns and fishing villages, while the Atlantic Coast is completely taken up by two very different beasts: the gloriously kitschy beach resort of **Ocean City** and the untrammeled wilds of **Assateague Island National Seashore.** Heading inland around Assateague, the highway passes by a number of historic small towns, including **Berlin** and captivating **Snow Hill.**

Ocean City

About the only place left on the entire East Coast that retains the carnival qualities of classic seaside resorts, **Ocean City** (pop. 7,102, swelling to almost 400,000 in summer) has by far the best array of old-time funfair attractions in the Mid-Atlantic (well, south of Wildwood, New Jersey, at least). On and around the main pier at the south end of the island, there are enough merry-go-rounds, Ferris wheels, roller coasters (including The Hurricane, which is illustrated with scenes from Ocean City

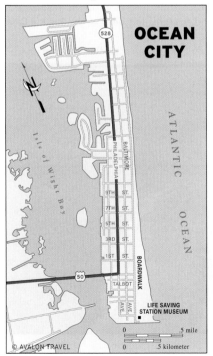

storms past), mini-golf courses, haunted houses, and bumper cars to divert a small army. A block inland, **Trimper's Rides and Amusements,** which has been operated by the same family for five generations, since the 1890s, has two more roller coasters, plus a Tilt-a-Whirl, a 100-year-old Herschell carousel, and a spooky haunted house. Places like Trimper's, and the sundry batting cages, go-kart tracks, and Whack-a-Mole games, are threatened by rising property values and property taxes and are increasingly close to becoming extinct, so enjoy them while you can. Trimper's Rides' local rival, Jolly Roger, also runs a big water park and another amusement park at the north end of town, along the bay at 30th Street.

Ocean City stretches for 10 miles along a broad clean white-sand beach. A wide, part-wooden 2.5-mile boardwalk lines the sands, packed with arcades full

To go along with its great beaches, Ocean City has a radio station, the excellent "Ocean 98" **WOCM 98.1 FM,** playing classic rock 'n' roll and broadcasting details of Ocean City's entertainment scene.

of video games and a few nearly forgotten old amusements like Skee-Ball, not to mention midway contests—the kind where, for $1 or $2 a try, you can win stuffed animals and other prizes by shooting baskets or squirting water into clowns' mouths. A ramshackle collection of fortune-tellers, T-shirt stands, and burger-and-beer bars completes the scene, forming a busy gauntlet that is among the nation's liveliest promenades.

On summer weekends, Ocean City becomes Maryland's second-largest city, and most of the fun is simply in getting caught up in the garish human spectacle of it all, but there are a couple of specific things worth searching out. For the price of a bumper car ride, you can enjoy the quirky collections of the **Life-Saving Station Museum** (daily May-Oct., Wed.-Sun. Apr. and Nov., hours vary Dec.-Mar., $3 adults), at the south end of the boardwalk, where alongside various exhibits you can compare and contrast bowls full of sand from 100 different beaches around the world. The museum also marks the starting point for the **open-air trams** ($3) that run north along the full length of the boardwalk.

Ocean City Practicalities

Much of Ocean City's charm is decidedly lowbrow, but the food is better than you might expect, with numerous places offering plates full of shrimp and pitchers of beer for under $10, and freshly fried chicken or crab cakes available from boardwalk stands. **Thrasher's Fries** are available (no ketchup; salt and vinegar only!) from one of the three counters along the boardwalk, and you can top them off with a cone or milk shake from **Dumser's Dairyland,** which runs several locations throughout Ocean City. Best breakfast for 30 years and counting has been at the **Sahara Café** (1900 N. Baltimore Ave., 410/289-5080).

Places to stay are also abundant. Built in 1875, the grand **Atlantic Hotel** (401 S.

aerial view of Ocean City

Running west from Ocean City across the Eastern Shore and then across the country to California is US-50 (see page 761). Full coverage of this **Loneliest Road** in America begins on page 670.

Haunted House at Trimper's Rides and Amusements

Baltimore Ave., 410/289-9111, $110 and up) is still open for business on the oceanfront. Modern motels like the **Hilton Suites** (3200 N. Baltimore Ave., 410/289-6444) often charge more than $300 a night for a room that goes for less than $200 off-season, so be sure to plan ahead. Many of the huge concrete towers you see are actually condominiums and not available for overnight stays.

For help finding lodgings and restaurants, contact the **Ocean City visitors center** (12320 Ocean Gateway, 410/213-0552), in the Conference Center.

Assateague Island National Seashore

At one time, Assateague Island, the long thin barrier island on which Ocean City sits, stretched in an unbroken line all the way into Virginia. In 1933, a major storm crashed through the sands and created the broad inlet that now divides Ocean City from the near-wilderness of **Assateague Island National Seashore.** Like its neighbor Chincoteague, the island is known for the wild ponies that live there. It's also one of the few areas of the Atlantic Coast protected from commercial development, with some 37 miles and 10,000 acres of hiking, swimming, camping, canoeing, bicycling, clamming, and bird-watching. Swarms of voracious mosquitoes and a lack of freshwater keep the crowds to a minimum.

To reach the island from Ocean City, follow US-50 west for two miles and turn south on Hwy-611, which loops around Sinepuxent Bay before arriving at the **visitor center** (410/641-1441, daily). The center has a small aquarium as well as maps, guides, and up-to-date information about the national seashore.

Berlin and Snow Hill

From Ocean City, the route turns inland around Assateague Island and Chincoteague Bay, following US-50 west for eight miles, then turning south on US-113 through the dark cypress swamps along the Pocomoke River. Just southwest of the US-50/113 junction, the remarkably well-preserved town of **Berlin** offers a look back at a slower-paced era. Redbrick buildings house antiques shops around the 1890s landmark **Atlantic Hotel** (2 N. Main St., 410/641-3589, $89 and up), where the rocking chairs along the open-air front porch all but demand that you sit and stay awhile. Inside, the stylish **Drummer's Café** (daily from 11am) may tempt you to alter your travel plans so you can enjoy the delicious local seafood.

Another 15 miles southwest of Ocean City, detour west from the highway to take a look at the 250-year-old town of **Snow Hill** (pop. 2,103). The **Julia A. Purnell Museum** (208 W. Market St., Tues.-Sun., $3 adults), housed in an old church, features a range of exhibits tracing Eastern Shore history, and around 10,000 artifacts and ephemera are on rotation. Pick up a walking-tour map of Snow Hill's many significant structures, or if the weather is fine, paddle a canoe or a kayak through the surrounding wild cypress swamps with the **Pocomoke River Canoe and Kayak** (2 River St., 410/632-3971), next to the drawbridge.

VIRGINIA

Virginia's Eastern Shore is among the most isolated regions of the country, and its dozens of small towns and villages remain much as they have for centuries. Everything on the Eastern Shore is on a much smaller scale than on the mainland, and the many stands selling fresh corn and tomatoes along the roadside attest to the important role farming plays in the local economy. Although fast-food places, chicken-processing plants, and a couple of modern malls dot US-13, the main route through Virginia's Eastern Shore, the area is still mostly rural and undeveloped, with business loops turning off through the many well-preserved old towns. The numerous historic sites include colonial-era plantations and archaeological remnants of Native American communities.

The highlight for most visitors is **Chincoteague,** a small commercial and sport-fishing port sitting at the entrance to massive Chincoteague National Wildlife Refuge, which faces the Atlantic Coast and offers the only ocean beaches in this part of the state. South of Chincoteague, US-13 runs down the center of the narrow Eastern Shore peninsula, giving access to the Chesapeake Bay waterfront at **Accomac,** then passing through numerous small towns like **Onancock** and **Eastville,** neither of which has changed much since Revolutionary times. Crossing the mouth of the Chesapeake Bay via a 23-mile-long bridge and tunnel brings you to maritime **Norfolk** and the state's main Atlantic resort, **Virginia Beach,** before the route turns inland and south into North Carolina.

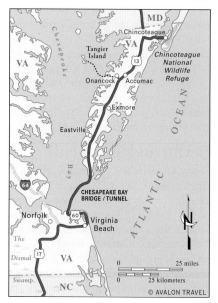

Chincoteague

The drive into **Chincoteague** (pop. 2,941; pronounced "SCHINK-a-teeg"), a low-key fishing village, takes you across miles of glowing gold and blue marshlands through a gauntlet of quirky billboards advertising local

wild ponies at Chincoteague National Wildlife Refuge

motels, restaurants, and sportfishing charters. This mix of natural beauty and tacky tourism aptly reflects the character of the town, which is totally dependent upon summertime visitors but seems to wish that we'd all just leave and let the locals go fishing.

A small bridge along Hwy-175, which runs 11 miles east from US-13, drops you at the heart of town, where casual seafood restaurants line the streets.

Among the many places to stay are several nice B&Bs and a handful of standard motels like the friendly and central **Birchwood Inn** (3650 Main St., 757/336-6133, $49 and up).

Chincoteague National Wildlife Refuge

Spreading east of town, the **Chincoteague National Wildlife Refuge** is one of the largest nature preserves along the Atlantic flyway, attracting hundreds of species of birds, including egrets, herons, geese, swans, and snow geese, not to mention thousands and thousands of migrating ducks. A continuation of the Assateague Island National Seashore across the Maryland border, the refuge contains thousands of acres of marshland, excellent beaches, and a number of hiking and cycling trails. The refuge **visitors center** (757/336-6122, daily) has detailed information on park activities as well as a small exhibit on Chincoteague's famous wild ponies, which can usually be seen from the Woodland Trail that loops south from Beach Road.

In summer, stands selling fresh fruit and vegetables—particularly sweet corn and tomatoes—dot roadsides all over the Eastern Shore.

The children's story *Misty of Chincoteague* is set in the area and tells how wild ponies—whose ancestors were sent here by English settlers in the late 1600s—are rounded up from the wildlife refuge on Assateague Island for a forced swim across to Chincoteague. The annual Pony Swim features a roundup, swim, and auction which benefits local firefighters and attracts thousands of spectators. The swim takes place the last Wednesday in July, and the auction follows the next day.

Accomac

One of the most photogenic spots on the Eastern Shore, **Accomac** (pop. 519) is centered on an ancient-looking redbrick courthouse. The library down the street, courthouse, and surrounding buildings together make for a great leg-stretch spot, midway along the Eastern Shore. By way of contrast, Accomac is also home to another Eastern Shore landmark: the huge Perdue Chicken processing plant, right along US-13, which produces and packs millions of birds every year.

Onancock and Tangier Island

The picturesque harbor town of **Onancock** (pop. 1,263; pronounced "o-NAN-cock"), on the Chesapeake Bay, two miles west of Accomac and US-13 via Hwy-179, is one of the nicest towns on the Eastern Shore. A short walking tour of over a dozen historical homes and churches begins at perhaps the finest mansion on the Eastern Shore, the **Ker Place** (69 Market St., 757/787-8012, Tues.-Sat. 11am-3pm Mar.-Dec., donation), built in 1799 and now home to the offices and museum of the Eastern Shore of Virginia Historical Society. Another historical curiosity is the 175-year-old Hopkins and Bros. General Store (2 Market St.), on the wharf, which in the past has sold everything from sweet potatoes to postcards—and now serves as the location for **Mallards at the Wharf** restaurant.

Ker Place in Onacock

A great taste of Onancock life awaits inside the **Corner Bakery** (36 Market St., 757/787-4520), where great doughnuts and fresh coffee are served up to a mostly local crowd. In the evening you can catch a flick at Onancock's nifty 1950s movie theater, the **Roseland** (48 Market St., 757/787-2010). Elegant dinners and nice rooms are available at the **Charlotte Hotel** (7 North St., 757/787-7400).

Onancock was born and grew up around its natural deep-water harbor, and the town wharf is still the place to catch the seasonal ferry across Chesapeake Bay to **Tangier Island,** an evocative old place where things seem to have hardly changed since colonial times. The seven hundred or so people who live here year-round have a unique and almost indecipherably archaic accent—which some trace back to 17th-century Cornwall, England—and earn their livelihoods catching crabs and the occasional oyster from Chesapeake Bay. Tangier Island is best known for its soft-shell crabs, which are sold all over the eastern United States.

Visiting Tangier Island is easy but takes some advance planning. From May until October, boats leave twice a day Tuesday-Sunday from **Onancock Wharf** (757/891-2505, about $25 round-trip); travel time is about one hour, leaving around 10am and 5pm and returning around 7:30am and 3:30pm. This means visitors departing on the 10am ferry and returning the same day by 3:30pm would have only about two hours on the island, so staying overnight at a homespun B&B like

Bay View Inn (757/891-2396) or **Hilda Crockett's Chesapeake House** (757/891-2331) is about the only way to have any kind of close encounter with the tourist-shy locals. Hilda's also serves meals, and good seafood can be had at a handful of unpretentious places like the **Fisherman's Corner Restaurant** (757/891-2900), where you may well be served by the person who caught your meal (or his wife).

Bike rentals are available on Tangier Island, no part of which is more than five feet above sea level.

Exmore and Eastville

Fifteen miles south of Accomac along US-13, the hamlet of **Exmore** has an architectural landmark that doubles as road-food stop: the **Exmore Diner** (4264 Main St., 757/422-2313), a streamlined Silk City prefab that has been in business here since 1954. Another 15 miles along, you can get a good idea of just how rural and quiet life is on Virginia's Eastern Shore by visiting **Eastville** (pop. 305), the seat of Northampton County. A mile west of US-13 on a well-marked business loop, Eastville centers on the redbrick courthouse and old county jail, with a handful of even older buildings dating back to the mid-1700s. Eastville also has an excellent roadside crab shack along US-13: **The Great Machipongo Clam Shack** (757/442-3800) has crabmeat sandwiches, fresh steamed clams, and an astonishing variety of shellfish, most of it grown, caught, or picked by locals.

Chesapeake Bay Bridge-Tunnel

One of the more impressive engineering feats on the East Coast is the **Chesapeake Bay Bridge-Tunnel** ($15 toll in peak season), which opened in 1964 at the mouth of the Chesapeake Bay and was effectively doubled in 1999 by the addition of an extra set of driving lanes. Almost 18 miles long, the structure consists of one high-level bridge, two deep tunnels, four islands, and many miles of raised causeway.

The Chesapeake Bay Bridge-Tunnel's unique design allows for ships to pass easily, and makes for a scenic drive, day or evening.

Before the Chesapeake Bay Bridge-Tunnel was completed in 1964, ferries linking the Eastern Shore with the mainland docked at Cape Charles, west of US-13 eight miles south of Eastville. Barges still use the harbor, ferrying freight trains across the bay.

Southernmost Sea Gull Island closed to the public in 2017 as the construction of a parallel tunnel began; completion is anticipated in 2022. The existing bridge-tunnel will remain open to road-trip traffic.

Virginia Beach

From the toll plaza at the southern end of the Chesapeake Bay Bridge, US-60 heads east along Atlantic Avenue, passing through the woodland waterfront of **First Landing State Park** before winding up at the ocean and **Virginia Beach** (pop. 437,994), the state's most populous city and its one and only beach resort. Hotels line the main drag, Atlantic Avenue, which is plastered with large signs banning cars from "cruising" the mile-long array of funfairs, surf shops, and nightclubs.

Unlike many coastal towns, Virginia Beach also boasts a significant history. Virginia's first colonists landed at Virginia Beach on April 26, 1607, before settling upriver at Jamestown; the site is marked by a stone cross at Cape Henry, at the southern lip of Chesapeake Bay. Five miles south, the excellent **Virginia Aquarium** (717 General Booth Blvd., 757/385-3474, daily, $25 adults, $30 combo ticket for admission and movie) holds nearly a million gallons with sharks, sting rays, seals, and sea turtles, plus an IMAX theater ($8).

Along with the beaches and the aquarium, one of the big attractions in Virginia Beach is breakfast, thanks to the fantastic range of places up and down Atlantic Avenue, like the awesome **Pocahontas Pancakes** (3420 Atlantic Ave., at 35th St., 757/428-6352).

Virginia Beach

Norfolk

During colonial times, **Norfolk** (pop. 242,803; pronounced "NAW-fik") was the largest city in Virginia and one of the busiest ports in North America. It's still much connected with the water, which you can experience firsthand at **Nauticus** (757/664-1000, daily summer, Tues.-Sun. fall-spring, $16 and up adults), where the engaging displays inside are dwarfed by the massive hulk of the battleship USS *Wisconsin* moored alongside. Away from the waterfront, Norfolk has a couple more worthwhile destinations, including the lovely **Chrysler Museum of Art** (1 Memorial Place, 757/664-6200, Tues.-Sun., free), on

downtown Norfolk

the north side of downtown off Duke Street. The personal art collection of Walter Chrysler, the self-educated engineer who created one of the "Big Three" car companies and built New York's Chrysler Building, is displayed inside a commodious Italianate building. Norfolk, a staunch Navy town, also holds the final resting place of controversial U.S. Army general Douglas MacArthur, preserved alongside his personal papers and his 1950 Chrysler Imperial limousine at the **MacArthur Memorial** (757/441-2965, Tues.-Sun., free), inside Norfolk's old City Hall building at Bank and Plume Streets downtown.

Even if you're just racing through, bound for the beach, Norfolk has one place where you really ought to stop and eat: **Doumar's Barbecue** (1919 Monticello Ave., 757/627-4163), a half mile north of downtown. Besides being a real old-fashioned drive-in, this place stakes a claim to having invented the ice cream waffle cone, since the owner's uncle, Abe Doumar, sold the first ones at the 1904 St. Louis World's Fair. Doumar's still sells great handmade cones, barbecue sandwiches, and a deliciously thirst-quenching limeade. Pass by at your peril.

From Norfolk, you can take US-17 south on the perimeter of the aptly named Great Dismal Swamp or follow the faster Hwy-168, which turns into US-158 and takes you past a feast of roadside fruit stands, barbecue shacks, and junk shops, straight down to Kitty Hawk and the Outer Banks of North Carolina.

Virginia Beach is home to the **Association for Research and Enlightenment** (215 67th St., 800/333-4499 or 757/428-3588), which is dedicated to continuing the legacy of early American psychic Edgar Cayce, offering casual classes as well as certification programs in hypnotherapy, massage, intuition, and holistic medicine.

The two deepwater harbors near Norfolk at the mouth of the Chesapeake Bay, **Newport News** and **Hampton Roads,** are the headquarters of the U.S. Navy's Atlantic Fleet and together form the world's largest naval base.

The **Norfolk Tides** (757/622-2222), Triple-A farm team of the Baltimore Orioles, play at beautiful **Harbor Park,** off I-264 at Waterside Drive, where you can watch big ships sail past. Games are broadcast on **ESPN 94.1 FM.**

Stop for a bite at Doumar's.

NORTH CAROLINA

Wild Atlantic beaches, a handful of tiny fishing villages, and some of the country's most significant historic sites make coastal North Carolina a great place to visit. A highlight for many vacationers are the **Outer Banks,** miles of barrier islands where busy resort towns like **Nags Head** contrast with the stretches of pristine beaches protected on the **Cape Hatteras National Seashore.** Besides golden sands, the Outer Banks area includes two evocative historic sites: the dunes at **Kitty Hawk,** where the Wright Brothers first took to the air, and **Roanoke Island,** site of the first ill-fated English effort to colonize the New World. Farther south, beyond the quirky small city of **Wilmington,** a movie-making mecca, the 300-mile coastal route turns inland around **Cape Fear,** heading toward the South Carolina border.

Warmed by the Gulf Stream currents, the **Outer Banks beaches** are some of the best in the world, but the waters do not warm up appreciably until south of Oregon Inlet, and swimming in the northern stretches remains quite invigorating until July.

Kitty Hawk: The Wright Brothers National Memorial

Alternately known as Killy Hauk, Kitty Hock, and Killy Honk before its current name came into general use, **Kitty Hawk** to most people means one thing: the Wright brothers' first powered airplane flight more than a century ago, on December 17, 1903. Lured by the steady winds that blow in from the Atlantic and by the high sand dunes that cover the shore, Wilbur and Orville Wright first came to the Outer Banks in 1900 and returned every year thereafter with prototype kites and gliders built out of bicycle parts, which they fine-tuned to create the world's first airplane. Their tale is truly one of the great adventure and success stories of the modern age, and the site of their experiments has been preserved as the **Wright Brothers National Memorial** ($7 adults). First stop is the **visitors center**

First flight: 120 feet in 12 seconds. Orville mans the plane, Wilbur runs alongside.

Orville Wright   Wilbur Wright

(252/473-2111, daily) which includes a number of exhibits tracing the history of human efforts to fly. There are daily ranger-led talks and tours that visit the site of the first flight.

The most affecting aspect of the memorial is the unchanged site where the brothers first flew. Each of the first four flights is marked by stones set on the grassy field. The first flight, with Orville at the controls flying into a 25-mph headwind, lasted 12 seconds and covered just 120 feet—barely more than a brisk walking pace. The 90-foot-high sand dune where Wilbur and Orville first took to the air has been planted over with grasses to keep it from blowing away. Paths climb to the top of the dune, where a 60-foot wing-shaped granite pylon is inscribed with these words:

In commemoration of the conquest of the air by the brothers Wilbur and Orville Wright. Conceived by genius, achieved by dauntless resolution and unconquerable faith.

Jockey's Ridge State Park

The windswept 110-foot-high twin sand dunes of **Jockey's Ridge State Park** (252/441-7132, daily, free) tower over US-158 between Kitty Hawk and Nags Head. The highest sand dunes on the East Coast, Jockey's Ridge barely survived being bulldozed in the 1970s to form yet another Outer Banks resort; it's now one of the prime hang-gliding spots in the country—remember the Wright brothers! Jockey's Ridge is also a nice place to wander the short boardwalk nature trail that points out the diverse plants and animals of the dune community. You may want to take your shoes off and scamper around the sands barefoot. If you feel especially daring, **Kitty Hawk Kites Hang Gliding School** (252/441-2426, $99 and up) in the park at milepost 12 dubs itself the "World's Largest Hang-Gliding School" and offers equipment rentals to certified pilots and lessons to those of all experience levels, plus anything else you might need to make the most of your time here.

Nags Head

The towns of the northern Outer Banks overlap each other so much it can be hard to tell you are in **Nags Head,** six miles south of Kitty Hawk. One of the oldest and most popular resorts in the region, Nags Head also offers the widest range of visitor facilities. Good places to spend a night or two include a beachfront roadside classic at milepost 16.5: the historic **Sea Foam Motel** (7111 S. Virginia Dare Trail, 252/441-7320, $130 and up), one of the last surviving 1940s motels on the Outer Banks. The pine-paneled walls, vivid tiles, and slamming screen doors will take you back to a simpler time. Nearby, the even more atmospheric **First Colony Inn** (6715 S. Croatan Hwy., 252/441-2343 or 800/368-9390, $89 and up), along US-158 at milepost 16, was moved from its valuable oceanfront location to the middle of the island, but it still offers oodles of old-fashioned charm along with a delicious breakfast and afternoon tea.

If you're traveling along the Carolina coast in summer, be aware that the hurricane season begins in June and lasts through the end of November. These are deadly serious storms, so take heed of any warnings, and follow the evacuation instructions broadcast over radio and TV networks.

The name Nags Head is derived from the practices of Outer Banks pirates, who tied lanterns around the heads of their horses to simulate boats bobbing at anchor. The lanterns lured passing ships onto shore, where they ran aground on the offshore sandbars.

One more long-standing local landmark, **Sam & Omie's** (7228 S. Virginia Dare Trail, 252/441-7366, closed for a few weeks in winter), near the east end of US-64, has featured inexpensive but well-prepared family fare, three meals a day plus a full bar, for 80 years.

Roanoke Island: Fort Raleigh

From an area known as Whalebone Junction at the south end of Nags Head, US-64 runs west over a causeway and bridge to **Roanoke Island,** site of the first English settlement in North America. The legendary "Lost Colony" was first established in 1584 by Walter Raleigh, but the effort was not a success, and the survivors returned to England. In 1587, a larger expedition of 117 colonists arrived, including women and children, but because of the outbreak of war with Spain and the manifold difficulties involved in crossing the Atlantic Ocean, there was no further contact with England until 1590.

By the time the next supply ship returned, the settlers had disappeared without a trace, which prompted numerous theories about their fate. Now, amid an eerily dark forest, the colony's original earthwork fortress has been excavated and reconstructed as the centerpiece of the **Fort Raleigh National Historic Site.** Exhibits inside the **visitors center** (252/473-2111, daily, free) include artifacts, displays, and a short video explaining the historical context of the colonial effort. There are also copies of the many beautiful watercolors and drawings of native plants, animals, and people produced by the original expedition's two immensely talented scientists, John White and Thomas Hariot.

Throughout the summer, a waterfront theater adjacent to Fort Raleigh presents a popular production of Lost Colony (252/473-2127, $20-35 adults, less for ages 6-18, free under age 6), which dramatizes the events of the ill-fated settlement. If the weather is fine, spare some time for the large and luscious landscape of the **Elizabethan Gardens** (252/473-3234, daily, $9), next to Fort Raleigh.

The historic port of **Manteo** (pop. 1,434; pronounced "MAN-tee-o"), in the middle of Roanoke Island between Fort Raleigh and the beach resorts of the Outer Banks, was named for the Native American who helped Walter Raleigh and the Lost Colony. Manteo is the only county seat in North Carolina that's located on an island. You can still

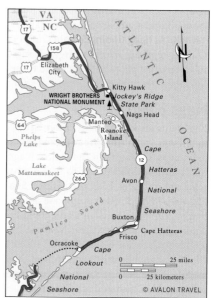

sense the town's proud seagoing history as you walk along the quiet streets near the tidied-up waterfront. Surrounded by pleasure boats, the main attraction here is the *Elizabeth II* (daily Mar.-Dec., $10 adults), a full-size square-rigged replica of the type of ship that carried colonists here from England 400-odd years ago.

Sir Walter Raleigh's flagship, *Ark Raleigh*

Cape Hatteras National Seashore

The first piece of coastline to be protected as a national park, **Cape Hatteras National Seashore** stretches for 75 miles along the Atlantic Ocean. Starting in the north at Nags Head, and continuing south along slender Bodie, Hatteras, and Ocracoke Islands, the area preserved within Cape Hatteras National Seashore is the largest undeveloped section of coastline on the East Coast, providing an increasingly rare glimpse of nature amid ever-encroaching development. The few old fishing villages that stood here when the seashore was set aside in the 1930s are unfortunately exempt from the antidevelopment prohibitions of the national seashore; these have grown ugly and unwieldy. Nevertheless, the many miles in between remain almost entirely untouched.

> Hundreds of ancient ships and unfortunate sailors met their watery end in the shallow waters off Cape Hatteras. The remains of over 1,000 vessels lie along the length of the Carolina coastline; a few are visible from shore at low tide.

For many visitors, the highlight of the national seashore is the historic **Cape Hatteras Lighthouse,** a mile south of Hwy-12 at the south end of Hatteras Island. Others come here to enjoy the warm waters and strong, steady winds—two areas of Pamlico Sound on the inland side of Cape Hatteras have been set aside for windsurfers, dozens of whom flock here on summer days to what's considered one of the finest sailboarding and kite-surfing spots in the United States. And, of course, there are miles of open beaches, perfect for aimless strolling.

Cape Hatteras Lighthouse

At the north end of Cape Hatteras, eight miles south of Nags Head, there's a national seashore **visitors center** (252/473-2111, daily) and a nature trail winding along Pamlico Sound at the foot of **Bodie Island Lighthouse,** the first of three historic towers along the Hatteras coast. On the ocean side of Hwy-12, **Coquina Beach** has a broad strand, lifeguards and outdoor showers in summer, and the remains of a wooden schooner that was wrecked here in the 1920s.

Continuing south, across the **Oregon Inlet** (where there's a first-come, first-served campground), Hwy-12 runs through the 5,800-acre **Pea Island National Wildlife Refuge,** which was established in 1937 to protect the nesting grounds of loggerhead sea turtles, as well as the coastal wetlands essential to the

THE OUTER BANKS

The geography of the Outer Banks, a series of barrier islands stretching for over 200 miles along the coast of North Carolina, has changed dramatically over time, thanks to hurricanes and winter storms, not to mention human hands. Until a series of lighthouses was built beginning in the late 18th century, the islands and the offshore shoals were so treacherous they became known as the "Graveyard of the Atlantic."

Nowadays, the same places where pirates once plundered are given over to windsurfing, hang-gliding, kite-surfing, sportfishing, and beachcombing, as the Outer Banks (sometimes abbreviated OBX) have become a tourist and recreation destination par excellence. The resident population of some 34,000 swells to accommodate over six million annual visitors, but unlike its nearest comparison, Cape Cod, the Outer Banks area boasts only a few historic towns. Instead, substantial development over the past 25 years has covered the sands with an ugly sprawl of vacation homes and time-share condos perched—often on stilts to protect them from storm damage—directly on the broad Atlantic beaches. Most of the development has taken place in the north along two parallel roads: US-158, usually called The Bypass but also known as Croatan Highway; and oceanfront Hwy-12, a.k.a. Virginia Dare Trail and Beach Road. Mileposts on both roads mark distances from north to south. There's plentiful lodging in the many little towns along Hwy-12; gas stations and fast-food restaurants line US-158. The exception to the commercial sprawl are the magical 75 miles of the Cape Hatteras National Seashore.

Along the northern Outer Banks, bridges link Nags Head and Kitty Hawk with the mainland, though access to the less-developed southern parts of the Outer Banks is limited to ferry boats, all of which carry cars.

The section of Pamlico Sound known as **Canadian Hole,** between the towns of Avon and Buxton, is rated as one of the best windsurfing spots on the East Coast.

survival of the greater snow goose and other migratory waterfowl. South of the refuge, a few short barrages of vacation condos and roadside sprawl—water sport rental shops, casual eateries, souvenir shops, and a KOA campground—line the highway between Rodanthe and Salvo, before the road reaches the heart of the park, where high sand dunes rise along 15 miles of undeveloped oceanfront.

Avon and Buxton: Cape Hatteras Lighthouse

At the rough midpoint of Hatteras Island, the vacation town of **Avon** stretches for a couple of miles along Hwy-12 before the road hits the Canadian Hole windsurfing area, two miles south of town. After another few miles of natural dunes, the road bends sharply to the west; continuing south here brings you to the main **Hatteras Island Visitor Center and Museum of the Sea** (252/473-2111, daily) and the famous **Cape Hatteras Lighthouse** (Apr.-Oct., $8). At 210 feet, the black-and-white-striped lighthouse is the tallest brick lighthouse in the United States, visible from as far as 25 miles. However, because the ocean here has been slowly eroding the beach (when the lighthouse was built in 1870, it was a quarter mile from the waves; by 1995 the coast was a mere 120 feet away from its base), in 1999 the National Park Service succeeded in lifting the 4,830-ton lighthouse onto rails and shifting it half a mile

inland. If you feel fit, climb the 257 stairs to the top of the lighthouse for a grand view—one that gives the clearest sense of just how narrow and transitive the Outer Banks are.

Farther along, at the end of this road, there's a campground open spring to fall.

From the Cape Hatteras Lighthouse, Hwy-12 bends west and south through **Buxton** and **Frisco.** The village of Frisco, five miles north of the Hatteras ferry terminal, holds the small but surprisingly good **Native American Museum** (252/995-4440, Tues.-Sun., $5), which boasts an extensive collection of artifacts from several indigenous nations, including those from the Cape Hatteras area, as well as Hopi and Navajo crafts.

In Buxton and Frisco you will find a gauntlet of motels, gas stations, and fast-food restaurants at the commercial center of Cape Hatteras. Buxton's motels, like the **Lighthouse View** (800/225-7651), which is right on the beach and also has a good-size swimming pool, are reasonably priced ($65 and up) and clean. Ocean beaches here at the tip of the cape are among the most spectacular anywhere. Swimmers should note that because they are south-facing, they tend to pick up some of the most extreme surf—especially when hurricanes hit—which is why Buxton and Frisco are the local surfing capitals.

More restaurants and motels await in **Hatteras,** at the southern end of the island. From here, state-run ferries (5am-midnight, free) shuttle at least once every hour across to Ocracoke Island, another mostly unspoiled barrier island where you'll find great beaches and the pretty village of Ocracoke, at the island's southern tip.

Ocracoke

About the only Outer Banks town that hasn't lost its small-scale charm, **Ocracoke** is a great place to spend an afternoon or two, walking or cycling along unpaved back streets lined by overgrown gardens and weathered old homes. Since it's easy to reach from the mainland, via ferries from Swan Quarter and from Cedar Island, Ocracoke is a popular destination, but the tourism here is so low-key it still feels like a place you can discover for yourself.

From Hwy-12, a number of small back roads are worth exploring, especially by bike, the best way to get around Ocracoke. These roads include oak-lined Howard Street and another called simply Back Road, which runs past **Teach's Hole,** a shop and exhibit ($4 for exhibit only) dedicated to the pirate Blackbeard. Just south of the harbor, Point Road runs west to the squat whitewashed 1823 **Ocracoke Lighthouse.**

Ocracoke Practicalities

The ferries from the mainland south of Ocracoke drop you at the heart of town, but coming in from the north on Hwy-12, you pass through a short strip of real estate agencies and restaurants like **Howard's Pub** (252/928-4441), a local institution whose rooftop ocean-view deck is a pleasant place to eat deep-fried local seafood and sample one or more of its 200-plus beers. A few doors down is the super-tasty

Eduardo's Tacos stand. First stop for those coming from the south, Ocracoke's small and photogenic harbor is ringed by low-key, low-rise restaurants, bike rental stands, hotels, bars, and B&Bs. Many of the restaurants ringing the Ocracoke harbor morph into bars after dark. All are friendly and informal, and most have some kind of live music during the summer season, making wandering around town a prime visitor activity.

There are no chain hotels on Ocracoke (which may in itself be reason enough to visit!), and local places are generally down-to-earth, not fancy. The oldest lodging option is **Blackbeard's Lodge** (111 Back Rd., 252/928-3421, $61 and up), a rambling old hotel with modern amenities.

Right across from the ferry landing, there's a helpful **visitors center** (252/928-4531) that has complete information on Ocracoke and the rest of Cape Hatteras. Running between Ocracoke on Cape Hatteras, and two places on the North Carolina mainland (Cedar Island and Swan Quarter), the state-run **ferry** (800/293-3779, around $15 per car, $30 RVs) departs approximately every few hours and takes just over 2.5 hours to get to Swan Quarter and 2 hours and 15 minutes to get to Cedar Island.

From Cedar Island, it's close to an hour's drive along US-70 to the next big city, Beaufort.

Cape Lookout National Seashore

If you like the look of Cape Hatteras but want to avoid the crowds, plan a visit to the much wilder **Cape Lookout National Seashore,** another series of barrier islands, which stretch for 56 miles from Ocracoke to the south near Beaufort. It's accessible only by boat (except for two sections that are accessible by car), and there are few roads or services once you're here, but it's a lovely place to hike or camp, collect seashells, or just wander along the peaceful shore, exploring the historic Portsmouth Village. Day trips to Point Lookout leave from Beaufort, or you can usually arrange a charter from Ocracoke.

Beaufort and Morehead City

Known as Fishtown until it was renamed in 1722, the charming 18th-century town of **Beaufort** (pop. 4,039) has quiet streets lined with churches, cemeteries filled with weather-stained monuments, and whitewashed houses with narrow porches. The nautical-themed shops and restaurants along the water on busy Front Street, three blocks south of US-70, attract tourists and boaters traveling along the Intracoastal Waterway. The spacious **North Carolina Maritime Museum**

BLACKBEARD THE PIRATE

Capture of the Pirate, Blackbeard, 1718

Wandering around the idyllic harbor of Ocracoke, it's hard to imagine that the waters offshore were once home to perhaps the most ferocious pirate who ever sailed the Seven Seas—Blackbeard. The archetypal pirate, even in his day, when piracy was common, Blackbeard was famous for his ruthlessness and violence as much as for his long black beard and exotic battle dress, wearing six pistols on twin gun belts slung over his shoulders and slashing hapless opponents with a mighty cutlass. His pirate flag featured a heart dripping blood and a skeleton toting an hourglass in one hand and a spear in the other.

For all his near-mythic status, Blackbeard's career as a pirate was fairly short. After serving as an English privateer in the Caribbean during Queen Anne's War, in 1713 Blackbeard (whose real name was Edward Teach) turned to piracy, learning his trade under the pirate Benjamin Hornigold. Outfitted with four stolen ships, 40 cannons, and a crew of 300 men, Blackbeard embarked on a reign of terror that took him up and down the Atlantic coast of the American colonies. After five years of thieving cargoes and torturing sailors, Blackbeard was confronted off Ocracoke by forces led by Lieutenant Robert Maynard of the Royal Navy, and during a ferocious battle on November 22, 1718, the pirate and most of his men were killed. Blackbeard himself was stabbed 25 times, and his head was sliced off and hung like a trophy on the bowsprit of his captor's ship.

Though there is no evidence that he ever buried any treasure anywhere near Ocracoke, Blackbeard's ship, the *Queen Anne's Revenge,* was discovered in 1996 off Bogue Bank, and some cannons and other objects recovered from the pirate's ship are being preserved by the North Carolina Maritime Museum in Beaufort. Blackbeard's legend, to be sure, lives on.

(315 Front St., 252/728-7317, daily, free) features many informative exhibits on the region's nautical and natural history. The museum also sponsors an annual **Wooden Boat Show,** held the first weekend in May.

If you're looking for a meal in Beaufort, try **Clawson's** (425 Front St., 252/728-2133), serving reliably great burgers, local seafood, and craft beers in an old grocery store that's been in business since 1905.

Inland from Front Street and the museum, a trio of historic churches surround the atmospheric **Old Burying Ground,** where grave markers track the town's residents from the 1700s to the early 1900s.

While Beaufort may be prettier, you'll find the best food in burly **Morehead City,** three miles west of Beaufort and across the bridge. Try the homemade seafood cocktail sauce and Tar Heel hushpuppies at the **Sanitary Fish Market and Restaurant**

Not surprisingly, Beaufort, North Carolina is often confused with Beaufort, South Carolina. The former is pronounced "BO-fort"; the latter is pronounced "BYOO-furd."

(501 Evans St., 252/247-3111), a local institution since 1938 and easy to find amid the sportfishing boats a block off US-70. For even more famous burgers (and shrimp burgers, and onion rings, and milk shakes, and more), head along to **El's Drive-In** (3706 Arendall St., 252/726-3002), open since 1959 on US-70, a mile west of the bridge to Atlantic Beach.

Bogue Banks: Fort Macon

North Carolina's beaches are prime nesting grounds for loggerhead sea turtles. These huge turtles come ashore from mid-May to late August by the light of the full moon. Females lay and bury as many as 100 eggs, then in September-October the tiny hatchlings scramble back into the sea.

More barrier island beach resorts line **Bogue Banks,** which runs south of Morehead City in a nearly east-west orientation for some 21 miles. The half-dozen family-oriented resort towns have freely accessible—but quite often crowded—beaches. The largest, **Atlantic Beach,** across a bridge from Morehead City, has a boardwalk backed by a mini-golf course and skateboard park. The enjoyable **North Carolina Aquarium** (daily, $13 adults), five miles west of town on Hwy-58 at Pine Knoll Shores, features extensive displays on the local loggerhead sea turtles as well as sharks and river otters.

At the northeast end of Bogue Banks stands **Fort Macon State Park** (daily, free), which centers on a massive pre-Civil War fortress overlooking the harbor entrance. The pentagon-shaped masonry fort, completed in 1834, was captured early in the Civil War by the Confederacy. In April 1862, Union forces retook Fort Mason after a bombardment and controlled Beaufort for the rest of the war.

Camp Lejeune and Jacksonville

Midway between Beaufort and Wilmington, much of the coastline is taken over by the 100,000-acre U.S. Marine Corps base of **Camp Lejeune,** established during World War II and now home to the Weapons Training Battalion.

At the northwest corner of Camp Lejeune, **Jacksonville** (pop. 70,145) is little more than a civilian adjunct to the base, with all the gas stations, fast-food franchises, and tattoo parlors Lejeune's 45,000-plus Marines and their dependents could want. One sobering sight is on the edge of town, just off Hwy-24 opposite a Sonic Drive-In: the 50-foot-long granite wall of the **Beirut Memorial** remembers the more than 220 Camp Lejeune Marines killed in Beirut in 1983 by a suicide bomber. Alongside a list of their names are the words "They Came in Peace."

Wrightsville Beach

South of Camp Lejeune, US-17 runs through the lushly forested lowlands around Holly Ridge, while Hwy-210 cuts across a series of narrow barrier islands. The waterfront is mostly private, backed by beach house after beach house (rentals aplenty, if you can manage to stay for a full week), but with a few parking areas for passing travelers. The clean strands and clear blue waters continue through sleepy **Surf City,** home to a homespun hospital for injured loggerhead turtles, cared for by volunteers at the **Karen Beasley Sea Turtle Rescue & Rehabilitation Center** (302 Tortuga Lane, 910/329-0222).

Most of this stretch of coastline is dedicated to low-key, by-the-week family vacation rentals, but the town of **Wrightsville Beach** has a bit more going on.

sunrise on Wrightsville Beach,
seen from Blockade Runner Beach Resort

Located about five miles east of US-17 via US-74 or US-76, it's not all that different from dozens of other coastal vacation communities, but proximity to the lively city of Wilmington makes it a great place to stop. Places to stay along the beach include the comfortable **Blockade Runner Beach Resort** (275 Waynick Blvd., 910/256-2251, $110 and up), which has a good restaurant, two bars, yoga classes, fishing trips, surf lessons, and various boat rentals. Nearby, located on the mainland overlooking the Intracoastal Waterway, the **Dockside Restaurant** (1308 Airlie Rd., 910/256-2752) serves thoughtfully prepared shrimp and Southern favorites like succotash in a relaxed waterside setting.

Wilmington

Though it's surrounded by the usual miles of highway sprawl, the downtown business district of **Wilmington** (pop. 112,067) is unusually attractive and well preserved, its many blocks of historic buildings stepping up from the Cape Fear River waterfront. The largest city on the North Carolina coast, Wilmington was of vital importance to the Confederate cause during the Civil War, when it was the only Southern port able to continue exporting income-earning cotton, mostly to England, in the face of the Union blockade. Wilmington also played an important role before and during the Revolution, first as a center of colonial resistance, and later as headquarters for British general Cornwallis.

In the book and movie *Gone with the Wind*, dashing southern hero Rhett Butler spent the Civil War as a Wilmington-based blockade runner, evading the U.S. Navy.

Despite its lengthy and involved military history, Wilmington itself has survived relatively unscathed and now possesses one of the country's more engaging

USS *North Carolina*

small-town streetscapes. Cobblestone wharves and brick warehouses line the Cape Fear River, which also provides moorage for the massive 35,000-ton battleship **USS North Carolina** (daily, $14 adults), across the river. A couple of the warehouses, like the Cotton Exchange at the north end, have been converted to house boutiques and restaurants. A block inland, Front Street is the lively heart of

HURRICANES

If you're traveling along the East Coast in late summer, be aware that the farther south you go, the more likely you are to encounter one of Mother Nature's most powerful phenomena, the hurricane. All across the southeastern United States, hurricane season begins in June and lasts through November, and the threat of a storm can put a sudden end to the summer fun. Hurricanes are tropical storms covering upward of 400 square miles, with winds reaching speeds of 75 to 150 mph or more. These storms form as far away as Africa. Sophisticated warning systems are in place to give coastal visitors plenty of time to get out of harm's way. Radio and TV stations broadcast storm watches and evacuation warnings, and if you hear one, heed it and head inland to higher ground.

Even more dangerous than the high winds of a hurricane is the storm surge—a dome of ocean water that can be 20 feet high at its peak, and 50 to 100 miles wide. Ninety percent of hurricane fatalities are attributable to the high waves of a storm surge, which can wash away entire beaches and intensify flooding in coastal rivers and bays many miles upstream from the shore. The strongest hurricane recorded in the United States was the Labor Day storm of 1935, which killed 500 people and destroyed the Florida Keys Railroad. More recent hurricanes include the destructive team of Harvey, Irma, and Maria which hit Texas, Florida, Puerto Rico, and the Virgin Islands in 2017, Superstorm Sandy, which devastated New Jersey and New York in 2012, and Katrina, which hit Louisiana in 2005. The deadliest hurricane on record hit Galveston Island, Texas, early in September 1900, killing more than 6,000 people—in human terms by far the worst natural disaster in United States history.

town, a franchise-free stretch of bookshops, art galleries, clothing stores, cafés, and other businesses that are often used by film crews attempting to recreate a typically American Main Street scene. Films like *Blue Velvet* and TV's teenage soap opera *Dawson's Creek* were shot at Wilmington's massive Screen Gems studio and in surrounding locales.

Thanks in large part to its significant TV and movie-making business, Wilmington has a number of excellent places to eat, like the welcoming **Black Sea Grill** (118 S. Front St., 910/254-9990), an excellent Eastern Mediterranean bistro serving juicy lamb kebabs and fresh fish dishes. Within stumbling distance are bars like the rough-hewn **Barbary Coast** (116 S. Front St., 910/762-8996). For a taste of top-quality traditional Southern food—grits with everything—try the **Dixie Grill** (116 Market St., 910/762-7280).

Rates at Wilmington's many chain motels and hotels are comparatively low; try the riverfront **Hilton** (301 N. Water St., 910/763-5900, $152 and up).

South of Wilmington, US-17 runs inland, so if you want to stick close to the coast, take Hwy-179, which curves along the shore past the rambling towns of **Ocean Isle Beach** and **Sunset Beach** before rejoining US-17 at the South Carolina border.

Cape Fear

Though it has lent its name to two of the most terrifying movies ever made, **Cape Fear** is not at all a scary place—as long as you stay on land. The name was given to it by sailors who feared its shipwrecking shoals, and hundreds of vessels have indeed been wrecked off the cape, including dozens of Confederate blockade-runners sunk during the Civil War embargo of Wilmington harbor.

South of Wilmington, US-421 runs along the east bank of the Cape Fear River through typical barrier island beach resort towns like Carolina Beach and Kure Beach. Near the south end of the island, **Fort Fisher State Historic Site** features remains of the earthen fortification that enabled Wilmington harbor to remain open to ships throughout most of the Civil War. The fortress looks more like a series of primitive mounds than an elaborate military installation, but its simple sand piles proved more durable against Union artillery than the heavy masonry of Fort Sumter and other traditional fortresses. A visitors center (910/458-5538, Tues.-Sun. summer, Tues.-Sat. fall-spring, free) describes the fort's role, with details of the war's heaviest sea battle, when Union ships bombarded Fort Fisher in January 1865. Surrounding lands have been left wild, apart from a nice outpost of the **NC State Aquarium** (910/772-0500, daily, $11) which has tanks of local sealife.

Transcontinental I-40 starts in Wilmington and runs west to Southern California. The first stretch is named in honor of local basketball superstar Michael Jordan. Another sign gives the mileage to the road's western terminus, Barstow: 2,554.

F.º FISHER. shewing Union Attack. JAN.ᵞ 15.º 1865.

On the west bank of the Cape Fear River, Hwy-133 winds up at the pleasure-craft harbor of **Southport,** which is the halfway point between New York City and Miami, attracting sailors traveling the Intracoastal Waterway. It's also the site of the large Brunswick nuclear power plant.

Between the east and west banks of the Cape Fear River, a **ferry** (910/458-3329, www.ncdot.org/ferry) runs about once an hour between Fort Fisher and Southport.

Cape Fear itself is formed by **Bald Head Island,** at the mouth of the Cape Fear River, reachable only by boat from Southport. The **Old Baldy Lighthouse** on the island is the state's oldest, built in 1817.

SOUTH CAROLINA

Just beyond the border into South Carolina, you suddenly hit the exuberant mega-tourism of the "Grand Strand," a 25-mile-long conglomeration of resort hotels, amusement arcades, and Coney Island-style Americana that centers on **Myrtle Beach,** the state's number-one tourist destination. South of here things quiet down considerably, as coastal US-17 winds past the lush lowland marshes, passing through historic **Georgetown** and numerous preserved plantations before reaching **Charleston,** one of the most gracious and engaging cities in the southern United States.

Myrtle Beach: The Grand Strand

Standing at the center of the Grand Strand, **Myrtle Beach** (pop. 27,109) is one of the largest and most popular beach resorts in the country, attracting some 13 million visitors every year. It's a huge place, with mile after mile of motels, Walmarts, and fast-food franchises lining all the main roads. Long famous for its golf courses (and for having the world's biggest collection of miniature golf courses), in recent years Myrtle Beach has matched roller coasters and beachfront fun for shopping and merchandising. In the 1950s, Myrtle Beach was the birthplace of "The Shag," a sexually charged slow jitterbug that is now the official South Carolina state dance.

The spring- and summer-blooming crepe myrtle trees, with long branches of purple and red flowers, gave Myrtle Beach its name.

The Carolina League **Myrtle Beach Pelicans** play baseball at **TicketReturn.Com Field at Pelicans Ballpark** (843/918-6000), off US-17 next to Broadway-at-the-Beach.

Myrtle Beach Practicalities

If you don't mind keeping your tongue wedged firmly in your cheek, the Myrtle Beach area can be fun, and it's definitely a mecca for fans of ersatz "themed" restaurants: Hard Rock Café, Johnny Rockets, and Margaritaville all vie for attention in the massive Broadway-at-the-Beach complex on Celebrity Circle, northeast of US-501. Owned by the same company that tore down the Pavilion, this is the biggest attraction in Myrtle Beach, but despite the name, Broadway-at-the-Beach is over a mile from the ocean.

If you want a more genuine taste of South Carolina, some of the best places to eat are in Murrells Inlet. That said, one nice old-time Myrtle Beach restaurant is the **Sea Captain's House** (3002 N. Ocean Blvd., 843/448-8082), which has survived the developers' blitz and is still serving three delicious meals a day, just as it has since 1954. The seafood is great, and just about every table has an ocean view.

Murrells Inlet

There *may* be more picturesque places elsewhere in the state, but the as-yet-unspoiled fishing village of **Murrells Inlet,** 10 miles south of Myrtle Beach, is definitely worth a stop for the chance to sample the dozens of excellent seafood restaurants lining a short business loop off US-17. For the best and freshest

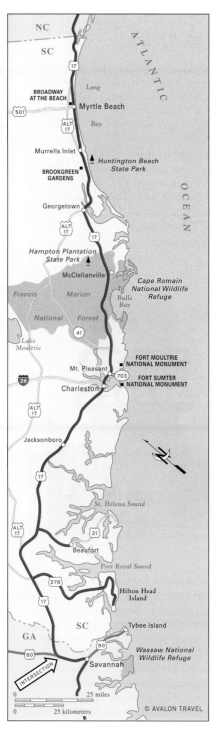

seafood and great key lime pie, head to **Flo's Place** (3797 US-17, 843/651-7222), at the north end of town, or the neon-signed **Lee's Inlet Kitchen** (4460 US-17, 843/651-2881), a mile south. And if you've got the time and inclination to catch your own seafood, you can charter a sportfishing boat from the marina, or put on some waders and head into the waters in search of clams, mussels, oysters, and crabs.

Myrtle Beach boasts more golf courses, including a bewildering array of miniature golf courses, than anywhere else in the country. Most have castaway or pirate themes; one is based upon the TV show *Gilligan's Island.*

Brookgreen Gardens and Huntington Beach State Park

One of the most popular and pleasant gardens in South Carolina, **Brookgreen Gardens** (daily, $16 adults), 18 miles south of Myrtle Beach, is a nonprofit 350-acre park on the 9,100 acres of lushly landscaped grounds of four colonial-era indigo and rice plantations. Oak trees laden with Spanish moss stand alongside palmettos, dogwoods, and azaleas, as well as hundreds of sculptures, including many done by the owner, Anna Hyatt Huntington, who developed the site in the 1930s. Alligators and otters play in the simulated swamp, and many species of birds fly around enclosed aviaries in a section of the gardens set aside as a wildlife park.

Across the highway is the 2,500-acre **Huntington Beach State Park** (843/237-4440, $5 adults), which sits on land carved out of the Huntington estate that is leased to South Carolina. Besides a nice beach and a popular campground, it features the Moorish-style castle called Atalaya ($2), Anna Huntington's winter home.

Pawleys Island and Hobcaw Barony

South of the commercial chaos of Myrtle Beach, travelers in search of serene tranquility have long appreciated **Pawleys Island.** The rope hammocks for which the island is

SOUTH OF THE BORDER

If the Grand Strand and Myrtle Beach haven't satisfied your need for roadside kitsch, or if you're bombing along I-95 looking for a place to take a break, head to **South of the Border,** the world's largest and most unapologetic tourist trap. Located just south of the North Carolina state line at I-95 exit 1, South of the Border is a crazy place with no real reason to exist, yet it draws many thousands of visitors every day to a 135-acre assembly of six restaurants, giant video arcades, souvenir shops, and innumerable signs and statues of the South of the Border mascot, Pedro.

Many roadside businesses suffered when a new interstate or bypass left them high and dry, but in the case of South of the Border, the opposite is true. It started as a fireworks and hot dog stand along US-301 in the early 1950s. But when highway engineers decided to locate I-95 here, its middle-of-nowhere locale suddenly became prime highway frontage. Owner Alan Shafer (who died in 2001 at the age of 87) made playful use of its location (50 feet south of the state line) to create this pseudo-Mexican "south of the border" village-cum-roadside rest stop. Though the complex itself is hard to miss, with its 50-foot-tall sombrero-clad Pedro and 200-foot Sombrero Observation Tower giving a panoramic view of the interstate, I-95 drivers from both directions get plenty of notice of their approach, thanks to the hundreds of garish billboards that line the road, saying silly things like "Chili Today, Hot Tamale." The subliminal messages all but force you to pull off and chow down on a taco or three and buy some mass-produced keepsake you'll throw away as soon as you get home.

South of the Border is open daily; each attraction has its own specific hours of operation. Along with the myriad tourist shlock, it also has two gas stations and a pleasant 300-room **motel** (843/774-2417, $90 and up).

Carry insect repellent and be prepared for mosquitoes, especially late in the afternoon, almost everywhere along the muggy South Carolina coast.

best known aptly symbolize this generally relaxed, weatherworn community, where a few traditional tin-roofed shacks mix with ever-increasing numbers of multimillion-dollar mock-antebellum mansions. The poet and novelist James Dickey, author of *Deliverance,* liked the island so much that he is buried in the small Pawleys Island cemetery, adjacent to All Saints Church.

An even more extensive and intimate (and affordable) taste of the old-fashioned Lowcountry life is available just down the road from Pawleys Island. Spreading along the north bank of the Pee Dee River, a mile north of Georgetown on US-17, **Hobcaw**

Greetings from SOUTH CAROLINA

Barony is a 16,000-acre estate that was once the winter hunting lodge of 1920s financier and New Deal-era statesman Bernard Baruch, who then sold it to his daughter, Belle. The extensive, mostly undeveloped grounds are home to two university research centers specializing in coastal ecology, and the main homes and plantation buildings have been kept in original condition, complete with one of only a few surviving slave villages. Along with preserving these historic quarters and the regional history they represent, the nonprofit educational foundation that runs Hobcaw Barony offers two-hour **tours** (843/546-4623, Tues.-Sat., $20, reservation required) to school groups and individuals. Tours start at the **Discovery Center Museum and Gift Shop** (Mon.-Sat., free) along US-17.

The carnivorous Venus flytrap, which Charles Darwin called "the most wonderful plant in the world," does not grow wild in any part of the world except the seacoast Carolinas.

One of the more unusual radio stations in the country, **WLGI 90.9 FM,** is operated by the Baha'i faith and broadcasts a commercial-free mix of classic 1970s soul, contemporary jazz, and messages of peace, love, and understanding. To learn more, or make a request, call 866/501-9544.

Georgetown

Site of a short-lived Spanish settlement in 1526, the first European outpost in North America, **Georgetown** later became the rice-growing center of colonial America. Bounded by the Sampit and Pee Dee Rivers and the narrow inlet of Winyah Bay, Georgetown is one of the state's few deepwater harbors and home to huge steel and paper mills along US-17. Its downtown district along Front Street is compact and comfortable, with dozens of day-to-day businesses and a few cafés and art galleries filling the many old buildings.

Three blocks south of US-17, at the east end of Front Street, there's a pleasant waterfront promenade, where the clock-towered old town market now houses the small but excellent **Rice Museum** (Mon.-Sat., $7 adults). Dioramas trace South Carolina's little-known history as the world's main rice and indigo producer, a past often overshadowed by the state's later tobacco and cotton trade. The rest of town holds many well-preserved colonial and antebellum houses, churches, and commercial buildings.

The original lyrics to Stephen Foster's song "The Old Folks at Home" began "Way down upon the Pee Dee River," though he quickly changed it to the more sonorous "Suwanee."

A couple of good places to eat in Georgetown include seafood specialties at the **River Room** (801 Front St., 843/527-4110) and the locals' favorite **Thomas Café** (703 Front St., 843/546-7776), next to the Rice Museum. For more information, or to pick up a self-guided-tour map of town, contact the **Georgetown County Chamber of Commerce** (531 Front St., 843/546-8436 or 800/777-7705), on the waterfront.

Hampton Plantation and McClellanville

The Santee Delta region along US-17 between Georgetown and Charleston once held dozens of large and hugely profitable plantations. One of the best preserved of these is now the **Hampton Plantation State Historic Site,** located 15 miles south of Georgetown, then 2 miles west of US-17. Spreading out along the northern edge of

the south facade of the Hampton Plantation house

Another South Carolina musical connection: Chubby Checker (of "The Twist" fame) was born inland from Georgetown in **Spring Gully,** near the town of Andrews.

Francis Marion National Forest, the 320-acre grounds feature a white-wood Greek Revival **manor house** (tours Fri. and Mon.-Tues. noon and 2pm, Sat.-Sun. 10am, noon, and 2pm, $7.50 adults) that once welcomed George Washington. The manor house was later home to Archibald Rutledge, poet laureate of South Carolina from 1934 until his death in 1973.

South from Hampton Plantation along US-17, a small sign marks the turnoff to the quaint Lowcountry fishing village of **McClellanville** (pop. 499). A short drive past moss-draped oak trees brings you to the town dock, where some of the last portions of South Carolina's shrimp and crab catch get unloaded and shipped to market. But some of the local shellfish doesn't travel far at all, ending up in the kitchens of **T.W. Graham & Co.** (810 Pinckney St., 843/887-4342, Tues.-Sun.), housed in a former general store just up from the docks. Graham & Co. also grills burgers and bakes great pies, so plan to stop and spend some time here.

Cape Romain National Wildlife Refuge

Dense forests stretch west from the highway, while the unspoiled **Cape Romain National Wildlife Refuge** stretches south of McClellanville nearly to Charleston, forming one of the largest and most important sanctuaries for migratory birds on the East Coast. Thousands of great blue herons, pelicans, terns, and ducks join the resident population of wild turkeys, feral pigs, deer, and alligators. To get a glimpse of the diverse life protected here, visit the **Sewee Visitor and Environmental Education Center** (843/928-3368, Wed.-Sat., free), on US-17 at Awendaw. Exhibits inside explain the natural and human history of the region, and trails outside lead to a boardwalk viewing area and an enclosure that's home to native red wolves.

Directly across from the refuge entrance on US-17, you can appreciate other aspects of the area's culture at the homey **SeeWee Restaurant** (4808 N. US-17,

843/928-3609), a general store turned restaurant serving homemade specialties, including a fabulously rich she-crab soup, served with a shot of sherry on the side. The ambience is perfect—tin cans and bottles still fill the shelves, and locals stop by to offer their catches—and the low prices and friendly people make it worth planning your trip around.

Fort Moultrie and Mount Pleasant

Sitting at the entrance to Charleston harbor, across from its better-known sibling, Fort Sumter, **Fort Moultrie** (daily, $3 adults) overlooks the Atlantic with good views of passing ships and the city of Charleston. The location alone would make Moultrie well worth a visit, but most come because of its vital role in American military history. Originally built from palmetto logs during the Revolutionary War, and since rebuilt many times, the fort is a testament to the development of coastal defenses.

Fort Moultire

Its well-preserved sections date from every major U.S. war between 1812 and World War II, when Fort Moultrie protected Charleston harbor from roving German U-boats. But the fort is most famous for its role in the events of April 1861, when Fort Moultrie touched off the Civil War by leading the bombardment of Fort Sumter.

Fort Moultrie is easy to reach. From **Mount Pleasant,** a suburban community on the north bank of the Cooper River across from Charleston, turn south from US-17 onto Hwy-703 and then follow signs along Middle Street to the fort. Along with Fort Moultrie, Mount Pleasant itself is worth visiting for the many African sweetgrass basket-makers who set up shop along US-17. While the roadside is rapidly filling up with suburban tract-house "plantations," in the warmer months women sit and weave these intricate baskets at their ramshackle stands. Like so many other Lowcountry traditions, sweetgrass weaving may soon be a lost art, as younger women are increasingly reluctant to take on this low-paid work; it can take four or five hours to weave a basket that may sell for less than $60.

You can also reach Fort Moultrie via the pleasant beach town of **Sullivan's Island,** home to two fine food stops, across the street from each other and two blocks from the beach: casual **Poe's Tavern** (2210 Middle St., 843/883-0083), where the menu includes fresh fish, beers, and burgers, and **Home Team BBQ** (2209 Middle St., 843/883-3131), for smoky ribs, moist pulled pork, and sports on TV.

Fort Sumter National Monument

Commanding an island at the mouth of Charleston Harbor, **Fort Sumter National Monument** marks the site of the first military engagement of the Civil War. On April 12, 1861, a month after Abraham Lincoln's inauguration and four months after South Carolina had seceded from the United States, Confederate guns bombarded the fort until the federal forces withdrew. The structure was badly damaged, but no one was killed and the fort was held by the Confederates for the next four years, by which time it had been almost completely flattened. Partly restored, but still a

Charleston

The Charleston accent is famous throughout the South. The word "garden" here is characteristically pronounced "gyarden," and "car" is "kyar," while the long "a" of Charleston (usually pronounced "Chaaahrleston") is as distinctive as JFK's "HAAH-vahd."

Established in 1670 as the capital of South Carolina, Charleston, more than any other Deep South city, proudly maintains the aristocratic traditions established during the plantation era. Then the elite would flee the heat, humidity, and mosquitoes of their lowland fiefdoms and come here to cavort in ballrooms and theaters. Still ruled by old money, though no longer the state capital, Charleston is both pretentious and provincial; locals like to say that Charleston is the place where the Ashley and Cooper Rivers meet to form the Atlantic Ocean. Though there are clear divides between the haves and have-nots, Charleston is surprisingly cosmopolitan, accommodating a historic ethnic mix of French Huguenots, Catholic Acadians, and Afro-Caribbeans, who collectively introduced the wrought-iron balconies and brightly colored cottages that give the city much of its charm. George Gershwin's opera *Porgy and Bess*, for example, was inspired by life in Charleston's Creole ghetto, specifically Cabbage Row, now a tidy brick-paved alley off Church Street.

Despite suffering through a devastating earthquake, two wars, and innumerable hurricanes, resilient Charleston remains one of the South's most beautiful cities. Impressive neoclassical buildings line the streets, especially in the older, upmarket sections of town south of Broad Street and along the waterfront Battery. Charleston's many small lush gardens and parks make it ideal for aimless exploring on foot rather than by car. If you'd like a friendly, intelligent guide to show you around, contact Ed Grimball (843/813-4447).

The Civil War Fort Sumter and many of the mansions and churches are all open to visitors, but it's the overall fabric of Charleston, rather than specific sites, that is

Edmondston-Alston House

C.T. 1—The Old Market, Charleston, S. C. "America's Must Historic City"

most memorable. That said, the 1828 Greek Revival **Edmondston-Alston House** (21 E. Battery, daily, $12) is definitely worth a look, as is the beautiful spire of **St. Michael's Episcopal Church** (71 Broad St., daily) which was modeled on the London churches of Christopher Wren. A quarter mile north, at Meeting and Market Streets, is the mostly open-air **City Market,** known as the "Ellis Island of Black America," since 40 to 60 percent of enslaved people arrived in the colonies here. The market now houses a range of souvenir shops and touristy restaurants.

The **Charleston RiverDogs** (843/723-7241), a Yankees farm team, play ball on the banks of the Ashley River.

Charleston's annual arts-and-opera **Spoleto Festival USA** (843/579-3100) is held over two weeks in May and June.

PRACTICALITIES

Charleston supports a number of excellent eateries at all price ranges. In the center of town, great meals are available at the popular **Hominy Grill** (207 Rutledge Ave., 843/937-0930) and **Toast** (155 Meeting St., 843/534-0043). Around the City Market, you'll find **Hyman's Seafood** (215 Meeting St., 843/723-6000), which has a variety of fresh fish entrées for around $15-20; expect a wait. More sedate and expensive dinner places include the stylish **SNOB** (Slightly North of Broad; 192 E. Bay St., 843/723-3424) and **Magnolias** (185 E. Bay St., 843/577-7771), serving inventive takes on traditional Lowcountry food.

Charleston's accommodations tend toward the luxurious and expensive. Dozens of old-fashioned but well-appointed B&Bs charge upward of $200. The elegant **John Rutledge House** (116 Broad St., 800/476-9741) offers four-star comfort in a converted 1763 house. Fronting the Battery, the romantic Queen Anne **Two Meeting Street Inn** (2 Meeting St., 843/723-7322) has been welcoming guests for over 50 years. Hotels in the historic district are similarly expensive, though you'll find a handy **Days Inn** (155 Meeting St., 843/371-3850, $101 and up) downtown. Families will appreciate the large rooms and big made-to-order breakfast at **Embassy Suites** (337 Meeting St., 843/723-6900, $129 and up), housed inside the original Citadel.

The **Charleston Visitor Center** (375 Meeting St., 800/774-0006, daily) is a good first stop. It is free to ride the DASH shuttle buses that follow several routes downtown.

powerful symbol of the destruction wrought by the war, Fort Sumter is a key stop on any tour of Civil War sites.

You can visit Fort Sumter by taking your personal boat or by taking a **ferry tour boat** (843/722-2628, $21); they leave from **Patriot's Point,** just off US-17's soaring cable-stayed bridge across the Cooper River. (Other boats to Fort Sumter dock at the Fort Sumter Visitor

the USS *Yorktown,* at Patriot's Point

Education Center in downtown Charleston.) Patriot's Point is also the anchorage of the aircraft carrier **USS Yorktown** (daily, $22), centerpiece of an excellent floating maritime museum that also includes World War II-era fighter planes, a destroyer that took part in D-Day, a River Patrol boat, and a Cold War-era submarine.

Beaufort

The second-oldest town in South Carolina, **Beaufort** (pop. 12,361; pronounced "BYOO-furd") is a well-preserved antebellum town stretching along a fine natural harbor. Established in 1710, Beaufort stands on the largest of some 75 islands near the Georgia border; the town is perhaps best known as the gateway to the massive U.S. Marine Corps Recruit Depot at nearby **Parris Island,** where new Marines undergo their basic training. Dozens of colonial-era and antebellum homes line Beaufort's quiet Bay Street waterfront, but only one, the **Verdier House,** is open to visitors. Perhaps the most significant home, once owned by slave-turned-Civil War naval hero and Reconstruction-era U. S. Congressman **Robert Smalls,** stands flanked by palmetto trees at 511 Prince Street; Smalls lived here as a slave, then later bought the house from his former owner. A memorial statue stands just north of downtown in the cemetery of Tabernacle Baptist Church (907 Craven St.), where Smalls is buried.

Beaufort is an enjoyable place to wander around and explore, and it has at least one great place to eat: **Blackstone's Café** (205 Scott St., 843/524-4330), where fans of the shrimp and grits and corned beef hash include local writer Pat Conroy. Places to stay include the waterfront **Best Western Sea Island Inn** (1015 Bay St., 843/522-2090) and one of the state's only recently awarded four-star B&Bs, the lovely **Rhett House Inn** (1009 Craven St., 843/524-9030, $179 and up), where the film *The Prince of Tides* was shot on location.

St. Helena Island

As recently as 1960, the population of South Carolina's rural Sea Islands was predominantly African American—10 to 1 on average. Now, with all the recent "plantation-style" vacation resorts, the proportions have effectively been reversed. As a last defense against the dark arts of resort developers, traditional African-American Gullah culture is celebrated in summer festivals and tourism literature promoting the **Gullah-Geechee Heritage Coast.** The centerpiece of Gullah cultural preservation is **St. Helena Island,** due east from Beaufort, where the Penn Center, a historic

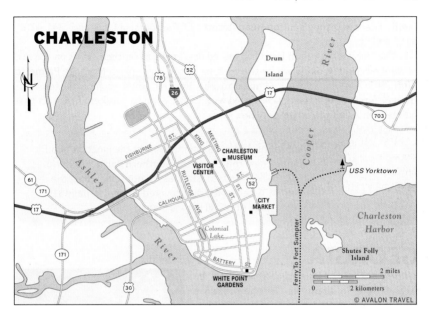

African-American educational center founded by abolitionists in 1862, was the first school in the Deep South dedicated to educating newly emancipated slaves. Recently awarded federal support as part of the new Reconstruction Era National Monument, the Penn Center has remained a vital contributor to civil rights and social justice. The Penn Center is open to the public, but until the new national monument is developed, the best taste of St. Helena may well be the **Gullah Grub Restaurant** (877 Sea Island Parkway, 843/838-3841, lunch and early dinner Sun.-Fri.), across from the Penn Center entrance. Dishes often include unusual strains of rice and other rare produce, through which chef Bill Green highlights links between Gullah heritage and the 400-plus-year story of African-American enslavement, freedom, and creativity. Menu items feature the whole Gullah taxonomy: local seafood, cornbread, and collard greens as well as more familiar mac 'n' cheese. Everything tastes good; Anthony Bourdain is a fan.

Along the Savannah River, which marks the boundary between South Carolina and Georgia, Eli Whitney invented the cotton gin in 1793 at **Mulberry Grove** plantation.

Hilton Head

From Beaufort, the easiest way south is to follow Hwy-170 all the way to Savannah or to detour east onto I-95. Otherwise, a pleasant but potentially confusing series of two-lane roads run around **Hilton Head Island** across the lowlands toward Georgia. Near the southern tip of South Carolina, Hilton Head Island is the largest ocean island between Florida and New Jersey. It was first settled in 1663, but only since the late 1950s, when a bridge to the mainland was completed, has it really been on the map. The deluxe 60-guest room, 5,000-acre **Sea Pines Resort** (32 Greenwood Dr., 866/561-8802, $161 and up) is an international destination. Upscale golf courses and plantation-style estates abound around the island's 30,000 acres, as do mini-malls and all the trappings of suburban America. There's also a popular family-friendly **Disney's Hilton Head Resort** (22 Harbourside Lane, 843/341-4100, $133 and up).

The "success" of Hilton Head has caused developers to set their sights on the rest of the Lowcountry, as shown by the opening of the super-plush **Montage Palmetto Bluff** (843/706-6500, $295 and up) at nearby Bluffton, where each of the 44 waterfront or forest-view cottages is outfitted with LCD TVs and a Sub-Zero fridge for that quintessential Lowcountry experience.

The beautiful city of Savannah marks the junction of our Atlantic Coast route with the **Southern Pacific** road trip along US-80. Some coastal destinations, including the excellent **Tybee Island,** are covered there (see page 818). Full coverage of US-80 begins on page 762.

GEORGIA

The marshes and barrier islands that line the Atlantic Ocean along the Georgia coast are among the lesser-known treasures of the eastern United States. Geographically, the coastline consists of mostly roadless and largely unconnected islands, which makes coastal driving nearly impossible; the nearest north-south routes, I-95 and the older US-17, run roughly 15 miles inland, and only a few roads head east to the Atlantic shore. The lack of access has kept development to a minimum and has also been a boon to wildlife—well over half the coastline is protected within state and federal parks, preserves, and refuges.

The "you can't get there from here" aspect can make it more than a little frustrating for casual visitors, but if you have the time and inclination, it also makes the Georgia coast a wonderful place to explore. One of the main car-friendly destinations along the Georgia coast is **Tybee Island** in the north, east of Savannah. Farther south, take time to explore the beautiful and history-rich **Golden Isles,** east of Brunswick. Both are great places to visit, and they offer an appetizing taste of the 100 miles of isolated shoreline Georgia otherwise keeps to itself.

Midway: The Smallest Church in America

The section of US-17 south of the Ogeechee River, off I-95 between exits 14 and 12, offers shunpikers (those who shun turnpikes) a 24-mile taste of old-style Lowland Georgia. Sometimes called the Old Atlantic Highway, it is a textbook example of how traveling the two-lane highways is superior in almost every way to hustling down the interstates. Midway along, the coincidentally named town of **Midway** (pop. 2,121) was founded back in 1754 by a band of New England colonists, two of whom (Lyman Hall and Button Guinett) went on to sign the Declaration of Independence as Georgia's self-declared representatives to the Continental Congress. The centerpiece of Midway, then and now, is 200-year-old **Midway Church,** which preserves the original pulpit and slave gallery; visitors are allowed only with a docent from the

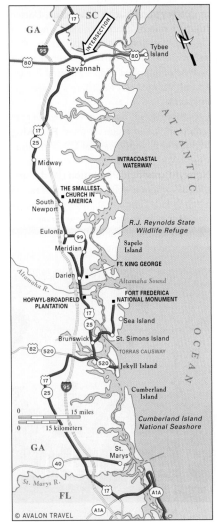

adjacent **Midway Museum** (912/884-5837, Tues.-Sat., $10 adults).

South of Midway along US-17, a small sign on the east side of the highway (a mile south of I-95 exit 67) points travelers toward the **"Smallest Church in America,"** a 12-seat cabin that's open 24 hours. (The original Smallest Church opened in the 1960s, burned down in 2015, and was quickly rebuilt.) Besides the kitsch value, there's another good reason to keep an eye out for the Smallest Church: six miles east of the church, a mile from the shore down Harris Neck Road, the wonderfully named and nearly world-famous **Old School Diner** (912/832-2136, Wed.-Sun., cash only) serves up generous portions of fantastically flavorful seafood, barbecue ribs, chicken, and more. Only a half hour from Savannah, it's worth a trip from just about anywhere.

Sapelo Island and Darien

Though coastal Georgia has by and large been spared the worst excesses of real estate development, for an unforgettable taste of the *real* pre-tourist industry Georgia culture, make your way east to **Sapelo Island,** which stretches offshore between Midway and Darien. The island is a stark, sparsely populated, mostly undeveloped, and generally fascinating place to spend some time, a truly wild landscape where alligators and ferocious feral pigs live free among remnants of colonial-era plantation agriculture and shell middens of the Muscogee people dating back 6,000 years. Once a cotton plantation, worked by enslaved people whose 70-odd descendants live in **Hog Hammock,** Sapelo's only permanent community, the island is now owned by the state of Georgia and used as a marine biology research center.

A compelling nonfiction account of 1970s Darien, Melissa Fay Greene's *Praying for Sheetrock* describes how locals and legal activists used federal lawsuits to overcome the corrupt regimes of local government and law enforcement officials.

There is no real commercial development on Sapelo Island—no stores and no restaurants, except for a small convenience store, so bring your own food and drink—just miles of beaches, marshlands, and open sea. Get here from the mainland hamlet of **Meridian,** where you can catch the state-run ferry for a four-hour **guided tour** (912/437-3224, reservations required, $15 adults, $10 children), which gives a full introduction to Sapelo Island life.

South of Sapelo Island near the mouth of the Altamaha River, which formed the rough and frequently fought-over boundary between British and Spanish parts of the New World, **Darien** (pop. 1,975) looks a lot like most other coastal Deep South towns, but it boasts a history to match many bigger or more famous destinations. After a small 16th-century Spanish mission near here was destroyed by Native Americans, Darien was founded in 1736 by Scottish colonists (many named McIntosh, now the name of the surrounding county) near Fort King George, the first British outpost in what became Georgia. Darien later became a center of the lucrative early-19th-century rice trade, surrounded by plantations where the abuse of enslaved people inspired British actress Fanny Kemble's book-length indictment, *Journal of a Residence on a Georgia Plantation in 1838-39,* an influential abolitionist text.

Despite the many claims it could make to importance, Darien preserves its past in a matter-of-fact manner. The main attraction is the reconstructed **Fort King George** (Tues.-Sun., $7.50 adults), a state historic site, a mile east of US-17 on Fort King George Drive.

Another intriguing place to visit is the **Hofwyl-Broadfield Plantation** (Wed.-Sun., $8 adults), five miles south of Darien along US-17, where a well-preserved plantation home is surrounded by 1,200 acres of one-time rice fields that have reverted to cypress swamps. Displays inside the visitors center tell the story of how slaves were forced to labor in the sweltering, mosquito-plagued summer heat, building levees and doing the backbreaking work of planting, growing, and harvesting the rice.

Brunswick: The Golden Isles

Along the southeast Georgia coast, a patchwork of islands known as the **Golden Isles** offer a wide range of images and experiences. The largest and best known, **St. Simons Island,** is a mini Hilton Head, with many vacation resorts and a sizable year-round community. At the south tip of the island is a central plaza and a few blocks of shops, saloons, and restaurants along Mallery Street, which leads down to the waterfront pier and a circa-1872 lighthouse. Sea kayaks, bicycles, and boats are available for rent, and there are a number of reasonable motels.

St. Simon's Island Light Station

Also on St. Simon's, right at the heart of the island, purist wood-smoke barbecue fans flock to **Southern Soul Barbeque** (2020 Demere Rd., 912/638-7685) for juicy melt-in-the-mouth ribs, pulled pork, sandwiches, and an excellent version of Brunswick stew (pork, chicken, beef, corn, beans, and more mixed up in a rich tomato barbecue sauce).

Apart from the excellent food, the one real "sight" on St. Simons Island is the **Fort Frederica National Monument,** at the northwest edge of the island, which protects the remains of the village surrounding what was once the largest fortress in the British colonies. Built in 1736 and abandoned in 1763, Fort Frederica played a vital role in keeping Georgia British rather than Spanish; in 1742 a key battle was fought six miles south of the fort at a site known as "Bloody Marsh."

> Georgia's most famous 19th-century poet, Sidney Lanier, settled near Brunswick after contracting tuberculosis as a POW during the Civil War. He wrote his most famous poems, including "The Marshes of Glynn," while he sat under an oak tree that stands along US-17, a mile north of town.

For the total Golden Isles experience, splurge on a night or two at one of the country's plushest resorts: the five-star **The Cloister at Sea Island** (855/572-4975, $395 and up), east of Fort Frederica, which covers adjacent Sea Island with three 18-hole of golf courses and 265 Spanish-style rooms. Presidents from Coolidge to Bush have vacationed here, and the G8 economic summit has been held here too, which should give you some idea of the elite character of the place.

Back on the mainland, heavily industrialized **Brunswick** (pop. 15,385) feels about as far from the genteel pleasures of the Golden Isles as you can be. Most vacationers pass through quickly on their way to and from the Golden Isles. Brunswick holds a road food attraction: **Willie's Wee-Nee Wagon** (3599 Altama Ave., 912/264-1146), a yellow-red-and-white candy-striped diner, a mile west of US-17 across from the College of Coastal Georgia. Famous for all sorts of good things—crunchy coleslaw, chili dogs, pork chops, steak sandwiches, and more—Willie's is something of a Georgia coast institution, and well worth searching for.

Jekyll Island

Southeast of Brunswick, and developed in the late 1880s as a private members-only resort for New York multimillionaires, **Jekyll Island** now offers a chance for those

not in control of a Fortune 500 company to enjoy a generous slice of Golden Isles life. Owned by the state of Georgia, a grand hotel and dozens of palatial vacation "cottages" that would look equally at home in Newport, Rhode Island, are accessible to anyone after a long life spent catering to the richest of the rich.

At the center of the island, and the best place

Georgia Sea Turtle Center, Jekyll Island

Savannah

Named the "Most Beautiful City in North America" by the Parisian newspaper and style arbiter *Le Monde,* Savannah (pop. 136,286) is a real jewel of a place. Founded in 1733 as the first settlement in Georgia, the 13th and final American colony, Savannah today preserves its original neoclassical, colonial, and antebellum self in a welcoming, unselfconscious way. Famous for having been spared by General Sherman on his destructive March to the Sea at the end of the Civil War, it was here that Sherman made his offering of "40 acres and a mule" to all freed slaves.

Bonaventure Cemetery

Before and after the war, Savannah was Georgia's main port, rivaling Charleston, South Carolina, for the enormously lucrative cotton trade, but as commercial shipping tailed off, the harbor became increasingly recreational—the yachting competitions of the 1996 Olympics were held offshore. Savannah, home of writer Flannery O'Connor and songsmith Johnny Mercer, also served as backdrop to the best-selling book *Midnight in the Garden of Good and Evil* and numerous movies, most famously *Forrest Gump,* but it has resisted urges to turn itself into an "Old South" theme park; you'll have to search hard to find souvenir shops or overpriced knickknack galleries. The city is in such good shape partly thanks to the Savannah College of Art and Design (SCAD), which has taken over many of the city's older buildings and converted them into art studios, galleries, and cafés.

At the center of Savannah, midway down Bull Street between the waterfront and spacious Forsyth Park, **Chippewa Square** was the site of Forrest Gump's bus bench; the movie prop was moved to the **Savannah History Museum** (303 MLK Jr. Blvd., 912/651-6825, daily 9am-5:30pm, $7) and may one day be erected in bronze. **Reynolds Square,** near the waterfront, has a statue of John Wesley, who lived in Savannah in 1736-1737 and established the world's first Sunday school here. **Wright Square** holds a monument to Chief Tomochichi, the Native American leader who allowed Georgia founder James Edward Oglethorpe to settle here. At the south edge of the historic center, **Forsyth Park,** inspired by the Place de la Concorde in Paris, is surrounded by richly scented magnolias.

Another great place to wander is **Factor's Walk,** a promontory along the Savannah River named for the "factors" who controlled Savannah's cotton trade. This area holds the Cotton Exchange and other historic buildings, many of them constructed from 18th-century ballast stones. Linked from the top of the bluffs by a network of steep stone stairways and cast-iron walkways, **River Street** is lined by restaurants, and at the east end there's a statue of a girl waving a cloth; it was erected in memory of Florence Martus, who for 44 years around the turn of the 20th century greeted every ship entering Savannah harbor in the vain hope that her boyfriend would be on board.

March is when things get crazy here in Savannah: Thousands of visitors come to the bars along Congress Street for what has grown into the world's second-largest **St. Patrick's Day** celebration—only New York City's is bigger.

One of Savannah's more unusual tourist attractions is the **Juliette Gordon Low Birthplace** (10 E. Oglethorpe Ave.), a circa-1820 house that was the childhood home of the woman who introduced Girl Scouts to America in 1912.

PRACTICALITIES

Getting around is blissfully easy: Savannah is the country's preeminent walkers' town, with a wealth of historic architecture and a checkerboard of 22 small squares shaded with centuries-old live oak trees draped with tendrils of Spanish moss, all packed together in a single square mile. Savannah's sensible and attractive modified grid plan makes finding your way so simple that it's almost fun to try to get lost.

For an unforgettable midday meal, be sure to stop at **Mrs. Wilkes' Dining Room** (107 W. Jones St., 912/232-5997, Mon.-Fri. 11am-2pm Feb.-Dec., all you can eat $22), a central Savannah home and former boardinghouse that still offers up seasonal, traditional family-style Southern cooking—varying from fried chicken to beef stews, with side dishes like okra gumbo, blueberry pie, red or brown rice, and cornbread. It's worth a trip from anywhere in the state—don't leave Savannah without eating here. For a more upscale take on these Deep South classics, make plans to have lunch or dinner at

St. Patrick's Day celebrators

The Olde Pink House (23 Abercorn St., 912/232-4286), on Reynolds Square. For an only-in-Savannah mix of Mississippi barbecue in a vintage New England diner, step inside the 1930s Worcester Lunch Car, housing the **Sandfly BBQ** (1220 Barnard St., 912/335-8058, Mon.-Sat.).

Places to stay in Savannah vary from quaint B&B inns to stale high-rise hotels. For the total Savannah experience, try the **Bed and Breakfast Inn** (117 W. Gordon St., 912/238-0518, $159 and up), which has nice rooms in an 1853 townhouse off Monterey Square. At the **River Street Inn** (124 E. Bay St., 912/234-6400, $149 and up), well-appointed rooms fill a converted antebellum cotton warehouse, right on Factor's Walk at the heart of the Savannah riverfront. Nearby, the large **Hotel Indigo** (201 W. Bay St., 912/236-4440, $124 and up) has good-size hotel rooms (in the former Inn at Ellis Square) a few blocks from Factor's Walk.

The main **Savannah visitors center** (301 Martin Luther King Blvd., 912/944-0455), in the old Georgia Central railroad terminal in the historic district, has free maps and brochures and other information on the city.

to start a visit, is the landmark **Jekyll Island Club Hotel** (855/535-9547, $129 and up). The pleasant rooms here aren't *all* that expensive, considering the luxury you're swaddled in, and the setting is superb. Majestic oak trees dangling garlands of Spanish moss cover the 240-acre grounds, and within a short walk, many of the grand old mansions are now open for **guided tours** ($16 adults). The nearby stables have been converted into a nice little **museum** (daily, free), which tells the whole Jekyll Island story.

One new development here has been the **Georgia Sea Turtle Center** (214 Stable Rd., 912/635-4444, $7 adults), housed in the old Jekyll Island power plant. This is one of the prime places for the study and rehabilitation of these lyrical swimmers, whose native habitats have been threatened by all the housing and resort development along the Atlantic shore.

Less than a mile east, the Atlantic oceanfront is lined by Beachview Drive and a five-mile-long beach—with the least developed stretches at the north and south ends of the island. **Bike rentals** (912/635-9801, $6 per hour)—which really provide the best way to see the island—are available along Beachview Drive at the Days Inn and Suites.

St. Marys, Georgia, the main access to Cumberland Island, is also home to the huge Kings Bay U.S. Navy Base, home port of the nuclear-powered and armed Atlantic submarine fleet.

Cumberland Island National Seashore

Right on the Florida border, and once the private reserve of the Carnegie family, the **Cumberland Island National Seashore** is a 99 percent uninhabited barrier island with miles of hiking trails and primitive backcountry camping along beaches and in palmetto forests. Also here is the unique **Greyfield Inn** (904/261-6408, around $425 and up), the Carnegie family mansion now operated by Carnegie heirs as an unpretentious 16-room historic lodge; a stay here includes gourmet meals, cocktail hour, gear rentals, and transportation from the mainland. (Bring your own bug spray!)

Unless you're a guest at the Greyfield, Cumberland Island is only accessible by a twice-daily **ferry** ($28 round-trip plus $7 entrance fee) from the town of **St. Marys,** 10 miles east of I-95 exit 3. For further details, contact the Cumberland Island National Seashore **information and reservations center** (877/860-6787).

FLORIDA

Stretching some 600 miles between the Georgia border and Key West at its far southern tip, Florida offers something for everyone, from unsullied nature to the tackiest tourist traps in the land, and everything imaginable in between. More than anywhere else in the United States, the Florida landscape has been designed for tourists, and no matter what your fancy or fantasy, you can live it here, under the semitropical sun. The many millions who visit Disney World or flock to fashionable Miami Beach each year are doing exactly what people have come to Florida to do for over a century—enjoy themselves.

In the 1930s, when car travel and Florida tourism were both reaching an early peak of popularity, the roadside landscape was, in the words of the WPA *Guide to Florida,* lined by

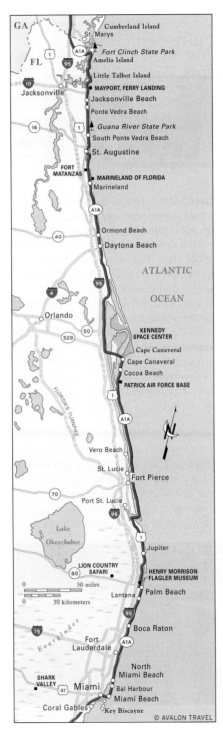

signs that turn like windmills; startling signs that resemble crashed airplanes; signs with glass lettering which blaze forth at night when automobile headlights strike them; flashing neon signs; signs painted with professional touch; signs crudely lettered and misspelled. They advertise hotels, tourist cabins, fishing camps, and eating places. They extol the virtues of ice creams, shoe creams, cold creams; proclaim the advantages of new cars and used cars; tell of 24-hour towing and ambulance service, Georgia pecans, Florida fruit and fruit juices, honey, soft drinks, and furniture. They urge the traveler to take designated tours, to visit certain cities, to stop at certain points he must see.

Despite the modern gloss of golf course estates and sprawling retirement communities, which tend to overshadow the substantial stretches of wide open beaches and coastal forest, Florida has a lengthy and fascinating history, with significant Native American cultures and, in **St. Augustine,** some of the oldest signs of European presence in North America, including the legendary Fountain of Youth. At the other end of the state, on the fringes of the Caribbean, **Key West** is a tropical paradise, founded by pirates four centuries ago and still one of the most lively and anarchic places in the United States. In between, our road-trip route passes through such diverse places as **Daytona Beach,** mecca for race car fans and a magnet for college kids on spring break; the launch

Of all the American colonies, only Florida remained loyal to the British crown during the Revolutionary War. After the war, the British ceded Florida to Spain, which eventually swapped it to the United States in 1821 in exchange for $5 million in assumed debt.

pads and mission control centers of the **Kennedy Space Center;** the multicultural melting pots of **Miami** and **Miami Beach;** and, of course, the "Happiest Place on Earth," **Disney World.**

There are three main routes running north-south along Florida's Atlantic coastline, and your travels will likely make use of at least a little of each one. The fastest route is the I-95 freeway, which races uneventfully along, linking the major cities. The most scenic route is Hwy-A1A, a mostly two-lane highway that runs as close as possible to the shoreline, linking many gorgeous beaches but, because of the flat topography and the extensive beachfront development, offering only rare glimpses of the open ocean. In between I-95 and Hwy-A1A runs historic US-1, part of the old Dixie Highway, which is lined by reminders of Florida's rich roadside heritage but which also passes through some of the state's less salubrious corners, especially in and around the larger cities. Our suggested route primarily follows coastal Hwy-A1A, but directions from other, faster routes are also given, so you can alternate freely and easily among them all.

Two men who made millions in the automobile industry have had immeasurable influence over the evolution of the Florida coast. Standard Oil baron Henry Flagler constructed the first railroad and built a chain of deluxe resort hotels from St. Augustine to Miami, while Carl Fisher, the developer of car headlights, promoted Florida's "Route 66," the Dixie Highway, and later helped to found Miami Beach. Their names reappear frequently wherever you travel along Florida's Atlantic Coast.

Amelia Island

Entering Florida from Georgia across the St. Marys River, which flows east out of the Okefenokee Swamp to the Atlantic Ocean, you may want to skirt around the metropolitan sprawl of Jacksonville by following old US-17, or getting off I-95 at exit 129, to Hwy-A1A, which runs due east to the brilliant white-sand beaches and picturesque historic buildings of **Amelia Island.** The main community on the island is **Fernandina Beach** (pop. 11,487), once the main port in northeast

Florida. The eastern terminus of the first trans-Florida railroad, and long a popular tourist destination, Fernandina Beach retains many late-Victorian buildings, collected together in a wanderable 50-block historic district along the Amelia Island bay front.

A local landmark, the **Florida House Inn** (22 S. 3rd St., 904/491-3322, $120 and

Forth Clinch State Park

An anhinga female guards a nest on Amelia Island.

up) is Florida's oldest hotel, welcoming travelers since 1857, while at the center of town the lively **Palace Saloon** (117 Centre St., 844/421-2444) is another of "Florida's Oldest," with a lovely carved wood bar, great punch, and regular live music.

More history has been preserved at the north end of Amelia Island, adjacent to Fernandina Beach, where the well-preserved remnants of a pre-Civil War brick fortress stand in **Fort Clinch State Park** (904/277-7274, daily, $6 per car, $2 per person for the fort), with over 1,400 acres of marshes, sand dunes, and coastal hammock forests, plus a nice campground, along the edge of Cumberland Sound.

South of Fernandina Beach, Hwy-A1A follows Fletcher Avenue along Amelia Island's gorgeous white beaches, passing upscale resorts (including a Ritz-Carlton) before crossing over a bridge onto Talbot Island. Amid the dense native jungles of **Little Talbot Island,** a large **state park** (904/251-2320, daily dawn-dusk, $5 per car) has hiking and cycling trails, a nice campground, and a magnificent beach. Four miles south of the bridge, there's a turnoff west to the 3,000-acre **Kingsley Plantation** (904/251-3537, daily, free), the last remaining antebellum plantation in Florida. You can explore the elegant old lodge and remains of more than 20 slave cabins on the grounds. The house is closed during the week for renovations but is open for tours on weekends with reservations. The scenic road, which has been dubbed the "Buccaneer Trail," eventually ends up at the terminal for the **ferry to Mayport** (every 30 minutes) across the St. Johns River.

Jacksonville Beach

East of Jacksonville, at the mouth of the St. Johns River, Hwy-A1A curves around a large U.S. Navy base (third largest in the country, specializing in helicopters, which you'll often see hovering overhead), past the busy Bath Iron Works shipyard and the sizable fishing port of **Mayport,** where you can enjoy a quick bite at **Singleton's Seafood Shack** (4728 Ocean St., 904/246-4442), about 170 yards west of the ferry landing. From Mayport, Hwy-A1A zigzags inland south and east, reaching the water again at **Jacksonville Beach,** a welcoming, family-oriented community with the usual gauntlet of cafés, mini-golf courses, and video arcades, and a nice beachfront centering on a small pier.

South of Jacksonville Beach spreads the enclave of **Ponte Vedra Beach,** where country club resorts replace roadside sprawl. Hwy-A1A bends inland through here,

Double-A farm club for the Miami Marlins, the **Jacksonville Jumbo Shrimp** play ball at a nice $35 million downtown stadium (904/358-2846).

Jacksonville, which covers over 840 square miles, is the largest city by area in the continental United States.

HENRY FLAGLER:
FATHER OF FLORIDA TOURISM

Though you've probably never heard of the man, you can't travel far along the east coast of Florida without coming under the influence of Henry Flagler, who almost single-handedly turned what had been swampy coastline into one of the world's most popular tourist destinations. After making a fortune as John D. Rockefeller's partner in the Standard Oil Company, in the early 1880s Flagler came to St. Augustine with his wife, who was suffering from health problems. He found the climate agreeable, but the facilities sorely lacking, so he embarked on construction of the 540-room Hotel Ponce de León, which opened in 1888. The hotel, the first major resort in Florida, was an instant success, and Flagler quickly expanded his operations, building the first railroad along the coast south to Palm Beach, where he opened the world's largest hotel, the now-demolished Royal Poinciana, in 1894, joined by The Breakers in 1901 and his own palatial home, Whitehall, in 1902.

Meanwhile, Flagler was busy extending his railroad south, effectively founding the new city of Miami in 1897 when he opened the deluxe Royal Palm Hotel. From Miami, he decided to extend his Florida East Coast Railway all the way to Key West, which at the time was Florida's most populous city and the American deep-water port closest to the proposed Panama Canal. At a cost of $50 million and hundreds of lives, this amazing railroad was completed in 1912, but it lasted only two decades before a hurricane destroyed the tracks in 1935. The remnants of Flagler's railroad were used as the foundation for today's Overseas Highway, US-1, but Flagler himself never lived to see it: In 1913, a year after his railroad reached Key West, Henry Flagler fell down a flight of stairs and died at age 84.

Whitehall, formerly Flagler's home in Palm Beach, is now the Henry Morrison Flagler Museum.

so if you want to keep close to the shore (most of which is private), follow Hwy-203 instead, rejoining Hwy-A1A on the edge of town.

South of Ponte Vedra, Hwy-A1A passes a pair of beachfront state parks: the marvelous 9,815-acre **Guana River** and smaller **South Ponte Vedra,** both of which give access to usually uncrowded sands.

Fountain of Youth

North of St. Augustine, Hwy-A1A cuts inland from the shore, crossing a bridge over the Tolomato River, then following San Marco Avenue south into the center of St. Augustine past the **Fountain of Youth** (904/829-3168, daily 9am-6pm, $15 adults). That's right, the Fountain of Youth. Though its efficacy has never been proven in court, there is an actual site where Spanish explorer Ponce de León, searching for a fabled spring that would keep him forever young, came ashore in 1513. Now a pleasant 20-acre park, facing Matanzas Bay about a mile north of central St. Augustine, the Fountain of Youth preserves a naturally sulfurous spring (which you can drink from using Dixie cups—though there are no guarantees of immortality!), a burial ground, and remnants of an indigenous Timucuan village and an early Spanish settlement.

St. Augustine

If you like history, architecture, sandy beaches, bizarre tourist attractions—or any combination of the above—you'll want to spend some time in **St. Augustine.** The oldest permanent settlement in the United States—though Santa Fe, New Mexico, makes a strong counterclaim to this title—St. Augustine was founded in 1565, half a century after Ponce de León first set foot here in 1513, looking for the Fountain of Youth. Under Spanish control, the town's early history was pretty lively, with Francis Drake leveling the place in 1586. The British, after trading Cuba for Florida at the end of the Seven Years' War, took control in 1763 and held St. Augustine throughout the American Revolution—during which Florida was staunchly loyal to King George. It served for many years as capital of Florida under both the British and Spanish, but after the Americans took over, the city lost that status to Tallahassee. St. Augustine subsequently missed out on much of Florida's 20th-century growth

and development, which has allowed the preservation of its substantial historical remnants.

The heart of St. Augustine is contained within a walkably small area, centered on the Plaza de la Constitución, which faces east onto Matanzas Bay. Pedestrianized St. George Street runs north and south from here through the heart of historic St. Augustine, while two blocks west stand the city's most prominent landmarks: two grand early 1900s hotels, the **Ponce de Leon** and the **Alcazar.** They were originally owned and operated as part of Henry Flagler's Florida empire, but now respectively house **Flagler College** and the decorative arts collections of the **Lightner Museum** (daily, $10 adults). Both are full of finely crafted interior spaces and well worth a look.

Quaint Old St. George Street, St. Augustine, Florida

The Oldest City in the United States

Though it's the compact size and overall historic sheen of St. Augustine that make it such a captivating place to spend some time, there are lots of individual attractions hawking themselves as important "historic sites," usually the oldest this-or-that in Florida, or even in the whole United States. The **Oldest Wooden Schoolhouse** (14 St. George St.), in the heart of historic St. Augustine, dates from 1750 and now features animatronic figures of the school teacher and students. The **Oldest Store Museum** (167 San Marco Ave.), has 100,000 items, all of them well past their turn-of-the-20th-century sell-by date. Continuing south down San Marco Avenue (Hwy-A1A) leads to another must-see tourist trap: the original **Ripley's Believe It or Not! Museum** (904/824-1606, daily, $16), an elaborate Spanish Revival mansion filled since 1950 with Robert Ripley's personal collection of oddities. Outside, in the parking lot, is a four-room "tree house," carved out of a California redwood tree in 1957.

Across the street from the Ripley's Believe It or Not!, a coquina stone ball known as the Zero Milepost marks the eastern end of the **Old Spanish Trail,** one of the earliest transcontinental highways. Marked and promoted from here west to San Diego, the Old Spanish Trail, like the Lincoln Highway and the Dixie Highway, preceded the system of numbered highways (Route 66 et al.) and provided a popular cross-country link.

These are fun in a tongue-in-cheek way, but the most impressive historic site is the remarkable **Castillo de San Marcos** (daily, $10 adults), which dominates the St. Augustine waterfront. Built by Spain between 1672 and 1695, the Castillo saw its first battle in 1702, when British forces laid siege for 50 days but were unable to capture it, though they did once again level the adjacent town of St. Augustine. The Castillo was later used by the British to house American POWs during the Revolutionary War, and by the United States to house Native American prisoners captured during the Seminole War of 1835-1842 as well as during the later Indian Wars of the Wild West. Since 1924 it has been a national monument and is open for walks along the ramparts and for frequent ranger-guided tours.

One of many attractive things about St. Augustine is the almost total lack of franchised fast-food restaurants, at least in the historic downtown area. Instead, you can choose from all sorts of local places, like the **Florida Cracker Café** (81 St. George St., 904/829-0397), a casual seafood grill where you can sample the local delicacy, alligator tail. Another fun place to while away an evening is **Scarlett O'Hara's** (70 Hypolita St., 904/824-6535), offering beers, burgers, and live music a block from Flagler College. Fun and fairly good value, east of the historic core but right on lovely St. Augustine Beach itself, **Paula's Beachside Grill** (6896 Hwy-A1A, 904/471-3463) is a popular tiki bar-style burger, hot dog, and beer stand.

Unfortunately for present-day visitors, the grand old Ponce de Léon Hotel no longer welcomes overnight guests, but contemporary St. Augustine does offer a wide variety of accommodations, including the imaginatively named **Beachfront B&B** (1 F St., 904/461-8727, adults only, $150 and up) in St. Augustine Beach. At Beachfront B&B you can spend the night in one of five tastefully decorated suites in a historic home, then wake up to watch the porpoises cavorting offshore. In the historic district, the **Kenwood Inn** (38 Marine St., 904/824-2116, $139 and up) has 14 rooms in a Victorian-era hotel along the Matanzas River.

Alligator Farm

Sulawesi red-knobbed hornbills at Alligator Farm

From the heart of St. Augustine, Hwy-A1A crosses over the Matanzas River on the lovely historic Bridge of Lions to **Anastasia Island,** bound for the Atlantic beaches three miles to the east. On the way to the beach, just two miles southeast of Old Town St. Augustine on Anastasia Boulevard (Hwy-A1A), sits one of the greatest of Florida's many tourist traps, **Alligator Farm** (904/824-3337, daily, $25 adults). Touted as the world's only complete collection of crocodilians, this was the first and is now one of the last of many such roadside menageries. A legitimate historical landmark, Alligator Farm is also a fun and informative place to spend some time—great for kids and anyone who finds gators and crocs (and turtles, iguanas, lemurs, and tropical birds, all of which are here) to be captivating creatures. Start at the mossy pond seething with gators (which you can feed), and be sure to pay your respects to Gomek, the Alligator Farm's massive taxidermied mascot, and to Maximo, a 15-foot Aussie crocodile.

Alligator Farm resident

Across from Alligator Farm, a road turns east from Hwy-A1A to **Anastasia State Park,** the site where the stone for Castillo de San Marcos was quarried, and where in addition to beaches there's an inlet set aside for surfing, hiking trails through coastal hammock forests, and a nice **campground** (904/461-2033) amid stately live oaks and magnolia trees.

Marineland

Eighteen miles south of St. Augustine, 35 miles north of Daytona Beach, the original sea-creature amusement park, **Marineland Dolphin Adventure** (904/471-1111, daily, $13 adults), opened with a splash in 1938 and is credited with the first performing dolphins. It later played a key role in the sci-fi movie *Creature from the Black Lagoon*. After struggling to compete with the much larger Sea World and Disney World, the park closed suddenly in 1998, but reopened in 2005 on a much smaller scale, with an "edutainment" focus on up-close encounters with its famous dolphins. It sounds like a magical experience, but be warned: pricing starts around $200 per person and continues upward depending on how much time you spend in the water.

About three miles north of Marineland, on the inland side of Hwy-A1A, you can see the 16-foot-thick stone walls of **Fort Matanzas,** built by the Spanish around 1736 and never conquered. Now a national historic site, it's open for free tours.

Continuing along the coast south of Marineland, you start to see roadside fruit stands advertising "Indian River Fruit"—something you'll see more of as you travel south. This is a major citrus-growing region. This stretch of Hwy-A1A, around the town of **Flagler Beach,** is also one of the few where you can actually see the ocean from the road.

Ormond Beach

Thirty miles south of Marineland, the town of **Ormond Beach,** which adjoins the northern fringes of more famous Daytona Beach, was also used by early speed-seekers. Prior to that, it was a winter playground of the rich and famous, richest and most famously John D. Rockefeller, who wintered here for years before his death in 1937 at age 97. His mansion, called **The Casements** (25 Riverside Dr., 386/676-3216), is now a museum along the east bank of the Halifax River. The beachfront park in Ormond Beach, midway along the town's four-lane stretch of Hwy-A1A, is as nice as any in Florida.

Daytona Beach

Offering a heady barrage of blue-collar beach culture, **Daytona Beach** (pop. 61,005) is a classic road-trip destination in every way, shape, and form. The beach here is huge—over 20 miles long, and 500 feet wide at low tide—and there's a small and recently pretty scruffy amusement pier at the foot of Main Street. The rest of Daytona Beach is rather rough at the edges, with boarded-up shops and some lively bars and nightclubs filling the few blocks between the beach area and the Halifax River, which separates the beach from the rest of the town.

Besides being a living museum of pop culture, Daytona Beach has long played an important role in car culture: In the first decades of the 20th century, a real who's who of international automotive pioneers—Henry Ford, R. E. Olds, Malford Duesenberg, and more—came here to test the upper limits of automotive performance. The first world land-speed record (a whopping 68 mph!) was set here in 1903, and by 1935 the ill-starred British racer Malcolm Campbell had raised it to 276 mph.

DETOUR: ORLANDO
AND WALT DISNEY WORLD

Entire guidebooks are devoted to covering the mind-boggling array of tourist attractions in and around Orlando, but three words would probably suffice: **Walt Disney World.** As many as 100,000 people come here during the winter and Spring Break peak seasons to experience the magic of the Magic Kingdom, which is divided into four main areas—the Magic Kingdom amusement park; the Animal Kingdom animal park, which is also home to Pandora—The World of Avatar; the once-futuristic 1980s-era Epcot; and the Disney Hollywood studio tours, which is also home to the Aerosmith-themed Rock and Rollercoaster, Disney World's second-fastest. The best way to see all of them is to get a Park Hopper pass ($162 and up), which allows entry to all four parks on every day covered by your ticket. Hard-core fans can buy an annual pass (around $779). For further information on admission and lodging packages, check online or call 407/939-5277.

At the time of this writing, there's still no law that says you have to go to Disney World just because you've come to Florida, but it is a cultural phenomenon and more than a little fun. While you're in Orlando, you may want to visit other big-time attractions like Sea World and Universal Studios, but there are also some funky, pre-Disney-era tourist traps, with ad budgets small enough that you won't have to fight the crowds. Best of this bunch is probably **Gatorland** (14501 S. Orange Blossom Trail, 800/393-5297, daily, $27), where thousands of alligators, crocodiles, snakes, and other reptiles are gathered together in a cypress swamp. Pass the original park entrance, shaped like a gator's gaping jaws, thankfully preserved for posterity. Inside, you can see such sights as live chickens being dangled over a pond, taunting the hungry carnivorous gators just out of reach below. Continuing south along US-441, past the world headquarters of Tupperware, another sight of offbeat interest is the 100-year-old historic district at the heart of **Kissimmee** (pop. 59,682), where The Monument of States, a 50-foot stone and concrete pyramid, constructed in 1943 with rocks from most states, as well as 21 countries, stands in Lakefront Park.

The entertaining design of Disney World doesn't stop at the park gates; *au contraire.* Perhaps the most memorable aspect of the Disney experience is seeing how the clever folks at Disney maximize their revenues, specifically by offering a full range of lodging, dining, shopping, and entertainment options around the park. Disney's extraordinary **Animal Kingdom Lodge** (407/938-3000, $319 and up), where a 43-acre savannah landscape, complete with roaming giraffes and zebras visible from your balconies, offers families and fans of *The Lion King* the chance to take an African safari—without the jet lag. And it's not all just for little kids: sports fans flock to the **All-Star Sports Resort,** a moderately priced sports-themed hotel near the ESPN/ABC Wide World of Sports complex, spring training home of the Atlanta Braves. For a Disneyfied view of the ideal American town, visit the Walt Disney Company's pleasant retro-Victorian planned community of **Celebration** (pop. 7,427 and growing), south of US-192 at the I-4 junction. Contrary to popular belief, this is not the town seen in the Jim Carrey movie *The Truman Show* (that was Seaside, in the Florida Panhandle), but it could have been.

Between Orlando and the Space Coast, the Beachline Expressway (Hwy-528) is a fast, flat toll road, with only four exits in the 30 miles between I-95 and greater Orlando.

The speed racers later moved west to Bonneville Salt Flats in Utah, and Daytona became the breeding ground for stock car racing—today's Daytona 500 started out as a series of 100- to 200-mile races around a rough 4-mile oval, half on the sands and half on a paved frontage road. The circuit races, both for cars and motorcycles, really came into their own after World War II. In 1947, NASCAR was founded here as the nascent sport's governing body. The races soon outgrew the sands, and in 1958 they were moved to the purpose-built **Daytona International Speedway,**

The winning car of each year's Daytona 500 remains on display until the following year's race.

on US-92 six miles west of the beach, right off I-95 exit 261A. Daytona offers "ride-alongs" and on-track driving experiences (for a mere $135 to $2,238). After a visit, you may want to spend some time practicing your skills at the **Speed Park Motorsports** (201 Fentress Blvd., 386/253-3278), the go-kart and drag racing track across the street.

It was at the **Daytona Beach baseball stadium** (105 E. Orange Ave., 386/257-3172) that **Jackie Robinson** broke through baseball's "color line," taking part in the first desegregated professional ball game during Spring Training on March 17th,

1946. He played for the Triple-A Montreal Royals against their parent club, the Brooklyn Dodgers. The stadium has been named in his honor, and hosts summer league Class A games for the Daytona Tortugas.

Daytona Beach is party central during March and April, when some 300,000 college kids escape from northern climes to defrost and unwind with a vengeance. There has been a concerted effort recently to keep a lid on things, but if you're after peace and quiet, you should head somewhere else. The same is true of the springtime **Bike Week** before the Daytona 200 in March, and again in fall during **Biketoberfest,** when thousands of motorcycling enthusiasts descend on Daytona for a week or more of partying in between races at Daytona Speedway. The granddaddy of all stock car races, the **Daytona 500,** is held around Valentine's Day, but getting one of the 101,000 tickets is all but impossible for casual fans.

A world apart from the spring break, biker, and race-car scenes, but just a block from the beach, the classic 1950s-themed **Starlite Diner** (401 N. Atlantic Ave., 386/301-5796) serves the expected range of breakfasts, burgers, and sandwiches. Daytona has a lot of low-rise motels as well as tons of high-rise hotels along the beachfront, like the large and spacious **Holiday Inn** (930 N. Atlantic Ave., 386/255-5494, $112 and up).

The Space Coast: Cape Canaveral

It's more than a little ironic that one of the most extensive sections of natural coastal wetlands left in Florida became home to the launch pads of the nation's space program. Though the natural aspects—thousands of

space shuttle *Endeavor*'s final launch, Cape Canaveral

seabirds and wide-open stretches of sandy beaches—are attractive enough in their own right to merit a visit, many people are drawn here by Cape Canaveral's **Kennedy Space Center.** All the big milestones in the history of the U.S. space program—the Mercury, Gemini, Apollo, and space shuttle launches—happened here, and if names like Alan Shepard, John Glenn, or Neil Armstrong mean anything to you, set aside time for a visit.

The Kennedy Space Center itself, eight miles west of US-1 via the NASA Parkway (Hwy-405), is open to the public, but only on guided tours. These tours require advance tickets, and all leave from the large **visitors complex** (855/433-4210, daily, $50 and up), where two IMAX theaters show films of outer space to get you in the mood. There are also some small museums, a simulated space shuttle mission control center, eight real rockets in the Rocket Garden, an actual space shuttle, and an exhibit previewing missions to Mars. The visitors center also has a couple of fast-food restaurants and a kennel for pets.

To see the Kennedy Space Center up close, board a bus for a tour; these leave every fifteen minutes and visit the Apollo and space shuttle launch pads and other sites, including the Vehicle Assembly Building. On other tours, you can visit the Cape Canaveral Air Force station or the Launch Control Center, or even have lunch with an astronaut and talk about outer space with someone who's actually been there (glass of Tang not included).

To witness a rocket launch at Kennedy Space Center, you can either watch from the main visitor center, get passes for entrance into a special viewing area, or simply watch from the many good vantage points: Playalinda Beach, in the Canaveral National Seashore at the west end of Hwy-402 from Titusville; across the Indian River, along US-1 in Titusville; or the beaches west of Hwy-A1A in Cocoa Beach.

One of the best places to eat in this part of Florida is west of the Space Center, in the town of **Titusville:** the immense and immensely popular **Dixie Crossroads** (1475 Garden St., 321/268-5000, daily) for seafood, especially the massive all-you-can-eat plates of small shrimp ($40). The Crossroads is away from the water, two miles east of I-95 exit 220.

> Inland from the Space Coast is Florida's biggest tourist attraction, **Orlando,** home of Walt Disney World.

> At the street entrance to the Kennedy Space Center visitors center, and visible from the Parkway, the **Astronaut Memorial** is a huge black granite block backed by high-tech mirrors that reflect sunlight onto the surface of the stone, illuminating the engraved names of the men and women who have given their lives exploring space.

Cocoa Beach

The town of **Cocoa Beach,** familiar to anyone who ever watched the 1960s space-age sitcom *I Dream of Jeannie,* sits south of the Kennedy Space Center. Long before there were space shuttles, or even NASA, Cocoa Beach was home to the **Cape Canaveral**

SPRING TRAINING: GRAPEFRUIT LEAGUE BASEBALL

Every February and March, hundreds of baseball players at all levels of expertise head to Florida to earn or keep their places on some 20 different major league teams and their farm club affiliates. The informality and ease of access during this spring training, which is known as the Grapefruit League, attracts thousands of baseball fans as well (more than a million spectators for the month-long "season"). Though they're not necessarily played to win, Grapefruit League games are played in modern 10,000-seat stadia that approach the major leagues in quality. The smaller size allows an up-close feel you'd have to pay much more for during the regular season (and your chances of snagging balls during batting practice, or the early morning training sessions, are infinitely better).

Most of the Grapefruit League teams make their springtime homes on the Gulf Coast, but many others locate in cities and towns along Florida's Atlantic coast, and some teams are in the Orlando area, including the Atlanta Braves and the Houston Astros. The teams move around from town to town depending on the deals they can finagle from local taxpayers, but at the time of writing, the New York Mets train in Port St. Lucie, the Washington Nationals in West Palm Beach, while the St. Louis Cardinals and Miami Marlins play in Jupiter.

East from Hwy-A1A on the south side of Cocoa Beach, I Dream of Jeannie Lane leads down to a nice beachfront park.

Air Station, the launch site for the unmanned space probes of the late 1950s, including the first U.S. satellite (Explorer 1), and the famous "astro chimps" (Gordo, Able, and Miss Baker, who were sent into orbit to test the effects of weightlessness). The air station, which is only accessible as part of the Kennedy Space Center's Cape Canaveral Early Space Tour, includes the launch complexes used for Mercury 7 and Project Gemini.

Though space travel is clearly on the minds of many residents, especially personnel stationed at Patrick Air Force Base here, another focus is catching the perfect wave: Cocoa Beach is surf center of the Space Coast. Along with a clean, 10-mile-long beach, the town also holds a batch of good-value motels, located within a short walk of the waves. Choose from chains (including a Motel 6), or check out the garish pink **Fawlty Towers** (100 E. Cocoa Beach Causeway/Hwy-520, 321/784-3870, $84 and up), which, for fans of the eponymous British sitcom, is sadly devoid of John Cleese or put-upon Juan. It is, however, cheap and walkably close to the beach, and right next door to Cocoa Beach's main event, the massive **Ron Jon Surf Shop** (4151 N. Atlantic Ave., 321/799-8888, daily 24 hours), *the* place to buy or rent surfboards, body boards, or bicycles.

Vero Beach

As a boy growing up in sunny Los Angeles, I could never understand why the Dodgers felt they had to disappear to distant Florida to get in shape during spring training. I knew the weather couldn't be so much better there (after all, didn't LA have the heavenly climate?), and I never quite figured out what the big attraction of Vero Beach, the Dodgers' historic off-season home, could be. But when I discovered that the Dodgers had started playing here way back in 1948—back when they still called Brooklyn home—it all began to make sense. But all that is in the past—after 60 years, the Dodgers moved west to Arizona in 2008, and the facility, called **Historic Dodgertown,** is used as training grounds for sports teams of all kinds.

With or without baseball, Vero Beach is a really nice place, with an excellent beach in South Beach Park at the end of the Palmetto Causeway. This South Beach is family-friendly and about as far as you can get from Miami's South Beach and still be in Florida: The sands here are clean, grainy, and golden, the waves are a good size, and there are showers and free parking. Vero Beach also has a nice place to stay and eat: the **Driftwood Resort** (3150 Ocean Dr., 772/231-0550), which has beachcomber-vibe motel rooms and villas, and the fun and good-value **Waldo's,** a poolside café and bar overlooking the ocean.

Fort Pierce and Jupiter

South of Vero Beach, Hwy-A1A continues along North Hutchinson Island past the **National Navy SEAL Museum** (772/595-5845, Tues.-Sun., $10 adults), which describes the various roles played by Navy SEAL units, whether it's serving as underwater divers in demolishing enemy property during wartime, or assassinating bad guys like Osama bin Laden. Among the displays of wetsuits and explosives is an Apollo capsule—it was Navy SEALs who rescued returning astronauts after they "splashed down" in the ocean. The most popular sight is the bright orange lifeboat in which the real-life Captain Phillips was held hostage in 2009 before being rescued, as depicted in the Tom Hanks film. On either side of the museum, undeveloped stretches of the coast have been preserved in a pair of parks, where you can enjoy uncrowded beaches or wander along boardwalks through thickly forested mangrove swamps.

South of Fort Pierce, **Port St. Lucie** is the spring training home of the **New York Mets** (525 NW Peacock Blvd., off I-95, 772/871-2115).

Bending inland across the North Bridge, Hwy-A1A links up briefly with US-1, the old Dixie Highway, through the town of **Fort Pierce** (pop. 41,590), a market center of the famous "Indian River" produce-growing district. After this half-mile detour, Hwy-A1A returns to the shore, passing along the way by the good **St. Lucie County Regional History Center** (Wed.-Sun., $4 adults), at the east end of the South Bridge, where broad-ranging displays tell the history of the region, showing off a hand-carved canoe and explaining the "fort" in Fort Pierce (it was built in 1835, during the Seminole Wars).

Heading south from Fort Pierce, Hwy-A1A embarks on a nearly 30-mile run along Hutchinson Island, where dense stands of pines block the views of largely undeveloped beachfront. On the coast just north of Palm Beach, the town of **Jupiter** has a landmark lighthouse, which you can climb inside for a grand view from the top. **Roger Dean Stadium** is spring training home of the Miami Marlins and St. Louis Cardinals, as well as their Class A Florida State League farm clubs.

Midway between Jupiter and Palm Beach, the hamlet of **Juno Beach** is home to the entertaining and educational **Loggerhead Marinelife Center** (14200 US-1, 561/627-8280).

Jupiter Inlet Lighthouse

Palm Beach

A South Florida sibling to the conspicuous consumption that once defined Newport, Rhode Island, **Palm Beach** (pop. 8,348) has been a winter refuge for the rich and famous since Henry Flagler started work on his fashionable long-vanished resort hotel, the 1,150-room Royal Poinciana. It was the world's largest wooden building when completed in 1894, but the site is now an upscale shopping district at the center of town. Away from here, most of Palm Beach is well-guarded private property, off-limits to most mere mortals. The best way for anyone not named Kennedy or Pierpont to get a look at Palm Beach life is to spend some time at the Hearst Castle of the East Coast, the **Henry Morrison Flagler Museum** (561/655-2833, Tues.-Sun., $18), on the inland side of downtown Palm Beach, at the north end of Cocoanut Row. Officially  known as Whitehall, this opulent 60,000-square-foot mansion was Flagler's private home, and the 50-plus rooms, many of which were taken from European buildings and reinstalled here, contain historical exhibits tracing the life of Flagler, the Standard Oil baron and John D. Rockefeller's right-hand man, who made a fortune while making Florida into an immensely popular vacation destination.

Inland from Palm Beach, you can wave at rhinos, lions, and wildebeests in a 500-plus-acre drive-through simulation of African ecosystems at **Lion Country Safari** (561/793-1084, $35), 18 miles west of I-95 via US-98. No convertibles allowed!

Not surprisingly, there are some good and expensive restaurants in and around Palm Beach, but happily there's also a nice all-American luncheonette, just two blocks north of The Breakers: **Green's Pharmacy Luncheonette** (151 N. County Rd., 561/832-0304) serves good diner-style meals.

Even bigger and better than Whitehall is **The Breakers** ($369 and up), a stately resort hotel that faces the ocean at the east end of Palm Beach and retains much of its 1920s Mediterranean style and grace. Even if you don't stay the night, you can enjoy the lobby, have a drink or afternoon tea, or take a **tour** (561/655-6611, Sat. 1pm, $15). At the south edge of town, along Hwy-A1A just north of the US-98 junction, stand the golden gates of another Palm Beach landmark: the private **Mar-A-Lago Club.**

Boca Raton

Whoever named **Boca Raton** (pop. 84,394), which translates literally as "Rat's Mouth," clearly didn't have an ear for future promotional bonanza. Despite the awkward name, the town has become one of the more chichi spots in the state. As in Palm Beach, Coral Gables, and Miami's South Beach, the best of Boca dates from the 1920s, when architect and real estate promoter Addison Mizner, flush from his success building Mediterranean-style manors in Palm Beach, created a mini Venice of resorts and canals, which survives mainly in the shocking pink palazzo of the **Boca Raton Resort** (501 E. Camino Real, 561/447-3000, $299 and up), on the southeast side of town.

Downtown Boca has been turned into a massive stucco shopping mall, but it's worth braving for a look inside the ornate Mizner-designed Town Hall, on US-1 (old Dixie Highway) downtown in Palmetto Park, which now houses the local **historical museum** (Mon.-Fri., $5).

Hwy-A1A misses most of Boca Raton, cruising past along the densely pine-forested coast. The beaches are accessible but hard to find; one well-marked stop along the way is the **Gumbo Limbo Nature Center** (561/544-8605, Mon.-Sat. 9am-4pm, Sun. noon-4pm, $5 donation) on the inland side of the highway, a mile north of Mizner Park. A variety of native Floridian landscapes have been recreated here, letting you wander at will past coastal dunes, mangrove wetlands, and rare sabal palm hammocks. Across Hwy-A1A, **Red Reef Park** is a popular surfing beach.

Fort Lauderdale

Once famed for wild spring break frolics that saw thousands of college kids descending here for an orgy of drunken round-the-clock partying, **Fort Lauderdale** (pop. 165,521) is a surprisingly residential city, brought to a more human scale by the many waterways that cut through it. One of the largest cargo ports in the state, Fort Lauderdale also boasts more boats per capita than just about anywhere else in the United States, and over 165 miles of canals, inlets, and other waterways flow through the city.

Fort Lauderdale is said to be one of the points that form the Bermuda Triangle, so of course there are numerous beachside bars where college kids try to simulate its supernatural effects by imbibing too many margaritas.

Downtown Fort Lauderdale has a few big, dull office towers, but along the New River there are some well-preserved historic buildings dating back to 1905, when the city first emerged from the swamps. Find out more by visiting the nifty **Stranahan House** (335 SE 6th Ave., daily, $12), off Las Olas Boulevard. This circa-1901 trading post and home, with broad verandas and high ceilings, is one of the most evocative historic places in the state.

Fort Lauderdale

Fort Lauderdale's main beachfront bar and nightclub district is along Atlantic Avenue and Las Olas Boulevard, where you'll find some nice sidewalk cafés and coastal-chic restaurants like **Wild Sea Oyster Bar and Grille** (620 E. Las Olas Blvd., 954/467-2555), a popular and stylish haunt where traditional seafood dishes are enlivened by a canny blend of exotic ingredients.

Miles of inexpensive motels line Hwy-A1A north of Fort Lauderdale, and unless there's something big going on, you shouldn't have trouble finding a room for under $100—half that in summer. One of the nicest places is the moderately priced, family-friendly **Premiere Hotel** (625 N. Fort Lauderdale Beach Blvd., 954/566-7676, $114 and up), with a pool, bar, and generally pleasant old-school 1960s vibe, just a short walk from the beach.

North of Fort Lauderdale, Hwy-A1A winds in along the coast through a series of funky, friendly beachside communities. South of Fort Lauderdale, Hwy-A1A heads inland and merges into US-1, returning to the coast for the run south to Miami Beach.

North Miami Beach

Between Fort Lauderdale and Miami Beach, Hwy-A1A runs along the shore, first as Ocean Drive and later as Collins Avenue, while US-1 runs inland parallel to (and sometimes as) the old Dixie Highway. There's nothing here to compare with the attractions farther south, but the town of **North Miami Beach** does have one oddity: the **Ancient Spanish Monastery** (16711 W. Dixie Hwy., 305/945-1461, Mon.-Sat. 10am-4:30pm, Sun. 11am-4:30pm, $10), a 12th-century monastery bought in the 1920s by William Randolph Hearst, who had it dismantled and shipped to the United States for his Hearst Castle complex in California. However, after U.S. Customs confiscated the stones, and Hearst lost his fortune in the Great Depression, the monastery was finally rebuilt here in Florida—as an Episcopal church.

On the coast, Hwy-A1A runs past a number of indistinct beach towns before hitting **Bal Harbour,** home to one of Miami's biggest and best shopping malls, and one of its biggest beaches, **Haulover Beach.** Besides having a café, lots of tennis

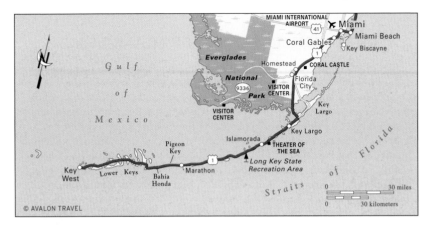

© AVALON TRAVEL

courts, and gorgeous sands, Haulover Beach is also famous for attracting the clothing-optional crowd.

From Haulover Beach south to Miami Beach, Collins Avenue (Hwy-A1A) used to be known as "Millionaire's Row" for all the huge estates here. Now the road is lined with towering concrete condos and hotels, including the landmark Morris Lapidus-designed complex of the **Fontainebleau** (4441 Collins Ave., 305/538-2000, $249 and up). It's been the setting for several movies: Jerry Lewis filmed *The Bellboy* here in 1959; Sean Connery checked in as James Bond, most famously in the 1964 film *Goldfinger;* and Al Pacino hung out by the pool in the quintessential 1980s Miami movie, *Scarface.*

Miami Beach

Covering a broad island separating downtown Miami from the open Atlantic Ocean, **Miami Beach** (pop. 87,779) has long been a mecca for fans of 1930s art deco architecture and design. More recently, it's also become one of the world's most fashionable and bacchanalian beach resorts, with A-List celebrity entertainers and artists preening around the deluxe hotels and high-style nightclubs and restaurants that line the broad white sands of **South Beach,** the relatively small corner of Miami Beach that gets 99 percent of the press and tourist attention. Here, along beachfront Ocean Drive and busier Collins Avenue (Hwy-A1A) a block inland, you'll find dozens of glorious art deco hotels, many lighted with elegant neon signs. Guided **walking tours** (daily, $25) of the district leave from the **Art Deco Welcome Center** (1001 Ocean Dr., 305/672-2014, daily), which also rents iPod-based self-guided tours and sells guidebooks, posters, postcards, and anything else you can think of that has to do with the art deco era.

No matter how intoxicating the architecture, beach life, and nightlife along South Beach are, while you're here, be sure to set aside an hour or two to explore the fascinating collection of pop culture artifacts on display two blocks inland at the **Wolfsonian** (1001 Washington Ave., 305/531-1001, Thurs.-Tues., $10 adults). One of the odder highbrow museums you'll find, the Wolfsonian (officially the Mitchell Wolfson Jr.

Because it is barely above sea level, Miami Beach frequently suffers from flooding, and not just during hurricanes: nearly every month, full-moon high tides wash over the streets, and the government is investing $400 million to install pumps and other protective measures to keep the tides at bay.

CARL FISHER: FATHER OF MIAMI BEACH

Fisher Park, on the bay side of Miami Beach on Alton Road at 51st Street, holds a small monument to the fascinating Carl Fisher, the man most responsible for turning Miami Beach from a mangrove swamp into America's favorite resort. Before building up Lincoln Avenue into Miami Beach's first commercial district, Carl Fisher had played an important role in America's early automotive history. Called the "P. T. Barnum of the Automobile Age," Fisher made millions through the Prest-O-Lite company, which in the early 1900s developed the first functioning car headlight. Around 1910, he invested this fortune in building and promoting the Indianapolis Motor Speedway, then went on to plan and publicize both the Lincoln Highway, America's first transcontinental road, and the Dixie Highway, the first main north-south route in the eastern United States. He invested heavily in Miami Beach property but was ruined by the Great Depression and the sudden drop in land values. He died here, nearly penniless, in 1939, just as the economy was rebounding and the art deco hotels of South Beach were bringing new life to Miami Beach.

Collection of Decorative and Propaganda Arts) fills a retrofitted 1920s building with seven floors of furniture, sculpture, architectural models, posters, and much more, almost all dating from the "modern era," roughly 1850 to 1950. Two areas of excellence are drawings and murals created under the New Deal auspices of the WPA, and similar agitprop artifacts created in Weimar, Germany. Only a small portion of the extensive collection is on display at any one time, and most of the floor space is given over to changing exhibitions—on anything from World's Fairs to Florida tourism to how children's books were used to indoctrinate future soldiers—but it's a thought-provoking and surprisingly fun place, with an unexpressed but overriding theme of how art can counterbalance, or at least respond to, the demands of industrial society.

Miami Beach Practicalities

Not surprisingly, there are scores of cafés and restaurants in and around Miami Beach. Just two blocks west of the beach, the **11th Street Diner** (305/534-6373) on 11th Street and Washington Avenue is a 1948 Paramount prefab diner, plunked down in 1992 and open 24 hours ever since.

For an unforgettably hedonistic experience, check into one of South Beach's great old art deco hotels, or at least saunter through the lobby and stop for a drink. The **Delano** (1685 Collins Ave., 305/672-2000, $309 and up) is a high-style Shrager-Starck symphony in white, while the **Raleigh** (1775 Collins Ave., 305/534-6300, $129 and up) has the coolest pool in South Beach—and that is really saying something. Dozens of these 1930s divas stand out along Ocean Drive and Collins Avenue, but the wonderful architecture, alas, doesn't always manage to mask their elderly

Miami

Equal parts jet-set glitz and multicultural grit, and with more than half its population coming here from other countries, Miami (pop. 399,457; metro pop. 5.5 million) embodies the transitive state of the nation in the 21st century. Having sprung up from swampland in the 1920s, Miami has weathered hurri-

the Domino Park, Calle Ocho

canes and race riots, real estate booms and busts, drug running, and endless political intrigue to become one of America's most energetic cities. In her book *Miami,* Joan Didion describes the city as an economically schizophrenic place where it's possible "to pass from walled enclaves to utter desolation while changing stations on the car radio."

Approaching from Miami Beach past the cruise ship docks along the MacArthur Causeway, or the older and more leisurely Venetian Causeway, you experience the view of Miami made famous by the 1980s television series *Miami Vice*—downtown towers rising above Biscayne Bay. West of downtown, Miami's most engaging district is Little Havana, which focuses along SW 8th Street (a.k.a. **Calle Ocho**) between 12th and 16th Avenues. Since the 1950s and 1960s, when refugees fleeing Fidel Castro's communist regime fetched up here, this neighborhood has been the heart of Cuban-American Miami. Hang out for a while with the old men who congregate in the **Domino Park** on 8th Street at 15th Avenue, or visit the **Martyrs of Giron** (a.k.a. Bay of Pigs) Monument along 8th Street at 13th Avenue; you'll definitely get a feel for it. Better yet, stop for something to eat or drink at one of Little Havana's many great Cuban cafés, like **Versailles** (3555 SW 8th St., 305/444-0240), a favorite haunt of Miami's politically potent anti-Castro Cuban-Americans. Enjoy good traditional Cuban food: toasted chorizo sandwiches, or perhaps a bowl of *ropa vieja* (tender threads of garlicky beef in a black bean soup), finished off with a creamy flan and a cup of super-strong Cuban coffee. Between US-1 and I-95 on the intriguingly edgy and increasingly arty north side of downtown Miami, an informal outdoor graffiti museum called "Wynwood Walls" covers the warehouses around the Latin-themed **Wynwood Kitchen and Bar** (2550 NW 2nd Ave., 305/722-8959).

For an entirely different aspect of Miami, check out the two-time wild card World Series champion **Miami Marlins** (305/480-1300), who play at a retractably roofed $700 million stadium on the site of the historic Orange Bowl.

Miami Beach has the best range of stylish hotels, but in downtown Miami the top end of the style and expense spectrum is the **Four Seasons** (1435 Brickell Ave., 305/358-3535, $259 and up), offering stunning views from a 70-story tower. Back down to earth, the major chains all have locations on the downtown waterfront; as at all South Florida accommodations, room rates tend to increase considerably during the peak season (Dec.-Apr.).

Two of Cuba's deposed presidents, Gerardo Machado and Carlos Prío Socarrás, are buried in Miami's **Woodlawn Park Cemetery,** a mile west of Little Havana. Former Nicaraguan dictator Anastasio Somoza is buried there too.

In 1983, the Bulgarian artist Christo wrapped 11 Biscayne Bay islands in bright pink plastic as part of his *Surrounded Islands* installation.

bones, nor is the 24-hour hubbub that surrounds them especially conducive to a good night's sleep. Ocean Drive, by the way, is undrivable on weekend nights, since so many cars cruise up and down it, stereos blasting.

Stylish though it is, South Beach is not frequented by many locals, who instead tend to spend time on **Lincoln Road,** a half mile north of South Beach. The Mediterranean Revival-style commercial district along Lincoln Road, developed in the 1920s by promoter Carl Fisher, was the original main drag of Miami Beach; it has been pedestrianized and nicely landscaped and is now packed with dozens of lively sidewalk cafés. Japanese refinement meets Brazilian passions at the iconoclastic **Sushi Samba** (600 Lincoln Rd., 305/673-5337), a fish lover's paradise, while designer tacos can be appreciated at **HuaHua** (1211 Lincoln Rd., 305/534-8226).

Across Miami

The I-95 freeway and the old main route, US-1, both enter Miami north of downtown in the rough but quickly changing Little Haiti neighborhood, while the infinitely more scenic Hwy-A1A crosses Biscayne Bay from Miami Beach. Around downtown, Biscayne Boulevard winds along the waterfront, merging into historic Brickell Avenue, now lined by flashy postmodern bank and condo towers. From here, detour west on the one-way system along 7th and 8th Streets through Little Havana, then south through Coral Gables, joining the old Dixie Highway (US-1) for the drive south through Homestead to the Florida Keys.

Coral Gables

South of Miami's Little Havana neighborhood, accessible through grand gates off the Tamiami Trail (8th Street), the stately community of **Coral Gables** is one of the few Florida resort towns that survives fairly unchanged since the boom years of the 1920s. Coral Gables boasts many grand boulevards, fine fountains, plazas, and lush gardens, but the landmark to look for is the 15-story **Biltmore Hotel** (1200 Anastasia Ave., 855/311-6903, $235 and up), off Granada Boulevard. This opulent hotel, which opened in 1926 and once boasted the world's largest swimming pool (Johnny Weissmuller was the original lifeguard!), has been restored to its original glory.

The southern edge of Coral Gables is occupied by the drab campus of the University of Miami, which is bounded by US-1, the old Dixie Highway.

Homestead: Coral Castle

One of the most diverting stops between Miami and the Florida Keys has to be the **Coral Castle Museum** (28655 S. Dixie Hwy., 305/248-6345, daily, $18 adults), an amazing house hand-carved out of huge blocks of oolitic coral from 1923 to 1951. Located right along the highway, two miles north of **Homestead,** the house is filled with furniture also carved from stone—a 3,000-pound sofa and a 500-pound rocking chair—and no one has figured how its enigmatic creator, Ed Leedskalnin, did it all without help or the use of any heavy machinery.

Homestead, along with neighboring Florida City farther south, forms the main gateway to Everglades National Park, and there are tons of reasonably priced motels hereabouts. All the usual suspects line up here along US-1, including the nice **Best Western Gateway to the Keys** (305/246-5100, $66 and up).

Florida's other big national park, **Biscayne National Park,** stretches east of Homestead from near Miami to the top of the Florida Keys, but it is almost completely underwater. Privately run **snorkeling and diving tours** ($129 per person) leave from behind the main **Convoy Point visitors center** (305/230-7275), nine miles east of US-1 at the end of 328th Street—near the huge Homestead-Miami Speedway (and a nuclear power plant).

Everglades National Park

Covering over 1.5 million acres at the far southwestern tip of mainland Florida, **Everglades National Park** protects the largest subtropical

the observation tower in Shark Valley

wilderness in the United States. A fair portion of the park is actually underwater, and the entire Everglades ecosystem is basically a giant slow-flowing river that is 50 miles wide but only a few inches deep. Fed by Lake Okeechobee, and under constant threat by irrigation in-flows and out-flows and by the redirection of water to Miami and other cities, the Everglades still seem to vibrate with life. Some 300 species of birds breed here, as do 600 different kinds of fish and animals, ranging from rare manatees to abundant alligators (not to mention the gazillions of mosquitoes).

The backcountry parts of the Everglades can be visited by boat, but by road there are only two main routes. In the north, the Tamiami Trail (the Tampa to Miami Trail, a.k.a. US-41) heads west from Miami to misnamed **Shark Valley** ($25 per car), where you can rent bikes or take a tram tour ($25) on a 15-mile loop through the sawgrass swamps that make up the heart of the Everglades. Gazing at the gators, eagles, and hawks here, it's hard to believe you're barely a half hour from South Beach. Just west of Shark Valley, the

Anywhere in Florida, mosquitoes are intensely annoying pests, so if you're here at any time but the dry middle of winter, bring strong insect repellent—and lots of it. In parts of the Everglades, the bugs are so bad that full-body cover is recommended, in addition to the most potent sprays and lotions you can lay your hands on.

Gators!

Miccosukee Indian Village is a somewhat poignant reminder of the plight of the Everglades indigenous people, the Seminoles, whose ancestors fought off the U.S. Army but who now wrestle alligators, run casinos and souvenir shops, and give airboat tours of their ancestral lands.

The main road access to the Everglades is via Palm Drive (Hwy-9336) from the Florida Turnpike or US-1. This route takes you past the **Ernest Coe Visitors Center** (305/242-7700), where interpretive displays and a pair of nature trails give an appetizing taste of the Everglades (and almost guaranteed sightings of alligators). The road continues nearly 40 miles west to the former town of **Flamingo.** Although both the residents and the namesake birds have moved on, there is a **visitor center** (1 Flamingo Lodge Hwy, Homestead, 239/695-2945) operated by the National Park Service.

Key Largo

The Overseas Highway (US-1) officially starts in Florida City, near the Everglades some 50 miles south of Miami, but doesn't really come alive until it leaves the mainland and lands at **Key Largo,** the first and largest of the dozens of "keys" (from the Spanish word *cayos,* meaning small islands) that the highway links together. The Overseas Highway reaches Key Largo at the popular **John Pennekamp Coral Reef State Park** (MM 102.5, 305/451-6300, daily, $8 per car). The first place where you can really get a feel for life on the keys, the park is the starting point for a variety of **guided tours** (scuba diving, snorkeling, or in glass-bottomed boats) that offer up-close looks at the only tropical coral reef in the continental United States and all but guarantee that you'll see enough sealife to fill a photo album or two. Along with the adjacent **Florida Keys National Marine Sanctuary,** the park gives access to more than 175 square miles of diving spots, including reefs, shipwrecks, and a nine-foot-high bronze statue called *Christ of the Deep.* The visitors center has a replica reef in a 30,000-gallon aquarium full of colorful fish, allowing a quick look at the fascinating underwater world without getting your feet wet; the park also has a pleasant campground.

Key Largo is home to the **Key Lime Products store** (305/853-0378) at mile marker 95, selling all manner of key lime pies, juice, cakes, cookies, suntan lotions—even key lime trees, though commercial key lime orchards are a thing of the past; most key limes today come from Mexico and Honduras.

sea sponges and tropical fish on the ocean floor in Key Largo

THE OVERSEAS HIGHWAY

Imagine a narrow ribbon of asphalt and concrete hovering between emerald seas and azure blue skies, and lined by swaying palm trees and gorgeous white-sand beaches. Add a generous taste of exotic wildlife, including alligators and dolphins; the country's only tropical coral reefs; and a romantic history rich with tales of buccaneering pirates and buried treasure. Hang it off the far southern tip of Florida, and you have the Overseas Highway, one of the country's most fascinating scenic drives.

Running for over 125 miles from the Everglades to the edge of the Caribbean, the **Overseas Highway** is the southernmost section of US-1, the historic route that

winds for over 2,400 miles along the full length of the East Coast. From its inception, the Overseas Highway has been unique. It was built on top of the legendary Florida and East Coast Railroad, which at the turn of the 20th century linked the great resort hotels of St. Augustine and Palm Beach with Key West and Cuba. An engineering masterpiece, the railroad cost $50 million and hundreds of lives to complete in 1912, but it lasted only two decades before the century's most powerful hurricane destroyed the tracks in September 1935. The state of Florida bought the remnants of the railroad for $650,000 and proceeded to convert it into a two-lane highway, the Overseas Highway, which opened to traffic in 1938. Most of the old road has since been superseded by a more modern highway, but many old bridges and causeways still stand as evocative remnants of an earlier era.

As in much of Florida, ramshackle roadside development has uglified much of the route—in the larger keys towns, like Key Largo, Islamorada, and Marathon, signs hawking restaurants, motels, and snorkel tours are more common than pelicans—but you can't help but be hypnotized by the scenic beauty of what pockets of nature still remain. Many of the best views are from the road itself, and specifically from the bridges, such as the Long Key Bridge and soaring Seven Mile Bridge, which run north and south of Marathon. Two state parks, John Pennecamp on Key Largo and Bahia Honda in the Lower Keys, offer a respite from the commercialism, and all along the Overseas Highways, unmarked roads and driveways lead across the narrow keys down to the waterside, where all manner of sportfishing marinas and Margaritaville-type bars give you another outlook on the true "key experience."

All the way along the Overseas Highway (US-1), the roadside is lined by mile marker (MM) posts counting down the miles from Florida City to Key West, starting at MM 127 and ending up at MM 0; addresses usually make reference to these numbers. Though it's only about 160 miles, be sure to allow at least four hours for the drive between Miami and Key West—plus however many hours you manage to spend out of the car, of course.

Film fans will know that Key Largo was the title and setting of a great 1948 film noir movie starring Bogie, Bacall, and Edward G. Robinson; these days, it's also home to the co-star of another classic, the boat from the *African Queen,* which is moored next to the Holiday Inn at mile marker 100 and provides daily canal cruises. Most of Key Largo today, however, is a rather tawdry four-mile stretch of seashell stands, dive shops, boat shops, and margarita bars; there are many good restaurants, including **Mrs. Mac's Kitchen** (MM 99.4, 305/451-3722, Mon.-Sat.), a small and friendly place with inexpensive food and more beers to drink than seats to sit on.

Key Largo also has many good places to stay, from the funky **Sunset Cove Beach Resort** (MM 99.3, 305/451-0705, $135 and up) to the boutique **Azul del Mar** (between MM 103 and MM 104, 305/451-0337, $179 and up), a relaxing small resort. Also here is the truly unique **Jules' Undersea Lodge** (305/451-2353, packages from $150 per person for a three-hour visit only), a two-room motel that is 21 feet beneath the sea—a quick scuba dive down from 51 Shoreland Drive, off mile marker 103.2.

Islamorada

Continuing south on US-1, Key Largo blends into **Islamorada** (pronounced "EYE-la-mo-RA-da"), the self-proclaimed "Sportfishing Capital of the World," where anglers from all over the world come to try their hand at catching the elusive, hard-fighting bonefish that dwell in the shallow saltwater "flats" and the deep-sea tarpon, marlin, and sailfish. Though now famous for its fishing and fun-in-the-sun, Islamorada (Purple Island) used to be synonymous with death and destruction: On September 2, 1935, a huge tidal wave, whipped up by 200-mile-per-hour hurricane winds, drowned over 400 people trying to escape on what turned out to be the last train ever to travel along the old Florida East Coast Railway. Most of the dead were World War I veterans, members of the "Bonus Army" who had marched on Washington DC, in 1934 and had been given jobs working to build the Overseas Highway. A stone pillar at the south end of Islamorada, along US-1 at mile marker 82, was erected by the WPA to remember the event.

At the center of Islamorada sits one of the older tourist traps in south Florida: the **Theater of the Sea** (MM 84.5, 305/664-2431, daily, $34 adults), a funky friendly place where you can watch performing sea animals or even swim with dolphins ($199).

Islamorada is also home to what may be the most pleasant and plushest lodging option in the Florida Keys: **The Moorings Village** (123 Beach Rd., 305/664-4708, $409 and up), on the ocean side of mile marker 81.5. The Moorings is an idyllic and much-loved retreat, with 18

a monument to sportfishing in Islamorada

Islamorada beach

self-sufficient wooden cottages on 18 acres, alongside a beautiful 1,100-foot white-sand beach.

The Moorings also have a nice restaurant and café, both at Morada Bay: **Pierre's** (81600 Overseas Hwy., 305/664-3225) which serves urbane renditions of traditional key favorites; and **The Beach Café & Bar,** both on US-1 at mile marker 81.6. For a more down-to-earth taste of the keys, try the nearby **Green Turtle Inn** (305/664-2006, Tues.-Sun.), where specialties include shrimp-and-grits and local fish.

Long Key State Park

South of Islamorada, up and over the high "Channel 5" bridge, the roadside scene gets pretty again fast, especially at the **Long Key State Park** (MM 67.5), where boardwalks wind through coastal hammocks (dense stands of mahogany and dogwood trees that bunch together on the small humps of land that lie above the tide line). There's a **campground** (305/664-4815, $36) in the park, with showers, and some nice but narrow beaches. Access may be affected by ongoing beach restoration.

Marathon and Pigeon Key

The second-longest of the many bridges that make up US-1, the elegant multi-arched **Long Key Bridge** supports a long flat causeway where the road finally earns its other name, the Overseas Highway. Unobstructed views of the distant horizon are yours in all directions, with the narrow ribbon of highway seemingly suspended between the sky and the sea. Fortunately, turnouts at both ends of the causeway let you take in the vista without worrying about oncoming traffic.

The Long Key Bridge marks the northern end of **Marathon,** a sprawling community that's the second largest in the keys, stretching between mile markers 60 and 47 over a series of islands. One of the visitor highlights of Marathon is on Grassy Key, where the **Dolphin Research Center** (MM 59, 305/289-0002, daily, $28 adults), a rescue and education facility for the study and care of marine mam-

mals, is marked by a 30-foot-tall statue of a dolphin mother and baby. You can swim with a dolphin for around $199.

Accessible by ferry from a visitors center in Marathon, **Pigeon Key** (MM 47, 305/743-5999, daily, $12 adults) is one of the least famous but perhaps most fascinating spots along the Overseas Highway. A national historic district, preserving substantial remnants of the clapboard

construction camp that housed some 400 workers employed on the original Seven Mile Bridge from 1912 to 1935, Pigeon Key offers a glimpse of blue-collar keys history the likes of which you'll find nowhere else.

Lower Keys: Bahia Honda

The old Seven Mile Bridge, which carried first the railroad and later US-1 over Pigeon Key between Marathon and Big Pine Key, was replaced in the early 1980s by a soaring new bridge that gives another batch of breathtaking ocean-to-gulf views. The old bridge, which was seen in the Arnold Schwarzenegger-Jamie Lee Curtis movie *True Lies,* still stands below the new one.

On Bahia Honda Key, near mile marker 37, you can see a double-decker remnant of the original keys railroad, with the 1938 Overseas Highway supported atop the trestle. Widening the rail bed to accommodate cars was impossible, so a new deck was added to the top of the bridge.

The west end of the **Seven Mile Bridge,** near mile marker 40, marks the start of the **Lower Keys,** which are considerably less commercial than the others. The best of the Lower Keys is yours to enjoy at mile marker 37, where the entrance to **Bahia Honda State Park** (305/872-2353) leaves the highway behind and brings you back to the way the keys used to be: covered in palms and coastal hardwood hammocks, with white-sand beaches stretching for miles along blue-water seas. Facilities include a few **cabins** (around $120-160), a general store, snorkel equipment and kayak rental, interpretive exhibits, hiking trails—and it's a great place to spend some time fishing, beachcombing, sunbathing, or swimming in the deep warm waters of the Atlantic Ocean or Gulf of Mexico. **Camping** (around $36) is the best way to enjoy the sunset, sunrise, and everything in between.

From Bahia Honda, US-1 bends along to **Big Pine Key,** second largest of the keys

Bahia Honda State Park

and suffering from a bout of suburban mini-mall sprawl. Though it looks about as far from natural as can be, Big Pine Key happens to be part of the **National Key Deer Refuge,** set up to protect the increasingly rare key deer, the "world's smallest deer" at around three feet tall. Some 800-1000 key deer now live on the island.

The last big key before Key West is **Sugarloaf Key,** formerly full of pineapple plantations but now known for its **Perky's Bat Tower** (MM 17), a national historic landmark off of US-1. Built by a man named Perky in 1929, the 35-foot tower was designed to house a colony of bats, who were supposed to feast on the plentiful mosquitoes here; however, the bats stayed away, and the mosquitoes stayed put. Sugarloaf Key is also home to the wild **Mangrove Mama's** (MM 20, 305/745-3030), a roadhouse tucked away west of the bridge. The seafood and key lime pie are as good as it gets, and there's often live music in the evenings.

Key West

Closer to Cuba than to the U.S. mainland, and still proudly preserving the anarchic spirit of a place that was founded by pirates, **Key West** (pop. 24,686) is definitely a world unto itself. The main drag, Duval Street, has been overrun by tacky souvenir shops, bars, eateries, and art galleries. The rest of Key West is also still a great place for aimless wandering.

At sunset over the Gulf of Mexico, keep your eyes open for the visual effect known as the "green flash," when the sky and the sea seem to explode in a bright flash of green.

Just so you know, the seashell that's been adopted as a Key West emblem, the conch, is pronounced "KONK."

Just a block from the official Mile Zero end of US-1, one of Key West's most popular stops is the **Ernest Hemingway Home & Museum** (907 Whitehead St., 305/294-1136, daily 9am-5pm, $14), an overgrown mansion on Hwy-A1A, where the burly writer produced some of his most popular works, including *To Have and Have Not* and *For Whom the Bell Tolls.* Writing in a small cabin connected to the main house by a rope bridge, and spending his nights in the roughneck **Capt. Tony's Saloon** (428 Greene St., originally called Sloppy Joe's), "Papa" Hemingway lived in Key West in the late 1920s and 1930s, and

Ernest Hemingway Home & Museum

BIRD'S EYE VIEW, SHOWING F. & O. DOCKS AND FLORIDA EAST COAST TERMINAL, KEY WEST, FLA.

Though Key West is the southwestern end of the Overseas Highway, the name is thought to derive from a corruption of the Spanish Cayo Hueso (Island of Bones). When the first explorers set foot here, they found piles of human bones.

owned this home from 1931 until his death in 1961.

A half mile away, at Whitehead and South Streets, a brightly painted buoy marks the **"Southernmost Point in the USA"**; next to this is the Southernmost House. (There's also a Southernmost Beach Resort.)

At the other end of Duval Street, one place you ought to go—especially if you can time it to be there around sunset—is **Mallory Square,** which faces west across the Gulf of Mexico and the open Caribbean Sea. Street performers juggle and play music on the broad, brick-paved plaza as evening approaches. This historic waterfront area is lined by old warehouses and the **Mel Fisher Maritime Museum** (200 Greene St., daily, $15), which displays many millions of dollars' worth of jewels, silver, and gold recovered from a pair of 17th-century Spanish shipwrecks.

Key West Practicalities

Amid the tourist clutter, Key West holds a range of fabulous restaurants, enough to suit all tastes and budgets. Capturing the eccentric Key West spirit for over 20 years, the kid-friendly but a little kinky **Camille's** (1202 Simonton St., 305/296-4811) serves crisp waffles, wraps, and delicious dinners every day. For a memorable dinner, **Antonia's** (615 Duval St., 305/294-6565) has truly excellent Italian food: great fresh pastas, perfect lasagnas, and awesome grilled meats.

Where would you like to go? A sign at Key West Marina on Duval Street gives directions and distances to dozens of places around the world.

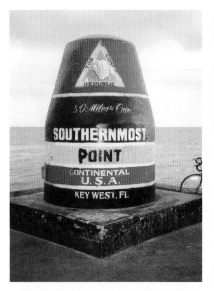

But for a real taste of Key West, you can't beat **B.O.'s Fish Wagon** (801 Caroline St., 305/294-9272), a ramshackle fish stand a block from the water and three blocks north of Duval—fish tacos and onion rings, fresh mahimahi sandwiches, cold beer, and frequent live blues bands make this a great place to soak up Key West's "party-hardy-at-the-end-of-the-world" ambience.

The **Southernmost Beach Resort** (1319 Duval St., 800/354-4455, $146 and up) has a poolside bar and AAA-rated rooms. Another desirable option is **La Concha Hotel & Spa** (430 Duval St., 305/296-2991, $187 and up); one of Key West's oldest and largest hotels, La Concha preserves the historic 1920s character, and you can't get more central than this. There are also many nice old B&Bs around Key West, like the landmark **Old Town Manor** (511 Eaton St., 305/292-2170, $135 and up), an 1880s Greek Revival mansion with a gorgeous garden.

Key West is the end of the Overseas Highway, but it's not the end of the sightseeing opportunities, so if you don't want to turn around and head home just yet, you don't have to. You can board a quick cruise, or take a seaplane tour or day-long guided tour on the **Yankee Freedom III** (800/634-0939, $175 per person) across the Caribbean to historic **Fort Jefferson,** a photogenic 150-year-old fortress and prison located on an island in **Dry Tortugas National Park,** 68 miles west of Key West. Prisoners held here included the hapless doctor Samuel Mudd, who set the broken leg of Lincoln assassin John Wilkes Booth.

> The official end and beginning of US-1 are marked by zero milepost signs at the corner of Fleming and Whitehead Streets, by the post office.

Fort Jefferson

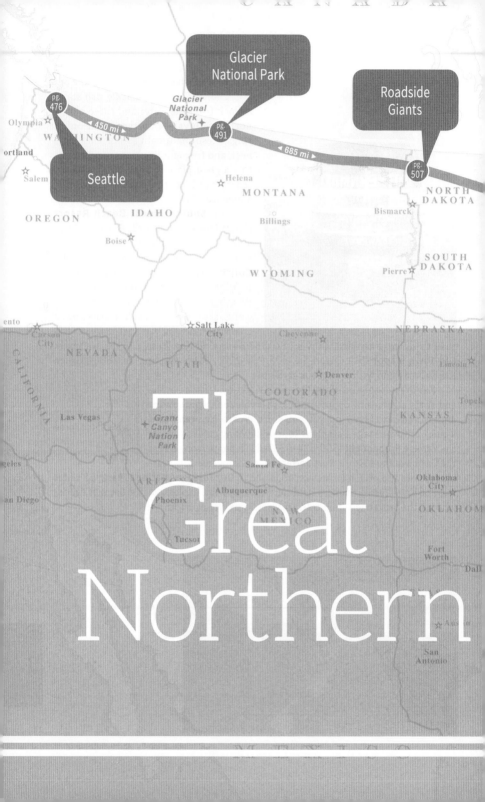

Seattle
pg. 476

Glacier
National Park
pg. 491

Roadside
Giants
pg. 507

◀ 450 mi ▶

◀ 685 mi ▶

The
Great
Northern

Michigan's Upper Peninsula

The Big Nickel

Acadia National Park

◀ 605 mi ▶

pg. 516

◀ 375 mi ▶

pg. 528

◀ 700 mi ▶

pg. 556

Montreal

OTTAWA

Montpelier ☆

Augusta ☆

Concord ☆

MINNESOTA

WISCONSIN

MICHIGAN

MAINE

VT NH

eapolis

☆ St. Paul

Madison ☆

Lansing ☆

Detroit

Cleveland

PENNSYLVANIA

NEW YORK

Alba

Chicago

Harrisburg ☆

Tre

Des Moines

ILLINOIS

INDIANA

Indianapolis ☆

OHIO

Columbus ☆

Baltimore

Annapolis

sas

☆ Springfield

Cincinnati

WEST VIRGINIA

WASHINGTON, D.C.

e City

St. Louis

Louisville ☆

Charleston ☆

Charlottesville ☆

INIA

MISSOURI

KENTUCKY

NORTH ☆ Raleigh

RINA

Charlotte

ARKANSAS

Memphis

Chattanooga

Columbia

Rock ☆

ALABAMA

Atlanta

Charleston

LOUISIANA

MISSISSIPPI

Mon

GEORGIA

allahassee

New Orleans

Orl

COOLER

NORTHERN VACATION
ROUTE

US

2

de St. May — Glacier National Park, Montana

THEODORE
ROOSEVELT
HIGHWAY

U. S. HIGHWAY 2 ASSOCIATION

Following US-2 through
wide-open spaces is
guaranteed to bring new
meaning to the expression
"getting away
from it all."

Between Seattle, Washington, and Acadia National Park

Though many come close, no other cross-country route takes in the variety and extremity of landscape that US-2 does. Dubbed the Great Northern in memory of the pioneer railroad that parallels the western half of the route, US-2 is truly the most stunning and unforgettable, not to mention longest, of all the great transcontinental road trips.

Starting in the west near the beautiful Pacific port city of Seattle, US-2 runs steeply up and over the volcanic **Cascade Range,** climbing from sea level to alpine splendor in around an hour. From the crest, the road drops down onto the otherworldly **Columbia Plateau,** a naturally arid region reclaimed from sagebrush into fertile farmland by New Deal public works projects like the great **Grand Coulee Dam,** one of the largest pieces of civil engineering on the planet. From **Washington,** US-2 bends north, clipping across the top of the **Idaho Panhandle** be-

fore climbing into western **Montana,** a land of forests, rivers, and wildlife that culminates in the bold granite spectacle of **Glacier National Park.**

On the eastern flank of the Rockies, the route drops suddenly to the windswept prairies of the northern **Great Plains.** Though empty to look at—especially when you're midway along the 1,000-mile beeline across Montana and **North Dakota,** wondering how long it will be until you see the next tree or peak—this is a land rich in history, where the buffalo once roamed freely, where Plains peoples like the Shoshone, Blackfeet, Sioux, and Cheyenne reigned supreme, and where the Lewis and Clark expedition followed the Mis-

Toboggan Slide—Château Frontenac et Glissoire, Québec, Canada.—47.

Mount Desert Island, Acadia National Park

souri River upstream in search of a way west to the Pacific.

Midway across the continent, the Great Plains give way to the **Great Northwoods** country of **Minnesota**—birthplace of both Paul Bunyan and Judy Garland—and then to the rugged lumber and mining country of **Wisconsin** and **Michigan's Upper Peninsula.** Continuing due east, the route

crosses the border into **Ontario, Canada,** running through the francophone environs of **Montreal** before returning to the United States near lovely **Lake Champlain** in upstate **New York.**

From there, US-2 passes through the hardwood forests of **Vermont's Green Mountains** and the rugged granite peaks of **New Hampshire's White Mountains,** two very different ranges, though only 50 miles apart. The route winds down to the coast of **Maine,** reaching the Atlantic Ocean at Bar Harbor and **Acadia National Park.**

Landscapes, rather than cities and towns, play the starring roles on this route. For nearly 2,000 miles at the heart of the route, between Seattle and the Canadian capital city of Ottawa, the biggest cities along the route are Spokane and Duluth. Still, after a few days spent following US-2 through small towns and wide-open spaces, you'll probably consider Duluth bustling and fast-paced; driving even a short stretch of the Great Northern highway is guaranteed to bring new meaning to the expression "getting away from it all."

WASHINGTON

The 350 miles of US-2 across Washington State contain enough contrasting landscapes to fill many states. West to east, the route begins at the industrial fringes of **Seattle** and Puget Sound, passing through a couple of Victorian-era towns before climbing steeply up toward the towering peaks, dense forests, and pristine lakes of the **Cascade Mountains.** East of the Cascade crest, the rugged volcanic landscape suddenly becomes drier and much sparser, the dense forests fading first into lush farmlands and orchards reclaimed from the natural desert, then continuing across increasingly barren sagebrush plains into Idaho.

Though traffic can be heavy on long summer weekends, and also in winter in the Cascades section, it is usually light along US-2, since most of the 18-wheelers and other heavy vehicles follow the parallel I-90 freeway, 25 miles to the south.

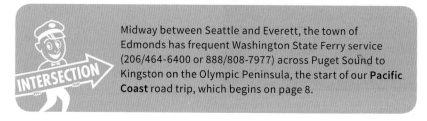

Midway between Seattle and Everett, the town of Edmonds has frequent Washington State Ferry service (206/464-6400 or 888/808-7977) across Puget Sound to Kingston on the Olympic Peninsula, the start of our **Pacific Coast** road trip, which begins on page 8.

Everett

Thirty-odd miles north of downtown Seattle via the I-5 freeway or the older, funkier Hwy-99, at the west end of transcontinental US-2, busy **Everett** (pop. 103,109) is a thoroughly blue-collar place that feels a lot farther from Seattle's high-tech flash than the mere half hour it is. A heavy industry center economically dependent on two of the largest livelihoods in the Pacific Northwest—wood products and aircraft manufacturing—Everett has a few large turn-of-the-20th-century mansions overlooking the all-business waterfront, home port to the aircraft carrier USS *Abraham Lincoln*,

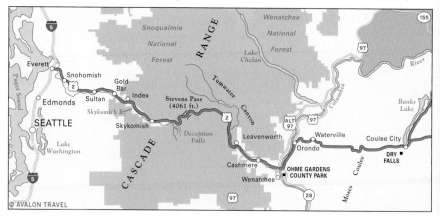

the ship on which George W. Bush made his "Mission Accomplished" speech during the Iraq War. The old-fashioned downtown, a half mile west of I-5 around Hewitt and Colby Avenues, has some neat antiques and junk shops, plus a dozen or so roughneck bars and taverns around the Historic **Everett Theatre** (2911 Colby Ave.). For milk shakes or great fish 'n' chips, stop by **Ray's Drive-In** (1401 Broadway, 425/252-3411), less than two miles north of downtown.

Everett's one big tourist draw is the huge **Boeing assembly plant** on the southwest edge of town, well-marked from I-5 exit 189, at the west end of Hwy-526. The factory, where they make some of the world's biggest planes—747s and 787 Dreamliners—is worth a look if only for the 11-story quarter-mile-long building, the largest in the world by volume. The on-site **Future of Flight Aviation Center and Boeing Tour** (800/464-1476 or 360/756-0086, daily 8am-5:30pm, $15-25) offers tours that leave on the hour 9am-5pm in summer.

US-2 leaves Everett on Hewitt Avenue, which crosses I-5

If a Boeing tour doesn't get your blood flowing, maybe a baseball game will: The always-entertaining **Everett AquaSox** (425/258-3673), Class A affiliate of the Seattle Mariners, play at the **Everett Memorial Stadium** on 39th Street and Broadway, off I-5 exit 192. Games are broadcast on **KRKO 1380 AM.**

then takes a historic old drawbridge over the Snohomish River before winding for a half dozen miles across low-lying fields toward the town of Snohomish.

Snohomish

Though they're spreading fast, Seattle's suburbs haven't yet reached the tidy Victorian town of **Snohomish** (pop. 9,098), a century-old former logging center that lines the north bank of the Snohomish River, 25 miles upstream from Puget Sound. Six blocks of well-preserved warehouses and commercial buildings stand along 1st Street, across the river from a whining old sawmill, while the blocks above hold dozens of charming homes and quite a few impressively steepled churches. One of these old homes has been restored and now houses the **Blackman House Museum** (118 Ave. B, 360/568-5235, Sun. 1pm-3pm, $5). The museum features period-style furnishings and displays on the town's early history. The range of antiques shops, taverns, and cafés in the historic center has made Snohomish a popular day trip from Seattle. Pastry fans come

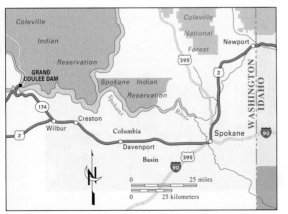

here for the fantastic apple, pecan, cherry, and other slices available at the Snohomish **Pie Company** (915 1st St., 360/568-3589), while beer-drinkers converge upon **Fred's Rivertown Alehouse** (1114 1st St., 360/568-5820), on the river. Snohomish has maintained an admirable balance of history and commerce and is well worth a short stop if you're passing by.

Seattle

The Two Sentries, The 42 story L. C. Smith Building and Mt. Rainier, SEATTLE U.S.A.

An engaging and energetic combination of scenic beauty, blue-collar grit, and high-tech panache has made Seattle one of the most popular cities in the United States, for visitors and residents alike. A young city, historically and demographically, Seattle has managed to preserve much of its heavy industrial heritage as parks and museums, if not as economic engines. The eco-conscious civic-minded city spreads over a series of hills, surrounded by the waters of Puget Sound (be sure to ride a ferry or two!), with a backdrop of the snow-capped Cascade and Olympic Mountains. The evergreen Seattle can be an entrancing city—at least when the sun comes out, which, no matter what people say, is likely to happen at least once during your stay.

The heart of downtown Seattle, **Pike Place Market** is a raucous fish, crafts, and farmers market with some 500 different stalls and stores, including the original branch of Starbucks, filling an early-1900s municipal-feeling building that steps along the waterfront. For a respite from the hubbub, head two blocks south to the post-modern **Seattle Art Museum** (1300 1st Ave., 206/654-3100, Wed.-Mon., $25-35) and enjoy the amazing collection of regional Native American art and artifacts on display. Much more memorable and enjoyable is the shiny **Seattle Central Library** (1000 4th Ave.), a fantastic (and free!) high-tech space whose multifaceted glass diamond exterior steps down between two city blocks.

At the south edge of downtown, a little under a mile from Pike Place Market, the 20-some-block **Pioneer Square** historic district preserves the original core of the city, which boomed in the late 1890s with the Klondike Gold Rush. Just south of

Seattle skyline

Pioneer Square, spectators can enjoy downtown views and Puget Sound sunsets at **Safeco Field** ballpark, where the **Seattle Mariners** (206/346-4001) play. The soccer **Seattle Sounders** and NFL champion **Seattle Seahawks** play next door at **CenturyLink Field,** cheered on by the world's loudest fans (136-plus decibels).

Another essential place to go is the **Seattle Center** (206/684-7200), a mile north of downtown at Broad Street and 5th Avenue North, built for the 1962 World's Fair and featuring Seattle's Space Age icon the **Space Needle** ($13-29). The Seattle Center, which you can reach via a quick ride on Seattle's short monorail, is the primary location for Seattle's excellent annual Labor Day arts and music festival, **Bumbershoot,** and is also home to the intriguing **Museum of Pop Culture** (206/770-2700, daily, $19-33), a hands-on musical exploration that includes a living memorial to the city's native-born guitar genius Jimi Hendrix. A don't-miss photo opportunity: a statue of Chief Seattle with the Space Needle rising behind him.

PRACTICALITIES

Seattle's main airport is Seattle-Tacoma International Airport ("Sea-Tac"), a half-hour drive south of downtown Seattle via the I-5 freeway. Seattle's freeways are often filled to capacity most of the day, especially with ongoing demolition and replacement of the old US-99 Alaskan Way Viaduct, which runs along the downtown waterfront, then follows Aurora Avenue on a soaring bridge over the west end of Lake Union. (By the way, under the Aurora Bridge sits one of Seattle's biggest pieces of auto-art: the **Fremont Troll,** caught in the act of capturing an old VW Beetle.)

Most everything of visitor interest in Seattle is within the compact, walkable downtown. There's also an extensive and expanding network of light-rail trams and trains run by SoundTransit, and a 1.2-mile-long **monorail** ($1-2.25) linking 5th Avenue and Pine Street downtown with the Seattle Center and Space Needle.

The niftiest place to stay is the **Hotel Ändra** (2000 4th Ave., 206/448-8600, $199 and up), a fully modernized 1920s hotel just a short walk from Pike Place Market. At the other end of the scale, the cheapest place to stay has to be the newly renovated **HI-Seattle at the American Hotel** (520 S. King St., 206/622-5443, dorm beds around $37), just east of Pioneer Square, which offers clean and comfortable dorm beds.

Seafood, not surprisingly, is the thing Seattle restaurants do best, and the city is full of great places to eat fish. The sushi here is as good as it gets outside Japan. Try **Maneki Restaurant** (304 6th Ave. S., 206/622-2631), which has been serving fresh sushi for over 100 years in the International District. For fish 'n' chips or cheap fresh oysters (and Washington produces more oysters than anywhere else in the United States), head down to **Emmett Watson's Oyster Bar** (206/448-7721) at the north end of Pike Place Market. More down-home fare is served up for breakfast, lunch, and dinner at the **5 Spot** (1502 Queen Anne Ave. N., 206/285-7768), in the residential Queen Anne district, about two miles northwest of downtown high above Lake Union.

East of Monroe, just west of the town of **Sultan,** a dollhouse-size church stands along US-2 as a roadside rest stop and mini shrine. Sultan is also home to an annual **Sultan Shindig and Logging Contest** every July.

Around Snohomish, the old US-2 road has been replaced by a four-lane freeway that loops around to the north, so follow signs for the "Historic Center."

Gold Bar and Index

Surprisingly little of the route traversed by US-2 on its way between the flatlands and Stevens Pass, high up in the Cascades, is given over to ski shops, bike shops, and espresso stands—except for the section around **Monroe,** where a mile-long gauntlet of mega-malls and fast-food franchises catering to Seattleites racing to and from the slopes comes as a shock to the system. East of Monroe, the onetime mining, logging, and railroad camp of **Gold Bar** stretches along US-2, halfway between Stevens Pass and Puget Sound. Besides all the gas stations and cafés you could want, Gold Bar also holds the well-posted trailhead (follow 1st Street north from the center of town) for the 3.5-mile hike to 265-foot **Wallace Falls,** one of the tallest in the northern Cascades, tantalizingly visible from US-2.

Farther east, **Index,** on a side road a mile north of US-2, sits at the western foot of the Cascade Mountains at the point where the scenery changes suddenly from pastoral to alpine. Besides The **River House Coffee Shop** (425/883-9039), you'll find a general store-post office, a neat little historical museum featuring Great Northern Railway photographs, and constant trains rumbling over the swimmably deep (but often freezing cold) Skykomish River.

You'll see reminders around town of Index's early industry: a granite quarry that cut the steps used in the state capitol. There's a giant saw blade in a park at the center of town and the **Index Town Wall,** a 1,200-foot sheer granite cliff that attracts Seattle rock climbers and quite a few peregrine falcons.

Wallace Falls

Skykomish and Deception Falls

Lining the busy Burlington Northern Santa Fe railroad tracks, a block south of US-2, **Skykomish** is a quirky and engaging place that seems to belong somewhere else, some long time ago. If you like the idea of being lulled to sleep by the rumble of trains, spend a night at the historic **Cascadia Inn** (210 Railroad Ave. E., 360/677-2030). The inn also has a café and a cocktail bar, popular with kayakers and trout-fishers who come for its access to the river, and with skiers who like its easy access to the slopes at Stevens Pass, 16 miles farther east.

Around eight miles east of Skykomish, midway to Stevens Pass, a well-marked

Cascadia Inn

turnout along US-2 gives access to one of the region's prettiest and most historically significant sites. On the north side of the highway, the parking area's interpretive exhibits tell the story of the Great Northern Railway, the transcontinental railroad that was completed on this spot in 1893. A plaque displays a photograph showing the driving of the traditional golden spike, while other exhibits discuss the construction and importance of the railroad in the growth of Puget Sound communities.

If you're not interested in railroad lore, head along the 100-yard-long paved trail that loops back under the highway to the powerful cascade of **Deception Falls.** If you can stand the usually bone-chilling snowmelt, you'll be pleased to find a number of deep and clean swimming holes in the area.

Stevens Pass

At the crest of the Cascades, US-2 climbs over 4,061-foot **Stevens Pass,** the highest and northernmost Cascade pass that's kept open year-round. Stevens Pass was also a historically vital railroad crossing, though Amtrak and other trains now avoid the pass, detouring instead through an eight-mile-long tunnel cut through the mountains in 1929. In 1910, before the completion of the tunnel—the longest still in use in the western hemisphere—the pass was the site of the worst avalanche disaster in U.S. history: 96 passengers and railroad workers were killed by a mile-long snow slide.

> **Stevens Pass** was named in honor of John F. Stevens, the Great Northern Railway engineer who also plotted the Panama Canal.

Besides providing grand views of the nearby peaks and more distant valleys, Stevens Pass is also a popular **ski area** (206/634-1645) with 10 chair lifts, reasonable rates, a terrain park, and a 1,800-foot vertical drop. In summer, the slopes convert to a mountain-biking terrain park.

Tumwater Canyon

Heading east through the Cascades from Stevens Pass, US-2 runs through the forests of **Tumwater Canyon,** a breathtaking place when fall color sweeps through it, and quite scenic any other time of year. Much of the surrounding wilderness was badly burned by wildfires, but most of the area right along US-2 survived pretty much unscathed.

All along this stretch, US-2 winds along the raging Wenatchee River through evergreen conifer forests highlighted by occasional aspens. The river is a popular rafting and kayaking spot, whose challenges vary with the water levels and intensity of the snowmelt. There are also some nice late-summer swimming holes, easily accessible from US-2, but the roadside is basically undeveloped, with one exception: At Coles Corner, 15 miles west of Leavenworth, the blue-roofed **'59er Diner** (509/763-2267) is a popular road-food restaurant, with great juicy burgers, crispy fries, milk shakes, and a jukebox.

Leavenworth

Sitting in the eastern foothills of the Cascades, 128 miles from Seattle, **Leavenworth** (pop. 1,965) has successfully transformed itself from an economically depressed railroad town into one of the most popular day-trip destinations in the Pacific Northwest. After the local lumber mills closed down in the mid-1960s, the town took advantage of its spectacular location and recreated itself as an ersatz Bavarian village; it has been drawing huge crowds of tourists ever since—over a million visitors annually. Check out the old photographs on the walls of **Stein** beer hall, on the corner of 8th and Commercial Streets, for the whole story.

Leavenworth

Over a dozen blocks of half-timbered pseudo-chalets and Tyrolean shopping malls house a range of low-budget craft galleries, sausage-and-beer gardens, and T-shirt stores, which you can escape by walking two blocks south to an attractively landscaped park along the Wenatchee River. Eat and drink at the **Heidleburger Drive-In** (12708 US-2, 509/548-5471), near the west end of town, or at the elaborate mock-Bavarian McDonald's. Perhaps the best place to eat and drink is the welcoming, popular, and inexpensive **München Haus** (709 Front St., 509/548-1158). Another pleasant and moderately priced place to stay is the **Linderhof Inn** (690 US-2, 509/548-5283 or 800/828-5680, $115 and up).

Cashmere

At the heart of the Wenatchee Valley, surrounded by apple orchards and bare-brown eastern Cascade foothills, **Cashmere** (pop. 3,063) has an attractive downtown district, its unusual red columns and brown-shingled awnings both shading the sidewalks and giving the town some visual identity. The main sight here is the large **Cashmere Museum and Pioneer Village** (daily Apr.-Oct., $7), off US-2 at the east end of town, with an excellent collection of Native American artifacts and an outdoor Pioneer Village made up of 20 different historic structures from around the county.

Four miles northwest of Cashmere, right along US-2, the sandstone slabs and spires of **Peshastin Pinnacles State Park** provide a popular rock-climbing spot—but no camping.

Cashmere is also the home of **Aplets and Cotlets,** fruit-and-nut candy, started here in the 1920s by two Armenian immigrants. These sweet treats are so dominant in the local scheme of things that the main route into town has been renamed Aplets Way. The **Liberty Orchards factory** (daily Apr.-Dec., Mon.-Fri. Jan.-Mar.), across from the railroad depot, is open for free tours and samples.

For road food (and good milk shakes!), stop by **Rusty's Drive-In** (700 Cotlets Way, 509/782-2425) at the east edge of town near the museum, or head to the block-long downtown district, where you'll find a handful of cafés and taverns and the **Village Inn** (229 Cottage Ave., 509/782-3522, $79-109).

Ohme Gardens County Park

Overlooking the confluence of the Wenatchee and Columbia Rivers on a bluff above the junction of US-2 and US-97, **Ohme Gardens County Park** (509/662-5785, daily Apr. 15-Oct. 15, $8) maintains nine acres of immaculate greenery that offer a cool contrast to eastern Washington's arid terrain. Created beginning in 1929 by the Ohme family, the lush plantings of ferns and evergreens have transformed an otherwise rugged Cascade crest. Stone pathways wind past waterfalls and rocky pools, culminating in a rustic lookout that gives sweeping views of Wenatchee and the surrounding Columbia River Valley.

Wenatchee

Just south of US-2, **Wenatchee** (pop. 31,925) is the commercial center of the Wenatchee Valley, one of the world's most productive apple- and pear-growing regions—it's responsible for about half the nation's annual crop. The **Washington Apple Commission Visitor Center,** a block south of US-2 below the Ohme Gardens, is the place to go to find out all about the state's apple industry, and to enjoy potent air-conditioning.

Wenatchee stretches south from US-2, with three miles of shopping malls, car dealerships, and anonymous highway sprawl before you reach the downtown business district. Many large fruit warehouses and a nice park line the railroad tracks along the riverfront. One place worth stopping is the excellent **Wenatchee Valley Museum and Cultural Center** (127 S. Mission St., Tues.-Sat., $5), which contains extensive displays tracing the region's prehistoric and pioneer past, from native rock art to a working HO-gauge model of the Great Northern Railway route over the Cascades. An adjacent building houses a large exhibit on Washington's apple industry, including an antique but fully functioning apple sorting and packing line.

Around the corner from the museum, **McGlinn's Public House** (111 Orondo Ave., 509/663-9073), has wood-fired pizzas and other good food. Along with every fast-food franchise known to humankind, Wenatchee also has some great local haunts, including **Dusty's In-N-Out** (1427 N. Wenatchee Ave., 509/662-7805), famous for burgers and shakes (and words of wisdom on its sign) since 1949. There are also lots of motels, ranging from the national chains to the business-oriented **Coast Wenatchee Center Hotel** (201 N. Wenatchee Ave., 509/662-1234, $109 and up).

Wenatchee apples

Lake Chelan

From Wenatchee, US-97A runs north along the west bank of the Columbia River to beautiful **Lake Chelan,** at the southern edge of the North Cascades National Park. Edged by wilderness and surrounded by tall mountain peaks, fjord-like Lake Chelan offers a quick and comfortable escape from the modern world, thanks to a pair of **Lady of the Lake tour boats** (509/682-4584, daily May-Oct. shorter hours Nov.-Apr., $36-61 round-trip), which cross the waters to the peaceful hamlet of **Stehekin,** on the lake's road-free northern shore. One Lady is faster than the other, so check the schedules.

Lake Chelan

North Cascades Lodge at Stehekin

From Stehekin, where there is a **national park visitors center** (509/699-2080), you can hike deep into the volcanic wilds of the North Cascades, ride bikes along old mining trails, fish or swim in the glacial lake, and stay the night at the 28-unit **North Cascades Lodge at Stehekin** (509/682-4494, $145 and up), one of a handful of tourist facilities in this delightfully isolated neck of the woods.

If you don't have much time but still want to savor the Lake Chelan experience, head to **Campbell's Resort** (509/682-2561), which has nice rooms and a great restaurant on the easier-to-reach south shore.

Waterville

Standing at the center of fertile wheat fields 10 miles east of the Columbia River, the compact farming town of **Waterville** (pop. 1,138) was laid out in 1885 around the stately whitewashed brick **Douglas County Courthouse,** which still stands at Birch and Rainier Streets. Most of downtown Waterville has been declared a national historic district, and the four franchise-free blocks of attractive brick buildings still house banks, cafés, and grocery stores—making it a nice place to stop on a journey across the state. There's a photogenic sign-painted barn at the west end of town, and midway along US-2's zigzag through town, the **Douglas County Museum and Historical Society** (124 W. Walnut St., 509/745-8435, Tues.-Sun. late May-early Oct., donation) has an intriguing display of objects tracing regional history, including Native American artifacts and a perfectly preserved pioneer post office.

Across US-2 from the museum, the attractive **Waterville Historic Hotel** (102 East Park St., 509/745-8695, $49-189) has been nicely restored and offers unexpectedly characterful and comfortable accommodations; it's like stepping back a century or so, to a time when Teddy Roosevelt was president. For a bite to eat, head a block north from the museum to the welcoming **Coyote Pass Café** (104 W. Locust St., 509/888-4189), on US-2.

Moses Coulee

One of the last vestiges of eastern Washington's natural, unirrigated landscape, protected in its untrammeled splendor by the nonprofit Nature Conservancy, **Moses Coulee** is an 800-foot-deep gorge bounded by vertical walls of ruddy brown volcanic basalt, brightened by splashes of green and orange lichen. From the rolling plains above, US-2 cuts down into the coulee, then back up the other side, passing through some of the Columbia River Basin's sole surviving sagebrush and giving a strong sense of how profoundly irrigation has changed the region.

Coulee City and Dry Falls

A shipping center for the wheat farms of eastern Washington, **Coulee City** (pop. 562) calls itself the "Friendliest Town in the West." Despite this claim, there's no more reason to stop now than there was during the pioneer days of the 1860s, when it was said that transfer times on stagecoaches and trains were arranged so that travelers were forced to spend the night in Coulee City, like it or not. If you find yourself here, you can choose from a pair of motels and three gas stations.

Northwest of Coulee City, the large **Dry Falls Dam** impounds Columbia River water to form Banks Lake; Hwy-155 runs along its sluggish shores on the way to the Grand Coulee Dam. Though you can see the coulee's towering basalt walls from this road, to get a sense of what the Grand Coulee looked like before the dams were built, follow Hwy-17 four miles south from Coulee City to where the **Dry Falls** escarpment stands out as the most impressive reminder of the region's tumultuous geology.

Interpretive exhibits along the highway explain that during the last ice age, when the Columbia River flowed over the falls, this was the most powerful waterfall on the planet: twice as high as Niagara, and over three miles across.

Grand Coulee Dam

The centerpiece of the massive project of dams and canals that have "reclaimed" the Columbia Basin, the **Grand Coulee Dam** is one of the civil engineering wonders of the world. Built from 1933 to 1941 under the auspices of FDR's New Deal, at a cost of many millions of dollars and 77 lives, the dam is one of the largest concrete structures in the world: 550 feet high, 500 feet thick at its base, and nearly a mile across. The combined generating capacity is more than 6,809 megawatts—half of which comes from the Third Power Plant, added in 1975. Exhibits on the construction and impact of the dam fill the large modern **Visitor Arrival Center** (509/633-9265, daily, free) just downstream. On summer evenings a free half-hour laser light show is projected onto the spillway of the dam.

In **Electric City,** along Hwy-155 about 2.5 miles southwest of Coulee Dam, take a look at the **Gehrke Windmill Garden,** a whimsical collection of whirligigs and windmills made by folk artist Emil Gehrke, who lived nearby until his death in 1979.

There are three small towns—Coulee Dam, Grand Coulee, and Electric City, respectively, east to west from the dam—all of which serve the needs of boaters, anglers, and other visitors. The best place to see the Grand Coulee Dam light show is the pleasant **Columbia River Inn** (509/633-2100 or 800/633-6421, $118 and up), across from the visitors center.

The Columbia Basin: Wilbur and Davenport

The 150-mile stretch of rolling farmland that lies to the east of the Cascades is a natural desert, receiving an average of 10 inches of annual rainfall. Though small-scale farming limped along here for over a century, the region underwent a whole-sale change after World War II, when irrigation water from reclamation projects along the Columbia River and its many tributaries turned the sagebrush plains into the proverbial amber waves of grain, spreading toward the horizon against an (almost) always-clear blue sky.

US-2 runs directly across the heart of this sparsely populated, nearly treeless region, passing through a few small towns. In **Wilbur,** at the turnoff to Coulee Dam, an old service station has been brought back to life as a drive-by espresso stand, and **Billy Burgers** (804 SE Main St., 509/647-5651) has good food and great milk shakes, right on US-2. Eight miles east is the blink-and-you'll-miss-it community of **Creston** ("Home of 1982 and 1984 Girls State B Champions"), where daily life revolves around the **Corner Café** at the center of town.

Twenty miles east of Creston, **Davenport,** one of the oldest towns in eastern Washington, has a nifty old courthouse on a hill just north of US-2, a handful of quaint old houses, and the small **Lincoln County Historical Museum** (509/725-6711), located a block south of US-2 at Park and 7th Streets. Davenport also boasts a burger-and-shake place along US-2 at the east end of town.

Spokane

The only real city in eastern Washington, **Spokane** (pop. 208,916) feels even bigger than it is thanks to its location amid the prosperous agricultural hinterlands of the Columbia River Basin. First established as a fur-trading outpost around 1810, Spokane began to grow when railroads arrived in the 1870s and has boomed since the advent of irrigation in the 1940s. The second largest city in Washington, and the biggest between Seattle and Minneapolis, Spokane is economically dependent on warehousing and transportation, taking advantage of its busy railroads as well as its location at the junction of US-2, US-395, and I-90.

Though downtown Spokane boasts a number of grand buildings—one guide-book calls Riverside Street between Jefferson and Lincoln "the loveliest three blocks in the Pacific Northwest"—Spokane came of age when it hosted the 1974 World's Fair, for which much of the riverfront was cleared and converted to the attractive 100-acre **Riverfront Park.** Designed by Frederick Law Olmsted a mere century earlier but never implemented, the park gives good views of tumbling **Spokane Falls,** which form a deep canyon at the center of downtown. Besides an opera house and a convention center, other remnants of the fair include a summer-only **gondola sky ride** (daily, $7.50) that drops down to the base of the falls, a 1909 **Looff Carousel** ($2) complete with hand-carved wooden horses, an IMAX theater, and a landmark sandstone clock tower that's the sole reminder of the Great Northern rail yards that lined the riverfront for most of the previous century.

Riverfront Park is right at the heart of downtown, and a quick walking tour can take in dozens of well-preserved, creatively reused architectural treats, like the Spokane **City Hall** (808 W. Spokane Falls Blvd.), which faces the southwest corner of Riverfront Park—the only government I know of that's housed in a converted Montgomery Ward department store, a cast concrete gem dating from 1929. Another worthwhile stop is **Auntie's Bookstore** (402 W. Main Ave., 509/838-0206), a full-service independent bookstore with a popular café next door.

Northeast of downtown, across the Spokane River via Division Street (US-2), the best-known dropout of **Gonzaga University,** Bing Crosby, is fondly remembered in a museum in the **Bing Crosby House** (508 E Sharp Ave.).

Spokane's other center of visitor interest is **Browne's Addition,** a turn-of-the-20th-century residential district a mile or so west of downtown with many stately homes. The highlight here is the wonderful MAC, the **Northwest Museum of Arts and Culture** (2316 W. 1st Ave., 509/456-3931, Tues.-Sun., $10), which houses extensive collections of artifacts tracing Native American and regional history and culture.

Spokane Practicalities

There's no shortage of good places to eat in Spokane, from hearty and homespun to eclectic and expensive. Spokane's best breakfast is served up in a unique setting: the former presidential carriage of the Northern Pacific Railroad is now **Frank's Diner** (1516 W. 2nd Ave., 509/747-8798) near downtown. Spokane's youthful, outdoorsy population also supports numerous bistro-style restaurants and brewpubs, like **Hills' Restaurant and Lounge** (401 W. Main Ave., 509/747-3946), serving great Reuben sandwiches and a full range of food and beer, across from Auntie's Bookstore. In Browne's Addition, west of downtown, another good bet is The **Elk Public House** (1931 W. Pacific Ave., 509/363-1973), with yet more good bistro-style food.

Motels line the main highways in and out of Spokane, especially along I-90. Spokane also has a great place to stay at the heart of downtown: The fabulous **Historic Davenport Hotel** (10 S. Post St., 800/899-1482, $150 and up) has luxurious rooms in the fully renovated circa-1914 original and in a brand-new tower.

In summer, enjoy a Class A **Spokane Indians** (509/535-2922) baseball game at **Avista Stadium,** on the county fairgrounds off Broadway. Games are broadcast on **KGA 1510 AM.**

One of Spokane's most popular roadside attractions is the giant **Radio Flyer wagon,** 12 feet tall with a slide down the "handle," near the clock tower in Riverfront Park.

Some people in Spokane insist that rather than dying in a shootout in South America, Wild West legend Butch Cassidy actually lived for years in Spokane, under the name William Phillips, until his death at age 70 in 1937.

Newport

Northeast of Spokane, US-2 crosses a few miles of suburban sprawl before winding through 35 miles of beautiful forested uplands and occasional crossroads communities on the Idaho border. Straddling the state line, **Newport** (pop. 2,126) began as a small trading post on the Idaho side in 1889, then moved to Washington when the Great Northern Railway arrived in 1892. The original town site, overlooking the Pend Oreille (pronounced "PON-duh-ray") River, holds the business district, while the railroad legacy still defines much of the main part of town. Two depots face each other along US-2 at the south end of the three-block main street, Washington Avenue, one holding the offices of a lumber company, the other housing the small but enjoyable **Pend Oreille County Museum** (daily May-Oct., $2), which has farming and mining artifacts—plus a pencil collection.

IDAHO

Even though the route zigzags for some 75 miles along the Kootenai and Pend Oreille Rivers, it doesn't take long for US-2 to cross the narrow neck, known as the Panhandle, of northern Idaho. Following the Pend Oreille River east from Washington, the route passes a pair of struggling but proud old logging communities, then pauses at the resort town of **Sandpoint** before threading the deep gorge of the Kootenai River upstream toward Montana.

Sandpoint

Located at the junction of US-2 and US-95 at the northern end of Idaho's largest lake, Pend Oreille, **Sandpoint** (pop. 7,365) is a resort community with a relaxed welcoming feel. The highly regarded **Schweitzer Mountain Resort** (208/263-9555 or 877/487-4643) north of Sandpoint attracts adventurous off-piste skiers in winter and daredevil mountain bikers in summer. The mix of Rocky Mountain scenery and abundant recreation has made Sandpoint a popular place to visit and live, yet despite the dozens of real estate agents and other signs of potential despoliation, it still feels like a small town.

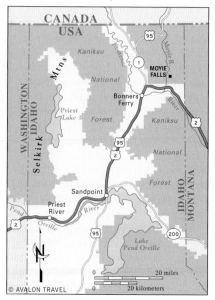

As you might guess from the name, Sandpoint boasts the fine quarter-mile-long **City Beach,** just a few blocks' walk from downtown at the east end of Bridge Street, complete with volleyball courts and a dock where you can board tour boats to cruise the lake.

South of downtown, summer

visitors in search of burgers and soft-serve cones flock to **Dub's Drive-In** (703 US-2, 208/263-4300). Downtown, the main business district along 1st Avenue fills a half-dozen blocks around the landmark **Panida Theater** (208/263-9191), where big names and locals still perform. You'll find a number of good cafés here, plus **Eichardt's** (212 Cedar St., 208/263-4005), a beer-drinker's delight with great food (burgers, sandwiches, fish 'n' chips). Two blocks east, the **Cedar Street Bridge** was rebuilt in 1983 to house a funky range of boutiques, cafés, and food stalls, inspired by the Ponte Vecchio in Florence. Besides the $150 rooms at Sandpoint's resorts, there are many more moderate motels, like the slightly faded but well-located **Best Western Edgewater Resort** (56 Bridge St., 208/263-3194, $109-279), right on the lakefront.

> The Idaho-Montana line marks the boundary between the Pacific and mountain time zones, so adjust your clocks and watches accordingly.

Naples and Bonners Ferry

North from Sandpoint, US-2 and US-95 run together through broad flat valleys dotted with small timber towns. The largest of these, **Naples,** is still a little bit notorious because of its connections to the 1990s battles between the FBI and local neo-Nazi sympathizers around nearby Ruby Ridge. These days things are pretty quiet, but travelers are drawn to Naples's friendly **Northwoods Tavern** (208/267-1094), on US-2, a great place to meet locals over a beer and a game of pool (or three). There's a handy general store, and not too far away is the **Naples Inn** (208/267-5964).

Ten miles north of Naples, and named after a ferry service across the Kootenai River that started here in 1864, **Bonners Ferry** (pop. 2,543) is a busy blue-collar town with a natural resource-based (read: logging and farming, especially hop-growing) economy. The **Kootenai River Inn** (7169 Plaza St., 208/267-8511, $99 and up) is an Native American-run casino and Best Western hotel.

Away from the highway, the Bonners Ferry area has an unusual lodging option: the **Shorty Peak Fire Lookout** (around $25), about 45 miles from town and a half-mile hike from the nearest road, way up in the wild Selkirk Mountains, where two people can spend the night and take in the panoramic views. For reservations and information on hiking in the surrounding wilderness, contact the **USFS ranger station** (208/267-5561) on US-2/95 at the south edge of town.

Between Bonners Ferry and the Montana state line, US-2 crosses the once-wild, now-dammed Moyie River on a 450-foot-high bridge.

MONTANA

Crossing northern Montana roughly 30 miles south of the Canadian border, US-2 gives an up-close look at two very different parts of this huge state. The western quarter, on the slopes of the Rocky Mountains, offers

incredible scenic beauty and innumerable options for outdoor recreation, culminating in magnificent **Glacier National Park.** East of Glacier, it's like a completely different world as two-lane US-2 (popularly known as the "Hi-Line") races across glaciated Great Plains rangelands along the many tributaries of the broad Missouri River. A few low buttes and cylindrical grain silos rise up in sharp silhouettes, but the horizon is the dominant aspect, stretching for what feels like hundreds of miles in all directions. Apart from dozens of one-side-of-the-road blink-stops, the towns along US-2 in the eastern stretches of Montana—Culbertson, Wolf Point, Glasgow, Malta, and Havre—are few and far between. It's here you realize what the "Big Sky Country" is all about: cruising along at 70 mph, pacing a freight train and waving at the engineer, and *never* passing a gas station when the tank is less than half full.

How big is Montana? It stretches for over 560 miles east to west, covering an area larger than New England and New York put together, but it has a total population smaller than that of Hartford, Connecticut.

The many roadside crosses you'll see while driving through Montana each mark a traffic fatality. Since 1953, they have been placed along the roads by the American Legion. Many are now elaborate shrines to lost loved ones.

Writer and resident Rick Bass has documented the isolated **Yaak River Valley,** north of US-2 via the scenic Hwy-508, in a trio of compelling books: the nonfiction titles *Winter: Notes from Montana* and *The Book of Yaak,* and a 1998 novel, *Where the Sea Used to Be.*

Troy: Kootenai Falls

On the banks of the broad Kootenai (pronounced "KOOT-nee") River, 14 miles east of the Idaho border, the mining and lumber-milling town of **Troy** (pop. 938) is at nearly the state's lowest elevation—1,892 feet above sea level. There's not a lot to the place, apart from a short stretch of motels, gas stations, taverns, churches, and cafés—the best of which is the family-friendly **Silver Spur** (13891 US-2, 406/295-2033), right in town—plus a small historical museum and visitor center at the east end of town. Some seven miles west of Troy, there's a nice USFS campground at the confluence of the Yaak and Kootenai Rivers.

Though the only sign says simply Historic Point, the nicest spot to stop is nine miles west of Libby, two miles east of Troy, where the thundering cascade of **Kootenai Falls** drops down a half-mile-long series of terraces. Two hiking trails leave from the well-marked roadside parking area, one leading 400 yards upstream to the main falls, the other heading downstream to a rickety old swinging bridge that sways from cables suspended 50 feet above the green water.

For most of the way between Troy and Libby, US-2 is bordered by marked turnouts where trails lead to the narrow, twisting old highway, preserved as a hiking and cross-country skiing trail through the dense forest.

Libby

The lumber town of **Libby** (pop. 2,628) was first founded as a gold-mining camp but grew into its present elongated form after the Great Northern Railway came through in 1892. On the south bank of the Kootenai River, Libby is just downstream from the Libby Dam, which was built in 1972 and forms the Lake Koocanusa Reservoir, stretching north into Canada. Despite the fact that Libby is the hometown of former Montana governor and Republican Party national chairman Marc Racicot, the town has suffered one of the worst cases of long-term toxic pollution in recent U.S. history. From the 1940s up until 1990, mining company W. R. Grace dug millions of tons of asbestos-laced vermiculite rock out of a local

Libby Dam on the Kootenai River

mountain, covering Libby in toxic dust that has caused more than 1,200 people (almost half the current population) to suffer from serious lung diseases. The EPA has taken 20 years and spent more than $600 million to clean up Libby's streets, gardens, and houses, and though company officials covered about half the costs, they were eventually cleared of all criminal charges.

Despite the occasional media interest in the asbestos case, Libby looks like a pretty typical Montana mountain town. Alongside the railroad tracks, Libby strings for a few miles along US-2 frontage, where you can find car washes and gas stations galore, plus a Subway, a Pizza Hut, and one good stop: the **Last Straw Café** (30890 US-2, 406/293-4000). A half dozen motels, including the **Sandman Motel** (31901 US-2, 406/293-8831, $65-105) offer rooms. Off the highway north of US-2 toward Libby Dam, the old center of town holds more cafés, a microbrewery, and the **Past Time Bar** (216 Mineral Ave., 406/293-6097).

A number of pleasant **campgrounds** operate in and around Libby, including excellent spots in the nearby **Cabinet Mountains Wilderness.** Libby's most interesting lodging option is spending a night or two in the **Big Creek Baldy Lookout** ($40), which is 20 miles north of town. The popular lookout sleeps up to four people; for details contact the Libby ranger station (406/293-7773) or Kootenai National Forest (406/293-6211).

Between Libby and the busy mini metropolis of the Columbia Falls-Whitefish-Kalispell area, US-2 traverses 70 miles of Kootenai National Forest, an all but uninhabited area, sections of which have been badly charred by forest fires. A small display at milepost 63 explains the role of fire in the natural scheme of things.

West of Glacier National Park, US-2 crosses US-93, the **Border to Border** route, which runs through the towns of **Whitefish** and **Kalispell** (see page 125). Full coverage of this route begins on page 110.

Columbia Falls and Hungry Horse

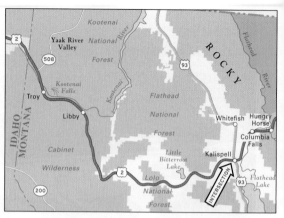

Two intriguingly named towns line US-2 between Kalispell and Glacier National Park. A roadside collection of gas stations and industrial plants, including a massive Plum Creek lumber mill, make up the much larger town of **Columbia Falls** (pop. 4,688), where, despite the name, there are no falls. There are, however, a ton of entertaining roadside attractions right on US-2, from go-karts to mini-golf, and a couple of good low-frills restaurants, including the MSG-free Chinese food at **Tien's Place** (329 W. 9th St., 406/892-1585) and great rotisserie chicken and ribs a block away at **The Back Room** (522 W. 9th St., 406/892-3131).

If you like homespun Americana and roadside kitsch, you're in for a big treat as you head east along US-2. The town of **Hungry Horse** (pop. 826), a service center for the large reservoir to the southeast, proclaims itself "The Friendliest Dam Town in the Whole World," and boasts ever bigger roadside attractions, starting with the **House of Mystery** (406/892-1210, daily Apr.-Oct., $12), "Montana's Only Vortex," on the north side of US-2. Located three miles east of Columbia Falls, along the Flathead River at the mouth of Bad Rock Canyon (which resident Native Americans thought was haunted), this is among the more credible of these places where, to quote from the brochure, "the laws of physics are bent, if not broken altogether . . . where birds won't fly and trees grow at odd angles. Could it be a bearing point for extraterrestrial visits centuries ago? . . . Nobody knows!" It's as fun as these places get (which is to say, very, if you get into the spirit of the place), and well worth the minimal admission fee; there's a good gift shop, too.

The stretch of US-2 between Hungry Horse and the turnoff to Glacier National Park holds one more "attraction" after another, but even if you're appalled by the brashness of all this hucksterism, you'll want to stop in Hungry Horse for a piece of pie or a milk shake at The **Huckleberry Patch** (8868 E. US-2, 406/387-5000 or 800/527-7340), at the center of town. In summer, it also has a full-service restaurant, boasting over 25 different fresh berry and cherry concoctions.

West Glacier

Like many tourist towns on the edges of our national parks, **West Glacier** has its share of tackiness, but here it's on a tolerably small scale and limited to the approach along US-2 from the west. After all the billboards advertising scenic helicopter rides, taxidermy museums, and "The World's Greatest Maze," the actual town of West Glacier seems serenely quiet and peaceful, with little more than a couple of restaurants and comfortable motels, including the **West Glacier Motel** (406/888-5662, $90 and up), right on the Flathead River (and the railroad tracks!). There's also a large visitors center for Glacier National Park.

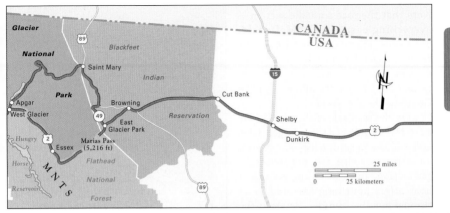

For many visitors, especially those who love trains, the main highlight in West Glacier is the landmark **Belton Chalet** (12575 E. US-2, 406/888-5000, $140 and up), built by the Great Northern in 1910 and fully, lovingly restored in 2000. Rooms are small but have balconies with nice views, and the restaurant is one of the best in the Glacier region.

Belton Chalet

Glacier National Park

The wildest and most rugged of all the Rocky Mountain national parks, **Glacier National Park** protects some 1,500 square miles of high-altitude scenery, including more than 200 lakes, and countless rivers and streams. Knifelike ridges of colorful sedimentary rock rise to over 10,000 feet, looming high above elongated glacier-carved valleys. Grizzly bears, black bears, bighorn sheep, mountain lions, and wolves roam the park's wild backcountry, which is crisscrossed by some 700 miles of hiking and riding trails. If you want to see the glaciers for which the park is named, you need to act fast: a warming climate has shrunk the glaciers to less than half their historic sizes, and forecasts say they may disappear completely with five years.

The park's main features are reached via 50-mile-long **Going-to-the-Sun Road**, a magnificent serpentine highway that is arguably the most scenic route on this planet. Climbing up from dense forests to the west and prairie grasslands to the east, this narrow road (built in 1932, and currently undergoing a multiyear rehabilitation project) is the only route across the park's million acres.

Note that the road's middle section—everything east of Lake McDonald, basically—is usually closed by snow from late October until early June. RV drivers note: No vehicles or combinations over 21 feet are allowed on the Going-to-the-Sun Road.

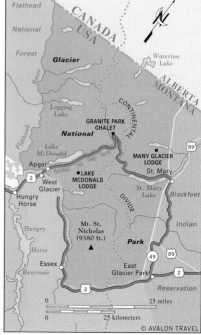

On the west side of the park, lovely Lake McDonald is Glacier's largest lake, and also the most developed area, with an attractive lodge, two restaurants, a gas station, and a nice campground. A boat offers hour-long narrated tours throughout the summer. Between the lake and Logan Pass, **Avalanche Creek** is the most beautiful short hike in the park, winding through dense groves of cedar and fir alongside a creek that cascades noisily down a sharp cleft in the deep red rock. The two-mile trail ends up at Avalanche Lake, hemmed in by 1,500-foot-high cliffs.

The heart of the park is **Logan Pass,** a 6,680-foot saddle straddling the Continental Divide, which comes alive when the snow melts to reveal a rainbow of brightly colored wildflowers. Two popular trails run from the large visitors center: The shorter but more strenuous one heads south on a wooden boardwalk across an alpine meadow to a viewpoint overlooking Hidden Lake, while the fairly flat Highline Trail

Going-to-the-Sun Road

Avalanche Creek

runs north, high above the Going-to-the-Sun Road, leading seven miles to the back-country **Granite Park Chalet** (888/345-2649, around $100 per person) where you can stay overnight in a spectacular setting. Bed linens and simple meals are available for additional fees, or you can bring your own sleeping bags and food.

Along with the extensive privately owned facilities just outside the park along US-2 at West Glacier, East Glacier, and St. Mary, there are a number of rustic lodges and motels within the park. Apart from the chalets, all lodging (and everything else) in Glacier is run by the same concessionaire, **Xanterra** (303/265-7010 or 855/733-4522). The nicest place to stay is the intimate, comfortable **Lake McDonald Lodge,** with a lovely lobby filled with comfy chairs arrayed around a fireplace, and lots of bearskin and

buffalo rugs. In the park's northeast corner, the **Many Glacier Lodge** is a circa-1915 pseudo-Swiss chalet on the shores of Swiftcurrent Lake, looking up at Grinnell Point. There are over a dozen campgrounds in Glacier, but they fill up fast.

Besides the grand lodges, a few other relics of Glacier Park's early days as a "Grand Tour" destination still survive: bright red, open-top, vintage 1930s touring buses, expensively overhauled to be as eco-friendly as possible, run along the Going-to-the-Sun Road, providing enjoyable guided tours as well as a shuttle service for hikers.

For a complete overview of the park, stop in at one of three main visitors centers, located in West Glacier, at Logan Pass (summer only), and at the eastern entrance in the town of St. Mary; or call the **park headquarters** (406/888-7800 or 406/888-7931).

Essex: The Izaak Walton Inn

Avoiding the most extreme alpine scenery and the heavy winter snows, US-2 winds around the southern edge of Glacier National Park, climbing over the Continental Divide at 5,216-foot **Marias Pass,** the lowest of the Rocky Mountain passes. Though the road and the railroad are kept open year-round, there's little visible development, and numerous trailheads access the southern reaches of the Glacier National Park backcountry.

One place that's well worth a stop, or better yet an extended stay, is the **Izaak Walton Inn** (406/888-5700, $109 and up), midway between East and West Glacier, a half mile south of US-2 in the railroad village of **Essex.** Especially in winter, when the inn overlooks miles of cross-country ski trails, this is one of the best stops in the state. A humbler version of the grand Glacier Park lodges, the inn was built to house railroad workers (which it still does) and is now a popular year-round alternative to the often overbooked accommodations within the park. The inn also serves good food for breakfast, lunch, and dinner (try the huckleberry desserts).

Another place worth a stop in early summer is the so-called **Goat Lick** on US-2, near milepost 182 about five miles east of the Essex turnoff, where, in April and May especially, dozens of shaggy white mountain goats congregate around a mineral-rich spring.

East Glacier Park

Situated along US-2 at the southwest edge of the Blackfeet Indian Reservation, the town of **East Glacier Park,** as the name suggests, is the eastern gateway to Glacier National Park. It has a number of services, including general stores and gas stations, plus **Serrano's** (29 Dawson Ave., 406/226-9392), a good Mexican restaurant just south of US-2. North of US-2, on the way to Glacier National Park, there's more good food available at the **Whistle Stop Restaurant** (1024 Hwy-49, 406/226-9292).

With the main park entrance over 30 miles northeast at St. Mary, East Glacier Park is not an especially convenient base, though it does have one compelling attraction: the **Glacier Park Lodge** (406/892-2525 or 406/226-5600), the grandest of all the historic park lodges. Built by the Great Northern Railway to attract visitors to the park (and to its trains), the lodge centers on a magnificent lobby built of 40-foot-tall Douglas fir logs—each of which runs floor to ceiling, with the bark still on it. It's an impressively rustic space, and well worth a look.

St. Mary

Located on the Blackfeet Indian Reservation, 30 miles north of US-2 at the east entrance to Glacier National Park, the town of **St. Mary** makes a great alternative to the in-park lodges. At the east end of the historic Going-to-the-Sun Road, St. Mary has a large Glacier National Park visitors center and the clean, modern **St. Mary Lodge & Resort** (406/732-4431, $76-499). Before or after a big day on the trails, you'll be pleased to find the excellent **Park Café and Grocery** (3147 US-89, 406/732-9979 or 406/732-9300), which serves mega-breakfasts and yet more great berry pies, a half mile north of the park turnoff. The Park Café is worth planning your day around, as the berry pies are every bit as amazing as Glacier's Rocky Mountain scenery.

St. Mary makes an especially handy base for visiting the comparatively quiet Many Glacier section of Glacier National Park, and for seeing the sights of adjacent **Waterton Lakes National Park,** across the border in Canada.

Blackfeet Indian Reservation

The 1.5-million-acre **Blackfeet Indian Reservation,** stretching north to the Canadian border along the eastern border of Glacier National Park, is a weather-beaten land home to 17,321 members of what was once the most powerful nation on the Northern Plains. The Blackfeet, whose nomadic lives took them all over the plains in pursuit of buffalo, were feared and respected for their fighting and hunting abilities, though contact with white traders brought smallpox, alcoholism, and other diseases that devastated the nation. Their strength in battle won the Blackfeet concessions from the encroaching U.S. government, including a huge swath of land that, in 1855, included everything north of the Yellowstone River between the Dakotas and the Continental Divide. Much of this land, including what's now the eastern half of Glacier

Thirteen miles east of Browning, or 22 miles west of Cut Bank, a much-abused monument along US-2 points out the most northerly point reached by Lewis and Clark on their cross-country expedition. On July 23, 1806, Meriwether Lewis, searching for the headwaters of the Marias River, made it to a spot four miles north of US-2, which he called **Camp Disappointment,** before turning back because of bad weather.

teepees in Browning

National Park, was later bought back or simply taken away; the Blackfeet Nation now earns most of its income from ranching and oil and natural gas leases.

The Blackfeet Nation's headquarters and main commercial center is **Browning** (pop. 1,061), located on US-2 near the eastern entrance to Glacier National Park. Like many reservation towns, Browning has a desolate and depressing feel to it, but there are a couple of places worth stopping, including the **Museum of the Plains Indian** (Tues.-Sat. summer, Mon.-Fri. fall-spring, $5), near the west end of town at the junction of US-2 and US-89. Operated by the U.S. government's Bureau of Indian Affairs, the bland building contains a small collection of Plains Indian arts and crafts, mostly blankets and jewelry. Browning, which comes alive during the annual **North American Indian Days Powwow** in early July, also has a couple of cafés, a small casino, and a large concrete tepee.

Cut Bank

It's hard for travelers heading west along US-2 to believe that, despite having covered over 1,000 miles of undulating Great Plains, they have yet to reach the mountains. It isn't until **Cut Bank** (pop. 2,820) that the see-forever glaciation looks like it might be waning. You crest a hill and suddenly there they are: the rugged Rocky Mountains. Popularly known as the coldest city in the United States, as measured at the local U.S. Weather Service monitoring station, Cut Bank is a friendly and pretty enough place, bisected neatly by US-2 and the railroad tracks.

Downtown, on US-2, the **Big Sky Café** (13 W. Main St., 406/873-4010) is great for rubbing shoulders with the locals at breakfast or lunch. At the east end of town, Cut Bank's iconic 27-foot-tall penguin stands next to the **Glacier Gateway Inn and Plaza** (1130 E. St., 406/873-5544 or 800/851-5541, $63-80), the town's nicest motel.

Shelby

By northern Great Plains standards, bustling **Shelby** (pop. 3,376) is a hive of activity, mainly due to the busy I-15 freeway, which crosses US-2 here, 25 miles south of the Canadian border. Even so, Shelby's activity—typical truck-jockey, blue-smoke activity—is relegated to the area immediately around the I-15 exit and to the busy multimodal depot along the Burlington Northern tracks. Otherwise, it's an oversize version of all the other Great Northern Railway towns, one that extends farther than most along the tracks, with wide streets and a much-appreciated hill flaring up to the south of downtown.

Shelby is not rowdy, but neither does it roll up its sidewalks by 8pm. Shelby has an impressive lineup of bars along Main Street (The Mint Club, the Montana Club,

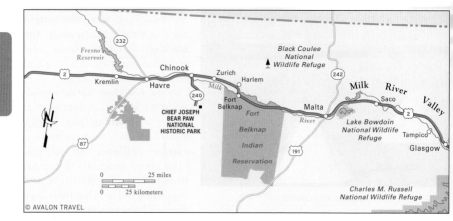

the Alibi Lounge, and the Tap Room, to name a few), but the town's major claim to fame is that it hosted the 1923 world heavyweight fight between Jack Dempsey and Tommy Gibbons, a 15-round decision for Dempsey that was closer than it should have been. The match was produced as a publicity stunt to lure people to the oil boomtown, and Shelby built a 40,000-seat arena, but after Dempsey's managers hemmed and hawed about canceling the bout, only 7,000 showed up.

A replica arena and a room full of artifacts from the fight are among the many intriguing items on display at the summer-only **Marias Museum of History and Art** (406/424-2551, Mon.-Sat., donation), in a former residence at the corner of 12th Avenue and 1st Street North. It feels much more like a home than a museum, which adds a welcome amount of weirdness to the usual battery of dusty old stuff. Best of all, the museum is across the street from the local **swimming pool,** an essential rest stop on a hot midsummer afternoon.

Shelby boasts the last good range of services for the 100-plus miles between here and Havre, so be sure to fill up the tank before setting off. There are a handful of cafés, like **The Griddle** (311 Main St., 406/434-7260), and an absolutely huge "Motel" sign marks the entrance to **O'Haire Manor** (204 S. 2nd St., 406/434-5555, $60 and up).

Heading east, US-2 eases into its long grind across the bare Great Plains, the level horizon broken by grain bins, wheat farms, and the occasional remnants of Cold War-era missile silos. Though the road meanders a little along the banks of the Milk and Mission Rivers, it's mostly a thumb-on-wheel, greased-lightning, straight-shot road, miles and miles of your own wandering thoughts.

Havre

The largest town along eastern US-2, **Havre** (pop. 9,310; pronounced "HAV-er") was founded by the Great Northern Railway and named, for no good reason, after the French port Le Havre, though you'd never tell by the pronunciation. Havre retains more than a little of its Wild West feel and has enough unusual attractions to merit an extended stop. West of town is a large area of eroded badlands, and just north of US-2, behind the Holiday Village Shopping Center, is **Wahkpa Chu'gn "Buffalo Jump" Archaeological Site** (406/265-6417, daily 9am-4pm June-Sept., $10). Dating to prehistoric times, the area was used by Plains people to drive bison to their deaths. Many of the artifacts recovered from the area are displayed inside nearby

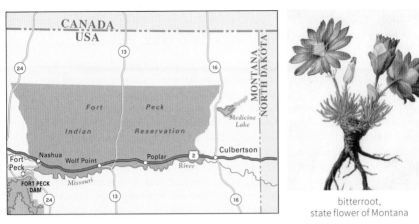

bitterroot,
state flower of Montana

H. Earl Clack Memorial Museum (406/265-4000, Tues.-Sat. 1pm-5pm Labor Day-Memorial Day, daily 11am-5pm Memorial Day-Labor Day, donation), which manages the site.

Havre itself, home to popular former governor Brian Schweitzer, is engaging and also a little rowdy. Numerous poker clubs (everything has "casino" tacked onto it) and cowboy bars line the compact downtown area, underneath which is a defunct underground world of illicit bordellos and opium dens, all part of the whiskey trail that flourished a century ago and again during Prohibition, when copious quantities of bathtub gin from Canada, a stone's throw north, were run through. Relaxed but informative tours ($15) are available through **Havre Beneath the Streets** (120 3rd Ave., 406/265-8888).

Along 1st Street (US-2) you'll find all the usual fast-food suspects, as well as a fresher deli-café, the **Lunch Box** (213 3rd Ave., 406/265-6588), south of US-2. For a place to stay, the plushest of Havre's handful of motels is the **Best Western PLUS Great Northern Inn** (1345 1st St., 406/265-4200, $90 and up).

For great shotgun-seat reading along the way, William Least Heat-Moon's *Blue Highways* contains an honest, lyrical account of the highs, lows, and endless in-betweens along this stretch, including a brief account of a day in Shelby.

SPEED LIMITS

DAY	REASONABLE & PRUDENT
TRUCK	60
NIGHT – ALL VEHICLES –	**55**

Chinook

Chinook (pop. 1,203) takes its name from the Northwest Native American patois for the warm southerly winds that rip through the area in January and February, raising temperatures some 50 degrees in a matter of hours, melting the winter snow, and allowing cattle to forage. Now a small cattle-ranching town, Chinook is best known for its proximity to the surrender site of Nez Percé Chief Joseph to the U.S. Army in 1877—which effectively marked the end of the Indian Wars of the Plains. The good

Until the oil crisis of 1974, when federal lawmakers enacted a national speed limit of 55 mph, Montana law stipulated only that drivers should travel at a reasonable and prudent speed, with no legal maximum. In 1996 federal legislation returned speed-limit control to the states, and for a few years—until Montana set a statewide 70-mph limit in 1999—this meant you could drive as fast as you wanted.

CHIEF JOSEPH AND THE NEZ PERCÉ

The odyssey of Chief Joseph and his 600 followers is perhaps the most familiar tale of the final days of freedom of indigenous people in the United States. Having led his band over 1,000 miles throughout the summer from their lands in Idaho, from which they were forcibly removed by the U.S. government (which had "renegotiated" an initial treaty, in effect reducing the Nez Percé's holdings by 90 percent), Joseph and the ragtag exhausted Nez Percé, thinking the cavalry farther south and Canada closer north than either really was, chose to camp and rest near Chinook, Montana, in 1877.

The U.S. Army, in hot pursuit, sent ahead a 400-man contingent, which reconnoitered the Nez Percé and camped 12 miles to the southeast on September 28. The Nez Percé awoke to attack on September 30. The Army, expecting to prevail on the basis of surprise, instead met fierce resistance, and a five-day siege ensued. After losing their herd of horses, 30 warriors, and three chiefs, and suffering high casualties among the women and children, the Nez Percé gave up. Chief Joseph's words upon surrendering were an eloquent and tragic encapsulation of the Native American experience:

Our chiefs are killed; the little children are freezing to death. My people have no blankets, no food. . . . I want to have time to look for my children and see how many I can find. . . . Hear me, my chiefs. I am tired. My heart is sick and sad. From where the sun now stands, I will fight no more forever.

After receiving promises from the U.S. commanders that the Nez Percé would be allowed to return to Idaho, Chief Joseph instead suffered the government's forked-tongue duplicity. Most of the Nez Percé were dispersed to several reservations, eventually winding up in Oklahoma. In 1885, through the Herculean efforts of Chief Joseph and with help from his old nemesis Colonel Miles, some 120 Nez Percé were allowed to return to Idaho. Chief Joseph, however, was never allowed to see his homeland again, finishing out his days in exile on the Colville Reservation in Washington, where he is buried.

Blaine County Museum (501 Indiana St., 406/357-2590, free), four blocks south of US-2, includes an impressive collection of fossils and local pioneer artifacts, as well as an informative multimedia presentation on the events leading up to the final surrender of Chief Joseph.

If the weather is fine and you can spare half a day, the actual site where the Nez Percé were captured is now preserved (with an interpretive trail and a few plaques, but otherwise unchanged) as **Nez Perce National Park and Nez Perce National Historic Trail,** 16 miles south of Chinook via Hwy-240.

Fort Belknap Indian Reservation

Between Chinook and Malta, US-2 runs along the northern border of the **Fort Belknap Indian Reservation,** which covers some 650,000 acres stretching south to near the Missouri Breaks, a rock-and-sagebrush landscape that provided perfect hiding spots for outlaws like Kid Curry, Butch Cassidy, and the Hole-in-the-Wall Gang.

The Fort Belknap reservation was established in 1888 to contain the surviving members of the once-feared Gros Ventre and Assiniboine nations, who, before siding with the U.S. Army against the Blackfeet, were one of the major powers on the northern Plains. The tiny town of **Fort Belknap,** just south of US-2 about 25 miles east of Chinook, is the main reservation crossroads. The town hosts the annual **Milk River Indian Days** at the end of July, featuring athletic contests as well as dances and country-fair festivities.

Butch Cassidy

Malta

Twenty miles east of the Fort Belknap reservation is **Malta,** named for the Mediterranean island but otherwise just another ranching town that grew up along the Great Northern Railway. Along with the above-average **Phillips County Museum** (431 US-2 E., 406/654-1037, Mon.-Sat. 10am-5pm Apr.-Dec., $5), Malta holds the region's best place to eat, drink, and sleep: the landmark **Great Northern Hotel** (2 S. 1st St. E., 406/654-2100, $69 and up), which has a bar-cum-steakhouse and a café with good breakfast specials.

Malta, where the eastbound and westbound trains of Amtrak's Empire Builder pass each other, is just one of dozens of flyspeck US-2 Montana towns with names borrowed at random by Great Northern Railway promoters from all over the globe. Heading along the highway, you pass near or through Dunkirk, Kremlin, Havre, Zurich, Harlem, and Tampico, all of which were founded by the railroad and settled in the main by Northern and Eastern European immigrants enticed here around the turn of the 20th century by the railroad's offers of farmlands and homesteads.

Milk River Valley

East of Malta, the road and the railroad cross and recross the banks of the sluggish and narrow **Milk River.** Highway signs proclaim your entrance to "Beef Country"; just check out the menu options in the cafés and you'll know you've arrived. US-2 continues its jaunt over the Milk River tributaries, winding along the swampy **Bowdoin National Wildlife Refuge,** once the state's best duck-hunting grounds and now warm-weather home to pheasant, grouse, and sage hens as well as pelicans, ibis, and herons.

Unless you're a keen bird-watcher, the main place worth stopping along this stretch is 10 miles west of Saco and 4 miles north of US-2. Here, the **Sleeping Buffalo Hot Springs & Resort** (406/527-3320, $50 and up) offers a huge naturally heated swimming pool, as well as hot tubs—as hot as 106°F!

At the tiny farming town of **Saco,** 28 miles east of Malta, pride of place is given to the one-room schoolhouse where TV journalist Chet Huntley received his education. Saco is also proud of the fact that, in 1999, the town cooked up a world-record-size hamburger, weighing in at more than three tons.

Glasgow

Glasgow (pop. 3,250), on the north banks of the Milk River 50 miles west of Wolf Point, is one of the few Hi-Line towns that's more than a collection of grain elevators, though its own dominant visual aspects are spreads of combines and threshers. Founded as a railroad town by the Great Northern Railway in 1889, Glasgow is now the largest town in northeastern Montana. In summer, stop in for a look at the tremendously cluttered, diorama-filled Valley County **Pioneer Museum** (54109 Treasure Trail US-2, 406/228-8692, $3), worth a look for the ornate Buffalo Bill Bar exhibit and the detailed story of New Deal-era Fort Peck Dam.

Fort Peck and Fort Peck Dam

Fifteen miles south of Glasgow and US-2 via Hwy-24, the enormous Fort Peck Lake collects the waters of the Missouri River behind massive **Fort Peck Dam,** one of the largest construction projects of the New Deal era and still the world's second-largest earthen dam. From 1933 until 1940, a friendly invasion of ultimately 10,000 civilian workers, earning between $0.50 and $1.20 per hour, hacked, dug, poured, sweat, and wrested a sea out of High Plains desolation. As a result, 20 million acre-feet of water can be impounded behind the nearly four-mile-long dam, corralled to a maximum depth of 220 feet and with a serpentine shoreline longer than California's—1,600 miles! Ongoing drought since 1998 means levels are well below average, hurting recreation and leaving boat ramps high and dry; the lake is also home to a huge array of wildlife, including elk, bighorn sheep, pronghorn, and migrating waterfowl, all protected within the **Charles M. Russell National Wildlife Refuge.** The Fort Peck area also has one of the world's biggest concentrations of fossils; dinosaur bones,

Roughly 20 miles north of US-2, the 15,500-acre **Black Coulee National Wildlife Refuge** shelters one of the few nesting areas of the white pelican in the northwestern United States.

Fort Peck Dam and the Missouri River

Fort Peck Theatre

including skulls of a triceratops and a T. rex, can be seen inside the **Fort Peck Dam Interpretive Center and Museum** (406/526-3493, daily summer, free), at the base of the dam. Fort Peck Lake is most easily approached via Hwy-117, driving 15 miles south from US-2 at the town of Nashua; you can also reach it from Glasgow via Hwy-24.

Besides the dam and the lake, the area's best surviving example of New Deal spirit is the snug town of **Fort Peck** (pop. 233), built from scratch to house the construction workers, though its current population is but a small fraction of the number that once called it home. In the premier issue of Life magazine (November 23, 1936), documentary photographer Margaret Bourke-White profiled the town of Fort Peck as well as the other 18 boomtowns that sprang up in the surrounding area during construction of **Fort Peck Dam.** A few of the old buildings still stand, including the landmark **Fort Peck Theatre** (406/526-9943) on Hwy-24, a huge draw in the area with its summertime plays and musicals. One of the greatest places to stay near US-2 in Montana is the original **Fort Peck Hotel** (175 S. Missouri St., 406/526-3266 or 800/560-4931, June-Nov.), long dormant but recently taken over and touchingly (with nary an ounce of avarice) brought back into a semblance of its classic old self. Rates are reasonable ($75 and up), and the restaurant is by far the best in the area.

Fort Peck Indian Reservation

The sprawling **Fort Peck Indian Reservation,** Montana's second largest, stretches for nearly 100 miles along US-2, and for 50 miles north. Although it is home to 6,800 Assiniboine and Yanktonai Sioux people, it is mostly owned by nonnatives as a result of unscrupulous land dealings encouraged by the 1887 Dawes Act. **Wolf Point,** the reservation's largest town (and location of the only Amtrak station for miles!), is also the site of the **Montana Cowboy Hall of Fame & Western Heritage Center** (218 3rd Ave. S., 406/653-3800) and home to cafés and taverns like the **Missouri Breaks Brewing Company** (326 Main St., 406/653-1467), where you can get a range of fresh-brewed micro beers. There are a few motels, including **Sherman Inn** (200 E. Main St., 406/653-1100, $8 and up), which has clean rooms and a decent restaurant.

Another 55 miles east of Wolf Point down US-2, nearly at the North Dakota border, **Culbertson** (pop. 714) is a quiet town with a disproportionate number of farm-implement and feed dealers. Located a mile east of town, the **Montana Visitor Center** (406/787-6320) houses a good local history museum.

In winter, northeastern Montana suffers some of the worst weather in the lower 48 states, as arctic storms cause wind chill to drop as low as -80°F.

Because trees are scarce on the eastern Montana plains, early settlers built homes by impaling slabs of sod over thin poles. A few of the museums in towns along US-2 display mock-ups of these sod houses.

The tiny hamlet of **Ismay** (pop. 22), 120 miles south of US-2, unofficially changed its name in 1993 to **Joe**, in honor of 1980s football superstar Joe Montana.

NORTH DAKOTA

Apart from the likeable small city of **Grand Forks,** at the state's eastern border, much of North Dakota's landscape lives up to those non-descript clichés from childhood family trips: It hems and rolls and yawns *forever.* If you tire of watching dancing golden wheat mirages, you can exercise your finger channel-surfing on the radio. It's a long, flat, and (dare we say it?) dull drive, divided four-lane almost all the way, with little but endless horizontal plains and the occasional frontier fortress to keep you company.

The state has done what it can to help out bored travelers by eliminating road-side mowing to encourage wildflowers for most of the trip across, opting for native prairie and a potential refuge for wildlife—and roadkill. That said, the 300 miles across the state do hold a few points of interest, including **Fort Union,** an evocative outpost of early fur-trapping explorers; popular **Devils Lake** recreational areas; and the geographical center of North America, marked by a stone monument in the town of **Rugby.**

Fort Union Trading Post

Astride the Montana-North Dakota border, standing proud atop the banks at the confluence of the Yellowstone and Missouri Rivers, the **Fort Union Trading Post National Historic Site** was once the largest and busiest outpost on the upper Missouri River. Despite the "fort" in its name, it was never a part of the U.S. military; it was, however, the most successful and longest-lived of all the frontier trading posts. In 1804, Lewis and Clark visited the site, which they called "a judicious position for the purpose of trade." Twenty-five years later, John Jacob Astor's American Fur Company proved them right, establishing an outpost here in a successful attempt to end the Hudson Bay Company's monopoly on northwest trade. Linked by steamboat with St. Louis some 1,800 miles away, Fort Union reigned over the northern plains. Its bon vivant overseer, Kenneth McKenzie, the "King of the

Fort Union Trading Post National Historic Site

Missouri," kept the fine china polished and the wines cool in the cellar, offering a taste of displaced civilization to such luminary explorers as George Catlin, Prince Maximilian, and John James Audubon.

The fort was abandoned as the fur trade declined in the 1850s, and portions of original buildings and walls were taken down by the U.S. Army in 1867 to construct Fort Buford, a mile to the east. In the late 1980s, the National Park Service reconstructed the buildings atop the original foundations, giving a palpable if somewhat overly polished idea of how the old fort looked. McKenzie's old home and office, **Bourgeois House,** is now a **visitors center** (701/572-9083, daily, donation) with some surprising artifacts. The fort hosts occasional reenactments of boisterous frontier life: Mid-June, for example, brings the annual **Fort Union Rendezvous,** a rollicking re-creation of fur-trapper gatherings to trade, talk, and compete in wilderness skills.

Fort Buford

Built in 1866 and now a state historic site, **Fort Buford** is eerily quiet, with only the stone powder magazine, a cemetery site, and a museum in an original soldiers' quarters open for viewing. South of Fort Union, and once home to a company of "Buffalo Soldiers," as the Sioux called the African-American cavalrymen, the fort is best known for its sad contribution to the U.S. campaign to exterminate Native Americans: It was here that Chief Sitting Bull surrendered to the U.S. Army in 1881, and here that Chief Joseph of the Nez Percé was brought after his "I will fight no more forever" surrender in Montana.

In the past, the historic sites of Fort Buford and neighboring Fort Union used to be more easily reached from Montana, though recent roadwork has made them accessible from either side of the border. Signs point the way south from US-2.

Williston

Just north of Lake Sakakawea and the Missouri River, a dozen miles east of the Montana line, **Williston** (pop. 14,716) has always been a boom or bust kind of place, and in recent years it has been enjoying a boom in its primary industries—wheat-growing and oil-pumping—which by some measures made it the fastest-growing small town in the USA. Motels are often booked up by crews of "fracking Bakken" oil field workers, but the downtown area is still an all-American scene straight out of *Our Town.*

Roughly 65 miles southeast of Williston via US-85, the north unit of **Theodore Roosevelt National Park** preserves one of the largest surviving contiguous areas of seminatural Great Plains landscape.

Apart from filling the tank before a trip to Fort Union or farther afield, one more good thing to do in Williston is eat: Responding to an impromptu poll, locals will likely recommend the classic truck stop **Lonnie's Road House** (226 42nd St., 701/774-1103), north of downtown, or will point you toward **Big Willy's Saloon & Grill** (3701 4th Ave. W., 701/577-3703) as the eatery of choice. Big Willy's is famous for its "Frack Attack": a double-height grilled cheese sandwich split by a full one-pound burger, all yours for $25. (You get a chance at a free T-Shirt if you finish it off in less than 30 minutes.)

Epping: Buffalo Trails Museum

Like many other North Dakota rural communities, the old Great Northern Railway town of **Epping** (pop. 100) has all but disappeared thanks to automobiles, changes in farming practices, the railroad's move to diesel instead of steam, and sundry

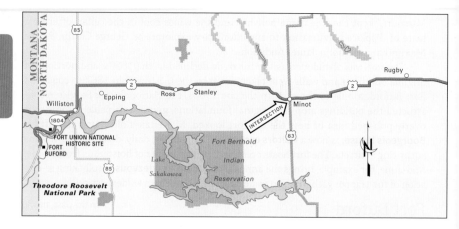

other common complaints. Here, however, the rapidly vanishing Great Plains lifeways have been partially preserved, thanks to the efforts of a local preacher who single-handedly preserved the abandoned buildings and artifacts as the **Buffalo Trails Museum** (701/859-4361 in season, Tues.-Sun., $5), which has grown to encompass almost the entire town. Main Street is still dusty dirt, lined by a general store, a hardware store, a pool hall, the Sons of Norway Hall, and other essential elements. Most of these old buildings have been converted to house an amazing array of animated dioramas (papier-mâché dummies dressed up like dentists and patients) and the usual old tools and other junk, but it's a great place to stop.

Ross and Stanley

East of Epping toward Minot, US-2 twists up and through a hundred miles of gentle chocolate-drop hillocks, residuals of great ice-age glaciers, with some beautiful rises and plateaus capped by an occasional abandoned squad of dwellings. Along the way, isolated villages whiz by, full of boarded-up buildings, grain silos, and occasional surprises: **Ross** (pop. 106), for example, is a typically funky old town with some dilapidated boarded-up buildings and huge grain elevators that look more like spacecraft engines. This unlikely looking place is home to the **first mosque built in the USA.** Constructed by a Syrian farmer back in 1929, the original mosque was replaced by a newer, nicer temple in 2005, next to a cemetery holding the remains of Ross's early Muslim settlers.

The one sizable place, **Stanley** (pop. 1,458), resting along the horizon-straight railroad tracks 7 miles east of Ross and 47 miles west of Minot, is worth a stop to sample the world's last working Whirl-a-Whip milk shake machine at the old-fashioned soda fountain inside the **Dakota Drug Store** (107 S. Main St., 701/628-2255), a mile north of US-2. This pure Americana is much appreciated on a hot summer day.

Minot, described on page 172, marks the junction of US-2 and US-83, **The Road to Nowhere.** Full coverage of this route, which runs from Canada to Mexico, begins on page 168.

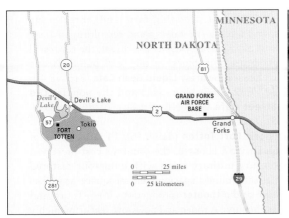

wild prairie rose,
state flower of North Dakota

Rugby: Geographical Center of North America

The landscape along the North Dakota stretch of US-2 consists of immense stretches of hay fields typical of the Great Plains, and only occasional highlights of miniature cattails, goldenrod, and sunflowers. The place-names here are decidedly Anglocentric, with towns named Leeds or York after the hometowns of English investors who, during the 1880s, pumped the fledgling towns full of cash. The general population, however, has always been decidedly Scandinavian.

Midway between Devils Lake and Minot, **Rugby** (pop. 2,876) is an important agricultural hamlet, known to road wanderers as the town nearest to the geographical center of North America. The exact spot is marked with a two-story stone cairn along the south side of US-2, in front of a café and gift shop (formerly the Conoco station) and across from a Dairy Queen. Nearby is the **Prairie Village Museum** (summer only, $7), featuring 20 restored buildings and six exhibit halls—a train depot, a schoolhouse, even a reconstruction of a railroad hobo camp—relocated here from around the county, as well as an exhibit on the life of an over-eight-foot-tall local man, Clifford Thompson.

Across western North Dakota, tune to **KMHA 91.3 FM** for commercial-free country music and rock alternative as well as community news and features from the **Fort Berthold Indian Reservation,** home to descendants of the Native American Mandan, Arikara, and Hidatsa peoples.

marker at the geographical center of North America

Devils Lake and Fort Totten

The wetlands south of the eponymous town of **Devils Lake** (pop. 7,141), which is 60 miles east of Rugby and 85 miles west of Grand Forks, are one of the biggest natural draws in the state, with bird-watching, hunting, and fishing opportunities aplenty. However, this largest body of water in North Dakota has no natural outlet, and true to its name, for the past 20 years Devils Lake has been wreaking havoc. Lake levels have risen by

Midway between Minot and Rugby, the tiny town of **Denbigh** is the burial site of Sondre Norheim, a Norwegian national hero who in the 1860s invented the telemark turn and introduced the words ski and slalom into the English language. Royals have paid their respects—you can too.

Many places along the Missouri River are named for the intrepid and enigmatic Shoshone woman who guided explorers Lewis and Clark across the Plains in 1804. Sacagawea is alternatively rendered as Sakakawea or Sacajawea and translated either as "Bird-Woman" or "Boat-Launcher."

more than 30 feet, flooding farmland, threatening homes, and forcing the raising and rebuilding of US-2 into a sort of causeway. Despite the threat, the town still takes good care of its blocks of tidy brick buildings, one of which houses the artsy **Liquid Bean Café** (316 NE 4th Ave., 701/662-1065, Mon.-Sat.) and the popular **Old Main Street Café** (416 NE 4th St., 701/662-8814), around the corner.

Historic **Fort Totten** (daily, $6), 14 miles south of town on Hwy-57, is one of the country's best-preserved 19th-century military forts, with numerous restored buildings set around a spacious central square, as well as a museum and a **theater** (productions Wed.-Thurs. and Sat.-Sun. in July). A rodeo and powwow, featuring highly competitive Native American dances, are held during **Fort Totten Days** (last weekend in July). Next to the fort is **Sullys Hill National Game Preserve,** a more-than-1,600-acre refuge for bison, elk, deer, and other wildlife, which you may spot while hiking the nature trail.

Both the fort and the nature preserve are located on the 137,000-acre reservation **Spirit Lake Nation,** centering on the mission village of **St. Michael's,** four miles east of the fort. The main attraction is the **Spirit Lake Casino and Resort,** formerly known as Dakotah Sioux Casino, "North Dakota's First and Finest," 18 miles southeast of downtown Devils Lake.

Grand Forks

The oldest and second-largest community in North Dakota, and frequently rated one of the "Top 10 Most Livable Places" in the country, **Grand Forks** (pop. 52,838) gained a place in the national headlines during the terrible floods that devastated

Long the commercial center of northern Great Plains agriculture, Grand Forks became the birthplace of Cream of Wheat cereal in 1893.

the city in April 1997. Following one of the worst winters on record, during which blizzard after blizzard dumped over eight feet of snow and ice on the surrounding plains, Grand Forks prepared for the North Plains' worst floods in living memory. The Red River of the North, which forms the state border between North Dakota and Minnesota, rose an inch every hour, two feet a day, day after day, while volunteers and relief workers struggled to protect the town.

Under the watchful eyes of the national news media, the river continued to rise, finally breaching its sand-bagged banks and inundating the town. The entire population was evacuated, and over 75 percent of the homes and buildings were flooded; many were partially submerged for more than a month until the waters finally receded and cleanup could begin. Total damage reached over $1 billion, but miraculously, not a single death was attributed to the floods. Grand Forks quickly and energetically set about rebuilding itself, and today a lone obelisk along the riverside shows the high-water mark.

Many century-old downtown buildings have been renovated, including the landmark **Empire Theater** (415 DeMers Ave., 701/746-5500), now an arts center.

ROADSIDE GIANTS OF NORTH DAKOTA

It may be the long cold winters, the endless flat landscape, or the incredible solitude of life on the northern Great Plains, but there's something about North Dakota that makes people do strange things. The most obvious signs of this odd behavior are the many giant sculptures that stand along roadsides all over the state. Bigger and better than their cousins elsewhere in the United States, the roadside giants of North Dakota quite simply have to be seen to be believed. Here are a few of the biggest and best:

World's Largest Turtle: Nicknamed W'eel, this giant turtle was made in 1982 out of more than 2,000 old steel wheels, and it stands along Hwy-5 near Dunseith, north of Rugby, near the Turtle Mountains.

World's Largest Cow: "Salem Sue" stands along I-94 in New Salem, 30 miles west of Bismarck.

World's Largest Buffalo: Built in 1959, and standing outside the National Buffalo Museum, this 60-ton giant looms over I-94 in Jamestown, 100 miles south of Devils Lake.

Another of Grand Forks's liveliest institutions is the 15,000-student University of North Dakota, whose pretty brick campus spreads north of DeMers Avenue (old US-2). A former campus gym is now home to the **North Dakota Museum of Art** (701/777-4159, daily, donation), which survived the flood unscathed and houses the state's only contemporary art collection.

Grand Forks Practicalities

For weary road-trippers, one place you'll definitely want to stop is legendary **Whitey's Café and Lounge** (121 DeMers Ave., 218/773-1831), across the river on the new "boardwalk" of East Grand Forks. Though legally in Minnesota, this is a true Grand Forks institution, a genuine speakeasy dominated by the fabulous art deco-style "Wonderbar"—a horseshoe-shaped stainless-steel sculpture that is surrounded by comfy booths and a jukebox. The food and drink—try the pan-fried walleye, best washed down with a bottle of microbrew Summit Ale—is excellent, but the ambience alone would be worth the visit. Another characterful old Grand Forks landmark, **The Kegs** (901 N. 5th St., 701/787-5347) is an outdoor root-beer stand supported by, you guessed it, a massive pair of bright orange wooden-looking kegs. Look for them north of downtown; order a sloppy joe and a side of onion rings, and people will think you belong here.

Right downtown, the best bet for food and drink is the **Toasted Frog** (124 N. 3rd St., 701/772-3764, Mon.-Thurs. 4pm-11pm, Fri.-Sat. 4pm-midnight), a popular sandwich and martini bar with an excellent range of beers, near the landmark Empire Theater.

Lodging options include the usual range of national chain motels out around the junction of US-2 and I-29; close to downtown there's also the attractive **Red Roof Inn Townhouse** (710 1st Ave. N, 701/746-5411 or 855/516-1090, $85 and up), with an indoor pool and on-site miniature golf course.

MINNESOTA

In its trek across northern Minnesota, US-2 offers nearly 250 miles of open road before winding up in the busy but surprisingly attractive lakefront city of **Duluth.** Midway across the state, after the endless wheat fields of the west, the scenery turns slightly turbid with the remnants of old iron mines and a series of still-busy lumber and paper mills. Opportunistic little cells of roadside community crop up to serve the beer-and-bait needs of those bound for the myriad recreational opportunities of Minnesota's Lake Country along the headwaters of the mighty Mississippi River. At either edge of this summertime playground, two largish towns, **Grand Rapids** and **Bemidji,** serve as gateways to the gaping spreads of **Chippewa National Forest** and many of Minnesota's 10,000 lakes.

The **Fisher's Landing Welcome Center** (May 15-Sept. 15), about 10 miles east of the North Dakota border on US-2, has a full range of maps and information on both states.

Fisher

The first town east of the North Dakota state line, tiny **Fisher** (pop. 435) doesn't look like much, but it was once a bustling frontier port, thanks to its location at the navigational headwaters of the Red River of the North. River traffic has all but disappeared, but the local sugar-beet industry pulls in a billion dollars a year, which may explain the town's prosperous air.

Near Fisher stretches the **Malmberg Prairie Preserve,** one of

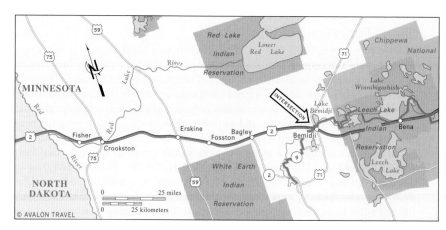

the few extant virgin prairies left. Preserved by early settlers and now protected by the Nature Conservancy, these 80 acres of wild prairie roses, blue gentians, and bright yellow sunflowers shine in late summer. Once home to herds of bison, the land here has never been plowed, and it looks all the more special, surrounded as it is by acres and acres of industrial-scale agriculture. To reach the preserve from US-2, take US-75 south to Hwy-9, then turn south onto Hwy-56 and drive for two miles until you see the Nature Conservancy sign.

Crookston and Erskine

Crookston (pop. 7,891), 25 miles east of the North Dakota border, has a series of bridges over the meandering and tree-lined Red Lake River, which winds along the south side of the compact downtown business district. The small **Polk County Historical Museum** (Tues.-Sun. Memorial Day-mid-Sept., donation) contains the usual slew of 19th-century stuff alongside the **"World's Largest Ox-Cart"** (celebrated in August's Ox-Cart Days).

In the 100 miles east of the North Dakota border, US-2 spreads into a divided four-lane highway, climbing out of the fecund Red River Valley of the North (which is not to be confused with the *other* Red River Valley, down in Texas) onto the flat glaciated plains, while the roadside colors alternate between the dark reds and greens of sugar beets and the buff and leafy tones of the wheat, soy beans, and potatoes for which the area is known.

Continuing east, US-2 passes occasional isolated pockets of trees, planted as windbreaks amid the furrowed fields. In the tiny village of **Erskine** (pop. 503), a classic one-horse Midwest town, you'll find **Joe DiMaggio's Grill and Pizza** (218/687-2100), southeast of downtown along the US-2 frontage, which is neither a misprint nor the genuine article. (The owner, Mr. D., used to get oodles of phone calls meant for the legendary Yankee Clipper. Not surprisingly, his place is full of baseball memorabilia.) Erskine also has a swimming beach on Lake Cameron and takes civic pride in being the home of the "World's Largest Northern Pike" (of whom there's a 40-foot-long statue on the pretty downtown lakefront).

The tiny town of **Fosston,** midway between Erskine and Bagley, holds one of two stoplights on this 100-mile stretch of US-2. Fosston also marks the sudden switch between the Great Plains and the Great North Woods. Appropriately, the town motto is "Fosston, Where the Prairie Meets the Pines."

pink and white lady slipper, state flower of Minnesota

Between **Bemidji** and **Grand Rapids**, US-2 runs parallel to the slower but more scenic **Great River Road** (see page 229). Coverage of the entire route, which winds along the Mississippi River from Lake Itasca all the way south to New Orleans, begins on page 224.

Skyline Parkway and Hwy-61

One of the greatest loop trips in the country, **Skyline Parkway** is a 25-mile (with side trips, over 30 miles) bucolic wind along the bluffs above Duluth. Accessed from West Duluth off I-35, the parkway takes in numerous historical sites, but it's mostly just jaw-dropping scenery, especially **Hawk Ridge,** which offers perfect wind conditions for viewing up to 30,000 hawks, eagles, and falcons daily in fall; also along the ridge is a fantastic network of trails, boarding stations, and observation posts. The parkway, which was started in 1889 and completed in 1929, connects at its north end with famed **Hwy-61,** which, if you've got the time to spend, is an even more beautiful jaunt along Lake Superior's granite cliffs to Grand Portage and Canada, 150 miles to the northeast. Along the way are some of the region's best places to eat: numerous smokehouses touting their smoked fish, plucked from the frigid waters of the great lake.

On Hwy-33, on the edge of the Fond Du Lac Indian Reservation, 11 miles south of US-2 and 15 miles west of Duluth, the town of **Cloquet** boasts the only gas station ever designed by famed architect Frank Lloyd Wright. Cloquet also has the large Fond-du-Luth Native American-owned casino.

Duluth

Though it doesn't get a lot of positive press, **Duluth** (pop. 86,265) has to be one of the most beautiful and underappreciated travel destinations in the Midwest, "a Lilliputian village in a mammoth rock garden," the old WPA *Guide to Minnesota*

aptly noted. Gracefully etched into the side of tough, 800-foot granite slopes and gazing over the dark harbor hues, Duluth, from the attractively redone redbrick paving of gentrified Superior and Michigan Streets downtown to the grittier heights atop the bluff, quietly goes about its business, usually with foghorns belching in the background. It is a city of maritime and timber history, but also a city of stunning, pervasive, pristine, *healthy* wilderness.

103-D   Bird's-Eye View from Skyline Drive, Duluth, Minn.

Tracts of forest, harbor preserves, shoreline, and parks flourish in the city, and there are dozens of interesting Great Lakes or historical museums, mansions, lakefront walks, boat or foot tours, and festivals—from Native American powwows (in the summer) to midwinter dogsled races. Many visitors start at Duluth's landmark, the **Aerial Lift Bridge,** a 386-foot-tall monster connecting the mainland to the

SS *William A. Irvin*

mouth of the harbor. The waterfront around here has been gently redeveloped into the popular Canal Park warehouse district, with restaurants, bars, and the **Lake Superior Maritime Visitor Center** (218/720-5260, daily, free), all within a short stroll. Best of all is another landmark of Great Lakes maritime industry, the truly huge hulk of the **SS William A. Irvin** (218/722-7876, daily, $12), a former U.S. Steel ore ship that stretches over two football fields long.

The Aerial Lift Bridge over Duluth's harbor can be raised 138 feet in under a minute to let ships pass underneath. When it's down, cross the bridge and continue for a quarter mile for a real treat: a long clean sandy beach stretching along the shores of Lake Superior.

Another good stop, the **St. Louis County Heritage and Arts Center** (506 W. Michigan St.), a.k.a. "The Depot," across I-35 but walkably close to the waterfront, is an enormous, magnificently restored example of early city architecture as well as home to many of the city's artistic and cultural centers. Around it are the historic locomotives of the Lake Superior Railroad Museum, and two dozen shops recreating early 20th-century Duluth, right down to the old ice cream parlor.

Legendary folk singer and Nobel laureate Bob Dylan is Duluth's most famous native son. Bob Dylan Way winds through downtown, but a more meaningful place of pilgrimage is the duplex house where Bob Dylan spent his childhood (519 N. 3rd Ave. E.), a mile northwest of The Depot.

Down in Canal Park, a fun and filling place to eat, **Grandma's Saloon & Grill** (522 S. Lake Ave., 218/727-4192) serves up heaps of Italian-American food at the foot of the Aerial Lift Bridge. Another excellent option is **Northern Waters**

In Minnesota and Wisconsin, the "On or Off" and "Off Sale" signs on many bars and roadhouse restaurants designate whether they can sell beer and wine for consumption on or off the premises.

While Bob Dylan was born in Duluth, he grew up in the nearby iron-mining town of **Hibbing,** which is also where Greyhound Bus Lines got its start, shuttling between the mines and the town. Home-run hitter Roger Maris was another Hibbing product.

Smokehaus (394 S Lake Ave., Suite 106, 218/724-7307), with a mind-boggling array of delicious smoked fish, ham, and pastrami sandwiches. The Canal Park area is a good bet for places to stay. Watch sunrise or sunset over the lake (while soaking in the rooftop swimming pool!) at the **Inn on Lake Superior** (350 Canal Park Dr., 218/726-1111, $130 and up).

WISCONSIN

US-2's brief stint across Wisconsin navigates wisely, for it takes in the lovely Lake Superior cap of Wisconsin's northern region and includes a majestic 140-mile detour along the rough-and-tumble **Lake Superior** shoreline, home of rich history, gorgeous boreal forest, and pastoral and littoral scenery.

Superior

Both rival and best friend of bigger Duluth across the harbor, despite the "superior" name, **Superior** (pop. 27,244) is often the butt of jokes, usually regarding its comparatively lower geography (which means Superior catches all of Duluth's flotsam), its blue-collar mentality, its forests of grain elevators rather than trees, and its mountains of coal. It is also proud, along with Duluth, of being one of the busiest harbors in the nation, shipping millions of tons of ore a year from the nation's most inland port.

Northern Wisconsin is in the heart of big snow country, a promontory jutting into the maw of bad-tempered Gitchee Gumee, where 35 inches of snow a month during the winter don't begin to crease a frown on a Wisconsinite's face. Play it safe if you're traveling along Lake Superior then.

Superior's lack of pretense is perhaps its biggest attraction. The route on US-2 through the city is decidedly industrialized, featuring a seemingly endless amount—almost 30 miles—of bay shore crowded with trains, tracks, elevators, and spindly working piers jutting out into the lake almost to the horizon. The city itself is sedate but offers a few things of historical or Great Lakes interest, including its biggest draw, **Fairlawn Mansion** (daily, $10 adults), the sprawling 42-room former

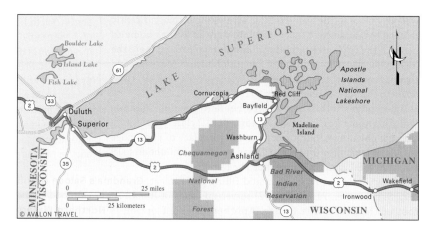

residence of a lumber and mining baron, once an orphanage and now the main local history museum. The main stretch of US-2 through town is looked over by a stern statue of an early industrial magnate, James J. Hill, "The Empire Builder," who made a fortune building and running the Great Northern Railway, whose tracks still parallel US-2 west to Puget Sound.

For food, try the **A & W Drive In** (701 Belknap St., 715/392-6125), a full service, family-oriented café on US-2, across from the UW-Superior campus, or the more local flavor of the **Anchor Bar & Grill** (413 Tower Ave., 715/394-9747), serving ice-cold beers and great cheap burgers since back when Nixon was in the White House. There are plenty of places to stay along the main strip through town.

After starring in the bodybuilding docudrama *Pumping Iron* in 1979, the future *Terminator* star and California governor Arnold Schwarzenegger got a BA degree from the UW-Superior business school.

Hwy-13 Loop: Cornucopia

One of the best alternative routes on the Upper Midwest stretch of US-2 is Hwy-13's 100-mile loop along the shores of Lake Superior. The 45 miles that this loop adds to your journey across the state are without question worth it, taking in the superlative Apostle Islands, charming peninsula communities, and unbeatable roadside vistas. Each little hill you climb reveals a new view of the expansive lake, groves of trees, or mosaics of farmland bordered by vacation cabins and archaic farming equipment. An occasional black bear may cross the road as you whiz by the tottering one-eyed cabins hardly larger than hunting shacks, their grainy weather-beaten shingled siding obscured by weeds.

Starting in the west at the blue-collar harbor town of Superior, Hwy-13 zigzags northeast to the lakeshore and follows it to picturesque **Cornucopia**, the northernmost community in Wisconsin.

East of Cornucopia, the road veers away from the water, emerging again onto the lakefront at the peninsula's main Ojibwa Native American town, **Red Cliff**, which has a marina and boat slip, a lakeside campground within view of Basswood and Madeline Islands, a big casino, and an annual summer powwow. The outskirts of Red Cliff include some lake views and some great views of open pastureland meshed with dense evergreen forests on what appears to be slight tableland. Boats and canoes are ever-present, scattered among rural jetsam, decades-old Chevys and Ford pickups, their sculpted sheet metal rusting mutely in the cattails.

From Red Cliff, Hwy-13 turns south, immediately entering the outskirts of Bayfield.

Bayfield and Apostle Islands National Lakeshore

The nerve center of Hwy-13's sinuous trip through the Apostle Islands region is the diminutive, laid-back resort village of **Bayfield** (pop. 487). Bayfield itself dates from 1856 and looks at first glance about as Lilliputian as you can get, with a curvy (10 mph on the corners) narrow road winding beside impeccably tailored cottages and modest local-brownstone mansions. Virtually every hairpin turn offers an

Apostle Islands National Lakeshore

outstanding glimpse of the Apostle Islands and the boats plying the waters, espe-cially on the far northern edge of town. While the waterfront area draws most visi-tors, the best views of the town and lake can be had from the blocks of dainty Victorian homes that line the hills above.

There are plenty of classy or quaint places to stay in Bayfield, from cottages and motels to the ritzy **Old Rittenhouse Inn** (301 Rittenhouse Ave., 715/779-5111, $140-335), famed for its comfy rooms and multicourse gastronomic feasts. Hearty meals for the common man and woman have been served up since the Civil War at **Greunke's Restaurant & First Street Inn** (17 Rittenhouse Ave., 715/779-5480), across from the marina, which is famous throughout the state for its whitefish livers, weekend fish boils, and gener-ally funky feel. From the marina, there are plenty of ferries (wind sleds over the ice in winter!) to Madeline Island or some of the Apostle Islands, which are sprinkled out to the north across the chilly waters of Lake Superior. The headquarters of the **Apostle Islands National Lakeshore** (715/779-3397, daily June-Sept.), located in the old Bayfield County Courthouse, offers the best intro-duction to these undeveloped islands, which are served by the **Apostle Island Cruises** (715/779-3925). The islands offer hiking trails, photogenic lighthouses, and wilderness camping. If you don't have time for an extended visit, you can hike along the Lakeshore Trail, which starts from Meyers Beach, 4 miles east of Cornucopia off Hwy-13.

A unique draw in the summer is Washburn's **Big Top Chautauqua** (715/373-5552 or 888/244-8368, $22-110), a revival of old traveling tent shows that offers great concerts, plays, and musical revues most evenings.

Ashland

It's not until you enter Ashland on US-2, roughly midway between the Minnesota and Michigan borders, that Lake Superior finally pokes its great nose at you. A big fish in sparsely populated north-woods Wisconsin, **Ashland** (pop. 8,216) likes to call itself the "Garland City of the Inland Seas," but it's really a town full of trestles, all the roads dipping and drooping under the mud-brown wood framework or plain faded steel of Soo Line bridges. Built up on an ever-so-slight rise above the lake, the town has an attractive Main Street with many well-preserved old buildings and a lakeshore lined with great parks and frigid-looking beaches. And you can walk on concrete base of the gargantuan **Soo Line Ore Dock,** the largest of its kind in the world.

Another sign of Ashland's historic importance is the grand Best Western **Hotel Chequamegon** (pronounced "shuh-WAH-muh-gun"; 101 W. Lake Shore Dr., 715/682-9095, $105-260), at the junction of US-2 and Hwy-13. Following a 1955 conflagration that destroyed the structure, the reconstruction has managed to capture the decorative charm and original grandeur, and it has a fine restaurant to boot.

Another big attraction, in interest if not actual size, is the newish **Northern Great Lakes Visitor Center** (715/685-9983, daily, free), 2.5 miles west of downtown, along US-2 at the Hwy-13 junction. The spacious building is full of interpretive exhibits tracing local history and industry; outside there's a nature trail through 180 acres of mixed forest and wetlands, and a five-story tower gives a panoramic view.

For a change of pace, head 50 miles south from Ashland to Phillips, where the **Wisconsin Concrete Park** (N8236 S. Hwy-13, 715/339-7282, free) preserves hundreds of creative concrete-and-glass sculptures of Paul Bunyan, Abe Lincoln, and lots of farm animals, all made in the 1950s by former logger and self-taught artist Fred Smith.

Bad River Indian Reservation and Superior Falls

Home to one of Wisconsin's six Ojibwa communities, the **Bad River Band Reservation** encompasses over 125,000 acres owned by descendants of the original Ojibwa Loon Clan who settled near the delta confluence of the Bad and White Rivers. The community holds its annual **Bad River Manomin Powwow** in late August, and of course there's a large casino.

From the eastern edge of the reservation, it's another 20 miles to the Michigan border. The main highlight of this stretch is about midway along: a nice vista point, overlooking the lakeshore from a parking area just west of the Hwy-122 junction. If you're up for a short detour, follow Hwy-122 north for a

Just west of the border with Michigan, a Wisconsin liquor store proffers travelers a giant corkscrew statue, beckoning you to imbibe.

half-dozen miles to the shores of Lake Superior, where beautiful **Superior Falls** plummet 90 feet at the end of the Montreal River. There's a parking area near the small power plant, and the sunsets here can be spectacular.

MICHIGAN

There are two main routes across **Michigan's Upper Peninsula** (the "UP"), which stretches for nearly 300 miles between Canada and Wisconsin, wedged between Lake Superior and Lake Michigan. Between Ironwood in the west and Sault Ste. Marie on the Canadian border in the east, you can choose **US-2** along the north shore of Lake Michigan or the slightly more direct option, **Hwy-28,** which runs near the south shore of Lake Superior near **Pictured Rocks National Lakeshore.** Either way takes most of a day, and this is not a place to try to make up time.

In either case, you're privy to one of the greater finds of the Midwest, the sparsely populated and thoroughly underappreciated (especially by the "trolls" of southern Michigan) land of the "Yoopers," as the proud residents have christened themselves, many still ensconced in the logging and mining enclaves their forebears founded. The UP is a surprisingly mountainous and larger-than-it-looks place, dotted with boom-to-bust towns relying on summer tourism and one or more of the industrial triumvirate up here: timber, mining, and fishing. More than three quarters of the land here is protected to varying degrees within national and state parks and forests, and it's no surprise that the best places tend to be farthest away from the main roads; though the roadside scenery is plenty pretty, the more remote areas are as wild and ruggedly beautiful as anywhere in North America.

Ironwood and Environs: The Gogebic Range

The westernmost UP town is **Ironwood** (pop. 5,387), which, along with sleepy **Bessemer** and rough-and-tumble **Hurley** over the Wisconsin border, was the center of the Gogebic Range iron-mining district. The area's population now is about a fifth of what it was during the 1920s peak, and these mountain towns have moved on from mining to a more leisurely occupation: downhill skiing. Within a few miles are some of the Midwest's largest ski resorts, all benefiting from the vertiginous topography and the average 200 inches of annual snowfall. Most of these ski areas, like **Indianhead** (906/229-5181 or 800/346-3426), Double-As summer mountain biking centers, and rental shops line US-2.

The center of Ironwood is easy to miss, but it's worth the quick trip along the US-2 Business Loop to see the old-fashioned business district, which fills a few blocks around the art deco Ironwood Theatre movie palace. In a small hillside park just south of downtown, don't miss the absolutely huge 52-foot-tall statue of **Hiawatha,** the fictional hero of Henry Wadsworth Longfellow's famous poem.

The place to eat in Ironwood is **Joe's Pasty Shop** (116 W Aurora St., 906/932-4412, daily breakfast and lunch), two blocks off US-2, serving pasties since 1946. For breakfast, try the pasties filled with eggs and cheese.

Besides ski areas, **Bessemer** is also home to what a large plaque claims is "The Most Scenic Little League Baseball Stadium in America," located just a block north of US-2.

Black River Road and the Porcupine Mountains Wilderness

From Hwy-28 at Bessemer, Hwy-513 heads north toward the shores of Lake Superior, forming one of the UP's many lovely scenic drives. Best known as the **Black River Road,** this 15-mile-long, densely wooded two-laner runs along the banks of the Black River, which drops over a series of well-signed waterfalls as it approaches the lakeshore; a good trail starts at a parking area about 13 miles from Bessemer. Nearby, the 26-story towers of **Copper Peak Ski Flying Hill** (906/932-3500) rise high above the forest. In summer, visitors with no fear of heights can take an "adventure ride" ($20) on the chairlift, then go up an elevator, then take stairs to the top for a great view of the forest, Lake Superior, three states, and Canada.

East of the Black River area, Michigan's largest state park, the **Porcupine Mountains Wilderness,** covers 60,000 acres of serrated ridges and dense pine forests, including the largest swaths of virgin forest in the Midwest. The main outposts of civilization here (motels, restaurants, bars, and more) are the lakefront towns of **Silver City** and **Ontonagon;** the latter is home to the **park headquarters** (906/885-5275). Both towns are about 20 miles north of Hwy-28 via Hwy-64 or US-45, respectively.

US-2: Crystal Falls

At the eastern edge of the vast Ottawa National Forest, **Crystal Falls** (pop. 1,469) is a charming, postcard kind of place built into a bluff near a rivulet waterfall on the Paint River. Time seems to stand still here, the town sporting original (read: *old*) street signs still pointing the way, and huge trees overhanging US-2 as it slowly hairpins through town. The only "sights" here are the local courthouse, won in a poker game in the 1880s, and a water-filled old pit mine outside of town.

All over the UP you'll see signs advertising pasties. The quintessential miner food, the Cornish pasty (which rhymes with "nasty," not "tasty"—hang onto the vowel a bit, like a true Yooper) was introduced to Copper Country 100-odd years ago by immigrant Cornish miners. These dense baked crust-pockets, stuffed with minced meat and vegetables, are ubiquitous in UP cafés and restaurants.

Southeast from Crystal Falls, US-2 passes numerous rock and ore formations jutting out of the hillsides. The road sweeps into the **Copper Country State Forest,** which gives every appearance of symmetrical reforestation, then flits through 15 miles of northern Wisconsin before reentering the UP just west of Iron Mountain.

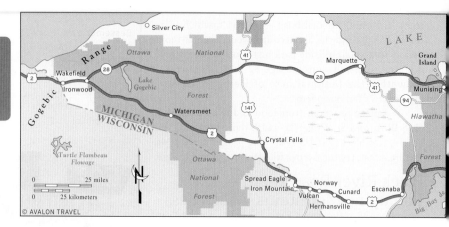

© AVALON TRAVEL

East of Ironwood, at the town of Wakefield, our route divides: US-2 runs south along Lake Michigan, while Hwy-28 veers north along Lake Superior.

Iron Mountain and Norway

Though separated by a half-dozen blacktop miles of US-2, the sister towns of **Norway** (pop. 2,845) and **Iron Mountain** (pop. 7,624) both grew up with the lumbering and iron-mining industry, producing over 300,000 tons annually from three big mines. The larger of the two towns, Iron Mountain, backs up against the easy grade of its eponymous mountain and seems casually strewn about in parts: The east side is mini-mall sprawl, while the west side is the older traditional "downtown."

The must-see here, everyone will tell you, is the **Cornish Pumping Engine and Mining Museum** (906/774-1086, daily June-Sept., $5), two blocks off US-2 on Kent Street. This comprehensive local-history museum has as its star attraction the most enormous steam-driven pump engine you could imagine—it's 54 feet tall and weighs over 700 tons. There are also displays about the old Ford Motor Company factory complex in Kingsford, which fabricated such innovations as the "Woody" station wagon, charcoal briquettes, and World War II gliders.

The *real* must-see is the freebie, the **Pine Mountain Ski Jump,** west of town off US-2 along Pine Mountain Road. This 120-meter jump hosts annual international competitions in late January or early February and is the site of the current U.S. distance record.

Around Iron Mountain in the 1920s, car maker Henry Ford created an industrial complex named **Kingsford** that supplied, among other products, fuel for his factories. This came in the form of charcoal briquettes, the same ones now essential for summer barbecues.

The mines at Norway were so close together and so active that the village once caved in and they had to rebuild it down the hill. Gritty Norway once produced more wood shingles than anywhere else, as shown by the numerous houses still coated with them. Norway also boasts the beautiful **Piers Gorge,** a couple of miles south via US-8, where the raging white water of the Menominee River scraped out this fascinating 70-foot-deep gorge on the border between Michigan and Wisconsin.

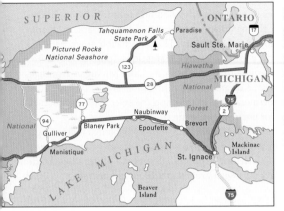

apple blosom,
state flower of Michigan

Escanaba

Midway along US-2's route across far northern Michigan, **Escanaba** (pop. 12,616)—with picture-perfect placement where the Escanaba River pours into the Little Bay de Noc—was born in typical UP fashion, out of the country's insatiable need for timber and ore. At one time its docks contributed to the largest ore-shipping operation of its kind in the United States, work that continues today as Escanaba feeds the steel mills of Indiana, across Lake Michigan. To get a feel for lake life, head to the renovated 1867 **Sand Point Lighthouse** (906/789-6790, $3) along the lushly landscaped waterfront. The annual **UP State Fair,** held here the third week in August, is great fun.

Hiawatha National Forest and Fayette Historic State Park

Between Escanaba and Manistique, US-2 broadens into a fast four-lane highway along both Big and Little Bay de Noc, where you'll pass through a slew of lakefront "resorts," some with their own beaches and all famous for their fishing. Between the bays, the landscape reverts to trees and more trees in the chevron conifers of the 879,000-acre **Hiawatha National Forest.** The flyspeck communities here haven't changed much—ubiquitous flashing yellow lights, matchbox dwellings attached to bulbous propane gas tanks, and, in a few communities, forlorn old Soo Line railcars aging gracelessly on the tracks right off the highway.

> Fifteen miles west of Escanaba, at the eastern edge of the tiny Potawatomi Reservation, you pass from the central to the eastern time zone. Adjust your clocks and watches accordingly.

Jutting south from US-2, two quiet peninsulas stick their thumbs out into Lake Michigan. Both have forests, fruit orchards, and a few lighthouses. The best destination here has to be **Fayette Historic State Park,** the extant ghost of an iron smelting community with a few dozen stone and wooden buildings kept almost totally in their original 1890s condition, not renovated but preserved in varying states of repair. The park is an impressive, sometimes eerie place, situated on sheer limestone cliffs along Hwy-183, about 17 miles south of US-2 from the crossroads community of Garden Corners.

US-2: Along Lake Michigan

The route that US-2 follows along Lake Michigan between Escanaba and St. Ignace is one of the UP's best autumn scenic drives. The true heart of the UP lies here, with

From the flyspeck town of Gulliver, 13 miles east of Manistique, a road leads southeast to Michigan's most picturesque lighthouse, at **Seul Choix Pointe.**

patches of pine or birch woodland followed by brief lakeshore, then a dormant ore mine, a trailer park, or a long-abandoned fishing camp. The only sizable town between St. Ignace and Escanaba, **Manistique** (pop. 3,097) tends to underwhelm, apart from its Lake Michigan frontage. Mountains of gravel and mini smokestacks line the road into town on the east side, and the sweetly pungent smell of paper permeates the air.

Driving between Manistique and St. Ignace, the scenery becomes increasingly gorgeous. Bay views give way only occasionally to small towns or groves of trees, but most of the way the lake breaks through fully as US-2 skims along a beachside causeway bordered by huge sand dunes with green tufts of mixed grasses.

St. Ignace

Coming into **St. Ignace** (pop. 2,452; pronounced "IG-nus," and sometimes "St. Iggy") from the west along US-2, travelers are tempted by a number of "scenic overlooks," each proffering a chance to stretch and view the often fog-shrouded Mackinac Bridge over blue Lake Michigan. Coming from the east, the approach is slightly diminished by the busy I-75 freeway, and from the south the buildup is truly unforgettable, riding high on the elegant Mackinac Bridge. No matter how you get here, picturesque St. Ignace is more important than its obviously tourism-contrived loveliness would indicate, situated as it is at the crossroads of the upper and lower regions of Michigan, with Mackinac Island just across the bay. The town is busy and cheerful, in places gentrified and meticulously maintained; downtown, you can stroll along a bright lake promenade lined with gift shops, motels, and restaurants.

Downtown, the city-run **Museum of Ojibwa Culture** (500 N. State St., 906/643-9161, daily May-Oct., donation) traces over three centuries of life along the Straits of Mackinac, detailing the lifeways of the indigenous Ojibwa and Huron peoples.

fall colors on Michigan's Upper Peninsula

The museum, on the site of Father Marquette's original mission, also hosts a summer powwow and a heritage day. Attending one is an unforgettable way to experience the community's heritage.

Sample yet more local culture by heading north from downtown along the lakeshore to **Bessie's Original Homemade Pasties** (1106 N. State St., 906/643-8487), where you can sample the UP's local delicacy, the Cornish pasty, brought over by immigrant miners from England over a century ago. Bessie's closest rival is **Famous Lehto's Pasties** (1983 W. US-2, 906/643-8542), west of the I-75 freeway, and between the two pasty stands is the blue mansard roof of an All-American classic: **Clyde's Drive In** (3 W. US-2, 906/643-8303), serving up good burgers, onion rings, and milk shakes since 1949.

Mackinac Island

The main attraction around St. Ignace is anachronistic **Mackinac Island,** one of the top draws in the Midwest. Pronounced "MACK-i-naw," this tiny island is almost completely car-free, and walking and cycling trails loop around its 2,200 acres (even UPS delivers parcels by bike!). Now billed as a sort of bygone-days living museum, during the early 19th century Mackinac Island was the headquarters of John Jacob Astor's early fur-trading empire. For two centuries before then, its coveted position at the heart of the Great Lakes meant that French, British, and later, Americans frequently fought over it. Historic sites and beauty spots abound, so be sure to move quickly through the Main Street commercial area around the ferry landing, which is oversupplied with fudge shops (an island specialty since Victorian times).

St. Ignace sits at the north end of what locals like to call the "Eighth Wonder of the World," the **Mackinac Bridge,** one of the longest suspension bridges in the world at 7,400 feet (with its approaches, the total length is over five miles). Lots of scenic views are found throughout St. Ignace and from **Straits State Park,** west of town.

Mackinac Island

Apart from slabs of fudge, the biggest tourist attraction on Mackinac has to be the aptly named **Grand Hotel** (906/847-3331, $275 and up, including breakfast and dinner), which has been in business since 1887. Famous for its 660-foot-long "World's Longest Front Porch," packed with potted plants and comfy chairs, the hotel is definitely deluxe; room rates are pretty high, but you can explore the place and enjoy a drink or high tea, or pay for a self-guided **tour** ($10 for nonguests). Room rates elsewhere on the island start around $150 at most of the many nice hotels and B&Bs, like the **Main Street Inn** (906/847-6530), at the heart of town. No matter where or how long you stay, Mackinac Island is a great place to rent a bike (or take a horse-and-buggy ride), cruise around, and forget about your daily grind.

GRAND HOTEL AND GROUNDS, MACKINAC ISLAND, MICH.

Passenger **ferry services** (about $26 round-trip) from the docks in St. Ignace are fast (20 minutes each way) and frequent from April through October; call **Star Line** (800/638-9892) or **Shepler's** (800/828-6157) for times and rates.

Hwy-28: Marquette

Midway across the Upper Peninsula along Hwy-28, the UP's biggest and, in many ways, most attractive city is **Marquette** (pop. 21,355), a Lake Superior ore port with a lovely lakeside setting. Blocks of 100-year-old beaux arts buildings fill the business district above the heavy industrial harbor, and the presence of government offices and the region's main college (Northern Michigan University) have given it a lively, prosperous feel. From downtown, you can follow the lakeshore drive 3 miles north to **Presque Isle Park,** 323 acres of pristine wilderness.

Every February, Marquette hosts the start and finish of the **UP 200,** a sled dog race to Grand Marais and back that draws some 15,000 spectators.

Other aspects of UP life are documented down the road in neighboring **Negaunee,** eight miles west along Hwy-28/US-41, where the excellent Michigan **Iron Industry Museum** (906/475-7857, daily May-Oct., Mon.-Fri. and first Sat. Nov.-Apr., free) tells the full story of the $48 billion Michigan iron mining industry. Farther west, the lighter side of UP life is the theme of **Yooperland** (906/485-5595, daily, free), a.k.a. "Da Yoopers Tourist Trap," a gigantic gift shop-cum-cultural museum along Hwy-28/US-41 in Ishpeming that features the "Largest Working Chainsaw in the World" and "The World's Largest Working Rifle." If you're looking for comic postcards of giant pasties and similar oddities, this is the place to come.

The Huron Mountains

Stretching north and west from the Marquette region, the **Huron Mountains** hold the highest point in Michigan (1,979-foot Mt. Arvon), but almost all of this rugged 50 by 25-mile area is privately owned and pretty much off-limits. It's also one of the wildest corners of a wild part of the country. The private owners (with last names like McCormick, founders of International Harvester, and Miller, of Miller Beer infamy) keep it pretty much as it has always been—before the miners and loggers had their way with the rest of the Upper Peninsula. The best place to get a feel for the Huron Mountains region is the hamlet of Big Bay on Lake Superior, 25 miles northwest of Marquette.

Pictured Rocks National Lakeshore

If travel time is not an issue for you, there is at least one excellent reason to bypass US-2 across the Upper Peninsula and to follow Hwy-28 instead. **Pictured**

Munising Falls is one of more than a dozen waterfalls in the Pictured Rocks region.

Rocks National Lakeshore, a lovely 40-mile-long stretch of undisturbed sand dunes, beaches, and colorful bluffs, lines Lake Superior in the northeastern quadrant of the Upper Peninsula. For casual visitors, the lakeshore is best visited by boat, since roads here are few, far between, mostly unpaved, and all but invisible; in summer, three-hour **cruises** leave about every two hours from the pier in **Munising,** right on Hwy-28 at the west edge of the park. Even better, if you're feeling fit, is a self-powered kayak trip; try **Northern Waters** (712 W. Munising Ave., 906/387-2323), which offers daylong, half-day, and evening guided tours.

Besides being the gateway to the Pictured Rocks, Munising is also the main departure point for glass-bottomed-boat tours of the many shipwrecks that lie along this treacherous stretch of coastline. Well preserved by the cold Lake Superior waters, the wrecks are also legally protected within the 113-square-mile **Alger Underwater Preserve.**

Tahquamenon Falls State Park and Paradise

East of the Pictured Rocks National Lakeshore, about 40 miles west of Sault Ste. Marie, you come to a real gem: **Hwy-123,** a must-do loop road (particularly during autumnal color sweeps) that heads north from Hwy-28 past the outstanding—and popular—**Tahquamenon Falls State Park.** The 50-foot-high, 200-foot-wide Upper

Tahquamenon Falls State Park

Falls here were mentioned in Longfellow's *Song of Hiawatha*. Hwy-123 also passes through the lakefront vacation village of **Paradise,** where Whitefish Point Road runs 11 miles north up to some of the best and most isolated beaches in the UP as well as the oldest lighthouse (circa 1849) on the Great Lakes.

From Longfellow to Lightfoot: In Whitefish Point, north of Paradise, visit the **Great Lakes Shipwreck Museum** (888/492-3747, daily May-Oct., $13) to learn about the wreck of the 725-foot lake freighter *Edmund Fitzgerald,* subject of Canadian balladeer Gordon Lightfoot's 1970s pop song. The ship suddenly went down 20 miles offshore—without a distress call, but with all 29 crew members on board—in November 1975.

Sault Ste. Marie, Michigan

Michigan's oldest community, **Sault Ste. Marie** (pop. 14,144; pronounced "SOO-saynt-muh-REE") was home to an Ojibwa community for hundreds of years before the first fur trappers and French Catholic colonists arrived in the late-17th century. Known historically for the tussles over the area between the French and British, and as the closest land link between the United States and Canada for hundreds of miles, "The Soo" is a great place to break a journey and catch up on the region's complicated past, present, and future.

Beneath the steel-span International Bridge, which links this Michigan town with Ontario's twin "Soo," the raging torrents that impelled French priest Jacques Marquette to dub the newly established mission Le Sault de Sainte Marie, literally "falling waters of Saint Mary," are no longer readily apparent.

The U.S. Army Corps of Engineers long ago corralled and tamed the rapids between 20-foot-higher Lake Superior and Lake Huron with four enormous locks, the largest and busiest in the world. During their 1920s mining heydays, the locks conveyed many times the tonnage of the Panama and Suez Canals combined—with no tolls paid. The locks area is worthy of at least an hour's siesta; lush parks and a walkway line the locks, with observation points letting you get within a few feet of the massive lake freighters that pass through around the clock. If you want to "lock through" yourself, join a **Soo Lock boat tour** (800/432-6301 or 906/632-6301, $29).

A handful of nice cafés and restaurants line Water Street and Portage Avenue within a few blocks of the locks, including the see-it-to-believe-it **Antlers Restaurant** (804 E. Portage Ave., 906/253-1728), where the fresh whitefish and other food is *almost* as memorable as the taxidermy decor. At the east end of the waterfront, in warmer months Sault Ste. Marie offers a chance to experience a rare treat: car-hop food service at the classic **Clyde's DriveIn** (1425 Riverside Dr., 906/632-2581). To stay the night, downtown is also where you'll find another Great Lakes classic: the art deco **Ramada Plaza Hotel Ojibway** (240 Portage Ave., 906/632-4100, $139 and up).

CANADA

Between **Sault Ste. Marie** and **Ottawa,** the capital of Canada, our route winds along the north shore of Lake Huron, then cuts inland to follow a series of broad rivers. The main highway here, Hwy-17, is a section of the busy Trans-Canada Highway. It is also part of the Voyageurs Trail, roughly retracing the route taken by the early fur traders between their winter trapping grounds—the wilderness of forests, lakes, and streams to the northwest—and Montreal, the summer fur market. The scenery varies from rivers and forests to paper mills and coal mines, and most of the way Hwy-17 is a two-lane road with a 90-km/h (55-mph) maximum and occasional passing lanes to help you get around the timber trucks. Towns here tend to sprawl along the roadside, with a few "chip stands," sell-ing fried potatoes, among the familiar franchised fast-food joints, but there are expansive sections of natural wilderness within easy reach.

the International Bridge that joins Sault Ste. Marie, Michigan and Sault Ste. Marie, Ontario

East of Ottawa, it's a short run to French-speaking **Montreal,** Canada's second-largest city and one of the most European places in North America. The change between bilingual Ontario and French-speaking Quebec is sudden and sometimes surreal, as if England and France were divided by a river, not the English Channel.

Sault Ste. Marie, Ontario

Across the busy harbor from Michigan, the "other" **Sault Ste. Marie** (pop. 66,313) is a much bigger, much grittier, and compara-tively depressed Canadian sibling. Fortunately, the main visitor attraction offers a quick escape from all the heavy industry. From the Algoma Central Railway Terminal, well signed downtown, the **Agawa Canyon Tour Train** (129 Bay St., 705/946-7300 or 800/242-9287, daily, C$91 and up) depart throughout the sum-mer and early fall (fall color season is the prime time to come). These daylong train trips take you north through a roadless wilderness featuring nar-row river canyons and spectacular views. An hour and a half stop above the canyon lets you get out and have a picnic or stretch your legs with a walk to a waterfall.

Unless otherwise noted, prices in the Canadian sections of this book are given in Canadian dollars (C$). The Canadian colloquial equivalent of "buck" (for a dollar) is "loonie," for the image of a bird (the loon) that adorns the dollar coin. The $2 coin is called a "toonie."

St. Joseph Island

East of Sault Ste. Marie, Hwy-17 winds along Lake Huron's North Channel water-front for most of the way to Sudbury. South and east of Bar River, a turnoff heads

DRIVING IN CANADA

Between the United States and Canada, the rules of the road don't really change, but the measurements do. Both countries drive on the right, and the speed limits are similar: In Canada it's generally 80 kilometers (50 miles) per hour on two-lane roads, 100 km/h (62 mph) on freeways. All cars are required to have their headlights illuminated night and day; to the unaccustomed, a daytime traffic jam can look like a massive funeral procession. Other rules: All passengers must wear seat belts, and turning right on red is no longer illegal in the Province of Quebec, but it is on Montreal Island; in

bilingual stop sign in Ottawa, near the Parliament Building

the rest of Canada, turning right on red is legal so long as you stop first. Deciphering parking zones, especially in French-speaking Quebec, can test your interpretive abilities.

Gas (*essence* in Quebec) north of the border tends to be more expensive than in the States, and it's priced by the liter (3.785 liters equal 1 U.S. gallon). Almost all gas stations accept credit cards, and some accept U.S. currency, but often they give you a less-than-favorable rate of exchange.

Crossing the border, there are brief checkpoints (and sundry duty-free shops) on both sides. Customs officers usually do a cursory check, asking your address, reason for travel, when you last visited the country, and whether you are carrying firearms, tobacco, or alcohol. The rules are subject to change, but all travelers need to have a passport, even U.S. or Canadian citizens. People of other nationalities should double-check their visa status well before attempting to cross the border, otherwise it may be difficult (or impossible) to return to the United States, and border officials have been known to confiscate vehicles and arrest people they suspect are trying to enter the United States illegally.

south to **St. Joseph Island,** part of the Manitoulin Island chain. The main sight here lies at the island's south end: **Fort St. Joseph National Historic Site.** When the fort was built by the British in 1796, it was the westernmost outpost of their Canadian empire. At first the fort protected the fur trade; it then served as a base for attacking the Americans during the War of 1812. The Americans burned the fort in 1814, and the park is built around its scenic remains.

At the island's north end is the tiny town of **Richards Landing;** the café at the dock serves good burgers and a variety of Italian-inspired entrées.

Along Lake Huron

Twelve miles east of the St. Joseph Island turnoff lies the town of **Bruce Mines,** founded in 1846 around some small copper mines. As in the UP, and mining areas all over the world, many of the earliest settlers were unemployed tin and copper miners from Cornwall in England. Two smaller islands offshore from Bruce Mines are home to the pleasant **Bruce Bay Cottages and Lighthouse** (705/785-3473, C$85 and up).

Following Hwy-17 east along the lakeshore toward Massey, the landscape is generally flat with occasional rocky outcrops. Just west of the settlements of Spanish and Serpent River, you have a great view across the North Channel, an arm of Lake Huron, to Manitoulin Island in the distance.

Massey and Manitoulin Island

Massey, "The Home of Chutes Provincial Park and Lots of Friendly People," sits at the confluence of the Sauble and Spanish Rivers. The main attraction hereabouts is just north of Hwy-17: **Chutes Provincial Park** offers swimming, camping, picnicking, and several scenic waterfalls along the Sauble River.

Twenty miles east of Massey, 40 miles west of Sudbury, Hwy-17 intersects with Hwy-6, which heads south toward **Manitoulin Island,** the world's largest freshwater island, set in the northern end of Lake Huron. Manitoulin is a popular vacation spot, ringed with picturesque harbors at Meldrum Bay, Providence Bay, and South Baymouth.

Sudbury

The biggest city between Ottawa and Duluth, **Sudbury** (pop. 164,689) lies in the middle of a geological basin that contains one of the world's largest concentrations of nickel, as well as numerous other precious metals. Originally an Ojibwa settlement, the town began to develop after the 1883 arrival of the railroad and boomed when nickel and copper were discovered here three years later. Uncontrolled development followed—mines and processing plants sprang up all over the landscape—and soon the area was a classic industrial-era ecological disaster. No trees grew for miles around, and a haze of toxic smoke choked the inhabitants, who lived in narrow valleys below the mine heads.

In the early 1950s, Sudbury undertook a massive urban renewal and land reclamation project to return the land to its original beauty and clean up the air, with great success. For older residents, the city has changed dramatically for the better; the air is cleaner and trees dot the landscape. Today, Sudbury is still Canada's most important mining community, producing tons of nickel and copper, but it's an infinitely healthier place than its polluted past may suggest.

As it passes around Sudbury, the Trans-Canada Highway (Hwy-17) bypasses the city's center, so turn north onto Hwy-80 toward Sudbury's real visitor draw: **Science North** (705/522-3701 or 800/461-4898, daily, C$26-50). Located at the edge of downtown Sudbury, along artificial Ramsey Lake, Science North is one of Canada's most popular attractions, a state-of-the-art science and technology museum featuring many hands-on displays for kids and adults alike.

The double suspension bridge linking the Canadian and American Sault Ste. Maries gives memorable views of the **Algoma Steel Mill,** one of the largest in Canada. Flags in the middle of the bridge mark the boundary between the two nations.

The highway town of Echo Bay is home to the Big Loonie, a very large statue of the Canadian dollar coin, right along Hwy-17B.

Manitoulin Island is one of the largest freshwater islands in the world, and it still has a substantial First Nations (indigenous) population.

Around Sudbury, a rare alternative to the often overearnest Canadian Broadcasting Corporation (CBC) radio is offered by Laurentian University's **CKLU 96.7 FM**— wacky and often funny college radio.

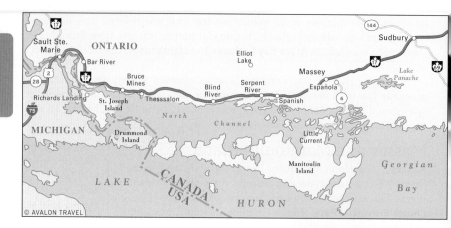

© AVALON TRAVEL

Inside the snowflake-shaped structure, exhibits have included solar system models, wave generators, a diffusion cloud chamber, a honeybee observation hive, and a flight simulator. The newest attraction in Sudbury is **Dynamic Earth,** which simulates an underground mine. Back in the open air, you can see Sudbury's famous **Big Nickel,** moved here in 2003—it's exactly what it sounds like, a 30-foot-tall replica of a Canadian nickel.

Among the many Sudbury hotels is **Travelodge Hotel Sudbury** (1401 Paris St., 705/522-1100 or 844/207-7302, C$83 and up), near Science North.

Big Nickel

North Bay

North Bay (pop. 5,533; "Gateway to the North") was originally a fur-trading post that boomed after the 1882 arrival of the railroad. These days North Bay is still a trade and transportation center, and its fur auctions are among the largest in the world. Many tourists use the city as a jumping-off point for wilderness expeditions.

East of Sudbury, Hwy-17 enters the narrow **Veuve River Valley,** lined with scraggly pines and picturesque rock outcroppings. Apart from a couple of small towns, it's mostly dairy farming country for the 130 kilometers (80 miles) of Hwy-17 between Sudbury and North Bay.

Just southeast of town, Hwy-17 joins Hwy-11, which runs south to Toronto. The main attractions of North Bay line up along the Lake Nipissing waterfront park. From here, the **Chief Commanda II cruises** (705/494-8167) follow the old voyageurs' route across the water. In midsummer, the guided tour will likely tell you all about the locally famous **shad flies,** mouthless, fish-smelly bugs (also known as mayflies) that swarm out of the water and make a nuisance of themselves on North Bay sidewalks in their short 24-hour lives.

Most of the motels are along Main Street and Lakeshore Drive, as are fast-food burger bars, pizza places, and a wide range

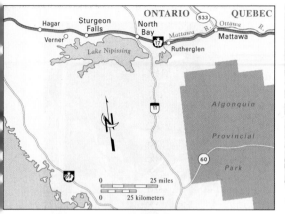

A beaver, national animal of Canada, adorns the Parliament Building.

of international places. Besides the good **Indra's Curry House** (454 Main St. E., 705/478-6000), check out Lebanese, Japanese, Thai, and more, all within a few blocks of each other.

Mattawa and the Ottawa River

East of North Bay, Trans-Canada Hwy-17 runs through its wildest and least populated stretch: scenic country largely empty of human habitation. The road hugs the riverside while rolling over steeper hills, past birch and pine forests and many lakes and ponds. In the midst of all this wilderness, the attractive and relatively large town of **Mattawa** (pop. 1,993; "There Is a Story Here Where Rivers Meet") lies at the confluence of the **Ottawa and Mattawa Rivers.** Surrounded by dense green forest, the riverfront is lined by a pleasant park (with free hot showers), and the town center is quaint and quiet, with two blocks of brick-fronted buildings along the river just north and west of the main highway.

The **Ottawa River** marks the border between Ontario and Quebec, the bluffs of which may be seen across the water.

The Mattawa River is the focus of the expansive **Samuel de Champlain Provincial Park** (705/744-2276), which offers campgrounds, canoeing, and hiking trails.

Algonquin Provincial Park

Between Mattawa and Deep River, Hwy-17 runs along the northern boundaries of the enormous **Algonquin Provincial Park,** which stretches for many miles to the south. Ontario's oldest and most popular park, Algonquin protects 3,000 square miles of almost untouched wilderness, offering a wide variety of wildlife (including moose, bears, beavers, and timber wolves), dozens of lakes, and hundreds of miles of backcountry hiking and canoeing trails. The main **visitors center** (705/633-5572) is at the park's far southwest corner, south of North Bay or west of Pembroke and Renfrew via Hwy-60, the Parkway Corridor, the only road through the park. Here you can get details on the park's abundant camping and cabins and pick up all the necessary permits.

Deep River and Chalk River

The first real town east of Mattawa is **Deep River** (pop. 4,109), Canada's first "Atomic Town," a planned community built for employees of the Chalk River labs just downstream.

Ottawa

Originally an Algonquin settlement, Ottawa (pop. 883,391) was a small fur-trading and lumber-milling outpost until the 1850s, when Queen Victoria chose the city to be the national capital, a compromise answer to the bitter rivalry between Montreal and Toronto. Construction of the Parliament buildings began the following year, but government only became the largest employer after World War II, when the lumber mills began to decline. Today the train tracks and factories have been replaced by telecom and computer companies. Miles of parks and greenbelts, and the boating (or ice skating) along the Rideau Canal, make Ottawa one of the most peaceable and pleasant of the world's capitals.

Royal Canadian Mounted Police

Orientation within Ottawa is easy: **Parliament Hill,** which holds the most prominent buildings, is on the north edge of town, with its back turned on the Ottawa River and the French-speaking province of Quebec. Getting around is easy, since most of the sights are gathered together around Parliament Hill and the adjacent ByWard Market. To see Ottawa, you should definitely park the car, get out, and walk (or bike, or rollerblade) around town.

Parliament Hill is home to the three buildings that compose Parliament, Canada's seat of federal government. The architecture is reminiscent of England's Houses of Parliament as redesigned by the cartoonist Charles Addams: Elegant, Gothic-style carved stone walls rise to copper mansard roofs topped with fantastically filigreed wrought iron. On the lawns of the Parliament buildings, the **Changing of the Guard ceremony** (daily at 10am late June or early July-late Aug., free) is extremely popular with tourists. On summer evenings, a **sound-and-light show** (10pm daily July, 9:30pm daily Aug., 9pm daily Sept., free) is projected onto the landmark facade.

East of Parliament Hill stands the **National Gallery of Canada** (380 Sussex Dr., daily May-Sept., Tues.-Sun. Oct.-Apr., C$15). Along with many floors of painting and sculpture from colonial times up to the present, including George Segal's automobilia assembly *The Gas Station,* there's also a large collection of Asian and Inuit art. Another striking piece of modern architecture stands upstream, west of Parliament Hill: the riverfront **Canadian War Museum** (daily, C$17), which documents Canadian soldiers' bravery in war and peacemaking.

PRACTICALITIES

Ottawa's airport, with flights from most major U.S. hubs, is 20 minutes south of the city. The major east-west access is via Hwy-17, the Trans-Canada Highway; within

Château Laurier

town, this becomes the Hwy-417 freeway. From the south, Hwy-31 links up with Hwy-401, the long-distance freeway along the north shore of Lake Ontario.

The **ByWard Market,** east of Parliament Hill across the Rideau Canal, is the place to go for food. The market stalls offer a variety of fresh produce, cafés are abundant, and the restaurants and bars are lively and generally pretty good. **Blue Cactus Bar & Grill** (2 ByWard Market, 613/241-7061) is one of many good restaurants here, featuring Southwestern food in a cheery ambience and a late-night supper club. There's a popular Streamline-style American diner, **Zak's** (14 ByWard Market, 613/241-2401, daily 24 hours), and the nice **Shafali** (308 Dalhousie St., 613/789-9188), on the east edge of ByWard Market, serving tandoori chicken, lamb madras, and other Indian specialties in a soothing saffron-colored room.

Places to stay in Ottawa are centrally located and not all that expensive—the capital of Canada is not a major tourist destination. **Fairmont Château Laurier** (1 Rideau St., 613/241-1414 or 866/540-4410, C$279 and up), situated in an opulent tower directly across from Parliament Hill, is a luxurious landmark. Finally, one of the most interesting budget options anywhere has to be the **HI-Ottawa Jail Hostel** (75 Nicholas St., 613/235-2595, C$27 and up), which occupies the old Ottawa jail, a 13-minute walk from Parliament Hill. Guests sleep on bunks in the old cells.

National War Memorial on Parliament Hill

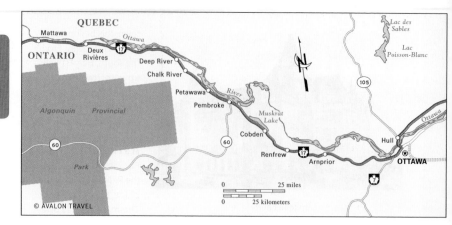

Nine miles farther east, you enter **Chalk River.** In 1945, this tiny logging center became the home of the first atomic reactor outside of the United States. Seven years later, Atomic Energy of Canada, Ltd. (AECL), a government-owned nuclear research organization, was founded here. It designs and sells commercial and research nuclear reactors around the world and produces most of the world's radioactive isotopes for medical use. In recent years, problems at the Chalk River plant, due to leaks, seismic improvements, and deferred maintenance, caused a serious worldwide shortage of these vital medical products, putting the Chalk River labs in the media spotlight.

Chalk River

Petawawa and Pembroke

Southeast of Chalk River, Hwy-17 crosses the namesake river of the town of **Petawawa,** home since 1905 to a Canadian Forces base. You can visit the small military museums on the base, including the **Garrison Petawawa Military Museums.** One exhibit, the **Canadian Airborne Forces Collection,** traces the history of Canadian paratroopers. There's also a riverfront beach and campground, but otherwise the area is strictly off-limits, as the numerous signs along the road warn.

The rather quaint, redbrick town of Petawawa itself is two miles north of Hwy-17 via Hwy-41, well worth the short trip through what seems like one big light-industrial park.

Wrapping around the eastern edge of Algonquin Provincial Park, Hwy-17 nears **Pembroke,** another timber town along the Ottawa River, north of the highway. The main sights here are the more than 30 history-themed murals painted on downtown buildings; the **Champlain Trail Museum** (1032 E. Pembroke St., May-Sept., C$7),

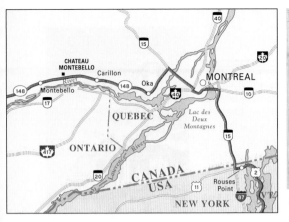

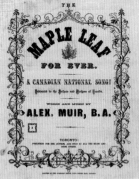

original cover sheet for *The Maple Leaf Forever,* 1867

with exhibits on local history; and the friendly ambience and awesome food at the **Nook Crêperie Inc.** (26 W. Pembroke St. W, 613/735-4800), right downtown.

Arnprior

Midway between Pembroke and **Renfrew,** you can see the Ottawa River loop north around **Cobden,** a little town on Muskrat Lake. Renfrew, another of Ontario's many Scots-founded towns, is now a center of high-tech industry.

> The Ottawa River marks the border between Ontario and Quebec, the bluffs of which may be seen across the water.

Twenty-seven miles east of Renfrew, Hwy-17 approaches the banks of the Ottawa near **Arnprior,** founded in 1823 by Archibald McNab, a despotic Scottish lord who imported dozens of his countrymen and women to the settlement and ruthlessly exploited them. This reign of terror ended when the townsfolk banded together and drove him away. There's a museum in the old stone post office building, and downtown boasts some moderately priced motels and, best of all, **Wes' Chips** (198 Madawaska Blvd., 613/623-5492, Mar.-Oct.), an open-air chip stand selling the exquisite Canadian delicacy Americans call french fries. Worth planning your day around, for sure!

East of Arnprior, Hwy-17 continues its trek toward Ottawa with a 90-km/h (55-mph) maximum speed posted; occasional passing lanes help you get around the timber trucks. The highway curves gradually southward, away from the Ottawa River, through mostly flat woodlands and a few farms, then converts to freeway for the run into Ottawa.

Gatineau

Offering the best views of Ottawa's dramatic riverside setting, the Francophone town of **Gatineau** (pop. 276,240) is a nice change of pace from the Canadian capital. Known as "Hull" until a civic reorganization in 2002, when it was renamed, Gatineau is older than Ottawa and is French-speaking despite having been founded in 1800 by an American Loyalist, Philemon Wright, fleeing the Revolution.

The best thing about Gatineau, apart from the chance to walk across the bridges and wander the riverside parks that link it to Ottawa, is the **Canadian Museum of History** (100 Laurier St., 819/776-7000 or 800/555-5621, daily, C\$20), a huge and fascinating institution, housed in two sinuously curving buildings that are a

Montreal

Located on an island in the St. Lawrence River, and first settled as a frontier outpost by fur-trapping French voyageurs, Montreal (pop. 1,866,481) has grown into Canada's second-largest city, and today is easily the most European city in North America, with the largest French-speaking population outside La France. Hotbed of the separatist movement, Montreal tolerates the polyglot federalism of Canada, but the accent here is most definitely on the "French" in French-Canadian; in a wide variety of gourmet restaurants, stylish boutiques, nightclubs, museums, and theaters, you can half-close your eyes and pretend you're in Paris.

Montreal City Hall

The city takes its name from a 700-foot-high hill, now the pleasant tree-covered **Mount Royal Park** just north of downtown. Planned by Frederick Law Olmsted and opened in 1876, the park's stairs and paths lead up to a belvedere, from which you have a sweeping view of the city, the St. Lawrence River, the southern suburbs, and, on the eastern slope, a huge steel cross that's lit up at night.

At the foot of Mount Royal Park runs Sherbrooke Street, Montreal's most prestigious and majestic street, lined with grand 1920s buildings as impressive as any on Park Avenue. Among the many posh boutiques (Chanel, Armani, et al.) and luxury hotels (like the Ritz-Carlton, where Richard Burton married Elizabeth Taylor), you'll find the **Montreal Museum of Fine Arts** (1380 Sherbrooke St., 514/285-2000 or 800/899-6873, daily, $0-15 for permanent displays, $15-23 for exhibitions). The oldest

Mount Royal Park

museum in Canada, and one of the finest in the world, the Museum of Fine Arts has a large permanent collection of European, Canadian, and American art as well as an extensive display of Inuit artifacts. A half mile east, the **McCord Museum** (690 Sherbrooke St. W., 514/398-7100 or 514/861-6701, daily summer, Tues.-Sun. winter, C$20) has a wonderful collection of art and artifacts related to Montreal, Quebec,

Dominion Square, Montreal

and Canada—everything from Victorian evening gowns to First Nation masks and carvings. South of the Museum of Fine Arts, the elegantly modern **Canadian Centre for Architecture** (1920 Rue Baile, 514/939-7000, Wed.-Sun., C$10) mounts fascinating shows devoted to the built environment.

About a mile southeast of Mount Royal, just off the riverfront, the two-block-long cobblestone square of **Place Jacques-Cartier** is the heart of Old Montreal, a picturesque neighborhood that was the site of the earliest European settlement. In the summer the square is transformed into an open-air market, and all year round you can sample the area's excellent cafés and restaurants.

PRACTICALITIES

Montreal's Pierre Elliot Trudeau airport lies 13 miles west of downtown. Numerous freeways crisscross Montreal, and driving around is pretty easy (though all signs, including the complicated parking rules, are in French), but if you want to escape from your car for a day or two, the city is eminently walkable.

For food, Montreal has something for everyone, thanks to the city's truly international population—sizable immigrant communities make Montreal a dining adventure. At lunchtime, workers from the Montreal financial district cram into **Chez Delmo** (275 Notre Dame St. W., 514/288-4288), a contemporary version of traditional Old Montreal seafood restaurants, where dishes are always fresh. There's a nice oyster bar too. You must eat French at least once while in Montreal, and French restaurants do not come more traditional. Another reliable bet is **L'Express** (3927 St. Denis St., 514/845-5333), east of Mount Royal Park, open from breakfast until after midnight.

For first-time visitors, one unexpected Montreal specialty is a taste of New York City: the deli sandwich, usually built of slices of rye bread around a classic version of Montreal's beloved "smoked meat," a.k.a. corned beef. Many of the great old delis have gone out of business; one survivor (since 1928!) is **Schwartz's Charcuterie Hebraique** (3895 St. Laurent Blvd., 514/842-4813), which is slightly touristy but serves some of the finest pastrami on the planet.

The best budget place to stay is the large **HI-Montreal** (1030 Mackay St., 514/843-3317, C$19 and up), which has dorm beds and private rooms a 20-minute walk south of Mount Royal Park. For something a bit more special, **Château Versailles** (1659 Sherbrooke St. W., 514/933-3611 or 888/933-8111, C$165 and up) is composed of four Victorian townhouses converted into one charming antiques-filled hotel.

THE DIONNE QUINTUPLETS

In 1934, during the depths of the Great Depression, in a small house deep in the wilds of northern Ontario, five baby girls were born to the Dionnes, a poor rural family. The fact that all the babies—Annette, Cécile, Yvonne, Marie, and Émilie—were born healthy despite being two months premature is noteworthy enough, but what happened in later years verges on the incredible. The babies were cared for at home for the difficult first weeks, but after that, the Ontario government took the infants away from their destitute family. Across from the family home, the government built a zoo-like environment called Quintland, and raised them in public—selling tickets for three shows daily and effectively doing everything possible to keep them from having a normal childhood. At age five (of course) they were introduced to the king and queen of England and later appeared in movies and "wrote" their own autobiography, *We Were Five*. The quints also did product endorsements, promoting soap, toothpaste, cereal, and Carnation milk. During the 1930s, the quintuplets were Canada's number-one tourist attraction—bigger than Niagara Falls, it was said—and by the time they turned 10 years old they had been visited by more than three million people.

After a long and bitter custody battle, the girls were eventually returned to their parents and faded from the public eye. The Ontario government, which earned an estimated half billion marketing the Quints, paid the surviving three girls a settlement of $4 million in 1998.

combined 100,000 square meters (more than one million square feet) on the banks of the Ottawa River, directly across the water from the Parliament Buildings at the foot of the Alexandria Bridge. The main lobby is filled with historic totem poles and canoes made by Canada's diverse indigenous peoples, and galleries elsewhere in the building highlight everything from whaling communities in Labrador to life on the vast western prairies. It's a fun and educational place, well worth half a day at least. It has the added bonus of a nice restaurant serving lunch.

Montebello and Carillon

East from Hull, Hwy-50 runs as a fast freeway along the north bank of the Ottawa River before calming down into a two-lane sojourn along Hwy-148. About an hour east of Ottawa, 80 miles west of Montreal, the town of **Montebello** holds one of the region's most famous landmarks: **Fairmont Le Château Montebello** (819/423-6341, C$249 and up), an enormous octagonal palace built of red cedar logs that has evolved into one of Canada's most exclusive hotels, frequently hosting international conferences by the likes of NATO, G7, and similar power brokers. The grounds of the hotel hold an even more historic landmark, Papineau Manor, a manor house completed in 1850 by a notable French-Canadian politician.

Farther east, 72 kilometers (45 miles) west of Montreal via sinuous Hwy-344, the roaring rapids at **Carillon** (pop. 207) have been harnessed by a massive hydropower facility and a lock system that provides the largest single lift of any in Canada—20 meters (65 feet). East of Carillon, Hwy-344 winds through sleepy farming country along the Ottawa River before ending up at the edge of the Montreal metropolis.

Driving Across Montreal

Montreal is as scythed by freeways as any U.S. city, and it helps to be prepared to deal with the sudden shift from quiet countryside to confusing urban madness. If you've followed the rural route across Quebec from Ottawa, you enter the city from the northwest, on the Hwy-640 Autoroute; the freeway route from Ottawa brings you in on the Hwy-40 Autoroute, straight into downtown.

Any east-west freeway you find yourself on will cross the Hwy-15 Autoroute, the main route between Montreal and the U.S. border. Vermont is a quick 30 miles south of Montreal; after crossing the U.S. border, take the second exit off the I-87 freeway and head east along US-11/US-2 to Rouses Point, New York, at the north end of Lake Champlain, to rejoin our two-lane road trip route. Between Vermont and the Canadian border, US-2 nips briefly and uneventfully across the northeast corner of New York State, crossing the international border on the I-87 freeway between the United States and Quebec.

Hwy-17 is fairly boring between Ottawa and Montreal, and you're better off taking the much faster Hwy-417, called the Queensway, or following our two-lane route across Quebec, along the north bank of the Ottawa River.

A quick Québécois sampler for travelers:
arrêt = stop
cul de sac = dead end
bar laitier = ice cream stand
poutine = chili cheese fries

A quiet town and provincial park along the Ottawa River, 32 kilometers (20 miles) west of Montreal, **Oka** gained international prominence in 1990, when indigenous Mohawk people, protesting plans to turn a burial ground into a golf course, blocked the main highway to and from Montreal.

VERMONT

Starting at the state's northwestern corner, US-2 crosses the heart of verdant Vermont. From the shores of **Lake Champlain,** our route winds south to the university town of **Burlington,** then east past Montpelier, the state capital, all the way to New Hampshire, some 150 miles in all. Paralleled for much of the way by the modern I-89 freeway, US-2 makes a slower but much more diverting alternative to the fast lane, passing through some of the state's most attractive small towns and giving an up-close look at its rural charms, not to mention Vermont's untrammeled mountains, forests, lakes, and rivers.

Lake Champlain Islands

After its brief jaunt across New York from the Canadian border, US-2 winds across the sleepy **Lake Champlain Islands.** Pancake-flat and covered with cows, orchards, and pick-your-own fruit farms, this trio of islands is pretty to drive across, with the

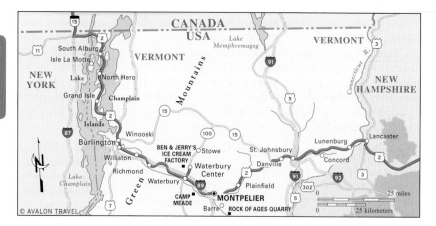

Adirondacks rising up to the west and the Green Mountains to the south and east, but there's not a lot to do; far more farm animals than people populate the route, and tractors clog the road, flinging clods of mud and manure (here pronounced "man-OO-ah") with abandon.

From the middle of the Alburgh Peninsula, where US-2 crosses from New York into Vermont, a turn west onto Route 129 leads to **Isle La Motte,** home of the first French settlement in Vermont, established in 1666. The site is now occupied by **Saint Anne's Shrine,** a popular pilgrimage destination featuring daily outdoor masses in summer and a granite statue of the explorer Samuel de Champlain, for whom the lake is named.

The roaring waterfalls that powered the Champlain Mill have been adapted with a fish lift; in spring and fall you can watch trout and salmon make their way upstream.

Continuing south on US-2, the town of **North Hero** (pop. 803) has a gas station, a stone courthouse, a number of quietly luxurious vacation homes dating from the early decades of the 20th century, and the handy **Hero's Welcome,** a café and general store at the center of the two-block-long town. A mile south along US-2, **Shore Acres Inn and Restaurant** (802/372-8722, $129 and up) offers tennis courts, boating and swimming, moderately priced lakeside rooms, and a restaurant.

Seven miles and another bridge to the south, the town of **Grand Isle** (pop. 2,067) ambitiously claims to be "The Beauty Spot of Vermont." A well-marked turn leads to tiny **Grand Isle State Park** (802/372-4300), on the shores of the lake, where there's a nice campground. At the other end of the island, connected by a causeway to the mainland, **South Hero** is another quaint little place; it and North Hero were named after those famous Vermont Revolutionary War heroes, the Green Mountain Boys, Ira and Ethan Allen.

From South Hero, US-2 rejoins the mainland at the entrance to **Sand Bar State Park,** set in a forest with picnic tables and bathing beaches, surrounded by sprawling, wildfowl-rich marshes on either side. From here US-2 heads east through rolling hills, linking up with the I-89 freeway for the fast route to Burlington, 10 miles to the south.

Winooski

If you have a little time or an abiding interest in America's industrial heritage, get off I-89 at exit 15, or follow Riverside Avenue (old US-2) north from Burlington to

Champlain Bridge connects New York and Vermont.

the center of **Winooski,** an old woolen mill town that provides a blue-collar balance to Burlington's somewhat upscale airs. Downtown, the restored **Champlain Mill** (20 Winooski Falls Way). This former woolen mill now houses cafés and specialty shops. The town green is marred by a bank and large parking lot, but the surrounding buildings hold some interesting spots, including **Sneakers Bistro** (28 Main St., 802/655-9081), which serves great breakfasts and lunches every day. Two doors down, the **Mule Bar** (38 Main St., 802/399-2020) serves more eclectic food and a great range of microbrew beers and ciders.

Another reason to visit Winooski is to tour the restored farm of Vermont patriot Ethan Allen, preserved as the **Ethan Allen Homestead Museum** (802/865-4556, daily 10am-4pm May-Oct., $10) along Route 127 two miles northeast of Winooski.

A mile north of the town of Grand Isle, along US-2 next to a school, stands the **Hyde Log Cabin,** considered by many to be the country's oldest log cabin, dating from 1783.

The worst floods in Vermont's history followed in the wake of Hurricane Irene in 2011. Streets and buildings were flooded, and many bridges damaged or destroyed, especially between Winooski and Montpelier.

Burlington

Best known these days as the home of Senator Bernie Sanders and countercultural icons Ben & Jerry's, **Burlington** (pop. 42,417) has a long tradition of independent and creative thinking. After the original French settlers were ejected from the Lake Champlain region at the end of the French and Indian Wars, Ethan Allen, leader of the Green Mountain Boys band of guerrillas, and his brothers took over huge tracts of land and, resisting competing claims from New York and New Hampshire, established the independent Republic of Vermont. When Vermont joined the Union as the 14th state in 1791, Burlington boomed, aided by its strategic position on Lake Champlain, which was the quickest route between New York's Hudson River and Montreal. While the political capital was established at nearby Montpelier,

Burlington became the center of Vermont industry, finance, education, and culture—a position it has held ever since.

US-2/US-7 passes right through the center of town, following Winooski Avenue to the north, then along Main Street, lined by motels and restaurants on the outskirts but eventually crossing the lively, sprawling campus of the **University of Vermont** (UVM), which stands on a shallow hill on the east side of town. Along Colchester Avenue on the north edge of campus, the **Fleming Museum of Art** (802/656-0750, Tues.-Sun. Sept.-mid-May, $5) is the main visitor attraction, with a small but varied collection of fine and applied arts from ancient Egypt to the present.

Midway between Lake Champlain and the UVM campus, downtown Burlington is anchored by the **Church Street Marketplace,** a pedestrianized and increasingly chain-dominated shopping district that lies perpendicular to Main Street, north from Burlington's stately old City Hall. From City Hall, Main Street continues west to **Lake Champlain,** where **Waterfront Park** has a strollable boardwalk linking up with Battery Park, home to a cannon pointing menacingly across the lake. In 1813, this cannon was used against British warships that bombarded the town. Bands frequently play here on summer evenings, and a bike path runs along the water. If you feel like getting out on the water, the Community Sailing Center north of the park rents kayaks, canoes and paddleboards. You can also hop a ferry across the lake to Port Kent, New York; or take a sunset cruise on board the **Spirit of Ethan Allen** (802/862-8300). Whatever you do, keep an eye out for Champ, Vermont's version of the Loch Ness monster, who dwells deep in the waters of Lake Champlain.

Just south of Burlington is one of the nation's great cultural institutions, the **Shelburne Museum** (802/985-3346, daily 10am-5pm May-Dec., Wed.-Sun. 10am-5pm Jan.-Apr., $10-24). See below for more.

Billings Library on the University of Vermont campus

Burlington Practicalities

Downtown Burlington offers all the delights of a typical college town: bookstores, bars, international food, and trendy shopping. For food, two local favorites—the popular **Penny Cluse Café** (169 Cherry St., 802/651-8834) and **The Daily Planet** (15 Center St., 802/862-9647), behind Church Street—stand out among the many offerings around the Church Street Marketplace.

Thanks to the many students and Vermonters' general love of live music, Burlington has some great nightclubs, ranging from the juke joint ambience of **Nectar's** (188 Main St., 802/658-4771), where the band Phish was born and bred, to the high-style art deco **Flynn Center for the Performing Arts** (153 Main St., 802/863-5966 or 802/652-4500), across from City Hall, where bigger-name bands perform.

East of the UVM campus, Winooski's historic **Centennial Field** is home to the Class A **Vermont Lake Monsters** (802/655-6611), farm club of the Oakland A's.

Places to stay, alas, don't come particularly cheap, especially during peak leaf-peeping season, when run-of-the-mill rooms can cost $250 or more. The historic and central **Willard Street Inn** (349 S. Willard St., 802/651-8710 or 800/577-8712, $150 and up) is a nice B&B in an 1880s home, and some rooms have views of Lake Champlain. There are also many motels along US-7 south of downtown Burlington.

Burlington was the home of Dr. Horatio Nelson Jackson, who, in 1903, along with his chauffeur and a stray dog they picked up along the way, became the first person to cross the country by automobile.

Church Street Marketplace

THE SHELBURNE MUSEUM AND SHELBURNE FARMS

One of the most popular and enjoyable stops in the state of Vermont is just six miles south of downtown Burlington, on the shores of Lake Champlain: the **Shelburne Museum** (802/985-3346, daily May-Dec., Wed.-Sun. 10am-5pm Jan.-Apr., $10-24). The museum presents perhaps the best, and certainly the most unusual, agglomeration of fine art, folk art, and general oddities you'll find anywhere. These toys, dolls, trade signs, and weathervanes (and much, much more) really do defy classification, but there's more here than a riot of garage-sale stuff. Assembled over a lifetime by heiress Electra Havemeyer Webb, whose parents introduced America to the art of the French impressionists, the Shelburne collection includes paintings by European and American masters (Rembrandt, Monet, Manet, and Winslow Homer, to drop a few of the famous names). However, it is most interesting for its unique Americana: old fire trucks, handmade quilts, and a collection of horse-powered vehicles.

There are also dozens of historic buildings brought here from all over New England: a covered bridge, a round barn, a lighthouse, a railroad depot, even a complete side-wheeled Lake Champlain steamboat, the *Ticonderoga*. The buildings, which all house different parts of the expansive collection, are spread over 45 acres of lawns and formal gardens, and there's so much to see you may want to save some for another visit, which you can do, since tickets are good for two days.

Northwest of the Shelburne Museum, just over a mile from US-7 via Bay and Harbor Roads, **Shelburne Farms** is a 1,400-acre farm and nonprofit environmental center with 10 miles of hiking trails on a promontory jutting out into Lake Champlain. The grounds were laid out by landscape architect Frederick Law Olmsted to take full advantage of the natural topography (and to maximize views across the lake toward the Adirondack Mountains). In recent years, Shelburne Farms has become a leading force in the movement toward sustainable agriculture, and you can taste the results in its fabulously flavorful cheddar cheeses, available nationwide. Free tastings are available here at the Farm Store, where you can also join a selection of **guided tours** (802/985-8686, times vary, $11) and explore the entire property. Included on the tour is a stop at the old mansion at the center of the estate, now the **Inn at Shelburne Farms** (802/985-8498, May-Oct., $160-525), where you can stay overnight or enjoy a wonderful meal (or three). There are also concerts, children's programs, and a variety of educational workshops held at Shelburne Farms throughout the summer.

Richmond and Williston

Between Montpelier and Burlington, US-2 follows the Winooski River Valley, lined with dairy farms. For most of the way, the road parallels the less-than-attractive concrete expanse of I-89, but a few sights along the "old road" make the two-lane route preferable. First and foremost of these is **Al's French Frys** (1251 Williston Rd., 802/862-9203), east of downtown Burlington on US-2, which has been churning out great fries (sold by the quart!), burgers, hot dogs, and shakes since the 1940s. Al's is open from lunchtime until late (midnight on summer weekends). For more architectural interest, slide in to the wooden booths of the 65-year-old Worcester Lunch Car classic **Parkway Diner** (1696 Williston Rd., 802/652-1155).

To escape the contemporary chaos, turn south from US-2 at the only stoplight in **Richmond,** where the National Historic Landmark **Old Round Church,** a 16-sided, two-story, white clapboard structure, stands just east of the road. The church was built in 1813 and is the communal effort of five different Protestant denominations. They eventually parted ways, and the structure lapsed into civic use, becoming the town hall. Today it is used as a meeting house, and during the summer the local **historical society** (802/434-2556) gives guided tours.

Williston (pop. 9,438) sits roughly 10 miles east of Burlington and less than a mile north of the freeway. Although large by local standards, Williston is a classic northern New England town, its streets lined by towering maple trees and white clapboard houses.

Waterbury Center: Ben & Jerry's

Though it's known for beautiful mountains and the brilliant fall color of its hardwood forests, Vermont's number-one tourist attraction is none other than **Ben & Jerry's Ice Cream Factory,** a kind of hippie Disneyland in **Waterbury Center,** on the hillside above Route 100, a mile or so north of I-89. The grounds of the brightly painted factory include a number of large cartoonish artifacts strewn outside to play on—weird vehicles, whimsical picnic tables, and the like. Ben and Jerry began making ice cream in 1978, becoming internationally famous for their ultrarich ice cream and for their activism, donating a percentage of profits to philanthropies supporting "progressive social change." Now part of Anglo-Dutch conglomerate Unilever, Ben & Jerry's is still a Vermont icon.

You can **tour the factory** (866/258-6877, daily, times vary, $4), although production is halted on weekends, holidays, and company celebration days—when you get a video presentation. The premises also feature a gift shop and the Scoop Shop, offering all of Ben & Jerry's ice cream, frozen yogurt, and sorbet flavors. Outside are many picnic tables where you can enjoy the ice cream and a view over the valley.

If Ben & Jerry's trademark black-and-white splotched ice cream packaging gets you interested in the different bovine breeds, here's a short primer to help you tell them apart:

black-and-white splotches = Holsteins
brown with white splotches = Guernseys
brown all over = Jerseys

North of Waterbury Junction on Route 100, the ski resort of **Stowe** was the post-World War II home of the musical Von Trapp family, whose escape from the Nazis inspired *The Sound of Music.* Running south, Route 100 travels through the heart of the **Green Mountains** all the way south to Massachusetts and is one of the state's most popular leaf-peeping drives.

Back on US-2, midway between Montpelier and Waterbury, right on US-2 just west of Middlesex, **Camp Meade** was a Depression-era Civilian Conservation Corps camp that was turned into a shrine to America in the 1930s and 1940s. The old barracks were turned into a motel, and a fighter plane, a tank, and military trucks once adorned the grounds, but in recent years Camp Meade has evolved into the Red Hen Baking Co., with a bakery and café.

Montpelier

The smallest capital in the country, and the only one without a McDonald's, Vermont's **Montpelier** (pop. 7,855) was settled in 1787 and designated the state capital in 1805. Today, Montpelier's economy is based on government, insurance, and tourism.

As you follow US-2 Business into town, the gold dome of the capitol building hovering over the valley ahead signals your arrival in Montpelier. Constrained by the Winooski River on one side and the narrow valley on the other, Montpelier is so compact that you can park your car and find all the sights within a 10-minute walk. (Thankfully, the I-89 freeway and the main US-2 bypass are well away from downtown.) A quick poll of shops along State and Main Streets reveals the cosmopolitan nature of the town: the magical **Bear Pond Books** (77 Main St., 802/229-0774), along with coffee bars, wine merchants, and multiple combinations of the same.

The north side of State Street opens up into a broad lawn fronting the capitol dome, the focal point of the Republic of Vermont—like Texas, the state takes some pride in the fact that it was an independent "country" before joining the rest of the United States. The state legislature is only in session a few months a year (typically from January to May), so being a Vermont politician is a part-time job. The rest

Vermont Historical Society Museum

of the year they go about being farmers, businesspeople, and so on, but you can **tour the state house** (Mon.-Fri.) year-round.

Near Montpelier, watch sap being turned into delicious maple syrup at the **Morse Farm Maple Sugarworks,** three miles northeast from the capitol dome along Main Street.

Above the state house rises **Hubbard Park,** a 118-year-old, 194-acre green space, with seven miles of hiking trails and a 54-foot observation tower atop the summit, the highest point in Montpelier.

Just west of the capitol is the **Vermont History Museum** (Tues.-Sat., $7), where permanent and temporary displays illustrate different aspects of Vermont's history, and you can also find lots of 19th-century furniture and a small bookstore and gift shop. Rising up a hill a few blocks farther west, the **Green Mount Cemetery** is filled with impressive granite monuments. Many of these were carved by the immigrant stonecutters of nearby Barre for their own family plots, and the well-groomed grounds make ideal picnic spots, especially on a summer afternoon.

Montpelier thrived off the granite quarries of the nearby town of **Barre.** The **Rock of Ages quarry** (802/476-3119, Mon.-Sat. June-Oct., free), four miles southeast of Barre, is the world's largest.

Montpelier Practicalities

Montpelier residents take their eating seriously. Very good and fairly inexpensive food is readily available, thanks to the local presence of the New England Culinary Institute, a cooking school that operates the **NECI on Main** (118 Main St.,

802/223-3188). Nearby, **The Blue Stone** (802/882-8188), on the corner of State and Main Streets, offers rustic pizza and craft beer. The **Skinny Pancake** (89 Main St., 802/262-2253) serves a huge variety of their crepes for breakfast, lunch, and dinner, with good coffee and sandwiches, too.

For upscale lodgings in period surroundings, go to the **Inn at Montpelier** (147 Main St., 802/223-2727, $150 and up), two renovated 1820s homes that have been joined into one hotel.

Plainfield

Hitchhikers are common on US-2 between Montpelier and **Plainfield,** thanks to the presence of **Goddard College,** one of the nation's most renowned countercultural institutes of higher learning. The tiny town of Plainfield also boasts the **Maple Valley Café** (802/454-8626, tie-dyes welcome), a combo deli-café that is the local hangout. The soups are fantastic, as are the veggie burgers. The store's parking area is built on a foundation of recycled granite, leftovers from the nearby quarries and stonecutters.

All along US-2, and all over New England for that matter, the old roads are lined by 1940s-style knotty-pine cabins and motor courts.

If you want to linger, consider a night on the farm: At **Hollister Hill Farm** (2193 Hollister Hill Rd., 802/454-7725, $100 and up), east of town, they make their own maple syrup (and serve it over pancakes at breakfast) and raise all sorts of organic produce (from vegetables to "beefalo" hybrids).

West Danville: Joe's Pond

West Danville, a summer community 20 lovely miles east of Plainfield on the edge of **Joe's Pond,** is ringed by rustic vacation cabins. The pond, which at sunset in summer is one of the more idyllic spots imaginable, was originally called Indian Joe's Pond. At the junction of US-2 and Route 15 in the center of town, you'll see a microsize covered bridge and the **Hastings Store** (802/684-3398), the local "if we ain't got it, we'll get it for you" emporium, selling cheddar cheese, maple syrup, fishing supplies, and other Vermont essentials.

Danville and Peacham

Heading east, the next place you'll pass is **Danville,** yet another picture-postcard Vermont town, set on a hill surrounded by farmland. The center of Danville is a classic New England village green, with a general store and the customary churches. Just off the green you'll find the headquarters of the **American Society of Dowsers** (184 Brainerd St., 802/684-3417, Mon.-Fri.), whose members have refined their talents for finding water or mineral deposits using a dowsing rod.

South of US-2 from the center of Danville, enjoy the lovely pastoral drive toward **Peacham,** a perennial contender for the "prettiest village in Vermont" title. During the fall color sweeps, the mountaintop village is likely to be crowded with sightseeing tourists, but most of the time it's a somnolent little place. In fact, Peacham is so timeless that the producers of the movie version of Edith Wharton's Victorian fable *Ethan Frome* filmed here, without having to remove any streetlights or other signs of modern life.

St. Johnsbury

In the 19th century, the economy of **St. Johnsbury** (pop. 6,193) was based on maple products and the manufacture of platform scales. Fairbanks Scales, founded by the inventor of platform scales, still operates a plant here. Today it is the pleasantly peaceful commercial center of Vermont's Northeast Kingdom, at the junction of the US-2 and US-5 highways, the I-91 and I-93 freeways, and the Canadian Pacific and old Maine Central railroad tracks. The economy never regained its Victorian-era prosperity, so the town's extensive stock of historic landmark architecture has been preserved almost totally unchanged. Elegant (and often empty) four- and five-story brick buildings line the riverfront and railroad line along US-2 and US-5. On the hill above the riverfront, a more genteel commercial district surrounded by massive trees and dozens of grand Victorian homes is highlighted by two of the most fascinating institutions in the state, both funded by the largess of the Fairbanks family.

At the center of town stands the **St. Johnsbury Athenaeum, Art Gallery, and Public Library** (1171 Main St., Mon.-Sat., free) in a redbrick 1871 building. The building houses a surprising collection of 19th-century paintings, the jewel of which is Albert Bierstadt's monumental *Domes of Yosemite*.

A block east down Main Street, you'll find my favorite museum in all New England: the **Fairbanks Museum and Planetarium** (802/748-2372, daily, $9), a charmingly quirky Victorian-era center of knowledge established by Franklin Fairbanks in 1889. Two menacing stuffed bears greet visitors inside the entrance, followed by a seemingly endless display of taxidermied wildlife—a veritable Noah's Ark of North American fauna. Climb the spiral stairs to the mezzanine of the main gallery, a grand Richardsonian Romanesque space topped by a coffered barrel vault and furnished with fireplaces and other homey touches. You'll find more fascinating oddities: arrowheads and other anthropological artifacts, rocks and fossils, and art made out of bugs (including a portrait of George Washington made out of dried insects!). View exhibits on local history, and a funny letter written by Robert Louis Stevenson in which he gifts his birthday (which he said he was too old to need anymore) to a family friend of the Fairbanks named Annie Ide (whose own birth fell on Christmas, meaning she effectively missed out).

St. Johnsbury's eating options include **Hilltopper Restaurant** (1216 Main St., 802/748-8964), a lunch spot, across the street from the Athenaeum, run by students at the St. Johnsbury Academy; the popular **Kingdom Taproom Restaurant** (397 Railroad St., 802/424-1355), serving good food and a remarkable range of Vermont beers; and the excellent **Anthony's Diner** (321 Railroad St.,

Fairbanks Museum and Planetarium

portrait of George Washington, made out of 6,399 dried insects by John Hampson in 1916

802/748-3613) at the junction of US-5 and US-2. There's also a good pizza place: the **House of Pizza** (287 Portland St., 802/748-5144).

For motels, try the **Fairbanks Inn** (401 Western Ave., 802/748-5666, $134 and up) on US-2.

Maple Grove Farms

Taking a scenic alternative to the I-93 freeway east from St. Johnsbury, US-2 passes over the Memorial Bridge (1943) spanning the Passumpsic River. One mile east of the bridge you'll find the **Maple Grove Farms** complex. Highlights include the maple museum (free samples!) and the so-called "World's Largest Maple Candy Factory." Vermont is the heart of maple-sugaring territory, which runs all the way from Maine to Michigan and up into Canada. Maple Grove Farms has been in business here since 1915, and it is the largest packager of maple syrup in the United States.

A marker along US-2 points out the site, in nearby **Concord Corner, Vermont,** where the **First Normal School,** America's first teachers' academy, was founded in 1823.

Concord and Lunenburg

Near the New Hampshire border, US-2 heads across rolling rocky hills covered with forests, largely pine and birch, with a few scattered farms. This corner of the state, a recreational paradise of hills and lakes and few year-round residents, is known as the Northeast Kingdom. The road drops down into the narrow, pastoral valley of the Moose River before reaching **Concord,** which features a country store and a small historical society.

Fifteen miles east of Concord, along the banks of the broad Connecticut River, **Lunenburg** is a perfect New England village of white clapboard houses clustered around a church—Vermont specializes in this species of quaintness.

From Lunenburg, you can take a highly recommended detour across the Connecticut River on the 266-foot-long **Mt. Orne covered bridge,** then proceed north along Route 135, rejoining US-2 at Lancaster.

NEW HAMPSHIRE

Crossing the broad Connecticut River, which forms Vermont's 200-mile-long border with New Hampshire, US-2 makes a short but scenic run across the state. From the historic commercial center of **Lancaster,** just east of the state border, US-2 winds along the wide valley of the Israel River before reaching **Jefferson,** home to two of the state's biggest tourist traps. Continuing east, US-2 curves around the northern flank of towering **Mt. Washington** and the rugged White Mountains, an area rich in outdoor recreation and scenic splendor. At **Gorham,** US-2 reaches the valley of the Androscoggin River, which it follows east into Maine.

Lancaster

Across the Connecticut River from Vermont, **Lancaster** (pop. 3,410) is a market town that was first settled in 1764. Through Lancaster US-2 becomes Main Street, lined with dozens of attractive old homes and churches, a cemetery on a knoll to the north, and on the south side a redbrick courthouse that dates from 1887.

A roadside marker along US-2 just west of Jefferson commemorates the birth nearby of inventor Thaddeus Lowe, who pioneered balloon aviation during the Civil War.

Two miles south of Lancaster via US-3, the mountaintop estate of the man who saved New Hampshire's forests from the lumber industry has been preserved as **John Wingate Weeks Historic Site** (Wed.-Sun. 10am-5pm summer, $5), complete with a tourable mansion and an observation tower giving grand views of Mt. Washington and Vermont's Green Mountains.

If you weren't thrilled by the modern bridge that carries US-2 into Lancaster, there are two historic covered bridges in Lancaster that will renew your appreciation of civil engineers. Five miles south of US-2 via Hwy-135 the Mt. Orne covered bridge spans the Connecticut River to Vermont, while just east of US-2 in Lancaster village there's the nifty 94-foot-long **Mechanic Street Covered Bridge** that spans the Israel River.

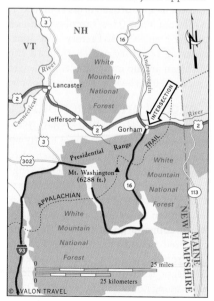

Jefferson

High above the Israel River on the slopes of the White Mountains, the small resort town of **Jefferson** (pop. 933) is a good base for exploring the surrounding peaks and is home to two big tourist draws, both ideal for the truly masochistic parent. About a mile west of Jefferson is **Santa's Village** (603/586-4445, daily summer, Sat.-Sun. fall, $32), with candy canes looming threateningly at the entrance, a Ferris wheel, a roller coaster, the Yule log flume, a "HoHoH2O" water park, and, of course, Santa himself.

Outside the town, along US-2 on a crest between Jefferson and Gorham, the **Grand View Lodge** (603/466-5715, $64 and up) has nice rooms and truly grand views. Two other accommodations in Jefferson deserve mention, starting with the historic **Jefferson Inn** (800/729-7908, $85-195), which has panoramic views and a swimming pond, right on US-2. A half mile south of Jefferson along Route 115A, the friendly **Applebrook B&B** (603/586-6008, $95 and up) sits on five acres and offers full Victorian splendor gilded with summer raspberries.

East of Jefferson the road ascends, the valley narrows, and the scenery becomes more spectacular with every mile, as the Presidential Range looms larger and larger to the south.

Gorham

Gorham (pop. 1,600), incorporated in 1836, was another early tourist town. Its boom began when the railroad came through in 1851; the train's story, and the town's, is told at the **Gorham Historical Society and Railroad Museum** (25 Railroad St., Wed.-Sat. 10am-3pm May-Oct., donation), which stands in the old depot, a half block off Main Street.

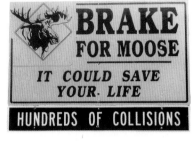

Your welcome to New Hampshire is a sign: Brake for Moose. Apparently, moose are hard to see at night because headlights shine through the legs of this towering beast, rather than reflecting off its body, leading to many serious collisions.

Just east of Gorham, the road passes through a famous grove of birch trees, the "world-renowned Shelburne birches." Here you find the big but pleasant **Town & Country Motor Inn** (603/466-3315, $129 and up) with some spa and resort facilities, such as saunas, a golf course, and a good dining room. This is also where the Appalachian Trail, which runs from Maine's Mt. Katahdin to northern Georgia, crosses US-2.

West of Gorham, right off US-2, the summer-only **Moose Brook State Park** (603/466-3860) has a campground and a swimming hole built back in the 1930s by the New Deal CCC.

MAINE

Following the Androscoggin River across the New Hampshire border, US-2 enters Maine at the forested eastern flank of the **White Mountains.** Winding east along the river, the route passes through alternating mountain resorts and mill towns, starting at sedate **Bethel** and ending up 135 miles later at **Bangor,** once one of the wildest lumber towns in the country. From Bangor the route veers south toward the coast, hitting the Atlantic Ocean at beautiful **Acadia National Park.**

Bethel

At the far west end of its run across Maine, US-2 winds along the south bank of the Androscoggin River through the dense pine and birch forests of the White

INTERSECTION Eight miles south of Gorham, towering Mt. Washington marks the start of our **Appalachian Trail** route (see page 298), which follows along these landmark mountains all the way south to Atlanta.

Mountains National Forest. Ten miles east of the New Hampshire border, along a placid stretch of the Androscoggin, **Bethel** (pop. 2,759) was first settled in 1774. At the tail end of the Revolutionary War, the town, then named Sudbury, suffered the last Native American raid inflicted on New England. The Gould Academy, one of Maine's oldest prep schools, was established at the west end of town in 1836. After the railroads came through, Bethel quickly became a center for White Mountain-area tourism. Founded in 1913, The **Bethel Inn Resort** (21 Broad St., 207/824-2175 or 800/654-0125, $139 and up) was one of New England's early health resorts, and it continues that tradition today. The inn is surrounded by 200 acres (including an 18-hole golf course), and if you're looking for upscale lodging at reasonable rates, this is the place to go. Information on Bethel's many other well-preserved old buildings can be found in the 200-year-old **Mason House,** facing the town common, which doubles as a small **museum** (15 Broad St., 207/824-2908, Thurs.-Sat. 1pm-4pm July-Aug., by appointment Sept.-June, $5).

Just east of the Maine border, 10 miles west of Bethel, a sign marks a turn south from US-2 onto Route 113 toward **Evans Notch.** This narrow, winding, motorcycle-friendly road runs along Wild River and Cold River up to a stunningly scenic mountain pass.

For outdoor enthusiasts, the **Sunday River Ski Area** (800/543-2754), six miles northeast of town, draws thousands of visitors to the area for Aspen-scale skiing in winter, and hiking and mountain biking in summer (there's also a popular "wife-carrying" contest in October). The après-ski party continues year-round, thanks to downtown Bethel's **Funky Red Barn** (19 Summer St., 207/824-3003), which has a pool table, food, drink, and good live music.

Back on US-2, which is also known as the Mayville Road, there are a couple of good brewpubs (the **Jolly Drayman Pub** and **Sunday River Brewing Company**), plus

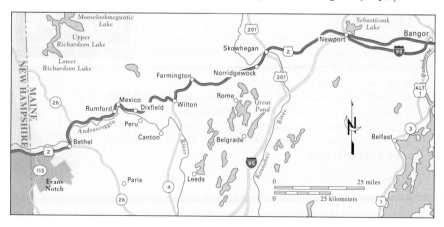

one unexpected treat. Whenever you see smoke—most likely on Sundays—**Smokin' Good Barbecue** (207/824-4744, Sun.) is cookin' up ribs and baked beans in a bright orange trailer along US-2, a mile north of town, next to the Good Food Store.

Near the well-marked turnoff to Sunday River, there's a nice picnic area with a covered bridge, along US-2 and the Androscoggin River. If you head north from here a mile or so past the ski area, another sign will point you toward the intricately constructed Sunday River **Artist's Covered Bridge,** which spans the Sunday River.

From US-2 at Bethel, Route 26 runs southeast toward Portland and the coast, passing through the spa town of **Poland Spring** and the world's last remaining intact Shaker community at **Sabbathday Lake** (207/926-4597, Mon.-Sat. May-Oct.), where a small museum gives tours ($10).

Rumford

The biggest and brawniest place along otherwise rural US-2, **Rumford** (pop. 4,218) is a definite change from the leisure-time orientation of many other places in New England. A historic paper-pulp mill town with low brick buildings and a downscale downtown along Waldo Street, Rumford grew up around Androscoggin River, which provided the hydropower that led to the original settlement of the town. Now, enormous steam-puffing smokestacks loom large at New Page, New England's largest paper mill, surrounded by huge piles of logs, chips, and wood residue.

> Rumford's main claim to fame is as the birthplace of Edmund Muskie, governor, U.S. senator, secretary of state, and vice-presidential and presidential candidate in 1968 and 1972, respectively.

The hard-working, perpetually underpaid realities of Rumford (and its next-door neighbor, **Mexico,** where the mill is located) are in many ways what makes it remarkable. Clearly this isn't a town designed for tourists, but if you're interested in how Americans live, work, and drink too much in places where heavy industry still rules the roost, Rumford is worth investigating. At the least, stop for a coffee at **Dick's** Restaurant (54 Main St.) on US-2 in Mexico.

Away from the center of town, the Rumford area is suddenly semi-pastoral and pretty. US-2 winds around the valley as the Androscoggin makes an oxbow, and an even nicer route heads north following Route 17 and the Swift River toward the popular Rangeley Lakes resort area.

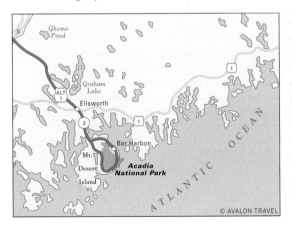

white pine cone and tassel, state flower of Maine

Wilton

West of Farmington and just north of US-2, the town of **Wilton** was the longtime home of famous shoe-maker G. H. Bass Company, makers of those leather "Weejuns" so loved by preppies. In 1998 the Bass Company abandoned Wilton for the lower-wage Dominican Republic, but its old mill is still standing. Next to the mill, an old boardinghouse holds

the **Wilton Farm and Home Museum** (207/645-2091, by appointment or Sat. 1pm-4pm July-Aug., donation), a fascinating museum with exhibits on G. H. Bass, its shoe-making operations, and everything from old bottles to the life of the Wilton-born "Maine Giantess," Sylvia Hardy, an 8-foot-tall, 400-pound woman who was a star of P. T. Barnum's famous freak shows.

Wilton is also where you'll find a large windmill marking the **Dutch Treat** (291 E. US-2) restaurant and ice cream stand, while one of the old G. H. Bass buildings in the historic core is now home to one of inland Maine's better restaurants: **Calzolaio Pasta Company** (248 Main St., 207/645-9500), which serves Maine seafood and brick-oven pizzas in its cozy dining room or on the outdoor deck.

Farmington

Like many other northern Maine towns, **Farmington** (pop. 4,288) was first settled by soldiers who fought in the Revolutionary War. The rolling hills that surround it still hold a few farms and orchards, but as elsewhere, the economy revolves around trees—both as tourist fodder during the fall color sweeps and as pulp for paper mills (there's a big pulp mill just south of town on US-201). US-2 bypasses the center, but the downtown area has a few blocks of tidy brick buildings housing barber shops, bookstores, and cafés—not to mention the too-cute **Narrow Gauge Cinema** (15 Front St., 207/778-2881 or 207/778-4877 for movie schedule)—supported in large part by the presence of the large Farmington campus of the University of Maine.

Farmington's main claim to fame is that way back in 1873, a local teenager, Chester Greenwood, rigged up a pair of beaver-skin pads on a piece of bent wire to create the world's first earmuffs.

On the south edge of downtown, at the junction of US-2 and Route 4, near where the Farmington Diner used to sit, family-run **Gifford's Famous Ice Cream** (293 Main St., 207/778-3617) serves silky-smooth "frappes" and luscious high-fat cones.

Between Skowhegan and Farmington, US-2 passes through a pair of quietly quaint places. **Norridgewock** is a historic hamlet, now home to a New Balance shoe factory. The region's real draw is south of US-2: the **Belgrade Lakes,** a chain of seven lakes circled by ageless vacation cabins and summer camps. It was this idyllic location that inspired Ernest Thompson to write the play *On Golden Pond,* later made into that weepy Fonda-family movie, though the movie was filmed at New Hampshire's Squam Lake, off US-3 in the White Mountains.

Skowhegan

First settled in 1771 on an island in the Kennebec River, the midsize mill town of **Skowhegan** (pop. 6,297) was the birthplace of Margaret Chase Smith (1897-1995),

one of Maine's most renowned politicians and a 36-year veteran of the U.S. House and Senate. Her home, set on 15 riverside acres, is now the **Margaret Chase Smith Library Center** (56 Norridgewock Ave., 207/474-7133, Mon.-Fri. 10am-4pm, donation). Northwest of town, the complex includes a museum depicting her life and Cold War times, when Smith was the first U.S. senator to stand up to the red-baiting character assassination of Joe McCarthy's Communist "witch trials."

Skowhegan's other larger-than-life character stands alongside US-201, just north of US-2: the **Skowhegan Indian,** a 62-foot statue sometimes billed as the "Largest Wooden Indian in the World."

North from Skowhegan, US-201 runs along the Kennebec River, offering some of Maine's greatest fall foliage vistas. One of the prettiest stretches is around the town of **Bingham,** about 25 miles north of Skowhegan. On US-201 a mile south of town, you can catch an alfresco movie at the **Skowhegan Drive-In** (207/474-9277) on weekend nights all summer long.

East of Skowhegan, US-2 veers away from the river across low, rolling hills covered with pine and birch forests, the only signs of habitation a few trailer homes and scraggly farms.

> In 1976, the Kennebec River at Skowhegan was the site of the last log drive in Maine.
>
> During the second week of August, Skowhegan is home to the **Maine State Fair.** Celebrated annually since 1818, it is one of the oldest state fairs in the country.

Bangor

Built on the banks of the Penobscot River, **Bangor** (pop. 33,039; pronounced "BANG-gor") is the largest city in northern Maine. This site was an important rendezvous for local Native Americans, who called it Kenduskeag ("eel-catching place"). In 1604 Samuel de Champlain sailed up the Penobscot River as far as Treats Falls here, but long-term settlement did not begin until 1769. Throughout the next century, Bangor was the most important lumber town in the eastern United States. It also developed into a shipbuilding center, and Bangor's lumber circled the globe. The people of Bangor were devoted to providing amusement for the loggers and sailors who would arrive in town with free time and fat wallets. In a riverside neighborhood called the Devil's Half Acre, dozens of bars, bordellos, and gambling dens competed to empty the men's pockets.

In the 19th century, Bangor was as wide-open as any town in the Wild West, but traces of rougher days have all but disappeared. Modern Bangor, once a supply center for the northern half of Maine, is still a center for the lumber industry. Coming into town across the Penobscot River, you'll turn right onto Main Street and see a 31-foot statue of a grinning **Paul Bunyan,** erected in 1959. The compact downtown area, impressive redbrick 19th-century buildings interspersed with church spires, lies a few blocks east of Paul Bunyan.

The **Bangor Historical Society Museum** (159 Union St., Mon.-Sat. 10am-4pm June-Sept., Tues. and Thurs. 10am-4pm fall, $5), housed in an 1836 Greek Revival mansion downtown, has exhibits, furnishings, and paintings reflecting 19th-century

Bangor, Maine

life. Away from the center of Bangor, car, truck, and tractor fans flock to the **Cole Land Transportation Museum** (405 Perry Rd., daily May-Nov., $7), off I-95 and I-395, which displays more than 200 historic vehicles, from wooden wagons to modern 18-wheelers.

Bangor Practicalities

Thanks to the nearby University of Maine, Bangor has a wide variety of places to eat and drink. Unexpectedly, there are a couple of inexpensive Indian and Pakistani places, including **Taste of India** (68 Main St., 207/945-6865), which gets annual "Best in New England" raves. For whiling away an evening, head down to the **Sea Dog Brewing Company** (26 Front St., 207/947-8009).

If you're just passing through Bangor on your way to or from Acadia National Park, you may want to turn off I-95 at exit 180, southwest from downtown (not far from the Land Museum), and soothe your white-line fever at the trucker's favorite stop, **Dysart's** (530 Coldbrook Rd., 207/942-4878). This around-the-clock fuel stop and café offers a place to rest where you can dig in to the world's largest sundae, the 18-scoop "18-Wheeler."

If you prefer character over spotlessness, the pick of Bangor-area lodging is the **Charles Inn** (20 Broad St., 207/992-2820, $120 and up), a restored 1873 hotel downtown. The national

Bangor is home to best-selling horror writer Stephen King, who lives in a suitably Gothic and surprisingly visible mansion on West Broadway.

Mt. Desert Island, Maine

111—Highest Headland on Atlantic Coast, Great Head, Bar Harbor

chains are out on US-2 near the airport and I-95, a mile or so west of downtown, which is also where the fast food is.

Ellsworth and Trenton

Ellsworth, chartered in 1763, began as a lumber town but is now a thriving commercial center, located southeast of Bangor at the junction of Route 3 and US-1. Downtown is marked by lots of redbrick buildings and the **Riverside Café** (151 Main St., 207/667-7220), an upscale retro diner that's famous for its weekend brunch and fine slices of pie. The rest of Ellsworth is full of malls and discount stores, car lots, chain motels, and gas stations—harsh reminders of the sprawling suburban America many Maine visitors are trying to escape.

Between Ellsworth and **Trenton,** gateway to Mount Desert Island and Acadia National Park, there's a short but bittersweet six-mile parade of tacky roadside attractions along Route 3. If you've got kids with you or are in the mood to act like one, you can consider such questionable pleasures as the Great Maine Lumberjack Show in Trenton, plus go-karts, trading posts, miniature golf courses—even a zoo. Just before the bridge, you pass many lobster pounds on this stretch of highway, the best of which is the **Trenton Bridge Lobster Pound** (207/667-2977, Mon.-Sat. and holiday weekends May-mid-Oct.), open since 1956; just look for the billowing clouds of steam.

From Bangor, US-2 winds northeast along the Penobscot River, ending up near the Canadian border at Houlton. We've opted to head "Down East," ending our cross-country odyssey at Acadia National Park.

At 1,530 feet, **Cadillac Mountain** on Mount Desert Island is the highest point on the Eastern seaboard of North America. It also shares a namesake with the classy automobile marque.

Bar Harbor

Once a semiprivate enclave of the very rich (can you say Rockefeller?), the town of **Bar Harbor** (pop. 2,552), the largest and busiest on Mount Desert Island, has turned to catering to the less-well-heeled visitor as the old money has retreated to more discreet settlements to the west, such as Northeast Harbor—a.k.a. Philadelphia on the Rocks. Bar Harbor's principal thoroughfares, lined with gift shops, art galleries, bike rental stands, hotels, and restaurants, intersect at the lively and pleasant village green. Since most of Bar Harbor's old mansions were destroyed in a 1947 fire, there aren't all that many sights to search out, although the Tiffany windows of lovely little **St. Saviour's Church** on the west side of the village green give some sense of the wealth that once lingered here.

There are dozens of generally good and relatively inexpensive restaurants clustered together in Bar Harbor's few short blocks, so wander around and take your pick. Many are clearly aimed at the tourist trade, none more so than the amiable **Route 66 Restaurant** (21 Cottage St., 207/288-3708), a pseudo-1950s diner that's absolutely packed with nostalgic memorabilia—jukeboxes, gas pumps, neon signs, you name it. There's a great range of good food, including fab blueberry pie, at **Poor Boy's Gourmet** (300 Main St., 207/288-4148). Another fun place is **Reel Pizza Cinerama** (33 Kennebec Place, 207/288-3828), across from the village green, where you can watch a classic or art-house film while kicking back in a recliner, waiting for your pizza. Lobsters, of course, are at the core of Maine cuisine; sample them at a half dozen places

MOUNT DESERT ISLAND

Mount Desert Island is an idyllic, 11-by-14-mile chunk of dense forests, barren peaks, and rocky inlets just off the coast of Maine. (The "desert" in Mount Desert Island is pronounced "dessert.") The island was first inhabited by the Penobscot people and was not explored by Europeans until 1604, when Samuel de Champlain named it Île des Monts Déserts (Isle of Bald Peaks) and claimed it for France. In 1844, Hudson River School artist Thomas Cole painted a stunning series of scenes featuring Mount Desert Island, which soon became a summer playground for elite Eastern families, many of whom built massive vacation "cottages" here, largely around Bar Harbor. In 1916, the Mount Desert colony, led by the Pulitzer and Rockefeller families, donated most of the island to the federal government to establish the first national park east of the Mississippi—Acadia National Park. The Great Depression and World War II effectively put an end to the Bar Harbor high life, and most traces of the summer colony were either torn down or destroyed by a huge fire that raged through Bar Harbor in 1947.

Today about half of Mount Desert Island remains in private hands, including the villages of Bass Harbor, Northeast Harbor, Seal Harbor, and Southwest Harbor, all of which are exclusive enclaves. These locales offer a much quieter version of island life than you'll get in Bar Harbor. Northeast Harbor is perhaps the most welcoming, with two public gardens, the genteel old **Asticou Inn** (207/276-3344, $145 and up) on Route 3, and some comparatively affordable cafés like the **Docksider** (207/276-3965) on Sea Street, where you can munch a lobster roll while waiting for the ferry boats that shuttle across to the picturesque Cranberry Isles.

The upscale environs of **Seal Harbor,** also on Mount Desert Island, are home to one of the country's great luxury car collections, on display inside the **Seal Cove Auto Museum** (207/244-9242, daily 10am-5pm May-Oct., $6) on Route 102.

on and around the West Street Pier. The most authentic lobster pound around has to be **Thurston's** (207/244-7600), on the water in tiny Bernard, south of Southwest Harbor.

The classic place to stay is the **Bar Harbor Inn** (1 Newport Dr., 207/288-3351, $105 and up), which has a lovely historic inn and standard rooms right on the water.

Acadia National Park

Mount Desert Island's natural glories are preserved in **Acadia National Park,** occupying 41,634 acres of the island's most scenic areas. Route 3 runs through the heart of the park, but the best way to appreciate Acadia is to track the 27-mile-long **Park Loop Road,** which circles the eastern side of the park. (Note that large campers and trailers are prohibited.) Midway along, the loop road pauses at Sand Beach, one of the few sandy beaches in Maine (get here early to find parking in summer), then passes the Thunder Hole tidal cavern before winding inland past Jordan Pond. If you want to get out and stretch your legs, the best way to see the fantastic ocean views and breathe the fresh ocean air is to walk along the two-mile trail that links Sand Beach, the Thunder Hole, and the 110-foot-high Otter Cliff. From Jordan Pond, the loop road continues past the turnoff (also accessible directly from Bar Harbor) for the drive to the top of Cadillac Mountain. Here, you'll experience a truly breathtaking panorama over Mount Desert Island, the surrounding inlets and

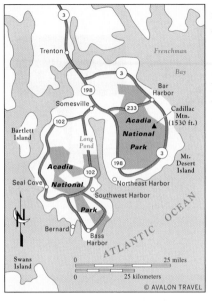

islands, and (on a fog-free day) miles and miles of the Maine coast.

In the summer and fall, when thousands clog the loop road and the streets of Bar Harbor, the most sensible visitors head to the park's hiking trails, which wind among the beautiful inland lakes and mountains. Approximately 57 miles of the unpaved, car-free "carriage roads" constructed (well, paid for) by Edsel Ford and John D. Rockefeller Jr. are open to walkers, bikers, wheelchairs, and baby strollers. Many of these roads leave directly from the main park visitors center, but some of the best (and least crowded) start from Jordan Pond, in the southwest corner of the park. Jordan Pond is also the site of the only restaurant within the park boundary, **Jordan Pond House** (207/276-3316), where you can reserve a table for an idyllic afternoon tea with popovers. In winter, when the park is virtually dormant, the carriage roads are kept open for cross-country skiing or snowshoeing, a magical way to get a feel for the place.

Acadia National Park also protects some exemplary places beyond Mount Desert Island, including the southern tip of Isle au Haut, tiny Baker Island (which you can visit on a ranger-guided tour), and the unforgettable Schoodic Peninsula across Frenchman Bay, accessible via US-1 just north of Ellsworth. Three miles northwest of Bar Harbor, on the edge of Hulls Cove, the main **Acadia National Park Visitors Center** (207/288-3338, daily May-Oct.) is a good place to start.

SCENE ON CADILLAC MOUNTAIN ROAD, ACADIA NATIONAL PARK, MT. DESERT ISLAND, MAINE

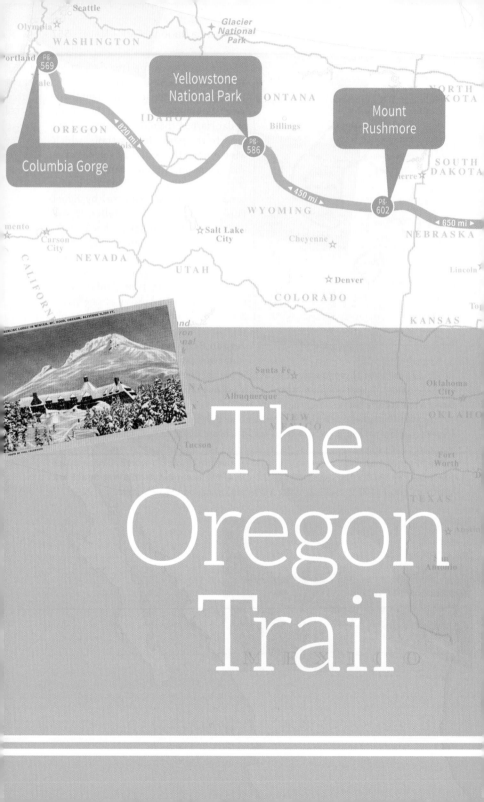

Columbia Gorge

pg. 569

820 mi

Yellowstone
National Park

pg. 586

Mount
Rushmore

450 mi

pg. 602

650 mi

The Oregon Trail

Field of Dreams

pg. 608

Niagara Falls

pg. 640

◄ 740 mi ►

◄ 480 mi ►

pg. 650

Cape Cod

pg. 665

Cooperstown: National Baseball Hall of Fame

Following in the footsteps of pilgrims and pioneers, US-20 takes in a little of everything during its two-lane trek from Oregon's rugged coast to the glorious sea and sand of Cape Cod.

Between the Oregon Coast and Provincetown, Massachusetts

From the wide-open spaces of the West to the dense urban chaos of the East, this route offers the longest and most involved road trip in this book. Connecting an exceedingly diverse range of places and totaling over 3,300 miles—many more if you count all the potential detours, side trips, and parallel routes—US-20 takes in a little of everything during its two-lane trek from Oregon's rugged coast to the glorious sea and sand of Cape Cod. Superlative sights include at least two wonders of the world, New York's **Niagara Falls** and Wyoming's **Yellowstone National Park**; the great cities of **Boston** and **Chicago**; and two halls of fame, one in Cleveland celebrating rock 'n' roll, the other in Cooperstown idolizing the national pastime, baseball. Odd museums, classic diners, idyllic towns, and poignant postindustrial decay—you'll find it all along this great cross-country highway.

Starting in the West, the route parallels, and in places runs right on top of, the broad path that formed the Oregon Trail. The landscape across **Oregon**, **Idaho**, and **Wyoming** along US-20 and a parallel highway, US-26, is still as lonesome as it was more than 150 years ago, when pioneer families followed this one-way route west to the promised lands of the Pacific Coast. Midway across the country you can visit two All-American monuments, **Mt. Rushmore** and **Carhenge.** You also can test the wisdom of Walt Whitman, who wrote, "While I know the standard claim is that Yosemite, Niagara Falls, the upper Yellowstone and the like afford the greatest natural shows, I am not so sure but the Prairies and Plains last longer, fill the aesthetic sense fuller, precede all the rest and make North America's characteristic landscape." Drive across the Sand Hills of northern **Nebraska**

Mt. Rushmore

on your way past Iowa's Field of Dreams, and see for yourself what's so great about the **Great Plains.**

US-20 crosses the Mississippi River at Dubuque, which, like Galena, on the Illinois side, was one of the oldest settlements on what was once the nation's western frontier. It then stops off for a look at Chicago before winding east through the newly resurgent, former "Rust Belt" along the Great Lakes. This densely populated region also holds some

perfectly preserved historic sites, ranging from rolling Amish farmlands to automobile plants responsible for the country's classiest cars.

In upstate **New York,** we follow US-20 across a historical middle ground, between the slow boats of the Erie Canal and the high-speed toll road of the I-90 New York Thruway, winding along the north edge of the lovely **Finger Lakes** before crossing the Hudson River into the Berkshires of western **Massachusetts.** The historic Mohawk Trail carries us past Lexington and Concord and into Boston, retracing Paul Revere's historic ride—in reverse—before following old US-6 to the tip of **Cape Cod** at the lovely and lively resort of Provincetown, where the Pilgrims *really* arrived in America, way back in 1620.

OREGON

Starting at one of the state's most enjoyable small towns, the arts-and-craftsy Pacific Ocean resort community of **Cannon Beach,** this route traverses the heart of Oregon. From the salty cow pastures along the Pacific Ocean, over the evergreen mantle of the Coast Range to culturally vibrant **Portland** and the lush Willamette Valley, the route starts where history says we should end up—amid the bountiful land at the west end of the Oregon Trail. From Portland, the state's largest city, you'll climb into the Cascade Mountains, through the amazing **Columbia Gorge** alongside its signature peak, Mt. Hood. East of the Cascades, the route drops down into the suddenly dry and desertlike landscape of the otherworldly Columbia Plateau, across which the highway rolls and rocks for 300 miles through old mining camps, fossil beds, and wide-open rolling ranch lands before crossing the Snake River into Idaho.

Most of the way across the USA, this Oregon Trail route follows US-20, but here in Oregon we've veered onto US-26, to follow the route of the original Oregon Trail and to visit the beauty spots of Columbia Gorge, Portland, and Cannon Beach.

US-20 runs farther south, across the center of the state, ending up at the coast at **Newport** (see page 33), which is covered in the **Pacific Coast** road trip. **Cannon Beach** (see page 29) is also part of the trip along scenic US-101's winding route. Full coverage of this route begins on page 8.

Cannon Beach

Unlike most Oregon coast towns, **Cannon Beach** (pop. 1,702) is hidden from the highway, but it's one place you won't want to miss. Though it has long been known as an artists' colony and has grown considerably in recent years thanks to its popularity as a weekend escape from Portland, Cannon Beach retains a rustic quality, a walkably small size, and a coastline that rates second to no other in the state.

Sunset Highway: Saddle Mountain State Park

Running over the coastal mountains between Cannon Beach and Portland, US-26 is known as the Sunset Highway. Climbing up from the coastal plain, two miles east of US-101, our first stop is the old-growth spruce and fir forest preserved in 25-acre **Klootchy Creek County Park.** Among the many huge firs and spruce trees was the Seaside Giant Spruce. More than 215 feet high, almost 16 feet in diameter, the tree was snapped in two by a storm in December 2007. Safety concerns caused officials to cut down the tree, but the huge stump and fallen sections have been left in place to show how massive the old-timer really was.

By state law, there is no self-service gasoline in Oregon; all stations have attendants who pump the gas for you. There's no sales tax either.

About 10 miles east of US-101, a seven-mile side trip to the northeast, along well-signed Saddle Mountain Road, will lift you quickly above the frequent coastal clouds and fog. Named for a geographical saddle that sits high above the surrounding forests, **Saddle Mountain State Natural Area** surrounds the highest point in the Coast Range. A steep 2.5-mile hiking trail climbs to the summit, with opportunities to view bleeding heart, Indian paintbrush, monkey flowers, and other rare wildflowers and other plants. From the 3,290-foot peak, you can often see the mouth of the Columbia River and the spine of the Coast Range. On a clear day, the panorama may include 50 miles of Pacific coastline and Mt. Hood, Mt. St. Helens, and Mt. Rainier (with more than a few ugly acres of clear-cuts in between). Ten primitive **campsites** (503/368-5943 or 800/551-6949, $11) are open April-October on a first-come, first-served basis; RVs should avoid this narrow road.

Cannon Beach marks the farthest point reached by the Lewis and Clark expedition to the West Coast. From here, they retreated back to their outpost at Fort Clatsop, near the mouth of the Columbia River, where they spent the winter of 1805-1806.

Camp 18

Continuing east on US-26, 60 miles from Portland, about 18 miles from the coast highway and a mile west of the hamlet of Elsie, the remarkable **Camp 18 Logging Museum and Restaurant** (503/755-1818 or 800/874-1810, daily) draws travelers for a variety of reasons. Some people come for the absolutely massive portions of good food, from the gigantic fresh-baked cinnamon rolls and quart jugs of coffee at breakfast to the steaks, chicken, and seafood served up at lunch and dinner. Others are drawn by the playful Paul Bunyan-esque scale of the place: The front door handle is a hefty old ax, the spacious dining room roof is held up by a single massive Douglas fir log—85 feet long, 8 feet thick, and weighing 50,000 pounds—and many of the tables are made from foot-thick planks of planed and polished wood.

The whole room is packed with an amazing collection of old logging gear, but best of all is the setting, overlooking a babbling brook, with dozens of bird-feeders attracting flocks of finches and other colorful songbirds. Outside, an extensive museum in the parking lot lets visitors examine more old logging equipment to get a feel for a bygone era of misery whips, 20-foot handsaws, and steam donkeys. (Surprise, surprise: There's also a good gift shop.)

Banks-Vernonia State Trail

Midway between the coast and Portland, US-26 reaches the 1,640-foot crest of Sunset Summit, then winds east through the verdant delights of the leeward Coast Range, zipping through tunnels and sliding down slopes to the farm country of northwest Willamette Valley. **Banks-Vernonia State Trail** (503/324-0606 or 800/551-6949, free), 26 miles or so from downtown Portland, is a 21-mile stretch of abandoned railroad that runs north from US-26 between the town of Banks and the tucked-away timber town of Vernonia. Six well-marked trailheads along Hwy-47 provide access to the fairly level gravel trail, Oregon's first rail-to-trail park. The park is especially lovely, and popular, during October's "fall color" season, when the many ash and maple trees turn gold and red, respectively, while the birds sing and the streams gurgle.

The town of **Vernonia** (pop. 2,143) has recently played another role in Pacific Northwest tourism, standing in for Forks, Washington, in the movie versions of the teenage vampire saga *Twilight*. (A paper mill credit union office at the center of

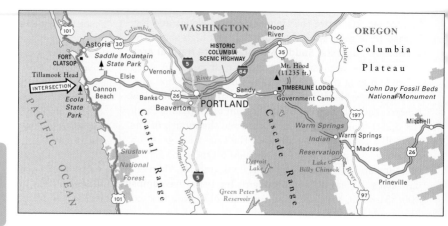

Vernonia stood in for the film's Forks Police Station, for example.) Vernonia is cute, having recovered from a bad flood some years ago, and is a nice destination whether or not you've seen the movies. After a day of hiking or cycling the Linear Trail, recharge your carb deficits with a Greek gyro and a hoppy pint of homebrew at the **Blue House Café** (919 Bridge St., 503/429-4350), in the center of town.

Across Portland

Coming in from the west on the Sunset Highway (US-26), our route enters Portland next to the Sylvan-Highlands neighborhood's Washington Park, then crosses the downtown area along Jefferson and Columbia Streets. Crossing the Willamette River, US-26 follows Powell Boulevard across East Portland.

Mount Hood Highway

Starting out along Powell Boulevard east from Portland, US-26—now dubbed the **Mount Hood Highway**—follows, albeit in reverse, the final leg of the historic Oregon Trail. Passing first through the comically named photo-stop town of **Boring,** the road some 20 miles east of Portland reaches **Sandy** (pop. 10,644), a boisterous gateway to the mountains. Nestled in berry-farm country, Sandy is full of ski shops, pizza parlors, and other enterprises geared for outdoor enthusiasts, but east of Sandy's lively commerce the road ambles through pastureland and into the foothills of the Cascades.

East of Sandy, oddly named towns along US-26 hold good places to eat and drink before or after a day out in the mountains. The **Barlow Trail Roadhouse** (69580 US-26, 503/622-1662), housed in

Mount Hood

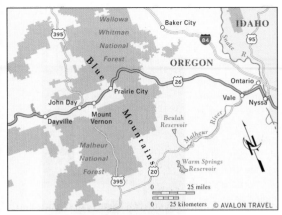

Oregon grape,
state flower of Oregon

The town of Boring inspires
some comical photos.

an old log cabin in Welches, is one of the many little wide spots clustered at the base of Mt. Hood, drawing day-tripping Portlanders for serious carbo-loading.

If you're planning to get out of your car and explore Mt. Hood, make sure you stop beforehand at the **Mount Hood National Forest ZigZag Ranger Station** (70220 E. US-26, 503/622-3191), in Zigzag, operated by the USFS and loaded with maps, brochures, and other information on the mountain and surrounding recreational hot spots.

Government Camp

Just off US-26 at the southern foot of Mt. Hood, **Government Camp** is but another wide spot in the road with a range of food and drink options. For espresso, microbrews, sandwiches, pizzas, and salads, stop at the **Mount Hood Brewing Company** (503/272-3172) at the west end of town. Another good stop is the **Huckleberry Inn** (503/272-3325), famous for its wild huckleberry pies, huckleberry pancakes, and huckleberry shakes. If you're unable to move after a berry feast, the inn also offers rooms for $90 and up.

Government Camp's main attraction is the **Mount Hood Skibowl** (503/222-3206), a year-round recreation center with skiing and snowboarding in winter and mountain biking and hiking in summer, plus guided horseback trips, go-karts, zip lines, and a 100-foot bungee jump.

Timberline Lodge

East of Government Camp, near the junction of US-26 and Hwy-35, which comes from Hood River and the Columbia Gorge, be sure to turn off north toward Mt. Hood to visit **Timberline Lodge** (503/272-3311 or 800/547-1406, $255 and up), an

Enticing though it is, snowcapped **Mt. Hood** is also a difficult and dangerous peak to climb—there is no trail to the 11,247-foot summit, and all routes require a high degree of technical ability and specialized equipment. There are lots of fine hikes around its base, however.

Portland

Portland, Oregon's largest city, is located inland from the coast near the confluence of the Willamette and Columbia Rivers. Due to its strategic location, the pioneer municipality grew so fast it was nicknamed Stumptown for the hundreds of fir stumps left by early loggers. While railroad tracks and other heavy industrial remnants are still visible around town, Portland's riverfront park and numerous winding greenways show that this mini-metropolis is a community that values art and nature as highly as commerce. Along with one of the largest (5,157-acre Forest Park) and the smallest (452-square-inch

Powell's City of Books

Mill Ends Park) urban parks in the nation, and one of the coolest urban skate parks anywhere (under the Burnside Bridge), Portland also has more movie theaters and restaurants per capita than any other U.S. city. It ranks high in microbreweries and bookstores per capita as well.

In the lively Old Town district, cast-iron facades of 120-year-old buildings hold some of the city's most popular bars, clubs, and cafés. South of Old Town along the river, an ugly freeway has been torn down to form the Governor Tom McCall Waterfront Park, and west of the river, downtown Portland centers on lively Pioneer Courthouse Square, at 6th Avenue and Yamhill Street. South of the square, the South Park Blocks between Park and 9th Avenues were set aside as parklands in 1852 and

Oaks Amusement Park

are now bounded by Portland's prime museums. One essential Portland place is north of the square: **Powell's City of Books** (1005 W. Burnside St., 800/878-7323) is the largest (and certainly among the best) new-and-used book-shop in the world.

One of the largest and oldest ballparks in the minor leagues, the 1926 **Providence Park,** a half mile west of downtown, saw one of the first outdoor rock concerts when Elvis Presley played here in 1957, and was home to the Portland Beavers ball club until 2010, when baseball was booted out to make room for Portland's pro soccer team, the Timbers.

Along the river 6.5 miles south of town is the wonderful circa-1905 **Oaks Amusement Park** (503/233-5777), with ancient and modern thrill rides and a roller-skating rink, all packed together in a sylvan oak tree-dotted park.

PRACTICALITIES

Air travelers can land at Portland International Airport (PDX), but most long-distance flights come and go via Seattle's Sea-Tac, which is only about a three-hour drive north, via the I-5 freeway. Getting around public-spirited Portland is a breeze thanks to the efficient **bus and light rail train system** (503/238-7433, from $2.50).

Portland has great places to eat and drink, in all stripes and sizes. **Screen Door** (2337 E. Burnside St., 503/542-0880) draws lines for its locally sourced organic versions of Deep South faves like fried chicken, shrimp 'n' grits, BBQ bris-ket, and apple rhubarb pies. Nothing beats the **RingSide Steakhouse** (2165 W. Burnside St., 503/223-1513), 1.5 miles west of downtown, famous for its beef, fried chicken, monster Walla Walla sweet onion rings, and Hemingway-esque ambience. For over a century, **Jake's Famous Crawfish** (401 SW 12th Ave., 503/226-1419) has been the place to go for the freshest seafood. If your taste happens to run more to Marilyn Manson than Marilyn Monroe, you'll prefer to eat across town at **Dot's Café** (2521 SE Clinton St., 503/235-0203), a late-night hangout that has comfy dark booths, great black-bean burrito bowls, brews, and a pool table. One last must-eat is **Voodoo Doughnut** (22 SW 3rd Ave., 503/241-4704); the original location is packed during Old Town Portland's popular Saturday Market but worth a visit any other time (it's open 24 hours).

There are all sorts of places to stay in Portland, starting with a pair of popular **HI-Portland Hostels,** one east of downtown (3031 SE Hawthorne Blvd., 503/236-3380) and another in the Northwest District (427 NW 18th Ave., 503/241-2783). **Hotel deLuxe** (729 SW 15th Ave., 503/219-2094, $135 and up) is stylish, comfort-able, and close to downtown. For a splurge, try **The Heathman Hotel** (1001 SW Broadway, 503/241-4100 or 855/516-1090, $209 and up), an impeccably restored downtown landmark, with an elegant lobby and sumptuously appointed (if some-what small) rooms.

elegantly rustic national landmark dedicated in 1937 by the Depression-era artisans of the Works Progress Administration. The actual hotel seen (from the outside, not the inside) in Stanley Kubrick's creepy 1980 film, *The Shining*, Timberline Lodge is an unforgettable place, with a humongous fireplace in the three-story main lobby, a cool pool, plus grand dining rooms and cozy guest rooms decorated in characterful Pacific Northwest motifs, not to mention an unbeatable setting high atop the Cascade Mountains. Even if you don't stay, check out the Cascade Dining Room's award-winning cuisine, the more-casual pizza and sandwiches at the Blue Ox, and the Ram's Head Bar, which has locally brewed beers and ales.

Timberline Lodge

South of US-26 on the western fringes of Portland, the mega-suburb of **Beaverton** is base camp for the high-tech companies of the Silicon Forest and, most famously, corporate headquarters for Nike, the international sports apparel giant.

The Columbia River Highway was built by millionaire lawyer Samuel Hill, who built the road to link Portland with the Quaker agricultural colony he planned at his 7,000-acre estate at Maryhill, Washington. **Maryhill Museum of Art** (509/773-3733, daily Mar. 15-Nov. 15, $9) is now a fascinatingly eclectic museum near the junction of I-84 and US-97. Three miles east of Maryhill, Hill also constructed a concrete replica of Stonehenge in memory of local men killed in World War I.

Warm Springs Indian Reservation

East of the Cascades crest, US-26 becomes the Warm Springs Highway as it angles down out of the mountains across the sage and juniper country of eastern Oregon. Most of the land between here and Madras is part of the more than 600,000-acre **Warm Springs Indian Reservation,** home to the Confederated Tribes of Warm Springs and their **Kah-Nee-Ta Resort** (800/554-4786; pronounced "ca-NEE-da," all run together despite the odd spelling), a 1970s complex that cheerfully blends ancient and mid-century modern lifestyles. You can soak in the famously soothing hot springs, camp in a tepee, play golf along the banks of the Warm Springs River, and savor salmon fillets cooked over an alderwood fire.

Back on US-26, the real attraction of the reservation is the modern 25,000-square-foot **Museum at Warm Springs** (541/553-3331, Tues.-Sat., $7). Check out exhibits of more than 20,000 artifacts, replicas of a Paiute mat lodge and a Wasco plank house, recordings of Native American languages, and a push-button-activated Wasco wedding scene. A mile east, at the edge of the reservation, US-26 bridges the deep canyon of the Deschutes River.

Madras

After crossing the Deschutes River from the Warm Springs reservation, US-26 climbs up a deep canyon, then plateaus at **Madras** (pop. 6,662), birthplace of the late actor River Phoenix and of Boston Red Sox baseball hero Jacoby Ellsbury. By strange coincidence, the town is named for a metropolis in Eastern India (the original Madras is now

DETOUR: COLUMBIA GORGE

Though our route across Oregon generally follows scenic US-26, the fastest route east from Portland is I-84, which races along the Columbia River, rejoining US-26 at the Idaho border. Freeway the whole way, I-84 is worth considering for its one incredible feature: the **Columbia Gorge,** the deep, verdant basalt canyon through which the mighty river and the freeway, not to mention a busy railroad, run. The heart of the Columbia Gorge is between the small towns of Sandy and Cascade Locks, some 28 and 43 or so miles east of Portland, respectively, and is best experienced by driving the **Historic Columbia River Highway**— the oldest scenic route in the country, built beginning in 1913 and still retaining all its old-road character.

Mushroom Rock along the Columbia River Highway, Ore.

The highlight (and approximate midpoint) of this historic highway, which here rises over 700 feet above the Columbia River, is the aptly named and recently renovated **Vista House,** built in 1917. East of Vista House, tremendous waterfalls drop down along the road: First comes **Latourell Falls,** with water dropping about 249 feet; then the 242-foot cascades of **Wahkeena Falls;** then, saving the best for last, famous **Multnomah Falls,** which drops around 620 feet into a densely forested canyon, bridged by a delicate concrete arch. Each of these waterfalls is within a short walk of parking areas along the scenic highway, and many smaller falls can be seen cascading from canyon walls.

The Columbia River Highway rejoins I-84 a few miles east of Multnomah Falls, at the town of Cascade Locks. Another 20 miles east, at the east end of the Columbia Gorge, the outdoorsy town of **Hood River** (pop. 7,624) is packed with brewpubs, espresso bars, bookshops, cafés, and moderate motels. Near the town of Hood River, the historic **Columbia Gorge Hotel** (4000 Westcliff Dr., 541/386-5566, $149 and up) preserves its Jazz Age elegance, with comfortable rooms and an excellent restaurant.

The **Columbia Gorge** west of Hood River is one of the world's best windsurfing spots. Throughout the summer dozens of brightly colored sails can usually be seen racing along the river.

Around the Warm Springs Reservation, tune to **KWSO 91.9 FM** for an intriguing array of music (from the Eagles to talking drums) and National Native News.

Vista House on its perch above the Columbia Gorge

called Chennai and has a population of seven million). In the 1980s thousands of orange- and red-clad followers of Indian guru Bhagwan Shree Rajneesh settled near and effectively took over this small Oregon town, but things here have been back to normal for a long while.

There's not a great deal to see or do in Madras, which stands at the junction of US-26 and busy US-97, but there are stores and gas stations and at least one good place to stay, on the south side of Madras: **Sonny's Motel** (1539 US-97, 541/475-7217, $80 and up), which has clean rooms and a pool. The best food is at the **Black Bear Diner** (237 SW 4th St., 541/475-6632), a block west of US-26.

One of eastern Oregon's landmarks, and a celebrated challenge to rock climbers, **Smith Rock State Park** (541/548-7501 or 800/551-6949, $5) is 28 miles south of Madras along US-97.

Prineville

East of Madras, US-26 veers farther away from the Cascades, crossing the **Crooked River National Grasslands,** which mark the geographical center of Oregon. Strolling the streets of **Prineville** (pop. 9,530), you'll notice plenty of cowboy hats (and "gimme" caps, emblazoned with the logo of the wearer's favorite fertilizer or tractor company) atop the heads of dusty citizens piloting dusty pickup trucks. It's been a ripsnorter of a town since Barney Prine built his black-smith shop and saloon here in 1868 following the discovery of gold in nearby hills. These days, the people of Prineville are still ranchers, loggers, and miners, plus perhaps 147 employees of social media company Facebook, which in 2011 established the first of a trio of data centers—the last, built in 2015, is a 487,000-square-foot "server farm." Tourism too is slowly but surely making its mark as an economic force.

You can learn more about the region's history at the **A. R. Bowman Museum** (246 N. Main St., 541/447-3715, Tues.-Fri. 10am-5pm and Sat. 11am-4pm winter, Mon.-Fri. 10am-5pm and Sat.-Sun. 11am-4pm summer), two blocks west of the landmark **Crook County Circuit Courthouse** (300 NE 3rd St.). Two floors of exhibits include a campfire setup, a moonshine still, and a country store with a pound of Bull Durham tobacco. A tastier way to get a handle on life here in the middle of Oregon is to chomp down on a juicy steak at **Barney Prine's Steakhouse and Saloon** (389 NW 4th St., 541/447-3333), known for its generous and eclectic

END OF THE OREGON TRAIL

After long months of hardship and danger, pioneers nearing the end of the Oregon Trail had two options when they reached the narrow gorge of the Columbia River: They could float their wagons down the perilous river to Fort Vancouver or climb over the Cascades to the Willamette Valley via the **Barlow Road,** a route that parallels today's US-26. While much safer than the river route, the Barlow Road had its own precarious moments—emigrants struggled down muddy declines, hanging onto ropes hitched around trees to keep wagons from runaway destruction. Such moments assuredly gave the pioneers second thoughts about their choice of passage. At $5 per wagon and 10 cents a head for cattle, horses, and mules, following the

privately owned Barlow Road was also expensive. Nonetheless, in 1845, the first year of operation, records report that 1,000 pioneers in 145 wagons traveled the route.

Heading east, you're going backward along the Barlow Road, so bear that in mind as you take in a few historical sites that record the struggles of pioneers on the last stretch of their 2,000-mile overland journey. The steepest section of the road was the **Laurel Hill Chute,** where wagons skidded down a treacherous grade; a sign and pull-out five miles east of Rhododendron mark the start of a short, steep hike up to the chute. Just west of Laurel Hill, at Tollgate Campground, you'll find a reproduction of the **Barlow Road Tollgate,** where the road's owner, Sam Barlow, stood with his hand out.

Look for other markers depicting Barlow Road history on Hwy-35, the loop road that traverses the eastern slope of Mt. Hood down to Hood River. The first, **Pioneer Woman's Grave,** is a quarter mile east of the junction with US-26; a sign marks a right turn onto Forest Road 3531 and points toward a gravesite with a brass plaque commemorating the women who traveled the Oregon Trail. Three miles east of the junction is 4,157-foot **Barlow Pass,** where ruts grooved in the Barlow Road lead downhill from a parking area, mute testament to the perseverance of westward-driven settlers.

The "official" western end of the Oregon Trail is at Oregon City, about 10 miles south of Portland in the Willamette Valley.

East of the Mt. Hood hamlet of **Zigzag,** US-26 drops to an old-fashioned, undivided two-lane road. Summer-only Lolo Pass Loop (Hwy-18) cuts off north from here on a scenic half-circle around the base of Mt. Hood to Hood River, on the Columbia River and I-84.

menu. Lodging choices include the **City Center Motel** (509 NE 3rd St., 541/447-5522, $74 and up), in the middle of the city.

The drive along US-26 east of Prineville takes you up into the Ochocos, a low-slung gem of a mountain range once the heartland of the Paiute people. Seven miles from Prineville, US-26 skirts **Ochoco Lake,** a popular recreational reservoir with fishing, boating, hiking, camping, and a picnic bench or two for travelers—but not a lot of shade. The rest of the Ochoco Range, which reaches heights of nearly 7,000 feet, holds acres and acres of lovely meadows, clear streams, pristine pine forests, and views of the jagged Cascade Range, rising on the western horizon.

Mitchell

The only concentration of human habitation near the John Day Fossil Beds National Monument is **Mitchell** (pop. 121), a semi-ghost town 45 miles or so east of Prineville and 2 miles east of the turnoff for the Painted Hills section of the fossil beds. The main "town" of Mitchell lines up along the three-block stretch of old road signed as the Business Loop, just south of US-26, where Main Street holds the old-fashioned general store **Wheeler County Trading Co.,** capturing the flavor of the 1870s, and a pair of pleasant cafés: The **Little Pine Café and Lodge** (100 E. Main St., 541/462-3532) and the **Sidewalk Café** (204 W. Main St., 541/462-3800) offer good food and great berry pies.

Mitchell also holds one of the more atmospheric old places to stay in this part of eastern Oregon: **The Oregon Hotel** (104 E. Main St., 541/462-3027, $20-110) has genuinely friendly owners and a comfy front porch overlooking the lazy old-road loop.

John Day Fossil Beds National Monument

East of the Ochocos, midway across Oregon, the **John Day Fossil Beds National Monument** documents many millions of years of prehistoric life, from just after the demise of the dinosaurs to delicate aquatic plants. In the 1860s, frontier preacher and amateur geologist Thomas Condon was the first to recognize the importance of the beds, which contain one of the world's richest and most diverse concentrations of mammalian and reptilian fossils, including saber-toothed cats. Offering a visually attractive and easily accessible record of life on earth, spanning the past 6 million to 54 million years (out of some 4.5 billion that our planet has existed), the monument is made up of three distinct units, totaling some 14,000 acres. Needless to say, fossil collecting is strictly prohibited in the park.

The eerie, empty moonscape can be easily toured from US-26. Start in the west with the **Painted Hills Unit,** just west of Mitchell, then six miles north of US-26, where trails and overlooks offer views of striated hills and bluffs formed by fallen ash and brilliantly colored in bands of red, pink, black, and bronze. A life-size Georgia O'Keeffe landscape, Painted Hills is a popular spot with photographers and painters, especially the short Painted Cove trail, which winds through the most intensely colored section.

About 35 miles east of Mitchell, 6 miles west of Dayville along US-26, then 2 miles north on Hwy-19, the **Sheep Rock Unit** (541/987-2333) is the best place to see

the Sheep Rock Unit

fossils up close. The monument headquarters and main paleontology museum are also here, housed inside an attractive modern building on the grounds of the historic Cant Ranch. East of the turnoff to the Sheep Rock fossil beds, US-26 runs right along the John Day River through the 500-foot-deep basalt canyon of Picture Gorge, so named because of the abundance of Native American pictographs.

A more distant section of the John Day Fossil Beds is the Clarno Unit, along the John Day River some 60 miles northwest of Painted Hills, near the aptly named town of **Fossil,** home of the fascinating **Oregon Paleo Lands Institute** (333 W. 4th St., 541/763-4480). This area includes the park's most ancient rocks—that formed 40 million to 54 million years ago—while the oldest rocks in Oregon, dating back 278 million years, can be seen atop volcanic Canyon Mountain, south of John Day village.

John Day

ammonite fossil

The namesake of the fossil beds, John Day, was a fur trapper who was robbed of everything, including clothing, near the mouth of a river. People would pass by and mention the incident, so it became known as the John Day River. The river flowed through the apparent wastelands of the fossil area, which were later named after John Day as well. These days, after gazing at striped hillsides and fossilized remains, regain some perspective by strolling through any of the towns that line the John Day River along this part of US-26—Dayville, Mount Vernon, John Day, and Canyon City. Founded as miners' camps after gold was discovered here in 1862, many now cater mostly to local ranchers—but offer a warm welcome to the few visitors who brave a trip through this uninviting but unforgettable part of the world.

Starting in the west, **Dayville** (pop. 146) has what has to be among the world's smallest city halls—a one-room shack at the east edge of town. The town of **John Day** (pop. 1,680), the metropolis in this chain of ghostly gold towns, holds the area's one not-to-be-missed attraction: **Kam Wah Chung State Heritage Site** (125 NW Canton St., 800/551-6949 or 541/575-2800, daily May-Oct., free), run by the state and located in a nice park just north of US-26 at the center of John Day. Built as a trading post in 1866-1867, in the late 1880s the Kam Wah Chung building became a general store and medical center for the Chinese workers who toiled in the mines, and for 60 years it continued to be the center of the almost exclusively male Chinese community of eastern Oregon, which at times made up a majority of the regional population. Most of the building is preserved intact, displaying a fascinating collection of items ranging from herbal remedies and ornate red Taoist shrines to gambling paraphernalia and ancient canned goods. There's also a bedroom with bunks and a wood stove left as they were by the last residents, Ing "Doc" Hay and Lung On, the herbalist and storekeeper who lived and worked here until the 1940s.

Right next to the museum is the town of John Day's **swimming pool,** where the chance to soak ($3) is much appreciated on a hot summer afternoon. For food, the **Grubsteak Mining Co.** (149 E. Main St., 541/575-1970) has a sumptuous menu of rib eyes and other beef entrées, while the **Squeeze Inn Restaurant** (423 W. Main St., 541/575-1045) has all-around good food all day long, with an especially tasty Reuben-and-fries combo. A block away, just north of US-26, the **Dreamers Lodge Motel** (144 N. Canyon Blvd., 800/654-2849 or 541/575-0526, $89-99) has nice rooms.

John Day made national news in connection with the January 2016 "occupation" of Malheur Wildlife Refuge, when leaders of the antifederal militants were arrested while driving to a public rally being held at the John Day Senior Center. During the arrest one of the militants, LaVoy Finicum, was shot and killed by law enforcement.

Prairie City

The first town east of John Day is tidy little **Prairie City** (pop. 880), an old-fashioned ranching community that is fast becoming a western false-front photo opportunity. For a taste of local life, stay at the 100-year-old **Riverside School House Bed and Breakfast** (28077 North River Rd., 541/820-4731, $150), a white-clapboard two-room schoolhouse, in use until the 1960s and now rented out as a one-of-a-kind B&B, located on a working cattle ranch with delightful views over the headwaters of the John Day River.

Halfway between Prairie City and Vale is the dividing line between Pacific and mountain time zones. Adjust clocks accordingly as you head over **Eldorado Pass.**

Leaving the John Day River watershed, US-26 heads east, climbing over mile-high Dixie Pass (which is just one yard shy of being one mile high—5,277 feet above sea level) while rambling through the **Malheur National Forest** (541/575-3000) and the **Wallowa-Whitman National Forest** (541/523-6391), where campgrounds, cool mountain lakes, natural hot springs, and dense forests abound.

East of the crest, dropping down from the mountains across the Snake River plain, US-26 crosses another 75 miles of rolling sagebrush, with little more than an occasional cattle ranch, or a golden eagle sitting atop a telephone pole, to attract your attention. Tiny little tavern-and-post-office towns like Unity, Ironside, Brogan, and Willow Creek will make you slow to 45 mph (or risk a ticket), while on a hot summer's day the smell of juniper and sage is so potent it perfumes the dry desert air, unmistakable even if you cruise through at 70 mph with the air-conditioning blasting.

Vale

The seat of Malheur ("Bad Smell" or "Bad Luck," depending upon who tells it) County, **Vale** (pop. 1,833) sits on the banks of the Malheur River at the junction of US-20 and US-26. The comparatively easy river crossing and the presence of a natural hot spring made it a prime stopping place on the Oregon Trail. Murals and markers around town explain something of the history and point out sights like the **Malheur Crossing,** next to the bridge on the eastern edge of the town, where pioneers dunked their aching bods in the still-hot Malheur River Springs; and Keeney Pass, just south of downtown Vale on Enterprise Avenue, where 150-year-old wagon ruts can still be seen along the roadside. There's more to see inside the **Rinehart Stone House Museum** (255 Main St. S., 541/473-2070, Tues.-Sat. 12:30pm-4pm Mar.-Oct.), housed inside a frontier-era stagecoach stop and hotel.

Taking a breather at Vale is an honored tradition—it was here that pioneers rested before climbing out of the Snake River Valley into the Blue Mountains.

Towns in eastern Oregon have taken to decorating their buildings with large and colorful murals, usually with historical or outdoorsy themes.

Toward Idaho: Ontario and Nyssa

Approaching the Idaho border, you have two choices: to follow I-84, heading east via **Ontario** (pop. 10,999), the largest of many midsize farming and ranching communities in the surrounding area; or to continue along the more atmospheric older roads. The official **Oregon Trail Auto Route** (US-20/26) bends to the south along the Snake River, passing one last Oregon town, **Nyssa,** before crossing into the Land of Famous Potatoes. Nyssa calls itself the "Thunderegg Capital of the World" because of the many geodes found there, but it's primarily a shipping point for the tons of spuds, onions, and sugar beets grown nearby—the different crops are even labeled along the highway for your edification.

IDAHO

US-20's route across southern Idaho cuts through one of the most magnificently empty American spaces, an arid, volcanic region cut by life-giving rivers and isolating mountain ranges, with strange geological outcrops that encourage travelers to stop and explore the inhospitable terrain. Irrigation has altered the look of the land considerably, so much so that vineyards and lush fields now thrive in the otherwise barren, gray-green sagebrush plains, but little else has changed since this region provided the greatest challenge to pioneers crossing the country along the Oregon Trail. The provision of

syringa, state flower of Idaho

visitor services has improved considerably in the intervening centuries, but southern Idaho is still a wild and demanding land. Like much of the American West, it's also an addictively satisfying place to explore.

Parma and Fort Boise

Just as US-20/26 does today, the historic Oregon Trail crosses between Idaho and Oregon at the confluence of the

Boise and Snake Rivers, southwest of I-84 at the town of **Parma.** Sugar beets and onions fill the fields around the tiny town, which takes pride in its replica of **Fort Boise,** one of the first European outposts in the Pacific Northwest. Originally established in 1834 by the Hudson's Bay Company, Fort Boise was famous for its frontier hospitality, entertaining and supplying travelers and traders until the mid-1850s, when it was closed because of declines in demand and an increase in Native American hostilities. The original Fort Boise stood along the banks of the river and was washed away long ago. The site is marked today by an odd horse-headed stone obelisk festooned with the Hudson's Bay Company flag, which stands along the Snake River at the end of Old Fort Boise Road, two miles west of US-20/26. The less-than-authentic steel-and-stucco reconstruction of the old fort that stands along US-20 near the center of town is the site of the annual **Old Fort Boise Days** in early summer.

> The quickest route across Idaho is the I-84 freeway, though the historic Oregon Trail route, marked by large highway signs, follows a much more scenic route along the Snake River.

Caldwell

East of Parma, US-20/26 runs along the north bank of the Boise River for more than a dozen miles before crossing I-84 at the city of **Caldwell**—home of the mid-August **Caldwell Night Rodeo** (208/459-2060). A century ago, Caldwell was the site of the 1905 bomb-blast murder of former Idaho governor Frank Steunenberg. Blamed on left-wing Wobbly union activists, including "Big Bill" Haywood, who'd been organizing Idaho's miners and loggers, the murder was the story behind J. Anthony Lukas's sprawling book *Big Trouble: A Murder in a Small Western Town Sets Off a Struggle for the Soul of America.*

From Caldwell, you can follow the freeway into Boise, but it's more interesting,

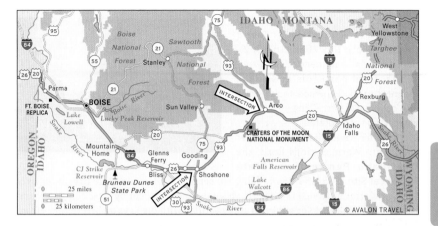

and depending on traffic possibly even quicker as well, to stay on US-20/26 (a.k.a. Chinden Boulevard), which runs right atop the old Oregon Trail into downtown, past corn and wheat fields that have been rapidly sprouting golf course estates, a Hewlett-Packard factory, car-parts stores, and the usual Asphalt Nation sprawl.

Boise

Capital of Idaho and perennial contender for the title of "most livable" city in the United States, **Boise** (pop. 218,281) is a lush green oasis in the middle of the barren lava lands of the Snake River

One fun spot out between Caldwell and Boise is the Western Idaho Fairgrounds, home to year-round events and the Class A baseball games of the **Boise Hawks** (208/322-5000).

plain. It was named by fur trappers for its dense groves of cottonwood trees (*bois* is French for "wood"), which made the area an especially welcome respite before irrigation turned the brown desert much greener than it naturally would be. The presence of the state government and the more than 22,000 students at Boise State University lend a degree of sophistication and vitality mixed in with the more usual Idaho trappings—more than anywhere else for miles, in-line skates and mountain bikes compete with pickup trucks as the main method of transportation here, and bookshops and espresso bars line the downtown streets.

Downtown Boise focuses on the **state capitol** (700 W. Jefferson St., daily, free), three blocks north of Main Street between 6th and 8th Streets, a typically grand neoclassical structure, built of local sandstone with a giant eagle atop its landmark dome. The usual exhibits of the state's produce fill display cases, and free guided tours are given upon request to groups of five or more.

South of the capitol, restaurants and cafés have reclaimed the blocks of hundred-year-old brick buildings around 6th and Main Streets, the historic center of Boise. In the heart of this lively pedestrian-friendly neighborhood, a block south of Main Street, the small but intriguing **Basque Museum and Cultural Center** (611 W. Grove St., 208/343-2671, Tues.-Sat., $5) documents the culture of the Basque people who work in Idaho's ranching industries. A block west stands **Grove Plaza,** home to Boise's convention center and main shopping complex, featuring a large fountain through which daredevils like to skate and cycle. Don't miss **Taters** (801 W. Main St., 208/338-1062), which sells all manner of Idaho souvenirs, from postcards and fridge magnets to spud-themed snow globes and cookbooks describing 100 things you can do with potatoes.

Farther east, where Main Street turns into Warm Springs Road, the **Old Idaho Penitentiary State Historical Site** (208/334-2844, daily, $6) served as the main state prison for over 100 years after it opened in 1872. High sandstone walls, cut by prisoners, surround the complex, and the old cellblocks are now filled with displays on prison life—from collections of tattoos to the gallows where many prisoners met their end.

Boise Practicalities

By Idaho standards, Boise has a truly exciting range of restaurants, with many good places around 6th and Main Streets and elsewhere in the compact downtown area. For a huge breakfast, or an out-of-this-world milk shake, stop by **Moon's Kitchen Café** (712 W. Idaho St., 208/385-0472, daily until 3pm), recently expanded after 50-plus years operating in the back room of a gift shop that used to be a gun shop. Another favorite stop is **Bar Gernika Basque Pub and Eatery** (202 S. Capitol Blvd., 208/344-2175, Mon.-Sat.), near the Basque Museum on the corner of Grove Street, which serves up delicious tastes of Basque-inspired food (lamb sandwiches, chorizo tapas, and out-of-this-world shoestring fries) plus Spanish wines in a friendly unpretentious room—with a sidewalk seating area in summer. And if this doesn't hit the spot, within a few blocks is the excellent **Guido's Pizzeria** (235 N. 5th St., 208/345-9011; 12375 Chinden Blvd., 208/376-1008), serving classic thin-crust New York-style pies.

*Northeast from Boise, Hwy-20 makes a scenic trip through the Sawtooth Mountains to **Stanley**.*

Boise's downtown restaurant district doubles as its nightlife zone as well, so after a meal you can stagger among old-fashioned carved-wood bars like **Pengilly's Saloon** (513 W. Main St., 208/345-6344).

Boise's former best place to stay, the wonderful old Idanha Hotel—built in 1901 and featuring ornate corner turrets, opulent public spaces, and Idaho's oldest elevator—has been converted into apartments but now holds the excellent **Guru Donuts** (928 Main St., 208/571-7792) on its ground floor. West of Boise, there's **Hostel Boise** (17322 Can-Ada Rd., 208/467-6858, $25-65) in Nampa.

Mountain Home and Bruneau Dunes

Across southern Idaho, the I-84 freeway has effectively replaced the older highways, especially in the area southeast of Boise. The huge **Mountain Home Air Force Base,** 50 miles or so southeast of Boise, is the only thing for miles, which is no doubt by design: The base is home to the latest high-tech weapons systems and aircraft, whose pilots train at the adjacent, 110,000-acre desert bombing range.

Eighteen miles south of Mountain Home and the I-84 freeway via Hwy-51, **Bruneau Dunes State Park** (208/366-7919) protects one of the highest

Bruneau Dunes State Park

free-standing sand dune in North America—rising over 470 feet above the Snake River plain. Since the temperatures can hit 100°F throughout the summer months, mornings or sunsets are the best times to exercise your legs by climbing up and careening back down the white sands.

Glenns Ferry

The tiny town of **Glenns Ferry,** 28 miles southeast of Mountain Home on the Snake River and I-84, would hardly rate a mention were it not the site of one of the most important crossings on the old Oregon Trail. This site, now preserved as **Three Island Crossing State Park** ($5 per vehicle), a mile southwest of town, gives one of the strongest impressions of the tough going for Oregon-bound pioneers. A good **visitors center** (208/366-2394, Memorial Day-Labor Day Tues.-Sun.), with a Conestoga wagon out front, has displays of trail lore and history. Go for a swim to cool off and feel the powerful currents—more placid here than most anywhere else, which is why it was considered the best place to ford the river. This is also a fine place to camp; the usually clear night sky makes for excellent stargazing.

At Mountain Home, US-20 cuts off northeast from I-84, following a branch of the Oregon Trail known as Goodale's Cut-off across the harsh volcanic plains. **Bliss** marks the turnoff onto US-30, which follows the old Oregon Trail along the banks of the Snake River along a lovely, waterfall-rich route known as **Thousand Springs Scenic Byway,** rejoining I-84 at Twin Falls.

Bliss and Hagerman

Along with providing the chance to add to your collection of city limits signs, or to send a postcard saying you're in **Bliss** (pop. 305), this idyllically named town is worth a stop to see the deep canyon of **Malad Gorge** (208/837-4505, daily dawn-dusk, $5), well signed southeast of town, off I-84 exit 147. Now part of Thousand Springs State Park, it doesn't look like much until you get out of the car and walk 100 feet down the trail, where you suddenly come upon a truly awesome sight: a 250-foot-deep gorge with a crashing waterfall. The freeway passes overhead, oblivious to the natural wonder directly below.

Across the Snake River from Malad Gorge, **Hagerman Fossil Beds National**

THE HISTORIC OREGON TRAIL

In 1993, the 150th anniversary of the opening of the Oregon Trail renewed interest in this best-known of emigrant trails across the Wild West. History buffs got together for summer-long reenactments of the arduous crossing, building authentic wagons and eating, dressing, and sleeping as the pioneers did—with the inestimable comfort of knowing that they, unlike their predecessors, could easily return home at any point.

From 1843 until the 1860s, some 400,000 men, women, and children followed this 2,000-mile trail, averaging four months to make the cross-country journey. Long followed by fur trappers and traders, and first charted by a series of U.S. Army expeditions led by Kit Carson and John C. Fremont in the early 1840s, the Oregon Trail followed the path of least resistance across the western half of the continent. Beginning at various points along the Missouri River, the trail followed the valley of the Platte River across the Great Plains, crossed the Rockies at Wyoming's gentle South Pass, then set off across the desert of southern Idaho. The most difficult parts were saved for the end, when emigrants had a choice of floating downstream on the turbulent Columbia River or struggling over the rugged Cascades to reach the Willamette Valley. Nearly half of the travelers who set off along the Oregon Trail from Missouri actually had other destinations in mind: More than 100,000 turned off south toward the California gold mines, and some 30,000 Mormons followed the route west to their new colony at Salt Lake City.

The Oregon Trail had many variants and shortcuts and was never a sharply defined track, but clear traces survive in a number of places along the route. Many evocative sites also survive, often as reconstructions of pioneer forts, trading posts, and river crossings. There are also many fine museums along the way.

Many Oregon Trail sites are covered in more detail under our Road Trip routes. As shown on the map, some of the most interesting Oregon Trail sites are:

The Barlow Road: To avoid the treacherous falls of the Columbia Gorge, many emigrants opted to follow this difficult toll road, which cuts inland around Mt. Hood (see page 571).

The National Historic Oregon Trail Interpretive Center: In eastern Oregon, off I-84 near Baker City, Oregon's biggest and most developed Oregon Trail historic site (541/523-1843, daily 9am-4pm fall-spring, daily 9am-6pm summer, $8) has an original Meeker Marker and a 15-mile-long set of well-preserved wagon ruts.

Fort Boise: This fortress, a reconstruction of a fur-trapping post built nearby in 1834, stands along the banks of the Snake River (see page 576).

covered wagon at The National Historic Oregon Trail Interpretive Center

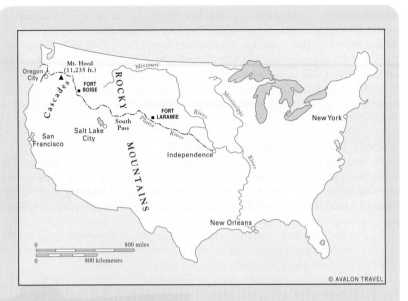

Three Island Crossing State Park: This is one of the best places to get a feel for life as an Oregon Trail pioneer. Camp where they camped and swim where they swam, at one of the most important crossings of the Snake River (see page 579).

Fort Caspar: A credible reconstruction of a frontier fort houses a good museum and the remains of an early ferry and bridge over the Platte River, while a new building in town houses the National Historic Trails Interpretive Center (see page 595).

Fort Laramie: Located 77 miles southeast of Douglas, Wyoming, this restored fort is among the best stops on the contemporary trail. The most impressive set of preserved wagon ruts survive in an evocative state park outside Guernsey, upstream from the fort (see page 598).

Santa Fe Trail Junction: For the first few miles, the Santa Fe and Oregon Trails coincided, and a sign here, at what is today the town of **La Junta,** pointed the way: right to Oregon, left to Santa Fe (see page 712).

Independence, Missouri: Where most travelers on the Oregon Trail began, this is also the site of one of the best museums on the subject of the westward migrations (see page 726).

Monument contains what's been called "the richest known deposit of Pliocene Age terrestrial fossils," mainly horses *(Equus simplicidens)* that roamed the area some 3.5 million years ago. The undeveloped monument also preserves one of the longest sections of visible wagon ruts in the entire length of the Oregon Trail. The **visitors center** (208/933-4105) is in Hagerman, 10 miles south of Bliss and across the river from the fossil beds. The center also has information on visiting the area's other national park property: the **Minidoka National Historic Site** (see page 139), north of Twin Falls.

US-26: Gooding and Shoshone

In the midst of inhospitable volcanic badlands, a pair of small towns that grew up along the railroad tracks have somehow survived to the present day. Coming from the west along US-26 from Bliss, the first one you reach is **Gooding** (pop. 3,509), named for local sheep rancher Frank Gooding, who went from being mayor to Idaho governor to U.S. senator before his death in 1928.

A straight shot east along the tracks brings you to **Shoshone** (pop. 1,488), another ranching and railroad center with a number of buildings that have been constructed from local volcanic rock. Though it's a fairly timeworn place, Shoshone looks great at sunset, when its steel water tower glows and places like the neon-signed **Manhattan Café** (208/886-2142), along the railroad tracks, look especially appealing.

Shoshone Falls, Idaho.

If you're hungry, thirsty, or low on gas, be sure to fill up here, as services are rare between Shoshone and Arco, 82 miles to the east.

INTERSECTION

Shoshone sits at the junction of US-26 and Hwy-75, which runs north to Sun Valley, and US-93, which runs south to **Twin Falls** (see page 139). Full coverage of this **Border to Border** route begins on page 110.

Craters of the Moon National Monument and Preserve

Described by writer Washington Irving as a place "where nothing meets the eye but a desolate and awful waste, where no grass grows nor water runs, and where nothing is to be seen but lava," the vast tracts of volcanic fields known as **Craters of the Moon National Monument and Preserve** aren't totally devoid of life—they just look that way. Covering some 750,000 acres at an average altitude of 6,000 feet, the lava fields are but a small part of the extensive Snake River volcanic plain, a 100-mile-wide, 400-mile-long crescent-shaped swath across southern Idaho from the border with Oregon to northwest Wyoming. The rounded cinder cones and acres of glassy black stone were formed between 2,000 and 15,000 years ago, and despite first impressions, they do shelter a wide variety of plant and animal life, from pines and prickly pears to various raptors and a population of mule deer. May and June see abundant wildflowers, and temperatures in the lava tubes are mild year-round, so any time of year is good for a visit.

Easily accessible from a seven-mile loop road that runs south from US-20/26, the most striking remnants of the region's volcanic activity are the huge cones that rise above the generally flat plain. These huge knolls of lightweight cinder give great views of the overall area, but they're not volcanoes, and there's no crater to look down into. The closest Craters of the Moon comes to real craters is the spatter cones midway along the loop, where the deep openings are often filled with snow late into summer. The most interesting section of the monument is at the end of the loop, where—provided you have a flashlight—you can wander through sub-surface **lava tubes** like Beauty Cave and Indian Tunnel. At about 800 feet, Indian Tunnel is the longest in the park. Before you enter the caves, however, check in with park rangers and pick up a permit at the small **visitors center** (208/527-1335, daily), where you can learn how to protect the health of cave-dwelling bats.

There are no real facilities at Craters of the Moon, but in summer there's a basic 42-site **campground** ($15), offering water and restrooms but no showers or hookups.

Arco

"The first city in the free world to be powered by nuclear-generated electricity," **Arco** (pop. 857) sits on the banks of the Big Lost River, so-called because it disappears a few miles downstream, vanishing into the volcanic labyrinth of the Snake River plain. Arco itself, a crossroads town straddling the junction of US-20, US-26, and US-93, is a handy stop for gas, supplies or a meal. Try **Atomic Burgers** (440 S. Front St., 208/527-9944), hard to miss thanks to the huge green "Eat!" sign. All over town, markers and historic plaques point out Arco's connections with the early days of nuclear power, including, most unexpectedly, the conning tower from a decommissioned nuclear-powered Cold War-era submarine, the USS *Hawkbill*, which is permanently moored along Front Street, a mere 1,000 miles from the nearest ocean.

> Northwest of Arco, the highest peak in Idaho, 12,662-foot **Mt. Borah,** was epicenter of a powerful 1983 earthquake that registered magnitude 7.3.

If you have more than a passing interest in nuclear fission, you'll want to check out the anonymous-looking redbrick structure 22 miles southeast of Arco on the south side of US-20, which holds the inoperative remains of **Experimental Breeder Reactor Number One** (208/526-0050, daily summer only, free). Sitting at the edge of

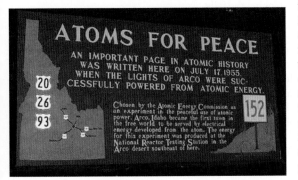

the massive Idaho National Engineering Lab (INEL), the deactivated reactor is open for self-guided tours, on which you can get an up-close glimpse of the turbines and control room, even the fuel rods that first produced nuclear power on December 20, 1951. (To put all this in context, the first reaction produced enough energy to power four small light bulbs.) By 1953 the reactor here was finally able to produce more energy through nuclear reactions than it consumed, a much more important achievement. Some 60 years later, INEL is now one of the nation's de facto repositories for nuclear waste and will remain so for the foreseeable future—with a half-life of more than 1,000 years, it will take the next 3 million years or so, by most estimates, until the waste loses its radioactive potency and decays to "safe" levels.

Idaho Falls

Taking its name from the wide but short waterfall completely tamed to form a pleasant green lake at the center of town, **Idaho Falls** (pop. 59,184), at the junction of US-20 and I-15, is a busy big city with an attractive Middle American downtown set along the banks of the Snake River. Grain elevators and stockyards stand along the railroad tracks, train whistles blow throughout the night, and all manner of neon signs line the

highways, offering a concentrated dose of rural Americana. The town's hotels, supermarkets, and restaurants make Idaho Falls a handy last stop before heading on to the diverse wilderness areas that rise to the north, east, and west. Apart from the chance to wander around a business district that's hardly changed since 1956, you can stroll along the waterfront park, feeding the geese or just watching the waters tumble over the weirs.

Though it's rich in small-town Americana, Idaho Falls also has a few pockets of big-city sophistication, no doubt thanks to the well-paid engineers employed at INEL west of town and the skiers bound for Grand Targhee in the mountains to the east. Cafés and bakeries crowd together around Park Avenue and A Street downtown, serving a wide enough range of pastries, coffees, and sandwiches to suit any palate. If you time it so you miss the crowds, the tiny but tasty **The SnakeBite Restaurant** (401 Park Ave., 208/525-2522, cash only) is excellent for everything from juicy steaks to chocolate cakes. West of downtown across the river, **Smitty's Pancake and Steakhouse** (645 W. Broadway, 208/523-6450) has been serving "IDF's Best Breakfast" for years, east of downtown along old US-20. For a place to stay, try **Residence Inn** (635 West Broadway, 208/542-0000, around $215), overlooking the falls.

Rexburg

First settled by Mormon homesteaders in the 1880s, the fast-growing town of **Rexburg** (pop. 27,663) still has a pronounced Mormon feel, thanks in part to the thousands of students attending Brigham Young University-Idaho. Apart from the BYU connections, Rexburg is best known for the near-disaster of 1976, when the huge Teton Dam collapsed and unleashed eight billion gallons of floodwater onto the valley below. Fortunately, engineers noticed the warning signs and were able to evacuate the area beforehand; though damage was extensive, fatalities were few.

Summer fun in Idaho Falls includes an **Idaho Falls Chukars** Pioneer League baseball game (208/522-8363), at **Melaleuca Field** along Jim Garchow Way west of I-15. Games are broadcast on **KSPZ 980 AM.**

Many of Idaho's famous potatoes are grown in the irrigated "Magic Valley" area along I-84 between Idaho Falls and Twin Falls. Planting takes place in April, while harvest season is usually in fall. To learn everything you ever wanted to know about spuds, take a 30-mile or so trip southwest from Idaho Falls to **Blackfoot** to see the unique **Idaho Potato Museum** (130 NW Main St., 208/785-2517, $4).

Housed in the basement of the old Mormon tabernacle, the **Museum of Rexburg** (51 W. Center St., 208/359-3063, Mon and Fri.-Sat., $2) has the usual displays of quilts and cattle brands tracing the history of the region, plus a large section devoted to the great flood of 1976. A short film shows the actual collapse of the dam.

In summer, make time for a stop at **Nielsen's Frozen Custard** (115 S. 2nd St. W., 208/356-3500), for refreshing cones, floats, and sundaes, plus a full range of burgers, hot dogs, and grilled cheese sandwiches.

Outside Rexburg, **Yellowstone Bear World** ($20 per person or $90 per vehicle, 208/359-9688) is a drive-through zoo featuring more than 200 captive-bred bears, representing all the native species. From Rexburg, US-20 runs northeast through the **Caribou-Targhee National Forest,** climbing from the Snake River plain along Henry's Fork River—one of the country's top fishing streams, loaded with cutthroat trout as big as 10 pounds—into the heart of the Rocky Mountains. On the Idaho-Montana border, 7,072-foot Targhee Pass marks the **Continental Divide.**

Midway between Idaho Falls and Rexburg, the sleepy town of **Rigby** played a hugely important role in the development of contemporary culture: It was here that young Philo T. Farnsworth, the inventor of the cathode-ray television, grew up and went to school.

Rising to the east of Idaho Falls, the serrated crest of the Grand Tetons stands out along the Idaho-Wyoming border. Though the US-20 route through Yellowstone National Park is closed in winter, you can get across the Rockies by detouring via US-26 through **Jackson Hole, Wyoming**— a beautiful drive.

West Yellowstone, Montana

Western gateway to Yellowstone National Park, the Montana town of **West Yellowstone** (pop. 1,339, elev. 6,667 feet) sits just over the Idaho border and nearly on the Wyoming border, offering all the motels, gas stations, and cafés you could ever want, plus a lot more. The primary access point for early tourists visiting Yellowstone on the Oregon Shortline and Union Pacific Railroad, West Yellowstone preserves a great deal of old-style tourist facilities. The rustic old railroad station is now an engaging museum, and the town's many roadside motels (there are more motel rooms than residents!) display a mouthwatering assembly of nifty 1950s-vintage neon signs.

vintage sign in West Yellowstone

There's also a huge **IMAX theater** (101 S. Canyon St., 406/646-4100, $9.75), in case you prefer the Memorex version to real-life Yellowstone. The IMAX theater is adjacent to the **Grizzly and Wolf Discovery Center** (201 S. Canyon St., 800/257-2570 or 406/646-7001, $13), which collects orphaned, abandoned, and "problem" bears and wolves and puts them on display rather than kill them, as is otherwise done.

West Yellowstone's main drag, Canyon Street (US-20), is lined by cafés and Wild West souvenir shops. The excellent **Book Peddler** (106 N. Canyon St., 406/646-9358) boasts an espresso bar along with a wide array of fiction and nonfiction titles.

In 1808, when fur trapper John Colter described the scenes he saw in what's now Yellowstone—gurgling, spouting steam vents and prismatic pools of sulfurous boiling water—nobody believed him, and many thought he was mad, calling the fantastic land "Colter's Hell."

Most of West Yellowstone's enviable collection of historic motels are off the main highway frontage, so drive around the back streets and take your pick. The arts-and-crafts-style **Stage Coach Inn** (209 Madison Ave., 800/842-2882 or 406/646-7381, $74 and up) has been charming visitors for more than half a century, as has the friendly and relaxing **Lazy G Motel** (123 N Hayden St., 406/646-7586, $89 and up), which has to be one of the world's nicest little motels.

WYOMING

Most visitors to Wyoming have one thing in mind: Yellowstone National Park. This amazing spectacle, which our route takes us right through, is deservedly the state's premier visitor attraction, but the rest of

Wyoming holds a surprising variety of interesting places, from Wild West cow towns to the wide open spaces of the Great Plains. The least populated of the 50 states, Wyoming has more wide-open space than just about anywhere else. If you like the idea of traveling for miles and miles without seeing anyone, then coming upon a crossroads outpost where the post office shares space with the general store and gas station, you'll want to take the time to explore Wyoming.

Yellowstone National Park

Sitting astride the Continental Divide, high up in the northern Rockies at the northwest corner of Wyoming, **Yellowstone National Park** is one of the true wonders of

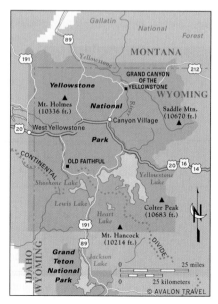

the natural world. A veritable greatest hits of Mother Nature, the park is packed full of burbling geysers, magnificent canyons, raging waterfalls, and still-wild wildlife. The country's (and the world's) oldest national park, established in 1872, Yellowstone was first explored by frontiersman John Colter, who passed through in 1807; it's also one of the largest parts of the lower 48 states never to be farmed or fenced.

You probably already know something about what Yellowstone has in store for you: The one essential Yellowstone sight is **Old Faithful Geyser,** in the southwest quarter of the park. One of the world's most famous natural features, Old Faithful is known for its clockwork eruptions, in which thousands of gallons of boiling water

the vivid colors of Grand Prismatic Spring in Yellowstone National Park

are sent over 100 feet into the air, forming a column of steam. Hundreds of people line up around the geyser waiting for it to blow, and rangers are able to predict it with a good deal of accuracy—the visitors center will list the expected times of the day's eruptions, which occur roughly every 35 to 120 minutes and last for another 2-5 minutes. In between eruptions, visit the impressive Old Faithful Visitor Education Center, opened in August 2010, or wander around the other features of the Old Faithful basin. These include a number of other geysers (the Old Faithful area has the greatest concentration in the world), as well as colorful pools and other geothermal features, all linked by well-marked boardwalks and trails along the Firehole River.

One rarely-mentioned aspect of life in Yellowstone is the profusion of bison (a.k.a. buffalo) droppings: Everywhere you look—all around the geysers, hot springs, etc.—they've made their mark. Although they may seem placid, bison can be dangerous, so keep your distance.

The other main sight is the **Grand Canyon of the Yellowstone River,** where a pair of powerful waterfalls cascade into a 20-mile-long, half-mile-wide, and more than 1,000-foot-deep canyon of eroding yellow stone. Parking areas line the north and south rims of the canyon, allowing access to trails along the edge of the gorge. A personal favorite is **Uncle Tom's Trail,** leaving from the south side of the falls. More a staircase than a trail, this route zigzags steeply down the walls of the canyon, bringing you face to face with the falls. Farther along the south rim is Artist's Point, which gives the classic view of the canyon. Also, two "Brink of the Falls" routes lead from the north side down to where the waters plunge.

Along with these two main attractions, there are many more sights to see, so take the time to visit the visitors centers, talk to the rangers, and find out what other wonders await. Covering more than 2.2 million acres, Yellowstone is a big place, plenty big enough to absorb the many tourists who come here during the peak summer season. Whatever you do, don't try to see it all in a day or two; if time is tight, choose one or two places and spend all your time there. Get out of the car, hike a few trails, and enjoy.

Yellowstone Practicalities

The $30 entry fee for each noncommercial vehicle covers seven days, opt for a combo pass for $50 to visit nearby Grand Teton National Park. (The America the Beautiful Annual Pass is a better value at around $80—it offers admission to all National Parks and Federal Recreational Lands for an entire family for a full year.) Yellowstone's visitor facilities book up well in advance (sometimes up to a year), so if you want the complete experience, it's best to plan ahead as much as possible. Accommodations are the

Yellowstone's Lower Falls

main thing you ought to sort out as soon as you can, as bed space is at a premium. The first choice is the wonderful **Old Faithful Inn,** next to the famous geyser. Built of split logs and huge boulders and exuding rough-hewn elegance, this delightful inn was completed in 1904. Rooms in the old lodge, without baths, start at about $120. A newer wing has larger rooms and modern conveniences for around $260-590 a night—some of these rooms have Old Faithful views. Another historic lodge, at Yellowstone Lake, is plusher but architecturally less distinctive. A half dozen other inns, cabins, and motels are scattered around the park, including the still-new **Dunraven Lodge** near the canyon, and the year-round **Snow Lodge** near Old Faithful, accessible in winter only by tank-like snow cat from West Yellowstone. All rooms are handled through park concessionaire **Xanterra** (307/344-7311, http://yellowstonenationalparklodges.com), which also handles reservations for the historic open-topped Yellow Bus tours and the park's campgrounds,

> Note that the Yellowstone visitor season is very short—roads are usually blocked by snow from November until April, May, or even June. US-26 is a year-round alternative through the Grand Tetons and Jackson Hole.

most of which operate on a first-come, first-served basis and tend to fill up by noon daily.

Places to eat include the usual cafeteria-type restaurants at all of the park's hotels and lodges, plus a truly remarkable restaurant at the classic Old Faithful Inn, with a three-story log-cabin dining room and food that's as good as it gets in the national parks.

You'll find gas stations, gift shops, and general stores at just about every road junction in the park. There are ranger stations at most main features and large visitors centers (307/344-7381) at Mammoth Hot Springs, Old Faithful, and the Canyon.

Cody

Eastern gateway to Yellowstone National Park, and an enjoyable overnight stop in its own right, **Cody** (pop. 9,792) is a self-conscious frontier town and a busy center for local ranching and wood products industries. The outskirts are lined by

Buffalo Bill Cody

Walmarts, Kmarts, and all the fast-food franchises you could name, but the town center along Sheridan Avenue (US-20) still looks like the Wild West town Cody was built to be.

The annual **Cody Stampede Rodeo** started in 1919 and has been a part of the town's 4th of July celebrations ever since, making it the nation's longest-running rodeo. It draws professional cowboys from across the continent. Equally impressive, The **Cody Nite Rodeo** (307/587-5155, 8pm daily June-Sept., $20), at the huge rodeo grounds at the west end of town, has been held since 1938. Get a seat in the "Buzzard's Roost," close to the chutes where the cowboys mount those bulls and buckin' broncos for this amateur event.

Sitting on the Big Horn Basin plains at the foot of the mountains, Cody was founded in the late 1890s by Wild West showman "Buffalo Bill" Cody, whose name graces most everything in town, including the **Buffalo Bill Center of the West** (720 Sheridan Ave., 307/587-4771, daily Mar.-Nov., Thurs.-Sun. Dec.-Feb., $19). One of the country's great museums, and certainly the best in the Wild West, this place tells all you could want to know about the American frontier. The center is divided into five main collections. First stop should be Buffalo Bill's boyhood home, which was moved here from LeClair, Iowa, in 1933; then move on to the Buffalo Bill Museum, which includes a battery of movies and artifacts from his famous Wild West Show, a circus-like extravaganza that toured the world. The Whitney Western Art Museum, one of the country's most extensive collections of western art, displays important works by George Catlin, Thomas Moran, Albert Bierstadt, and Frederic Remington, plus some fine contemporary works. Gun freaks will enjoy the Cody Firearms Museum, which displays more than 7,000 historic weapons. Saving the biggest and best for last, the Plains Indian Museum has an amazing collection of art and artifacts created by the diverse Plains peoples, from beadwork dresses to a reconstructed Sioux tepee. Pride of place is given to an extraordinary buffalo robe painted with scenes of the legendary Battle of Little Big Horn.

At the west edge of Cody is **Old Trail Town** (307/587-5302, daily mid-May-mid-Sept., $9), a low-key but engaging collection of old buildings moved here from northwestern Wyoming and southern Montana. Wagons, buffalo robes, and other relics are on display. A memorial cemetery holds the remains of Wild West figures, including John Jeremiah "Liver Eating" Johnston, played as Jeremiah Johnson—with no t—by Robert Redford in the 1972 movie named for the man.

Between Yellowstone and Cody, US-20 drops steeply through lovely **Wapiti Valley.** Teddy Roosevelt supposedly called this area "the most scenic 50 miles in America." Another scenic route, the **Beartooth Highway** (US-212), runs northeast to Red Lodge, Montana, and was rated by Charles Kuralt as "the most beautiful roadway in America."

Though Buffalo Bill gets most of the publicists' ink, another famous Cody figure is the abstract impressionist "action painter" Jackson Pollock, who was born here in 1912.

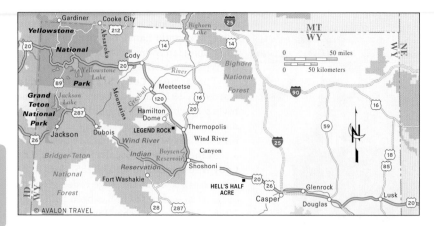

Cody Practicalities

You'll find most of Cody's good places to eat on Sheridan Avenue, the main drag. The Wild West-themed **Proud Cut Saloon** (1227 Sheridan Ave., 307/527-6905) has taxidermy heads of megafauna on the walls. The menu ranges from burgers at lunch to great steaks at dinner. A restaurant and rooms are available at the historic **Irma Hotel** (1192 Sheridan Ave., 800/745-4762 or 307/587-4221, around $150), which was built by "Buffalo Bill" Cody and named for his daughter; it still features a lovely cherrywood bar given by Queen Victoria, and there's an evening gunfight on the front porch. Fans of vernacular roadside Americana may want to have a look at the **Buffalo Bill Village** (1701 Sheridan Ave., 800/527-5544 or 307/587-5555, $120 and up), which started life in 1914 as a cowboy campout, was developed in the 1930s as a log cabin motor court, and now stands in the heart of Cody amid the full-service Holiday Inn family resort. The nicest place to stay in Cody may well be the **Big Bear Motel** (139 W. Yellowstone Ave., 800/325-7163 or 307/587-3117, $79-169) near Trail Town.

Aviator Amelia Earhart was having a cabin built for her near Meeteetse along the Greybull River, but construction stopped in 1937 after she disappeared on her round-the-world flight.

Hwy-120: Meeteetse

Southeast of Cody, Hwy-120, a prettier alternative to US-20, angles south over the rugged foothill badlands of the Absaroka ("ab-SAR-uh-kuh") Mountains, historic homeland of the Crow people but now equal parts cattle ranches and oil wells. Thirty miles along this lonely highway brings you to **Meeteetse** (pop. 326), one of the oldest settlements in central Wyoming and still much the same after 125 years. The broad Greybull River—and an occasional cattle drive—runs right through town, which still retains wooden boardwalks and hitching posts for cowboys' horses.

Besides being wonderfully evocative of an earlier era, Meeteetse also has a great museum documenting diverse aspects of the region's past: the **Belden Museum** (1947 State St., 307/868-2423, Tues.-Sat. 10am-4pm, free), which holds an extraordinary collection of cowboy photography that includes the first Marlboro Man ads, shot on the nearby Pitchfork Ranch by Charles Belden, a local rancher and commercial photographer. The building also houses the Meeteetse Museum, which has the stuffed remains of an eight-foot-tall **grizzly bear,** one of the largest ever found in the area.

Along with an old but fully stocked general store, tiny Meeteetse has a pair of saloons side by side on State Street as well as the **Oasis Motel and RV Park** (1702 State St., 307/868-2551, $60 and up, $30 and up for an RV space), with camping and a Conestoga wagon, right on the Greybull River. The Oasis also owns the **Vision Quest Motel** (2207 State St.), with the same rates and phone numbers.

Legend Rock

One of Wyoming's most significant collections of petroglyphs, **Legend Rock State Petroglyph Site** contains over 300 images dating back some 2,000 to 10,000 years, carved into sandstone cliffs in the oil-rich foothills of the Owl Creek Mountains. Legend Rock is administered by **Hot Springs State Park** (538 N. Park St.) in Thermopolis. A series of road signs make the petroglyphs pretty easy to find. That said, getting there requires a serious investment of time and attention. Follow US-120 for 21 miles from Thermopolis, or 33 miles from Meeteetse, then turn south at the Hamilton Dome turnoff and follow the dirt road for 8.5 miles. You will arrive at an unforgettable scene: High above Cottonwood Creek, hundreds of images cover a 400-meter long sandstone wall, connecting contemporary visitors with the ancestors of the Shoshone people who lived here millennia ago.

Thermopolis

Despite the highfalutin resonance of its classical-sounding name, **Thermopolis** (pop. 2,974) is a sleepy little retirement town, surrounded by red-rock canyons and centered among a remarkable set of natural hot springs. The land was bought in 1896 from local Shoshone chief Washakie and Arapaho chief Sharp Nose on the understanding that the spring waters be kept open to the public, indigenous and

Hot Springs State Park

newcomer alike. This spring, which flows at a rate of 18,000 gallons of 135°F water daily, was the basis of Wyoming's first state park, **Hot Springs State Park** (538 N. Park St., 307/864-2176, daily, free), which still covers the east bank of the Bighorn River. A state-run bathhouse has showers and changing rooms—you can rent towels and bathing suits for a nominal charge. There are two commercial enterprises in the park— **Hellie's Tepee Pools** and **Star**

velociraptor skeleton at the Wyoming Dinosaur Center

Plunge—with water slides, saunas, and so on, perfect for families with littler kids.

Across the river in the center of town, the enjoyable **Hot Springs County Historical Museum and Cultural Center** (700 Broadway St., 307/864-5183, Mon.-Sat. summer, Tues.-Sat. winter, $5) has a wide-ranging collection of historic photos, farming and oil-drilling implements, and even the cherrywood bar from the Hole-in-the-Wall Saloon where Butch and Sundance supposedly bellied up for a drink or two. The final big draw in Thermopolis—and I mean *big*—is the **Wyoming Dinosaur Center** (110 Carter Ranch Rd., 307/864-2997, daily, $10), on the east side of town. Wyoming is one of the world's most abundant sources of fossils. Follow the green dinosaur footprints from the center of town to a paleontology dig that's open to the public. Finds on display include a full T. rex and a triceratops.

The friendly Thermopolis **visitors center** (220 Park St., 877/864-3192) has more information on the area, including details about the intriguing Legend Rock petroglyphs north of town.

Wind River Canyon

South of Thermopolis, US-20 winds through **Wind River Canyon,** one of the most memorable drives in a state of memorable drives. The 2,500-foot-deep canyon, with the highway on one side of the broad river and the railroad on the other, reveals millions of years of sedimentary rock. As you drive along heading south, you reach deeper and deeper into the earth; each layer is labeled with signs explaining its geological age and significance, with the oldest layers dating back to the Precambrian era, some 2.5 billion years ago.

Due in part to the visual effect of the uplifted sedimentary layers, the river at times gives the illusion of flowing uphill; this may explain why Indians and early explorers thought there were two distinct rivers and called the canyon itself the "Wedding of the Waters." The river still has two distinct names: Upstream from Wind River Canyon, it is called the Wind River; downstream from the canyon, it's called the Bighorn River.

Driving along US-20 between the Wind River Canyon and Shoshoni, keep an eye out for the many pronghorn antelope that play on the rolling rangeland.

At the south end of the Wind River, **Boysen State Park,** a popular place for fishing and waterskiing, backs up behind Boysen Dam, which was built from 1947 to 1952. The land west of the reservoir forms the 2.2-million-acre **Wind River Indian Reservation,** home to descendants of the Eastern Shoshone and Northern Arapahoe peoples. A woman thought by some to be Sacagawea (the Shoshone guide of Lewis and Clark fame) is buried on the reservation, along the Wind River near Fort Washakie.

Jackson Hole

In winter, Yellowstone is closed to cars, and the only road kept open is US-212 between Gardiner and Cooke City, Montana, at the northern edge of the park. But if you're here anytime but summer, don't despair: US-26, a very different but still unforgettable route, is open year-round, running south of Yellowstone between Idaho Falls and Casper, through **Jackson Hole** and the spectacular scenery of Grand Teton National Park.

Climbing up from Idaho Falls along the banks of the Snake River, US-26 crosses into Wyoming on a sinuously scenic route, past cottonwood trees and white-water-running kayakers, before linking up with north-south US-89. The tourist mecca of Jackson Hole, one of the country's most popular "wilderness" destinations, takes its name from the main town, **Jackson** (pop. 10,523), which sits at the center of a broad, mountain-ringed valley. Drawing upward of 35,000 visitors on a summer day, Jackson isn't exactly an idyllic spot, but it has managed to retain its Wild West character, especially in the few blocks around the lively Town Square. Here, false-fronted buildings linked by a raised wooden sidewalk hold upscale boutiques and the wonderfully kitsch likes of the **Million Dollar Cowboy Bar** (25 N. Cache St., 307/733-2207) on the west side of the square, a huge and always lively hangout with silver dollars implanted in the bar top and real leather saddles instead of bar stools. There are free dance lessons on Thursday nights!

Jackson has many very good (and very expensive) restaurants, like **E. Leaven Food Co.** (175 Center St., 307/733-5600), a spacious and unpretentious pre-ski breakfast spot serving house-made omelets, soups, and salads. Jackson caters to so many visitors that accommodations, however plentiful, can be booked solid in summer. There's something for everyone here: campgrounds and RV parks; $4,000-a-week dude ranches; B&Bs; and highway motels, including an affordable Motel 6 along US-89, about two miles south of town.

The Jackson Hole area is one of the country's most exclusive winter resorts, with world-class ski areas including **Grand Targhee Resort** (800/827-4433 or 307/353-2300), powder-hound heaven on the Idaho border; and **Jackson Hole Mountain Resort** (888/333-7766 or 307/733-2292), which boasts one of the longest vertical drops in the United States: an astounding 4,139 feet!

Grand Teton National Park

North of Jackson, south of Yellowstone, the silver peaks of **Grand Teton National Park** cut into the sky, their slopes offering some of the best hiking and mountaineering in the lower 48 states. US-26/89 runs right along the base of the mountains,

From Grand Teton National Park, US-89/191 runs north to the heart of Yellowstone National Park.

the Grand Tetons from Snake River Overlook

giving grand views and tempting travelers to stop and explore. West of the main highway, Teton Park Road winds past **Jenny Lake,** where you can rent a kayak or board a boat ($15 round trip) and ride across to a short trail that leads up past Hidden Falls to **Inspiration Point,** at the foot of 13,776-foot Grand Teton.

Details on the abundant hiking, skiing, fishing, and other recreational activities, as well as camping and lodging options, are available by contacting the main Grand Teton National Park **visitors center** (307/739-3300), a mile west of US-26 on Teton Park Road.

Dubois and the National Bighorn Sheep Center

Between Casper and the Grand Tetons, US-26 is a mostly scenic highway, crossing the Continental Divide at 9,659-foot Togwotee Pass before winding along the Wind River through the multicolored badlands that surround the town of **Dubois** (pop. 987; pronounced "dew-BOYS"). A low-key ranching and logging center that's still in its infancy as a tourist destination, Dubois does have one unique attraction: the **National Bighorn Sheep Center** (307/455-3429 or 888/209-2795, daily spring-fall, Mon.-Sat. winter, $4), right on US-26 at the west edge of town, documenting the life and times of the thousands of elusive bighorn sheep that congregate in the winter months around Whisky Mountain, south of Dubois.

On US-26, about 18 miles west of Dubois, a roadside monument remembers the work of the "tie hacks," who, from the 1870s until World War II, cut down lodgepole pines to form railroad ties.

There are a few saloons, steakhouses, and fly-fishing shops, and one great place to stay in Dubois. For full Wild West immersion, book a room at the log-cabin **Twin Pines Lodge** (218 W. Ramshorn, 800/550-6332, $80 and up), in business since 1934.

Shoshoni: Hell's Half Acre

Named for the Shoshone people who once held sway over this part of the Great Plains, the town of **Shoshoni** (pop. 648) now sits somewhat forlornly at the junction

The Mushroom, Hell's Half Acre, Wyoming.

of US-20 and US-26, at the southeast edge of the Boysen Reservoir.

Between Shoshoni and Casper, the only attraction worth mentioning is the odd geology of **Hell's Half Acre,** a more than 300-acre concentration of grotesquely eroded stone south of US-20 amid the arid badlands landscape. Scenes in the cult-classic late-1990s Neil Patrick Harris military sci-fi movie *Starship Troopers* were filmed here in 1996.

Casper

Like other towns in southern Wyoming, **Casper** (pop. 60,285) began as a way station on the many frontier trails that followed the North Platte River, first as a ferry crossing (log rafts were run by Salt Lake City-bound Mormons from 1847 to 1852; non-Mormons were charged $1.50) and later toll bridges, culminating with an elaborate plank bridge built by Louis Guinard in 1859. The second-largest city in Wyoming, only slightly smaller than capital city Cheyenne, Casper is still dependent on passing trade. Casper's key location along the I-25 corridor has enabled the local economy to survive the boom-and-bust-and-boom-again variations in its other main industry, oil.

Most of the places of interest in Casper (which was originally spelled Caspar) have to do with the westward migration. Your first stop should be the wonderful **National Historic Trails Interpretive Center** (1501 N. Poplar St., 307/265-8030, daily summer, Tues.-Sat. Sept.-May, free), a cooperative venture between the Bureau of Land Management, the National Historic Trails Center Foundation, and the City of Casper, which opened in 2002, just north of I-25 exit 189. High-tech exhibits are good for younger folks, giving a sight-and-sound tour along the historic Oregon Trail and Pony Express routes, which passed through here on their way west. **Fort Caspar Museum** (307/235-8462, daily summer, Tues.-Sat. Oct.-Apr., $3), west of downtown off Hwy-220, is a New Deal-era replica of the original rough log fort and Pony Express station. There's also a reconstruction of the Mormon-operated ferry and displays of pioneer artifacts in the small museum.

While the rest of the city has a definite roughneck feel, downtown Casper is also rich in 1920s Americana, with a pair of great old movie theaters, rusty neon signs, and art deco storefronts, plus one of the country's largest cowboy clothing stores: **Lou Taubert Ranch Outfitters** (125 E. 2nd St., 307/234-2500 or 800/447-9378) has over 10,000 pairs of boots and nine floors of blue jeans, rhinestones, and other essential range-riding gear.

East of downtown, one place you really ought to visit is the **Nicolaysen Art Museum and Discovery Center** (400 E. Collins St., 307/235-5247, Tues.-Sun., $5, free on Sun.), housed in an imaginatively converted old power plant, along the railroad tracks. The finest contemporary art museum in Wyoming, the Nicolaysen also has a hands-on art center for children.

Casper was the heart of the oil fields that led to the notorious Teapot Dome scandal of the 1920s, in which Secretary of the Interior Albert Fall went to prison for accepting $400,000 in bribes. It is also the hometown of oil magnate and former vice president Dick Cheney and his high school sweetheart (and wife), Lynne.

JACKALOPES 'R' US

Traveling around the Great Plains, you're bound to come across all sorts of oversize wildlife—giant fish, giant cows, giant bison—plus some more that defy anatomical description. Most of the latter—fur-bearing trout, in particular—are seen primarily on postcards, but at least one species can usually be found mounted on the wall of any self-respecting saloon or taxidermist's shop: the jackalope, Wyoming's "Official State Mythical Creature." So rare that one has never been seen in the wild, the jackalope has the body of a jackrabbit and the horns of an antelope. Dozens of examples are displayed around the Wyoming town of Douglas, with the "world's largest" standing over eight feet head-to-tail in Jackalope Square at 3rd and Center Streets downtown (an even larger one, sometimes wearing a saddle, has been spotted along US-20, a quarter mile west). The enigmatic creature is also celebrated all over Douglas during Douglas Railroad Days in the middle of June.

Not far from the Nicolaysen museum, the homespun **Cottage Café** (116 S. Lincoln St., 307/234-1157) has good coffees and filling meals for lunch. Best breakfast: **Eggington's** (229 E. 2nd St., 307/265-8700). Casper's lodging options along the I-25 frontage include most of the national chains.

Glenrock: Ayres Natural Bridge

Midway between Casper and Douglas along the south bank of the North Platte River, **Glenrock** (pop. 2,598) was a vital rest stop and supply station on the Oregon and other emigrant trails. Several downtown buildings have endured since its heyday, when Glenrock was known as Deer Creek Station and some 20,000 migrants came through each year, many of them camping overnight at the "rock in the glen" on the west side of town, where a sandstone boulder still holds the names of passing pioneers. Nowadays, Glenrock is known for its massive 800-megawatt coal-fired power plant, one of the largest in the country; a pair of wind farms intended to generate 100 megawatts of electricity are under construction nearby.

Between Casper and Glenrock, US-26 winds along the river, but between Glenrock and Douglas the old road has been replaced by the I-25 freeway. A dozen miles east of Glenrock, midway to Douglas, turn off I-25 onto Natural Bridge Road and drive five miles south of the freeway to visit one of Wyoming's unsung beauty spots, **Ayres Natural Bridge,** which arches 30 feet above peaceful La Prele Creek, next to a small campground in a pleasant county park.

Douglas

Situated far enough off I-25 to retain its Wild West cowboy character, the enjoyable town of **Douglas** (pop. 6,531) was founded in 1886 across the river from Fort Fetterman, which for the previous 25 years had protected traffic on the old Oregon and Bozeman Trails along the North Platte River. The setting of Owen Wister's genre-inventing Western novel *The Virginian* and, more recently, birthplace of that other Wild West icon, the jackalope, Douglas is a quietly picturesque small town with a wild history, and a great place to break your long-distance road trip.

Douglas's own **KKTY 1470 AM** plays local news, country hits, and regional college sports.

1158 — Tombstone of George W. Pike

GEORGE W. PIKE

Underneath this stone in eternal rest Sleeps the wildest one of the wayward west He was gambler and sport and cowboy too And he led the pace in an outlaw crew And he was sore on the trigger and stuck to the end But he was never known to quit on a friend In the relations of death all mankind is alike But in life there was only one George W. Pike

Famous Character of the Early Days in the Wild West

The **Wyoming State Fairgrounds,** along the river at the west end of Center Street, host a livestock-frenzied fair at the end of August. The fairgrounds also feature the year-round **Wyoming Pioneer Museum** (307/358-9288, Mon.-Fri. Oct.-May, Mon.-Sat. June-Sept., free), packed full of artifacts from the late 1800s—everything from rifles and a roulette table to fossils and farm implements. It also houses a Sioux-style hide tepee made for the movie *Dances with Wolves.* The wilder side of Douglas history is perhaps most vividly apparent in tombstones in the **cemetery** on the east edge of town at the end of Pine Street, where legendary cattle rustler George Pike is interred beneath an impressive marker that reads, in part:

Underneath this stone in eternal rest sleeps the wildest one of the wayward west.

Lusk

A cattle-ranching and farming center, **Lusk** (pop. 1,628) is the largest town in the least-populated county in the country's least-populated state. It also boasts the only traffic light on US-20 between Douglas, Wyoming, and Chadron, Nebraska. And if those claims to fame don't make you want to stop, the **Stagecoach Museum** (322 S. Main St., 307/334-3444, Mon.-Fri., by appointment Sat.-Sun., $2) definitely will, if only to see the sole authentic 1880s Cheyenne-Deadwood Stagecoach—the one Doris Day sang about in *Calamity Jane.* (The only other stagecoach from this legendary route is now in the Smithsonian.) Behind the museum building is another frontier icon—a one-room schoolhouse—and along US-20 at the east edge of town, a plaque points out a redwood water tower dating from 1886, when steam locomotives still chugged across the plains.

A marker on the south side of US-20, a mile east of Lusk, stands where US-20 intersects the Texas Trail: In the 1870s over 500,000 head of cattle were driven each year between Fort Worth and the open range of Wyoming and Montana along this route.

Lusk also has a good range of motels, including the **Covered Wagon Motel** (730 S. Main St., 307/334-2836, $100 and up).

Guernsey

A worthwhile detour from Douglas or Lusk via I-15 and US-26 takes you 40-plus miles south to the town of **Guernsey** (pop. 1,195) on the North Platte River, where you can visit two of the most evocative Oregon Trail historic sites. The Oregon Trail passed through along the south bank of the river and the well-signed Guernsey State Park. A mile south of town via Wyoming Avenue you'll find the best surviving set of Oregon Trail **wagon ruts,** cut shoulder-deep in the soft sandstone. Nearby is a small obelisk marking the grave of an unfortunate pioneer, and three miles to the southeast along the same road, **Register Cliff** is carved with the names of over a thousand pioneers and explorers, many dating back to 1840-1860, the heyday of the trail. **Fort Laramie National Historic Site,** another frontier landmark, is 15 miles east of Guernsey via US-26.

NEBRASKA

In its 430-mile or so trek across Nebraska, US-20 passes through a surprising variety of landscapes. In the

Oregon Trail wagon tracks across Guernsey

west, the highway skirts the edge of the huge and desolate **Sand Hills,** where North America's largest system of sand dunes underlies a grassy pastoral scene. Across

the midsection, the road runs parallel to the broad **Niobrara River,** one of the few rivers in the Great Plains not blocked behind a dam, before reaching the bluffs above the Missouri River.

One of the last reaches of the country to be settled and domesticated, northern Nebraska is still sparsely populated and looks like the Great Plains are *supposed* to look. Towns are few and far between, and come and go in the proverbial blink of an eye; the rolling ranch lands are marked every mile or so by spinning Aermotor windmills pumping up water for wandering cattle herds, while historical plaques point out the sites where, barely a century ago, cowboys rode and Native Americans did battle with the U.S. Cavalry. Besides being rich in Wild West history—and in prehistoric fossil beds—the region has a strong literary tradition, thanks to writers such as Mari Sandoz and John G. Neihardt. All in all, few corners of the country pay back time spent with as much interest as does northern Nebraska—hard to believe, perhaps, but true.

Harrison and Agate Fossil Beds National Monument

Just over the Wyoming border, the tiny town of **Harrison** (pop. 238, elev. 4,878 feet; "Nebraska's Top Town") is an attractive wide spot in the road located near the highest point in the state. The spirit of old-time hospitality is kept alive by a pair of welcoming haunts: the **Longhorn Saloon** (168 Main St.) and the **Harrison House Hotel** (115 Main St., 308/668-2166, rooms $50-95) in an 1886 building. The hotel also includes a breakfast-only restaurant that serves brunch on Sunday. Outside town, on the banks of the Niobrara River, 23 miles south of Harrison, the **Agate Fossil Beds National Monument** (308/436-9760, daily, free) contains the 19- to 21-million-year-old

remains of bison-size pigs, twin-horned proto-rhinos, and other van-ished Miocene-era creatures. The acres of grassland here are good for wildflowers and bird-watching, even if you aren't fascinated by old bones. If you are interested in paleontology, the Agate Fossil Beds National Monument and the Hudson-Meng Bison Bone Bed in nearby Crawford are both stops along what is being marketed as the "Fossil Freeway" collection of historic sites in Nebraska and South Dakota.

The US-20 highway alignment through Harrison was unpaved up until 1941.

Fort Robinson

Thirty miles east from the Wyoming border, **Fort Robinson State Park** (308/665-2900) was established in 1874 to control the Red Cloud and Pine Ridge Sioux people. Now a state park and planted with groves of mature trees where 100 years ago all was grassland prairie, Fort Robinson has perhaps the most tragic and uncomfortable history of all the many old forts on the Wild West frontier: This is where, in 1877, the unarmed Sioux chief Crazy Horse was stabbed to death with bayonets while in the custody of the U.S. Army. In 1879, the last of the Cheyenne people under Morning Star (a.k.a. Chief Dull Knife) escaped from prison and were killed in battle here rather than be taken away to a reservation in Oklahoma.

Knowing this history, it can be hard to take Fort Robinson as the enjoyable respite it is today. The hundreds of hardwood trees make it an oasis on the generally treeless plains, and the whitewashed wooden barracks, many now converted to cultural centers and museums, give it the air of a college campus—especially on summer weekends, when the park turns into a living history museum, complete with cookouts, carriage rides, and evening melodramas.

The only part of the park open year-round is the **Fort Robinson Museum** (308/665-2919, $2) in the old headquarters building, with full displays on the fort's history, plus walking-tour maps of the entire post. Accommodations are offered in the officers' quarters, and there are many good camping spots.

Crawford

Three miles east of Fort Robinson, **Crawford** (pop. 973) has settled into a sedate life as a ranching and farming center. Pines and cottonwoods line the White River at the foot of the weirdly eroded Legend Buttes, making a pretty scene. Even prettier are the

Fort Robinson State Park

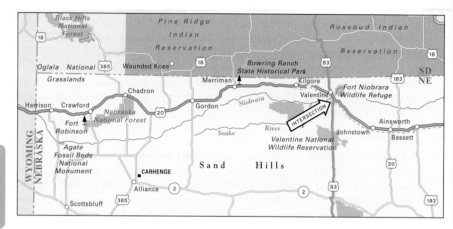

Oglala National Grasslands, which start eight miles north of Crawford via Hwy-2 and occupy 94,000 acres along the Nebraska, Wyoming, and South Dakota borders. The grasslands are home to hawks, eagles, and antelope and are highlighted by the eerie landscape of **Toadstool Geological Park,** where ancient fossils can be found among weirdly eroded figures. The grasslands also protect an archaeological site known as the **Hudson-Meng Bison Bone Bed** (308/432-0300), a shallow arroyo holding the enigmatic remains of over 600 bison spread over an area the size of a football field. Displays on the site include stone tools and arrowheads dating from approximately 10,000 years ago and a small garden growing native preconquest crops.

Back in the present day, you can dig into juicy chicken sandwiches and other timeless fast food at Crawford's **Staab's Drive In** (110 McPherson St., 308/665-1210), right on US-20.

Chadron

The largest town in northwest Nebraska, **Chadron** (pop. 5,775) sits at the northern edge of the Sand Hills region, bounded by pine forests to the south and the Pine Ridge Sioux Reservation to the north, across the South Dakota border. The highway frontage along US-20 isn't especially inviting, but the two-block town center preserves its turn-of-the-20th-century character with sandstone and brick-fronted buildings along the south side of the still-used railroad tracks.

In 1893, Chadron's early boosters found a perfect way to get their town in the news: They sponsored a 1,000-mile horse race from Chadron to Chicago, which made front pages across the country. A plaque in front of the black-and-white Blaine Hotel, a block east of Main Street, marks the start of the race.

Chadron may feel livelier and younger than other Nebraska towns, thanks to the energetic presence of Chadron State College, which has 3,000 students and an intriguing museum, the **Mari Sandoz High Plains Heritage Center** (1000 Main St., 308/432-6401, free). Known as the "The Story Catcher," Sandoz (1896-1966) wrote about growing up on a nearby ranch in her first book, the haunting classic *Old Jules,* and captured the spirit and history of the Great Plains in her many later works of fiction and nonfiction. The museum has extensive displays of her personal effects and free pamphlets describing a driving tour of Sandoz-related sites in the area.

Besides giving a good look at the diverse heritage of the Sand Hills region, Chadron makes a handy base for trips north to the

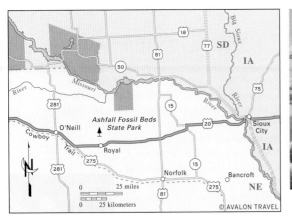

goldenrod,
state flower of Nebraska

Pine Ridge lands and the Black Hills of South Dakota, or south to the marvelous Carhenge. Motels include a Best Western and a Super 8, but **The Olde Main Street Inn** (115 Main St., 308/432-3380, $65-95) has the most character. Part old railroad hotel, part cozy B&B, the inn has rooms, a popular restaurant and a saloon downstairs, and Chadron's only espresso machine. The hotel has a historical dark side as well: In 1890, General Nelson Miles stayed at this hotel when his soldiers massacred Sioux women and children at Wounded Knee.

Even if you're just passing through, don't miss one of the great stops on the Great Plains, the excellent **Museum of the Fur Trade** (308/432-3843, daily May-Oct., by appointment rest of the year, $5), on US-20 three miles east of downtown Chadron. One of the great small museums in the United States, this privately run collection focuses on the material culture of the North American frontier. Its extensive displays bring to life the first few centuries of interaction between Native Americans and Europeans. Besides giving the overall historical context of the fur trade and its many related enterprises, the collection emphasizes the day-to-day realities of life on the Great Plains in the 18th and 19th centuries. Walls decked with weapons and bottles of whiskey (from the Americans), rum (from the English), and brandy (from the French) document the better-known aspects, but what captures your attention are the little things: packs of playing cards, a checkerboard—even a waterproof parka made out of seal intestines by the Inuit.

Merriman

East of Chadron, US-20 winds along the northern edge of the Sand Hills, coming within a few miles of the South Dakota border. The town of **Merriman** (pop. 131) may not look like much, but it does mark the turnoff north to the nearby **Bowring Ranch State Historical Park** (308/684-3428, Thurs.-Tues., $2), a working cattle ranch preserved pretty much as it was at the turn of the 20th century. The site is lovely, with a sod house surrounded (in springtime, at least) by rolling green hills. A modern visitors center has displays on windmills and other facts of Sand Hills life, plus biographical displays on the politically powerful Bowring family, who lived and worked here from 1895 until 1985. To get there, head 1.3 miles north of town on Hwy-61, then 2 miles northeast following good signs.

In Merriman, a block south of US-20, a roadside display shows the many different cattle brands used by Sand Hills ranches.

MT. RUSHMORE, CRAZY HORSE, AND CARHENGE

Three of the nation's most distinctive outdoor sculptures stand along US-385 within a manageable drive from US-20. One is perhaps the best-known artwork in the United States: the giant presidential memorial at **Mt. Rushmore.** Roughly 100 miles north from Chadron, at the far eastern side of the beautiful Black Hills, Mt. Rushmore is graced by the 60-foot heads of four U.S. Presidents—Washington, Jefferson, Lincoln, and Teddy Roosevelt—carved into a granite peak. It's equal parts impressive monument and kitschy Americana, and one of those places you really have to see to believe.

On the way to Mt. Rushmore, be sure to stop and see the ambitious **Crazy Horse Memorial,** the world's largest work-in-progress, along US-385 five miles north of Custer, South Dakota. When completed, Crazy Horse will be 563 feet tall and 641 feet long—10 times the size of Mt. Rushmore. For now, it's worth a visit for the panoramic views over the Black Hills.

Another newer, less-famous monument to America sits in a flat field off US-385, outside the town of Alliance, 55 miles south of Chadron. Built in 1987 as part of a local family reunion, **Carhenge** is a giant replica of the famous ruins of Stonehenge; this one, however, is built entirely out of three dozen American cars, stacked on top of one another to form a semicircular temple.

Between Merriman and Valentine, US-20 passes through flyspeck former railroad towns including Kilgore (pop. 79), Crookston (pop. 71), and Cody (pop. 157). Kilgore marks the dividing line between central and mountain time zones; adjust your clocks and watches accordingly.

Johnstown

In the village of **Johnstown** (pop. 61), 35 miles southeast of Valentine and 10 miles west of Ainsworth, a block of wooden storefronts and boardwalks was gussied up as a backdrop for a TV production of Willa Cather's *O Pioneers!* Behind the contrived facades you'll find a dusty old general store and a beer bar and pool hall complete with a backyard privy.

Off Norden Road, 17 miles north of Johnstown, the Nature Conservancy protects the nearly 56,000-acre **Niobrara Valley Preserve** (402/722-4440), which has

Valentine marks the junction of the Oregon Trail with US-83, **The Road to Nowhere** (see page 192). Full coverage of this route begins on page 168.

both sand hills and riparian ecosystems stretching west to the Niobrara reserve on the outskirts of Valentine. Self-guided trails wind through the preserve past a slowly expanding herd of some 500 bison, and early spring sees the annual migration of sandhill cranes, some 500,000 of whom rest here and at sites along the North Platte River before continuing north to Canada.

Nearly completed after decades of negotiation and hard labor, the 321-mile-long **Cowboy Trail** is the nation's longest rail-to-trail conversion, following the crushed gravel bed of the old Chicago and Northwestern Railroad along US-20 almost all the way across northern Nebraska, with especially nice sections around Valentine.

Ainsworth

Roughly the midway point of US-20's long cruise across Nebraska, **Ainsworth** (pop. 1,635) has something of an identity problem, if its slogans ("Welcome to the Middle of Nowhere" and "Where the Sandhills Meet the Niobrara") are any guide. Ainsworth also calls itself the state's "Country Music Capital" and hosts a popular concert and festival in early August. Ainsworth's **Middle of Nowhere Festival,** held in June, is celebrated with a Main Street parade, a Wild West-style trail ride, and a black-powder rendezvous—where living-history fans reenact the muzzle-loading, fur-trapping frontier era. Whenever you come, eat big burgers at **Big John's Restaurant** (1110 E. 4th St., 402/387-0500), along US-20.

windmills in Ainsworth

O'Neill

East of Ainsworth, US-20 runs through an especially scenic section of the Sand Hills around the artsy hamlet of Bassett before following the Elkhorn River 66 miles downstream to the town of **O'Neill** (pop. 3,663). Nebraska's official "Irish Capital," O'Neill hosts a popular St. Patrick's Day parade and celebration (the town paints shamrocks on the side of the police station and at the intersection of US-20 and US-281). It also has a fascinating history: The town was founded in 1880 by Irish settlers led by John O'Neill, who commanded a brigade of black infantrymen during the Civil War and afterward became involved in the Fenian raids on still-British Canada.

Northeast Nebraska

Because it's a fascinating part of the country, fairly detailed coverage has been directed at the places along US-20 across most of northern Nebraska. The same cannot be said of Nebraska's far northeast quarter, but there are a couple of interesting detours.

Six miles north of US-20 via Hwy-59, from a well-signed junction two miles west of the tiny village of Royal (pop. 60), you can watch paleontologists at work uncovering giant fossils at **Ashfall Fossil Beds State Historical Park** (402/893-2000, daily May-Oct., $7 entry plus $6 per day Nebraska Park permit). Unusual for a fossil bed, the skeletons here are preserved completely intact because the original residents—including prehistoric herds of rhinoceros, camels, and saber-toothed deer—got caught in a volcanic eruption some 12 million years ago. Since the bones haven't been disturbed, you can get a clear sense of the creatures' size and the sheer numbers of their populations around a prehistoric watering hole.

If you want to learn more about the fascinating human histories and cultures of the Great Plains, head south of US-20 across the Winnebago and Omaha Indian Reservations to the tiny town of **Bancroft,** where the **John G. Neihardt Center** (888/777-4667 or 402/648-3388, daily, free) exhibits the personal collection of Nebraska's poet laureate and writer of the Native American classic *Black Elk Speaks.*

IOWA

US-20 cuts straight across the midsection of Iowa between the Missouri and the Mississippi Rivers, running along the invisible border that divides the flat agricultural tableland that distinguishes the northern half of the state from the more heavily industrialized south. The first industry here was lead mining in the 1840s, but the predominant activity these days is livestock raising. Cows and pigs feed on the abundant corn that grows in fields all along the highway. Popcorn is also a major crop.

More than on any other section of its cross-country trek, US-20 across Iowa has been "upgraded" into a fast four-lane freeway, so you may well want to consider alternative routes like old US-30, which preserves some fine stretches of the historic **Lincoln Highway,** the country's first transcontinental road.

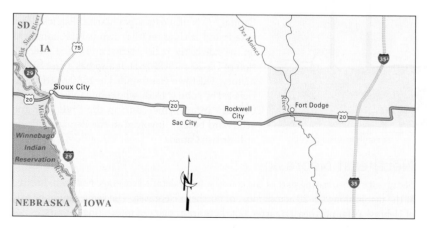

Sioux City

The honey-producing and hog-butchering center of **Sioux City** (pop. 82,872) is not most people's idea of a vacation treat, but it does offer a few diversions to the road-tripping traveler. Grain elevators and huge brick warehouses fill the riverfront district, an immaculately restored City Hall dominates downtown, and the gorgeous brick and glass-block **Sioux City Art Center** (225 Nebraska St., 712/279-6272, Tues.-Sun., free) includes pieces by Grant Wood, Salvador Dalí, David Hockney, and James McNeill Whistler. Downtown Sioux City has recently been enhanced by the move here of the **Sioux City Public Museum** (607 4th St., 712/279-6174, Tues.-Sun., free), which fills a nicely converted former JCPenney store with comprehensive and engaging displays tracing the Native American, pioneer, and agricultural histories of the area.

Lewis and Clark buffs will also want to stop south of Sioux City at the **Sergeant Floyd Monument Historical Marker,** where a 100-foot stone obelisk marks the place where expedition member Sgt. Charles Floyd—the Corps of Discovery's only fatality—died

> Over 90 percent of Iowa is cultivated farmland—the highest percentage of any U.S. state.

of appendicitis in August 1804, two months after setting off from St. Louis. Besides the historical homage, the site offers a great panorama of the Missouri River. Fact collectors might want to know that this little-known marker was the first official National Historic Landmark in the United States. The nearby **Interpretive Center** (daily, free), built in 2002 to honor the 200th anniversary of Lewis and Clark, offers an excellent introduction to the fascinating story of the expedition.

Sioux City Practicalities

Part of the general renaissance of midsize American downtowns, the newly renovated two-block section of Sioux City known as **Fourth Street Historic District,** just east of the railroad yards around the intersection of 4th and Court Streets, boasts a

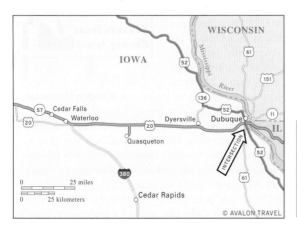

Sioux City's unaffiliated American Association baseball team, the **Explorers,** plays throughout the summer in modern **Lewis & Clark Park** (712/277-9467, $6-12). Games are broadcast on **KSCJ 1360 AM.**

Sioux City's favorite daughters were the identical twin sisters and rival advice columnists Ann Landers and Abigail "Dear Abby" Van Buren.

large selection of restaurants, brewpubs, live-music clubs, and specialty shops in a restored commercial district built between 1889 and 1915, many in the Richardson Romanesque style. Just south of historic 4th Street, dine on delicious hot dogs at the beloved **Milwaukee Wiener House** (301 Douglas St., 712/277-3449). The best in-town lodging option is probably the pleasant, clean, and modern **Stoney Creek Hotel** (300 3rd St., 712/234-1100, $90 and up). The usual chains line the I-29 exits north and south of town, and there is also the chance to get lucky at the **Hard Rock Hotel Casino** (111 3rd St., 712/226-7600, $150 and up).

Sergeant Floyd Monument in Sioux City

Sac City and Rockwell City

East of Sioux City, US-20 is pretty much a four-lane freeway all the way, racing past acres of farmland and occasional towns. **Sac City** (pop. 2,105) is one of the few places along this stretch where the road is still old-school two-lane, and the town itself seems to want to preserve its past, with a log cabin and preserved Chautauqua Building along US-20 and a small historical museum on Main Street. It also has the nicely maintained **Sac City Motel** (103 Ash Ave., 712/662-7109), right off Main Street.

Nineteen miles farther east, in **Rockwell City** (pop. 2,137, "The Golden Buckle on the Corn Belt"), the **Leist Oil Company** (705 High St., 712/297-8631) has an incredible collection of old neon and enameled metal roadside signs advertising cars, car parts, soda pop, and sundry other things. Downtown also has a Carnegie Library, a railroad station, and some nifty little shops, well worth a few minutes of wandering.

Fort Dodge

Founded in 1850 to protect settlers from Sauk and Black Hawk people, **Fort Dodge** (pop. 24,441) is today a sleepy Midwestern town, economically dependent on local farms, gypsum wallboard plants, and a huge Friskies cat food factory. Amid many stately homes on

the south side of downtown, one place really worth a look is the **Blanden Memorial Art Museum** (920 3rd Ave. S., 515/573-2316, Tues.-Sat., free). Housed inside a grand neoclassical 1930s building, the collections of "Iowa's Oldest Museum" include examples of pre-Columbian pottery, Renaissance sculpture, and Japanese prints. Modern paintings include works by people you wouldn't expect to find in the middle of the Midwest—Max Beckmann, Marc Chagall, and Rufino Tamayo, to name three—along with works by Grant Wood and other Iowa artists.

The famous **Cardiff Giant,** a 10-foot-tall "petrified man" supposedly unearthed in New York in 1869, was thought by experts to be the body of a prehistoric man.

You've kept up with the Joneses —

You've been in Jones County!

However, the figure, which was kept on prominent display by showman P. T. Barnum for the next 35 years, was later proven to be a hoax, carved from a slab of gypsum quarried at Fort Dodge. A duplicate is on display at the **Fort Museum and Frontier Village** (515/573-4231, daily May-mid-Oct., $7) along US-20 on the southwest edge of town.

Cedar Falls and Waterloo

For the eastern half of its run across Iowa, US-20 has been "upgraded" to fast four-lane freeway most of the way between Dubuque and **Cedar Falls,** a historic industrial town founded in 1845 along the Cedar River. Now home to the University of Northern Iowa, Cedar Falls (pop. 41,390) preserves the remnants of its manufacturing heritage and has a lively collection of pubs and bistros tucked away along the cobbled streets of its tidy six-block downtown. For die-hard road-food types, there is a vintage **Maid-Rite Diner** (116 E. 4th St., 319/277-9748), serving up classic Iowa-style "loose meat sandwiches" in the small industrial section of downtown "CF." Also good, and one of the key forces driving the reawakening of downtown Cedar Falls, is a 1950s-style chrome diner at the heart of downtown: the **Cup of Joe** (102 Main St., 319/277-1596), whose strong coffee is guaranteed to revive even the most exhausted road-tripper.

For a place to stay in the historic core of Cedar Falls, check out the lovely **Blackhawk Hotel** (115 Main St., 319/277-1161, $129 and up), which has a great lobby and oodles of charm.

Downstream from Cedar Falls, and similarly bypassed by the modern US-20 freeway, **Waterloo** (pop. 37,934) is a bigger and busier city, with an almost urban feel and an unexpected ethnic diversity, thanks in particular to the estimated 3,500 Bosnian Muslim refugees who were resettled here by the U.S. government after escaping the genocidal 1990s wars in the Balkans. Waterloo also has a good museum, the **Grout Museum of History and Science** (503 South St., 319/234-6357, Tues.-Sat., $10). Despite the name, it's a general science and history museum—not a collection of great tile-setting materials!

Though it now employs less than half the 25,000 workers it did at its 1960s peak, Waterloo is also home to a massive **John Deere Tractor assembly plant** (3500 E. Donald St., 319/292-7668 or 888/453-5804, Mon.-Fri.) on the outskirts of town. The plant is open for free tours and has a small shop where you can stock up on their trademark caps and souvenirs.

Waterloo is worth a look if you can be here on Memorial Day weekend, when vintage car enthusiasts from around the Midwest participate in the **Fourth Street Cruise.**

Memorial Day is especially significant in Waterloo, since this was the hometown of the "fighting Sullivan brothers," five young men who were all killed at the World War II Battle of Guadalcanal. The U.S. Navy has named a series of ships after them.

Quasqueton: Cedar Rock

Midway between Waterloo and Dyersville, the tiny town of **Quasqueton** (pop. 544) holds **Cedar Rock,** a wonderful riverside house completed in 1950 by architect Frank Lloyd Wright for local-boy-done-good businessman Lowell Walter, who got rich by developing and patenting a method of sealing highway surfaces. Walter died in 1981, and his wife, Agnes, donated it to the state. It is now a state park. Cedar Rock is one of 10 houses Wright built in Iowa, and one of only 17 of the 1,000-plus houses

THE LINCOLN HIGHWAY IN IOWA

Iowa may not be near the top of everybody's vacation bucket list, but fans of old highways are in for a treat here: The state has some of the best-preserved remnants of the nation's first cross-country route, the Lincoln Highway. Running between New York and San Francisco, the Lincoln Highway was the main transcontinental road from its opening in 1915 until 1927, when it was converted to the less-inspiring US-30, which, improvements notwithstanding, it still is today. Much of the original alignment survives, especially in small towns, and the old road makes a fascinating alternative across the state.

Thanks to its many dedicated devotees, the old route is well-marked all across Iowa—just keep an eye out for the red, white, and blue markers, and the giant "L." Two of the many evocative sites on the Lincoln Highway in Iowa are in the midsection, between Ames and Cedar Rapids. The city of **Belle Plaine** (pop. 2,454), for example, has hardly changed since its 1915 heyday. In the town of **Tama** (pop. 2,803), a historic bridge with the words *Lincoln Highway* spelled out in the concrete guardrails has been preserved as a riverside park, on 5th Street, a block west of the US-30 bypass.

Wright built that he signed with a signature tile. Cedar Rock is an excellent and complete example of his "Usonian" ideals, and everything in the house—from the soaring roof, the smooth flow of interior space, and the signature hearth, right down to the designs of the carpets and cutlery—embodies Wright's idealized vision of middle-class American houses, designed for simple and stylish living in close accord with nature.

Carved into a limestone ridge overlooking a bend in the Wapsipinicon River, Cedar Rock is five miles south of US-20 and surrounded by acres of rolling woodland. The house and grounds are now owned and managed by the state of Iowa and are open for **guided tours** (319/934-3572, Thurs.-Sun. summer only, $5).

Dyersville: The Field of Dreams

"If you build it, they will come. . . . " Ever since *Field of Dreams* came out in 1989, as many as 100,000 people have flocked each year to **Dyersville** (27 miles west of Dubuque) to reenact the fairy-tale baseball movie, major scenes from which were filmed just outside of town. Acres of cornfield surround the diamond, where people can play for free. The privately owned **Field of Dreams Movie Site** (28995 Lansing Rd., 888/875-8404, field tours daily Apr.-Oct., home tours daily) was thoroughly upgraded to celebrate the film's 25th Anniversary in 2014. To get here, take Hwy-136 north from US-20, then follow signs northeast along 3rd Avenue and Field of Dreams Road for about 3.5 miles from US-20. "Is this heaven? No, it's Iowa."

Field of Dreams Movie Site

Considering it's such a small town, Dyersville has a lot in store. It boasts one of only a handful of Roman Catholic basilicas in the United States (St. Francis Xavier, that can't-miss Gothic pile in the center of town). The **National Farm Toy Museum** (1110 16th Ave., 563/875-2727, daily, $5), right off US-20, has over 30,000 miniature tractors and plows showcasing 100 years of toys—from horse-drawn wooden ones to die-cast modern ones—many of them made here in Dyersville by the Ertl Toy Company, which has moved most of its operations overseas.

Dubuque (see page 245) marks the junction with our road trip along **The Great River Road.** Full coverage of this route begins on page 224.

ILLINOIS

ILLINOIS

US-20 angles across northern Illinois from the Mississippi River to Lake Michigan, bringing you from the unglaciated scenery of the Driftless Region to the towering city of **Chicago** in less than 200 miles. The western stretches pass through hill-and-valley regions where water power and mineral deposits were harnessed by early industry. Especially around **Galena,** the old two-lane road is still in use, climbing onto stony ridges, then dropping into hardwood-forested valleys across the undulating region that stretches east from the Iowa border. This stretch of old road, officially named and signed as the General Grant Highway, has as great a variety of barns and grain bins as anywhere in the country. However, there's considerable pressure to widen and "improve" it into a four-lane freeway, so enjoy it while you can.

Galena

If ever there's a place where you can truly step back in time, **Galena** (pop. 3,255) is it: Pass through the floodgates that protect the town from the namesake river (and the US-20 highway), and it's like entering Brigadoon. Spawned by Wisconsin's mid-19th-century lead-mining rush, Galena became the social and cultural capital of the Upper Mississippi basin. In the 1840s, while Chicago was still a mean collection of tents in a swamp around Fort Dearborn, and the Twin Cities were but a trading post in the woods around Fort Snelling, Galena was producing upward of 75 percent of the world's lead,

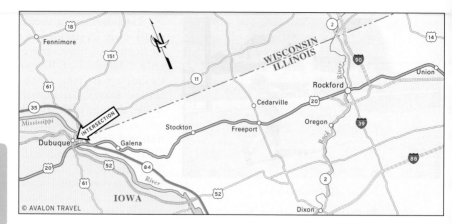

and the town was filled with bankers, merchants, and speculators who built mansions, hotels, and emporiums stuffed with fine goods and furnishings from around the world. This part of the Driftless Region saw some of the greatest wealth and commerce of the upper Mississippi, with Galena alone higher in population—some 15,000 lived here during the Civil War—than the entire Minnesota Territory.

But the California gold rush, played-out lead mines, a river silting up from miner-induced erosion, and a national economic panic all drove Galena to become a handsome ghost town that nobody bothered to tear down. For 100 years it slumbered, but beginning in the 1980s Galena was resurrected as a quaint tourist town. The brick warehouses were converted into shops and galleries, and anything but the most subtle, hand-carved signage

Commander of the Union Army and President of the United States
1822 - 1885

was banned: In Galena, preserving the historical complexion of the streetscape isn't just a good idea, it's the law. The outskirts, especially along the US-20 frontage, are fairly typical roadside sprawl, and there are still a few everyday businesses in the historic core (including a funeral parlor and a large and busy metal foundry), but the overall feel is of a long-ago era. Even the innumerable galleries and shops selling T-shirts and "collectibles" can't spoil the remarkable effect of the place. One essential: Park the car and *stroll*.

Besides the integrity of its mid-19th century buildings, Galena is famous as the town that saw a local store clerk win both the Civil War and the presidency. The modest **Ulysses S. Grant Home** (815/777-3310, 9am-4:45pm Wed.-Sun. except major holidays, $5) sits up Bouthillier Street in a quiet residential neighborhood across the river from downtown. Given to the general by a grateful group of local Republicans, the house is now a state historic site restored to the period immediately preceding Grant's move to the White House. A small museum behind the house traces Grant's life, from the Civil War to the presidency to his burial in Grant's Tomb.

From the end of November to the beginning of March, the American bald eagle nests along the middle and upper Mississippi. The best place to catch sight of one is below any of the dams, where turbulence keeps the river from icing over and fish injured or stunned by the dams make easy prey for the great bird.

common blue violet,
state flower of Illinois

Galena Practicalities

Even if you're somehow blind to Galena's manifold aesthetic and historical delights, you'll probably enjoy its wide variety of food and lodging options. Unless you're fortunate enough to be staying at one of Galena's many B&Bs, the best choice for a good breakfast comes down to the **Victory Café** (200 N. Main St., 815/777-4407). Downtown also has at least one place for a reliably good and always cheerful dinner: the **Log Cabin** (201 N. Main St., 815/777-0393). Galena's oldest restaurant, with a great big green-and-red sign that predates the town's anti-neon ordinance, the Log Cabin is also known as "The House of Plenty" and has been serving up great steaks and a mix of industrial-strength Greco-Italian food since 1937. Galena also has a pair of great pizza places: **Cannova's** (247 N. Main St., 815/777-3735) and **Procento's** (105 Franklin St., 815/777-1640).

There are some 60-odd hotels, guest homes, and historic inns here in "the B&B capital of the Midwest." The central **DeSoto House** (230 S. Main St., 815/777-0090 or 800/343-6562, $140 and up) was Ulysses S. Grant's headquarters during his 1868 presidential campaign; the entire place was tastefully modernized during an $7.8 million renovation back in 1986. Smaller and perhaps more relaxing, the friendly **Farmers Guest House** (334 Spring St., 815/777-3456, $165 and up) is also right downtown. If you're just passing through, the cheapest decent sleep is at the friendly and affordable **Grant Hills Motel** (9372 E. US-20, 815/777-2116 or 877/421-0924, $69 and up) east of town.

The Galena-Jo Daviess County Convention and Visitors Bureau operates an excellent **visitors center** (815/777-3557 or 800/747-9377), across the river via a pedestrian-only bridge, in the old Illinois Central Railroad depot at the base of Bouthillier Street. Stacks of brochures cover everything from accommodations to bike tours. This is also the best place to park the car, as spaces are at a premium in the often-crowded downtown area.

Galena is also a part of our **Great River Road** trip. Full coverage of this journey along the mighty Mississippi begins on page 224.

Freeport

Midway between Galena and Rockford, the oddly named town of **Freeport** (pop. 24,392) is neither a port nor even near any body of water. According to the WPA *Guide to Illinois,* the name was bestowed by Elizabeth Baker, the wife of the community's founder, William "Tutty" Baker, to satirize his fondness for providing free river ferry passage and even free room and board to passersby.

There's no free lunch here today, but Freeport does offer at least one good reason to stop: The **Alber Ice Cream Parlor at the Union Dairy** (126 E. Douglas St., 815/232-7099), two blocks north of the US-20 Business Loop, has been serving ice cream since 1914. In the small park next door, an oddly distorted statue marks the site of the second **Lincoln-Douglas debate,** held here on August 27, 1858. A plaque quotes both men equally, with Lincoln's "This government cannot endure permanently half-slave and half-free" opposing Douglas saying, "I am not for the dissolution of the Union under any circumstance."

Rockford

Spreading haphazardly along the leafy banks of the Rock River, **Rockford** (pop. 147,651) is a big, somewhat sprawling postindustrial city five miles west of the busy I-90 toll road from Chicago. US-20 bypasses the down-at-heel downtown area that, if the denizens wore more hats, would look like a film set on Main Street of industrial America circa 1949. Unfortunately, many of the classy office buildings and storefronts here have been abandoned in favor of anonymous office parks and shopping malls closer to the I-90 corridor.

North of downtown, along the west bank of the river and away from the frantic highways, one great place to check out (especially if you have creature-loving youngsters with you!) is the **Burpee Museum of Natural History** (737 N. Main St., 815/965-3433, Tues.-Sun., $10), where an entire floor of paleontology exhibits is highlighted by the skeleton of a 21-foot-tall, 65-million-year-old T. rex called "Jane."

a Thescelosaurus at the Burpee Museum of Natural History

Further north along the riverside, if the weather is nice, take time to stretch your legs while exploring the manicured grounds of **Anderson Japanese Gardens** (318 Spring St., 815/229-9390, daily, $9.50).

After exploring Rockford's nooks and crannies, reward yourself with lunch or dinner at one of Illinois's great road-food haunts, **Der Rathskeller** (1132 Auburn St., 815/963-2922), off Main Street a mile north of downtown Rockford. Since 1931, this Teutonic institution has been serving up skillets of sausage and potatoes, corned beef sandwiches, good desserts, and live accordion music on weekends! For something a bit more light and contemporary, taste your way through the tapas-style small dishes at **Abreo** (515 E. State St., 815/968-9463). If you're in the mood for something hoppy, malty, and liquid, try the **Carlyle Brewing** pub (215 E. State St., 815/963-2739).

Rockford has lots of places to stay, from all the main chains along the interstate to old US-20's **Alpine Inn** (4404 E. State St., 815/399-1890, $50 and up), a still-thriving icon of kitschy 1950s roadside Americana.

The transnational corporation Kraft Foods got its start in **Stockton, Illinois,** and thanks to the three large cheese plants along US-20. Illinois is the top-ranked Swiss cheese producer in the United States.

Dixon and the Rock River

If you have the time, Hwy-2 follows a lovely route from Rockford along the Rock River southwest to the quaint old town of **Dixon,** where the **Ronald Reagan Boyhood Home** (816 S. Hennepin Ave., 815/288-5176, $5) preserves the house where in the early 1920s the late "Great Communicator" (1911-2004) spent his preteen years. Midway between Rockford and Dixon, in Lowden State Park, a rather majestic Eternal Indian statue inspired by the great chief Black Hawk stands high above the river outside the town of Oregon.

Ronald Reagan in Dixon, 1922

Union: Illinois Railway Museum

Between Rockford and Chicago, US-20 is a slow, winding, and poorly signposted alternative to the high-speed I-90/Jane Addams Memorial Tollway. It's a leisurely route, with few identifiable attractions except for the road itself, which cruises through small towns surrounded by farmlands and lined by fruit-and-vegetable stands. The one real draw here is a mile east of the tiny town of **Union** (pop. 562), where the sprawling **Illinois Railway Museum** (815/923-4000, daily, $10 and up) displays the country's widest range of track-based transportation: streetcars, interurban trolleys, and railroad cars, with historic engines running weekends throughout the year.

Chicago

New York may have bigger and better museums, shops, and restaurants, and even Los Angeles has more people, but Chicago is still the most all-American city, and one of the most exciting and enjoyable places to visit in the world. After shrinking for decades as its suburbs grew and grew, Chicago seems to have stabilized. The city reinvents and reinvests in itself, with new parks, art galleries, and condo towers, as a new generation discovers the pleasures of urban life. Commerce capital of Middle America, Chicago's location at the crossroads between the settled East and the wide-open West has helped it to give birth to many new things we now take for granted: the skyscraper, the blues, and the atomic bomb (not to mention Oprah and Obama!).

Michigan Avenue Bridge
and skyscrapers

Away from the Loop, the skyscraper-spiked lakefront business district that holds North America's tallest and most impressive collection of modern architecture in its oblong square mile, much of Chicago is surprisingly low-rise and residential. Also surprising, considering its inland location, is that Chicago has a high percentage of immigrants—nearly 200,000 Poles form one of the largest communities outside Poland, and Hispanics constitute nearly 29 percent of Chicago's population of close to three million—with a multiethnic character readily apparent in numerous enclaves all over the city. Whatever their origin, however, residents take a particular pride in identifying themselves as Chicagoans, and despite the city's rusting infrastructure, their good-natured enthusiasm for the place can be contagious.

For an unbeatable introduction to Chicago, hop aboard a river cruise offered by the **Chicago Architecture Foundation** (312/922-8687, daily Apr.-Nov., $46). Departing from where the Michigan Avenue Bridge crosses the river and Wacker Drive, these informative and enjoyable tours offer an unusual look up at the city's magnificent towers. If you can't join a tour, enjoy the **RiverWalk** park and promenade, which fronts the river on both sides of the bridge. North from the river, the "Magnificent Mile" of Michigan Avenue is a bustling shopping strip that holds yet more distinctive towers, along with many of the city's top shops, restaurants, and hotels. Starting with the Gothic-style Tribune Tower—decorated with bits of famous buildings and monuments stolen by *Tribune* staffers from around the globe—and running past the circa-1869 Historic Water Tower at its midpoint, the "Mag Mile" ends in the north with the 100-story John Hancock Center.

Along the lakefront at the heart of downtown, the **Art Institute of Chicago** (111 S. Michigan Ave., 312/443-3600, $25) boasts one of the world's great collections of 19th- and 20th-century French painting and a broad survey of fine art from all over the world. Among its many fine paintings, the institute gives pride of place to Grant Wood's *American Gothic,* which he painted as a student and sold to the institute for $300. North and east of the museum's beautiful Modern Wing is Chicago's latest great claim to fame: **Millennium Park,** a 25-acre public garden full of fabulous sculptures and a magical Frank Gehry-designed outdoor concert pavilion that's home to numerous summer concerts and events.

More than just another baseball game, watching the **Chicago Cubs** play at **Wrigley Field** (1060 Addison St., 773/404-2827) is a rite of passage that taps into the deepest meanings of the national pastime. Ivy covers the redbrick outfield walls, and Chicagoans of all stripes were relieved to exorcise a century-long curse with a 2016 World Series win. The other Chicago baseball team, the **White Sox,** play at modern **Guaranteed Rate Field** (333 W. 35th St., 312/674-1000), south of the Loop alongside I-94.

PRACTICALITIES

Chicago is home to one of America's busiest and most infuriating airports, O'Hare (ORD), 17 miles northwest of the Loop and well served by Chicago Transit Authority (CTA) subway trains, shuttle services, and taxis. Chicago's other airport, Midway, is closer to the center of town, and Chicago is also the hub of the national Amtrak system, with trains pulling in to Union Station from all over the country. To get around, you're better off leaving the car behind and riding the CTA elevated train—better known as the "L"—which serves the entire city almost around the clock.

Chicago has all sorts of top-quality, cutting-edge-cuisine restaurants, but to get a feel for the city, you'll be better off stopping at the many older places that have

catered to Chicagoans forever. Near the start of old Route 66, **Lou Mitchell's** (565 W. Jackson Blvd., 312/939-3111) is one of the greatest breakfast and lunch places on the planet. Along with deep-dish pizza (as served at Uno's, Pizzeria Due, etc.), hot dogs, a.k.a. red hots, a.k.a. Polish sausages, are a real Chicago specialty that can be sampled at a dozen world-class spots. Try them at **Jim's Original** (1250 S. Union Ave., 312/733-7820, daily 24 hours), just west of the I-90 Dan Ryan Expressway. Farther from downtown, toward O'Hare, there's **Superdawg Drive-In** (6363 N. Milwaukee Ave., 773/763-0660), where you can soak up the 1940s character.

Places to stay in Chicago include the moderate likes of the **Best Western River North** (125 W. Ohio St., 312/467-0800, $189 and up), in the trendy River North gallery district, which offers free parking within a quick walk of the Magnificent Mile along Michigan Avenue. Chicago's classiest older hotel is the **Drake Hotel** (140 E. Walton Place, 312/787-2200, $269 and up), just off the lake, with elegant public areas and gracious staff. Even if you only soak up the exuberant 1920s Moorish-style lobby, or go for a swim in the palatial 14th-floor pool, the most fabulous place to stay could be the **InterContinental** (505 N. Michigan Ave., 312/944-4100, $180 and up), though the smallish rooms expose the truth that the building started life as a Shriner's health club.

The small town of **Woodstock,** 10 miles northeast of Union, stood in for the Pennsylvania town of Punxsutawney in my favorite Bill Murray movie, *Groundhog Day.*

Oak Park

Running parallel to and south of the I-90 Northwest Tollway, old US-20 approaches Chicago from the northwest past Schaumberg and O'Hare Airport before bending south near **Oak Park** (pop. 51,774), Chicago's most interesting suburb. Just 10 miles west of the Loop, easily reachable at the end of the Lake-Dan Ryan CTA "L" line, this sleepy but well-heeled neighborhood was the boyhood home of Ernest Hemingway, and before that Oak Park was the home and proving ground of America's best-known architect, Frank Lloyd Wright. Visit the **Frank Lloyd Wright Home and Studio** (951 Chicago Ave., 312/994-4000, daily, $18) for a fascinating look into the life and work of the great architect. Take a guided tour of the house he designed, remodeling almost constantly between 1889 and 1909 as his practice, and his family, grew. He also completed many other buildings in this turn-of-the-20th-century suburb, including the austere classic Unity Temple.

Oak Park has good transit connections to Chicago and makes a pretty good alternative base, thanks to the **Harvey House B&B** (107 S. Scoville Ave., 708/848-6810, $199 and up), which is no relation to the famous 1920s railroad hotels but offers comfortable rooms within walking distance of Frank Lloyd Wright's Unity Temple and the Oak Park CTA "L" station.

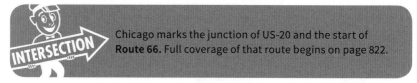

Chicago marks the junction of US-20 and the start of **Route 66.** Full coverage of that route begins on page 822.

US-20 Across Chicago

From Oak Park, US-20—which somehow has managed not to be diverted onto one of Chicago's many freeways—crosses the Des Plaines River and the Chicago Sanitary and Ship Canal, then bends east onto 95th Street, following that road all the way across Chicago to the Lake Michigan waterfront. East of downtown, US-20 bends south along Lake Michigan into Hammond, Indiana, and the industrial districts along the Calumet River.

INDIANA

So close and yet so far away from the excitement of Chicago, northern Indiana can't help but seem a little bit boring. In the northwest, the state is bounded by Lake Michigan, along whose shores Rust Belt hulks of derelict heavy industry stand side by side with the pristine sands of the fascinating and beautiful **Indiana Dunes National Lakeshore.** The northeastern corner, even in the estimation of the state tourist office, offers little more than a few lakes and the so-called "muck lands" around the Fighting Irish homeland of Notre Dame University at **South Bend.** In between stretch endless acres of rolling farmland, Amish homes, and

DETOUR: INDIANAPOLIS

Before Detroit came to dominate the industry, **Indianapolis**, a 2.5-hour drive south of South Bend, was an early center of American automobile manufacturing, home to such classy marques as Stutz, Marmon, and Duesenberg, and of course the Indianapolis 500, perhaps the most famous car race in the world. Held the Sunday before Memorial Day almost every year since 1911, the Indianapolis 500 is still the biggest thing in town, drawing upward of a half million spectators to "The Brickyard," the oldest racetrack in the country. The rest of the year, the speedway is open for tours ($30), on a bus that cruises around the legendary 2.5-mile oval. Tours leave from the excellent **Indianapolis Motor Speedway Hall of Fame Museum** (4790 W. 16th St., 317/492-6784, daily, $10), which displays some 75 racing cars, from the Marmon "Wasp," which won the inaugural **Indy 500** race, to the latest Indy champions. The museum is located on the speedway grounds at in the city of **Speedway** (pop. 12,102), an enclave in the northwest quarter of Indianapolis's pancake-flat sprawl.

1911: the first Indy 500

other tourist-attractive agricultural communities, as well as some of the most important sites in early American automotive history: the homes of Studebaker, Cord, Duesenberg, and other now-defunct car companies.

Gary

If you ever watched and enjoyed the Hollywood musical *The Music Man*—in which the song "Gary, Indiana" paints a picture of idyllic homespun Americana—you'll be surprised by the reality of the place. In contrast to the rural rest of the state, this far northwest corner of Indiana is among the most heavily industrialized and impoverished areas of the country. Developed beginning in 1910 around a huge U.S. Steel mill (the largest in the world for much of the 20th century, and still the biggest in North America), **Gary** (pop. 76,424, down from a circa-1960 peak of 178,320) epitomizes the boom and bust cycle of the single industry "company town." Surrounded by block after block of decaying houses, the streets are lined by empty strip malls, strip clubs, and stripped-down cars—with road signs directing you toward the waterfront casinos along the Calumet River. During the region's heyday around the middle of the 20th century, the Gary mill employed more than 30,000 workers and pumped out millions of dollars' worth of products every day. The town's more recent products include musical family The Jackson 5, born and raised here in the late 1950s, but nowadays half the homes have been abandoned and economic times are so hard that local authorities have had to call in the National Guard to police the streets.

One bright spot: Gary's steel heritage is kept alive by the local Northern League baseball team, the **RailCats** (219/882-2255, $6-10), who play at **U.S. Steel Yard.** The outfield fences back onto US-20 and the tracks of the South Shore Line, America's oldest inter-urban streetcar system, creating a slightly surreal view. Trains from Gary to Chicago's Millennium Station take about an hour and cost $6.

Indiana Dunes National Lakeshore

Covering 15,000 acres along 15 miles of Lake Michigan shoreline, 25 miles or so east of Chicago, **Indiana Dunes National Lakeshore** is a striking and surprising collection of golden sand dunes, freshwater beaches, and dense forests. Chicago poet Carl Sandburg said the dunes "are to the Midwest what the Grand Canyon is to Arizona." Dedicated in 1972, the park includes a huge variety of plantlife— groves of maples and red oaks, pine trees and prickly pear cactus, grasslands and berry bushes—linked by many miles of hiking trails and highlighted by

Indiana Dunes National Lakeshore

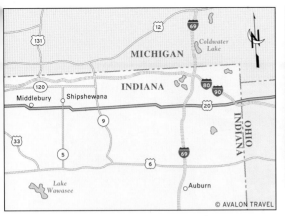

peony,
state flower of Indiana

126-foot Mt. Baldy at the far northeast corner of the park. When the weather cooperates, you can see the skyline of Chicago shimmering across Lake Michigan like the Emerald City in the Land of Oz.

Huge steel mills and a number of small vacation home communities share space among the dunes. Also here, two miles northeast of the main visitors center, is the unusual **Beverly Shores,** a model community constructed for the "Century of Progress" World's Fair in Chicago in 1933 and reassembled here soon after in an attempt to attract buyers to a new resort community. Six of these then-futuristic structures survive along Lakefront Drive, including three steel-framed, enamel-paneled "Lustron" houses, designed to provide low-cost housing during the Great Depression. Next door is the "House of Tomorrow," an ordinary-looking house designed with an additional garage to hold the private plane every future family was sure to have.

Pick up maps, guides, and other information at the **visitors center** (219/926-7561, daily, free) on Highway 49, midway between US-20 and I-94 exit 26.

South Bend

The largest city in Indiana's northern tier, **South Bend** (pop. 101,735) is probably best known as the home of the "Fighting Irish" of **Notre Dame University,** and home of the car- and carriage-making Studebaker Company. The Notre Dame campus is most visitors' destination, whether or not it's a Saturday during football season. The 1,250-acre campus, along Michigan Street a mile north of downtown, is worth a stroll to see its many Roman Catholic icons, including a replica of the grotto of Lourdes and the famous "Touchdown Jesus."

For fans of classic cars, the **Studebaker National Museum** (201 S. Chapin St., 888/391-5600 or 574/235-9714, daily, $8) is maybe the bigger draw, displaying a comprehensive survey of

Though its etymology sparks heated debates, the nickname "Hoosier" has come to connote all that is Middle American about Indianans—their independence, their practicality, and their thrift (or is it their cussedness, conservatism, and cheapness?).

The 5,000-seat **Four Winds Field** (574/235-9988) hosts Midwest League Class A baseball games of the **South Bend Cubs.** Tickets to see these potential Chicago Cubs cost $11-13. On "Belly Buster Mondays" they offer a place to sit plus an all-you-can-eat barrage of hot dogs, hamburgers, and popcorn for $15.

1953 Commander Starliner

horseless carriages, stylish cars, fire trucks, and other motor vehicles produced by the South Bend-based company before the factory closed in 1963.

One of South Bend's best restaurants, **Tippecanoe Place** (620 W. Washington St., 574/234-9077), is housed in the old Studebaker Mansion. One final piece of car culture history: Washington Street was part of the historic Lincoln Highway, which first crossed the USA in 1915.

Peru was the birthplace of songwriter Cole Porter, who is buried in the town's Mount Hope Cemetery.

The small town of **Peru,** on US-31 midway between South Bend and Indianapolis, was the home base of many traveling circuses during the mid-19th century, an era remembered in the **Circus City Museum** (154 N. Broadway, 765/472-3918), downtown.

Elkhart

A light industrial center, once famous for producing over half the brass-band instruments made in America, **Elkhart** was founded in the 1830s along the banks of the St. Joseph River and now makes RVs, Humvees, and pharmaceutical products. Drug giant Miles Laboratories was founded here in 1884 and still has a major presence as the American HQ of its parent company, Bayer. In many ways Elkhart is a quintessential sleepy Midwest town, with an abundance of pleasant parks lining the riverbanks and a historic downtown hosting the energetic little **Midwest Museum of American Art** (429 S. Main St., 574/293-6660, Tues.-Sun., $10). There's also an appreciation of the industrial heritage, on display at the **National New York Central Railroad Museum** (721 South Main St., 574/294-3001), where model train layouts and a number of full-size locomotives are displayed around what was once the largest rail yard east of the Mississippi River.

Northern Indiana is one of the country's main centers for the manufacture of recreational vehicles, so don't be surprised to find that Elkhart is home to the **RV/ MH Hall of Fame** (574/293-2344 or 800/378-8694, daily, $10), located east of Elkhart off I-90. If you like old machines, it's definitely worth an hour or more, if only for the chance to admire Mae West's deep blue 1930s Chevrolet Housecar, the

1950s "canned ham" trailers, the first Winnebago motor home (circa 1967), and the creativity and ingenuity of early handmade conversions.

Indiana's Amish Country: Middlebury and Shipshewana

East of South Bend, US-20 again becomes a road worth traveling, especially through the quiet agricultural expanses around the towns of **Middlebury** and **Shipshewana,** heartland of Indiana's sizable Amish population. As in other Amish areas, it's the general look of the land, rather than specific attractions, that make it enjoyable to visit; as elsewhere, the few attractions that offer an "authentic Amish experience" leave a lot to be desired. One of the largest tourist traps, the 1,100-seat **Das Dutchman Essenhaus,** offers groaning all-you-can-eat buffets at the west edge of Middlebury, but rather than fight your way through the bus-tour hordes, turn north here into the quiet town center and stop by the **Village Inn** (107 S. Main St., 574/825-2043). This perfect little country café is run by, and popular with, local Amish and Mennonites, who, along with everyone else, enjoy the hearty coffee-shop food—not to mention great handmade pies for around $3 a slice. If you need to work off the calories, head a block west of Main Street to walk the **Pumpkinvine Nature Trail,** an old railroad line transformed into an arboretum of fruit trees.

Back on US-20, seven miles east of Middlebury, Hwy-5 runs north just short of a mile to the intriguing **Menno-Hof Mennonite-Amish Visitor Center** (510 S. Van Buren St., 260/768-4117, Mon.-Sat., $7), outside the hamlet of Shipshewana. Operated by the local Amish and Mennonite communities, who built the large barn that houses the center during a six-day barn-raising, the center gives an overall introduction to the Amish and Mennonite beliefs and lifeways. Surprisingly high-tech multimedia exhibits also tell of their resistance to modern technology, their long struggle for religious freedom, and their love of peace, which has helped them through centuries of torture and abuse—so often, as in the "Dungeon Room" recreated here, at the hands of fellow Christians.

Ten miles or so south of Shipshewana via Hwy-5, the tiny town of **Topeka** holds the **Yoder Popcorn Shoppe** (800/892-2170 or 260/768-4051), one of many popcorn sellers whose signs you'll see all around this part of Indiana.

Auburn-Cord-Duesenberg Museum

Though it's a bit out of the way (20 miles or so south of US-20 via the I-69 freeway), lovers of vintage American cars will want to make the effort to visit the elegant **Auburn-Cord-Duesenberg Automobile Museum** (1600 S. Wayne St., 260/925-1444, daily, $12.50), in a lovely art deco showroom in the town of Auburn. Considered by

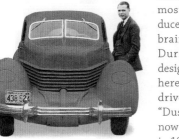

most aficionados the finest, most innovative, and most all-around gorgeous automobiles ever produced in America, these instant classics were the brainchild of Auburn industrialist Errett Cord. During the 1920s and 1930s, Cord's company designed and produced the covetable cruisers right here in Indiana—Auburns and the front-wheel-drive Cords were produced in Auburn, while the "Dusies" were made in Indianapolis—and they're now on display inside the original showroom, built in 1930 and immaculately preserved.

Detour: Detroit

PENOBSCOT BUILDING

Though Detroit (pop. 672,795, down from a 1950 peak population of 1,849,568!) is a ways off our route, no guidebook enamored with American car culture could feel complete without covering the "Motor City," heart of America's automotive industry. Once among the biggest, brawniest, and busiest American cities, Detroit has lost nearly two-thirds of its population to suburban sprawl, sub-prime foreclosure, and out-migration, leading the city to declare bankruptcy in 2013, with debts of $20 billion. Numerous efforts to "renew" the city by replacing the historic urban fabric with megalithic casinos, sports stadiums, and (more recently) urban farms and artisanal manufacturing have resulted in a cityscape that at times resembles a war zone, but there are plenty of places where Detroit's positive energy and creativity holds back the decline.

One of the best ways to get a sense of Detroit, past and present, is at the **Detroit Institute of the Arts** (5200 Woodward Ave., 313/833-7900, Tues.-Sun., $12.50), two miles north of downtown on the city's once-proud main drag. The DIA is home to a massive collection of art from around the world as well as a huge and powerful Diego Rivera mural, *Detroit Industry,* celebrating the workers behind the wheels. Across the street is the worthwhile **Detroit Historical Museum** (Tues.-Sun., free).

Another must-see is the **Motown Museum** (2648 W. Grand Blvd., 313/875-2264, Tues.-Sat., $15), about three miles northwest of downtown, contained in the very house where Berry Gordy Jr. produced so many great dance hits in the 1960s by the likes of Smokey Robinson, Martha Reeves, Marvin Gaye, Stevie Wonder, the Temptations, and Diana Ross and the Supremes. Detroit also remembers Joe Louis, 1930s-era boxer known as the "Brown Bomber," with the 25-foot-high Big Fist, looming over the city's main thoroughfare, in the middle of Woodward Avenue at Jefferson Avenue, across from the Renaissance Center downtown.

Baseball fans will want to take in a **Detroit Tigers** (313/962-4000) game in the fan-friendly, faux-retro surrounds

Motown Museum

the bus made famous when Rosa Parks refused to give up her seat, outside of the Henry Ford Museum

of downtown's **Comerica Park,** where a Ferris wheel and a carousel entertain between pitches.

In the southwestern suburbs of Detroit, pay homage to the man who made your car affordable at **The Henry Ford: America's Greatest History Attraction** (20900 Oakwood Blvd., 800/835-5237 or 313/982-6001, daily Apr. 15-Nov., about $38 for both museum and village), located just off US-12 in Dearborn, about 10 miles southwest of downtown Detroit. The complex comprises the Henry Ford Museum, Greenfield Village, and a Ford factory, and its incredible collection of cars and car-related objects certainly illustrates the massive impact the automobile has had on American history and American life. The adjacent open-air complex of Greenfield Village is a virtual microcosm of American history, holding everything from Abe Lincoln's law office and Thomas Edison's workshop to the Montgomery, Alabama, bus on which longtime Detroit resident Rosa Parks refused to give up her seat in 1955, sparking the Civil Rights-era bus boycott.

PRACTICALITIES

The downtown riverfront has been the focus of much of Detroit's reinvention, but the best places to stay, eat, and generally spend time are in smaller neighborhoods around the city. One welcome sign of Detroit's potential future has been the success of artisanal food like that sold on Saturday in and around the historic **Eastern Market** and every day at **Slow's Bar-B-Q** (2138 Michigan Ave., 313/962-9828) in the trendy Corktown district west of downtown. To gain a deeper appreciation of Detroit's past, stay overnight near the Detroit Institute of the Arts and lively Wayne State University at one of the

restored Victorian-era homes that make up the **Inn on Ferry Street** (84 E. Ferry St., 313/871-6000, $159 and up), a comfortable property that feels like a B&B.

The collection here, valued at some $600 million, includes beautifully restored examples of all these classic makes, plus representatives of other classic roadsters—Packards, Cadillacs, even a Rolls-Royce or two—numbering more than 120 altogether, and making this one of the top auto museums in the world. It also hosts one of the country's most popular classic car festivals, every Labor Day weekend.

Another lost American industry is remembered near Auburn in **Kendallville,** along US-6: the **Mid-America Windmill Museum** (260/347-2334, Tues.-Sun. Apr.-Nov., $5), where 40 acres of grounds display over 52 whirring Aermotors, Flint & Wallings, Elgins, and more—the largest collection in the country.

OHIO

The many routes across Ohio along the Lake Erie shore have long been major thoroughfares. Traders and war parties of Iroquois and other Native Americans regularly passed this way hundreds of years before European and American pioneers started coming through in Conestoga wagons. Nowadays, historical survivors, including colonial-era taverns and other early roadside Americana, and a rapidly decreasing number of vegetable farms and greenhouses fill the flatlands, threatened by ever-expanding suburbia. All over northern Ohio you'll also see Rust Belt remnants of massive industrial activity that took place here from the 1880s to the 1950s, when the Great Lakes were the "Anvil of America," producing the bulk of the nation's—and the world's—iron, steel, and petroleum products.

Rather than try to follow one or another of the many old roads that crisscross the state, it's best to alternate between a variety of routes to either side of the part-tollway, part-freeway known as I-90. In the western half of the state, we follow US-20 from **Toledo** through a rural landscape of gambrel-roofed, red-painted barns, daubed with Chew Mail Pouch signs and made immortal by Sherwood Anderson's classic portrayal in his book *Winesburg, Ohio.* In the middle, we detour north to the lakeshore along US-6, which passes through idyllic summer home communities, gritty old ports, and one of the country's great old amusement parks, **Cedar Point.** East of the metropolitan **Cleveland** area, US-20 veers north along the **Lake Erie** shore, while US-6 zigzags south through the fertile farming country of northeastern Ohio—a region accurately described by the 1939 WPA *Guide to Ohio* as an "enchanting country of tumbling hills, valleys, and forests."

On I-90 at the Indiana-Ohio border, the World's Largest Fireworks Stand also hypes itself as the "8th Wonder of the World."

Toledo

One of Ohio's most important industrial centers, **Toledo** (pop. 278,508) is the third-busiest Great Lakes port, with many miles of docks, bridges, warehouses, factories, refineries, and power plants lining the mouth of the Maumee River. That may not sound like a good reason to visit, but Toledo is a fascinating place, big enough to be impressive but small enough to get

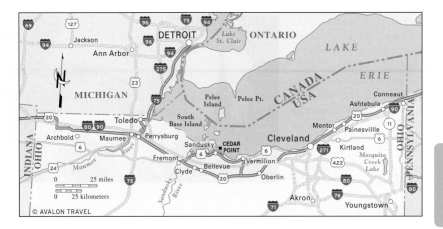

around and get a feel for. Downtown Toledo has long been a rather anonymous place that empties after 5pm (that world-renowned expert on tedium, the late John Denver, went so far as to write a song saying, "Saturday night in Toledo, Ohio, is like being nowhere at all"), but the streets just south hold dozens of gorgeous old cast-iron warehouses and commercial buildings. Downtown Toledo has been given a boost of energy and invest-ment by the delightful **Fifth Third Field** baseball stadium, home of the lovable **Toledo Mud Hens** (419/725-4367), Triple-A International League affiliate of the Detroit Tigers. The stadium is located not at 5th and 3rd Streets (the name comes from a Cleveland bank) but along Huron and Washington Streets. Unlike most ballparks, the playing field is visible from the streets (although tickets are pretty cheap, $12 for good seats).

A mile west of downtown, among the stately homes of the Old West End neigh-borhood, Toledo's pride and joy is the excellent **The Toledo Museum of Art** (2445 Monroe St., 419/255-8000, Tues.-Sun., free). Works by El Greco (who lived and worked in Toledo, Spain) are a highlight of one of the country's most comprehensive collections of art and sculpture from all around the world, with ancient Egyptian and Greek masterpieces, and paintings by the likes of Rembrandt, Peter Paul Rubens, the British pre-Raphaelites, and Americans Thomas Cole and Willem de Kooning. The singular strength of the collection is its glassware, a craft at which Toledo once excelled. Across the street from the neoclassical main building, doz-ens of beautiful goblets and vases, dating from Roman times to the present day, are housed in a transparent pavilion designed by the Pritzker Prize-winning archi-tects Sanaa.

Another truly not-to-be-missed Toledo stop offers a different feast for the senses: **Tony Packo's café** (1902 Front St., 419/691-6054), whose original loca-tion sits at the foot of a gorgeous new Toledo Skyway bridge soaring over the Maumee River (and lit at night by 200 feet of colorful LED lamps). Packo's addic-tive chili dogs, made famous by Corporal Klinger (played by real-life Toledo native Jamie Farr) on the long-running TV series *M.A.S.H.*, still pack the crowds into this East Toledo haunt. Tony Packo's also offers some delicious Hungarian specialties, and other signs of Toledo's ethnic mix are on the menu at **Byblos**

(1050 S. Reynolds Rd., 419/382-1600), an excellent Lebanese restaurant right on US-20.

A good-value place to stay in the region is the **Radisson at the University of Toledo** (3100 Glendale Ave., 419/381-6800 or 800/333-3333, from $79) on the southwest edge of downtown.

Architect's Fantasy at The Toledo Museum of Art

Maumee and Perrysburg

South of Toledo along the Maumee River, a pair of towns preserve important parts of western Ohio's early history. On the west bank of the river, **Maumee** (pop. 13,874, pronounced "MAH-mee") was founded in 1817 at the western edge of settled territory and holds remnants of the Miami and Erie Canal.

Across the river, **Perrysburg** (pop. 21,592) is a pretty little town of white colonial-style houses, with a nice waterfront park and a short strip of restaurants and bars running east along Louisiana Street. A mile upstream from town, **Fort Meigs** (419/874-4121 or 800/283-8916, Wed.-Sun. summer, $8) is a full-scale reconstruction of the wooden fortress that played a key role in defending the frontier against British and Native American attacks during the War of 1812.

Fremont

In **Fremont** (pop. 16,309), where indigenous Wyandot people established a village along the main trail between Pittsburgh and Detroit in the 1700s, the main attraction is the **Rutherford B. Hayes Presidential Center** (Spiegel Grove., 419/332-2081, Tues.-Sun. Jan.-Mar., $13), southwest of US-20, which encompasses the 25-acre estate of Civil War general and former U.S. president Rutherford B. Hayes, who lived here 1873-1893 and served as president 1877-1881. The nation's first presidential library, the Hayes center includes the rather plain redbrick family house and a large museum displaying his public and private papers, sundry mementos, and his daughter Fanny's dollhouse collection. Hayes is buried on a wooded knoll on the grounds, alongside his wife and their favorite horses.

Clyde: *Winesburg, Ohio*

Eight miles east of Fremont, the town of **Clyde** (pop. 6,221) is a perfect little place, still the typical farm town that the New Deal-era WPA *Guide to Ohio* said might well have served as a model for one of Thomas Hart Benton's murals of rural America: "Old Indian paths and sand ridges are now angular streets; cheek by jowl with an odd assortment of business houses is the railroad cutting across Main Street, gyved with station, elevator, and spur track; around the decorous houses are gardens, flowerbeds, and shrubbery tended by friendly and loquacious folk."

Clyde's brick-paved streets are still quiet, lined by mature trees and most of the same houses as when writer Sherwood Anderson, who was born in southern Ohio in

1876, grew up here in the 1880s and 1890s. Because the people of Clyde took offense at Anderson's sharply drawn and only slightly disguised portraits of them in his groundbreaking book, *Winesburg, Ohio*—which was published in 1919, 20 years after Anderson left Clyde for Chicago—the town doesn't celebrate him in any obvious way. The only real sign of Anderson is in the local **library** (222 W. Buckeye St., 419/547-7174, Mon.-Sat.), a block west of the town center, where visitors can examine a collection of his books and a short documentary video of his life and times. The library is also the best place to pick up the pamphlet that points out Anderson's home and the sites of many scenes from *Winesburg*.

While downtown "Winesburg" is still a low-key place, the US-20 frontage west of Clyde is dominated by a truly massive factory and distribution center for Whirlpool Maytag and Kenmore brand washing machines.

Besides the Winesburg legacy, Clyde also offers one very good road-food stop: the photogenic **Twistee Treat** (419/547-6996, daily), shaped like an ice-cream cone.

Sandusky and the Lake Erie Islands

Midway between Toledo and Cleveland, a fine natural harbor has enabled **Sandusky** (pop. 25,006) to remain a busy port, albeit now more for recreational ferries to the offshore islands than for the coal and iron ore it once handled. The waterfront is good for a short stroll, and the town is rich in elaborate mid-1800s houses like the **Follett House Museum** (404 Wayne St., 419/625-3834, Apr.-Dec., free), a well-preserved 1827 Greek Revival house filled with period artifacts and a few displays on the area's history. Sandusky also offers a magical old-fashioned ice-cream parlor: **Toft Dairy** (3717 Venice Rd., 419/625-5490). Five scoops for $3!

In Clyde, the **McPherson Cemetery** along US-20 holds the remains of Brigadier General James "Birdseye" McPherson, the highest-ranking Union officer killed in the Civil War.

On **South Bass Island** in Lake Erie, 22 miles from Sandusky, the 352-foot **Perry's Victory and International Peace Memorial** (419/285-2184) commemorates the victory of Admiral Oliver Perry, who defeated a British fleet here on September 10, 1813, announcing his success with the laconic words, "We have met the enemy, and they are ours." The second biggest thing on the island, which is a popular vacation spot, may well be the "World's Longest Bar," a 405-footer running inside the **Beer Barrel Saloon** (324 Delaware Ave., 419/285-2337) in the town of Put-in-Bay.

If the weather's too bad to brave a boat trip or a ride on the roller coasters of Cedar Point, families may want to head to the **Great Wolf Lodge** (4600 Milan Rd., 800/641-9653 or 419/609-6000, family suites $170 and up), a kid-friendly hotel and massive indoor water park (open to guests only) south of Sandusky.

Cedar Point

Northern Ohio's number-one summer attraction is the wonderful old-time amusement park of **Cedar Point** (419/627-2350, hours vary, $69 adults, $49 children under four feet tall), just north of Sandusky. Open since 1892, Cedar Point has the country's biggest and best collection of roller coasters, 16 in all, ranging from fragile-looking old wooden ones to high-speed modern monsters like the **Magnum XL-200,** a 15-story colossus; the terrifying **Raptor,** in which riders swing on benches hanging from the track; the 90-plus-mph **Millennium Force,** which features a stomach-levitating 300-foot drop; and the 42-story **Top Thrill Dragster,** which accelerates from 0 to 120 mph in four seconds. Cedar Point is definitely one of the most popular destinations in the Midwest (and is regularly voted "Best Amusement Park in the World" by its many fans), so expect crowds if you come on summer weekends. The 364-acre park sits on a peninsula across the water from downtown Sandusky and has animal shows, a Lake Erie beach, and a water park, as well as restaurants, on-site camping, and comfortable accommodations in the retro Gilded Age Hotel Breakers.

Vermilion

One of the more attractive resorts on Ohio's Lake Erie frontage, **Vermilion** (pop. 10,409) took its name from the rich red clay that colors the soil. Along with a fine

beach backed by dozens of attractive summer homes, the town also holds a great old-fashioned ice cream and sandwich parlor, **Granny Joe's Ice Creamatorium** (5598 Liberty Ave., 440/967-3663), which stands at the center of town. For a more complete meal, try the comfortable **Old Prague Restaurant** (440/967-7182) next door.

Oberlin

Away from the lakeshore, 35 miles southwest of Cleveland between I-90 and US-20, the attractive college town of **Oberlin** (pop. 8,331) serves up an idyllic slice of Middle Americana. Founded along with the surrounding town in 1833, Oberlin College has a history of being at the leading edge of American education, despite (or perhaps because of) its location far from the madding crowds. In 1837 Oberlin became the country's first coed college. It was also among the first to embrace the education of African Americans: In the 19th century, Oberlin awarded more degrees to black students than all other mainstream American colleges combined. Today, it's on the cutting edge of creating a sustainable, renewable future.

The lovely little town of **Milan** (pop. 1,343), two miles south of I-90 via US-250, was the birthplace in 1847 of the great inventor Thomas Edison. His childhood home at 9 Edison Drive is preserved as a museum.

The Oberlin College campus spreads west of the town's green main square, which is also graced on the east side by the neoclassical facade of the **Allen Art Museum** (87 N. Main St., 440/775-8665, Tues.-Sun., free). The museum displays an overall survey of world art—Japanese prints, Islamic carpets, and modern painting by the likes of Cézanne and Diebenkorn. Architecture fans should take note: The old gallery was designed by Cass Gilbert, who also planned a handful of Romanesque buildings on campus; a new wing was added in 1976 by Robert Venturi. The museum also offers guided tours on the first Sunday of each month ($5) of a nearby house designed in 1947 by Frank Lloyd Wright.

The town of Oberlin seems preserved in a time warp, mostly avoiding the trend-swapping café culture of many college towns. Its few blocks are lined by an old five-and-dime, an Army surplus store, a hardware store, and a bookstore, all along the south side of the broad town square. Another block south holds a spacious, modern library (with free Internet access) and a nice Mediterranean-flavored café, **The Feve** (30 S. Main St., 440/774-1978), which has fresh hummus, good coffee, and cold Guinness on tap. For a place to stay, try the comfortable and historic B&B **Buckeye and the Frog** (171 Elm St., 440/990-6500), or the turquoise-green motor-court cabins of the **Sunset Motel** (44077 Oberlin-Elyria Rd., 440/375-0808, $55 and up), due east of downtown.

US-20 Across Cleveland

The nicest old-road route into Cleveland from the west is US-6, which winds along Lake Erie as Sandusky Road, Lake Avenue, and Clifton Boulevard. Running right

The Cleveland Municipal Airport, Cleveland, Ohio

through downtown, past "The Flats" along Shoreway, then east along Superior Avenue, US-6 gives a great taste of the city.

US-20, on the other hand, diverges slightly east of downtown Cleveland, following Euclid Avenue past the Cleveland Museum of Art, then crosses to the north of US-6, following the lakeshore all the way into Pennsylvania.

Kirtland and Mentor

The rolling farmlands of northeastern Ohio around **Kirtland** (pop. 6,773) were, from 1831 to 1837, the center of the Mormon religion. Joseph Smith Jr., along with 1,000 of his followers, settled here and built a large temple—the first Mormon temple anywhere—and developed industries and a bank (known as the "Kirtland anti-BANK-ing Company"). The bank failed in 1838 and Smith fled, first to Liberty, Missouri, and later to Nauvoo, Illinois. He surrendered to the governor in 1844 and was killed by a mob in Carthage, Illinois.

The **Kirtland Temple** (9020 Chillicothe Rd., 440/256-1830, guided tours daily May-Oct., less frequently Feb.-Apr. and Nov.-Dec., $5), just south of I-90, is surrounded by pleasant gardens and open to the public on guided tours. The stately Greek Revival structure has a gleaming white interior built in part by Brigham Young, with elaborately crafted woodwork pulpits (one at each end) and an upstairs classroom with more of the unusual double pulpits. The temple and most of the town have been preserved under the auspices of the Reorganized Church of Jesus Christ of Latter-day Saints, now called Community of Christ, which was set up in 1852 by Joseph Smith Jr.'s oldest son and the Mormons who didn't go west to Salt Lake City with Brigham Young.

In the past 30 years, much of Ohio has been turned from farmland to suburbia, a development that inspired Pretenders singer and Ohio native Chrissie Hynde to write "My City is Gone"—the beginning strains of which serve as the theme song for Rush Limbaugh's radio program.

Much of Oberlin's endowment comes from the bequest of Oberlin graduate Charles Hall, who in 1886, a year after graduating, discovered a viable process for refining aluminum and later founded Alcoa Corporation.

Cleveland

Night Scene, Hotel Cleveland and Terminal Tower.

Cleveland, Ohio

Once the home base of John D. Rockefeller's Standard Oil monopoly, for decades on either side of the turn of the 20th century Cleveland was among the biggest and most prosperous of the Great Lakes industrial giants. A century later, the city has lost more than half its population (down from its 1949 peak of almost a million) and spent much of the past 60 years reeling from Rust Belt decay. The first sign of the city's renaissance came in the 1990s, when the opening of downtown's **Progressive Field,** where the **Cleveland Indians** (216/420-4487), sold out every game for its first five years. The more recent return of Ohio-born basketball star LeBron James to the Cleveland Cavaliers seems to have fully restored civic pride.

Within walking distance of the sports arenas, Cleveland's old lakefront industrial district, known as "The Flats," has undergone a successful face-lift, overlaid by a network of bridges (drawbridges, lift bridges, swing bridges) that form a feast for the eyes. Water taxis run back and forth across the river, linking the bars and restaurants that fill gigantic old mills, factories, and warehouses. Another primal force behind the area's rebirth has been the **Rock & Roll Hall of Fame and Museum** (1100 E. 9th St., 216/781-7625, daily, $23.50), housed in a striking I. M. Pei-designed building. Multimedia exhibits trace the roots and branches of the rock family tree, filling 55,000 square feet of galleries in a 162-foot tower. (Why Cleveland? The Hall of Fame was located here because Cleveland DJ Alan Freed is credited with naming the music "rock 'n' roll," way back in 1951.)

Rock and Roll Hall of Fame and Museum

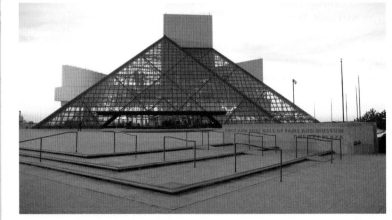

East of downtown, in the sedate University Circle neighborhood, some of the best things about Cleveland survive from its early 20th century heyday. Most notable is the **Cleveland Museum of Art** (11150 East Blvd., 216/421-7350, Tues.-Sun., free), just north of US-20/Euclid Avenue. Building on a long tradition of excellence in Egyptian and Asian art and sculpture, the museum now fills more than 500,000 square feet with memorable works, including paintings by Caravaggio, Zurbarán, and Picasso.

Just east of the museum, at Cleveland's **Lake View Cemetery** (12316 Euclid Ave., 216/421-2665) many of the grandees from Cleveland's Gilded Age prime, including "America's First Billionaire" John D. Rockefeller and U.S. President James Garfield, assassinated by a disgruntled bureaucrat in 1881, rest in peace among a landscaped forest of hardwood trees.

PRACTICALITIES

The Cleveland airport, Hopkins International, is 12 miles southwest of downtown, linked by I-71 and the RTA subway (216/621-9500) to central Cleveland. To get a feel for the place, a car is hard to beat, especially since the city sprawls sideways rather

than concentrating vertically. Downtown, finding your way around the Cuyahoga River waterfront takes patience, as many roads dead-end and some of the old bridges are closed to traffic; on foot, the Ohio City RTA stop is a good place to start exploring.

In the artsy, low-rent neighborhood of Ohio City, just west of the Cuyahoga River, the **West Side Market Café** (1979 W. 25th St., 216/579-6800) serves delicious breakfast and lunch meals with most ingredients sourced from the adjacent and always lively **West Side Farmers Market.** Also here: the **Great Lakes Brewing Company** (2516 Market Ave., 216/771-4404), which has good food, great beer, and a convivial crowd. While you're here, check out the Allstate Barber College across the street on 26th and Lorain Avenue—20 chairs, no waiting!

For a place to stay, the **DoubleTree Cleveland Downtown-Lakeside** (1111 Lakeside Ave., 216/241-5100, $169 and up) is hard to beat. It offers the usual comforts and is near the Rock & Roll Hall of Fame. Right downtown, across from Claes Oldenburg's **World's Largest Rubber Stamp** statue, the **Renaissance Cleveland Hotel** (24 Public Square, 216/696-5600, $165 and up) is a 1920s classic that has been immaculately updated.

For complete visitor information, contact the **Cleveland Convention and Visitors Bureau** (216/875-6680 or 800/321-1001).

North of I-90 along US-20, a half mile from the center of **Mentor,** a large white Gothic-style house is preserved much as it was when James Garfield lived here before assuming the presidency in 1881. Garfield served for only a few months before being assassinated, but **Garfield's home** (440/255-8722, daily 10am-5pm May-Oct., Fri.-Sun. Nov.-Apr., $7) is now preserved as a national historic site.

Eight miles to the northeast in **Painesville,** the **Rider's Inn** (792 Mentor Ave., 440/354-8200) is another historic landmark, built in 1812 along the stagecoach route between Buffalo and Cleveland. It still offers good food and a warm bed to passing travelers.

Ashtabula

On the shores of Lake Erie, 18 miles from the Pennsylvania border, **Ashtabula** (pop. 18,311) is a large and busy port, first dredged at the mouth of the Ashtabula River in 1826 and later home to some of the biggest shipyards on the Great Lakes. Now primarily recreation-oriented, Ashtabula still has more than a few signs of its industrial past, including the massive coal conveyor that forms an archway over the river, next to a squat lighthouse and a small local history **museum** housed in the old lighthouse keeper's quarters. Pride of place goes to a burly bascule drawbridge over the Ashtabula River. The many turn-of-the-20th-century industrial buildings along Bridge Street form a three-block parade of gift shops, bars, and restaurants.

The town's lakeside location made it a key transit point for enslaved people escaping on the Underground Railroad, a history recounted inside the **Hubbard House Museum** (1603 Walnut Blvd., 440/964-8168, Fri.-Sun. afternoons Memorial Day-Labor Day, $5).

One last local landmark is a half mile south of the harbor: **Tony's Dog House** (528 Lake Ave., 440/964-0202), a friendly indoor-outdoor hangout serving well-prepared all-beef dog with a huge variety of toppings, plus delicate ribbon-fried potatoes and soft-serve cones.

Conneaut

The dozen miles between Ashtabula and the Pennsylvania border offer a full range of Great Lakes scenery, from pristine waterfront forests and lakeside vacation cabins to historic covered bridges and massive power plants, best seen by following Lake Road, which runs right along the shore. Close to the state line, the historic town of **Conneaut** (pop. 12,708, pronounced "KAH-nee-ot") is home to an engineering landmark, the 136-foot-long **Middle Road Covered Bridge,** built in the 1860s and restored in the 1980s, five miles south of downtown. It also has an art director's dream of a road-food restaurant, the **White Turkey Drive-In** (388 E. Main Rd., 440/593-2209), on US-20. Owned and run by the Tuttle family since 1952, this place serves burgers and has a fantastic ambience but is truly famous for shredded turkey sandwiches, root beer floats, and chili-cheese fries. Between Mother's Day and Labor Day, sit outside under the red canopy on a warm summer evening watching the fireflies, and everything is guaranteed to feel right with the world.

PENNSYLVANIA

US-20 takes little more than the proverbial blink of an eye to cross the 45 miles of northwestern Pennsylvania, which is part of Pennsylvania only because the country's founding fathers thought it was unfair to deny the Keystone State a share of the Lake Erie shoreline. I-90 is most travelers' route of choice, but US-20 does have a couple of worthwhile stops.

Erie

Midway across Pennsylvania's short Lake Erie shoreline, the biggest city in these parts, **Erie** (pop. 98,593), is a heavy industrial powerhouse that seems to have escaped the downward spiraling fate of many other Rust Belt cities. Home to the heaviest of heavy industry, the factory where General Electric produces the world's most powerful locomotives, Erie is recreating itself around a nice new downtown ballpark, with a replica of Commodore Perry's flagship *Niagara* moored along the Lake Erie waterfront, where the 10-story Bicentennial Tower offers an impressive panorama.

A mile south of the waterfront, along the still-busy train tracks, the art deco Union Pacific depot is now home to a popular brewpub and restaurant, **The Brewerie** (123 W. 14th St., 814/454-2200). The opulent **Warner Theater** (811 State St.) is a picture palace par excellence, its 2,250-seat auditorium still in regular use.

Ten miles east of the Ohio border, the town of **Girard** (pop. 2,996) has one of the country's oldest Civil War memorials, an eagle-topped obelisk dedicated with great fanfare in November 1865.

marquee of the restored Warner Theater

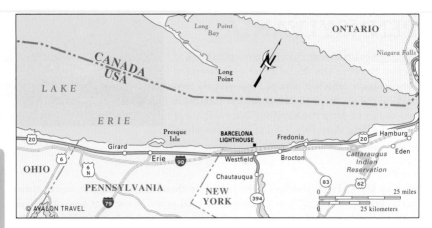

Erie has a Double-A baseball team, the Detroit Tigers-affiliated **Erie SeaWolves** (110 E. 10th St., 814/456-1300), who play at a neighborly downtown stadium, two blocks east of State Street. Games are broadcast on **WFNN 1330 AM.**

For a taste of old-fashioned, blue-collar, working-class Erie, take a trip four miles east of downtown, past the massive GE locomotive works, to a classic All-American diner. Recently added to the National Register of Historic Places, the **Lawrence Park Dinor** (4019 Main St., 814/899-4390, Tues.-Sun.) is an elegantly streamlined 1940s Silk City, serving high-quality locally sourced breakfast and lunch meals at fair prices.

One more reason to spend time here, especially in the depths of winter, is **Splash Lagoon** (8091 Peach St., 814/217-1111 or 866/377-5274, around $45), an 80,000-square-foot indoor water park, just south of the I-90 Erie exit. Package deals at the trio of attached chain hotels (around $110 and up) include admission to the slides.

NEW YORK

From inauspicious beginnings in the marshlands and vineyards of the Lake Erie "grape belt" at the state's far western tip, the portion of US-20 that runs across upstate New York cuts a wide scenic swath through a diverse terrain of flatlands, rippling hills, and spring-fed lakes. This well-maintained, mostly four-lane road glides surreptitiously through four centuries of history, slicing through vast Dutch patroonships, serene Shaker colonies, blood-soaked Revolutionary War battlefields, Native American hunting grounds, the birthplace of the women's movement, Underground Railroad hideouts, and the long-calmed waters of the once-mighty Erie Canal. Sparkling baseball diamonds, dairy bars by the dozen, petrified creatures, stately longhouses, abandoned motor courts, prancing wooden horses, off-key nose whistles, and succulent grill-toughened hot dogs are just a few of the countless other reasons to slow down and pull over early and often as you cross the Empire State.

The "Romance Road," as labeled by a 1940s travel writer, follows several old

Iroquois trails as it nudges its way through the western Niagara Frontier, then traces the 19th-century Great Western Turnpike through the **Finger Lakes** region before easing down into the historically rich Hudson Valley near **Albany,** where it begins a gradual ascent of the Taconic Mountains and Berkshire foothills that hug the Massachusetts border. All the way across the state, US-20 roughly parallels the crowded, rumbling I-90 New York Thruway toll road—a necessary evil that lures most of the diesel-spewing, view-obscuring 18-wheel traffic away from placid US-20 with a 65-mph speed limit and the promise of uneventful, predictable fast-food rest-stop dining experiences and fluorescent-lit motels.

rose, state flower of New York

Westfield: New York's Wine Country

While it's unlikely to be mistaken for the timeless landscapes of Tuscany, or even the nearby Finger Lakes, the rolling hills of westernmost New York have more than a few moments of picturesque perfection. Rows of craggy vines surround an endless parade of 150-year-old farmhouses, all topped by delightful bell tower-like cupolas, and all in varying stages of repair and oblivion. Signs for "Indian Cigarettes" interrupt the idyll, but the shaggy vineyards are still productive and profitable, especially around **Westfield** (pop. 3,054), known locally as Vine City because of its large Italian American grape-growing community.

The tangy Concord grape was introduced to the region in 1859, but it wasn't until 1896 that Charles Welch and his father moved to Westfield and founded the factory that led to Westfield's long-standing nickname, the "Grape Juice Capital of the World." Westfield is also in the history books thanks to a local 11-year-old girl who, during the presidential campaign of 1860, urged candidate Abraham Lincoln to grow a beard, which he did to iconic effect. A statue on Main Street commemorates the scene.

Only a mile south of the I-90 Thruway, Westfield offers a quick but satisfying taste of what old road travel is all about: a spacious central park surrounded by church spires, and a compact Main Street lined by brick buildings housing antiques shops and thrift shops. Best of all, the no-frills **Main Diner** (40 E. Main St., 716/326-4351, daily 6am-2:30pm, plus Fri. evening), right in the heart of downtown, is a pleasant place to grab a cup of coffee and sandwich while watching the pickup trucks cruise past. (For all you diner mavens, the building is a 1929 Ward & Dickinson, originally fabricated in neighboring Silver Creek.)

Across I-90 from Westfield along waterfront Hwy-5, Lake Erie's Barcelona Harbor is home to the landmark **Barcelona Lighthouse,** which was constructed in 1829 and two years later was the first lighthouse in the world to be lit by natural gas. There are a couple of nice cafés nearby, and though the lighthouse itself is prominent even from the road, it stands on private property and is not accessible to visitors.

Fredonia

East of Westfield, US-20 trucks through cherry orchards, vineyards, and dozens of U-pick fruit stands before ebbing into the center of neatly maintained **Fredonia** (pop. 10,639), possible namesake for the Marx Brothers' beloved *Duck Soup* homeland. Site of the first natural gas well in the United States (1821), Fredonia was also—ironically, for a town in the heart of the western New York Wine Belt—the home of one of the earliest chapters of the Women's Christian Temperance Union.

Downtown Fredonia boasts the gracefully shaded New England-style town square, bordered by a restored opera house and a host of Greek Revival, Italianate, Victorian, and Gothic 19th-century commercial buildings. A stroll down tree-lined Central Avenue to the north of Main Street (US-20) reveals an equally diverse array of turn-of-the-20th-century homes, which stand in marked contrast to the sterile modernity you encounter up the road in the several I. M. Pei-designed buildings that define the State University of New York (SUNY) Fredonia campus.

The veranda-fronted **White Inn** (52 E. Main St., 716/672-2103, $75 and up) has been open so long it still boasts of recommendations by 1930s road-food writer Duncan Hines.

East of Fredonia, the vineyards vanish, replaced by the thick stands of scruffy pine trees, used car lots, and cheap-cigarette stands that crowd the roadside along US-20's two-mile passage through the northeastern corner of the Cattaraugus Reservation.

Comedian Lucille Ball grew up in **Jamestown,** south of Fredonia, at the southeast end of Chautauqua Lake. The **Lucille Ball Desi Arnaz Museum & Center for Comedy** (2 W. 3rd St., 716/484-0800, $15) displays lots of *I Love Lucy* memorabilia.

West of Fredonia, in the town of **Brocton** ("Home of Don Reinhoudt, World's Strongest Man"), a unique green arch has been hovering over US-20 at the main downtown intersection since 1910.

Eden:
Original American Kazoo Company

US-20 bumps up north along the lakeshore through several miles of scraggly forest, and you won't miss a thing by taking the I-90/NY Thruway to exit 57A, which lands you on a two-lane back road bound right for sleepy downtown **Eden** (pop. 7,688). Eden, a make-your-own-music lovers' paradise that lays claim to an annual summer Eden Corn Festival, is home to the one-and-only **Original American Kazoo Company museum, gift shop, and factory** (8703 S. Main St., 716/992-3960, Mon.-Sat., free). Established in 1916, the company boasts the world's only still-operating metal kazoo factory (most of the ones now made in China and Hong Kong are plastic). A restored two-story clapboard house contains a gift shop and museum offering an up-close-and-personal view of the factory's belt-and-pulley metal kazoo production line and the opportunity to sign a petition aimed at getting the kazoo declared America's national instrument.

After viewing a video extolling the virtues of one of the few musical instruments invented in the United States, visitors can gaze at a display of antique kazoos, ranging from an original wooden model to the bottle-shaped kazoos churned out to celebrate the repeal of Prohibition. A large sign chimes in with some fascinating kazoo-related trivia, describing the most popular kazoo (the slide trombone), the largest kazoo ever made (the 43-pound Kazoophony), and

DETOUR: CHAUTAUQUA

One of the few utopian-minded 19th-century communities to survive to the present day, Chautauqua (pop. 4,464) is an idyllic 750-acre Victorian village of quaint pastel cottages, tidy flower gardens, and pedestrian-friendly streets—a genteel model of middle-class, small-town civilization. Chautauqua was founded in 1874 by Lewis Miller, inventor Thomas Edison's father-in-law. It was established as a summer training ground for Methodist Sunday school teachers and is now preserved as a nonprofit, nonsectarian cooperative foundation. In the first decades of the 20th century, Chautauqua had an immeasurable effect on American culture, sponsoring correspondence courses and cross-country lecture tours that brought liberal arts education to the masses, especially in the rural Midwest.

Chautauqua, located along Hwy-394 about 11 miles south of Westfield on US-20 (off I-90 exit 60), has hardly changed since its heyday and still welcomes all comers to its summer-long series of lectures and concerts. Though the emphasis is on education, Chautauqua is not entirely academic: In between broadening their minds, visitors can relax on the white-sand beaches that line the lakeshore. Day visitors to **Chautauqua** (716/357-6250) have to pay an admission fee ($41 morning and afternoon) and pass through a set of ancient turnstiles, as if entering a mind-improving amusement park. Others come for a week or two, renting a cottage or staying at the wonderful old **Athenaeum Hotel** (800/821-1881 or 716/357-4444, $270 and up, with all meals included), built in 1881.

For further information, or to request a schedule of Chautauqua classes, lectures, and events, call 800/836-2787.

idyllic Chautauqua

the number of kazoo bands registered in the United States (15,000 and still counting). You can pick up an adenoid-popping nose flute, a trombone kazoo, and a variety of noisemakers in the gift shop on your way out, or grab some wax paper, rubber bands, and an empty toilet paper roll and create your own kazoo.

Buffalo

Founded as a Niagara frontier outpost in the early 1800s, **Buffalo** (pop. 256,902) exploded into a bustling shipping, manufacturing, and railroad center after the 1825 opening of the Erie Canal. For over a century, especially around World War I, Buffalo was the commercial and industrial linchpin between the Great Lakes, Canada, and the eastern United States. A shrinking population and the continuing departure of many factories and corporate headquarters to warmer cheap-labor climes has dented Buffaloans' self-confidence over the past several decades. Still, the optimistic, made-in-Buffalo spirit captured so eloquently in nonfiction

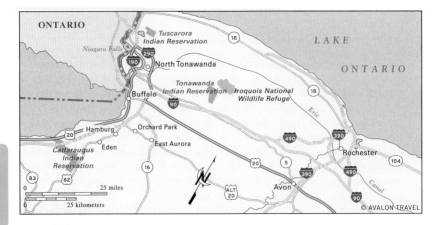

The **Buffalo Bisons,** the Toronto Blue Jays Triple-A farm team, play right downtown at 16,907-seat **Coca-Cola Field** (716/846-2000, $10.50 and up). Games are broadcast play-by-play on **WWKB 1520 AM.**

writer Verlyn Klinkenborg's portrait of Polish-American bartender Eddie Wenzek, *The Last Fine Time,* lives on. Creative investment has adapted the city's industrial infrastructure to modern times. Art studios and coffee shops have opened in old warehouse buildings, and the landmark grain elevators along the waterfront have been converted into an indoor rock-climbing gym. An excellent range of walking and kayaking tours are offered by the non-profit **Explore Buffalo.Org** (716/245-3032).

A 15-minute drive from downtown up tree-lined Elmwood Avenue takes you to Buffalo's premier attraction, the extensive collection of Picassos, de Koonings, Pollocks, and other important modern masterpieces inside the **Albright-Knox Art Gallery** (1285 Elmwood Ave., 716/882-8700, Tues.-Sun., $12). This world-class museum stands adjacent to the grassy expanses and ponds of **Delaware Park,** designed by Frederick Law Olmsted, the landscape architect of New York City's Central Park and Brooklyn's Prospect Park. Across the road you'll see the marble neoclassical structure that has housed the **Buffalo and Erie County Historical Society Museum** (716/873-9644, Tues.-Sun., $7) since its construction in 1901 for the historic Pan-American Exposition. The non-air-conditioned gallery can be a bit stifling on hot summer afternoons, but the wonderful Made in Buffalo exhibit, on local manufacturing, and Dividing the Land, about immigration, should satisfy most of your local-history thirsts.

A short walk from the Delaware Park brings you to the Frank Lloyd Wright-designed **Darwin D. Martin House** (125 Jewett Parkway, 716/856-3858, tours $19 and up), well worth a look for anyone interested in American architecture, especially after its recent restoration.

Between Buffalo and Niagara Falls, **North Tonawanda** (pop. 30,607) is a tough-looking factory town concealing one of the Buffalo area's best-kept secrets, the **Herschell Carrousel Factory Museum** (180 Thompson St., 716/693-1885, May-Dec., $7) a half mile east of Hwy-265. Creator of much-loved landmarks at amusement parks from the Jersey Shore to Santa Monica, the barn-like factory houses a restored

1916 pulley-driven carousel and a stable of immaculately painted wooden steeds, zebras, roosters, ostriches, frogs, bears, and bulls hand-carved by the factory's immigrant artisans for the countless carousels and kiddie rides turned out by the factory in its 1920s to 1940s heyday.

Buffalo Practicalities

Most of Buffalo's many local clubs, films, and offbeat attractions are found in the funky, historic Allentown neighborhood around the junction of Elmwood Avenue and Allen Street, just north of downtown. The "World Famous" **Anchor Bar** (1047 Main St., 716/886-8920), "Birthplace of Buffalo Wings," is here. Skip the bland Italian entrées in favor of the bar's much-hyped specialty—the saucy, fiery, deep-fried chicken wings, served here since 1964. A long way out on Main Street, about three miles from downtown near the SUNY Buffalo campus, are a pair of perfect Buffalo pit stops. Get breakfast (or veggie-friendly Lebanese lunch and dinner) at **Amy's Place** (3234 Main St., 716/832-6666), or feast on delicious hot fudge sundaes or housemade candies at **Parkside Candy** (3208 Main St., 716/833-7540), an opulently decorated 1930s space that looks like a ballroom out of a Jane Austen novel.

Downtown Buffalo is energized by Bisons baseball and Sabres hockey games. During these games, the always-enjoyable **Pearl Street Grill & Brewery** (76 Pearl St., 716/856-2337) is even more packed than usual. There frequent farmers markets around the **Filling Station at Larkin Square** (745 Seneca St., 716/362-2665), in a resurgent industrial district about two miles east of downtown.

Southeast of downtown, another unique Buffalo treat—the Beef on Weck sandwich, a moist and meaty version of a French dip, best eaten with a dash of horseradish—can be sampled at **Schwabl's** (789 Center Rd., 716/675-2333) in West Seneca.

East of Buffalo, US-20 makes a rigidly straight run through the flat corn and hay fields that climb the gradually rising plateau toward the Finger Lakes. This 40-mile-or-so stretch is virtually devoid of traffic, thanks to the faster-moving New York Thruway and serpentine Hwy-5, which links up with US-20 at Avon.

Anchor Bar, home of the original Buffalo Wings

For a place to stay, most of the national chain motels are clustered east of town around I-90 and the Buffalo airport. The in-town **Best Western** (510 Delaware Ave., 800/780-7234 or 716/886-8333, $125 and up) is a bit higher-priced, but its central location saves driving time and grounds you smack in the middle of the city's Allentown bar, restaurant, and club district; there's also a comfy **Hampton Inn** (220 Delaware Ave., 716/855-2223, $157 and up) nearby. Downtown has the spacious **Lofts on Pearl** (92 Pearl St., 716/856-0098) in a wonderfully ornate old factory, while solo travelers on a smaller budget will appreciate the immaculate **Hostel Buffalo-Niagara** (667 Main St., 716/852-5222, $30 and up), with dorm beds in a historic downtown building.

Another arts-and-crafts aesthetic treasure is tucked away in the south Buffalo suburb of East Aurora. In the early 1900s, East Aurora was home of Roycroft Campus, a turn-of-the-20th-century arts-and-crafts community of furniture shops and studios, the crown jewel of which was recently restored and opened as **The Roycroft Inn** (40 S. Grove St., 716/652-5552 or 877/652-5552, $145 and up), a lovely hotel and restaurant.

For additional information and maps of Buffalo's wealth of significant architecture (Louis Sullivan, H. H. Richardson, Eliel Saarinen, and Frank Lloyd Wright all completed major buildings here), contact the Buffalo-Niagara County **visitors center** (403 Main St., 716/852-2356 or 800/283-3256).

Niagara Falls

One of the most famous sights in the world, the **Niagara Falls** are a quick trip upriver from Buffalo. They're not the biggest or most powerful waterfall in the world, but they're easy to reach and very easy to get up close and personal with. Once you venture underneath the falls on the famous **Maid of the Mist boat ride** (716/284-8897, $18), or even stand on the brink at Prospect Park or Goat Island, you won't soon forget the awesome force of the water tumbling in twin torrents. One is 167 feet; the other is 176 feet.

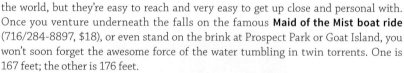

The power of Niagara Falls was first used to generate electricity by the remarkable inventor Nikola Tesla in 1896. A monument to him stands near the falls in Prospect Point.

Much to the despair of the tourism authorities on the U.S. side, where the surprisingly postindustrial town has long suffered from economic decline, the best views are across a bridge on the Canadian side, where all the major hotels join the Las Vegas-scale **Fallsview Casino Resort** (888/325-5788, $165 and up) among a barrage of wax museums, water parks, and a Ripley's Believe It or Not! Museum, fronted by a 25-foot statue of King Kong.

Rochester

There's plenty of culture in the sprawling Genesee River manufacturing center of **Rochester** (pop. 208,880), and the best of it is of the vernacular variety, making the 25-mile detour off US-20 well worth your time and effort. With impressive **High Falls,** a mini Niagara right at the center of town; numerous historic sights (the Erie Canal passed right through Rochester, and Susan B. Anthony and

Frederick Douglass both lived here for many years); and an expansive Lake Ontario shoreline boasting long beaches, Rochester is a fine example of how much fun one can have in a smaller U.S. city. The best road trip-worthy attraction is historic **Seabreeze Amusement Park** (585/323-1900, around $30), which sits on the Lake Ontario shore, complete with the ancient wooden Jack Rabbit roller coaster, the third oldest operating in the USA, and a fun water park.

Start your visit with the vast holdings of the Americana-rich **Strong National Museum of Play** (585/263-2700, daily, $14.50), clearly marked off I-490 downtown. This impressive collection includes Victorian-era toys, appliances, dolls, perfume bottles, marbles, salt-and-pepper shakers, and classic board games. It's a must-visit for closet pack rats, pop culture fanatics, and anyone with children in tow. Just inside, but accessible without paying admission, is a lovely circa-1918 Herschell hand-carved carousel (made in nearby North Tonawanda), as well as a fully restored 1956 Skyliner diner, serving lunch all day.

The **George Eastman House** (900 East Ave., 585/271-3361, Tues.-Sun., $15) is a 10-minute drive along Rochester's fashionable mansion-lined main boulevard. In addition to relaying the Horatio Alger-like story of workaholic Eastman's success and philanthropy as the founder of the Eastman Kodak Company, the 50-room Colonial Revival mansion in which he lived before his 1932 suicide also houses a fascinating exhibit, Enhancing the Illusion, on the history of photography.

The **Rochester Red Wings** Triple-A baseball team play at friendly **Frontier Field** (585/454-1001, around $12) downtown. The team had been the Baltimore Orioles' prime farm team since the 1960s (ironman Cal Ripken played for Rochester as a teenager) but now feeds the Minnesota Twins.

South of Rochester, I-390 runs alongside a still-intact section of the original Erie Canal waterway. In other places, the freeway runs right over the old canal, with the old stone locks still visible on the side of the road. Iroquois legend has it that the **Finger Lakes** (five of which—Cayuga, Onondaga, Oneida, Seneca, and Tuscarora—bear names of the Six Nations of the Iroquois Confederacy) were created by the handprint of God.

Geneva and Waterloo

Geneva (pop. 12,988) sits at the head of Seneca Lake, the largest of the Finger Lakes, and is linked to this sailboat-flecked jewel by a long green linear park. For a worthwhile detour off the busy four-lane highway, take a quick pass through the lively downtown along Main Street, perhaps wandering around the twin campuses of Hobart and William Smith Colleges to take in a more long-distance view of the lake. The waterfront is dominated by a solitary high-rise housing the **Ramada Inn** (41 Lakefront Dr., 315/789-0400, $110-265), but a much more interesting place to stay is a half mile south of town: the historic **Belhurst Castle** (4069 West Lake Rd., 315/781-0201, $150 and up), a 100-year-old, 11-room B&B and restaurant.

Near the conservatory in Rochester's Frederick Law Olmsted-designed Highland Park, the 1898 memorial to antislavery activist Frederick Douglass was the first public statue of an African American erected in the United States.

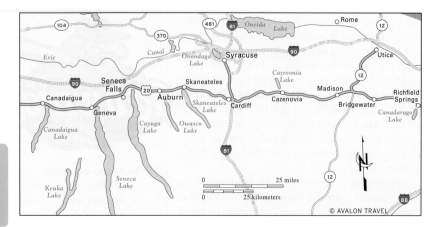

Seven miles east of Geneva, picturesque, flag-draped downtown **Waterloo** (pop. 5,019) has an all-American feel. It was the site of the nation's first observance (in May 1866) of **Memorial Day.** A small **museum** (35 E. Main St., Apr.-Oct., 315/539-9611) evokes the somber postwar roots of what is now the start of summer. At the edge of town, the unprepossessing **Mac's Drive-In Curb Service Restaurant** (1180 Waterloo-Geneva Rd., 315/539-3064) has been open every summer since 1961, dishing out creamy Richardson's root beer floats, frosty 16-ounce mugs of Pabst Blue Ribbon, and burgers-in-a-basket at an awning-covered counter or right at your car window.

Seneca Falls: Women's Rights National Historical Park

You'd never think that the diminutive redbrick blue-collar town of **Seneca Falls** saw the birth of the American women's movement. The first women's rights convention, spearheaded by Lucretia Mott and Elizabeth Cady Stanton, took place here in July 1848. The remains of the Wesleyan Chapel where the convention was held can still be viewed at the center of town, on a guided tour from the **Women's Rights National Historical Park** (136 Fall St., 315/568-2991, Fri.-Sun., free), right on US-20. A brief exhibit on the scandalous pants-like "bloomers" popularized in 1851 by local feminist

organizers of the first women's rights convention, in 1848 in Seneca Falls

Amelia Bloomer combines with displays on transcendentalism, abolitionism, temperance, and phrenology to place the rise of this revolutionary movement in historical context.

A block away, the **National Women's Hall of Fame** (76 Fall St., 315/568-8060) is a reading-intensive monument to the likes of Georgia O'Keeffe, Harriet Tubman, Emily Dickinson, Billie Jean King, and Jane Addams. You can listen to a saucy blues selection from Bessie Smith while dodging an endless stream of group tours.

And if the extensive architectural and historic landmarks are not enough, Seneca Falls also inspired the cinematic Bedford Falls in the classic Frank Capra film It's a Wonderful Life. The 1946 film was made on a Hollywood set, not here, but it's easy to imagine Jimmy Stewart meeting his guardian angel when you see the quaint bridge over the river. Every Christmas there are celebratory events, and year-round you can learn more about the story at a small **It's a Wonderful Life Museum** (32 Fall St., 315/568-5838, Wed.-Sun., free), housed appropriately enough in the town's old movie theater.

At the west edge of Seneca Falls, the emblematic landmark of the long-vanished 1920s-era Windmill Tourist Camp has been kept alive as the local chamber of commerce and visitor information center.

Auburn

Auburn (pop. 26,821) is a proud industrial city with a solid, hilly downtown and a rich stock of historical homes, including that of William H. Seward, the antislavery Whig governor of New York. Seward founded the Republican Party, was a U.S. senator, served as secretary of state under presidents Abraham Lincoln and Andrew Johnson, and single-handedly negotiated the purchase of Alaska from Russia in 1867. The **William Seward House Museum** (33 South St., 315/252-1283, Tues.-Sat. 10am-5pm, $12), on Hwy-34 a block south of US-20, contains all the original furniture and many fascinating historic exhibits. Down the street from the Seward home, you can also tour the home of the once enslaved underground railroad heroine Harriet Tubman, who, from before the Civil War until her death in 1913, lived in the tidy white house that was recently protected as part of the **Harriet Tubman National Historical Park** (180 South St., 315/882-8060, Thurs.-Sat., donation). In 1859, William Seward, then a U.S. senator, quietly sold Harriet Tubman the home for almost no money, which was both generous and illegal, and he and Tubman are both buried in the town's Fort Hill cemetery, west of South Street between their two homes.

Right downtown, the sparkling streamlined **Hunter's Dinerant** (18 Genesee St., 315/255-2282, Fri.-Sat. 24 hours), a 1950s O'Mahony, offers great greasy-spoon breakfasts, slices of thick lemon meringue pie, and a panoramic view of the aging Genesee Beer sign that watches over the wide streets of the hill-hugging downtown.

North of Auburn, the Class A **Auburn Doubledays** (315/255-2489) play at friendly **Falcon Park.**

Along US-20 on the western outskirts of Auburn, keep your eyes peeled and your camera at the ready as you pass the **Finger Lakes Drive-In Theater** (315/370-7780, summer only).

Along US-20, just west of the I-81 interchange, the tiny crossroads of **Cardiff** is where the 10-foot 2,990-pound "fossil" of the P. T. Barnum-hyped Cardiff Giant was "unearthed" in 1869.

Skaneateles

Roughly midway across New York State, **Skaneateles** (pop. 2,487, pronounced "scan-ee-AT-less") is a pristine sun-dappled resort nestled on the north shore of shimmering Skaneateles Lake. This popular summer family escape houses arts, crafts, and antiques stores along its immaculate Genesee Street (US-20), which fronts a lovely lakeside park where you can enjoy free **summer concerts** (7:30pm Fri.) on the quaint bandstand, watch the boats come and go, or hop on board a historic lake steamer for a scenic tour offered by **Mid-Lakes Navigation** (11 Jordan St., 800/545-4318 or 315/685-8500).

Stroll up the main downtown north-south drag and you'll notice the smell of fresh bread (and delicious doughnuts!) at the unadorned **Skaneateles Bakery** (19 Jordan St., 315/685-3538) before reaching the Skaneateles Historical Society's **Creamery Museum** (315/685-1360, Fri.-Sat. 1pm-4pm, donation). Elm-lined side streets are full of well-maintained Greek Revival homes.

If you're hungry for more than a pastry or piece of cake, wait in line at the high-quality but self-effacing **Doug's Fish Fry** (8 Jordan St., 315/685-3288, daily), "Not Famous since 1982," for its fried haddock sandwiches, fried clams, Coney Island hot dogs, and ice-cold beer. Doug's also has creamy thick Perry's ice cream and milk shakes, plus fresh strawberry sundaes in season. Buy a postcard for a nickel and Doug's will slap on a stamp and send it on its way.

Right in the center of Skaneateles, the **Sherwood Inn** (26 W. Genesee St., 800/374-3796 or 315/685-3405, $175 and up) along US-20 has been welcoming travelers to its lakeside restaurant, good bar, and comfortable rooms since it was built as a stagecoach stop back in 1807.

Syracuse and Utica

Sliced and diced by a half-dozen freeways at the I-90 Thruway junction with I-81, and just a short side trip from US-20, **Syracuse** (pop. 143,378) embodies the ups and downs of upstate New York's connections, both literal and creative, with the wider world, mainly via transportation infrastructure. Start your visit where it all began, with an informative tour of the fascinating **Erie Canal Museum** (318 E. Erie Blvd., 315/471-0593, daily, $5 donation) in the shadow of I-690. Facing City Hall, the museum is housed in a delicate 1850s "Weighlock" building straddling the mostly paved-over original route of the Erie Canal, which now sadly cowers in the shadow of I-81. The museum is the primary repository of objects related to the original canal, displaying a restored 65-foot-long canal boat and numerous interpretive exhibits. A short film describes the staggering impact of the canal's 1825 opening on the city, still visible in the cast-iron commercial districts of its historic, still lively downtown. Walk two blocks west from the museum to Clinton Square, where a shallow fountain (and winter ice-skating rink) reflects the former canal, the surrounding architecture, and a Sailors and Soldiers war memorial.

West of downtown Syracuse, the sizable Irish immigrant population of the

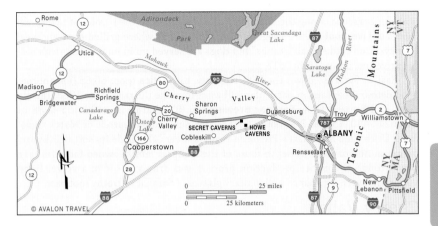

© AVALON TRAVEL

Tipperary Hill neighborhood insisted that traffic lights in their neighborhood be turned upside-down so that the "British" red did not sit above the "Irish" green. One traffic light is still "upside down," and a statue at the corner of Tompkins and Milton streets evokes the whole story.

In downtown Syracuse, treat yourself to a plate of some of New York's finest ribs at **Dinosaur Bar-B-Que** (246 W. Willow St., 315/476-4937), a biker-friendly haunt housed in a brick tavern dating from the last days of the Erie Canal. This is the original incarnation of what is now a major East Coast institution. Another local culinary landmark sits a few miles

One of the oldest baseball clubs in existence, the **Syracuse Chiefs** (315/474-7833) have been around in various forms since 1858. Now the top farm club for the Washington Nationals, they play at modern **NBT Bank Stadium** north of downtown off I-81 exit 25.

Saranac Brewing Co. in Utica

north of Syracuse, along the shores of Lake Onondaga in the hamlet of Liverpool: **Heid's of Liverpool** (305 Oswego St., 315/451-0786), where grilled pork-and-veal "Coneys" and traditional "Franks" hot dogs are served up in one of America's oldest drive-ins, dating from 1917.

East of Syracuse down the I-90 Thruway, hilly **Utica** (pop. 60,652) is another good detour. Beer fans in particular will want to make the trip: Since 1888, the old West End Brewery, now **Saranac Brewing Co.** (830 Varick St., 800/765-6288 or 315/624-2490, $5), on Brewhouse Square, has pumped out barrels of Matt's trademark Utica Club and Matt's Premium regional beers alongside its soft drinks and premium microbrews. In-depth tours of the compact family-owned facilities take you through the entire production process and drop you off in a velvet-lined Victorian tavern for your complimentary glasses of Saranac or frothy root beer.

Cherry Valley

East of I-81, all the way to Albany, US-20 follows the route blazed by the old Great Western Turnpike over gradually steepening roller-coaster hills, past sweet-corn stands, dairy bars, and cabbage fields, and into the western reaches of picture-perfect Cherry Valley. Just south of the highway, the attractive little hamlet of **Cherry Valley** (pop. 497) contains a small local history museum. **Cherry Valley Museum** (49 Main St., 607/264-3303, daily summer-fall, $6) recalls this tiny crossroads' early-19th-century boom period as a rowdy turnpike stagecoach stop. A small monument in the village cemetery on South Main Street pays homage to the residents killed in 1779 in the Cherry Valley Massacre, a British-backed Iroquois raid during the Revolutionary War.

Cherry Valley also holds a more recent landmark: **The Tepee** (7632 E. US-20, 607/264-3987), a 50-foot-tall tepee-shaped attraction, which has lured souvenir-starved travelers since 1950 with its array of Native American trinkets, famous TePee Taffy, and "Grand Panoramic View" telescope. A snack bar, a.k.a. TePee Pete's Chow Wagon, has hot dogs and good chili.

Sharon Springs

The 19th-century spa and resort community of **Sharon Springs** (pop. 530), about 50 miles west of Albany, was once on a par with Saratoga Springs, its spas attracting as many as 10,000 visitors at a time. But for most of the past 75-plus years, the silent streets have been lined by the slowly crumbling remains of once-grand Victorian-era hotels. Sharon Springs has been kept alive thanks to its unlikely role as a seasonal escape for Orthodox Hasidic Jews fleeing the heat of New York City summers. Throughout the ups and downs, the sulfurous, supposedly health-giving waters have continued to flow, bubbling up into a small fountain in the small park at the center of town.

Sharon Springs seems ready for a revival. On Main Street, the white-columned hotels have been undergoing total overhauls. The stately **American Hotel** (192 Main St., 518/284-2105, $170 and up) has a good restaurant with a stylish cocktail bar. Guests can settle into comfy chairs lined up along the spacious front porch and watch the world go by.

Howes Cave: Iroquois Indian Museum

If you're interested in the Native American history of upstate New York, detour southeast along I-88 to tidy **Howes Cave** (pop. 4,533) and the **Iroquois Indian Museum** (324 Caverns Rd., 518/296-8949, Tues.-Sat. 10am-4pm, Sun. noon-4pm Apr.-Nov., 10am-5pm, Sun. noon-5pm May-Oct., $8). The imposing longhouse-shaped structure contains artifacts, arrowheads, and more recent works of art associated with the Native Americans descended from the Six Nations of the Iroquois Confederacy, as well as an interactive hands-on children's museum. The museum's collection of contemporary Native American painting and sculpture also asks tough probing questions about the one-dimensional casino culture that has recently come to dominate reservation life across the United States.

All over this part of New York, massive roadside billboards blare out the competitive presence of **Howe Caverns** (518/296-8900, daily, $25 and up), marked by simple yellow-and-black Howe Caverns directional signs, and **Secret Caverns** (518/296-8558, daily Apr.-Dec., $18), on which a Deadhead-ish wizard beckons you onward with pesky lines like "If you haven't seen the underground waterfall, you ain't seen guano!" Though located within two miles of each other, these two tourist attractions are about as far apart as Pat Boone and Jimi Hendrix.

The sanitized-for-your-protection Howe Caverns boast a well-lit, guided elevator and flat-bottomed boat tour of a 156-foot-deep underground cave. Along the same road, you know you're in for something completely different the moment you approach the dark foreboding Secret Caverns and enter through the mouth of a giant leering bat. Don't let the "Abandon Hope All Ye Who Enter Here" sign scare you off from taking the twisting (and twisted) 1.5-hour guided trek down into the clammy 180-foot-deep innards along a narrow, randomly lit footpath, which terminates at an impressive 100-foot waterfall.

Albany

The New York state capital, **Albany** (pop. 308,846) was founded in 1609 when Dutch traders traveling up the Hudson River from New Amsterdam on Henry Hudson's ship *Half Moon* went ashore and established a fur-trading post. As the gateway between upstate New York and the increasingly powerful New York City port, Albany remained an important trading center through the 1820s and 1830s, extending its reach with the opening of the Erie Canal and the city's growth as a central railroad terminus and manufacturing center. Nowadays, the legendary canal has long since vanished, and the glamorous New York Central railroad's French renaissance-style, turn-of-the-20th-century Union Station, at Broadway and Clinton Street, has sat mostly empty since being bypassed in favor of a lonely platform on the opposite side of the Hudson River.

NEW YORK STATE CAPITOL, ALBANY.

As the seat of the New York state government, however, Albany still wields major political power, most visibly in the towering granite slabs and flying saucer-like structures of the 98-acre Empire State Plaza government center, home to exhibition halls, theaters, a 42-story observation tower, and the excellent **New York State Museum** (518/474-5877, Tues.-Sun., free). The State Museum, Albany's main attraction, includes a sensitively organized exhibit on the state's Iroquois and Mohawk Native American cultures, centering on a reconstructed longhouse, and a fully functioning (and rideable!) Herschell-Spillman carousel. The huge area devoted to the history of New York City is as good or better than anything in "the city that never sleeps," with a recreated Upper West Side Hispanic barber shop, a Horn and Hardart Automat food dispenser, a restored 1940s car from the A-train subway line, and a solemn gallery documenting the September 11, 2001, destruction of the World Trade Center.

facade of the cottage at Springside, on exhibit in the New York State Museum

Albany Practicalities

If all the high culture and power politics leave you hungry for a back-to-basics road-food experience, head west from downtown to **Jack's Diner** (547 Central Ave., 518/482-9807). This New Jersey-built 1930s chrome-plated diner car attracts a diverse batch of families, local crazies, beat cops, and fellow travelers who come for its hearty breakfast and burgers, bottomless cups of coffee, and friendly, loquacious staff. In between Jack's and the downtown museums, the blue-collar bohemian Lark Street neighborhood is Albany's answer to Greenwich Village, sporting several cafés and a number of good international restaurants. Albany's motels congregate off the I-90 Everett Road exit.

Troy

The grave of Uncle Sam and the birthplace of the detachable shirt collar are both across the river in **Troy** (pop. 49,702), eight miles north via the I-787 freeway. A world removed from downtown Albany, this narrow riverfront city was strategically situated at the point where the Erie Canal headed west from the Hudson River. It rose to national prominence as a manufacturing center in the 19th century, when its foundries and factories cranked out iron for stoves, stagecoaches, bells, and battleships.

Troy's burly factories have given way to a quietly picturesque college town, with Rensselaer Polytechnic Institute rising on the steep hill to the east above the cast-iron business district downtown. In addition to its many impressive buildings, Troy's dense downtown has two great road-food finds: **Manory's Restaurant** (99 Congress St., 518/272-2422) doles out stuffed combo sandwiches, home-cooked pasta, and really, really big breakfasts, while **The Famous Lunch** (111 Congress St., 518/272-9481) is a delightfully worn-down greasy spoon with

UNCLE SAM

Troy's prominent Uncle Sam monument, along the waterfront at River and Fulton Streets, memorializes bearded local meat-packer Samuel Wilson, who supplied beef to the soldiers quartered at the local Watervliet Arsenal during the War of 1812. Wilson's donations were quickly dubbed "Uncle Sam's beef," and the nickname and character have become the finger-pointing stuff of legend. Wilson himself is buried in the macabre Gothic hillside Oakwood Cemetery, at the head of 101st Street north of Troy via Oakwood Avenue. A health food store around the corner from the monument admonishes passersby with an "I want you . . . to enjoy good health" window poster.

hand-lettered signs, tall wooden booths, and an eye-opening clientele of cops, winos, RPI students, and local businesspeople. From noon until late every day but Sunday, nearly all the clientele chow down on multiple four-inch-long chili-doused hot dogs served on Styrofoam plates with cold RC Colas on the side.

Mount Lebanon Shaker Village

Heading east from Albany across the Hudson River toward the Massachusetts state line, US-20 follows Columbia Avenue through the warehouse and factory town of **Rensselaer,** then climbs a long retail-lined hill past innumerable liquor stores, mini-marts, gas stations, and motels into the Taconic Mountains. Also here is the full-throttle dirt oval of the **Lebanon Valley Speedway** (518/794-9606), with racing throughout the summer.

After this barrage of contemporary culture, the tranquil hillside remains of **Mount Lebanon Shaker Village,** on the south side of US-20 a few hundred yards west of the Massachusetts border, come as a welcome relief. Of the 20 Shaker communities once scattered over the eastern United States, practicing a passionate but celibate form of Christianity, Mount Lebanon was the head ministry, founded here in 1785. The community endured until 1947, and some two dozen historic buildings still stand, including a 192-foot stone barn—the largest stone barn in the world when constructed in 1859—and a no-frills but cleverly constructed 1854 washhouse boasting hidden wall drawers and

Troy's Astros-affiliated Class A **Tri-City ValleyCats** (518/629-2287), transplanted from Pittsfield, Massachusetts, play on the campus of Hudson Valley Community College.

Downtown Troy's cast-iron buildings are popular with set designers, who transform them into backdrops for films like Martin Scorsese's 1992 adaptation of Edith Wharton's *The Age of Innocence.*

DETOUR: COOPERSTOWN

The neat, prosperous village of **Cooperstown** (pop. 1,770), founded in 1786 by the father of *Last of the Mohicans* novelist James Fenimore Cooper, was transformed into a family tourist mecca thanks to the **National Baseball Hall of Fame** (25 Main St., 888/425-5633 or 607/547-7200, daily, $23), which opened here in 1939. Recently expanded and upgraded, the Hall of Fame revolves around a beautifully organized time line of dioramas and display cases that walk you through the sport's greatest—and most embarrassing—moments. You'll see Babe Ruth's bat, the pair of cracked black leather shoes worn by the ill-fated and latterly famous 1919 "Black Sox" player Shoeless Joe Jackson, and rows and rows of bronze plaques naming all the greats of the game. Special exhibits highlight the Negro Leagues, women in baseball, and, of course, baseball cards, all amid a voluminous collection of uniforms, periodicals, programs, player records, scrapbooks, and film and audio holdings. The combination admission ticket (around $37) to the Baseball Hall of Fame also gains you entrance to the other Cooperstown museums.

Cooperstown's many attractions are augmented by the subtler delights of the **Fenimore Art Museum** (888/547-1450 or 607/547-1400, daily summer, Tues.-Sun. Apr. and Sept.-Dec., $12), which, along with memorabilia of the writer, has engaging displays of Native American artifacts, folk art, and Hudson River School paintings. The Fenimore House is on Lake Street, a mile north of town along the shores of Otsego Lake, which is the source of the Susquehanna River, known locally as "Glimmerglass" for its spectacular sparkling appearance.

Near the Fenimore House, the **Farmers' Museum** (888/547-1450 or 607/547-1450, daily summer, Tues.-Sun. spring and fall, special programs only in winter, $12) has illuminating exhibits on 19th-century rural life, with dignified agricultural and local history exhibits occupying most of the sturdy stone structures speckling this 1918 farm. The "remains" of the previously encountered Cardiff Giant lie in stony silence.

Avoid the in-town parking hassles and stash your car in one of the free lots near the Fenimore House. Then catch a city-operated **trolley** ($2 for an unlimited day pass) to downtown.

In the several-block central business district, every other bookstore, restaurant, and variety store seems to be cashing in on their tourist customers' insatiable appetite for baseball-related camp and nostalgia. For example, the **Doubleday Café** (93 Main St., 607/547-5468) has above-average food and a Father-of-the-National-Pastime theme.

There are dozens of hotels and motels from which to choose in the Cooperstown area, and the Hall of Fame offers many package deals; be sure to make your reservations far in advance to beat the summer rush. The **Lake Front Motel, Restaurant and Marina** (10 Fair St., 607/547-9511, $95-270) has a lakefront beach within walking distance of downtown, while in-town lodging options include the grand **Otesaga Resort Hotel** (60 Lake St., 607/547-9931, $320 and up).

For more information on Cooperstown, including details on the popular summertime **Glimmerglass Opera Festival**, contact the **visitors bureau** (31 Chestnut St., 607/322-4046).

Irving, - Photographer, - Troy.

Mt. Lebanon. Columbia Co., N. Y.

Shaker Church.

perfectly fitted floorboards. All the craftsmanship is testimony to the Shaker edict, "Hands to work, hearts to God."

The **Shaker Museum** (202 Shaker Rd., 518/794-9100, Fri.-Mon. 11am-4pm mid-June-mid-Oct.) has the world's most extensive collection of Shaker-related items, from Shaker seed catalogs and pieces of Shaker furniture to the woodworking tools and devices used to make them.

The quickest route east from Troy is Hwy-2, a rural back road across the Taconic Mountains to Williamstown, Massachusetts. Alternatively, you can follow old US-20 east through New Lebanon to Pittsfield, Massachusetts, then follow a short stretch of the **Appalachian Trail** route along US-7 north to **Williamstown** and **North Adams** (see page 325). Coverage of that route begins on page 298.

MASSACHUSETTS

Across Massachusetts, we follow the scenic Route 2, also known as the **Mohawk Trail,** across the state's northern tier, rather than US-20, which runs more or less underneath the Massachusetts Turnpike, I-90. Passing across some of the least populous and most deeply forested acres in the whole Commonwealth of Massachusetts, you can easily imagine you're in Vermont rather than the so-called Bay State. Picking its way over the flattened summits of the Hoosac Range foothills to the Green Mountains in the north, Route 2 follows rock-strewn trout streams flecked with white water and shaded by boreal forests of hemlock, yellow birch, and red spruce—including some of the state's only remaining stands of old growth. Midway across Massachusetts, Route 2 bridges the Connecticut River above Turners Falls, lopes through the

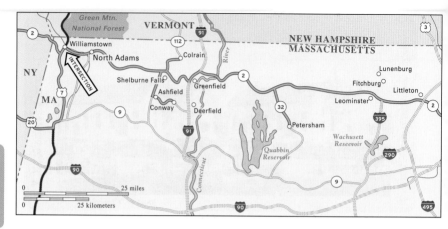

In Massachusetts and the rest of New England, we have adopted the use of "Route" instead of "Hwy," in keeping with regional practice.

trees, and emerges at historic **Lexington** and **Concord,** at **Boston**'s back door.

The Mohawk Trail

Running east from North Adams toward Greenfield and I-91, and taking its name from the warpath used for raids against Algonquin settlements along the upper Connecticut River Valley, the **Mohawk Trail** (Route 2) was one of the nation's first scenic highways, improved and paved as early as 1914 as part of a massive state effort to lure tourists into this cash-deprived farm belt of New England. If you're driving an overloaded or underpowered vehicle, you'll appreciate the thrill and radiator-popping risks that once attended the slow switchback grind up around the attention-getting Hairpin Turn at the edge of the Western Summit. The turn is so tight that signs insist on a 15-mph speed limit, and people who don't abide by the rules are likely to find themselves screeching around past the sightseers at the friendly **Golden Eagle Restaurant** (1935 Mohawk Trail, 413/663-9834).

Farther up, at the top of the hill, the tidy **Whitcomb Summit Retreat** (413/664-0007, $109-149) is in the best shape of the many photogenic old motor courts along this route. It has been taking in guests since 1914. One of the original cottages has been left untouched, but the rest of the resort has been fully modernized.

Don't be fooled by the short stretch of gentle ups and downs east of the summit over the glacier-flattened mountain peaks: The route east along the tortuous Cold River ravine quickens the pulse, even in these days of power steering and antilock brakes, especially if you get sandwiched between a pair of 18-wheelers, whose burning brake pads sometimes scent the air all the way down the valley.

East of the summit, dropping down into the valley of the Deerfield River, you pass groups of kayakers and some roadside stands offering rentals of inner tubes—the white-water equivalent of a recliner, and the preferred

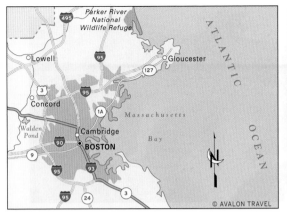

mayflower,
state flower of Massachussetts

Native View

mode of transport for those interested in relaxing and enjoying the ride. More serious river runners may want to sign up for one of the trips offered by **Zoar Outdoor** (800/532-7483), who also welcome travelers with a range of cabins, yurts, and camping options. The Mohawk Trail area is also home to some enticingly kitschy old "Indian Trading Post"-style tourist attractions and souvenir shops, all packed full of postcards, plastic tomahawks, and moccasins; my personal favorite is the **Native View,** formerly known as the Big Indian Shop because it's fronted by a historically inaccurate, politically incorrect, and photogenically irresistible 35-foot-tall statue of a Plains man. Another giant Native American statue, a half-ton bronze titled *Hail to the Sunrise,* stands along Route 2 just west of the town of Charlemont.

You'll find excellent wooded hiking trails and streamside campsites in **Mohawk Trail State Forest** (413/339-5504), just above where the Cold River empties into Deerfield. There are six year-round rustic log cabins too, but make reservations well in advance if you have your heart set on staying in one.

Shelburne Falls

Travelers in search of variety should head farther along the historic Mohawk Trail, Route 2, and take a turn at the signs for the lively, artsy little town of **Shelburne Falls,** which is actually two towns, Shelburne and Buckland (combined pop. 1,731), facing one another across the Deerfield River. The two are linked by the **Bridge of Flowers,** a former electric trolley bridge that was converted to a linear display garden after the trolleys closed down in the 1920s. Four score and a few years later, there are mature trees growing out of the concrete arches. Every spring local gardeners add rich displays of annual color. The story of the trolleys is told and rides are sometimes offered at the **Shelburne Falls Trolley Museum** (14 Depot Rd., 413/625-9443, free), in walking distance south of the bridge.

Bridge of Flowers in Shelburne Falls

Nearby food and beverage options include vegetarian-friendly sandwiches and espresso concoctions from the cooperatively run **McCusker's Market** (3 State St., 413/625-9411), facing the south end of the iron bridge. Two candidates for best grub in town face off along Bridge Street: the homey **Fox Towne Diner** (413/625-6606), where you can feast on a short stack of pancakes with real maple syrup or enjoy a fresh BLT with a packet of potato chips and a pickle on the side, across from the locally sourced, sustainably armed fare at **Hearty Eats** (413/625-6460). At the west end of the bridge, there's a third way, the burgers and salads and beers at the **West End Pub.**

Scenic Route 116: Ashfield and Conway

Come fall, the sugar maples in the surrounding mixed hardwood forest add a blaze of brilliant orange to the landscape, making Route 2 a favorite of leaf-peepers between the end of September and Columbus Day weekend. But if sharing the two-lane road with thousands of rubbernecking drivers becomes wearisome, consider taking a road less traveled. Almost any road will do, but a loop along Route 116 through **Ashfield** and **Conway,** a few miles south of Route 2, passes over several historic covered bridges and offers enough pastoral beauty to more than compensate for the detours.

Greenfield and Deerfield

As Route 2 speeds down into the Connecticut River Valley, it veers along I-91 just long enough to skirt the county seat of **Greenfield,** a place once known for its cutlery, tap-and-die, and other metals-related manufacturing. The proximity of the interstate has endowed Greenfield with some of the few chain motels in western Massachusetts, but it also supports the warm hospitality of the **People's Pint** (24 Federal St., 413/773-0333), serving up good food and pints of New England's most interesting locally-brewed beer.

A world away from the modern interstate aesthetic, but just three miles south of Greenfield along Route 5, **Historic Deerfield** (413/774-5581, daily Apr.-Dec., $18) is an immaculately preserved ensemble of architecture and agriculture dating back over 350 years. More than a dozen clapboard buildings, shaded by a canopy of stately old elm trees, form a mile-long reminder of the time when this part of Massachusetts formed the western frontier of "civilization," and English settlers waged bloody war against the native Pocumtuck people. The adjacent town of Deerfield, and the famous Deerfield Academy prep school, hardly intrude, leaving Historic Deerfield to stand as it was—fanlight windows, wrought iron, well-worn stones and all. Inside each house, guides discuss the lives, belongings, and historical contexts of the former inhabitants, often with such parental intimacy that you half-expect these long-dead Ebenezers, Jonathans, and Marys to be napping upstairs. One of the finest surviving colonial townscapes in America, Historic Deerfield is well worth a visit, no matter how brief.

Historic Deerfield also offers the **Flynt Center of Early New England Life** at the edge of a field behind Main Street. The 27,000-square-foot museum, designed to look like a colonial tobacco barn, displays thousands of "fancy goods" and other consumer treasures—pewter teapots, silk waistcoats, and the like—that were keys to civilized life here on the edge of wilderness. For the full historic experience, stay for dinner or overnight at the **Deerfield Inn** (413/774-5587, $235 and up), right in the historic core.

It's outside the historic core of Deerfield, and not technically in the Berkshires for that matter, but one of New England's great beermakers, **Berkshire Brewing Company** (12 Railroad St., 413/665-6600), offers tours and tastings in South Deerfield.

Although early spring is aptly known as mud season throughout New England's backcountry, it's also when the sugar maple sap starts to flow. Boil away nearly 98 percent of the sap and you have genuine maple syrup delicious enough to make muddy frost-heaved farm roads positively inviting.

Northeast of Deerfield, near the Vermont border, the town of **Northfield** had the first youth hostel in the United States in 1934. Unfortunately, the hostel closed in 1998, taken over as dormitories by a local college.

Route 2: Gardner

About 10 miles east of I-91, Route 2 crosses high over the Connecticut River atop the huge art deco French King Bridge, giving grand views over the surrounding landscape. From here east, the route becomes a mini freeway as it launches into a 40-mile stretch of almost nothing but forest; though nearly unimaginable today, some two-thirds of the landscape you see out your windows was totally deforested in the early 1800s. After some 150 years, that statistic has been reversed, although much of the forest along this stretch is relatively young, having grown up since a devastating hurricane in 1938 blew down nearly every pine tree in its path.

For most of the way across this part of central Massachusetts, the older two-lane alignment of the Mohawk Trail (Route 2) is still in use as Route 2A, running

through a series of small towns like Orange, Athol, Templeton, and **Gardner** (pop. 20,430), which was once one of the busiest chair-making centers in the United States. The area's industrial history is remembered by the town's pride and joy, the onetime **World's Largest Chair,** which sits on the front lawn of Gardner's Elm Street elementary school.

Leominster

As you approach the Tri-Town area of **Leominster** (pronounced "LEH-min-ster"), **Fitchburg,** and **Lunenburg,** rooftops begin to supplant treetops and Boston radio stations crowd the dial. Although "The Hub" is still some 30 miles away, its gravitational attraction seems to compel a majority of cars to exceed the speed limit. If you already know that you would rather walk barefoot over hot coals than be caught driving in Boston, you can start looking for accommodations now, as you are within the sphere of the **MBTA Commuter Rail service** (617/222-3200) to downtown. Purely by way of an example, the 90-minute journey from end-of-the-line Fitchburg to Boston's North Station, made 10 times daily on weekdays, five times daily on weekends, costs around $22 round-trip—equivalent to a couple of hours' parking in most Boston lots.

Accommodations here, along I-495 on the perimeter of the Boston metropolitan area, are largely geared toward business travelers, though the aptly named **Friendly Crossways Hostel** (247 Littleton County Rd., 978/456-9386), just north of the Route 2/I-495 junction in the hamlet (not the college) of Harvard, has HI-approved dorm beds and a few private rooms.

Practicalities aside, one positive reason to spend time out here is the presence of **Fruitlands** (102 Prospect Hill Rd., 978/456-3924, Wed.-Mon. Apr.-Nov., $14), a 210-acre indoor-outdoor art center. Spiritual heir to the historic Utopian colony that started (and failed) here in 1843, Fruitlands now houses the Harvard College museum of American arts and crafts, Native American lifeways, and Shaker design.

Lowell

At "five o'clock of a red-all-over suppertime" on March 12, 1922, Jack Kerouac—baptized John L. (Jean-Louis) Kirouac by his French-Canadian parents—was born in **Lowell** (pop. 110,558), a city sincerely regarded as one of the wonders of the world back when the Industrial Revolution was as fascinating as the Internet is now. Although this original dharma bum is more widely remembered for hanging out with Ferlinghetti in San Francisco and Ginsberg in New York, and for pasting the beat generation firmly across the map of American culture, Kerouac also wrote five novels based on friends and familiar places in his native city. His fictional work, from *On the Road* on, is that much more interesting when read in the context of his real life in this Merrimack River mill town.

Though Lowell is doubtless best known as the home of Jack Kerouac, in recent years the town made the news as the home of boxing brothers Micky Ward and Dicky Ecklund, whose story was the basis of the 2010 film *The Fighter,* which was set and filmed here.

Reciprocating Kerouac's lifelong love for Lowell, the National Park Service publishes a walking-tour brochure on Jack and his life in Lowell. It also helps sponsor the annual **Lowell Celebrates Kerouac!** festival in early October. Maps and guides to the man and the town are available from the **Lowell National Historical Park visitors center** (67 Kirk St., 978/970-5000); **parking** (304 Dutton St.) is a block west.

If you want to pay your respects to Kerouac, who died in Florida in 1969, he is buried in **Edson Cemetery,** two miles south of downtown Lowell via Gorham Street. Fans by the hundreds beat a path to his grave, which is on Lincoln Avenue between 7th and 8th Streets, marked by a pile of beer cans and other ritual offerings.

Even without the Kerouac connection, Lowell—with its working water-powered looms, canal tours, and engaging interpretive tours—would deserve attention.

Befitting its blue-collar past, Lowell is home to several classic diners. The best of the diners is the excellent **Arthur's Paradise Diner** (112 Bridge St., 978/452-8647), a 1937 Worcester diner where the house specialty is the great big Boot Mill sandwich, a two-hands-full combination of eggs, cheese, potatoes, and meat—lots of meat.

Lowell's other legendary blue-collar landmarks include the **Club Diner** (145 Dutton St., 978/452-1679) and the **Four Sisters' Owl Diner** (244 Appleton St., 978/453-8321, daily).

Concord: The Shot Heard Round the World

Route 2 feels increasingly freeway-like the closer you get to Boston, but there are a few things in the neighborhood you may want to check out if you're not in a hurry to hit "The Hub." A good example is lovely little **Concord** (pop. 17,669), the destination of British Redcoats that fabled day in April 1775 when the war for American independence began. A reconstructed **Old North Bridge,** site of the "shot heard round the world," still arches over the placid Concord River next to open fields and dry stone walls. The superb setting draws artists and picnickers as well as history buffs, and if the crowds aren't too bad, the scene ranks among the most evocative in New England. The **Minute Man National Historical Park** (978/369-6993) maintains a free year-round visitors center on the hillside overlooking the famous site. Stop in and pick up a guide to the rest of the park's 900-acre holdings along the "Battle Road" (a.k.a. Lexington Road and Route 2A) between Concord and Lexington. (And try to turn a deaf ear to the constant stream of small planes flying in and out of nearby Hanscom Field.)

Get to know life in Lowell by watching a Class A baseball game at downtown's riverside **LeLacheur Park,** home to the Red Sox-affiliated **Lowell Spinners** (978/459-1702).

Although it often seems as if you can't toss a stick anywhere in eastern Massachusetts without hitting something of historic significance, this is especially true in and around Concord, where some of the most influential American writers—Ralph Waldo Emerson, Nathaniel Hawthorne, Henry David Thoreau, and Louisa May Alcott, to name the most famous four—lived or worked. To get a sense of the lives of these influential and interconnected writers, head to that ancient-looking parsonage alongside the famous Old North Bridge, **The Old Manse** (269 Monument St., 978/369-3909, daily, grounds free, house $10), whose study window views are not so different from what they were when Ralph Waldo Emerson and Nathaniel Hawthorne lived here. And if the mood strikes you, you can visit the final resting place of these literary lions along Author's Ridge in **Sleepy Hollow Cemetery,** off Bedford Street northeast of the town center.

the Minute Man National Historical Park

Visitors may be struck by the quantity of "No Parking" signs lining the streets of Concord. The reason for this barrage of apparent inhospitality may be seen on any sun-drenched summer weekend, when long columns of cars bound for the beach at nearby **Walden Pond** jam Route 126. Serious fans of Henry David Thoreau and his little experiment of simple living may be able to overlook its overstressed condition, but more than likely you'll be taken aback by the erosion, the crowds, and the racket of passing commuter trains. Of course, there is still some magic to the place, although it usually takes a near-dawn in late spring or near-dusk in late fall to find any hint of peace or magnificence along the pond's well-worn peripheral path.

For a quick introduction to all this and more, stop by the **Concord Museum** (978/369-9763, daily, $10), just east of the town green, where the collection contains everything from the lantern used in Paul Revere's famous ride to dozens of household objects (beds, chairs, desks, etc.) belonging to Emerson and Thoreau.

If you want to linger in Concord long enough to have some transcendent moments of your own, stay the night at one of many nice B&Bs, like the **Hawthorne Inn** (462 Lexington Rd., 978/369-5610, $199 and up), across from Hawthorne's home, The Wayside, which is part of the Minute Man National Park.

Perhaps you haven't got a week—like Thoreau did—to paddle down the Concord River. You can still make your own, albeit abbreviated, journey with a summer or fall canoe rental from **South Bridge Boat House** (496 Main St., 978/369-9438, around $18 per hour).

Ralph Waldo Emerson's marker in Sleepy Hollow Cemetery

PATRIOTS AND POETS

One of the more enjoyable rites of springtime in and around Boston is the annual celebration of the events leading up to the American Revolution. Now held on the third Monday in April, but originally occurring on April 18, the state holiday known as Patriot's Day sees all kinds of special events. Most famous is the Boston Marathon, which since 1897 has been run from Hopkinton southwest of the city through Newton to its finish at Copley Square. Although the marathon follows a different route, it is held on the anniversary of another famous race, the one between British soldiers and patriot Paul Revere, who made his legendary ride on the night of April 18, 1775, to warn his fellow minutemen of the British march on Lexington and Concord.

At the end of his ride, on the morning of April 19, Paul Revere reached the Buckman Tavern in Lexington, where fellow revolutionaries John Hancock and Samuel Adams (he of boutique beer fame) were asleep, awaiting word of the British advance. Revere woke them (and some 70 others), and at 5:30am they assembled to meet the redcoats. Although the minutemen backed off, shots were fired and eight Americans were killed. Three hours later, when the British moved on to Concord, they were met by a much larger and better organized force of minutemen, who fired back and started what we now know as the Revolutionary War. This battle, which raged all day and followed the overwhelmed British all the way back to Boston, was remembered in another oft-recited patriotic poem by Concord writer Ralph Waldo Emerson, words from which are inscribed on the base of Concord's statue *The Minute Man*:

By the rude bridge that arched the flood
Their flag to April's breeze unfurled
Here once the embattled farmers stood
And fired the shot heard round the world.

These events and many related ones are all reenacted each year, either on their actual anniversary or on Patriot's Day, and usually at the historically accurate crack of dawn.

Cambridge

One last stop before you hit Boston proper is erudite **Cambridge** (pop. 110,651). The inseparable sibling to the big city is best known for its top universities, **Harvard** and **Massachusetts Institute of Technology.** Cambridge is a liberal, earthy, and open-minded foil to the big money and social pretension that so often characterize its big brother across the water.

The two universities and their many fine museums (especially Harvard, which boasts world-class collections in the Fogg Art Museum, the Arthur M. Sackler Museum of Far Eastern Art, and the Peabody Museum of Archaeology and Ethnology) are the main draws for visitors, but the "town" away from the "gown" is equally worth exploring, despite the recent outbreak of chain-store disease around Harvard Square. One of the most beautiful gardens in the Boston area is **Mount Auburn Cemetery,** along the Charles River in western Cambridge: 170 acres of trees, hills, paths, and

Not far from Thoreau's reconstructed cabin at Walden Pond, a different philosophy of simplicity may be found in the design of the **Gropius House** (781/259-8098, Wed.-Sun. 11am-5pm summer, Sat.-Sun. 11am-5pm fall-spring, $15), on Baker Bridge Road in **Lincoln.** Built in 1937-1938 by and for Bauhaus founder Walter Gropius, this small showcase blends Bauhaus form-is-function precepts with traditional New England simplicity.

Driving Across Boston

From Concord, the remaining dozen miles to Boston are most quickly devoured along Route 2, although you can take slower Route 2A if you wish to follow the footsteps of those retreating British redcoats. Either way will bring you to the same gateway for the metropolitan area. Following US-3 will bring you in through wealthy Winchester and eventually onto Memorial Drive along the Charles River, past the campuses of Harvard and MIT. But unless it's 3am and the roads are all clear, you would be well-advised to leave your car in the gigantic **Alewife T subway station commuter parking garage** (about $15 a day) at the junction of Route 2, US-3, and Route 16 in Arlington, and use the subway to get around the city. (Cyclists note: From the Alewife T, the nice **Minuteman Bikeway** follows the bed of the old Boston & Lowell Railroad between Cambridge and the edge of Concord—10 idyllic car-free miles.)

Driving directions across downtown Boston are basically a waste of paper; signs are few and traffic is chaotic, and anyway you'll need to keep your eyes firmly on the road.

Quincy: The Adams Family

South of Boston, Route 3 reemerges from the I-93 freeway at **Quincy** (pop. 93,688), home of the Adams family, the political dynasty that helped shape the early republic. John Adams (1735-1826) signed the Declaration of Independence, served as a diplomat during the Revolutionary War, helped negotiate the Treaty of Paris, then returned home to become George Washington's vice president and successor. His son, John Quincy Adams (1767-1848), served as president from 1825 to 1829. Rather than quit politics after losing the election in 1828, he returned to Washington, serving in the House of Representatives for the next 16 years. The rather modest houses where both men were born, plus a nice garden and a historic church, are preserved as part of the **Adams National Historic Site** (1250 Hancock St., 617/770-1175, daily, $10), which covers 13 downtown acres starting at a visitors center.

More recently, Quincy has been home to the truly huge Fore River Shipyard. This dense forest of cranes, derricks, and scaffolding rises along the south side of the 1930s Fore River Bridge, along Route 3A at the south edge of town.

Plymouth Rock and Plimoth Plantation

Although the Pilgrims are often given credit for establishing the first permanent European settlement in what later became the United States, they arrived a

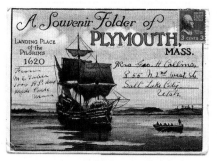

dozen years after other English settlers established Jamestown, Virginia. There's even less evidence to back up the story of **Plymouth Rock,** the supposed landing site of those weary *Mayflower* passengers back in 1620, but like the Liberty Bell and Mt. Rushmore, it's something every red-blooded American tourist has to see.

Now protected by a neoclassical granite portico and inscribed with the date 1620, Plymouth Rock is right on the waterfront, off Water Street at the south end of North Street in **Plymouth.** The rock is part of pleasant **Pilgrim Memorial State Park,** which also includes the *Mayflower II* (daily Apr.-Nov., $10), a replica of the Pilgrims' ship, where an onboard exhibit describes the Pilgrims' two-month transatlantic journey. The *Mayflower* is about the only sign of Plymouth being a potential tourist trap; the whole place is actually fairly low-key, with a couple of gift shops and snack bars across from the rock. Two blocks inland, downtown Plymouth looks like any other pleasant New England suburb, with no tacky T-shirt shops to be found.

Two miles south from Plymouth Rock along Route 3A, or off the Route 3 freeway at exit 5, **Plimoth Plantation** (508/746-1622, daily, $28) is a living history re-creation of the original Pilgrim colony and features costumed interpreters taking part in planting, harvesting, and other daily chores.

> Playing on the common perception of the Pilgrims as thrifty, reliable, and steadfast, in 1928 the automobile company Chrysler named its now-defunct line of low-priced cars Plymouth.

New Bedford

Predominantly Portuguese **New Bedford** (pop. 95,032) is remembered as a capital of the whaling industry back in the days when spermaceti candles and whale oil lamps were necessities, not antiques. The city's harbor at the mile-wide mouth of the Acushnet River was home port for the East Coast's largest commercial fishing fleet until nearly two decades of flagrant overfishing brought the industry to collapse. The **New Bedford Whaling National Historical Park** showcases the cobblestone streets and brick facades, virtually unaltered since Herman Melville shipped out of here in 1840 aboard a whaler bound for the Pacific. For a good orientation, drop by the well-stocked **visitors center** (508/996-4095), at the corner of William Street and North 2nd Street, and join one

> New Bedford's Acushnet Avenue has a significant place in the world of late-19th-century American art: Albert Pinkham Ryder, visionary "painter of dreams," was born here, across from the childhood home of Albert Bierstadt, Romantic painter of the American West.

of the free hour-long guided walking tours. Before or after a stroll around town, head to the top of Johnny Cake Hill and visit the excellent **New Bedford Whaling Museum** (508/997-0046, daily, $17). Scrimshaw (carved whale ivory), tools of the whaling trade, historic photos, special maritime exhibits, and an 89-foot ship model are a few of the artifacts found in the not-to-be-missed museum collection maintained by the Old Dartmouth Historical Society. Across the street from the museum, the gorgeous little

painting by a New Bedford whaleman, 1840

Boston

In the nearly 400 years since its founding, Boston (pop. 673,184) has witnessed more historically significant events than any American city even twice its size. The youthful energy of the city's many college students certainly helps cloak its traditional Puritan parochialism, while the high-tech economic boom and the breaking of the "Curse of the Bambino" by the 2004 World Series-champion Boston Red Sox baseball team have helped loosen up a city previously best known for baked beans and banning sexy books.

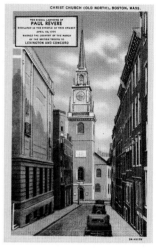

There are lots of places to start a Boston tour, but a personal favorite is the **Old North Church** (193 Salem St., 617/523-6676, daily, donation), a Boston landmark since well before Paul Revere set off on his midnight ride. The steeple has been rebuilt, but almost everything else dates back to colonial times. The **Paul Revere House** (19 North Square, 617/523-2338, daily Apr.-Dec., Tues.-Sun. Jan.-Mar., $5), the oldest in Boston, is a few blocks away. The surrounding neighborhood, the predominantly Italian North End, is the city's oldest and most pedestrian-friendly quarter. Its narrow streets jut out toward Boston harbor.

With its abundance of universities, museums, and cultural centers, Boston is packed with places to improve your mind. One of the nicest has to be the **Isabella Stuart Gardner Museum** (25 Evans Way, 617/566-1401, Wed.-Mon., $15). In the late 19th century, "Mrs. Jack" Gardner built her home in the style of a Venetian palazzo, crammed it with exquisite art, and then opened it as a museum. And what a museum, now better than ever thanks to the copper-and-glass Renzo Piano-designed addition fronting the lushly landscaped interior courtyard. (Note: Anyone named "Isabella" gets in free!) The much bigger **Museum of Fine Arts** (465 Huntington Ave., 617/267-9300, daily, $25) is only a short walk away and has more

night game at Fenway Park

than 200 world-class galleries of just about every type and era of fine art, including world-class Impressionists and perhaps the best Japanese art collection in the United States.

For baseball fans, Boston's must-see is **Fenway Park** (4 Yawkey Way, tickets 877/733-7699), home of the Red Sox. Located off Boylston Street, this is the oldest, smallest, and arguably most entertaining stadium in the nation.

PRACTICALITIES

Boston, a.k.a. "The Hub," sits spider-like at the center of a web of major highways. Air travelers get to deal with the chaos and malfunction of Logan International Airport, the major gateway to New England for U.S. and overseas flights. Logan is central—just a seven-minute ride across Boston Harbor to downtown if you take the Water Shuttle. Logan is also connected to the city by the Blue Line subway run by **Massachusetts Bay Transportation Authority** (800/392-6100 or 617/222-3200), the "T," a well-run and nearly comprehensive network of subways, buses, trams, ferries, and commuter trains. Despite the completion of the $15 billion Big Dig, Boston's 21st-century traffic and 17th-century streets are not for faint-hearted drivers. Narrow, often unidentified, poorly maintained, and laid out in irregular patterns conforming to long-buried topography, the streets of Boston are also home to aggressive bumper-riding red light-runners. So park your car, take public transit, and walk.

While nightly rates at top-end hotels run well over $400 a night, places to stay in Boston start with the budget **HI-Boston Hostel** (19 Stuart St., 617/536-9455, $44 per person, higher for a private room). As befitting a historical city such as Boston, the hostel is in a National Register of Historic Places building; as befitting the times, it is a green LEED-certified building as well. For a moderate price and a great location, right at the Copley Square finish line of the Boston Marathon, try the popular **Charlesmark Hotel** (655 Boylston, 617/247-1212, around $250 and up).

Thanks no doubt to Boston's Puritan past, the city has never had a great reputation for its food, but things have definitely changed. For an old-fashioned Boston meal, you could go to **Durgin-Park** (617/227-2038, daily), open since 1827 in what's now Faneuil Hall Market Place, or opt for the casual and popular **James Hook & Company** (15 Northern Ave., 617/423-5501), serving up delicious lobster rolls on the downtown waterfront since the 1920s. Boston also has more than a few great Mexican, Japanese, and Chinese places. For another only-in-Boston experience, head to **The Daily Catch** (323 Hanover St., 617/523-8567, daily, cash only), in the old North End within walking distance of the Haymarket T. This family-run place, started in 1973, is so tiny that the cook could shake hands with half his customers without leaving his stove. Calamari (squid) is the house specialty, but the menu's mainstay is Sicilian seafood over linguine (with red or white sauce), served in sauté pans instead of on plates. It doesn't take reservations, so expect a wait after 6pm.

Every year, on the anniversary of the **Boston Tea Party** (December 16, 1773), reenactors dressed as Native Americans, mimicking the colonists, who disguised themselves as Native Americans, throw bales of tea into the harbor from the decks of the Boston Tea Party Ship.

Massachusetts is one of two states that recognizes private property ownership down to the low tide line, which is why you should respect the "No Trespassing" signs you may encounter on some beaches. Fortunately, plenty are amended with the words "Walkers Welcome."

Seamen's Bethel, dedicated in 1832 and featuring a pulpit shaped like a ship's bow, was featured in a chapter of Herman Melville's classic, *Moby Dick*.

Diner fans will appreciate New Bedford's offerings too. The easiest diner to find is **Angelo's Orchid Diner** (805 Rockdale Ave., 508/993-3172), on old US-6, a 1953 O'Mahony serving solid short-order cookery enlivened by—you guessed it—a Portuguese influence.

Cape Cod: Sandwich

Although it rides the ridge of Cape Cod's glacial moraine, the forest-clad US-6 freeway (called Mid-Cape Highway) affords few good vistas. Traffic willing, you'll sail between the Sagamore Bridge and the Outer Cape in about 30 minutes, surrounded by more green than blue. One preferred route is parallel Route 6A. Never more than a mile or two from US-6, this slower road is a good introduction to a part of the Cape that does its utmost to stay quaint without being too cute. Generally, it succeeds.

Take **Sandwich,** for example. When you reach the center of town, you'll come across a small irregular green bordered by a tall white church, a stately carriage-stop inn, and the Historical Society's **Sandwich Glass Museum** (129 Main St., 508/888-0251, daily Apr.-Dec., Wed.-Sun. Feb.-Mar., $9). Although the town's various glassworks could and did produce consummate extravagant vases and other artistic pieces, they mostly created inexpensive mass-market stuff—such as 10-cent oil-lamp chimneys and pressed plates and saucers, hundreds of which are on display.

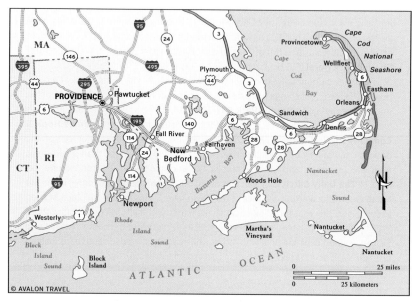

Nearby on Pine and Grove Streets (follow signs from Route 130) is a more diverse collection of Americana, the **Heritage Museums and Gardens** (508/888-3300, daily Apr.-Oct., $18). Here, 100 acres of landscaped gardens surround collections of Currier & Ives prints, military miniatures, antique cars, cigar store figures, American primitive portraiture—more unflattering likenesses of children have never been conceived—and even a working 1912 carousel.

Bayside Route 6A

In total contrast to the high-speed US-6 freeway or the traffic-clogged, overdeveloped, and frequently ugly Route 28 along the south shore, **Route 6A** along Cape Cod Bay shows off the Cape as it should be seen. Route 6A's winding back roads pass through small historic town after small historic town, and they are lined by seafood shacks, ice cream stands, high-style restaurants, colonial-era homes, village greens, and stately churches—backed all the way by miles of bay-front beaches.

If you can't get a ticket to Fenway Park, get a feel for New England baseball by catching a Triple-A **Pawtucket Red Sox** game at **McCoy Stadium** (401/724-7300), right in the heart of this historic mill town.

From Sandwich in the west to Brewster in the east, Route 6A offers a taste of what the Cape is all about. **Barnstable** (pop. 45,193), for example, is the second-oldest community on Cape Cod (founded in 1639) and has managed to retain its historic core through the years. A series of quaint villages line the bay between here and **Brewster** (pop. 9,820), which has 85 acres of coastal marshlands outside the **Cape Cod Museum of Natural History** (869 Main St., 508/896-3867, daily, $15) and the old-fashioned **Brewster Store** (1935 Main St., 508/896-3744), in a building originally built as a church in 1852.

Midway along, **Dennis** is home to the nation's oldest professional summer-stock theater, the **Cape Playhouse** (box office 508/385-3911). If you prefer film over stage, the **Cape Cinema** (508/385-2503), on the grounds behind the playhouse, specializes in movies you won't find at the multiplex; if you arrive late, stick around until the lights go up after the credits or you'll miss one of the Cape's best public artworks, Rockwell Kent's brightly colored Zodiac-themed mural of Prometheus on the cinema's ceiling.

Dennis also offers the chance to take in excellent Cape Cod views from atop **Scargo Tower,** built of local stone atop Cape Cod's highest point.

Cape Cod National Seashore

The outermost stretch of Cape Cod, from Orleans to Provincetown, is protected from commercial development within the **Cape Cod National Seashore,** a 40-mile-long National Park Service property encompassing the whole of the coast.

The park's highlights include miles of gorgeous beaches, harbor seals, and some of the Cape's best waves, which occur here because the south-facing beaches are blocked by the islands of Nantucket and Martha's Vineyard, and the bayside is sheltered by the Cape itself. Pick up information detailing the various nature trails and interpretive programs at the **Salt Pond Visitor Center** (508/255-3421, daily, free) in Eastham or **Province Lands Visitor Center** (508/487-1256) in Provincetown.

A CAPE COD PRIMER

To avoid frustration and confusion when visiting Cape Cod, it helps to understand its basic directions and seasons. The compass isn't your friend here, as you will discover when faced with highway signs stubbornly directing you south to Provincetown—when heading south would bring you sooner to Venezuela than to the Cape's north-ernmost town. Instead, the principal directions are up and down: "Up-Cape" means generally westward, toward the mainland, while "Down-Cape" means roughly east, toward the Outer Cape and Provincetown.

Further confusion arises with the distinctions among the various coasts: "Bayside" faces inward onto Cape Cod Bay, the "South Shore" faces Nantucket Sound, and the "Backside" braves the open Atlantic to the east.

It's a little easier to keep track of Cape Cod's seasons. High season, when Cape-bound traffic can be bumper-to-bumper from near Boston all the way to Hyannis, is basically from Memorial Day to Labor Day. The summer vacation months of July and August see the highest hotel rates, the most crowded beaches, and abysmal traffic on Fridays especially, when most vacation rentals "turn over."

That said, even at the worst of times you can still find peace and quiet if you're willing to walk, paddle, or bike a little way from your car. Cycling is especially attractive thanks to the 22-mile Cape Cod Rail Trail, which follows an old train route between Dennis and Wellfleet. Rentals are available all along the route, at places like **Barb's Bikes** (430 Route 134, 508/760-4723), off US-6 in South Dennis.

Wellfleet

The town of **Wellfleet** (pop. 2,750) is one of the Cape's most picturesque communities, favored for some reason by writers, psychiatrists, and oysters. Although home to a cluster of fine-art galleries, crafts and clothing shops, clam shacks, and pricey restaurants, the place succeeds handsomely in finding a niche between self-conscious quaintness and residential seclusion. It's also blessed by **Mac's Seafood** (508/349-0404), just west of the town pier, which sells fresh fish, shellfish, and ice cream cones, best eaten just before a glorious sunset over the bay.

If you've never watched a movie in the comfort of your own car, it's time you caught up with lost pleasures at the **Wellfleet Drive-In and Cinemas** (508/349-7176, $11, cash only), on US-6 four miles north of Eastham. The drive-in is a genuine throwback to the late 1950s era of roller-skating carhops and T-bird convertibles. There's also a four-screen indoor cinema, open year-round.

Wellfleet also has some of the Outer Cape's more affordable rooms, at the historic **Holden Inn** (140 Commercial St., 508/349-3450, $115 and up), where you share baths, the front porch, and yet more bay views.

Truro

One of the finest biking or scenic driving routes on Cape Cod is the stretch of Old County Road that winds between Wellfleet and **Truro** (pop. 2,003), on the bay side of US-6. Topography is varied, with hills and dunes, and traffic is minimal, so you can get a full sense of what the Cape is like beyond parking hassles and bijou restaurants. Like Wellfleet, Truro is well off the beaten track and has little commercial development. From the 1940s through the 1960s, Truro attracted a significant summer artists' colony whose members included painter Edward Hopper. These days, Truro is perhaps best known for the **Head of the Meadow** beach, just north of the landmark Highland Lighthouse on the Atlantic side of the Cape.

The classic Cape Cod dwelling—a porchless, rectangular, peak-roofed shed, not unlike an oversize shingle or clapboard Monopoly piece—is a familiar feature of the Outer Cape landscape.

The fury of the Atlantic constantly reworks Cape topography, borrowing up to 10 feet from the Outer Cape's cliffs each year, and stealing over 30 acres annually through erosion and rising sea levels.

The Truro area also has one of Cape Cod's most appealing low-cost lodging options: the **HI-Truro Hostel** (508/349-3889, late June-Aug. only), beautifully situated between cranberry bogs and ocean beach in a former Coast Guard station on North Pamet Road.

Provincetown

If not for its lack of freshwater, **Provincetown,** not Plymouth, would be the place we immediately equate with the Pilgrims. Way back in 1620, the band of religious travelers and fortune-seeking shipmates aboard the *Mayflower* landed here, expecting warm weather (in November, of all times) and good water. Neither was to be found, and the Pilgrims sailed on, disembarking across the bay at Plymouth Rock. Thus, P-town (as natives and in-the-know locals call it) lost its chance to be enshrined as the cornerstone of Anglo-American civilization and has had to butter its bread with something other than the national creation story.

So P-town took to the water. For much of its history, the sea sustained the town, which became a trading spot, whaling village, and fishing port. As those industries tapered off, new ones arose to take their place. Art and tourism now keep P-town busy.

In 1899 Charles Hawthorne opened an art school here, and the town earned the art colony status that persists to this day. Bohemians followed. Among the artists and writers were John Reed, Eugene O'Neill, and George Cram Cook, whose Provincetown Players made theater history. And on the heels of Greenwich Village's fashionable flock came the car-borne tourists, who have proven themselves as faithful as Capistrano swallows, returning year after year to this tip of the Cape. Provincetown is a particularly strong magnet for East Coast gays and lesbians, so don't be surprised to see as many rainbow flags as Stars and Stripes waving in the breeze.

That 252-foot tower jutting up over Provincetown is the **Pilgrim Monument and Museum** (daily 9am-7pm May-Aug., daily 9am-5pm Apr. and Sept.-Nov., $12), with the best panorama on the Cape: In clear weather the entire peninsula can be seen, as well as the Massachusetts coast at Plymouth.

The summer trade prompts P-town to do its beach-boardwalk strut, as boatloads of day-trippers from Boston mob aptly named Commercial Street each afternoon, tanned couples mingle among the restaurants and outdoor cafés each evening, and fun-seekers fill up the bars and clubs each night. During any other season, however, the beach shuttle becomes a school bus, the wait for a table is negligible, and there's actually a chance that you'll find a place to park. Meanwhile, the

Provincetown shops

off-season sunsets are still worth a visit to Race Point or Herring Cove Beach, even if they come at an earlier hour and require extra layers of clothing.

Because Cape Cod juts out into the Atlantic, Provincetown is one of the best spots on the East Coast for whale-watching trips. From April through mid-October, boats of the **Dolphin Fleet of Provincetown** (800/826-9300 or 508/240-3636) leave many times a day on four-hour trips, traveling out to feeding areas off Stellwagen Bank to see humpback, minke, and finback whales.

Provincetown Practicalities

After a day spent cycling amid dunes speckled with wild roses and beach grasses, or admiring the handiwork of window-box gardeners in P-town's cottage-lined lanes, you'll probably get hungry. Snackers may want to try the sugar-coated *malasadas* from the **Portuguese Bakery** (299 Commercial St., 508/487-1803). However, if you have a bigger appetite and want a harborside table, consider the moderately priced **Lobster Pot** (321 Commercial St., 508/487-0842), just east of MacMillan Wharf, for heaping portions of time-tested local favorites such as cioppino or *sopa do mar,* veggie pastas, and, of course, lobster every which way you want it. It's open year-round too—an exception in these parts. Enter through the kitchen.

For livelier, less-expensive dining, check out the multicultural menu—one of the few to please

vegetarians—at **Napi's** (7 Freeman St., 508/487-1145), tucked away behind Tedeschi's. **Spiritus Café & Pizzeria** (190 Commercial St., 508/487-2808) is another good low-cost savior, dishing up pizza, ice cream, and lattes to a steady clientele of tattooed young smokers and slackers until 2am on summer weekends.

Planning to spend the night? If it's a summer weekend, make reservations or you may spend your time searching for a bed rather than basking on the beach. If you don't mind the occasional bout of late-night laughter from Commercial Street carousers, the **Somerset House Inn** (378 Commercial St., 800/575-1850 or 508/487-0383, $135 and up) has comfortable rooms and a central location in an old Cape Cod manse. Quieter and calmer, the **Inn at Cook Street** (7 Cook St., 508/487-3894, $219 and up), in the East End, offers relaxing decks and gardens, and a great breakfast.

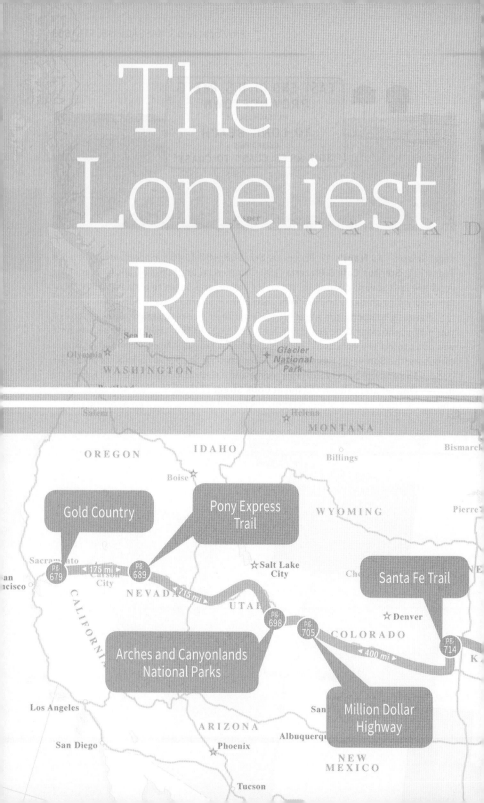

The backbone of America runs from sea to shining sea, passing through 11 states and some of the country's most magnificent landscapes.

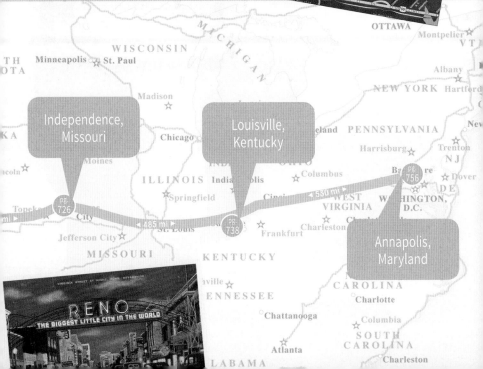

Between San Francisco and the Chesapeake Bay

Running coast-to-coast through the heart of America on a 3,200-mile odyssey from sea to shining sea, US-50 passes through a dozen different states and four state capitals, as well as the nation's capital, Washington DC. Along the route are some of the country's most magnificent landscapes: the **Sierra Nevada** and the **Appalachian** and **Rocky Mountains**, the endless farmlands of the **Great Plains**, and the desiccated deserts of **Utah** and **Nevada**. It follows the footsteps of pioneers and gives a reverse time line of national development. Heading west to east, you can travel back in history from the cutting-edge high tech of contemporary Silicon Valley, across the Wild West frontier of the mid-1800s, and through lands the likes of Daniel Boone and countless others pioneered in the 1700s, before arriving at the Atlantic Ocean near some of the oldest and best-preserved colonial-era landscapes in the United States.

Pony Express silhouette in Schellbourne, Nevada

All the way across the country, US-50 passes through literally hundreds of timeworn small towns, the great majority of which have survived despite the modern onslaught of Walmarts and fast-food franchises. *Blue Highways* author William Least Heat-Moon writes about US-50, "for the unhurried, this little-known highway is the best national road across the middle of the United States." The route offers such a compelling cross-section of the nation that *Time* magazine once devoted an entire issue to telling the story

551—Suspension Bridge over the Royal Gorge, Canon City, Colorado

World's Highest Bridge over one of the World's Most Stupendous Chasms

of the road it called the "Backbone of America."

From its start at **San Francisco,** the route cuts across California's midsection, passing the state capital of Sacramento before following the route of the old Pony Express up into the Sierra Nevada to the shores of **Lake Tahoe** and into Nevada. The Nevada portion of the route, dubbed "The Loneliest Road in America" by travel writers and tourist boards, is one of the most compelling long-distance drives in the country—provided you find miles and miles of little more than mountains, sagebrush, and blue sky compelling. **The Great Basin** desert continues across half of Utah, but then the route climbs over the Wasatch Front and onto the national park-packed red-rock country of the Colorado Plateau.

Continuing east, you cross the Continental Divide atop the Rockies, then follow the Arkansas River along the historic Santa Fe Trail. For fans of vanishing Americana, the route comes into its own here across the Great Plains, with its hypnotically repetitive landscape of water towers, windmills, railroad tracks, and one small town after another.

After bisecting **Missouri** from Kansas City to St. Louis, US-50 crosses the Mississippi River into a much older and more settled landscape, through the agricultural heartlands of **Illinois, Indiana,** and **Ohio.** After climbing into the Appalachian backwoods of **West Virginia,** US-50 emerges suddenly into the wealth and power of downtown **Washington DC** before passing through the still perfectly picturesque fishing and farming communities of **Maryland's Eastern Shore.**

Thomas Jefferson Memorial at Night, Washington, D. C.

CALIFORNIA

Heading east from San Francisco across the heavy-duty Oakland Bay Bridge, the route across California starts off along the busy I-80 freeway through the urbanized San Francisco Bay Area. Passing diverse bay-front towns, including blue-collar **Oakland** and collegiate **Berkeley,** the busy and often congested eight-lane highway heads northeast across the historically important but increasingly suburbanized flatlands of the Sacramento Delta. Beyond **Sacramento,** the state capital of California, US-50 finally emerges, first as a freeway but later as a two-lane mountain road climbing through the heart of the **Sierra Nevada** foothills, where many of the small towns slumber in a gold-rush dream of the 1850s. Continuing east, US-50 winds through endless tracts of pine forest before cresting the Sierra to reach alpine **Lake Tahoe,** a year-round resort lying astride the California-Nevada border.

San Francisco (see page 62) is also a stop along our **Pacific Coast** road trip. Full coverage of that route begins on page 8.

Oakland

Though it sometimes suffers in comparisons with its richer and better-looking sibling across San Francisco Bay, the hardworking city of **Oakland** (pop. 390,724) is a lively and intriguing place, with a nearly perfect climate and a proudly liberal political heritage. The main attraction for visitors is its waterfront **Jack London Square,** honoring the city's favorite prodigal son. Covering a few blocks at the foot of Broadway, the complex contains a couple of good restaurants and nightclubs, a re-creation of the log cabin where Jack London lived when he was in the Yukon Territory, and, last but not least, the truly funky **Heinold's First and Last Chance.** This rickety old saloon,

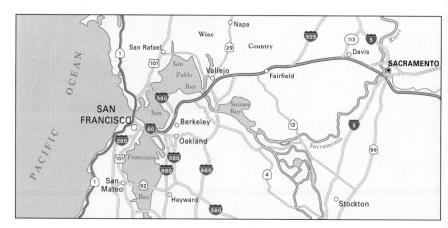

serving a wide variety of good beer, is just about the only survivor from Oakland's wild and woolly past. Jack London Square is pleasant to wander, with a handsome yacht formerly used by President Franklin D. Roosevelt, and **ferries** ($13 round-trip) head across the bay to San Francisco.

Oakland's other main draw is the excellent **Oakland Museum of California** (1000 Oak St., 510/318-8400, Wed.-Sun., $16), housed in a landmark modernist ziggurat on the east edge of downtown, a block from Lake Merritt. Inside, exhibits cover everything from California's natural history to the photography of Dorothea Lange. An in-depth look at the state's popular culture is highlighted by a lively display of Hollywood movie posters, neon signs, jukeboxes, and classic cars and motorcycles.

Berkeley

The intellectual, literary, and political nexus of the San Francisco Bay Area, left-leaning **Berkeley** (pop. 112,580) enjoys an international reputation that overshadows its suburban appearance. The town grew up around the attractively landscaped **University of California** campus, which, during the 1960s and early 1970s, was the scene of ongoing battles between "The Establishment" and unwashed hordes of antiwar, "sex, drugs, and rock 'n' roll-crazed" youth. Today, while its antiauthoritarian traditions are less in-your-face, Berkeley still maintains a typical college town mix of cafés and vinyl stores, and its site is superb, looking out across the bay to the Golden Gate and San Francisco.

The city's low-budget but high-achieving baseball club, the **Oakland A's** (510/568-5600), play their home games at **Oakland-Alameda County Coliseum,** south of downtown.

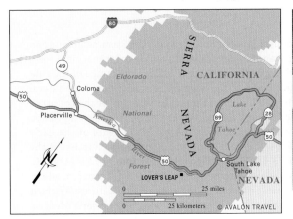

golden poppy,
state flower of California

The big "C" above the University of California campus is over 100 years old. It was the first of these giant letters, which have since been repeated on hillsides all over the country.

In the 1940s, to help ease the pain of his baby son's arthritis, a Berkeley machinist named Candido Jacuzzi created the air-bubbling hydrotherapy device that bears his name.

The square-mile University of California Berkeley campus sits at the foot of eucalyptus-covered hills a mile east of the University Avenue exit off the I-80 freeway. Wander along Strawberry Creek, admiring the mix of neoclassical and post-modern buildings. Berkeley's cacophonous main drag, Telegraph Avenue, runs south from the heart of campus in a crazy array of tie-dye and tarot.

There are dozens of great places to eat and drink in Berkeley, including one of the best breakfast joints on the planet, **Bette's Oceanview Diner** (1807 4th St., 510/644-3932), two blocks north of the I-80 University Avenue exit at the center of a boutique shopping district. Berkeley also has many top-rated restaurants, including world-renowned **Chez Panisse** (1517 Shattuck Ave., 510/548-5525, reservations essential), birthplace of California cuisine, located in the heart of Berkeley's gourmet ghetto. Chez Panisse is, not surprisingly, *très cher,* so mere mortals may decide to take advantage of the more affordable gourmet cheese, bread, and out-of-this-world pizzas made and sold across the street at **The Cheese Board Collective** (1512 Shattuck Ave., 510/549-3183), where the California cuisine revolution started way back in 1967.

If you want to take the slow road north from Berkeley, follow San Pablo Avenue (Hwy-123), the old US-40-Lincoln Highway-Victory Highway route, which winds uneventfully along the bay front through **El Cerrito** (birthplace of 1960s pop group Creedence Clearwater Revival) and industrial **Richmond,** where the new **Rosie the Riveter National Historical Park** preserves the waterfront's vital World War II-era heritage.

Vallejo

On the north side of the Carquinez Straits, through which the Sacramento and San Joaquin Rivers flow into San Francisco Bay, **Vallejo** is a blue-collar maritime town that made national news by declaring bankruptcy in 2008, in the wake of the sub-prime housing crash. Longtime home of the huge and historic Mare Island naval shipyard, which from 1854 to 1994 built and maintained many of the country's fighting ships and submarines, Vallejo also served as California's state capital on two different occasions in the gold rush years of the early 1850s. These days, Vallejo's one bona fide attraction is the theme park **Six Flags Discovery Kingdom** (707/644-4000, hours vary, daily summer, around $68), on the north side of town just west of I-80. Along with one of California's most intense arrays of high-speed thrill rides (like 65-mph Medusa,

Vallejo marks the turnoff for Hwy-12, which runs north and west through the Wine Country of the Napa and Sonoma Valleys.

the Medusa rollercoaster at Six Flags Discovery Kingdom in Vallejo

or the even-faster Vertical Velocity), Six Flags is surrounded by more than 135 acres of kid-friendly animal attractions, so you can admire tigers, elephants, and dolphins, or feed the tropical birds and butterflies.

I-80 Towns

Between the San Francisco Bay Area and Sacramento, I-80 passes through an ever more suburbanized corridor, where towns like Fairfield and Vacaville have grown almost exponentially, from a few hundred residents in the 1950s to more than 100,000 today. **Fairfield** (pop. 10,321) grew up around busy Travis Air Force Base, and more enjoyably is also home to the **Jelly Belly Jelly Bean Factory** (800/522-3267 or 800/953-5592, self-guided tours daily, free) and a large **Anheuser-Busch beer refinery** (707/429-7595, Thurs.-Tues. 10am-5pm June-Aug., Thurs.-Tues. 10am-4pm Sept.-May, $5).

From the coastal hills the landscape flattens out into the endless plain of the Sacramento Delta, and 80-mph I-80 crosses an unstintingly flat landscape of farmland, housing tracts, and big-box shopping centers. Just before Sacramento, I-80 reaches bike-friendly **Davis,** a former Lincoln Highway town that's home to a University of California campus, renowned for its winemaking school and creative fine art faculty, including pop art legend Wayne Thiebaud, celebrated in the stunning **Manetti Shrem Museum of Art** (254 Old Davis Rd., www.manettishremmuseum.ucdavis.edu).

East of Davis, I-80 is raised on stilts across the Yolo Bypass wetlands, one of the last signs of the natural delta that covered this part of California before the water supply was diverted to other parts of California.

Sacramento

Spreading for miles at the heart of California's 500-mile-long agriculturally rich Central Valley, **Sacramento** (pop. 466,488) is not what most would expect of the capital of the Golden State. Green and suburban, with only the state capitol and a few modern towers rising over fine Victorian houses that line the leafy downtown streets, Sacramento is a relatively quiet backwater that effectively embodies California's bipolar politics, forming a sort of neutral ground between the liberal urban centers, which contain 90 percent of the state's population, and the conservative rural rest, which covers 90 percent of the land.

Now scythed by freeways and stretching for miles along the banks of the Sacramento and American Rivers, the city was chosen as the state capital during the gold rush era, when Sacramento was the main jumping-off point for the Sierra Nevada mines. Dozens of buildings dating from that era have been restored to form **Old Sacramento,** a diverting shopping complex and tourist trap along the riverfront, where yachts offer sightseeing cruises and the **California State Railroad Museum** (916/323-9280, daily, $12), boasting one of the world's largest collections,

documents the history of western railroads. Along
with the wealth of gold rush architecture, "Old
Sac" also has memorials to the Pony Express and
the Transcontinental Railroad, both of which had
primary stations here.

Two other museums are nearby. The **Crocker
Art Museum** (216 O St., 916/808-7000, Tues.-
Sun., $10), two blocks from the riverfront, is the
oldest art gallery west of the Mississippi, with a
broad range of European and California paintings.

California's capitol as it appeared
in the early 1900s

A half mile south of Old Sacramento, underneath
the interchange of I-80 and I-5 at Front and V Streets, the **California Automobile
Museum** (916/442-6802, Wed.-Mon. 10am-5pm, $10) displays hot rods and muscle
cars (from Corvettes to a Lamborghini Countach), alongside examples of just about
every Ford made before 1952, from Model Ts to massive Ford V-8s.

A half mile inland from the riverfront, standing at the west end of a pleasantly
landscaped park, the impressive **California State Capitol** (daily, free) has publicly
accessible legislative chambers of the state's Senate and Assembly, and hallways full
of exhibits on the Golden State's diverse counties.

Two miles east of the waterfront, at 27th and L Streets, Sacramento's main historic attraction is **Sutter's Fort** (916/445-4422, daily, $5), a reconstruction of the
frontier outpost established here in 1839 by Swiss settler Johann Sutter. The first
commercial, as opposed to religious, settlement in Alta California, Sutter's Fort
played a vital role in early West Coast history—this is where the Donner Party was
headed, and where the gold rush began, when Sutter's employee James Marshall discovered flakes of gold at Sutter's Mill, in the Sierra Nevada foothills above
Sacramento. The grounds of Sutter's Fort also hold the small but interesting
California State Indian Museum ($5), which has displays of baskets and other
California Native American handicrafts.

During Memorial Day weekend, Old Sacramento hosts the **Sacramento Music
Festival** (916/444-2004), which draws an enormous crowd intent on hearing the
dozens of jazz bands—everything from Dixieland and "trad" bands to cutting-edge
contemporary players.

Sacramento Practicalities

The Old Sacramento area has some good but touristy restaurants and bars, but the
Midtown neighborhood south of Sutter's Fort holds Sacramento's best range of restaurants, including the tasty but inexpensive **Paesanos** (1806 Capitol Ave.,
916/447-8646), which has great cheap pizzas and a nice sidewalk terrace. Another
lively spot is the **Tower Café** (1518 Broadway, 916/441-0222), attached to the landmark 1920s Tower Theater (which plays art-house hits) and serving healthy multiethnic food with a world-beat attitude. (The café is where the now-defunct Tower
Records got its start.)

Places to stay include the wonderful **HI-Sacramento Hostel** (925 H St.,
916/668-6631, $33), in a fabulous Victorian mansion right downtown. For an
unusual experience, how about staying the night in a 1920s paddlewheel riverboat? The **Delta King** (916/444-5464, $148 and up) is permanently moored on the
Old Sacramento riverfront.

Placerville and Coloma: Gold Country

The main US-50 stop in the Sierra Nevada foothills, **Placerville** (pop. 10,389; elev. 2,585) takes its name from the placer gold deposits recovered from the South Fork of the American River, which flows just north of town. The historic core of Placerville is well preserved, with a few cafés and bars paying homage to its rough-and-tumble past. A reminder of the town's gold-rush heritage is the nation's only municipally owned gold mine: **Gold Bug Park and Mine** (530/642-5207, daily summer, Sat.-Sun. fall-spring, $7), a mile north of US-50 off the Bedford Avenue exit. A stamp mill and other mining equipment stand outside the entrance to the mine tunnel, which you can explore on a self-guided tour.

The Oakland A's Triple-A farm club, the **Sacramento River Cats** (916/371-4487), plays all summer long at **Raley Field,** across the bridge from Old Sacramento. Games, which frequently sell out, are broadcast on **KCTC 1320 AM.**

If you want to explore the region's many evocative gold rush-era remnants, Placerville makes a good base, with its handful of motels (including a Best Western and a Days Inn) fronting the highway. Placerville also has the **Old Town Grill** (444 Main St., 530/622-2631), serving up world-class shoestring french fries along with chili dogs and refreshing milk shakes.

Between Sacramento and Placerville, US-50 is an eight-lane freeway—and one of the California Highway Patrol's most lucrative speed traps, especially for westbound (downhill) travelers.

North and south of Placerville, Hwy-49 runs along the Sierra Nevada foothills through the heart of the Gold Country. Starting in the north beyond beautiful Nevada City, Hwy-49 winds through one historic town after another, all the way to the gates of Yosemite National Park, 150 miles to the south. One great old Gold Country haunt can be reached

Throughout the gold-rush era, Placerville was known as Hangtown, with a reputation for stringing up petty thieves and other law-breakers. An effigy still hangs at the center of town, in front of a bar.

within a short drive of US-50 from Placerville. The ancient and still popular **Poor Red's Bar-B-Q** (530/622-2901), housed in a gold-rush-era stagecoach station in the hamlet of El Dorado, five miles south of Placerville on Hwy-49, has full lunches and dinners (and great margaritas) for little money. If you have the time and inclination to take a longer detour, head south along Hwy-49 to the stately

town of Sutter Creek, then climb up into the mountains via winding Hwy-88, which passes by the intriguing semi-ghost town of Volcano before linking up again with US-50 near Lake Tahoe and Carson City.

A half-hour north of Placerville via Hwy-49, the original site of the discovery of gold, **Sutter's Mill,** has been reconstructed as part of **Marshall Gold Discovery State**

Historic Park (530/622-3470, daily, $8 per car) in **Coloma,** now an idyllic place along the banks of the American River, nine miles north of Placerville along Hwy-49. The 273-acre park, set aside in 1890 as the state's first historic monument, is also a prime spot for white-water rafting and kayaking, especially on weekends, so don't be surprised to find the place thronged with wet-suited and Teva-shod hordes.

The American River and Lover's Leap

Some 20 miles east of Placerville, US-50 changes suddenly from a four-lane freeway into a twisting, narrow, two-lane road over the crest of the Sierra Nevada. The usually busy highway, which every year is battered and frequently closed by winter storms, runs right alongside the steep banks of the **American River.** The lushness of the western Sierra Nevada is immediately apparent as the road passes luxuriant groves of pine, fir, and cedar, with numerous old resorts and vacation cabins lining the highway.

About six miles west of the summit, the towering granite cliff of **Lover's Leap** stands out to the south of the highway, its 1,300-foot face attracting rock climbers, while to the north the delicate cascade of **Horsetail Falls** offers a more serene pit stop. Climbing east up US-50's steepest set of hairpin turns, you'll reach 7,365-foot **Echo Summit,** which gives great views of the Lake Tahoe basin—the shining blue waters beckoning you along another steep stretch of US-50, downhill to the lake-shore itself.

South Lake Tahoe

One of the biggest (12 miles wide, 22 miles long, and 72 miles of coastline) and deepest (over 1,000 feet in places) lakes in the country, straddling the Nevada/California border at 6,220 feet above sea level, **Lake Tahoe** is a beautiful sight from any angle—from the crest of the alpine peaks surrounding it, from a car or bicycle as you cruise along the shoreline roads, or from a boat out on the lake itself.

Sitting, as the name suggests, at the southern end of Lake Tahoe, the ungainly resort community of **South Lake Tahoe** is a place of multiple personalities. On the California side, low-rise motels line the US-50 frontage, and the atmosphere is that of a family-oriented summer resort, with bike-rental stands and T-shirt shops clogging the roadside. Across the Nevada border, glitzy 20-story casinos rise up in a sudden wall of concrete and glass, ignoring the surrounding beauty in favor of round-the-clock "adult fun"—gambling, fine dining, racy nightclub revues, and more gambling. A few strategically placed pine trees work hard

to retain a semblance of the natural splendor, but in peak summer season it's a *very* busy stretch of road, on both sides of the state line.

To get away from it all, head along Hwy-89 around the west side of the lake to the magnificent state parks around **Emerald Bay.** Acres of shoreline forest and numerous mansions built as summer resorts back around the turn of the 20th century, like the **Tallac Historic Site** (530/541-5227, $5-15), three miles west of US-50, have been preserved and are open for tours. In winter, the Tahoe area turns into an extremely popular ski resort—**Heavenly** (775/586-7000) on the south shore and **Squaw Valley** (530/583-6985) in the north are among the largest and busiest ski areas in the United States; both have sightseeing chair lifts in summer.

Despite the lake's great popularity, year-round prices for Tahoe accommodations can be surprisingly low; with a **Best Western Station House Inn** (530/542-1101) and dozens of others to choose from, you shouldn't have trouble finding something suitable. For a carb-loading breakfast, head to the circa-1959 **Red Hut Waffle Shop** (2723 Lake Tahoe Blvd., 530/541-9024) on US-50. Red Hut has three other locations along US-50 in South Lake Tahoe, but this is the original.

NEVADA

Between Lake Tahoe in the west and **Great Basin National Park** on the Utah border, US-50 crosses more than 400 miles of Nevada's corrugated country, climbing up and over a dozen distinct mountain ranges while passing through four classic mining towns and the state capital, **Carson City.** Early explorers mapped this region, Pony Express riders raced across it, and the long-distance Lincoln Highway finally tamed it, but the US-50 byway has always played second fiddle to the I-80 freeway, the more popular northern route across the state. Besides being a more scenic alternative to the mind-numbing, and therefore accident-prone, I-80, US-50 across Nevada has gained a measure of notoriety in its own right—it's known as the "Loneliest Road in America." As you travel along it you'll see road signs, T-shirts, and bumper stickers proclaiming it as such.

Inspired by the July 1987 story in *Life* magazine that dubbed US-50 "The Loneliest Road," the state-run **Nevada Commission on Tourism** (775/687-4322 or 800/NEVADA-8—800/638-2328) sponsors a tongue-in-cheek promotion in which trans-Nevada travelers can earn themselves a certificate saying "I Survived the Loneliest Road in America." Get your official US-50 travel passport stamped at visitors centers along the highway.

Stateline

Right where US-50 crosses from California into Nevada, the casino complex at **Stateline** forms, for a few short blocks, a mini Las Vegas, with four 20-story resort hotels towering over the lakeshore. **Harveys** (775/588-2411, $89 and up), the largest with 742 rooms, started it all in the 1940s with six nickel slot machines. **Harrah's** (775/588-6611, $9 and up), across US-50, is the most opulent, with luxurious 500- to 800-square-foot suites. Altogether, over 2,000 rooms are available, combined with at least that many more across the California border. The multitudes of game-hungry

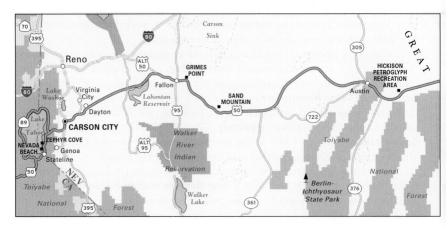

visitors that converge here create a definite charge in
the rarefied atmosphere when the casino tables are
turning at full speed, and it's also a great place to
catch your favorite slightly aging music and comedy
performers or a Vegas-style floor show.

Nevada Beach and Zephyr Cove

From the casino district at Stateline, US-50 winds
along Lake Tahoe's southeastern shore for over 20
miles, passing by a pair of waterfront parks at
Nevada Beach and **Zephyr Cove,** where you can ride
the faux paddle-wheeler **MS *Dixie II*** (775/589-4906
or 800/238-2463, $59 and up) on a variety of
cruises across the lake. Otherwise, lakeshore access
is severely limited, since most of the waterfront is
privately owned, though numerous roadside turnouts (most easily accessible to westbound, lakeside
travelers) offer ample opportunities to take in
unforgettable views.

Midway along the lake's eastern shore, US-50 turns sharply and begins climbing
up and over the 7,140-foot crest of **Spooner Summit,** all the way giving great views
of the tantalizing blue gleam below. At the summit, stretch your legs on the **Tahoe
Rim Trail** (http://tahoerimtrail.org), which circumnavigates the entire Lake Tahoe
basin. Dropping down swiftly from Spooner Summit into the Great Basin desert,
US-50 links up with US-395 for the final few miles into Carson City.

Genoa

Between Stateline and Carson City, a delightful little back-door route takes you
through **Genoa,** the oldest city in Nevada. Founded by Mormon farmers way back in
1851, Genoa still retains its rural frontier feel, especially since most of the 20th-cen-
tury development was focused elsewhere, leaving Genoa pleasantly far behind the
times—for the time being, at least, though new faux-Victorian houses for Carson
City commuters have been springing up around the historic downtown.

sagebrush,
state flower of Nevada

At the center of town is **Mormon Station State Historic Park** (775/782-2590, daily 10am-4pm, May-Sept., Thurs.-Mon. 11am-3pm Oct.-Apr., $1), which has a small museum and a stockade dating back to the 1850s. Across the way, at Main and 5th Streets, the **Genoa Courthouse Museum** (775/782-4325, daily May-Oct., $5) has more comprehensive displays of historical items—everything from Native American baskets to the keys of the old jail, with an especially interesting exhibition on Wild West legend John A. "Snowshoe" Thompson, who carried the mail over the mountains between Genoa and Placerville. There's also a little tidbit on mining engineer and native son George Ferris, who designed and built the first of his namesake Ferris wheels for the 1893 World's Fair in Chicago. Much of old Genoa has burned down over the years, but the **Genoa Bar** (2282 Main St., 775/782-3870) is full of character and fairly claims to be the oldest bar in the state.

To get to Genoa from Stateline and Lake Tahoe, go east on Hwy-207, down the steep Kingsbury Grade, then turn north on Hwy-206. From Carson City, turn off US-395 south of the US-50 junction onto Jacks Valley Road (Hwy-206), and follow that for 12 miles.

Carson City

Nevada's state capital and 10th largest city, **Carson City** (pop. 55,274) was named in honor of Wild West explorer Kit Carson. Nestled at the base of the sheer eastern scarp of the Sierra Nevada, the city was founded in 1858—just a year before the discovery of the Comstock Lode riches, and six years before Nevada became a state.

Carson City is a hard place to characterize. Considering it's the capital, life is slow, with the main buzz being the **Carson Nugget** (507 N. Carson St., 775/882-1626) on the main US-50/395 route through town. It features roulette, craps, and blackjack tables, and an army of senior citizens feeding banks of slot machines.

Gambling aside, the one place to stop in Carson City is the excellent **Nevada State Museum** (600 N. Carson St., Tues.-Sun., $8), which stands four blocks north of the state capitol—and catercorner from the Nugget. The solid old U.S. Mint, built in

In 1861, Orion Clemens was appointed secretary to the governor of Nevada Territory, and his younger brother Sam came with him to Nevada. Sam submitted dispatches of his mining and travel adventures to Virginia City's largest daily newspaper, the *Territorial Enterprise,* and began perfecting his unique brand of humor under the pen name Mark Twain.

Nevada State Railroad Museum

1870 to make coins from Comstock silver, houses displays on mining (including a full-scale mock-up of a working mine), features a Native American gallery called Under One Sky, and gives an overview of Great Basin natural history. Also worth a look: the old Virginia & Truckee steam engines at **Nevada State Railroad Museum** (2180 S. Carson St., Thurs.-Mon. 9am-4pm, $6), south of town along US-50/395, where vintage trains run on warm-weather weekends and some holidays.

Good Mexican meals are the order of the day at **El Charro Avitia** (4389 S. Carson St., 775/883-6261), south of town, while the best and most expensive fare is served at **Adele's** (1112 N. Carson St., 775/882-3353), where power brokers broker their power. Motels line Carson Street north and south of the capitol; try the classic 1950s-style **Frontier Motel** (1718 N. Carson St., 775/882-1377).

Virginia City

In 1859, prospectors following the gold deposits up the slopes of Mt. Davidson discovered one of the richest strikes in world history: the **Comstock Lode.** Almost overnight, the bustling camp of Virginia City grew into the largest settlement between Chicago and San Francisco, and over the next 20 years nearly a billion dollars in gold and silver (in 19th-century dollars!) was grubbed from deep underground. Afterward the town nearly dried up and blew away, but thanks in part to the 1960s TV show

The dress of the Silver Queen in Virginia City contains over 3,000 silver dollars.

Bonanza, in which Hoss and company were always heading over to Virginia City for supplies or to fetch the sheriff, tourists discovered the town and gave it a new lease on life.

These days **Virginia City** (pop. 855) is both a tacky tourist trap and one of the most satisfying destinations in the state. It is reachable via a steep (grades in excess of 15 percent) eight-mile drive up Hwy-341 from US-50. Dozens of hokey but enjoyable attractions—like the amiable **Bucket of Blood Saloon,** which offers a panoramic view down the mountain—line the five-block-long main drag, C Street. The streets above and below—and I do mean above and below: the town clings to such a steep slope that C Street is a good three stories higher than neighboring D Street—hold some of the most authentic sites. B Street, for example, has the elegant **Castle,** Nevada's premier mansion, with all the original furnishings and fittings, a block south of the ornate Victorian **Storey County Courthouse** and the landmark **Piper's Opera House.** Down the hill on D Street was once a more raucous quarter, where brothels and opium dens shared space with railroad tracks, cemeteries, and the mines themselves: the Gould, Curry, the Ophir, and the Consolidated Virginia.

Before or after a wander around town, be sure to stop in to the excellent museum on the ground floor of the **Fourth Ward School** (775/847-0975, daily May-Oct., $6), the Victorian Gothic landmark at the south end of C Street. Exhibits inside recount the lively history of Virginia City, from mining technology to Mark Twain, who made his start as a journalist with Virginia City's *Territorial Enterprise.* An intact classroom is preserved as it was in its heyday through the late 1880s to 1936, when the last class graduated.

Other intriguing stops are the handful of historic fraternal, civic, and religious cemeteries at the north end of Virginia City, where delicate wrought-iron fences surround elaborate tombstones. The oddest stop has to be the **Red Light Museum** (5 N. C St., 775/847-4188, daily), where an amazing barrage of sexually explicit historical oddities is displayed. Located in the basement of a former saloon, now the Virginia City Bar & Grill, the museum has been undergoing renovations.

Unless you're tempted by the many places to eat hot dogs and drink sarsaparilla along C Street, food options in Virginia City are limited. C Street is home to the **Red Dog Saloon** (76 N. C St., 775/847-7474), where tasty bar food is served up in an historic space that played a crucial role in the development of West Coast psychedelic music in the years b the Summer of Love.

Reno

Nothing helps heighten the contrast between the rest of the world and life along the "Loneliest Road" more than making a stop in **Reno** (pop. 231,027), "The Biggest Little City in the World," as the bold archway over Virginia Street downtown proclaims. An ancient city by Nevada standards, dating back to pioneer days (the Donner Party camped here on their ill-fated way west), Reno first came to national prominence in the 1930s as a center for quickie divorces. It now has all the gambling of its much-larger sibling, Las Vegas, but at a pleasantly homey, settled-down scale.

Just east of the downtown casinos, the **Reno Aces** (775/334-4700) play Triple-A baseball all summer long.

Besides taking advantage of Reno's cheap hotel rooms, cheap food deals, and 24-hour fun, car culture fans may want to visit the $10 million, 100,000-square foot **National Automobile Museum** (10 Lake St., 775/333-9300, daily, $12), on the south bank of the Truckee River, perhaps the best and probably the most extensive car collection in the country, assembled primarily by casino magnate William Harrah. Over 200 classic cars, including the 1949 Mercury James Dean drove in *Rebel Without a Cause,* are on display, and there's a great gift shop too. Reno's other national attraction is the **National Bowling Stadium** (300 N. Center St.), a state-of-the-art 78-lane extravaganza. The parking garage is at Center and 4th Streets.

Reno's famous arch, which spans Virginia Street at 3rd Street downtown, was first erected in 1926 to mark the Lincoln Highway route through town. The current arch, the third to stand on the site, was built in 1987; an older version has been rebuilt next to the National Auto Museum.

Dayton

Though the roadside east of Carson City is increasingly lined by trailer parks and convenience stores, just a half block north of the highway sits **Dayton,** one of the oldest settlements in Nevada. Gold was first discovered here in 1849, and later the town's massive stamp mills pounded the ore carried through the massive Sutro Tunnel from the fabulous Comstock Lode in the mountains above. The historic town center is little more than the two blocks of Main Street north from the traffic light on US-50; choose from a couple of combination café-saloons, including the nicely renovated **J's Old Town Bistro** (30 Pike St., 775/246-4400). Formerly named the Old Corner Bar, it was the rumored hangout of John Huston, Marilyn Monroe, and Arthur Miller when they were in Dayton in 1960 during the filming of *The Misfits.*

Fallon

Coming into **Fallon,** especially after crossing the Great Basin deserts of Utah and Nevada that stretch to the east, can be a shock to the system. First, relative to Nevada's

National Automobile Museum in Reno

other US-50 towns, Fallon is big: upward of 8,000 residents, with all the attendant shopping malls, traffic lights, and fast-food franchises. Second, but perhaps more striking, Fallon is green: alfalfa, onions, garlic, and cantaloupe grow as far as the eye can see. Otherwise, Fallon offers ATMs, gas stations, and motels lining US-50, as well as the usual Pizza Huts and Subways, and a handy 24-hour Safeway.

Besides agriculture, Fallon's main employer is the U.S. Navy, whose air base and target range is an important training center for carrier-based fighters and bombers—the "Top Guns" made famous by the Tom Cruise movie.

While it's not an especially attractive place, Fallon does have what they accurately call "The Best Little Museum on the Loneliest Road in America," the eclectic and engaging **Churchill County Museum** (1050 S. Maine St., 775/423-3677, Tues.-Sun., hours vary, free), less than a mile south of US-50. Exhibits contain native Paiute basketry, clothing, and hunting gear, and the usual array of pioneer quilts and clothing. The gift shop sells a wide range of books and historical postcards. A second building contains the transportation collection of old buggies, cars, and trucks.

Forty-five miles east of Fallon, Hwy-361 heads south to the magnesium-mining company town of Gabbs. East of Gabbs lies fascinating **Berlin-Ichthyosaur State Park** (775/964-2440), which holds an only-in-Nevada combination: the over 100-year-old ghost town of Berlin and a 225-million-year-old marine fossil quarry. Camping is available mid-April to October, and guided tours of the mine, town and the fossil beds are given weekends in summer.

Grimes Point and Sand Mountain

The 110 miles of US-50 between Fallon and Austin, the next town to the east, look pretty empty on most maps, but there's more to see than you might think. In the midst of a U.S. Navy target range, where supersonic fighters play electronic wargames across the alkali flats, there are historical plaques marking Pony Express and Butterfield Stage way stations, a dusty old brothel, and two unique attractions—a singing sand dune and an extensive petroglyph site.

Grimes Point petroglyphs

Ten miles east of Fallon, the extraordinary grouping of petroglyphs at **Grimes Point** is not to be missed. Just 100 yards north of US-50, a self-guided trail leads past hundreds of images etched into the lichen-covered, espresso-brown basalt boulders. Some 6,000 years ago, when the carvings were made, Grimes Point was on the shores of now-vanished Lake Lahontan, a prime hunting and fishing ground for prehistoric Great Basin peoples. These days, fast and fierce lizards, and the occasional antelope, share the arid setting with the shiny rocks, into which a huge array of abstract and figurative images have been pecked and chiseled. If you're intrigued and want to know more, stop by the excellent Churchill County Museum in Fallon; guided **tours** (every other Sat.) are available of nearby **Hidden Cave,** where significant archaeological remains have been uncovered.

Sand Mountain, 15 miles east of Grimes Point, 84 miles west of Austin, and just a half mile north of US-50, is a giant sword-edged sand dune that makes a deep booming sound when the cascading crystals oscillate at the proper frequency—somewhere between 50 and 100 hertz. On weekends you're more likely to hear the sound of unmuffled dirt bikes and dune buggies, but at other times the half-hour trudge to the top is well worth making to watch the swirls of sand dance along the ridges.

Austin

At the turnoff to Sand Mountain, a battered sign marks the official (solar-powered!) "Loneliest Phone on the Loneliest Road in America."

Some 110 miles east of Fallon and 70 miles west of Eureka, tiny **Austin** (pop. 192) huddles well above 6,000 feet on the north slope of the mighty Toiyabe Mountains. The steep incline of Main Street (US-50) as it passes through town attests to the precariousness with which Austin has clung to life since its 10-year mining boom ended—in 1873. Austin hangs on to the rustic, steadfastly unwhitewashed nature that was once—and in some places, remains—central to Nevada's character. Austin takes its central assignment seriously, since the state's exact geographical center is a mere 12 miles to the south (near the hard-to-find but pleasant Spencer Hot Springs).

According to local legend, a Pony Express rider accidentally discovered silver ore here in 1862, and the rush was on. Prospectors fanned out from Austin, which was named after the Texas hometown of one of its founders, to establish Belmont, Berlin, Grantsville, Ione, and dozens of other boomtowns-turned-ghost towns; roughly $50 million in gold and silver was shipped out over the next 10 years. Since then Austin has experienced a long, melancholy decline, though recent efforts to mine the abundant turquoise in the region have met with some success.

A two-minute drive (at 10 mph) along Main Street takes you past all there is to

THE PONY EXPRESS

Of all the larger-than-life legends that animate the annals of the Wild West, none looms larger than that of the Pony Express. As is typical of frontier adventures, accounts of the Pony Express are often laced with considerable exaggeration, but in this case the facts are unusually impressive. Beginning in April 1860, running twice a week between St. Joseph, Missouri, and Sacramento, California, where it was linked with San Francisco by steamship, the Pony Express halved the time it took to carry news to and from the West Coast, making the 1,966-mile trek in just 10 days. Eighty riders (including teenaged William "Buffalo Bill" Cody, who made the record single run of 322 miles) were employed to race between the 190 stations en route, switching horses every 10 to 15 miles and averaging 75 miles per run—day or night, in all kinds of weather, across 120°F deserts or snowbound Sierra passes.

Covering nearly 2,000 miles of the wildest and ruggedest land on the frontier, the Pony Express established the first high-speed link between the two coasts. At a time when the nation was divided against itself, with the Civil War looming on the horizon, the Pony Express connection played a key role in keeping the valuable mines of California and Nevada in Union hands. A private enterprise that lasted just 18 months and lost considerable amounts of money before being put out of business for good, the Pony Express proved that overland connections across the still-wild western United States were both necessary and possible.

The completion on October 28, 1861, of the transcontinental telegraph made the Pony Express obsolete overnight, and not so much as a saddle survives from this legendary endeavor, apart from a few postmarked letters. Along with the various statues and plaques marking the Pony Express route, the most evocative sites survive in the dry Nevada desert, within easy access of the US-50 highway. East of Fallon, for example, the highway runs right on top of the old Pony Express route, and the remains of two relay stations can still be seen. One is at **Sand Springs,** at the foot of Sand Mountain. More substantial remains survive at **Cold Springs,** 32 miles east, where plaques recount the history and a trail brings you to what was once among the most isolated and dangerous of the Pony Express stations.

1860 1861

PONY EXPRESS TRAIL

Every June, Wild West aficionados recreate the era in the **Pony Express Re-Ride,** in which a team of over 700 riders follows the old route as closely as possible, alternating direction each year.

see in Austin today, but you could easily spend hours wandering around the place or hanging out in its quirkily populated junk shops, cafés, and bars. The impressive steeples of the Roman Catholic, Methodist, and Episcopal churches dominate the townscape, while at the western (downhill) end of town you can glimpse **Stokes Castle,** a three-story stone sentinel built in 1897 and lived in for all of a month. It looks best from a distance, looming over the nearby cemeteries, but if you want to get closer, follow Castle Road for about a half mile south from US-50.

If the "Loneliest Road" nickname makes you think that road maintenance may have suffered, it hasn't: the road surface is mostly smooth champagne asphalt, much to the delight of the hundreds of motorcyclists who ride the road every summer.

For its 300 or so residents, Austin has two gas stations (it's a long way to the next town, so fill up here) and three motels—including the clean but basic mobile home trailers of the **Cozy Mountain Motel** (40 Main St., 775/964-2471, $55 and up). Two cafés are right on US-50/Main Street; both open early (around 6am) and both close around 8pm: the ancient **International Café and Bar,** moved here board by board from Virginia City in 1863, and the **Toiyabe Café.**

Get a great feel for Great Basin life by spending some time at **Miles End Ranch B&B** (107 Del Dr., 775/964-1046), about 30 miles south and east of Austin via Hwy-376, with a wood-fired hot tub and all the stars you can ever want to see.

Hickison Petroglyph Recreation Area

Bookended by 7,000-foot mountain ranges at either end, the route between Austin and Eureka is perhaps the longest, flattest, straightest stretch of the entire trans-Nevada length of US-50—over 70 miles of Great Basin nothingness. Cattle ranches fill the plains, which were crisscrossed by early explorers like John C. Fremont, who passed through in 1845, as well as by the Pony Express and the Butterfield Stage. Such recent history, however, pales in comparison to the relics from the region's prehistoric past, particularly the fine petroglyphs carved into the rocks on the eastern side of 6,594-foot Hickison Summit, 28 miles east of Austin and 46 miles west of Eureka.

Now protected as part of the BLM-operated **Hickison Petroglyph Recreation Area,** the petroglyphs stand in a shallow sandstone draw on the north side of the highway. A half-mile trail loops through sagebrush, junipers, and piñon pines from the parking area and campground past dozens of these enigmatic figures, some of which are thought to date back as far as 10,000 BC. Somewhat surprisingly, so far they are graffiti-free.

Eureka

Right in the middle of a 100-mile stretch of spectacular Great Basin scenery, **Eureka** is one of the most engaging and enjoyable stops in the state. Unlike a lot of places along the Loneliest Road, Eureka is fairly thriving, thanks to numerous gold mines still in operation in Eureka County.

The four blocks of 100-year-old buildings lining the steeply sloping, franchise-free Main Street (US-50) are a mix of well-restored brick and wood storefronts alongside less fortunate ruins, some merely sets of cast-iron pilasters holding up false fronts. The focal point, the grand 1879 **Eureka County Courthouse,** is still in use. Behind it, the **Eureka Sentinel Museum** (775/237-5010, Tues.-Sat., free) has displays tracing the lively local history as well as typesetting equipment and printing presses of the newspaper published here from 1870 to 1960.

Besides being an intriguing place to stroll around (walking-tour booklets are available from the Sentinel Museum and many local shops), Eureka is also a good place to break a journey. A **Eureka Gold Country Inn** (775/237-5247, $102 and up) has modern rooms and is conveniently located on Main Street. Good food and drink can be had at **DJ's Diner & Drive In** (501 S. Main St., 775/237-5356) and from the **Owl Club Bar & Steakhouse** (61 N. Main St., 775/237-5280), which has been in business forever.

historic Eureka

Ely

Ely (pop. 4,255; pronounced "EE-lee") is a sprawling crossroads community where US-6, US-50, and US-93 all intersect. For nearly 100 years, Ely was a boomtown flush with the wealth from the massive Kennecott-owned Liberty Pit copper mines, Nevada's largest and longest-lived mining venture, which produced over a billion dollars' worth of ore while employing nearly 10,000 people at its peak during the 1950s. After the main mines closed down in 1982, the railroad that had shuttled pay dirt from the mines to the smelter was abandoned—track, stock, and depot. In 1985 the entire railroad operation was turned into **Nevada Northern Railway Museum** (775/289-2085, Wed.-Mon.), and now you can take a 90-minute tour aboard the **Ghost Train** (around $31), pulled by a 1910 Baldwin Steamer locomotive. The train leaves from the depot at the north end of East 11th Street and uses a ton of coal and 1,000 gallons of water.

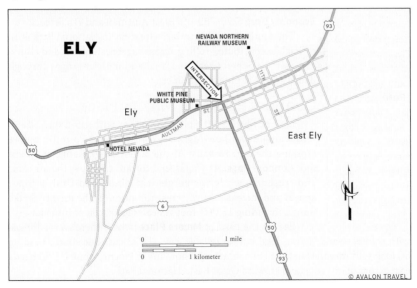

mural of macho miners in Ely

Ely's other main stop is the **White Pine Public Museum** (2000 Aultman St./ US-50, 775/289-4710, seasonal hours, free), which has a wide-ranging collection of minerals, mining implements, and Pony Express memorabilia on display.

Along with extensive mining history, Ely has motels, gas stations, the only supermarket for the next 153 miles east, and dozens of vivid, building-size **murals** depicting various aspects of the town's heritage. The heart of town is a neon-rich few blocks of Aultman Street (US-50) west of the US-93 junction, centering on the landmark **Hotel Nevada** (775/289-6665 or 888/406-3055, $64 and up), with its giant miner and neon-lit slot machines. Inside there are real (as opposed to video) slot machines, pool tables, a café, and a bar. For a bit more peace and quiet, try **Jailhouse Motel** (211 5th St., 775/289-3033, $53 and up), a block north of Aultman Street.

For food, Ely has three coffee shops along US-50, plus the chance to down a milk shake at the soda fountain inside **Economy Drug** (775/289-4929), at Aultman and 7th Streets.

The route east of Ely toward Great Basin National Park is an official "scenic route," rolling across sagebrush plains and climbing over the Schell Creek and Snake Mountain ranges through dense groves of pine and juniper.

> Across Nevada, US-50 follows the route of the Lincoln Highway, the nation's first transcontinental route.
>
> Mountains of mine tailings tower over US-50 west of Ely, and five miles west of town a short detour south takes you to **Ruth,** which sits alongside the huge crater where hundreds of tons of ore were dug. A mining company is currently leaching the metal out of the previously discarded ore, so there's no longer access to the crater itself.

Connors Pass and Majors Place

East of Ely, US-50, spliced together with US-6 and US-93 into a single two-lane highway, continues for 25 miles before crossing the narrow waist of the Schell Creek Range at 7,729-foot **Connors Pass.** As you ascend toward the pass, the air cools and freshens, while the single-leaf piñon and Utah juniper appear and increase. As you crest the summit, the mighty Snake Range, including 13,063-foot Wheeler Peak, comes into view.

East of the pass, at **Majors Place** (where there's a roadhouse with cold beer and "loose slots" but no reliable gas), US-93 cuts due south, heading 80 long solitary miles to the next contact with humans at Pioche, while US-50 heads east across open rangelands toward Great Basin National Park.

Ely marks the junction of US-50 and our **Border to Border** route along US-93 (see page 145). Full coverage of that route, running between the Canadian Rockies and the desert Southwest, begins on page 110.

Great Basin National Park

Approaching Nevada from the east, travelers are greeted by the towering silhouette of **Wheeler Peak,** at 13,063 feet the second-highest and most impressive mountain in the state; from the west, similarly sheer escarpments tower over lush green open range for miles and miles along US-50. In 1987 the 77,000 acres around Wheeler Peak were designated **Great Basin National Park,** but its remote location has made it one of the least-visited national parks in the United States. Hikers and campers will have no trouble finding solitude amid the alpine forests, ancient bristlecone pines, delightful annual wildflowers, glacial lakes, and a small ice field.

Thanks to the well-maintained **Wheeler Peak Scenic Drive** climbing to over 10,000 feet, the wilderness areas are easily accessible to people willing to take a short hike, though many visitors go no farther than the park's centerpiece, **Lehman Caves.**

The world's oldest known bristlecone pine, dubbed Prometheus, was cut down on **Wheeler Peak** in 1964 by a graduate student researcher who discovered too late that, at 4,900 years old, the tree had been the oldest living thing on earth.

A cross-section of the trunk is displayed at the **Bristlecone Convention Center** (150 6th St.) in Ely.

Geological forces have been sculpting Lehman Caves for roughly 70 million years, but they weren't noticed until homesteader Absalom Lehman stumbled upon the small entrance to the caves in 1885. They were declared a national monument in 1922, and since then only minor improvements have been made, leaving the mind-bending limestone formations alone—no flashy light-and-sound show, just hundreds of delicate

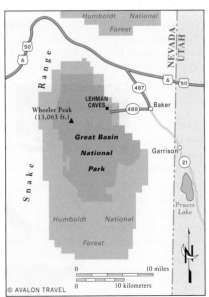

Wheeler Peak in Great Basin National Park

Lehman Caves, Great Basin National Park

stalagmites, stalactites, helictites, aragonites, and the like. A variety of guided tours are conducted at intervals throughout the day; on some holidays and special events on summer evenings at 4:30pm, there's a memorable candlelight tour. Tours leave from the small **visitor center** (775/234-7331, tours $8-10), which has details of hiking and camping options as well as exhibits on Great Basin wildlife—from birds and bats to mountain lions. There's even a small summer-only café.

If you're not camping and self-relying, or if you are and want a break, the nearest food and drink are at the foot of the park in the tiny, artsy, and friendly "town" of **Baker** (pop. 66), which boasts a gas station, a great place to stay—the nine-room **Stargazer Inn** (775/234-7323, $72-and up)—as well as good food, beer, wine, and at **Kerouac's Restaurant & Bar** (Wed.-Mon.). Baker is also home to the main Great Basin National Park **visitor center** (775/234-7331), on the north side of town.

Back on US-50, straddling the Utah-Nevada border, the **Border Inn Casino** (775/234-7300) is a much more functional café-gas station-motel, open daily 24 hours. From here, the only other reliable services are in Ely, 70 miles west, or in Delta, Utah, 85 miles to the east, so pass by at your peril.

UTAH

For most of the way across Utah, the high-speed I-70 freeway has replaced US-50, but if you have time to take a couple of detours, you'll be rewarded with some of the most incredible scenery in the world. Most of this is concentrated in the southeastern corner of the state, where a number of national parks, including **Canyonlands** and **Arches,** preserve the sandstone Canyon Country of the Colorado Plateau. In the west a few old mining towns stand amid the arid desert of the Great Basin. Distances are huge and services few and far between, but if you have the time and plan ahead, this is one of the most satisfying and memorable corners of the country.

Delta

The striking silhouette of North Peak rises above US-50 about 85 miles east of the Nevada border, as the landscape changes suddenly from sagebrush desert to lush pastures around the town of **Delta,** which is irrigated by the green Sevier River. Delta bills itself the "Gateway to Great Basin National Park," and it does have a **Days Inn** and other motels, gas stations, and grocery stores—but little else to attract visitors. One place worth a stop is the small **Great Basin Museum** (45 W. Main St., 435/864-5013, Mon.-Sat., free), which features minerals, arrowheads, and local history exhibits. Next door, the **Topaz Museum** (435/864-2514) includes a thoughtful display of artifacts relating to Topaz Camp, a World War II internment camp set up in the desert 16 miles northwest of Delta by the U.S. government to imprison more than 8,000 American men, women, and children of Japanese descent.

North of Delta, the horizon is split by the belching smokestack of the 1,800-megawatt coal-fired Intermountain Power Plant, operated by the distant city of Los Angeles.

From Delta, US-50 officially cuts southeast across I-15, linking up with I-70 at Salina for the trip east to Grand Junction. Our route, however, follows US-6 (old US-50) toward the Great Salt Lake area, then east over the Wasatch Front, rejoining official US-50 (now I-70) at Green River.

Little Sahara Recreation Area

From Delta, the route follows the Sevier River northwest, racing across the featureless desert for 32 miles before reaching the well-posted turnoff north to the **Little Sahara Recreation Area.** Visible from the highway, to the north of US-6, the Little Sahara Recreation Area holds 60,000 acres of sand dunes and sagebrush flats, the prettiest parts of which are preserved for hikers and campers, though motorcyclists and ATVers can overwhelm any sense of peace and tranquility, turning it into a campground from hell.

Eureka

Fifty miles east of Delta, 20 miles west of the I-15 freeway, the weather-beaten town of **Eureka** (pop. 669) climbs steeply up surrounding mountainsides at the heart of the once-thriving Tintic Mining District, where, as recently as the 1930s, thousands of miners dug millions of dollars' worth of gold, silver, copper, and lead out of the ground every year. Now the massive wooden head-frames of long-closed mine shafts stand high above the houses and prefab trailers that cling to the slopes, while fading signs advertise abandoned businesses along Main Street.

Though diehard residents still speak of plans to reopen one or more of the mines, prosperity seems a distant dream in Eureka, and while it's not quite a ghost town, it seems well on its way there. The glory days are recounted in the small **Tintic Mining Museum** (435/433-6842), next to city hall on Main Street. At the west edge of town a historical plaque stands alongside the heavy timber head-frame of the Bullion-Beck Mine, one of the area's most productive.

Heading east from Eureka, our route bends across rock-strewn sagebrush hills around the southern shore of **Utah Lake** toward I-15. Utah Lake, which is freshwater in contrast to the briny expanse of the Great Salt Lake to the north, used to be much larger than it is now, before so much of it was diverted to water the apple, peach, and cherry orchards that line US-6 around **Santaquin**—whose gas stations are a reliable source of fuel for westbound travelers heading to Delta, 70 miles to the southwest.

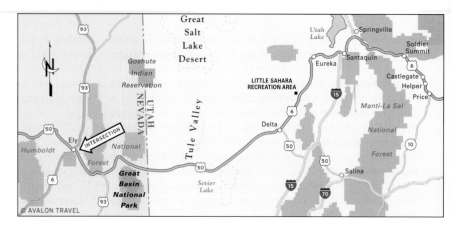

From Santaquin, follow the I-15 freeway north to **Springville,** from where the Salt Lake City megalopolis stretches north along I-15 for nearly 100 miles.

Castle Gate and Helper

Heading east from Springville, the drive along US-6 (old US-50) up and over 7,477-foot **Soldier Summit** is truly beautiful, as the two-lane highway twists alongside pines and cottonwoods to the crest, then passes through bright red sandstone canyons along the stark eastern side of the towering Wasatch Range. Dropping down from Soldier Summit, US-6/191 winds along the Price River through **Castle Gate,** a steeply walled sandstone canyon lined with working coal mines, many of which you see from the highway. While most now rely on heavy machinery to do the dirty work of digging out the coal, the Castle Gate area has been the site of the two worst mining disasters in Utah history: 171 men and boys killed in a 1924 explosion, and 200 killed at nearby Scofield on May Day, 1900.

Park City, in the mountains above Salt Lake City, is home to the annual Sundance Film Festival. Nearby ski resorts hosted the 2002 Winter Olympics.

Tiny **Helper** (pop. 2,201), at the downstream edge of Castle Gate, six miles northwest of Price, is a classic railroad town preserved almost unchanged for nearly a century. Helper earned its name in 1892 when the Denver and Rio Grande Railroad built a depot and roundhouse here to hold the "helper" engines that were added to trains to help push them over Soldier Summit, 25 miles to the west. The six-block downtown area, fronting onto the tracks, includes so many turn-of-the-20th-century brick-and stone-fronted buildings that it's been declared a National Historic District—although the sad truth is that most of these have stood abandoned since the railroad switched to diesel power in the 1950s.

Relive the glory days at the excellent **Western Mining & Railroad Museum** (294 S. Main St., 435/472-3009, Tues.-Sat. winter, Mon.-Sat. summer), which contains enough raw material on railroading and coal mining, not to mention the region's diverse immigrant cultures, to keep you occupied for an hour or more. There's also a display recounting the exploits of Butch Cassidy and his gang, who raided banks and rustled cattle throughout the region in the late 1890s, hiding out in the surrounding hills. Behind the museum, an outdoor lot displays some of the giant machines used in the coal mines, which, unlike the railroad, still employ a large number of local people.

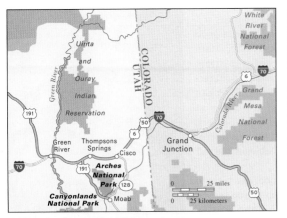

sego lily,
state flower of Utah

Helper, Utah

Price

The largest city in eastern Utah, **Price** (pop. 8,715) is located roughly midway between the I-15 and I-70 freeways, 65 miles northwest of Green River. Coal is so prevalent in the area that road cuts reveal solid black seams, but the town itself is lush and green thanks to irrigation provided by the Price River, which flows south from town into the Green and Colorado Rivers.

Coal mining and, to a lesser extent, agriculture still power Price, where the kid-friendly **Utah State University Eastern Prehistoric Museum** (155 E. Main St., 435/613-5060, Mon.-Sat. 9am-5pm, $6) is worth a look for its extensive displays on the Native American cultures of the region, and for its range of full-size dinosaur skeletons, including a stegosaur and a Utahraptor. Many of these were reassembled from fossils collected from the **Cleveland-Lloyd Dinosaur Quarry,** 30 miles south of town.

Price also has all the highway services travelers might need: numerous gas stations, places to eat, and nine motels, including the nice **Quality Inn** (435/637-5660, $80 and up).

Southwest from Price, bound for Green River and the I-70 freeway, US-6/191 runs alongside the busy Denver and Rio Grande main-line railroad through a region of arid plateaus highlighted every few miles by brilliantly colorful, weirdly sculpted sandstone mesas. Though barren and empty at first glance, the region is particularly rich in two things: coal mines and, more unusually, dinosaur bones. (Why do you think they call them fossil fuels?)

Green River

Straddling the eponymous river on the north side of I-70, **Green River** (pop. 952) makes a handy base for exploring southeastern Utah, but it offers little in and of itself. The town holds numerous 24-hour gas stations, a handful of motels, and a couple of good places to eat—try the **Tamarisk** (1710 E. Main St., 435/564-8109), overlooking the Green River.

Just south of Main Street, the most characterful place to eat and drink in Green River can be found under the unmissable neon sign at **Ray's Tavern** (25 S. Broadway, 435/564-3511), with excellent burgers, a wide range of microbrews, a pool table, and dining tables made out of tree trunks.

Even if you don't need fuel, food, or a place to sleep, Green River offers one compelling reason to stop: the spacious, modern **John Wesley Powell River History Museum** (1765 E. Main St., 435/564-3427, Mon.-Sat. 9am-7pm, Sun. 12pm-5pm summer, Tues.-Sat. 9am-5pm, Sun. 12pm-5pm winter, $6), above the east bank of the river. In 1869 Powell and his crew were the first to

aerial view of the Green River

travel the length of the Colorado River through the Grand Canyon. Though the legendary explorers started their epic adventure in Green River, Wyoming, not here in Utah, the spacious modern museum, on old US-50 along the east bank of the Green River, is the best single repository of artifacts relating to their feat. The collection concentrates on Powell in particular and on waterborne transport in general, but there are also displays chronicling the adventures of other early explorers (including Juan de Oñate in 1605 and the Domínguez and Escalante expedition of 1776), and of fur-trappers, miners, and Mormons—all of whom contributed to the exploration and mapping of the American West.

The otherworldly aspects of the Utah landscape south of Green River have tempted would-be space colonizers to establish the **Mars Desert Research Station** here, to test equipment and train potential Mars-bound astronauts.

To get some sense of what Powell and crew experienced, take a raft, canoe, or kayak trip down the Green or Colorado River. Dozens of outfitters offer equipment rentals, shuttles, and guided trips, from all-day to weeklong tours.

Canyonlands National Park

The largest and least-visited park in the Southwest, **Canyonlands National Park** is both breathtakingly beautiful and totally inhospitable, an arid wilderness of high plateaus and deep canyon carved by the mighty Green and Colorado Rivers. The park is divided into several different areas, each of which is at least a 100-mile drive from the others, so it pays to plan ahead. The most popular section, the **Island in the Sky,** stands high above the confluence of the rivers and gives the most sweeping panoramas—100 miles in every direction from over 6,000 feet above sea level. South of the rivers, **The Needles** district holds 50 square miles of spires, arches, and canyons and is the best place to undertake lengthy hikes. One trail leads from the end of the road down to the mouth of Cataract Canyon on the Colorado River. Another area of Canyonlands, **The Maze,** is west of the rivers and virtually inaccessible.

DETOUR: SALT LAKE CITY

With no other city for some 500 miles in any direction, Salt Lake City (pop. 186,440, metro pop. 1.2 million) looks and feels like the oasis it naturally is. Taking its name from the undrinkable alkaline Great Salt Lake, the city is actually blessed with abundant freshwater, thanks to the rain- and snow-making properties of the Wasatch Range, which rises knifelike to the east. Founded by Mormons in 1847, and effectively controlled by Mormon elders ever since, Salt Lake City is clean and pleasant, and unusual enough to merit a detour. Most of what there is to see has to do with the Mormons, better known as the Church of Latter-Day Saints, which has its worldwide headquarters at **Temple Square** downtown (street numbers and addresses are measured from here, not the nearby state capitol, which goes to show just how predominant the LDS church is in local life). On the west side of Temple Square are the amazing genealogical libraries the Mormons maintain; a block east of Temple Square is the **Beehive House,** preserved as it was in the 1850s, when early Mormon leader Brigham Young lived here.

Given its Mormon roots and Midwest temperament, Salt Lake City is not exactly a food-lover's paradise, but there are a number of good restaurants. One truly fine place to dine is **Bambara** (202 S. Main St., 801/363-5454), whose eclectic menu and stylish decor would feel at home in New Orleans or San Francisco. The same 1920s building houses a nice place to stay: the boutique Kimpton **Hotel Monaco** (801/546-7866, $136 and up).

For more information, contact the **Salt Lake City visitors bureau** (800/541-4955).

There's one **visitors center** near the entrance to Island in the Sky and another near the entrance to the Needles. The **Canyonlands Park Headquarters** (2282 SW Resource Blvd., 435/719-2313 or 435/259-7164) in Moab also has extensive information. Adjacent to Canyonlands are two state parks, **Dead Horse Point** in the north and **Newspaper Rock** in the south, both of which are also well worth a look.

Arches National Park

Taking its name from the hundreds of naturally formed sandstone arches scattered here, **Arches National Park** is the most feature-packed of southern Utah's national parks. Ranging in size from around 3 feet to nearly 300 feet in span, the arches are the result of erosion over millions of years, the same agent that formed the thousands of brilliantly colored spires, pinnacles, and canyons that cover southeast Utah. Piñon pines and junipers add a splash

The LA Angels Triple-A farm club **Salt Lake Bees** (801/325-2337) play right in downtown Salt Lake City at West Temple and 1300 South Street.

Uranium mined from **Temple Mountain,** west of Canyonlands, was used to make the first atomic bombs.

BUTCH BUTCH CASSIDY AND THE HOLE-IN-THE-WALL GANG

Long before Paul Newman played him alongside Robert Redford's Sundance Kid, Butch Cassidy was one of the great outlaw legends of the Wild West. Thanks to his habit of sharing the proceeds from his crimes with the widows and children of men killed or ruined by bankers and cattle barons, Butch Cassidy earned a reputation as the Robin Hood of the Wild West. That, plus the fact that he never killed anyone while committing his crimes, gained him popularity and admiration from the cowboys, miners, and homesteading pioneers among whom he worked his trade.

Born Robert Leroy Parker to a family of Mormon farmers in Beaver, Utah, on Friday the 13th of April, 1866, the man who came to be known as Butch Cassidy spent his youth as a ranch hand in Utah, Colorado, and southern Wyoming. The first major crime attributed to Butch Cassidy is the robbery of a bank in Telluride, Colorado, in 1889, which netted him and his three accomplices some $20,000. From 1894 to 1896 he was imprisoned in Wyoming for cattle theft, and following this he joined up with Harry Longabaugh (a.k.a. The Sundance Kid) and the rest of the gang. Together they robbed over a dozen banks, trains, and stagecoaches throughout the West, netting an estimated $350,000 in five years. One of their many daring heists was the daylight robbery of a coal-mining company in Castle Gate, Utah, in April 1897; while the pay-roll was being taken from a train, Butch simply grabbed the satchel and rode off in a cloud of dust, $9,000 richer.

According to many sources, Butch and Sundance died in 1908, in a shoot-out in South America (as depicted in the 1969 movie *Butch Cassidy and the Sundance Kid*). But some people (including his sister, who lived until the 1970s) say that Butch survived to a ripe old age, living in Spokane, Washington, under the name William T. Phillips until his death in 1937.

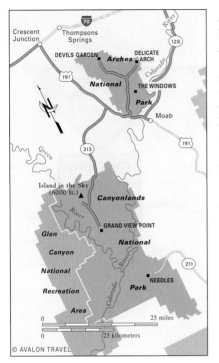

of green to the red and brown backdrop, but mostly what you see are red stone and blue sky—lots and lots of both.

The park's highlights can be easily reached from the 18-mile paved road that runs through the center of the park. A **visitors center** (435/719-2299, hours vary seasonally) at the entrance, east of US-191 and five miles north of Moab, has maps, pamphlets, and displays on the geology and natural history of Arches.

From the entrance, the road switchbacks uphill past the sandstone skyline of "Park Avenue" before reaching a turnoff east to **The Windows,** whose dense concentration of arches and spires is required viewing, no matter how little time you have. Four miles beyond The Windows, a dirt road leads east to Wolfe Ranch, trailhead for **Delicate Arch,** the park's most postcard-worthy feature, a three-mile round-trip hike. Three miles farther along the main road, **Fiery Furnace** is an otherworldly collection of narrow canyons that, despite the name, is quite cool and shady; park rangers give guided walks here throughout the summer. At the far end of the road there's a two-mile trail leading to **Devils Garden,** where

Arches National Park

you can see **Landscape Arch,** the park's and the world's largest arch—291 feet across and 105 feet high.

Moab

Driving across southern Utah, you have two main options: Race along I-70 and get somewhere else in a hurry, or slow down and search out the truly unforgettable scenery the state has to offer. One of the best places to base yourself for an exploration of the region is **Moab** (pop. 5,046), an old uranium mining town located 30 miles south of the freeway, surrounded by two national parks (Arches and Canyonlands) and hundreds of thousands of acres of desert wilderness.

Arches National Park

Thanks to *Outside* magazine and the recent mania for outdoor athleticism, Moab has experienced a massive tourist boom in the past decades—Edward Abbey, cantankerous poet of the Southwest who wrote his first book, *Desert Solitaire,* about a season he spent at nearby Arches National Park, would probably turn in his grave if he saw the gangs of Lycra-clad mountain bikers milling around Moab's Main Street T-shirt stores and brewpubs. But despite the addition of fast-food franchises and hundreds of new motel rooms, Moab is still a dusty little back-of-beyond hamlet, albeit one that gives easy access to the wilds nearby.

If you're not prepared to camp out in the backcountry (if you are, the nearby state and national parks have a full range of possibilities), Moab has the usual

landscape surrounding Moab

national motels plus local ones like the **Apache Motel** (166 S. 400 E., 435/259-5727 or 800/228-6882, $45 and up), where John Wayne slept while filming *Rio Bravo* near Moab in 1958.

For breakfast or lunch, try the excellent **Jailhouse Café** (101 N. Main St., 435/259-3900) or the **Moab Diner** (189 S. Main St., 435/259-4006), two blocks away. For a treat after a day on the trails, enjoy a gourmet dinner at the **Desert Bistro** (36 S. 100 W., 435/259-0756), in the heart of downtown.

For more information on visiting the Moab area, including all the surrounding parks, contact the helpful **Moab Information Center** (435/259-8825 or 800/635-6622, daily) at Main and Center Streets in the middle of town.

The prettiest route east from Moab, Hwy-128, winds along the broad and brown Colorado River past 25 miles of swimming, kayaking, and camping spots. Hwy-128 links up with I-70 about 23 miles west of the Colorado border at junction 212, near the former sheep-ranching center of **Cisco,** a ghostly old US-50 crossroads abandoned after completion of the interstate, where old gas station buildings are slowly decaying into a post-apocalyptic art installation.

The annual Fat Tire Festival, which is now the **Moab Ho-Down Mountain Bike Festival,** held the week before Halloween, brings mountain bikers from all over the world to Moab.

A word of warning: Even if you're not planning to venture from your car, it's a good idea to carry at least a gallon of water per person when traveling in the desert.

Fifteen miles south of Moab along US-191, one of Utah's oddest attractions is the **Hole N" The Rock** (435/686-2250, daily, $6), a 5,000-square-foot home carved out of a sandstone cliff over a 20-year period, beginning in the 1940s, by Albert and Gladys Christensen. Now open to tourists, the site also includes a large carving of FDR's face.

COLORADO

Driving across southern Colorado on US-50 takes you through almost every landscape landlocked North America has to offer. From the geological wonderland of the Colorado River plateau, which stretches west into Utah, the route climbs up and over the 14,000-foot **Rocky Mountains,** which form a formidable wall down the center of the state. Continuing east, the alpine meadows, deeply etched river canyons, and snow-covered peaks of the southern Rockies fade away into the flat agricultural prairies that stretch east across the middle of the country. While there is considerable ranching and farming, outdoor recreation—fishing, hiking, skiing, and mountain biking—is the basis for the economy, and the region is well provided with tourist facilities, especially in the mountainous middle.

Grand Junction

Thirty miles east of the Utah border, US-50 diverges from high-speed I-70 at the city of **Grand Junction** (pop. 58,566) on the Colorado River. After all the desert that

surrounds it, Grand Junction feels much bigger than you'd expect, with its thriving old downtown, complete with cobblestone streets, odd bits of outdoor sculpture, great antiques shops, neon signs—and tons of free parking. Catering to passing traffic, Grand Junction's I-70 frontage has all the motels and places to eat you could want, but downtown holds one really nice older place, the clean and comfortable **Historic Melrose Hotel** (337 Colorado Ave., 970/242-9636, hostel bunks $33, rooms $67 and up), a block south of Main Street—just look for the red neon sign.

Like the rest of western Colorado and eastern Utah, the Grand Junction area is rich in two things: the scenic splendor of rivers and red-rock canyons, and fossilized dinosaurs. The scenery is everywhere, and a fine array of the latter are on display west of town along I-70 at Fruita, in the Museum of Western Colorado's wonderful **Dinosaur Journey** (970/858-7282, daily, $9). Kids can have fun pushing buttons to control gigantic audio-animatronic mechanical critters while learning a little about Triassic, Jurassic, and other period details.

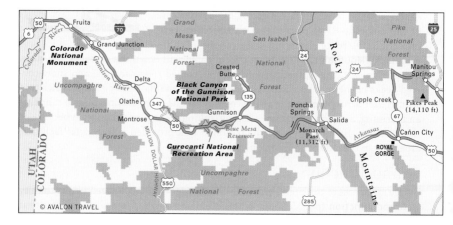

fresh peaches at a roadside market east of Grand Junction

Colorado National Monument

Rising south and west of Grand Junction, nearly 2,000 feet above the Colorado River, the brilliantly colored cliffs of **Colorado National Monument** are simply impossible to miss. Deep canyons, alive with piñon pines and cottonwood trees, nestle at the foot of sheer rock walls, at the top of which you get panoramic views over miles and miles of the Colorado Plateau. The 23-mile-long **Rim Rock Drive** winds along the tops of the cliffs, giving quick access to numerous trails for up-close looks at the various layers and hues of sandstone and shale, which have eroded over the eons into masses of sculpted stone.

© AVALON TRAVEL

Colorado National Monument

There's a large **visitors center** (970/858-3617) at the main entrance, four miles southeast of town, and there's another entrance off I-70 in Fruita, at the northern end of the park.

Delta

From Grand Junction, US-50 briefly becomes a four-lane freeway, then reverts to two lanes following the Gunnison River as far as **Delta** (pop. 8,915). The half-dozen building-size murals of elk and local agricultural products support Delta's claim that it is "The City of Murals."

Delta has one great old landmark, the 1920s **Egyptian Theater Movie Palace** (452 Main St., 970/874-9770), along with its fair share of motels (including a Days Inn) and fast-food places. It's also home to a classic piece of roadside Americana: the log-and-stone cabins of the **Westways Court Motel** (1030 Main St., 970/874-4415, $65 and up), on US-50 in the center of town.

Montrose: The Million Dollar Highway

With the San Juan Mountains standing out to the south, and Black Canyon just up the road, **Montrose,** a fast-growing farming community of over 19,000 that spreads from the heart of the fertile Uncompahgre Valley, makes a good base for exploring the region. The town itself has an appealing, still-in-business business district and a historical museum housed in the old railroad depot; the US-50 frontage has plenty of motels and places to eat.

Eight miles east of Montrose, Hwy-347 turns off north from US-50 toward the Black Canyon of the Gunnison National Park, but Montrose also marks the start of one of the best-loved roads in the country, the **Million Dollar Highway,** a classic

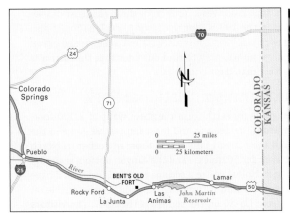

Rocky Mountain columbine, state flower of Colorado

stretch of two-lane blacktop that forms a swirling ribbon through the San Juan Mountains, the wildest and ruggedest peaks in the Colorado Rockies. Marked on maps and by road signs as US-550, which runs south from the Gunnison River ranch lands around Montrose to the Southern Ute Indian Reservation, the "Million Dollar" tag is generally applied to the 25 steep and twisting miles that link Ouray and Silverton, a pair of remote gold- and silver-mining communities, but it's also an appropriate nickname for the entire 110 miles of US-550 that link US-50 with Ouray and Durango.

memorial to snowplow drivers killed on the Million Dollar Highway

No matter what you want from a scenic drive, the Million Dollar Highway has it in spades. Loaded with sublime natural scenery, historically fascinating and visually appealing small towns, and, most of all, sheer driving pleasure, the road more than lives up to its name. As you might expect of a road born in a Wild West mining country animated by tales of million-dollar fortunes earned, lost, and hoped for, the history of the Million Dollar Highway is rife with legend. The route was first blazed by the so-called "Pathfinder of the San Juans," a five-foot-tall Russian immigrant named Otto Mears who was working as a U.S. mail carrier between Silverton and Telluride. By 1882 Mears had created a lucrative toll road that he parlayed into a sizable empire of roads and railroads, but his original hand-carved route through the mountains formed the basis of today's Million Dollar Highway.

> The New Deal-era documentary photography project, which produced many indelible images from the likes of Walker Evans and Dorothea Lange, was directed by Roy Stryker, who spent his youth on a ranch outside Montrose.

Even the origin of the "Million Dollar" name is clouded in myth. Some say it was first used after an early traveler, complaining of the vertigo-inducing steepness of the route, said, "I wouldn't go that way again if you paid me a million dollars." Others claim that it derives simply from the actual cost of paving the route in the 1930s. But the favorite explanation is also the most likely: When the highway was first constructed, the builders used gravel discarded by nearby gold and silver mines, only to find out later that this dirt was actually rich in ore and worth an estimated million dollars.

Black Canyon of the Gunnison National Park

Some of the hardest and oldest rocks on earth form the sheer walls of 2,000-foot-deep **Black Canyon of the Gunnison,** the deepest and most impressive gorge in the state. The river cutting through the canyon falls faster than any other in North America—dropping 2,150 feet in under 50 miles—and the canyon bottom is so rugged that there are no trails along it. Unless you're a serious mountaineer, you'll have to content yourself with looking down into it from the rim, which is accessible on the north side via Hwy-92 and from US-50 on the south via Hwy-347. The **visitors**

DETOUR:
MOVIE MANOR, GREAT SAND DUNES, AND COLORADO GATORS

Some 75 miles southwest of US-50, the potato-farming town of Monte Vista is home to the **Movie Manor** (2830 US-160 W., 719/852-5921, $90 and up), a unique combination of drive-in movie theater, restaurant, and Best Western motel. You can watch movies (for free!) from the comfort of your motel room, though the screen is so far away it's about the same size as watching movies on TV. It's fun, though, and unique, for sure—where else can you snuggle down beneath the covers, gazing out the window as the sun sets and the lights come up on the big-screen figures swaggering through their latest Hollywood hits against a backdrop of snowcapped 14,000-foot peaks?

Other good reasons to loop south from US-50 include the **Great Sand Dunes National Park & Preserve** and the even more unlikely sight of some 400 alligators enjoying the geothermal hot springs at **Colorado Gators Reptile Park** (719/378-2612, daily, $15), an hour south of US-50 on Hwy-17, near the turnoff east to the Great Sand Dunes.

Great Sand Dunes National Park

center (970/249-1914 or 970/641-2337) on the south rim provides details on hiking trails and camping and can tell you more than you ever wanted to know about the canyon's unique geology: For instance, unlike the Grand Canyon, with its layers of exposed rock, the Black Canyon is basically one solid hunk of stone, a half-mile-thick chunk of two-billion-year-old Precambrian gneiss (pronounced "nice").

Upstream from the Black Canyon, US-50 parallels the Gunnison River, renowned for its excellent trout and landlocked salmon fishing, though sadly the once-raging waters have been backed up behind dams to form a series of reservoirs, jointly managed as the **Curecanti National Recreation Area.**

Gunnison and Crested Butte

A crossroads cattle town with a rapidly growing recreational aspect and the only commercial airport for miles, **Gunnison** (pop. 5,854; elev. 7,703) is made livelier than many Colorado towns by the presence of Western State Colorado University, whose ski-bumming students are responsible for the town's many bike shops and Internet cafés, not to mention the huge "W" that marks a mountainside south of town. To get a feel for Gunnison, stop by the lively **W Café** (114 N. Main St.,

The first European explorers to pass through this part of the Rockies were the Spanish missionaries Domínguez and Escalante, in 1776.

970/641-1744), marked by a nifty neon sign, or the nearby coffeehouse, **The Bean** (120 N. Main St.), a half block north of US-50, which runs through the redbrick heart of old downtown Gunnison. Motels line up along US-50, making Gunnison a handy base for exploring the region.

If you're taken with the scenery around Gunnison and want to see more, head north along Hwy-135 and the Gunnison River to the area's skiing and mountain biking center, **Crested Butte** (pop. 1,487), about 25 miles away. As in Telluride and Aspen, this 100-year-old gold-mining camp won a second lease on life thanks to tourism, though compared to other Colorado places, Crested Butte is low-key and somewhat off the beaten path. Skiers in search of solitude flock here in winter to cruise the 1,100-plus acres of Mt. Crested Butte, while in summer Crested Butte is a mountain-bike mecca, home to miles upon miles of mining roads and single-track trails winding through the mountains. (The ski lifts convert to bike lifts, to save you suffering on the climb back uphill.)

Relax while you recharge your batteries with a burger and a beer or two at the **Wooden Nickel** (222 Elk Ave., 970/349-6350).

Three blocks north of Elk Avenue, the **Crested Butte International Lodge & Hostel** (615 Teocalli Ave., 888/412-7087, hostel bunks $23-35, rooms $65 and up) has dorm beds and family rooms. There are also hotels and condos available through the **ski resort** (970/349-2262 or 877/547-5143).

Monarch Pass

East of Gunnison, the landscape changes swiftly as US-50, along with a few masochistic cyclists, climbs steeply through a gorgeous alpine landscape of meadows and cattle ranches toward 11,312-foot **Monarch Pass.** The pass marks the highest point on US-50 and straddles the Continental Divide: The 30 feet of annual snowfall on the east side of the pass end up in the Atlantic, while (in theory, at least) moisture falling farther west makes its way to the Pacific. There's a ski and snowboarding area here in winter, and in summer you can ride a tram or hike to a nearby summit for a 360-degree view over the Rocky and Sangre de Cristo Mountains.

Salida

Sitting alongside the Arkansas River east of Monarch Pass, **Salida** (pop. 5,236; elev. 7,083) is a one-time railroad town gradually and prosperously switching over to the tourist trade. Close your eyes to the sprawl of Walmart and McDonald's along US-50, and head a dozen blocks north to the historic downtown, where dozens of historic brick buildings line up around a spacious riverfront park. Outdoor recreation shops like **Absolute Bikes** (330 W. Sackett Ave., 719/539-9295) and **Salida Mountain Sports** (110 N. F St., 719/539-4400) sell all the gear and clothing you could need, and can provide bikes and useful information on the area's wealth of recreational opportunities. Historic downtown Salida also has some great food and drink options, including **Currents** (122 N. F St., 719/539-9514), serving grilled steaks, fish-and-chips, and veggie-friendly sandwiches along with good beers and cocktails.

The **Salida Hot Springs Aquatic Center** (410 W. Rainbow Blvd./US-50, 719/539-6738, $11), next to the visitors bureau, is the largest hot springs in the state. The naturally heated WPA-built indoor pool and baths are open year-round.

East of Salida, river rafters can be seen riding the rapids of the Arkansas River for most of the next 45 miles. Over a dozen different rafting companies have operations along this beautifully scenic stretch, where steeply walled sandstone gorges alternate with broad meadows and sagebrush plains all the way to Royal Gorge and Cañon City.

Every December, Salida lights up a tree on **Christmas Mountain** with 10,000 bulbs.

Royal Gorge

It would be easy to object to the rampant commercialism of **Royal Gorge** (719/275-7507 or 888/333-5597, $26), owned and operated by Cañon City, but if you don't mind seeing impressive works of humankind amid a stupendous show of nature's prowess, I heartily recommend a visit. The gorge itself is unforgettable, its sheer red granite cliffs dropping over 1,000 feet straight down to the Arkansas River. The experience is enhanced by a barrage of civil engineering feats, including aerial trams, incline railroads, and an impossibly delicate suspension bridge, all enabling visitors to experience the area in diverse ways. You can look down from the rim, dangle from a gondola on your way across to the other side, and from there follow a short nature trail that offers good views of Pike's Peak. Walk back across the wooden planks of the bridge—the highest in the world, feeling uncomfortably like a rickety old seaside pier.

Cañon City

One of the last remaining Wild West towns in the lower 48 states, **Cañon City** (pop. 16,400) is carved out of the eastern flank of the Rocky Mountains. Over a mile high and surrounded by a ring of 14,000-foot peaks, Cañon City's short Main Street, a block north of US-50, is lined by workaday gun shops, bookshops, and saloons. But the local economy prospers not so much from tourism as from prisons—a dozen in all, including a notorious federal maximum-security "supermax" penitentiary. Built in the 1990s, the top-security supermax prison has held some 500 of the nation's most notorious inmates, including numerous organized crime kingpins and terrorists like Oklahoma City bomber Terry Nichols; Atlanta Olympics bomber Eric

bridge over Royal Gorge

River rafters and a railroad share Royal Gorge.

All along US-50 west of Cañon City, you can see rafters racing along the wild Arkansas River. Many companies offer guided trips, including **Royal Gorge Rafting** (719/722-2731).

Rudolph; the "Unabomber," Ted Kaczynski; and Al Qaeda "Shoe Bomber" Richard Reid.

Despite the notoriety of its many prisons, Cañon City's main attraction is the surrounding scenery, particularly the views along **Skyline Drive,** accessible from just west of town. It's a three-mile, one-way drive across the top of an 800-foot hill, as close to riding a roller coaster as you're ever likely to get while inside a passenger car. Royal Gorge to the west is another major draw, and Cañon City makes a good base for explorations, with a few moderately priced motels. The best place for cheap food and drink is **The Owl** (626 Main St., 719/275-9946), a combo soda fountain, diner, and pool hall at the heart of the lively Main Street business district just north of US-50.

Pike's Peak and Manitou Springs

One of the highest points you can drive to in the continental United States, **Pike's Peak** has been a road trip destination since 1901 when the first car (a two-cylinder Locomobile Steamer) made its way to the 14,110-foot summit. Opened as a toll road in 1915, the **Pike's Peak Highway** ($10-15 toll per person, depending on the season) now winds its way to the top—climbing nearly 7,000 vertical feet in under 20 miles, with no guardrails to comfort you or block the amazing 360-degree Rocky Mountain panorama. The road is now owned and operated by the city of Colorado Springs; go early, before the clouds and haze build up, for the best long-distance views.

And if the views aren't enough, another good reason to climb Pike's Peak is that to get there you pass through the delightful old resort town of **Manitou Springs.** A national historic district, Manitou Springs has all the grand hotels, hot springs, tourist traps, and cave tours you could want, plus what may be my favorite pinball arcade in the entire world: The barely advertised **Arcade Amusement Inc.** (930 Manitou Ave.,

Pike's Peak

719/685-9815, free) whose penny arcade houses dozens of ancient machines in perfect working order, some still charging the same penny, nickel, or dime that they did in the 1920s, '30s, and '40s. The nearby **Sahara Café** (954 Manitou Ave., 719/685-2303) is a great Middle Eastern place, open more than 20 years, and the **Cliff House Hotel** (306 Canon Ave., 719/785-1000) is a gorgeous Victorian-era landmark, one of the nation's classic old hotels.

Besides the Victoriana, Manitou Springs is also the home of the classic "car culture" motor courts cabins of the **El Colorado Lodge** (23 Manitou Ave., 719/685-5485, $60 and up), arrayed around four acres of pine trees, with fireplaces, a pool, and a horseshoe pit.

North of Manitou Springs, the 1,350-acre **Garden of the Gods** (daily, free) is a photogenic geological outcropping of red sandstone spires, some rising to heights of 300 feet.

Pueblo

At the foot of the mountains, 38 miles east of Cañon City and 150 miles west of the Kansas border, the heavily industrialized city of **Pueblo** (pop. 106,595) spreads to both sides of the Arkansas River. Colorado's seventh-largest city, Pueblo was founded by legendary black fur-trapper Jim Beckwourth in 1842, but the town really grew in the 1870s following the arrival of the railroad and the discovery nearby of vast amounts of coal. Steel mills, including some of the largest west of the Mississippi, still stand around the fringes of the pleasant tree-lined downtown area, but Pueblo is increasingly more bucolic than brawny, and the historic areas are slowly filling up with artsy cafés, bookshops, and antiques stores, especially along Union Avenue and the "Riverwalk" promenade along the Arkansas River. For great fresh-made Mexican food, try **Papa Jose's Union Café** (320 S. Union Ave., 719/545-7476); for pizza, go to **Angelo's** (105 E. Riverwalk, 719/544-8588).

After a visit to the top of Pike's Peak in 1893, Katharine Lee Bates wrote the words to "America the Beautiful."

The **Pike's Peak International Hill Climb** has been held in late June or early July almost every year since 1916. Top drivers often compete, hitting speeds of up to 100 mph on the twisting mountain road.

DETOUR: DENVER

Though it is 100 miles north of Pueblo via the I-25 freeway, Denver (pop. 683,096) has the biggest, newest, and coolest airport in the Rockies, which may make it a handy starting or stopping point. The airport, which opened in 1995, is in the middle of nowhere, 25 miles northeast of town. The main lobby has a soaring fabric roof that from the outside looks like a Plains Indian encampment; inside is a pair of artworks, called *America: Why I Love Her,* which trace artist Gary Sweeney's childhood memories of road trips to see the "World's Largest Ball of Twine" and other all-American icons.

Other reasons to visit Denver include the **U.S. Mint** (320 W. Colfax Ave., Mon.-Thurs., free), right downtown, where you can watch and hear coins being pressed into shape; **Coors Field** (303/ROCKIES—303/762-5437 or 800/388-7625), lively home of the Colorado Rockies baseball team; and **Lakeside Amusement Park** (4601 Sheridan Blvd., off I-70, 303/477-1621, $4 admission, unlimited ride passes around $17 Mon.-Fri., $26 Sat.-Sun. and holidays), a nifty and not expensive summer-only amusement park with art deco architecture, a wooden Cyclone roller coaster, and other rides dating back over 100 years.

On the west side of the **Colorado State Capitol,** a benchmark at the unlucky 13th step lets you stand exactly 5,280 feet above sea level—a mile high.

In downtown Denver, eat at **Snooze** (2262 Larimer St., 303/297-0700), a family-friendly haunt serving great breakfasts, including a spicy corned beef hash. There is the usual range of hotels and motels in and around Denver, plus one unforgettable classic dating from the 1890s: President Dwight Eisenhower's favorite hotel, The **Brown Palace** (321 17th St., 303/297-3111, $283 and up). The lobby is worth a look even if you stay the night somewhere else.

For details on these or anything else to do with Denver, contact the **visitor information center** (1575 California St., 303/892-1505 or 800/233-6837).

La Junta

For eastbound travelers, **La Junta** (pop. 7,077), a busy railroad town on the banks of the Arkansas River, is where we begin tracing the historic Santa Fe Trail. The name La Junta, which means "the junction," is apt, since the town has long been a key crossroads, first on the Santa Fe Trail and now as the main Amtrak stop south of Denver. The town's excellent **Koshare Indian Museum** (115 W. 18th St., 719/384-4411, daily, $5) is housed in a giant kiva-shaped structure on the campus of Otero Junior College, on the south side of town. It's a local tradition for Boy Scouts to don Native American regalia and perform interpretive dances on-site (Sat. June-July, $12).

La Junta also offers gas stations, a good range of places to eat (Mexican restaurants are a particular strength), a two-screen movie theater, and an ancient-looking barber shop. Sleep cheap at the clean and friendly **Midtown Motel** (215 E. 3rd St., 719/384-7741, $50-75).

La Junta also marks the spot where the Mountain Branch of the Santa Fe Trail finally cuts away to the south, following what's now US-350 through the Comanche National Grassland and continuing over Raton Pass into New Mexico and on to Santa Fe. Eastbound travelers are in luck, as we follow this historic route all the way to the other side of Kansas City.

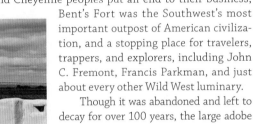

From US-50, one of the West's most scenic drives (unpaved but easily passable), **Phantom Canyon Road,** 25 miles west of Pueblo and 7 miles east of Cañon City, winds north to the old mining camp, and now prosperous gambling town, of **Cripple Creek.**

Bent's Old Fort

From La Junta, an interesting quick detour off US-50, Hwy-194 runs along the north bank of the Arkansas River to one of Colorado's most evocative historic sites, **Bent's Old Fort** (719/383-5010, daily, $3). It lies 8 miles east of La Junta, or 15 miles west of Las Animas. From 1833, when it was built by the fur traders William and Charles Bent, until 1848, when war with Mexico and increasing unrest among the local Arapahoe, Apache, and Cheyenne peoples put an end to their business,

Bent's Fort was the Southwest's most important outpost of American civilization, and a stopping place for travelers, trappers, and explorers, including John C. Fremont, Francis Parkman, and just about every other Wild West luminary.

Though it was abandoned and left to decay for over 100 years, the large adobe fort was authentically rebuilt by the National Park Service in 1976 and now stands as a palpable reminder of the early years of the frontier era. Thick adobe walls, 15 feet tall with circular bastions at the corners, protect a roughly 100-square-foot compound. Rangers, dressed in period clothing during special events, work as wheelwrights, coopers, and carpenters, or process the many buffalo robes and beaver pelts piled up in storerooms.

Bent's Old Fort

Las Animas

The farming community of **Las Animas** (pop. 2,410) takes its name from the Arkansas River tributary originally known as Río de las Animas Perdidas en Purgatorio (River of Lost Souls). Las Animas is also the place where, on November 15, 1806, Lieutenant Zebulon Pike first laid eyes on the Rocky Mountain peak that now bears his name—Pike's Peak, 120 miles to the northwest.

Beyond Las Animas, US-50 continues its gradual descent across the Rocky Mountains foothills. The area was first known as Big Timbers for the tall cottonwoods that grew here along the Arkansas River, though most of these trees were cut down soon after the arrival of white settlers. In the 1840s and 1850s, local Cheyenne, Arapahoe, Kiowa, and Apache peoples bartered bison hides at William Bent's trading post, and Wild West explorer Kit Carson died here on May 23, 1868, in his family home at what was then the U.S. Army's Fort Lyon, south of present-day

SANTA FE TRAIL

For over half a century, beginning in the 1820s and lasting until the railroads were completed in the 1880s, the Santa Fe Trail was the primary link between the United States and the Spanish and Mexican Southwest. Running from the Missouri River ports around present-day Kansas City, the trail angled along the banks of the Arkansas River, splitting west of what's now Dodge City into two routes: the Mountain Branch, which US-50 follows, and the quicker but more dangerous Cimarron Cutoff, across the arid plains of the Jornado del Muerto. The two branches rejoined before climbing the Sangre de Cristo Mountains into what was then, as it is now, the capital of the Southwest, Santa Fe.

Unlike many of the routes across the Wild West frontier, the Santa Fe Trail was established by commercial traders rather than emigrant pioneers, and travel along it was active in both directions: Merchants from the United States brought manufactured goods by the wagonload, which they exchanged for Mexican silver. First blazed by trader William Becknell in 1821, the year the newly independent Republic of Mexico opened the border (which Spain had kept closed), the 750-mile-long trail was surveyed by the U.S. government in 1826, and traffic increased slowly until the Mexican-American War brought Santa Fe, and all the land in between, under U.S. control. Military forts were established to protect traders from marauding Comanche and other Native Americans; at the time of the Civil War, commerce along the trail reached a peak, with over 5,000 wagons making the trek to Santa Fe, carrying over $50 million worth of trade goods. The extension of the railroads across the Great Plains in the 1870s diminished the importance of the trail, and by 1880, when the Santa Fe railroad reached Santa Fe itself, the trail became a part of history.

Though US-50 follows the Santa Fe Trail almost exactly, from Las Animas east to Kansas City, little remains, apart from outposts like Bent's Fort and Fort Larned, and a few all-but-invisible stretches of old wagon ruts. Numerous plaques mark historic sites, and it's still possible to get a powerful sense of what the trail might have been like—provided you take the time to park the car and walk even a few hundred yards in the footsteps that crossed here a century ago.

The following are some of the most evocative sites along the Santa Fe Trail, west to east.

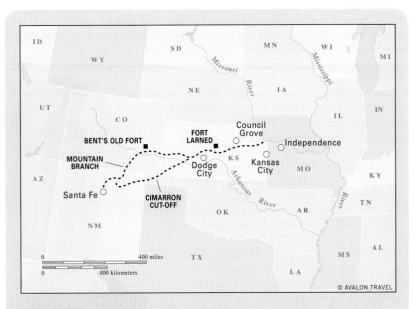

Santa Fe, New Mexico: The second-oldest city in North America preserves a vivid taste of its Spanish, Mexican, and American past (see page 868).

Bent's Old Fort, Colorado: A reconstructed adobe trading post sits along the banks of the Arkansas River in the Rocky Mountain foothills (see page 713).

Dodge City, Kansas: On one of the best-preserved remnants of the original Santa Fe Trail, wagon ruts stretch across the rolling farmlands just west of this Wild West landmark town (see page 717).

Fort Larned, Kansas: This well-preserved U.S. Army fortress, intact since the 1850s, protects a fine set of wagon ruts (see page 719).

Council Grove, Kansas: The last American town on the trail west has hardly changed since the heyday of the trail (see page 723).

Westport, Missouri: Now surrounded by suburban Kansas City, this was the real start of the trail from the 1840s on (see page 728).

Independence, Missouri: The original start of the Santa Fe and Oregon Trails offers a fine museum detailing the westward frontier movements (see page 726).

US-50. Carson's remains were later moved to Taos, New Mexico, and his lands were flooded after the Arkansas River was dammed to form the large John Martin Reservoir, which stretches most of the way downstream to Lamar.

Lamar

Following the Arkansas River downstream toward the Kansas border, US-50 runs along what was known as the Mountain Branch of the Santa Fe Trail, a longer but safer alternative to the main route along the Cimarron Cutoff. Massive truck stops and acres and acres of irrigated farmlands, feedlots, and cattle ranches greet you in

Lamar's **KLMR 93.5 FM** plays a broad mix of classic hits music.

Lamar (pop. 7,804). It's worth a stop, if only to admire the "World's Oldest Gas Station" (501 N. Main St.). Built out of blocks of 175-million-year-old petrified wood, the structure opened as a gas station in 1932. Although the building still attracts tourists, it is now used for storage.

Lamar's *Madonna of the Trail*

At the heart of town, next to the Old Depot, a stately *Madonna of the Trail* stands as a reminder of the indefatigable spirit of the pioneers. Standing nearly 20 feet tall atop an engraved plinth, this statue is one of 12 identical memorials erected in the 1920s by the Daughters of the American Revolution (DAR). From Bethesda, Maryland, to Upland, California, the memorials were placed along the original National Old Trails Highway, which followed the National Road (US-40) and later Route 66 on the westward path of Manifest Destiny.

North of Lamar, then east of US-287, the **Sand Creek Massacre National Historic Site** (719/729-3003, daily Apr.-Nov., Mon.-Fri. Dec.-Mar., free) preserves and interprets the place where, in November 1864, volunteer U.S. soldiers opened fire on a camp of Cheyenne and Arapahoe people, killing more than 100 unarmed women and children. An investigation by the U.S. Congress vilified the cowardly and racist murders, saying that while "wearing the uniform of the United States, which should be the emblem of justice and humanity" the soldiers "deliberately planned and executed a foul and dastardly massacre." There's not a lot to see or do, but standing on the site is at once profound, symbolic, and deeply disturbing.

KANSAS

All the way across Kansas, we follow almost exactly in the footsteps of the trappers and traders who braved the Santa Fe Trail along the western frontier, stopping at preserved old outposts like Fort Larned and Council Grove while tracking the few more evocative remnants of this pioneer Wild West corridor. In its nearly 500 miles across Kansas, US-50 and its selected variants pass across the agricultural heartland of America, winding

At **Garden City** (see page 202), 50 miles west of Dodge City, US-50 crosses US-83, **The Road to Nowhere,** which follows the 100th meridian from Canada to Mexico. Full coverage of this route begins on page 168.

through dozens of small farming towns that dot the generally level landscape. (Locals definitely seem to prefer the word "level" to the equally accurate "flat," if only because it sounds less boring.) This is the heart of the "Wheat Belt," where most of the country's grain is grown—as much as half the bread baked in America is made from Kansas wheat—and it's also prime cattle country, with towns like **Dodge City** maintaining their historic dependence on cows and cowboys, producing and packing much of the nation's beef supply.

The dividing line between the central and mountain time zones is 15 miles west of **Garden City.** Set your clocks and watches accordingly.

Holcomb

Apart from numerous feedlots fattening cattle for slaughter and a few wheat, corn, and beet farms fed by water diverted from the Arkansas River, there's not much to see in the 120 miles of barren plains that stretch east from the Colorado border. On the western outskirts of **Garden City,** the region's biggest town, US-50 runs through the meat-packing town of **Holcomb,** notorious as the site of the *In Cold Blood* murders documented by Truman Capote and in a pair of mid-2000s Hollywood bio-pics (*Capote* and *Infamous*). In 1959, Perry Smith and Richard Hickock ruthlessly killed all four members of the Clutter family during a robbery attempt. Both killers were eventually captured, convicted, and executed.

Santa Fe Trail Tracks

One of the best-preserved sections of **Santa Fe Trail wagon tracks** is 10 miles west of Dodge City along this stretch of US-50. Marked by a large sign, just west of the Howell grain elevator, these wheel tracks, or ruts, lie in a rolling field 100 yards north of the parking area and are basically a broad depression in the soil, approximately 800 yards wide and two miles long. Farther west, at **Cimarron,** 32 miles east of Garden City and 1 miles west of Dodge City, the main track of the Santa Fe Trail crossed the Arkansas River and headed southwest across the waterless plain of the Jornada del Muerto on what was known as the **Cimarron Cutoff.** This desolate region is also where, in 1831 during the earliest days of the trail, legendary mountain man Jedediah Strong Smith was killed by a band of Comanche warriors.

Dodge City

One of the most notorious places on the Wild West frontier, **Dodge City** (pop. 27,340) can be something of a disappointment if you come here looking for a rip-roaring frontier town. In its heyday, which lasted roughly from 1872, when the railroad arrived, to 1884, when the cattle drives were effectively banned, Dodge City was the undisputed capital of the buffalo-hunting, cattle-driving Wild West, with as many as 100 million bison hides and seven million head of cattle shipped out from here in that decade alone. At the same

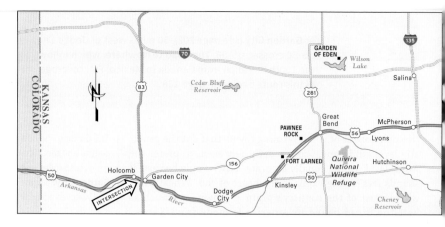

time, Dodge City was known as "Hell on the Plains," famous for its gunfights and general lawlessness, despite marshals like Bat Masterson and Wyatt Earp keeping order and planting bad guys in the Boot Hill cemetery above town.

However, almost nothing in Dodge City survives from that era. Boot Hill, for example, was bought by the city and is now the site of a small office building. (A statue of a cowboy, erected in 1927, says somewhat mournfully: "On the ashes of my campfire this city is built.") Most of what you see in Dodge City dates from the 1920s at the earliest, and Dodge City is by and large a busy farming and cattle-ranching community, with extensive stock-yards surrounding the small downtown area. Because of the low-profit economics of the beef industry, most of the 4,000 to 5,000 people who work in the feedlots and slaughterhouses today are immigrant workers from Mexico—which explains the predominance of Mexican cafés and grocery stores around town.

For travelers, there's little here apart from one of the Midwest's more heavily hyped tourist attractions, the fake but fun **Boot Hill Museum** (620/227-8188, daily, $12) and its recreated Front Street, where actors stage gunfights and "medicine shows"

throughout the day. There's also an evening burlesque show, featuring Miss Kitty and her Can-Can Girls; a reconstructed sod house; the old (circa-1865) jail; and a one-room schoolhouse. A historic Santa Fe locomotive completes the Boot Hill collection; not surprisingly, Boot Hill is hard to miss, well marked on the west side of town, just north of the railroad tracks along Wyatt Earp Boulevard (US-50/56), the main route through town.

sunflower,
state flower of Kansas

Kinsley: Midway USA

Paralleling the main line of the Santa Fe Railroad across the flattest, emptiest 50 miles of Kansas cornfields, east of Dodge City we follow US-50 as far as **Kinsley,** where we switch onto US-56 (which used to be known as "US-50 North") to follow the Santa Fe Trail. Kinsley, which calls itself "Midway USA," lies equidistant from New York and San Francisco: 1,561 miles from either place. This geographical fact is pointed out by a large sign outside the entertaining (and free!) **Edwards County Historical Society Museum,** at the US-50/56 junction on the west side of town, surrounded by an old locomotive and a variety of old farming and ranching equipment.

Fort Larned

One of the best-preserved vestiges of the Santa Fe Trail, and the whole "Wild West" for that matter, **Fort Larned** (620/285-6911, daily, free), six miles west of US-56 via Hwy-156, was established in 1859, and for the next 20 years the troops stationed here protected travelers on the Santa Fe Trail from the threat of attack by local Arapahoe and Cheyenne people. The fort also served a vital role in the many Indian Wars of the 1860s, but by 1878, when the trail was no longer in active use, the fort was deactivated. It was sold and used as a ranch until 1960, but has survived the intervening years in excellent condition. Careful restoration by the National Park Service has made Fort Larned an excellent place to understand what the frontier was really like, albeit from the U.S. military perspective.

Sandstone buildings, which replaced the original adobe after the end of the Civil War, surround a 400-square-foot parade ground, and interior rooms have been filled with accurate reproductions of original fixtures and fittings, ranging from barracks to blacksmith shops to a large storehouse. A nearby farm preserves a set of ruts surviving from the Santa Fe Trail days, though you need to have an active imagination to get much from them.

In between Fort Larned and US-56, the **Santa Fe Trail Center** (620/285-2054, Tues.-Sat., $6) is a private nonprofit museum focusing on the overall history of the Santa Fe Trail region. Diorama-like exhibits feature full-scale mock-ups of wagons and frontier trading posts, and behind the main building are a sod house and a one-room schoolhouse.

TORNADOES

Driving across the Great Plains heartland, especially in late spring and early summer, be prepared to encounter Mother Nature's most potent force: a tornado, whose swirling winds can reach 150-300 mph or more. The Midwest has been dubbed Tornado Alley, for the frequency of storms that can hit the region. While the tornado at the start of *The Wizard of Oz* touched down in Dorothy's home state, Kansas, they are just as likely to occur in Michigan, Missouri, or Alabama.

Each year there are more than 1,000 tornadoes across the United States, and on average 50 or so people are killed by them, though in recent years storms seem to have become more frequent and more deadly: More than 500 people were killed by tornadoes in the U.S. in 2011. The powerful tornado that tore through Joplin, Missouri, in May of that year killed more than 150 people. Tornadoes can last from several seconds to more than an hour, but most last around 10 minutes.

If confronted by a tornado, you can greatly reduce the chance of injury by doing a few simple things. First, be aware of the possibility of severe weather; most tornado-related deaths and injuries happen to people who are caught unaware and uninformed, so tune into local TV and radio stations for current information. If a **tornado watch** has been issued, it means that a tornado is considered likely. Once a **tornado warning** is issued, it means that a tornado has actually been spotted, and if you are nearby, you should seek shelter immediately.

If you are in a car and spot a tornado, it is not a good idea to try to escape by driving away from it. Tornadoes have been known to blow cars off the road or hurl them hundreds of feet in the air. If there is no time to find shelter somewhere solid and indoors, get out of the car and lie down in a ditch or low-lying area, away from the vehicle. Though it might look safe, experts say it's best not to seek shelter under a highway overpass, which can act like a wind tunnel, making the winds even stronger.

Pawnee Rock

Just eight miles northeast of Larned, a half mile north of US-56 and the Arkansas River, **Pawnee Rock** was once one of the most important landmarks on the Santa Fe Trail. However, so much of the original 60-foot-high tower of Dakota sandstone has been quarried—to build houses as well as the rail bed of the Santa Fe railroad—that it's little more than a stubby hump. But you can still get a grand view of the surrounding countryside from the easy trail that leads to the rock's much-diminished summit.

Great Bend

Spreading along the northern bank of the Arkansas River at the northernmost point on its sweep across central Kansas, **Great Bend** (pop. 15,955) was originally established as a fort along the Santa Fe Trail, but it really began to grow after the railroad came through. As with Dodge City to the southwest, the arrival of the railroad in 1872 attracted cattle drovers from the Chisholm Trail, who turned Great Bend into a raucous Wild West town. It's now a quiet, rural city, earning its livelihood from wheat farms and, since the 1930s, oil.

Downtown Great Bend has a number of building-size murals, especially the blocks along Main Street perpendicular to US-56. The outskirts of town have the engaging **Barton County Historical Society Museum** (620/793-5125, Tues.-Sun. summer, Tues.-Fri. winter, $4), just south of the railroad tracks and the river along US-281. Farther afield, the Great Bend area holds two of the largest wildlife refuges in Kansas: **Cheyenne Bottoms** to the northeast and **Quivira** to the southeast, both of which offer excellent bird-watching and hunting opportunities.

Great Bend does have a fairly good range of places to eat, with franchise fast food supplemented by a handful of local restaurants like **Granny's Kitchen** (925 10th St., 620/793-7441). Along with the national chains, one reliable place to stay in Great Bend is the **Travelers Budget Inn** (4200 10th St., 620/793-5448, $40 and up).

The next town east of Great Bend along US-50 is **Ellinwood,** where a couple of antiques shops mark the historic downtown area. Ellinwood sits atop a series of tunnels used as tornado shelters and occasionally as storerooms for contraband. These tunnels are open for guided tours by **Ellinwood Underground** (620/617-6915, Thurs.-Mon. $10).

Great Bend was the boyhood hometown of Jack Kilby, the Texas Instruments electrical engineer who helped invent the integrated circuit and the pocket calculator. Kilby was awarded the Nobel Prize for Physics in 2000, and he died in 2005.

Public auctions are held irregularly in towns across the rural Midwest. Fast-talking auctioneers take bids on various lots, ranging from real antiques to boxes of junk and cast-off clothes. If you happen upon one, check it out!

Lyons

The farming, oil-drilling, and salt-mining town of **Lyons** (pop. 3,739), about 30 miles due east of Great Bend, doesn't look much different from most other Kansas towns, but it has an unusually impressive history—and a nice courthouse square downtown. There's a 150-foot-long intaglio serpent carved into the prairie eight miles northeast of town, and some Santa Fe Trail ruts, but the most compelling remains are those left behind by Coronado's expedition through the region in 1541, in search of the fabled Golden City of Quivira. Exhibits on all of these, as well as on Native American and pioneer cultures, are displayed inside the modern purpose-built **Coronado-Quivira Museum** (105 W. Lyon St., 620/257-3941, Tues.-Sat., $3), two blocks south of the landmark county courthouse off US-56.

Two miles west of Lyons along US-56, a large cross marks the site where the priest Juan de Padilla, who accompanied Coronado on his expedition and returned the following year to convert the locals, was killed by unreceptive Native Americans, thereby becoming the first Christian martyr in what is now United States.

US-50: Hutchinson

If you've opted to follow US-50 rather than the Santa Fe Trail tour along US-56, be sure to check out **Hutchinson** (pop. 42,080), a large and lively city that's home to the world's second longest grain elevator (over a half mile long). The town's old salt mines, some 600 feet below ground, are now used for storage of important archives, including the original negatives of many classic Hollywood films. The mines are open to visitors via the **Strataca Kansas Underground Salt Museum** (3650 E. Ave. G, 620/662-1425 or 866/755-3450, daily, $19).

Another surprising attraction, the **Kansas Cosmosphere and Space Center**

DETOUR: THE GARDEN OF EDEN

If you're one of those bicoastal types who thinks the Midwest is full of conventional-minded folks leading ordinary lives as contented consumers, you owe it to yourself to visit the **Garden of Eden** (305 E. 2nd St., 785/525-6395, daily summer, Sat.-Sun. winter, $7), one of the country's oldest and oddest folk-art environments. Located in the tiny town of **Lucas, Kansas** (pop. 393), the Garden of Eden is the sort of place that puts the Gothic back in American Gothic, a front-yard forest of biblical scenes and populist political allegories—*Adam and Eve, Cain and Abel,* and the *Crucifixion of Labor at the Hands of Preachers, Bankers, and Lawyers*—created out of concrete from around 1910 to 1930 by one Samuel Perry Dinsmoor. An Ohio native and Civil War veteran, Dinsmoor actively promoted his garden as a tourist attraction, managing to draw many hundreds of visitors to this distant and fairly inaccessible corner of Kansas. Dinsmoor died at age 89 in 1932 and is preserved in a glass-covered tomb on the property, yet he carried on his hucksterism even after death, insisting in his will that no one be allowed "to go in and see me for less than $1."

This all-American Garden of Eden is at the corner of 2nd Street and Kansas Avenue in Lucas, which is on Hwy-18 north of Great Bend and 15 miles north of I-70. Homespun Lucas is also home to the **Grassroots Art Center** (213 S. Main St., 785/525-6118), a gallery showing and selling artworks created by other self-taught "outsider" artists. Outside the gallery is a courtyard full of carved limestone masonry sculptures, many salvaged from demolished buildings around the area.

(1100 N. Plum St., 620/662-2305 or 800/397-0330, daily, $13.50-26 depending on the venue) boasts a great collection of historic air- and spacecraft, including Mercury, Gemini, and Apollo capsules; a Redstone nuclear warhead; and a pair of German V-1 and V-2 rockets, plus two planetarium shows and an IMAX theater.

McPherson

From a distance across the flat plains, the towering grain elevators make **McPherson** (pop. 13,155), about 30 miles east of Lyons and marking the junction of US-56 and I-135 between Salina and Wichita, look more impressive than it really is. You can fill the gas tank or get a bite to eat (all the usual franchise food places and gas stations are here) or just stretch your legs wandering around the four-block Main Street business district.

The small **McPherson Museum** (11 E. Kansas Ave., 620/241-8464, Tues.-Fri. 8am-5pm, Sat.-Sun. 1pm-5pm, $5), well marked in a residential district, displays rooms furnished in typical turn-of-the-20th-century Kansas style. It also holds the world's first artificial diamond, produced by Willard Hershey, a local chemistry teacher.

Mennonite Country

One of the centers of the sizable local Mennonite community, **Hillsboro** (pop. 2,993), 13 miles west of US-77, serves as market center for the area's highly productive farmlands. Tabor College, on the east side of town, is the most visible sign of the Mennonite presence; although it's a coed nondenominational college, about half the students are local Mennonites.

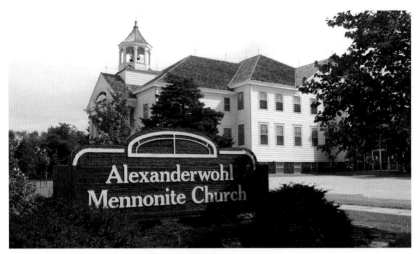

Mennonite church in Goessel

The tidy town of **Goessel** (pop. 539), about 15 miles southwest of Hillsboro, was also founded by Mennonite farmers and now holds the worthwhile **Mennonite Heritage and Agricultural Museum** (200 N. Poplar St., 620/367-8200, Tues.-Sat., $4), where numerous buildings, including two schools, a barn, and a bank, have been moved for preservation. The flat black earth around Goessel is among the world's greatest producers of wheat, in particular the hardy hybrids able to withstand the Midwestern winter. The original seed, known as "Turkey Red," was brought to Kansas in the early 1870s by Russian Mennonites who immigrated here after their 100-year exclusion from military service was rescinded.

Zigzagging east from Hillsboro and then north along US-77/US-56, after another 37 "level" miles, US-56 reaches the town of **Herington,** whose central square holds a monument to Juan de Padilla, who passed through southern Kansas in search of the mythical Golden City of Quivira as part of Coronado's expedition.

The **Kaw Mission State Historic Site,** in Council Grove, five blocks north of Main on Mission Street, was built by Methodist missionaries in 1851 as a school for local Native American children. Students included Charles Curtis, who served as U.S. vice president from 1929 to 1933.

Council Grove

Just 75 miles southwest of the suburban sprawl of Kansas City, 25 miles west of the I-335 Kansas Turnpike, **Council Grove** (pop. 2,182) still looks much as it did over a century ago, when, from the 1830s to the 1860s, it was the most important of all way stations on the Santa Fe Trail. Council Grove's lush maples and oaks were the last hardwoods available on the long route west across the treeless plain, which meant traders and travelers could make final repairs and stock up on spare axles and other essentials. It was also the western extent of "safe territory"; beyond here travelers were subject to frequent attacks by hostile Native Americans.

Nowadays the town proudly preserves its many historic sites, and in many ways serves as the most not-to-be-missed stop for modern travelers heading along the Santa Fe Trail. Though by now the trees themselves are little more than desiccated stumps, the sites of two of the most important trail icons are marked along Main

BLUE HIGHWAYS TO PRAIRYERTH

Writing about US-50, author William Least Heat-Moon has said that "for the unhurried, this little-known highway is the best national road across the middle of the United States." After traveling 13,000 miles of back road through the nooks and crannies of 38 states to write his first book, the road-trip classic *Blue Highways*, Heat-Moon began work on a very different study. Straying no farther than the 744 square miles of Chase County, Kansas, he embarked upon what he termed a "deep map" of the area that sits atop the lush rolling Flint Hills, the nation's last remaining grand expanse of tallgrass prairie, split by US-50 and the Santa Fe Railroad.

The result was the 1991 book *PrairyErth*, a 600-plus-page evocation of history and contemporary life in this otherwise unremarkable corner of the country, which Heat-Moon describes as being "five hours by interstates from home, eight hours if I follow a route of good café food." Combining folk history and contemporary anecdotes with captivating quotes from sundry novels, Native American legends, travel guides, essays, and old newspaper clippings, this unique project—which has been described as the nonfiction equivalent of the Great American Novel—manages to capture the rhythms of ranching life here in the middle of the great American nowhere.

Street (US-56), east of the bridge over the small Neosho River: the **Council Oak,** under which, in 1825, the indigenous Kansa and Osage people agreed to allow Americans to cross their territory, and the **Post Office Oak,** which served as a natural message center for early travelers. Four blocks west, the **Last Chance Store** at Main and Chautauqua Streets has served as a bank and a post office since it was built in 1857.

The banks, cafés, and stores along Main Street, which the Santa Fe Trail followed through town, make little obvious effort to cater to tourists. The town basically goes about its day-to-day business without forgetting its extraordinary past. The **Hays House** (112 W. Main St., 620/767-5911), in the center of town, lays fair claim to being the oldest restaurant west of the Mississippi; originally built as a frontier home, and later serving as a saloon, supply post, courthouse, and hotel, it has stood on this site since 1847. Now modernized, it is still the focus of the town's social and political life and is open all day—with excellent fried chicken. Across Main, the soda fountain inside the **Aldrich Apothecary** (115 W. Main St., 620/767-6731) serves famous "Santa Fe Trail" root beer floats, and ice cream. The best place to stay is the comfortable **Cottage House Hotel** (25 N. Neosho St., 620/767-6828, $60 and up).

US-50: Tallgrass Prairie National Preserve

The delights of the Flint Hills landscape are pastoral in the extreme, with few roaring waterfalls or towering cliffs to take your breath away or make you pull out the camera, but the unique ecosystem has enough admirers that a section of it was recently set aside as the **Tallgrass Prairie National Preserve.** Located along Hwy-177 about 17 miles south of Council Grove, or 2 miles north of Strong City and US-50, the 11,000-acre preserve protects a large remaining portion of the extensive tallgrass prairie that once covered the Great Plains—most of the present-day Midwest. Native grasses form a naturally insulating sod roof atop the eco-friendly **visitors center** (620/273-8494, daily) which has exhibits and videos on the natural flora,

Chase County Courthouse

fauna, and geography of the preserve and the surrounding area. A 1.5-mile nature trail starts here, winding along to the historic one-room Fox Creek Schoolhouse while giving an up-close look at the head-high (or taller) flowering grasses that give the tallgrass prairie its name. Park rangers also guide bus tours of the grassland ecosystem.

The best base for a visit to the Tallgrass Prairie National Preserve is **Cottonwood Falls,** two miles south of Strong City and US-50 via Hwy-177. The town boasts the beautiful **Chase County Courthouse,** the oldest still in use in the state, standing like a French château at the south end of a sleepy Main Street business district. In the business district, you'll also find a couple of cafés and crafts shops, and the elegant 10-room **Grand Central Hotel** (215 Broadway, 620/273-6763, $160 and up), which has a fine, subtly Western-themed restaurant.

Burlingame and Baldwin City

Between Council Grove and Kansas City, US-56 passes through the lovely cattle-ranching grasslands of the northern Flint Hills, zigzagging at 90-degree angles through onetime coal-mining towns like Worden, Overbrook, and Scranton. **Burlingame** (pop. 934), the largest of this bunch, is noteworthy for its broad, brick-paved, 20-mph Main Street (US-56), lined by diverse 100-year-old buildings painted with a barrage of signs advertising the usual liquor, food, and auto parts.

At the northeast edge of the Flint Hills, 13 miles west of the I-35 freeway from Kansas City, US-56 skirts the leafy brick-paved streets of **Baldwin City** (pop. 4,515), a small town that was once a main rest-and-repair stop on the Santa Fe Trail—four days' travel west of Independence, Missouri. In 1858, the first college on the western frontier was founded here in a three-story sandstone building now preserved as "The Old Castle," alongside a combination general store and post office on the east side of the pleasant campus of Methodist-run Baker University. The **library** (785/594-8414, by appointment, free), three blocks west, displays the Quayle Collection of rare religious texts, including clay tablets dating from Old Testament times and a range of hand-bound bibles, arranged to trace the development of printing techniques and typography styles.

For the rest of the way east to Kansas City, US-56 parallels I-35 across lush rolling grassland pastures and farms, marked in places by signs reading "Old US-50." Along this route, two miles west of Gardner, a historical marker stands on the site where the Santa Fe and Oregon Trails once divided. For many years, a crude wooden sign pointed westbound travelers in the proper direction: left to Santa Fe, right to Oregon.

MISSOURI

From **Kansas City,** and its noteworthy neighboring towns of Independence and Liberty, US-50 makes a lazy trek across Missouri's rolling-prairie farmlands, stopping at the historic railroad town of **Sedalia** before reaching the state capital, **Jefferson City,** roughly midway across.

Continuing east, climbing through hardwood forests of the Ozark uplands, US-50 leads to a number of similarly slow but more interesting old roads like Hwy-100, which winds through a number of historic towns along the banks of the Missouri River before approaching **St. Louis,** at the eastern edge of the state.

US-50: Across Kansas City

US-50 is now submerged beneath the interstates and runs west-east around Kansas City via I-35, I-435, and I-470. The older pre-interstate route also avoided downtown, following what's now signed as US-169 along Park Avenue and 47th Street, past the Country Club Plaza and the Nelson-Atkins Museum of Art, before dipping south again on the Swope Parkway to Lee's Summit, where the old alignment rejoins the current US-50 routing.

To reach the downtown area from US-50, you can follow any of many north-south streets, like Troost Avenue, the down-at-the-heels old main drag, or the parkway-like El Paseo.

Independence

A quiet suburb lying on the eastern fringe of greater Kansas City, **Independence** (pop. 116,830) doesn't look like a special place, but it is. One of the country's most history-rich small cities, Independence came to life during the early years of the westward expansion, serving as the jumping-off point for the Santa Fe and, later, Oregon and California Trails. A century later, Independence again gained prominence as the hometown of President Harry Truman, who lived here from boyhood until his death in 1972.

The city-run **National Frontier Trails Museum** (318 W. Pacific Ave., daily, $6), four blocks south of the town square, is one of the best museums dedicated to America's pioneers. Beginning with a brief account of Lewis and Clark, the exhibits explore the heyday of the Santa Fe Trail, which throughout the 1820s and 1830s made Independence the leading town on the western frontier. The later Oregon Trail, on which some 300,000 people left Independence for the West Coast, is recounted through an engagingly displayed series of diary entries and drawings made by pioneers.

While little remains from the pioneer days, Independence has hardly changed since Harry Truman grew up here around the turn of the 20th century. The soda fountain where he held his first job, and the courtroom where he presided as judge, still stand in the town square. His home, northwest of the square, is open for **tours** (219 N. Delaware St., Tues.-Sat., $5), and the large **Harry S Truman Library and Museum** (daily, $8), four blocks north, contains his presidential papers, a replica of his White House office, and the gravesites of Truman and his wife, Bess.

Clinton's Soda Fountain (100 W. Maple St., 816/833-2046), "Where Harry Had His First Job," still serves milk shakes and phosphates.

Liberty

Outlaw Jesse James grew up near Liberty.

Another ideally named small town on the suburban fringes of Kansas City, **Liberty** (pop. 29,149) is worth a visit for rather different reasons. This is where, having finished fighting for the Confederacy in the Civil War, on February 13, 1866, **Jesse James** and his brother Frank staged the first-ever daylight bank robbery, getting away with over $60,000. The bank building itself, on the northwest corner of the preserved-in-amber town square, is pretty much as it was, complete with the vault, safe, and banknotes; it's now a small **museum** (103 N. Water St., Mon.-Sat., $6.50).

A block north of the square stands another historic site, the oxymoronic **Liberty Jail** (216 N. Main St., daily, free), where Mormon prophet Joseph Smith and his followers were imprisoned during the winter of 1838-1839. It's a significant site for Mormons and has been faithfully reconstructed.

Sedalia

East of Kansas City, the roadside along fast, four-lane US-50 is endless open rolling prairie, most of it planted in wheat and corn. As in most of the West, early development here occurred along the railroad lines, which were constructed beginning in the 1850s. Towns boomed when the trains arrived, but most went bust as the tracks were extended westward to Kansas City and beyond.

Sedalia (pop. 21,387), which is 75 miles east of Kansas City, was one of the few that survived, growing into a small city thanks to its position straddling the main line between St. Louis and Kansas City. Sedalia reached its peak of prosperity around 1900, an era evoked by the

In 1867, the militant prohibitionist Carrie Nation moved to the village of **Holden,** nine miles south of US-50 via Hwy-131, with her alcoholic first husband, the doctor William Gloyd, who died the following year.

the site of Jesse James' first bank robbery in Liberty

Kansas City

Country Club Plaza

Though it covers a huge area, stretching for some 20 miles on both sides of the Missouri-Kansas border, and nearly 30 miles north to south, Kansas City (pop. 459,787) never feels like a big city. It's more like a conglomeration of small towns, once separate from each other but now joined together by tract-house sprawl and the 100-mile-long I-435 Beltway. The historic center of Kansas City lines the south bank of the Missouri River, where 30-story skyscrapers stand above hefty brick warehouses, huge stockyards, railroad tracks, and banks of grain elevators, all testifying to Kansas City's role as the main distribution point for Midwestern farm products.

Southwest of the city center, off Main and 40th Streets, **Westport** is the birthplace of Kansas City. Before the Kansas River switched course and left it high and dry, Westport was the westernmost steamboat landing in the United States, and it quickly grew into a prime supply point on the Santa Fe and Oregon Trails. For a better taste of old-time riverfront Kansas City, head downtown to the **Steamboat Arabia Museum** (400 Grand Blvd., 816/471-1856, daily, $14.50), in the historic City Market, which displays the fascinating contents of a steamboat that sank in 1856: hardware, guns, clothes, booze, canned and bottled food, and all sorts of things that made life on the western frontier livable.

Located on the south side of Westport, the remarkable **NelsonAtkins Museum of Art** (4525 Oak St., 816/561-4000 or 816/751-1278, Wed.-Sun., free) would do any city proud, with a little of everything from Caravaggio's brooding masterpiece *St. John the Baptist* to in-depth coverage of KC-based Thomas Hart Benton. The nation's coolest parking structure sits underneath the museum's translucent Bloch Building. Two blocks west is another architectural innovation: **Country Club Plaza,** one of the country's first shopping malls, its opulent Spanish Revival styling still attracting the upscale likes of Tiffany & Co. and Burberry.

At the south edge of downtown, the historic tower of the Liberty Memorial has been joined by the thought-provoking **National World War I Museum** (816/888-8100, daily summer, Tues.-Sat. fall-spring, $16), which pays tribute to the soldiers while putting the conflict into its complicated political context.

A mile east of downtown KC is the revitalizing 18th and Vine neighborhood, heartland of Kansas City's prolific 1930s and 1940s African American music scene, a golden age that spawned jazz greats Charlie Parker, Lester Young, and Count Basie, all of whom are honored in the **American Jazz Museum** (1616 E. 18th St.), which shares space with the marvelous **Negro Baseball Leagues Museum** (1616 E. 18th St., 816/221-1920, Tues.-Sun., $10 each or $15 for both), dedicated to documenting the players and culture of the various professional baseball leagues that existed side-by-side with the "majors" before the color barriers began to be broken down in the late 1940s.

PRACTICALITIES

To get around Kansas City, drive. As in Los Angeles, which Kansas City resembles more than residents of either city are likely to admit, cars rule the roads. Distances are huge and public transportation is basically nonexistent.

In downtown Kansas City, there are a number of nicely restored grand 1920s hotels: the **Hilton President** (1329 Baltimore Ave., 816/221-9490, $259 and up) is a block away from the **Holiday Inn Aladdin** (1215 Wyandotte St., 816/421-8888, $162 and up). Budget-conscious travelers can choose from a slew of highway motels lining the interstates.

For food, there's no better introduction to the delights of KC cuisine than **Arthur Bryant's** (1727 Brooklyn Ave., 816/231-1123), east of downtown near the Negro Baseball Leagues Museum. Meat-eaters drive for miles to eat at this classic no-frills rib shack, where heavenly barbecue sauces come in plain plastic bottles. More world-class barbecue is on the menu (along with delicious steaks, seafood, and salads) in the fancy environs of **Fiorella's Jack Stack Barbecue** (101 W. 22nd St.,

816/472-7427) in KC's lively and history-rich Crossroads Arts district, south of downtown. For burgers, fries, malts, and shakes (and a killer cherry limeade!), look no farther than **Winstead's** (101 Emanuel Cleaver III Blvd., 816/753-2244), across from the art museum, near Country Club Plaza.

Kansas City's once-vaunted nightlife is nothing like it was during the jazz and R&B heyday of the 1940s and 1950s, though there's always something going on in the ambitious **"P&L,"** the Power and Light District, where bars, clubs, restaurants, and street performers cover eight downtown blocks around 13th and Main Street. One other place to go: The historic **Kelly's Westport Inn** (500 Westport Rd., 816/561-5800) is a great place to enjoy a budget-priced beer while soaking up some old KC ambience.

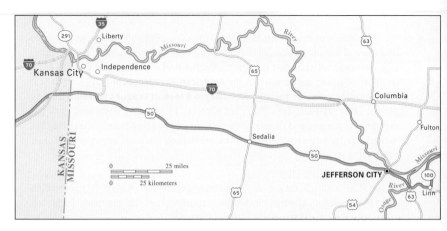

Twenty miles west of Sedalia, south of US-50 near the town of Knob Noster, **Whiteman Air Force Base** is the home of the 509th Bomb Wing, which operates and maintains the entire fleet of B-2 Stealth bombers. Whiteman AFB was named after 2nd Lieutenant George A. Whiteman, a Sedalia resident and fighter pilot who was killed in action during the attack on Pearl Harbor.

ragtime music of Sedalia's own Scott Joplin. The tracks through town, and most of the way across Missouri, have been converted into the hiking and bicycling Katy Trail.

Along with ragtime music and railroad history, Sedalia offers an unexpected treat: modern galleries of excellent contemporary art, courtesy of the **Daum Museum** (3201 W. 16th St., Tues.-Sun., free) on the campus of the local community college, a half mile south of US-50.

At the heart of the historic downtown, a few blocks from the Katy Trail, **Fitters 5th Street Pub** (500 S. Ohio Ave., 660/827-6500) has pizzas and sandwiches across from the courthouse, while the **Hotel Bothwell** (103 E. 4th St., 660/826-5588, $90 and up) is a nicely restored 1920s hotel, now part of the Choice Hotels group.

The old railroad depot downtown has been brought back to life as the town's **visitors bureau** (600 E. 3rd St., 800/827-5295 or 660/826-2222).

Jefferson City

Roughly at the center of the state, 130 miles west of St. Louis and 140 miles east of Kansas City on the south bank of the Missouri River, **Jefferson City** (pop. 43,079) is a strangely small and somnolent place. The handsome neoclassical **state capitol** (daily, free), modeled on the U.S. Capitol and completed in 1917, is the central landmark, rising above the river at the heart of town. Inside, the rotunda and ground floor area are packed with informative exhibits tracing the state's political and natural history, while one-hour **guided tours** take in the entire building, including a famous mural by Thomas Hart Benton on the walls of the third-floor House Lounge.

The small, surprisingly quiet downtown area has a couple of places worth searching out: start with **Arris' Pizza Palace** (117 W. High St., 573/635-9225), which has been serving great pizzas and a range of Greek specialties since 1961.

common hawthorn,
state flower of Missouri

Afterward, enjoy freshly churned ice cream at **Central Dairy** (610 Madison St., 573/635-6148). And if all that makes you want to linger, stay the night at the historic but recently remodeled **Baymont Inn and Suites** (319 W. Miller St., 573/636-5231, $84 and up), right downtown, a block off US-50, the main alternative to the national chains.

Hwy-100: Hermann and Washington

Running along the south bank of the Missouri River, Hwy-100 is the most interesting route between Jefferson City and St. Louis. Midway along, the town of **Hermann** (pop. 2,431) was founded by German immigrants in 1837. Surrounded by small wineries and standing right on the riverfront, Hermann reminds some visitors of a Rhine Valley village, its German heritage kept alive at the **German School Museum** (312 Schiller St., 573/486-2017, Thurs.-Tues. Apr.-Oct., Sat.-Sun. Nov. and 1st two weekends of Dec., $5) downtown.

Roughly 50 miles from the Gateway Arch at downtown St. Louis, the redbrick town of **Washington** (pop. 13,982) rises on narrow streets above the broad Missouri River. Like Hermann, the town was settled by German immigrants in the mid-1800s and is now full of restaurants and B&B inns catering to weekend visitors. The small **Washington Historical Society Museum** at 4th and Market Streets has exhibits on early settlers and the town's current main industry (after tourism, that is): manufacturing corncob pipes.

St. Louis is the only city where three of our routes coincide—US-50, The **Great River Road** (page 264), and **Route 66** (page 835). For details on visiting **St. Louis,** see page 262.

SCOTT JOPLIN: THE KING OF RAGTIME

Music is among the most mobile of the arts, equally affecting anywhere and anytime, but many forms are strongly identified with a given place and era. New Orleans means jazz, the Delta has the blues, Detroit will always be equated with the Motown sound, and if credit were given where credit is due, Sedalia, Missouri, would join the above places as the source of another classic African American musical genre—ragtime. The first ragtime tunes, so-called because of their ragged, syncopated rhythms, were played in the early 1890s but later came into full flower out of the musical mind of Scott Joplin, the universally acclaimed king of ragtime.

Born in 1868 near Texarkana, Texas, to a formerly enslaved father and a freeborn mother, Scott Joplin was one of six children in a musical family. After moving around the Midwest throughout his youth, in the late 1890s Joplin settled in Sedalia, which was then a raucous railroad town, where he studied music theory at Sedalia's small black college. To pay his way, Joplin played piano at many of the clubs that lined Main Street in Sedalia, which had a reputation both for multiracial harmony and as an adult playground of bars and brothels catering to the many itinerant men passing through. One of these nightclubs gave its name to the "Maple Leaf Rag," the composition that made Joplin's reputation and which, at a penny-per-sheet royalty, earned around $500 a year—enough to support him, but far from a fortune. As late as 1940, *Life* magazine said Sedalia still had one of the "most notorious red-light districts" in the Midwest, but little remains here today to give a taste of the rowdy ragtime era. Sedalia remembers its favorite son with a **Scott Joplin Ragtime Festival** (660/826-2271) every June. There's also a Scott Joplin mural, downtown at Ohio and 2nd Streets, near the site of the Maple Leaf club.

It was at Westminster College in the town of **Fulton,** 20 miles northeast of Jefferson City, that Winston Churchill made his famous "Iron Curtain" speech in 1946.

The great frontiersman Daniel Boone settled along the northern banks of the Missouri River in 1799 and lived near what's now the town of **Defiance** for the next 20 years until his death in 1820. His home, five well-signed miles outside Defiance, is now open for **tours** (636/798-2005, Mon.-Fri. 8:30am-5pm, Sat.-Sun. 11:30am-5pm, $8).

West of St. Louis, Hwy-100 and US-50 merge into the high-speed I-44 freeway in Eureka, near the massive **Six Flags amusement park** (636/938-5300, $66), which has great roller coasters. Near the wooden Colossus Ferris wheel is a mural with scenes from the 1904 World's Fair.

ILLINOIS

US-50 runs straight across over 150 miles of southern Illinois's pancake-flat farmlands—acres of corn and soybeans as far as the eye can see, with small towns dotting the roadside every 10 or so miles. For much of the way, US-50 follows the Trace Road, a slightly raised causeway originally traced across the swampy marshlands by the same prehistoric people who built the enigmatic mounds at Cahokia, which still stand in the eastern suburbs of St. Louis. Midway across Illinois, US-50 passes through the quirkily historic town of **Salem** (birthplace of two American icons: William Jennings Bryan and Miracle Whip), then crosses over the Wabash River into Indiana.

Lebanon

US-50 follows I-64 east from St. Louis across the flat prairie, whose fertile alluvial soil has earned it the nickname Little Egypt. The highway parallels the Illinois Central Railroad through a dozen small towns, the most significant of which is **Lebanon** (pop. 4,418), about 20 miles east of the Mississippi River. An attractive town with a number of stately, mansard-roofed, Victorian-era commercial buildings now housing antiques shops near downtown (US-50), Lebanon grew up around the bucolic campus of McKendree University, founded here in 1828, making it one of the oldest in Illinois.

The best reason to stop, however, is the small museum at the **Mermaid House Inn** (114 E. St. Louis St., 618/537-8420; tours by appointment, donation), on US-50. Charles Dickens, who visited the area to see the rich but muddy prairie east of town, stayed here for a night in 1842 and described it in *American Notes* as comparing "favorably with any village ale house of a homely kind in England."

Bible-packing 18th-century settlers of the uplands opposite St. Louis referred to their chosen homesteads as "Goshen" and the flood-prone flats to the south as "Egypt." Comparisons between the Mississippi and Nile rivers were reinforced with place-names like Karnak, Joppa, Thebes, and Cairo.

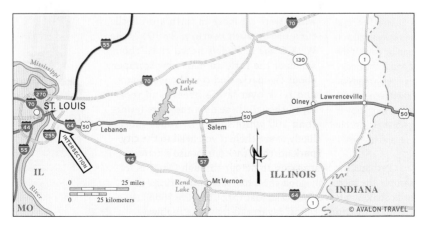

© AVALON TRAVEL

Salem

Halfway across Illinois, just east of the busy I-57 freeway, US-50 cuts through the center of **Salem** (pop. 7,485), a historically fascinating if visually less-than-thrilling city best known as the birthplace and boyhood home of William Jennings Bryan. The turn-of-the-20th-century politician and orator, who served as leader of the Democratic Party for 15 years, prosecuted the so-called "Monkey Trial" of 1925 and led the successful attack on Tennessee schoolteacher John Scopes (who, coinciden-tally, was also born and raised in Salem) for breaking a local ban on teaching evolution. Bryan was born in 1860 in a small frame house, four blocks south of Main Street (US-50). It has been preserved as a small **museum** (408 S. Broadway, 618/547-2222, by appointment, free). There's a statue of Bryan, crafted by Mt. Rushmore sculptor Gutzon Borglum, on Broadway a half mile north of Main Street, across from the **Bryan Memorial Park.**

> Miracle Whip was created at Max Crosset's café on Main Street before being sold to Kraft Foods (for $300!) in 1931. The birthplace of Miracle Whip is now a parking lot at the center of Salem.

Salem has also given America the **G.I. Bill of Rights.** Also known as the G.I. Bill, this law entitles military veterans to sub-sidized education and other services. It was first proposed by the local American Legion branch before being signed into law in 1944.

Salem is an interesting place to linger, and if you want to stay overnight, try the inexpensive **Continental Motel** (1600 E. Main St., 618/548-3090, $38 and up), on US-50, next door to an enjoyable bowling alley.

> On the east side of Carlyle, 22 miles west of Salem, the delicate **General Dean Suspension Bridge** was built in 1859 and has been preserved in a riverside park, on the northeast side of where US-50 crosses the Kaskaskia River.

Olney and Lawrenceville

The flat farmlands of southeast Illinois are dotted with occa-sional oil wells and signs painted on barn sides encouraging travelers to "Chew Mail Pouch Tobacco" or "See Rock City," but towns are few and far between. The first of these is the attractive town of **Olney** (pop. 9,115). Besides boasting a large number of grand old mansions set behind broad green lawns along quiet leafy streets, Olney has the singular attraction of **albino squirrels,** which were set loose in town around the turn of the 20th century. By 1940, the WPA *Guide to Illinois* noted that "thou-sands of the little animals now scamper about the parks and courthouse square, and frisk over lawns, trees, and roof-tops," though these days there are fewer than 100 white squirrels. You're most likely to see them if you head to the **city park** north of the courthouse square.

> The **Wabash River** between Indiana and Illinois marks the boundary between the central and eastern time zones. Subtract an hour heading west; add an hour heading east. At the west end of the bridge over the river, a roadside memorial recounts the westward migration of young Abraham Lincoln and his family.

WILLIAM JENNINGS
BRYAN

1860 1925

"YOU SHALL NOT PRESS DOWN UPON THE BROW OF LABOR THIS CROWN OF THORNS YOU SHALL NOT CRUCIFY MANKIND UPON A CROSS OF GOLD"

Perhaps the best reason to detour through Olney is to sample the incredibly good cheeseburgers, onion rings, and milk shakes at **Hovey's** (412 E. Main St., 618/395-4683).

East of Olney, US-50 reverts to two-lane highway,

running for 23 miles before passing by **Lawrenceville** (pop. 4,348), which was named for U.S. Navy Captain James Lawrence, best remembered for his dying words, "Don't give up the ship," during the War of 1812.

East of Lawrenceville, follow the old road south of the modern freeway, crossing the Wabash River into Indiana at historic Vincennes.

INDIANA

From the Wabash River at its western end to the Ohio River in the east, the 170 miles of southern Indiana that lie between present an immensely varied landscape. The hilly eastern sections are surprisingly rugged, though the central and western reaches are comparatively flat and largely agricultural. Besides numerous well-preserved historic Ohio River towns like **Madison** and **Aurora,** there are a number of unlovely industrial sections, especially around **Bedford** and the famous limestone quarries in the central parts of the state.

Vincennes

First settled by the French in 1732, and intensely fought over during the Revolutionary War, **Vincennes** (pop. 18,423) remained a lawless frontier until 1803, when it was named the territorial capital. A handful of early buildings, including a bank, a church, and a newspaper office, have been restored at 1st and Harrison Streets in the historic downtown area. Nearby, overlooking the Wabash River, the **George Rogers Clark National Historical Park** (free) is a classical dome honoring

George Rogers Clark Memorial

Revolutionary War general George Rogers Clark, who led local militiamen in the capture of Vincennes from the British in 1779. (George Rogers Clark was the older brother of William Clark, of Lewis and Clark fame.)

The monument, built as a WPA project during the Great Depression, wouldn't look out of place in DC, but the rest of Vincennes is decidedly down-to-earth, with grain elevators, five-and-dime stores, and cafés along the busy railroad tracks.

The area around Vincennes is flat farming country, notable for its large Amish communities (and numerous roadside "Amish Kountry Korner" stores and cafés), especially around **Loogootee,** 30 miles east of Vincennes.

French Lick and Mitchell

Between Vincennes and Bedford, US-50 winds its way through the hilly groves of the Hoosier National Forest. A worthwhile detour heads south through the hometowns of two of Indiana's best-known sons. The first of these, on Hwy-56 just south of US-150, is **French Lick** (pop. 1,807), where 1980s Boston Celtics basketball star Larry Bird, who famously called himself "The Hick from French Lick," learned to

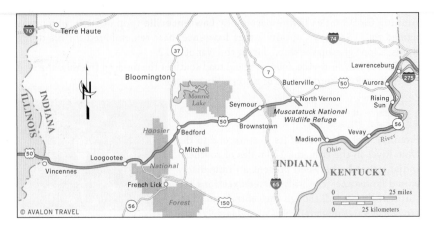

play. A century ago the surrounding area was a popular vacation resort, as thousands of Midwesterners (including Al Capone and other Chicago mobsters) came here to stay and play. After many years of neglect, the resorts have been reborn as part of the inevitable casino complex but still retain oodles of historic character. The fabulous **West Baden Springs Hotel** closed decades ago but was fully restored and reopened in 2007; it is now operated as part of the opulent **French Lick Resort Casino** (812/936-1902, $209 and up), where you can take the mineral-rich waters that still flow from local Pluto Springs.

The whole story of regional development and personality is conveyed inside the **French Lick West Baden Museum** (469 S. Maple St., 812/936-3592, $8), which also displays a 1,110-square-foot diorama of circus tents, elephants, and a carnival midway dating from the early 1900s, when West Baden was home to the nationally acclaimed Hagenbeck-Wallace Circus. French Lick also celebrates its favorite son with a Bird-themed (and Bird-owned!) sports bar called **33 Brick Street** (480 Maple St., 812/936-3370).

West Baden Springs Hotel's atrium

West Baden Spring No. 5

The other famous southern Indiana hometown, **Mitchell,** is about six miles south of Bedford and was the boyhood home of astronaut Virgil "Gus" Grissom, who captained Mercury and Gemini space flights before dying in the Apollo 1 disaster. There's an impressive memorial—a 44-foot-high limestone statue of a Redstone rocket—to Grissom south of Main Street on 6th Street, next to the police station.

Bedford

Nicknamed "Stone City" because it holds some of the largest and most famous limestone quarries in the country, **Bedford** (pop. 13,413) is a busy industrial-looking city, the largest on the Indiana stretch of US-50. The quarries that earned Bedford's reputation are still in use, producing the durable stone that has clad many high-profile structures, including the Empire State Building. Though you can see the limestone in situ at many road cuts along US-50, perhaps the most prominent examples in Bedford are the monuments and gravestones in the cemeteries lining the highway through town.

Bedford's main hard-rock attraction is **Bluespring Caverns** (812/279-9471, daily mid-Mar.-Oct., $18), five miles west of downtown on US-50, where you can descend into a cave and take an hour-long boat tour along the largest underground river in the United States.

Brownstown, Seymour, and North Vernon

Roughly 27 miles east of Bedford and 10 miles west of the I-65 freeway, **Brownstown** (pop. 2,947) is an unusually pretty Indiana town set around a large central square shaded by 100-year-old maple trees—and a war-surplus tank. An old-fashioned general store and a couple of down-home restaurants make it worth a brief stop.

East of Brownstown, it's a scenic 10 miles to **Seymour** (pop. 1,503), with its many motels (including a Holiday Inn Express & Suites and an EconoLodge), fast-food franchises, 24-hour gas stations, and an absolutely *huge* Walmart distribution center marking the junction with I-65. Blue-collar Seymour is the birthplace of rock star John Mellencamp and Indiana's first Miss America (2009 winner Katie Stam). You can get a good feel for the place by stopping for a meal at the **Townhouse Café** (206 E. 4th St., 812/522-1099).

One thing to see along US-50 is 10 miles east of North Vernon, in **Butlerville,** where a roadside plaque marks the 1885 birthplace of Hannah Milhous Nixon, Richard's mother.

Twelve miles east of Seymour, turn south from US-50 at neat little **North Vernon** onto Hwy-7, which runs toward the Ohio River town of Madison, across miles of rolling farmland, closely paralleling the route of Morgan's Raid, when General John Morgan and 2,000 Confederate soldiers invaded Indiana during the Civil War.

Madison and the Ohio River Towns

The route east along US-50 is uneventful, so if you have some time, loop to the south along **Hwy-56,** which curves along the north bank of the broad Ohio River. The riverside here is rich in history, and the 60-mile drive passes by modest tobacco farms and timeless small towns, the pastoral scene marred only by occasional power plants, most of them across the water on the Kentucky side.

DETOUR: LOUISVILLE

Home of the world's greatest horse race (the Kentucky Derby), the world's biggest baseball bat (a 120-foot-tall Louisville Slugger), and the man who was simply "The Greatest" (boxer Muhammad Ali, who grew up here, and whose life and times are featured in a riverfront museum), Louisville (pronounced "LOO-a-vil") is a characterful midsize city on the south bank of the Ohio River. During Kentucky Derby week, the mint julep-fueled party leading up to the first Saturday in May, the whole city comes alive, but Louisville is an enjoyable place to explore any time of year. Within a short walk of the **Muhammad Ali Museum** (144 N. 6th St., 502/584-9254, Tues.-Sun., $12) is another of the country's top pop-culture destinations: the **Louisville Slugger Museum** (800 W. Main St., 502/588-7228 or 877/775-8443, daily, $14), marked by that giant baseball bat and full of memorabilia on big hitters from Babe Ruth to Hank Aaron. Thanks to the Louisville Slugger connection, the local baseball team is called the **Louisville Bats** (401 E. Main St., 502/212-2287), a Triple-A farm club for the Cincinnati Reds. Games are broadcast on **WKRD 790 AM.** The Bats play at **Louisville Slugger Field,** right downtown. It's across from the 85-acre Waterfront Park, which has an authentic 100-year-old steam-powered paddlewheel **riverboat** (502/574-2992, $15-43). From here, the newly restored "Big Four" railroad bridge reaches across the Ohio River to the historic town of Jeffersonville, Indiana.

Louisville has managed to preserve a great number of its fine old homes. Unusual brick-built mansions from the 1870s now form the heart of the **Old Louisville** neighborhood, south of downtown along 4th Street, near the expansive University of Louisville campus. Around the historic and lushly landscaped **Cave Hill cemetery** (701 Baxter Ave., 502/451-5630, free), southeast of downtown, you can pay your respects to diverse luminaries, including frontier soldier George Rogers Clark, early settler George Keats (brother of the English poet John Keats), and Kentucky's chicken-frying "Colonel" Harland Sanders.

Adventurous eaters will be rewarded with lots of good food all over Louisville. If you want a sure thing, head three miles east of downtown via old US-60 to **Momma's Mustard, Pickles & BBQ** (102 Bauer Ave., 502/938-6262), for authentic smoked beef brisket, pork ribs, creamy mac 'n' cheese, and health-restoring side dishes (green beans, cole slaw—you name it).

Outside Louisville, along US-31 about 30 miles to the southwest, you can cruise past another icon, **Fort Knox,** and dream about the 10 million pounds of pure gold locked inside.

Louisville Slugger Museum

Though the drive is nice enough in itself, it's most worthwhile because it brings you to **Madison** (pop. 12,247), one of the best-preserved historic Ohio River towns, thanks in large part to the National Trust for Historic Preservation, which used Madison as a case study in how to keep small-town America alive and well in the modern age. Now a popular vacation destination, especially during the **Chautauqua Arts Festival** in late September and the rowdier **Madison Regatta** around the 4th of July, when 200-mph hydroplanes race along the river, Madison has managed to stay alive economically without sacrificing its small-town charms. Wandering around a few blocks of the franchise-free Main Street, you can enjoy a meal, listen to the town gossip while getting a haircut at the chrome and red-leather barbershop, or tour the many historic homes. The best of these is the impressive Greek Revival **mansion** (601 W. 1st St., $10) of Civil War financier James Lanier, near the river. Also worth a look is the perfectly preserved **Victorian-era doctor's office** (120 W. 3rd St., $4), which served as the only hospital between Cincinnati and Louisville.

The quaint town of **Vevay,** 20 miles east of Madison, was the birthplace of Edward Eggleston, author of *The Hoosier Schoolmaster.* Another important area native was engineer Elwood Mead, the man for whom Lake Mead is named.

Along with its wealth of Americana, Madison has a number of good places to eat along the three blocks of Main Street, including the 1930s-era **Hinkle's** (204 W. Main St., 812/265-3919, Mon.-Tues. 6am-10pm, Wed.-Thurs. 6am-midnight, Fri.-Sat. 24 hours), featuring great greasy-spoon burgers, traditional breakfasts, and fresh fried fish. There's the romantic **Riverboat Inn and Suites** (906 E. 1st St., 812/265-2361, $75 and up). Best value are the motel-type rooms at the **Clifty Inn** (812/265-4135, $115-185) in wooded Clifty Falls State Park, a mile west of town on Hwy-56.

Grand Victoria

Rising Sun

Farther along Hwy-56, nine miles south of Aurora and US-50, the village of **Rising Sun** holds a handful of frontier-era structures as well the **Rising Star Casino Resort** ($79 and up). The historic parts of town have managed to stay quaint despite the influx of gamblers, and the old-fashioned (but newly repaved) downtown area has the good **Ohio County Historical Museum** (212 S. Walnut St.). Along with the usual array of local history, the museum also recounts the Ohio River's unique heritage of hydroplane racing.

Aurora and Lawrenceburg

Our Ohio River detour along Hwy-56 rejoins US-50 at **Aurora** (pop. 3,750), a small riverside town that's well worth at least a brief stop. The highlight here is the handsome **Hillforest Mansion** (213 5th St., Tues.-Sun. Apr.-Dec., closed major holidays, $10), an exuberant survivor from the steamboat era whose colonnaded facade is topped by a circular lookout tower from which residents could gaze out at river traffic up and down the Ohio. Built in 1852 and preserved in fine condition, the hillside mansion gives a strong sense of how comfortable and sophisticated life was for the wealthy, even on the so-called frontier.

East from Aurora, approaching the Ohio state line, US-50 forms a busy gauntlet of roadside motels, diners, cut-rate liquor stores, and fireworks stands, all competing via giant billboards for the tristate trade. **Lawrenceburg** (pop. 5,042), along the I-275 freeway three miles west of the Indiana-Ohio-Kentucky border, seems to revolve around the sale of cheap booze, perhaps because for years the main employer was

Hillforest Mansion

the massive redbrick **Seagram's** distillery at the north end of Main Street—among the largest and oldest in the United States, dating from 1847. Nowadays Lawrenceburg embraces another vice, gambling, as evidenced by the sprawling Hollywood Casino & Hotel that spreads south of US-50 on the east side of town.

Lawrenceburg as seen from US-50 is less than scenic, with railroad tracks and a huge levee cutting off the town from the waterfront. However, the historic town center, south of the highway along Walnut Street, holds a number of interesting old buildings dating from the steamboat era of the early 1800s, when Lawrenceburg was a favorite Ohio River port of call. Among the many church spires competing for preeminence is that of the Presbyterian church, where in 1837 orator Henry Ward Beecher (brother of Harriet Beecher Stowe, she of *Uncle Tom's Cabin* fame) held his first pastorate.

Places to eat in old-town Lawrenceburg emphasize the 80-proof aspects of local life: **Whisky's** (334 Front St., 812/537-4239), for example, serves steaks in an old button factory on Front Street.

While Lawrenceburg embraces its heritage of gambling and booze, a detour across the river into Kentucky will bring you to a very different place: the fundamentalist **Creation Museum** (888/582-4253, $30), near the Cincinnati airport along I-275 in Petersburg. Its 70,000 square feet of high-tech galleries let you walk through a biblical history of the world.

Lawrenceburg's signs of the old road

OHIO

Winding along the Ohio River from Indiana, US-50 cuts east from Cincinnati across the hill-and-valley country of southern Ohio before finally crossing the Ohio River into West Virginia. The 220 miles US-50 takes to cross the state are a fairly constant mix of upland forest and bottomland farms, with a single industrial district in the middle around **Chillicothe,** and a refreshing small college town, **Athens,** farther east.

North Bend

East from the Indiana line, US-50 winds along the partly industrial, partly rural Ohio River waterfront, without much to detain you before Cincinnati. The one place worth a stop is the hamlet of **North Bend** (pop. 857), five miles east of the state border. A tall sandstone obelisk, overlooking the river and US-50 amid a 14-acre park, marks the final resting place of William Henry Harrison (1773-1841), the ninth president of the United States, who lived here for many years when North Bend was a thriving frontier port. Born in Virginia, Harrison came to fame fighting Shawnee people in and around the Ohio Valley, and he served in Congress for many years before he was elected president; he died of pneumonia after only a month in office. His grandson Benjamin Harrison, who became president in 1889, was born in the nearby family home in 1833.

Continuing along US-50, five miles west of downtown Cincinnati and just three miles north of the main Cincy airport, the tiny **Anderson Ferry** ($5 per car, $0.50 foot passengers) has been chugging back and forth since 1817, though the broad Ohio River is nothing like the busy river it was back then. But as recently as 1940, the WPA *Guide to Ohio* wrote that "fleets of barges pushed by snub-nosed towboats crawl along the motionless water; and now and then appears one of the Greene Line packets, all white and triple-decked."

US-50: Across Cincinnati

US-50 survives pretty much intact across Cincinnati, though most of its former traffic now follows the freeways that loop around and cut through the city. West of downtown, US-50 follows the Ohio River along River Road, but the old alignment veers away from the freeway-sliced waterfront along State Avenue, running through downtown along 7th, 8th, and 9th Streets. East of downtown, old US-50 rejoins the riverfront around Mt. Adams, then follows the Columbia Parkway east to the garden city of Mariemont, where we rejoin it.

Mariemont

From Cincinnati, US-50 follows surface streets through the warehouse and residential districts along the Ohio River before becoming a freeway for the quick drive east to **Mariemont** (pop. 3,403). Built in the mid-1920s as one of the nation's first planned "Garden City" communities, Mariemont's mock-Tudor downtown centers on the historic and comfortable **Best Western Premier Mariemont Inn** (6880 Wooster Pike, 513/271-2100, $174 and up), right on US-50. Across the street there's a branch of the excellent local ice cream chain, **Graeter's.** The sole surviving neighborhood of Mariemont's original 1920s half-timbered arts-and-crafts homes is an easily walkable block to the southeast. On the east edge of Mariemont, the legacy of old US-50 is celebrated right along the old highway at the popular **50 West Brewing Company** (7668 Wooster Pike, 513/834-8789), where good food and a range of local beers are served in a former roadside speakeasy. In summer, you can also rent kayaks or inner tubes for a leisurely float along the Little Miami River, on the south side of the highway, and the old railroad route is a rail trail running all the way from Cincinnati to Cleveland.

East of Mariemont, US-50 crosses the Little Miami River again at the scenic, 25-mph town of **Milford** before racing east across 40 miles of flat and sparsely settled farming country to Hillsboro. In Milford, there's a **Frisch's Big Boy** restaurant (840 Lila Ave., 513/831-0111), with a great old Big Boy sign, straight out of *American Graffiti*.

Cincinnati

Spreading along the north bank of the Ohio River, Cincinnati, whose nicknames range from "Queen City" to "Porkopolis," was once the largest and busiest city on the western frontier. During the heyday of steamboat travel in the first half of the 19th century, the city's riverside location made it a prime transportation center, but as the railroad networks converged on Chicago, Cincinnati was eclipsed as the prime gateway to the western United States. Procter & Gamble, the world's largest consumer products company, started here in the 1830s, making soap out of the abundant animal fat from the city's hundreds of slaughterhouses. In recent years, the city has welcomed some cutting-edge art and architecture, most notably in the angular forms of Zaha Hadid's **Contemporary Arts Center** (44 E. 6th St., 513/345-8400, Wed.-Mon., free), downtown. But Cincy is also known for a variety of less salubrious things: race riots, the fall from grace of baseball hero Pete Rose, and the TV antics of talk show host Jerry Springer. (Onetime mayor of Cincinnati, Springer started his media career here in the 1970s as a hard-rock radio DJ.)

Cincinnati's modest population, just under 300,000 people, ranks it just ahead of Toledo as Ohio's third largest city, which from a traveler's point of view makes it an easily manageable and usually stress-free place to visit. A good first stop in Cincy is the **Museum Center** (513/287-7000 or 800/733-2077, daily, $24),

45.—Aeroplane View, Ohio River and Bridges connecting Kentucky and Cincinnati, Ohio.

west of downtown in the former Union Terminal off I-75 exit 1. This 1930s art deco railroad station has been converted into an enjoyable complex of science and history museums, plus an Omnimax Theater. Nearby Eden Park holds the respected **Cincinnati Art Museum** (513/721-2787, Tues.-Sun., free), amid acres of greenery.

Unfortunately, most of Cincinnati's once vibrant waterfront area, known as "The Basin," has been torn down in the name of urban renewal. What the 1940 WPA *Guide to Ohio* called "a museum of city history and the building styles of the past century" has been demolished in favor of a stadium each for the **Reds** (513/381-7337) and **Bengals** (513/621-8383), standing on either side of an open-air riverfront mall called "The Banks." The other main attraction along the Ohio River (which until the Civil War marked the dividing line between slave and free states) is the **National Underground Railroad Freedom Center** (513/333-7500, Tues.-Sun., $15), a flashy, $110-million museum drawing links between slavery, the abolitionist movement, the Underground Railroad, and the spread of free-market democracy worldwide. The sole survivors of old Cincinnati are found in the expansive and rapidly gentrifying

"Over the Rhine" neighborhood, north of Liberty Street around historic **Findlay Market** (1801 Race St.), and across the river in Covington, Kentucky, which you can reach by walking or driving across the **Roebling Bridge**, built in 1867 as a precursor to the more famous Brooklyn Bridge.

Along with art and history, Cincinnati is also home to a marvelous museum embracing a more unusual subject: the **American Sign Museum** (1330 Monmouth St., 513/541-6366, Wed.-Sun., $15), housed in an old parachute factory in the Camp Washington area. The high ceilings provide plenty of room to display hundreds of painted signs, sculpted signs, neon signs—you name it, they're here.

PRACTICALITIES

Most major airlines fly into the Cincinnati-Northern Kentucky International Airport, which lies southwest of downtown in Kentucky. Getting around town is best done by car, if only so you can drive back and forth across the Ohio River on the Roebling Bridge.

No road-tripper in his or her right mind should pass through Cincinnati without sampling its excellent road food—mounds of chili and stacks of melt-in-your-mouth ribs, finished off with a scoop or two of Graeter's ice cream (available all over the city, both at its own parlors and at most good restaurants). Cincinnati-style chili is poured over spaghetti and served either "3-way" (spaghetti, chili, and grated cheese); "4-way" (add onions); or "5-way" (add beans). One road-food landmark, **Camp Washington Chili** (3005 Colerain Ave., 513/541-0061), three miles north of downtown, right off I-75 exit 3, is famous for it. Over 100 other places around town serve this subtly spiced local specialty. Downtown, **Arnold's** (210 E. 8th St., 513/421-6234) is a fine old place, a cozy circa-1860 tavern and deli that also features good live music. Just east of downtown along the river, **Montgomery Inn Boathouse** (925 Riverside Dr., 513/721-7427) serves some of the best barbecue ribs in America in a pleasant river-view setting.

From the neon signs to the peanut shells on the floor, one place that turns on the retro-nostalgia charms is **Terry's Turf Club** (4618 Eastern Ave., 513/533-4222), always packed with families and friends enjoying pretty good burgers in a roadhouse right on old US-50, east of downtown. Closer in, at the foot of Mt. Washington, the hickory smoked barbecue ribs and pulled pork sandwiches at **Eli's BBQ** (3313 Riverside Dr., 513/533-1957) have earned it awards and fans all over the Ohio River Valley.

Thanks to all the suppliers, retailers, and advertising execs courting Procter & Gamble business, there are hundreds of rooms available in national chain hotels and motels along Cincinnati's I-71 and I-75 freeways, so finding a place to stay shouldn't be a problem. The handy and spacious **Best Western Plus Cincinnati Riverfront** (200 Crescent Ave., 859/581-7800, $139 and up) overlooks the Ohio River from Covington on the Kentucky side of the Roebling Bridge. Downtown, the nicest place to stay is the art deco **Hilton Netherland Plaza** (35 W. 5th St., 513/421-9100, $149 and up), one of the country's grandest old hotels.

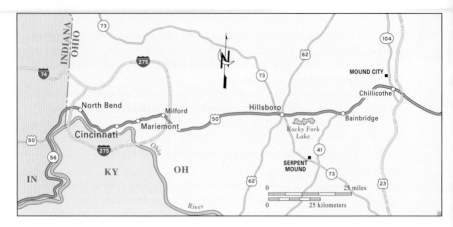

Hillsboro

Hillsboro (pop. 6,605), 60 miles east of Cincinnati and 40 miles west of Chillicothe, is the biggest and busiest town along the way. Besides the Greek Revival landmark **Highland County Courthouse,** second oldest in Ohio, Hillsboro has a unique alcohol-related history: During Christmas in 1873, the town's 13 saloons were closed down by one of the country's earliest temperance movements, and more recently, late great country singer Johnny "Take This Job and Shove It" Paycheck did time in prison for shooting a man in Hillsboro's North High Saloon. (Even more recently, that saloon was torn down to make way for a new city office building.)

Serpent Mound

Across southwestern Ohio, US-50 winds past whitewashed farmhouses and broad cornfields flanked by low hills. The region also holds two fascinating remnants of the Mound Builder people who once lived here. Just west of the sleepy village of Bainbridge, heading 20 miles south onto Hwy-41 (or following Hwy-73 south from Hillsboro) brings you to the **Serpent Mound** (800/752-2757, daily 9am-dusk, museum daily 10am-4pm Apr.-Oct., Sat.-Sun. Mar. and Nov.-Dec., $8 per car), which stretches in seven sinuous curves alongside a creek for nearly a quarter mile. There's a small museum on the site. To see the snake-shaped earthworks—the largest and finest effigy mound in the country—visitors climb up a turn-of-the-20th-century vintage lookout tower.

Midway between Chillicothe and Hillsboro, the nice little town of **Bainbridge** was the site of the first dental school in the United States, now a **Dental Museum** (208 W. Main St.) along US-50.

Chillicothe served as capital of the Northwest Territory from 1800 to 1802, and later as the first capital of Ohio.

Another of these prehistoric sites, the **Seip Earthworks,** 2 miles east of Bainbridge and 14 miles west of Chillicothe, is over 200 feet long and 30 feet tall, surrounded by 10 acres of pasture. To prevent early farmers from plowing them into oblivion in the 1880s, many of these evocative monuments were purchased and preserved through the efforts of Harvard University archaeologists. Harvard owned the land for many years and later donated the sites to the state of Ohio.

Chillicothe and Mound City

In the middle of the state, **Chillicothe** (pop. 21,901; pronounced "chill-a-COTH-ee") comes as a sudden surprise after the pastoral

red carnation,
state flower of Ohio

Hopewell Culture National Historical Park

landscape that surrounds it. It is one of the state's oldest industrial centers; since 1812 Chillicothe's economy has revolved around the massive paper mill on the south side of town, whose red-and-white striped smokestack belches a pungently steaming white cloud around the clock.

Heavy industry aside, Chillicothe has done an admirable job of preserving its history, most notably in the recently spruced-up "First Capital" district along Main Street (US-50) downtown. Dozens of elaborate late-Victorian commercial buildings and Greek Revival-style mansions, mostly dating from the mid-1850s, surround the overwrought Ross County Courthouse, which has a different entrance for each government department.

While the downtown area is worth a quick stroll, specific sights are few, and the area's real attraction is three miles north of town via Hwy-104. Officially known as the **Hopewell Culture National Historical Park,** but usually called **Mound City,** this complex of prehistoric burial sites sits on the west bank of the Scioto River, just beyond a huge prison complex. Some two dozen distinct, grass-covered mounds, the largest of which is about 19 feet high, are reachable on a mile-long trail that starts at the **visitors center** (16062 Hwy-104, 740/774-1126, daily, free), where films and exhibits explore aspects of this 2,000-year-old culture.

Chillicothe is known throughout Ohio as the site of **Tecumseh** (740/775-0700 or 888/775-0700, Mon.-Sat. 8pm summer, $24), an outdoor pageant dramatizing the life of the Shawnee warrior.

Athens

East of Chillicothe, US-50 passes through Vinton County, one of the state's poorest and least-developed regions. Hidden amid forested hills, the remains of coal mines and overgrown rail-fenced cornfields line the next 50 miles, and little has changed (for the better, at least) since the WPA *Guide to Ohio* described the scene in 1939: "Abruptly the

THE MOUND BUILDERS

The broad area between the Mississippi River and the Appalachian crest is rich in early American history, but the human story here goes back way beyond Daniel Boone and Abraham Lincoln to an era not often discussed in textbooks. From around 800 BC until AD 1500, this region was home to two successive prehistoric cultures that were roughly simultaneous with the legendary Maya and Aztecs of Mexico but are now all but forgotten, remembered solely for the massive earthen mounds they left behind.

The older of these two prehistoric peoples is known as the Hopewell culture, since the first scientific studies were conducted in 1891 at a farm owned by a man named Hopewell. Some 50 years earlier, the mounds had already become famous, as stories spread tracing their construction back to a "lost race" of mysterious origin, not unlike the Ancestral Puebloans of the desert Southwest. As the Hopewell culture began to decline, around AD 500 another culture, called the Mississippian, rose. Similarities between these two hunter-gatherer cultures, with their far-flung trading networks and hierarchical societies, are much greater than their differences, but archaeologists consider them to be completely distinct from one another. A key difference: Almost all of the Hopewell mounds were rounded or conical and built as burial sites, while Mississippian sites tended to be more rectilinear, with the mounds serving not as interments but as bases for long-vanished wooden structures built atop them. In Hopewell sites, buried along with the usually cremated human 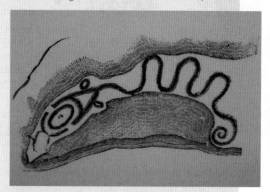 remains, archaeologists have recovered a compelling array of artifacts—obsidian tools from the Pacific Northwest, shell beads from the Gulf of Mexico, and silver and copper objects from the Great Lakes, which give some hint of the quality of ancient Native American life.

Ohio is particularly well provided with these enigmatic earthworks. At the **Hopewell Culture National Historical Park** near Chillicothe, five prehistoric earthworks complexes, with two dozen mounds, have been preserved by the National Park Service. West of Chillicothe, the low-lying **Serpent Mound** stretches for a quarter mile along a river, and over 100 other sites have been identified across the state.

Farther west on US-50, along the Mississippi at **Cahokia Mounds State Historic Site** (see page 833), the remnants of the largest prehistoric city in North America now sit across the river from St. Louis. North along the river, the **Effigy Mounds National Monument** (see page 242) in Iowa, across from Prairie du Chien, preserves yet more burial mounds, while down south, the Natchez Trace Parkway features the prehistoric **Emerald Mound** (see page 285).

the Ohio University campus

road sweeps into a rock-bound gorge dotted with the rickety houses of hill-folk . . . who make a living by seasonal mining, moonshining, trapping, or on Government relief projects."

After all this rural poverty, US-50 finally arrives at **Athens** (pop. 23,832), one of the most attractive small towns in Ohio. Set, like its classical namesake, on a series of hills, Athens is an idyllic little town that has grown up around the leafy campus of Ohio University, which opened here in 1809. It's a pretty place, with brick-paved streets, bookstores, copy shops, and clothing stores filling the eight-block Uptown neighborhood along College and Court Streets on the north side of the neoclassical college green.

US-50 follows the Hocking River and bypasses the heart of town, so follow Stimson Avenue or State Street from the highway, past the cafés and shops that fill the few blocks around the campus, where the **Union Street Diner** (70 W. Union St., 740/594-6007) has Athens's best cheap burgers and sandwiches. A cone or cup of **Whit's Frozen Custard** (49 S. Court St., 740/594-7375) will help you cool down on a hot summer's day. Accommodations in Athens include a **Hampton Inn** (986 E. State St., 740/593-5600), just east of campus, and many other motels along Columbus Road (US-33) on the north side of town.

East of the Athens area, US-50 passes through 40 miles of scrubby second-growth forests and the abandoned but enticingly named coal-mining towns of Guysville and Coolville, before reaching the West Virginia border at the Ohio River and Parkersburg.

> Southeastern Ohio has one of the country's greatest concentrations of barns painted with signs reading "Chew Mail Pouch Tobacco."

WEST VIRGINIA

The slowest part of US-50's transcontinental crossing is the 150-mile section across West Virginia, which twists and turns its way over the rugged **Allegheny Mountains.** Starting along the Ohio River in the western, more-developed half of the state, US-50 runs briefly as a fairly fast freeway before beginning its climb into the rugged hill country. Across West Virginia, US-50 follows the approximate route of the colonial-era Northwest Turnpike, which was surveyed in 1748 by a 16-year-old George Washington.

Though there are many fine hardwood forests and white-water rivers, including some of the most extensive semi-wilderness areas left in the eastern states, this part of West Virginia is mostly rural, with more than a few corners where things seem

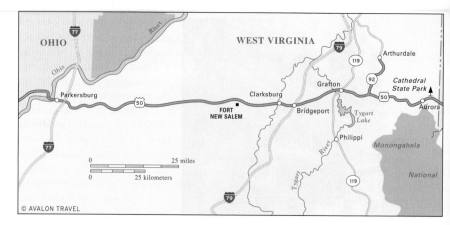

straight out of a Depression-era Walker Evans photograph. Rusting appliances and broken-down cars fill more than a few front yards, but around the next bend you may come across a lovely old covered bridge, or a waterfall that takes your breath away. The few towns along the route, formerly bustling thanks to the railroads or coal mines, are still dominated by the empty remnants of industries that have vanished, never to return. Most places are populated by people who seem to have lived there forever. The self-reliant "mountaineer" ethos still runs strong in West Virginia, but the lingering impression of a visit is of taking a step back in time to a world where men work hard in mines and mills, women raise the kids, and everybody goes to church on Sunday.

Parkersburg

Northern West Virginia's largest and most heavily industrialized city, **Parkersburg** (pop. 31,492) is located strategically at the junction of the Ohio and Little Kanawha Rivers. The town's economy is based on an unusual pair of employers: the federal Bureau of the Public Debt, which redeems U.S. Savings Bonds, and a massive DuPont Teflon factory.

Though the first impression can be fairly bleak, Parkersburg does merit a closer look. The **Blennerhassett Museum of Regional History** (304/420-4800, Tues.-Sun., $4), housed in a turn-of-the-20th-century brick warehouse at 2nd and Juliana Streets, traces regional history, with a focus on the escapades of the Irish aristocrat Harman Blennerhassett, who in 1806 conspired with Aaron Burr to establish an independent fiefdom in Texas and the Southwest. If you're interested, you can ride a sternwheeler to and from the Ohio River island on which Blennerhassett built the palatial home where the plot was hatched. The house has been reconstructed as a **state park** (tours $5). **Boats** ($10) leave hourly for the island from Point Park, which is two blocks west of the museum, under the railroad bridges and on the far side of the 25-foot concrete flood walls at the confluence of the rivers.

Parkersburg also has a good range of motels and a couple of coffee shops along US-50, like the **Mountaineer Family Restaurant** (4006 E. 7th St., 304/422-0101, daily 6am-10pm), near I-77 on the east side of town. If you want to linger, stay overnight at the delightful **Blennerhassett Hotel** (320 Market St., 304/422-3131 or 800/262-2536, $99 and up).

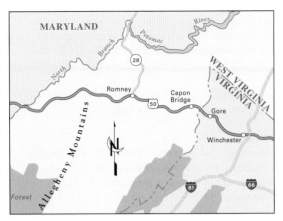

rhododendron,
state flower of West Virginia

Fort New Salem

Between Parkersburg and Clarksburg, US-50 winds along as a fast four-lane freeway through a mountainous onetime oil- and gas-producing region dotted with tiny all-but-forgotten towns. The small farms are cultivated by descendants of Scotch-Irish immigrants who settled here in the late 18th century. One place that's well worth a short stop is **Fort New Salem** (304/695-2220, $5-7), which is 14 miles west of Clarksburg. Just south of US-50, near the campus of Salem International University, the fort consists of 18 historic log cabins relocated here in the 1970s.

Clarksburg

Clarksburg (pop. 16,578) is a tidy railroad town sitting on a branch of the Monongahela River. The downtown area is a sampler of turn-of-the-20th-century commercial buildings, great for taking pictures of old signs and brick walls. It's also the birthplace of Confederate Civil War hero Thomas "Stonewall" Jackson, commemorated by a plaque on the house where he was born, at 326 Main Street.

The town's large Italian population, estimated at around 40 percent, supports numerous good restaurants, like **Minard's Spaghetti Inn** (813 E. Pike St., 304/623-1711) on old US-50, at the Joyce Street exit off the US-50 freeway. Another good old-fashioned place to eat is the **Ritzy Lunch** (456 W. Pike St., 304/622-3600), selling famous chili dogs since 1933.

> Clarksburg houses the FBI's national center for fingerprint and high-tech biometric security operations, located here thanks to West Virginia's U.S. Senator Robert Byrd, in office from 1959 until his death in 2010.

On the east side of Clarksburg, US-50 climbs a steep hill before becoming suddenly busy at **Bridgeport,** which straddles the I-79 freeway, around which the highway is lined by a two-mile sprawl of motels and fast food.

Grafton: International Mother's Day Shrine

Grafton (pop. 5,164), the first large town west of Winchester, Virginia, grew up as a bustling B&O railroad town beginning in the 1850s but is now among the most economically and socially depressed places in the state. Dozens of architecturally interesting but run-down houses and churches on brick-paved streets descend the steep hills to the Tygart River and the railroad tracks, where a monumental station and a grand but boarded-up hotel are grim reminders of Grafton's formerly busy self.

Besides its impressive physical setting, Grafton's main claim to fame is as the birthplace of Mother's Day, first celebrated here in 1908 in a Methodist church that's now been converted into the **International Mother's Day Shrine** (11 E. Main St., 304/265-1589 or 304/265-0583, call for hours or to schedule a tour, $5), across from the old train station.

East of Grafton, the landscape becomes more mountainous, and isolated villages replace the small towns that line the western half of the route.

South of Grafton, US-119 passes through the town of **Philippi,** where the largest covered bridge in West Virginia spans the Tygart River. Originally constructed in 1852, the 286-foot-long red-and-white bridge was badly burned in 1989 but has been totally restored.

Arthurdale

Northeast of Grafton, a half hour north of US-50 via Hwy-92, the homestead community of **Arthurdale** was the first and perhaps the most important of the many antipoverty rural resettlement projects initiated during the Depression-era New Deal. Though not the largest, Arthurdale was prominent because of the personal involvement of First Lady Eleanor Roosevelt, who not only helped plan the project but also visited many times, handing out diplomas at school graduations.

Beginning in 1934 with the construction of some 165 homes, plus schools and factories, a cooperative farm, a health center, and a small hotel, Arthurdale was an ideal community set up to relieve the dire living conditions of unemployed Morgantown coal miners. Most of the houses are still intact and still inhabited by the original homesteaders or their descendants. The old community center is being restored and now holds a small **museum** (18 Q Rd., 304/864-3959, $11) that chronicles the whole story.

Cathedral State Park

Four miles west of the Maryland border, US-50 runs right through **Cathedral State Park,** where over 133 acres of stately maples and hemlocks constitute one of the few first-growth stands left in this lumber-hungry state. Beyond here, US-50 makes a quick seven-mile jaunt across a corner of Maryland before crossing the north branch of the Potomac River back into West Virginia.

From the bridge, US-50 climbs steeply up the densely wooded Alleghenies, twisting over 3,000-foot-high ridges with turns so tight the posted speed limit is 15 mph—the going is slow, and not much fun if you're prone to car sickness.

Romney and the Eastern Gateway

The oddly shaped arm of eastern West Virginia, which juts between Maryland and Virginia at the headwaters of the Potomac River, is promoted as the **"Eastern Gateway"** and offers quick access to the mountainous wilderness of **Monongahela National Forest** that stretches south of US-50, and to the raging white water of the Cheat and Gauley Rivers. Originally inhabited by the Shawnee people, the region was settled during colonial times as part of the six-million-acre Virginia estate of Lord Fairfax.

The B&O Railroad came through in the 1850s, which made the region strategically important during the Civil War, nowhere more so than around **Romney** (pop. 2,009), the Eastern Gateway's largest town, which changed hands over 50 times in four years of fighting. In the center of Romney, at the corner of Main Street and Bolton, the **Davis History House** (304/822-3185, hours vary) is a well-restored log cabin packed full of pioneer and Civil War artifacts. Romney also has the oldest Confederate War Memorial, erected on the west side of town in Indian Mound Cemetery semi-secretly in 1866, since West Virginia was officially a "northern" state.

Heading east toward Winchester, US-50 passes through mountain hamlets like **Capon Bridge** (on the West Virginia side) and **Gore** (on the Virginia side), which consist of little more than a tavern and a post office, plus one or two antiques stores selling everything from colonial-era furniture to old highway signs. It's hard to help feeling light years from the modern world, even though Washington DC is only 90 miles away.

VIRGINIA

Dropping from the Allegheny and Appalachian Mountains of West Virginia, US-50 enters Virginia at the northern tip of the **Shenandoah Valley,** passing through the center of the quietly attractive small city of **Winchester.** Continuing east, in short order the road climbs the foothills of the Blue Ridge Mountains and crosses the Shenandoah River, delighting John Denver fans and carrying travelers through the heart of the ultra-wealthy "Hunt Country" of northern Virginia, a rural and unspoiled landscape of small towns, horse farms, and vineyards that's home to more well-connected millionaires than just about anywhere in the United States.

Approaching the outer suburbs of the nation's capital, however, US-50 swiftly loses its luster, and while you *can* follow it through miles of suburban sprawl on both sides of the I-495 Beltway, you might prefer to follow the misleadingly numbered I-66 freeway—which has nothing at all to do with the real Route 66—into the city. US-50's final approach takes you past the powerful Iwo Jima Memorial, arriving in **Washington DC** at the Lincoln Memorial.

Winchester

Northern Virginia's largest city, **Winchester** (pop. 26,203) is a surprisingly quiet and pleasant small city, best known for the

On Winchester's town square you'll find the **"World's Largest Apple,"** a 5,200-pound rival to another "World's Largest Apple" in Cornelia, Georgia, which was actually a 1926 gift from the city of Winchester.

© AVALON TRAVEL

extensive apple orchards that fill the surrounding countryside. The I-81 freeway, complete with the usual sprawl of shopping malls and fast-food franchises, cuts across US-50 along the east side of Winchester, but the downtown district is eminently strollable, especially the pedestrianized Old Town area around Loudoun Street, between Piccadilly (US-50) and Cork Streets, where you can visit George Washington's office or Stonewall Jackson's Civil War headquarters.

Patsy Cline

After apples and American history, Winchester is probably most famous as the hometown of Patsy Cline, the inimitable country singer who died in a plane crash in 1963 at age 30. Cline, whose greatest hits include "Crazy," "Sweet Dreams," and "Walkin' after Midnight," lived in Winchester from ages 3 to 16 in what's now the **Patsy Cline Historic House** (608 S. Kent St., 540/662-5555, $8) near downtown. She's buried in **Shenandoah Memorial Park,** a mile southeast of town.

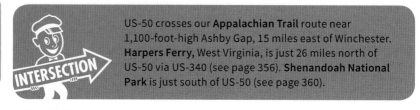

US-50 crosses our **Appalachian Trail** route near 1,100-foot-high Ashby Gap, 15 miles east of Winchester. **Harpers Ferry,** West Virginia, is just 26 miles north of US-50 via US-340 (see page 356). **Shenandoah National Park** is just south of US-50 (see page 360).

Middleburg

Located at the heart of northern Virginia's "Hunt Country," where senators, ambassadors, and aristocrats mix at multimillion-dollar country estates, **Middleburg** (pop. 673) is a small but immaculate town with a four-block business district packed with antiques shops, art galleries, and real estate agencies.

Many of Middleburg's brick- and stone-fronted buildings date from colonial times, including the **Red Fox Inn and Tavern** (2 E. Washington St., 540/687-6301 or 800/223-1728, $195 and up), on US-50 at the center of town. Originally built in 1728 as a coach inn and tavern, it's now a comfortable and upscale B&B and restaurant. There are a couple of other good places to eat, including the **Upper Crust Bakery** (2 N. Pendleton St., 540/687-5666), a local favorite offering cookies and sandwiches among the usual array of baked goods.

East of Middleburg, US-50 winds through gently rolling farmlands for a dozen miles before hitting the outlying suburbs of Washington DC.

Manassas National Battlefield Park

Site of the first major land battle of the Civil War, **Manassas National Battlefield Park** has been preserved intact despite the suburbanizing pressures of the surrounding towns. The prospect of battle-view executive homes still looms in the future, but for now, Manassas (which in the North was also known as Bull Run) is among the most evocative of all the Civil War sites, its five square miles of rolling hills and woodlands kept as they were, with few intrusions of modern life.

Manassas, which controlled transportation links between Washington DC and the Shenandoah Valley, was the site of two major battles. The first battle, fought here on July 21, 1861, was strategically inconclusive, though the fact that the Confederates forced the overconfident Union army into a panicked retreat surprised the many onlookers who had traveled out from Washington to watch the fighting, and it foreshadowed the next four years of war. The second battle, fought August 28-30, 1862, followed the instatement of Robert E. Lee as commander of the Confederate forces. That conflict marked the beginning of the bloodiest year of fighting, culminating in the battle of Gettysburg the following July.

Monuments and memorials dot the grassy hills, pointing out the many key moments of the battles, and rows of artillery are set up along battle lines. A loosely structured 1.4-mile walking tour begins at the **Henry Hill Visitor Center** (703/361-1339, free), where audiovisual displays and collections of military artifacts give a sense of what the war was like.

To reach Manassas Battlefield, follow the I-66 freeway from Washington DC or the Lee Highway (US-29) west from Fairfax. From US-50, follow US-15 or the smaller Hwy-659 south.

Arlington National Cemetery

Across the Potomac River from Washington DC, one of the most compelling and thought-provoking places in the capital region is **Arlington National Cemetery** (daily, free), a 600-acre hillside that contains the mortal remains of over 250,000 U.S. soldiers, sailors, and public servants. Row after row of nearly identical unadorned white tablets cover most of the cemetery, but special plots are dedicated to the most prominent people, such as John F. and Jacqueline Kennedy, who are buried together beneath an eternal flame, 200 yards straight beyond the main gate. Bobby Kennedy's grave is adjacent.

Located high on a ridge at the top of Arlington Cemetery, the neoclassical mansion of **Arlington House** was the antebellum home of Confederate general Robert E. Lee. Besides providing great views of the Mall and the heart of monumental Washington, the house serves as a vivid reminder of the deep rift caused by the Civil War. During the war, the grounds of the house were made into a cemetery for war dead, which formed the basis for Arlington National Cemetery. Washington's French-born designer, Pierre L'Enfant, lies in front of the mansion

Confederate hero Thomas "Stonewall" Jackson earned his nickname at the first battle of Manassas, where his steadfastness under fire helped rally rebel troops.

A dozen miles north of Manassas, just north of US-50 on the western fringes of Washington DC, the grounds of Dulles International Airport are home to the Smithsonian Air and Space Museum's **Udvar-Hazy Center** (703/572-4118, free), which displays hundreds of oversize airplanes and spaceships that cannot be exhibited on the National Mall. The two sites together showcase the largest collection of aviation and space artifacts in the world.

Tomb of the Unknown Soldier, Arlington National Cemetery, Va.

in a tomb marked by his plan for the city. The somber **Tomb of the Unknown Soldier** is a quarter mile south of Arlington House, where a U.S. Army honor guard is formally "changed" every half hour during hot summer days, every hour on cold winter nights.

To explore Arlington Cemetery more completely, stop first at the **welcome center**

Washington, D.C.

Even if you slept through high school history and have zero interest in politics, visiting Washington DC (pop. 672,228), is an unforgettable experience. The monuments that line the city's many grand avenues embody nearly two centuries of American political history, and museums show off everything from ancient art to the first flying machines. Best of all, almost everything is free, though there are a few caveats every would-be tourist should know: Parts of DC can be dangerous after dark, and the weather varies tremendously, from freezing cold in winter to swelteringly hot and humid in summer (though both spring and fall can be lovely).

You'll probably spend the bulk of your time at the many fine art and history museums that line the National Mall, at the center of town, all run by the Smithsonian Institution (daily, free, 202/633-1000). The huge and endearingly quirky **National Museum of American History** (202/633-1000, daily, free), on the north side of the Mall between 12th and 14th Streets, is sometimes called the "Nation's Attic," displaying a little of everything: the giant flag that inspired Francis Scott Key to write the "Star-Spangled Banner"; a pair of ruby slippers Judy Garland wore in *The Wizard of Oz;* even a 40-foot stretch of historic Route 66, part of the massive "America on the Move" transportation exhibit.

In recent years, a trio of impressive museums and monuments have opened along the National Mall. Closest to the Capitol is the **National Museum of the American Indian.** At the west end of the Mall is the **FDR Memorial,** which traces the journey of our longest-serving U.S. president from his elite childhood, through his midlife affliction by polio, up through the Great Depression, the New Deal, and World War II. The newest museum is the intensely moving **National Museum of African American History and Culture** between the Washington Monument and the White House.

National Museum of the American Indian

Your favorite memory of visiting Washington may be watching workers pushing wheelbarrows full of money across the floors of the **Bureau of Engraving and Printing** (14th St. and C St. SW, 202/874-2330, Mon.-Fri., free, tickets required in peak season), south of the United States Holocaust Memorial Museum. This high-security printing plant is where your hard-earned cash—some $300 billion a year—is born, along with postage stamps.

Washington's baseball team, the **Nationals** (888/632-6287), play at the $611-million stadium on the Anacostia River, near the Navy Yard metro station.

PRACTICALITIES

Ronald Reagan National Airport (DCA) is DC's main airport, near downtown and easily accessible on the Metro subway system. The second DC airport is Dulles (IAD), way out in the western suburbs, which handles most international flights (and has a large branch of the Smithsonian Air and Space Museum nearby). By road, DC lies on the busy north-south I-95 corridor, encircled by the I-495 Beltway. US-50, redubbed I-595 east of DC and supplemented in the west by the I-66 freeway, is the main east-west artery.

The basic layout of DC is fairly simple, as the entire diamond-shaped city is divided into four quadrants (NE, NW, SE, and SW) with the Capitol at the center. However, because of DC's baroque street plan, with its extensive one-way systems, driving can be confusing. Avail yourself of the handy Metro subway, which serves most of the places you'll want to go. It may also help to know that the Mall, where most of the museums and memorials are located, is roughly two miles long, from the Capitol west to the Potomac River.

The cheapest and most convenient place to sleep is the modern **HI Washington DC Hostel** (1009 11th St. NW, 202/737-2333, dorm around $33-50, private rooms $90-120), within walking distance of the White House. It has amenities like Wi-Fi and air-conditioning (essential in a DC summer). At the plushest end of the price and comfort spectrum, the **Hay-Adams Hotel** (800 16 St. NW, 202/638-6600, $329 and up), directly across from the White House, is luxurious and old-fashioned, with a grand lobby and discreet Off the Record cocktail bar full of expense-account lobbyists. The nicest midrange place to stay is the **Woodley Park Guest House** (2647 Woodley Rd. NW, 202/667-0218, $175 and up), which has clean, nicely furnished rooms and helpful staff in a convenient location near the Zoo Metro stop and trendy Adams-Morgan neighborhood.

To wine and dine with the movers, shakers, and wannabes, head to Wisconsin Avenue in Georgetown, at the northwest edge of the district, or leap back to a time when polished wood bars and brass spittoons were the order of the day at the **Old Ebbitt Grill** (675 15th St. NW, 202/347-4800), east of the White House. Open early until late, this casual grill serves everything from breakfasts and burgers to oysters and filet mignon. Along the canal, Georgetown's **Pizzeria Paradiso** (3282 M St. NW, 202/337-1245) has wood-fired pies and a fine range of beers (there's a bigger branch in Dupont Circle as well). For a more down-home taste, head north on the Green Line Metro to the U Street station, near which you can enjoy chili dogs at **Ben's Chili Bowl** (1213 U St. NW, 202/667-0909); Ben's also has a stand at the Nationals ballpark.

(877/907-8585, daily) near the cemetery entrance for a map of the grounds that identifies the gravesites of many other famous people interred here, including boxer Joe Louis, explorer Robert Peary, civil rights martyr Medgar Evers, and writer Dashiell Hammett.

Driving DC

Following US-50 across Washington DC takes you through the heart of the nation's capital. Starting in the west, alongside Arlington National Cemetery at the **Iwo Jima Memorial** (which sits in the middle of a traffic circle and is all but impossible to reach), US-50 crosses the Potomac River, entering "The District" on the Theodore Roosevelt Bridge—making a beeline toward the State Department. US-50 then follows Constitution Avenue along the north side of The Mall, running past the Lincoln and Vietnam Veterans Memorials and between the White House and the Washington Monument, before zigzagging northeast along 7th Street and New York Avenue. Heading east of DC, US-50 turns into a freeway and runs east to Annapolis and the Chesapeake Bay.

> Some versions of DC license plates read "Taxation without Representation," a symbol of the District's quest for full representation in the U.S. Congress.

MARYLAND

Racing out of Washington DC on a high-speed multilane freeway, US-50 accesses one of the state's most popular destinations, the colonial Chesapeake Bay port town of **Annapolis.** From Annapolis, heading toward the Atlantic coast and the massively popular beach resort of **Ocean City,** the final leg of US-50's 3,200-mile transcontinental trek is a mad dash across 100 miles of Maryland's Eastern Shore. This is one of the more captivating areas in the northeastern United States, but the four-lane US-50 freeway doesn't encourage sightseeing. If you want to get a feel for the *real* Eastern Shore of piney woods, cornfields, and fishing fleets, you'll have to follow the many back roads and search out the many historic towns and villages—many of which we point out as worthwhile detours, including some that are among the oldest and most carefully preserved in the nation.

Annapolis

State capital of Maryland, and one of the most attractive and well-preserved historic cities in the United States, **Annapolis** (pop. 39,958) is one place you won't want to miss. First settled in 1649 and chartered in 1708, Annapolis makes fair claim to being the oldest city in the country. The nation's first capital, it's now best known for its maritime heritage, both as a yachting center and as home of the U.S. Naval Academy, which stands guard along the Chesapeake Bay waterfront.

The historic center of Annapolis is just south of US-50 via Hwy-70, which leads straight to the **State House** (daily, free), where the U.S. Congress met in 1783-1784 and ratified the Treaty of Paris, ending the Revolutionary War. The west facade is fronted by a memorial to Supreme Court Justice Thurgood Marshall. From the State House, Main Street drops downhill to the City Dock waterfront, where a **visitors center** has walking-tour maps and guides to the wealth of historic buildings, including

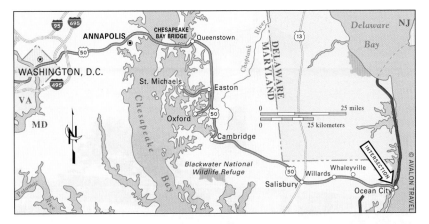

the beautiful colonial-era **Hammond Harwood House** (19 Maryland Ave., 410/263-4683, Tues.-Sun., $10).

Annapolis has a number of good places to eat, including the venerable **Chick & Ruth's Delly** (165 Main St., 410/269-6737), and **Iron Rooster** (12 Market Space, 410/990-1600), a popular breakfast, lunch, and brunch place near the waterfront, and the fancy yachts moored along "Ego Alley."

To fully absorb the colonial-era ambience, stay a night or two at the **Historic Inns of Annapolis** (410/263-2641 or 800/847-8882, $130 and up), a trio of historic homes right across from the State House, or any of the town's many characterful B&Bs.

Between DC and Annapolis, the town of **Bowie** is home to the Baltimore Orioles' Double-A farm team, the **Bowie Baysox** (301/464-4865).

Bay Bridge

Before the four-mile-long **Bay Bridge** was completed in the early 1950s, Maryland's Eastern Shore was physically and spiritually an island, protected by the broad Chesapeake Bay from the sprawling modern cities of Washington and Baltimore, and cut off at its neck by the Chesapeake and Delaware Canal. Despite

In Annapolis, **WRNR 103.1 FM** is an anarchic rock station, playing everything from The Animals to Frank Zappa.

the completion of a parallel span in the 1970s, the bridge gets clogged solid each summer by vehicles headed for coastal resorts like Rehoboth Beach ("The Beltway by the Bay") and Ocean City.

At the west end of the bridge, US-50 lands at **Sandy Point State Park,** where you can swim, hike, or launch a boat. At the eastern end, US-50 is joined by US-301, and together the two roads race along as a six-lane freeway as far as **Queenstown,** a busy port in the early 1800s but now little more than an upscale suburb of the greater Baltimore-Washington urban area.

Easton

Midway across Maryland, 20 miles southeast of the Chesapeake Bay Bridge, turn off the freeway and head a half mile west to explore the well-preserved heart of **Easton** (pop. 15,945), where the stately Talbot County Courthouse overlooks a compact

the Chesapeake Bay Maritime Museum

business district that could easily pass as an English country high street. Besides the many 18th-century structures, the most interesting place to stop is the white wood-frame **Third Haven Friends Meeting House,** on the edge of town on South Washington Street, built in 1684 and still in use by a Quaker congregation.

The most impressive place to stay in Easton is the stately **Tidewater Inn** (101 E. Dover St., 410/822-1300 or 800/678-8946, $149 and up), a well restored landmark in the center of town, which offers guests free carriage rides around town on Saturdays in December. Easton also holds the comfortable (and bike-friendly!) **Bishop's House** B&B (214 Goldsborough St., 410/820-7290, $185 and up) and the usual range of motels and fast-food places along the US-50 frontage.

> Maryland's Eastern Shore is excellent bicycling country, with generally flat quiet roads winding through farmlands, forests, and waterfront fishing villages.

St. Michaels and Oxford

The pride and joy of the Eastern Shore is the Chesapeake Bay village of **St. Michaels,** a colonial-era shipbuilding center turned yachting haven that's home to the excellent **Chesapeake Bay Maritime Museum** (410/745-2916, daily, $15). Located right on the waterfront at the center of town, the museum has extensive displays of skipjacks and other historic sailing vessels, which you can watch being restored in the museum workshops. There are also diverse pieces of fishing and hunting gear, plus a working lighthouse, all displayed to conjure up traditional Eastern Shore maritime life.

> West of St. Michaels, at the far end of Hwy-33, **Tilghman Island** is home port for Chesapeake Bay's sole surviving fleet of skipjacks, the unique sail-powered vessels used to harvest oysters from the bay.

Although it's full of lovingly maintained old houses and commercial buildings as well as working wharves, chandlers, and sail lofts, St. Michaels is also a major tourist trap, with all the souvenir shops you could want. The lovely harbor is lined with restaurants like the **St. Michaels Crab and Steakhouse** (305 Mulberry St., 410/745-3737, Thurs.-Mon.).

DETOUR: BALTIMORE

The best description of Baltimore's quirky charms came from film director John Waters, who has drawn considerable inspiration from his offbeat hometown. In his book *Shock Value*, Waters wrote: "I would never want to live anywhere but Baltimore. You can look far and wide, but you'll never discover a stranger city with such extreme style. It's as if every eccentric in the South decided to move north, ran out of gas in Baltimore, and decided to stay." Signs of this can be seen at the **American Visionary Art Museum** (800 Key Hwy., 410/244-1900, Tues.-Sun. 10am-6pm, $16), which displays an array of works by outsider and self-taught artists in every medium imaginable—painted packing crates, "art cars," and so on—south of the popular Inner Harbor waterfront redevelopment.

Location for the nostalgic 1980s film *Diner*, as well as the acclaimed TV shows *Homicide* and *The Wire*, Baltimore is not as faded or gritty as that might sound. For typically Baltimorean food and drink, head to historic **Fell's Point**, a mile east of the Inner Harbor. One of a dozen good places to eat here is **Bertha's** (734 S. Broadway, 410/327-5795), a friendly little café famed for (grit-free!) mussels and other seafood specialties. To sample the other local specialty, Chesapeake Bay crab, head down to the Patapsco waterfront to **Nick's Fish House** (2600 Insulator Dr., 410/347-4123).

If you're interested in catching a ball game, the **Baltimore Orioles** play at Camden Yards (888/848-2473) right downtown.

art car at the American Visionary Art Museum

Salisbury

After seeing the museum and wandering around the town, if you want to get a feel for the unspoiled Chesapeake, follow the signs southeast from St. Michaels to the historic **ferry** (daily 9am-sunset, $20 per car round-trip, $5 pedestrians round-trip) that shuttles across the Tred Avon River every half hour or so between **Bellevue** and **Oxford** (pop. 651). Oxford, a truly sleepy little Eastern Shore town, has hardly changed since the 1760s, when it was one of two authorized ports-of-entry into colonial-era Maryland. Wander along the waterfront or south along Morris Street to the village center, through what may be the best-preserved colonial townscape left in America. No less an authority than James Michener, who lived in St. Michaels for many years, went so far as to say that the crab cakes served inside the circa-1710 **Robert Morris Inn** (410/226-5111, $145 and up), opposite the ferry dock, were among the best he'd ever tasted.

Cambridge

Founded in 1684 on the south bank of the broad Choptank River, busy **Cambridge** (pop. 12,326), unlike sleepy Oxford, is a market town for the surrounding farmlands. Still somewhat industrial in feel, thanks to its now-closed canning and packing plants, Cambridge has some attractive corners, and is also home to the Eastern Shore's most bizarre range of annual festivals, from February's **World Champion Muskrat Skinning Contest** to powerboat regattas and antique-airplane fly-ins held throughout the summer. You can get a good sense of Cambridge character by stopping for a meal at downtown's popular brew-pub **RAR Brewing** (504 Poplar St., 443/225-5664), west of US-50, or at **Cindy's Eastside Kitchen** (3127 Aireys Rd., 410/228-3830), a cozy breakfast café along the old US-50 frontage east of town.

US-50 through Cambridge has been named the **Harriet Tubman Highway,** in memory of the Underground Railroad leader who was born enslaved and lived much of her life in this part of Maryland. Her birthplace and other significant

Ocean City is also a stop along the **Atlantic Coast** route (see page 390). Full coverage of **Ocean City** begins on page 403.

locations are being preserved as part of the new **Harriet Tubman Underground Railroad National Historic Park** (4068 Golden Hill Rd., 410/221-2290), which opened in 2017 at the heart of the extensive marshlands and natural areas of the Blackwater National Wildlife Refuge. It has extensive exhibits about her life and work as well as self-guided cycling and driving tours on the Tubman Byway to help understand her political and personal contexts.

HARRIET TUBMAN.

Salisbury

Though largely modern and commercial, **Salisbury** (pop. 30,343) has preserved part of its older townscape in a pedestrianized downtown shopping district and in the Newton Historic District, a collection of dainty Victorian-era houses along Elizabeth Street. The one place to stop is the **Ward Museum of Wildfowl Art** (909 S. Schumaker Dr., daily, $7), on the Salisbury University campus, which has a comprehensive collection of carved decoys and other hunting-related arts and crafts. Though this may not sound immediately enticing, the museum does explore varying aspects of the engagement between people and the "natural" world, and the items on display, ranging from Native American reed figures to highly collectible decoys, are all beautifully crafted.

TM

Crossing the coastal wetlands and estuaries, US-50 races east from Salisbury, bypassing a few small towns like Willards and Whaleyville, which are best seen by following the Hwy-346 frontage road. The two routes run parallel, joining each other 30 miles east in the old-time beach resort of **Ocean City.**

Throughout the summer, Salisbury is home to the popular **Delmarva Shorebirds,** the Baltimore Orioles' Class A farm team, who play at the modern **Perdue Stadium** (410/219-3112, $8 and up) off US-50 on Hobbs Road.

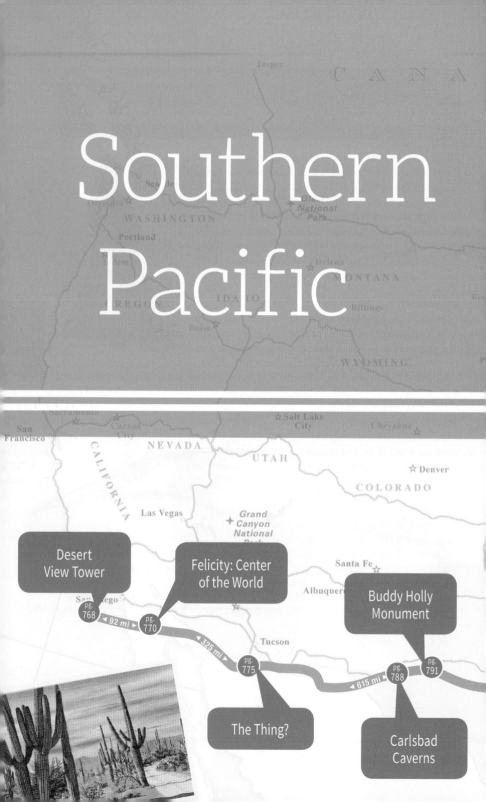

Southern
Pacific

Desert
View Tower
pg. 768

◄ 92 mi ►

Felicity: Center
of the World
pg. 770

◄ 325 mi ►

The Thing?
pg. 775

Buddy Holly
Monument
pg. 788

◄ 615 mi ►

Carlsbad
Caverns
pg. 788

pg. 791

From deserts to bayou swamps and Tex-Mex to barbecue, this route offers a full-flavored taste of America.

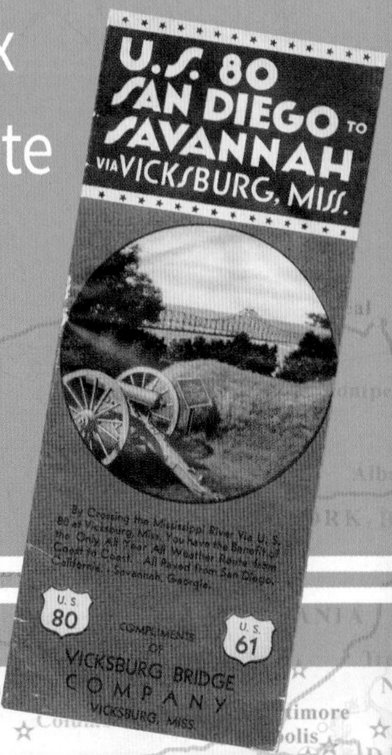
U.S. 80
SAN DIEGO TO SAVANNAH
VIA VICKSBURG, MISS.
By Crossing the Mississippi River Via U.S. 80 at Vicksburg, Miss. You have the Benefit of the Only All Year All Weather Route from Coast to Coast. All Paved from San Diego, California, to Savannah, Georgia.
U.S. 80
COMPLIMENTS OF
VICKSBURG BRIDGE COMPANY
VICKSBURG, MISS.
U.S. 61

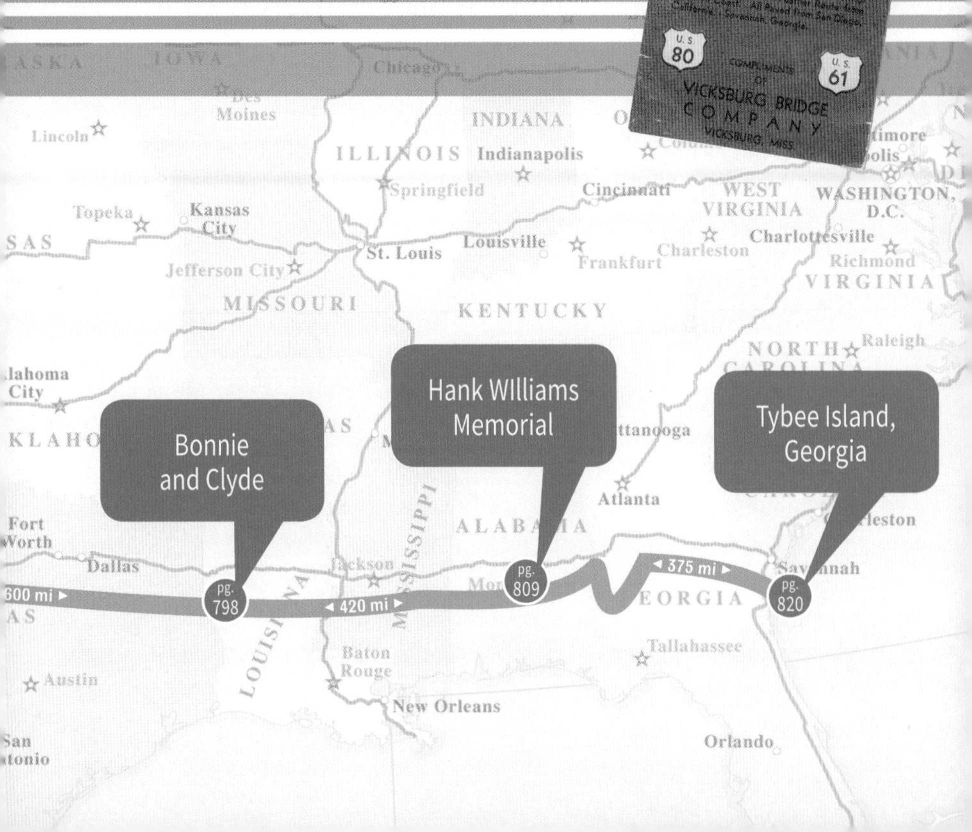
Bonnie and Clyde
pg. 798
Hank WIlliams Memorial
pg. 809
Tybee Island, Georgia
pg. 820
600 mi
420 mi
375 mi
Lincoln
Des Moines
IOWA
Chicago
INDIANA
ILLINOIS
Indianapolis
Springfield
Cincinnati
WEST VIRGINIA
WASHINGTON, D.C.
Topeka
Kansas City
St. Louis
Louisville
Frankfurt
Charleston
Charlottesville
Richmond
VIRGINIA
Jefferson City
MISSOURI
KENTUCKY
NORTH CAROLINA
Raleigh
Atlanta
ALABAMA
MISSISSIPPI
Dallas
Jackson
Savannah
GEORGIA
LOUISIANA
Baton Rouge
New Orleans
Tallahassee
Austin
Orlando

Between San Diego, California, and Savannah, Georgia

Following old US-80 and its contemporary equivalents across the nation's southern tier takes you through more varied cultural and physical landscapes than you'll find along any other cross-country route. Throughout this roughly 3,000-mile journey, you can shift from one world to another in the time it takes to play a baseball game. Heading east from the golden sands of San Diego, within a few hours you reach the harshly beautiful Southwestern deserts, their trademark saguaro cacti creating a backdrop straight out of a Road Runner cartoon. The route's central segment crosses the thousand-mile "you can see it for two days" plains of New Mexico and West Texas, where pump jacks jig for oil and cattle graze beneath a limitless sky. To the east spreads yet another land, starting at the cotton-rich Mississippi Delta and continuing along the foot of the Appalachians to the bayous and sea islands surrounding the country's grandest little city, Savannah.

Especially memorable is the diversity of people and prevailing customs along the route, all highlighted by a range of accents and lingos. For travelers, this cultural diversity is perhaps most accessible in the food. Many regional American cuisines—Tex-Mex, Cajun, Creole, and barbecue, to name a few—were originally developed somewhere along this route, and roadside restaurants continue to serve up local specialties that lend new meaning to the word "authentic." Along the open borders between Texas and New and old Mexico, in unselfconscious adobe sheds with corrugated metal roofs, chili-powered salsa accompanies roast-steak fajitas; in Louisiana, entrées featuring catfish fillets or bright-red boiled shrimp grace most menus; and everywhere you turn, roadside stands dish out reputedly the best barbecue in the universe.

ding, or pay your respects at the final resting places of Hank Williams, Jimmie Rodgers, and Duane Allman. After dark, listen to the current and next generation making music in roadside bars and clubs.

A wealth of distinctive literature has grown out of these regions, and you can visit dozens of characteristic literary scenes, live and in the flesh: Carson McCullers's "Ballad of the Sad Café" and other tales, which capture 1920s life in Columbus, Georgia; Cormac McCarthy's wide-open tales of the Texas frontier; the diner from *Fried Green Tomatoes;* and the original God's Little Acre and Tobacco Road. But there's also sober history, from Wild West Tombstone and Bonnie and Clyde's death site, to the Dallas intersection where JFK was assassinated, to the streets of Selma, where the civil rights movement burst forth onto the nation's front pages. Best of all, many of the most fascinating places along the way remain refreshingly free of the slick promotion that greets you in more established tourist destinations. The relatively low profile of tourism here, and the fact that only a few big cities lie in wait to swallow your vacation dollars, help make this part of the country relatively inexpensive for visitors—but even at twice the price, it would be well worth experiencing.

We've noted favorite places along the route, but all you need to do is follow your nose, or look for a line of pickup trucks, and you'll find yourself in culinary heaven.

On an equal footing with the fine food is the incredible variety of music you'll hear, whether it's in a Texas honky-tonk or in the juke joints and gospel-spreading churches of Mississippi and Alabama. Along the Mexican border, from San Diego well past El Paso, radio stations blast out an anarchic mix of multilingual music, part country-western, part traditional Mexican, with accordions and guitars and lyrics flowing seamlessly from one language to the other and back—often in a single line of a song. Along the way, you can visit the hometowns of Buddy Holly, Little Richard, and Otis Red-

CALIFORNIA

From the Pacific bays and golden beaches of **San Diego,** you can choose between two routes as you head east across Southern California: the high-speed I-8 freeway up and over pine-forested mountains, or a winding drive along the Mexican border. We've covered the slower, more southerly route that follows the remnants of old US-80 through sleepy border towns and past a pair of unique roadside attractions—the funky old **Desert View Tower** and the oddly endearing "Official Center of the World" at tiny **Felicity.** Also included is a quick side trip south of the border to beer-making **Tecate.** But no matter which way you choose, eventually you'll have to cross many monotonous miles of the **Mojave Desert,** a barren, dry, and inhospitable land.

San Diego (see page 106) is at the southern end of our **Pacific Coast** road trip. Full coverage of that route begins on page 8.

Point Loma: Cabrillo National Monument

The sturdy headland that protects San Diego's extensive harbor from the open Pacific Ocean, **Point Loma** has long been occupied by the military, whose many fences, radio towers, and gun emplacements all seem to disappear at the tip, where the **Cabrillo National Monument** (619/557-5450, daily 9am-5pm, $10 per car) protects a breathtaking 160 acres of cliffs and tide pools. It was set aside in 1913 to remember the efforts of conquistador Juan Rodríguez Cabrillo, who explored the California coast in 1542, sailing under a Spanish flag. There's also an old lighthouse, some nice trails, and a visitor center describing the whole shebang.

Across San Diego: Old US-80

From Point Loma and the Pacific Ocean, old US-80 bends south past the San Diego

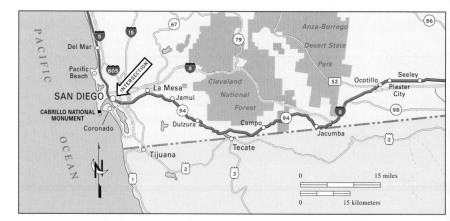

International Airport (sometimes referred to as Lindbergh Field, named for Charles Lindbergh and featuring one of the most hair-raising landing patterns of any big American airport) and through downtown along 12th Avenue and Market Street. Old US-80 then veers north again along the Cabrillo Freeway (one of the oldest in the country) through historic **Balboa Park,** home to the San Diego Zoo, a replica of London's Old Globe Theater, and many grand Spanish colonial buildings that have been standing here since the 1915 Panama-California Exposition.

East of San Diego, old US-80 follows El Cajon Boulevard past San Diego State University and a dozen miles of old motels, cafés, and gas stations before it reaches the foothill town of **La Mesa,** where you can leave old US-80 (which runs alongside the high-speed I-8 freeway) and turn onto the two-lane blacktop of Hwy-94. Twisting to the southeast around the 4,000-foot peaks of this part of the **Cleveland National Forest,** Hwy-94 traverses classic Southern California landscape: rolling, chaparral-covered hillsides rising above grassy ranch lands and stately valley oaks.

Tecate, Mexico

After passing through **Jamul** and **Dulzura,** two quiet ranching towns that appear on the verge of extinction due to San Diego's rapidly approaching sprawl, some 40 miles east of downtown San Diego along Hwy-94, you'll spot a sign marking the turnoff south to the Mexican border town of **Tecate** (pop. 64,764). Known around the world as the source of tangy Tecate beer—by most accounts, the brew that started people drinking beer with a squeeze of fresh lime—Tecate is in the top tier of enjoyable border towns, if only by virtue of being cleaner, quieter, safer, and much less "touristy" than Tijuana. Potential stops include a nice park, four blocks south of the border; the usual restaurants, cantinas, and souvenir shops; plus two special stops: the idyllic and rejuvenating **Rancho la Puerta spa resort** (858/764-5500 or 800/443-7565), and the historic **Tecate Brewery** (+52-665/654-9490, Mon.-Sat.). The brewery, now part of the Dutch megabrewer Heineken, offers free tours by appointment; call ahead for a reservation.

border crossing at Tecate

Because of insurance concerns and Homeland Security hassles, it's a good idea to leave your car on the U.S. side of the border and cross into Mexico on foot, passport in hand. East of the Tecate area, Hwy-94 runs along the U.S. side of the border for 41 miles before joining the I-8 freeway.

Campo

Set in a broad valley midway between Tecate and the I-8 freeway, tiny **Campo** (pop. 2,684) has one main attraction, the **Pacific Southwest Railway Museum** (619/478-9937, Sat.-Sun. and holidays 9am-5pm, $5 adults, $2.50 children), at the west end of town on Forrest Gate Road. Along with an extensive outdoor collection of old locomotives and carriages, the museum offers **train rides** (11am and 2:30pm, $15 adults, $5 children) on restored steam- and diesel-powered trains, including a 12-mile round-trip through the surrounding countryside. Campo also marks the southern end of the Pacific Crest Trail, which winds for 2,650 or so miles between Canada and Mexico.

Jacumba and the Desert View Tower

South of the I-8 freeway on a surviving stretch of the old US-80 highway, **Jacumba** (pop. 561) is a former spa and resort town where Clark Gable, Marlene Dietrich, and countless others soaked themselves silly in the free-flowing natural hot springs. Established in 1852 as a station on the stagecoach mail route across the desert, Jacumba had its heyday during the 1920s. While little remains apart from the water, it makes a great place to stop. The mineral-rich hot springs still flow into outdoor pools and private hot tubs at **Jacumba Hot Springs Spa & Resort** (44500 Old US-80, 619/766-4333, $25 per day), which includes motel rooms for$99 and up, a good on-site restaurant, and a popular "locals" bar.

Southern gateway to the splendid 600,000-acre **Anza-Borrego Desert State Park,** one of the largest and wildest desert parks in the country, the Jacumba area is also home to one of the great road-trip stops in southern California: the **Desert View**

Anza-Borrego Desert State Park

Tower (619/766-9139, daily 8:30am-dusk, $6.50). The four-story cut-stone structure was built in 1923 to commemorate the pioneers who struggled across the arid desert.

Inside the tower, a small but interesting museum displays a haphazard collection of desert Americana, such as Navajo blankets and Native American artifacts, with similar items on sale in the gift shop. At the top of the tower, an observation platform offers views across 100 miles of desert landscape, sliced by the I-8 freeway. (You can also see places where the excavations for I-8 have left sections of the old US-80 roadway stranded on artificially constructed mesas, 50 feet or so higher than the modern freeway.)

Across the parking lot from the Desert View Tower, a hillside of quartzite granite boulders has been carved with dozens of three-dimensional figures. Most of the figures are of skulls, snakes, and lizards—with real lizards sometimes racing each other across the rocks. The whole ensemble was created during the Great Depression by an out-of-work engineer named W. T. Ratcliffe.

The Desert View Tower stands at a cool 3,000 feet above sea level, seven miles east of Jacumba, on the north side of I-8 at the In-Ko-Pah Road exit; billboards point the way. For more information on visiting Anza-Borrego Desert State Park, which covers some 600,000 acres of desiccated desert, contact the **ranger station** (760/767-4205) in Borrego Springs.

> When driving in the desert, always keep the gas tank as full as possible, and always carry at least one gallon of drinking water per person. In case of trouble, stay with your car. Don't walk off in search of help; let it find you.

El Centro

Located some 50 feet below sea level, midway across California at the heart of the agricultural Coachella Valley, **El Centro** (pop. 44,201) was founded in 1906 and has since bloomed into a bustling small city, thanks to irrigation water diverted from the Colorado River. Melons, grapefruit, and dates are the region's prime agricultural products, along with alfalfa grown to feed the many dairy cows. There's not a lot here that doesn't depend on farming.

> **El Centro** is the winter home of the aerial acrobats of the U.S. Navy's Blue Angels, who can sometimes be spotted practicing their loops and rolls in the skies around the city. It is also the birthplace of Cher.

Though not much of a destination, El Centro is still the best place to break a journey between San Diego and the Arizona border, so fill your gas tank, if nothing else. All the national food and lodging chains are here, along with neon-signed local ones along the I-8 Business Loop. Local character and tasty Mexican food abound at the good **Sobe's** (1151 S. 4th St., 760/352-6838), three blocks north of I-8.

Algodones Dunes

In the middle of the southern Mojave Desert, 42 miles east of El Centro, a rest area south of the I-8 freeway at the Gray's Well Road exit gives access to the enticing pink-hued sands of the **Algodones Dunes,** which stretch on both sides of the freeway for

From 1857 to 1861 the original Butterfield Stage, which carried mail and passengers from St. Louis to San Francisco, followed the approximate route of I-8 across Southern California. The route was originally blazed by Spanish explorer Juan de Anza, on his way to found San Francisco in 1775.

over 40 miles. The slender dunes, which measure at most eight miles wide and reach heights of 200 to 300 feet, have been seen in Hollywood movies from *Beau Geste* to *Star Wars* and often cover the highway in blowing sandstorms. Though you can amble around on foot, be aware that the dunes themselves are under constant abuse from hordes of motorcycles and dune buggies.

If you're really, really interested in old highways, you won't want to miss the reconstructed remnants of a wooden plank road, built across the sands in 1915 and later replaced by the original US-80 highway. Preserved by the dry desert air and arranged to form a 100-foot section across the dunes, this fenced-off museum piece is along the south side of I-8, two miles west of the Gray's Well Road exit. The All-American Canal, which waters the Coachella Valley, snakes alongside the freeway.

Felicity: The Center of the World Pyramid

One of the odder sites in the Southwestern deserts—and competition for this title is pretty fierce—sits just north of the I-8 freeway in the tiny but happily named town of **Felicity** (pop. 2). Local resident Jacques-André Istel—author of a children's fairy tale concerning a scholarly fire-breathing dragon named Coe who lives at the center of the world reading fireproof books and eating the nearby Chocolate Mountains—named the "town" after his wife Felicia and somehow convinced France, China, and Imperial County to recognize that Felicity is, legally and officially, the center of the world.

A 21-foot-high pink terrazzo pyramid stands above the exact spot, which you can

I STOOD AT THE OFFICIAL
CENTER OF THE WORLD
FELICITY, CALIFORNIA USA

visit on regular **guided tours** (760/572-0100, daily late Nov.-mid-Apr., $3). The fee also buys a certificate saying you've stood at "The Official Center of the World." You can climb a set of stairs that used to belong to the Eiffel Tower and sift through sundry souvenirs in the gift shop.

ARIZONA

Between the Colorado River, which divides Arizona from California, and the Phoenix-Tucson megalopolis in the middle of the state, there is not much to attract the traveler off the freeway. However, the rather complete absence of interesting places in southwestern Arizona is more than made up for by the wealth of fascinating things to see in the state's southeast corner. Here you'll find such legendary sites as **Tombstone**—home of the O.K. Corral—and other finely presented reminders of the state's Wild West heritage, along with some of Arizona's most beautiful natural scenery.

Yuma

Among the hottest, driest, and fastest-growing areas in the country, **Yuma** (pop. 94,906) was first settled in the 1770s at the site of one of the few good crossings

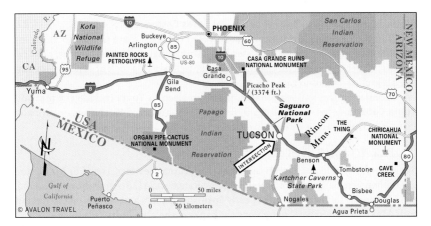

along the Colorado River. Dozens of decaying old adobe buildings around town testify to Yuma's lengthy history, and a select few places are preserved as historic parks. The **Yuma Quartermaster Depot State Historic Park** (928/783-0071, daily Oct.-May, Tues.-Sun. June-Sept. $4), along the river and I-8 at the north end of 4th Avenue, includes buildings that have been restored to their appearance prior to the arrival of the railroad in 1877, when supplies for U.S. troops throughout the Southwest arrived here by steamboat from the Gulf of California.

Around the time the railroad arrived, a full century after its founding by Spanish missionaries, Yuma was the site of Arizona Territory's main prison. Convicts struggled in the 120°F heat to build the stone and adobe prison, which earned a reputation as the "Hellhole of Arizona," due in large part to the summer heat and the brutality of its regime, though park rangers emphasize the fact that prisoners had access to a library and other facilities unusual at the time. It operated 33 years until it was closed in 1909 and is now preserved as the state-run **Yuma Territorial Prison State Historic Park** (928/783-4771, daily 9am-5pm Oct.-May, Thurs.-Mon. June-Sept., $6), well posted along the north side of I-8 at the North 4th Avenue exit; the site consists of a few of the cells and the main gate, as well as a small museum.

From the prison, a rickety pedestrian-only steel bridge (formerly part of US-80)

leads across the Colorado River to California and the **St. Thomas Indian Mission Church** on the Fort Yuma Quechan Indian Reservation.

Along with the usual national franchises, Yuma has a number of decent places to eat, ranging from world-class chorizo-and-eggs and chicken fried steak at **Brownie's Restaurant** (1145 S. 4th Ave./old US-80, 928/783-7911) to the pool

The Colorado River forms the border between California and Arizona, and it marks the line between the Pacific and mountain time zones. Most of Arizona, however, doesn't observe daylight saving time, so in summer both states are on the same time.

Yuma's **KBLU 560 AM** offers round-the-clock news and talk radio.

tables, burgers, and sandwiches at ancient **Lutes Casino** (221 S. Main St., 928/782-2192) in the historic old downtown area. Voted the "Best Place to Stop in Yuma" by the *Arizona Republic* newspaper, Lutes is a barnlike hall full of old photos, political posters, street signs, and all manner of junk, well worth a look at least for its passionately played domino games.

Along with the national chains, places to sleep in Yuma include the pleasant **Yuma Cabana** (2151 S. 4th Ave., 928/783-8311, around $40 and up), with palm trees, a nice pool, and a recliner in every room.

Yuma to Gila Bend: I-8

Spanning 110 miles of barren desert east of Yuma, between the U.S. Air Force's 2.7-million-acre Barry M. Goldwater Bombing Range and a U.S. Army Proving Ground, the I-8 freeway follows the route of early Spanish explorers and settlers on the flat but forbidding El Camino del Diablo, along the banks of the usually dry Gila River.

Twelve miles or so west of Gila Bend, off I-8 at exit 102, Painted Rocks Road leads 11 miles north to a Bureau of Land Management-run site where petroglyphs, carved into the boulders by the Hohokam people around AD 1400 and earlier, cover the rocks.

East of 787-foot-high Telegraph Pass, 20 miles outside Yuma, the old US-80 highway reappears along the north side of the freeway, running through old-time desert outposts. If you're hungry, the flyspeck ranching community of **Tacna** has a great place to eat burgers, lamb chops, and a full menu of other Spanish and American dishes: **Basque Etchea** (928/785-4027, Tues.-Sun.). Take I-8 exit 42, then head north across the railroad tracks.

Another great middle-of-nowhere desert oasis, along I-8 at milepost 67, is **Dateland**, 67 miles east of Yuma and 49 miles west of Gila Bend. Dateland has a 24-hour gas station, a **café** (928/454-2772), an RV park, and a gift shop selling dates in all possible forms, including refreshing date milk shakes. The top-quality, hand-pollinated Medjool dates are grown in the adjacent nine-acre grove.

Gila Bend

The only place approaching a town between Yuma and Phoenix or Tucson, **Gila Bend** (pop. 2,071) is regularly the "Hottest Spot in the Country"—a title of which it is so proud that, more than once, it's been caught inflating the numbers. First settled as a main stop on the Butterfield Stage route, Gila Bend doesn't offer much relief for the senses, though it does have some photogenic old motels and all the gas stations, restrooms, and restaurants you could reasonably expect to find in the middle of the Arizona desert.

From Gila Bend, Hwy-85 runs south to the beautiful and totally deserted **Organ Pipe Cactus National Monument** (520/387-6849, daily, $12) before linking up with Hwy-86 to loop east to Tucson. Be aware that the area is subject to road closures.

One place to eat is the **Space Age Restaurant** (401 E. Pima Ave., 928/683-2761), downtown off exit 115. Marked by a flying-saucer-shaped sign, it's part of the **Best Western Space Age Lodge** motel (928/683-2273, $80 and up). Both are essential stops for any *Jetsons*-age traveler, though the refurbishment after a fire has diminished the 1960s Space Age charm.

Old US-80 via Phoenix

I-8 is by far the fastest way east from Gila Bend to Tucson and beyond, but if you have the time and inclination to follow the old road, it took the long way around: From Gila Bend, US-80 veers north across the usually dry Gila River along what's now an unmarked county road, then east through the towns of Arlington, Palo Verde, and **Buckeye,** where a 25-odd-foot statue of "Hobo Joe" stands along East Monroe Avenue downtown. US-80 runs through downtown Phoenix on Van Buren Street (which was also US-60 and US-70) before heading south to Tucson.

Saguaro National Park and Tucson Mountain Park

Northwest of Tucson, the more popular half of **Saguaro National Park** protects extensive stands of saguaro cactus as well as ancient petroglyphs, spring wildflowers, and generally gorgeous desert scenery. From I-10 at Cortaro (exit 246), a loop road runs southwest, then back east through rugged mountainous terrain,

The saguaro cactus, whose creamy white blossoms are the Arizona state flower, blooms in May-June, depending on the year's rainfall and high temperatures.

which, though popular, is a great place to get a feel for the Sonora Desert landscape. A **visitor center** (520/733-5158, daily, $15 per vehicle) has details of the many hikes here, like the popular Hugh Norris Trail, which winds along a mountain ridge to the 4,687-foot summit of Wasson Peak.

There's more hiking, plus camping and the excellent **Arizona-Sonora Desert Museum** (520/883-2702, daily, $21) in the adjacent **Tucson Mountain Park.**

Across Tucson: Old US-80

From the north and west, the best old road introduction to Tucson is the so-called **Miracle Mile,** a few blocks of slightly seedy old neon-signed motels, right off the I-10 freeway at exit 255. From here, old US-80 follows a series of one-way surface streets into compact downtown Tucson, first following 5th Avenue, then 6th Avenue, the pre-interstate main highway.

Saguaro National Park

Cactus Forest Scenic Loop

About a dozen miles east of Tucson, on the slopes of the Tanque Verde and Rincon Mountains, the eastern half of **Saguaro National Park** covers nearly 58,000 acres of rolling desert landscape. Named in honor of the anthropomorphic saguaro cactus, which here reaches heights up to 60 feet and lives as long as 175 years, the park is best seen by following eight-mile **Cactus Forest Scenic Loop Drive**, along which numerous hiking trails give close-up looks at the multilimbed succulents. For more information and details of hiking opportunities, stop at the **visitors center** (520/733-5153).

Tucson (see page 162) marks the junction with our **Border to Border** road trip along US-93. Full coverage of that route begins on page 110.

Colossal Cave

Beyond the Rincon Mountains section of Saguaro National Park, 25 miles or so from downtown Tucson via the Old Spanish Trail, **Colossal Cave** (520/647-7275, daily, $5 per car, plus $16 and up per tour) is another great place to stop. A huge old limestone cavern that offers a cool (in every sense of the word!) escape from the sweltering summer heat, this is one of the state's

most enduring tourist attractions. (Avid cavers will appreciate comparing Colossal Cave, a "dry" cave, with the newly opened Kartchner Caverns, a "wet" cave where the humidity will have you dripping with perspiration.) Colossal Cave was used in Wild West times by train robbers who escaped here with $72,000 in gold and currency. Most of the limited "development" here (footpaths, a museum, and a gift shop) was done as a Civilian Conservation Corps project during the New Deal 1930s.

The surrounding ranch land has been opened as a nature reserve with hiking, horseback riding, and mountain-bike trails. The ranch buildings have been preserved as a museum of early Arizona life.

Kartchner Caverns State Park

On the other side of I-10 from Colossal Cave, one of Arizona's most long-awaited "openings" was that of **Kartchner Caverns State Park** (520/586-4100), a massive limestone cavern—over 2.5 miles long—that is rated by experts as one of the 10 most beautiful in the world. It was discovered by a pair of avid cavers, Randy Tufts and Gary Tenen, back in 1974. It then took 25 years of negotiation and more than $28 million worth of careful construction of tunnels and facilities before the cave was opened to the public. Advance reservations for one of the **guided tours** (around $25) are all but required if you want to enter the cave to see the 150-foot-square Throne Room, with its 60-foot ceiling, or the larger but less lofty Rotunda Room, or any of the other phantasmagorical sights. The caverns, which are kept at near 100 percent humidity by a set of airlocks at the entrance, are remarkable for their diverse and delicate formations, including over 30 different types of stalactites, stalagmites, columns, draperies, shields, and helictites, not to mention

the longest "soda straw" in the United States—a thin tube of limestone over 21 feet long but only a quarter-inch in diameter.

Kartchner Caverns State Park is just west of Benson, nine miles south of I-10 exit 302, along Hwy-90. If you don't manage to join a tour, it's still worth stopping at the 23,000-square-foot **visitors center** (520/586-4100, daily, $7 per vehicle) to see the movie describing the cave and its discovery. There are also some full-scale replicas of the cave's features, along with an above-ground hiking trail through native hummingbird habitat, a 62-site campground with full hookups, and four camping cabins.

Benson and the Amerind Foundation

Off I-10 along the banks of the San Pedro River, **Benson** (pop. 4,870) was founded as a Santa Fe railroad connection to booming Tombstone and the Mexican harbor town of Guaymas. Trains still rumble through town, but there's not much to see apart from fading roadside signs. **Reb's Café and Coffee Shop** (1020 W. 4th St., 520/586-3856) and the **Horseshoe Café and Bakery** (154 E. 4th St., 520/586-2872), across from the railroad tracks, are where locals go to eat. Thanks in part to the popularity of Kartchner Caverns, Benson has a number of motels congregating around I-10 exit 304.

Benson radio station **KAVV 97.7 FM** plays lots of good Waylon-and-Willie-type country hits, plus captivating accounts of local news and activities.

From Benson, our route cuts south on old US-80 (now Hwy-80), while I-10 races east over the mountains that 100-plus years ago were a stronghold of Apache warriors under Geronimo and Cochise. If you're following the interstate, a couple of sights are worth looking for. The more satisfying of these, the **Amerind Foundation Museum** (520/586-3666, Tues.-Sun., $10), lies 13 miles or so east of Benson, off Dragoon Road a mile southeast of I-10 exit 318. Started in 1937, the private nonprofit museum is devoted to the study of local Native American cultures, with everything from ancient arrowheads to contemporary Pueblo pottery on display in the spacious mission-style buildings. Not surprisingly, the best collections are of Hopi, Navajo, and Apache artifacts, with well-presented exhibits of ceremonial and domestic objects—kachina dolls, rugs, and ritual costumes.

I-10: The Thing?

Advertised by signs all along the freeway, one of the country's odder roadside attractions stands atop 5,013-foot Texas Summit, along I-10 at exit 322: **The Thing** (520/586-2581, $2). A gas station, a gift shop, and a Dairy Queen stand in front of a prefab shed full of stuff ranging from a Rolls Royce said to have been used by Adolf Hitler to The Thing itself, a mummified corpse whose "secret identity" has yet to be revealed. "What is it?" the signs ask.

Tombstone

While I-10 races east over the mountains, our more scenic route, promoted by tourism authorities as the "Cochise Trail," winds south on old US-80 through the Wild West town of **Tombstone** (pop. 1,300), "The Town Too Tough to Die." The route loops along the Mexican border before rejoining I-10 across the New Mexico border.

Tombstone's famous shoot-out is re-enacted.

Though it's just 24 miles south of the freeway, and regularly inundated by bikers, RVers, and busloads of tourists, the rough-and-ready mining town of Tombstone has kept itself looking pretty much as it did back in the 1880s, when 7,500 miners called it home and one of the more mythic events of the Wild West took place here: the shootout at the **O.K. Corral.**

Historians, and everyone in Tombstone, still debate the chain of events of October 26, 1881. Was Wyatt Earp a sharpshooting savior, out to make Tombstone safe for decent society? Or was he a grandstanding cowboy whom history has romanticized? Decide for yourself after hearing all sides of the story. The O.K. Corral is still here, a block south of Fremont Street (old US-80), on Allen Street between 3rd and 4th Streets, with life-size black leather-clad statues taking the places of Virgil and Wyatt Earp facing down the Clanton brothers. Nearby, in a fenced-off outdoor theater, gun-slinging actors stage re-creations of the shootout. To see any or all of this, you have to buy a ticket at the entertaining **Historama** (520/457-3456, daily, around $10), adjacent to the OK Corral.

The dead men, and many hundreds of others, ended up at **Boothill Graveyard** (520/457-3300, daily, free), along the highway at the northwestern edge of town, where you can wander among 300 wooden grave markers inscribed with all manner of rhyming epitaphs. The Boothill cemetery is the real thing, and the souvenirs in the large gift shop at the entrance are as wonderfully tacky as they come.

Though the OK Corral and Boothill are both fun, the best place to learn about Tombstone's real, as opposed to mythic, history is at the **Tombstone Courthouse State Historic Park** (520/457-3311, $5), at 3rd and Toughnut Streets. Built in 1882, this old courthouse building holds 12,000 square feet of artifacts documenting and describing the *real* Wild West.

Despite the huge numbers of people who descend on Tombstone every day, and the gauntlet of T-shirt and knickknack shops catering to them, the town is still an appealing place to visit. Enjoy a cool drink at the truly historic **Big Nose Kate's Saloon** (417 E. Allen St., 520/457-3107), named for, owned, and run by Doc

Holliday's brothel-keeper girlfriend. The authentic old saloon now hosts live music and serves the tasty "Goldie's Famous Overstuffed Reuben."

Every day in summer, just about every hour on the hour, historic gunfights are reenacted all around Tombstone. During the third week in October, the whole town comes alive with a weekend of shootouts and parades during **Helldorado Days.** Places to stay are not extensive, nor expensive: Try the centrally located **Tombstone Motel** (502 E. Fremont St., 888/455-3478 or 520/457-3478, $50 and up), on the main road.

Bisbee

A classic boom-and-bust mining town, **Bisbee** (pop. 5,221) is one of the most satisfying offbeat destinations in Arizona, combining scenic beauty, palpable history, and a good range of places to eat, drink, and enjoy yourself. Climbing up winding streets lined by 100-year-old structures—Victorian cottages, board shacks, and stately brick churches—Bisbee has attracted a diverse population of desert rats, bikers, working artists, and New Age apostles, all of whom mix amiably in the town's cafés and bars. One of the more infamous events in Bisbee's busy history occurred in July 1917, when Industrial Workers of the World representatives presented demands for better conditions. Tensions grew, and a few weeks later 1,186 men—not all of them miners on strike for better pay and conditions—were forcibly deported and literally railroaded out of town and dumped in the desert outside Hermanas, New Mexico.

Almost every summer for more than a century, the streets of Bisbee have hosted the 4th of July **Bisbee Coaster Race Soap Box Derby,** part of a generally excellent Independence Day party.

The heart of Bisbee lies north of old US-80 along Main Street, stretching west from the **Bisbee Mining and Historical Museum** (daily 10am-4pm, $8), which displays dioramas, old photos, and sundry artifacts inside the old Phelps Dodge company headquarters.

For visitors, the main event in Bisbee is the **Queen Mine** (866/432-2071 or 520/432-2071, tours daily, $13). Put on a hard hat and a miner's lamp and take a train ride down into the mine shafts and tunnels, which were in operation until 1975. Call for times for the hour-long tours, leaving from the Queen Mine building, just south of downtown along old US-80. Temperature down in the mine is a cool 47°F, so dress appropriately.

One of Arizona's most unforgettable sights, the massive **Lavender Open Pit Mine** forms a gigantic polychrome crater along Hwy-80, just south of the Queen Mine. Named not for its color—which is more rusty red than purple—but for a mine superintendent, Harrison Lavender, its ore deposits provided the bulk of Bisbee's eight billion pounds of copper before being shut down in 1974.

About two miles west of Bisbee at the 6,030-foot Mule Pass summit of old US-80, a much-abused **stone obelisk** commemorates the convict-laborers who first constructed the road in 1913. The monument stands in a somewhat scruffy parking area directly above the modern tunnel, and from it you get a great panoramic view of the surrounding Mule Mountains.

FLY'S PHOTOS

The work of Wild West photographer Camillus S. Fly (1849-1901) forms one of the primary records of life in frontier Arizona. Fly was born in Missouri and raised in Napa, California, then moved to Arizona to open a portrait studio in Tombstone, which has been restored as part of the O.K. Corral Historama complex. His iconic images, preserved in the Library of Congress and here displayed in the small gallery, include some of the earliest photos taken of Chiricahua Apache warrior Geronimo, photographed soon after his 1886 surrender. Fly's studio also displays his images of Wyatt Earp, "Doc" Holliday, and many others. What Matthew Brady was to the Civil War, Camillus S. Fly was to Tombstone in its 1880s heyday.

Bisbee Practicalities

Lined by characterful old brick buildings, Bisbee's winding Main Street has many cafés, antiques shops, art galleries, and restaurants. At the center of town, the **Copper Queen Hotel** (520/432-2216, $165 and up), looming over downtown along Howell Street, has been the best place to stay since it opened in 1902. Most of the rooms have been upgraded to include modern conveniences without losing their old-fashioned charm.

Bisbee also offers what has to be the most unusual lodging option in Arizona: the **Shady Dell RV Park** (1 Old Douglas Rd., 520/432-3567, $85-145), located just under two miles east of downtown, behind the gas station at the Hwy-80/Hwy-92 traffic circle. The Shady Dell welcomes you to stay the night—or longer—in one of eight well-restored 1940s and 1950s Airstream, Royal Mansion, and Spartanette trailers, or a pleasure boat, all filled with period furnishings. Rates are reasonable and include use of a VCR stocked with classic B-movies. Across old Hwy-80 from the Shady Dell, a few blocks of ramshackle buildings are coming back to life, hosting the healthy **Bisbee Food Coop** (72 Erie St., 520/432-4011) and the even tastier **Bisbee Breakfast Club** (75A Erie St., 520/432-5885), known for its corned beef hash-and-eggs and creamy cheesecake.

Back in Bisbee proper, the Copper Queen Hotel has a good restaurant and popular bar, while the nicest place in town is the gourmet **Café Roka** (35 Main St., 520/432-5153). Brewery Gulch, which runs north from Main Street at the east side of downtown Bisbee, once held over 50 different saloons and gambling parlors. It's considerably quieter now but still tolerates crazy drunken fun at haunts like **The Stock Exchange Saloon** (15 Brewery Ave., 520/432-1333), inside the old Bisbee

Stock Exchange, and the ancient **St. Elmo Bar** (36 Brewery Ave., 520/432-5578), which has live music most weekend nights.

The Border: Douglas and Agua Prieta

Like Bisbee, the border town of **Douglas** (pop. 16,604) grew up on copper mining, which here lasted until fairly recently: The Phelps-Dodge smelter a mile west of town was in operation until 1987, processing ores from mines in Bisbee and Mexico. Now most of the economy revolves around the many *maquiladora* plants in its much larger Mexican neighbor, **Agua Prieta** (pop. 79,138), which feels surprisingly calm and quiet, considering its border-town location.

There's not a lot to see in either Douglas or Agua Prieta, though Douglas does boast one fabulous attraction: the landmark **Gadsden Hotel** (1046 G Ave., 520/364-4481, $69 and up). Rebuilt in 1929 after a fire destroyed the 1907 original, the spacious gold-leafed lobby—one of the grandest public spaces in the state—has a pretty Tiffany-style stained-glass mural decorating its mezzanine. The small and basic rooms are bargain-priced. The hotel also has a good Mexican-American restaurant, the Casa Segovia, and a popular bar, the Saddle & Spur Tavern, its walls decorated with over 200 cattle brands from area ranches.

Much of southeastern Arizona is still open range, so keep an eye out for wildlife and livestock on the highway. At the end of summer, you're likely to see tarantulas crossing roads in search of a mate.

Cave Creek Canyon and Chiricahua National Monument

For the 50-odd miles between Douglas and the New Mexico state line, old US-80 cuts diagonally across the southeast corner of Arizona, a rugged country of mountains, canyons, and volcanic outcrops rising above sagebrush plains. There's not much to see along the highway, but to the northwest rise the enticing Pedregosa Mountains, whose forested peaks, now protected as part of the Coronado National Forest, long served as sanctuary to Chiricahua Apache people and sundry outlaws and wanted men. While you can also reach them from the north off I-10, the best access to the mountains from the south is via the aptly named hamlet of **Portal,** west of old US-80 from the New Mexico state line. In Portal, the **Portal Peak Lodge** (2358 Rock House Rd., 520/558-2223, around $85) is a welcoming oasis, offering peace and quiet, fresh food, and comfortable rooms, plus a handful of nearby cabins.

Agua Prieta was the site of skirmishes between revolutionary Pancho Villa and the Mexican army.

Above Portal to the west rise the sheer cliffs of **Cave Creek Canyon,** which writer William Least Heat-Moon described in *Blue Highways* as "one of the strangest pieces of topography I've ever seen," its pale sandstone walls looking like a sun-bleached twin of Utah's Zion National Park. Fitting in well with its astounding natural setting, Cave Creek Canyon draws visitors who come to enjoy its superb bird-watching, with more species in one place than you can find anywhere else in the United States, including hummingbirds, bright red cardinals, tanagers, and raptors. Birds and bird watchers flock to **Cave Creek Ranch** ($125 and up, 520/558-2334).

A narrow but passable (except in winter) 20-mile dirt road from Cave Creek climbs over the mountains' pine-covered 7,975-foot-high crest, ending up in the west at the foot of intriguing **Chiricahua National Monument,** a veritable "Wonderland of Rocks" whose contorted shapes were formed out of soft volcanic rhyolite by eons of erosion.

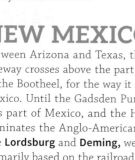

Chiricahua National Monument

NEW MEXICO

Between Arizona and Texas, the I-10 freeway crosses above the part of New Mexico known as the Bootheel, for the way it steps down toward Old Mexico. Until the Gadsden Purchase of 1854, all this was part of Mexico, and the Hispanic influence still dominates the Anglo-American. The few towns here, like **Lordsburg** and **Deming,** were founded and remain primarily based on the railroad and offer little for the passing traveler. However, at least one place is definitely worth a stop: the historic village of **Mesilla,** set around a dusty plaza just south of the region's one big city, **Las Cruces.**

Lordsburg, Silver City, and Shakespeare

Coming in from southeastern Arizona, old US-80 rejoins I-10 at a crossroads community aptly called Road Forks, near the tin-roofed ghost town of Steins. Eighteen miles farther east, the freeway swerves south to bypass the town of **Lordsburg** (pop. 2,463), named not from any religious conviction but in honor of the Southern Pacific railroad engineer who plotted it in 1880.

After delving into Texas at El Paso, this route enters New Mexico again near Carlsbad Caverns National Park.

Silver City, an evocative old mining town high in the mountains 44 miles northeast of Lordsburg, was another early stomping ground of Wild West outlaw Billy the Kid. It makes an excellent detour from the I-10 freeway between Lordsburg and Deming. If you have a taste for enigmatic ancient ruins, the **Gila Cliff Dwellings National Monument** (575/536-9461) in the wilderness north of Silver City are well worth setting aside a full day.

New Mexico's best-preserved ghost town, **Shakespeare,** is three miles south of Lordsburg on a well-marked dirt road. Briefly home to some 3,000 silver miners during the early 1870s, Shakespeare was abandoned when the mines dried up, only to be reborn during another brief mining boom in the 1880s. By the 1930s it was turned into a ranch by the Hill family, whose descendants have lived there for more than 80 years, caring for the buildings. They conduct **guided tours**

(575/542-9034, selected dates each month, $4) of the Grant House saloon, a former Butterfield Stagecoach station, and the Stratford Hotel, where Billy the Kid washed dishes as a young boy.

Deming

Some 60 miles east of Lordsburg, halfway to Las Cruces, the dusty ranching and farming community of **Deming** (pop. 14,488) advertises itself as "Deming—Home of Pure Water and Fast Ducks." This odd motto makes more sense than it may at first seem: Deming's water comes from the underground Mimbres River, and every year at the end of August the town hosts the **Great American Duck Race** (575/567-1469) for living ducks, not the rubber kind, racing 20 feet on dry land and in water—in less than two seconds!

All this may be little more than a cheap ploy to get hapless (or bored stiff, or both) travelers to turn off tedious I-10 and visit the city, but fortunately, Deming's not a bad place, boasting the excellent **Deming Luna Mimbres Museum** (301 S. Silver Ave., 575/546-2382, Mon.-Sat., free), three blocks south of Pine Street (old US-80), Deming's main drag. Besides the usual range of old pottery, sparkling rocks, and pioneer artifacts, the museum displays an endearing collection of old toys, dolls, quilts, and dental equipment—well worth at least a quick look. Don't be worried by the big tank parked out front—the museum is housed in the old Armory building.

Deming also offers great Mexican food (*chorizo y huevos*, fajitas, etc.) at **El Mirador** (510 E. Pine St., 575/544-7340).

Rooms are available at Hampton Inn and other national chains. The best place to camp is southeast of town in **Rockhound State Park** (575/546-6182, $5 day use, $8 primitive campsites, $10 developed sites), where, besides finding nice sites with hot showers, you can take home up to 15 pounds of geodes, agates, or quartz crystals.

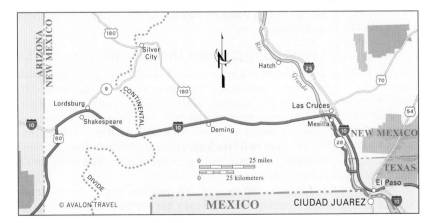

Las Cruces

Spreading along the eastern banks of the Rio Grande, at the foot of one of the country's newest national monuments, the angular Organ Mountains, **Las Cruces** (pop. 101,759) is the commercial center of a prosperous agricultural and recreational region. Named for a concentration of pioneer grave markers, Las Cruces was first settled by Spanish missionaries but is now a thoroughly modern American-looking place, with all the motels you could want and a youthful vitality made possible by the presence of the large New Mexico State University campus. One place worth searching out is **Nellie's café** (1226 W. Hadley St., 575/524-9982), a Mexican restaurant famed for spicy salsas and delicious green chiles rellenos, housed in a little brown box off Valley Boulevard on the northwest edge of downtown.

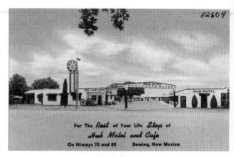

One more rare treat: West of town along I-10, the Las Cruces rest area is home to a giant statue of the New Mexico state bird, the roadrunner, crafted entirely from recycled material (or what used to be called "trash").

Along US-70 some 50 miles northeast of Las Cruces, **White Sands National Monument** protects over some 142,00 acres of gleaming white gypsum dunes.

Mesilla

The historic village of **Mesilla,** six miles southwest of downtown Las Cruces via Hwy-28, was founded across the Rio Grande on the Mexican side of the border in 1848, after the agreement of the Mexican-American War gave everything north of the river to the United States. Six years later, Mesilla became (legally at least) American again, after the Gadsden Purchase bought the entire nearly 30,000-square-mile "Bootheel" region for $10 million.

And not much has changed in the past 160-odd years: Low-slung adobe buildings set around a shady central plaza include the landmark 1855 adobe Basilica of San Albino, an old jail from which Billy the Kid escaped in 1881, and a former Butterfield Stage station that's now home to the popular restaurant **La Posta de Mesilla** (575/524-3524, daily lunch and dinner).

Juan de Oñate, for whom Hwy-28 and numerous other places in the Southwest are named, was a Spanish conquistador and colonial commander. His name is infamous in Native American circles because of his role in ordering the mutilation of 24 captive warriors from Acoma, whose right feet were cut off in 1599.

Hwy-28: Juan de Oñate Trail

Southeast from Las Cruces and Mesilla, our route dips south across the Texas border to El Paso, then continues on US-180 for some 150 miles east before reentering New Mexico at Carlsbad Caverns National Park. For the run to El Paso, you have your choice between I-10 or slower and more scenic Hwy-28, the **Juan de Oñate Trail,** which avoids the freeway and runs through the pecan groves, pepper fields, and dusty small towns that spread along the west bank of the Rio Grande.

This part of New Mexico is chili country, and there's no better place to sample the great variety of spicy peppers than at **Chope's Bar and Café** (16145 S. Hwy-28,

A TORTILLA BY ANY OTHER NAME

Carne adovada, calabacitas, posole, sopapillas . . . Menu items like these put you squarely in the lower left-hand quadrant of any U.S. map. But how do you know whether you're eating traditional New Mexican cooking, Southwestern cuisine, or the popular hybrid known as Tex-Mex? Truth is, they're all hybrids, launched more than 500 years ago when the Spanish brought European spices and domestic animals to combine with indigenous ingredients. As Spanish and Mexican settlers followed El Camino Real north from Chihuahua to Santa Fe, culinary distinctions grew out of regional variations in locally grown products along the way.

What's new is the categories: A generation ago, folks just helped themselves to

"Mexican food." Tex-Mex, as its name implies, draws from both sides of the international border, from grazing lands where vaqueros roast meat over mesquite fires. In New Mexico, it's the chilies that set the dishes apart—and set your taste buds afire. When you order a local specialty, the server may ask, "Red or green?"—referring to red or green chilies. Red chilies are usually sun-dried, while green chilies are fresh, but the flavor and spiciness varies depending on which of the 200 or more different chili varieties are used to make it. Try a little of each, a.k.a. "Christmas," and enjoy.

575/233-3420), an unpretentious cinderblock café along Hwy-28 in La Mesa, roughly midway between Mesilla and El Paso. The house specialty here is *chiles rellenos*—whole chilies stuffed with cheese and deep-fried.

TEXAS AND NEW MEXICO

Mileage-wise, the haul across Texas is the longest part of this coast-to-coast route, but as far as things to see, the state doesn't offer a high quotient per gallon. In the far-western stretches near **El Paso,** to maximize scenic interest, follow the slower but significantly more attractive route along US-180 past the beautiful **Guadalupe Mountains,** and veer across a corner of New Mexico to see the remarkable **Carlsbad Caverns.**

From Carlsbad it's a straight shot across the painfully flat **Llano Estacado,** or Staked Plains, which stretches on both sides of the New Mexico-Texas border. This section of the route is one of the least action-packed in the country—there's almost nothing for miles on end, apart from oil derricks, cattle ranches, and cotton plantations. Only a few of the sporadic towns here have any historic claim or aesthetic interest; it's basically a long day's drive across the open plains.

If you're in a hurry, you won't miss much by following the route of old US-80, alongside the I-20 freeway between El Paso and the **Dallas-Fort Worth** metropolitan area, through roughneck oil towns like **Odessa** and **Midland.**

In eastern Texas, the landscape gradually evolves into that of the Deep South, the dense pine woods doing their best to disguise the historic dependence on the oil industry—with profits far more apparent in the towers of Dallas than here at the often poverty-stricken source. Again, the interstates offer a faster way across, and you can turn off where you want to visit the few sites of interest, like tiny **Kilgore,** home of the "World's Richest Acre."

El Paso

Part of the largest and fastest-growing international community in North America, **El Paso** (pop. 683,080) was originally settled because of its site at one of the safest crossings of the Rio Grande. It later grew into a vital way station on the transcontinental Butterfield Stage and Southern Pacific Railroad. As its name suggests, for most people El Paso is a place to pass through, but there are many things here for visitors to enjoy, particularly in the wake of the thoughtful revival of the historic downtown district. In 2014 the aging City Hall was replaced with a brand-new, $75 million, 7,500-seat baseball stadium, home to the Triple-A **El Paso Chihuahuas** (1 Ballpark Plaza, 915/533-2273), top farm club for the San Diego Padres.

El Paso's hard-to-find **Concordia Cemetery** (it's just northwest of the junction of I-10 and US-54) is the final resting place of John Wesley Hardin, the "Fastest Gun in the West" before he got killed in 1895.

One of the most interesting aspects of El Paso is the border itself, which for years followed the Rio Grande (known as the Río Bravo in Mexico), whose frequent changes in course caused innumerable problems for the two governments. Finally, in 1968, the river was run through a concrete channel so it could not change course. El Paso has at least three other unique claims to fame: It's the home of Tony Lama boots, which are available at significant discounts at three showrooms around town;

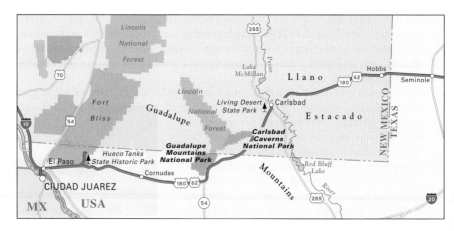

the "World's Largest Harley-Davidson Dealership," **Barnett's** (8272 Gateway Blvd. E., 915/592-5804), is along I-10; and the University of Texas El Paso (UTEP) campus, along I-10 west of town, has the only buildings in North America designed to look like Bhutanese monasteries. College basketball fans may also know that in 1965-1966 UTEP, then called Texas Western, became the first all-black team to win the NCAA championships, a story told in the book and film *Glory Road*.

Hidden away amid El Paso's horizontal sprawl are the oldest Spanish colonial missions that still stand in what is now the United States. These three churches—Ysleta, Socorro, and San Elizario—stand along the well-signed "Mission Trail," southeast of downtown between the Rio Grande and I-10.

Places to eat in and around El Paso tend, not surprisingly, to specialize in Tex-Mex food. One unique stop for breakfast or lunch is at the friendly **H&H Car Wash and Coffee Shop** (701 E. Yandell Dr., 915/533-1144), just north of downtown, where you can enjoy delicious scrambled eggs and chorizo or chile relleno burritos while getting your car cleaned at the adjacent car wash. Another classic is **Forti's Mexican Elder Restaurant** (321 Chelsea St., 915/772-0066), east of downtown near the Paisano Avenue exit off I-10.

El Paso's grand old **Camino Real Hotel** (101 S. El Paso St., 915/534-3050, $89 and up) has a beautiful bar off the lobby with a Tiffany-glass dome. Once in dire need of renovation, the rooms are slated to get a $70-million facelift in 2017-2018. In the meantime, choose from the usual midrange chains, including a downtown **Doubletree** (600 N. El Paso St., 915/532-8733, $179 and up), a block from the ballpark.

Hueco Tanks State Historic Park

In the 100 miles of arid West Texas desert between El Paso and the Guadalupe Mountains, don't miss tiny

For the first 35 miles east of El Paso, US-180/62 runs along the southern edge of gigantic **Fort Bliss,** which stretches north for 50 miles into New Mexico and is home to about 27,000 active-duty U.S. troops.

From 1858 to 1861, the legendary Butterfield Overland Mail ran between St. Louis and San Francisco by way of El Paso, carrying mail and passengers across the country in 24 days. Running twice a week in both directions, the Butterfield line had some 140 relay stations along the route, each supplied with a Concord stagecoach and a fresh team of horses.

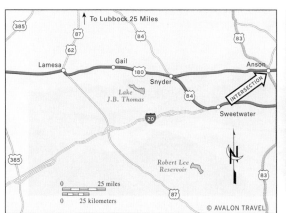

bluebonnet,
state flower of Texas

The 70-mph section of US-180 east of El Paso is also signed as Camino Buena Suerte, the "Good Luck Highway."

Q: Why do they call it Texas? A: Because it "Texas" so long to drive across.

Hueco Tanks State Historic Park (915/857-1135, daily 8am-dusk Oct.-Apr., daily 7am-dusk May-Sept., $7). Located on the eastern fringes of sprawling Fort Bliss, some 25 miles east of El Paso, then eight miles north on Hwy-2775, the 860-acre park was established to preserve the approximately 3,000 pictographs painted on the syenite basalt boulders. The "hueco tanks" of the title are naturally formed rock basins that collect rainwater, making the site a natural stop for passing travelers, from prehistoric Native Americans to the Butterfield stagecoach in the 1850s. Unfortunately, sometimes the historic pictograph graffiti is overwhelmed by more contemporary spray-paint versions. But the site is pleasant enough, with a popular campground and excellent opportunities for bird-watching and rock climbing.

Some 36 miles east of the Hueco Tanks turnoff the tiny highway town of **Cornudas** has the welcome middle-of-nowhere **May's Café** (915/964-2508), "Home of the World Famous Cornudas Burger." At mile marker 82.5, there's a row of false-fronted Wild West buildings.

Guadalupe Mountains National Park

One of the few unhyped wonders of Texas, **Guadalupe Mountains National Park** covers the rugged peaks that rise along the New Mexico border, 110 miles east of El Paso. Formed as part of the same Capitan Reef of 250 million-year-old limestone as the great caverns of Carlsbad, the Guadalupe Mountains, a cool contrast to the surrounding desert, rise in sheer faces more than 2,000 feet above the desert floor and offer the chance to experience many different and contrasting ecosystems side by side, within easy reach of the highway.

Even if you're not prepared to do any serious hiking—which is the best way to experience the grandeur of the park or to see signs of the abundant wildlife (including mountain lions)—the quickest way to get a feel for the Guadalupes is to walk the half-mile **nature trail** that runs between the main **visitor center**

Guadalupe Mountains National Park

DETOUR: CIUDAD JUÁREZ

Largest by far of the Mexican border cities, **Ciudad Juárez** (pop. 1.6 million, and growing fast) is a compelling, disturbing, exciting, and unforgettable place to visit, although the ongoing drug-related violence (and an annual average of 2,500 murders) has made the city off-limits to most sensible travelers. The city sprawls through miles and miles of some of the worst pollution and direst poverty in Mexico. If you feel brave, a half-hour walk can take you far away from the United States. From the El Paso side, don't drive; park and walk down El Paso Street from downtown and cross the bridge on foot. This crossing drops you at the head of Avenida Juárez, the main drag, lined by cantinas, nightclubs, stalls, and stores selling everything from mass-produced "crafts" to knock-off designer goods and Cuban cigars, which will likely be confiscated if you try to bring them back into the United States.

About a half mile south of the border, at the junction with Avenida 16 de Septiembre, Avenida Juárez brings you to the heart of Juárez, where the good historical museum, housed in the old customs building, and a large often packed cathedral give glimpses into the city's history and culture. Among the many restaurants and bars along Avenida Juárez, the one to check out is the **Kentucky Club** (643 Ave. Benito Juárez), a 1930s-looking bar that could be used as a set for some Raymond Chandler underworld adventure. Legend has it that Marilyn Monroe got drunk here, celebrating her Juárez divorce from playwright Arthur Miller. The Kentucky Club is also the setting of an eponymous 2012 PEN/Faulkner Award-winning novel by Benjamin Alire Sáenz.

Food and drink aside, the best thing about a trip south is the chance to enjoy some **Lucha Libre** (about US$8)—professional wrestling, Mexican style. Theatrical and impassioned bouts are often held on Sunday nights, in the large municipal auditorium near the cathedral, and there's been talk of someone establishing a *salón de fama* or Wrestling Hall of Fame.

(915/828-3251, daily, $5 park entry fee) and the remains of a Butterfield stagecoach station, passing well-signed specimens of all the major desert flora. If you have more time, head to **McKittrick Canyon,** off US-62/180 in the northeast corner of the park. From the ranger station at the end of the road, a well-marked, well-maintained, and generally flat trail

Along with New Mexico, El Paso and the Guadalupe Mountains area are in the mountain time zone. The rest of Texas is on central time.

winds along a stream, through a green landscape that changes gradually from the cacti of the Chihuahuan Desert to the oaks, madrones, and maples of the inner canyon. Rated by many as the most beautiful spot in Texas, it is best in spring, when the desert wildflowers bloom, or in autumn, when the big-leaf maple hardwoods turn color.

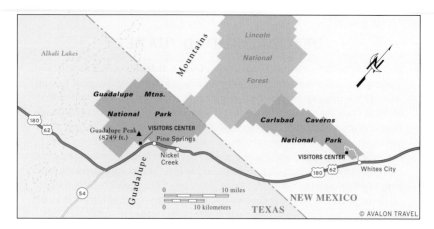

If you're feeling fit, climb **Guadalupe Peak,** at 8,750 feet the highest point in Texas, via a steep 8.4-mile round-trip trail from the main visitors center. Be aware that the change in elevation makes the mountains subject to serious weather, with great booming thunderstorms in late summer.

Camping is available on a first-come, first-served basis at **Pine Springs Campground,** near the main visitors center, and at numerous sites in the backcountry.

Carlsbad Caverns National Park

Carved out of the solid limestone of Capitan Reef by immersion in a bath of sulfuric acid some 5 million years ago, the **Carlsbad Caverns National Park** (575/785-2232, daily, $10 park entrance and self-guided tours, more for ranger-guided tours) contains over 119 underground caves, some 1,500 feet deep. A 1.25-mile trail drops steeply from the large visitors center, or you can board an elevator and ride 750 feet

Carlsbad Caverns National Park

ROSWELL: UFO CENTRAL

Seventy-five miles or so north of Carlsbad, the New Mexico ranching town of Roswell (pop. 48,184) has become a catch-word for flying saucers, UFOs, extraterrestrials, and a complicated U.S. government cover-up of all the above. The cover-up is the one thing that's pretty much a given, since the Air Force has gone so far as to deny officially that anything ever happened in Roswell—which is equivalent to a confession, in the minds of UFO believers. Everything else about Roswell is, so to speak, up in the air.

The Roswell story goes something like this: In 1947, at the start of Cold War hysteria, something strange and metallic crashed into a field outside town, and the Army Air Corps (teams of tight-lipped operatives wearing special suits and dark glasses, no doubt) came and recovered it. Reports to the effect that a flying saucer had landed in Roswell appeared in the local paper, and then quickly spread around the globe, only to be denied by the government, which claimed the "flying saucers" were actually weather balloons.

Thirty-three years later, a retired military intelligence officer from the Roswell base sold a story to the *National Enquirer,* repeating details of the 1947 "flying saucer" crash and telling of his subsequent capture of extraterrestrial beings. This in turn spawned countless other stories, books, and videos, and spurred the growth of a

battery of tourist attractions and souvenir stores in and around Roswell. To learn more, stop at the **International UFO Museum and Research Center** (114 N. Main St., 575/625-9495, $5), which fills an old movie theater in downtown Roswell. Several blocks north is the only UFO-themed McDonald's in the world.

straight down to the Big Room, where the floor area totals more than eight acres. After wandering among the countless stalactites, stalagmites, and other formations, you can chow down on sandwiches at a snack bar.

The Big Room is only one of many cave formations protected at Carlsbad; some more delicate features can be found in the King's Palace, and the park also has many more exotic and hard-to-reach caves (like Spider Cave, which you have to explore on hands and knees, or Slaughter Canyon, which is 23 miles away). These other caves can be enjoyed (if that's the word) on the many longer guided **tours** (877/444-6777, $7-20, advance reservations recommended) available. These ranger-guided tours provide all the specialist caving gear (helmets, headlamps, knee pads, etc.) that you'll need if you want to explore some of the more delicate features of the caverns or clamber around through more confined reaches of the caves.

Even if you just opt for the main cavern, be aware that the trail down to the Big Room closes early in the afternoon (usually around 3:30pm) so that visitors don't interrupt the increasingly popular spectacle of the **Bat Flight,** in which hundreds of thousands of Brazilian free-tailed bats swirl out of the caverns at sunset. Every summer evening, rangers give a brief **talk about bats** (575/236-1374, around daily 7:30pm summer, free with park admission)—proselytizing about how great and harmless they are—while waiting for them to set off into the night. (You won't catch sight of the bats here in winter, when they migrate to Mexico.)

Along Hwy-180 at the turnoff to the park stands **White's City Resort & Water Park** (575/785-2291), a complex of motels, restaurants, pinball arcades, and souvenir shops. The most reliable places to stay and eat are 20 miles to the northeast, in the town of Carlsbad.

Carlsbad

Twenty miles or so northeast of the turnoff to Carlsbad Caverns, the town of **Carlsbad** (pop. 28,914) makes its living from the 380,000 tourists who visit the caves every year. Lining Canal Street (a.k.a. US-180, the National Parks Highway), the main road through Carlsbad, you'll find most national motel chains along with funkier local counterparts. There's also one good Mexican-American restaurant, the **Pecos River Café** (409 S. Canal St., 575/887-8882), where locals come for early-morning short-order breakfasts and lunchtime enchiladas.

Apart from the caverns, the one other wonderful thing to see in the Carlsbad area is the **Living Desert Zoo and Gardens State Park** (575/887-5516, daily, $5), five miles northwest along US-285, which shows off the plant and animal life of the arid Chihuahuan Desert region. Foxes, wolves, hawks, and eagles are kept in re-creations of their natural environments and can be seen along a 1.3-mile nature trail.

US-180: The Llano Estacado

From Carlsbad, US-180 crosses the Pecos River, then snakes across the barren **Llano Estacado** (Staked Plains), which covers most of eastern New Mexico and the Texas Panhandle. Supposedly named by early explorers who drove wooden stakes into the ground to mark their way, the Llano Estacado area is pretty much the same on both sides of the border—flat, dry, and mostly devoid of settlement. For eastbound travelers, this is the place where oil first becomes importantly noticeable. Pump jacks can be seen pumping away from here all the way to Alabama.

This is also cowboy country, thanks to the extensive pastures irrigated by water pumped up from aquifers deep underground. For travelers, however, the dominant image is of land stretching out far and wide: mile after mile after mile of endless flat cotton fields, interrupted every now and then by brilliant green alfalfa fields and a few surprisingly large towns, like **Hobbs** (pop. 38,143), New Mexico. Right on the border, Hobbs's main street is lined with drilling supply and hydraulic fracturing ("fracking") companies, as well as front yards filled by huge piles of steel pipe. Because the plains get a huge amount of summer sunshine, which generates a lot of thermal lift, this part of the world is also ideal for gliding, which may be why the **Soaring Society of America** (575/392-1177) is located here.

As part of a federal program known as the **Waste Isolation Pilot Plant**—WIPP—the 250 million-year-old salt beds east of Carlsbad have been adapted into a contentious disposal site for some of the nation's nuclear waste. You can't visit the plant itself, 2,133 feet below the desert, but there is a small museum describing the project at the **WIPP Information Center** (4021 National Parks Hwy., 800/336-9477) in Carlsbad.

LUBBOCK: PANHANDLE MUSIC MECCA

The largest city in northwest Texas, Lubbock (pop. 252,506) is a busy agricultural center, best known for having given the world Buddy Holly, whose songs ("Peggy Sue," "That'll Be The Day," "Rave On") helped pave the way for rock 'n' roll. Music fans make the trip downtown to pay homage at the statue of Buddy and to learn about his brief but influential life in the **Buddy Holly Center** (1801 Crickets Ave., 806/775-3560, Tues.-Sat. 10am-5pm, Sun. 1pm-5pm, $8), just west of I-27, off 19th Street. Across the street is a statue of Buddy and a "West Texas Walk of Fame," remembering the lives and times of Lubbock's other musical boys and girls made good, including Bob Wills, Roy Orbison, Waylon Jennings, Tanya Tucker, Terry Allen, and Joe Ely.

Buddy Holly's tragic sudden death at age 22 in a 1959 plane crash also took the lives of fellow American rock-and-roll pioneers Ritchie Valens and J. P. "The Big Bopper" Richardson, and inspired the Don McLean song "American Pie," remembering "the day the music died." Holly is buried near the entrance of Lubbock Cemetery, at the east end of 31st Street (his gravestone uses the "real" spelling of his family name, "Buddy Holley").

The Texas part of the drive is dotted with towns like **Lamesa** (pop. 9,461; pronounced "la-MEE-sa"), which, after the miles of open red-earth prairie around it, can seem like a bustling hive of activity. Lamesa also has all the all-American makings of a location from the high-school-football TV show *Friday Night Lights,* which was inspired by real-life Odessa, Texas, an hour to the southwest. Sports-mad families enjoy the old **Dairy Queen drive-in** (512 N. 4th St., 806/872-8155), right on the main drag.

The Llano Estacado town of **Gail** and the county **(Borden)** are named in memory of pioneer surveyor and newspaper editor Gail Borden, who is perhaps best known as the inventor of condensed milk and founder of Borden Foods.

At the town of **Anson** (see page 209), US-180 crosses US-83, **The Road to Nowhere.** Full coverage of that route begins on page 168.

Albany

Albany (pop. 1,983), one of the more interesting-looking towns in this part of Texas, started as a stagecoach stop on the Butterfield Overland Mail in 1854. It's still a tiny place, but it has a lively feel, the oldest county courthouse in the state, and more surprisingly, a small but intriguing **Old Jail Art Center** (201 S. 2nd St., 325/762-2269, Tues.-Sat., free) in the Old City Jail. A big surprise in the middle of the ranch lands, the museum contains an outstanding permanent collection of art by Modigliani, Renoir, and others, and also displays Chinese ceramics from the Tang and Ming dynasties, among others. If you're here the last two full weekends in June, make plans to see a production of the oldest outdoor musical in Texas, the Fort Griffin Fandangle (325/762-3838, around $15), which began as a school play in 1938 and has grown to involve a cast of some 300 mostly local performers and live longhorn steer.

Coming from the west, US-80/180 makes one last small-town stop in **Weatherford** (pop. 29,969), where an opulent old courthouse anchors a lively town square. For a last taste of small-town Americana before or after a trip across Dallas, stop for breakfast, a bite of chicken-fried steak, or just a cup of coffee at the **Weatherford Downtown Café** (101 W. Church St., 817/594-8717), a block south of the square.

I-20: Sweetwater and Cisco

If you've decided to take the high-speed route along I-20, midway across Texas you'll pass **Sweetwater** (pop. 10,755), where, every March during the **Sweetwater Jaycees Rattlesnake Roundup,** townspeople get together and collect hundreds of rattlers from the surrounding ranch lands, winning prizes for the biggest, shortest, and most snakes handed in. The town, 41 miles or so west of Abilene, also has shops selling all manner of rattlesnake-related souvenirs. Sweetwater was first settled in the 1870s and now earns its livelihood mining gypsum for use in wallboard. Any time of year, it

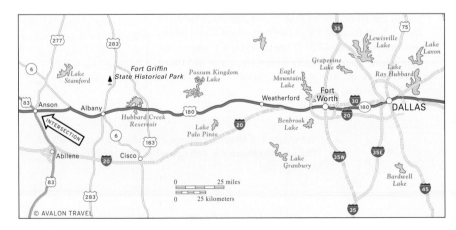

is worth a stop for some of the best fried chicken in West Texas at **Allen Family Style Meals** (1301 E. Broadway, 325/235-2060, lunch and dinner Tues.-Sun.), along old US-80.

The I-20 town of **Cisco** (pop. 3,804), about 45 miles east of Abilene, is where Conrad Hilton bought and ran his first hotel, the Mobley, in 1919; the hotel is now the chamber of commerce office, and a couple of rooms have been restored to their circa-1919 appearance.

East of Cisco, the town of **Eastland** (pop. 3,889) is proud of its two world-class oddities. The middle entrance to the county courthouse displays the embalmed body of "Old Rip," the horny toad who supposedly survived 30 years embedded as a living time capsule in the cornerstone of the old courthouse before being discovered, still alive, when the building was being torn down. A few blocks away, in the town **post office** (411 W. Main St.), a 10 feet tall and 6 feet wide mosaic mural composed of some 11,217 postage stamps depicts American legends like Abe Lincoln, Ben Franklin, and Martha Washington. It was constructed in the early 1960s by former postmistress Marene Johnson.

Northwest of Fort Worth, 26 miles south of Wichita Falls, writer Larry McMurtry turned his hometown of **Archer City** (pop. 1,746) into the world's largest used-book store. Housed in a number of downtown buildings, many of which are featured in McMurtry's *The Last Picture Show* and other works, his **Booked Up** (940/574-2511, Thurs.-Sat., by appointment Mon.-Wed.) carries old and out-of-print editions.

Old US-80 Across Fort Worth and Dallas

From Weatherford and the west, it's easiest to approach Fort Worth and Dallas via I-20 and I-30, which separate west of the city. From I-30, old US-80 enters Fort Worth on Camp Bowie Boulevard, running right past the museums of the Cultural District to the heart of downtown. East of Fort Worth, the older roads disappear under the modern freeways, so hop onto I-30 and beeline past Arlington, where the stadia for the Texas Rangers and Dallas Cowboys stand around the Six Flags over Texas amusement park before reaching Dallas.

The old road between Fort Worth and Dallas, now signed as Hwy-180, approaches downtown Dallas on Commerce Street, passing the notorious Texas School Book Depository before heading down Main Street. Southwest of downtown, a great stretch of roadside Americana has been reborn as the **Bishop**

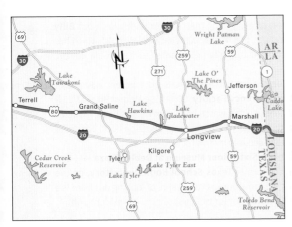

Dallas and Fort Worth

Like warring branches of an extended family, Dallas and Fort Worth are inseparable arch-rivals. Both towns lay fair claim to being capitals of their respective industries. Fort Worth (pop. 854,113) calls itself "Cowtown" but has a surprisingly sophisticated range of cultural centers and feels like an altogether more "Texan" place; it was founded during the heyday of the Chisholm Trail and still retains much of its Wild West past. Meanwhile, Dallas (pop. 1,317,929) boomed after the discovery of oil in east Texas during the 1930s and has remained a fossil fuels powerhouse, becoming famous around the world for the Dallas Cowboys football team, its luxury department store Neiman Marcus, and the eponymous 1980s TV soap opera.

In terms of things to see and do, Fort Worth may hold the winning hand. The wonderful **Kimbell Art Museum** (3333 Camp Bowie Blvd., 817/332-8451, Tues.-Sun., permanent collection free, special collections $18) is one of the most perfectly beautiful modern buildings on the planet, designed as a series of vaulted galleries by Louis Kahn. This small museum, which includes a Renzo Piano-designed pavilion, stands at the heart of the Fort Worth Cultural District, which also includes the Tadao Ando-designed **Modern Art Museum of Fort Worth** (3200 Darnell St., 817/738-9215, Tues.-Sun., $10) and, across the street, the **Amon Carter Museum** (3501 Camp Bowie Blvd., 817/738-1933, Tues.-Sun., free), displaying the country's finest collection of Wild West and other American art.

Two miles north of downtown Fort Worth, head to the **Stockyards** (817/624-4741), on Main and Exchange Streets. For a taste of how Texas used to be, spend some time wandering these two short blocks of turn-of-the-20th-century buildings, stretching west from the still-busy Fort Worth Stockyards and housing some of the city's most popular places to eat, drink, and be merry. After dark, check out **Billy Bob's Texas** (817/624-7117, $2 and up), the "World's Largest Honky-Tonk," which has live music almost every night, often featuring famous names such as Willie Nelson, Merle Haggard, and Ted Nugent.

Farther out on the north side of Fort Worth is the U.S. government's Bureau of Engraving and Printing's **Western Currency Facility** (9000 Blue Mound Rd., 817/231-4000 or 866/865-1194, daily), where you can watch billions of dollars being made as you walk along an enclosed walkway suspended over the production floor. Be sure to factor in time needed to get through security for this tour.

In Dallas, sightseers head to **The Sixth Floor Museum at Dealey Plaza** (411 Elm St., 214/747-6660, daily, $16) in the former **Texas School Book Depository,** on the west side of downtown. Besides the gruesome novelty value of looking out from the same place where Lee Harvey Oswald shot (or didn't shoot . . .) President John F.

Dallas skyline at dusk

Kennedy on November 22, 1963, this extensive museum describes the historical context and discusses the myriad conspiracy theories. Amidst the forest of skyscrapers downtown, the **Dallas Museum of Art** (1717 N. Harwood St., 214/922-1200, Tues.-Sun., free) and the elegant **Nasher Sculpture Center** (2001 Flora St., 214/242-5100, Tues.-Sun., $10) are soothing refuges from all the Texas-size commerce.

Between Dallas and Fort Worth, the **Texas Rangers** (817/972-RANGERS—817/972-7264) play at retro-modern Globe Life Park, off I-30 at the Ballpark Way exit in Arlington. Games are broadcast on **103.3 ESPN.**

PRACTICALITIES

Linked (or is it divided?) by a trio of fast freeways (I-20, I-30, and Hwy-183), Dallas and Fort Worth lie some 30 miles or so apart across the plains of northeast Texas. Each city is circled by its own ring road. Two north-south freeways (I-35W through Fort Worth and I-35E through downtown Dallas) complete the high-speed network.

Food in Fort Worth, not surprisingly, tends to the beefy. **Cattlemen's Steak House** (2458 N. Main St., 817/624-3945), in the historic Stockyards, has steaks of all cuts and sizes, plus barbecue and some seafood. **Joe T. Garcia's** (2201 N. Commerce St., 817/626-4356, cash only) may or may not be the world's biggest Tex-Mex restaurant. Its outdoor patio and roving mariachi bands have kept it popular for decades. Another Fort Worth institution, the 1950s landmark **Paris Coffee Shop** (704 W. Magnolia, 817/335-2041, Mon.-Sat.) has big breakfasts, chicken-fried steak, and delicious fresh fruit pies.

In Dallas, east of the I-35E Central Expressway from downtown, "Deep Ellum" is a slightly scruffy-looking post-industrial district of boutiques, restaurants, and nightclubs and biker bars like **Reno's Chop Shop Saloon** (210 N. Crowdus St., 214/744-1200), a block north of Elm Street. North of downtown, upscale Uptown has a popular hiking-biking rail-trail and the **Katy Trail Ice House** (3127 Routh St., 214/468-0600), a relaxing outdoor beer garden, perfect for eating burgers and drinking a few cold ones after a long day on the trail. The historic four-star **Adolphus Hotel** (1321 Commerce St., 214/742-8200, $170 and up) in downtown, built in 1912 by beer magnate Adolphus Busch, is a stylish place to stay.

In Fort Worth, the **Embassy Suites** (600 Commerce St., 817/332-6900, $180 and up) is centrally located near Sundance Square. Bonnie and Clyde (both of whom grew up and are buried in Dallas, in different cemeteries) stayed in the **Stockyards Hotel** (109 E. Exchange Ave., 817/625-6427, $219 and up), a turn-of-the-20th-century hotel that has been restored and redecorated according to various themes, including the Depression-era bank robbers. The downstairs bar is fun too: It has saddles instead of bar stools.

The salt deposits under **Grand Saline,** 70 miles east of Dallas, are estimated to be over 20,000 feet thick and nearly 1.5 miles across, enough to supply the world's needs for the next 20,000 years.

South of I-20, the city of **Tyler** grows thousands and thousands of roses, including the famous yellow ones.

Another highlight of the drive west of Dallas is **Snyder** (pop. 11,472), where a life-size statue of an albino buffalo stands on the courthouse square.

Arts District, a lively mix of art galleries, boutiques, and restaurants like the wonderful **Lockhart Smokehouse BBQ** (400 W. Davis St., 214/944-5521). East of Dallas, the old main road passes through Deep Ellum neighborhood before leaving town past the historic Cotton Bowl football stadium, on the grounds of the **Texas State Fair** (held here in late September or early October).

Kilgore: Oil!

The pine-covered red-earth hills of East Texas are covered with creaking old pump jacks, still sucking up the crude oil that has kept the region economically afloat since the 1930s. The oil business here has gone through numerous booms and busts since it gushed into existence in December 1930 at a well outside **Kilgore** (pop. 14,839), on the south side of I-20, about 12 miles southwest of Longview via US-259. This comparatively small and quiet oil town has street lamps disguised as oil rigs and a set of 100-foot-tall derricks standing along the railroad tracks in memory of the "World's Richest Acre," a plot of downtown land that produced over 2.5 million barrels of oil through the 1960s. The site was so productive and so valuable that one of the wells was drilled through the terrazzo floor of a local bank, and over a thousand derricks once loomed over the downtown area.

The history of the local petroleum industry is recounted in entertaining detail at the **East Texas Oil Museum** (Hwy-259 at Ross St., 903/983-8295, Tues.-Sat., $8) on the campus of Kilgore College, off US-259. The museum includes displays of drilling equipment and old gas stations, plus a simulated "elevator ride" a mile deep into the earth to show off the oil-bearing geology. Also on the Kilgore College campus, in the Physical Education Complex, is a small free museum devoted to the **Kilgore Rangerettes** (1100 Broadway, 903/983-8265), a highly trained precision drill and dance cheerleading team that performs at college and professional football games.

Back on US-80, well north of the I-20 freeway, the booming oil-fueled city of **Longview** (pop. 82,055) holds one of the best places to eat in East Texas. Longview is also where actor Matthew McConaughey went to high school. In between his role in the stoner comedy *Dazed and Confused* and his Academy Award-winning performance in *Dallas Buyers Club,* McConaughey appeared in Richard Linklater's East Texas film *Bernie.*

Marshall and Jefferson

North of I-20 some 20 miles west of the Louisiana state line, **Marshall** (pop. 23,561) is one of the older towns in Texas, and was once among its wealthiest. Now a fairly quiet place, in its early years Marshall was the commercial capital of the East Texas cotton country. During the Civil War, two local residences served as the Confederate capital— of Missouri. This anomaly, along with general regional history, is chronicled in the **Harrison County Historical Museum** (903/935-8417, Tues.-Sat., $6), housed in the supremely ornate yellow Old Harrison County Courthouse on Peter Whetstone Square.

If you have the time and inclination to get a more palpable sense of the varied culture and history of East Texas, take US-59 for 17 miles or so north of Marshall to **Jefferson** (pop. 2,043), an almost perfectly preserved bayou town that looks much as it did during the 1870s when, with a population of nearly 7,300, it was the busiest inland port west of the Mississippi. Among the most prominent of the hundreds of historic structures here is the 1858 **Excelsior House** (211 W. Austin St., 903/665-2513, $120 and up), a favorite stopover for President Ulysses S. Grant and later First Lady Lady Bird Johnson. Across the street, if there are guides available, you can tour Jay Gould's private railroad car, the Atalanta, or simply wander the charming old town, exploring the many good antiques shops, cafés, and restaurants.

LOUISIANA

Northern Louisiana, which covers some 200 miles of forested, rolling hills between Texas and Mississippi, is a far cry from the Cajun fun of the southern half of the state. A Baptist-dominated Bible Belt heartland, it's also a diverse place—part heavily industrial, part poor rural backwater, with a mix of people and products that encapsulates its transitional position between the agricultural Deep South and the petrochemical plants of Texas.

The main city here is the oil town of **Shreveport,** which has recently become a prime place for gamblers, with flashy casinos lining the riverfront. However, you'll mostly find small towns ranging from **Gibsland** (where Bonnie and Clyde met their doom) to the college town of **Ruston** (home to Louisiana Tech University).

Shreveport and Bossier City

Shreveport (pop. 194,920) is named in honor of Capt. Henry Shreve, who in the 1830s cleared the Red River of a 165-mile-long logjam known as the Great Raft that had blocked navigation. He then "bought" the land from native Caddo people. A King Cotton town that thrived in the antebellum years and survived the war physically, though not economically, unscathed, it is now a busy industrial city rising on the west bank of the Red River. Along with its stepbrother across the river, **Bossier City** (pop. 68,485; pronounced "BO-zher"), Shreveport is a center of the Louisiana oil business, which is small only when compared to that of Texas and is still hugely important. The two cities are hot spots of Louisiana's nascent gambling industry, with a line of major resort-casinos along the riverfront attracting people from all over the tristate "Ark-La-Tex" region—including the lively

> North of Shreveport on Hwy-1, **Oil City** has one of the region's better history museums, housed next to the old railroad depot and displaying a wonderful collection of old postcards.

Horseshoe (711 Horseshoe Blvd., 800/895-0711), a 24-story Caesars hotel and 4-story faux riverboat floating in a shallow pond on the Bossier City side.

Downtown Shreveport is the usual mix of turn-of-the-20th-century brick buildings and boarded-up shop fronts, with a handful of interesting structures surviving near the river, facing the casinos and shopping malls of Bossier City on the other side.

The nicest part of town is the leafy **Highland Historic District,** stretching south from the end of Market Street, south of I-20 between the river and the I-49 freeway. This is where you'll find the grand old houses of the landed gentry, many of which

From 1948 to 1969 and again from 1973 to 1987, Shreveport and Bossier City hosted the *Louisiana Hayride*, a country-western radio program (and later television show) on which Hank Williams and Elvis Presley both started their careers.

look like they belong in *Gone With the Wind*, despite the fact that almost all of them date from the 20th century. While you're in the area, stop at the homey **Strawn's Eat Shop** (125 Kings Hwy., 318/868-0634) for yummy hash browns, biscuits, fried chicken, and seasonal strawberry pies.

The Bossier City casinos sometimes offer good deals on accommodations. All the usual hotel and motel chains line I-20.

Gibsland: Bonnie and Clyde

East of Shreveport, the old US-80 highway winds through dozens of somnolent little towns, following the rolling land while crisscrossing back and forth under the high-speed I-20 freeway. After passing the pawnshops and strip clubs outside Barksdale Air Force Base, the route parallels railroad tracks along the remains of a historic log turnpike, built in the 1870s to provide all-weather passage across the muddy bogs and bayous.

Apart from the usual barrage of roadside businesses, there's not a lot to stop for until you reach the tiny town of **Gibsland** (pop. 947), just south of I-20, about 45 miles east of Shreveport. This pleasantly unremarkable little hamlet has one unique claim to fame: It was here, on May 23, 1934, that the notorious Depression-era criminals Clyde Barrow and Bonnie Parker were ambushed and killed by a posse of police. A small **Bonnie and Clyde Ambush Museum** (2419 Main St., 318/843-1934, daily, $7) and gift shop tells their story and sells postcards of their bullet-riddled bodies. Every May on the gruesome anniversary locals dress up for the Bonnie and Clyde Festival and stage gun battles and car chases, as much for cops-and-robbers fun as any real dedication to historical accuracy.

Clyde and Bonnie, circa 1933

A battered stone marker, eight miles south of Gibsland along Hwy-154, stands on the site where the desperate duo were riddled with bullets by Texas and Louisiana law enforcement officers. The late-1960s

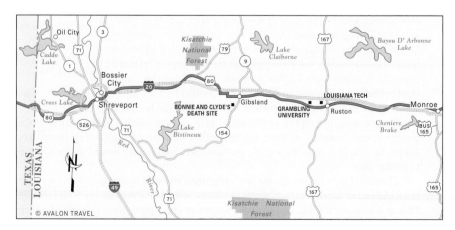

Arthur Penn movie *Bonnie and Clyde* enveloped Clyde in Hollywood glamour, but as far as most accounts describe him, the real-life Clyde was a nasty, twisted, cold-blooded murderer, nothing like the romantic hero played by Warren Beatty. Bonnie, who, like Clyde, grew up desperately poor, may or may not have ever shot anyone, and she definitely was a romantic figure; at her funeral, the newspapers of Dallas donated the most impressive floral tribute, and some 20,000 people lined the streets to say farewell.

Ruston and Monroe

Roughly halfway across the state, **Ruston** (pop. 22,370) calls itself the "Peach City." It's best known for two major colleges: Louisiana Tech (where local boy Terry Bradshaw played college football) and smaller Grambling University, one of the nation's top historically African American schools, six miles west in the town of Grambling (pop. 5,217), just south of I-20.

Considering that it is one of the largest towns in northern Louisiana, **Monroe** (pop. 49,297) feels strangely abandoned, even though the downtown area has a number of classic commercial buildings dating from the period between the two world wars, and Victorian-era warehouses and hundreds of ancient-looking shotgun shacks line the railroad tracks and US-80. Celtics basketball star Bill Russell, in 2011 awarded the Presidential Medal of Freedom for his role in desegregating professional sports, was born in Monroe, as was Black Panther Huey Newton.

Apart from its photogenic architecture and fading roadside signs, Monroe doesn't offer much reason to stop, though the gorgeous greenery of the **Louisiana Purchase Gardens and Zoo** (1405 Bernstein Park Rd., 318/329-2400, daily, $6), south of I-20 off US-165, makes it a great place to stretch your legs, ride a steam train, or go for a **boat ride** (Mar.-Oct., $3) among the moss-draped oaks and cypress trees.

East of Monroe, it's an hour's drive across the bayous before you reach the fascinating city of Vicksburg, across the Mississippi River.

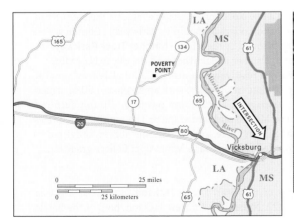

magnolia, the state flower of Louisiana and of Mississippi

One of the oldest, largest, and most significant concentrations of archaeological remains in North America has been protected as **Poverty Point National Monument** (888/926-5462 or 318/926-5492, $4), 18 miles north of I-20 off Hwy-17 near **Epps,** Louisiana. These 3,000-year-old burial mounds are jointly managed by federal and state authorities.

MISSISSIPPI

US-80, which for much of the way has been replaced by the I-20 freeway, cuts across the middle of Mississippi, passing through Meridian, Jackson, and Vicksburg. Only Jackson, the capital and by far the biggest city in the state, is anything like an urban center, with a couple of "skyscrapers" and nearly 200,000 people. Along this stretch you will mostly see small farms and Civil War battlefields, the most extensive and important of which rises above the Mississippi River in Vicksburg.

The Mississippi River town of **Vicksburg** (see page 281) marks the junction with **The Great River Road.** Full coverage of that route begins on page 224.

Clinton and the Natchez Trace

The onetime Choctaw Indian agency town of **Clinton** (pop. 25,211), north of I-20, about 10 miles west of Jackson, was renamed in 1828 in honor of New York governor DeWitt Clinton, who oversaw construction of the Erie Canal. It is now a small cotton-growing and shipping center, with a few blocks of "olde towne" around the Baptist-run Mississippi College along Hwy-80 and College Street. In its early years, Clinton sat on the notorious Natchez Trace, now followed by the blissful **Natchez Trace Parkway** (see page 288), which runs southwest to Natchez and northeast all the way to Nashville.

Though it survived the Civil War relatively unscathed, Clinton later saw some of the worst Reconstruction-era race riots in the state, with an estimated 50 unarmed blacks killed during a single rampage in 1875. More recently, Clinton suffered through the painful fallout of the MCI/WorldCom scandal: The multinational telecom company had its world headquarters here, and CEO Bernie Ebbers, convicted in 2005 of overseeing a multibillion-dollar fraud, was a Mississippi College graduate.

Jackson

Spreading west from the banks of the Pearl River, **Jackson** (pop. 169,148) was established as state capital in 1822. Named for Andrew Jackson, hero of the Battle

FATHER OF COUNTRY MUSIC

The collision of Mississippi's rural past with the early stages of industrial development was embodied in the life and work of Meridian's favorite son, Jimmie Rodgers, whose original mixing of black Delta blues and white Appalachian folk songs earned him the title "Father of Country Music." What Elvis Presley was to the 1950s, Rodgers was to the previous generation. Born in Meridian on September 8, 1897, Rodgers worked briefly on the railroad, lost his job after coming down with tuberculosis, then became the original overnight success. After he was discovered by an RCA talent scout in 1927, Rodgers's first record, "Sleep, Baby, Sleep," sold over a million copies. For the next five years he called himself the "Singing Brakeman" and was the world's best-selling recording artist. Rodgers's life and legend are honored in the small **Jimmie Rodgers Museum** (1725 Jimmie Rodgers Dr., 601/485-1808, Tues.-Fri. 10am-4pm, Sat. 10am-

1pm Mar.-Nov., $10) in Highland Park, well signed two miles northwest of downtown. It contains all manner of odd Rodgers-related memorabilia, plus his boots and his custom Martin guitar. Jimmie Rodgers died of tuberculosis in May 1933 and is buried alongside his wife in Oak Grove Cemetery, five miles east of downtown Meridian. On the centenary of Rodgers's birth, an excellent tribute album of his songs was recorded by the likes of Bono, Bob Dylan, Jerry Garcia, and Willie Nelson, all of whom rated Rodgers as a major influence on their music.

of New Orleans during the War of 1812 and later president of the United States, it was destroyed during the Civil War but is now Mississippi's political and commercial heart and its biggest city—though you wouldn't know it by the somnolent look of the place.

The attractive Greek Revival **Old State Capitol** (601/576-6920, Tues.-Sun.), built in 1839 and used until 1903, rises at the center of Jackson at State and Capitol Streets and is open for free self-guided tours of the building and the well-presented historical exhibits that fill it. The few other fine old antebellum buildings—under a dozen altogether—that survive around Jackson were used by Union forces and were thus spared destruction. These include the art-filled **Governor's Mansion** (300 E. Capitol St., 601/359-6421, Tues.-Fri. 9:30am-11am, free), a short walk west of the old capitol, and **The Oaks House Museum** (823 N. Jefferson St., 601/353-9339, by appointment only, $4.50), in which General Sherman lived. Restored to prewar splendor, The Oaks is furnished with period antiques and, surprisingly for the South, a sofa from Abraham Lincoln's law office.

On the south side of downtown Jackson, the new home of the **Mississippi Museum of Art** (380 S. Lamar St., 601/960-1515, Tues.-Sun., admission varies) has

The tiny town of **Vaughan,** 39 miles north of Jackson via the I-55 freeway, was the site of the crash that killed legendary train engineer John Luther "Casey" Jones.

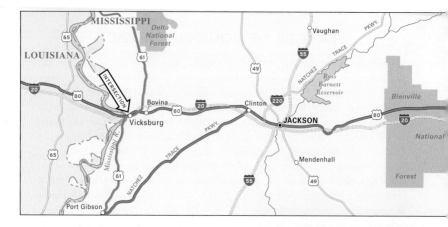

established an international reputation as one of the top museums in the USA. Even if you don't spend the time to appreciate the paintings and sculptures, a visit will give you a chance to stretch your legs while appreciating the well-landscaped and inviting gardens, fountains, and performance spaces, not to mention the welcoming and reasonably-priced café.

Away from downtown, the main attraction is the **Mississippi Agriculture and Forestry Museum** (601/432-4500, Mon.-Sat., $5), a 39-acre complex on Lakeland Drive northeast of downtown, off I-55 exit 96A. Despite the dull name, it's a hugely engaging and entertaining place, with a composite "Small Town" made up of authentic buildings, including a general store, filling station, and sawmill brought here from all over Mississippi.

the Old State Capitol building in Jackson

For more local flavor, head to the north side of Jackson, east of US-51/State Street, where the **Eudora Welty House** (1119 Pinehurst St., 601/353-7762, Tues.-Fri., $5), home of Pulitzer Prize-winning writer Eudora Welty (1909-2001), is now open as an atmospheric museum of her life and work. For more than 76 years, Welty lived and worked here.

Jackson Practicalities

For food and drink, a good place to get a taste of Jackson is the **Elite Restaurant** (141 E. Capitol St., 601/352-5606) near the Mississippi Museum of Art, a friendly 1940s-era local favorite serving up a wide range of inexpensive, great-tasting food. For fried catfish or hot tamales (two contenders for Mississippi's state dish), cold beer, and great live music, make your way to **Hal & Mal's** (200 S. Commerce St., 601/948-0888, Mon.-Sat.), in an old warehouse perched along the abandoned railroad tracks above the Pascagoula Street underpass.

© AVALON TRAVEL

Double-A-affiliate of the Atlanta Braves, the **Mississippi Braves** (601/932-8788) play baseball in Pearl, just east of Jackson between I-20 and US-80.

How times change, Mississippi style: Jackson's main streets have been renamed to honor civil rights movement martyrs Martin Luther King Jr. and Medgar Evers.

Places to stay in Jackson tend to be either rough-but-cheap highway motels lining old US-80 or anodyne chains along the I-20 and I-55 frontages. One grand exception is the 1920s beaux arts classicism of the **King Edward Hotel,** now operated as a **Hilton Garden Inn** (235 W. Capitol St., 601/353-5464, $120 and up). After nearly 40 years of neglect, the hotel has been reborn, with a great bar, good food, and oodles of ambience. For complete information, or details on driving the nearby Natchez Trace Parkway, contact the **visitors bureau** (111 E. Capitol St., Suite 102, 601/960-1891 or 800/354-7695).

Meridian

At the junction of US-80, I-20, and I-59, the main route to and from New Orleans, modern **Meridian** (pop. 39,113) is a medium-size industrial center that started from rubble in the aftermath of the Civil War, and owes its existence to strategic geography. After the native Choctaw people were removed in 1831, Meridian became a railroad junction and served as a Confederate stronghold until General Sherman destroyed it in February 1864, saying afterward, "Meridian with its depots, storehouses, arsenals, hospitals, offices, hotels, and cantonments no longer exists." Despite this, the town

Meridian's former Public Library now houses the Meridian Museum of Art.

recovered with a vengeance. From the 1890s until the 1930s Meridian was the largest and most prosperous city in this very poor state, as shown by the many fine Victorian and art deco buildings that still stand (in varying stages of repair) around the leafy and clean downtown area.

Two of Meridian's most intriguing stops are two miles northwest of downtown, in **Highland Park,** on 41st Avenue at State Boulevard/Highland Park Drive. First is the **Dentzel Carousel** (daily 1pm-5pm June-July, Sat.-Sun. 1pm-5pm Aug.-Oct., Sat. 1pm-5pm Nov.-Mar., $0.50 per ride), a cheerful and historic wooden merry-go-round manufactured in 1896 by Gustav Dentzel of Philadelphia, Pennsylvania, for the 1904 St. Louis Exposition. It was later sold to the City of Meridian, preserved in its original condition. Nearby is the **Jimmie Rodgers**

Museum (1725 Jimmie Rodgers Dr., 601/485-1808, Tues.-Sat. 10am-4pm, Mar.-Nov., $10). Another offbeat but interesting Meridian "attraction" is the grave site of the "King and Queen of the Gypsies," Emil and Kelly Mitchell, whose 1915 plot in **Rose Hill Cemetery** (40th Ave., between 8th St. and Davis St., west of downtown) is a place of pilgrimage for Gypsies from all over America. Marked by a set of wrought-iron patio furniture and traditional headstones, the grave is often piled high with strands of beads, fruit, and other offerings.

> The incidents recounted in the film *Mississippi Burning* (the murders of civil rights activists by Ku Klux Klan members in June 1964) took place in the small town of **Philadelphia,** 40 miles northwest of Meridian.

Thanks to its location at the I-20 and I-59 junction, there's no shortage of places to eat and sleep in Meridian.

> Continuing its musical traditions, Meridian is also the birthplace and corporate headquarters of Peavey Electronics, amplifier- and instrument-makers to the stars.

ALABAMA

Our route across the midsection of Alabama cuts through the rural Black Belt, a name that comes from the richly fertile but often swampy lowland soil, but which also reflects its predominantly African American population. Prime cotton-growing country, central Alabama was feverishly supportive of slavery and secession—Montgomery, the state capital, was also the first capital of the Confederacy. Central Alabama later became a crucible in the civil rights battles of the 1950s and 1960s.

Events of both of these historical moments provide most of what there is to see and do in the state. The intimate scale of things—even t h e biggest city, **Montgomery,** feels like a sleepy small town—makes for an enjoyable tour, as does the fact that for most of its 230-odd miles, US-80 alternates between old-style two-lane and newer-style four-lane freeway. It is far away from the interstates, passing through some of the South's most interesting places.

Demopolis and Faunsdale

Standing just north of US-80 on a bluff at the confluence of the Black Warrior and Tombigbee Rivers, **Demopolis** (pop. 7,019) has an interesting history to explain its unusual name—which means "City of the People" in Greek. In 1817, a band of French aristocrats in exile for their allegiance to Napoleon arrived here after the U.S. Congress

Gaineswood antebellum mansion

granted them the land to found a colony based on growing grapes and olives. Not surprisingly, the colonists, a group of soldiers and courtiers whom the WPA *Guide to Alabama* described as "cultured people . . . from the glittering drawing rooms of the French aristocracy . . . none of whom had ever set foot in a plowed field," failed miserably; they survived thanks only to the local Choctaw people, who gave them food and taught them to grow viable crops.

By the 1820s the last of the French had quit and the lands were swiftly taken over by slave-owning American cotton planters, whose mansions still stand in and around town. Although it's not overly imposing from the outside, the biggest and best of these is **Gaineswood** (805 S. Cedar St., 334/289-4846, Tues.-Fri. 10am-4pm, Sat. 10am-2pm, Sun. 2pm-4pm, $7), just north of US-80. The finest antebellum mansion in Alabama, and one of the top three in the country according to the *Smithsonian Guide to Historic America,* Gaineswood began as a rough cabin in 1821 and over the next 40 years grew into a classic Greek Revival manor, built by enslaved laborers according to pattern-book designs. Most unusually, it is still decorated with the original furniture, fixtures, and fittings. Today it is a national historic landmark owned and operated by the Alabama Historical Commission.

The other well-maintained plantation home still standing in Demopolis is **Bluff Hall** (407 N. Commissioners Ave., 334/289-9644, Tues.-Sun., $5), overlooking the river at the west edge of town. Smaller than Gaineswood but more attractively situated, Bluff Hall contains a wider array of furniture, with pieces dating from throughout the 19th century; the kitchen in particular is packed with Victorian-era gadgets.

Demopolis's franchise-free downtown fills four blocks of Washington Street east from Bluff Hall and the river. It's centered upon one of the South's oldest public squares, with a cast-iron fountain and many comfy benches.

The Tombigbee River at Demopolis comes to life the first weekend of December for **Christmas on the River,** when lighted, animated "floats that really float" parade downstream.

The most enjoyable place to eat near Demopolis is about 16 miles east of town in tiny **Faunsdale** (pop. 92), on the south side of US-80. Though little more than a speck on the map, Faunsdale is worth a stop to enjoy the good food and frequent live music at the **Ca-John's Faunsdale Bar and Grill** (334/628-3240, Wed.-Sat. 5pm-9pm) in the block-long center of town.

Selma

A full century before it played a seminal role in the civil rights movement of the 1960s, **Selma** (pop. 18,983) was second only to Richmond as an industrial arsenal for Confederate forces. Selma's foundries and forges produced weapons, ammunition, and ironclad warships, including the legendary *CSS Tennessee*—and altogether accounted for nearly half of Confederate-made munitions. As in Richmond, the factories were destroyed by Union forces toward the end of the war in April 1865, but a few blocks of downtown's Water Avenue were spared and now form one of the few intact antebellum business districts left in the

Edmund Pettus Bridge

South. Hundreds of Civil War-era houses line Selma's streets, marked by blue shields and forming one of the largest collections of historic houses in the country.

Along the north bank of the broad Alabama River, Water Avenue's five blocks of well-maintained commercial structures, many now housing antiques shops, include the **St. James Hotel** (1200 Water Ave., 334/872-0332, $115 and up), the oldest hotel still standing in the South. It was built in 1837 and restored in 1997, with wrought-iron balconies and rooms arrayed around a garden atrium. At the west end of Water Avenue, the hump-backed landmark **Edmund Pettus Bridge** still carries old US-80 over the river. At the north foot of the bridge, the small but significant **National Voting Rights Museum** (6 US-80 E., 334/418-0800, Mon.-Thurs. 10am-4pm, Fri.-Sun. by appointment, $6.50), near the US-80 intersection with Cosby Avenue, uses personal artifacts, photographs, and handbills to tell the story of the civil rights struggles of the 1950s and 1960s. While most accounts focus on the high-profile political leaders, the story here is of the local grassroots activists and

Alabama's original state capital, **Cahawba,** was founded along the Alabama River in 1820 but was totally abandoned by the 1860s. Its few buildings and other remains are preserved as the **Old Cahawba Archaeological Park** (334/872-8058, Thurs.-Sun. 9am-5pm, free), 13 miles southwest of Selma via Hwy-22 and Hwy-9.

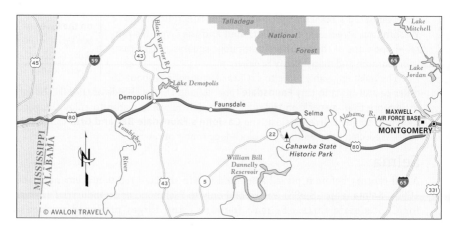

organizers who struggled for years to win the right to vote. The big names, particularly Martin Luther King Jr., clearly played key roles, but the sense you get from visiting the Voting Rights Museum is that it was the many brave but uncelebrated heroes who really made the civil rights movement happen.

Five blocks east, at the other end of the Water Avenue historic district, on the site of Selma's largest Civil War foundry, the **Old Depot Museum** (4 Martin Luther King Jr. St., 334/874-2197, Mon.-Fri., Sat. by appointment, $5) traces regional history from before the Civil War up through the civil rights movement and features a large selection of Confederate currency, much of which was printed in Selma. The depot also marks the juncture of Selma's Civil War history with the more recent battles for civil rights: North along Martin Luther King Jr. (formerly Sylvan) Street, markers point out the unchanged sites of key moments in the civil rights movement up to the 1965 March to Montgomery fronted by Martin Luther King. Twenty different displays explain the significance of Selma and point out the historic importance of such sites as the Brown Chapel AME church, where marchers set off toward Montgomery before being violently turned back at the Edmund Pettus Bridge, and the simple brick public housing of the George Washington Carver Homes, where most of the original activists lived.

Responding to the civil rights marches of 1965, President Lyndon Johnson said, "At times, history and fate meet at a single time, in a single place to shape a turning point in man's unending search for freedom. So it was at Lexington and Concord. So it was a century ago at Appomattox. So it was last week in Selma, Alabama."

Civil Rights Movement National Historic Trail

Dozens of sites in Selma and Montgomery, and the entire 50-some-mile length of US-80 between them, are being documented, preserved, and protected as part of the **Civil Rights Movement National Historic Trail.** It's a challenging story to tell, and so far two of three planned **National Park Service interpretive centers** are opened, on the north side of US-80 near **White Hall** (334/877-1983, Mon.-Sat., free) and in **Selma** (2 Broad St., 334/872-0509, Mon.-Sat., free). The centers have information on the Selma-to-Montgomery marches and explore the larger context of the civil rights movement through interactive displays and a film.

Just east of Hayneville is the place where Viola Liuzzo, a white homemaker

camelia, the state flower of Louisiana and of Alabama

from Detroit who volunteered to help shuttle marchers between Montgomery and Selma, was murdered by the KKK. A small memorial stands on the site, on the south side of US-80 between Petronia and Lowndesboro.

Montgomery

Original capital of the Confederate States of America, and now the state capital of Alabama, **Montgomery** (pop. 226,329) is among the more engaging destinations in the Deep South. Not surprisingly, much of what there is to see has to do with the Civil War, which officially started here when Jefferson Davis gave the order to fire on Fort Sumter. Montgomery survived the war more or less unscathed and is now a pleasant little city with lovely houses lining leafy streets and an above-

Dexter Avenue King Memorial Baptist Church

average range of restaurants, thanks to the presence of politicos and the nearly 5,000 undergrads at Alabama State College.

Montgomery's landmark is the circa-1851 **Alabama State Capitol** (334/242-3935, Mon.-Sat., free), which served as the Confederate capitol for four months in 1861 and is still in use. A bronze star on the west portico marks the spot where Jefferson Davis took the oath of office as President of the Confederate States of America on February 18, 1861. Twin cantilevered spiral staircases surrounded by historical murals climb the three-story domed rotunda. Moved to a site across the street from the capitol in 1921, the first **White House of the Confederacy** is where Jeff Davis and family lived before moving from Montgomery to Richmond. Yet more Confederate memorabilia is on display next door at the **Museum of Alabama** (334/242-4364, Mon.-Sat., free), which has displays tracing Alabama history from the Creek people and pioneer times up through today.

A single block west of the state capitol complex—mind-bogglingly close, considering the historically huge gulf between whites and blacks in Alabama—stands the **Dexter Avenue King Memorial Baptist Church & Parsonage,** a simple brick building where Martin Luther King Jr. served as pastor from 1954 to 1960. One of the key landmarks of the civil rights movement, it was here that supporters rallied around Rosa Parks in the Montgomery bus boycott of

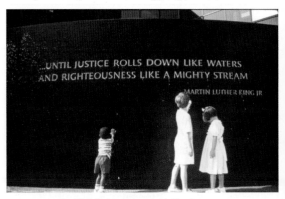

the Civil Rights Memorial in Montgomery

1955-1956, eventually leading to an end to official segregation. You can visit and tour the **Parsonage** (309 S. Jackson St., 334/261-3270, Tues.-Sat.), where King and his family lived during the Montgomery years. Right downtown, the small **Rosa Parks Library and Museum** (252 Montgomery St., 334/241-8615, Mon.-Sat., $7.50), dedicated to Parks and the bus boycott, is open in the new Troy University library, next to the site of the bus stop where she refused to give up her seat for a white passenger, sparking the struggle.

Montgomery's Maxwell-Gunter Air Force Base, occupying the same site as the Wright Brothers' 1910 flight school, is now home to the **Air War College at The Air University,** national finishing school for fighter pilots and military tacticians. Tuskegee, just east, was the training base of the Tuskegee Airmen, black pilots who fought in World War II.

Right around the corner from the Dexter Avenue King Memorial Baptist Church, Montgomery's most powerful site may be the **Civil Rights Memorial** (400 Washington Ave., Mon.-Sat., $2), two blocks west of the state capitol at the entrance to the Southern Poverty Law Center. Designed by Vietnam Veterans Memorial architect Maya Lin, the monument consists of a circular black granite table inscribed with the names of 40 people killed in the struggle for civil rights. A brief description of how and when they died radiates like the hands of a clock from a central water source, which flows gently over the edges of the stone. Behind the table, a waterfall tumbles over a marble wall inscribed with Martin Luther King's favorite biblical passage, which says that we will not be satisfied "until Justice rolls down like water, and righteousness like a mighty stream." The building behind the Civil Rights Memorial houses the non-

profit Southern Poverty Law Center, a nationally important force for fighting all forms of racial and religious hatred. Along with numerous legal battles, the center has targeted racism on the Internet via its website, www.tolerance.org.

Montgomery also has sights to see that have nothing at all to do with the Civil War or the civil rights movement. The first of these is the **Hank Williams Memorial,** marking his final resting place on the northeast side of downtown in **Oakwood Cemetery Annex** (1304 Upper Wetumptka Rd.). Hank Williams was an Alabama native, and singer and writer of such enduring classics as "Your Cheating Heart," "Jambalaya," "Hey, Good Lookin'," "I'm So Lonesome I Could Cry," and "Lost Highway." Williams's last concert in Montgomery took place on December 28, 1952, three days before his death; he died in the back of his Cadillac while en route from Knoxville, Tennessee, to a scheduled New Year's Day concert in Canton, Ohio. His song, "I'll Never Get Out of This World Alive," was rising up the charts at the time of his demise. His grave is on the east side of the central circle. Back downtown, his baby blue 1952 Cadillac convertible is one of the prime exhibits inside the **Hank Williams Museum** (118 Commerce St., 334/262-3600, daily, $10), across from City Hall.

Another notable local was Zelda Fitzgerald, who was born and raised in Montgomery and later lived here with her husband, F. Scott, while he wrote *Tender Is the Night* during the winter of 1931-1932. The house they shared, south of downtown, has been converted into apartments, one of which (apartment B, on the ground floor) is now the small **Fitzgerald Museum** (919 Felder Ave., 334/264-4222, Tues.-Sat. 10am-3pm, Sun. 12pm-5pm, $10) that details their lives and works through videos and memorabilia—press clippings, twin typewriters, first editions, photographs, and more. It's the only museum anywhere dedicated to either of them.

Montgomery Practicalities

At the east end of downtown, there's a clutch of good "authentic Southern" restaurants within a short walk of the state capitol, including the cacophonously huge, and hugely popular, cafeteria-style **Farmers Market Café** (315 N. McDonough St., 334/262-1970). Another great traditional Deep South place is on the south side of town: **Martin's Restaurant** (1796 Carter Hill Rd., 334/265-1767, Sun.-Fri.), southeast of the Alabama State University campus, gets votes for making the "World's Best Fried Chicken," and they also bake some pretty fine pies.

The **Montgomery Biscuits,** Double-A farm club of the Tampa Bay Rays, play at a nice new riverfront stadium (200 Coosa St., 334/323-2255), right downtown.

Montgomery even has great fast food: **Chris' Hot Dogs** (138 Dexter Ave., 334/265-6850, Mon.-Sat.), located three blocks west of Martin Luther King's church, is famous across the state for its spicy chili dogs and crispy fries. If you've got a hankering for juicy ribs and a slice of banana cream pie, visit **Dreamland BBQ** (101 Tallappoosa St., 334/273-7427), between the ballpark and the Hank Williams Museum.

Places to stay in Montgomery include the usual national chains, plus two good choices in downtown: a comfy **Hampton Inn** (100 Commerce St., 334/265-1010, around $140 and up), in a restored older building, and the luxurious **Renaissance** (201 Tallapoosa St., 334/481-5000, $160 and up). For more peace, quiet, and comfort, consider a night at the **Lattice Inn** (1414 S. Hull St., 334/263-1414), Montgomery's nicest B&B.

Tuskegee

Midway between Montgomery and the Georgia border, **Tuskegee** (pop. 8,722) is a medium-size town that has grown up around **Tuskegee University** (334/727-8011). Founded in 1881 by former slave Booker T. Washington to help black Americans rise up the economic ladder, it's now a national historic site. Many of the early buildings built by student laborers still stand around the university's 5,000 acres, which include the campus, farm, and forest land. The main points of interest are close to the entrance off Old Montgomery Road. Here you'll find the **George Washington Carver Museum** (334/727-3200, Mon.-Sat., free), which is part of the Tuskegee Institute National Historic Site and traces the career of Tuskegee teacher George Washington Carver, with displays of the various products Carver developed during his lifelong tenure at Tuskegee.

Across the Chattahoochee River from Georgia, the oddly spelled **Phenix City** is where, in 1836, thousands of native Creek people were forced west to new territory in Oklahoma, along what became known as the **Trail of Tears.**

Facing the Carver Museum across the lawn is the strikingly modern Tuskegee University Chapel, designed by noted architect Paul Rudolph and built from 1967 to 1969. The graves of both Booker T. Washington and George Washington Carver are next to the chapel.

Southeast of the college campus, the center of Tuskegee is a broad square dominated by the large Macon County Courthouse.

East of Tuskegee, the I-85 freeway races up to Atlanta, while US-80 rolls east to the engaging old industrial city of Columbus, across the Georgia border.

GEORGIA

Running across the middle of Georgia, US-80 follows the "fall line," a geological divide where rivers drop in a series of rapids from the higher Piedmont Plateau to the lower coastal plain. Because the fall line marked the limits of navigation in from the sea, settlements naturally sprung up along it: **Columbus** was founded on the banks of the falling Chattahoochee, while in the middle of the state, **Macon** was built along the Ocmulgee River. These, the second- and sixth-biggest cities, respectively, in this still-rural state, are the only real cities our route passes through, and both are fascinating places in different ways.

For the rest of its trip across Georgia, US-80 takes in more than 300 miles of rolling countryside, speckled here and there with dozens and dozens of small towns. Runs along ancient-looking two-lane blacktop wind through thick hardwood-and-pine forests, past stately white-columned farmhouses with wide lawns and run-down tin-roofed shacks with yards full of rusting refrigerators and old bangers on blocks. Especially in the western half of the state, US-80 runs across rolling Piedmont countryside past extensive orchards at the heart of Georgia peach country. Follow U-pick signs in early summer for a field-fresh selection, or stop at roadside stands selling the Georgia specialty along with other local fruits and vegetables, including, of course, peanuts. You can detour to explore the surprisingly simple homes of two U.S. presidents, Franklin Delano Roosevelt's at **Warm Springs** and Jimmy Carter's at **Plains.**

Continuing east toward Savannah and the Atlantic Coast, US-80 has been replaced by the much faster I-16 freeway, bypassing numerous small towns across an agricultural region that was devastated during General Sherman's Civil War "March to the Sea." Fortunately, Sherman spared the colonial capital, **Savannah,** a lushly verdant gem generally considered among the most beautiful cities in North America.

Columbus

Crossing the Chattahoochee River between Alabama and Georgia, look north to see the rushing waterfalls around which the city of **Columbus** (pop. 197,485) grew. Built on the site of a Creek Native American village, Columbus ("Home of the 2006 Little League World Series Champions") is now Georgia's second-largest city and home of the brutal Army Ranger training school at Fort Benning. During the Civil War, its iron foundries and water-powered factories converted to munitions production, but Columbus was untouched until Union general James H. Wilson stormed across the Chattahoochee in 1865. Unaware that the treaty of Appomattox had already ended the war, "Wilson's Raiders" destroyed much of the city. The huge brick textile mills now lining the river's eastern bank date from the post-Reconstruction years up through the turn of the 20th century, when Columbus emerged as an industrial giant, an era captured in the stories of Columbus author Carson McCullers and in the recordings of blues singer Gertrude "Ma" Rainey. Her home has been preserved,

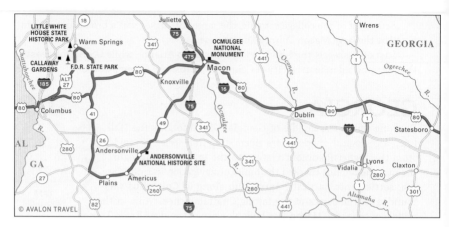

The Chattahoochee River between Alabama and Georgia officially marks the line between the central and eastern time zones, though Phenix City, Alabama, also observes eastern time.

and now houses **The Gertrude "Ma" Rainey House and Blues Museum** (805 5th Ave., 706/653-4960, Tues.-Sat.).

Most city sights are conveniently located in a compact riverside district. Stroll along the Riverwalk promenade for a close-up look at the river (or the kid-friendly science museum), or rumble down the cobblestone lanes of Broadway and Front Street past block after block of graceful old homes and fountain-studded parks. The elegant little **Springer Opera House** (103 E. 10th St.) is the highlight of the adjacent commercial district, where beautifully renovated buildings mix with funky shops selling wigs and voodoo trinkets.

On a hill east of downtown, a half mile from the river, the **Columbus Museum** (1251 Wynnton Rd., 706/748-2562, Tues.-Sun., free) is the major cultural center for the region, with engaging displays tracing the history of the river valley from the time of the Creek people—don't miss the 20-minute movie *Chattahoochee Legacy*, which screens frequently throughout the day. A wide-ranging collection of fine and folk art is on display in the spacious galleries. Overall, this is one of the state's more captivating small museums, well worth an hour at least.

On the site of the former Confederate shipyard at Port Columbus, south of downtown at the foot of 4th Street, the **National Civil War Naval Museum** (1002 Victory Dr., 706/327-9798, daily, $7.50) contains the charred remnants of two Civil War ironclad ships, mock-ups of early submarines and mines, and tons of naval memorabilia.

Columbus Practicalities

At either end of historic downtown, restaurants span the range from down-home to upper-crust. **Country's on Broad** (1329 Broadway, 706/596-8910) serves up classic country cookin' and fabulous hickory-smoked barbecue in a spruced-up 1930s bus depot, complete with an old bus used as a dining area. A step or two down the street and up the style scales is **The Loft** (1032 Broadway, 706/596-8141), a lively bistro with good food and west Georgia's best range of music and comedy. For a midday treat, before or after a visit to the Columbus Museum, head east from downtown along old US-80 to the **Dinglewood Pharmacy** (1939

azalea,
state wildflower of Georgia

Wynnton Rd., 706/322-0616), for a Scrambled Dog, a hot dog buried under chili, onions, and Oysterette crackers.

Most of the national chains line up along the I-185 freeway, but the nicest place to stay in Columbus is the **Marriott** (800 Front Ave., 706/324-1800, $160 and up) downtown, impressively carved out of a former foundry. The former Iron Works next door has been converted into a convention center and performance space and is the site of the city's major festival, the **RiverFest,** in late April or early May. Southeast from downtown, Victory Drive winds toward Fort Benning, passing most of Columbus's budget accommodations.

Warm Springs: FDR's Little White House

About 40 miles north of Columbus, an hour southwest of Atlanta, the rising, forested flanks of Pine Mountain attract flatlanders in search of cooler temperatures and an overlook of the surrounding countryside. In 1924, the therapeutic natural hot springs here also drew the future president Franklin Delano Roosevelt, who, in between losing the election for vice president in 1920 and winning the governorship of New York in 1928, was struck with polio and left unable to walk. Roosevelt loved the area so much he built a wooded three-bedroom retreat here later called the **Little White House** (706/655-5870, daily, $12). He established a treatment center nearby for himself and fellow polio sufferers, funded a charity that grew into today's March of Dimes, and returned regularly over the next two decades. After being elected president in 1932 he formulated much of the "New Deal" and managed the conduct of World War II while staying here. And on the afternoon of April 12, 1945, FDR collapsed suddenly and died at Warm Springs, leaving an unfinished portrait propped on an easel.

The surprisingly small and unpretentious house is as it was when Roosevelt died. The recent addition of an excellent 11,000-square-foot museum tells all about Roosevelt's life and times. Many of the displays concentrate on his political career, but many of the objects are personal and vividly moving, such as the heavy leg braces FDR wore during public appearances, the wall full of walking canes crafted for FDR by disabled people all over the world, and the dark-blue Ford V-8 convertible (with hand controls) that he drove around the Warm Springs countryside.

At nearby 9,049-acre **F. D. Roosevelt State Park,** on land donated by Roosevelt, you can take in the terrific views, swim at the pool, hike a portion of the 23-mile

FDR's Little White House

Pine Mountain Trail, or stay the night in one of the many rustic **cottages** (reservations 800/864-7275, http://gastateparks.org/FDRoosevelt). In the small town of **Warm Springs** (pop. 401), a half mile north of the Little White House park, **Mac's Barbeque** (5711 Spring St., 706/655-2472, daily), at Main Street a block east of Hwy-41, has hickory-smoked ribs and chicken. Home-style comfort food is on the menu at warm and friendly **Bulloch House Restaurant** (70 Broad St., 706/655-9068), in a gorgeous old Victorian home a short walk down Spring Street. Right in the heart of Warm Springs, the historic **Hotel Warm Springs Bed and Breakfast Inn** (47 Broad St., 800/366-7616 or 706/655-2114, $85-195) offers B&B accommodations (with 12-foot ceilings!). There are also plenty of craft, gift, and antiques stores to browse through.

One last area attraction, west of Warm Springs off US-27, is perhaps the biggest draw in north Georgia: **Callaway Gardens** (800/852-3810, daily, $20 adults), which has 14,000 lushly landscaped acres covered in topiary gardens, a lakeside swimming beach, and dazzling displays of colorful flowers. The **Day Butterfly Center,** a 7,000-square-foot atrium with more than 50 exotic species of free-flying butterflies, is surrounded by 1.5 acres of butterfly-friendly gardens. Restaurants, a golf course, and overnight accommodations are also available.

Plains: Jimmy Carter

Another stop along central Georgia's "Presidential Trail," 53 miles southeast of Columbus via US-280, **Plains** (pop. 734), the home of former president Jimmy Carter, stands as a living monument to small-town America. Here, in a town that's small and remote even by South Georgia standards, the 39th president of the United States was raised, mounted his presidential campaign, and now officiates on matters of international diplomacy—that is, when he isn't teaching Sunday School at the Maranatha Baptist Church. Though the Carter family compound is off-limits, visitors can see Carter's high school, stop by late brother Billy's old gas station (the only one in town), and buy a bag of peanuts at the general store.

the 39th president and former first lady in their hometown

Much of Plains has been proclaimed the **Jimmy Carter National Historic Site,** and self-guided touring maps are available at the **visitors center** (300 N. Bond St., 229/824-4104, daily), inside the old Plains High School. Another major part of the Plains experience is the family farm, preserved in the pre-electricity circa-1937 state described in Carter's evocative memoir, *An Hour Before Daylight: Memories of a Rural Boyhood.* Finally, there's the old train depot downtown, which served as Carter's campaign headquarters in 1976 and again in 1980, when he was trounced by Ronald Reagan.

The town of **Americus** is the worldwide operational headquarters of **Habitat for Humanity,** which helps provide basic shelter for people all over the world.

Thirteen miles northeast of Plains is the market town of **Americus** (pop. 15,854). The wealth generated by the region's cotton plantations is embodied in the towering brick **Windsor Hotel** (125 W. Lamar St., 229/924-1555, $85-200). A truly elegant Victorian-era hotel with a three-story atrium lobby—one of the grandest interior spaces in the state—the Windsor is worth a look and makes a great base for exploring central Georgia.

Andersonville Prison

A dozen miles northeast of Americus via Hwy-49, the **Andersonville National Historic Site** (229/924-0343, daily, free) stands on the site of the largest and most notorious Confederate military prison. During the 14 months the prison existed, 45,000 Union soldiers were imprisoned here in overcrowded conditions, and 13,000 died as a result of disease, poor sanitation, and exposure. Once this was uncovered, public outrage was so great that the camp's commandant, Captain Henry Wirz, the only Confederate officer tried for war crimes, was convicted of murder and hanged in Washington DC. Historians generally agree that there was little he could have done to alleviate the suffering. Thousands of closely packed gravestones fill the Andersonville National Cemetery, just north of the prison site.

Only a few parts of the prison have been reconstructed, but the prisoners' harrowing stories are told in one part of the adjacent **National Prisoner of War Museum,** which was dedicated in 1998 and recounts the stories of American POWs during wars up through the present day. Perhaps surprisingly, the tone of the museum is neither vindictive nor especially patriotic, focusing instead on the instances of individual bravery in the face of impossible difficulties.

Macon

Near the geographic center of the state, the city of **Macon** (pop. 92,582) was founded along the Ocmulgee (pronounced "oak-MUL-gee") River in 1823, and flourished with the cotton trade. The downtown area was energized by the opening of the Georgia Music Hall of Fame, which stood alongside dozens of well-preserved

historically significant public buildings, including the 110-year-old **Grand Opera House** (651 Mulberry St.) and the turn-of-the-20th-century **Douglass Theater** (355 Martin Luther King Jr. Blvd.) west of Mulberry Street, where such Macon-born music legends as Lena Horne, Otis Redding, and Little Richard got their start. A generation later, the Allman Brothers' "Ramblin' Man" was "born in the back seat of a Greyhound Bus, rolling down Highway 41." Old US-41 is now home to the **Allman Brothers Big House Museum** (2321 Vineville Ave., 478/741-5551, Thurs.-Sat. 11am-6pm, Sun. 11am-4pm, $10), a mile west of downtown Macon, where a museum and memorial occupy the same 16-bedroom mansion the innovative bluesy, jazzy rock-and-roll band called home during their 1970s heyday. Band members Greg Allman, Duane Allman, and Berry Oakley are buried in Rose Hill Cemetery, off Riverside Drive. Oakley's epitaph (and the wrought iron front gate of the Big House Museum) reads "and the road goes on forever."

> In early spring, **Macon**'s more than 300,000 cherry trees come into bloom, drawing flower lovers from all over the region.

Another aspect of Macon heritage, the city's collection of well-preserved antebellum mansions, stands on a low hill at the north end of downtown, having survived the Civil War unscathed apart from one brief battle: While most of Sherman's troops skirted by to the north, a band of Union soldiers engaged young Confederate soldiers at the city limits and fired a cannonball that landed in the foyer of a stately residence, now known as the **Cannonball House** (856 Mulberry St., 478/745-5982, Mon.-Sat., $8). A small museum behind the house displays the usual barrage of Confederate memorabilia, and inside the house you can see the dented floor and original cannonball. A few blocks away, the stunning **Hay House** (934 Georgia Ave., 478/742-8155, daily, $11) is among the most beautiful antebellum houses in the state. You can see these two and many more on a meandering walk led by a Macon tour guide posing as Sidney Lanier, the city's famous 19th-century poet; call the **visitors bureau** (478/743-1074 or 800/768-3401) for details.

> **Knoxville,** Georgia, 25 miles west of Macon and just north of US-80, holds a unique monument to local woman Joanna Troutman, who designed the Lone Star flag of Texas. She gave the flag, which featured a blue star on a white background but which was otherwise identical to the current one, to a battalion of Macon volunteers heading west to fight for the Texas Republic.

Macon Practicalities

One of the nation's oldest fast-food restaurants is a Macon institution: the original **Nu-Way Weiners,** with six locations, has been in business since 1916.

For a place to stay, choose from the many motels lining

Riverside Drive north of town along the I-75 frontage, or splurge a little on the comfortable **1842 Inn** (353 College St., 877/452-6599 or 478/741-1842, $189-255), a white-columned antebellum mansion converted into a bed-and-breakfast with tons of historical ambience.

Ocmulgee National Monument

Across the Ocmulgee River, well signed from I-16 exit 4, two miles east of Macon along the Emory Highway (US-23/80), the settlement now preserved as the **Ocmulgee National Monument** was a center of preconquest Native American culture. By the mid-

entrance to the earth lodge at Ocmulgee National Monument

1500s, when DeSoto and the first European colonists arrived, Ocmulgee had already been inhabited for over 800 years, with some remains dating from AD 900.

From the small WPA-era **visitors center** (478/752-8257, ext. 222, daily, free), where you can watch a short film and admire pieces of elaborate pottery found on the site, a short trail leads to a restored earthen lodge (complete with thinly disguised air-conditioning ducts!), where you walk through a narrow tunnel to the center of the circular kiva-like interior. The trail continues past the excavated remains of a Creek trading post, then crosses a set of railroad tracks before climbing a 45-foot-high Great Temple Mound, where you can see downtown Macon across the rumbling I-16 freeway—2,000 years of culture in one pleasant half-mile walk.

Juliette: the Whistle Stop Café

Tucked away upriver on the Ocmulgee, in the heart of the Piedmont forests of middle Georgia, sits the town of **Juliette,** somewhat revived after a long slumber because of its **Whistle Stop Café** (443 McCrackin St., 478/992-8886). The café, town, and river were the backdrop for the 1991 film *Fried Green Tomatoes,* based on Fannie Flagg's novel. (The novel, it should be said, was based on the Irondale Café outside Birmingham, Alabama.) You can taste Whistle Stop barbecue, along with a plate of fried green tomatoes, every day of the week. Juliette is due north of Macon along US-23, or 10 miles east of the I-75 town of Forsyth via Juliette Road.

Off I-16: Dublin and Vidalia

Named by its Irish founders in 1812, **Dublin** (pop. 16,104) continues to celebrate its Irish heritage with shamrocks painted on the center dividers, and an all-out St. Patrick's Day festival that lasts most of a month. The historic district is centered along Bellevue Avenue, where you can note the prominent Confederate Memorial, glimpse the town's many graceful old homes, and look inside the local **historical museum** (702 Bellevue Ave., 478/272-9242, Tues.-Fri. 10am-5pm, free) at Bellevue and Academy Streets.

All across the Deep South, but across Georgia in particular, US-80 is lined by the photogenic remains of long-abandoned filling stations, many of them built with accommodations on the upper floor—right above the old gas pumps.

Southeast of Dublin, around 24 miles south of I-16, **Vidalia** (pop. 10,703) is known to food-lovers around the world as the home of the delectable Vidalia onion, so sweet it can be eaten raw, like an apple. In late April and early May, follow the scent to the **Vidalia Onion Festival** (912/538-8687) for taste treats.

Statesboro and Claxton

Twelve miles north of I-16, **Statesboro** (pop. 31,419) was also one of Sherman's stops on his notorious March to the Sea. Here in 1864 his troops torched the courthouse; today's historic courthouse dates from the late-19th century. Georgia Southern University, with an enrollment of more than 19,000, dominates the town, especially during the fall football season. In Statesboro, Main Street runs in four different directions: north, east, south, and west. In the late 1920s, the town inspired Georgia-born Blind Willie McTell to write "Statesboro Blues," a blues classic that was later recorded by Taj Mahal and the Allman Brothers.

For barbecue, head over to **Vandy's Barbecue** (22 W. Vine St., 912/764-2444, Mon.-Sat.), a white-painted breezeblock local landmark a block south from the center of Statesboro on that omnidirectional Main Street, then a block west.

Ten miles south of I-16 at the intersection of US-280 and US-301, the town of **Claxton** (pop. 2,297) bills itself as the "Fruitcake Capital of the World." In the fall fruitcake-making season, the **Claxton Bakery** (800/841-4211 or 912/739-3441), right along the railroad tracks in the center of town, offers free samples of the 3,000 tons of fruitcake it pounds out each year.

INTERSECTION The beautiful city of **Savannah** (see page 438) marks the junction of our US-80 route with the **Atlantic Coast** road trip. Full coverage of that route begins on page 390.

US-80 across Savannah

Old US-80 comes into Savannah on Louisville Road, past the Savannah-Hilton Head International Airport on the northwest edge of town. The old road turns into Bay Street for the final approach, then runs south across the historic downtown area before turning east onto Victory Drive, which runs along the southern foot of Savannah, then across to the barrier islands. If you'd rather save Savannah for another day, you can follow I-16 and Victory Drive around the south side of downtown.

The drive east from Savannah to the Atlantic Ocean passes by the beautiful Bonaventure Cemetery, a stately Civil War fort, and a number of

Bonaventure Cemetery

picturesque fishing villages on its way across the serene marshlands, where a maze of small rivers and creeks weaves through the tall green reeds. Fishing boats bob along the tidal waters as they head off to harvest shrimp and oysters.

Bonaventure Cemetery

Whether or not you got obsessed with *Midnight in the Garden of Good and Evil,* the book that put Savannah back on the map in the 1990s, you'll enjoy visiting **Bonaventure Cemetery** (330 Bonaventure Rd., daily, free), which features prominently in the story. Located east of Savannah proper, north of US-80 via Whatley Avenue, it is simply one of the most evocative corners of this characterful part of the country, where majestic old trees draped in mossy strands stand over abundant azaleas and all manner of monuments and memorials. No less a figure than naturalist John Muir, who camped here for a while immediately after the Civil War, called it "one of the most impressive assemblages of animal and plant creatures I have ever met." Songwriter Johnny Mercer of "Moon River" fame is buried here, along with centuries' worth of other Savannahians.

Fort Pulaski

East of Savannah the landscape gets peaceful quickly. Amid the contemporary calm stands **Fort Pulaski National Monument** (912/786-5787, daily, $7), 14 miles east of Savannah on US-80, a well-preserved stone-and-brick fortress completed in 1848 at a commanding site at the mouth of the Savannah River. Its prominent island site originally held colonial-era fortifications, which were demolished by a hurricane in 1804 and replaced by the architecturally impressive pentagon-shaped bulwark that survives in its battered and breached state today, surrounded by a moat and many acres of grassy lawn.

Beginning in 1829, construction of Fort Pulaski, proclaimed "as strong as the Rocky Mountains," took 18 years, used 25 million bricks, and cost just over a million

Fort Pulaski

dollars (which is equivalent to something close to $5 billion these days, as a share of the U.S. GDP!). During the Civil War, its seven-foot-thick walls withstood bombardment by the Union forces' new rifled cannon for only 30 hours, prompting the fort's surrender in April 1862.

Beautiful and endlessly photogenic, besides the military history Fort Pulaski preserves abundant natural habitat for all sorts of splendid creatures. Eagles, falcons, and songbirds fly about, while alligators, manatees, and turtles cruise through the lazy waters of the moat and nearby wetlands.

Tybee Island

Less than 20 miles southeast of central Savannah, spreading lazily over the eastern-most of many islands filling the delta at the mouth of the Savannah River, the town of **Tybee Island** (pop. 3,113) is a funky old family-oriented resort, with four blocks of burger stands, taverns, and broad clean sands at the eastern end of US-80. Increasingly grown-up and genteel, Tybee still has one last remnant of a rowdier era, in a fun amusement arcade, batting cage, go-kart, and mini-golf combo: **Island Miniature Golf and Games** (912/898-3833), on US-80 just west of the Bull River Bridge. Locally famous for the annual **Beach Bum Parade** (912/786-5444 or 800/868-2322) and riotous water fight to kick off summer, Tybee Island's main attraction is its endless, and usually uncrowded, powdery white-sand beaches, which spread from either side of the pier and pavilion at the east end of 16th Street.

At the north end of Tybee Island, from whence the Union forces bombarded Fort Pulaski during the Civil War, a centuries-old lighthouse stands next to the World War II-era concrete bunkers that house the **Tybee Island Light Station and Museum** (912/786-5801, Wed.-Mon., $9), which includes the old lighthouse keeper's cottage among its collections tracing the island's history.

Other draws here are the wacky, slightly ersatz diner-style **Breakfast Club**

Tybee Island Light Station and Museum

(1500 Butler Ave., 912/786-5984), right at the center of things, open daily for breakfast or an early lunch; if the line is too long, head across the road to the **Sunrise Restaurant** (1511 Butler Ave., 912/786-7473).

Tybee Island's stretch of US-80, Butler Avenue, was home to the world's first Days Inn motel, but these days inexpensive accommodations can be hard to find. There's an older but comfortable (and pet-friendly!) **Dunes Inn & Suites** (1409 Butler Ave., 912/786-4591, $100 and up) near the beach and breakfast club. For a more memorable stay, try the **Tybee Island Bed and Breakfast Inn** (24 Van Horne Ave., 912/786-9255, $189 and up), built in 1902 and set in lovely gardens at the north end of the island, near the grounds of historic Fort Screven.

Route 66

1933 Road Map
CHICAGO METROPOLITAN AREA
A CENTURY OF PROGRESS EXPOSITION

B

HISTORIC
NEW MEXICO
66
ROUTE

BARNSDALL
THE WORLD'S FIRST REFINED

The Grand Canyon — pg. 881

◄ 420 mi ►

pg. 891

◄ 400 mi ►

pg. 900

pg. 864

◄ 250 mi ►

pg. 858

Hollywood Forever

London Bridge

Tinkertown

Cadillac Ranch

If you're looking for great displays of neon signs, mom 'n' pop motels in the middle of nowhere, or kitschy Americana, do as the song says and "get your kicks on Route 66."

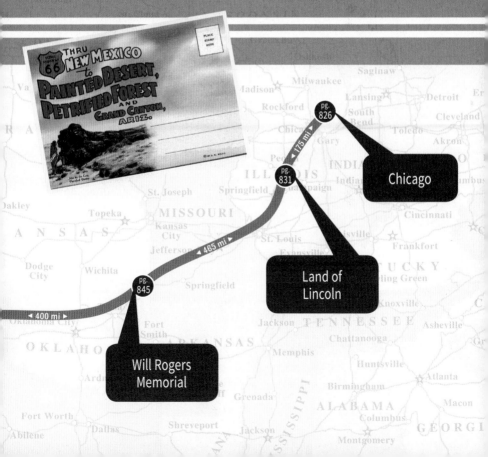

Between Chicago, Illinois, and Los Angeles, California

The romance of Route 66 continues to captivate people around the world. Running between Chicago and Los Angeles, "over two thousand miles all the way" in the words of the popular R&B anthem, this legendary old road passes through the heart of the United States on a diagonal trip that takes in some of the country's most archetypal roadside scenes. If you're looking for great displays of neon signs, rusty middle-of-nowhere truck stops, or kitschy Americana, do as the song says and "get your kicks on Route 66."

But perhaps the most compelling reason to follow Route 66 is to experience the road's ingrained time line of contemporary America. Before it was called Route 66, and long before it was even paved in 1926, this corridor was traversed by the National Old Trails Highway, one of the country's first transcontinental highways. For three decades before and after World War II, Route 66 earned the title **"Main Street of America"** because it wound through small towns across the Midwest and Southwest, lined by hundreds of cafés, motels, gas stations, and tourist attractions. During the Great Depression, hundreds of thousands of farm families, displaced from the Dust Bowl, made their way west along Route 66 to California, following what John Steinbeck called **"The Mother Road"** in his vivid portrait, *The Grapes of Wrath*. After World War II, many thousands more expressed their upward mobility by leaving the industrial East, bound for good jobs in the suburban idyll of Southern California—again following Route 66, which came to embody the demographic shift from the Rust Belt to the Sun Belt.

Beginning in the late 1950s and

continuing gradually over the next 25 years, old Route 66 was bypassed section by section as the high-speed interstate highways were completed. Finally, after the last stretch of freeway was completed in 1984, Route 66 was officially decommissioned. The old route is now designated Historic Route 66.

Though it is no longer a main route across the country, Route 66 has retained its mystique in part due to the same effective hype, hucksterism, and boosterism that animated it through its half-century heyday. It was a Route 66 sight, the marvelous **Meramec Caverns,** that gave the world the bumper sticker. And it was here on Route 66 that the great American driving vacation first flourished. Billboards and giant statues along the highway still hawk a baffling array of roadside attractions, tempting passing travelers to view giant blue whales, to see live rattlesnakes and other wild creatures on display in roadside menageries, or to stay at "Tucumcari Tonite."

The same commercial know-how and shameless self-promotion has helped the towns along the old route stay alive. Diners and motels play up their Route 66 connections, and many bona fide Route 66 landmarks are kept in business by nostalgic travelers intent on experiencing a taste of this endlessly endangered American experience. That said, many quirky old motels and cafés hang on by a thread of hope, sit vacant, or survive in memory only—all for want of an interstate exit. In fact, of all the roads covered in this book, Route 66 has perhaps felt the greatest impact from the modern interstate world; for many stretches you'll be forced to leave the old two-lane and follow the super slabs that have been built right on top of the old road.

Route 66 passes through a marvelous cross-section of American scenes, from the cornfields of Illinois all the way to the golden sands and sunshine of Los Angeles, passing by such diverse environs as the **Grand Canyon,** the Native American communities of the desert Southwest, the small-town Midwest heartlands of **Oklahoma** and **the Ozarks,** and the gritty streets of **St. Louis** and **Chicago.** Whether you are motivated by an interest in history, feel a nostalgic yearning for the "good old days" Route 66 has come to represent, or simply want to experience firsthand the amazing diversity of people and landscapes that line its path, Route 66 offers an unforgettable journey into America, then and now.

ILLINOIS

Heading diagonally across the state between Chicago and St. Louis, what remains of Route 66 is a surprisingly rural cruise through endless fields of corn. Despite the urban conglomerations at both ends, for most of its nearly 300-mile trek here, Route 66 and its modern usurper, I-55, pass along flat prairies with nary a smokestack or skyscraper as far as the eye can see.

The heavy industrial and poverty-stricken hinterlands of Chicago and East St. Louis aren't terribly rewarding for travelers in search of the Mother Road, but a couple of intriguing attractions—one a prehistoric city, the other a water tower shaped like a catsup bottle—are worth searching out. The only real city along Route 66 is the Illinois state capital, **Springfield,** which has preserved its sections of Route 66 alongside a wealth of places connected to the namesake president here in the "Land of Lincoln." Dozens of small towns across the state play up their Route 66 connections, and most boast at least one true old-road landmark.

> A little piece of highway history happened in 1926 when the original alignment of Route 66 crossed the even older Lincoln Highway, America's first transcontinental road, later marked on maps as US-30. The Lincoln Highway and Route 66 intersected first at Joliet and later farther west at Plainfield.

Route 66 Across Chicagoland

Following the first (or last) leg of Route 66 across Chicago and its hinterlands is not worth the effort for anyone except the most die-hard end-to-ender—even Jack Rittenhouse, in his original 1946 *A Guide Book to Highway 66,* didn't bother to describe the route until it reached Plainfield, 35 miles southwest of the Loop, and these days the Chicagoland suburbs don't fade away until you get beyond Joliet.

For a symbolic starting point, you can use the grand old Art Institute of Chicago in Grant Park along the lakeshore, since the last US-66 shield used to hang from a streetlight just south of the gallery. If Chicago is your "end of the road," you'll probably prefer to avoid the final few miles of surface streets and make your way to town as quickly as possible via I-55, celebrating your arrival with a cup of coffee at **Lou Mitchell's** restaurant and bakery.

From Lake Michigan, the old road ran westbound through the Loop via Adams Street (take Jackson Boulevard eastbound; both are one-way) before angling southwest along Ogden Avenue—a long diagonal exception to the city's main grid of streets.

Ogden Avenue, which carries Route 66 in and out of Chicago, is not one of the world's scenic wonders, but it can reveal a lot about the places it passes through. Located just south of Frank Lloyd Wright's hometown of Oak Park, **Cicero** is notorious for its connections to another local legend: mobster Al Capone, who took refuge here outside the jurisdiction of the Chicago police. Cicero's main Route 66 connection is the fine sign—"It's a Meal in Itself"—marking **Henry's Drive-In** (6031 W. Ogden Ave., 708/656-9344), where you can snack on excellent Polish hot dogs smothered with a pile of french fries. And crisp pickles, if you want them.

Bounded by the I-55 freeway, **Berwyn** effectively marks one end of this first or last stretch of Route 66 with the unusual **Chicago Portage National Historic Site.** This nearly 100-acre semi-wilderness, surrounded by decrepit and abandoned industrial lands, preserves the place where early explorers learned to carry their canoes and boats between the Chicago and Des Plaines water-sheds, linking the Atlantic Ocean and Gulf of Mexico via the Great Lakes and Mississippi River. (Today, the euphemistically named Chicago Sanitary and Ship Canal serves a similar role, running via Lockport and Joliet.)

One longstanding Route 66 landmark stands about 20 miles outside Chicago in Willowbrook, off Hwy-83 on the north side of I-55: **Dell Rhea's Chicken Basket** (645 Joliet Rd., 630/325-0780) is a welcoming old roadside tavern, with famously fabulous chicken dinners and frequent live music.

Joliet

Joliet, the "City of Steel and Stone," has a rough reputation that dates back long before the 1970s, when Saturday Night Live star John Belushi sang in the Blues Brothers band as paroled convict "Joliet Jake." Route 66 through this once-mighty industrial enclave is a feast for fans of postindustrial scenery. Along the Des Plaines River north of downtown is the now-closed state prison from which "Joliet Jake" is released at the beginning of the 1980 movie, which was filmed on location here and in Chicago.

Stalwart bridges cross the Des Plaines River and historic Illinois & Michigan Canal, which, beginning in the 1840s, connected Chicago with the Mississippi River before being replaced by the less salubrious Sanitary and Ship Canal. Old warehouse and commercial buildings survive all over town. The most notable is the lovely Rialto Theater

Chicago (see page 614) marks the junction of Route 66 and our cross-country route along **The Oregon Trail.** Full coverage of that route begins on page 558.

on Chicago Street, where you'll also find the original home of fast-food megacorp Dairy Queen. It's now an official landmark—but it's occupied by a storefront church (501 N. Chicago St.) signed "Jesuscristo es el Señor," which seems all too appropriate.

While the suburbs grow and grow, efforts to reverse downtown Joliet's long economic downturn by embracing casino gambling have not had much success. The large **Harrah's Joliet Casino** (151 N. Joliet St., 815/740-7800) draws gamblers but has not done much to revive the waterfront or the surrounding streets.

South of Joliet, following old Route 66 (Hwy-53) across the I-80 superslab brings you past the massive **Chicagoland Speedway** and the **Route 66 Raceway** (888/629-7223), where NHRA drag races, NASCAR stock car races, and occasional pop music concerts are held.

Midewin National Tallgrass Prairie Preserve

Along Route 66 between Joliet and Wilmington, a unique partnership between environmentalists and the U.S. military is working to recreate the natural ecosystem on one of the most environmentally damaged areas imaginable: more than 19,000 acres of the old Joliet ammunition factory are being converted into the **Midewin National Tallgrass Prairie Preserve** (815/423-6370, trails open daily, welcome center Mon.-Sat. summer, Mon.-Fri. winter). Since 1996, when the land was transferred from the U.S. Army to the U.S. Forest Service, the change from producing TNT to regrowing the native tallgrass prairie has been slow and steady. After years of toxic cleanups and careful husbandry, more than half the old plant has been returned to its natural state and now offers more than 34 miles of hiking and biking trails on both sides of Hwy-53 (old Route 66). Midewin (pronounced "mi-DAY-win") is an indigenous Potawatomi word meaning "healthy balance," and a visit here gives a good feeling for the flora and fauna that would have existed naturally in places like this all over the Midwest.

Hwy-53: Wilmington and Dwight

From Joliet, you can follow old Route 66 southwest through a series of nice small towns along Hwy-53, which runs along the southeast side of I-55. Though the route is sometimes a bit obscure and not all that rich in history or aesthetic delights, the towns here offer a pleasant taste of what old Route 66 had to offer. **Wilmington** is semi-famous for its photogenic 30-foottall, bright green **Gemini Giant** statue, which stands in front of the former Launching Pad Drive-In (810 E. Baltimore St.). The Gemini Giant is in fine shape, but not its host; the Launching Pad has been closed and put up for sale for a number of years. Fortunately, for hungry road-trippers, the neighboring town of **Braidwood** has the popular retro-1950s **Polk-A-Dot Drive-In** (222

N. Front St., 815/458-3377) along old Route 66, and the Polk-A-Dot has a giant of its own: a 9-foot-tall guitar-wielding 1970s-era Elvis Presley.

Continuing along Hwy-53, there are a couple more classic Route 66 scenes along the old road northwest of Pontiac, the next biggish town. **Dwight** is leafy and quaint, well known a century ago for its Keeley Institute treatment center for alcoholics, and now famous for its fine old Texaco station, which stands at the main crossroads (near the reliable Old Route 66 Family Restaurant). The Dwight Texaco station opened in 1933 and managed to stay in business until 1999, earning it a reputation as the oldest continually operating gas station on the Mother Road (retiring at the ripe old age of 66 was a clever marketing move!). The station has been restored to its original look and now serves as Dwight's welcome center. To my eye, an even more picturesque old Standard Oil gas station stands just down Hwy-53 in the next Route 66 town, **Odell.**

Pontiac: Route 66 Hall of Fame

Some 90 miles southeast of Lake Michigan, the former coal-mining town of **Pontiac** (pop. 11,827) surrounds the stately 1875 Livingston County Courthouse. The courthouse's green lawns hold the usual battery of monuments, including one to the namesake Ottawa chief whose visage also graced the General Motors "Pontiac" models, which were discontinued and abandoned in 2010. According to the WPA *Guide to Illinois,* another of these monuments, the Soldiers and Sailors Monument, received the shortest presidential dedication in history when, in 1902, it was "dedicated with a few hasty words by President Theodore Roosevelt, before an audience of less than a dozen people, who congregated briefly under a terrific downpour."

A short stretch of original, circa 1926-era Route 66 near **Lexington,** right off the south side of I-55 exit 178, has been decorated with replicas of old billboards and Burma-Shave advertisements and dubbed **Memory Lane.** It's officially a pedestrian and bike-only section of Morris Street.

Though the old road ran around rather than right through Pontiac, the town has become one of the main stops on the Illinois Route 66 tour, thanks to the presence here of the **Route 66 Association Hall of Fame Museum** (110 W. Howard St., 815/844-4566, daily, free), in the old main fire station. Along with the usual displays of gas pumps, enamel and neon advertising signs, and old photos documenting the road's heritage, the Pontiac museum is worth a look for its tribute to iconic Route 66 artist Bob

Welcome to Downtown Pontiac!

Waldmire (1945-2009), whose delicate line drawings were instrumental in nurturing national enthusiasm for preserving and protecting the unique legacy of Route 66. Many of Bob's drawing and mural paintings and large murals are reproduced here, alongside the 1972 VW camper and the big old Chevy school bus RV in which Bob traveled and lived for much of his prolific life. Bob's VW van and his hippy-dippy appreciation of the human and natural history of Route 66 inspired the countercultural character Fillmore in the movie *Cars,* voiced by comedian George Carlin. Adding to the aesthetic experience, the engaging **International Wall Dogs Sign and Mural Museum** (217 N. Mill St., 815/842-1848, daily, free) is in the same building. The Wall Dogs are an international collective who get together in places around the world to paint large signs and public murals, including most of those lining the streets of downtown.

Pontiac is also home to two more excellent attractions. Facing the west side of the landmark Livingston County Courthouse, the world's greatest car museum, officially known as the **Pontiac-Oakland Museum** (205 N. Mill St., 815/842-2345, daily, free), displays immaculately preserved Firebirds and Bonnevilles amid a Smithsonian-worthy array of advertising and related memorabilia, all in a beautifully designed and maintained space reclaimed from a historic showroom.

One more long-lived Route 66 landmark to experience: the **Old Log Cabin Inn** (18700 Old Route 66, 815/842-2908) on the north edge of town. When Route 66 was redirected behind the original location, this restaurant was jacked up and flipped around. The older old road, which dates from 1918, is still there, behind the café along the railroad tracks. The old log building doesn't catch the eye like some other more exuberant Route 66 icons, but the good food and warm hospitality on offer inside are the essence of the old road—especially if you visit before they've run out of coconut cream pie!

Bloomington-Normal

Hometown of politician Adlai Stevenson (and Colonel Henry Blake of TV's *M*A*S*H*), **Bloomington-Normal** sits at the middle of Illinois, surrounded by five different freeways and miles of cornfields. Its main claim to fame is in being the only place in the world where that classic bar snack, Beer Nuts, is made; for a free sample (but no tour, alas), stop by the **Beer Nuts factory** (103 N. Robinson St., 800/BEER-NUTS—800/233-7688 or 309/827-8580, Mon.-Fri.). The "Twin Cities" are also the corporate home of insurance company State Farm and birthplace of another all-American icon, the Midwest-based burger chain Steak 'n Shake, which started here in 1934. Good food is available downtown at **Lucca Grill** (116 E. Market St., 309/828-7521), which has been serving pizza and pasta dishes since the 1930s.

Funks Grove

Heading on from Bloomington-Normal, westbound drivers will encounter the next two towns in sonorous order—Shirley and McLean. Wordplay aside, the stretch of Illinois farmland between Bloomington and Springfield is rich in Route 66-related heritage. In McLean, 55 miles from Springfield and 16 miles southwest from Bloomington, old Route 66 emerges from the shadow of I-55. You can follow old Route 66 along the west side of the freeway for just over four miles past the delightful anachronism of **Funks Grove** (309/874-3360), where the friendly Funk family has been tapping trees and selling delicious maple "sirup" (that's how they spell it) since 1891. If you're here in late winter or early spring, you can watch them tap the trees and hammer in the spouts; each tree can produce up to 4 gallons of sap a day, but it takes 35 to 50 gallons of sap for each gallon of the final product. Free tastings are available, and a full range of bottles is on sale.

Logan County Courthouse in Lincoln

Lincoln

The only town named for Honest Abe in his lifetime, **Lincoln** (pop. 13,969) took his name before he became a famous figure. As a young lawyer, Abraham Lincoln drew up the legal documents for founding the town but warned developers that he "never knew of anything named Lincoln that amounted to much." At the dedication ceremonies, Lincoln supposedly "baptized" the place by spitting out a mouthful of watermelon seeds—hence the plaster watermelon and historical plaque commemorating the great event, next to the Amtrak-serviced train station at Broadway and Chicago Streets in the center of town. Lincoln was also home to Harlem Renaissance poet Langston Hughes (1902-1967), who was elected Class Poet while in the eighth grade here.

Lincoln's Tomb in Springfield

Springfield

As the Illinois state capital, **Springfield** (pop. 115,715) embodies the rural small-town character of most of the state and feels much farther away from Chicago than the three-plus-hour drive it actually is, traffic willing. Springfield is also the place that takes the "Land of Lincoln" state's obsession with Abraham Lincoln to its greatest extreme, for it was here that Honest Abe worked and lived from 1837 to 1861. He left Springfield after being elected president and was buried here after his assassination at the end of the Civil War.

There are all manner of Lincoln sights to see all over Springfield, but the newest and best place to start your homage is at the state-run **Abraham Lincoln Presidential Library and Museum** (112 N. 6th St., 217/558-8934, daily, $15), across from the Old State Capitol. Once you've toured this comprehensive, reverential yet thought-provoking, over $100 million, 200,000-square-foot complex, other sights include the only home Lincoln ever owned, his law offices, and, of course, his tomb. Located in Oak Ridge Cemetery, two miles north of downtown, Lincoln's tomb also includes the remains of his wife and three of four children. Legend has it that if you touch the nose on the bronze bust of Lincoln, good luck will follow.

Though quite sincere and understated, the Lincoln homage can overwhelm. If you need a change of pace from Lincoln Land there is the beautiful **Dana-Thomas House** (301 E. Lawrence Ave., 217/782-6776, Wed.-Sun., $10), a half mile south of

LOCATED ON HISTORIC ROUTE 66 SINCE 1949, SPRINGFIELD, ILLINOIS

South of Springfield, on the stretch of old Route 66 that forms the frontage road at I-55 exit 63, near the town of **Raymond**, a marble statue of the Virgin Mary forms a shrine that has become known as **Our Lady of the Highways**.

the state capitol. Designed by Frank Lloyd Wright in 1902 for socialite Susan Dana, who lived here until the late 1940s, it is the most luxurious, best preserved, and most fully furnished of his houses.

Springfield also has a favorite Route 66 watering hole, the **Cozy Dog Drive-In** (2935 S. 6th St., 217/525-1992), on the old road south of downtown. The birthplace of the corn dog, which here goes by the nicer name "Cozy," was founded in 1949 by Ed Waldmire, father of noted Route 66 artist Bob Waldmire. So come on in and chow down—four Cozy Dogs and a big basket of fries cost around $11.

Complete your Route 66 Americana tour by taking in a flick or two at the **Route 66 Twin Drive-In** (1700 Recreation Dr., 217/698-0066), west of 6th Street southwest of the junction of I-72 and I-55.

Almost all the national chain hotels and motels have operations in Springfield, so you shouldn't have trouble finding a room. For genuine character in a convenient location, consider the elegant **Inn at 835** (835 S. 2nd St., 217/523-4466, $125 and up), near the Dana-Thomas House.

Litchfield and Mount Olive

Between Springfield and Cahokia Mounds, the most interesting stretch of old Route 66 runs along the east side of the freeway for about a dozen miles, between Litchfield and Mount Olive. The first stop is **Litchfield** (pop. 6,812), an old coal-mining center that is home to a lively downtown flea market (Sat.-Sun. summer) and one of the best and most stylish Route 66 restaurants: the **Ariston Café** (413 N. Old Route 66, 217/324-2023, Wed.-Sun.), right in the heart of town at the junction of old Route 66 and Hwy-16. The menu is a step or two up from the usual roadside fare, with excellent fried chicken, while the white linen and refined decor have earned it a spot in the Route 66 Hall of Fame. The rest of Litchfield reeks of the old road, with cafés, motor courts, and old billboards aplenty, plus another old "ozoner," the **Sky View Drive-In** (217/324-4451) on old Route 66 one mile north of town.

Parts of the old road survive between Springfield and Litchfield, but the route is incomplete and can be confusing to follow. I-55 makes much shorter work of the 45-mile drive.

Some seven miles southwest of Litchfield, the hamlet of **Mount Olive** (pop. 2,002) was a bustling coal-mining center in the early 20th century. It's now a sleepy little community, where the only signs of its mining past are in the Union Miners Cemetery, along old Route 66 at the northwest edge of town. Near the rear is a granite shaft rising from an elaborate pedestal, which serves as a memorial to Mary Harris "Mother" Jones (1837-1930), the celebrated union activist (and namesake of the liberal-minded magazine) who was famous for her passionate oratory, like the phrase "Pray for the dead, and fight like hell for the living." She died here, possibly aged 100, while supporting a miners' strike, and is buried nearby. Her grave is marked by a simple headstone.

For old-road fans, Mount Olive is also home to the oldest surviving service station on Route 66, the immaculate, restored (but no longer in business) Shell station downtown, long owned by Russell Soulsby.

Collinsville: Cahokia Mounds

Old Route 66 followed today's I-270 around the north side of St. Louis, crossing the Mississippi River on the restored Chain of Rocks Bridge, but one of southern Illinois's biggest attractions sits directly east of the Gateway Arch, off the I-55/70 freeway at exit 6. Clearly visible to the south side of the interstate, the enigmatic humps of **Cahokia Mounds State Historic Site** are the remains of a city larger than London was in AD 1250. Over 100 earthen mounds of various sizes were built here by the indigenous Mississippian people while Europe was in the Dark Ages. The largest covers 14 acres—more ground than the Great Pyramid of Cheops. But don't expect the works of the pharaohs: Symmetrical, grass-covered hills sitting in flat, lightly wooded bottomlands are what you'll find here. The view of the Gateway Arch in distant St. Louis from the 100-foot top of Monks Mound lends an odd sense of grandeur to the site. A sophisticated **Interpretive Center** (618/346-5160, daily, $7) is a recommended first stop for its exhibits, award-winning multimedia orientation show, and guided and self-guided tours.

The Cahokia Mounds sit in the middle of the American Bottom, a broad floodplain whose gunpowder-black alluvial soils have long been considered among the richest and most productive in the world. However, Charles Dickens was not impressed; after enduring its mud, he wrote in American Notes that the region was an "ill-favored black hollow" which had "no variety but in depth."

The nearest town to the Cahokia Mounds is **Collinsville,** a pleasant little place that's nearly world-famous for its 170-foot-high **World's Largest Catsup Bottle,** which rises high above Hwy-159 a half mile south of Main Street, on the grounds of what used to be the **Brooks Catsup Company** (800 S. Morrison Ave.). This decorated water tower was constructed in 1949 and restored by the people of Collinsville in 1993; it has since been adopted by Collinsville as a supersize symbol of local pride and perseverance.

Chain of Rocks Bridge

If you have the time and the inclination to stretch your legs and breathe deeply, make your way to the northeast edge of St. Louis, where, instead of following the 75-mph I-270 freeway, you can cross the Mississippi between Illinois and Missouri on the historic **Chain of Rocks Bridge.** The bridge has been renovated for use as a mile-long **bike and hiking trail** (314/416-9930, daily dawn-dusk), decorated with an array of old gas pumps and signs, just south of the modern I-270 freeway. If you're driving, the best parking is on the Illinois side of the bridge, but cyclists or energetic walkers can cross the surprisingly narrow bridge and continue all the way to the Gateway Arch in St.

Louis, following an 11-mile Riverfront Trail that snakes between the flood walls, the river, and acres of heavy (and sometimes smelly) industry.

Not quite on the same scale as the Cahokia Mounds, the Chain of Rocks Bridge, or even the Collinsville catsup bottle, the nearby Route 66 town of **Mitchell** holds one more Route 66 landmark: **Luna Café** (201 E. Chain of Rocks Rd., 618/931-3152), a one-time casino, speakeasy, and brothel built in 1924 that's now a pretty seedy but atmospheric bar, north of the I-270 freeway exit 6, along old Route 66.

MISSOURI

The Ozark Highlands of southern Missouri, which Route 66 crosses in its 300-odd-mile journey between Illinois and Kansas, are about the only significant hills the road crosses east of the Sandia Mountains in New Mexico. This plateau region, though not by any means alpine or breathtaking, is visually dynamic in a way the broad flatlands of Illinois or Oklahoma rarely are. Though the I-44 freeway has replaced the old road all the way across the state, there are many signs of older alignments, and just about every interstate exit drops you within a moment's drive of the Mother Road. Missouri also holds some great old motels and one of the greatest of the old Route 66 tourist attractions—**Meramec Caverns,** an extensive set of limestone caves offering the most over-the-top underground tour you can take.

Route 66 Across St. Louis

It can be maddening to follow old Route 66 across St. Louis, but its many great spots—Ted Drewes Frozen Custard stand, in particular—make it well worth the effort. One route crossed the Mississippi River right into downtown from Collinsville, Illinois, while another "City 66" route headed across the Chain of Rocks Bridge before running into downtown St. Louis along Florissant Avenue and Riverview Drive.

Heading southwest out of downtown, the old road followed Gravois Avenue, Chippewa Street, and Watson Road, just south of the parallel I-44 freeway.

Times Beach: Route 66 State Park

There's no plaque or notice proudly marking the spot, but the story of **Times Beach** (pop. 0) deserves mention. Founded in the 1920s as a weekend getaway a dozen miles west of St. Louis along the Meramec River, the town grew into a working-class commuter suburb of some 2,000 people, thanks to Route 66. But there were no paved streets except for the not-yet-famous highway that passed through the center of town. Times Beach remained a quiet hamlet until 1982, when the federal government discovered that the industrial oil sprayed on streets to keep down dust had in fact been contaminated with toxic dioxin. The toxic waste, combined with a Meramec River flood that buried the town for over a week, made Times Beach uninhabitable.

In 1983 the government paid $33 million to buy Times Beach and tear it down, and 15 years later the cleanup was declared complete. Four hundred acres of what was

St. Louis, the only place where three of our routes coincide, marks the junction of old Route 66; US-50, the cross-country **Loneliest Road** (page 731); and **The Great River Road** (page 264). **St. Louis** itself is covered on page 262.

once Times Beach have since been reopened as the **Route 66 State Park** (636/938-7198, daily, free), north of I-44 exits 265 and 266, with hiking trails, river access, and a nice little museum on Times Beach and Route 66, housed in a 1930s roadhouse.

Eureka and Gray Summit: I-44

Heading south and west out of St. Louis, the I-44 freeway has pretty well obliterated old Route 66 as far as **Eureka,** where the sprawling amusement park **Six Flags St. Louis** (636/938-5300, around $65) effectively marks the city's suburban edge. The park has all the thrill rides and water park fun you could want, and often hosts concerts and special events.

A different experience can be had at **Gray Summit,** just west of Six Flags, where the Missouri Botanical Garden tends to the magical **Shaw Nature Reserve** (636/451-3512, daily, $5), a 2,400-acre semi-wilderness of native plants, cultivated orchards, and wildflower meadows, just 40 miles from the Gateway Arch. And if you like animals, especially dogs and cats, you'll want to check out the well-trained pets showcased across I-44 at **Purina Farms** (314/982-3232, Tues.-Sun. May-Aug., Wed.-Mon. Mar.-Apr. and Sept.-Nov., free). Dogs catch Frisbees and do all sorts of amazing tricks, while cats sit there and look pretty.

Between Six Flags and the Shaw Nature Reserve, Route 66 reemerges from the shadows of I-44, winding through the hamlet of **Pacific.** West of Pacific, Route 66 climbs toward Gray Summit past the faded old Route 66 sign for the shuttered Diamonds Truck Stop and long-gone Gardenway Motel.

For most of the 30 miles between Gray Summit and Meramec Caverns, old Route 66 is overwhelmed by the I-44 freeway, so most Route 66 aficionados opt for the freeway and save their exploring for better stretches, like Devil's Elbow.

Meramec Caverns

The best stop along old Route 66's trek across Missouri, and one of the most enjoyable and charming roadside attractions along the entire Mother Road, **Meramec Caverns** (573/468-2283, daily, $21) is a set of limestone caves advertised by signs on barns and buildings all along the route, and all over the Midwest. First developed during the Civil War, when the natural saltpeter was mined for use in manufacturing gunpowder, the caves were later popularized as a place for local farmers to get

From Gray Summit, Hwy-100 runs northwest from I-44 toward the Missouri River to the historic towns of **Hermann** and **Washington** (see page 731), which are covered in our US-50 road trip, **The Loneliest Road.** Full coverage of that route begins on page 670.

Meramec Caverns: nature's best sculpture and a disco light show!

Among its many other claims to fame, **Meramec Caverns** is known as the birthplace of the bumper sticker.

together for dances. The largest room in the caves is still used for Easter services, arts and crafts shows, and even the occasional chamber of commerce meeting. An hour west of St. Louis, Meramec Caverns was opened as a tourist attraction in 1935 by Lester Dill, who guided visitors through the elaborate chambers and, more importantly, was a true master of the art of garnering cheap but effective publicity for his tourist attraction. An example: After World War II, Dill sent his son-in-law to the top of the Empire State Building dressed up as a caveman and had him threaten to jump off unless everyone in the world visited Meramec Caverns.

Fact and fiction mix freely at Meramec Caverns, adding to the pleasures of seeing the massive caves. Jesse James used these caverns as a hideout, and at least once took advantage of the underground river to escape through the secret "back door." Though Meramec is not huge compared to other caves, the natural formations are among the most sculptural and delicate of any cave you can visit, and the artificial additions are all low-tech and kitschy enough to be charming. The hand-operated sound-and-light show ends with a grand finale of Kate Smith singing "God Bless America," while the red, white, and blue of Old Glory is projected onto a limestone curtain. For the full Meramec experience, add in a canoe ride or a zip-line ride, or stay the night in the pleasant riverside campground.

Meramec Caverns is near the town of **Stanton,** 60 miles west of St. Louis, 3 miles south of I-44 exit 230. There's a small café and a motel on the grounds, which spread along the banks of the Meramec River. At the I-44 exit, the odd little **Jesse James Wax Museum** (573/927-5233, daily June-Aug., Sat.-Sun. Apr.-May and Sept.-Oct., $8) insists, despite all evidence to the contrary, that a 100-year-old man who turned up in Stanton in 1948 was in fact Jesse James.

DETOUR: BRANSON

A middle-American mecca, mixing equal parts Las Vegas glitz and Myrtle Beach summer fun, Branson is a century-old Ozark resort town that hit the big time in the 1980s through clever promotion and cunning repackaging of country-and-western music and God-fearing recreation. There are well over 50 major performance venues in Branson, and looking down the list of luminaries who have played here—the Osmond Brothers, Tony Orlando, and Jim "I Don't Like Spiders and Snakes" Stafford—you'd think that anyone who had a hit record or a TV show, or can still sing and smile at the same time, can have their own showcase theater. To cater to the estimated 7.2 million annual visitors, the range of shows keeps expanding, at times including such exotic offerings as Acrobats of China or the Beatles-themed Liverpool Legends.

What originally put Branson on the tourist map was not music but a book: *The Shepherd of the Hills,* by Harold Bell Wright. Set in and around Branson and published in 1907, it was a huge best-seller, adapted in the 1930s into an outdoor stage play, with performances continuing into the 21st century.

The Ozark Mountains around Branson are lovely to explore; just about any road south, east, or west will take you through beautifully scenic mountain landscapes. And if scenery is not enough, one of the most popular spots in Branson is **Silver Dollar City** (800/475-9370 or 417/336-7100, daily, $62 and up), nine miles west of Branson via Hwy-76, a turn-of-the-20th-century theme park devoted to Ozark arts, crafts, and music—and roller coasters.

Cuba

Along I-44 west of Meramec Caverns, the old Route 66 roadside is lined by ramshackle wooden stands, which, toward the end of summer, sell sweet Concord grapes from local Rosati vineyards. The stands are located along the frontage roads (which in many cases are the remnants of the original Route 66), but people park along the freeway and walk to them. At the eastern edge of this grape-growing district, the small town of **Cuba** has a vintage Phillips 66 gas station and a dozen colorful murals covering large areas of downtown buildings with scenes from Cuba's history, depicting everything from the Civil War to the day in 1928 when Amelia Earhart made an emergency landing in a farmer's field.

Cuba also makes it onto many Route 66 itineraries thanks to the friendly **Wagon Wheel Motel** (901 E. Washington St., 573/885-3411, $66 and up), which, for many years, was famous for offering 1930s charm at 1970s prices. Although it has been remodeled, the Wagon Wheel still allows travelers to sample a kinder, gentler, less complicated era—even while taking advantage of clean comfy beds and free Wi-Fi. The Wagon Wheel Motel is right on Route 66. An added bonus: good barbecue is right next door at the **Missouri Hick BBQ** (573/885-6791).

The route west from Cuba to Rolla, along what's now marked as Hwy-ZZ, offers a fine stretch of unsullied Route 66 scenery, made all the more enticing by the presence of the **World's Largest Rocker,** a Guinness-sanctioned champion chair (not a musician!) standing more than 40-feet tall, four miles west of Cuba outside the Fanning Outpost souvenir stand and archery supply store.

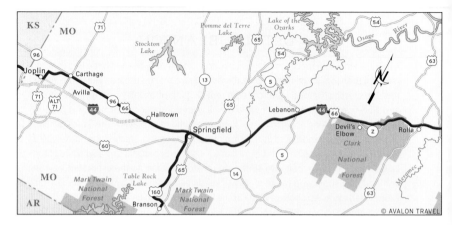

Rolla

Twenty miles west of Cuba, about midway between St. Louis and Springfield, one of the liveliest towns along the Ozark Mountains stretch of Route 66 is **Rolla** (pop. 20,075; pronounced "RAW-la"). In the center of town, right along old Route 66 on the campus of the Missouri University of Science and Technology (MUST), one big draw is the half-scale replica of that ancient Druidical observatory, **Stonehenge,** created in 1984 to show off the high-tech stone carving capabilities of MUST's High Pressure Water Jet Lab.

Adding to the surprising mix of international flavors is another Rolla tradition: a wild and crazy St. Patrick's Day party, held every year since 1908, during which students paint the streets of Rolla green, slay rubber snakes, and drink just about anything they can find, all in homage to the Emerald Isle.

Among the I-44 freeway clutter of Waffle Houses and Shoney's at the west end of Rolla, there's still a sign for the fireworks and moccasins on sale at the landmark **Totem Pole Trading Post.** Once you've got your fill of T-shirts and postcards, head up the hill to Rolla's most popular watering hole, **Rob and Kricket's Tater Patch** (103 Bridge School Rd., 573/368-3111). It's on the south side of Route 66 across from the Rolla visitors center. Try one of their signature baked potatoes topped with pulled pork for a unique taste treat. They've also been serving big breakfasts, pork tenderloins, delicious onion rings, and ice-cold beer for more than 40 years. And anytime you're near Rolla, make sure to set aside enough appetite and enough time to enjoy **A Slice of Pie** (601 Kingshighway St., 573/364-6203), on old Route 66 south of downtown, where two former schoolteachers bake an amazing array of fruit, nut, cream, and meringue pies, and even a few creamy quiches.

Old Route 66: Devil's Elbow

West of Rolla toward Springfield, I-44 has been built right on top of the old Route 66 corridor. Dozens of mostly abandoned old motels, motor courts, gas stations, and other highway-dependent businesses line the remains of the old road, which still serves as a freeway frontage road for most of the way. There are plenty of antiques shops and cafés to make detours interesting, and the longish detour along old Route 66 through the **Devil's Elbow** district is especially memorable. But if you're pressed for time, even the interstate superslab offers a plenty-scenic drive through these

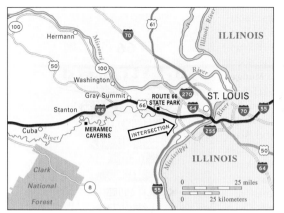

white hawthorn,
state flower of Missouri

upland Ozark Mountains, much of which are protected from development within the Mark Twain National Forest.

This is the most ruggedly picturesque stretch of Route 66 across Missouri; the name "Devil's Elbow" comes from a section of the Big Piney River that turns so acutely it caused repeated logjams. The earliest incarnations of Route 66 followed what's now signed as "Teardrop Road," and up until 1981 the last alignment of Route 66 followed what's now the hilly, four-lane **Hwy-Z,** some of the last Missouri sections of the old road to be bypassed by I-44 (all this is between I-44 exits 163 and 169).

Besides the old road itself, a great reason to tour this 10-mile stretch of old Route 66 is the chance to sample some fine Missouri brisket and pulled pork barbecue at the **Elbow Inn** (573/336-5375), just south of the junction of Hwy-Z and Teardrop Road, a lively good-natured biker bar with cans of cold beer and lots of abandoned bras pinned to the ceiling. If you're a real barbecue fan, you can vote for mid-Missouri's best ribs by comparing the Elbow Inn with its nearest competitor, the **Sweetwater BBQ** (573/336-8830), on Hwy-Z just southeast of I-44 exit 163.

West of here, the scenic old road crashes suddenly back into the franchised fast

food of I-44 at the twin towns of St. Robert and Waynesville, where 30,000-plus soldiers and dependents at the nearby Fort Leonard Wood U.S. Army base, headquarters of the U.S. Army military police school (and a small museum), have generated a rash of Walmarts and shopping malls.

Lebanon: Munger Moss

The stretch of old Route 66 running through **Lebanon** (pop. 14,709) holds more than its fair share of sights, so make sure you slow down and soak it all in. The most worthwhile but easiest-to-miss sight is the excellent **Route 66 Museum** (915 S. Jefferson St., 417/532-2148), tucked away inside the Lebanon-Laclede County Public Library, next door to the Ritz 8 Cineplex. Here the whole history of the U.S. highway systems is conveyed through maps, post-cards, promotional posters, and life-size dioramas. The stretch of old Route 66 running from the museum along the north side of I-44 holds the marvelous **Munger Moss Motel** (1336 E. Route 66, 417/532-3111, $45), where Ramona Lehman and family have been offering clean rooms, a swimming pool, and a wonderful neon sign since 1946. Across from the Munger Moss is a bowling alley with a snack bar and a set of batting cages (5 cents a pitch!), making it a perfect Route 66 destination.

Follow Elm Street (old Route 66) east from downtown Lebanon, past the Munger Moss and along the north side of I-44, to two more highlights. On weekend nights, noisy NASCAR stock cars race around the asphalt oval of the **Lebanon I-44 Speedway** (417/532-2060, $12).

Detour: Mansfield and the Laura Ingalls Wilder Museum

While the good food and warm Munger Moss hospitality is more than reason enough to visit Lebanon, the town also marks the turnoff for a trip to visit another American institution, the Ozark Mountain homestead where author Laura Ingalls Wilder wrote the famous *Little House* books. Though it's an hour detour south via Hwy-5, or 52 miles due east of Springfield via US-60, Wilder's Rocky Ridge Farm has been preserved as the **Laura Ingalls Wilder Home and Museum** (3060 Hwy-A, 877/924-7126, daily Mar.-Nov. 15, $14), on a hill a mile southeast of the town of Mansfield. Unlike the many reconstructed Little House sights elsewhere, this museum has a direct and intimate connection with the woman who, for generations of readers, brought the American frontier to life. Born in 1867, Wilder grew up with the country, her iconic "little house" moving ever westward from the "big woods" of Wisconsin on to the "prairie" of Kansas and South Dakota. Wilder moved to the Ozarks in 1894 and worked to establish a successful apple and dairy farm. It was not until the economic downturn of the 1930s, when Wilder was in her 60s, that she began publishing her books, which have since sold millions (some of the royalties go to support the Mansfield library, where there is also a small museum). The home the Wilders lived in most of their adult lives forms the heart of the museum. They are buried in the town cemetery, alongside their daughter Rose, who urged on (and some say collaborated on) Laura's autobiographical stories.

Springfield

The largest city in southern Missouri, **Springfield** (pop. 167,319) doesn't feel nearly as big as it is, though it does sprawl for many miles in all directions. Despite the ongoing growth and development, most notably the green and pleasant **Jordan**

Valley Park surrounding the attractive downtown baseball stadium and sports complex, Springfield has preserved much of its old Route 66 frontage, along St. Louis Street east of downtown, as well as the grandly named Chestnut Expressway west of downtown. The 20-mph speed limit on downtown streets—along with tons of free parking—enables Route 66 pilgrims to pay homage to the town's Arabesque landmark **Shrine Mosque theater** (601 E. Saint Louis St., 417/869-9164), which still hosts occasional concerts.

Springfield is also celebrated as the place where "Wild Bill" Hickok killed fellow gambler Dave Tutt, apparently because Tutt wore the watch he'd won from Hickok playing cards. A plaque in the central square, just west of the Shrine Mosque, tells one of many variations on the tale.

Springfield has at least one fine old Route 66 motel: the **Route 66 Rail Haven** (203 S. Glenstone Ave., 417/866-1963 or 800/670-7234, $79 and up), on the corner of old Route 66 and US-65. Open since 1938, it has been fully modernized and now is a Best Western affiliate with a railroad theme. A mile away on old Route 66 is one of the earliest and most stylish models of the **Steak 'n Shake** burger chain (1158 St. Louis St., 417/866-6109, daily 24 hours). This is one of the last ones where carhops still bring your food to your car (during daylight hours).

Carthage

Just shy of the Kansas border, six miles north of I-44 and right on old Route 66, **Carthage** (pop. 14,309) is a perfect little town, looking for all the world like the model for the idyllic-though-fictional town of Hill Valley from the *Back to the Future* movies. The center of Carthage, three blocks south of Route 66, is dominated by the outrageously ornate circa-1895 limestone **Jasper County Courthouse,** which features a local history mural and an open-cage elevator in the lobby. (On Thursdays and Fridays the elevator is hand-operated by a charming and friendly woman, Geraldine Bunn, who serves as Carthage's unofficial ambassador.) Carthage was the boyhood home of naturalist Marlin Perkins, host of Mutual of Omaha's long-running Wild Kingdom TV show, and a life-size statue of him stands in Central Park, three blocks southwest of the courthouse square. Carthage was also the girlhood home of Wild West outlaw Belle Starr.

Springfield is home to the Double-A Texas League **Springfield Cardinals,** who play off US-65 at one of the country's most attractive ballparks, **Hammons Field** (417/863-2143).

Across the street from the central courthouse there's a good place to eat: the **Carthage Deli** (301 S. Main St., 417/358-8820, Mon.-Sat.), which serves sandwiches and milk shakes in a 1950s-style soda fountain on the northwest corner of the courthouse square. Two blocks east is a bowling alley, **Star Lanes** (219 E. 3rd St., 417/358-2144). Also in Carthage is an old Route 66 landmark: the glowing pink-and-green 1940s neon sign of the **Boots Court Motel** (107 S. Garrison St., 417/310-2989, $66) has welcomed Clark Gable and hundreds of other weary travelers over the years. Local preservationists and Route 66 fans renovated the property and kindly offer a few clean, comfortable rooms for retro-minded road-tripping guests.

A mile or so west of downtown on Old Route 66, enjoy a double feature of Hollywood blockbusters in the comfort of your car at the **66 Drive-In** (17231 Old 66 Blvd., 417/359-5959, Thurs.-Sun.).

Finally, if you have a soft spot for hyperbolic sentimentality, don't miss the **Precious Moments Chapel** (800/543-7975, daily, free), featuring the wide-eyed characters from the religious figurine series. The chapel is well signed, west of US-71 on the southwest edge of Carthage.

About 16 miles southeast of Joplin, **George Washington Carver National Monument** (417/325-4151, daily, free) preserves the farm where the eminent agricultural scientist, educator, and self-sufficiency advocate grew up in the 1860s.

Joplin

If you want to travel the old Route 66 alignment across Kansas, you'll also pass through **Joplin** (pop. 52,195), a border town that's the industrial center of the tristate region. Formerly a lead- and zinc-mining town, in May 2011 Joplin made the national news in the worst possible way when it was hit by one of the most powerful tornados in recent U.S. history, 200-mph winds tearing a swath of destruction and killing more than 150 people in less than 10 minutes of terror. Before the tornado, Joplin was better known for its high-quality limestone quarries than for its history, though highway heritage is well served at **Schifferdecker Park,** west of downtown off 7th Street, a pre-Route 66 rest area that now has a mining museum, a small historical museum, and a public **swimming pool** (417/625-4750, daily, $5) that is much appreciated on a sweltering late-summer day. Though the tornado destroyed dozens of homes and businesses, Joplin's downtown area does hold one unlikely attraction: a vibrant mural by artist Thomas Hart Benton depicting life in Joplin at the turn of the 20th century. The over-70-square-foot mural, which turned out to be the artist's final complete work, is in the lobby of the **Joplin City Hall** (602 S. Main St.).

Joplin has a number of good places to eat. Try the excellent barbecue at **Big R's** (1220 E. 15th St., 417/781-5959). The smoky brisket and juicy ribs make it hard to leave room for the tasty fresh-fruit pies. The popular **Eagle Drive-In** (4224 S. Hearnes Blvd., 417/623-2228) serves up a delicious short-rib chili along with a wide range of burgers: veggie burgers, bison burgers, lamb burgers, tuna burgers, you name it.

One of the Lead and Zinc Mines in the Tri-State Mining District of Missouri-Kansas-Oklahoma

Massive lead mines like this have disappeared from Kansas.

KANSAS

The shortest but perhaps best-signed stretch of Route 66's eight-state run is its 13.2-mile slice across the southeast corner of Kansas. Be careful not to blink your eyes, or you'll be saying, as Dorothy did in *The Wizard of Oz*, "I have a feeling we're not in Kansas anymore."

Coming from Missouri, your first town in Kansas is **Galena,** where the funky **Galena Mining and Historical Museum** (319 W. 7th St., 620/783-2192, hours vary, free), just off the main drag and marked by a big Old 66 sign, is stuffed with old newspaper clippings and other items that give a glimpse of town life during its 1920s-era mining heyday. At its peak, Galena had a population near 30,000, which was 10 times the current number. Various rusting tools and machines testify to the work that once went on here. That said, the hospitable Route 66 spirit lives on, most obviously at **Cars on the Route** (119 N. Main St., 620/783-1366), inside the old Kan-O-Tex gas station, now serving sandwiches and selling souvenirs related to Pixar's animated Route 66 movie *Cars*. The early 1950s International Harvester tow truck that apparently inspired the *Cars* character "Tow Mater" is parked outside.

Another appetizing attraction awaits in **Riverton,** the next town to the west, where the **Old Riverton Store** (7109 SE Route 66, 620/848-3330), a.k.a. "Eisler Brothers," has been open since the 1920s. Across the highway from a big power plant, the old store has a good deli counter, with good handmade sandwiches. The last of the Eislers passed away in 2009, but the store is still in good hands, headquarters of the small but active Kansas Route 66 Association and owned by its president. It's an essential stop for fans of the old road.

Heading west toward Oklahoma, the newer highway bypasses a fine old rainbow-arched Route 66 concrete bridge, well-signed on the northeast side of **Baxter Springs.** Locals point with pride at the circa-1870 **Crowell Bank** in the historic three-block downtown, which was said to have been robbed by Jesse James. A block away, the nicely restored 1930s Phillips 66 filling station is now a useful museum and Baxter Springs **information center** (620/856-2385, Mar.-Nov.) at 10th Street and Military Avenue (a.k.a. Route 66).

Though it's pretty quiet these days, during the Civil War Baxter Springs saw one of the worst massacres in the country's history, when more than 100 unarmed Union soldiers, including many African Americans, were captured and killed by William Quantrill's rebel Confederate raiders (including the aforementioned Jesse James), who had disguised themselves by wearing blue Union uniforms. A monument to the murdered soldiers stands in **Baxter Springs Soldiers' Lot** in the Baxter City Cemetery, off US-166 two miles west of town.

While the soda fountain is no more, this enticing sign remains.

Baxter Springs information center

OKLAHOMA

Apart from occasional college football teams, Oklahoma doesn't often get to crow about being the best in the country, but as far as Route 66 is concerned, the state is definitely number one. Containing more still-drivable miles of the old highway than any other state, Oklahoma is a Middle American mecca for old-roads fans.

Oklahoma has the longest and most intact stretches of old Route 66. If you want to explore it to the fullest, get your hands on a copy of the essential map-packed road guide *Oklahoma Route 66*, by Arcadia, Oklahoma's own Jim Ross.

The Dust Bowl exodus of the 1930s uprooted thousands of families who headed west on Route 66, and today many of the towns along the road take bittersweet pride in their *The Grapes of Wrath* connections. You can also still see signs that go back farther into the state's history, just over a century ago, when all of Oklahoma was Indian Territory. It was the last refuge of Kiowa, Apache, Comanche, and other nations before the U.S. government took even this land away from them during "land rushes" in the 1890s. Today, some nations have retained enough legal autonomy to issue license plates and run casinos.

Northeast Oklahoma: The Sidewalk Highway

In the far northeastern corner of Oklahoma, old Route 66 runs through a hardscrabble former lead- and zinc-mining region, from the Kansas border to Vinita on the I-44 turnpike. Three miles southwest of the Kansas border, **Quapaw** could be the first or last Oklahoma town you visit, depending on your direction, but either way it's worth a look for the many murals painted on the walls of downtown businesses. The next town along, **Commerce** (pop. 2,460), was another old mining town, noteworthy as the boyhood home of the late, great Yankee switch-hitter Mickey Mantle, in whose honor the old Route 66 alignment down Main Street has been renamed. A statue of Mantle graces the Commerce high school baseball field, right off Route 66.

Five miles to the south via old Route 66 (now signed as US-69), **Miami** holds the magnificent Spanish Revival-style Coleman Theater, built in 1929 when the town was still luxuriating in the riches coming out of the surrounding mines.

Still following US-69, now roughly parallel to (and eventually crossing under) I-44 between Miami and Afton, some of the earliest paved stretches of old Route 66 were constructed only one lane wide, because in 1926 the state of Oklahoma did not have enough money to build a full-width version. Not surprisingly, these lengths of the road became known as the **"Sidewalk Highway."** The easiest stretch to find runs parallel

old-style Conoco station, Commerce

to US-69: Turn west at the Northeast Technology Center vocational school along an increasingly narrow country lane, and look out for the 66 shields painted on the pavement. This "Sidewalk Highway" rejoins the main Route 66 alignment at Afton, where a convenience store now stands on the site of the fabled Buffalo Ranch Trading Post. For more on Afton, the Buffalo Ranch, Route 66, or help finding the Sidewalk Highway, head down to **Afton Station** (12 SE 1st St., 918/284-3829), a nicely renovated 1930s-era gas station that has been brought back to life as a gift shop and museum of mostly old Packard cars.

Vinita

Old Route 66 crosses the interstate (a.k.a. the Will Rogers Turnpike) again at **Vinita,** where the region's Native American heritage is brought into focus at the **Eastern Trails Museum** (215 W. Illinois St., 918/256-2115, Mon.-Fri. 11am-4pm, Sat. 11am-3pm, free), next to the public library. The exhibits center on the Cherokee Trail of Tears, which brought the Cherokee people here after a forced march from North Carolina in the 1830s, but the museum also covers the general history of the surrounding area.

Vinita is home to the **Will Rogers Memorial Rodeo,** held here each August since 1935, the year he died. Rogers attended secondary school in Vinita after growing up near Claremore. Vinita also hosts the annual **World's Largest Calf Fry Festival and Cook-Off** in late June. (Calf fries are prairie oysters, otherwise known as beef testicles. Just so you know.) Contact the **chamber of commerce** (918/256-7133) for details on any of these.

Vinita also has a great old Route 66 restaurant: **Clanton's Café** (319 E. Illinois Ave., 918/256-9053), right at the center of town. "Oklahoma's oldest family-owned and operated restaurant," Clanton's has been famous for its chicken-fried beefsteak, served here with mashed potatoes and slathered in peppery white gravy, since 1927. Clanton's also has good burgers and, in case you miss the festival, calf fries (see above for a disclaimer).

Foyil

Between Vinita and Claremore, old Route 66 survives in regular use as the "free road" alternative to the I-44 Turnpike, alternating between two-lane and divided four-lane highway. The most interesting wide spot along this stretch of hallowed road is **Foyil,** where in the 1940s and 1950s retired fiddle-maker and folk artist Ed Galloway sculpted an outdoor garden of giant totem poles—the tallest is over 90 feet—and other Native American-inspired objects out of concrete. After fading and weathering for many years, the poles, four miles east of town via Hwy-28A, have been restored and maintained as **Totem Pole Park** (918/342-9149, daily dawn-dusk, free). It's now a fascinating place to stop for a picnic or to simply admire the effort that went into these "Watts Towers of the Plains."

Foyil was also the hometown of Andy Payne, the Cherokee youth who in 1928 won the "Bunion Derby," a coast-to-coast foot race that followed Route 66 from Los Angeles to Chicago, then headed east to New York City—equivalent to running a marathon and a half every day for the 84 days it took him to finish.

Claremore: Will Rogers Memorial

Twenty miles northeast of Tulsa, **Claremore** (pop. 19,069) is a bigger-than-average Route 66 town, one that will be forever connected with its favorite son, Will Rogers

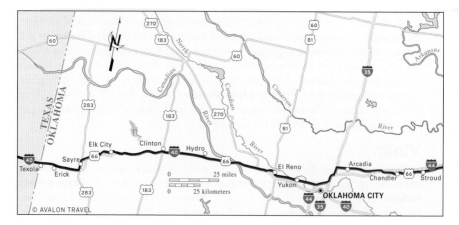

(1879-1935). Rogers was born nearby in a rough log cabin "halfway between Claremore and Oologah before there was a town at either place." He rose from a vaudeville career as a sideshow rope-tricks artist to become one of the most popular figures in America, thanks to his folksy humor.

Will Rogers starred on Broadway for 10 years in the *Ziegfield Follies*, wrote an immensely popular national newspaper column, and acted in more than 70 Hollywood movies. Sadly, before he could retire back home to Claremore, Rogers was killed in a plane crash in 1935; his land here was later turned into the **Will Rogers Memorial** (918/341-0719, daily, $7), a mile northwest of downtown Claremore on a hill overlooking the town. A statue of Rogers greets visitors at the front door, and his tomb is here, along with a small archive and museum that recounts his life story, showing off his collections of saddles, lariats, and other cowboy gear.

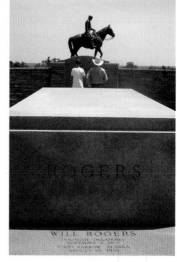
Will Rogers Memorial

Another popular Claremore stop is the **J. M. Davis Arms and Historical Museum** (330 N. J. M. Davis Blvd., 918/341-5707, Tues.-Sat., donation), right off Route 66. Besides housing one of the largest and most comprehensive gun collections anywhere in the world (just under 12,000 firearms!), the museum has antique musical instruments, hundreds of posters dating back to World War I, and 1,200 German beer steins.

For good food and out-of-this-world pies (over a dozen different kinds), stop by the **Hammett House Restaurant** (1616 W. Will Rogers, 918/341-7333), west of downtown next to the Rogers Memorial.

Catoosa: The Blue Whale

One of Tulsa's premier Route 66 attractions was the giant **Blue Whale sculpture**, in the suburb of **Catoosa**, northeast of Tulsa along the stretch of the old road that runs from I-44 exit 240. The park, built as an animal-themed tourist attraction in

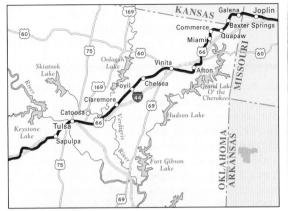

Totem Pole Park in Foyil

the 1970s by Hugh Davis, a curator at the Tulsa Zoo, closed down long ago and was left to crumble. Unlike so many other long-suffering Route 66 landmarks, however, the Blue Whale has been lovingly restored by the family of its original creators (with a little help from the Hampton Inn brand of Hilton Hotels).

Catoosa, surprisingly, is also a major port, linked, by way of impressively engineered improvements to the Arkansas River system, to the Gulf of Mexico. Even more surprising may be the presence in Catoosa of the 20-story **Hard Rock Casino** (800/760-6700), where there are three acres of gaming, a 24-hour Route 66 Diner, and 454 plush rooms, plus big-name entertainers performing in the state-of-the-art concert hall.

Tulsa

Home to fine art deco buildings built during the 1920s boom years of the Oklahoma oil industry, **Tulsa** (pop. 403,090) is a bustling big city that doesn't make a song-and-dance out of its many treasures. It's a fascinating place to explore. If your time is limited, spend it at one of the country's top art museums, the **Gilcrease Museum** (918/596-2700, Tues.-Sun., $8), on the northwest edge of town. Bought with the fortune benefactor Thomas Gilcrease made when oil was discovered on his land, the collection includes some of the most important works of Western American art and sculpture, with major works by Thomas Moran, George Catlin, and others, plus Native American artifacts and early maps that put the frontier region into its historical context. The expansive grounds include a lovely series of gardens and Mr. Gilcrease's old house.

Tulsa is the home of **Oral Roberts University,** marked by a futuristic, 15-story tower and a 60-foot-high pair of praying hands along Lewis Avenue, 10 miles south of downtown.

Due south of downtown Tulsa, the art deco spire of the **Boston Avenue Methodist Church** (1301 S. Boston Ave.) is a national landmark tower rising over Route 66. South of the Tulsa airport, a few blocks north of Route 66's run along 11th Street, is a different sort of landmark: the **Admiral Twin Drive-In** (7355 E. Easton St., 918/878-8099,

A Double-A affiliate of the LA Dodgers, the **Tulsa Drillers** play Texas League baseball on the north side of downtown at **ONEOK Field** (201 N. Elgin Ave., 918/744-5901).

$3), which was a key setting in S. E. Hinton's best-selling coming-of-age novel *The Outsiders*.

For dinner or a drink, the liveliest part of Tulsa is the Brookside district, south of downtown around 34th Street and Peoria Avenue, where there's a handful of trendy cafés, nightclubs, and restaurants, including the **R Bar and Grill** (3421 S. Peoria Ave., 918/392-4811). Downtown, you can get a feel for the old days at the retro 1920s **New Atlas Grill** (415 S. Boston Ave., 918/583-3111), serving full breakfasts plus soups, salads, and lunchtime sandwiches in an art deco tower. Much of the old Route 66 frontage along 11th Street near the University of Tulsa has been rediscovered by retro-minded revivalists who enjoy the good honest food at **Tally's Café** (1102 S. Yale Ave., 918/835-8039). Another fixture on Route 66 since the early 1950s is the **El Rancho Grande** (1629 E. 11th St., 918/584-0816), which still offers unreconstructed Mexican food.

The usual chain hotels and motels line all the freeways around Tulsa. There is a big **Holiday Inn Tulsa City Center** (17 W. 7th St., 918/585-5898, $80 and up) downtown. For the full Route 66 experience, try the renovated and stylish **Campbell Hotel** (2636 E. 11th St., 855/744-5500, $135 and up).

Old Route 66: Stroud

Between Sapulpa, on the suburban fringes of southwest Tulsa, and the next main stop, Chandler, old Route 66 zigzags back and forth along the freeway for the next 50 miles. Near the east end of this stretch, two miles west of Sapulpa, the 1924 **Rock Creek Bridge** is a reminder of what the old roads were really like: 120 feet long yet only 12 feet wide. The truss is rusty but the bridge

still stands as a proud reminder of the original 1920s Route 66. Across the bridge is another evocative reminder: an abandoned drive-in movie theater, long closed but with the screen and the fan-shaped parking lot still intact.

Continuing west, old-roads fanatics will probably want to follow the winding alignment of Route 66, which continues along the south side of the turnpike for nearly 40 miles. On the west side of **Stroud** (pop. 2,778; "Home of Daneka Allen, Miss OK 1999"), check out the **Rock Café** (114 W. Main St., 918/968-3990), a Route 66 relic built in 1939 out of local stone quarried when the original highway was cut in the 1920s. The Rock Café (whose restroom featured original graffiti by *Toy Story* creator John Lasseter, who modeled some scenes in his Route 66 movie *Cars* on the Rock Café's inimitable architecture) suffered from a fire in 2008 but got back up and running in no time and still churns out its better-than-average roadside fare. Stroud also has the classic old **Skyliner Motel** (717 W. Main St., 918/968-9556, $50 and up).

Chandler and Warwick

West of Stroud, as for most of the way between Tulsa and Oklahoma City, old Route 66 continues along the south side of the I-44 turnpike, which has another of its rare

READING UP ON ROUTE 66

Considering the old road's great fame, it's hardly surprising that over a dozen different books in print deal with the Route 66 experience. Some are travel guides, some folk histories, others nostalgic rambles down what was and what's left along the Mother Road. Photographic essays document the rapidly disappearing architecture and signage, and at least one cookbook catalogs recipes of dishes served in cafés on the route. Even in the age of GPS coordinates, online maps, and Twitter feeds (like the timely and accurate Route 66 News), nothing beats a good book. The following is a sampling of favorite titles, most of which can be found in stores along the route if not in your local bookstore.

The Grapes of Wrath, John Steinbeck (Penguin Books). The first and still most compelling Route 66-related story traces the traumatic travels of the Joad family from Dust Bowl Oklahoma to the illusive Promised Land of California. Brutally vivid, *The Grapes of Wrath* was an instant best-seller at the tail end of the Depression and was the source of Route 66's appellation "The Mother Road."

A Guide Book to Highway 66, Jack D. Rittenhouse (University of New Mexico Press). A facsimile reprinting of the self-published 1946 book that the late author sold door-to-door at truck stops, motor courts, and cafés along the route.

EZ 66: Route 66 Guide for Travelers, Jerry McClanahan (National Historic Route 66 Federation). The most-detailed driver's guide to old Route 66, packed with maps and mile-by-mile instructions and information, spiral-bound for on-the-road ease of use.

Route 66: The Mother Road, Michael Wallis (St. Martin's Press, 1987). This richly illustrated and thoroughly researched guide to the old road is more armchair companion than practical aid, but the book captures the spirit of Route 66, and the writer has been a key promotional force behind the road's preservation and rediscovery. (Wallis also does the voice of the sheriff in *Cars.*)

Route 66 Sightings, Jerry McClanahan, Jim Ross, and Shellee Graham (Ghost Town Press, 2011). By far the best Route 66 photo book, this lush volume captures the Mother Road in all its moods.

Searching for 66, Tom Teague (Samizdat House, 1996). More personal than other titles on Route 66, this poignant book of vignettes, illustrated with the fine pen-and-ink drawings of Route 66 artist Bob Waldmire, describes the author's interactions with the many people along Route 66 who made it what it was. Sadly, both the author and the artist (and almost everyone profiled) have since died, making the stories here all the more important and affecting.

exits at **Chandler** (pop. 3,181). Chandler is one of the most pleasant old Route 66 towns in Oklahoma, with a wealth of well-preserved sandstone-and-brick buildings, a trio of which house an enjoyable local history center. It stands out for a number of good reasons, not least of which is the classic **Lincoln Motel** (740 E. 1st St., 405/258-0200, $55 and up), along old Route 66 at the east edge of town. It's a little time-worn, for sure, but still as neat and tidy as the day it opened in 1939 with two dozen two-room cabins, each with a green bench for watching the world whiz by. Chandler's solid-looking WPA-era Armory has been done up to house the lively and engaging **Route 66 Interpretive Center** (400 E. Route 66/1st St., 405/258-1300, Tues.-Sun. year-round, $5), which gives an eye-opening introduction to the enterprising and welcoming Route 66 spirit. There's a public swimming pool (summer only), a gallery run by Route 66 artist and guidebook writer Jerry McClanahan (306 Manvel St., 405/240-7659), and a well-restored cottage-style Phillips 66 station.

Heading west toward Oklahoma City, old Route 66 continues along the south side of I-44, passing a metal-roofed barn emblazoned with a photogenic "Meramec Caverns—Stanton MO" sign west of Chandler and crossing under the freeway about three miles west of **Warwick.** From here, one of the state's best surviving stretches of Route 66, known locally as the "free road," runs for over 30 miles along the north side of the turnpike, passing by horse and cattle ranches as it rolls across the red earth.

On old Route 66, about seven miles west of Chandler and a few miles east of where Route 66 again crosses the I-44 Turnpike (at exit 158), the old highway town of Warwick has a small gem: the **Seaba Station Motorcycle Museum** (405/258-9141, Thurs.-Tues., free), a simple 1920s filling station, recently and thoughtfully renovated to house a covetable collection of motorcycles, memorabilia, fan magazines, and more. My favorite item is a 1970s Evel Knievel pinball machine. Altogether there are around 60 motorbikes on display, mostly one-of-a-kind racing and moto-cross machines.

Arcadia

About six miles east of the I-35 freeway through OKC, the main stop along this idyllic rural cruise is the old highway town of **Arcadia** (pop. 269), which holds a wonderfully restored, very large, red **round barn** (405/396-0824). The ground floor of this much-loved landmark, originally built way back in 1898, is now a mini museum and gift shop, selling some highly collectible original Route 66 memorabilia.

A half mile west of the round barn, Arcadia's other Route 66 landmark is bright, shiny, and comparatively new: **Pops** (405/928-7677), a gas station and small café fronted by a giant (66-foot-tall) soda pop bottle-shaped sign (not neon, but multicolored, energy-efficient LEDs). Built by Aubrey McClendon, an Oklahoma-born natural gas billionaire, Pops opened in 2007 and sells over 500 different varieties of soda pop (including around 100 brands of root beer!) as well as the requisite burgers and fuel, plus silky milk shakes. Even if you're not all that hungry

Following old Route 66 across Oklahoma City can be confusing, but keep an eye peeled for a bottle-shaped building on Classen Boulevard at 23rd Street.

or thirsty, the exuberant bottle-shaped tower, with its rainbow of colors, makes it worth hanging around till nightfall.

Between Arcadia and Oklahoma City, Route 66 ran through the town of **Edmond,** the place where aviator Wiley Post is buried (he was the pilot killed in the same crash as Will Rogers). Edmond is also notorious for the fact that a disgruntled post office employee killed 14 of his coworkers here in 1986, inspiring the expression "going postal."

Oklahoma City

Long one of the primary stops along the Mother Road, **Oklahoma City** (pop. 638,367) is the only place along the route singled out for praise in the Bobby Troup song ("Oklahoma City is mighty pretty"), no doubt thanks to the easy rhyme. Its wealth of "City Beautiful" era avenues and neighborhoods makes it not only mighty pretty but enjoyable. The city was the biggest boomtown of the 1889 Land Rush, when Oklahoma was opened for white settlement after being set aside "for eternity" as Indian Territory. Between noon and sundown on April 22, some 50,000 people raced here to claim the new lands—many of them having illegally camped out beforehand, earning the nickname "Sooner," which is still applied to the state's college football team.

A second boom took place during the Great Depression years, when oil was struck. There are still producing wells in the center of the city, including some on the grounds of the state capitol. The collapse of the oil industry in the 1980s hit hard, then the shock of the 1995 antigovernment terrorist bombing carried out by Timothy McVeigh in 1995 hit even harder. The city has since revitalized itself, with a gorgeous new baseball stadium, an exciting NBA basketball team, a concert arena, and canal-side cafés, all collected in the compact walkable "Bricktown" warehouse district.

Just off old Route 66 across from the capitol, a good first stop is the **Oklahoma History Center** (800 Nazih Zuhdi Dr., 405/522-0765, Mon.-Sat., $7), which has exhibits tracing the state's growth, with special collections on the Native American presence and on pioneers. There's also a wide-ranging oral history of the Mother Road.

For poignant balance to a nostalgic Route 66 tour, pay your respects to the 168 men, women, and children killed in the April 19, 1995, bombing of the Alfred P. Murrah Federal Building. Between the capitol and Bricktown, the site of the bombing has been preserved as a **memorial park** (620 N. Harvey Ave., daily 24 hours, free), landscaped with a shallow pool around which are arrayed a series of 168 sculpted chairs. Each chair represents a person killed in the blast, and the chairs range from small to full-size, marking the varying ages of the dead (who included 19 kids from the building's day-care center). An adjacent **museum** (405/235-3313, daily, $12) tells the story of the bombing, its perpetrators, and its victims.

The Triple-A **Oklahoma City Dodgers** (405/218-1000) play at ever-pleasant **Chickasaw Bricktown Ballpark,** south of downtown near the junction of I-235 and I-40.

The exciting NBA basketball team **Oklahoma City Thunder** (405/208-4800) plays at **Chesapeake Energy Arena,** on the west side of the railroad tracks from Bricktown.

Oklahoma City Practicalities

The downtown Bricktown district is home to a lively concentration of restaurants and bars, many lined up along the attractively landscaped Bricktown Canal. Near the north edge of Bricktown, **Tapwerks Ale House** (121 E. Sheridan Ave.,

West of Oklahoma City, the first real town beyond the OKC suburbs is **Yukon,** hometown of country crooner Garth Brooks and of a giant "Yukon's Best Flour" grain mill, whose huge sign lights up the night sky and draws shutterbugs off the highway.

405/319-9599) has great beers, good food, and frequent live music. Oklahoma City also has more barbecue stands and steakhouses than just about anywhere in the country. On the old Route 66 landmark alignment northwest of downtown, head to **Jack's BBQ** (4418 NW 39th St., 405/605-7790), a traditional cafeteria-style barbecue joint with good brisket sandwiches, best washed down with a cold drink next door at the Hideaway Club sports bar. Other good OKC barbecue bets include the bigger and more accessible **Iron Starr Urban BBQ** (3700 N. Shartel Ave., 405/524-5925), just off 36th Street; or **Earl's Rib Palace** (216 Johnny Bench Dr., 405/272-9898), with six locations, including one right on the Bricktown Canal. For great nonbarbecue food right on old Route 66, go to the popular **Ann's Chicken Fry House** (4106 NW 39th St., 405/943-8915)—look for the classic Caddies and fake police cars in the parking lot.

Lodging options in and around OKC are provided by the usual motel chains, plus a nice **Hampton Inn** (300 E. Sheridan Ave., 405/232-3600, $140 and up) in Bricktown.

El Reno: Hamburger City

Established as Fort El Reno in 1874 as part of U.S. Army efforts to subdue the Cheyenne people, **El Reno** (pop. 18,786) later saw duty as a POW camp during World War II, then earned a measure of fame as the site of a motel seen in the offbeat road movie *Rain Man*. (In the movie, the motel was in Amarillo, but the "real" one, called the Big Eight, sat along old Route 66 at the east edge of El Reno.)

For hungry road-trippers, especially those fond of all-American burger joints, El Reno offers an abundance of choices. Three great old places stand within a block of

each other along old Route 66. The oldest, **Robert's Grill** (300 S. Bickford St., 405/262-1262), has been cooking since 1926 and should be a national model for short-order cooking. A block to the west is **Sid's Diner** (300 S. Choctaw Ave., 405/262-7757), which became insanely popular after it was featured on the TV show *Man v. Food*. Finally, a block to the east is **Johnnie's Grill** (301 S. Rock Island Ave., 405/262-4721, daily), with the biggest menu and most spacious dining room. All three El Reno burger joints are famous for putting fried onions in and on their burgers. On the first weekend in May, El Reno gets together to cook up the "World's Largest Fried Onion Hamburger," a 750-pound behemoth that inspires an all-day festival.

Hydro

There's no clearer contrast between the charms of the old road and the anonymity of the interstate than tiny **Hydro,** about midway between Oklahoma City and Clinton on the west bank of the Canadian River. A wonderful length of old Route 66 runs along the north side of I-40 exit 89, right past the ancient service station and souvenir stand operated by Lucille Hamons from 1941 until her death in 2000. Though it's just 50 yards from the fast lane of the freeway, visiting Lucille's place to buy a soda or a postcard and have a quick hello with the energetic proprietor was a Route 66 rite of passage. Lucille's inspired the creation of a replica roadhouse on the north side of I-40 in the next town to the west, Weatherford, called **Lucille's Roadhouse** (580/772-8808).

West of Lucille's, a surviving six-mile stretch of old Route 66 pavement follows the lay of the land up and down, offering a better sense of the landscape than does the faster but duller new road, which was completed in 1966.

Clinton

Named for Judge Clinton Irwin and not for former president Bill, **Clinton** (pop. 9,393) started life as a trading post for local Cheyenne Arapahoe people and is now in the spotlight as home of the official **Oklahoma Route 66 Museum** (2229 W. Gary Blvd., 580/323-7866, daily, Tues.-Sat. Dec.-Jan., $7), near the west end of town. Unlike many other "museums" along the route, this one is a true showcase and not just another souvenir stand. Funded by a variety of state and local sources, the museum opened in 1995 after undergoing a massive million-dollar expansion and improvement. Collectors from all over the coun-

try, including Clinton's own Gladys Cuthbert, whose husband, Jack Cuthbert, was the primary promoter of Route 66 throughout its glory years, donated signs, artifacts, and memorabilia that have been organized into a comprehensive exhibition of Mother Road history and culture not to be missed by any Route 66 aficionado. (There's a good gift shop, too.)

Childhood home of country-western star Toby Keith, Clinton also has the nice **McLain Rogers public park,** with a swimming pool and water slide, at the center of town along 10th Street (old Route 66).

Welcome to Texola!

For food, west of town along the I-40 frontage, just north of exit 62, **Jigg's Smoke House** (580/323-5641) is a tiny cabin specializing in travel-friendly beef jerky. The slightly faded **Trade Winds Inn** (2128 W. Gary Blvd., 580/323-2610, $50 and up), across from the Route 66 museum, played host to Elvis Presley at least four times. Elvis's room has been "preserved" as a mini shrine, and you can stay in it (for around $100) and experience a time warp back to the mid-1960s. There's also a Hampton Inn and many other national chains.

Just east of the Texas-Oklahoma border, **Texola** (pop. 35) has dried up and all but blown away since it was bypassed by I-40, but a few remnants still stand, awaiting nostalgic photographers.

Elk City

The last—or first, depending on your direction—sizable town east of the Texas border is **Elk City** (pop. 11,997), "Home of Susan Powell, Miss America 1981," and also childhood home of songwriter Jimmy Webb, who penned such all-time classics as "Galveston," "Wichita Lineman," "MacArthur Park," and "Up, Up and Away." Elk City was a popular stopover on Route 66, as evidenced by the many old motels along the various alignments of the old highway through town. Long before Elk City had its Route 66 heyday, it was a wild frontier town along the cattle trails from Texas to Dodge City, Kansas. The area's cowboy and pioneer history is recounted in the **Old Town Museum** (2717 W. 3rd St., 580/225-2207, daily May-Dec., Mon.-Sat. Jan.-Apr., $5), on the far west side of town, where there's a recreated Wild West town, complete with a doctor's office, a schoolhouse, a tepee, and a rodeo museum. A newer addition to Old Town Museum is the official **National Route 66 Museum,** which has a *huge* Route 66 shield outside; inside there's an old pickup truck decorated to look like the one from *The Grapes of Wrath* and lots of other old-road memorabilia.

During the 1940s, oil and gas were discovered underground in the Anadarko Basin, and the town experienced another short boom, a time remembered by the towering **"Rig 114,"** a record-breaking, 180-foot-tall drilling rig, installed after its retirement in the park next to the closed Casa Grande Hotel. Though fossil fuels have had their ups and downs, in recent years the industry has been on the upswing, leading city fathers to proclaim Elk City the "Natural Gas Capital of the World."

Elk City has one more surefire Route 66 attraction: the delectable French Silk pie (butter, sugar, and vanilla served in a graham cracker crust) baked at the **Country Dove Tea Room** (610 W. 3rd St., 580/225-7028).

Sayre

If you want a quick flashback to the dark days of Steinbeck's *The Grapes of Wrath*, turn north off I-40 into sleepy **Sayre** (pop. 4,603). The landmark **Beckham County Courthouse,** which looms over the east end of Main Street, was prominently featured in the movie version as Henry Fonda and the rest of the Joads rattled down Route 66 toward California. The Depression era also lives on in the cool and pleasant

WPA-era swimming pool in **Sayre City Park,** between the old Route 66 alignments. Just off the old road, take a look in the ever-expanding **Shortgrass Country Museum** (106 E. Poplar Ave., 580/928-5757, Tues.-Fri. 9am-noon, free), housed in the old Rock Island Line railroad depot, with changing displays documenting regional history from Cheyenne times to the arrival of homesteading settlers during the great Land Rush of 1892. East of the museum stands a giant grain elevator that has rusted into a gorgeous orange glow.

Erick

In Jack D. Rittenhouse's original *A Guide Book to Highway 66,* published in 1946 and now widely available in reprinted versions, he described **Erick** (pop. 1,036) as "the first town you encounter, going west, which has any of the true western look, with its wide, sunbaked street, frequent horsemen, occasional sidewalk awnings, and similar touches." His description still rings true today (apart from the horses, which have been replaced by pickup trucks). Along with main streets named for hometown musical heroes Sheb "Flying Purple People Eater" Wooley and Roger "King of the Road" Miller, Erick has another unique draw: All the buildings at the main intersection, and the only stoplight in town, have chamfered corners, filed off to give a sense of consistency and improve the view. One of the original buildings is gone, so it's not perfect, but another has been resuscitated to house the **Roger Miller Museum** (101 S. Sheb Wooley Ave., 580/526-3833, Wed.-Sun.). Established by the widow of the original "King of the Road," it shows off many old photos, posters, and personal items.

Erick is a quiet but welcoming little town, especially if you walk around the corner from the Miller Museum to the **Sandhills Curiosity Shop** (201 S. Sheb Wooley Ave., 580/526-3738, hours vary, free). Marked by the dozens of old signs hanging outside the old City Meat Market, this old curiosity shop is owned and curated by Harley Russell, an energetic pack rat of a man whose guitar-playing, singing, and story-telling has entertained Route 66 travelers for years.

A mile south of the I-40 freeway (exit 7), a nice stretch of late-model Route 66 continues west from Erick as a four-lane divided highway, all the way to Texas through the borderline ghost town of Texola.

Sandhills Curiosity Shop

TEXAS

Known as the Panhandle because of the way it juts north from the rest of Texas, this part of the route is a nearly 200-mile stretch of pancake-flat plains. Almost devoid of trees or other features, the western half, stretching into New Mexico, is also known as the Llano Estacado or "Staked Plains," possibly because early travelers marked their route by driving stakes into the earth. The Texas Panhandle was the southern extent of the buffalo-rich grasslands of the Great Plains, populated by roving bands of Kiowa and Comanche people as recently as 100 years ago. Now oil and gas production, as well as trucking and Route 66 tourism, have joined ranching as the region's economic basis.

Even more than in New Mexico or Oklahoma, old Route 66 has been replaced by I-40 most of the way across Texas, though in many of the ghostly towns, like **McLean, Shamrock,** or **Vega,** and the sole city, **Amarillo,** old US-66 survives as the main business strip, lined by the empty remains of roadside businesses. A select few are still open for a cup of coffee and a sharp taste of the living past.

Midway between McLean and the Oklahoma border, the town of **Shamrock** (see page 207) marks the junction of Route 66 and US-83, **The Road to Nowhere** along the 100th meridian. Full coverage of that route begins on page 168.

McLean

McLean (pop. 775) was founded around the turn of the 20th century by an English rancher, Alfred Rowe, who later lost his life on the *Titanic* in 1912. Considering its minimal size, McLean is now perhaps the most evocative town along the Texas stretch of Route 66. Bypassed only in the early 1980s, the old main drag is eerily silent, with a few businesses—such as a boot shop—and a fine Texas-shaped neon sign still standing despite the near-total drop in passing trade.

McLean is headquarters of the state's Old Route 66 Association, and efforts are being made to preserve the town in prime condition, which explains the lovingly restored Phillips 66 station at 1st and Gray Streets (on the westbound stretch of old Route 66—the pumps price gas at 19 cents a gallon!) and the many other odds and ends on display around town. The center of activity here is the wonderful **Devil's Rope Museum** (100 S. Kingsley St., 806/779-2225, Mon.-Sat. Mar.-Nov., free), at the east end of downtown, which has a huge room full of barbed wire—the "devil's rope"—and some of the most

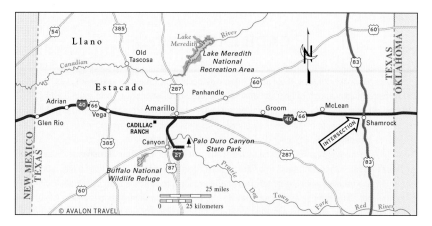

entertaining and educational collections of Route 66 memorabilia you'll find anywhere. No hype, just lots of good stuff and friendly people telling you all about it.

Besides the barbed wire museum, a pair of places next to each other at the west end of McLean offer good food and reliably clean and pleasant rooms: Try the thick steaks, juicy catfish, and weekend barbecue at the **Red River Steak House** (101 W. Route 66, 806/779-8940), then sleep at the **Cactus Inn** (101 Pine St., 806/779-2346).

Groom

The town of **Groom** (pop. 565), which is 45 miles east of Amarillo on the north side of I-40 at exit 113, holds two of the more eye-catching sights along old Route 66. One of these is a water tower on the north side of I-40 that leans like the Tower of Pisa, causing drivers to stop and rub their eyes, then stop and pull out

the camera to take some snapshots to show the folks back home. The other landmark is even harder to miss: a gigantic stainless steel cross—just shy of 200 feet tall and weighing 1.25 tons. This was the largest cross in the western hemisphere until a competitive copycat erected a slightly taller one along I-70 in Effingham, Illinois. Erected by a religious group in 1995, the Groom cross stands above a series of sculptures depicting biblical scenes and the evils of abortion.

Amarillo

At the heart of the Llano Estacado, midway across the Texas Panhandle, **Amarillo** (pop. 199,582; pronounced "am-uh-RILL-o") is a busy big city that retains its cowboy roots. Center of the

leaning water tower near Groom

CADILLAC RANCH

No, you're not seeing things—there really are nearly a dozen Cadillacs upended in the Texas plain west of Amarillo, roughly midway between Chicago and Los Angeles. Two hundred yards south of I-40 between the Hope Road and Arnot Road exits (exits 62 and 60, respectively), some 10 miles west of Amarillo where old US-66 rejoins the interstate, the rusting hulks of 10 classic Caddies are buried nose-down in the dirt, their upended tail fins tracing design changes from 1949 to 1964.

A popular shrine to America's love of the open road, **Cadillac Ranch** was created by the San Francisco-based Ant Farm artists' and architects' collective in May 1974, under the patronage of the eccentric Amarillo helium millionaire Stanley Marsh III. The cars were all bought, some running, some not, from local junkyards and used car lots at an average cost of $200 each. Before the Cadillacs were planted in the ground, all the hubcaps and wheels were welded on, a good idea since most of the time the cars are in a badly vandalized state. Tagging the cars with spray-paint graffiti has become a popular activity, but every once in a while advertising agencies and rock bands tidy them up for use as backdrops during photo shoots. In the late 1990s, Cadillac Ranch got

another 15 minutes of fame when Marsh decided to dig them up and move them two miles west from where they'd been—to escape the ever-expanding Amarillo sprawl and preserve the natural horizon. Marsh's death in 2014 has made the site's future less secure, so see it while you can.

There's a well-worn path from the frontage road if you want a closer look. Visitors are allowed any time, day or night.

local ranching industry that handles some two million head of cattle each year, Amarillo handles nearly 90 percent of all the beef in Texas and some 30 percent of the national total.

Old Route 66 followed 6th Street through Amarillo, past the brick-paved streets of the Old San Jacinto district around Western Avenue, where you can wander among ancient-looking gun and saddle shops, numerous Wild West-themed clothing shops, and kitsch-minded antiques shops. To eat and drink with the Coors-drinking cowboys and cowgirls of Amarillo, head west to the **GoldenLight Café** (2906 SW. 6th Ave., 806/374-9237), a fairly funky roadhouse famed for burgers, homemade hot sauce, green-chili stew, and Frito pies. Next door, the GoldenLight Cantina hosts frequent live music. Amarillo is best known for its many good steakhouses, the most famous of which has to be the 450-seat **Big Texan Steak Ranch** (7701 I-40 East, 806/372-6000), which started in 1960 along historic Route 66 and now stands on the east side of Amarillo, off I-40 exit 74, marked by a false-front Wild West town and a giant cowboy atop a billboard. This is the place where they offer a free 72-ounce steak, provided you eat it all—plus a table full of salad, baked potato, and dessert—in under an hour. If you don't finish everything, the cost is $72; regular meals and good "normal" steaks are available as well.

There's a Texas-shaped swimming pool at the **Big Texan Motel** (806/372-5000, $79 and up), and dozens of moderate chain motels stand along the I-40 and I-27 frontages, so rooms shouldn't be hard to find.

Palo Duro Canyon State Park

Lovely **Palo Duro Canyon State Park** (daily, $5), one of the most beautiful places in all of Texas, is just 35 miles southeast of Amarillo, east of the town of Canyon off the I-27 freeway. Cut into the Texas plain by the Prairie Dog Town Fork of the Red River, Palo Duro has more than 60 miles of ravines, with canyon walls climbing to 800 feet. Coronado and company were the first Europeans to lay eyes on the area, and numerous Plains people, including Apache, Kiowa, and Comanche, later took refuge here. From the end of Hwy-217, a well-paved road winds past the Palo Duro park **visitors center** (806/488-2227, daily), from where a short trail leads to a canyon overlook. Beyond here, more than 30 miles of hiking extend through the canyon's heart. It's prettiest in spring and fall, and fairly popular year-round.

On your way to or from Palo Duro Canyon, be sure to stop by the excellent **Panhandle-Plains Historical Museum**

Dynamite Museum consists of a series of mock street signs placed around Amarillo that say things like "Road Does Not End," "Lubbock is a Grease Spot," and "Remember You Promised Yourself This Would Be a Good Day."

Most of the Texas Panhandle's 22 inches of annual rain falls during summer thunderstorms that sweep across the plains between May and August.

The Great Plains region, and Amarillo in particular, was one of the few places on earth where lighter-than-air helium has been found in an easily recoverable form. An estimated 90 percent of the world's supply once came from here. Today, the Amarillo region is home to the largest wind farms in the USA.

Palo Duro Canyon State Park

(2503 4th Ave., 806/651-2244, Tues.-Sat. Sept.-May, $10) in the neighboring town of **Canyon.** One of the state's great museums, this has extensive exhibits on the cultural and economic life of the Panhandle region and its relations with Mexico, the Texas Republic, and the United States. The museum, which is housed in a WPA-era building on the campus of West Texas A&M University, has a special section on rancher Charles Goodnight (1836-1929), who once owned a half-million acres here, invented the chuck wagon, and was an early advocate of saving the bison from extinction.

Vega and Adrian: Midpoint Café

Between Amarillo and the New Mexico border, the landscape is made up of endless flat plains dotted with occasional oil derricks and Aermotor windmills. The one biggish town, **Vega** (pop. 906), has a photogenic collection of former and still-functioning businesses, including a nicely preserved 1920s Magnolia service station.

West of Vega, the main event hereabouts is both a geographical and culinary magnet: the hamlet of **Adrian** (pop. 167) and the unmissable **Midpoint Café** (806/538-6379, daily Apr.-Nov.). One of the route's most enjoyable places to eat, located more or less at the halfway point in Route 66's long ride between Chicago and Los Angeles—both of which are some 1,105 miles away—the Midpoint is friendly, has great food, and basically epitomizes all that old-fashioned hospitality that makes Route 66 such a special experience. Be sure to check out the fine selection of Route 66 books and "midpoint" souvenirs, or just stop by for a piece of baked-from-scratch Ugly Crust pie. As more than one satisfied customer has said, you can taste the happiness.

NEW MEXICO

Following old Route 66 across New Mexico gives you a great taste of the Land of Enchantment, as the state calls itself on its license plates. There is less of the actual "old road" here than in other places, but the many towns and ghost towns along I-40, built more or less on top of Route 66, still stand. Route 66 runs around the historic heart of the state's cultural and political capital, **Santa Fe,** and right through the heart of its sprawling Sun Belt commercial center, **Albuquerque.** In other places finding the old road and bypassed towns can take some time, though the effort is usually well rewarded.

Western New Mexico has the most to see and the most interesting topography, with sandstone mesas looming in the foreground and high pine-forested peaks rising in the distance. Paralleling the Burlington Northern Santa Fe Railway, the route passes through the heart of this region. Numerous detours—to **El Morro National Monument** and **Chaco Culture National Historical Park,** among others—make unforgettable stops along the way. In the east, the land is flatter and the landscape drier as the road transitions from the Great Plains.

GET YOUR KICKS

If you ever plan to motor west
Travel my way, that's the highway that's the best
Get your kicks on Route 66.
It winds from Chicago to L.A.
More than 2,000 miles all the way
Get your kicks on Route 66
Now you go through St. Looey, Joplin, Missouri
And Oklahoma City is mighty pretty.
You'll see Amarillo, Gallup, New Mexico,
Flagstaff, Arizona, don't forget Winona,
Kingman, Barstow, San Bernardino.
Won't you get hip to this timely tip:
When you make that California trip
Get your kicks on Route 66.
Get your kicks on Route 66.
—Bobby Troup

One of the most popular road songs ever written, and a prime force behind the international popularity of Route 66, **"Get Your Kicks on Route 66"** was penned by jazz musician Bobby Troup in 1946 while he was driving west to seek fame and fortune in Los Angeles. Troup consistently credited his former wife Cynthia, with whom he was traveling, for the half dozen words of the title and refrain. The rest of the song simply rattled off the rhyming place-names along the way, but despite its apparent simplicity, it caught the ear of Nat King Cole, who made it into a hit record and also established the pronunciation as "root" rather than "rout," as repeated in later renditions by everyone from Bob Wills to the Rolling Stones.

If you haven't heard the song for a while, there's a jazzy version by Bobby Troup himself, along with some lively Route 66-related songs, on the compilation CD, *The Songs of Route 66—Music from the All-American Highway,* available at souvenir stores en route.

Tucumcari

Subject of one of the most successful advertising campaigns in Route 66's long history of roadside hype, **Tucumcari** (pop. 4,975) looks and sounds like a much bigger place than it is. Also known as "the town that's two blocks wide and two miles long" (though Tucumcari Boulevard, which follows the route blazed by old Route 66 through town, stretches for closer to seven miles

The border between Texas and New Mexico marks the boundary between the central and mountain time zones. Set your clocks and watches accordingly.

between interstate exits), Tucumcari does have a little of everything, including a great range of neon signs, but it can be hard to explain the attraction of the town that hundreds of signs along the highways once trumpeted as "Tucumcari Tonite—2,000 Motel Rooms." (A new ad campaign plays on this legacy, but signs now say "Tucumcari Tonite—1,200 Motel Rooms.")

Hype or no hype, Tucumcari is a handy place to break a journey, and even if you think you can make it to the next town, you will never regret stopping here for a night. Especially if you stop at the famous **Blue Swallow Motel** (815 E. Route 66, 575/461-9849, $90 and up), which no less an authority than *Smithsonian* magazine called "the last, best, and friendliest of the old-time motels." Thanks to the warm hospitality of longtime owner Lillian Redman, few who stayed there during her long reign 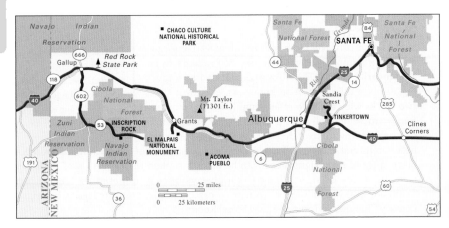 would disagree, and more recent owners have kept up the old spirit while improving the plumbing and replacing the mattresses. Many rooms come with their own garage, and the neon sign alone is worth staying awake for. If the Blue Swallow is full, as it often is, try one of Tucumcari's other old-fashioned motels: The **Motel Safari** (722 E. Route 66, 575/461-1048, $55 and up), a block away, has Wi-Fi and flat-screen TVs, while the **Historic Route 66 Motel** (1620 E. Route 66, 575/461-1212, $40 and up) is clean and stylish, with a Rat Pack-era Palm Springs vibe and Tucumcari's best espresso bar.

Across Route 66 from the Blue Swallow stands another survivor, the landmark tepee fronting the historic **Tee Pee Curios** (924 E. Route 66, 575/461-3773), where friendly owners Gar and Heidi Engman will tempt you to add to your collection of Southwest or Route 66 souvenirs (or "Damn Fine Stuff," as their business cards have it). The Tee Pee has one of the coolest neon signs anywhere, so time your visit to see it in its full glory.

To enjoy the Mexican food as well as a photo opportunity, head to **La Cita** (575/461-7866), under the turquoise, yellow, and brown sombrero on the corner of 1st Street and old Route 66. A few blocks east is the popular **Del's Restaurant** (1202 E. Route 66, 575/461-1740). Three blocks north of Route 66, next to Tucumcari Ranch and Farm Supply is **Watson's Bar-B-Que** (502 S. Lake St., 575/461-9620), a trailer-and-picnic-tables place. It's worth the 60-second detour for the smoky but juicy beef brisket, pinto beans, and green-chili stew.

Three newer additions fill out Tucumcari's roster of attractions: one is a

BUDDY HOLLY, CLOVIS MAN

South of Tucumcari, at the edge of the desolate Llano Estacado that stretches south and east across the Texas Panhandle, the city of Clovis is a large railroad and ranching town that has two unique claims to fame. It is the site where some of the oldest archaeological remains ever found in North America were unearthed: In the 1930s, archaeologists dug up bones and arrowheads that proved human habitation dating back as early as 11,000 BC. Some of these artifacts, belonging to what archaeologists have dubbed "Clovis Man," are on display at the **Blackwater Draw Museum** (575/562-2202, Tues.-Sun., $3), on US-70 about 20 miles south of Clovis.

Clovis also played a part in early rock 'n' roll: Buddy Holly came here from Lubbock, across the Texas border, in the late 1950s to record "Peggy Sue," "That'll Be The Day," and other early classics. You can tour the restored **Norman Petty Recording Studios** (1313 W. 7th St., 575/356-6422), open only by appointment. Buddy's contributions to Western culture are also well documented in his hometown of **Lubbock,** which is described on page 791.

chromed steel **Route 66 sculpture,** welcoming travelers at the west edge of town; another is the vivid Route 66 mural painted on the corner of 2nd Street. The third is the unique **Mesalands Dinosaur Museum** (222 E. Laughlin Ave., 575/461-3466, Tues.-Sat., $6.50), two blocks north of Route 66. Housed inside Mesa Community College, the museum boasts "the largest collection of life-size bronze prehistoric skeletons in the world," plus real fossils, unusual minerals, and a full-size skeleton of the rare *Torvosaurus,* a cousin of legendary *Tyrannosaurus rex.*

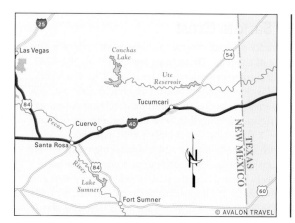

Along the Pecos River via US-84, some 50 miles southeast of Santa Rosa, the gravesite of Wild West legend Billy the Kid lies just steps from the **Old Fort Sumner Museum** (575/355-2942, $5) in Fort Sumner, where 9,500 Navajo and 500 Mescalero Apache people were imprisoned from 1863 to 1869. A visit to the grave is free. To learn more about the Kid, stop by the private museum about three miles from downtown Fort Sumner.

Clines Corners, midway between Albuquerque and Santa Rosa off I-40 exit 218, is a truck stop café that dates back to 1934 and is, as the signs say, "Worth Waiting For"—for the huge gift shop and the "Cleanest Restrooms on I-40."

Santa Rosa

The I-40 freeway has bisected the town of **Santa Rosa** (pop. 2,680) and cut its old Route 66 frontage in two, but for over 65 years, travelers crossing New Mexico along Route 66 and I-40 made a point of stopping here for a meal at Club Café, "The Original Route 66 Restaurant Since 1935." Thanks to signs lining the road for miles in both directions, emblazoned with the smiling face of the "Fat Man," the Club Café was nationally famous for its always-fresh food until it closed in 1992.

Just off the freeway, east of downtown on Route 66 and marked by a hard-to-miss bright-yellow hot rod perched atop a 30-foot pole, the **Route 66 Auto Museum** (2866 Historic Route 66, 575/472-1966, $5) has a wide-ranging exhibit on "anything to do with wheels," highlighted by some tricked-out old Fords and Chevys.

Santa Rosa's other main attraction is unique: the **Blue Hole,** an 80-foot-wide, 80-foot-deep artesian well filled with water so crystal-clear that it draws scuba divers from all over the Western states to practice their underwater techniques here. The water of the Blue Hole, at around 62°F, is too cold for casual swimming, but in the summer heat

scuba diver in the Blue Hole

it's a great place to cool your heels. The Blue Hole is well signed at the end of Blue Hole Road, a half mile south of old Route 66; for purists, Blue Hole Road is *old, old* Route 66, since it formed the early (pre-1937) alignment of the Mother Road across Santa Rosa, the rest of which is used as a runway at the city's airport (no cars allowed!). East of here, running along the south side of I-40, one of the oldest stretches of Route 66 is only partly paved and best done in a 4WD or on a mountain bike. Here you get an indelible sense of what travel was like in the early days, when less than half of the route's 2,400-odd miles were paved.

Tinkertown and the Sandia Crest

Not that there's any shortage of wacky roadside Americana along what's left of Route 66, but one of the most endearing of them all, **Tinkertown Museum** (505/281-5233, daily Apr.-Oct., $3.75), is a quick 10-minute drive north of the old road in Sandia Park, east of Albuquerque. Like an old-fashioned penny arcade run riot, Tinkertown is a

Though most people associate computer giant Microsoft with Seattle, the company actually began here in Albuquerque in 1975, in an office building along Route 66.

marvelous assembly of over a thousand delicately carved miniature wooden figures, arranged in tiny stage sets to act out animated scenes—a circus Big Top complete with side show, a Wild West town with dance-hall girls and a squawking vulture—all housed in a ramshackle building made in part out of glass bottles and bicycle wheels, created over the past 50-odd years by Ross and Carla Ward and family. It's impossible to describe the many odds and ends on show here—one display case holds over 100 plastic

Tinkertown Museum

figures taken from the tops of wedding cakes, for example—especially since the whole thing is always being improved and "tinkered" with. The spirit of the place is aptly summed up in the Tinkertown motto: "We Did All This While You Were Watching TV." The Dalai Lama loved it, and so will you.

To get to Tinkertown, turn off I-40 at exit 175, six miles east of Albuquerque, and follow Hwy-14 for six miles, toward Sandia Crest. Tinkertown is on Hwy-536, 1.5 miles west of the Hwy-14 junction, hidden off the highway among the juniper trees.

Sandia Crest itself is another 12 miles uphill at the end of Hwy-536 National Scenic Byway. This ridge at the top of the Sandia Mountains offers a phenomenal panorama from an elevation of 10,679 feet.

Albuquerque

Roughly located at the center of New Mexico, the sprawling city of **Albuquerque** (pop. 559,277) spreads along the banks of the Rio Grande and east to the foothills of more than 10,000-foot Sandia Crest. By far the state's biggest city, and in the spotlight as location of the TV show *Breaking Bad,* Albuquerque is a young, energetic, and vibrantly multicultural community, which, among many features, boasts a great stretch of old Route 66 along Central Avenue through the heart of the city—18 miles of diners, motels, and sparkling neon signs.

One of the best parts of town is **Old Town,** the historic heart of Albuquerque. Located a block north of Central Avenue, at the west end of Route 66's cruise through downtown, Old Town offers a quick taste of New Mexico's Spanish colonial past, with a lovely old church, the 200-year-old **San Felipe de Neri,** as well as shops and restaurants set around a leafy green park. An information booth just off the park has maps of Old Town and other information about the city. Another Old Town attraction, one that carries on the Route 66 tradition of reptile farms and private zoos, is the **American International Rattlesnake Museum** (202 San Felipe St., 505/242-6569, daily, $5),

Albuquerque was also the home of the great travel writer and World War II war correspondent Ernie Pyle. His old house at 900 Girard Avenue, a half mile north of Central Avenue, is now the city's oldest public library, which includes his collected works and a few personal items in a small display.

New Mexico's long relationship with radioactivity is reflected in the name of Albuquerque's popular Colorado Rockies–affiliated Triple-A baseball club, the **Isotopes** (505/924-2255, $11 and up), who play just south of downtown. Games are broadcast on **KNML 610 AM.**

southeast of the main square, where you can see a range of rattlers from tiny babies to full-size diamondbacks, about 50 altogether, plus fellow desert-dwellers like tarantulas and a giant Gila monster.

A different look into New Mexico's varied cultural makeup is offered at the **Indian Pueblo Cultural Center** (2401 12th St., 505/843-7270, daily, $8.40), a block north of I-40 exit 158. The center is owned and operated by the state's 19 different Pueblo communities. Its highlight is a fine museum tracing the history of the region's Native American cultures, told by the pueblo people (including in their native languages). It touches on the Indian School era, fitting given the center sits on formerly Indian school grounds. On most weekends ceremonial dances are held in the central courtyard, open to the general public. There's also a restaurant where you can sample traditional food like fry bread and atole, and a gift shop with pueblo pottery and jewelry.

Downtown Albuquerque has been under reconstruction seemingly forever, with an ambitious mixed-use project surrounding the train station and massive old Santa Fe Railroad yards. Despite budget shortfalls, the state has pledged money for it, so someday the area may feature the enticingly named **Wheels Museum** (1100 2nd St. SW., 505/243-6269), tracing (surprise, surprise) transportation in New Mexico, inside the sprawling complex of train repair sheds.

Albuquerque Practicalities

The largest city in New Mexico, Albuquerque makes a handy point of entry for tours of the southwestern United States. For old-road fans, the best stretch of Route 66 through Albuquerque is probably the section along Nob Hill, east of downtown near the University of New Mexico. Here you'll find vintage neon and some great places to eat and drink, including **Kelly's Brew Pub** (3222 Central Ave. NE, 505/262-2739), housed in a 1930s Streamline Moderne auto dealership, and the original **Flying Star** (3416 Central Ave. NE, 505/255-6633), famous for its grilled cheese sandwiches.

Between Nob Hill and downtown, the excellent **66 Diner** (1405 Central Ave. NE, 505/247-1421) serves top-quality burgers and shakes, and regional specialties like green-chili chicken enchiladas. Perhaps the best breakfasts are at the super stylish **Grove Café & Market** (600 Central Ave. SE, 505/248-9800) in downtown's Huning Highland Historic District.

Another good range of places to eat lies within walking distance of Old Town, close to the Rio Grande. Enjoy a delicious mix of Mexican and American diner food at **Garcia's Kitchen** (1736 Central Ave. SW, 505/842-0273), beneath a glorious neon sign. Fans of the TV show *Breaking Bad* may want to pay their respects to Walt and Jesse at the **Dog House Drive In** (1216 Central Ave. SW, 505/243-1019), whose blinking neon sign appeared in a number of episodes. Another old Route 66 landmark, **Mac's La Sierra** (6217 Central Ave. NW, 505/836-1212), serves up steak fingers and other beefy specialties in a cozy dark-wood dining room a long ways west of town.

Like most of New Mexico, Albuquerque has a ton of inexpensive accommodations, with all the usual chain motels represented near the airport and along the interstate

San Felipe de Neri church in Old Town, Albuquerque

frontage roads, plus a lot of fading or extinguished old stars of the Route 66 era, like the famous **El Vado** (2500 W. Central Ave.), which has been in redevelopment limbo for decades. Purchased by the city of Albuquerque, the El Vado likely will be redeveloped, perhaps as live-work spaces. For a place with oodles of Route 66 character, stay at the neat and tidy Del Webb-built **Hiway House Motel** (3200 Central Ave. SE, 505/268-3971, $62 and up), in the Nob Hill district, or the unimaginatively but accurately named **Monterey Non-Smokers Motel** (2402 Central Ave. SW, 505/243-3554, $78 and up), near Old Town. The nicest hotel has got to be the grand old **Hotel Andaluz** (125 2nd St., 505/388-0038, $180 and up), a block off old Route 66 in the heart of the lively downtown nightlife district. One of the first inns built by New Mexico-born hotel magnate Conrad Hilton, the Andaluz has been thoughtfully and completely restored and updated, and is now the most comfortable and gracious place to stay, with an entrancing second-story open-air bar.

Old Route 66: Bernalillo

True fans of the full Route 66 tour, and anyone interested in the art and architecture (and food!) of the American Southwest, will want to make the trip to the state capital, Santa Fe. The original Route 66 alignment ran north from Albuquerque along the I-25 corridor through Las Vegas, then curved back south from Santa Fe along what's now US-84, to rejoin I-40 west of Santa Rosa.

The best sense of this old route across old New Mexico comes just north of Albuquerque, at the historic town of **Bernalillo.** Route 66 here follows the much older El Camino Real, which linked these Spanish colonies 400 years ago. The heart of Bernalillo contains two great stops, poles apart from each other in ambience but together capturing the essence of the place. First of these is ancient-feeling **Silva's Saloon** (955 S. Camino del Pueblo, 505/867-9976), whose walls, coated in layers of newspaper clippings, old snapshots, and other mementos, form a fabulously funky backdrop for a cold beer alongside cowboys, bikers, and other characters. Just up the street is the stylish **Range Café** (925 S. Camino del Pueblo, 505/867-1700), where a spacious dining room has good "New New Mexican" food (try the bread pudding!) and a sophisticated big-city air.

Rio Puerco and the Route 66 Casino

Between Albuquerque and Acoma Pueblo, a fine old stretch of old Route 66 survives, passing crumbling tourist courts and service stations across the Laguna Indian Reservation. The photogenic Route 66 highlight here is the graceful old steel truss **Rio Puerco Bridge,** which spans a usually dry river, right alongside the I-40 superslab about 10 miles west of Albuquerque. The old-road ambience is also overwhelmed by the huge new **Route 66 Casino,** south of the freeway, one of the largest of many gambling complexes that have sprung up on Native American reservations across this part of New Mexico. Besides the jinglingly huge 50,000-square-foot

Santa Fe

An hour away from Albuquerque via I-25 or its old road equivalents, Santa Fe (pop. 83,875) is one of the prime vacation destinations in the country. New Mexico's state capital has been at the center of Southwestern life for centuries, and the cultural crossroads of a region that has been settled for thousands of years. From the east, detour north from Clines Corners via

US-285, or for the full "Historic Route 66" tour, follow US-84 north near Santa Rosa toward Las Vegas (the original one, here in New Mexico), then continue west on I-25, parallel to the pioneer-era Santa Fe Trail.

Despite its swirling hordes of vacationers, and its vast infrastructure of hotels, restaurants, art galleries, and souvenir shops, Santa Fe remains one of the most enjoyably un-American small cities. It makes the most sense to begin your tour of Santa Fe at its center, the **Plaza.** This will help you get not only your geographical bearings but also a historical context with which to appreciate the rest of Santa Fe. On the north side of the Plaza, the **Palace of the Governors** (105 W. Palace Ave., Tues.-Sun. Nov.-Apr., $12) is the oldest continuously used public building in America. Dating from 1610, the palace served as residence for Spanish, Mexican, and, later, American territorial governors until 1909, when the New Mexico legislature voted to turn the building into the Museum of New Mexico (it's now the New Mexico History Museum's largest artifact). The museum contains an excellent overview of the building's and the city's tumultuous history, numerous artifacts and documents, and an exhaustive collection of regional photographs.

To get a sense of the life and work of the woman who did as much as anyone to fix Santa Fe in the American mind, walk two blocks west and one block north from the Plaza to the **Georgia O'Keeffe Museum** (217 Johnson St., 505/946-1000, daily, $13), whose collection contains 1,149 pieces of the late artist's work. Many of the paintings here depict the landscape in and around her home at Abiquiú, north of Santa Fe, where she lived for 40 years.

Shops, shops, and more shops (plus a few cafés and restaurants) line the streets emanating from the Plaza. Many of these have a decidedly upscale bent; there are about 200 art galleries alone in Santa Fe, for instance (though the most engaging and scenic stretch of them is found along narrow and tree-lined Canyon Road, which runs east from Paseo de Peralta up into the foothills above town). Once you penetrate Santa Fe's Paseo de Peralta, the historic ring road encircling the 17th-century city center, leave your car at one of the many parking lots or garages and see Santa Fe on foot. Another downtown street, Old Pecos Trail, carried Route 66 for its first dozen years before Santa Fe was bypassed in favor of Albuquerque in 1937.

If you're interested in classical music, the **Santa Fe Chamber Music Festival** (505/982-1890 or 888/221-9836) performances take place in July and August in a variety of atmospheric old Santa Fe buildings.

PRACTICALITIES

It's a pleasant surprise that only moderately deep pockets are needed to find good food or memorable accommodations in Santa Fe. With recipes that show the influence of more than 2,000 years of Native American culture (which contributed three major staples: beans, corn, and squash), some 400 years of Roman Catholic inclusion (chilies, cilantro, cumin, onions, garlic, wheat, rice, and both beef and pork), and a liberal dash of American inventiveness, Santa Fe restaurants serve the world's oldest, newest, and, some say, tastiest cuisines—often all side by side on the same plates. Menu offerings include dishes like a buttermilk corn cake with smoky chipotle-chili shrimp (and a side of red-chili onion rings), chiles rellenos stuffed with roast duck and black bean mole sauce, or blue corn turkey enchiladas. Santa Fe's fine food is at least as much a draw as its rich history and magical mountain light.

To ease your way into Santa Fe food, start on the Plaza at the **Plaza Café** (54 Lincoln Ave., 505/982-1664), which has been serving no-nonsense meals since it opened in 1918. Part of the fun here is the constant clatter of dishes and silverware, the old-fashioned tile floor, and a rear wall with a giant map of the Southwest. If you don't have time for a full meal (the green-chili meatloaf is a specialty), pop in for a helping of Frito pie, which is quite the local delicacy (although the recipe allegedly originated in Texas in the 1930s, when Daisy Doolin, the mother of the Dallas-based founder of Frito-Lay, poured chili over her Fritos and found that she liked it).

Just off the Plaza, and well worth a visit for its addictive breakfast quesadilla (with scrambled eggs, applewood-smoked bacon, Jack cheese, and guacamole), is

Café Pasqual's (121 Don Gaspar Ave., 505/983-9340), which has deliciously inventive dishes at lunch and dinner too. After a meal elsewhere (unless someone else is paying your expenses!), join Santa Fe's old guard at the **Pink Adobe** (406 Old Santa Fe Trail, 505/983-7712), also known as simply "The Pink," a deluxe retro-minded supper club that's also home to the kitschy Dragon Room bar, a popular late-night hangout.

For a convenient and memorable place to stay, a pair of small B&B gems are within a short walk of the Plaza. **Adobe Abode** (202 Chapelle St., 505/983-3133, $135 and up), as the name suggests, consists of several large adobe-style rooms and casitas, and the **Casa del Toro** (229 McKenzie St., 505/455-6140, $88 and up) has modern baths, upscale amenities, and eclectic antiques and folk furnishings.

If you prefer to park within sight of your room, there's a nice motor inn with a location that's hard to beat: **Garrett's Desert Inn** (311 Old Santa Fe Trail, 505/982-1851, $95 and up), a few blocks off the Plaza. If all the desirable places are full, or if you're tight on funds, cruise along busy Cerrillos Road (Hwy-14), where you'll find all the major chains.

casino, which has the usual card tables, craps, and roulette, the complex also has a 2,800-seat theater, a roadside café, a smoke shop offering cheap (tax-free) tobacco, and a large hotel (866/711-7829, $89 and up).

The heart of the historic Laguna Pueblo, where some 500 people live in adobe buildings around a church that dates from 1699, is not open to travelers, but just west of the pueblo the old Route 66 frontage runs past an old road landmark: **Budville,** where the remnants of an old trading post and café still stand in atmospheric silence along the south side of the highway.

Acoma Pueblo: Sky City

A dozen miles east of Grants and 50 miles west of Albuquerque, one of the Southwest's most intriguing sites, **Acoma Pueblo,** stands atop a more than 350-foot-high sandstone mesa. Long known as "Sky City," Acoma is one of the oldest communities in North America, inhabited since AD 1150. The views out across the plains are unforgettable, especially toward Enchanted Mesa on the horizon to the northeast.

Acoma Pueblo

Few people live on the mesa today, though the many adobe houses are used by Pueblo craftspeople, who live down below but come up to the mesa-top to sell their pottery and other crafts to tourists. To visit this amazing place, you have to join a guided **tour** (800/747-0181, daily, call ahead for closures for cultural observances, $25), which begins with a bus ride to the mesa-top and ends with a visit to **San Esteban del Rey Mission,** the largest Spanish colonial church in the state. Built in 1629, the church features a roof constructed of huge timbers that were carried from the top of Mt. Taylor on the backs of local Native Americans—a distance of nearly 50 miles.

Acoma Pueblo is 15 miles south of I-40, from exit 108 (westbound) or exit 96 (eastbound). Start your visit by appreciating the artifacts displayed in the beautiful **Haak'u Museum,** at the base of the mesa, where tours of the ancient Sky City begin.

Acoma Pueblo, or "Sky City"

The Acoma community also operates the money-spinning **Sky City Casino and Hotel** (888/759-2489, $89 and up), sited well away from the historic core of the pueblo, right off I-40 exit 102.

US-60: Pie Town and the Lightning Field

A long way south of Grants, an old mining camp was so famous for fine desserts that it became known as **Pie Town.** After many years of pielessness, local meringue-lovers lucked out when baker Kathy Knapp opened the **Pie-O-Neer Café** (575/772-2711, Thurs.-Sat.), on old US-60 at milepost 59.

East of Pie Town off US-60, more than 40 miles outside Quemado (the next "town" to the west), the **Lightning Field** (May-Oct.) is an outdoor "land art" installation by the late great Walter De Maria, who implanted a grid of steel tubes into the high-elevation (7,200 feet above sea level) New Mexico plain with the intention of attracting lightning strikes. The sculpture consists of 400 stainless steel poles, ranging in height from 16 to 27 feet, placed 200 feet apart in a roughly 1-by-0.6-mile rectangular grid. The engineering feat here was to set the poles so that their tops form an exactly level plane. Despite the name, the experience is meant to be about contemplation, rather than spectacle; casual visitors are not allowed, and for the full Lightning Field experience you have to stay overnight in a nearby cabin; meals and transportation to the site are included in the $150-250 per person rates. The Lightning Field is maintained by the same foundation that curates the intriguing Dia-Beacon museum, north of New York City.

Midway between Grants and Gallup, I-40 crosses the approximately 7,250-foot Continental Divide, where the Top O' the World dance hall used to tempt travelers off old Route 66. From here (exit 47), it's possible to follow the old road for 30 miles, running east along I-40 as far as Grants.

Much less developed, but every bit as memorable as the cliff dwellings of Mesa Verde, the extensive archaeological remains protected inside **Chaco Culture National Historical Park** are well worth your time. Though it's a two-hour drive from I-40 via unpaved roads, the park is one of the wonders of the Southwestern desert.

Grants

Along with the usual Route 66 range of funky motels and rusty neon signs, the former mining boomtown of **Grants** (pop. 9,298) has the unique attraction of the **New Mexico Mining Museum** (505/287-4802, Mon.-Sat., $5), right downtown on old Route 66 (Santa Fe Avenue) at the corner of Iron Avenue. Most of the exhibits trace the short history of local uranium mining, which began in 1950 when a local Navajo rancher, Paddy Martinez, discovered an odd yellow rock that turned out to be high-grade ura-

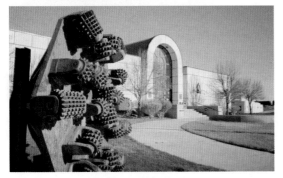
New Mexico Mining Museum

nium ore. Mines around Grants once produced half the ore mined in the United States, but production has ceased, pending renewed interest in nuclear power. From the main gallery, ride the elevator down (only one floor, but it feels like 900 feet) to the highlight of the mining museum: a credible re-creation of a uranium mine, complete with an underground lunch room emblazoned with all manner of warning signs.

The landmark Uranium Café, with its atomic neon sign across Route 66 from the mining museum, has been going in and out of business for years.

Inscription Rock and El Malpais: Hwy-53

Western New Mexico is among the most beautiful places on the planet. South of I-40 and Route 66, one of the best drives through it, Hwy-53, loops between Gallup and Grants across the Zuni and Navajo Nation reservations. Hwy-53 skirts the southern foothills of the more than 9,000-foot Zuni Mountains, along the edge of the massive **El Malpais** lava flow—thousands of acres of pitch-black, concrete-hard, glassy sharp rock sliced and diced by lava tubes and collapsing craters. Formed between 10,000 and 115,000 years ago, most of the Malpais is wild and undeveloped, but on the slopes of Bandera Volcano, you can tour the privately run **Ice Cave** (888/423-2283, daily, $12), where the cool temperatures are welcome on a hot summer's day.

West from El Malpais, the route follows ancient Native American trails that Coronado used on his ill-fated 1540 explorations, winding past piñon-covered hills, open grasslands, and the fascinating graffiti collection of **El Morro National Monument.** Better known as **Inscription Rock,** the 200-foot-high sandstone cliffs of El Morro have been inscribed by travelers like Juan de Oñate, who wrote his name with a flourish in 1605, after he "discovered" the Gulf of California.

Atop the cliffs are the partially excavated remains of a small pueblo dating from around AD 1200. A two-mile loop trail to the inscriptions and the ruins starts from a small **visitors center** (505/783-4226, ext. 801, daily, free), where exhibits outline the history of the site. The trails are closed an hour before sunset, so get here early enough in the day to enjoy the beautiful scenery. There is also a small campground (no showers; pit toilets) amid the junipers.

Southwest of Inscription Rock, animal lovers may want to visit the **Wild Spirit Wolf Sanctuary** (505/775-3304, Tues.-Sun., $10), where over three dozen wolves and wolf-dogs live on a 100-year-old moonshiner's ranch.

Gallup

Though it's not exactly scenic, **Gallup** (pop. 22,670) is a fascinating place. Founded in 1881 when the Santa Fe Railroad first rumbled through, and calling itself "The Gateway to Indian Country" because it's the largest town near the huge Navajo and other Native American reservations of the Four

Corners region, Gallup has some of the Southwest's largest trading posts and one of the best strips of neon signs you'll see anywhere on old Route 66.

For travelers intent on experiencing a little of the charms of old Route 66, Gallup also has **El Rancho Hotel** (1000 E. Route 66, 505/863-9311, $115 and up), a delightful old hotel lovingly preserved in its 1930s glory. Built by a brother of movie director D. W. Griffiths, El Rancho feels like a national park lodge, with a large but welcoming lobby dominated by a huge stone fireplace. All the rooms in the old wing are named for the movie stars who have stayed here over the years—the W. C. Fields Room, the John Wayne Room, the Marx Brothers Room (which sleeps six), even the Ronald Reagan Suite—and signed glossies of these and many more actors and actresses adorn the halls. El Rancho also has a good restaurant serving regional food, and a gift shop selling souvenirs and locally crafted jewelry, pottery, and rugs.

Gallup hosts the annual **Inter-Tribal Ceremonial** (505/863-3896), perhaps the largest Native American gathering in the country, held early in August at **Red Rock Park,** nine miles east of Gallup, and culminating in a parade that brings some 30,000 people out to line old Route 66 through town. Festivities include a rodeo, powwows, and a beauty show.

In the heart of historic downtown, the old Santa Fe train depot (still in use by Amtrak), houses the **Gallup Cultural Center** (201 E. Route 66, 505/863-4131). Free dances are staged at the nearby courthouse square nightly in summer, next to a statue of a World War II Navajo Code Talker. Another place worth spending some time is **Richardson's Cash Pawn and Trading Post** (223 W. Route 66, 505/722-4762). Family-run since 1913, this busy but friendly space is crammed to the rafters with arts, crafts, and pawned goods—Navajo rugs and jewelry, ornately tooled leather saddles, pearl-inlaid guitars, and more—that give a better sense of local lifestyles (and all their ups and downs) than any museum ever could.

If you like huevos rancheros, breakfast burritos, or even diner stand-bys like french toast, you can sample some of the best at the unpretentious but excellent **Plaza Café** (1501 W. Route 66, 505/722-6240), which is way better than it looks amid the neighboring gas stations and car repair shops.

I-40 and old Route 66 trace the southern edge of the massive Navajo Nation reservation, home to radio station **KTNN 660 AM,** which broadcasts a fascinating mélange of Navajo chants and Jimi Hendrix riffs on a "clear" signal that (especially at night) reaches all over the western USA. KTNN is also the only station in the United States that broadcasts pro football games in Navajo.

ARIZONA

If you're not yet a die-hard Route 66 fan, traveling the old route across Arizona is bound to convert you. The high-speed I-40 freeway gives quick access to some of the best surviving stretches of the old road, and these are some of the most captivating parts of Route 66 anywhere. Between the red-rock mesas of New Mexico and the arid desert along the

Colorado River, the route runs past dozens of remarkable old highway towns along some of the oldest and longest still-drivable stretches of the Mother Road.

East of **Flagstaff,** the old road is effectively submerged beneath the freeway,

In and around Holbrook, you'll come across a series of concrete dinosaurs rescued from the old International Petrified Forest Dinosaur Park, which used to stand along I-40 near exit 289.

which drops down to cross desolate desert, passing through desiccated towns and **Petrified Forest National Park.** Remnants of numerous old roadside attractions—Native American trading posts, wild animal menageries, and **Holbrook**'s famous "Sleep in a Teepee" Wigwam Village—all survive in varying degrees of preservation along Arizona's section of Route 66.

Midway across the state, the route climbs onto the forested (and often snowy) Kaibab Plateau for a look at the mighty **Grand Canyon,** one of the true wonders of the natural world.

Painted Desert and Petrified Forest National Park

Right along the New Mexico border, Arizona welcomes westbound travelers with an overwhelming display of trading-post tackiness—huge concrete tepees stand at the foot of brilliant red-rock mesas, while gift shops hawk their souvenirs to passing travelers. The gift shops themselves may not be all that attractive, but the old Route 66 frontage road along here, a.k.a. Hwy-118 between exit 8 in New Mexico and exit 357 in Arizona, is truly spectacular, running at the foot of red-rock cliffs. If you like rocks, gems, and petrified wood, a fine collection is for sale at the endearingly strange **Stewart's Petrified Wood Trading Post,** marked by a family of animated dinosaurs at I-40 exit 303.

A great introduction to the Four Corners region, the **Hubbell Trading Post National Historic Site** (928/755-3254, $5), 38 miles north of I-40 from exit 333 and a mile west of the town of Ganado, is a frontier store preserved as it was in the 1870s, when trader John Hubbell began buying the beautiful rugs made by local Navajo weavers.

The easternmost 60-mile stretch of I-40 across Arizona is little more than one long speedway, since almost any sign of the old road has been lost beneath the four-lane interstate. One place that's worth a stop here is **Petrified Forest National Park**

the Painted Desert

Petrified Forest National Park

(928/524-6228, daily dawn-dusk, $20 per car). The polished petrified wood on display in the visitors center is gorgeous to look at, but seeing 146,930 acres of the stuff in its raw natural state is not, to be honest, particularly thrilling. The story of how the wood got petrified is interesting, though: About 225 million years ago, a forest was buried in volcanic ash, then slowly embalmed with silica and effectively turned to stone. Alongside the visitors center at the entrance to the park, there's a handy restaurant and a gas station.

While the park contains a vast array of prehistoric fossils and pictographs as well as the petrified wood, one of the more interesting sights is the old **Painted Desert Inn,** a Route 66 landmark during the 1920s and 1930s that was converted into a museum and bookstore after the National Park Service took it over in the 1960s. The pueblo-style building, now restored to its 1920s splendor with lovely murals, Navajo rugs and sand paintings, and handcrafted furnishings, is perched on a plateau overlooking the spectacularly colored **Painted Desert** that stretches off toward the northern horizon.

Holbrook: Wigwam Village

Holding a concentrated dose of old Route 66 character, **Holbrook** (pop. 5,074) is definitely worth a quick detour off the I-40 freeway. More than the other Route 66 towns in the eastern half of Arizona, it still feels like a real place, with lively cafés and some endearing roadside attractions around the center of town, where Route 66 alternates between Hopi Drive and Navajo Boulevard. Along with the many rock shops—be sure to check out the huge dinosaur collection outside the **Rainbow Rock Shop,** a block south on Navajo Boulevard near the railroad tracks—and trading post tourist traps, another worthwhile place to stop is the **Navajo County Historical Museum** (daily, free) in the old Navajo County Courthouse, about a quarter mile south of I-40 at the corner of Navajo Boulevard (old Route 66) and Arizona Street. The collections are wide-ranging and include a walk downstairs to the old county jail, in use from 1898 until 1976 (the graffiti is great).

Best of all, stop for the night at the marvelous **Wigwam Village Motel** (811 W. Hopi Dr., 928/524-3048, around $70) at the western edge of town and sleep in a concrete tepee. Based on the original circa-1936 Wigwam Village motor court built in Cave City, Kentucky, Holbrook's was one of seven franchises across the country; this one opened in 1950 but closed down

West of Holbrook along I-40, **Joseph City** is noteworthy for two things. East of town, the giant 995-megawatt Cholla power plant consumes more than 100 tons of coal every hour. At the west end of town, on the south side of I-40 at exit 269, there's the **Jackrabbit Trading Post,** the one whose signs you've probably noticed over the past hundred miles—take a picture or buy a postcard of the giant jackrabbit, one of a long line of creatures who have stood here since 1949.

saguaro cactus blossom,
state flower of Arizona

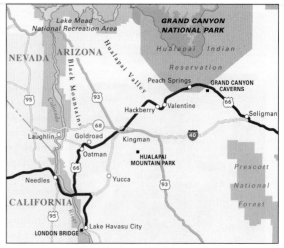

when the interstate came through in 1974. The family of original owner Chester Lewis fully renovated the buildings and reopened the place after his death in 1988. Original bentwood hickory furniture, a small curio shop, and a handful of historic American cars parked outside help complete the ambience of classic roadside Americana. Especially if you want to introduce the younger generations to the joys of old-road travel, you should stay here at least once in your life.

After you've checked in to the Wigwam, be sure to wander down the road for a friendly, filling Route 66 meal at **Joe and Aggie's Café** (120 W. Hopi Dr., 928/524-6540).

Winslow

Winslow, Arizona, didn't make it into Bobby Troup's original Route 66 hit list, but the town more than made it a generation later when Glenn Frey and the Eagles recorded the Jackson Browne tune "Take It Easy," whose second verse starts with "Standin' on a corner in Winslow, Arizona," a line that has caused more people to turn off in search of the place than anything else. Right downtown between the two strips of Route 66, which runs one-way in each direction down 2nd and 3rd Streets, the funky **Old Trails Museum** (212 N. Kinsley Ave., 928/289-5861, Tues.-Sat., free) sells a range of "Standin' on the Corner" T-shirts, and displays a few reminders of Winslow in its heyday. Standing on the corner of 2nd and Kinsley, where a little sign stakes a claim to being *the* corner the Eagles sang about, there's a statue of a guy with a guitar and a mural of a girl (my lord!) in a flatbed Ford, slowing down to take a look.

The usual chain motels and fast-food franchises stand at either end of town around Winslow's I-40 exits, but in between is a great landmark of Southwest style: the elegant **La Posada Hotel** (303 E. 2nd St., 928/289-4366, $120 and up). Designed in the late 1920s for Fred Harvey by architect Mary Colter, who considered it her masterpiece, the hotel was closed for 40 years before being fully and lovingly restored and reopened in 1998. Near a busy rail line but surrounded by pleasant gardens, the luxurious hotel is also home to a stylish cocktail bar and one

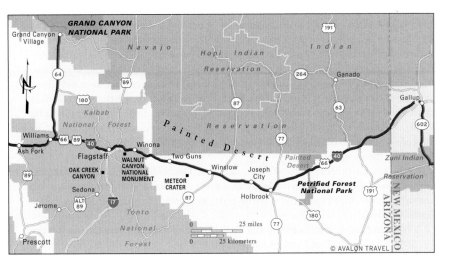

of the finest restaurants for miles, the Turquoise Room. If you have the time and inclination to appreciate its old-fashioned, handcrafted charms, La Posada is an unforgettable stop.

Meteor Crater

Between Winslow and Winona, three miles east of Two Guns and six miles south of I-40 exit 233, sits **Meteor Crater** (928/289-2362, daily, $18), Arizona's second-most-

aerial view of Meteor Crater

distinctive hole in the ground. Formed by a meteorite some 50,000 years ago and measuring more than 550 feet deep and nearly a mile across, the crater is a privately owned tourist attraction. The Astronaut Wall of Fame plays up the crater's resemblance to the surface of the moon (Apollo moon-walkers practiced here). You can't climb down into it, but (weather permitting) you can join a guided rim tour, walking a half mile there and back across the desert to gaze down into the crater.

Two Guns and Twin Arrows

Heading west from Meteor Crater toward Flagstaff, the route climbs swiftly from the hot red desert up into the cool green pines. Old-road fanatics will want to take the time to explore what remains of two old-time tourist traps lining the next 20 miles of highway. Keep your eyes peeled approaching I-40 exit 230: The freeway crosses deep Diablo Canyon, where an old Route 66 bridge still spans the dry wash, and the walls of a half dozen bleached buildings are all that's left of the **Two Guns Trading Post.** A roadside attraction par excellence, Two Guns had a zoo full of road-runners, Gila monsters, and coyotes, and one building still has a sign saying

Mountain Lions—all for the entertainment of passing travelers. For a while in the 1970s, Two Guns was a KOA Kampground (with a swimming pool!), and according to various reports down the Route 66 grapevine, Two Guns has been on the verge of reopening many times, most recently after reports circulated that the whole she-bang had been purchased by Australian actor Russell Crowe so that he could film a remake of the classic Yul Brynner film *Westworld*. But most of the time Two Guns is dead quiet, with the old access road blocked by a sign reading "No Trespassing by Order of Two Guns Sheriff Department." Probably a good thing, since the old buildings are all dangerously close to collapse. It's an evocative site, nonetheless, and photogenic in the right light.

A dozen miles west of Two Guns is another Double-Attraction: **Twin Arrows,** where a pair of giant and surprisingly well-preserved red and yellow arrows point toward a long-closed café and trading post, last seen alive in the 1990s movie *Forrest Gump.*

Twin Arrows is also home to the Navajo-owned **Twin Arrows Casino Resort** (928/856-7200, $127 and up), the largest of the four casinos the Navajo Nation runs. Now if only they'd spend some of that money fixing up Route 66 landmarks, starting with those Twin Arrows . . .

Don't Forget: Winona

East of Flagstaff, in fact across most of eastern Arizona, following old Route 66 can be a frustrating task, since much of the roadway is blocked, discontinuous, torn up, or all three. Unlike the long stretches found in the western half of the state, here the old road exists only as short segments running through towns, and most of the way you're forced to follow the freeway, stopping at exit after exit to get on and off the old road. Among the places worth considering is the one town mentioned out of sequence in the Route 66 song: "Flagstaff, Arizona, don't forget Winona," which, alas, is now little more than a name on the exit sign along I-40.

Walnut Canyon National Monument

The most easily accessible of the hundreds of different prehistoric settlements all over the southwestern United States, **Walnut Canyon National Monument** (928/526-3367, daily 9am-5pm fall-spring, daily 8am-5pm summer, $8) is also one of the prettiest places imaginable, with piñon pines and junipers clinging to the canyon walls, and walnut trees filling the canyon floor. On the edge of the canyon, a small visitors center gives the historical background, but the real interest lies below, on the short but steep Island Trail, which winds through cliff dwellings tucked into overhangs and ledges 400 feet above the canyon floor. Winter storms sometimes dislodge boulders that wipe out parts of the trail. Check with the rangers to make sure the trail is open, and ask about weather, water supplies, and other safety issues. The rim of Walnut Canyon is nearly 7,000 feet above sea level, and the altitude can make the climbing especially strenuous.

The entrance to the Walnut Canyon monument, which contains some 80 dwellings, lies nine miles east of Flagstaff, accessible from I-40 exit 204.

Flagstaff

An old railroad and lumber-mill town given a new lease on life by an influx of students at Northern Arizona University, and by the usual array of ski bums and mountain bikers attracted by the surrounding high mountain wilderness, **Flagstaff** (pop. 71,459) is an enjoyable, energetic town high up on the Colorado Plateau. The natural beauty of its forested location has meant that, compared to other Route 66 towns, Flagstaff was less affected by the demise of the old road. That said, it still takes pride in the past, notably in the form of the **Museum Club** (3404 E. Route 66, 928/526-9434), an old roadhouse brought back to life as a country-western nightclub and ad hoc nostalgia museum.

Along with a great but slowly shrinking range of classic neon signs, Flagstaff also has a pair of non-Route 66 related attractions. First and foremost of these stands high on a hill on the west side of downtown Flagstaff, reachable from the west end of Santa Fe Avenue (old Route 66): the **Lowell Observatory,** established in 1894 by Percival Lowell and best known as the place where, in 1930, the onetime planet Pluto was discovered. A **visitors center** (928/774-3358, daily, $15) has descriptions of the science behind what goes on here—spectroscopy, red shifts, and expanding universes, for example—and the old telescope, a 24-inch refractor, is open for viewings 8pm-9:30pm most nights in summer. Not exactly consistent with its neon-lit Route 66 reputation, since the 1950s Flagstaff has been a pioneer in combating light pollution. To help preserve the dark sky at night, here at the observatory and also at the surrounding natural sights, Flagstaff is an official International Dark Sky Community.

Flagstaff's other main draw, the **Museum of Northern Arizona** (928/774-5213, daily, $12), perches at the edge of a pine-forested canyon three miles northwest of downtown via US-180, the main road to the Grand Canyon. Extensive exhibits detail the vibrant cultures of northern Arizona, from prehistoric Ancestral Puebloans to contemporary Hopi, Navajo, and Zuni peoples.

Downtown Flagstaff has more than enough espresso bars—probably a half dozen within a two-block radius of the train station—to satisfy its many multiply pierced

Way back in 1946, in his classic *A Guide Book to Highway 66,* Jack Rittenhouse wrote that "Cowboys and Indians can be seen in their picturesque dress on Flagstaff streets year-round," but these days he'd probably notice the Lycra-clad cyclists who crowd into the college town's many cafés.

Flagstaff's San Francisco Street was named not for the California city but for the nearby volcanic peaks, so called by early Spanish missionaries and still held sacred by the indigenous Hopi people.

Flagstaff nearly became an early movie center, when young Cecil B. DeMille stopped here briefly while scouting locations to shoot the world's first feature-length film, a Western called *The Squaw Man.* It was snowing in Flagstaff that day, so he moved on to Los Angeles.

20-something residents. There are also ethnic restaurants specializing in Greek, Thai,
German, or Indian cuisine, so finding suitable places to eat and drink will not be a
problem. Grab a cup of good coffee, a pastry,
or a sandwich at **Macy's European
Coffeehouse & Bakery** (14 S. Beaver St.,
928/774-2243), a cozy café two blocks north
of the Northern Arizona University campus,
or wander two blocks farther north and east,
past the train station and across Route 66 to
MartAnne's Burrito Palace (112 E. Route 66,
928/773-4701), a popular little hole-in-the-
wall serving authentic Mexican specialties
(*posole, chilaquiles,* etc.) alongside more
Americanized palate-pleasers like burritos.
Hungry road-food fans may prefer to cruise
west down Route 66 to the authentic-feeling
Galaxy Diner (931 W. Route 66, 928/774-
2466), open since the 1950s.

the telescope that discovered Pluto,
Lowell Observatory

Step back into an even earlier time and
stay at the classy (and possibly haunted) railroad-era **Hotel Monte Vista** (100 N. San
Francisco St., 928/779-6971, $105 and up), right off old Route 66. It was good
enough for Gary Cooper, and it has been restored to its Roaring '20s splendor. For
value and convenience, top marks go to the **Budget Inn** (913 S Milton Rd., 928/774-
5038, $150 and up); it's a block south of Route 66, behind the Galaxy Diner.
Accommodations are plentiful; if you can't decide, pick the motel with the most
appealing sign.

Sunset Crater

While 90 percent of visitors approach the Grand Canyon from the south, a better and
less crowded approach follows US-89 and Hwy-64, climbing up from the Navajo
Nation deserts onto the Kaibab Plateau. The views are amazing in any direction—
north across the desiccated Colorado Plateau, east across the colorful Painted Desert,
west to the forests of the Kaibab Plateau, or south to the angular San Francisco Peaks,
including 12,635-foot Mt. Humphreys, the highest point in Arizona.

This route is somewhat longer than the US-180 route to the Grand Canyon, but
in most other ways it's far superior—not least because it gives access to a huge variety of scenery and historic sites. The first of these, 12 miles north of Flagstaff and 4
miles east of US-89, is **Sunset Crater,** a 1,000-foot-tall black basalt cone tinged with
streaks of oranges and reds and capped by a sulfur-yellow rim—hence the name,
which was bestowed by explorer John Wesley Powell in 1892. You can hike through
the lava field that surrounds the cone, but the cone itself is off limits.

Sunset Crater marks the start of a scenic loop that winds around for some 30
miles through neighboring **Wupatki National Monument** (928/679-2365, daily, $20
per vehicle). The monument protects the remains of a prehistoric Native American
community, thought to have been ancestors of the Hopi, who lived here between
AD 1100 and 1250 and now inhabit the broad mesas rising to the northeast.

Hundreds of ruins—most in fine condition—are spread over the 35,000-acre monument. The largest ruin, 100-room **Tall House,** stands near a ceremonial amphitheater and a rare ball court, which may indicate a link with the Maya culture of Central America.

Back on US-89, 35 miles north of the north entrance to Wupatki, the crossroads settlement of **Cameron** stands at the junction with Hwy-64, which heads up (and up) to the east entrance of **Grand Canyon National Park.** A mile north of the Hwy-64 junction, along the south bank of the Little Colorado River is historic **Cameron Trading Post** (800/338-7385, $79-169), which includes a motel and an RV park. It stands next to an equally historic one-lane suspension bridge, built in 1911 (and now carrying an oil pipeline). Cameron makes a good alternative to Tusayan, in case all the Grand Canyon's in-park accommodations are full.

From Cameron, Hwy-64 runs west along the Little Colorado River Gorge, which Hopi cosmology considers to be the place where the human race emerged into the present world. This deep canyon leads into the much larger Grand Canyon, while Hwy-64 climbs up the plateau for 32 miles to the east entrance of Grand Canyon National Park. Your first overlook is a desert view, where the photogenic 1930s Watchtower gives a great taste of the canyon from the highest point on the South Rim.

> Cameron is named in memory of a cantankerous prospector turned early promoter of the Grand Canyon. Ralph Cameron blazed the Bright Angel Trail, then charged tourists $1 to use it, and did everything he could to obstruct the government from taking over "his" canyon—even going so far as to get elected U.S. Senator in 1920 so he could try to eliminate the newly established national park.

Detour: Grand Canyon National Park

One of the wonders of the natural world, the **Grand Canyon** of the Colorado River—277 miles long, more than a mile deep, and anywhere from 5 to 18 miles across—defies description, and if you're anywhere nearby, you owe it to yourself to stop for a look. The most amazing thing about the Grand Canyon, apart from its sheer size and incredible variety of shapes and colors, is how different it looks when viewed from different places (artist David Hockney has said that the Grand Canyon is the only place on Earth that makes you want to look in all directions—up, down, and side to side—at the same time). Be sure to check it out from as many angles, and at as many

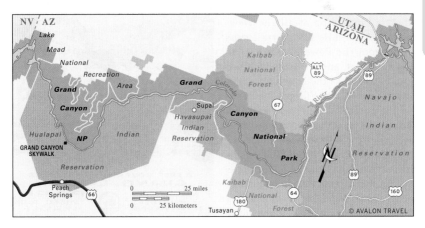

view of the Grand Canyon looking to the North Rim

different times of day, as you can. A book like this one can do little more than hint at all there is to see and do, but if you have time for nothing else, take a quick hike down into the canyon to get a real sense of its truly awesome scale.

The great majority of the five million people who visit the Grand Canyon each year arrive at the **South Rim** and gaze down into the Grand Canyon from **Mather Point,** where the entrance road hits the edge of the gorge. The park visitors center and most of the food and lodging are located two miles west at **Grand Canyon Village.** Beyond Grand Canyon Village, **West Rim Drive** winds west, leading past the **J. W. Powell Memorial** at Hopi Point (from where you get great views of the Colorado River, which otherwise can be surprisingly hard to see) and a series of other viewpoints before ending up at **Hermit's Rest,** eight miles from Grand Canyon Village—where there are yet more stupendous views as well as restrooms, drinking fountains, and a gift shop.

The West Rim Drive, which was built for tourists by the Santa Fe Railroad in 1912, is closed to cars throughout summer, but frequent shuttle buses stop at all the viewpoints. A six-mile hiking trail runs west from the Powell Memorial to Hermit's Rest, and a three-mile paved nature trail links the Powell Memorial with Grand Canyon Village.

East from Mather Point, **East Rim Drive** runs for 25 miles, stopping first at aptly named **Grandview Point,** 12 miles from Grand Canyon Village and a half mile north of the East Rim Drive. This is, literally and figuratively, a high point of any Grand Canyon tour, giving a 270-degree panorama over the entire

A FREE GOVERNMENT SERVICE
GRAND CANYON
NATIONAL PARK
U.S. DEPARTMENT OF THE INTERIOR · NATIONAL PARK SERVICE

gorge. Continuing east, the road passes a small prehistoric pueblo at **Tusayan Ruins** before ending with a bang at **Desert View Watchtower,** an Ancestral Puebloan-style tower set right at the edge of the canyon. Though it looks ancient, the tower was created for tourists in 1932, designed by Mary Colter, also the architect of the Bright Angel Lodge and most of the wonderful old Harvey House hotels that lined Route 66 across the Southwest.

From the watchtower, the road continues along the rim through the east entrance, then drops down to the crossroads town of Cameron and the Little Colorado River.

Grand Canyon Hikes

To get a real feel for the Grand Canyon, you have to get out of the car, get beyond the often overcrowded viewpoints that line the South Rim, and take a walk down into the depths of the canyon itself. The most popular and best-maintained path, the **Bright Angel Trail,** descends from the west end of Grand Canyon Village, following a route blazed by prospectors in the 1890s. It's a 19-mile hike down to the Colorado River and back. There are rest stops (with water) along the way; however, the park does not recommend anyone walking from rim to river in one day. A shorter day hike cuts off to **Plateau Point,** 1,300 feet above the river and a 13-mile round-trip from the South Rim. If you can finagle a reservation, you can stay overnight at **Phantom Ranch,** on the north side of the Colorado River, which is accessed from the South Rim by a pair of suspension bridges. Camping at nearby **Bright Angel Campground,** which has space for more than 100 people, requires an advance permit from the park. Permit information is available at www.nps.gov/grca or by calling the main visitors center for details.

Another interesting old trail drops down from Grandview Point to **Horseshoe Mesa,** where you can still see the remnants of an old copper mine that closed in 1907. This is a six-mile round-trip and gives an unforgettable introduction to the Grand Canyon.

No matter where you go, when hiking down into the canyon, remember that it will take you twice as long to hike back up again, that the rim can be covered in snow and ice as late as June, and *always carry water*—especially in summer—at least a quart for every hour you're on the trail. The good **visitors center** (928/638-7888) in Grand Canyon Village has information about the park's many hiking trails, the canyon's geology, the burro rides that take you down and back up again, and anything else to do with the Grand Canyon.

Practicalities

It may give a sense of the immensity of the Grand Canyon to know that, while the North Rim is a mere 6-10 miles from the South Rim as the crow flies, to get there by road requires a drive of at least 215 miles.

Most of what you'll need to know to enjoy your Grand Canyon visit is contained in the brochure you're given at the entrance, where you pay the $30-per-car fee (national parks passes are accepted).

To make advance reservations for accommodations—a good idea at any time of year but essential in the peak summer months—phone the park concessionaire, **Xanterra** (888/297-2757 in advance, 928/638-2631 for same-day cancellations), which handles reservations for the six different lodges in Grand Canyon Village. The most characterful and best-value place to stay is the **Bright Angel Lodge,** which overlooks the canyon; the cheapest rooms share baths, while others have canyon views and fireplaces. The coffee shop here is open all day, there's a pretty nifty soda fountain right on the edge of the canyon, and the lobby fireplace shows off the rock strata, in proper chronological order, that form the walls of the Grand Canyon. The other historic lodge is the **El Tovar Hotel,** opened in 1905 but recently renovated; rooms here start around $200 and top out at more than $400 a night for suites. The El Tovar also has the park's best restaurant—and a comfy piano bar to help while away the night.

For a basic motel bed, there are four other lodges in Grand Canyon Village, offering more than 750 rooms altogether, costing $90-210. There's also a nice lodge at the North Rim, open usually mid-May to mid-October.

Lower Ribbon Falls

It's more of an effort to reach, but the best place to get a feel for the Grand Canyon is splendid **Phantom Ranch,** a rustic complex of cabins and dormitories way down in the canyon, on the north side of the Colorado River. Space here is usually taken up by people on overnight burro-ride packages (which cost around $575). But, particularly in the off-season, you may be able to get a bed without the standard six months (or more) advance reservation. Ask at the desk in the Bright Angel Lodge, or call 303/297-2757.

Reservations for **camping** (877/444-6777, www.recreation.gov) at the South Rim are also essential in summer. The largest facility, **Mather Campground** (no hookups, $18), is near Market Plaza, the park's general store and commerce area, and is open year-round, with more than more than 300 sites and coin-operated showers. Sites with RV hookups are available nearby at the Delaware North-run **Trailer Village.** There's another National Park Service campground at **Desert View,** near the east entrance. Backcountry camping (overnight permits required) is available at established sites down in the canyon.

If all the in-park accommodations are full, thousands of rooms are available in Williams, Flagstaff, and right outside the park's southern boundary at **Tusayan,** where you can choose from a Best Western, a Holiday Inn Express, and a Quality Inn.

Williams

The last Route 66 town to be bypassed by I-40, **Williams** (pop. 3,159; elev. 6,765 feet) held out until the bitter end, waging court battle after court battle before finally surrendering on October 13, 1984. Despite the town's long opposition, in the end Williams gave in gracefully, going so far as to hold a celebration-cum-wake for the old road, highlighted by a performance atop a new freeway overpass by none other than Mr. Route 66 himself, Bobby "Get Your Kicks" Troup.

Williams today is primarily a gateway to the Grand Canyon, but it also takes full tourist advantage of its Route 66 heritage: The downtown streets sport old-fashioned street lamps, and every other store sells a variety of Route 66 souvenirs,

Grand Canyon Railway

making the town much more than a pit stop for Grand Canyon-bound travelers. Apart from the Route 66 connections, Williams's pride and joy is the vintage **Grand Canyon Railway** (800/843-8724, round-trip $70 and up), which whistles and steams its way north to the canyon every morning, taking roughly two hours each way. Call for current schedules and fares, or stop by the historic depot, a former Harvey House hotel restored in 1990.

If you hanker after a slice of pie and a cup of coffee, or simply appreciate good food and a warm welcome, you'll want to save time and space for the **Pine Country Restaurant** (107 N. Grand Canyon Blvd., 928/635-9718), serving breakfast, lunch, dinner, and famous fresh pies near the train station. Williams is also home to a landmark old Route 66 restaurant, **Rod's Steak House** (301 E. Route 66, 928/635-2671), in business since 1946.

For a place to stay—and there are many, thanks to the nearby Grand Canyon—there are a couple of old motor court motels, one disguised as an  **EconoLodge** (302 E. Route 66, 928/635-4085, $127 and up), another branded as a **Rodeway Inn** (928/635-4041, $150 and up). At the upper end of the scale, try the plushly renovated **Lodge on Route 66** (200 E. Route 66, 877/563-4366, $140 and up), or look into that historic Harvey House hotel, now known as the **Grand Canyon Railway Hotel** (800/843-8724, $219 and up), a plush overnight that's ideal for passengers taking the vintage train to the Grand Canyon with packages available for coupling the hotel and train.

Sedona

Most Arizona visitors head for the Grand Canyon, but smaller and still scenic **Oak Creek Canyon,** just south of Flagstaff, has one great advantage over its world-famous neighbor: You can drive through it, on scenic Hwy-89A. Starting right at the edge of Flagstaff, this red sandstone gorge has been cut into the surrounding pine and juniper forests by eons of erosion. The most popular place to enjoy Oak

Creek Canyon, **Slide Rock State Park** (928/282-3034, daily, $20), which is 22 miles south of Flagstaff and 7 miles north of Sedona, is a 43-acre, day-use-only area focused on the long natural rock chute for which the park is named.

At the south end of Oak Creek Canyon, 25 miles from Flagstaff, the otherworldly landscape surrounding **Sedona** (pop. 10,397) has made it one of the nation's most popular vacation destinations, particularly for New Agey visitors, who in the past 20 years have made Sedona into an upmarket center for psychic channeling, astral travel, and the like. Sedona first came to attention in the 1950s, when the red-rock spires that dominate the local landscape were seen in a wide variety of Hollywood westerns (including *Johnny Guitar*). Despite the rampant sprawl—and the high hotel rates, which can reach $200 a night—Sedona is still well worth a look, especially if you can get away from the town and explore some of the surrounding wilderness.

Cathedral Rock, on the Sedona Skyline

Jerome

South of Route 66 and I-40 from Ash Fork, or west from Sedona, Hwy-89A makes a wonderfully scenic loop, winding past 7,815-foot Mingus Mountain into photogenic **Jerome** (pop. 455; elev. 5,066 feet), the liveliest and most interesting "ghost town" in Arizona. Set on steep streets that switchback up the mountainside, Jerome is an old copper mining camp that has turned itself into a thriving artists community, with many nice shops, galleries, and cafés, and almost no touristy schlock. Park wherever you can and walk around, enjoying the incredible views out over the Verde Valley to the San Francisco Peaks and beyond.

At the north (uphill) edge of town, a mile off Hwy-89 at the end of fairly rough Perkinsville Road, the **Gold King Mine** (928/634-0053, daily 10am-5pm, $5) has a misleading name but is still a great place to go. It's not so much a mine as an anarchic collection of ancient-looking machinery (sawmills, pumps, hoists, trucks, cars, and ore cars), most of which is kept in working order, plus an intact old gas station dating from Jerome's 1920s heyday.

At the heart of Jerome, enjoy food or a fine shot of espresso at the **Flatiron Café** (416 Main St., 928/634-2733), or for a full meal with a great view, try the delicious Asylum dining room inside the huge old **Jerome Grand Hotel** (200 Hill St., 928/634-8200, $155 and up), a former hospital.

Seligman

From I-40 exit 139, just west of Ash Fork, a nice section of the old Route 66 two-lane runs along the railroad tracks just north of, and parallel to, the I-40 freeway all the way to the sleep little town of Seligman. One of best places to stop and get a feel for the spirit of old Route 66, **Seligman** (pop. 456; pronounced "suh-LIG-muhn") is a perfect place to take a break before or after rejoining the interstate hordes. The town retains a lot of its historic character—old sidewalk awnings and even a few hitching rails—and offers lots of reasons to stop. Coming into

Delgadillo's Snow Cap Drive-In

Seligman on this stretch of Route 66, you'll be greeted by **The Rusty Bolt** (115 Route 66, 928/422-0106), a fantastic junk shop and oddball emporium that's impossible to miss along the north side of the old highway. A pilgrimage point for old-roads fans for decades, Angel Delgadillo's barber shop now hosts the **Route 66 Gift Shop and Museum** (22265 W. Route 66). Angel's brother, Juan Delgadillo, created and ran the wacky **Snow Cap Drive-In** (301 E. Route 66, 928/422-3291) a half block to the east, where the sign says "Sorry, We're Open," and the menu advertises "Hamburgers without Ham." Behind the restaurant, in snow, rain, or shine, sits a roofless old Chevy decorated with fake flowers and an artificial Christmas tree. Juan's family carries on the Snow Cap traditions. The burgers, fries, and milk shakes (not to mention the jokes!) are worth driving miles for.

Another good place to eat is the kitschy **Road Kill Café** (502 W. Route 66, 928/422-3554) near the OK Saloon and Rusty Bolt junk shop. Find German-American barbecue at **Westside Lilo's** (22855 W. Route 66, 928/422-5456); good coffee served behind the bright-green facade of **Seligman Sundries,** a half mile farther west; and the cold beer typically downed by cowboys and truckers across the road at the **Black Cat Bar.**

For an overnight, choose from a half dozen motels like the nice, clean, and friendly **Historic Route 66 Motel** (22750 W. Route 66, 928/422-3204, $75 and up).

The longest and probably the most evocative stretch of old Route 66 runs between Seligman and Kingman through the high-desert **Hualapai Indian Reservation** (pronounced "WALL-ah-pie"), along the Santa Fe Railroad tracks through all-but-abandoned towns bypassed by the "modern" interstate world. Save the stretch between here and Needles for daytime, as it's one of the most memorable of the Mother Road's whole cross-country haul.

Grand Canyon Caverns

Far, far away from the high-speed freeway frontage, midway between Williams and Kingman, 22 miles northwest of Seligman and a dozen miles east of Peach Springs, a large green sign marks the entrance to **Grand Canyon Caverns** (928/422-3223, daily, $20-100), which has somehow managed to survive despite being bypassed by the I-40 superslab. Once one of the prime tourist draws on the Arizona stretch of Route 66, the Grand Canyon Caverns were discovered and developed in the late 1920s and still have the feel of an old-time roadside attraction.

Peach Springs is the starting point for the 19-mile drive along Diamond Creek Road—all the way to the "bottom" of the Grand Canyon. Get a permit and detailed info at the Hualapai Lodge.

Just west of the Grand Canyon Caverns, Hwy-18 cuts off 65 miles to the northeast toward the **Havasupai Indian Reservation,** which includes one of the most beautiful and untrammeled corners of the Grand Canyon. No roads, just red rocks, green canyons, cobalt-blue waterfalls, and the **Havasupai Lodge** (928/448-2111, $145 and up).

Tours start every half hour at the gift shop, where you hop on the elevator that drops you 200-300 feet to underground chambers, including the 18,000-square-foot Chapel of the Ages. Regular tours last around 45 minutes. Back above ground, there's also a gas station and a motel. If you want a truly unique experience, ask about staying overnight in the **Cavern Suite,** a fully furnished two-bed suite dating back to the 1962 Cuban Missile Crisis, when a corner of the caverns was set up as a fallout shelter.

Old Route 66 Loop: Grand Canyon Skywalk

Midway along the Historic Route 66 loop between Seligman and Kingman, the road comes close to the Grand Canyon as it passes through the large and lonely Hualapai Indian Reservation. The 2,300-strong Hualapai tribe has its community center at the town of **Peach Springs,** which marks the halfway point of this 87-mile old-roads loop and offers at least one reason to stop: the comfortable **Hualapai Lodge** (888/868-9378, $134 and up) and Diamond Creek restaurant, right on Route 66. Apart from this, Peach Springs is mostly a prefab Bureau of Indian Affairs housing project with few services, though there is a photogenic old Route 66 filling station at the center of town.

The lodge was the first sign of tourism in Peach Springs, but the Hualapai community seems to have embraced commerce in a big way: 2007 saw the opening of the much-hyped (and much-troubled) **Grand Canyon Skywalk,** a glass-floored steel horseshoe that juts out from the edge of the Grand Canyon, 4,000 feet above the Colorado River. Installed at a cost of $30 million, the daring and impressive Skywalk is certainly unique, but it's also expensive (count on it costing close to $80 per person, including lots of annoying fees and charges to park and ride the bus out to the Skywalk itself). The Skywalk is most popular as a day-trip destination from Las Vegas, but you can get here from Peach Springs via 91 miles of rough roads. The recommended route is to take I-40 or Route 66 to Kingman (50 miles southwest of Peach Springs), then head north via US-93, Pierce Ferry Road, and Diamond Bar Road, sections of which are still unpaved, though that extends the route to 132 miles.

A museum is planned and facilities are supposed to start being improved once the money rolls in, but for now there isn't much apart from the Skywalk itself. There's an ambitious long-term plan to develop the entire western end of the

Grand Canyon Skywalk

Hualapai Reservation into "Grand Canyon West," with all sorts of water-rafting tours and outdoor activities on offer; time will tell if the Skywalk endures once the novelty wears off.

West of Peach Springs, Route 66 winds along the railroad tracks, passing through a few ghost towns (like Hackberry, where the old gas station still stands in rusting splendor) before zooming into Kingman.

Kingman

The only town for miles in any direction since its founding as a railroad center in 1882, **Kingman** (pop. 29,029) has always depended on passing travelers for its livelihood. Long a main stopping place on Route 66, and still providing the only all-night services on US-93 between Las Vegas and Phoenix, and along I-40 between Flagstaff and Needles, the town remains more a way station than a destination despite the increasing number of people who have relocated here in recent years, attracted by the open space, high desert air, and low cost of living. The stretch of Route 66 through Kingman has been renamed in memory of favorite son Andy Devine, who was born in Flagstaff in 1905 but grew up here, where his parents ran the Beale Hotel. One of the best-known character actors of Hollywood's classic era, the raspy-voiced Devine usually played a devoted sidekick. His most famous role was as the wagon driver in the classic 1939 John Ford western Stagecoach.

The best first stop in Kingman is **The Powerhouse** (120 W. Andy Devine Ave., 928/753-9889, $4), a hulking old power plant that's been inventively repurposed to house a good Route 66 museum, with galleries full of enough old cars, postcards, and mementos to occupy you for an hour or more. Best of the bunch is a nifty relief map of the entire path of Route 66 (the many mountain ranges make you realize why old cars needed so many service stations!). The displays do a good job of evoking and exploring the deep romance many Americans seem to feel for the old Mother Road.

Be sure to contact the **visitors center** (928/753-6106) here to pick up a copy of the town's good Route 66 brochure. Then pop across Route 66 for a burger, some fries, and a milk shake at **Mr. D'z Route 66 Diner** (105 E. Andy Devine Ave., 928/718-0066), impossible to miss thanks to its bank of neon.

The blocks off Route 66 hold Kingman's most interesting older buildings—Beale Street, north of Route 66, has dozens of 100-year-old railroad-era storefronts now housing an array of junk and antiques shops. Besides the usual chain motels along I-40, lodging options in Kingman include the pleasant **Hill Top Motel** (1901 E. Andy Devine Ave., 928/753-2198, $55 and up), forever infamous as the place where evil Timothy McVeigh stayed for a week before blowing up the Federal Building in Oklahoma City.

To escape the summer heat, Kingmanites head east and south along a well-marked 14-mile road to **Hualapai Mountain Park,** where pines and firs cover the slopes of the 8,417-foot peak. Hiking trails wind through the wilderness, where there's a campground and a few rustic **cabins** ($65-130) built by the Civilian Conservation Corps during the New Deal 1930s. Contact the **ranger station** (928/757-0915) near the park entrance for detailed information or to make reservations.

Crossing the Colorado River between Arizona and California, look downstream (south) from the I-40 freeway to see the arching silver steel bridge that carried Route 66 up until 1966. It's still in use, supporting a natural gas pipeline; beyond it, the red-rock spires for which Needles is named rise sharply out of the desert plains.

The crossing over the Colorado River at the California-Arizona border was the site of illegal but effective roadblocks during the Dust Bowl era, when vigilante mobs turned back migrant Okies if they didn't have much money.

The main road between Las Vegas and Phoenix, US-93 crosses I-40 and Route 66 at Kingman. Starting high up in the Canadian Rockies and running across the Great Basin and Sonora Desert all the way to Mexico, the drive along US-93 is the heart of our "Border-to-Border" road trip. **Las Vegas** is covered on page 148, **Phoenix** on page 158, and full coverage of the entire route begins on page 110.

Cool Springs and Black Mountains

Midway between Kingman and Oatman, set against the angular **Black Mountains** high above the desert plain, **Cool Springs** is a nifty old rough stone service station resurrected as a Route 66 gift shop and mini museum. Built in the 1920s, abandoned in the 1960s, and brought back to life in 2005, Cool Springs is a nice place to stop, buy a soda, and soak up the Route 66 spirit.

Between Cool Springs and Oatman, old Route 66 twists and turns past recently reactivated gold mine workings while climbing up and over the angular Black Mountains. Steep switchbacks and 15-mph hairpin turns carry the old road on a breathtaking more than 2,100-foot change in elevation over a short eight miles of blacktop.

Old Route 66: Oatman

One of the most demanding, desolate, and awesomely satisfying stretches of the old road loops north from the I-40 freeway, between Kingman and the California border. Climbing over steep mountains while cutting across a stretch of desert that brings new meaning to the word "harsh," the narrow roadway passes few signs of life on this 50-mile loop, so be sure you and your car are prepared for the rigors of desert driving.

Westbound drivers have it the easiest—simply follow the well-signed Historic Route 66 west from Kingman, exit 44 off I-40. From the west heading east, take exit 1 on the Arizona side of the river, then head north. Whichever way you go, you can't avoid the steep hills that lead to **Oatman** (elev. 2,700 feet), an odd mix of ghost town and tourist draw that's one of the top stops along Route 66. A gold mining town whose glory days had long faded by the time I-40 passed it by way back in 1952, Oatman looks like a Wild West stage set, but it's the real thing—awnings over the plank sidewalks, bearded roughnecks (and a few burros) wandering the streets, lots of rust, and slumping old buildings. The gold mines here produced some two million ounces from their start in 1904 until they panned out in the mid-1930s; at its peak, Oatman had a population of over 10,000, with 20 saloons lining the three-block Main Street. One of these, the old **Oatman Hotel** (181 N. Main St.), was where Clark Gable and Carole Lombard were said to have spent their first night after getting married in Kingman in 1939. You can sample some highly recommended Navajo tacos and have a beer in the downstairs bar (which is thickly wallpapered in years and years' worth of dollar bills!), or peer through a Plexiglas door at the room where Clark and Carole slept, hardly changed for half a century.

Saloons and T-shirt shops line the rest of Main Street, where Wild West enthusiasts act out the shootouts that took place here only in the movies. Oatman does get a considerable tourist trade, but after dark and outside of the peak summer

LONDON BRIDGE

It may not have stood out as the finest piece of engineering art when it spanned the Thames, but London Bridge is a marvelous sight in the middle of the Arizona desert. A replacement for a series of bridges that date back to medieval times, inspiring the children's rhyme, "London Bridge Is Falling Down," this version of London Bridge was constructed in the 1830s. When it was no longer able to handle the demands of London traffic, the old bridge was replaced by a modern concrete span and its stones were put up for sale in 1967.

Bought by property developer Robert McCulloch for $2.4 million, the 10,247 blocks of stone were shipped here and reassembled at a cost of another $7 million. After a channel was cut under the bridge to bring water from the Colorado River, the Lord Mayor of London flew in to attend the rededication ceremonies in October 1971. The bridge now stands as the centerpiece of Lake Havasu City, a fast-growing retirement and resort community that's home to more than 53,000 residents.

There's no admission charge to see this oddly compelling sight. If you have a taste for surreal experiences, walk across the bridge and sample the Ye Olde England ambience of Barley Brothers brewery. Even more schizoid is the adjacent, all-suite **London Bridge Resort** (928/855-0888, $139 and up), where the "original" medieval turrets and Arthurian design flourishes have been redecorated with palm trees for that unforgettable tropical island experience.

tourist season, the town reverts to its rough-and-tumble ways. The conservative libertarian bent of most of the local population ensures that nothing is likely to change Oatman's crusty charms.

Lake Havasu City

The first stop east of the Colorado River, just across the state border and 20 miles south of I-40, **Lake Havasu City** is a thoroughly modern vacation town built around a thoroughly odd centerpiece: **London Bridge,** brought here stone by stone between 1967 and 1971. Terribly tacky souvenir shops and faux London pubs congregate around the foot of the bridge, which spans an artificial channel to a large island, but the bridge itself is an impressive sight.

Unless you plan to retire here—or simply rent a houseboat and relax on the water—there's not a lot to do at Lake Havasu. That said, the area has become a popular spring break destination for Western college kids, thousands of whom flock to **Lake Havasu State Park** (928/855-2784) for fun-in-the-sun and who-knows-what after dark. For the rest of us—have an English muffin and a cup of tea, pay your respects and take a photograph or two, then hit the road again.

CALIFORNIA

From the demanding **Mojave Desert,** over mountains and through lush inland valleys, to the beautiful beaches of **Santa Monica,** Route 66 passes through every type of Southern California landscape. The old road, which survives intact almost all the way across the state, is marked for most of its 315 miles by signs declaring it Historic Route 66. Across the Mojave Desert the route is also marked as the National Old Trails Highway, its title before the national numbering system was put into effect in the late 1920s.

Needles

Founded soon after the Santa Fe Railroad came through in 1883 and named for the group of sharp stone spires that stand near where I-40 crosses the Colorado River

> Needles was the boyhood home of *Peanuts* cartoonist Charles Schulz and is featured in the comic strips as the desert home of Snoopy's raffish sibling, Spike. Needles now features Spike and Snoopy in a series of Route 66-themed murals around town, as at the gas station on Needles Highway.

from Arizona, **Needles** (pop. 4,988) is one of the hottest places in the country, with summertime highs hovering between 100°F and 120°F for months on end. Though often unbearable in summer, Needles is a popular place with winter snowbirds escaping colder climes; it also has a very rich Route 66 heritage. The stretch of old Route 66 through Needles runs along Broadway, alternating along either side of the freeway. The best place to stop and soak some Route 66 personality is the **Wagon Wheel Restaurant** (2420 Needles Hwy., 760/326-4305), west of downtown, open all day for good, fresh food, and on Friday nights for all-you-can-eat fish 'n' chips. The magnificent El Garces Hotel reopened as a transportation facility in 2014.

If you're set on traveling as much of the old road as possible, another stretch of Route 66 runs west of Needles and north of I-40 through the near-ghost towns of **Goffs** and **Fenner,** on a roller coaster of undulating two-lane blacktop, parallel to the railroad tracks.

Old Route 66 Loop: Ludlow and Amboy

Thanks to the orderly planners of the Santa Fe Railroad, which first blazed this

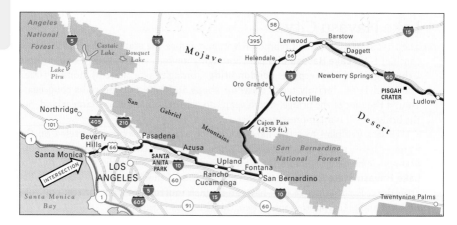

route across the desert in 1883, many of the place-names on this old Route 66 loop come in alphabetical order: from west to east, you have Amboy, Bristol, Cadiz, Danby, Essex, Fenner, Goffs, Home, Ibis, Java, and Klinefelter. Yes, Klinefelter.

If you want a quick and convincing taste of what traveling across the Mojave Desert was like in the days before air-conditioning and cellular phones, keep your eyes peeled for Historic Route 66 signs, and turn south off I-40 and follow the National Old Trails Highway, one of the many monikers Route 66 has carried over the years, on a 75-mile loop along the old road. Heading west, the loop leaves I-40 about 25 miles beyond Needles; heading east, the old road turns off I-40 at **Ludlow,** 50 miles east of Barstow, where two gas stations, a coffee shop, and a motel represent a major outpost of civilization.

While the drive alone is worth the extra time it takes, the real attraction comes midway along this old road loop: **Amboy** is synonymous with **Roy's Motel and Café,** a museum-worthy assembly of roadside architecture that has survived solely due to the willpower of its longtime lord and master, Buster Burris, who ran the place from 1938 (when he married the daughter of owner Roy Crowl) until 2000, when Buster died at the age of 92. In the late 1940s, Roy's was the prime stop between Needles and Barstow, and as many as 90 people staffed the café, the motel, and the car repair shop, working around the clock to cater to the thousands of passing cars. Roy's fell on hard times after the opening of I-40 in 1974, but the whole town—complete with a huge "Roy's" sign, a set of simple motor court cabins, and a pair of gas pumps—has hung on. Now, thanks to owner Albert Okura (who also owns the San Bernardino-based restaurant chain Juan Pollo and the "First McDonald's" museum), Amboy is used as a film and photo-shoot location as well as being a photogenic reminder of the heyday of Route 66.

From Amboy, you can leave Route 66 and head south to the lovely high desert of **Joshua Tree National Park** and the newly reenergized 1950s Rat Pack-era resorts of **Palm Springs.** Staying on Route 66, you'll pass the lava flows around **Amboy Crater,**

From Needles, it's a quick 30-mile drive north along the Colorado River into Nevada to visit the gambling center of **Laughlin,** a sparkling city with huge casinos and over 10,700 cheap rooms.

Huge chunks of the Mojave Desert have been used as military training grounds since World War II, when General George Patton commandeered this area to prepare his tank battalions for battle in the North African desert. The remains of the camp can still be seen in the desert along Crucero Road, just north of the I-40 Ludlow exit.

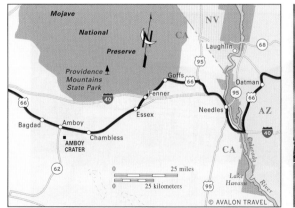

The Mojave Desert is one of the driest places on the planet. Parts of it receive less than three inches of rainfall in an average year, sometimes going for more than two years without getting a drop.

and you may see and hear helicopters and Warthog fighters playing war games on the huge **Twentynine Palms Marine Corps Base,** which stretches off to the south. At nearly 58 square miles, it has a population of 11,000 and is often the last U.S. stop for personnel bound for battle in the Middle East.

Mojave National Preserve

Spreading north of old Route 66, more than 1.6 million acres between I-40 and I-15 have been set aside as the **Mojave National Preserve,** a harsh desert landscape of volcanic cinder cones and sand dunes, desert tortoises, and Joshua trees. One evocative landmark here in the middle of the desert is the **Kelso Depot** (760/252-6100), a restored train station that sits on the main LA-to-Las Vegas Union Pacific Railroad line. Trains still rumble past, and the depot, featuring a variety of interpretive exhibits, recreates the sense of life here in the 1920s, before air-conditioning and cell phones made life in the desert so much more agreeable. Kelso is on Kelbaker Road, about 22 miles north of I-40, midway between Fenner and Ludlow.

Another of the many places in the Mojave Preserve that's worth the trip is **Mitchell Caverns** (760/928-2586) at the center of **Providence Mountains State Recreation Area,** 25 miles north of I-40 at the end of Essex Road. At the time of this writing, the park was closed due to infrastructure issues. Call before you make the drive.

Newberry Springs: Bagdad Café

Running alongside the I-40 freeway for about 50 miles east of Barstow, old Route 66 survives as a sort of frontage road, passing little more than an occasional lava flow (like Pisgah Crater, where there's a pair of I-40 rest areas).

About 25 miles east of Barstow is the place that for many people symbolizes the quirky personality of Route 66: **Newberry Springs.** The cult classic Percy Adlon movie *Bagdad Café* was shot at the town's one and only café, now also known as the **Bagdad Café** (760/257-3101). Considering its connections with the oddly endearing movie (which features a cast of drifters, an obese German magician, and Jack Palance!), the real-life Bagdad Café is welcoming and appropriately weird, not so much a restaurant as it is a semi-catered film set. It stays in business as a pit stop for fans of offbeat European cinema who happen to find themselves in the middle of the Mojave Desert.

Be sure to read and sign the guest book, which features heartfelt comments from hundreds of people who've made the trek here from all over the world; Scandinavians and Teutonic types seem especially well represented.

Between the Bagdad Café and Barstow, old Route 66 runs past the region's other unique claim to fame: The semi-successful **Solar One** power plant, an experimental 10-megawatt electricity generating station north of I-40, was built in the 1980s and is now used as an astronomical gamma-ray observatory. If you like shiny cutting-edge technology, you may want to detour from Barstow to Las Vegas along I-15 to see the nearly 400-megawatt **Ivanpah Solar Power Facility,** one of the world's largest solar thermal plant, which is clearly visible from the freeway.

Northeast of Barstow, **Calico Ghost Town** is an enjoyable resurrection of the silver mining camp that boomed here during the 1890s.

Barstow

The burly railroad and transportation center of **Barstow** (pop. 23,835) is located in the middle of the Mojave Desert, at the point where I-40 disappears into I-15, approximately midway between Los Angeles and Las Vegas. Trucks and trains are the main business in town—even the McDonald's pays homage to trains, with its dining rooms housed in old passenger cars from a train. Barstow is scruffy and a little scary in the way railroad towns can be. Along Main Street, the old Route 66 corridor, many of the old cafés and motels are now closed and boarded up, but there's an unexplained copy of the Amboy "Roy's" sign, and just north of old Route 66, the 1911 **Barstow Harvey House** hotel next to the train station is a survivor from an earlier age. Looking like the Doge's Palace in Venice (if the Doge's Palace faced the wide-open desert instead of an intricate network of canals), the Gothic-style arcades are a substantial reminder of a time when travel meant more than just getting somewhere. The long-abandoned building has been brought back to use as the railroad and Route 66 **Mother Road Museum** (760/255-1890, Fri.-Sun. 10am-4pm, free).

Outside Barstow at the west end of Main Street, keep an eye out for the Christian Motorcycle Club sign welcoming you to **Lenwood,** a crossroads near where the old road reconnects with I-15.

Oro Grande: Bottle Tree Ranch

Between Barstow and Victorville, old Route 66 survives as an old-roads trek across the Mojave Desert. The 32-mile route, called the National Old Trails Highway, parallels the railroad tracks and the usually parched Mojave River, passing through odd little towns like **Oro Grande,** which is still home to a huge cement plant and an array of roadside junk shops. The cement plant, processing local limestone, follows on from the optimistic prospectors who gave the town its "Big Gold" name back in the 1850s. The cemetery here is one of the oldest in southern California. Oro Grande is also home to some long-abandoned roadside businesses, relics of Route 66. One relic lives on: A 1930s tractor dealership now houses the popular **Iron Hog Saloon** (20848 National Trails Hwy., 760/843-0609), which serves cold beers and big steaks.

The Oro Grande boasts an impressive silver steel bridge over the bed of the Mojave River and is getting famous for another more colorful sight: the hard-to-miss **Elmer's Bottle Tree Ranch** (24266 Route 66), where thousands of green, blue, brown, and clear glass bottles have been dangled from a forest of mostly metal "trees" by a white-bearded local retiree named Elmer Long. There's no admission charge for the Bottle Tree Ranch, which Elmer has dedicated to "those who have lived and died on the Mother Road." Elmer is not shy (he has his own Facebook page!), so stop and say "hi."

Victorville

Take the "old road" between Barstow and **Victorville** to be sure to enter Victorville on old Route 66 and see Victorville at its best. At the **California Route 66 Museum** (16825 S. D St., 760/951-0436, Mon. and Thurs.-Sat. 10am-4pm, Sun. 11am-3pm, free), right on old Route 66, in Old Town across from the train station, a small but growing collection of road signs, photographs, and reminiscences help preserve the life and times of this great old highway. The museum also holds most of the surviving pieces of Hula Ville, an outdoor sculpture park and oddball art gallery that once stood west of Victorville. Most of its paintings and hand-lettered memorials to sundry bums,

pointing the way in Victorville

hobos, and other travelers were moved here after Hula Ville's 100-year-old creator and caretaker, former carnival worker "Fry Pan" Miles Mahan, died in 1996.

Without its Route 66 connections, Victorville would be just another distant SoCal commuter suburb. In fact, ever since the departure of Hula Ville, not to mention the wonderful Roy Rogers and Dale Evans Museum, which—along with its much-loved celebrity subjects—had a home here, Victorville just hasn't seemed the same. Fortunately, old Route 66 can still be traced through town: From the Route 66 Museum, turn south onto 7th Street, which runs past a few neon-signed old motels like the **New Corral** (14643 7th St., 760/245-9378, $64 and up) with its animated bucking bronco.

There's also a worthwhile stop two miles east of downtown: Join the truckers and bikers at family-run **Emma Jean's Holland Burger Café** (17143 N. D St., 760/243-9938), featured on *Diners, Drive-Ins and Dives* TV show.

South and west of Victorville, heading toward Los Angeles and the seemingly distant Pacific Ocean, a number of picturesque but generally dead-end stretches of old Route 66 go over **Cajon Pass,** but the main road is definitely I-15.

the first McDonald's, now a museum

San Bernardino

Sometimes known as "San Berdoo," in the 1940s and 1950s the city of **San Bernardino** (pop. 216,239) was where Maurice and Richard McDonald perfected the burger-making restaurant chain that bears their name. In 1961 the McDonald brothers sold their company to Ray Kroc, and the rest is

San Bernardino County, which covers over 20,000 square miles (most of it desert), is the largest in the United States.

fast-food history. Though the original buildings were demolished decades ago, the location is now home to the unofficial ad hoc **First Original McDonald's Museum** (1398 N. E St., 909/885-6324, daily, free), displaying McDonalds and Route 66 memorabilia.

From downtown San Bernardino, which somewhat confusingly is actually a dozen miles east of the I-15 freeway, the old

Route 66 alignment headed west along Foothill Boulevard, where a remnant of old Route 66 road culture still survives: the 19 concrete tepees that form the **Wigwam Motel** (2728 E. Foothill Blvd., 909/875-3005, around $79 and up). Once as seedy as its "Do It in a TeePee" sign suggested, this Wigwam (one of three in the world—another sits along Route 66 in Holbrook, Arizona) has been fully updated and once again welcomes travelers interested in offbeat accommodations (with free Wi-Fi, a swimming pool, and barbecue grills).

From the Wigwam Motel, Foothill Boulevard runs west through the postindustrial city of **Fontana,** birthplace of the Hells Angels Motorcycle Club (and LA culture critic Mike Davis), before passing by another great old road landmark: **Bono's Giant Orange** (15395 Foothill Blvd.), an orange-shaped stand that, during the 1920s, offered thirsty Route 66 travelers "All the Orange Juice You Can Drink—10¢." The original orange grove is now a Walmart, and the Giant Orange was moved next to the now-closed Bono's Restaurant and Deli, where it still stands—for now (it's been endangered by ongoing road improvements).

San Bernardino is home to the Class A farm club of the Anaheim Angels. The team name plays up the Route 66 connections: They're called the **San Bernardino 66ers of the Inland Empire** (San Manual Stadium, 280 S. E St., 909/888-9922, $8 and up). The stadium is right off the old road. Games are broadcast on **KCAA 1050 AM.**

San Gabriel Valley

Though it's now effectively swallowed up in Southern California's never-ending sprawl, the **San Gabriel Valley** used to be the westbound traveler's first taste of Southern California. After crossing the Mojave Desert and the high mountains, Route 66 dropped down into what might have seemed like paradise: orange groves as far as the eye could see, a few tidy towns linked by streetcars, and houses draped in climbing roses and bougainvillea. The valley takes its name from old **Mission San Gabriel Arcángel** (428 S. Mission Dr., San Gabriel, 626/457-3035, Mon.-Sat. 9am-4:30pm, Sun. 10am-4pm, $6), which still stands. Despite suffering extensive earthquake damage, the mission is an interesting spot, though not as evocative as others in the chain.

Winding between Pasadena and San Bernardino, along the foothills of the sometimes snowcapped San Gabriel Mountains, old Route 66 links a number of once-distinct communities. In **Upland,** where the old road features a number of recently installed retro-Route 66 streetlamps, there's a grass median strip graced by a statue one of the 12 Madonna of the Trail statues, which officially marked the western end of the National Old Trails Highway, the immediate precursor to Route 66. **Glendora** is home to a great old-fashioned 24-hour doughnut shop, the **Donut Man** (915 E. Route 66, 626/335-9111), while **Azusa** is home of the classic Foothill Drive-In, whose marquee was saved when the land was developed as a college campus.

The city of **Monrovia** (pop. 37,126) holds another Route 66 survivor: the **Aztec Hotel** (311 W. Foothill Blvd., 626/358-3231), known more for its groovy Mesoamerican-style art deco exuberance than for its rooms, but well worth a look. Monrovia was home for

Rancho Cucamonga (pop. 176,534) is the home of the popular **Rancho Cucamonga Quakes** (909/481-5000), an LA Dodgers farm club that plays Class A baseball at **LoanMart Field.**

many years to quixotic author Upton Sinclair (1878-1968) and is now the headquarters of the cult-favorite grocery store Trader Joe's. The company, which started in 1958 as Pronto Markets and is now owned by the transnational corporation Aldi, opened its first Trader Joe's store in Pasadena in 1967.

Aztec Hotel in Monrovia

In the next town to the west, **Sierra Madre,** Foothill Boulevard runs past the landmark racetrack at **Santa Anita,** designed by Hoover Dam stylist Gordon Kaufmann. In 1937 the Marx Brothers filmed *A Day at the Races* here, but the art deco facades have been ruined by the track's ongoing "development" into a Las Vegas-scale gaming and shopping complex.

Huntington Library, Museum, and Gardens

East of Pasadena, at the west end of the San Gabriel Valley, old Route 66 runs along Huntington Drive, which takes its name from one of the most important figures in early Los Angeles, Henry Huntington. nephew of Southern Pacific Railroad baron Collis P. Huntington, from whom Henry inherited a huge fortune (as well as a wife, Arabella). Henry Huntington controlled most of Southern California's once extensive public transit system. He is now most remembered for creating and endowing one of the world's great museums, the **Huntington Library, Art Collections, and Botanical Gardens** (1151 Oxford Rd., 626/405-2100, Wed.-Mon., $23 and up), located in the upscale community of San Marino.

The Huntington Library contains all sorts of unique books and documents and preserves thousands more for the benefit of scholars, but the real draw is the art gallery, which displays an excellent collection of British and European painting and sculpture, with major works by Reynolds, Gainsborough, and others. There are also

the Huntington Library's desert garden

fine assemblages of American art, including Gilbert Stuart's familiar portrait of George Washington. Perhaps the best part of the Huntington is its splendid gardens, which cover 120 acres in a series of mini ecosystems, distilling the essence of Australia, Japan, South America, and, in one of the country's largest cactus gardens, the American Southwest.

Colorado Boulevard in Pasadena holds the annual **Tournament of Roses Parade,** every New Year's Day before the famous Rose Bowl football game.

Pasadena

Heading out of downtown Los Angeles, the historic Pasadena Freeway (Hwy-110) drops you off unceremoniously short of **Pasadena,** but following Figueroa Street brings you in with a bang on the soaring **Colorado Boulevard Bridge,** an elegantly arching circa-1913 concrete bridge at the western edge of Pasadena, which long marked the symbolic entrance to Los Angeles from the east.

Recently restored, the bridge spans the **Arroyo Seco** along the south side of the Ventura Freeway (Hwy-134). The Arroyo Seco itself is full of significant sights, including college football's **Rose Bowl Stadium** and some of the most important architecture in Southern California, notably the **Gamble House** (4 Westmoreland Place, 626/793-3334, Thurs.-Sun. afternoons, $15), a 100-year-old arts-and-crafts gem. Above the arroyo, on old Route 66, the **Norton Simon Museum** (411 W. Colorado Blvd., 626/449-6840, Wed.-Mon., $12) has a medium-size but impeccably chosen collection of Western and Southeast Asian art, ranging from Hindu sculpture to one of the world's foremost collections of Edgar Degas paintings, drawings, and sculptures.

Just a few blocks east of the Arroyo Seco and the Norton Simon Museum, down old Route 66, **Old Pasadena** is the name for the old center of town, where locals congregate for evening fun and daytime shopping. Start your morning with breakfast at **Marston's** (151 E. Walnut St., 626/796-2459), just north of Old Pasadena, or detour two blocks south of old Route 66 to enjoy the fine neon sign and classic soda-fountain milk shakes at the **Fair Oaks Pharmacy and Soda Fountain** (1526 Mission St., 626/799-1414). There are quite a few old motels along this stretch of Route 66; one good bet is the **Saga Motor Hotel** (1633 E. Colorado Blvd., 626/795-0431, $89 and up).

INTERSECTION

Los Angeles (see page 96) is a stop along our **Pacific Coast** route, which begins on page 8.

Route 66 Across Los Angeles

Diehard old-road fans will be pleasantly surprised to know that Route 66 across Los Angeles still exists, almost completely intact. West from Pasadena into downtown LA, you have your choice of Route 66 routings. You can hop onto the Arroyo Seco Parkway (Hwy-110) for a trip back to freeways past: Opened in 1939, this was California's first freeway and featured such novel (and never repeated) concepts as 15-mph exit ramps and stop signs at the entrances. Or you can follow Figueroa, which in LA lingo is known as a "surface street," running parallel to the freeway past some fascinating pieces of Los Angeles new and old, including the concrete-lined Los Angeles River, hilltop **Dodger Stadium,** and the excellent **Autry National Center** (323/667-2000, Tues.-Sun., $14) at Griffith Park, a phenomenally wide-ranging collection featuring Native American art and artifacts from all over western North America, as well as Wild West ephemera and pop culture icons. (The center is the result of a merger between the Southwest Museum of the American Indian and the

Autry Museum of Western Heritage, established by Hollywood's "Singing Cowboy," Gene Autry, a media magnate who is the only person with five different stars on the Hollywood Walk of Fame.)

Now marked by prominent beige road signs reading "Historic Route 66 1935-1964," old Route 66 follows Sunset Boulevard from the historic core of the city, starting at Olvera Street and

Johnny Ramone's final resting place in the Hollywood Forever cemetery

the **El Pueblo de Los Angeles State Historic Park** before winding west to **Hollywood.** In Hollywood itself, Route 66 turns onto Santa Monica Boulevard, then runs past the cemetery-cum-theme park **Hollywood Forever** (323/469-1181, daily, free), where such luminaries as Rudolph Valentino and Mel Blanc are entombed, overlooked by the water tower of legendary Paramount Studios. It's a unique experience by day, and even more so on summer nights when the cemetery is host to outdoor screenings of its residents' works.

Besides all the sights, Route 66 across LA also holds two of the city's best bookshops: **Vroman's** (695 E. Colorado Blvd.), in Pasadena, and **Book Soup** (8818 Sunset Blvd.), in West Hollywood.

Continuing west to the Pacific, old Route 66 follows Santa Monica Boulevard through the heart of **West Hollywood** and **Beverly Hills,** where "Mr. Route 66" himself, the Oklahoma-born comedian Will Rogers, once was honorary mayor.

Santa Monica

Old Route 66 had its western terminus at the edge of the Pacific Ocean in **Santa Monica,** on a palm-lined bluff a few blocks north of the city's landmark **pier.** The pier holds a small amusement park and a lovely old Looff carousel (as seen in the movie *The Sting*). A beachfront walkway heads south of the pier to **Venice Beach,**

carousel at the Santa Monica Pier

heart of bohemian LA. Near where Santa Monica Boulevard dead-ends at Ocean Avenue, a brass plaque marks the official end of Route 66, the "Main Street of America," also remembered as the Will Rogers Highway, one of many names the old road earned in its half century of existence. The plaque remembers Rogers as a "Humorist, World Traveler, Good Neighbor"—not bad for an Okie from the middle of nowhere.

Two blocks east of the ocean, stretch your legs at **Santa Monica Place** and the adjacent **Third Street Promenade,** an indoor-outdoor shopping area and icon of contemporary Southern California (sub)urban culture. The surrounding streets are among the liveliest in Southern California; people actually walk, enjoying street performers, trendy cafés, bookshops, and movie theaters.

Enjoyable in its own right, Santa Monica also makes a good base for seeing the rest of the LA area. For the full retro-luxury experience, check in to the art deco

Georgian Hotel (1415 Ocean Ave., 800/538-8147, $300 and up). Or you can save your money for food and fun by staying at the popular **HI-Santa Monica Hostel** (1436 2nd St., 310/393-9913, around $45).

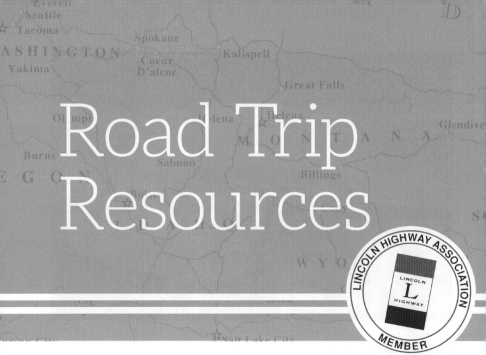

Road Trip
Resources

ORGANIZATIONS

The American Automobile Association (AAA, 1000 AAA Dr., Heathrow, FL 32746, 800/922-8228, www.aaa.com) is an indispensable resource. No traveler in his or her right mind should hit the road without a membership card. Besides the free roadside assistance (daily 24 hours across the country), AAA also offers free maps, useful guidebooks, and tons of related information. Check their website or look in the Yellow Pages to find a local office.

The Lincoln Highway Association (136 N. Elm St., P.O. Box 308, Franklin Grove, IL 61031, 815/456-3030, www.lincolnhighwayassoc.org) is a group of old-roads aficionados who work to preserve remnants of the nation's first coast-to-coast highway and to promote its memory. They also get together for annual meetings to retrace the route.

The National Historic Route 66 Federation (P.O. Box 1848, Lake Arrowhead, CA 92352-1848, 909/336-6131, http://national66.org) is the only nationwide nonprofit organization committed to revitalizing Route 66 and to promoting awareness of its historic role as the Main Street of America. Members receive a high-quality quarterly magazine. All dues go directly toward lobbying governments to preserve what's left of Route 66.

The National Trust for Historic Preservation (2600 Virginia Ave. NW, Suite 1000, Washington, DC 20037, 800/944-6847, http://savingplaces.org) is a nonprofit organization dedicated to protecting the irreplaceable historic buildings and the neighborhoods and landscapes they anchor. One of the benefits of membership ($20 a year) is a subscription to the wonderful bimonthly magazine Preservation.

The Society for Commercial Archeology (P.O. Box 2500, Little Rock, AR 72203, http://sca-roadside.org) is an all-volunteer organization working to preserve and interpret 20th-century roadside culture. Anyone interested in the cultural landscape lining America's highways and byways will want to join the SCA. The enterprise is geared toward appreciation and enjoyment of quirks and crannies of the highway environment. Studies cover everything from diners to giant roadside dinosaurs. Dues are $45 a year, and members receive a full-color magazine twice a year and a quarterly newsletter that details preservation efforts as well as get-togethers for annual tours of different regions.

PRACTICALITIES
Hotel and Motel Chains

Best Western: 800/780-7234, www.bestwestern.com
Clarion: 877/424-6423, www.choicehotels.com/clarion
Comfort Inn: 877/424-6423, www.choicehotels.com/comfort-inn
CourtyardMarriott: 888/236-2427, wwwcourtyard.marriott.com
Days Inn: 800/225-3297, www.wyndhamhotels.com/days-inn
Econo Lodge: 877/424-6423, www.choicehotels.com/econo-lodge
Embassy Suites: 800/EMBASSY—800/362-2779, http://embassysuites3.hilton.com
Hampton Inn: 800/HAMPTON—800/426-7866, http://hamptoninn3.hilton.com
Hilton: 800/HILTONS—800/445-8667, www3.hilton.com
Holiday Inn: 800/HOLIDAY—800/465-4329, www.holidayinn.com
Howard Johnson: 800/221-5801, www.wyndhamhotels.com/hojo
Hyatt: 800/233-1234, www.hyatt.com
Marriott: 888/236-2427, www.marriott.com
Motel 6: 800/4-MOTEL-6—800/466-8356, www.motel6.com
Radisson: 800/967-9033, www.radisson.com
Ramada Inn: 800/854-9517, www.wyndhamhotels.com/ramada
The Ritz-Carlton: 800/542-8680, www.ritzcarlton.com
Rodeway Inn: 877/424-6423, www.choicehotels.com/rodeway-inn
Sheraton: 800/325-3535, www.starwoodhotels.com/sheraton
Super 8: 800/454-3213, www.wyndhamhotels.com/super-8
Westin: 800/937-8461, www.starwoodhotels.com/westin
W Hotels: 877/946-8357, www.starwoodhotels.com/whotels
Wyndham: 877/999-3223, www.wyndham.com/wyndham

Camping

One essential purchase for anyone traveling around the USA, especially in the western states, is a pass from the **National Parks Service** (www.nps.gov). The cost for a general **InterAgency Annual Pass** is around $80. This card gives free admission for an entire family for a full year to all National Parks and National Historic Sites. The **Senior Pass** is a $10 lifetime pass that gives free admission to any U.S. citizen or permanent resident over the age of 62. The free **Access Pass** makes the National

Parks available to people with permanent disabilities. Other passes offer discounts on campgrounds. For information on camping and recreation in other federal lands, a great starting point is the www.recreation.gov website.

Car Rental Companies

Alamo: 877/222-9075, www.alamo.com
Avis: 800/230-4898, www.avis.com
Budget: 800/218-7992, www.budget.com
Enterprise: 800/261-7331, www.enterprise.com
Hertz: 800/654-3131, www.hertz.com
National: 877/222-9058, www.nationalcar.com
Thrifty: 800/367-2277, www.thrifty.com

U.S. STATE TOURISM AND ROAD CONDITIONS

Alabama
Tourism Info: 334/242-4169,
http://alabama.travel
Road Conditions: www.dot.state.al.us

Arizona
Tourism Info: 602/364-3700,
http://tourism.az.gov
Road Conditions: 888/411-7623,
www.az511.com/traffic or www.high-wayconditions.com/az

Arkansas
Tourism Info: 501/682-7777,
www.arkansas.com
Road Conditions: 800/245-1672,
www.arkansashighways.com and
http://idrivearkansas.com

California
Tourism Info: 877/225-4367,
www.visitcalifornia.com
Road Conditions: 800/427-7623,
www.dot.ca.gov

Colorado
Tourism Info: 800/
COLORADO—800/265-6723,
www.colorado.com
Road Conditions: 303/639-1111,
www.cotrip.org

Connecticut
Tourism Info:
888/CT-VISIT—888/288-4748,
www.ctvisit.com
Road Conditions: 860/594-2650

Delaware
Tourism Info: 866/284-7483,
www.visitdelaware.com
Road Conditions: 302/659-4600,
www.deldot.gov

Florida
Tourism Info:
888/7-FLA-USA—888/735-2872,
www.visitflorida.com
Road Conditions: 800/475-0044,
http://fl511.com or
www.usroadconditions.com/fl

Georgia
Tourism Info:
800/VISIT-GA—800/847-4842,
www.exploregeorgia.org
Road Conditions: 404/635-8000,
www.511ga.org

Idaho
Tourism Info:
800/VISIT-ID—800/847-4843,
http://visitidaho.org

Illinois

Tourism Info: 800/226-6632,
www.enjoyillinois.com
Road Conditions: 800/452-4368,
www.idot.illinois.gov

Indiana

Tourism Info: 800/677-9800,
http://visitindiana.com
Road Conditions: 800/261-7623,
www.in.gov/indot

Iowa

Tourism Info:
800/345-IOWA—800/345-4692,
www.traveliowa.com
Road Conditions: 800/288-1047,
www.511ia.org

Kansas

Tourism Info: 785/296-2009,
www.travelks.com
Road Conditions: 800/585-7623,
www.kandrive.org

Kentucky

Tourism Info: 800/225-TRIP—
800/225-8747,
www.kentuckytourism.com
Road Conditions: 509/564-4890,
http://transportation.ky.gov/sites/GoKY

Louisiana

Tourism Info: 800/677-4082,
www.louisianatravel.com
Road Conditions: 877/452-3683,
http://511la.org

Maine

Tourism Info: 888/624-6345,
http://visitmaine.com
Road Conditions: 206/624-3000,
http://govnewengland511.org

Maryland

Tourism Info: 866/639-3526,
www.visitmaryland.org
Road Conditions: 855/GO-MD-511—
855/466-3511, www.md511.org

Massachusetts

Tourism Info: 800/227-MASS—
800/227-6277, www.massvacation.com
Road Conditions: 617/986-5511,
http://mass511.com

Michigan

Tourism Info: 888/78-GREAT—
888/784-7328, www.michigan.org
Road Conditions: 517/373-2090,
http://mdotnetpublic.state.mi.us/drive

Minnesota

Tourism Info: 888/VISIT-MN—
888/847-4866,
www.exploreminnesota.com
Road Conditions: 800/542-0220,
www.511mn.org

Mississippi

Tourism Info:
866/SEE-MISS—866/733-6477,
www.visitmississippi.org
Road Conditions:
www.modottraffic.com/ms511

Missouri

Tourism Info: 800/519-2100,
www.visitmo.com
Road Conditions:
800/ASK-MODOT—800/275-6636,
www.modot.org

Montana

Tourism Info: 800/VISIT-MT—
800/847-4868, www.visitmt.com
Road Conditions: 800/226-7623,
www.mdt.mt.gov/traveninfo

Nebraska

Tourism Info: 800/228-4307,
http://visitnebraska.com
Road Conditions: 402/471-4567,
www.511.nebraska.gov

Nevada

Tourism Info: 800/
NEVADA-8—800/638-2328,
http://travelnevada.com
Road Conditions: 877/687-6237,
http://nvroads.com

New Hampshire
Tourism Info: 603/271-2665, www.visitnh.gov
Road Conditions: 603/271-6862, www.nh.gov/dot

New Jersey
Tourism Info: 800/VISITNJ—800/847-4865, www.visitnj.org
Road Conditions: 866/511-6538, www.511nj.org

New Mexico
Tourism Info: 505/827-7336, www.newmexico.org
Road Conditions: 800/432-4269, http://nmroads.com

New York
Tourism Info: 800/CALL-NYS—800/225-5697, www.iloveny.com
Road Conditions: 800/847-8929, http://511ny.org

North Carolina
Tourism Info: 800/VISIT-NC—800/847-4862, www.visitnc.com
Road Conditions: 877/511-4662, www.ncdot.gov/travel/511

North Dakota
Tourism Info: 800/435-5663, www.ndtourism.com
Road Conditions: 866/696-3511, www.dot.nd.gov/travel-info

Ohio
Tourism Info: 800/BUCKEYE—800/282-5393, www.ohio.org
Road Conditions: www.ohgo.com

Oklahoma
Tourism Info: 800/652-6552, www.travelok.com
Road Conditions: 844/465-4997, http://ok.gov/odot

Oregon
Tourism Info: 800/547-7842, www.traveloregon.com
Road Conditions: 800/977-ODOT—800/977-6368, http://tripcheck.com

Pennsylvania
Tourism Info: 800/VISIT-PA—800/847-4872, http://visitpa.com
Road Conditions: 888/783-6783, www.511pa.com

Rhode Island
Tourism Info: 800/556-2484, www.visitrhodeisland.com
Road Conditions: 401/222-3005, www.dot.ri.gov/travel

South Carolina
Tourism Info: 803/734-0124, http://discoversouthcarolina.com
Road Conditions: 877/511-4672, www.511.sc.org

South Dakota
Tourism Info: 800/S-DAKOTA—800/732-5682, www.travelsd.com
Road Conditions: 866/697-3511, www.safetravelusa.com/sd

Tennessee
Tourism Info: 800/GO-2-TENN—800/462-8366, www.tnvacation.com
Road Conditions: 877/244-0065, www.tn.gov/tdot/section/tn511

Texas
Tourism Info: 800/452-9292, www.traveltexas.com
Road Conditions: 800/452-9292

Utah
Tourism Info: 800/200-1160, www.visitutah.gov
Road Conditions: 866/511-8824, www.udot.utah.gov

Vermont
Tourism Info: 800/VERMONT—800/837-6668, www.vermontvacation.com
Road Conditions: http://511vt.com

Virginia
Tourism Info: 800/VISIT-VA—800/847-4882, www.virginia.org

Road Conditions: 800/367-7623, www.511virginia.org

Washington
Tourism Info: 800/554-1800, www.experiencewa.com
Road Conditions: 800/695-7623, www.wsdot.wa.gov/traffic/511

West Virginia
Tourism Info: 800/225-5982, www.gotowv.com
Road Conditions: 855/699-8511, www.wv511.org

Wisconsin
Tourism Info: 800/432-TRIP— 800/432-8747, www.travelwisconsin.org
Road Conditions: 866/511-9472, www.511.wi.gov

Wyoming
Tourism Info: 800/225-5996, www.travelwyoming.com
Road Conditions: 888/996-7623, www.wyoroad.info

CANADIAN PROVINCIAL TOURISM AND ROAD CONDITIONS

Alberta
Tourism Info: 800/661-8888, www.travelalberta.com/ca
Road Conditions: 855/391-9743, http://511.alberta.ca

British Columbia
Tourism Info: 800/HELLO-BC— 800/435-5622, www.hellobc.com
Road Conditions: 800/550-4997, www.drivebc.com

Ontario
Tourism Info: 800/ONTARIO— 800/668-2746, www.ontariotravel.net
Road Conditions: 416/235-4686 or 866/929-4257, www.mto.gov.on.ca/english.traveller/trip/

Quebec
Tourism Info: 800/363-7777
Road Conditions: 888/355-0511, www.quebec511.info

RECOMMENDED READING
Roadside America

American Diner: Then and Now by Richard J. S. Gutman (Johns Hopkins University, 2000): Lushly illustrated, encyclopedic history of that great American roadside institution, from its humble beginnings in the lunch wagons of the late 1880s to the streamlined stainless-steel models so beloved by art directors everywhere.

Asphalt Nation: How the Automobile Took Over America and How We Can Take It Back by Jane Holtz Kay (University of California, 1998): An enthusiastic and informative account of how cars, and the commuter culture they've spawned, have sapped the strength of the nation's communities. Not as histrionic as the title might lead you to believe, this is an engaging and insightful book that aims to help us cut down on the billions of annual hours Americans spend stuck in traffic.

The Colossus of Roads: Myth and Symbol along the American Highway by Karal Ann Marling (University of Minnesota Press, 2000): If you're interested in the stories behind America's many roadside giants—Paul Bunyan statues, supersize fruits and vegetables, and myriad concrete dinosaurs—you'll love this informative and funny study. Packed with pictures, but a little lacking in details on how to find these giant figures in the flesh, it's bound to inspire more than a few detours.

Flattened Fauna: A Field Guide to Common Animals of Roads, Streets, and Highways by Roger M. Knutson (Ten Speed Press, 1987): Lighthearted look at that under-studied ecosystem, the highway. Besides being a helpful guide to identifying the sundry dead objects along the roadside, the book also details the natural life and habitats of the unfortunate road-killed creatures.

The Lincoln Highway: Main Street Across America by Drake Hokanson (University of Iowa Press, 1999): The bible of Lincoln Highway history, tracing America's first transcontinental highway from its beginnings in 1915 to its gradual fadeout in the post-interstate world. If you want to travel along the granddaddy of old roads, look for **Greetings from the Lincoln Highway,** a fully illustrated mile-by-mile guide by Brian Butko (Stackpole Books, 2005).

Main Street to Miracle Mile: American Roadside Architecture by Chester H. Liebs (John Hopkins University Press, reprint, 1995): This lushly illustrated historical survey of roadside design is the best single introduction to the familiar yet fascinating environment that lines the nation's highways.

Open Road: A Celebration of the American Highway by Phil Patton (Simon and Schuster, 1986): An energetic account of how the American roadside landscape came to look the way it does today, masterfully blending a discussion of the economic and political forces behind the nation's highway network with a contagious enthusiasm for the inherent democracy the automobile embodies.

Pump and Circumstance: Glory Days of the Gas Station by John Margolies (Bulfinch Press, 1993): Profusely illustrated coffee-table book that uses photographs, advertising, enamel signs, road maps, and brief but revealing text to track the development of that essential feature of the American highway landscape, the gas station. Margolies, who died in 2016, also produced many other great books, including **Hitting the Road,** about road maps; **Fun Along the Road,** about roadside amusements; and **See the USA,** which explores the graphic world of travel brochures and posters.

New Roadside America: The Modern Traveler's Guide to the Wild and Wonderful World of America's Tourist Attractions by Doug Kirby et al. (Fireside Books, 1992): The best guidebook to the wackiest and weirdest attractions along the Great American Roadside. Organized by theme rather than by location, but still an entertaining and agreeable travel companion; check it out "live" at www.roadsideamerica.com.

Travelogues

Blue Highways: A Journey into America by William Least Heat-Moon (Back Bay Books, reprint, 1999): One of the best-selling travel books ever written, this intensely personal yet openhearted tale traces the path of a part-Native American

English teacher who travels the back roads "in search of places where change did not mean ruin and where time and men and deeds connected."

Drive, They Said: Poems about Americans and Their Cars edited by Kurt Brown (Milkweed Editions, 1994): If you like to drive, and like to read or write poetry, you'll love this thick volume of contemporary verse, which samples the work of over 100 poets.

Elvis Presley Boulevard: From Sea to Shining Sea, Almost by Mark Winegardner (Atlantic Monthly Press, 1987): An energetic mix of road trip journal and coming-of-age autobiography, this short book recounts a summer-long tour around the southern and central United States. The Elvis obsession hinted at by the title is only a small part of the book, which looks at many of the odder corners of America.

Fear and Loathing in Las Vegas by Hunter S. Thompson (Random House, 1972): Subtitled "A Savage Journey to the Heart of the American Dream," this riotous blast of a book starts with the words "We were somewhere around Barstow on the edge of the desert when the drugs began to take hold," and goes on to tell the story of a lost weekend in Sin City, and much, much more.

Great Plains by Ian Frazier (Farrar, Straus and Giroux, 1989): In-depth, top-to-bottom study of the wide-open land where the buffalo roamed, tracing historical themes like water, cowboys, and Native Americans, while capturing the contemporary scene.

Let Us Now Praise Famous Men by James Agee, photographs by Walker Evans (Mariner Books, 2001): A classic. The talented collaborators spent the summer of 1936 living with three families of poor white cotton sharecroppers in the Appalachian foothills of northwest Alabama, and together created a vivid and compassionate portrait of rural America during the depths of the Great Depression.

The Lost Continent: Travels in Small Town America by Bill Bryson (Harper Perennial, reprint, 2001): Iowa-born British transplant returns to America in search of material for his sarcastic commentary on contemporary life. Hilariously funny in parts, mean-spirited in others, and packed with trivial truths about life in the land of liberty.

On the Road by Jack Kerouac (Viking, 1957): What the Beatles were to music, the Beats were to literature, and this wild ramble of a road story was Kerouac's first number-one hit, inspiring a generation or two to hightail it along America's highways in the tracks of Sal Paradise and Dean Moriarty.

Out West: American Journey along the Lewis and Clark Trail by Dayton Duncan (Viking Penguin, 1987): The best travel book since Blue Highways, this marvelous tale retraces the route blazed by the Corps of Discovery on their epic adventure. With a combination of concise history lessons, captivating storytelling, and wry humor, Duncan vividly points out what has and hasn't changed in the 200-odd years since the captains first trekked across the country and back.

Spirit of Place: The Making of an American Literary Landscape by Frederick Turner (Sierra Club Books, 1989): A multilayered tapestry of biography, travel writing, and literary criticism, this wonderful book explores how different locales have inspired and defined many of America's greatest writers.

Travels with Charley: In Search of America by John Steinbeck (Viking, 1962): Rambling around "this monster of a land" in his camper, Rocinante, accompanied only by the eponymous French poodle, Steinbeck returns to his California haunts from self-imposed exile in New York to find that, even if you can't go home again, there are many intriguing things along the way.

Zen and the Art of Motorcycle Maintenance: An Inquiry into Values by Robert M. Pirsig (Prerenial Classics, reprint, 1999): The subtitle points out this big book's more ponderous aspects, but at its best this is a captivating, full-throttle ride down America's back roads in search of meaning in the modern age.

INDEX

Photo and Illustration Credits

Road Trip USA and the Moon Logo are the property of Avalon Travel, a member of the Perseus Books Group. All other marks and logos depicted are the property of the original owners. All rights reserved.

All vintage postcards, photographs, and maps in this book are from the private collection of Jamie Jensen, unless otherwise credited.

Photos © Jamie Jensen pages 17, 19, 34, 42, 44, 46, 89, 105, 124, 135, 140, 167, 174, 176 (bottom), 183 (top), 205, 212, 216, 232 (top), 237, 238, 265, 284, 296, 318, 319, 322, 341 (bottom), 346, 388, 399, 412 (top), 435, 469, 483, 495 (botom), 497, 505 (bottom), 515, 517, 528, 549, 565 (bottom), 571 (bottom), 583, 593, 603, 608, 624, 637, 653 (bottom), 657, 669, 679, 688, 689, 706, 718, 734, 738, 740 (middle), 772, 774, 775, 779, 781, 791, 809, 815 (right), 826, 829, 833, 839 (bottom), 840, 844, 847 (bottom), 848, 852, 854, 855, 857, 860 862, 872, 878, 893.

United States Quarter-Dollar Coin Images

State quarter-dollar coin images from the United States Mint. Used with permission.
page 392: 2007 Presidential $1 Coin image from the United States Mint. (www.usmint.gov/pressroom/index.cfm?flash=no&action=photo#Pres)

United States Postage Stamps

Pages 12, 25, 40, 125, 132, 141, 154, 172, 185, 192, 198, 205, 228, 238, 242, 247, 268, 272, 288, 302, 315, 324, 334, 337, 342, 354, 356, 358, 370, 383, 394, 401, 424, 440, 516, 549, 586, 616, 624, 694, 703, 780, and 804 "Greetings from America Series # 3561 – #3610 © 2000 United States Postal Service. All Rights Reserved. Used with Permission."

Minor League Baseball Logos

© 2018. All Minor League Baseball copyrights, trademarks and service marks are used with permission and under license from MiLB. All Rights Reserved. Visit www.MiLB.com. Pages 129, 150, 251, 253, 271, 295, 339, 346, 347, 376, 382, 388, 411, 424, 431, 443, 450, 453, 454, 475, 485, 541, 577, 584, 605, 619, 625, 634, 638, 641, 643, 645, 649, 657, 665, 679, 685, 699, 738, 757, 761, 784, 803, 810, 841, 848, 851, 866, and 897.

The following images were sourced from www.123rf.com:

11 © iofoto, 13 © Travis Manley, 18 © Harry Hu, 28 (top) © Steve Estvanik, 36 © Shirley Palmer, 38 © Jill Battaglia, 56 © Julia Nelson, 61 © Mariusz Jurgielewicz, 66 © Mariusz Jurgielewicz, 77 © Chee-Onn Long, 78 © Mariusz Jurgielewicz, 80 © Mike Norton, 85 © Charles Shapiro, 93 © Byron Moore, 96 © StrangerView, 97 © Andrew Kazmierski, 98 © Randy Hines, 101 © Kan Khampanya, 103 © Spectruminfo, 106 (top) © Deepa Vaswani, 106 (bottom) © Andrew Zarivny, 112 © Rieke Photo, 113 © Paul Moore, 119 © Jennifer Barrow, 120 © Elena Elisseeva, 123 © Alberto Loyo, 129 © Sergey Andrianov, 136 © FredyFish4, 148 (bottom) © Songquan Deng, 150 © Cecilia Lim, 152 © Amy Harris, 153 © Andrew Zarivny, 155 © Dave Broberg, 156 © Joerg Hackermann, 161 © William Silver, 171 (top) © Visions of America LLC, 171 (bottom) © Woody Pipatchaisiri, 195 © George Burba, 199 © Tommy Brisson, 200 © Deron Rodehaver, 217 © Brandon Seidel, 222 (bottom) © Mike Norton, 226 © Steven Gaertner, 227 (top) © Anton Foltin, 227 (bottom) © Dan Thornberg, 234 © Bill5md, 262 (top) © Henryk Sadura, 262 (bottom) © Carlos Santa Maria, 273 © Steve Kingsman, 285 © Visions of America LLC, 300 © Jon Bilous, 301 © William Silver, 307 © Richard Semik, 308 © Patricia Hofmeester, 309 © Chee-Onn Leong, 353 © Todd Thatcher, 360 © S. Borisov, 363 © Amnuaiphorn Boonjamras, 364 © Rollie, 374 © Timothy Mainiero, 375 © Jon Bilous, 393 (bottom) © Timothy Mainiero, 394 © P. Orbital, 410 © Tom McNemar, 411 © Henryk Sadura, 429 © Katie Smith, 442 (bottom) © Iofoto, 443 © Carolina K. Smith, M.D., 447 (bottom) © Rui Dios Aidos, 454 © William Silver, 456 © Ivan Cholakov, 461 (top) © William Silver, 461 (bottom) © Oleg Zinkovetsky, 462 © Vilaine Crevette, 466 (top) © Natalia Bratslavsky, 466 (bottom) © Varina and Jay Patel, 467 © Gino Rigucci, 468 © Chris Cifatte, 473 © Eric Metzler, 476 © Gino Rigucci, 478 © Matt Ragan, 480 © William Perry, 482 (top) © Travis Manley, 482 (bottom) © Frank L. Junior, 492 © Snehit, 493 © Robert Brown, 514 © Scott Nesvold, 520 © Snehit, 521 © Michael G. Smith, 523 (bottom) © Snehit, 525 © Phillip O'Brien, 526 © Keith Levit, 529 © CityLights, 530 © Mark Spowart, 531 (bottom) © Steve Kingsman, 534 (top) © CityLights, 534 (bottom) © Stefanos Kyriazis, 539 © Jan Gorzynik, 544 © Richard Semik, 561 ©

State flag and Canadian flag images:

Public Domain images:

and Photographs division (Lincoln: digital ID cph.3a53289, Lee: Brady-Handy Photograph Collection, LC-BH82-4430, Meade: digital ID cwpb.04402); 354 Courtesy of Boston Public Library Tichnor Brothers Collection; 356 Courtesy National Park Service, original photo by Mathew Brady, c. 1865; 357 Courtesy National Park Service/Doug Coldwell; 366 (top) Courtesy Library of Congress's Prints & Photographs Division (digital ID cph.3a04218), original photograph by Pach Brothers, New York, 1912; 368 Courtesy Library of Congress's Prints & Photographs Division (digital ID ppmsca.23961), original photograph by Harris & Ewing, 1905; 376 Courtesy of Ken Thomas/Wikimedia Commons (http://kenthomas.us); 389 (photo) Courtesy of Bloodfox at en.Wikipedia; 393 (middle) National Archives and Records Administration, ARC Identifier 200542; 404 (bottom) Courtesy Tex Jobe, U.S. Army Corps of Engineers/Wikimedia Commons; 407 (bottom) Courtesy United States Coast Guard, PA2 Christopher Evanson; 408 Courtesy of Joel Bradshaw/Wikimedia Commons; 412 (bottom) Courtesy Library of Congress's Prints & Photographs Division (LC-DIG-ppprs-00626), original authors: Orville Wright and John T. Daniels, 1903; 413 (both) Courtesy Library of Congress's Prints & Photographs Division (LC-DIG-ppprs-00680 and LC-DIG-ppprs-00683); 419 Courtesy of www.neatorama.com, original painting: *Capture of the Pirate, Blackbeard, 1718* by Jean Leon Gerome Ferris, 1920; 421 (top) Courtesy of Ken Thomas/Wikimedia Commons (http://kenthomas.us), 421 Courtesy US Navy, USN photo # DN-ST-89-00322, by Don S. Montgomery; 422 Courtesy FEMA Photo Library/Cynthia Hunter; 423 Courtesy www.learnnc.org/lp/multimedia/12418, original map by Union soldier Robert Knox Sneden, 1865; 444 (top) Courtesy of Mike Horn/Wikimedia Commons; 451 Courtesy NASA/Tony Gray and Tom Farrar/Wikimedia Commons; 464 Courtesy of Mr. William Folsom, NOAA, NMFS; 465 Courtesy of Piehoney/Wikimedia Commons; 468 (top) digital file Courtesy of Downtowngal/Wikimedia Commons; 469 (bottom) digital file Courtesy Domini Dragoone; 471 digital file courtesy Doug Pappas; 481 (middle) Courtesy Wenatchee Valley Museum & Cultural Center; 489 Courtesy of the U.S. Army Corps of Engineers Digital Visual Library; 497, 576, 719, 749 "Our State Flowers: The Floral Emblems Chosen by the Commonwealths", *National Geographic Magazine*, XXXI (June 1917), paintings by Mary E. Eaton; 498 Courtesy National Archives, photo by William H. Jackson, before 1877; 499 Courtesy Wyoming State Museum; 500 Courtesy Harry Weddington, U.S. Army Corps of Engineers; 507 (bottom) Courtesy Only/Wikimedia Commons; 523 (top) Courtesy Brenda St. Martin/National Park Service; 532 Photo provided courtesy of Atomic Energy of Canada Limited, Chalk River Laboratories.; 533 Courtesy Toronto Public Library; 546 & 547 Courtesy of Daderot/Wikimedia Commons; 589 from Wikimedia Commons, photo by Burke, c. 1892; 598 (bottom) from Wikimedia Commons; 599 Courtesy Ammodramus/Wikimedia Commons; 613 Courtesy Ronald Reagan Presidnetial Library; 618 Courtesy of Visviva/Wikimedia Commons; 622 Courtesy of TMPeukert/Wikimedia Commons; 628 Courtesy Library of Congress's Prints & Photographs Division (digital ID cph.3c31044), original photo by Hunt, Ft. Myers, FL, 1914; 630 Courtesy Derek Jensen/Wikimedia Commons; 645 Courtesy F.X. Matt Brewing Company/Wikimedia Commons; 649 Courtesy Library of Congress's Prints & Photographs Division (LC-USZC4-3859), poster by James Montgomery Flagg; 651 Courtesy New York Public Library Digital Library (ID G91F085_024F), photo by James E. Irving, c. 1880; 658 (bottom) © Allowishus/Wikimedia Commons; 663 Courtesy Boston Public Library; 671 digital file Coutesy Doug Pappas; 672 Courtesy National Park Service; 705 (bottom) Wikimedia Commons; 730 Courtesy U.S. Air Force; 732 from Wikimedia Commons, originally published by Seminary Music Co., New York, 1908; 737 (bottom) from Wikimedia Commons, originally published Baker-Meyer & Co., Importers & Publishers, West Baden, Ind.; 747 Courtesy Leslie K. Dellovade/Wikimedia Commons; 752 Courtesy of Decca Records; 761 originally printed by W.J. Moses in *Scenes from the Life of Harriet Tubman*, pre 1869; 763 digital file Courtesy Doug Pappas; 765 Courtesy Library of Congress's Prints and Photographs division under the digital ID highsm.04384; 773 Courtesy Jörn Napp/Wikimedia Commons; 774 Courtesy of Boston Public Library Tichnor Brothers Collection; 778 (both) Courtesy National Archives, photos by Camillus S. Fly; 782 and 783 Courtesy Boston Public Library; 789 Courtesy J. Dykstra/Wikimedia Commons; 793 Courtesy Bob Smith/EPA/Wikimedia Commons; 798 United States Library of Congress's Prints & Photographs Division (digital ID cph.3c34474); 803 Courtesy of the Mississippi Department of Archives and History; 805 © Carol Highsmith/Wikimedia Commons; 806 Library of Congress's Prints & Photographs Division (digital ID highsm.07312), photo by Carol Highsmith; 831 University of Maryland Digital Collections; 846 (top) Courtesy OkiefromOkla/Wikimedia Commons; 853 Courtesy Count Calen/Wikimedia Commons; 859 Courtesy Leaflet/Wikimedia Commons; 868 (top) Courtesy Boston Public Library, Prints Division; 871 Courtesy Anna Foxlover/Wikimedia Commons; 882 (bottom) Courtesy Library of Congress's Prints & Photographs Division (digital ID ppmsca.13397), original poster by NPS employee, 1938, 884 Courtesy Kkaufman11/Wikimedia Commons.

GNU and/or Creative Commons images:

21 photo © Miso Beno (http://commons.wikimedia.org/wiki/File:Lady_Washington_Commencement_Bay.jpg), 33 © PFFY (http://commons.wikimedia.org/wiki/File:Aquarium_tunnel.jpg), 52 © Robert Campbell/www.chamoismoon.com (http://commons.wikimedia.org/wiki/File:Fort_Bragg_California_aerial_view.jpg), 54 © Naotake Murayama (http:// http://commons.wikimedia.org/wiki/File:Vineyard_in_Anderson_Valley.jpg), 81 (top photo) © Urban (http://commons.wikimedia.org/wiki/File:Hearst_Castle_Casa_Grande1.jpg), 84 © Omar Bárcena (http:// commons.wikimedia.org/wiki/File:Madonna_0069_(2837851311).jpg), 92 (bottom photo) © Los Angeles/Wikimedia Commons (http://commons.wikimedia.org/wiki/File:Grandma_Prisbrey%27s_Bottle_Village_(3).jpg), 109 © David S. Roberts (http://commons.wikimedia.org/wiki/File:Belmont_Park_with_Giant_Dipper.jpg), 138 © Acroterian (http://commons.wikimedia.org/wiki/File:Hailey-Rialto_Hotel_ID1.jpg), 146 © Frank K. from Anchorage, Alaska, USA (http://commons.wikimedia.org/wiki/File:Colored_eroded_landscapes_in_Cathedral_Gorge_State_Park_(3193579244).jpg), 166 © Jeff Keyzer (http://commons.wikimedia.org/wiki/File:Titan_II_missile,_Titan_Missile_Museum_.jpg), 176 (top) © Nakor (http://commons.wikimedia.org/wiki/File:Knife_River_Earthen_Lodge_Exterior.JPG), 190 © Coemgenus (http://commons.wikimedia.org/wiki/File:Wall_Drug.JPG), 204 © Billy Hathorn (https://commons.wikimedia.org/wiki/File:Liberal,_KS,_welcome_sign_IMG_5968.JPG), 215 © Zereshk (http://commons.wikimedia.org/wiki/File:Lost_maple_Nima_(2).JPG), 220 (bottom) © Kati Fleming (http://commons.wikimedia.org/wiki/File:Altamira_Oriole_icterus_gularis_Bentsen_State_Park,_South_Texas.jpg), 234 (top) © T. Loewen (http://commons.wikimedia.org/wiki/File:WalkerArt.jpg), 241 © Ivo Shandor (http://commons.wikimedia.org/wiki/File:Oregon_Il_Lowden_State_Park10.jpg), 249 © Kepper66 (https://commons.wikimedia.org/wiki/File:Buffalo_Bill_Museum.jpg), 260 © Kbh3rd (http://commons.wikimedia.org/wiki/File:IllinoisGreatRiverRoad_north_of_Alton_20091122.jpg), 269 © Jeremy Atherton, 2001. (http://commons.wikimedia.org/wiki/File:Reelfoot_Lake.jpg), 270 (top) © D.B. King (http://commons.wikimedia.org/wiki/File:Sun_Studio,_Memphis,_TN_(3636820842).jpg), 277 © Steve Bott (http://commons.wikimedia.org/wiki/File:Ground_Zero_Blues_Club_Sign.jpg), 278 © Wescbel (http://commons.wikimedia.org/wiki/File:Rowan_Oak.JPG), 284 (large image) © Galen Parks Smith (http://commons.wikimedia.org/wiki/File:Port_Gibson_steeple2.JPG), 292 © SewTex at en.wikipedia (http://commons.wikimedia.org/wiki/File:Sunshine_Bridge_2.jpg), 294 © Daniel Schwen (http://commons.wikimedia.org/wiki/File:Jackson_Square.jpg), 297 © Ebyabe (http://commons.wikimedia.org/wiki/File:GA_Savannah_Fort_Jackson_inside02.jpg), 311 © Clark's Trading Post (https://commons.wikimedia.org/wiki/File:Clark%E2%80%99s_Trading_Post_(2877777326).jpg), 316 © Alexius Horatius (https://commons.wikimedia.org/wiki/File:Downtown_Woodstock_Vermont_5.JPG), 321 © Seth Tisue (http://commons.wikimedia.org/wiki/File:Gifford_woods_state_park_(2601284043).jpg), 328 (bottom) © Daderot (http://commons.wikimedia.org/wiki/File:Arrowhead_(Herman_Melville),_Pittsfield,_Massachusetts.JPG), 330 (bottom) © Richard Taylor (http://commons.wikimedia.org/wiki/File:Shaker_Kitchen.jpg), 331 © Midnightdreary (http://commons.wikimedia.org/wiki/File:TheMount_garden.jpg), 332 © John Pehlan (http://commons.wikimedia.org/wiki/File:Santarella,_Tyringham_MA.jpg), 333 © Anc516 (http://commons.wikimedia.org/wiki/File:Great_Barrington_2.jpg), 336 © Wikipedia at the English Language Wikipedia (http://commons.wikimedia.org/wiki/File:Kent_Falls.jpg.pg), 340 © Beyond My Ken (http://commons.wikimedia.org/wiki/File:High_Line_20th_Street_looking_downtown.jpg), 345 (bottom) © Alex Hardin (http://commons.wikimedia.org/wiki/File:C.F.Martin_Tour-04.jpg), 349 © Hermann Luyken (http://commons.wikimedia.org/wiki/File:2003.09.20_46_Ephrata_Cloister_Pennsylvania.jpg), 351 © CrazyLegsKC (http://commons.wikimedia.org/wiki/File:Shoehouse.jpg), 366 © Woody Hibbard (http://commons.wikimedia.org/wiki/File:Shenandoah_Homestead_(6613546223).jpg), 383 © Mimi L. Cunningham (https://commons.wikimedia.org/wiki/File:Folk_Art_Chapel.JPG), 384 © Zac Wolf at en.wikipedia (http://commons.wikimedia.org/wiki/File:Male_whale_shark_at_Georgia_Aquarium.jpg), 387 © Mike Gonzalez (TheCoffee) (http://commons.wikimedia.org/wiki/File:Helen_Georgia.jpg), 400 © CaptAdam at en.wikipedia (http://commons.wikimedia.org/wiki/File:MVCapeMay.jpg), 405 © Mttbme (http://commons.wikimedia.org/wiki/File:HauntedHouseTrimpers.jpg), 407 (top) © Rachel Tayse (http://commons.wikimedia.org/wiki/File:Chincoteague_Ponys.jpg), 415 © Jim Gordon (http://commons.wikimedia.org/wiki/File:Cape_Hatteras_Lighthouse.jpg), 426 © Leonard J. DeFrancisci (http://commons.wikimedia.org/wiki/File:South_of_the_Bor-

der_(attraction)_1.jpg), 428 © Brian Stansberry (http://commons.wikimedia.org/wiki/File:Hampton-plantation-south-facade-sc1.jpg), 430 © Brian Stansberry (http://commons.wikimedia.org/wiki/File:Edmonston-alston-house-sc1.jpg), 436 © Ebyabe (http://commons.wikimedia.org/wiki/File:GA_St_Simons_Lighthouse_and_Keepers_Bldg01.jpg), 444 (bottom) © Ebyabe (http://commons.wikimedia.org/wiki/File:PB_FL_Flagler_Whitehall01.jpg), 447 (top) © Gregory Moine (http://commons.wikimedia.org/wiki/File:Aceros_cassidix_-St_Augustine_Alligator_Farm_Zoological_Park-8a.jpg), 450 © Brian Cantoni (http://commons.wikimedia.org/wiki/File:Ryan_Newman_2008_Daytona_500_Winning_Car_at_Daytona_500_Experience.jpg), 459 © Infrogmation (http://commons.wikimedia.org/wiki/File:Little_Havana_Dominos_Park.JPG), 467 © Andreas Lamecker (http://commons.wikimedia.org/wiki/File:Hemingwayhouse.jpg), 479 © Konrad Roeder/Wikimedia Commons, 481 (bottom) © Stemilt Growers (http://commons.wikimedia.org/wiki/File:SweeTango%27s_Await_Picking.jpg), 491 © Acroterion (http://commons.wikimedia.org/wiki/File:Belton_Chalet_main_1.jpg), 505 (top) © Alex W. Covington (http://commons.wikimedia.org/wiki/File:Rosa_arkansana.jpg), 509 © Bouba (http://en.wikipedia.org/wiki/File:Cypripedium_reginae.jpg), 511 (top) © Elkman (http://commons.wikimedia.org/wiki/File:Appletree_bloom_l.jpg), 519 © Krzysztof P. Jasiutowicz (http://commons.wikimedia.org/wiki/File:Appletree_bloom_l.jpg), 540 © Jonathan Leo Connor (Gopats92) (http://commons.wikimedia.org/wiki/File:BillingsLibraryUVM.jpg), 541 © Mfwills (http://commons.wikimedia.org/wiki/File:Head_of_Church_Street_HD.JPG), 554 (top) © Denis Santerre/Slashinme (http://commons.wikimedia.org/wiki/File:Bangor_Maine.JPG), 554 (bottom) © Julia Ess (http://commons.wikimedia.org/wiki/File:Stephenking_house.JPG), 565 (top) © Jean Tosti (http://commons.wikimedia.org/wiki/File:Mahonia_aquifolium3.jpg), 566 (top) © Visitor7 (http://commons.wikimedia.org/wiki/File:Powells.jpg), 566 (bottom) © Tedder (http://commons.wikimedia.org/wiki/File:Oaks_Amusement_Park_entrance_Portland_Oregon.jpg), 568 © EncMstr (http://commons.wikimedia.org/wiki/File:Timberline_lodge_lobby_art_level3.jpeg), 571 © Chris Murphy (http://commons.wikimedia.org/wiki/File:Barlow_road.jpg), 573 © Finetooth (http://commons.wikimedia.org/wiki/File:Sheep_Rock_near_sunset.jpg), 579 © Lazarus-long (http://commons.wikimedia.org/wiki/File:Bruneau_sand_dunes.jpg), 592 © Ben Townsend (http://commons.wikimedia.org/wiki/File:Velociraptor_Wyoming_Dinosaur_Center.jpg), 601 © Daryl Mitchell (http://commons.wikimedia.org/wiki/File:Goldenrod_Flowers.jpg), 612 © Ben Jacobson (Kranar Drogin (http://commons.wikimedia.org/wiki/File:Burpee_-_Thescelosaurus.jpg), 623 © femaletrumpet02 (http://commons.wikimedia.org/wiki/File:Rosa_Parks_bus_full_shot_by_femaletrumpet02.jpg), 633 © Pat Noble (http://commons.wikimedia.org/wiki/File:Warner_Theatre_Erie_Marquee.jpg), 639 © Darmon (http://commons.wikimedia.org/wiki/File:AnchorBar.jpg), 648 © UpstateNYer (http://commons.wikimedia.org/wiki/File:SpringsideCottageFacade2.jpg), 653 (top) © Nancy (http://commons.wikimedia.org/wiki/File:Epigaea_repens.jpg), 654 © ToddC4176 (http://commons.wikimedia.org/wiki/File:Bridge_of_Flowers.JPG), 658 (top) © Daderot at en.wikipedia (http://commons.wikimedia.org/wiki/File:Hartwell_Tavern_Lexington_Massachusetts.jpg), 662 © werkunz1 on Flickr (http://commons.wikimedia.org/wiki/File:Fanway_Park_2009.jpg), 675 (top) © Calibas (http://commons.wikimedia.org/wiki/File:Heinolds.jpg), 675 (bottom) © Magnus Manske (http://commons.wikimedia.org/wiki/File:Eschscholzia_californica_%27californian_poppy%27_2007-06-02_%28flower%29.jpg), 677 (top) © Tinned Elk (http://commons.wikimedia.org/wiki/File:Medusa_%28Six_Flags_Discovery_Kingdom%29_01.JPG), 683 © Ragesoss (http://commons.wikimedia.org/wiki/File:Small_twisted_sagebrush.jpg), 687 © Tobias (http://commons.wikimedia.org/wiki/File:USA_2005_%28October_1st%29_Nevada,_Reno,_National_Automobile_Museum.jpg), 691 (top) © Davemeistermoab (http://commons.wikimedia.org/wiki/File:Eurekanv.JPG), 694 © Wing-Chi-Poon (http://commons.wikimedia.org/wiki/File:Calabash_Shaped_Stalactites_that_Resemble_Chinese_Red_Lanterns.jpg), 697 (top) © Maylett (http://commons.wikimedia.org/wiki/File:Sego_lily_cm.jpg), 697 (bottom) © Tricia Simpson (http://commons.wikimedia.org/wiki/File:HelperUtah.jpeg), 698 © Signalhead (http://commons.wikimedia.org/wiki/File:Green_river_utah_from_sky.jpg), 709 © Hustvedt (http://commons.wikimedia.org/wiki/File:Royal_Gorge_Bridge_2010.jpg), 711 © MarekWK (http://commons.wikimedia.org/wiki/File:Pike_Peak_1.JPG), 713 © Ealdgyth (http://commons.wikimedia.org/wiki/File:Bent%27s_Old_Fort_buildings.jpg), 723 © Jon Harder (http://commons.wikimedia.org/wiki/File:Alexanderwohl-church-2.jpg), 725 © Ichabod (http://commons.wikimedia.org/wiki/File:Chase_county_kansas_courthouse_sideview_2009.jpg), 727 (bottom) © Americasroof at en.wikipedia (http://commons.wikimedia.org/wiki/File:Clay-savings.png), 731 (http://commons.wikimedia.org/wiki/File:Common_hawthorn_flowers.jpg) 736 © Sarah Wilkerson Poole from Bedford, USA (http://commons.wikimedia.org/wiki/File:West_Baden_Springs_Hotel_atrium.jpg), 740 © Cédric Boismain from France (http://commons.wikimedia.org/wiki/File:Thomas_Gaff_House_%28Hillforest%29.jpg), 745 (top) © Rick Kimpel (http://commons.wikimedia.org/wiki/File:Red_Carnation_Flower.jpg), 745 (bottom) © Rdikeman at en.wikipedia (http://commons.wikimedia.org/wiki/File:Hopewell_culture_nhp_mounds_chillicothe_ohio_2006.jpg), 751 © Albert Herring (http://commons.wikimedia.org/wiki/File:Virginia_State_Capitol_complex_-_state_seal_on_doorknob.jpg), 754 © Phillip Ritz (http://commons.wikimedia.org/wiki/File:National_Museum_of_the_American_Indian_in_Washington,_D.C.jpg), 758 © Acroterion (http://

Cover Artwork:

Acknowledgments

Keeping tabs on the life and times along more than 40,000 miles of all-American highways is a lot of fun—and a lot of work. For those who've helped make this latest edition more of the former than the latter, I'd like to send out a huge and heartfelt thank you.

First and foremost I'd like to acknowledge the tremendous contributions from the whole team at Avalon Travel for their usual but nonetheless extraordinary efforts in fact-checking and map-making. Specific shout-outs go to ace designer Domini Dragoone and eagle-eyed editor Kevin McLain, without whom this book would not be the attractive and engaging object you're holding in your hands.

Special thanks also go to Sandra Hebert and the whole team at Minor League Baseball.

To all of you who have gotten in touch (via Facebook, or even in person!) with suggestions, ideas and intriguing questions: Please keep those trip reports, postcards, and cherry pie pointers coming!

After more than 20 years of wanderlust, there's still no place I'd rather be than alongside my wife Catherine Robson and our boys Tom and Alex, with whom I always look forward to our next trip.

Getting to know these miles of highways and the wonderful places they can take us has been a dream come true, but tracking the changes has a bittersweet side as well. While researching this edition, I mourned the loss of three heroes: songwriter Chuck Berry, photographer John Margolies, and the inimitable Yogi Berra. I would like to dedicate this edition to the memory of my late father Bob Jensen, who woke me up for many a roadside sunrise, taught me to read and understand road maps, and helped open my eyes (and ears, and taste buds!) to the abundance of good things along the Great American Highway.

Keep up with Jamie online:

RoadTripUSA.com
facebook.com/RoadTripUSAguide
instagram.com/RoadTripUSAguide
twitter.com/RTUSAguide

Moon Road Trip Guides

BLUE RIDGE PARKWAY Road Trip
INCLUDING SHENANDOAH & GREAT SMOKY MOUNTAINS NATIONAL PARKS
JASON FRYE

CALIFORNIA Road Trip
SAN FRANCISCO, YOSEMITE, LAS VEGAS, GRAND CANYON, LOS ANGELES, & THE PACIFIC COAST HIGHWAY
STUART THORNTON

NASHVILLE TO NEW ORLEANS Road Trip
NATCHEZ TRACE PARKWAY · MEMPHIS · TUPELO · MISSISSIPPI BLUES TRAIL
MARGARET LITTMAN

NEW ENGLAND Road Trip
BOSTON, ACADIA NATIONAL PARK, WHITE MOUNTAINS, BERKSHIRES, NEWPORT, AND CAPE COD
JEN ROSE SMITH

PACIFIC COAST HIGHWAY Road Trip
CALIFORNIA, OREGON & WASHINGTON
IAN ANDERSON

PACIFIC NORTHWEST Road Trip
SEATTLE, VANCOUVER, VICTORIA, THE OLYMPIC PENINSULA, PORTLAND, THE OREGON COAST & MOUNT RAINIER
ALLISON WILLIAMS

Also Available:

Popular chapters of Road Trip USA are available excerpted in these smaller, individual guides.

Road Trip USA JAMIE JENSEN — Route 66

Road Trip USA — Appalachian Trail — JAMIE JENSEN

Road Trip USA — Atlantic Coast — JAMIE JENSEN

Road Trip USA — Great River Road — JAMIE JENSEN

Road Trip USA — Pacific Coast Highway — JAMIE JENSEN

Advice on where to sleep, eat, and explore

Detailed driving directions including mileage and drive times

Itineraries for a range of timelines

Moon Travel Guides are available from your favorite bookseller.

MOON
ROUTE 66
Road Trip
MIDPOINT CAFE
CANDACY TAYLOR

MOON
SOUTHWEST
Road Trip
LAS VEGAS, ZION & BRYCE, MONUMENT VALLEY,
SANTA FE & TAOS, AND THE GRAND CANYON
TIM HULL

MOON
VANCOUVER &
CANADIAN ROCKIES
Road Trip
VICTORIA, BANFF, JASPER, CALGARY,
THE OKANAGAN, WHISTLER &
THE SEA-TO-SKY HIGHWAY
CAROLYN B. HELLER

National Parks Guides

A memorable road trip includes stunning stops. Craft a personalized journey through the top National Parks in the U.S. and Canada with Moon Travel Guides.

MOON

ACADIA
NATIONAL PARK
HILARY NANGLE

MOON

ARCHES &
CANYONLANDS
NATIONAL PARKS
W.C. BURGE & JUDY JEWELL

MOON

BANFF
NATIONAL PARK
ANDREW HEMPSTEAD

MOON

DEATH VALLEY
NATIONAL PARK
JENNA BLOUGH

MOON

GLACIER
NATIONAL PARK
BECKY LOMAX

MOON

GRAND
CANYON
KATHLEEN BRYANT

MOON

GREAT SMOKY
MOUNTAINS
NATIONAL PARK
JASON FRYE

MOON

MOUNT RUSHMORE
& THE BLACK HILLS
Including the Badlands
LAURAL A. BIDWELL

MOON

ROCKY MOUNTAIN
NATIONAL PARK
ERIN ENGLISH

MOON

YELLOWSTONE
& GRAND TETON
Jeff Bishop, Jackson Hole
BECKY LOMAX

MOON

YOSEMITE,
SEQUOIA &
KINGS CANYON
ANN MARIE BROWN

MOON

ZION &
BRYCE
Including Arches,
Canyonlands, Capitol Reef,
Escalante, Cedar Cedar Breaks & Moab
W.C. BURGE & JUDY JEWELL

In these books:

- Full coverage of gateway cities and towns
- Itineraries from one day to multiple weeks
- Advice on where to stay in and around the park, including campgrounds

Road Trip USA

Cross-Country Adventures on America's Two-Lane Highways

Avalon Travel
Hachette Book Group
1700 Fourth Street
Berkeley, CA 94710, USA
www.moon.com

Editor: Kevin McLain
Fact Checkers: Ashley Biggers, Lara Dunning, Sonia Weiser
Copy Editor: Christopher Church
Graphics and Production Coordinator: Domini Dragoone
Cover Design: Erin Seaward-Hiatt
Interior Design: Domini Dragoone
Moon Logo: Tim McGrath
Map Editor: Mike Morgenfeld
Cartographers: Mike Morgenfeld, Stephanie Poulain
Indexer: Greg Jewett

ISBN-13: 978-1-64049-384-1

Printing History
1st Edition – 2005
8th Edition – March 2018
5 4 3

Printed in China by RRD Shenzhen